RAND McNALLY

Road Atlas

2017 LARGE SCALE

CONTENTS

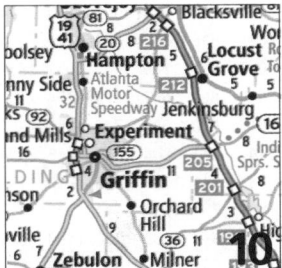

TRAVEL INFORMATION

Mileage Chart 2
Driving distances between 77 North American cities.

Best of the Road® Trips 3-7
Our editor's five favorite road trips from our Best of the Road® collection

Mileage and Driving Times Map inside back cover
Distances and driving times between hundreds of North American cities and national parks.

MAPS

Map Legend inside front cover

United States Overview Map 8-9

States and Cities 10-235

INDEX 236-264

D0904615

Quick Map References

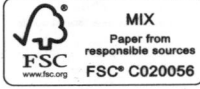

MIX
Paper from responsible sources
FSC® C020056

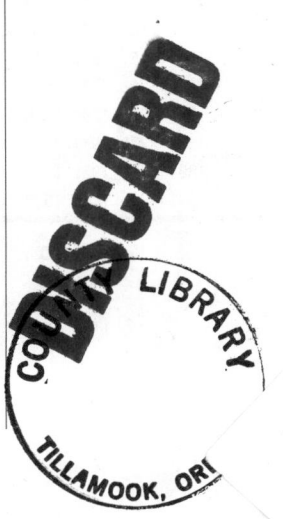

Mileage Chart

This handy chart offers more than 2,400 mileages covering 77 North American cities and U.S. national parks. Want more mileages? Visit **randmcnally.com/MC** and type in any two cities or addresses.

	Albuquerque, NM	Atlanta, GA	Billings, MT	Boston, MA	Charlotte, NC	Chicago, IL	Cincinnati, OH	Dallas, TX	Denver, CO	Detroit, MI	Houston, TX	Indianapolis, IN	Kansas City, MO	Los Angeles, CA	Memphis, TN	Miami, FL	Milwaukee, WI	Minneapolis, MN	New Orleans, LA	New York, NY	Omaha, NE	Orlando, FL	Philadelphia, PA	Phoenix, AZ	Pittsburgh, PA	Portland, OR	Saint Louis, MO	Salt Lake City, UT	San Francisco, CA	Seattle, WA	Washington, DC	Wichita, KS
Albuquerque, NM		1386	998	2219	1626	1333	1387	647	446	1570	884	1279	784	786	1008	1952	1354	1225	1165	2001	863	1730	1924	462	1641	1363	1037	599	1086	1438	1885	591
Amarillo, TX	284	1102	965	1935	1342	1049	1103	363	424	1286	589	995	570	1072	720	1668	1132	1009	881	1716	647	1446	1640	746	1357	1669	752	883	1370	1743	1600	382
Atlanta, GA	1386		1831	1095	244	715	461	780	1404	722	794	533	800	2174	379	661	809	1127	468	882	992	440	780	1844	684	2603	555	1878	2472	2649	637	955
Atlantic City, NJ	1985	831	2072	338	590	818	632	1518	1792	644	1598	703	1187	2774	1063	1248	910	1232	1273	126	1272	1038	60	2447	365	2922	948	2201	2934	2889	188	1379
Austin, TX	705	920	1495	1959	1164	1121	1128	193	950	1358	157	1067	702	1381	643	1341	1204	1136	503	1737	839	1124	1658	1010	1411	2068	825	1304	1760	2143	1524	542
Baltimore, MD	1887	683	1953	400	442	699	513	1368	1673	524	1448	584	1068	2670	914	1082	792	1112	1124	192	1153	889	98	2349	246	2804	829	2081	2816	2771	39	1260
Billings, MT	998	1831		2236	1990	1246	1546	1425	551	1535	1652	1435	1026	1240	1477	2497	1173	838	1868	2041	845	2275	2011	1210	1713	891	1278	552	1173	818	1951	1064
Birmingham, AL	1241	146	1780	1177	390	660	466	636	1329	724	668	478	749	2030	235	746	754	1072	343	960	939	534	880	1700	748	2551	502	1826	2327	2598	745	810
Boise, ID	938	2177	621	2660	2336	1693	1943	1702	830	1960	1930	1835	1372	842	1825	2844	1732	1461	2216	2465	1225	2622	2435	914	2137	428	1622	339	639	503	2375	1338
Boston, MA	2219	1095	2236		841	983	870	1764	1970	724	1844	937	1421	2983	1312	1482	1074	1396	1520	207	1436	1288	306	2681	570	3086	1182	2365	3098	3054	439	1613
Branson, MO	864	652	1241	1433	868	545	601	435	806	784	602	493	209	1651	274	1284	630	643	597	1201	402	1062	1138	1326	851	2013	249	1288	1950	2060	1081	292
Calgary, AB	1542	2357	541	2615	2400	1627	1925	1967	1096	1916	2209	1814	1567	1557	2028	3018	1555	1221	2419	2439	1387	2797	2391	1524	2093	787	1820	869	1500	678	2334	1606
Charleston, SC	1703	317	2133	970	207	908	620	1099	1706	826	1105	726	1103	2491	696	583	1002	1324	742	768	1294	380	668	2165	654	2904	857	2180	2789	2951	532	1272
Charlotte, NC	1626	244	1990	841		769	477	1023	1566	616	1038	583	961	2414	619	728	867	1180	712	641	1151	526	539	2088	446	2761	714	2037	2712	2808	398	1092
Chicago, IL	1333	715	1246	983	769		289	926	1002	280	1085	181	526	2015	531	1381	90	408	923	787	470	1153	757	1795	459	2118	296	1398	2130	2063	697	724
Cincinnati, OH	1387	461	1546	870	477	289		934	1187	259	1055	108	584	2172	482	1127	381	703	804	637	722	905	571	1849	288	2369	348	1647	2380	2363	512	779
Cleveland, OH	1598	714	1597	638	514	342	248	1194	1330	168	1315	315	799	2342	729	1240	434	756	1057	460	797	1043	428	2060	131	2446	560	1725	2458	2414	370	992
Columbus, OH	1457	567	1606	763	426	354	106	1039	1261	191	1174	176	657	2244	587	1164	445	766	910	533	792	954	468	1920	184	2439	421	1718	2451	2425	411	851
Corpus Christi, TX	855	1001	1622	2051	1244	1338	1262	410	1077	1542	207	1228	919	1494	782	1394	1421	1353	554	1844	1056	1172	1754	1122	1561	2218	1042	1454	1873	2292	1619	758
Dallas, TX	647	780	1425	1764	1023	926	934		880	1163	228	873	489	1437	453	1307	1010	928	519	1548	656	1086	1467	1066	1221	2128	630	1403	1734	2193	1332	361
Denver, CO	446	1404	551	1970	1566	1002	1187	880		1270	1035	1083	603	1015	1097	2069	1042	913	1398	1775	534	1851	1732	908	1447	1256	854	533	1268	1320	1671	519
Des Moines, IA	983	902	946	1299	1057	332	580	683	670	599	938	474	193	1682	617	1567	371	242	1008	1105	137	1339	1074	1445	777	1786	354	1065	1798	1764	1015	391
Detroit, MI	1570	722	1535	724	616	280	259	1163	1270		1319	288	764	2281	742	1354	374	696	1066	613	736	1144	583	2032	285	2385	533	1664	2397	2353	522	964
Duluth, MN	1375	1187	860	1370	1239	466	760	1092	1063	754	1331	651	586	2076	963	1852	394	152	1354	1264	530	1632	1230	1838	932	1749	679	1458	2033	1677	1171	785
Edmonton, AB	1724	2391	722	2549	2443	1670	1968	2149	1278	1958	2391	1857	1626	1755	2147	3058	1598	1264	2538	2482	1445	2836	2434	1721	2136	966	1878	1069	1695	793	2377	1787
El Paso, TX	260	1418	1257	2373	1662	1455	1569	635	707	1702	744	1398	929	796	1089	1934	1497	1377	1095	2202	1004	1712	2102	424	1774	1630	1157	866	1175	1705	1967	730
Fargo, ND	1318	1361	607	1629	1414	641	937	1079	873	930	1321	825	600	1848	1054	2025	569	235	1445	1438	420	1807	1405	1780	1107	1497	841	1160	1781	1424	1348	685
Gatlinburg, TN	1439	196	1803	922	202	578	290	884	1376	552	964	396	773	2226	431	865	672	994	640	707	964	640	625	1901	493	2574	527	1850	2525	2621	490	905
Guadalajara, JA	1194	1739	2194	2789	1982	1954	1962	1028	1639	2191	948	1901	1535	1501	1482	2131	2037	1969	1292	2592	1672	1910	2492	1212	2261	2545	1658	1792	1963	2631	2356	1377
Gulfport, MS	1221	399	1912	1482	643	896	767	562	1386	1025	403	780	883	1949	365	792	988	1196	78	1266	1073	572	1180	1577	1052	2633	647	1909	2307	2730	1036	867
Houston, TX	884	794	1652	1844	1038	1085	1055	228	1035	1319		1021	732	1550	575	1186	1163	1171	347	1632	898	965	1547	1178	1354	2356	784	1634	1929	2431	1411	595
Indianapolis, IN	1279	533	1435	937	583	181	108	873	1083	288	1021		482	2068	464	1198	272	591	818	707	613	968	643	1742	359	2260	243	1541	2273	2253	582	674
Jacksonville, FL	1636	346	2183	1146	379	1068	796	992	1756	1002	871	874	1152	2421	677	349	1163	1474	547	939	1344	141	844	2050	825	2954	907	2230	2723	3001	706	1272
Kansas City, MO	784	800	1026	1421	961	526	584	489	603	764	732	482		1616	451	1466	565	436	844	1196	187	1246	1127	1246	840	1797	250	1073	1808	1844	1066	193
Key West, FL	2099	809	2646	1659	886	1534	1275	1455	2222	1515	1334	1348	1617	2884	1159	162	1632	1944	1010	1446	1807	387	1357	2514	1332	3417	1370	2693	3186	3464	1213	1735
Las Vegas, NV	572	1959	973	2714	2199	1746	1932	1220	747	2013	1457	1828	1349	270	1581	2525	1786	1656	1739	2518	1278	2303	2480	286	2190	1023	1600	419	569	1128	2428	1164
Lexington, KY	1371	369	1610	917	400	370	83	876	1186	344	996	184	581	2158	423	1030	464	782	745	701	771	817	638	1833	370	2381	334	1657	2392	2428	533	773
Little Rock, AR	877	515	1407	1447	754	650	617	319	965	885	439	583	381	1666	137	1147	724	815	425	1230	574	925	1150	1340	905	2211	345	1488	1963	2275	1015	446
Los Angeles, CA	786	2174	1240	2983	2414	2015	2172	1437	1015	2281	1550	2068	1616		1794	2735	2055	1925	1894	2787	1546	2515	2713	370	2428	963	1821	688	380	1134	2670	1377
Memphis, TN	1008	379	1477	1312	619	531	482	453	1097	742	575	464	451	1794		1012	622	831	394	1094	641	778	1014	1471	768	2245	283	1524	2095	2299	879	577
Mexico City, DF	1404	1718	2301	2768	1962	2017	1979	1090	1756	2254	924	1963	1598	1839	1500	2111	2100	2032	1272	2571	1735	1889	2471	1469	2279	2768	1721	2003	2218	2842	2336	1440
Miami, FL	1952	661	2497	1482	728	1381	1127	1307	2069	1354	1186	1198	1466	2735	1012		1475	1791	861	1288	1658	229	1180	2362	1173	3260	1221	2544	3038	3315	1044	1587
Milwaukee, WI	1354	809	1173	1074	867	90	381	1010	1042	374	1163	272	565	2055	622	1475		336	1015	879	509	1258	849	1817	551	2062	379	1437	2170	1990	788	763
Minneapolis, MN	1225	1127	838	1396	1180	408	703	928	913	696	1171	591	436	1925	831	1791	336		1223	1204	372	1573	1171	1687	874	1727	563	1308	2040	1655	1110	634
Mobile, AL	1234	328	1874	1427	571	917	721	589	1414	978	468	733	850	2014	382	719	1011	1224	144	1202	1038	497	1101	1643	1000	2661	645	1936	2320	2727	965	894
Montréal, QC	2129	1218	2099	310	980	847	824	1722	1832	560	1884	847	1330	2845	1314	1647	938	1262	1640	382	1302	1437	454	2591	603	2948	1092	2228	2960	2916	587	1529
Nashville, TN	1219	248	1586	1099	407	469	273	664	1158	534	786	287	555	2006	212	913	564	881	532	884	747	692	802	1682	560	2357	310	1633	2306	2404	667	688
New Orleans, LA	1165	468	1868	1520	712	923	804	519	1398	1066	347	818	844	1894	394	861	1015	1223		1304	1032	641	1222	1523	1090	2642	675	1920	2252	2716	1087	880
New York, NY	2001	882	2041	207	641	787	637	1548	1775	613	1632	707	1196	2787	1094	1288	879	1204	1304		1245	1089	97	2463	369	2891	954	2170	2902	2858	228	1391
Norfolk, VA	1910	558	2132	569	328	878	605	1350	1758	704	1362	720	1155	2707	898	950	969	1295	1026	370	1335	755	271	2373	425	2962	911	2238	2973	2949	189	1349
Oklahoma City, OK	542	844	1203	1678	1084	792	846	204	631	1029	437	739	348	1326	466	1476	876	788	722	1460	452	1254	1384	1005	1101	1922	496	1200	1627	1948	1344	158
Omaha, NE	863	992	845	1436	1151	470	722	656	534	736	898	613	187	1546	641	1658	509	372	1032	1245		1436	1212	1325	914	1650	439	930	1662	1663	1151	298
Orlando, FL	1730	440	2275	1288	526	1153	905	1086	1851	1144	965	968	1246	2515	778	229	1258	1573	641	1089	1436		986	2145	975	3048	999	2323	2816	3093	849	1365
Ottawa, ON	2039	1158	1768	428	920	760	732	1632	1748	471	1804	757	1240	2763	1230	1618	859	1032	1582	440	1213	1408	447	2501	546	2660	1002	2142	2877	2586	566	1439
Philadelphia, PA	1924	780	2011	306	539	757	571	1467	1732	583	1547	643	1127	2713	1014	1180	849	1171	1222	97	1212	986		2387	304	2861	888	2140	2873	2828	137	1319
Phoenix, AZ	462	1844	1210	2681	2088	1795	1849	1066	908	2032	1178	1742	1246	370	1471	2362	1817	1687	1523	2463	1325	2145	2387		2104	1332	1499	653	749	1414	2348	1053
Pittsburgh, PA	1641	684	1713	570	446	459	288	1221	1447	285	1354	359	840	2428	768	1173	551	874	1090	369	914	975	304	2104		2563	604	1842	2574	2530	244	1035
Portland, ME	2315	1192	2333	110	938	1079	967	1861	2067	825	1940	1034	1518	3082	1408	1585	1176	1492	1616	304	1533	1385	402	2778	666	3186	1279	2461	3196	3151	535	1710
Portland, OR	1363	2603	891	3086	2761	2118	2369	2128	1256	2385	2356	2260	1797	963	2245	3260	2062	1727	2642	2891	1650	3048	2861	1332	2563		2050	765	635	172	2800	1764
Rapid City, SD	843	1508	323	1900	1670	912	1208	1061	397	1200	1291	1100	704	1312	1160	2173	840	575	1551	1708	525	1956	1675	1305	1378	1215	959	649	1384	1142	1618	699
Reno, NV	1019	2396	958	2881	2555	1913	2163	1668	1051	2180	1904	2056	1591	470	2029	3063	1953	1818	2186	2685	1445	2841	2656	733	2357	578	1844	518	217	720	2595	1558
Richmond, VA	1832	532	2051	547	293	797	512	1278	1671	622	1329	627	1069	2620	824	944	888	1210	1002	334	1259	742	245	2294	344	2869	822	2145	2880	2868	108	1261
Saint Louis, MO	1037	555	1278	1182	714	296	348	630	854	533	784	243	250	1821	283	1221	379	563	675	954	439	999	888	1499	604	2050		1326	2061	2096	827	442
Salt Lake City, UT	599	1878	552	2365	2037	1398	1647	1403	533	1664	1634	1541	1073	688	1524	2544	1437	1308	1920	2170	930	2323	2140	653	1842	765	1326		735	839	2079	1042
San Antonio, TX	712	986	1480	2039	1230	1202	1210	276	935	1439	197	1149	766	1357	727	1379	1285	1205	541	1822	920	1160	1742	985	1495	2076	906	1311	1736	2150	1607	625
San Diego, CA	810	2138	1302	3046	2381	2080	2196	1359	1077	2346	1472	2089	1597	120	1819	2656	2118	1986	1816	2809	1613	2436	2738	352	2452	1083	1845	750	501	1256	2693	1401
San Francisco, CA	1086	2472	1173	3098	2712	2130	2380	1734	1268	2397	1929	2273	1808	380	2095	3038	2170	2040	2252	2902	1662	2816	2873	749	2574	635	2061	735		807	2812	1775
Santa Fe, NM	58	1379	943	2212	1618	1313	1379	640	391	1562	877	1272	766	846	998	1944	1336	1207	1158	1994	891	1723	1917	520	1634	1388	1029	625	1144	1463	1879	572
Sault Ste. Marie, ON	1777	1040	1273	923	947	471	577	1370	1428	347	1527	540	951	2465	972	1685	398	538	1355	921	850	1475	911	2240	614	2166	740	1848	2581	2090	854	1150
Seattle, WA	1438	2649	818	3054	2808	2063	2363	2193	1320	2353	2431	2253	1844	1134	2299	3315	1990	1655	2716	2858	1663	3093	2828	1414	2530	172	2096	839	807		2768	1828
Spokane, WA	1320	2369	541	2774	2528	1785	2084	1964	1091	2075	2192	1973	1564	1216	2018	3035	1712	1377	2409	2580	1383	2814	2550	1381	2252	351	1817	720	874	278	2490	1600
Tampa, FL	1746	451	2293	1342	578	1166	916	1102	1860	1178	980	984	1252	2525	779	255	1260	1578	651	1138	1445	84	1040	2153	1023	3064	1008	2340	2832	3111	904	1381
Toronto, ON	1800	963	1771	548	756	519	493	1393	1504	232	1551	518	1001	2517	983	1483	609	933	1306	489	974	1284	497	2262	316	2620	763	1899	2632	2588	486	1188
Tulsa, OK	645	782	1234	1576	1022	687	738	258	692	927	487	635	243	1433	402	1414	773	704	671	1350	380	1192	1282	1107	994	1938	392	1215	1731	2012	1234	173
Vancouver, BC	1575	2785	953	3188	2944	2198	2499	2338	1465	2487	2565	2389	1980	1275	2437	3451	2125	1790	2851	2993	1799	3229	2963	1550	2665	313	2232	973	947	141	2903	1973
Washington, DC	1885	637	1951	439	398	697	512	1332	1671	522	1411	582	1066	2670	879	1044	788	1110	1087	228	1151	849	137	2348	244	2800	827	2079	2812	2768		1258
Wichita, KS	591	955	1064	1613	1092	724	779	361	519	964	595	674	193	1377	577	1587	763	634	880	1391	298	1365	1319	1053	1035	1764	442	1042	1775	1828	1258	

Mileages in this chart are based upon the routes usually followed by motorists. Highway systems include interstate, U.S., and state highways.

Ohiopyle State Park

BEST OF THE ROAD® TRIPS

If you're like us, you love road trips. Here are some favorites from our Best of the Road collection. They follow scenic routes along stretches of coastline—both east and west—to forests and mountains, and through small towns and big cities.

Western Pennsylvania Town & Country

From Pittsburgh's steel heritage to Fallingwater's architectural wonder to Gettysburg's Civil War history, a trip through western Pennsylvania will satisfy your craving for urban adventure, natural serenity, and Americana in one succinct weekend.

Outside Pittsburgh city limits, the scenery quickly changes to tree-lined streets, town squares, and state routes that have become hallmarks of rural Pennsylvania. Along the way you can immerse yourself in Colonial history as well as that of the Civil War. And, at a national memorial in a field in Stoystown, you can also pay homage to some of the victims of the tragic events on September 11, 2001.

Statue of General Gouverneur Kemble Warren at Little Round Top, Gettysburg National Military Park

Pittsburgh

Andy Warhol Museum. Each floor of this seven-story building follows a decade of the life and art of Andy Warhol, who was born in Pittsburgh in 1928. In addition to the well-known Pop Art collection and portraits, the museum has extensive archives and about a half-million bits of ephemera: from Warhol's party invitations and scrapbooks to his trademark silver-white wigs. *117 Sandusky St., (412) 237-8300, www.warhol.org.*

Duquesne Incline. It was built to haul freight and passengers up Mount Washington, and today its century-old, full restored wooden cable cars carry commuters as well as visitors. Don't miss the views from the Upper Station observation deck or one of the restaurants along Grandview Avenue. *1197 W. Carson St., (412) 381-1665, www.duquesneincline.org.*

Station Square. This 52-acre complex on the Monongahela River was once the hub of the Pittsburgh and Lake Erie Railroad. Some of the remaining boxcars have been converted into shops, and the station houses the Grand Concourse restaurant. There are also more than 40 shops and 20 restaurants, a riverboat cruise line, amusements, entertainment venues, and nightclubs—all just a 5-minute walk from downtown Pittsburgh. *125 W. Station Square Dr., (412) 261-2811, www.stationsquare.com.*

Latrobe

Steelers Training Camp. Grab your Terrible Towel and head to St. Vincent College, the summer retreat and training ground of the Pittsburgh Steelers. (Coincidentally, it's the alma mater of team co-owner Art Rooney, Jr.) The camp is open to the public, and offers Steelers history and merchandise as well as daily fan activities such as field-goal kicks and quarterback tosses. *300 Fraser Purchase Rd., (412) 432-7800, www.steelers. com/schedule-and-events.*

Mill Run

Fallingwater. Designed by Frank Lloyd Wright in 1935 for the Kaufmanns, the prominent Pittsburgh family that owned Kaufmann's department store, this house is built on cantilevers over a 30-foot waterfall, so it becomes one with its natural setting. It was used

PENNSYLVANIA

Atlas map WM-4, p. 176
Distance: 291 miles point to point.

as a summer retreat until 1963, when Edgar Kaufmann Jr. gave the home to the Western Pennsylvania Conservancy. It's the only Wright-designed house open to the public with its original furnishings, artwork, and setting intact; it's now a National Historic Landmark. (Advance tickets recommended.) *1491 Mill Run Rd., (724) 329-8501, www.fallingwater.org.*

Stoystown

Flight 93 National Memorial. On Tuesday morning, September 11, 2001, United Airlines Flight 93 was hijacked. Realizing the goal was to destroy the U.S. Capitol, the 40 passengers and crew devised a plan to crash the plane into a field before it reached Washington. The field is now home to a 2,200-acre National Park Site, where a Wall of Names honors those aboard the flight and marks a portion of the flight path. The mile-wide Field of Honor is viewable from the crash site. There's also a Visitor Center and a Learning Center. *6424 Lincoln Hwy., (814) 893-6322, www.nps.gov.*

Gettysburg

Gettysburg National Military Park and Cemetery. Portions of the Gettysburg battlefield are much as they were that fateful July day in 1863. You can explore more than 1,300 monuments along 40 miles of scenic roadways on bus tours or self-guided drives. The National Park Service Museum and Visitor Center has a huge collection of Civil War relics, interactive exhibits, a 22-minute film, and the fully restored *Gettysburg Cyclorama* mural. There's also a bookstore, a café that serves Civil War–era cuisine, a campground, and several miles of bike paths and hiking or bridle trails. The adjoining, 17-acre Gettysburg National Cemetery is the final resting place of more than 6,000 soldiers, including 3,512 from the Civil War. This is also where President Lincoln delivered his famous address. *1195 Baltimore Pike (Rte. 97), (717) 334-1124, www.nps.gov/gett.*

Duquesne Incline

Forsyth Park, Savannah

Historic Georgia

This is the perfect weekend escape for, well, anyone: couples, families, best friends, beach lovers, history buffs. Although it takes you on side trips south and east of Savannah, it centers on the city's 2.2-square-mile Historic District. Amid streets lined with 18th- and 19th-century buildings and trees draped in Spanish moss, you truly feel transported back in time.

The city that was the only one to survive General Sherman's March to the Sea was founded in 1733 and has sites dating from the Colonial and Federal periods as well as those related to the Civil War and Underground Railway. Savannah is also a bustling port, so be sure to see it from the water aboard a riverboat.

Savannah

Savannah History Museum. Housed in a converted railway station in Tricentennial Park, this museum offers a great introduction to the city's rich legacy. Exhibits highlight English settlement in 1733, the 1779 Siege of Savannah, the Civil War, the Industrial Revolution, and Savannah's arts scene. Across the street, Battlefield Memorial Park honors those who fought in the American Revolution's second-bloodiest battle. The site is also home to the Georgia State Railroad Museum and the **Savannah Children's Museum** (912/651-4292). *303 Martin Luther King, Jr. Blvd., (912) 651-6825, www.chsgeorgia.org.*

Green-Meldrim House. Among the noteworthy Historic District buildings you can tour is the 1850 Green-Meldrim House, where General William Tecumseh Sherman stayed during Union occupation on the March to the Sea. Sherman considered Savannah too pretty to burn. Instead, he sent a letter to Abraham Lincoln giving him the city as a Christmas gift in 1864. *14 W. Macon St., Madison Sq., (912) 233-3845, www. stjohnssav.org.*

Forsyth Park. The southern edge of the Historic District is home to a 30-acre park with one of Savannah's most photographed attractions—the white, two-tiered, cast-iron fountain made famous in *Midnight in the Garden of Good and Evil.* Adults love the peacefulness of the park; kids love the open space. *Drayton St., (912) 651-6610, visithistoricsavannah. com/forsyth-park.*

Telfair Museums. Founded in 1883, the South's oldest art museum has three buildings, each containing works that correspond to the era in which it was built. Telfair Academy is home to 19th- and 20th-century American and European art; the Owens-Thomas House has a collection of late 18th- to early 19th-century decorative arts and an exhibit featuring an intact urban slave quarters; and the contemporary Jepson Center has the Glass House and the Sculpture Terrace. Another highlight is Sylvia Shaw Judson's *Bird Girl,* a statue made famous on the cover of *Midnight in the Garden of Good and Evil. 121 Barnard St., (912) 790-8800, www.telfair.org.*

Pin Point

Pin Point Heritage Museum. About 11 miles southeast of downtown Savannah, Pin Point is one of the Georgia coast's few remaining traditional Gullah-Geechee communities, where residents are descendants of first-generation freed slaves. From 1926 until 1985, A.S. Varn & Son Oyster Seafood Factory was the area's main employer. Its closure threatened not only the community but also a way of life. This museum, however, helps to preserve the area's unique culture. *9924 Pin Point Ave., (912) 667-9176, www. pinpointheritagemuseum.com.*

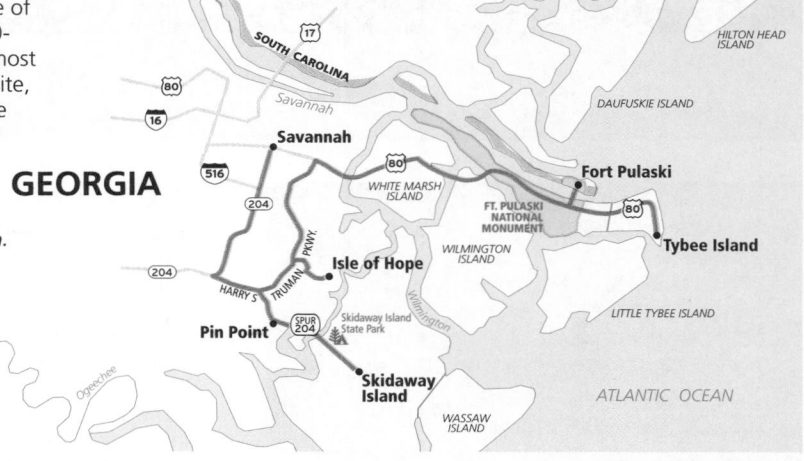

Atlas map K-13, p. 61

Distance: 45 miles point to point (i.e., Savannah to Tybee Island via sights south of the city).

Skidaway Island

Skidaway Island State Park. You can follow stretches of the Colonial Coast Birding Trail, along which more than 300 species have been spotted, through this 588-acre site about 13 miles southeast of downtown Savannah. It's also home to the 1-mile Sandpiper and 3-mile Big Ferry trails as well as a boardwalk that leads to a wildlife observation tower. An interpretive center has reference materials and ranger programs. *52 Diamond Causeway, (912) 598-2300, www.gastateparks.org/SkidawayIsland.*

Isle of Hope

Wormsloe State Historic Site. In the 1730s, colonist Noble Jones carved out an impressive plantation. Today, a 1.5-mile, oak-lined avenue leads to what's left of the house, which remained in the Jones family until 1973. Like many residences along the Georgia and South Carolina coast, it was a "tabby house," built using cement that's a mixture of sand, water, lime, wood ash, and oyster shells. The on-site museum has excavated artifacts and a short film; the Colonial Life Area often has costumed docents demonstrating period crafts and trades. *7601 Skidaway Rd., (912) 353-3023, www.gastateparks.org/Wormsloe.*

Fort Pulaski

Fort Pulaski National Monument. Although it predates the Civil War, this fort is most famous for a 30-hour 1862 bombardment that resulted in Union forces seizing it from the Confederates. The visitors center has historical exhibits, a bookstore, and a gift shop. Ranger-led walks through the fort's interior are available. *U.S. Hwy. 80 E., (912) 786-5787, www.nps.gov/fopu.*

Tybee Island

Tybee Light Station and Museum. Given its 3-mile strand of gorgeous white sand and a location just 18 miles east of Hostess City, this barrier island serves as Savannah's public beach. The island is also home to Georgia's oldest (circa 1732) and tallest lighthouse, **Tybee Light Station and Museum** (30 Meddin Ave., 912/786-5801, www. tybeelighthouse.org). Climb the tower's 178 steps for a view of the entire island. *802 1st St., (877) 344-3361, tybeeisland.com.*

Tybee Island

Ozark Mountain fall scenery

Missouri Family Fun & Fine Fiddling

The middle of Missouri offers plenty of family fun, down-home food, and lake and Ozark Mountain scenery. And, of course there's Branson, the hub for fine music—on the fiddle and other instruments. In Jefferson City, the majesty of the Missouri River and its tree-lined bluffs is captivating, and so is the capitol itself.

South of the state capital is the Lake of the Ozarks, where you can swim, paddle, fish, or just relax waterside. The region also has several caves to explore and a Civil War battlefield to tour. Highway 65 south takes you to the Tri-Lakes Area (Table Rock Lake, Lake Taneycomo, and Bull Shoals Lake) and Branson, playgrounds for the child in everyone.

Jefferson City

Missouri State Capitol & Museum. The third Missouri State Capitol on this downtown site was modeled after the U.S. Capitol, built of Missouri-quarried marble, and completed in 1917. A tour of its grounds, interior, and on-site state history museum provides a great overview of both Missouri and Jefferson City. Admission is free, and so are the 45-minute guided tours, which take place on each hour (except for noon) Monday through Saturday 9–4 and Sunday at 10, 11, 2, and 3. *201 W. Capitol Ave., (573) 751-2854 or (573) 751-4127 (tour info), mostateparks.com.*

Jefferson Landing State Historic Site. The Lohman Building, a one-time warehouse, is set up just as it would have been in the days when river boats and, later, the railroads, stopped here. The Rozier Gallery, inside the landing's Union Hotel, has rotating exhibits of memorabilia, photographs, and art. Admission to the site is free. *100 Jefferson St., (573) 751-2854, mostateparks.com.*

Missouri State Penitentiary & Museum. Before being decommissioned in 2004, this was the oldest continuously operating prison west of the Mississippi. In 1836, when it opened, the Battle of the Alamo was going on, and Andrew Jackson was in his second term. By the time Alcatraz began accepting prisoners, MSP

was 100 years old—and well on its way to infamy. Buy advance tickets for the history, ghost, and other prison tours, and be sure to visit the nearby **Missouri State Penitentiary Museum** (100 High St.), where admission is free. *115 Lafayette St., (866) 998-6998, www.missouripentours.com.*

Lake of the Ozarks Area

Lake of the Ozarks State Park & Ozark Cavern. Missouri's largest state park comprises 17,626 acres. It has 89 miles of shoreline, two swimming beaches, horseback riding, and more than 10 developed trails—one of which, the Ozarks Aquatic Trail, is designed for boaters, with 14 designated buoy stops along the shore. Take time for a guided tour of the park-operated Ozark Caverns, where a highlight is the unusual Angel Showers formation. *403 Hwy. 134, Kaiser, (573) 348-2694, mostateparks.com.*

Springfield

Fantastic Caverns. The temperature in Fantastic Caverns is a constant 60 degrees, and the trip through them is easy because all the work is done by a Jeep-drawn tram. Along the way, you'll see limestone stalactites, stalagmites, and other formations. You'll learn about cavern inhabitants, like the blind Ozarks cave fish, and past cavern uses—as a place to grow mushrooms, a fallout shelter, and a music hall. *4872 N. Farm Rd. 125, (417) 833-2010, www.fantasticcaverns.com.*

Republic

Wilson's Creek National Battlefield. The first major Civil War battle west of the Mississippi River claimed the life of Nathaniel Lyon, the first Union general to die in the conflict. Although it was considered a Confederate victory, they suffered heavy losses and were prevented from making inroads into Missouri. The land around the so-called Bloody Hill remains much as it was when the battle raged here on August 10, 1861. The visitors center has military exhibits and a well-stocked bookstore. You can take a self- or cell-phone-guided 4.9-mile driving tour, featuring 8 interpretive sites, or explore on foot along one of 5 short trails off the tour road. *6424 W. Farm Rd. 182, (417) 732-2662, ext. 227, www.nps.gov/wicr.*

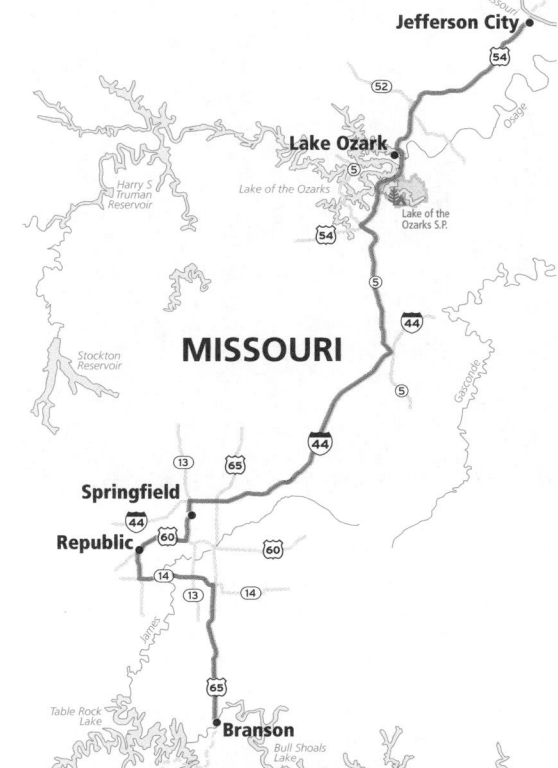

Atlas map G-14, p. 118
Distance: 210 miles point to point.

Silver Dollar City

Branson

Silver Dollar City. Folksy, 1880s-themed Silver Dollar City, 5 miles west of Branson off Highway 76, emphasizes Ozark crafts and culture. The entertainment complex has more than 40 rides; historic structures like a 19th-century homestead, school, and church; and a colony of 100 resident artisans. Affiliated with Silver Dollar City are the White Water Park, with its watery rides and slides, and the 278-foot *Branson Belle* paddle-wheeler, which sails from the shop-lined boardwalk at White River Landing, just south of Branson. *399 Silver Dollar City Pkwy., (800) 475-9370, www.silverdollarcity.com.*

Dick's Old Time 5&10. With an inventory of 50,000 items—give or take—you could explore this store for hours. Shelves are packed with toys, gifts, housewares, and hardware. If you're not a collector, you might just become one after seeing the aviation, train, sports, and other memorabilia. And it's hard to resist picking up a few sweets in the old-time candy aisle. *103 W. Main St., (417) 334-2410, dicksoldtime5and10.com.*

Showboat *Branson Belle* paddle-wheeler

Hot Springs National Park

Arkansas Springs Eternal

This trip starts and ends in towns known for their curative waters. In the hillside resort of Eureka Springs, the Victorian architecture is so well preserved that the entire downtown district is on the National Register of Historic Places. There are more than 60 springs in the town itself, including the Blue, Basin, Grotto, and Crescent.

To the south and east is Hot Springs, whose thermal waters put it on the map first as a healing center, then as a national park, and then as a gangster getaway. There's a lot of colorful history in and between these communities. And then there's all that nature along and through swatches of the vast Ozark and Ouachita national forests.

Eureka Springs

Eureka Springs Tram Tours. Narrated, 90-minute tours take you up and down the town's hilly streets lined with always-stately and often-colorful Victorian architecture. Stops include the Crescent Hotel and Grotto Spring. Tours often sell out; reserve ahead. *137 W. Van Buren St., (800) 386-8711, www. eurekaspringstramtours.com.*

Quicksilver Gallery. This two-floor shop sells works by about 120 of the more than 200 working artists, artisans, and craftspeople that call this historic town home. *73 Spring St., (479) 253-7679, quicksilvergallery.com.*

Thorncrown Chapel. The gabled, 48-foot-high, sky-lighted roof seems to balance atop a frame of pine columns and latticework beams. The walls are made of glass—6,000 square feet of it. The result is a soaring,

Fort Smith

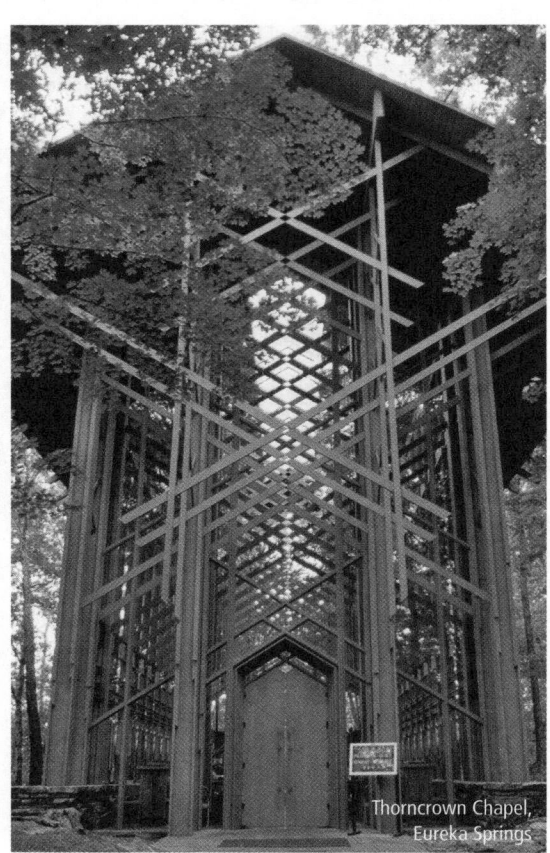

Thorncrown Chapel, Eureka Springs

light-filled Ozark Gothic building that's perfectly at home amid the surrounding hardwood forest. *12968 Hwy. 62 W., (479) 253-7401, www.thorncrown.com.*

Bentonville

Crystal Bridges Museum of American Art. Alice Walton, longtime art collector and daughter of the Walmart founder, was instrumental in establishing this truly special place. The galleries—filled with works by the likes of Winslow Homer, Georgia O'Keeffe, and Edward Hopper—are as compelling as the wooded and watery views through the window-lined corridors. In addition to taking in the art, you can hike or bike the 120-acre site along seven short trails. *600 Museum Way, (479) 418-5700, crystalbridges.org.*

Fort Smith

Fort Smith National Historic Site. Established in 1817 to protect the area's few settlers, Fort Smith was briefly abandoned and later rebuilt to serve as a military supply depot. In 1872, it was transformed from fort to court as an attempt instill order in what was still a rough-and-tumble, far western outpost. Exhibits in restored buildings cover the military; area outlaws; the U.S. Marshal Service; and the Trail of Tears, an 1838–39 forced march west during which thousands of Native Americans died. Be sure to see the courthouse's basement jail; the reproduction gallows; and the displays of handcuffs, leg irons, and guns—all testaments to life on the edge of lawlessness. *301 Parker Ave., (479) 783-3961, www.nps.gov/fosm.*

Atlas map B-3, p. 22
Distance: 280 miles point to point.

Fort Smith Museum of History. Fascinating exhibits take you from Fort Smith's days as a frontier town in Indian Territory to its post–Civil War federal-court period and beyond. Highlights include a re-creation of the courtroom presided over by Judge Isaac C. Parker (aka the Hanging Judge) and a 1920s drugstore with a working soda fountain. *320 Rogers Ave., (479) 783-7841, www.fortsmithmuseum.com.*

Hot Springs

Hot Springs National Park. The resort community of Hot Springs has been a national park since 1921. Several of the opulent bathhouses along Central Avenue (aka Bathhouse Row) have been restored, including the Fordyce which contains a park visitors center and museum. To take the waters yourself, head to the Buckstaff—the only functioning bathhouse open within the national park—or the Quapaw Bath & Spa. *369 Central Ave., (501) 620-6715, www.nps.gov/hosp.*

The Gangster Museum of America. Ah, the good old bad old days, when gambling and booze were illegal—but that didn't stop anyone from enjoying them—and Hot Springs was a hot attraction for ne'er-do-wells. Memorabilia, photographs, and recorded accounts in exhibits here highlight many of them, including Al Capone. *510 Central Ave., (501) 318-1717, www.tgmoa.com.*

Fox Pass Pottery. This studio and shop, founded in 1973, features pieces by Jim and Barbara Larkin. He works at the potter's wheel, while she hand-builds her pieces. Although they're known for their unique glazes, the wood-fired salt kiln they use can create a pleasing finish without a traditionally applied glaze. *379 Fox Pass Cutoff, (501) 623-9906, foxpasspottery.com.*

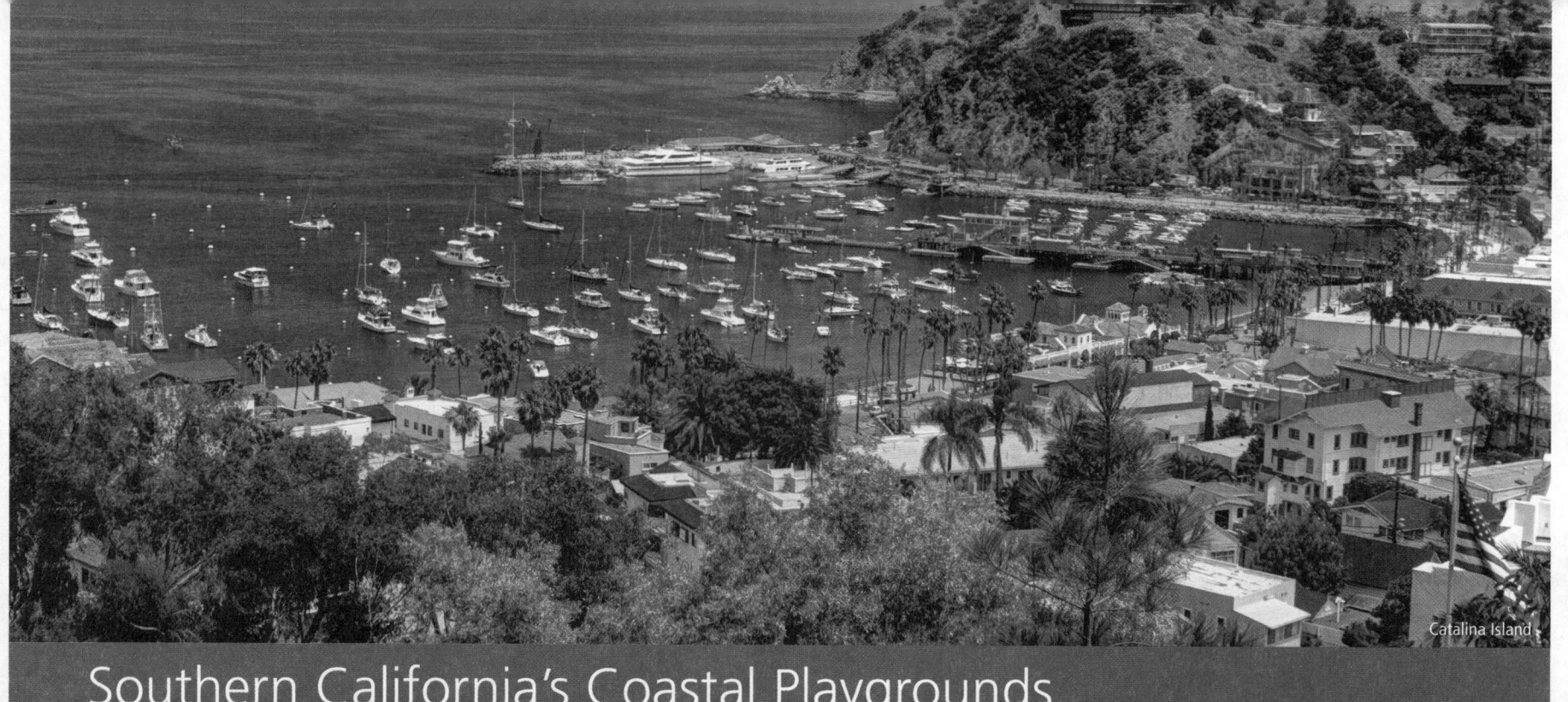
Catalina Island

Southern California's Coastal Playgrounds

South of Los Angeles, the California coast is a veritable playground of natural and man-made attractions. This trip launches in Anaheim, home to Disney's first theme park, and continues south along the Pacific Coast Highway. It takes you through the breezy port of Long Beach and into ritzy surf towns like Huntington Beach.

Farther south, you'll motor through state parks, perhaps stopping at the mission in San Juan Capistrano (to uncover regional history) or Legoland (to find your inner child). You'll end the drive in San Diego, a large, culturally rich beach city with fantastic weather all year, a buzzing Old Town, and one of the country's best zoos.

Huntington Beach

Huntington City Beach. Known for its dependable surf, thin blonde sand, and miles of uninterrupted coastline, this iconic beach hosts its share of surf and volleyball contests year round. Take a surf lesson from one of the instructors hanging out by the pier, shop for souvenirs at Kite Connection, or grab a cocktail on the patio of the Shorebreak Hotel. *Hwy. 1 and 2nd St., (714) 969-3492, www.surfcityusa.com.*

San Juan Capistrano

Mission San Juan Capistrano. Founded in 1775, this mission brought religious settlers to San Juan Capistrano. After almost a century of decay, Catholic conservationists refurbished the original Great Stone Church, Serra Chapel, and acres of lush grounds. You can picnic in the gardens, or join activities like fish feeding, basket weaving, gold panning, and crafting. *26801 Ortega Hwy., (949) 234-1300, www.missionsjc.com.*

CALIFORNIA

Atlas map SK-11, p. 37
Distance: 132 miles point to point.

Globe Theater, a carousel, gardens, and trails. Pick up a Museum Pass for entry to multiple sites. *2001 Pan American Plaza, (619) 234-8291, www.sandiegoairandspace.org.*

San Diego Zoo. Considered by many to be the country's finest zoo, this spectacular 100-acre destination houses more than 3,700 animals from more than 650 species—including the largest collection of koalas outside of Australia and a Giant Panda from China. *2920 Zoo Dr., (619) 231-1515, zoo.sandiegozoo.org.*

Old Town San Diego State Historic Park. Stroll through California's first Spanish settlement, where original structures still stand and others have been restored. Costumed volunteers depict the history and culture and give cooking demonstrations. Most people stroll through the park and end up exploring the shops, restaurants, art galleries, and museums of nearby Old Town. *San Diego Ave. at Twiggs St., (619) 220-5422, www.parks.ca.gov.*

Torrey Pines State Natural Reserve & Beach. Oceanfront bluffs at this 2,000-acre reserve are dotted with wildflowers as well as fine examples of one of the rarest types of pine on the planet. Trails weave down to quiet beaches along sandstone shelves and offer peeks of gray whales migrating between Mexico and Alaska. *12600 N. Torrey Pines Rd., (858) 755-2063, torreypine.org.*

Sunset in San Clemente

Anaheim

Disneyland. Disneyland's Magic Kingdom, the first theme park of its kind, has staples like It's a Small World and Jungle Cruise for the whole family and thrill rides like Space Mountain and Matterhorn for older visitors. Then there are live performances, character breakfasts, princess makeovers, light shows, parades, and fireworks. *1313 S. Harbor Blvd., (714) 781-4000, disneyland.disney.go.com.*

Long Beach

Queen Mary. In service as an ocean liner from the 1930s to the '60s, the *Queen Mary* now sits in Long Beach harbor, attracting thousands of guests each year to its museum, restaurants, shops, and hotel rooms. Tour the historic cruise ship while learning all about the restoration project that landed it on the National Register of Historic Places. *1126 Queens Hwy., (877) 342-0738, www.queenmary.com.*

Catalina Island Ferry. Hop on an express ferry—you might see dolphins and whales in winter—to arrive at majestic Catalina Island in about an hour. Just 22 miles from the mainland, it seems worlds away with its bird sanctuaries, active bison population, and pristine beaches. (Reservations recommended.) *320 Golden Shore, (800) 481-3470, catalinaexpress.com.*

San Clemente

San Clemente State Beach. Near the south end of San Clemente, this camping beach is popular with surfboarders and body surfers. There are a few notable surf breaks in the park, including a nice easy beach break right in front of the campground. More advanced surfers should walk about 15 minutes south of the parking area to Cottons, a local favorite. *225 Avenida Califia, (949) 492-3156, www.parks.ca.gov.*

Carlsbad

Legoland California Resort. More than 60 million Lego bricks are artfully arranged throughout both the park and the resort. You'll also find over 60 rides as well as water adventures, an aquarium, and Lego Minilands depicting everything from *Star Wars* scenes to cities like Las Vegas. Weekend fireworks displays add to the dazzle. *One Legoland Dr., (760) 918-5346, california.legoland.com.*

San Diego

San Diego Air and Space Museum. Highlights here include full-scale mock-ups of NASA spacecraft and nearly 70 flying machines, including replicas of Wright gliders from 1901 and 1902. It's in Balboa Park, also home to the San Diego Museum of Art, the Old

Selected National Park Service locations

- Acadia National Park, C-20
- Arches National Park, G-6
- Badlands National Park, E-9
- Big Bend National Park, L-8
- Biscayne National Park, M-18
- Bryce Canyon National Park, G-5
- Canyonlands National Park, G-6
- Capitol Reef National Park, G-5
- Carlsbad Caverns National Park, J-7
- Channel Islands National Park, H-1
- Congaree National Park, I-17
- Crater Lake National Park, D-2
- Cuyahoga Valley National Park, F-16
- Death Valley National Park, G-3
- Denali National Park, L-4
- Dry Tortugas National Park, M-17
- Everglades National Park, M-17
- Glacier Bay National Park, M-5
- Glen Canyon National Recreation Area, G-5
- Grand Canyon National Park, H-4
- Grand Teton National Park, E-6
- Great Sand Dunes Nat'l Park & Pres., H-7
- Great Smoky Mountains Nat'l Park, H-15
- Guadalupe Mountains National Park, J-7

Land area:	Population:	Largest city:
3,531,905 sq. mi.	308,745,538	New York, 8,175,133

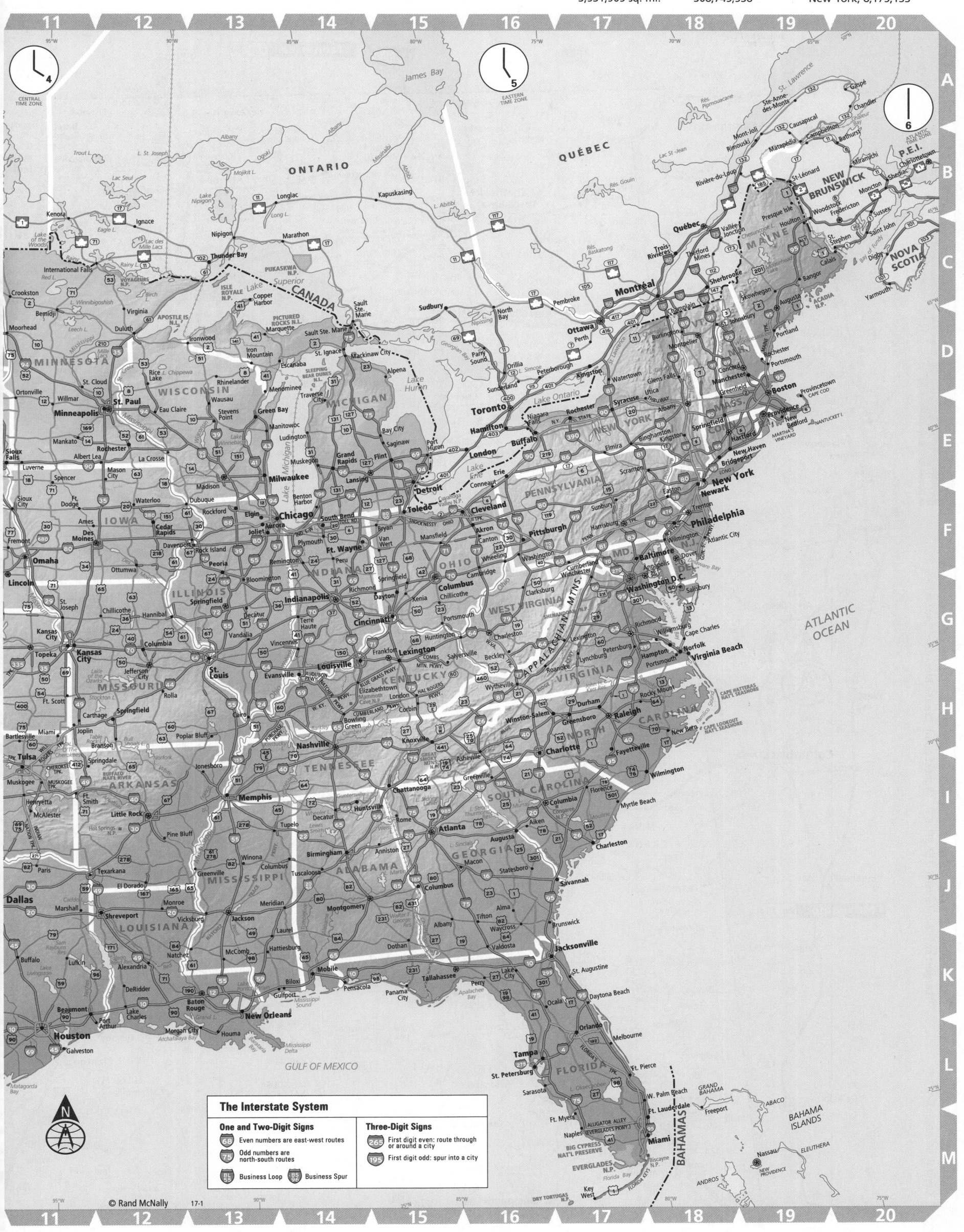

- Haleakalā National Park, K-2
- Hawai'i Volcanoes National Park, L-3
- Hot Springs National Park, I-12
- Isle Royale National Park, C-13
- Kings Canyon National Park, G-2
- Lake Mead National Recreation Area, H-4

- Lassen Volcanic National Park, E-2
- Mammoth Cave National Park, H-14
- Mesa Verde National Park, H-6
- Mount Rainier National Park, B-3
- North Cascades National Park, B-4
- Olympic National Park, B-3

- Petrified Forest National Park, I-5
- Redwood National Park, D-1
- Rocky Mountain National Park, F-7
- Sequoia National Park, G-2
- Shenandoah National Park, G-17
- Theodore Roosevelt National Park, D-8

- Voyageurs National Park, C-12
- Waterton-Glacier Int'l Peace Park, B-5
- Wind Cave National Park, E-8
- Yellowstone National Park, D-6
- Yosemite National Park, F-2
- Zion National Park, G-5

The Interstate System

One and Two-Digit Signs
- Even numbers are east-west routes
- Odd numbers are north-south routes
- Business Loop
- Business Spur

Three-Digit Signs
- First digit even: route through or around a city
- First digit odd: spur into a city

© Rand McNally 17-1

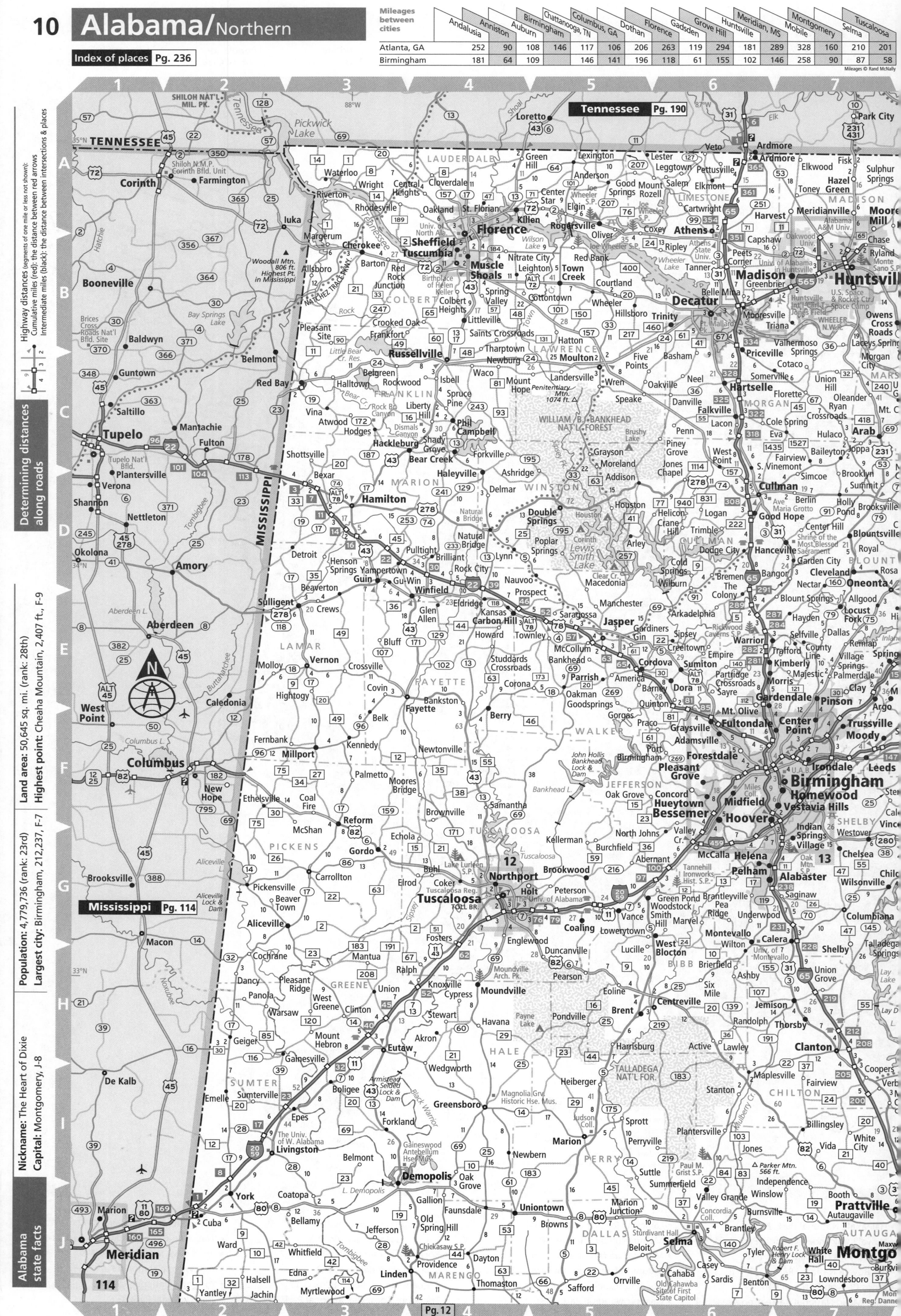

Mileages between cities	Andalusia	Anniston	Auburn	Birmingham	Chattanooga, TN	Columbus, GA	Dothan	Florence	Gadsden	Grove Hill	Huntsville	Meridian, MS	Mobile	Montgomery	Selma	Tuscaloosa
Chattanooga, TN	322	119	221	146		219	319	166	89	300	102	291	399	232	228	203
Dothan	74	207	118	196	319	99		311	252	169	294	253	196	103	148	210

continued p. 12

Mileages by Rand McNally

Total mileages through Alabama

10 66 miles   59 241 miles
26 215 miles   65 367 miles

More mileages at www.randmcnally.com/MC

Huntsville

Florence

Toll Road Information: (all use FreedomPass)
Foley Beach Expressway (Baldwin Co.): (251) 968-3415; www.beachexpress.com
Montgomery Expressway (Montgomery): (334) 290-2002; www.montgomeryexpressway.com
Tuscaloosa By-Pass (Tuscaloosa): (205) 752-2003; www.tuscaloosabypass.com

Road Conditions & Construction: (888) 588-2848
www.dot.state.al.us
alitsweb2.dot.state.al.us/RoadConditions

Tourism Information: Alabama Tourism
(800) 252-2262, (334) 242-4169
www.alabama.travel

Travel planning & on-the-road resources

© Rand McNally

One inch represents approx. 15 miles

Georgia Pg. 58

Pg. 13

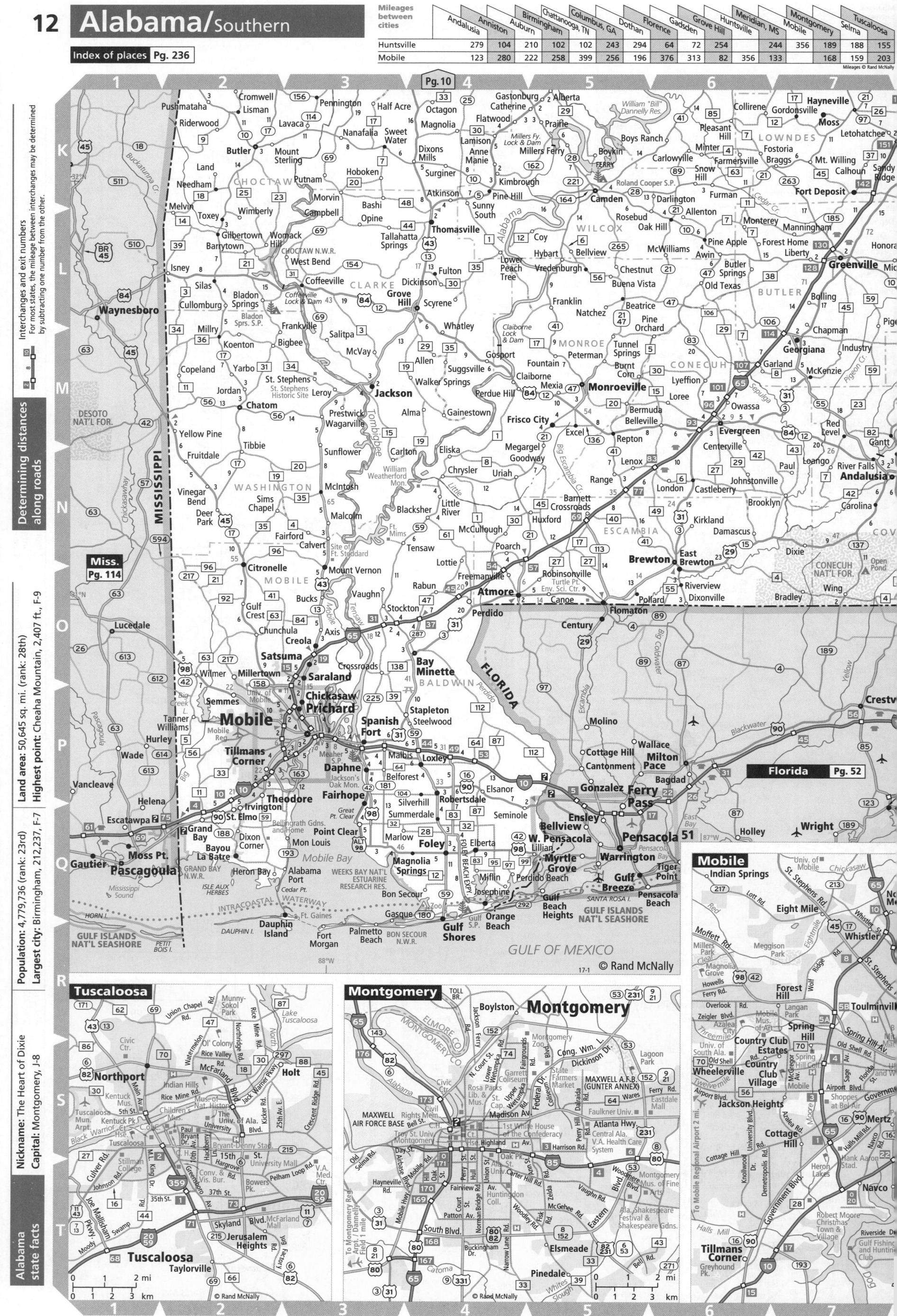

Mileages between cities	Andalusia	Anniston	Auburn	Birmingham	Chattanooga, TN	Columbus, GA	Dothan	Florence	Gadsden	Grove Hill	Huntsville	Meridian, MS	Mobile	Montgomery	Selma	Tuscaloosa
Montgomery	91	110	54	90	232	87	103	205	148	134	189	153	168		50	104
Tuscaloosa	194	118	159	58	203	192	210	123	118	121	155	93	203	104	75	

Mileages by Rand McNally

Total mileages through Alabama
More mileages at www.randmcnally.com/MC

[10] 66 miles [59] 241 miles
[20] 215 miles [65] 367 miles

One inch represents approx. 15 miles
0   5   10   15   20 mi
0   5 10 15 20 25 30 km

Georgia Pg. 58

Toll Road Information:
Foley Beach Expressway (Baldwin Co.): (251) 968-3415; www.beachexpress.com
Montgomery Expressway (Montgomery): (334) 290-2002; www.montgomeryexpressway.com
(all use FreedomePass) Tuscaloosa By-Pass (Tuscaloosa): (205) 752-2003; www.tuscaloosabypass.com

Road Conditions & Construction:
(888) 588-2848
www.dot.state.al.us
alitsweb2.dot.state.al.us/RoadConditions

Tourism Information:
Alabama Tourism
(800) 252-2262, (334) 242-4169
www.alabama.travel

Travel planning & on-the-road resources

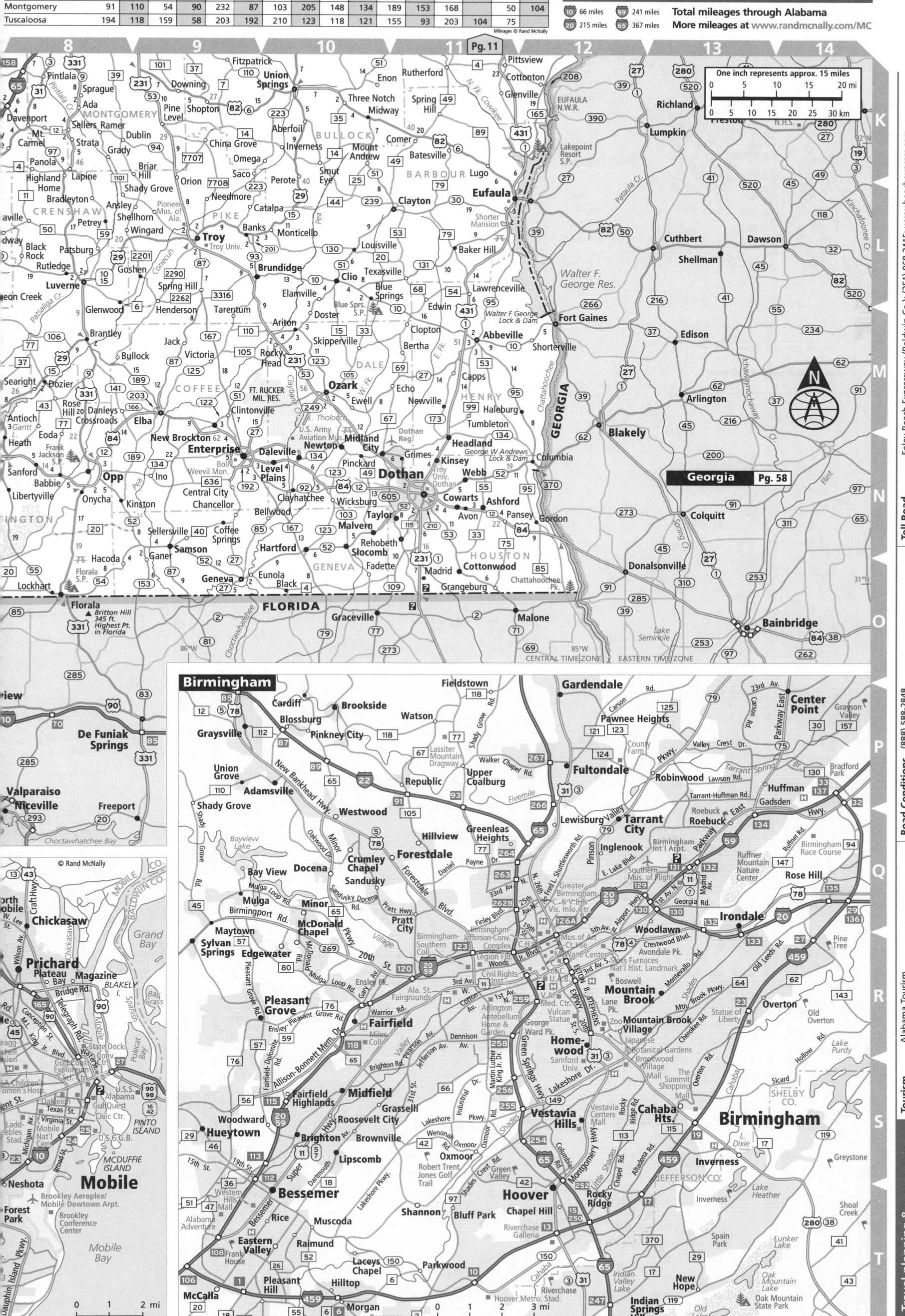

Birmingham

Mobile

© Rand McNally

Index of places **Pg. 236**

Mileages between cities

	Anchorage	Denali N.P.	Fairbanks	Haines	Homer	Prince Rupert, BC	Tok	Valdez		Anchorage	Denali N.P.	Fairbanks	Haines	Homer	Prince Rupert, BC	Tok	Valdez
Anchorage		236	358	756	221	1557	317	297	Haines	756	762	640		975	919	438	691
Fairbanks	358	122		640	578	1441	202	362	Homer	221	457	578	975		1776	537	277

Mileages © Rand McNally

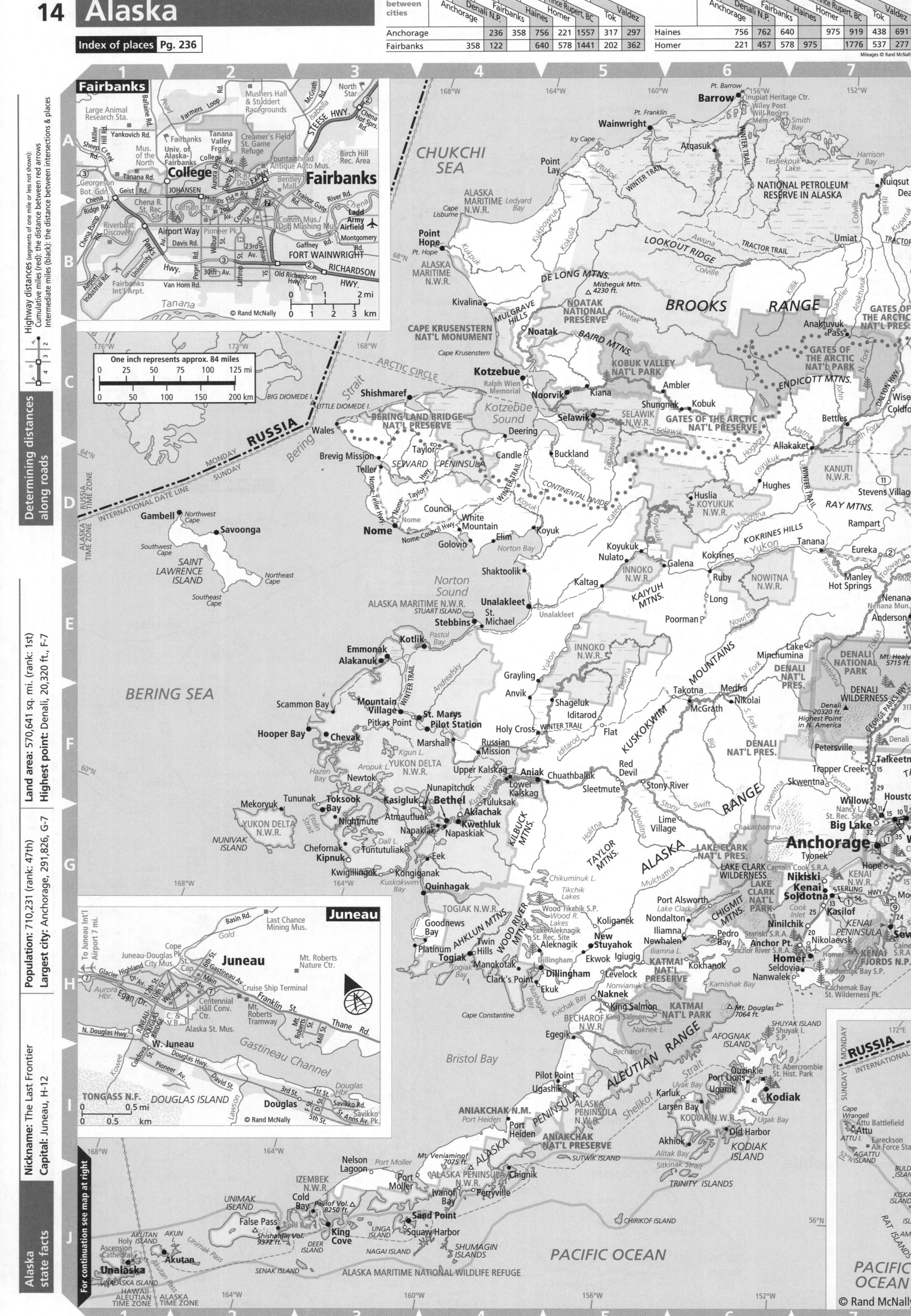

Fairbanks (inset map)

© Rand McNally

Juneau (inset map)

© Rand McNally

One inch represents approx. 84 miles

Highway distances (segments of one mile or less are not shown)
Cumulative miles (red): the distance between red arrows
Intermediate miles (black); the distance between intersections & places

Determining distances along roads

Nickname: The Last Frontier
Capital: Juneau, H-12
Population: 710,231 (rank: 47th)
Largest city: Anchorage, 291,826, G-7
Land area: 570,641 sq. mi. (rank: 1st)
Highest point: Denali, 20,320 ft., F-7

Alaska state facts

For continuation see map at right

© Rand McNally

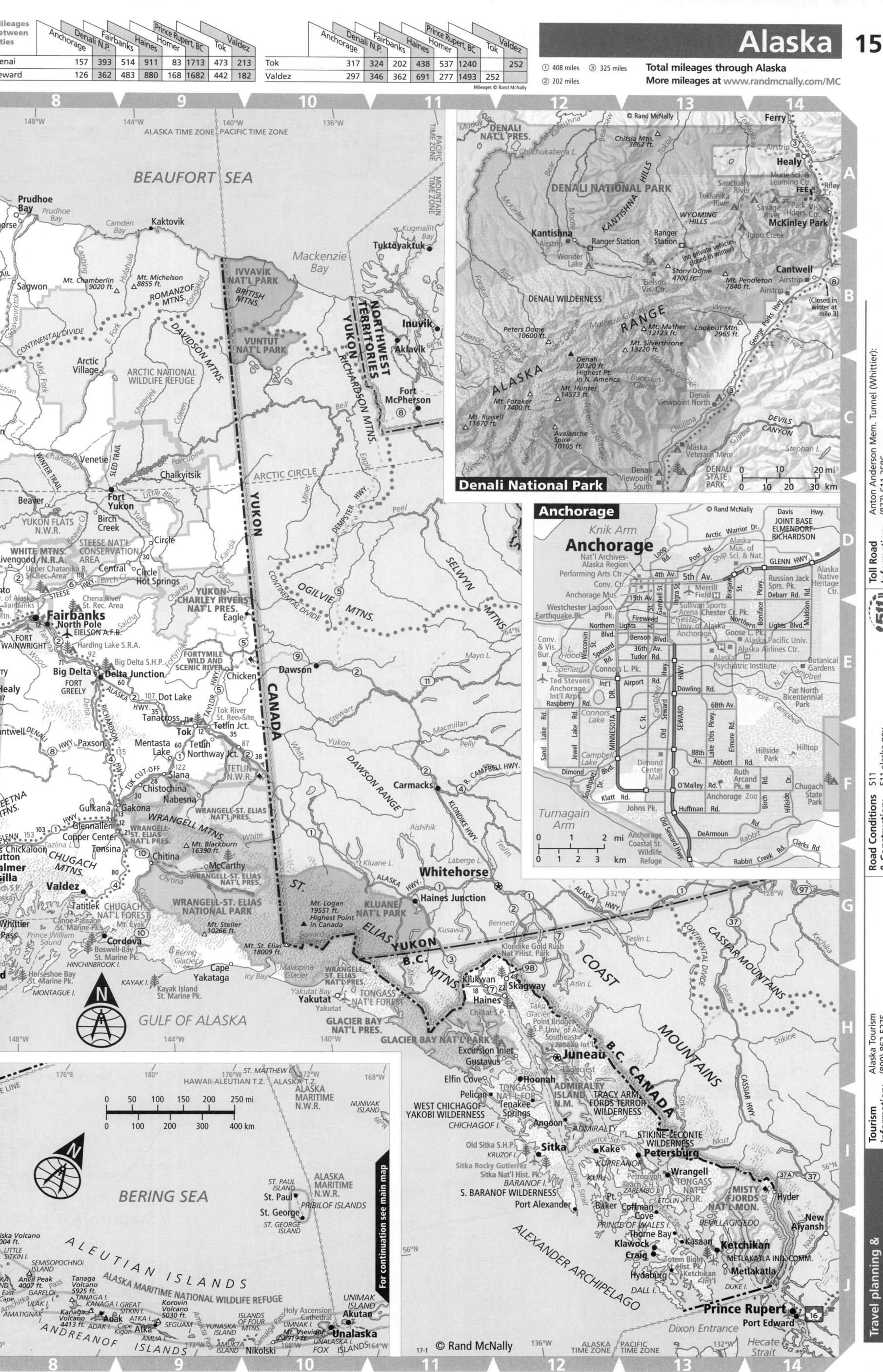

Mileages between cities	Anchorage	Denali N.P.	Fairbanks	Haines	Homer	Prince Rupert, BC	Tok	Valdez		Anchorage	Denali N.P.	Fairbanks	Haines	Homer	Prince Rupert, BC	Tok	Valdez
Kenai	157	393	514	911	83	1713	473	213	Tok	317	324	202	438	537	1240		252
Seward	126	362	483	880	168	1682	442	182	Valdez	297	346	362	691	277	1493	252	

Mileages © Rand McNally

① 408 miles ③ 325 miles
② 202 miles

Total mileages through Alaska
More mileages at www.randmcnally.com/MC

Denali National Park

Anchorage

Travel planning & on-the-road resources

Tourism Information: Alaska Tourism (800) 862-5275 www.travelalaska.com

Road Conditions & Construction: 511 511.alaska.gov www.dot.state.ak.us

Toll Road Information: Anton Anderson Mem. Tunnel (Whittier): (877) 611-2586 www.dot.state.ak.us/creg/whittiertunnel/index.shtml

© Rand McNally

Mileages between cities	Casa Grande	Chinle	Eagar	Flagstaff	Gallup, NM	Grand Canyon	Holbrook	Kingman	Lake Havasu City	Las Vegas, NV	Lordsburg, NM	Nogales	Page	Phoenix	Tucson	Yuma
Flagstaff	191	213	176		185	79	90	146	204	250	374	321	133	139	255	318
Holbrook	220	123	86	90	94	167		237	295	340	264	304	214	230	238	409

Mileages © Rand McNally

Arizona state facts

Nickname: The Grand Canyon State

Capital: Phoenix; J-7

Population: 6,392,017 (rank: 16th)

Largest city: Phoenix, 1,445,632, J-7

Land area: 113,594 sq. mi. (rank: 6th)

Highest point: Humphreys Peak, 12,633 ft., E-8

Determining distances along roads

Highway distances (segments of one mile or less not shown):
Cumulative miles (red): the distance between red arrows
Intermediate miles (black): the distance between intersections & places

One inch represents approximately 20 miles
0 10 20 30 mi
0 10 20 30 40 km

Nevada **Pg. 130**

Utah **Pg. 206**

California **Pg. 26**

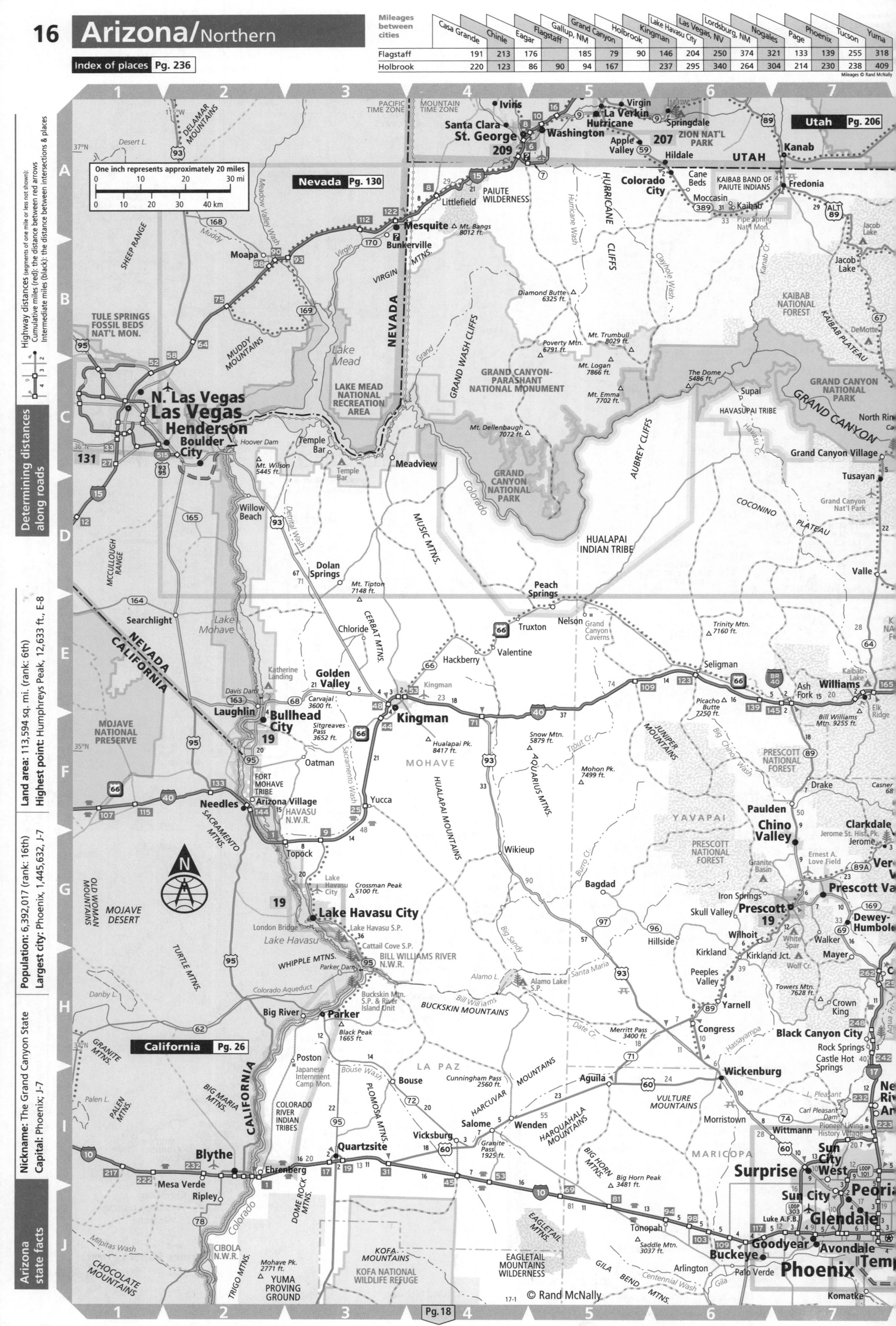

© Rand McNally

Pg. 18

17-1

Mileages between cities	Casa Grande	Chinle	Eagar	Flagstaff	Gallup, NM	Grand Canyon	Holbrook	Kingman	Lake Havasu City	Las Vegas, NV	Lordsburg, NM	Nogales	Page	Phoenix	Tucson	Yuma
Las Vegas, NV	336	463	427	250	435	275	340	104	152		558	467	271	285	401	292
Page	324	204	301	133	255	137	214	281	340	271	499	455		275	390	453

Mileages © Rand McNally

continued p. 18

Total mileages through Arizona

8	178 miles	17	146 miles
10	392 miles	40	359 miles

More mileages at www.randmcnally.com/MC

No toll roads

Toll Road Information: 511

Road Conditions & Construction: 511, (888) 411-7623 www.az511.com www.azdot.gov

Tourism Information: Arizona Office of Tourism (866) 275-5816, (602) 364-3700 www.arizonaguide.com

Travel planning & on-the-road resources

Colo. Pg. 42

N.M. Pg. 138

Pg. 19

Index of places Pg. 236

Mileages between cities

	Casa Grande	Chinle	Eagar	Flagstaff	Gallup, NM	Grand Canyon	Holbrook	Kingman	Lake Havasu City	Las Vegas, NV	Lordsburg, NM	Nogales	Page	Phoenix	Tucson	Yuma
Phoenix	48	353	226	139	324	218	230	182	198	285	268	179	275		116	181
Prescott	148	306	270	93	278	126	184	148	206	251	368	278	227	97	213	214

Interchanges and exit numbers
For most states, the mileage between interchanges may be determined by subtracting one number from the other.

Determining distances along roads

Nickname: The Grand Canyon State
Capital: Phoenix, J-7
Population: 6,392,017 (rank: 16th)
Largest city: Phoenix, 1,445,632, J-7
Land area: 113,594 sq. mi. (rank: 6th)
Highest point: Humphreys Peak, 12,633 ft., E-8

Arizona state facts

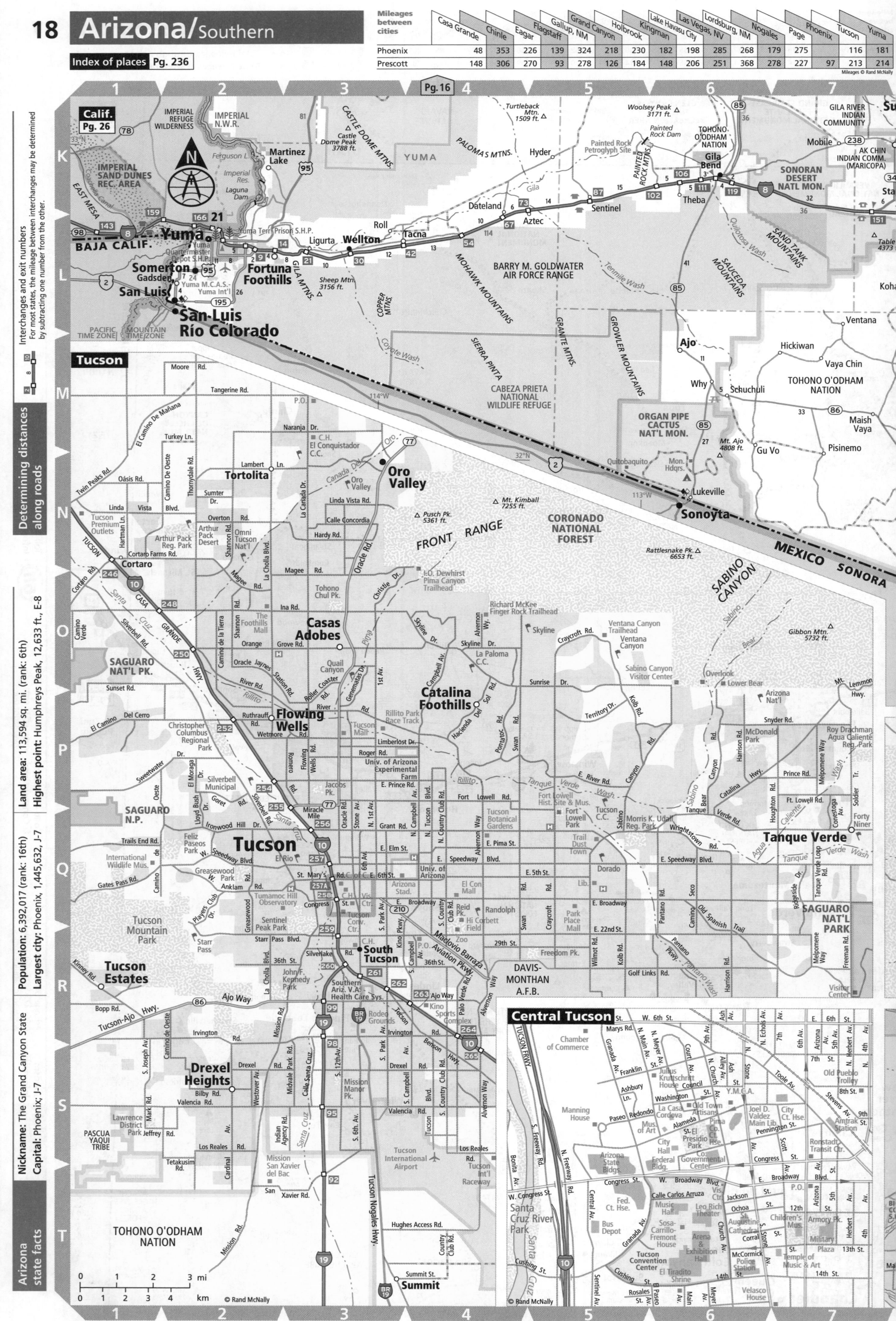

Mileages between cities

	Casa Grande	Chinle	Eagar	Flagstaff	Gallup, NM	Grand Canyon	Holbrook	Kingman	Lake Havasu City	Las Vegas, NV	Lordsburg, NM	Nogales	Page	Phoenix	Tucson	Yuma
Tucson	66	361	238	255	333	334	238	297	314	401	156	66	390	116		236
Yuma	172	532	399	318	502	397	409	213	155	292	392	301	453	181	236	

Total mileages through Arizona

8	178 miles	17	146 miles
10	392 miles	40	359 miles

More mileages at www.randmcnally.com/MC

© Rand McNally

One inch represents approximately 20 miles

0   10   20   30 mi
0   10   20   30   40 km

I-19 uses metric mileposts. Exit numbers are in kilometers. On this map, distances along I-19 are shown in miles.

Prescott

Flagstaff

Bullhead City

Lake Havasu City

Sierra Vista

No toll roads

Toll Road Information:

511

511, (888) 411-7623
www.az511.com
www.azdot.gov

Road Conditions & Construction:

Arizona Office of Tourism
(866) 275-5816, (602) 364-3700
www.arizonaguide.com

Tourism Information:

Travel planning & on-the-road resources

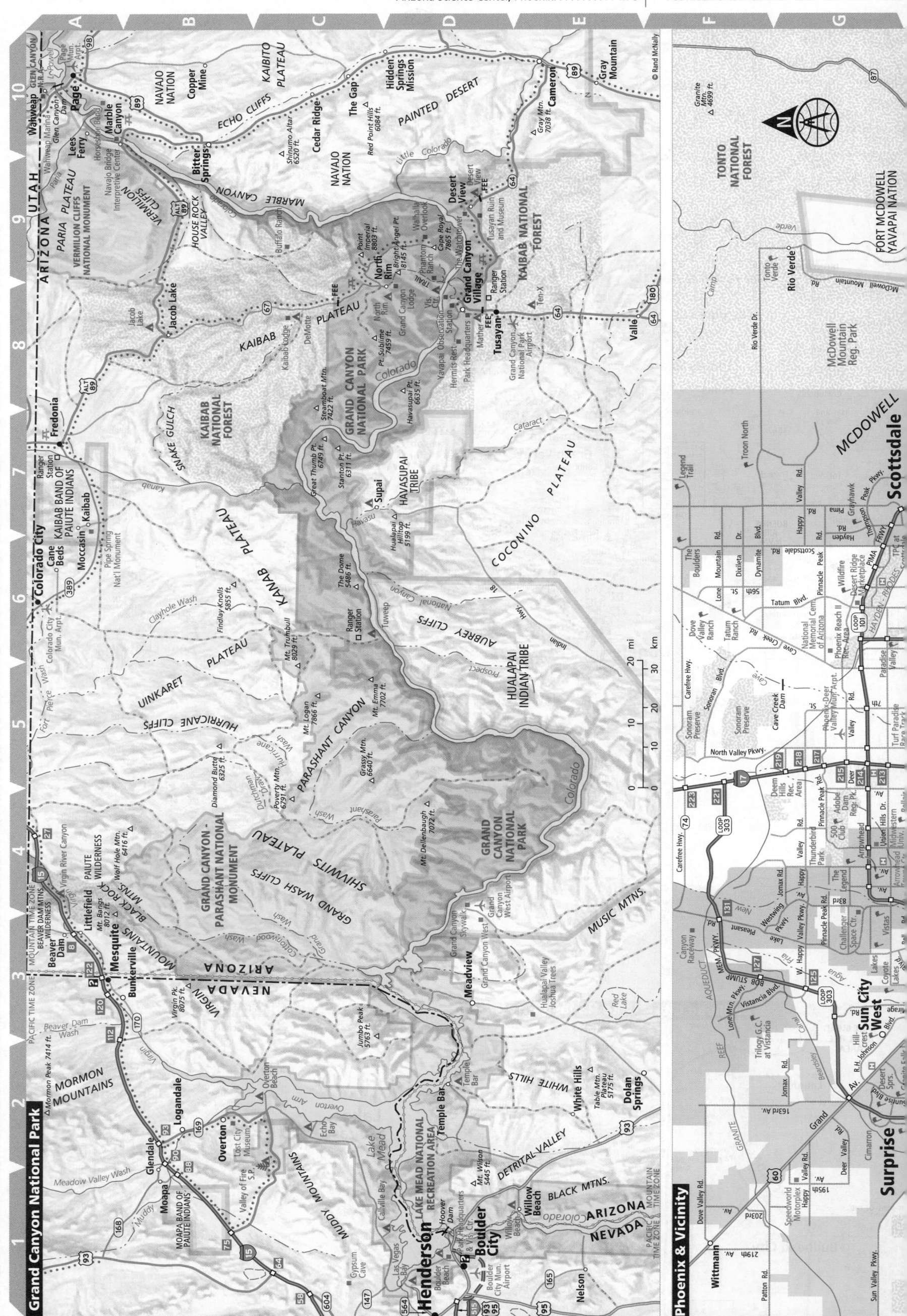

Sights to see

- Phoenix Art Museum, Phoenix L-2
- Taliesin West, Scottsdale H-7
- Tusayan Ruin and Museum, Grand Canyon National Park D-9
- Yavapai Observation Station, Grand Canyon National Park D-8
- Yuma Territorial Prison State Historic Park, Yuma L-6

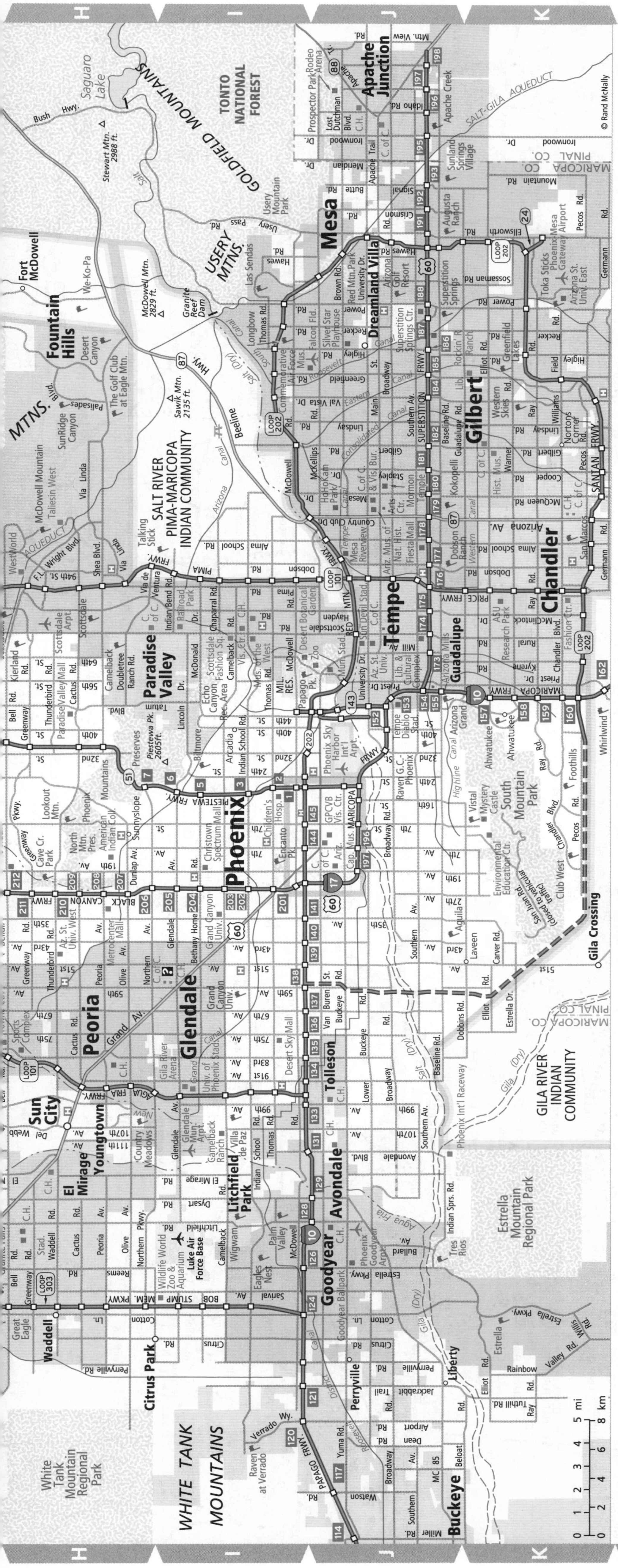
Phoenix
Mesa
Tempe
Chandler
Gilbert
Glendale
Scottsdale
© Rand McNally

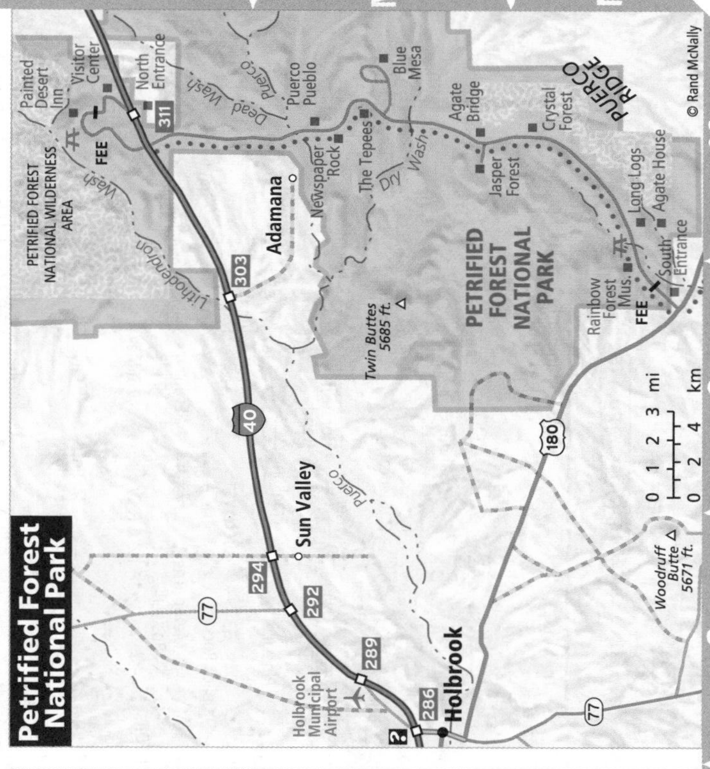
Petrified Forest National Park
Holbrook
© Rand McNally

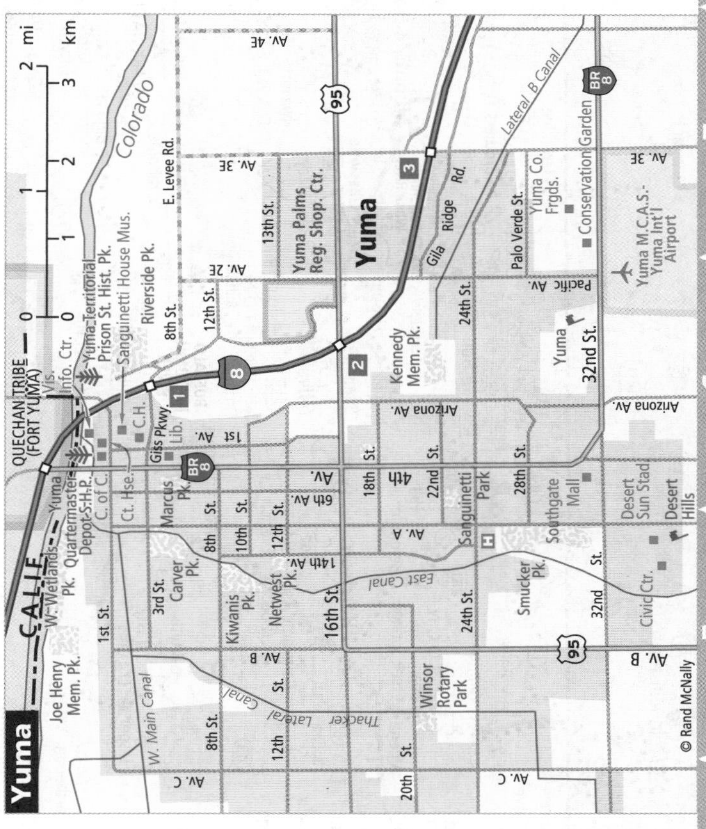
Yuma
© Rand McNally

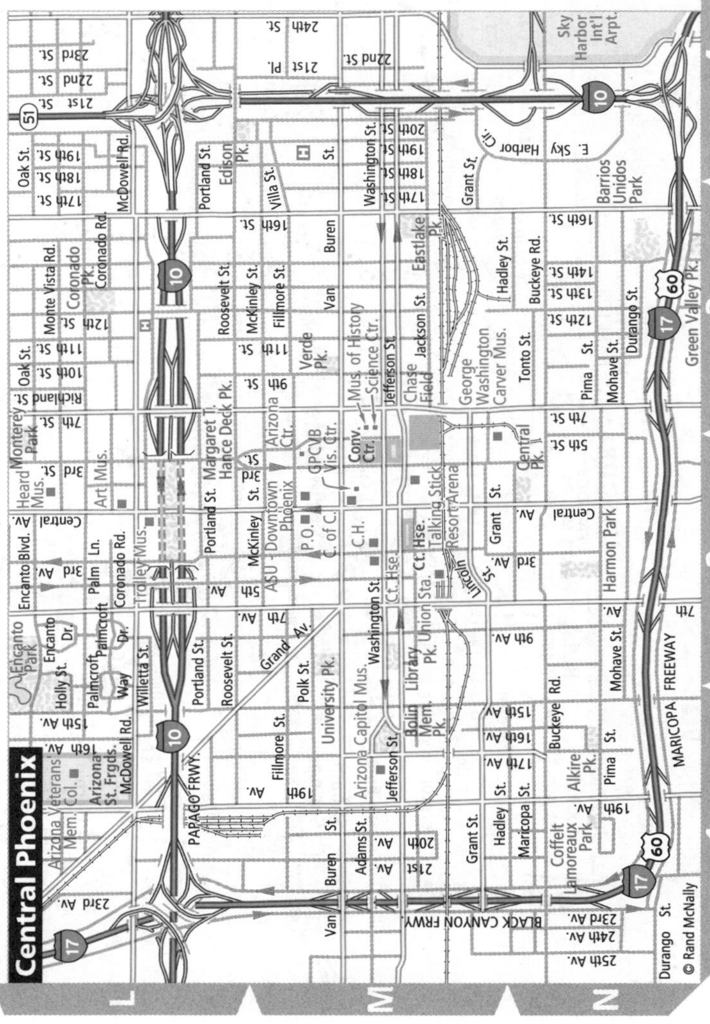
Central Phoenix
© Rand McNally

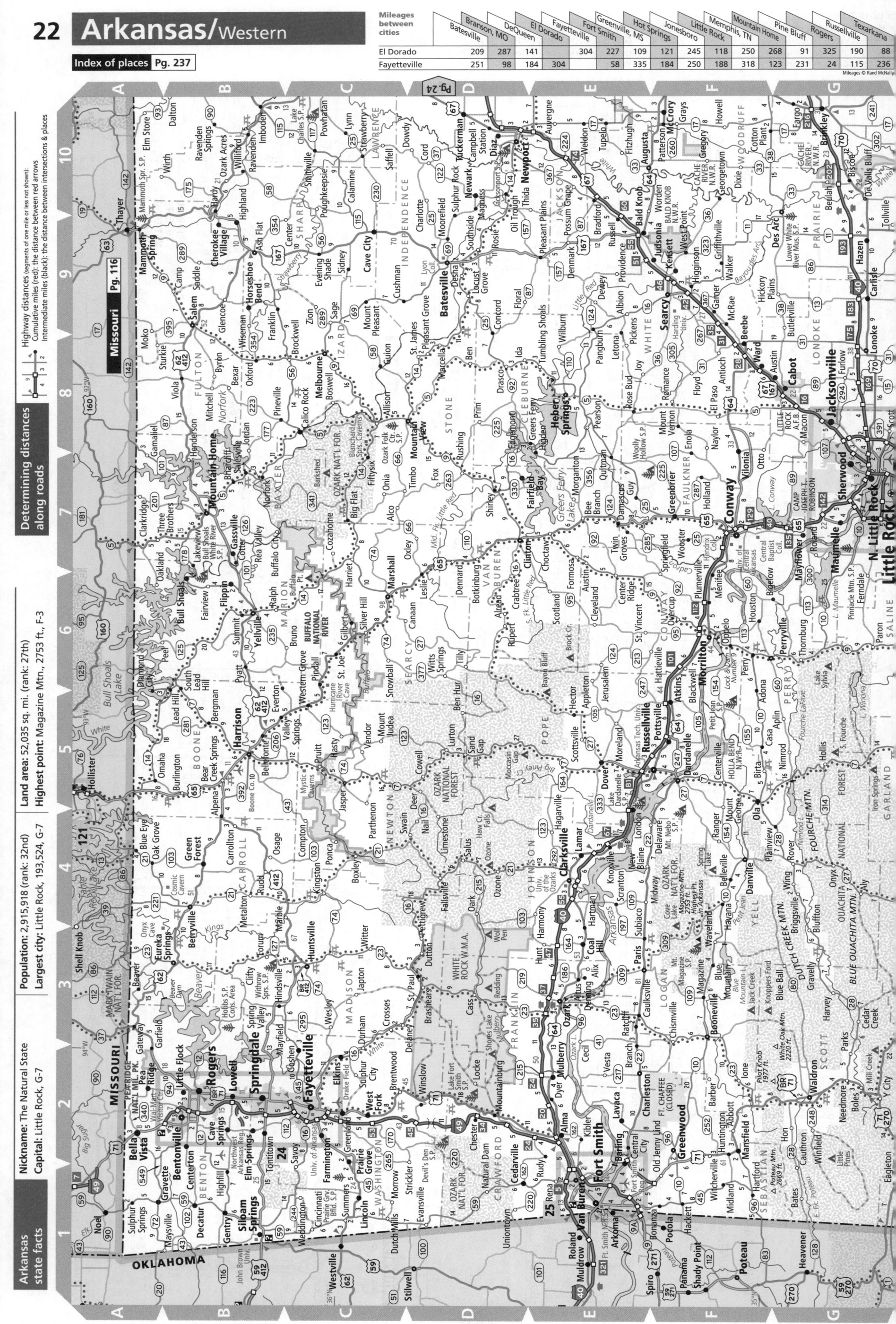

Mileages between cities	Batesville	Branson, MO	DeQueen	El Dorado	Fayetteville	Fort Smith	Greenville, MS	Hot Springs	Jonesboro	Little Rock	Memphis, TN	Mountain Home	Pine Bluff	Rogers	Russellville	Texarkana
El Dorado	209	287	141		304	227	109	121	245	118	250	268	91	325	190	88
Fayetteville	251	98	184	304		58	335	184	250	188	318	123	231	24	115	236

Mileages © Rand McNally

Arkansas state facts

Nickname: The Natural State
Capital: Little Rock, G-7

Population: 2,915,918 (rank: 32nd)
Largest city: Little Rock, G-7

Land area: 52,035 sq. mi. (rank: 27th)
Highest point: Magazine Mtn., 2753 ft., F-3

Determining distances along roads

Highway distances (segments of one mile or less not shown):
Cumulative miles (red): the distance between red arrows
Intermediate miles (black): the distance between intersections & places

Mileages between cities	Batesville	Branson, MO	DeQueen	El Dorado	Fayetteville	Fort Smith	Greenville, MS	Hot Springs	Jonesboro	Little Rock	Memphis, TN	Mountain Home	Pine Bluff	Rogers	Russellville	Texarkana	continued p. 24
Fort Smith	219	158	130	227	58		304	130	261	158	286	187	199	81	84	182	
Jonesboro	68	203	272	245	250	261	219	182		130	70	126	171	253	173	270	

Mileages by Rand McNally

30 143 miles	55 72 miles	**Total mileages through Arkansas**
40 284 miles	65 309 miles	**More mileages at** www.randmcnally.com/MC

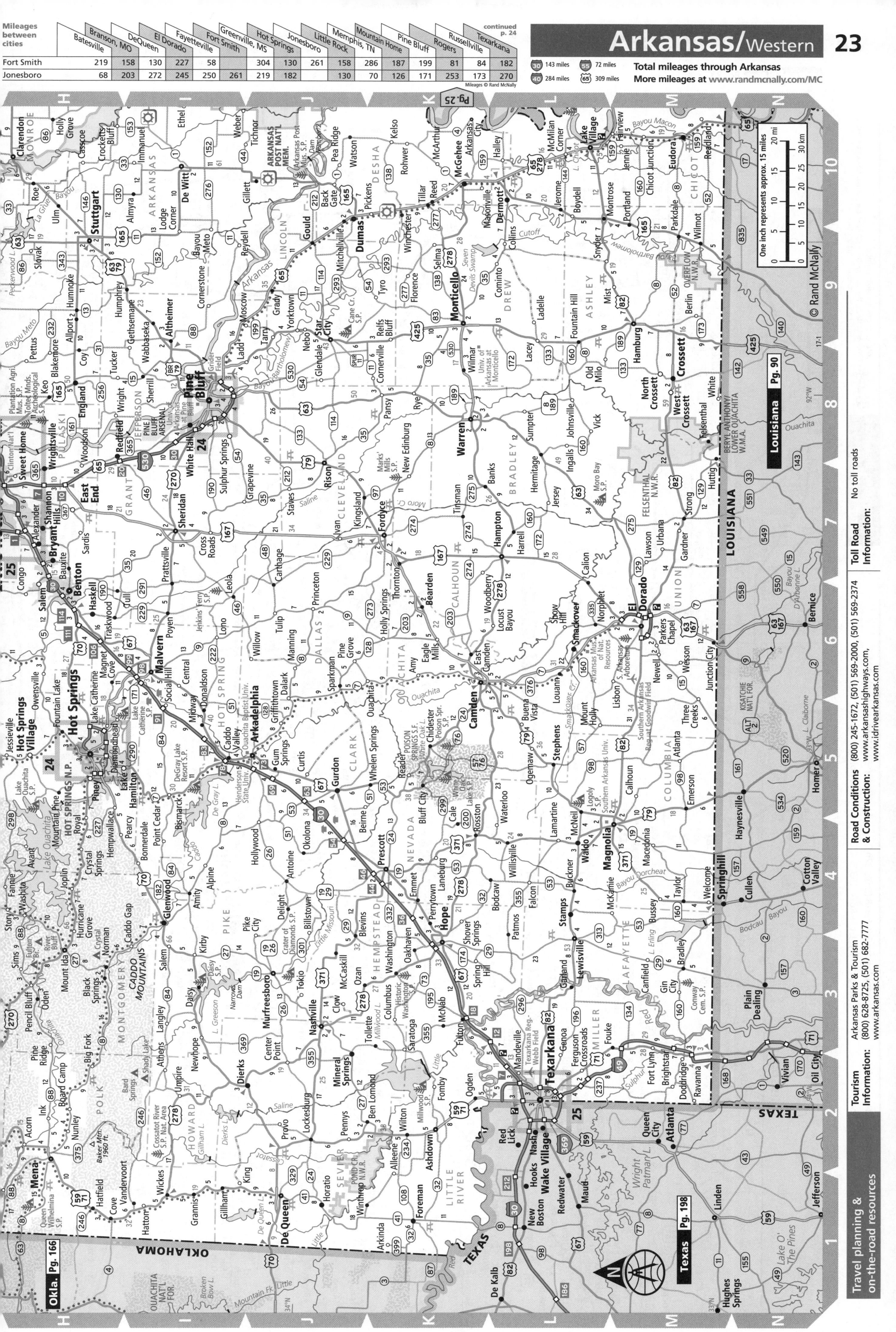

One inch represents approx. 15 miles
20 mi
0 5 10 15 20 25 30 km

© Rand McNally

Louisiana Pg. 90

Texas Pg. 198

Okla. Pg. 166

Road Conditions & Construction: (800) 245-1672, (501) 569-2000, (501) 569-2374 www.arkansashighways.com, www.idrivearkansas.com

Tourism Information: Arkansas Parks & Tourism (800) 628-8725, (501) 682-7777 www.arkansas.com

Toll Road Information: No toll roads

Travel planning & on-the-road resources

Mileages between cities	Batesville	Branson, MO	DeQueen	El Dorado	Fayetteville	Fort Smith	Greenville, MS	Hot Springs	Jonesboro	Little Rock	Memphis, TN	Mountain Home	Pine Bluff	Rogers	Russellville	Texarkana
Little Rock	94	172	143	118	188	158	147	54	130		137	151	43	208	74	142
Memphis, TN	119	274	278	250	318	286	152	188	70	137		195	152	339	204	276

Mileages © Rand McNally

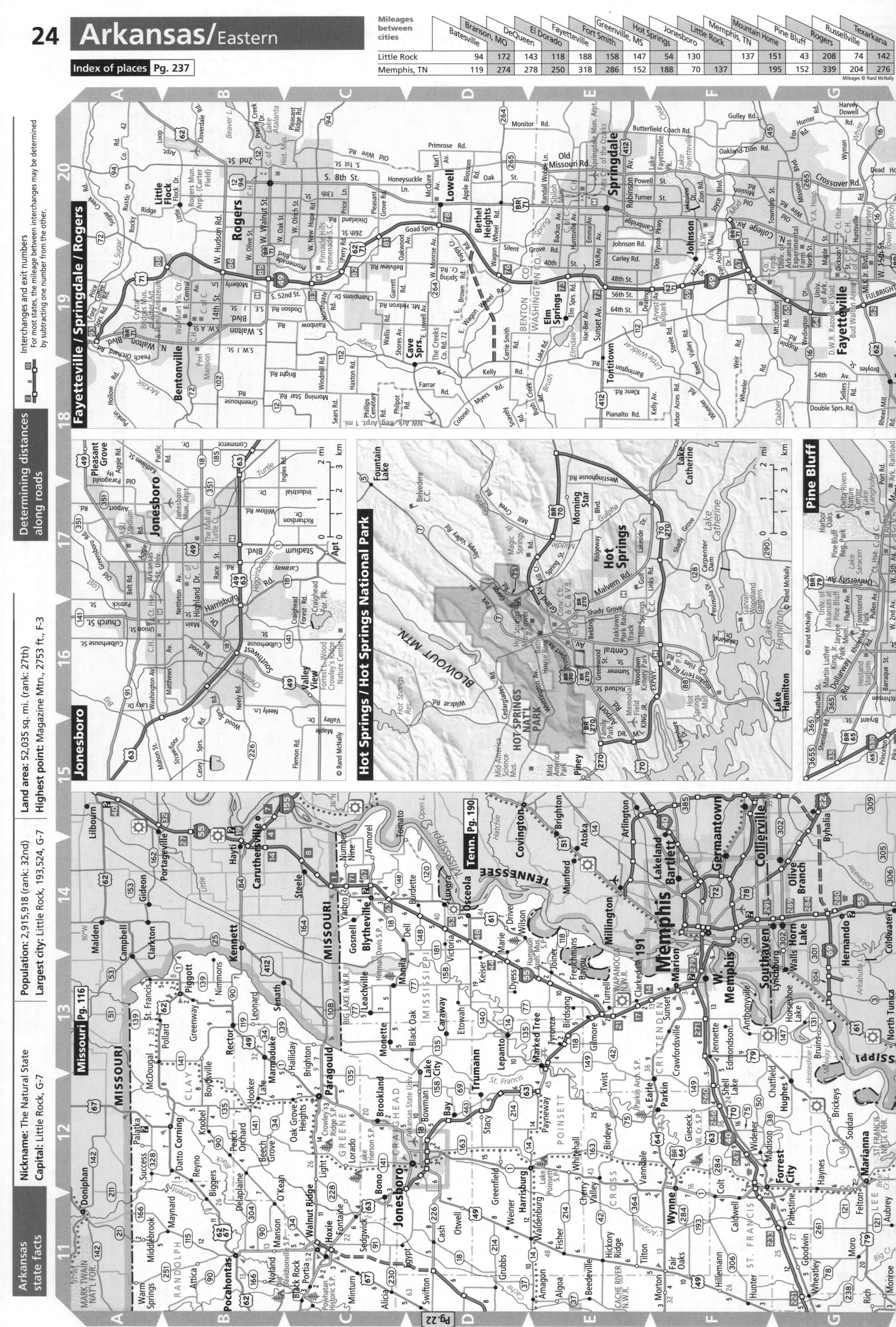

Mileages between cities	Batesville	Branson, MO	DeQueen	El Dorado	Fayetteville	Fort Smith	Greenville, MS	Hot Springs	Jonesboro	Little Rock	Memphis, TN	Mountain Home	Pine Bluff	Rogers	Russellville	Texarkana
Mountain Home	78	83	287	268	123	187	298	198	126	151	195		194	126	125	287
Texarkana	234	306	54	88	236	182	198	110	270	142	276	287	152	258	209	

Mileages © Rand McNally

Total mileages through Arkansas
More mileages at www.randmcnally.com/MC

- 30 143 miles
- 55 72 miles
- 40 284 miles
- 65 309 miles

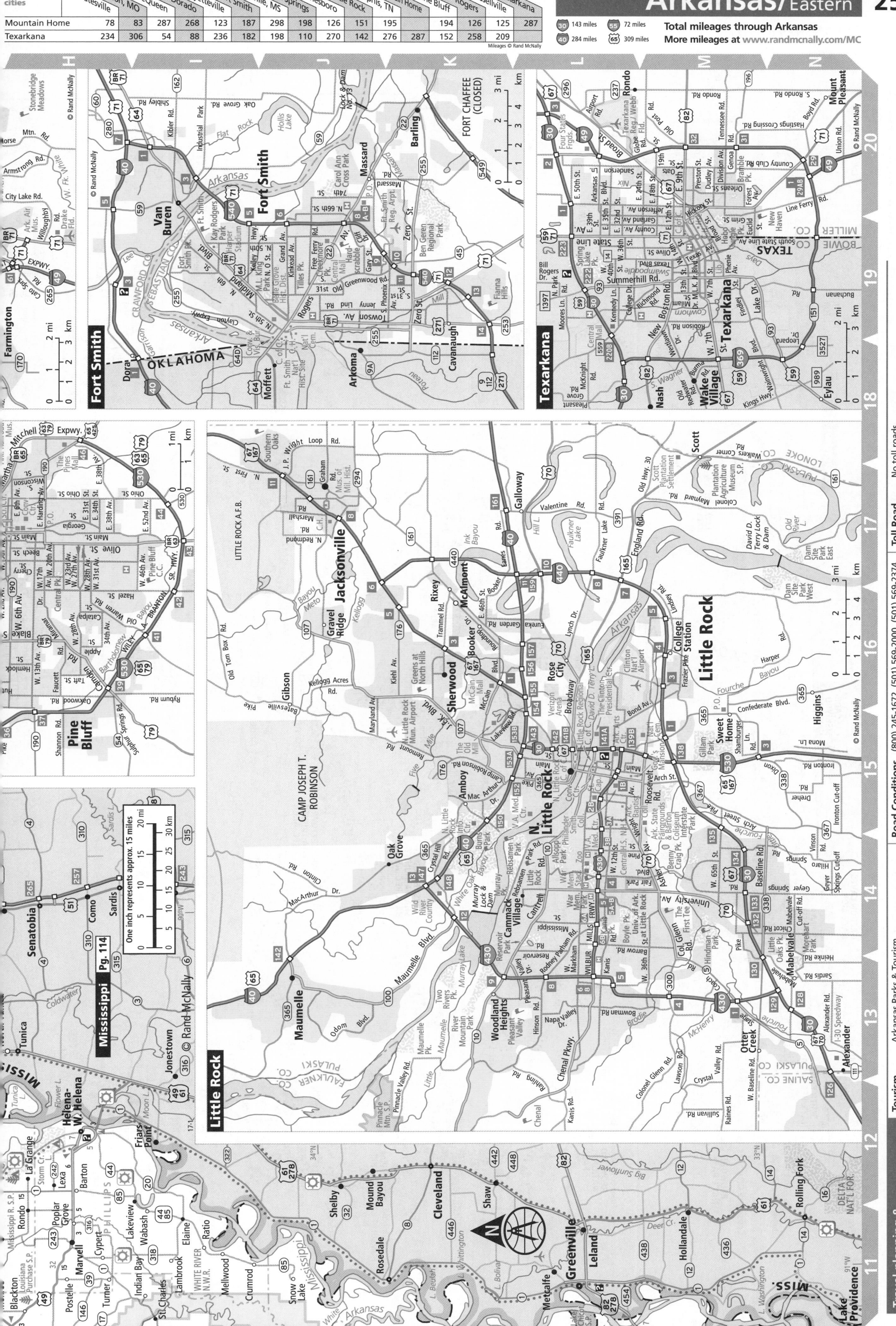

Tourism Information: Arkansas Parks & Tourism (800) 628-8725, (501) 682-7777 www.arkansas.com

Road Conditions & Construction: (800) 245-1672, (501) 569-2000, (501) 569-2374 www.arkansashighways.com, www.idrivearkansas.com

Toll Road Information: No toll roads

Travel planning & on-the-road resources

Index of places **Pg. 237**

Mileages © Rand McNally

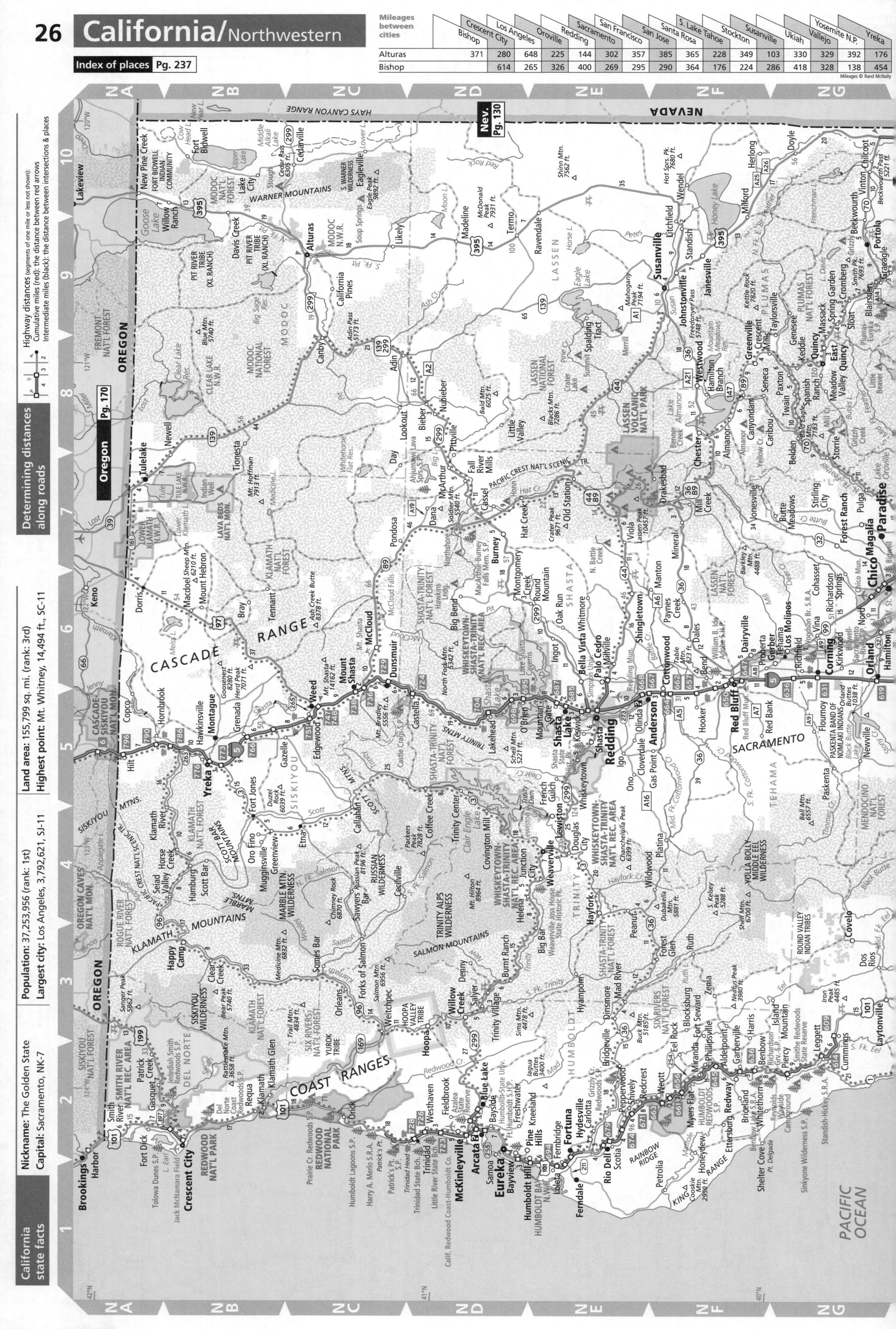

California state facts

Nickname: The Golden State
Capital: Sacramento, NK-7
Population: 37,253,956 (rank: 1st)
Largest city: Los Angeles, 3,792,621, SJ-11
Land area: 155,779 sq. mi. (rank: 3rd)
Highest point: Mt. Whitney, 14,494 ft., SC-11

Determining distances along roads

Highway distances (segments of one mile or less not shown):
Cumulative miles (red): the distance between red arrows
Intermediate miles (black): the distance between intersections & places

Oregon Pg. 170

Nev. Pg. 130

Mileages between cities	Bishop	Crescent City	Los Angeles	Oroville	Redding	Sacramento	San Francisco	San Jose	Santa Rosa	S. Lake Tahoe	Stockton	Susanville	Ukiah	Vallejo	Yosemite N.P.	Yreka
Eureka	546	81	644	222	146	289	272	315	217	392	325	259	158	262	454	198
Redding	400	208	544	94		161	216	244	198	264	209	112	188	187	332	98

continued p. 28

Mileages © Rand McNally

797 miles [I-5] 791 miles [101]
199 miles [80]

Total mileages through California
More mileages at www.randmcnally.com/MC

Yosemite National Park (inset map)

One inch represents approximately 18 miles

© Rand McNally

Travel planning & on-the-road resources

Golden Gate Bridge (San Francisco Bay area): (415) 921-5858; www.goldengatebridge.org
Bay Area Toll Authority (all other San Francisco Bay area bridges) (FasTrak): (510) 817-5700; bata.mtc.ca.gov

Toll Road Information:

511
Sacramento region: 511; www.sacregion511.org
San Francisco Bay area: 511; www.511.org

Road Conditions & Construction: (800) 427-7623; www.dot.ca.gov
Sacramento region: 511; www.sacregion511.org
San Francisco Bay area: 511; www.511.org

Tourism Information: California Tourism (877) 225-4367, (916) 444-4429 www.visitcalifornia.com

Mileages between cities	Bishop	Crescent City	Los Angeles	Oroville	Redding	Sacramento	San Francisco	San Jose	Santa Rosa	S. Lake Tahoe	Stockton	Susanville	Ukiah	Vallejo	Yosemite N.P.	Yreka
Sacramento	269	372	383	68	161		87	115	95	100	47	217	145	58	160	257
San Francisco	295	355	380	150	216	87		45	55	187	82	303	115	30	189	312

Mileages © Rand McNally

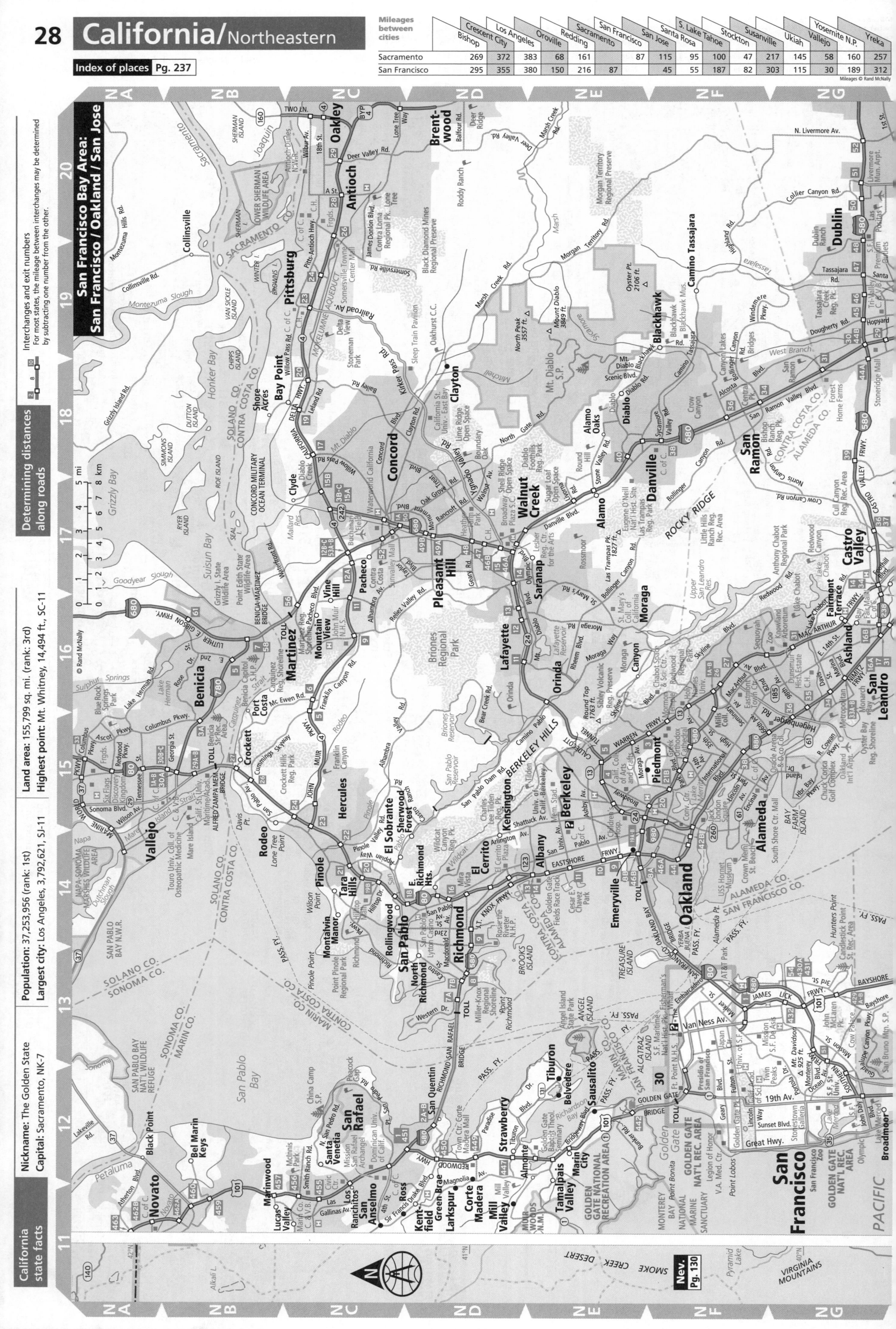

San Francisco Bay Area:
San Francisco / Oakland / San Jose

California state facts

Nickname: The Golden State
Capital: Sacramento, NK-7

Population: 37,253,956 (rank: 1st)
Largest city: Los Angeles, 3,792,621, SJ-11

Land area: 155,799 sq. mi. (rank: 3rd)
Highest point: Mt. Whitney, 14,494 ft., SC-11

Determining distances along roads

Interchanges and exit numbers
For most states, the mileage between interchanges may be determined by subtracting one number from the other.

Mileages between cities	Bishop	Crescent City	Los Angeles	Oroville	Redding	Sacramento	San Francisco	San Jose	Santa Rosa	S. Lake Tahoe	Stockton	Susanville	Ukiah	Vallejo	Yosemite N.P.	Yreka
San Jose	290	396	340	178	244	115	45		96	215	74	330	156	64	182	340
S. Lake Tahoe	176	472	445	157	264	100	187	215	195		147	143	248	159	189	311

Mileages © Rand McNally

5 797 miles 101 791 miles **Total mileages through California**
80 199 miles More mileages at www.randmcnally.com/MC

Toll Road Information: Golden Gate Bridge (San Francisco Bay area): (415) 921-5858; www.goldengatebridge.org
Bay Area Toll Authority (all other San Francisco Bay area bridges) (FasTrak):
(510) 817-5700; bata.mtc.ca.gov

Road Conditions & Construction: (800) 427-7623; www.dot.ca.gov
Sacramento region: 511; www.sacregion511.org
San Francisco Bay area: 511; www.511.org

Tourism Information: California Tourism
(877) 225-4367, (916) 444-4429
www.visitcalifornia.com

FasTrak: 511

Travel planning & on-the-road resources

© Rand McNally

Central San Francisco

Sacramento

© Rand McNally

Sights to see
- Ghirardelli Square, San Francisco B-7
- Golden Gate Bridge, San Francisco. A-2
- Monterey Bay Aquarium, Monterey M-1
- National Steinbeck Center, Salinas K-5
- Pier 39, San Francisco. A-8
- San Francisco Cable Car Museum,
  San Francisco. C-8
- Squaw Valley U.S.A., Olympic Valley F-8

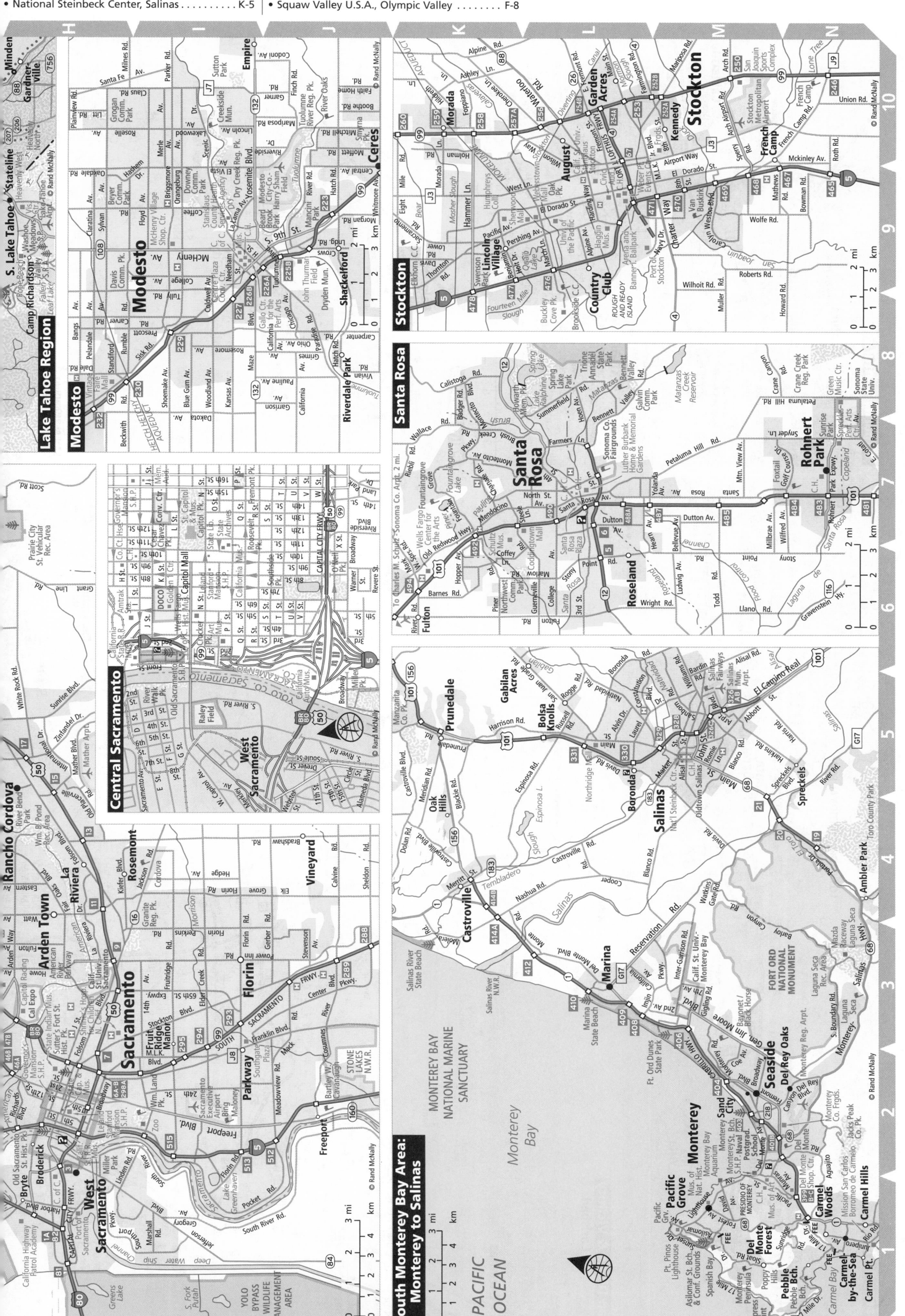

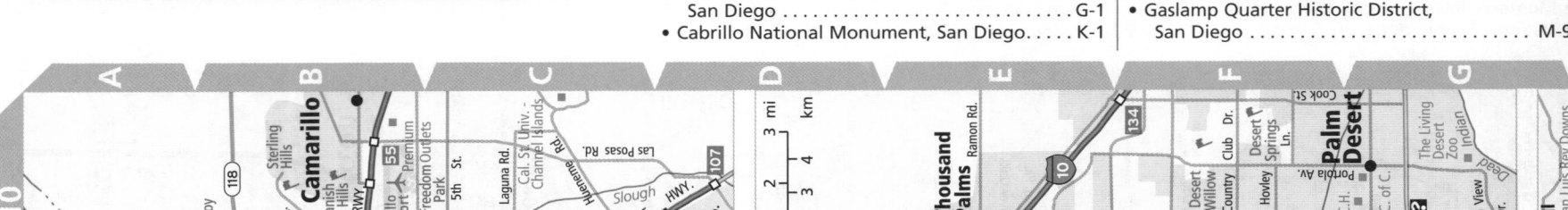

Sights to see
- Balboa Park, San Diego K-10
- Birch Aquarium at Scripps Institute,
  San Diego G-1
- Cabrillo National Monument, San Diego K-1
- Channel Islands National Park Visitor Center
  & Headquarters, Ventura B-8
- Gaslamp Quarter Historic District,
  San Diego M-9

Sights to see
- Legoland California, Carlsbad J-8
- The Living Desert Nature Preserve, Palm Desert G-10
- Museum of Contemporary Art, San Diego . . . L-8
- Palm Springs Desert Museum, Palm Springs . . E-7
- San Diego Zoo, San Diego J-3
- SeaWorld, San Diego I-1
- Stearns Wharf, Santa Barbara B-5

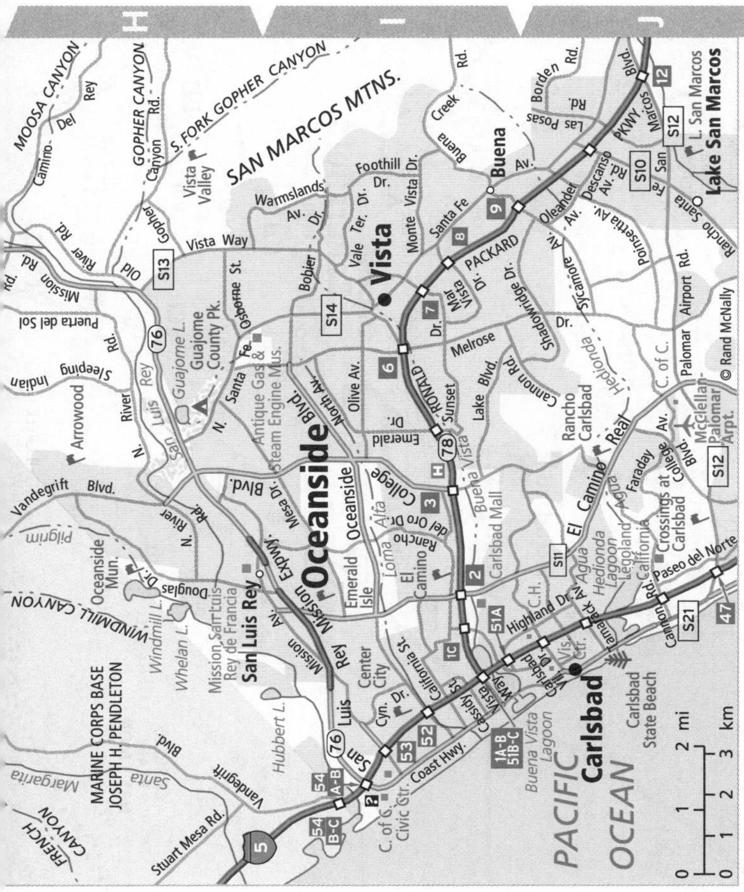

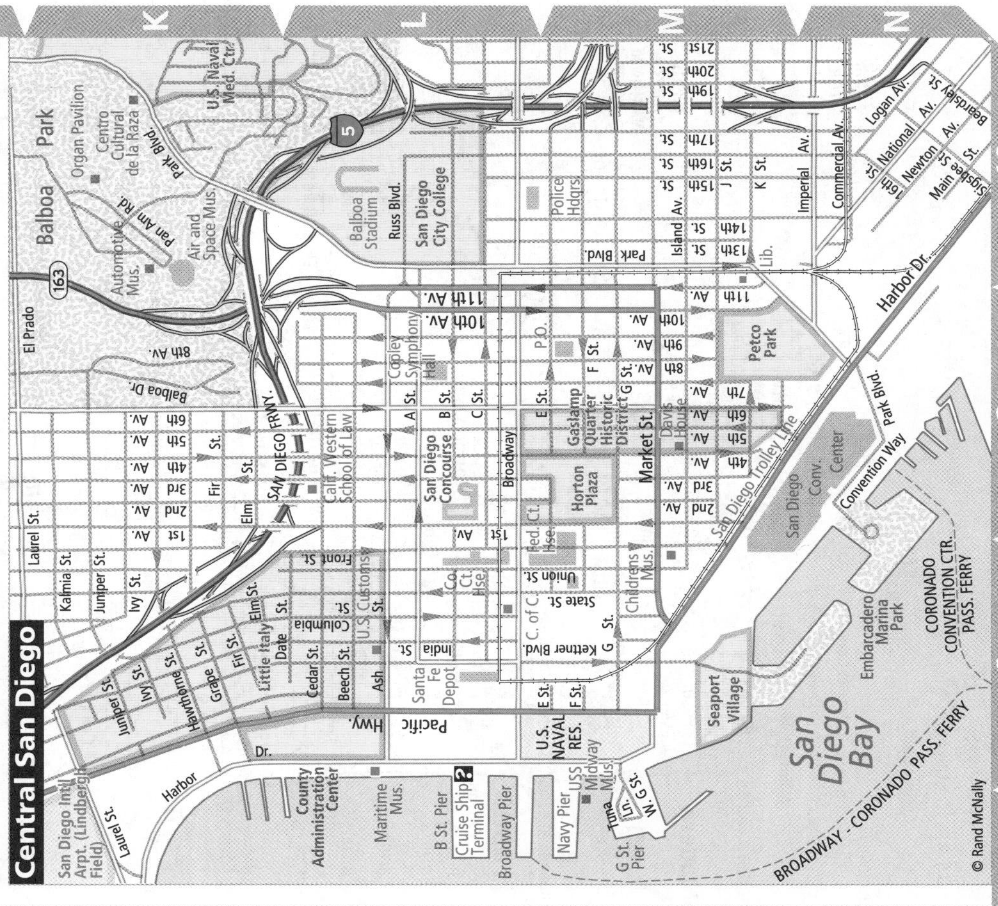

Central San Diego

© Rand McNally

Index of places   Pg. 237

Mileages between cities	Bakersfield	Barstow	El Centro	Fresno	Las Vegas, NV	Los Angeles	Monterey	Needles	Palm Springs	Riverside	San Bernardino	San Diego	San Francisco	San Luis Obispo	Santa Barbara	Sequoia N.P.
Bakersfield		129	322	109	286	112	222	272	216	166	166	232	284	130	147	122
Fresno	109	239	429		395	218	150	381	323	271	273	339	183	130	254	77

Mileages © Rand McNally

California state facts

Nickname: The Golden State
Capital: Sacramento, NK-7
Land area: 155,799 sq. mi. (rank: 3rd)
Population: 37,253,956 (rank: 1st)
Largest city: Los Angeles, 3,792,621, SJ-11
Highest point: Mt. Whitney, 14,494 ft., SC-11

Determining distances along roads

Highway distances (segments of one mile or less not shown):
Cumulative miles (red): the distance between red arrows
Intermediate miles (black): the distance between intersections & places

One inch represents approximately 18 miles

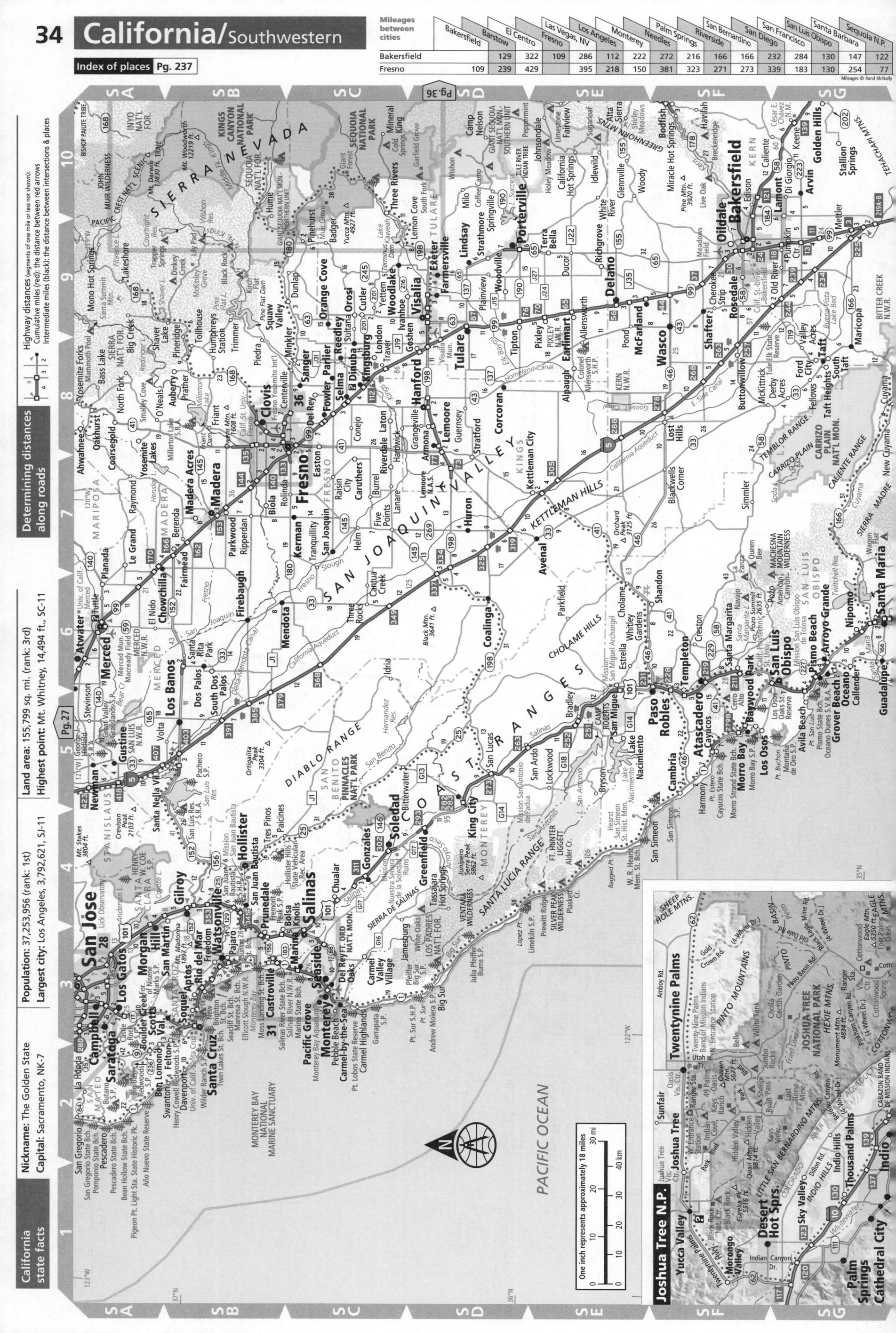

Mileages between cities

continued p. 36

	Bakersfield	Barstow	El Centro	Fresno	Las Vegas, NV	Los Angeles	Monterey	Needles	Palm Springs	Riverside	San Bernardino	San Diego	San Francisco	San Luis Obispo	Santa Barbara	Sequoia N.P.
Las Vegas, NV	286	156	312	395		270	507	110	278	234	225	331	569	415	358	410
Los Angeles	112	114	212	218	270		319	256	107	54	60	120	380	189	94	232

Mileages at www.randmcnally.com

Total mileages through California

5	797 miles	15	287 miles
10	243 miles	40	155 miles

More mileages at www.randmcnally.com/MC

Bakersfield

Sequoia & Kings Canyon National Parks

© Rand McNally

Tourism Information:
California Tourism
(877) 225-4367, (916) 444-4429
www.visitcalifornia.com

Road Conditions & Construction:
(800) 427-7623, www.dot.ca.gov
Los Angeles metro area: 511; www.go511.com
San Diego area: 511, www.511sd.com

Toll Road Information:
The Toll Roads (Orange Co.) (FasTrak): (949) 727-4800; www.thetollroads.com
South Bay Expressway (San Diego Co.) (FasTrak):
(619) 661-7070; www.southbayexpressway.com

Travel planning & on-the-road resources

Mileages between cities	Bakersfield	Barstow	El Centro	Fresno	Las Vegas, NV	Los Angeles	Monterey	Needles	Palm Springs	Riverside	San Bernardino	San Diego	San Francisco	San Luis Obispo	Santa Barbara	Sequoia N.P.
Monterey	222	350	530	150	507	319		494	424	372	373	439	112	142	237	226
Palm Springs	216	123	108	323	278	107	424	188		52	54	139	486	296	201	338

Mileages © Rand McNally

Determining distances along roads

Interchanges and exit numbers
For most states, the mileage between interchanges may be determined by subtracting one number from the other.

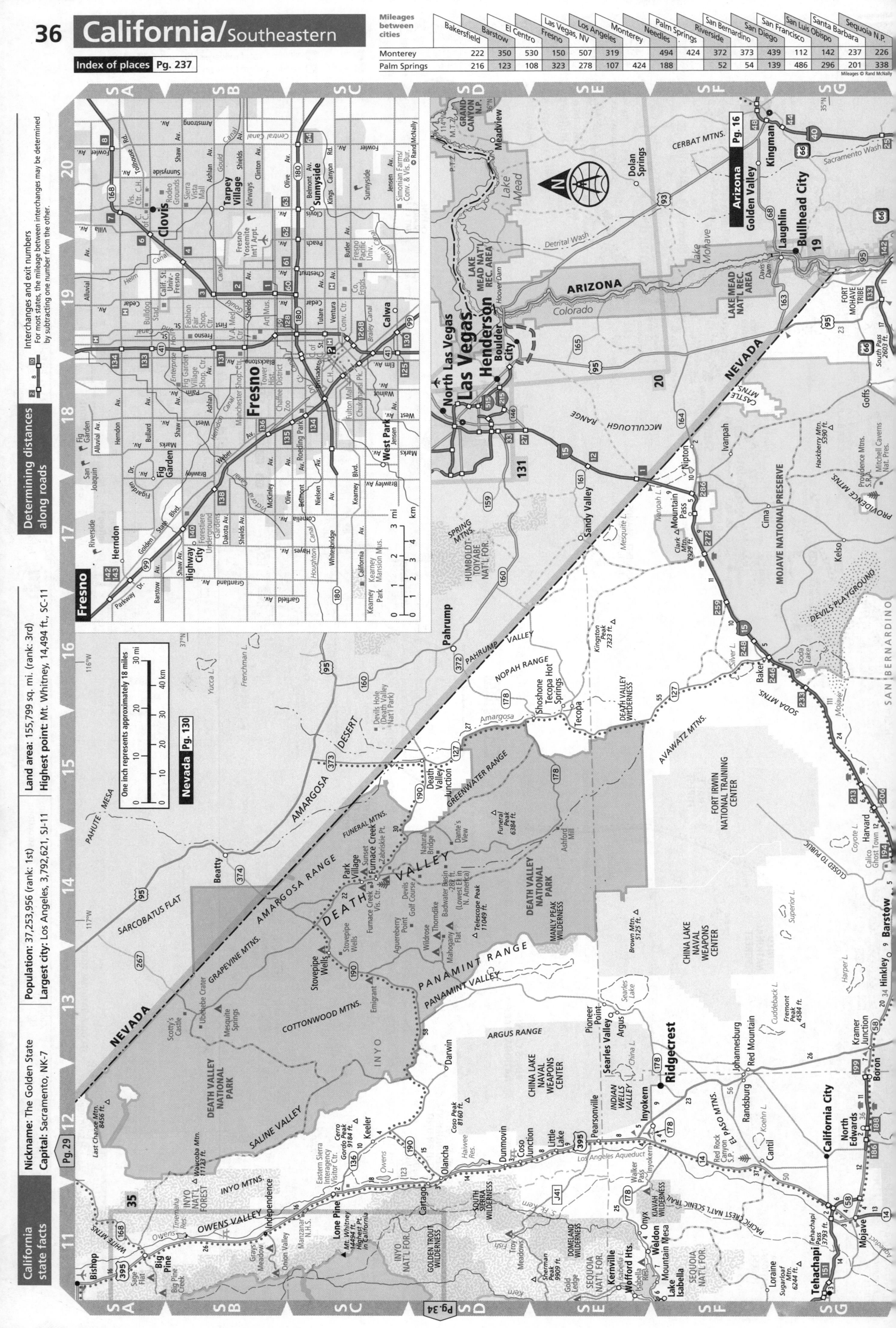

One inch represents approximately 18 miles

Nevada Pg. 130

Mileages between cities	Bakersfield	Barstow	El Centro	Fresno	Las Vegas, NV	Los Angeles	Monterey	Needles	Palm Springs	Riverside	San Bernardino	San Diego	San Francisco	San Luis Obispo	Santa Barbara	Sequoia N.P.
San Diego	232	176	113	339	331	120	439	317	139	97	106		501	313	214	352
Santa Barbara	147	203	306	254	358	94	237	345	201	148	150	214	325	94		268

Mileages © Rand McNally

Total mileages through California

5	797 miles
10	243 miles
15	287 miles
40	155 miles

More mileages at www.randmcnally.com/MC

Tourism Information:
California Tourism
(877) 225-4367, (916) 444-4429
www.visitcalifornia.com

Road Conditions & Construction:
(800) 427-7623, www.dot.ca.gov
Los Angeles metro area: 511; www.go511.com
San Diego area: 511, www.511sd.com

Toll Road Information:
The Toll Roads (Orange Co.) (FasTrak): (949) 727-4800; www.thetollroads.com
South Bay Expressway (San Diego Co.) (FasTrak):
(619) 661-7070; www.southbayexpressway.com

Travel planning & on-the-road resources

© Rand McNally

Sights to see

(located on pages 38-41)

Los Angeles & Vicinity

Central Los Angeles

Sights to see

list continued on p.40

Lancaster / Palmdale

PACIFIC OCEAN

© Rand McNally

Sights to see (located on pages 38-41)

- Mission San Juan Capistrano, San Juan Capistrano. M-14
- Mount Wilson Observatory, Mt. Wilson. C-9
- Old Pasadena, Pasadena D-8
- Oldest Winery in Calif., Rancho Cucamonga. . D-15
- The Queen Mary, Long Beach. J-8
- Richard M. Nixon Library & Birthplace, Yorba Linda. H-12

Sights to see

(located on pages 38–41)

- Rose Bowl, Pasadena D-8
- Santa Monica Pier, Santa Monica F-4
- Universal City, Los Angeles D-6
- Venice Boardwalk, Los Angeles F-4
- Walt Disney Concert Hall, Los Angeles K-2
- Warner Bros. Studio, Burbank. D-6
- Will Rogers State Historic Park, Pacific Palisades E-4

© Rand McNally

Mileages between cities	Alamosa	Aspen	Burlington	Colorado Springs	Craig	Denver	Durango	Estes Park	Fort Collins	Grand Junction	Gunnison	Lamar	Leadville	Pueblo	Sterling	Trinidad
Burlington	311	363		151	363	166	460	222	220	408	324	108	265	189	142	230
Colorado Springs	163	155	151		264	69	313	133	133	309	166	158	121	42	194	128

Mileages © Rand McNally

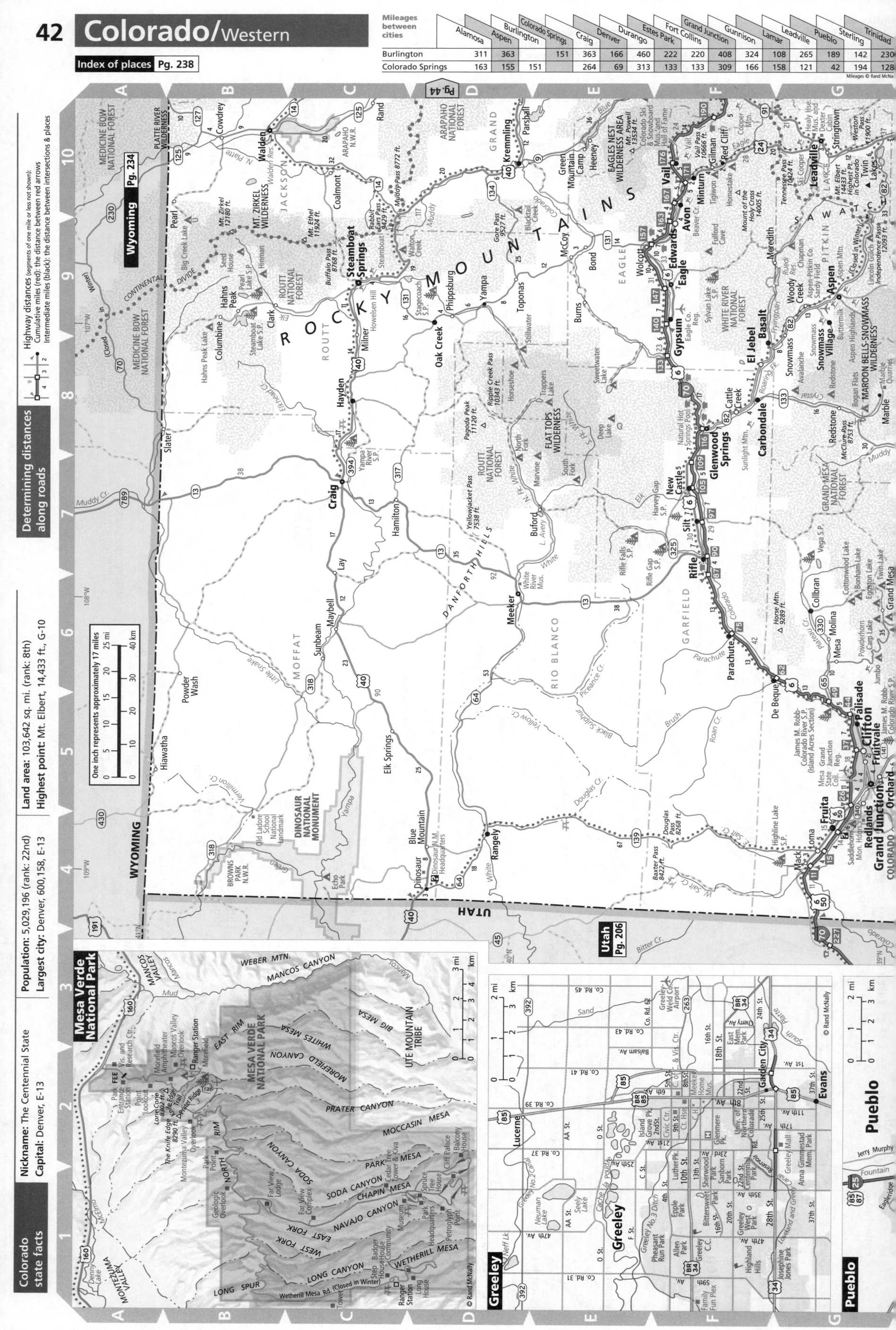

Colorado state facts

Nickname: The Centennial State

Capital: Denver, E-13

Population: 5,029,196 (rank: 22nd)

Largest city: Denver, 600,158, E-13

Land area: 103,642 sq. mi. (rank: 8th)

Highest point: Mt. Elbert, 14,433 ft., G-10

Determining distances along roads

Highway distances (segments of one mile or less not shown)
Cumulative miles (red): the distance between red arrows
Intermediate miles (black): the distance between intersections & places

One inch represents approximately 17 miles

Pg. 44
Pg. 234
Utah Pg. 206

Mesa Verde National Park

Greeley

Pueblo

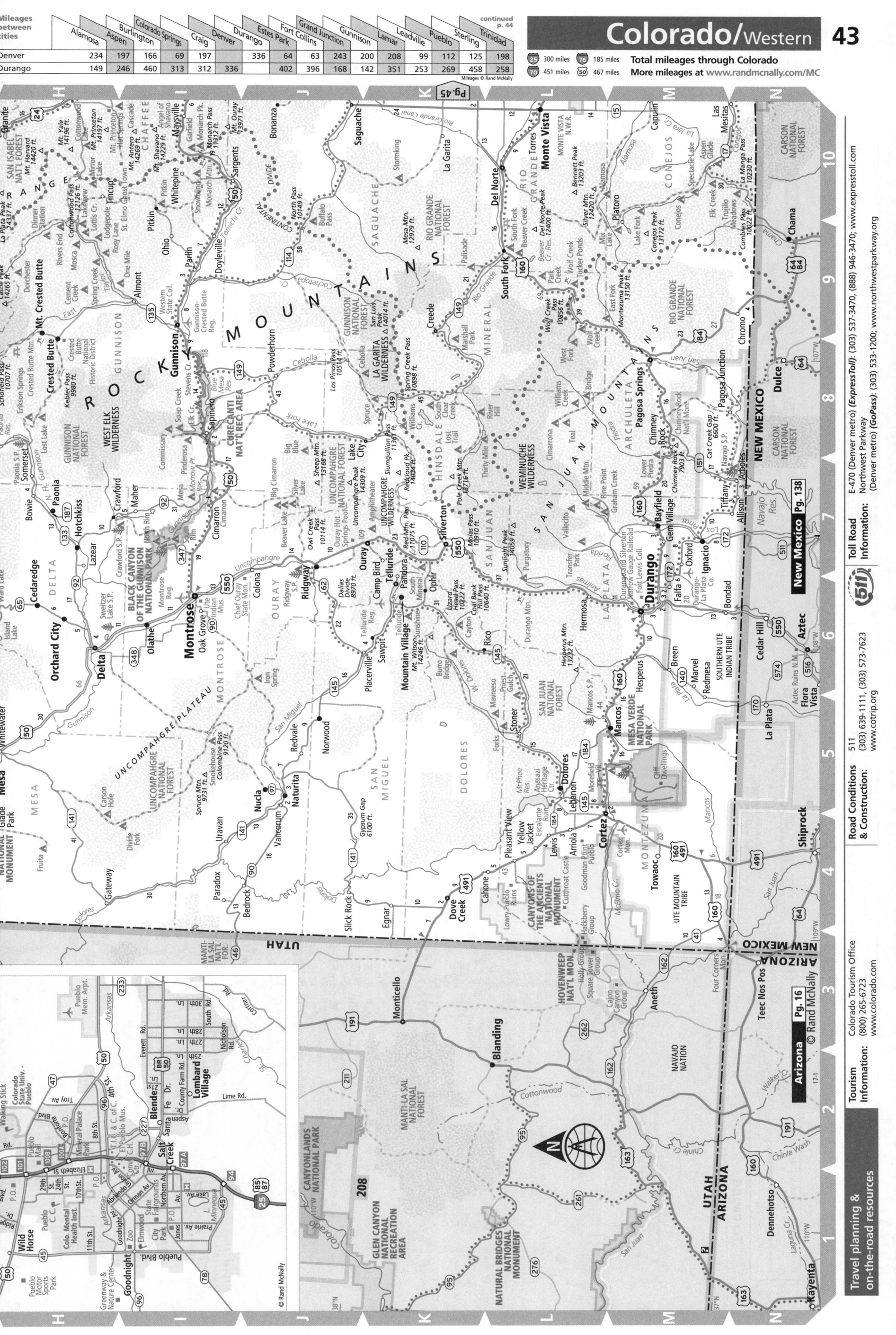

Mileages between cities

	Alamosa	Aspen	Burlington	Colorado Springs	Craig	Denver	Durango	Estes Park	Fort Collins	Grand Junction	Gunnison	Lamar	Leadville	Pueblo	Sterling	Trinidad
Denver	234	197	166	69	197		336	64	63	243	200	208	99	112	125	198
Durango	149	246	460	313	312	336		402	396	168	142	351	253	269	458	258

Mileages © Rand McNally

Total mileages through Colorado

25 = 300 miles 76 = 185 miles
70 = 451 miles 50 = 467 miles

More mileages at www.randmcnally.com/MC

Travel planning & on-the-road resources

Toll Road Information:	E-470 (Denver metro) (ExpressToll): (303) 537-3470, (888) 946-3470; www.expresstoll.com Northwest Parkway (Denver metro) (GoPass): (303) 533-1200; www.northwestparkway.org
Road Conditions & Construction:	511 (303) 639-1111, (303) 573-7623 www.cotrip.org
Tourism Information:	Colorado Tourism Office (800) 265-6723 www.colorado.com

New Mexico Pg. 138
Arizona Pg. 16
511

© Rand McNally

Mileages between cities	Alamosa	Aspen	Burlington	Colorado Springs	Craig	Denver	Durango	Estes Park	Fort Collins	Grand Junction	Gunnison	Lamar	Leadville	Pueblo	Sterling	Trinidad
Fort Collins	296	258	220	133	201	63	396	42		303	260	261	160	175	102	261
Grand Junction	247	128	408	309	151	243	168	258	303		126	448	174	287	364	370

Mileages © Rand McNally

Colorado state facts

Nickname: The Centennial State
Capital: Denver, E-13

Population: 5,029,196 (rank: 22nd)
Largest city: Denver, E-13

Land area: 103,642 sq. mi. (rank: 8th)
Highest point: Mt. Elbert, 14,433 ft., G-10

Determining distances along roads

Interchanges and exit numbers For most states, the mileage between interchanges may be determined by subtracting one number from the other.

One inch represents approximately 17 miles

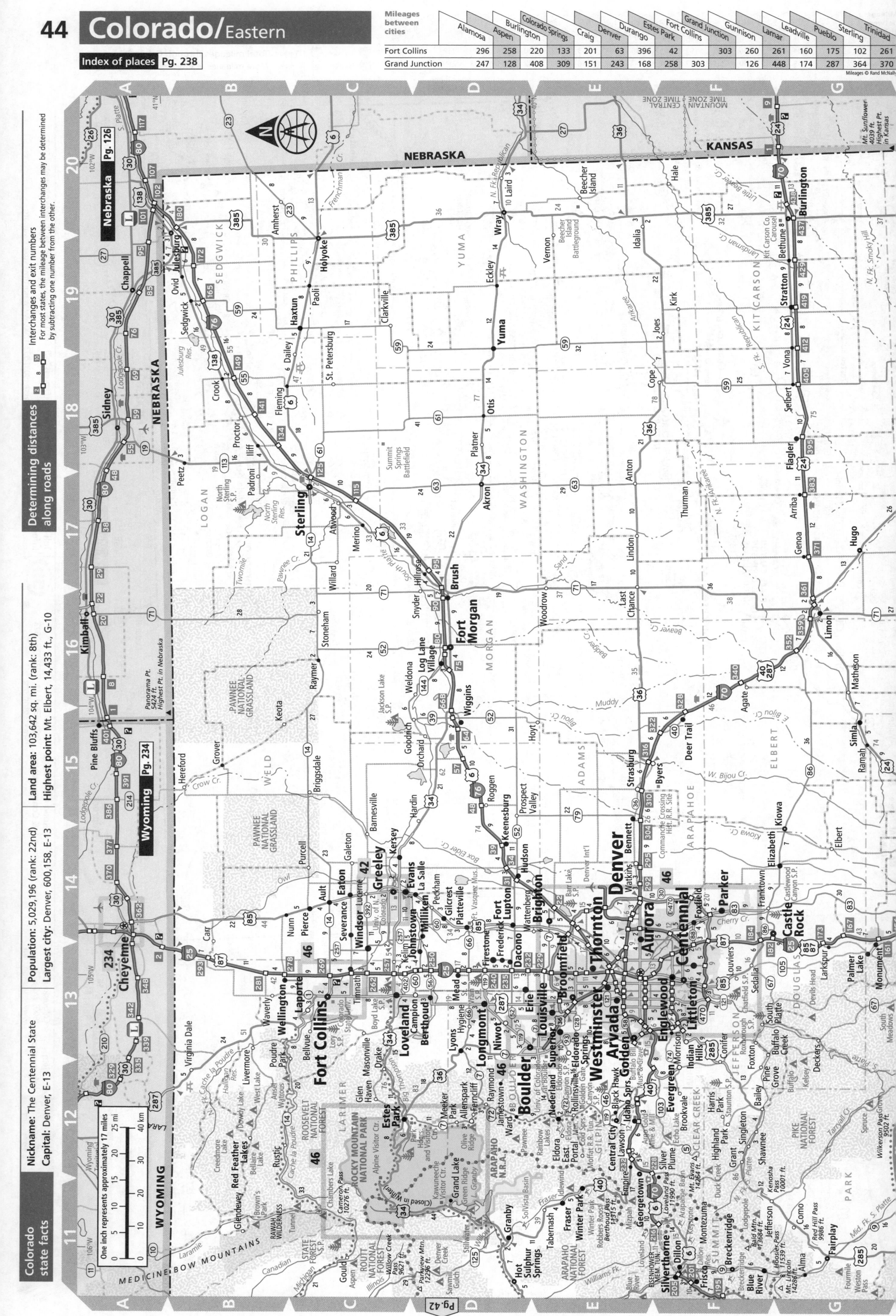

Pg. 126
Pg. 234
Pg. 42

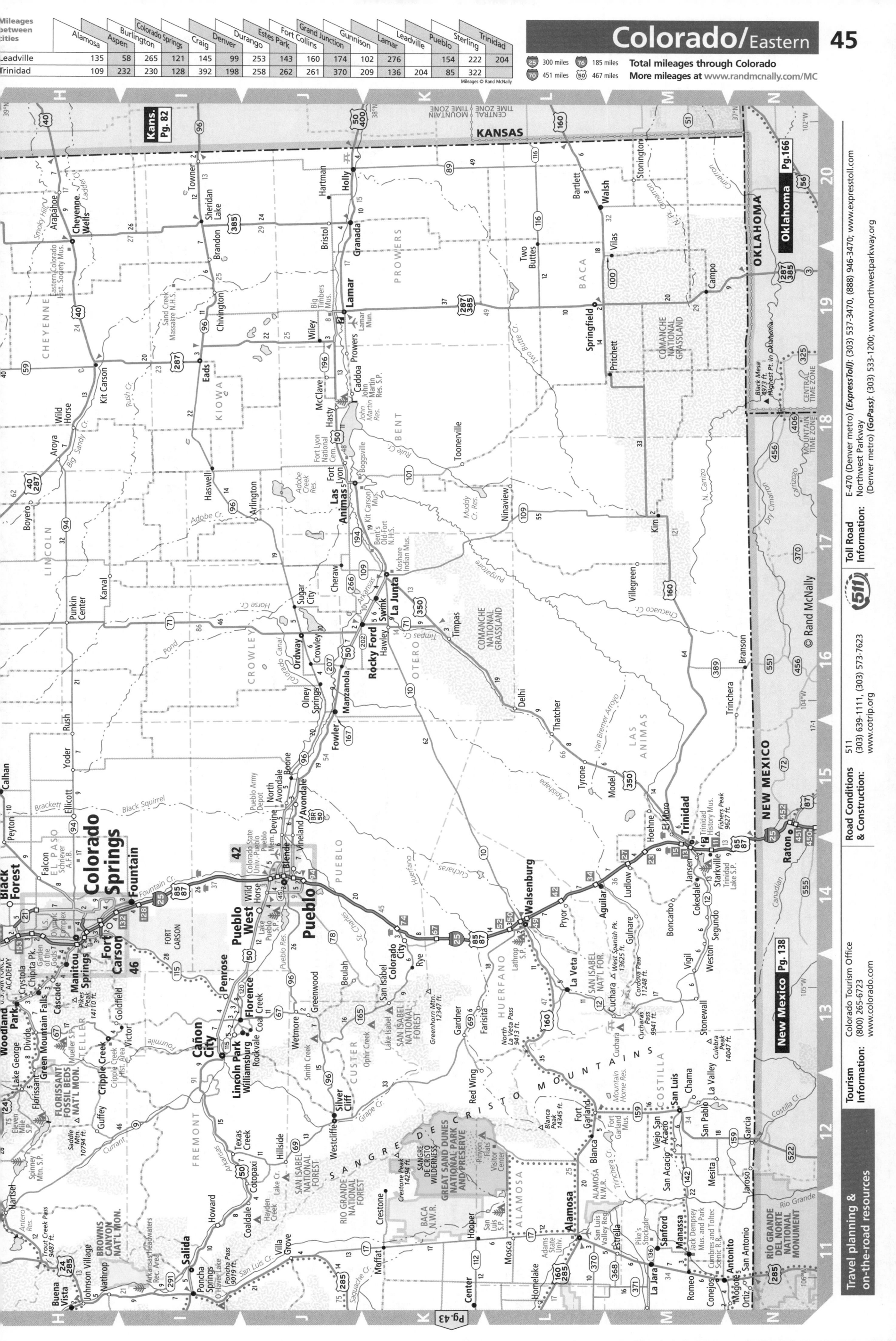

Mileages between cities	Alamosa	Aspen	Burlington	Colorado Springs	Craig	Denver	Durango	Estes Park	Fort Collins	Grand Junction	Gunnison	Lamar	Leadville	Pueblo	Sterling	Trinidad
Leadville	135	58	265	121	145	99	253	143	160	174	102	276		154	222	204
Trinidad	109	232	230	128	392	198	258	262	261	370	209	136	204	85	322	

Mileages © Rand McNally

Kans. Pg. 82

Kansas Pg. 82

New Mexico Pg. 138

New Mexico Pg. 166

Oklahoma Pg. 166

Pg. 42

Pg. 43

Pg. 46

© Rand McNally

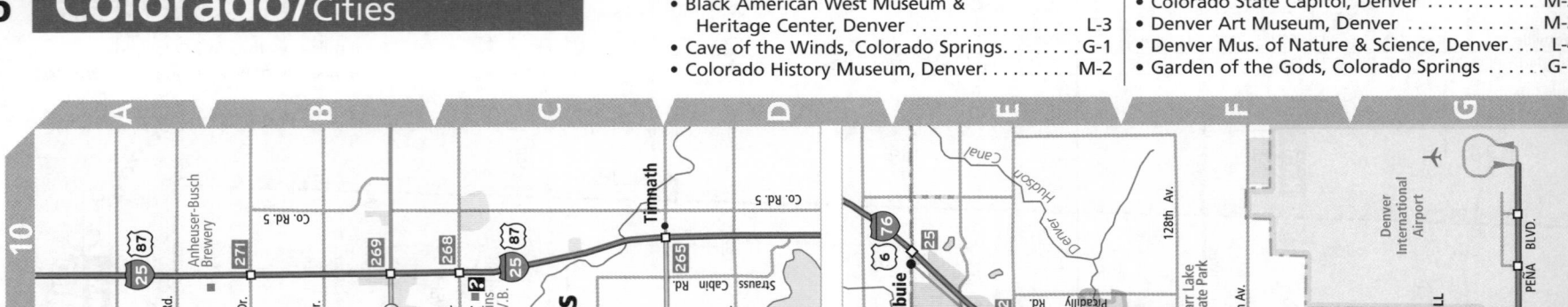

Sights to see

- Black American West Museum & Heritage Center, Denver L-3
- Cave of the Winds, Colorado Springs. G-1
- Colorado History Museum, Denver. M-2
- Colorado State Capitol, Denver M-2
- Denver Art Museum, Denver M-2
- Denver Mus. of Nature & Science, Denver. L-4
- Garden of the Gods, Colorado Springs G-1

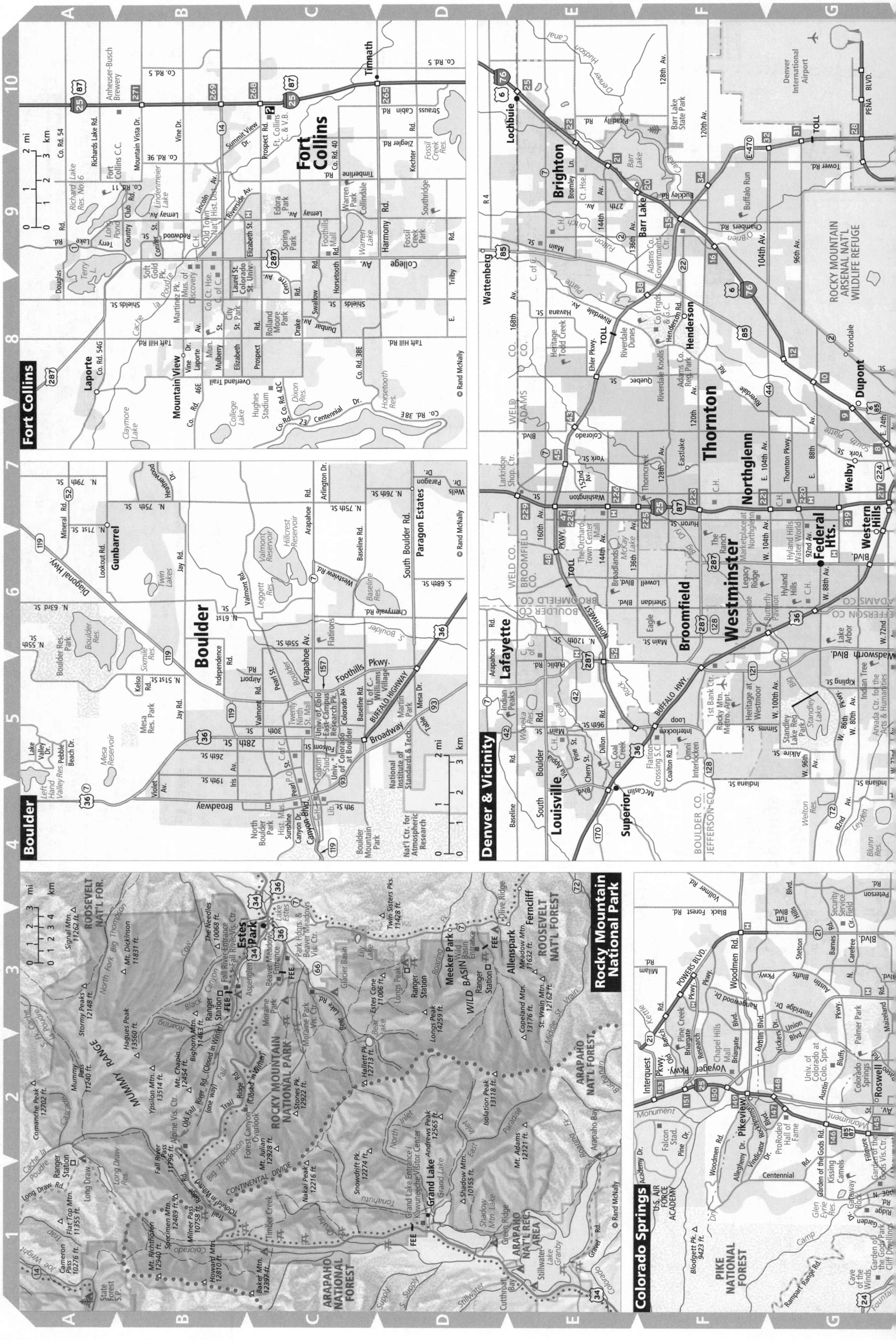

Fort Collins
Boulder
Denver & Vicinity
Rocky Mountain National Park
Colorado Springs
Fort Collins
Boulder
Lafayette
Louisville
Superior
Broomfield
Westminster
Thornton
Northglenn
Brighton
Federal Hts.
Estes Park
ROCKY MOUNTAIN NATIONAL PARK
ROCKY MOUNTAIN ARSENAL NAT'L WILDLIFE REFUGE
Denver International Airport
PIKE NATIONAL FOREST
ARAPAHO NATIONAL FOREST
ROOSEVELT NAT'L FOREST
© Rand McNally

Sights to see
- Nat'l Ctr. for Atmospheric Research, Boulder . . D-4
- Old Town Nat'l Historic District, Fort Collins . . B-9
- ProRodeo Hall of Fame, Colorado Springs G-2
- Red Rocks Amphitheatre, Morrison J-4
- U.S. Airforce Academy, Colorado Springs F-1
- United States Mint, Denver M-2
- World Figure Skating Hall of Fame, Colorado Springs I-2

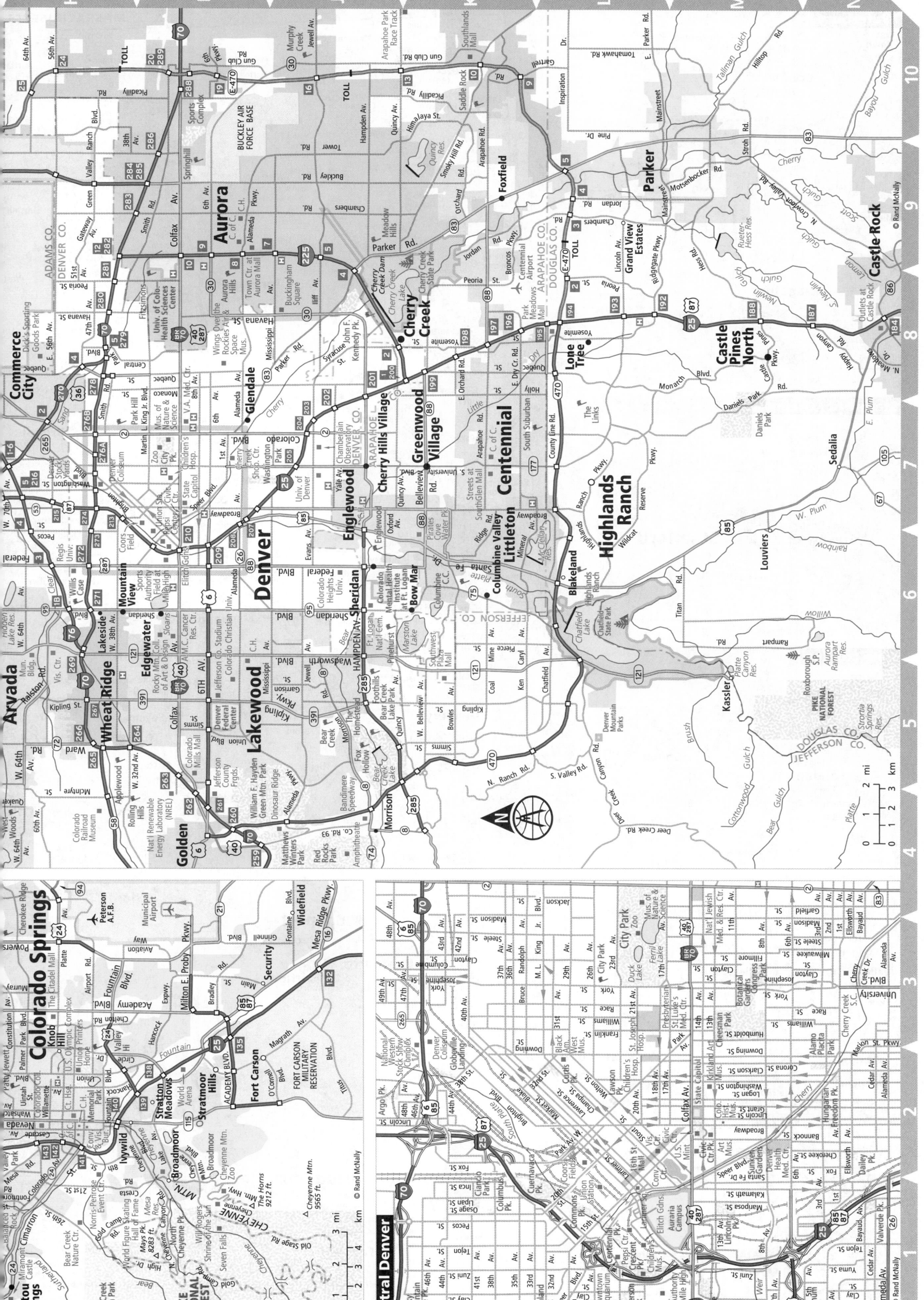

Mileages © Rand McNally

Mileages between cities	Bridgeport	Hartford	New Haven	New London	New York, NY	Putnam	Torrington	Waterbury
Bridgeport		55	18	64	54	107	50	30
Danbury	29	57	35	81	62	104	47	27

	Bridgeport	Hartford	New Haven	New London	New York, NY	Putnam	Torrington	Waterbury
Hartford	55		38	45	108	47	26	30
New Haven	18	38		46	72	89	43	22

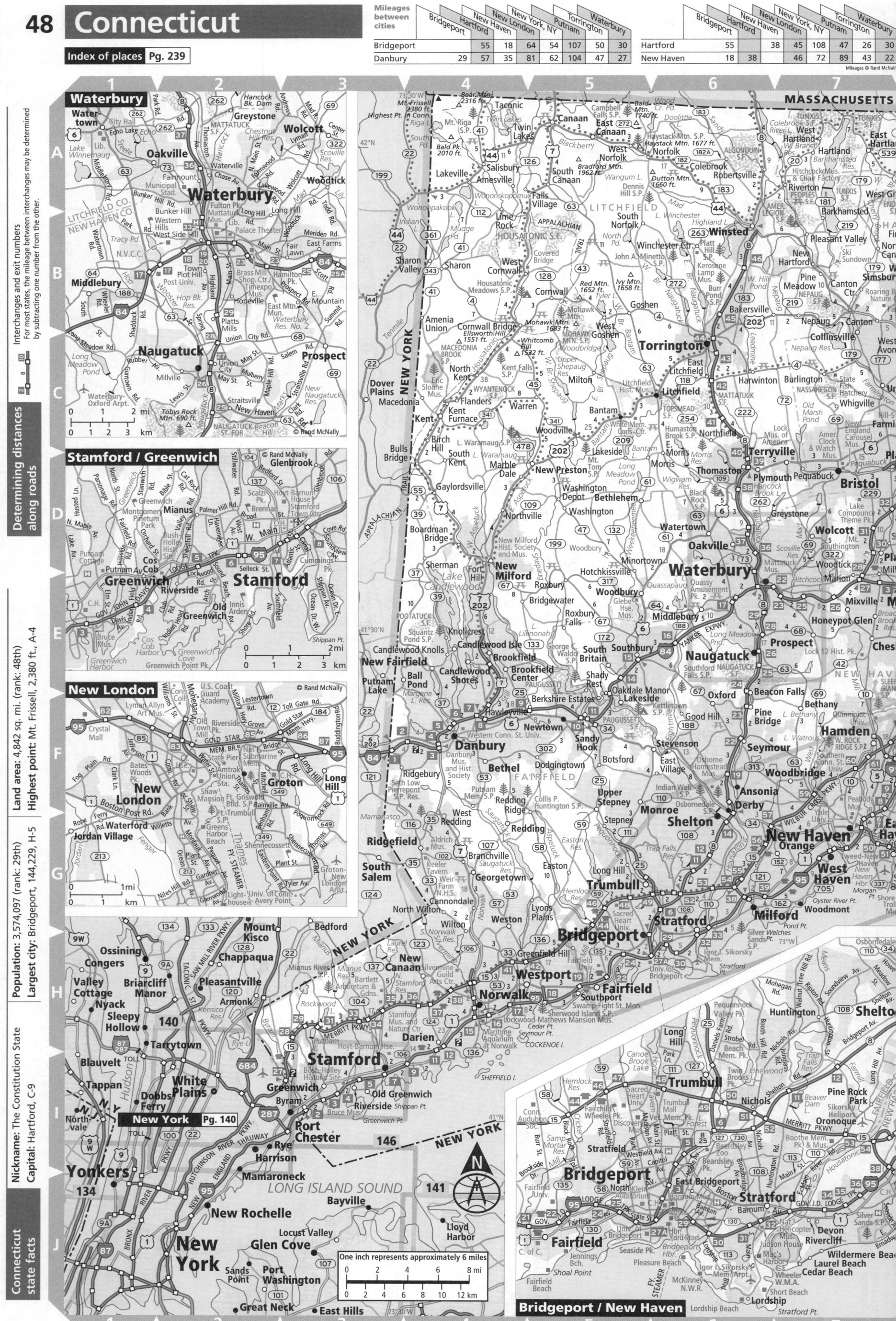

One inch represents approximately 6 miles

Mileages between cities

	Bridgeport	Hartford	New Haven	New London	New York, NY	Putnam	Torrington	Waterbury
New London	64	45	46		118	47	79	63
Putnam	107	47	89	47	162		73	78

	Bridgeport	Hartford	New Haven	New London	New York, NY	Putnam	Torrington	Waterbury
Torrington	50	26	43	79	109	73		20
Waterbury	30	30	22	63	89	78	20	

Mileages © Rand McNally

Total mileages through Connecticut

84 — 98 miles 95 — 112 miles
91 — 58 miles 395 — 55 miles

More mileages at www.randmcnally.com/MC

© Rand McNally

Long Island Sound

Block Island Sound

FISHERS I.

Hartford / Bloomfield (inset)

New Haven (inset)

No toll roads

Toll Road Information:

Road Conditions & Construction: (860) 594-2000, (860) 594-2650 www.ct.gov/dot

Tourism Information: Connecticut Office of Tourism (860) 256-2800 www.ctvisit.com

Travel planning & on-the-road resources

Index of places Pg. 239

Mileages between cities	Georgetown Dover	Lewes	Philadelphia, PA Milford	Salisbury, MD	Wilmington Selbyville				Georgetown Dover	Lewes	Philadelphia, PA Milford	Salisbury, MD	Wilmington Selbyville		
Dover		36	40	20	80	56	55	50	Lewes	40	15		21	119	43	29	90
Georgetown	36		15	16	114	27	20	85	Middletown	26	62	66	46	56	84	81	27

Mileages © Rand McNally

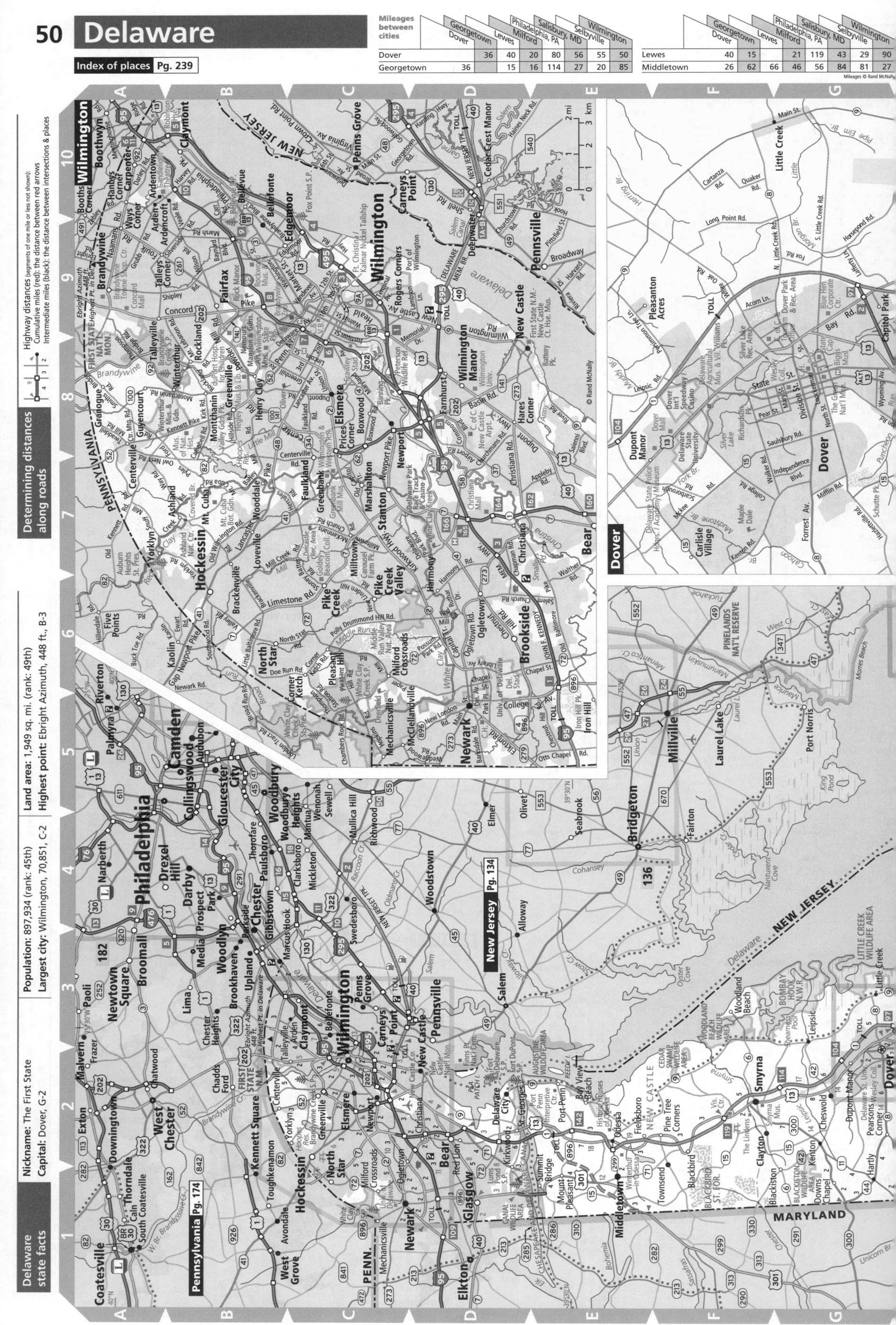

Delaware state facts

Nickname: The First State
Capital: Dover, G-2
Population: 897,934 (rank: 45th)
Land area: 1,949 sq. mi. (rank: 49th)
Highest point: Ebright Azimuth, 448 ft., B-3

Determining distances along roads

Highway distances (segments of one mile or less not shown):
Cumulative miles (red); the distance between red arrows
Intermediate miles (black); the distance between intersections & places

Dover

Mileages between cities

	Dover	Georgetown	Lewes	Milford	Philadelphia, PA	Salisbury, MD	Selbyville	Wilmington
Millville, NJ	94	124	128	108	45	147	143	53
Newark	46	80	85	64	43	102	99	14

	Dover	Georgetown	Lewes	Milford	Philadelphia, PA	Salisbury, MD	Selbyville	Wilmington
Selbyville	55	20	29	36	133	24		104
Wilmington	50	85	90	70	29	107	104	

Mileages © Rand McNally

95 23 miles   1 104 miles
13 108 miles

Total mileages through Delaware
More mileages at www.randmcnally.com/MC

© Rand McNally

Travel planning & on-the-road resources

Tourism Information: Delaware Tourism (866) 284-7483 www.visitdelaware.com

Road Conditions & Construction: (800) 652-5600, (302) 760-2080 www.deldot.gov

Toll Road Information: Delaware River & Bay Authority (Del. Memorial Bridge & Lewes-Cape May Ferry) (E-ZPass): (302) 571-6300; www.drba.net
Del. Dept. of Trans. (all other toll roads) (E-ZPass): (888) 397-2773, (302) 678-7000; www.ezpassde.com

Pensacola

Tallahassee

Maryland Pg. 94

One inch represents approximately 7 miles

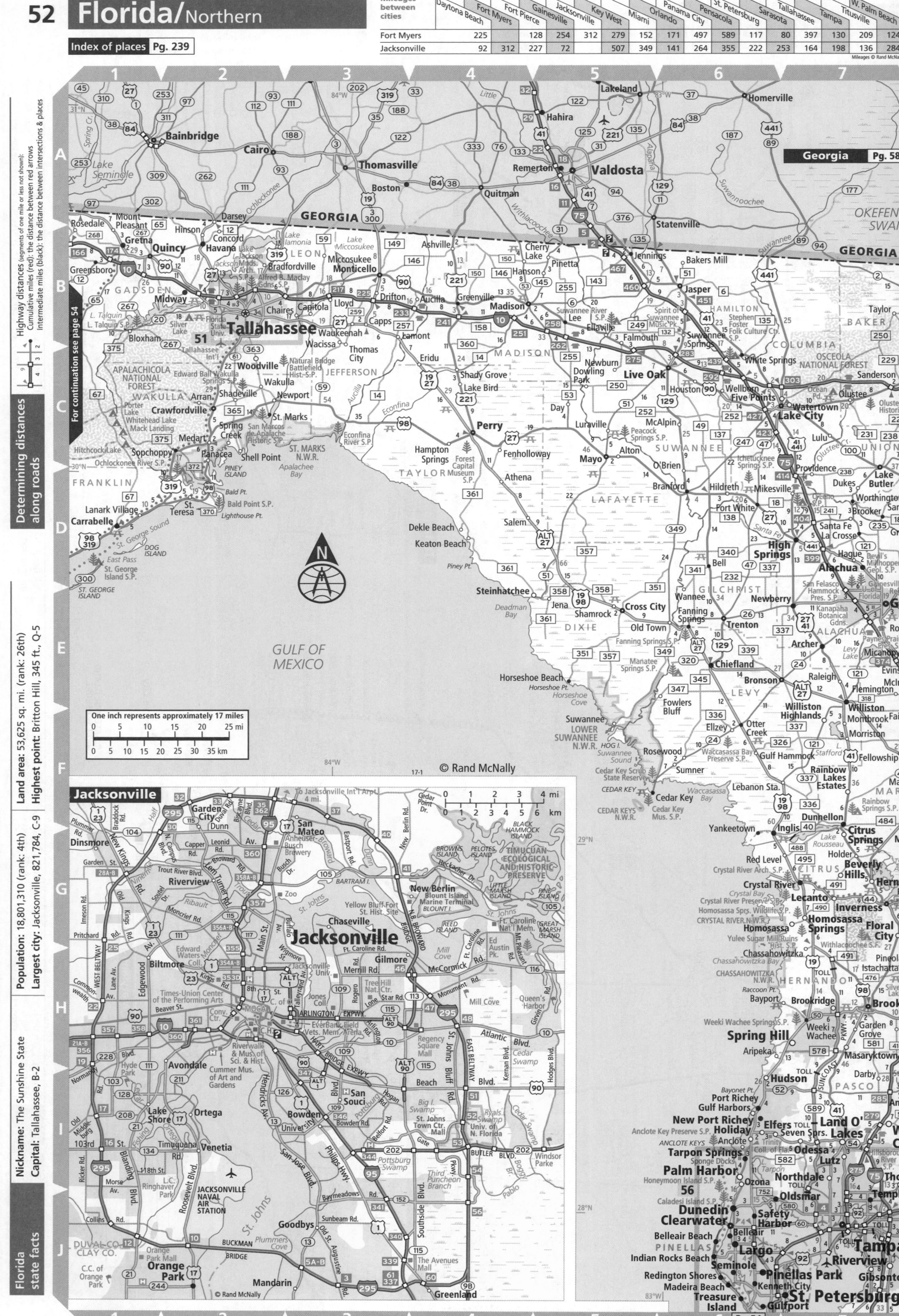

Mileages between cities

	Daytona Beach	Fort Myers	Fort Pierce	Gainesville	Jacksonville	Key West	Miami	Orlando	Panama City	Pensacola	St. Petersburg	Sarasota	Tallahassee	Tampa	Titusville	W. Palm Beach
Fort Myers	225		128	254	312	279	152	171	497	589	117	80	397	130	209	124
Jacksonville	92	312	227	72		507	349	141	264	355	222	253	164	198	136	284

Mileages © Rand McNally

Florida state facts

Nickname: The Sunshine State

Capital: Tallahassee, B-2

Population: 18,801,310 (rank: 4th)

Largest city: Jacksonville, 821,784, C-9

Land area: 53,625 sq. mi. (rank: 26th)

Highest point: Britton Hill, 345 ft., Q-5

Determining distances along roads

Highway distances (segments of one mile or less not shown)
Cumulative miles (red): the distance between red arrows
Intermediate miles (black): the distance between intersections & places

For continuation see page 54

One inch represents approximately 17 miles

0 5 10 15 20 25 mi
0 5 10 15 20 25 30 35 km

GULF OF MEXICO

© Rand McNally

Jacksonville

Pg. 54

Mileages between cities

	Daytona Beach	Fort Myers	Fort Pierce	Gainesville	Jacksonville	Key West	Miami	Orlando	Panama City	Pensacola	St. Petersburg	Sarasota	Tallahassee	Tampa	Titusville	W. Palm Beach
Key West	414	279	284	483	507		162	387	727	821	390	352	627	402	371	231
Miami	256	152	123	336	349	162		229	579	663	262	225	479	255	213	68

Mileages © Rand McNally

continued p. 54

Daytona Beach

Melbourne / Titusville

Florida's Turnpike (SunPass):
(800) 749-7453
Toll Road Information:
floridasturnpike.com

Road Conditions & Construction:
511
(866) 374-3368
fl511.com, www.dot.state.fl.us

Tourism Information:
Visit Florida
(888) 735-2872, (850) 488-5607
www.visitflorida.com

Travel planning & on-the-road resources

© Rand McNally

Mileages between cities

	Daytona Beach	Fort Myers	Fort Pierce	Gainesville	Jacksonville	Key West	Miami	Orlando	Panama City	Pensacola	St. Petersburg	Sarasota	Tallahassee	Tampa	Titusville	W. Palm Beach
Tallahassee	253	397	364	148	164	627	479	257	96	193	257	328		273	295	413
Tampa	137	130	151	127	198	402	255	84	373	459	23	60	273		124	202

Mileages © Rand McNally

Total mileages through Florida
- ④ 132 miles
- ⑦⑤ 471 miles
- ⑩ 362 miles
- ⑨⑤ 382 miles

More mileages at www.randmcnally.com/MC

Florida's Turnpike (SunPass):
(800) 749-7453 floridasturnpike.com

Toll Road Information:

511

Road Conditions & Construction: 511 (866) 374-3368 www.fl511.com, www.dot.state.fl.us

Tourism Information: Visit Florida (888) 735-2872, (850) 488-5607 www.visitflorida.com

Travel planning & on-the-road resources

ATLANTIC OCEAN

Ga. Pg. 58

For continuation see page 52

Pg. 53

Sights to see

- Art Deco National Historic District,
  Miami Beach........................ L-9
- Busch Gardens, Tampa................. B-4
- Goodyear Blimp Base, Pompano Beach...... G-9
- Hugh Taylor Birch State Park,
  Fort Lauderdale H-9
- Marie Selby Botanical Gardens, Sarasota..... H-3
- Miami Seaquarium, Miami M-9

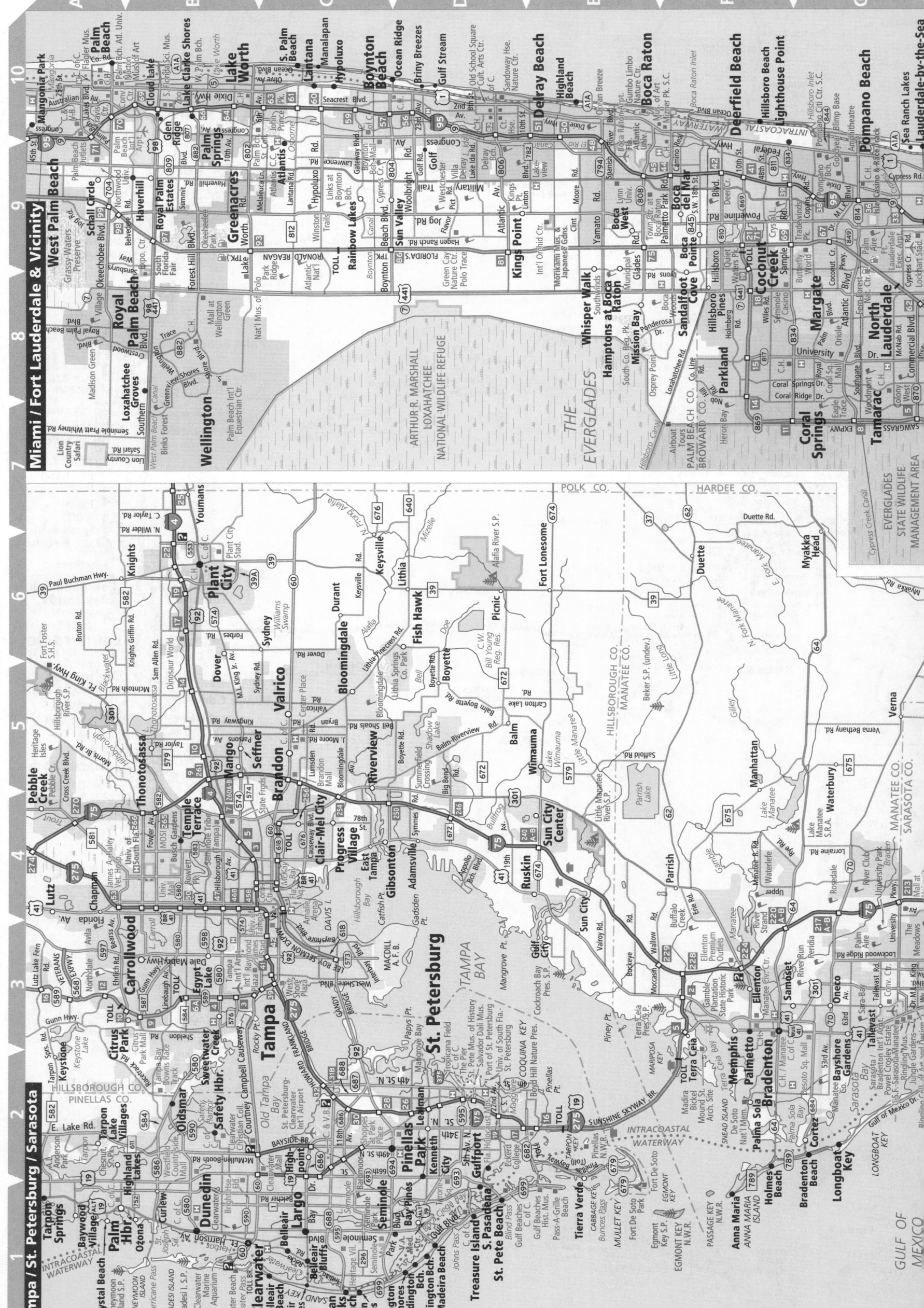

Miami / Fort Lauderdale & Vicinity

Tampa / St. Petersburg / Sarasota

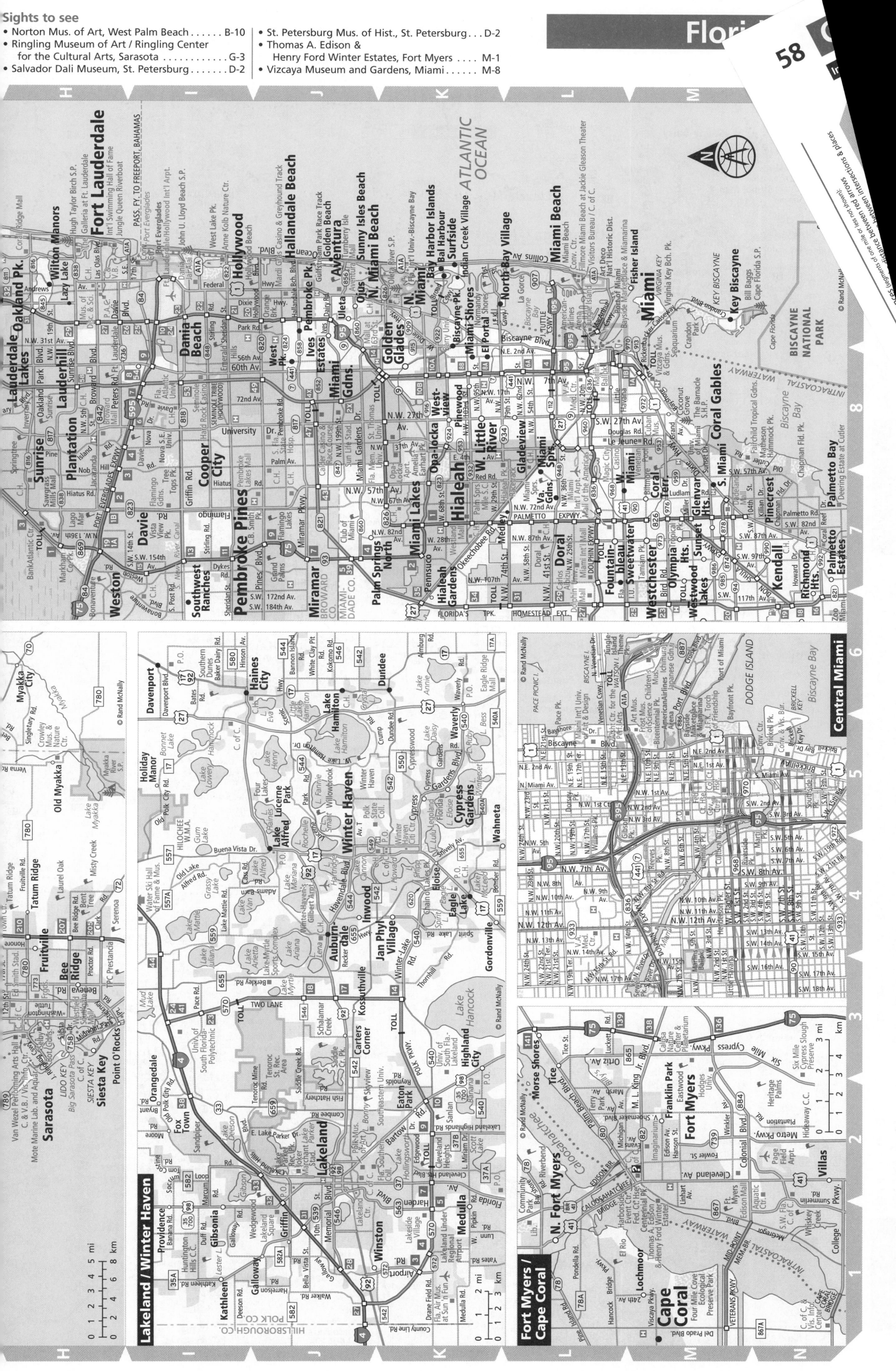

Sights to see

- Norton Mus. of Art, West Palm Beach B-10
- Ringling Museum of Art / Ringling Center
  for the Cultural Arts, Sarasota G-3
- Salvador Dali Museum, St. Petersburg D-2
- St. Petersburg Mus. of Hist., St. Petersburg . . . D-2
- Thomas A. Edison &
  Henry Ford Winter Estates, Fort Myers M-1
- Vizcaya Museum and Gardens, Miami M-8

Fort Lauderdale

Lakeland / Winter Haven

Sarasota

Fort Myers / Cape Coral

Central Miami

ATLANTIC OCEAN

Mileages between cities	Albany	Athens	Atlanta	Augusta	Bainbridge	Brunswick	Chattanooga, TN	Columbus	Gainesville	Jacksonville, FL	Macon	Rome	Savannah	Toccoa	Valdosta	Vidalia
Atlanta	182	69		148	240	275	117	106	54	346	82	70	247	94	228	172
Augusta	211	98	148		268	193	265	249	140	254	123	217	134	132	217	99

Mileages © Rand McNally

© Rand McNally

Tennessee Pg. 190

Alabama Pg. 10

Pg. 60

continued p. 60

Mileages © Rand McNally

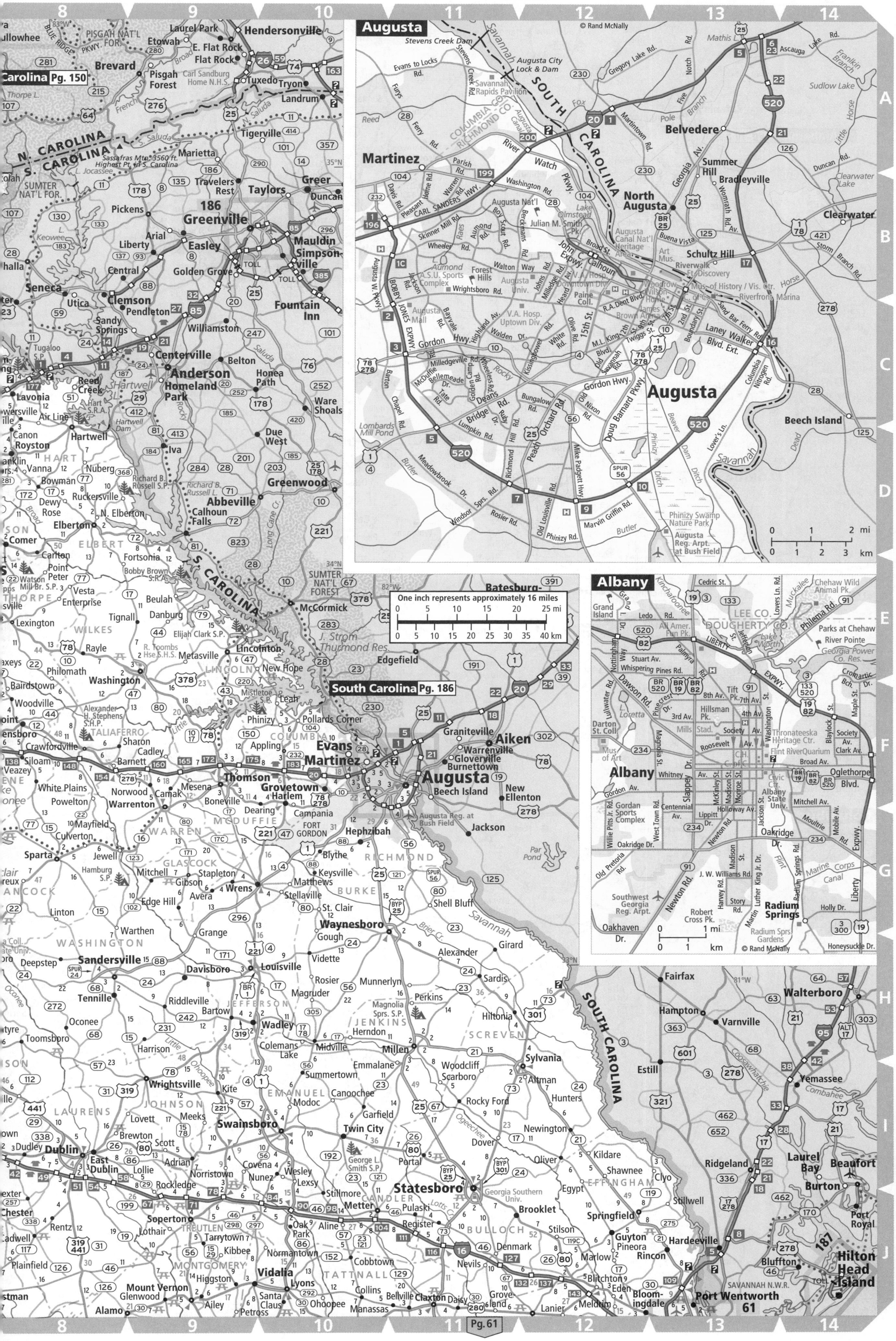

Total mileages through Georgia

20 203 miles   85 180 miles
75 355 miles   95 112 miles

More mileages at www.randmcnally.com/MC

© Rand McNally

Augusta

Albany

One inch represents approximately 16 miles

0 5 10 15 20 25 mi
0 5 10 15 20 25 30 35 40 km

Carolina Pg. 150

South Carolina Pg. 186

Pg. 61

Pg. 61

511 Road Conditions & Construction: 511, (888) 635-8287, (877) 694-2511, (404) 635-8000 www.511ga.org

Toll Road Information: No toll roads

Tourism Information: Visit Georgia (800) 847-4842 www.exploregeorgia.org

Travel planning & on-the-road resources

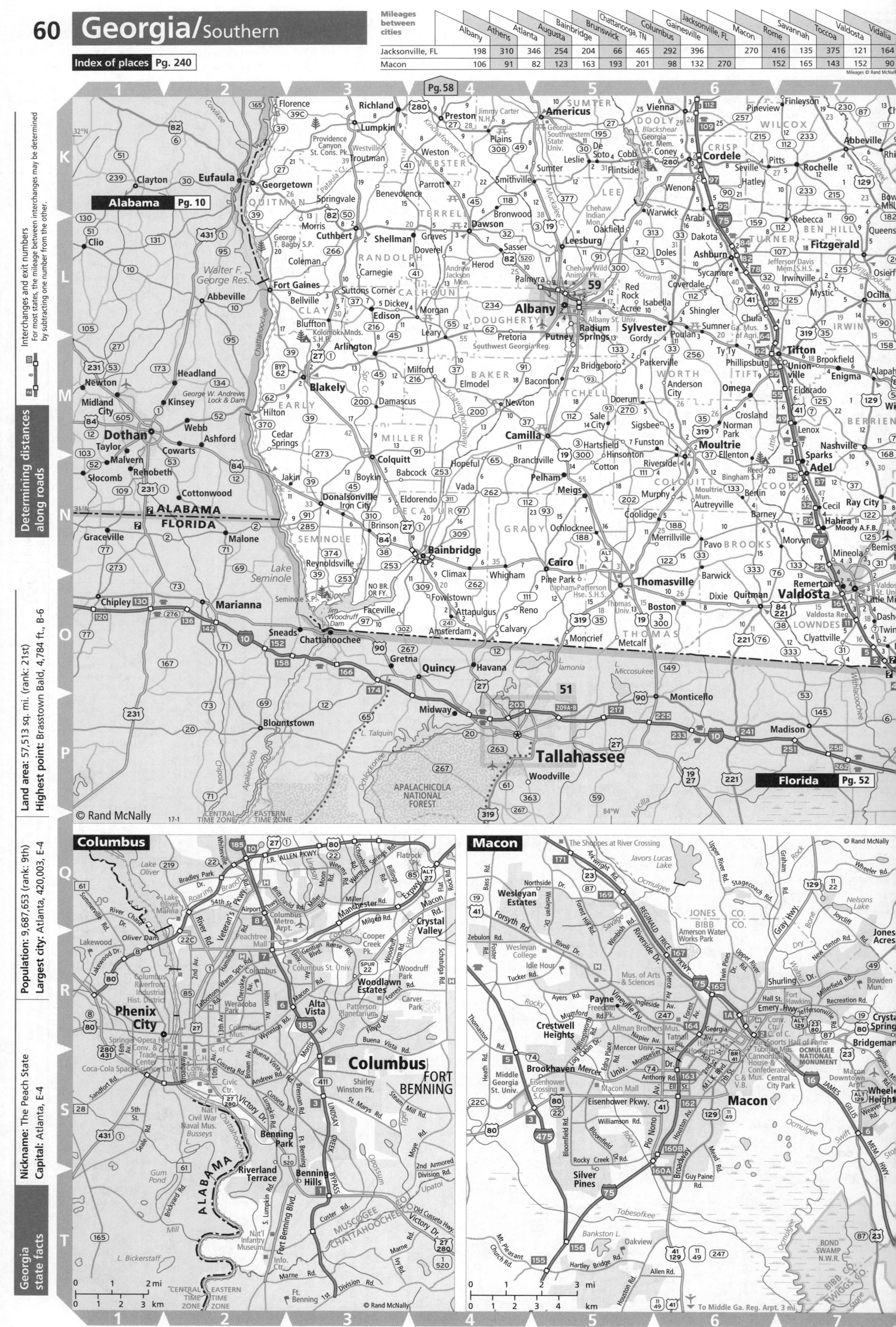

Mileages between cities	Albany	Athens	Atlanta	Augusta	Bainbridge	Brunswick	Chattanooga, TN	Columbus	Gainesville	Jacksonville, FL	Macon	Rome	Savannah	Toccoa	Valdosta	Vidalia
Jacksonville, FL	198	310	346	254	204	66	465	292	396		270	416	135	375	121	164
Macon	106	91	82	123	163	193	201	98	132	270		152	165	143	152	90

Mileages © Rand McNally

Columbus

Macon

© Rand McNally

Georgia state facts

Nickname: The Peach State
Capital: Atlanta, E-4

Population: 9,687,653 (rank: 9th)
Largest city: Atlanta, 420,003, E-4

Land area: 57,513 sq. mi. (rank: 21st)
Highest point: Brasstown Bald, 4,784 ft., B-6

Determining distances along roads

Interchanges and exit numbers
For most states, the mileage between interchanges may be determined by subtracting one number from the other.

Mileages between cities	Albany	Athens	Atlanta	Augusta	Bainbridge	Brunswick	Chattanooga, TN	Columbus	Gainesville	Jacksonville, FL	Macon	Rome	Savannah	Toccoa	Valdosta	Vidalia
Savannah	226	222	247	134	249	77	364	249	297	135	165	317		255	167	90
Valdosta	79	243	228	217	83	120	346	173	278	121	152	298	167	317		118

Mileages © Rand McNally

20 203 miles 85 180 miles **Total mileages through Georgia**
75 355 miles 95 112 miles More mileages at www.randmcnally.com/MC

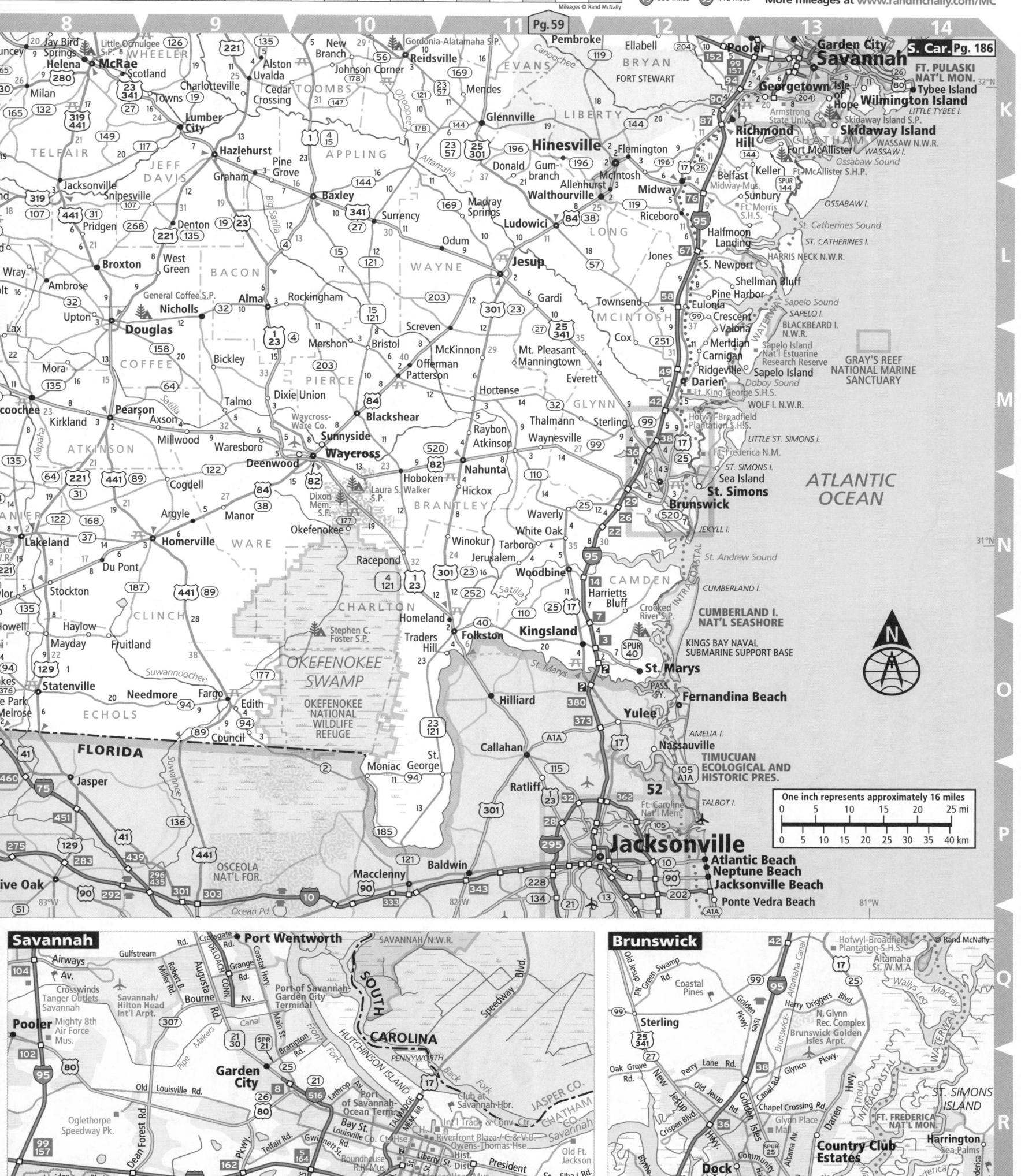

One inch represents approximately 16 miles

No toll roads

Toll Road Information:

511
511ga.org

Road Conditions & Construction: 511, (888) 635-8287, (877) 694-2511, (404) 635-8000 www.511ga.org

Tourism Information: Visit Georgia (800) 847-4842 www.exploregeorgia.org

Travel planning & on-the-road resources

© Rand McNally

*via plane

Mileages between cities	Honolulu Hilo	Kahului	Kailua	Kailua Kona	Kapa'a	Lahaina	Wahiawa
Hilo	225*	127*	237*	74	337*	149*	236*
Honolulu	225*	108*	11	177*	116*	130*	20

	Honolulu Hilo	Kahului	Kailua	Kailua Kona	Kapa'a	Lahaina	Wahiawa
Kahului	127*	108*	22*	93*	214*	22	119*
Kailua Kona	74	177*	93*	188*	283*	116*	188*

Mileages © Rand McNally

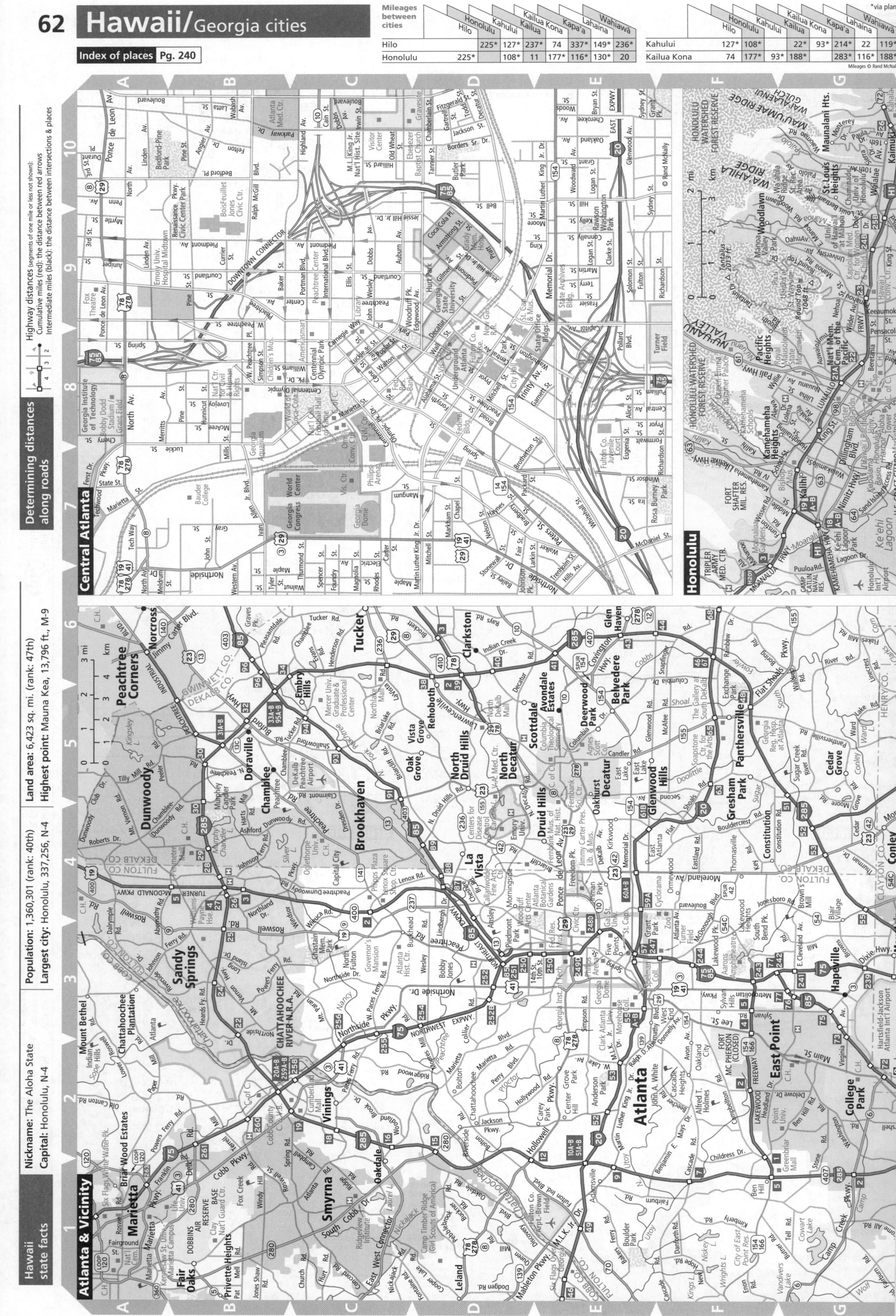

Hawaii state facts

Nickname: The Aloha State
Capital: Honolulu
Population: 1,360,301 (rank: 40th)
Land area: 6,423 sq. mi. (rank: 47th)
Largest city: Honolulu, 337,256, N-4
Highest point: Mauna Kea, 13,796 ft., M-9

Determining distances along roads

Highway distances (segments of one mile or less not shown):
Cumulative miles (red): the distance between red arrows
Intermediate miles (black): the distance between intersections & places

Central Atlanta

Honolulu

Atlanta & Vicinity

Mileages between cities	Honolulu / Hilo	Kahului	Kailua Kona / Kailua	Kapa'a	Lahaina / Wahiawā
Kapa'a	337*	116*	214* 128*	283*	236* 128*
Kaunakakai	177*	68*	55* 79*	144*	174* 77* 79*

	Honolulu / Hilo	Kahului	Kailua Kona / Kailua	Kapa'a	Lahaina / Wahiawā
Lahaina	149*	130* 22	43* 116*		236* 141*
Wahiawā	236*	20 119*	26 188*		128* 141*

*via plane

Mileages © Rand McNally

Total mileages through Hawaii
More mileages at www.randmcnally.com/MC

H1 27 miles H3 15 miles
H2 8 miles

No toll roads

Index of places Pg. 241

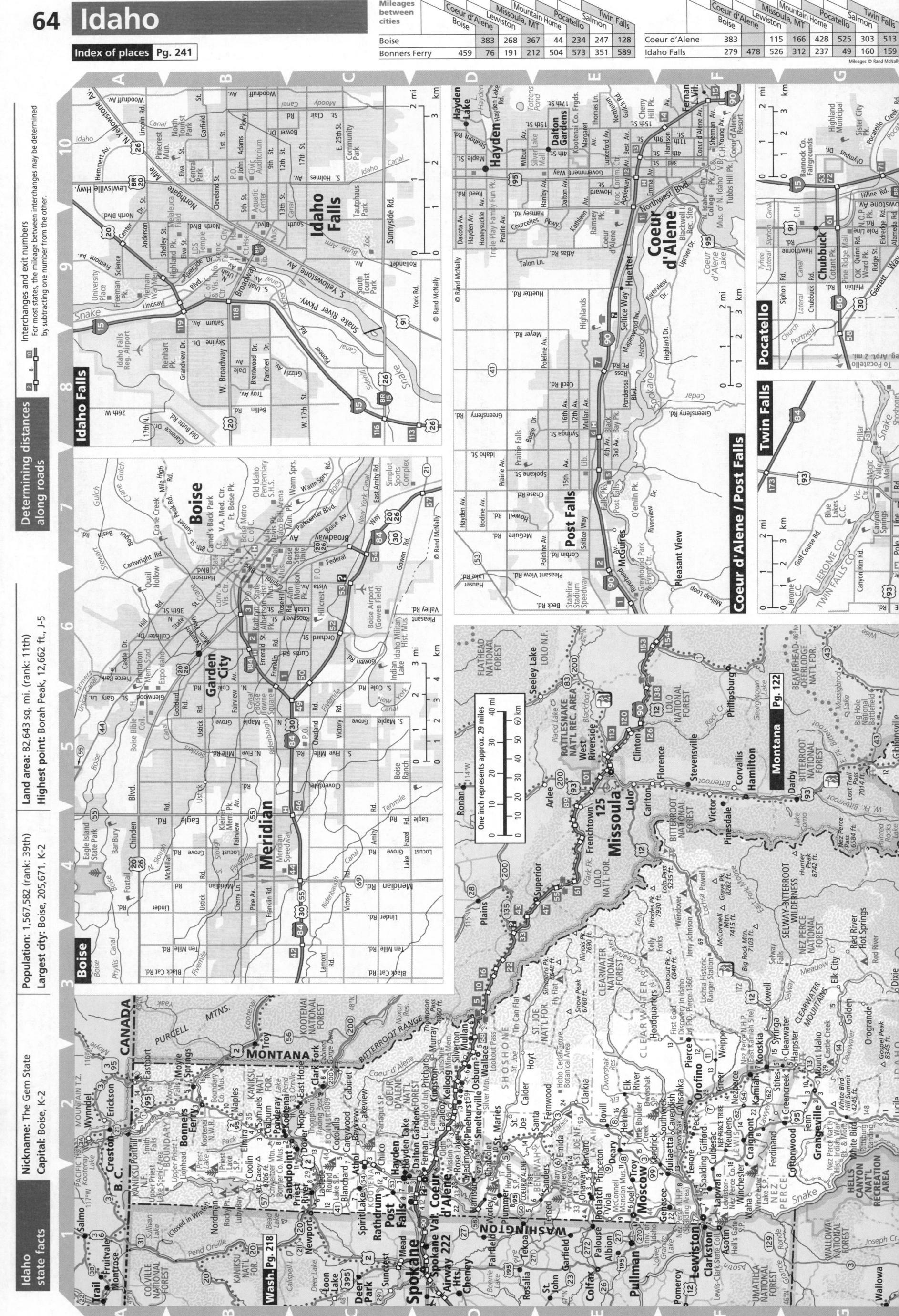

Mileages between cities	Boise	Coeur d'Alene	Lewiston	Missoula, MT	Mountain Home	Pocatello	Salmon	Twin Falls
Boise		383	268	367	44	234	247	128
Bonners Ferry	459	76	191	212	504	573	351	589
Coeur d'Alene	383		115	166	428	525	303	513
Idaho Falls	279	478	526	312	237	49	160	159

Mileages © Rand McNally

Idaho state facts

Nickname: The Gem State
Capital: Boise, K-2
Population: 1,567,582 (rank: 39th)
Land area: 82,643 sq. mi. (rank: 11th)
Highest point: Borah Peak, 12,662 ft., J-5
Largest city: Boise, 205,671, K-2

Determining distances along roads

Interchanges and exit numbers — For most states, the mileage between interchanges may be determined by subtracting one number from the other.

Mileages between cities

	Boise	Coeur d'Alene	Lewiston	Missoula, MT	Mountain Home	Pocatello	Salmon	Twin Falls
Lewiston	268	115		214	313	504	332	398
Pocatello	234	525	504	361	191		209	114
Salmon	247	303	332	138	287	209		247
Twin Falls	128	513	398	384	85	114	247	

Mileages © Rand McNally

15 196 miles 86 63 miles
84 276 miles 90 74 miles

Total mileages through Idaho
More mileages at www.randmcnally.com/MC

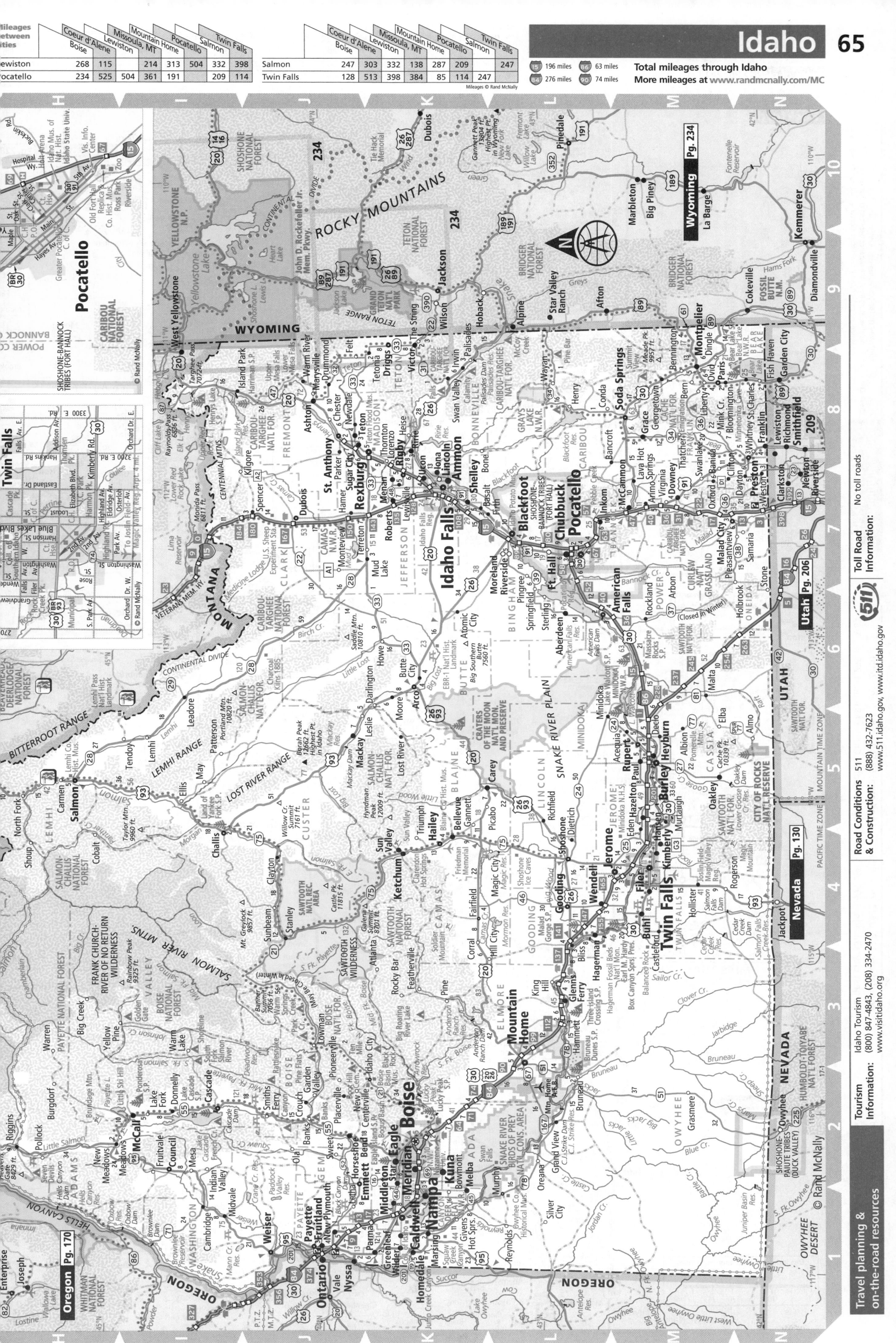

Travel planning & on-the-road resources

Tourism Information: Idaho Tourism (800) 847-4843, (208) 334-2470 www.visitidaho.org

Road Conditions & Construction: 511 (888) 432-7623 www.511.idaho.gov, www.itd.idaho.gov

Toll Road Information: No toll roads

Index of places Pg. 241

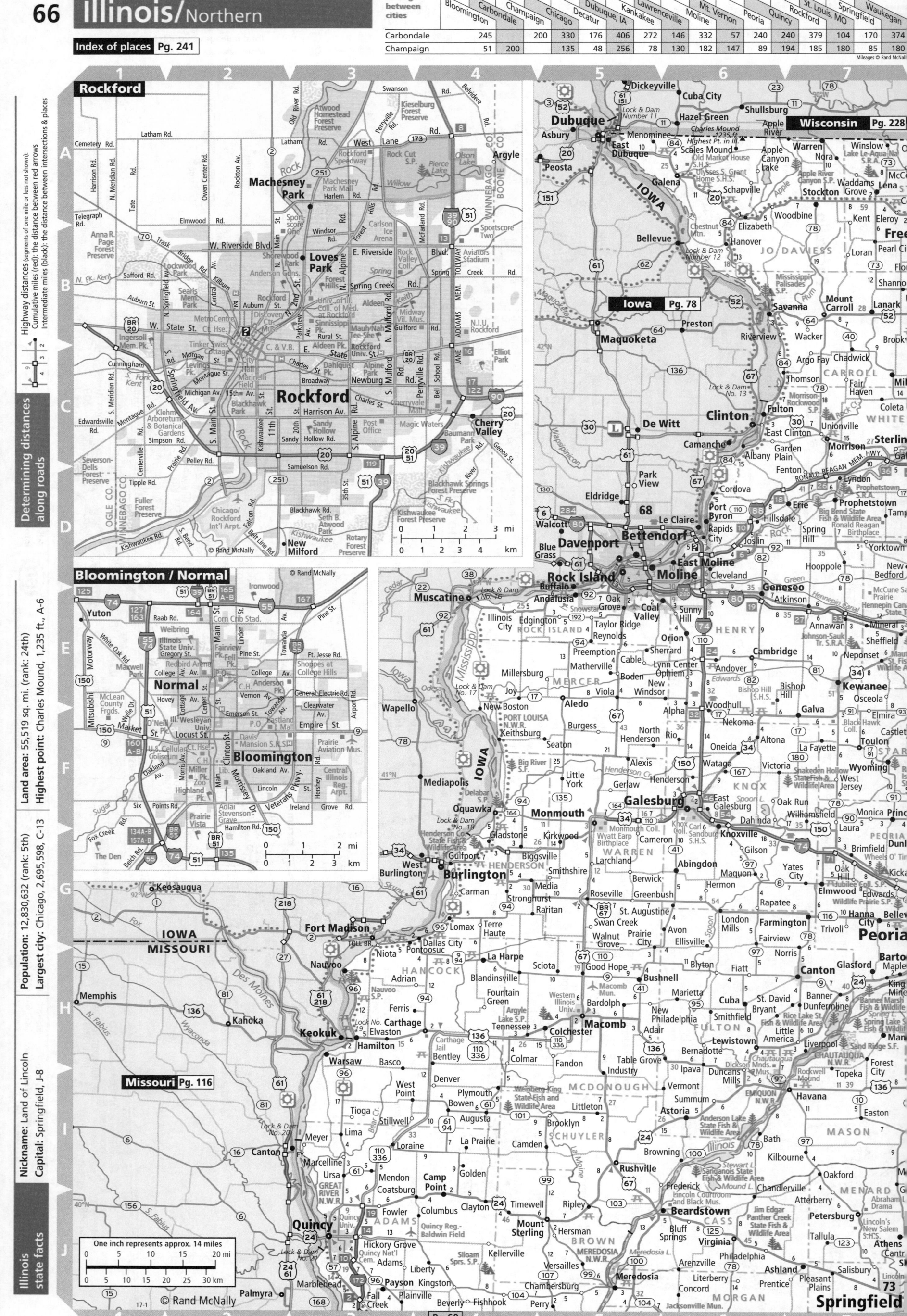

Mileages between cities	Bloomington	Carbondale	Champaign	Chicago	Decatur	Dubuque, IA	Kankakee	Lawrenceville	Moline	Mt. Vernon	Peoria	Quincy	Rockford	St. Louis, MO	Springfield	Waukegan
Carbondale	245		200	330	176	406	272	146	332	57	240	240	379	104	170	374
Champaign	51	200		135	48	256	78	130	182	147	89	194	185	180	85	180

Mileages © Rand McNally

Illinois state facts

Nickname: Land of Lincoln
Capital: Springfield, J-8

Population: 12,830,632 (rank: 5th)
Largest city: Chicago, 2,695,598, C-13

Land area: 55,519 sq. mi. (rank: 24th)
Highest point: Charles Mound, 1,235 ft., A-6

Determining distances along roads

Highway distances (segments of one mile or less not shown):
Cumulative miles (red): the distance between red arrows
Intermediate miles (black): the distance between intersections & places

One inch represents approx. 14 miles

© Rand McNally

continued p. 6B

Mileages between cities	Bloomington	Carbondale	Champaign	Chicago	Decatur	Dubuque, IA	Kankakee	Lawrenceville	Moline	Mt. Vernon	Peoria	Quincy	Rockford	St. Louis, MO	Springfield	Waukegan
Chicago	132	330	135		179	177	58	247	166	277	154	309	84	296	198	38
Moline	131	332	182	166	171	75	158	307		308	93	148	120	261	164	190

Mileages © Rand McNally

Total mileages through Illinois
313 miles · 164 miles
156 miles · 124 miles
More mileages at www.randmcnally.com/MC

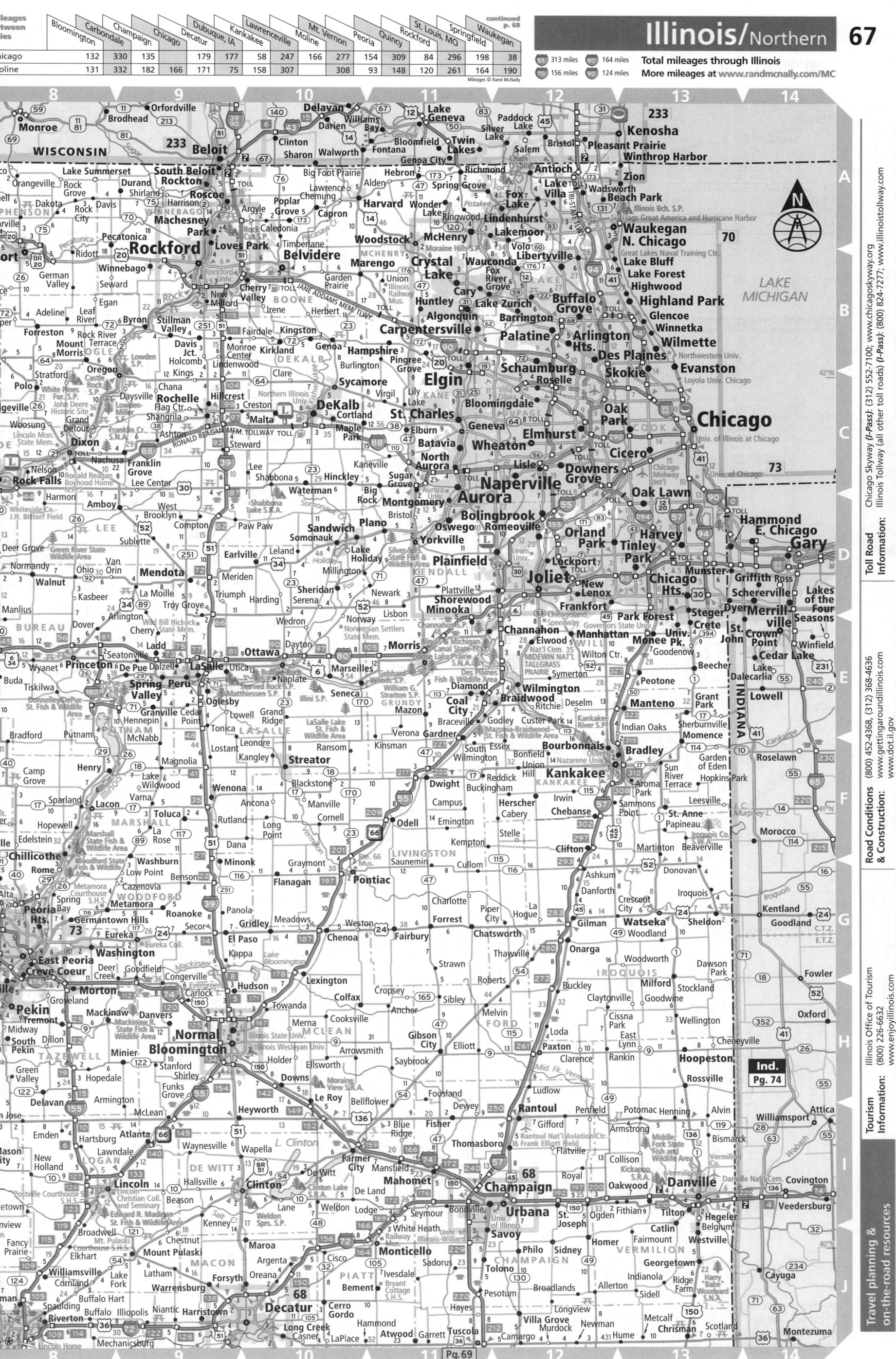

Ind. Pg. 74

Index of places Pg. 241

Mileages between cities	Bloomington	Carbondale	Champaign	Chicago	Decatur	Dubuque, IA	Kankakee	Lawrenceville	Moline	Mt. Vernon	Peoria	Quincy	Rockford	St. Louis, MO	Springfield	Waukegan
Peoria	38	240	89	154	78	167	108	214	93	215		130	138	168	71	184
Rockford	132	379	185	84	180	93	139	309	120	326	138	268		294	197	73

Mileages © Rand McNally

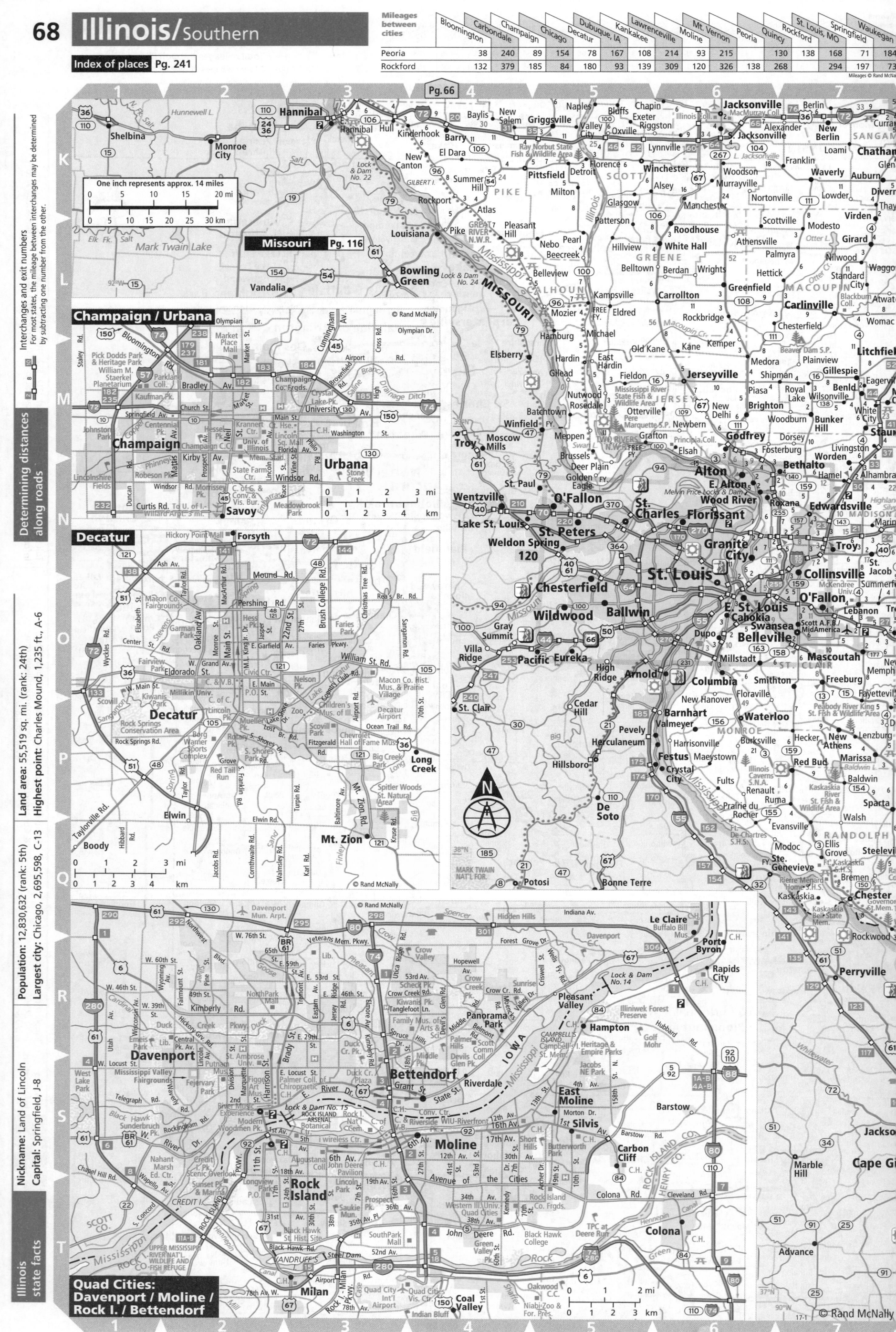

Mileages between Cities

	Bloomington	Carbondale	Champaign	Chicago	Decatur	Dubuque, IA	Kankakee	Lawrenceville	Moline	Mt. Vernon	Peoria	Quincy	Rockford	St. Louis, MO	Springfield	Waukegan
St. Louis, MO	162	104	180	296	135	335	252	144	261	79	168	139	294		98	326
Springfield	66	170	85	198	38	238	157	153	164	138	71	112	197	98		229

Mileages © Rand McNally

Total mileages through Illinois

55 — 313 miles	80 — 164 miles	70 — 156 miles	90 — 124 miles

More mileages at www.randmcnally.com/MC

Toll Road Information: Chicago Skyway (I-Pass): (312) 552-7100; www.chicagoskyway.org — Illinois Tollway (all other toll roads) (I-Pass): (800) 824-7277; www.illinoistollway.com

Road Conditions & Construction: (800) 452-4368, (312) 368-4636 — www.gettingaroundillinois.com — www.dot.il.gov

Tourism Information: Illinois Office of Tourism (800) 226-6632 — www.enjoyillinois.com

Travel planning & on-the-road resources

Indiana Pg. 74

Kentucky Pg. 86

Pg. 67

Sights to see

(located on pages 70-73)

Chicago & Vicinity

© Rand McNally

LAKE MICHIGAN
El. 579 ft. above sea level

Sights to see (located on pages 70-73)

- John G. Shedd Aquarium, Chicago........G-14
- John Hancock Center, Chicago............C-13
- Lincoln Park Zoo, Chicago................H-9
- Millennium Park, Chicago................E-13
- Museum of Science & Industry, Chicago.....J-10
- Navy Pier, Chicago.....................D-14
- Willis Tower, Chicago..................E-12
- Wrigley Field, Chicago.................G-9

Sights to see

- Abraham Lincoln Presidential Library & Museum, Springfield M-16
- Children's Museum of Indianapolis, Indianapolis. D-18
- Eiteljorg Museum, Indianapolis E-17
- Fort Wayne Children's Zoo, Fort Wayne L-19
- Illinois State Capitol Complex, Springfield. . M-16

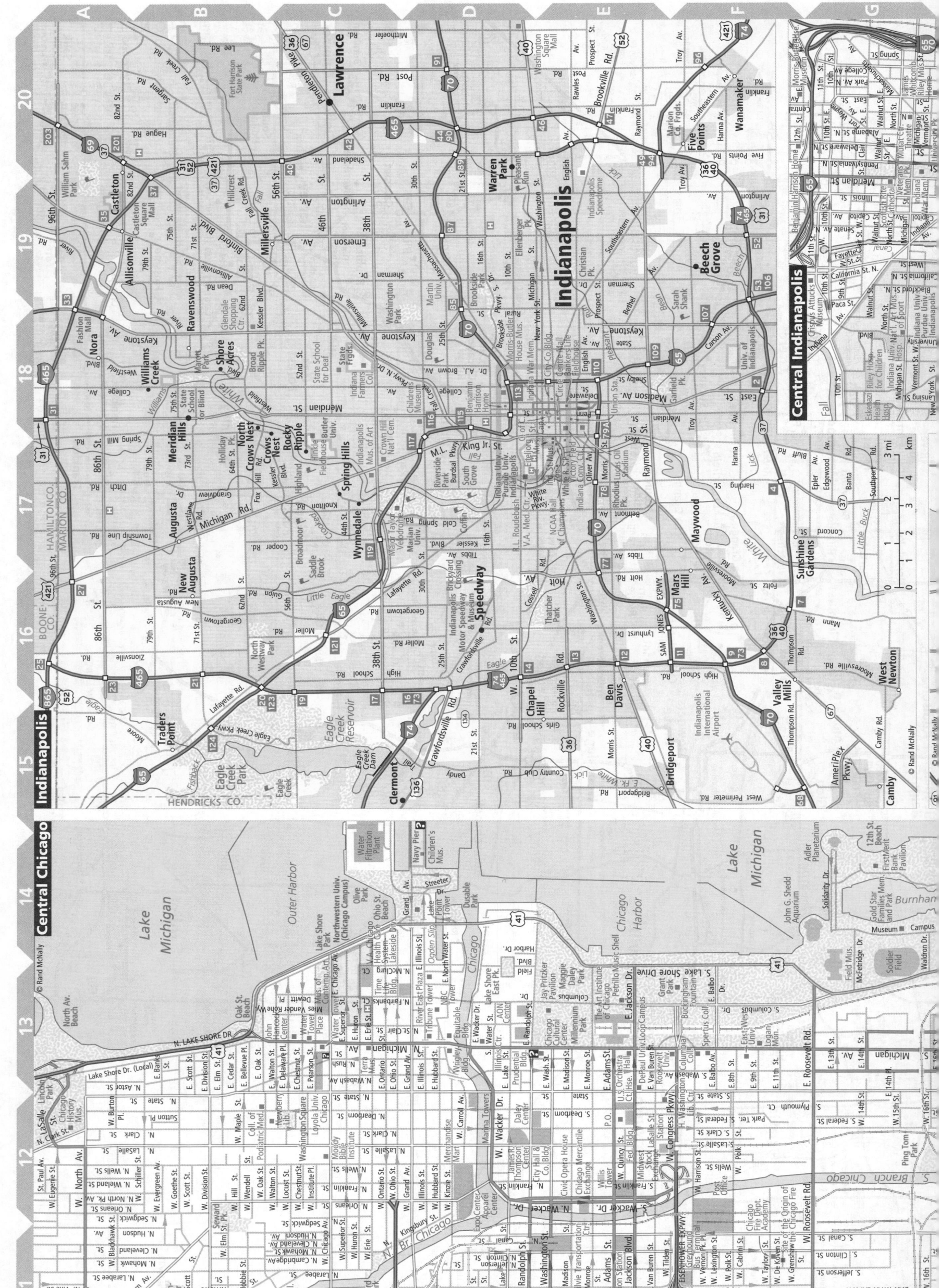

Sights to see

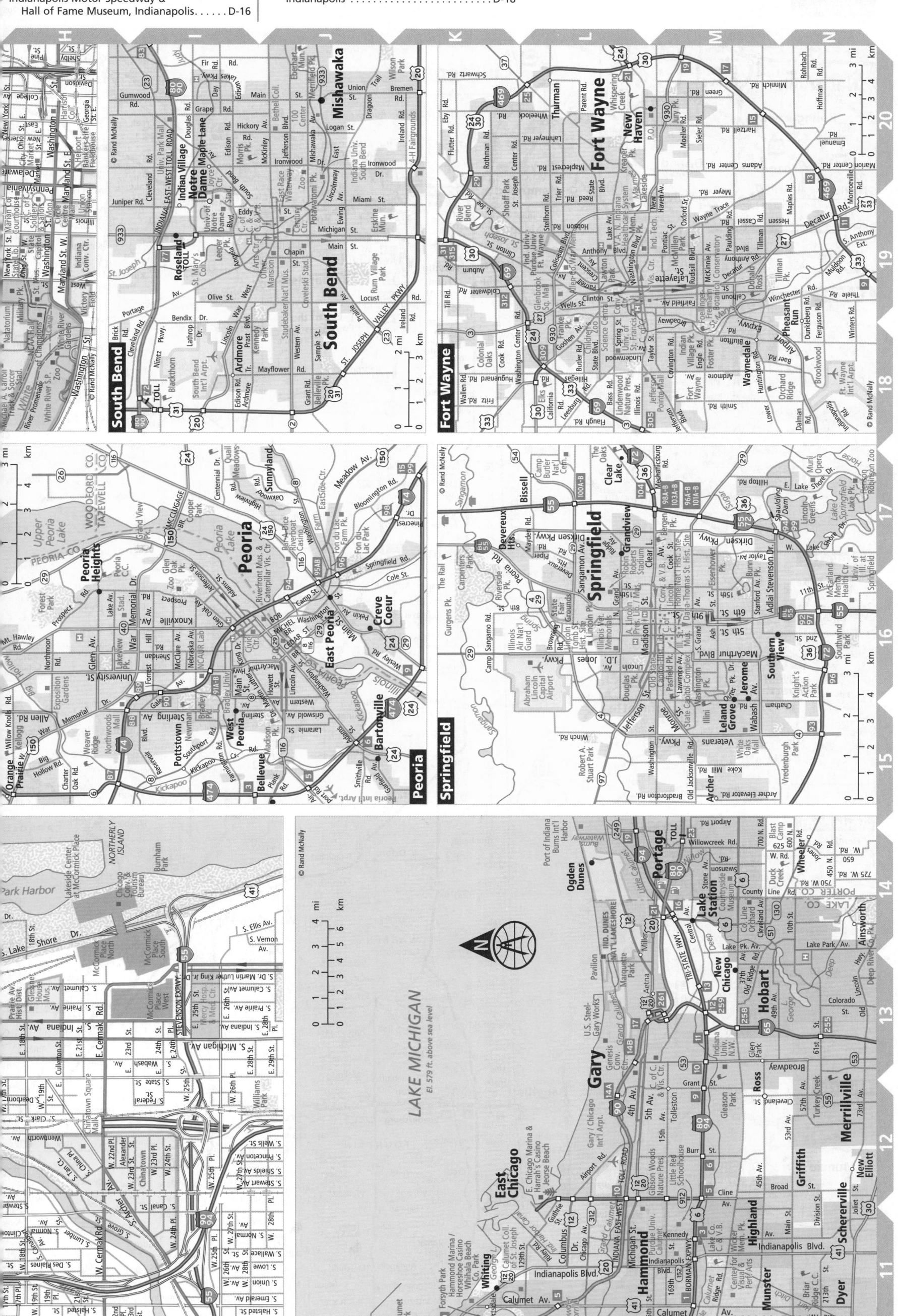

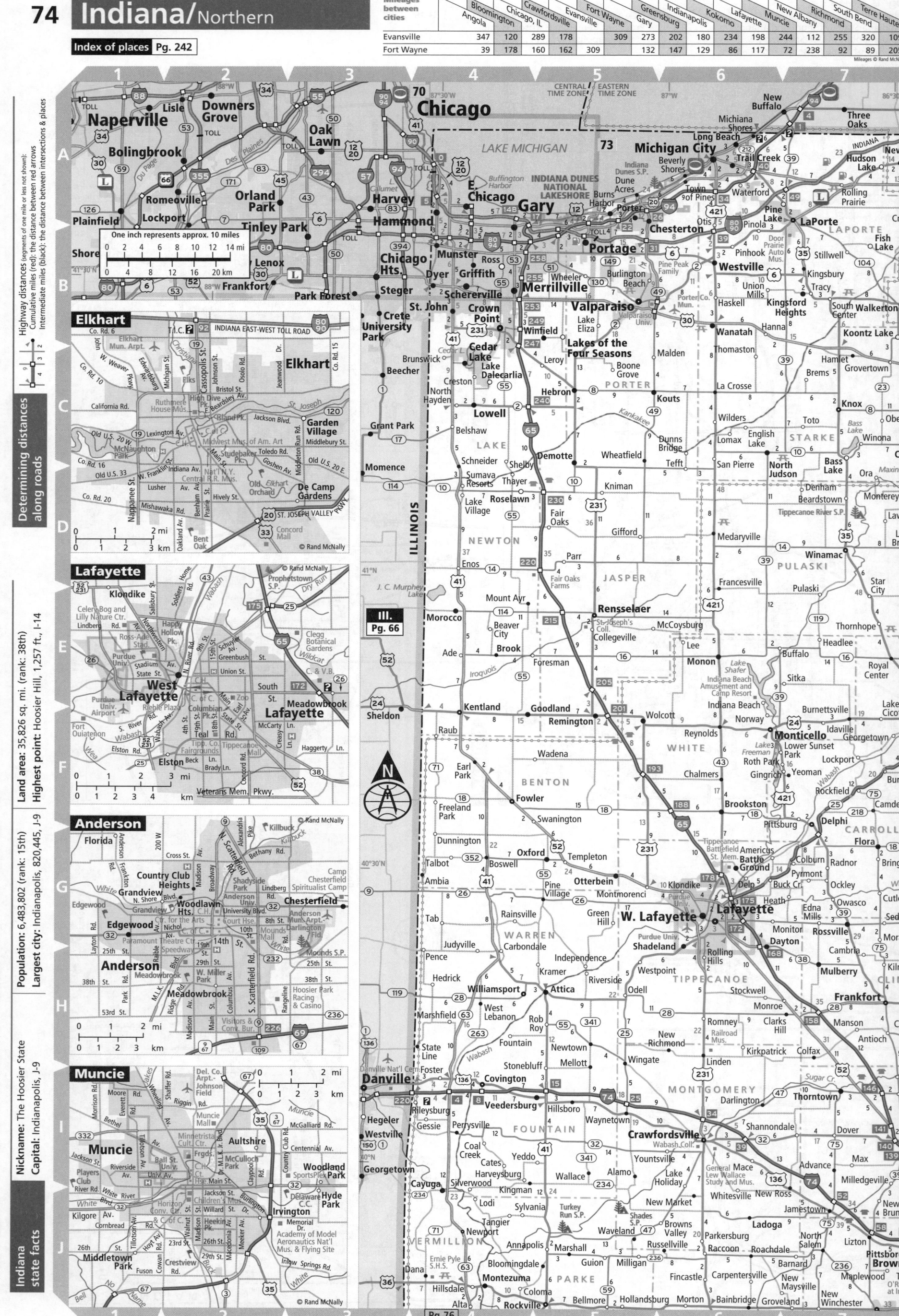

Mileages between cities	Angola	Bloomington	Chicago, IL	Crawfordsville	Evansville	Fort Wayne	Gary	Greensburg	Indianapolis	Kokomo	Lafayette	Muncie	New Albany	Richmond	South Bend	Terre Haute
Evansville	347	120	289	178		309	273	202	180	234	198	244	112	255	320	109
Fort Wayne	39	178	160	162	309		132	147	129	86	117	72	238	92	89	205

Mileages © Rand McNally

State facts

Nickname: The Hoosier State
Capital: Indianapolis, J-9

Land area: 35,826 sq. mi. (rank: 38th)
Highest point: Hoosier Hill, 1,257 ft., I-14
Population: 6,483,802 (rank: 15th)
Largest city: Indianapolis, 820,445, J-9

Determining distances along roads

Highway distances (segments of one mile or less not shown)
Cumulative miles (red): the distance between red arrows
Intermediate miles (black): the distance between intersections & places

One inch represents approx. 10 miles
0 2 4 6 8 10 12 14 mi
0 4 8 12 16 20 km

continued p. 76

Mileages between cities	Angola	Bloomington	Chicago, IL	Crawfordsville	Evansville	Fort Wayne	Gary	Greensburg	Indianapolis	Kokomo	Lafayette	Muncie	New Albany	Richmond	South Bend	Terre Haute
Gary	135	200	30	118	273	132		203	151	127	91	196	266	222	64	164
Indianapolis	166	52	181	49	180	129	151	50		51	63	61	114	73	145	76

Mileages © Rand McNally

55 261 miles 74 172 miles **Total mileages through Indiana**
70 157 miles 80 156 miles More mileages at www.randmcnally.com/MC

Toll Road Information: Indiana Toll Road (E-ZPass) (888) 496-6690 www.ezpassin.com

Road Conditions & Construction: (866) 849-1368, (317) 232-5533 www.in.gov/dot

Tourism Information: Indiana Office of Tourism Development (800) 677-9800 www.visitindiana.com

Travel planning & on-the-road resources

Michigan Pg. 102

Pg. 77

Ohio Pg. 158

© Rand McNally

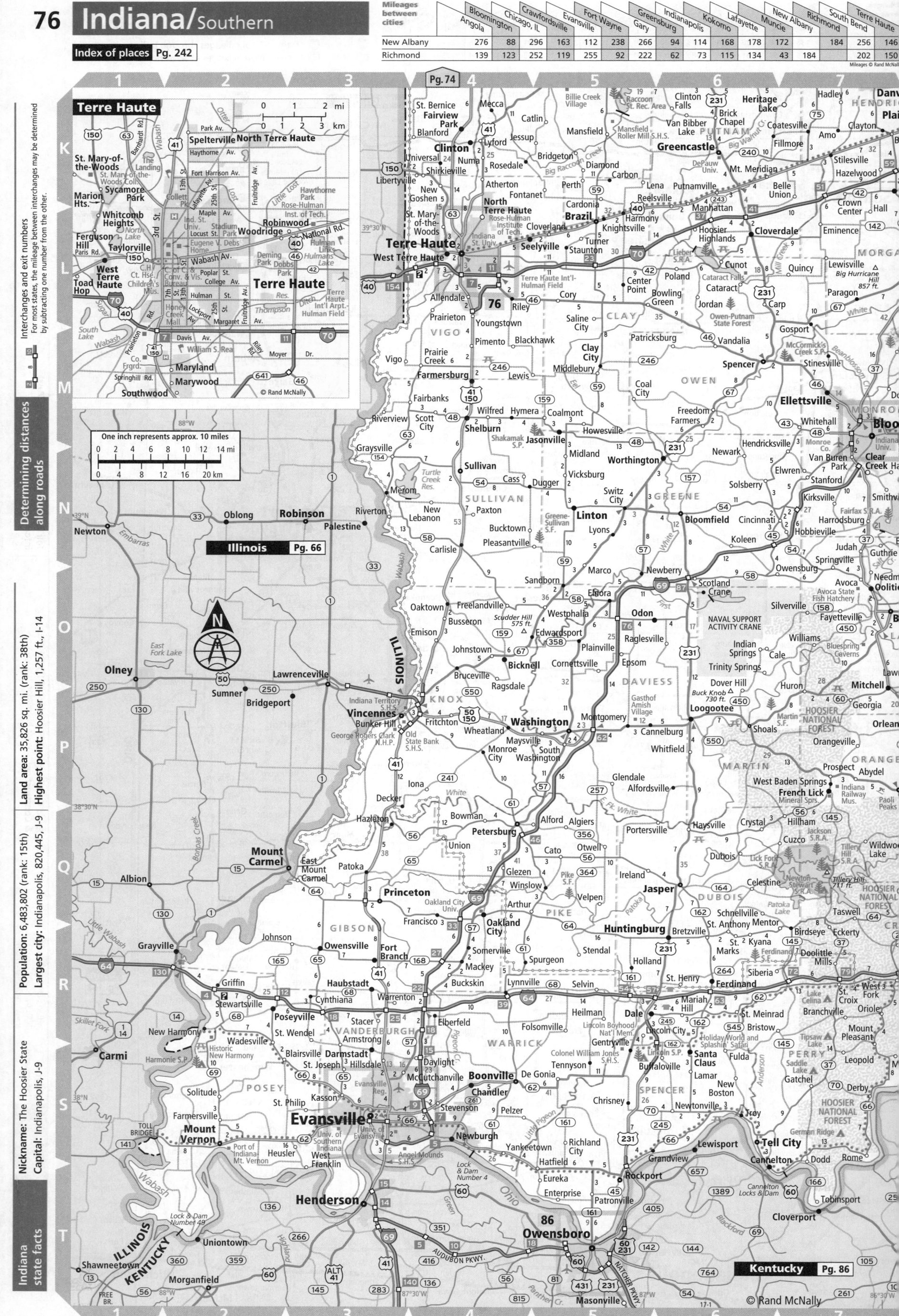

Mileages between cities	Angola	Bloomington	Chicago, IL	Crawfordsville	Evansville	Fort Wayne	Gary	Greensburg	Indianapolis	Kokomo	Lafayette	Muncie	New Albany	Richmond	South Bend	Terre Haute
South Bend	77	195	93	135	320	89	64	183	145	87	106	143	256	202		216
Terre Haute	242	58	180	58	109	205	164	123	76	129	89	139	146	150	216	

Mileages © Rand McNally

Total mileages through Indiana
- 65 – 261 miles
- 74 – 172 miles
- 70 – 157 miles
- 90 – 156 miles

More mileages at www.randmcnally.com/MC

Toll Road Information: Indiana Toll Road (E-ZPass) (888) 496-6690 www.ezpassin.com

Road Conditions & Construction: (866) 849-1368, (317) 232-5533 www.in.gov/dot

Tourism Information: Indiana Office of Tourism Development (800) 677-9800 www.visitindiana.com

Travel planning & on-the-road resources

Bloomington

Evansville

© Rand McNally

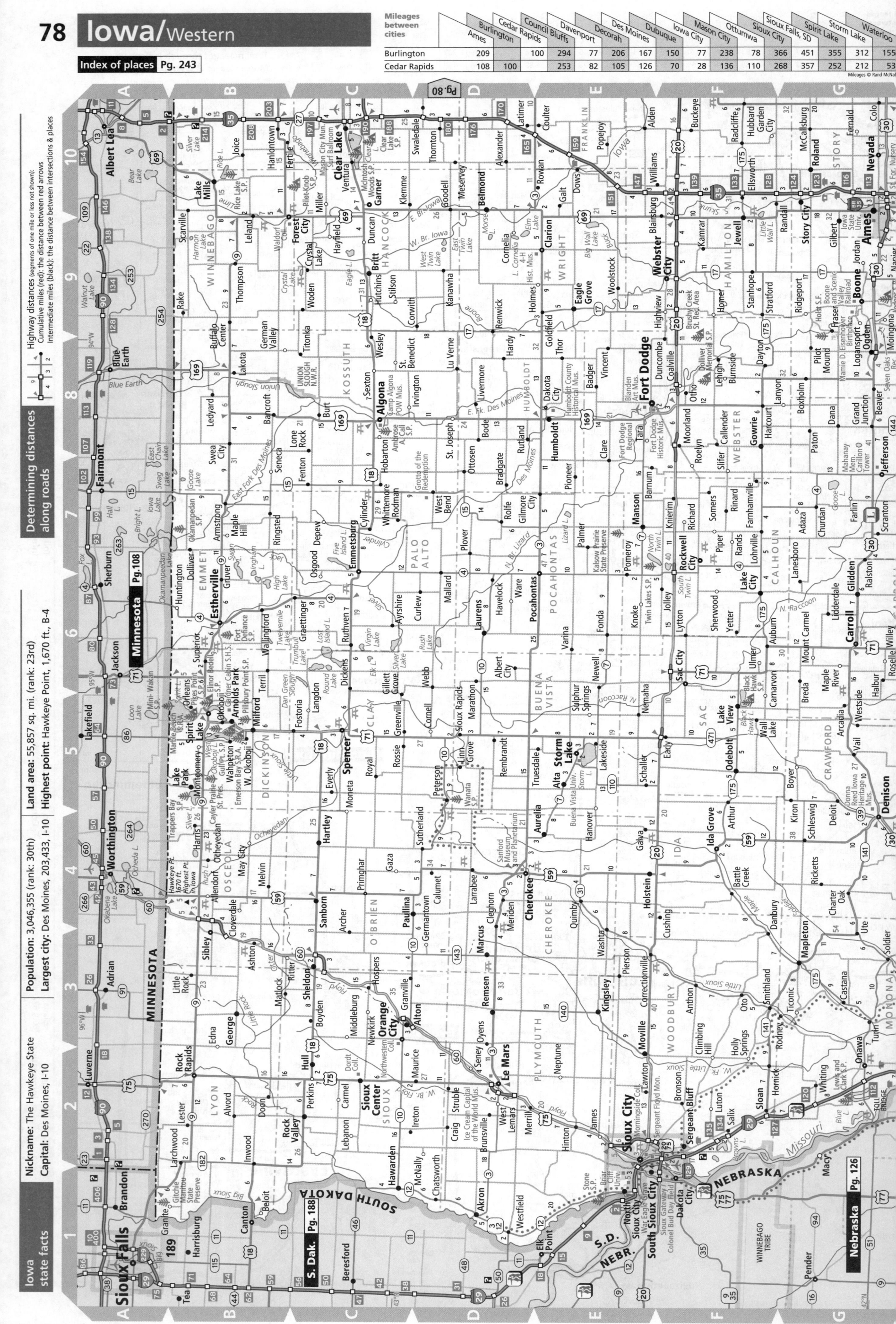

Mileages between cities		Ames	Burlington	Cedar Rapids	Council Bluffs	Davenport	Decorah	Des Moines	Dubuque	Iowa City	Mason City	Ottumwa	Sioux Falls, SD	Sioux City	Spirit Lake	Storm Lake	Waterloo
Council Bluffs		160	294	253		295	328	127	327	241	246	213	94	180	176	122	253
Davenport		191	77	82	295		167	167	71	57	220	133	366	441	336	294	136

Mileages © Rand McNally

continued p. 80

| 29 | 155 miles | 80 | 303 miles |
| 35 | 218 miles | 218 | 257 miles |

Total mileages through Iowa
More mileages at www.randmcnally.com/MC

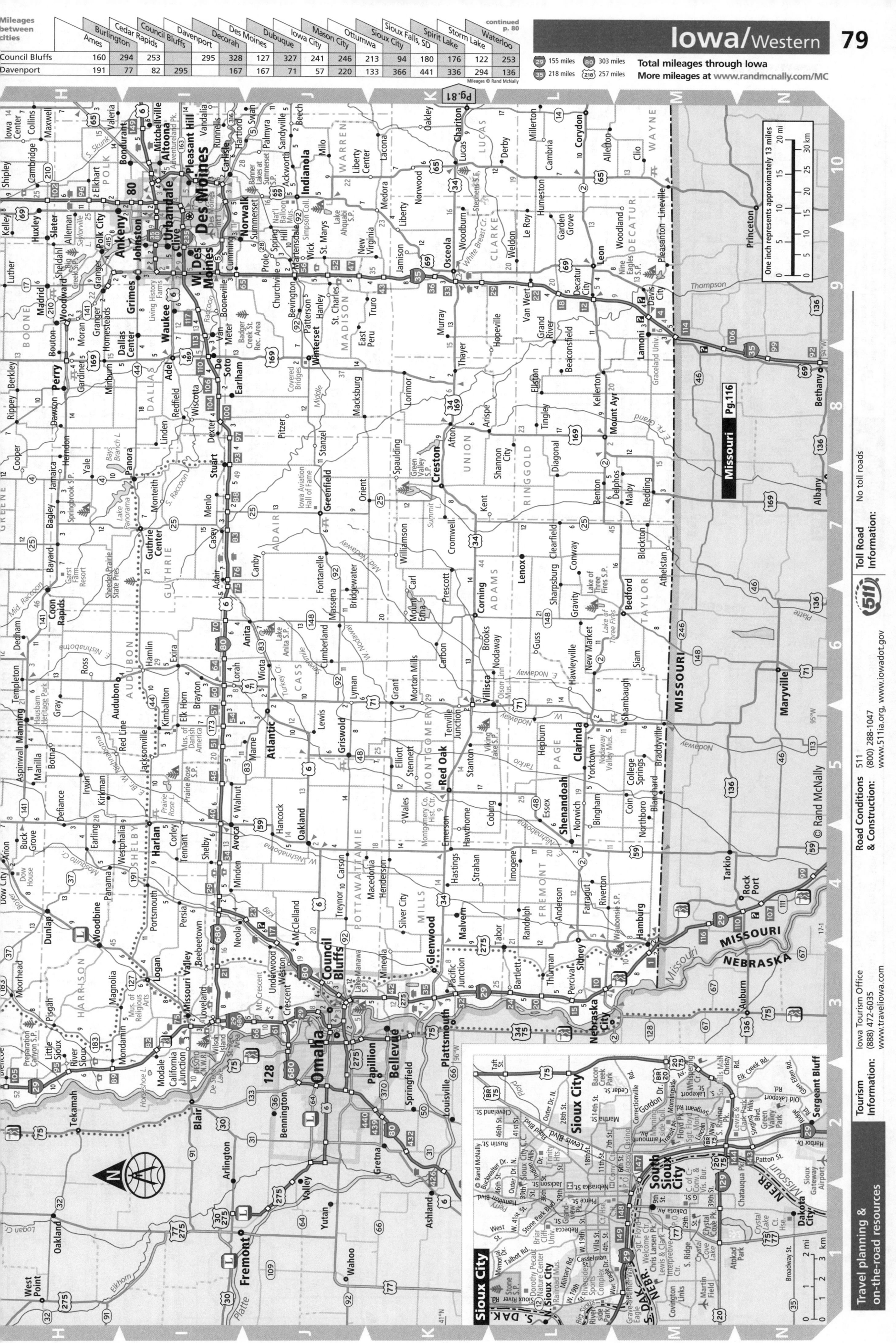

One inch represents approximately 13 miles

Tourism Information:
Iowa Tourism Office
(888) 472-6035
www.traveliowa.com

Road Conditions & Construction:
511
(800) 288-1047
www.511ia.org, www.iowadot.gov

Toll Road Information:
No toll roads

Travel planning & on-the-road resources

© Rand McNally

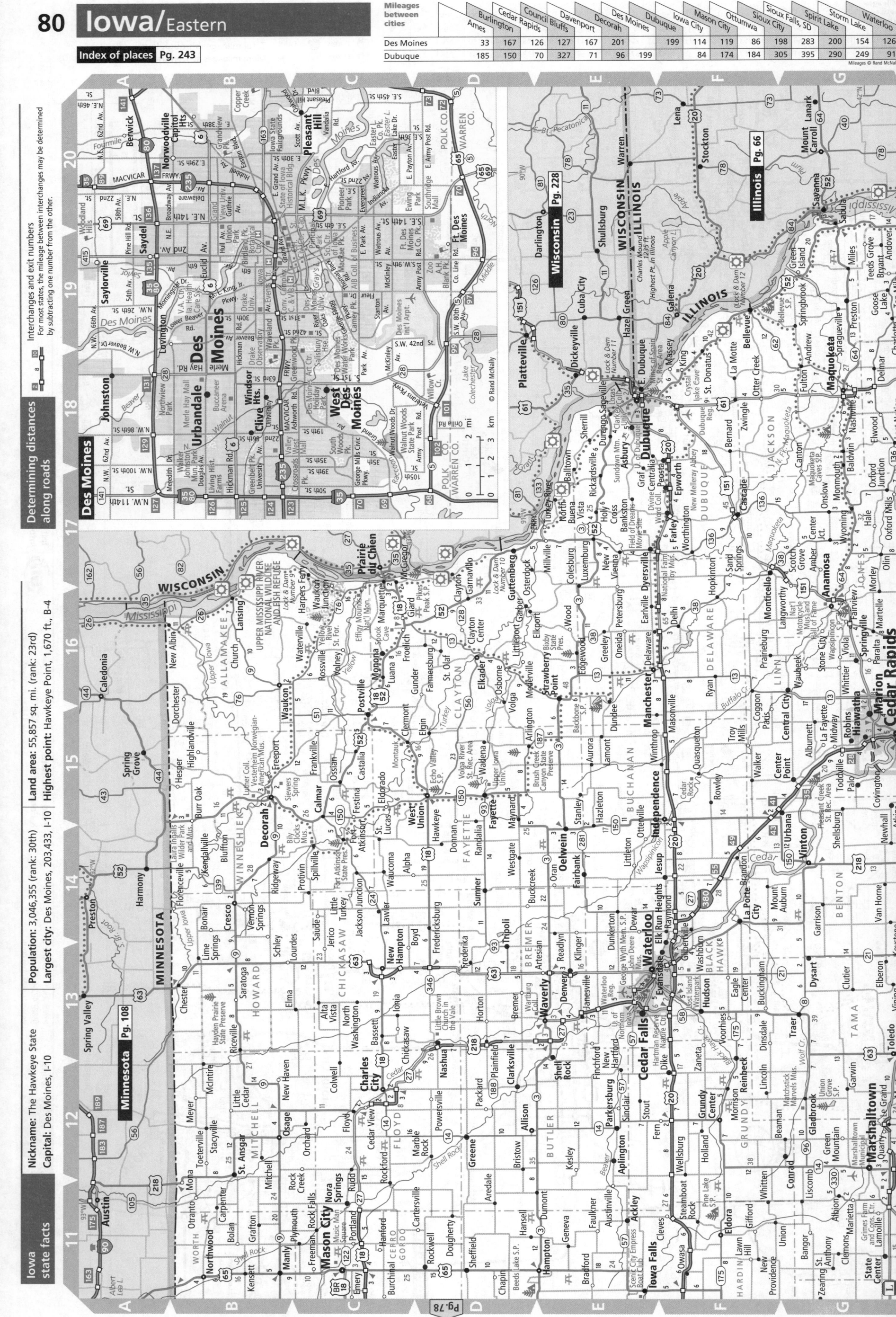

Interchanges and exit numbers
For most states, the mileage between interchanges may be determined by subtracting one number from the other.

Determining distances along roads

Iowa state facts

Nickname: The Hawkeye State
Capital: Des Moines

Population: 3,046,355 (rank: 30th)
Largest city: Des Moines, 203,433, I-10

Land area: 55,857 sq. mi. (rank: 23rd)
Highest point: Hawkeye Point, 1,670 ft., B-4

Des Moines

© Rand McNally

Mileages between cities

	Ames	Burlington	Cedar Rapids	Council Bluffs	Davenport	Decorah	Des Moines	Dubuque	Iowa City	Mason City	Ottumwa	Sioux City	Sioux Falls, SD	Spirit Lake	Storm Lake	Waterloo
Mason City	91	238	136	246	220	88	119	174	165		203	200	222	118	135	83
Sioux City	175	366	268	94	366	304	198	305	312	200	285		85	109	78	218

Mileages by Rand McNally

Total mileages through Iowa
More mileages at www.randmcnally.com/MC

29 155 miles   80 303 miles
35 218 miles   218 257 miles

Cedar Rapids

Iowa City

Coralville

Travel planning & on-the-road resources

Tourism Information: Iowa Tourism Office (888) 472-6035 www.traveliowa.com

Road Conditions & Construction: 511 (800) 288-1047 www.511ia.org, www.iowadot.gov

Toll Road Information:

Missouri Pg.116

© Rand McNally

Pg.79

Index of places Pg. 244

Mileages between cities	Arkansas City	Atchison	Coffeyville	Dodge City	Emporia	Fort Scott	Goodland	Hays	Hutchinson	Joplin, MO	Kansas City	Liberal	Manhattan	Salina	Topeka	Wichita
Dodge City	212	323	288		240	304	192	104	122	337	333	82	227	164	273	154
Goodland	384	395	455	192	349	472		144	268	505	406	209	299	235	344	323

Mileages © Rand McNally

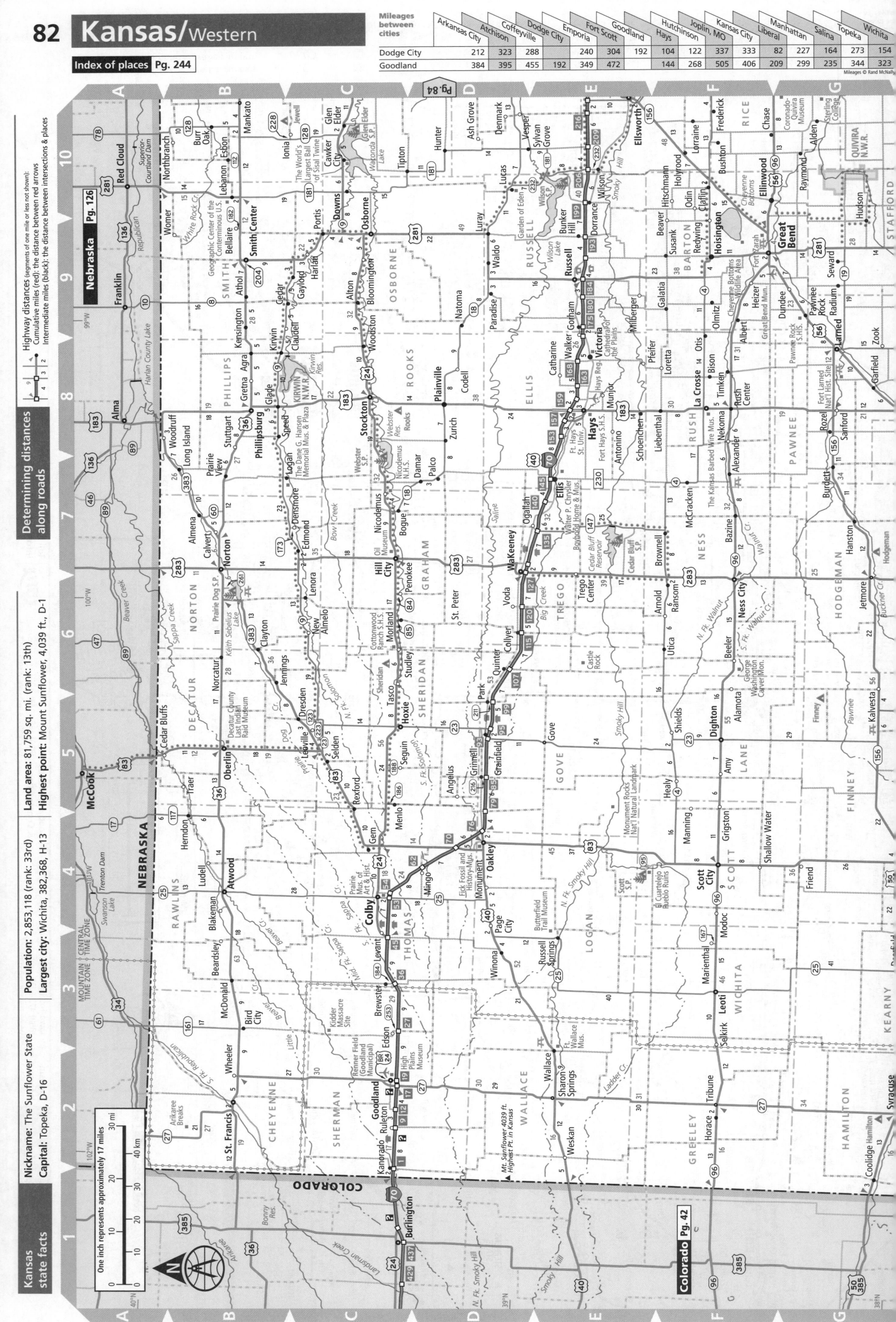

Pg. 84 · Pg. 126 · Colorado Pg. 42

Mileages between cities	Arkansas City	Atchison	Coffeyville	Dodge City	Emporia	Fort Scott	Goodland	Hays	Hutchinson	Joplin, MO	Kansas City	Liberal	Manhattan	Salina	Topeka	Wichita
Joplin, MO	150	196	65	337	177	60	505	366	233		154	395	252	274	196	183
Kansas City	228	58	172	333	109	94	406	266	220	154		406	117	173	62	196

continued p. 84

Mileages © Rand McNally

Total mileages through Kansas

35 235 miles 56 464 miles
70 424 miles 81 220 miles

More mileages at www.randmcnally.com/MC

Pg. 85

Oklahoma Pg. 166

Wichita

Hutchinson

Salina

Travel planning & on-the-road resources

Tourism Information: Kansas Dept. of Wildlife, Parks & Tourism (800) 252-6727, (785) 296-2009 www.travelks.com

Road Conditions & Construction: 511 (866) 511-5368, (785) 296-3566 511.ksdot.org, www.ksdot.org

511 Toll Road Information: Kansas Turnpike Authority (K-TAG) (316) 682-4537 www.ksturnpike.com

© Rand McNally

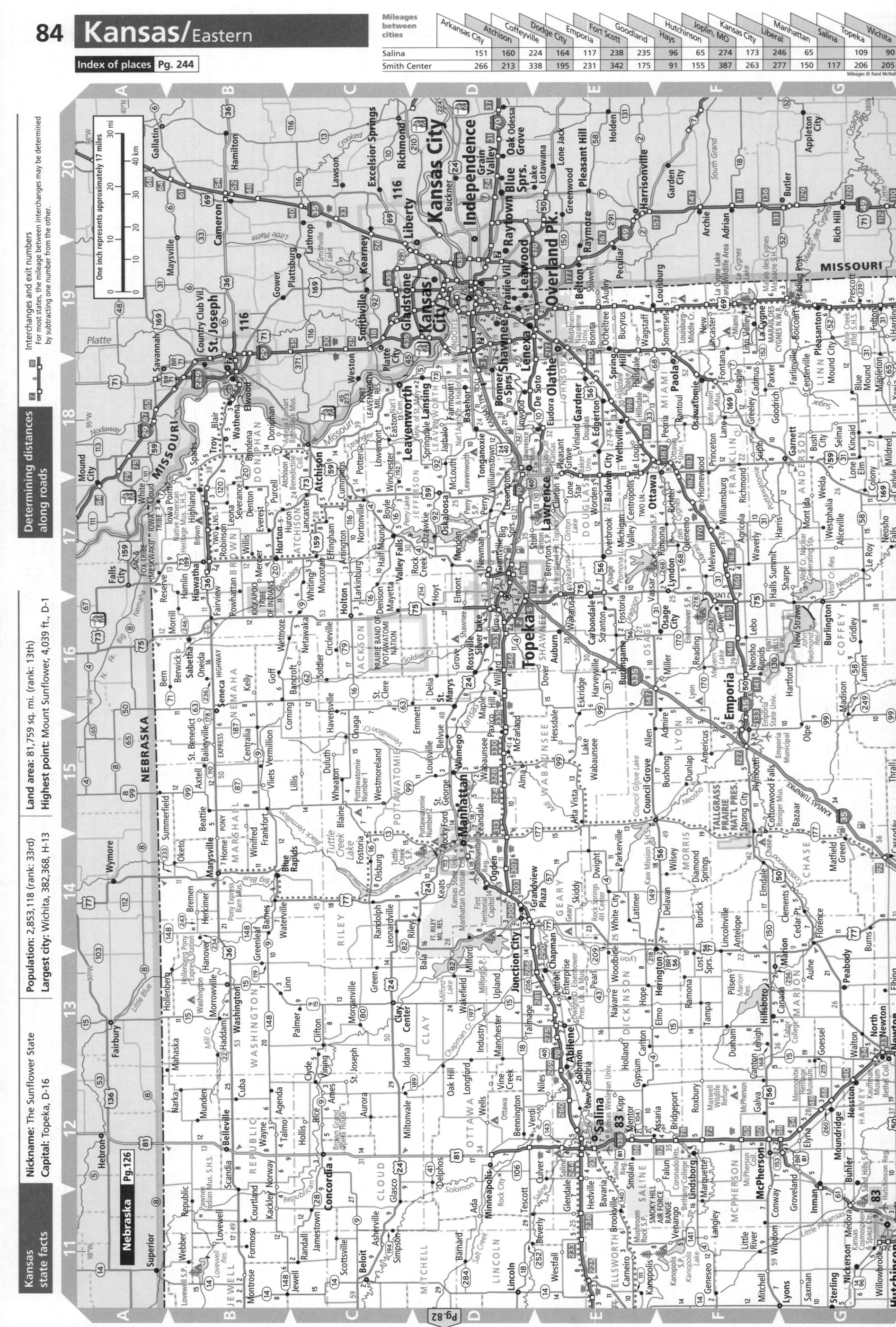

Kansas state facts

Nickname: The Sunflower State
Capital: Topeka, D-1

Population: 2,853,118 (rank: 33rd)
Largest city: Wichita, 382,368, H-13

Land area: 81,759 sq. mi. (rank: 13th)
Highest point: Mount Sunflower, 4,039 ft., D-1

Interchanges and exit numbers
For most states, the mileage between interchanges may be determined by subtracting one number from the other.

Determining distances along roads

One inch represents approximately 17 miles

Mileages between cities	Arkansas City	Atchison	Coffeyville	Dodge City	Emporia	Fort Scott	Goodland	Hays	Hutchinson	Joplin, MO	Kansas City	Liberal	Manhattan	Salina	Topeka	Wichita
Topeka	170	55	155	273	58	136	344	204	162	196	62	349	56	109		137
Wichita	61	188	134	154	85	149	323	183	51	183	196	212	130	90	137	

Mileages © Rand McNally

Total mileages through Kansas

35 — 235 miles · 56 — 464 miles
70 — 424 miles · 81 — 220 miles

More mileages at www.randmcnally.com/MC

Travel planning & on-the-road resources

Tourism Information: Kansas Dept. of Wildlife, Parks & Tourism
(800) 252-6727, (785) 296-2009
www.travelks.com

Road Conditions & Construction: 511
(866) 511-5368, (785) 296-3566
511.ksdot.org, www.ksdot.org

Toll Road Information: Kansas Turnpike Authority (K-TAG)
(316) 682-4537
www.ksturnpike.com

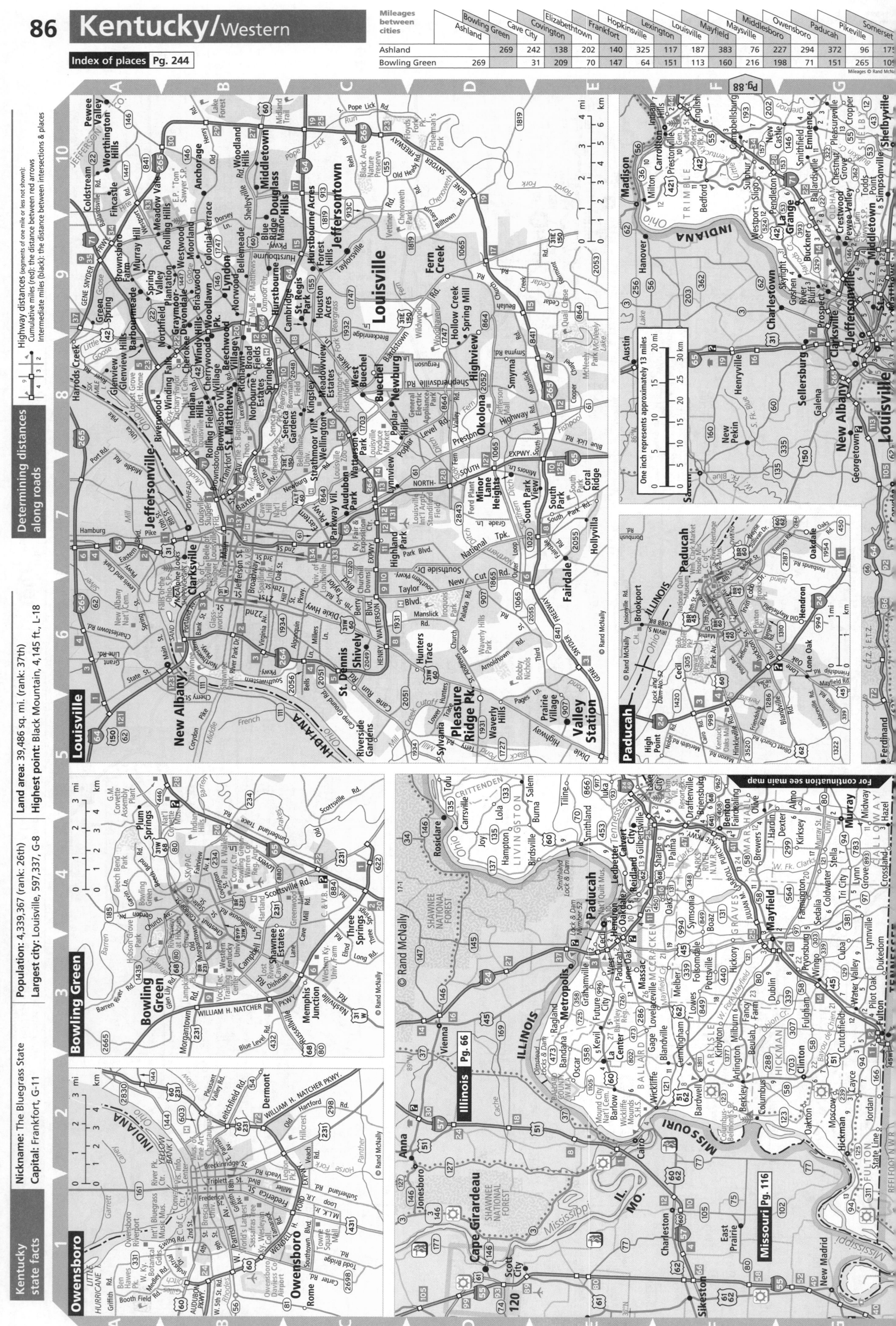

Kentucky state facts

Nickname: The Bluegrass State
Capital: Frankfort, G-11

Population: 4,339,367 (rank: 26th)
Largest city: Louisville, 597,337, G-8

Land area: 39,486 sq. mi. (rank: 37th)
Highest point: Black Mountain, 4,145 ft., L-18

Determining distances along roads

Highway distances (segments of one mile or less not shown)
Cumulative miles (red): the distance between red arrows
Intermediate miles (black): the distance between intersections & places

Mileages between cities	Ashland	Bowling Green	Cave City	Covington	Elizabethtown	Frankfort	Hopkinsville	Lexington	Louisville	Mayfield	Maysville	Middlesboro	Owensboro	Paducah	Pikeville	Somerset	continued p. 88
Covington	138	209	181		140	78	265	81	97	322	59	208	203	312	216	157	
Lexington	117	151	124	81	84	29	207		76	266	63	130	177	256	140	78	

Mileages © Rand McNally

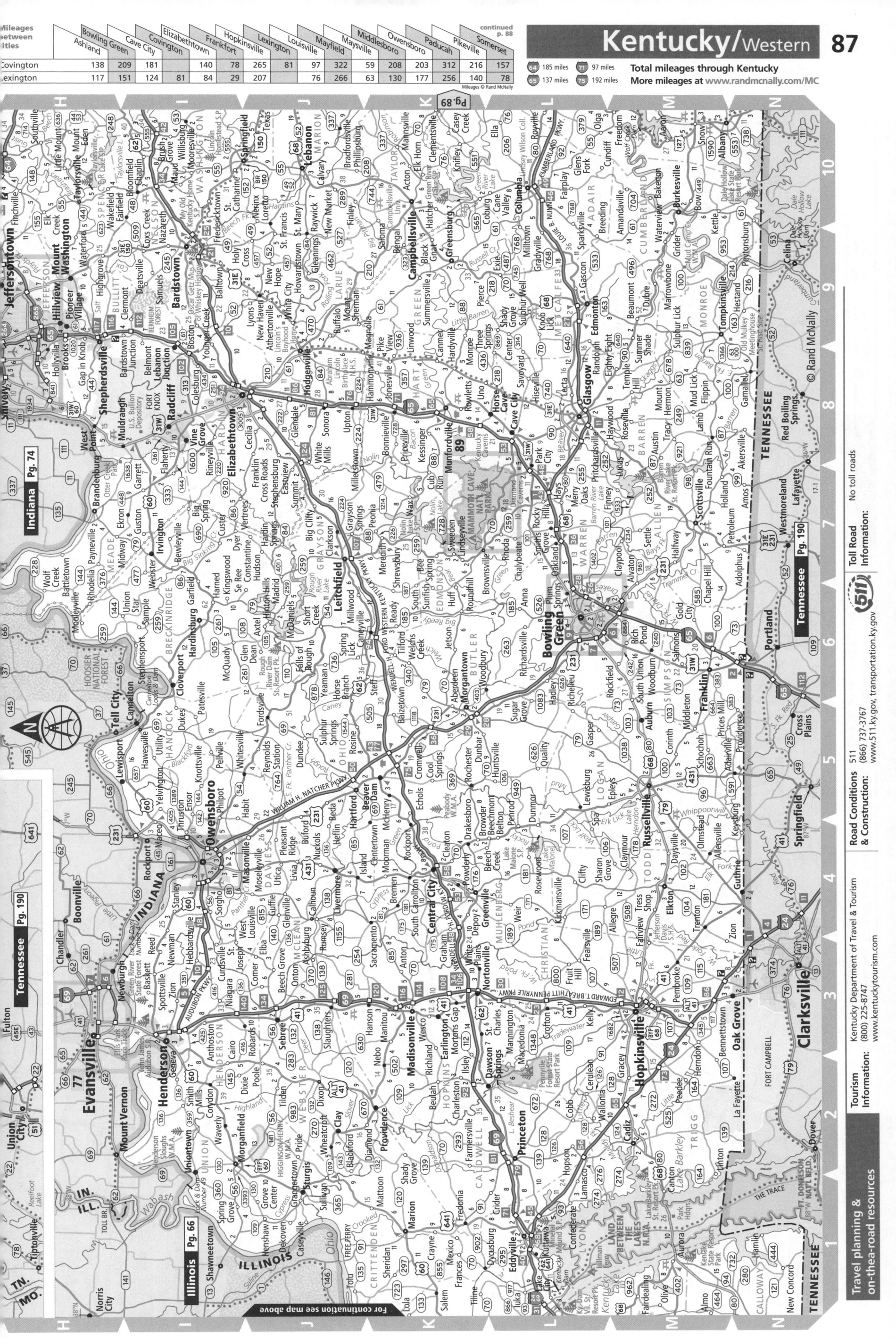

Pg. 89

For continuation see map above

Travel planning & on-thea-road resources

| Tourism Information: | Kentucky Department of Travel & Tourism (800) 225-8747 www.kentuckytourism.com | Road Conditions & Construction: | 511 (866) 737-3767 www.511.ky.gov, transportation.ky.gov | 511 | Toll Road Information: | No toll roads |

© Rand McNally

Index of places Pg. 244

Kentucky state facts

Nickname: The Bluegrass State
Capital: Frankfort, G-11

Population: 4,339,367 (rank: 26th)
Largest city: Louisville, 597,337, G-8

Land area: 39,486 sq. mi. (rank: 37th)
Highest point: Black Mountain, 4,145 ft., L-18

Determining distances along roads

Interchanges and exit numbers
For most states, the mileage between interchanges may be determined by subtracting one number from the other.

Frankfort

Covington

Lexington

Frankfort

Ohio Pg. 158

Ohio Pg. 163

Ind. Pg. 74

West Virginia Pg. 226

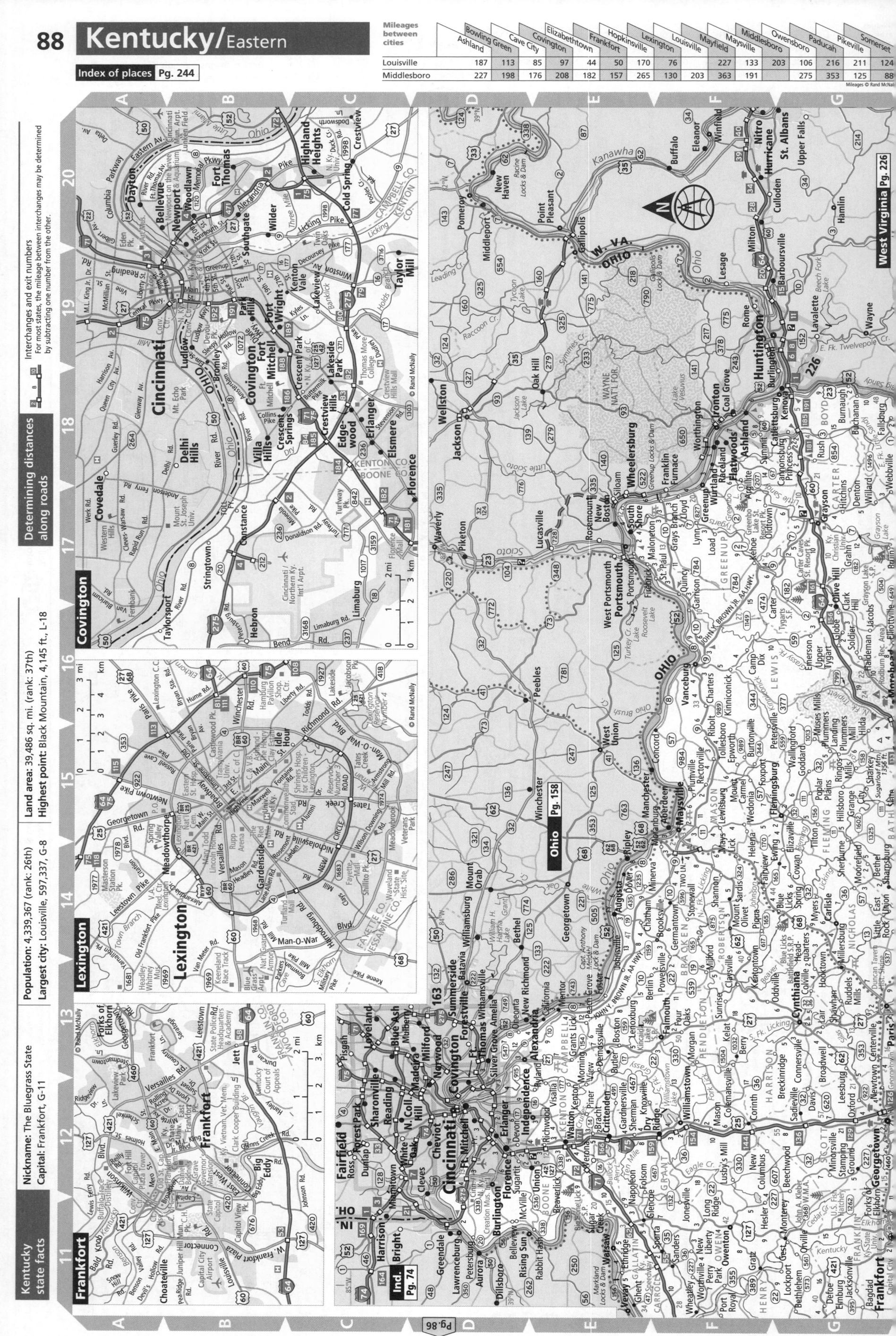

Mileages between cities	Ashland	Bowling Green	Cave City	Covington	Elizabethtown	Frankfort	Hopkinsville	Lexington	Louisville	Mayfield	Maysville	Middlesboro	Owensboro	Paducah	Pikeville	Somerset
Owensboro	294	71	108	203	94	159	96	177	106	154	242	275		143	318	187
Paducah	372	151	186	312	172	250	72	256	216	24	319	353	143		396	265

Mileages © Rand McNally

Total mileages through Kentucky
More mileages at www.randmcnally.com/MC

64	185 miles
65	137 miles
71	97 miles
75	192 miles

Virginia Pg. 212

One inch represents approximately 13 miles

Mammoth Cave National Park

© Rand McNally

Tennessee Pg. 190

Tourism Information: Kentucky Department of Travel & Tourism (800) 225-8747 www.kentuckytourism.com

Road Conditions & Construction: 511 (866) 737-3767 www.511.ky.gov, transportation.ky.gov

Toll Road Information: No toll roads

Travel planning & on-the-road resources

Mileages © Rand McNally

Louisiana state facts

Nickname: The Pelican State
Capital: Baton Rouge, G-7

Population: 4,533,372 (rank: 25th)
Land area: 43,204 sq. mi. (rank: 33rd)
Highest point: Driskill Mountain, 535 ft., B-3
Largest city: New Orleans, 343,829, H-9

Determining distances along roads

Highway distances
Cumulative miles (red): the distance between red arrows
Intermediate miles (black): the distance between intersections & places

One inch represents approx. 21 miles
0 10 20 30 mi
0 10 20 30 40 km

GULF OF MEXICO

© Rand McNally

17-1

Mileages between cities	Baton Rouge	Beaumont, TX	Houma	Lake Charles	Monroe	New Orleans	Shreveport	Vicksburg, MS
Lake Charles	124	60	177		190	203	184	243
New Orleans	79	262	56	203	281		340	207
Shreveport	250	206	314	184	98	340		171
Vicksburg, MS	157	301	234	243	74	207	171	

Mileages © Rand McNally

Interstate	Miles
10	274 miles
20	190 miles
49	208 miles
55	66 miles

Total mileages through Louisiana
More mileages at www.randmcnally.com/MC

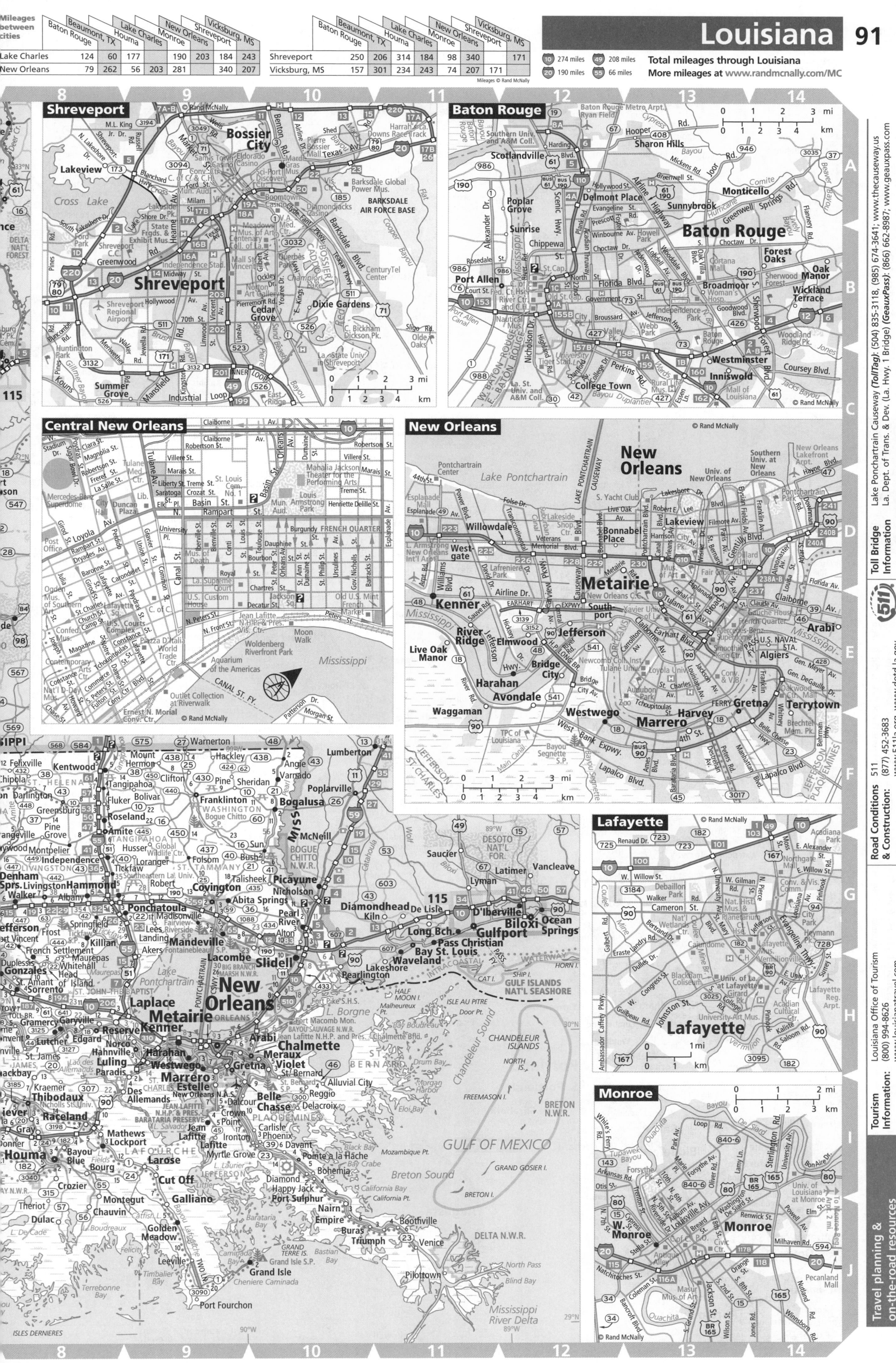

Toll Bridge Information
Lake Ponchartrain Causeway (*TollTag*): (504) 835-3118, (985) 674-3641; www.thecauseway.us
La. Dept. of Trans. & Dev. (La. Hwy. 1 Bridge) (*GeauxPass*): (866) 662-8987; www.geauxpass.com

Road Conditions & Construction: 511
(877) 452-3683
www.511la.org, www.dotd.la.gov

Tourism Information: Louisiana Office of Tourism
(800) 994-8626
www.louisianatravel.com

Travel planning & on-the-road resources

Mileages © Rand McNally

Mileages between cities	Auburn	Bangor	Bar Harbor	Eastport	Houlton	Millinocket	Portland	Rangeley
Bangor	107		47	120	118	72	128	120
Eastport	226	120	118		115	125	247	242

Mileages between cities	Auburn	Bangor	Bar Harbor	Eastport	Houlton	Millinocket	Portland	Rangeley
Houlton	225	118	167	115		69	246	238
Madawaska	326	219	267	218	102	170	347	339

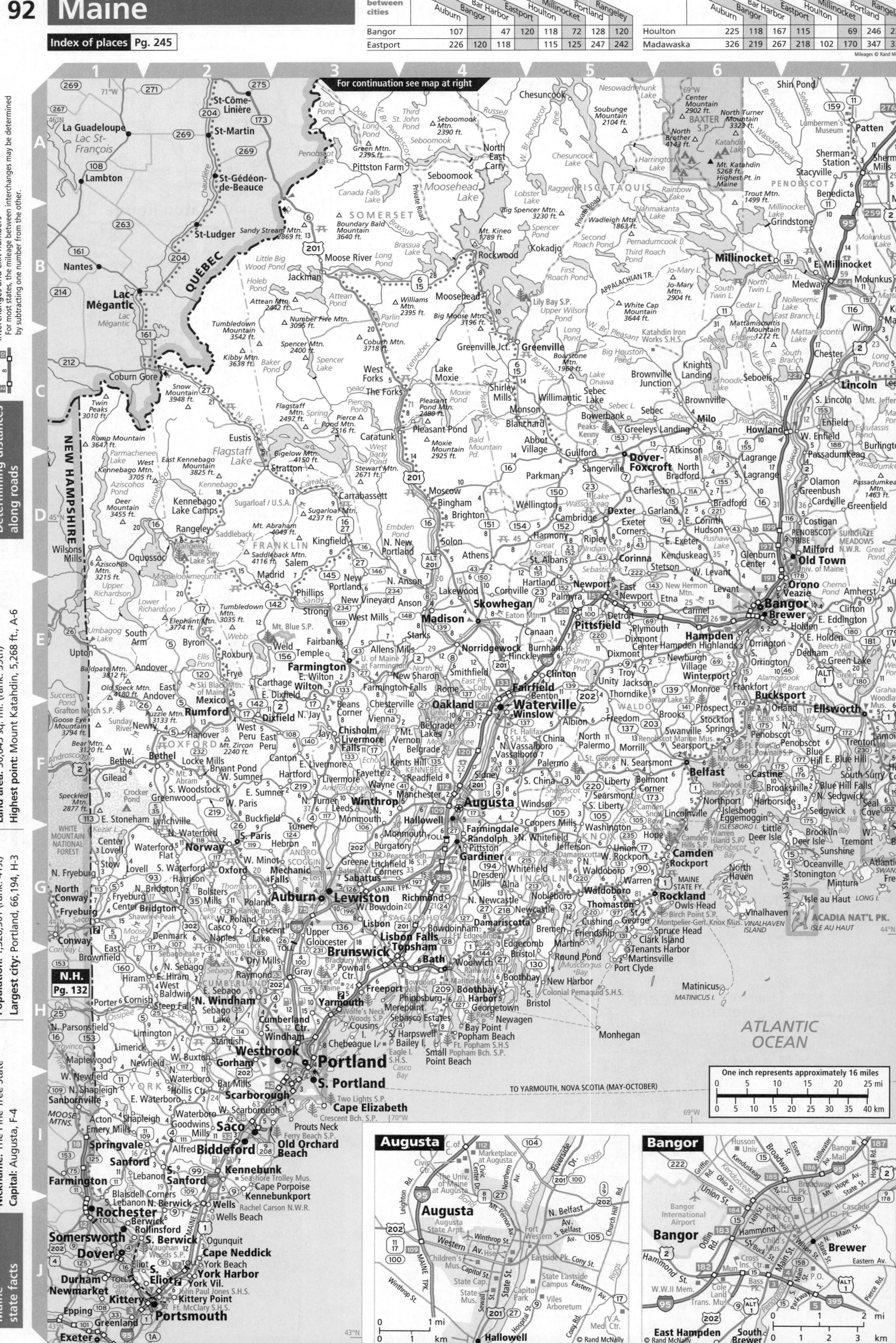

For continuation see map at right

Maine state facts

Land area: 30,843 sq. mi. (rank: 39th)

Highest point: Mount Katahdin, 5,268 ft., A-6

Population: 1,328,361 (rank: 41st)

Largest city: Portland, 66,194, H-3

Nickname: The Pine Tree State

Capital: Augusta, F-4

Determining distances along roads

Interchanges and exit numbers
For most states, the mileage between interchanges may be determined by subtracting one number from the other.

N.H. Pg. 132

N.H. Pg. 132

Augusta

Bangor

One inch represents approximately 16 miles

ATLANTIC OCEAN

TO YARMOUTH, NOVA SCOTIA (MAY-OCTOBER)

ACADIA NAT'L PK.

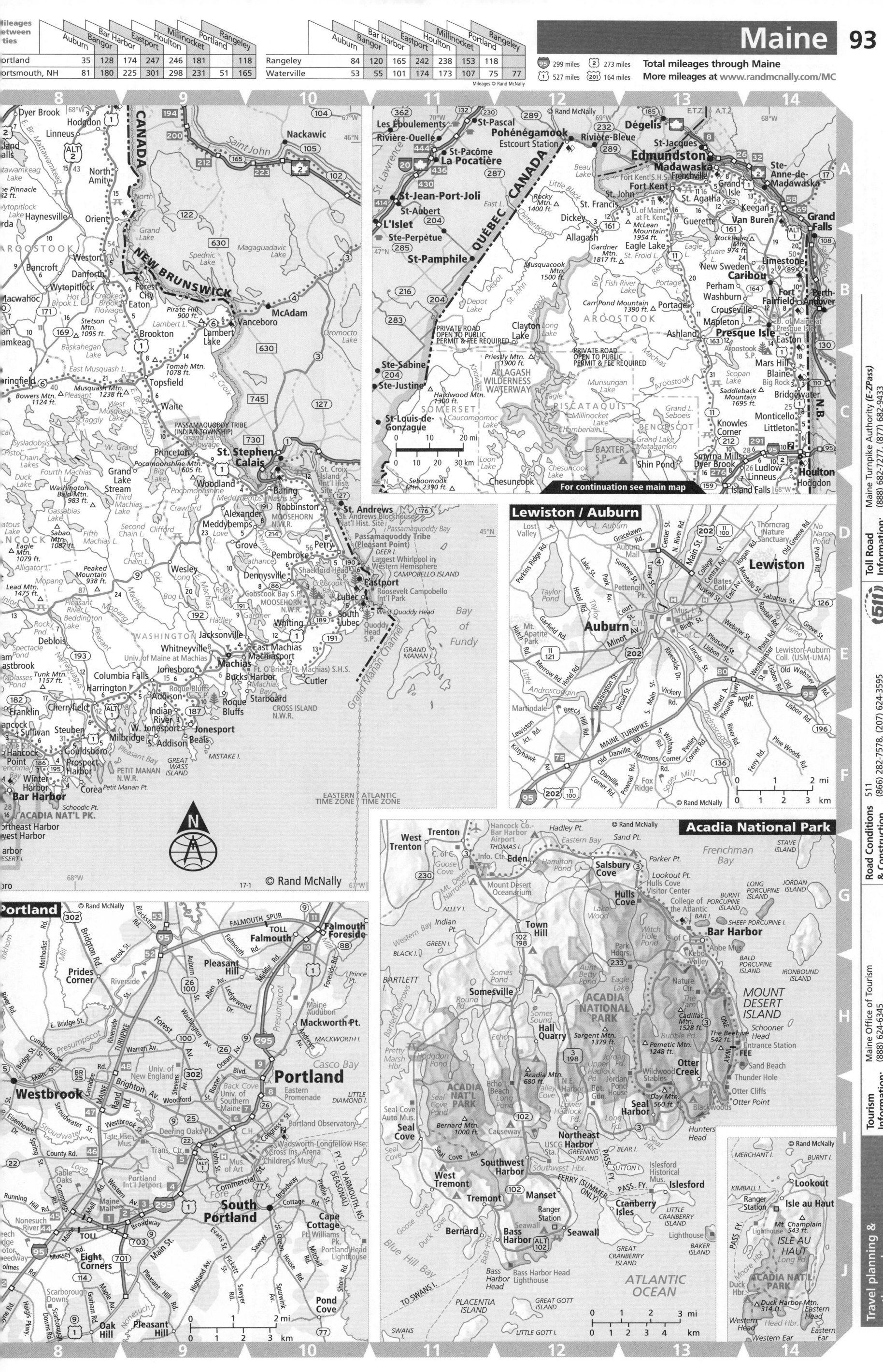

Mileages between cities

	Auburn	Bangor	Bar Harbor	Eastport	Houlton	Millinocket	Portland	Rangeley
Portland	35	128	174	247	246	181		118
Portsmouth, NH	81	180	225	301	298	231	51	165

	Auburn	Bangor	Bar Harbor	Eastport	Houlton	Millinocket	Portland	Rangeley
Rangeley	84	120	165	242	238	153	118	
Waterville	53	55	101	174	173	107	75	77

Mileages © Rand McNally

Total mileages through Maine
- 95 — 299 miles
- 2 — 273 miles
- 1 — 527 miles
- 201 — 164 miles

More mileages at www.randmcnally.com/MC

Lewiston / Auburn

Acadia National Park

© Rand McNally

Maine Turnpike Authority (E-ZPass)
(888) 682-7277, (877) 682-9433
www.maineturnpike.com

Road Conditions & Construction
511
(866) 282-7578, (207) 624-3595
www.maine.gov, www.maine.gov/mdot

Maine Office of Tourism
(888) 624-6345
www.visitmaine.com

Mileages between cities	Aberdeen	Annapolis	Baltimore	Cambridge	Chestertown	Cumberland	Frederick	Hagerstown	Lexington Park	Ocean City	Pocomoke City	Rockville	St. Charles	Salisbury	Washington, DC	Wilmington, DE
Aberdeen		58	31	113	65	171	83	107	122	134	152	74	90	122	70	42
Annapolis	58		28	57	47	157	68	93	73	108	120	42	41	89	30	96

Mileages © Rand McNally

Maryland state facts

Nickname: The Old Line State
Capital: Annapolis, E-14

Population: 5,773,552 (rank: 19th)
Largest city: Baltimore, 620,961, C-13

Land area: 9,707 sq. mi. (rank: 42nd)
Highest point: Backbone Mountain, 3,360 ft., D-1

Determining distances along roads

Highway distances (segments of one mile or less not shown)
Cumulative miles (red): the distance between red arrows
Intermediate miles (black): the distance between intersections & places

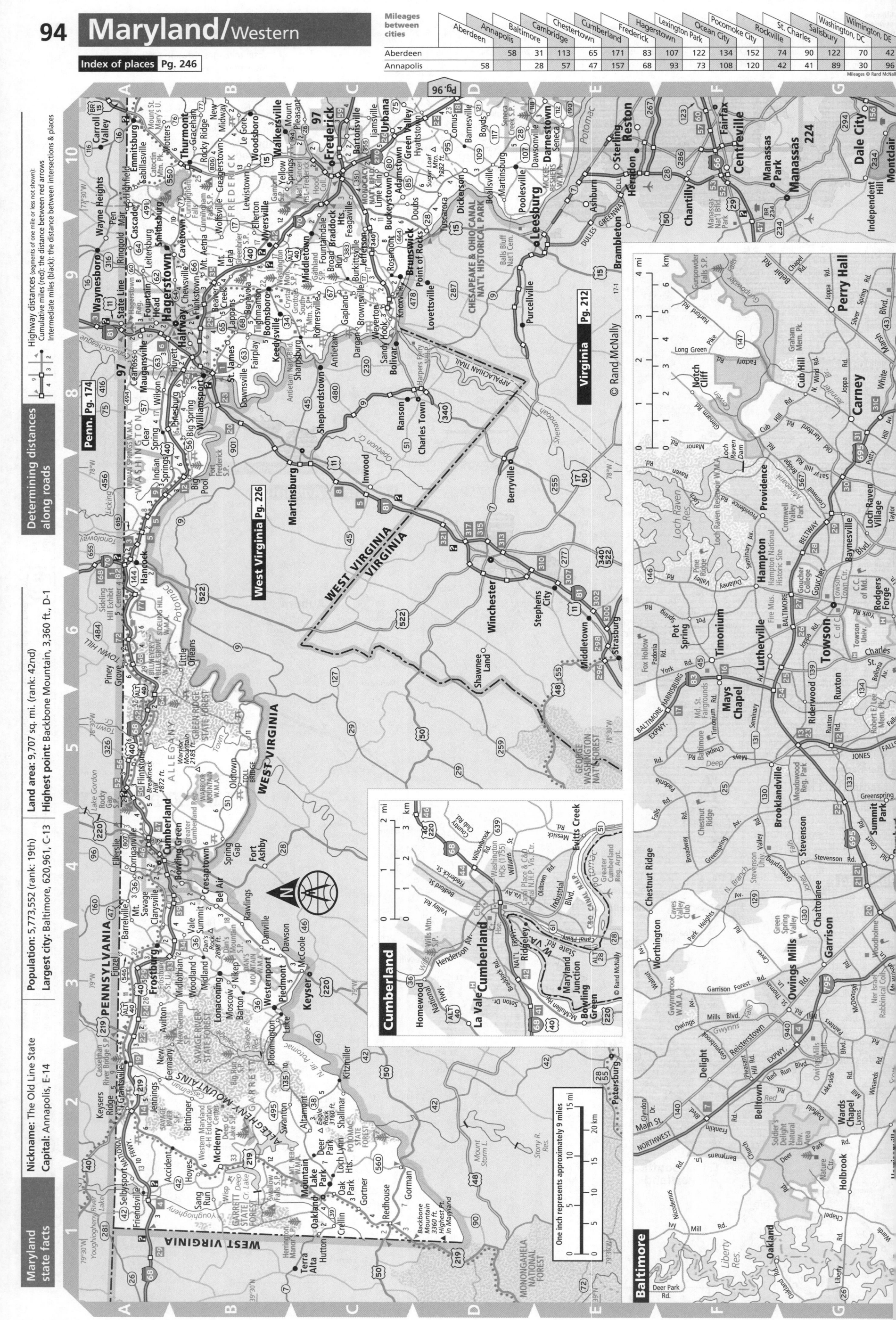

Mileages © Rand McNally

continued p. 96

Total mileages through Maryland
More mileages at www.randmcnally.com/MC

56 81 miles	81 12 miles
70 94 miles	95 110 miles

Travel planning & on-the-road resources

Tourism Information:
Maryland Office of Tourism
(866) 639-3526
www.visitmaryland.org

Road Conditions & Construction
511, (800) 323-6742, (410) 582-5650,
In Maryland: (800) 543-2515;
www.md511.org, www.roads.maryland.gov

Toll Road Information:
Maryland Transportation Authority (E-ZPass)
(866) 713-1596, In Maryland: (410) 537-1000;
www.mdta.maryland.gov

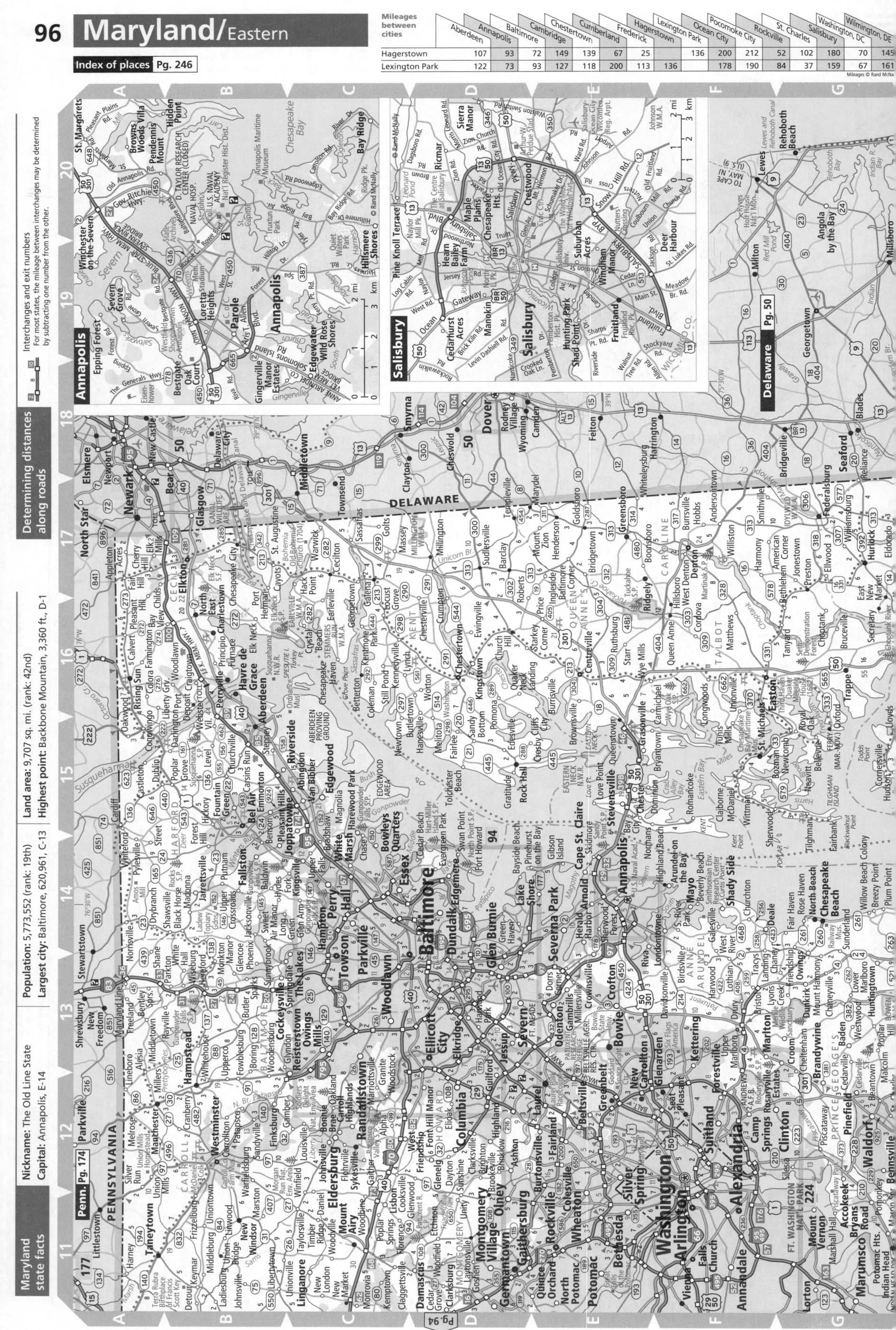

Mileages between cities	Aberdeen	Annapolis	Baltimore	Cambridge	Chestertown	Cumberland	Frederick	Hagerstown	Lexington Park	Ocean City	Pocomoke City	Rockville	St. Charles	Salisbury	Washington, DC	Wilmington, DE
Hagerstown	107	93	72	149	139	67	25		136	200	212	52	102	180	70	145
Lexington Park	122	73	93	127	118	200	113	136		178	190	84	37	159	67	161

Mileages © Rand McNa

Maryland state facts

Nickname: The Old Line State
Capital: Annapolis, E-14

Population: 5,773,552 (rank: 19th)
Largest city: Baltimore, 620,961, C-13

Land area: 9,707 sq. mi. (rank: 42nd)
Highest point: Backbone Mountain, 3,360 ft, D-1

Determining distances along roads

Interchanges and exit numbers
For most states, the mileage between interchanges may be determined by subtracting one number from the other.

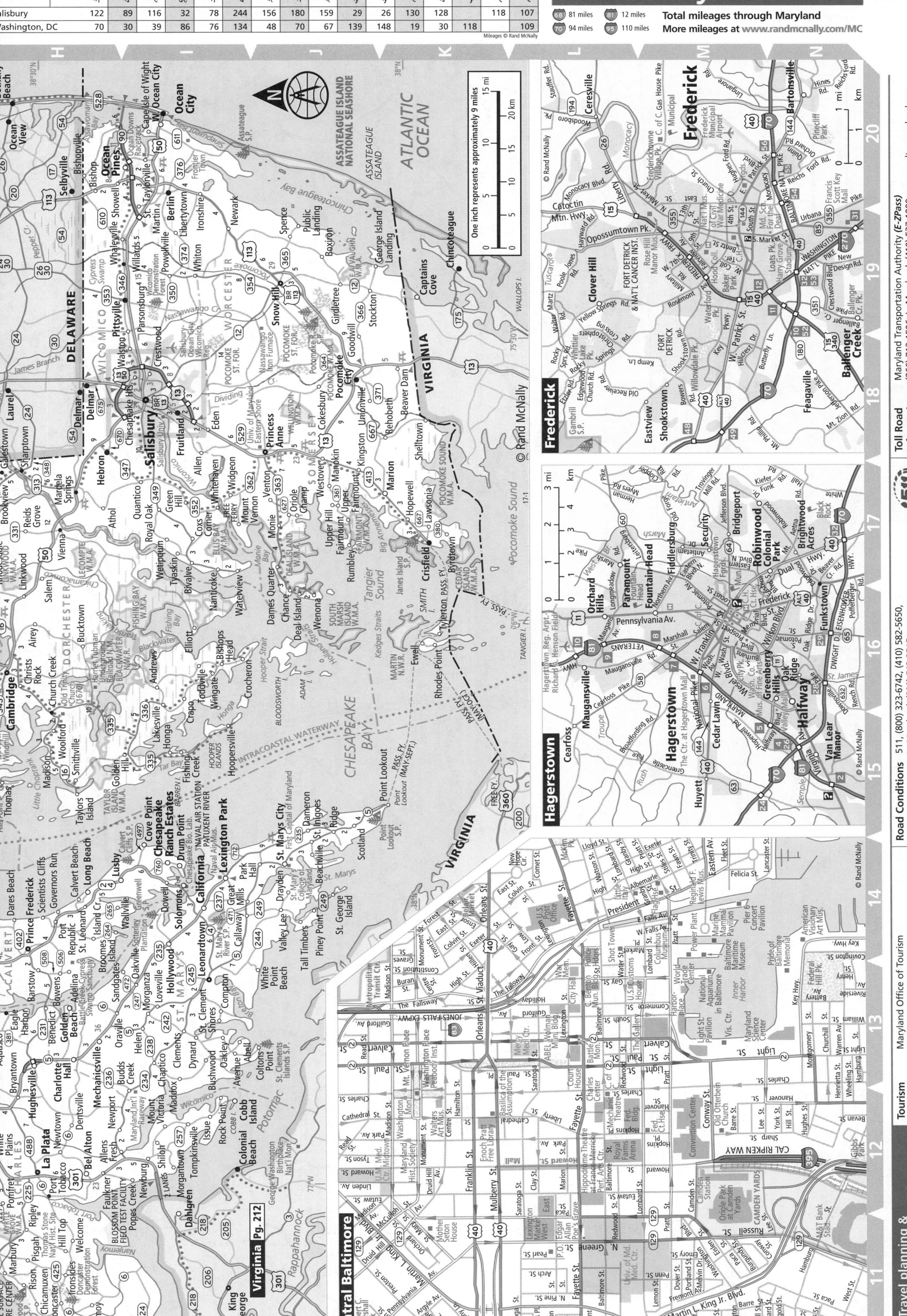

Mileages between Cities

	Aberdeen	Annapolis	Baltimore	Cambridge	Chestertown	Cumberland	Frederick	Hagerstown	Lexington Park	Ocean City	Pocomoke City	Rockville	St. Charles	Salisbury	Washington, DC	Wilmington, DE
Salisbury	122	89	116	32	78	244	156	180	159	29	26	130	128		118	107
Washington, DC	70	30	39	86	76	134	48	70	67	139	148	19	30	118		109

Mileages © Rand McNally

Maryland/Eastern

Total mileages through Maryland
More mileages at www.randmcnally.com/MC

68 81 miles	81 12 miles
70 94 miles	95 110 miles

Travel planning & on-the-road resources

Tourism Information: Maryland Office of Tourism (866) 639-3526 www.visitmaryland.org

Road Conditions & Construction 511, (800) 323-6742, (410) 582-5650, In Maryland, (800) 543-2515; www.md511.org, www.roads.maryland.gov

Toll Road Information: Maryland Transportation Authority (E-ZPass) www.mdta.maryland.gov (866) 713-1596. In Maryland (410) 537-1000; www.roads.maryland.gov

Virginia Pg. 212

Pg. 95

Mileages between cities	Boston	Brockton	Falmouth	Fitchburg	Gloucester	Greenfield	Lowell	Nantucket	New Bedford	North Adams	Pittsfield	Plymouth	Providence, RI	Provincetown	Springfield	Worcester
Boston		24	76	47	39	94	29	101*	58	157	136	40	50	116	90	43
Gloucester	39	63	114	74		120	47	140*	97	157	169	78	90	154	122	75

*via ferry

Mileages © Rand McNally

Massachusetts state facts

Nickname: The Bay State

Capital: Boston, E-14

Population: 6,547,629 (rank: 14th)

Largest city: Boston, 617,594, E-14

Land area: 7,800 sq. mi. (rank: 45th)

Highest point: Mount Greylock, 3,491 ft., C-2

Determining distances along roads

Highway distances (segments of one mile or less not shown):
Cumulative miles (red): the distance between red arrows
Intermediate miles (black): the distance between intersections & places

One inch represents approximately 7 miles

© Rand McNally

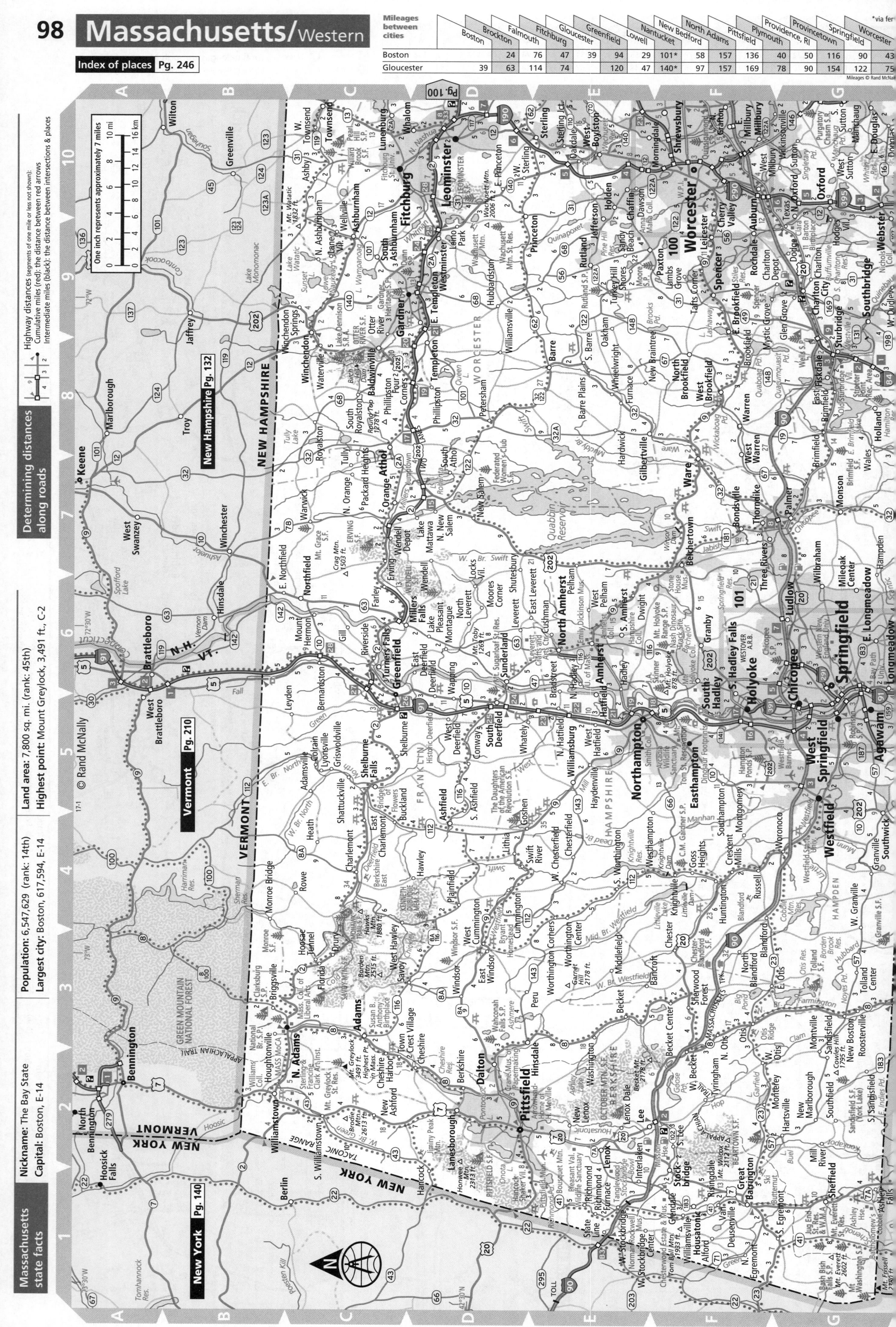

Mileages between cities

	Boston	Brockton	Falmouth	Fitchburg	Gloucester	Greenfield	Lowell	Nantucket	New Bedford	North Adams	Pittsfield	Plymouth	Providence, RI	Provincetown	Springfield	Worcester
Lowell	29	50	102	32	47	78		130*	84	115	139	69	69	145	92	41
New Bedford	58	37	40	94	97	148	84	77*		182	161	37	31	91	114	71

Mileages © Rand McNally

Total mileages through Massachusetts

- 90 = 136 miles
- 93 = 47 miles
- 91 = 55 miles
- 95 = 92 miles

More mileages at www.randmcnally.com/MC

Boston & Vicinity

Central Boston

Pg. 101
Pg. 48

Conn. Pg. 48

Travel planning & on-the-road resources

Tourism Information: Massachusetts Office of Travel & Tourism (800) 227-6277, (617) 973-8500 www.massvacation.com

Road Conditions & Construction: 511, Metro Boston: (617) 986-5511, Central: (508) 499-5511, Western: (413) 754-5511 www.mass511.com, www.mhd.state.ma.us

Massachusetts Dept. of Transportation (E-ZPass): (877) 627-7745, (857) 368-4636 www.massdot.state.ma.us/highway

Toll Road Information: 511 www.massdot.state.ma.us/highway

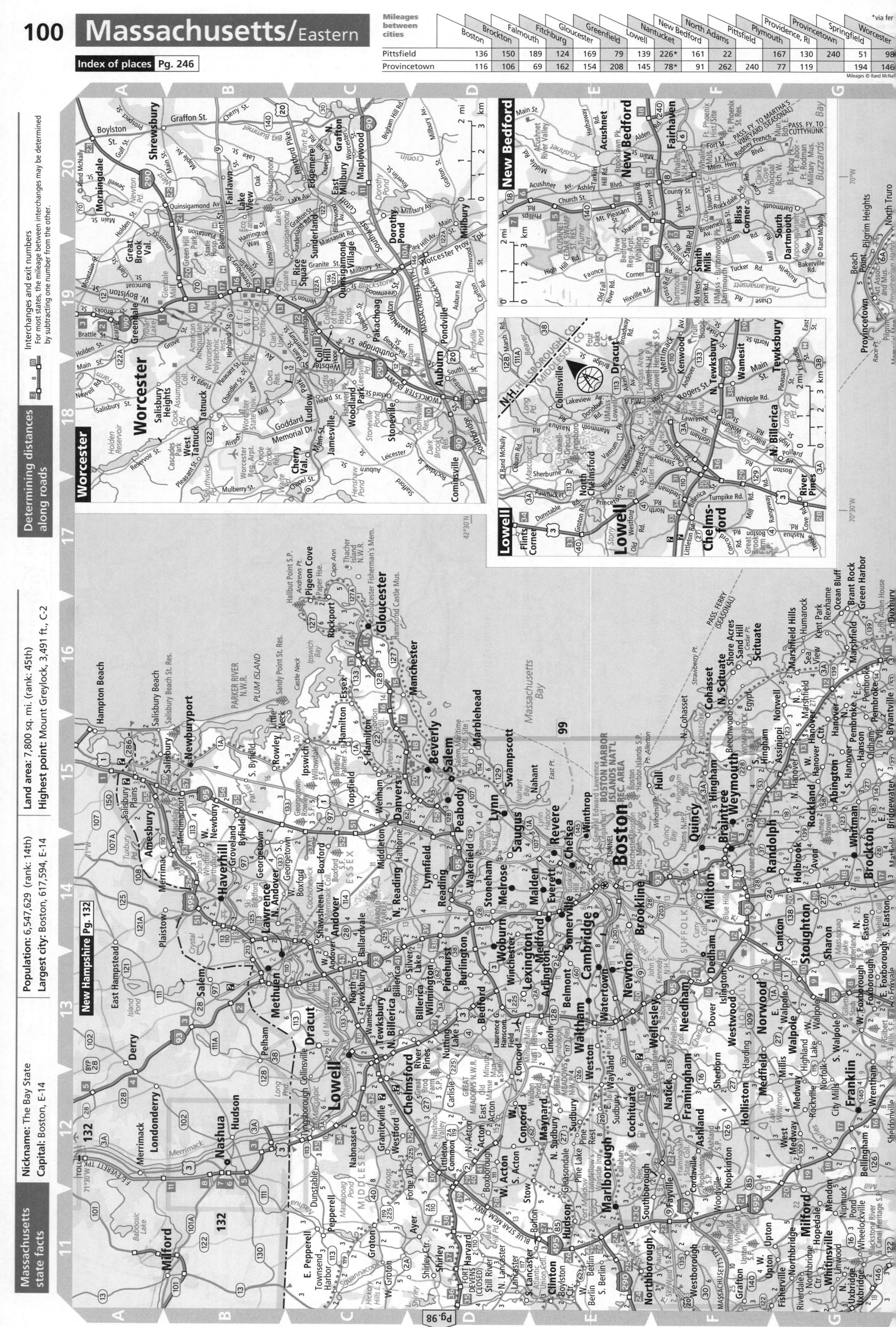

Mileages between cities	Boston	Brockton	Falmouth	Fitchburg	Gloucester	Greenfield	Lowell	Nantucket	New Bedford	North Adams	Pittsfield	Plymouth	Providence, RI	Provincetown	Springfield	Worcester
Pittsfield	136	150	189	124	169	79	139	226*	161	22		167	130	240	51	98
Provincetown	116	106	69	162	154	208	145	78*	91	262	240	77	119		194	146

*via ferry

Mileages © Rand McNally

Massachusetts state facts

Nickname: The Bay State
Capital: Boston, E-14

Population: 6,547,629 (rank: 14th)
Largest city: Boston, E-14

Land area: 7,800 sq. mi. (rank: 45th)
Highest point: Mount Greylock, 3,491 ft., C-2

Determining distances along roads

Interchanges and exit numbers
For most states, the mileage between interchanges may be determined by subtracting one number from the other.

Mileages between cities

	Boston	Brockton	Falmouth	Fitchburg	Gloucester	Greenfield	Lowell	Nantucket	New Bedford	North Adams	Pittsfield	Plymouth	Providence, RI	Provincetown	Springfield	Worcester *via ferry
Springfield	90	103	143	77	122	38	92	180*	114	73	51	121	83	194		51
Worcester	43	56	96	26	75	72	41	133*	71	120	98	74	40	146	51	

Mileages © Rand McNally

Total mileages through Massachusetts

90 136 miles   93 47 miles
91 55 miles   95 92 miles

More mileages at www.randmcnally.com/MC

© Rand McNally

One inch represents approximately 7 miles

Travel planning & on-the-road resources

Tourism Information: Massachusetts Office of Travel & Tourism (800) 227-6277, (617) 973-8500 www.massvacation.com

Road Conditions & Construction 511; Metro Boston: (617) 986-5511; Central: (508) 499-5511; Western: (413) 754-5511 www.mass511.com, www.mhd.state.ma.us

Toll Road Information: Massachusetts Dept. of Transportation (E-ZPass) (877) 627-7745, (857) 368-4636 www.massdot.state.ma.us/highway

Pg. 99

Pg. 184

Mileages between cities	Alpena	Chicago, IL	Detroit	Grand Rapids	Houghton	Ironwood	Kalamazoo	Ludington	Mackinaw City	Menominee	Muskegon	Port Huron	Saginaw	Sault Ste. Marie	Toledo, OH	Traverse City
Ann Arbor	227	240	43	132	538	584	98	228	272	473	172	102	86	329	51	238
Detroit	244	280		157	553	599	140	252	290	488	197	62	102	345	59	255

Mileages © Rand McNally

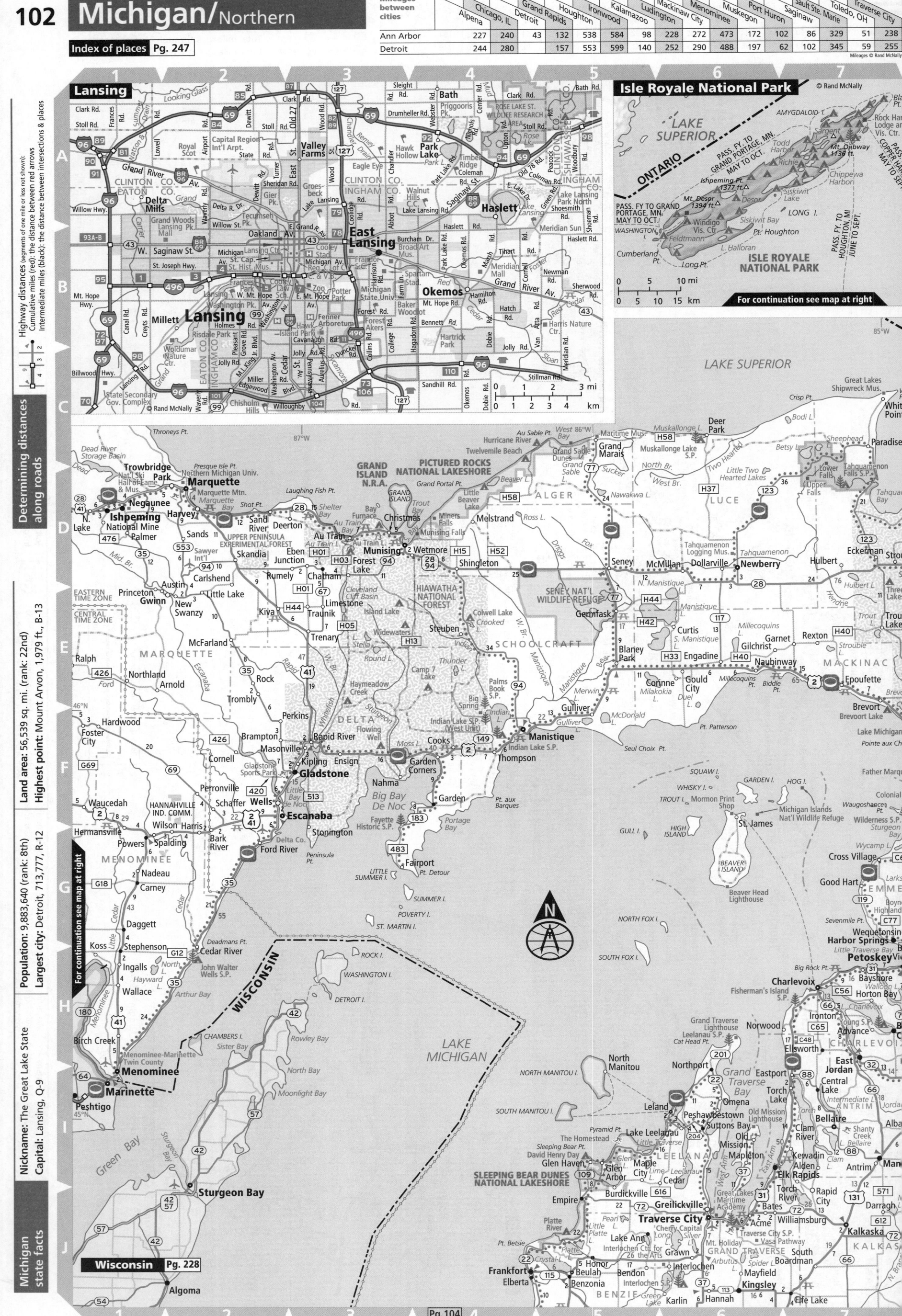

Lansing

Isle Royale National Park

© Rand McNally

For continuation see map at right

Wisconsin Pg. 228

Pg.104

Michigan state facts

Nickname: The Great Lake State
Capital: Lansing, Q-9

Population: 9,883,640 (rank: 8th)
Largest city: Detroit, 713,777, R-12

Land area: 56,539 sq. mi. (rank: 22nd)
Highest point: Mount Arvon, 1,979 ft., B-13

Determining distances along roads

Highway distances
(segments of one mile or less shown)
Cumulative miles (red): the distance between arrows
Intermediate miles (black): the distance between intersections & places

Mileages between cities	Alpena	Chicago, IL	Detroit	Grand Rapids	Houghton	Ironwood	Kalamazoo	Ludington	Mackinaw City	Menominee	Muskegon	Port Huron	Saginaw	Sault Ste. Marie	Toledo, OH	Traverse City
Flint	178	271	68	113	489	534	130	186	224	423	152	66	37	280	107	188
Grand Rapids	249	177	157		502	552	50	97	236	438	41	180	115	292	185	140

continued p. 104

Mileages © Rand McNally

	Total mileages through Michigan
69 199 miles	94 275 miles
75 396 miles	96 192 miles

More mileages at www.randmcnally.com/MC

Continued on next page

Toll Road Information: Mackinac Bridge Authority (Mac Pass): (906) 643-7600; www.mackinacbridge.org
Michigan Department of Transportation (all other toll bridges):
(517) 373-2090; www.michigan.gov/mdot

Road Conditions & Construction: (800) 381-8477, (517) 373-2090
www.michigan.gov/drive

Tourism Information: Travel Michigan (888) 784-7328 www.michigan.org

Travel planning & on-the-road resources

© Rand McNally

One inch represents approx. 15 miles

17-1

Pg. 105

Michigan state facts

Nickname: The Great Lake State
Capital: Lansing, Q-9

Population: 9,883,640 (rank: 8th)
Land area: 56,539 sq. mi. (rank: 22nd)
Highest point: Mount Arvon, 1,979 ft., B-13
Largest city: Detroit, 713,777, R-12

Determining distances along roads

Interchanges and exit numbers
For most states, the mileage between interchanges may be determined by subtracting one number from the other.

Mileages between cities	Alpena	Chicago, IL	Detroit	Grand Rapids	Houghton	Ironwood	Kalamazoo	Ludington	Mackinaw City	Menominee	Muskegon	Port Huron	Saginaw	Sault Ste. Marie	Toledo, OH	Traverse City
Lansing	228	216	90	68	494	539	75	162	228	429	107	122	88	284	118	180
Mackinaw City	94	412	290	236	266	311	287	218		200	251	290	188	56	327	102

Total mileages through Michigan
- 69 : 199 miles
- 75 : 396 miles
- 94 : 275 miles
- 96 : 192 miles

More mileages at www.randmcnally.com/MC

One inch represents approx. 15 miles
0 5 10 20 mi
0 5 10 15 20 25 30 km

Ambassador Bridge (Detroit): (800) 462-7434; www.ambassadorbridge.com
Detroit-Windsor Tunnel (NEXPRESS or NEXUS): (313) 567-4422 ext. 200, (519) 258-7424 ext. 200; www.dwtunnel.com

Toll Road Information:

Road Conditions & Construction: (800) 381-8477, (517) 373-2090; www.michigan.gov/drive

Tourism Information: Travel Michigan (888) 784-7328; www.michigan.org

Travel planning & on-the-road resources

Continued from previous page

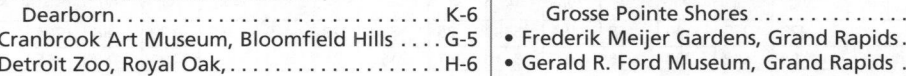

Sights to see
- Arab American National Museum,
  Dearborn K-6
- Cranbrook Art Museum, Bloomfield Hills G-5
- Detroit Zoo, Royal Oak, ... H-6
- Edsel & Eleanor Ford House,
  Grosse Pointe Shores I-9
- Frederik Meijer Gardens, Grand Rapids A-3
- Gerald R. Ford Museum, Grand Rapids B-2

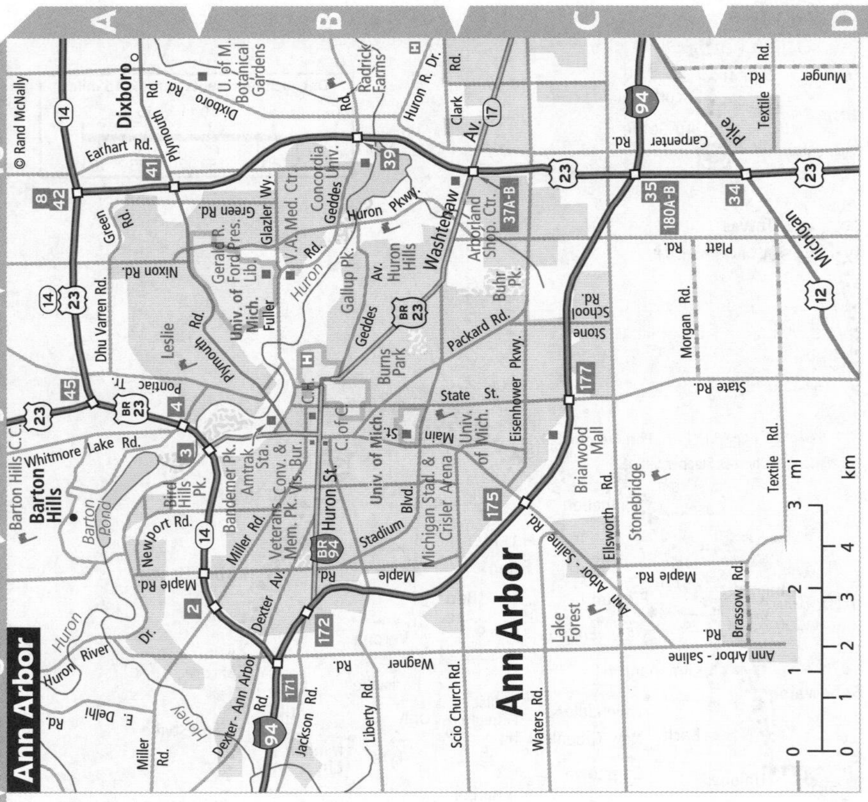

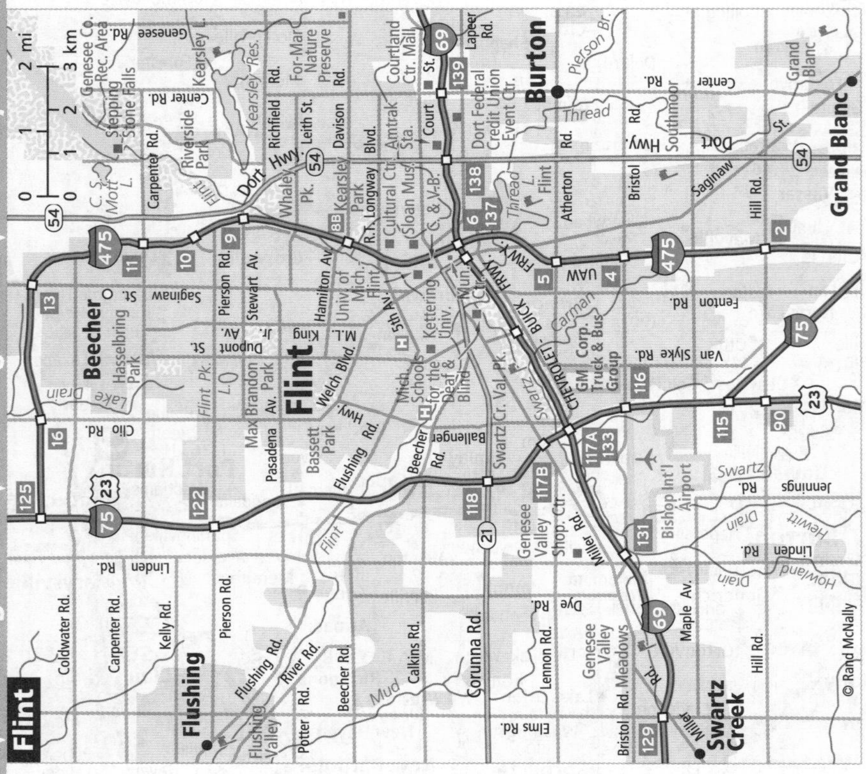

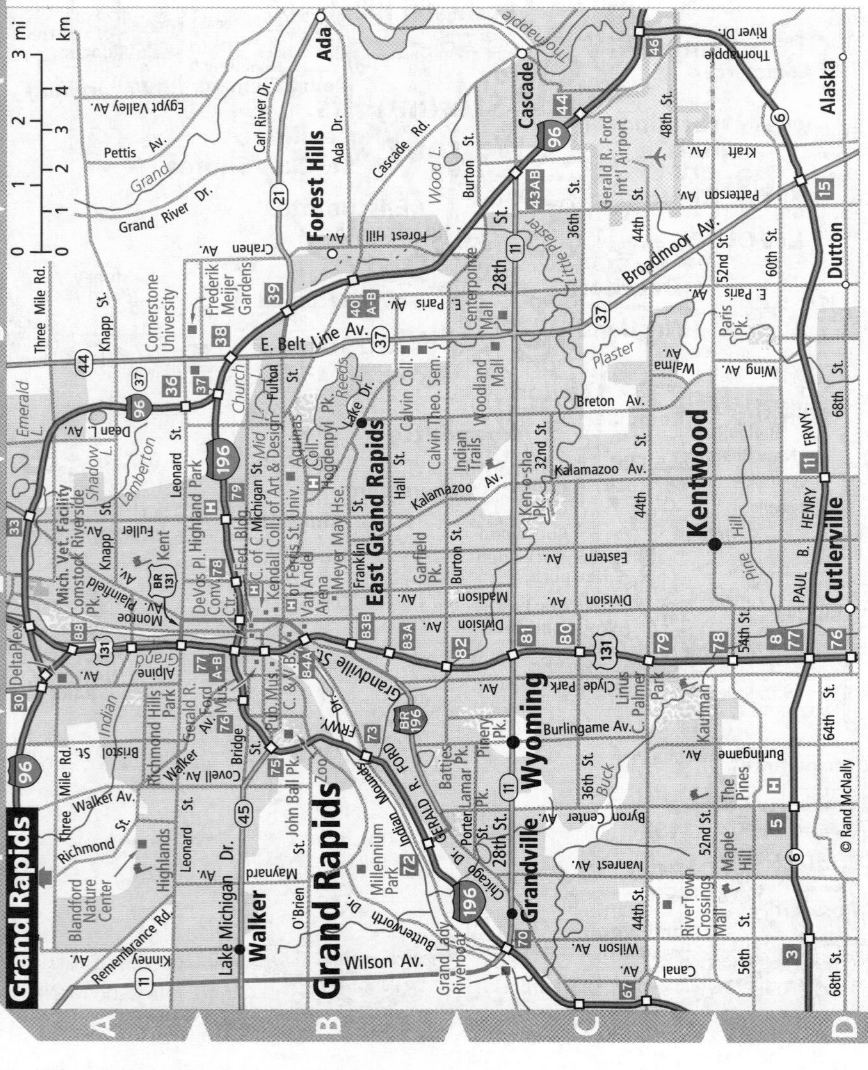

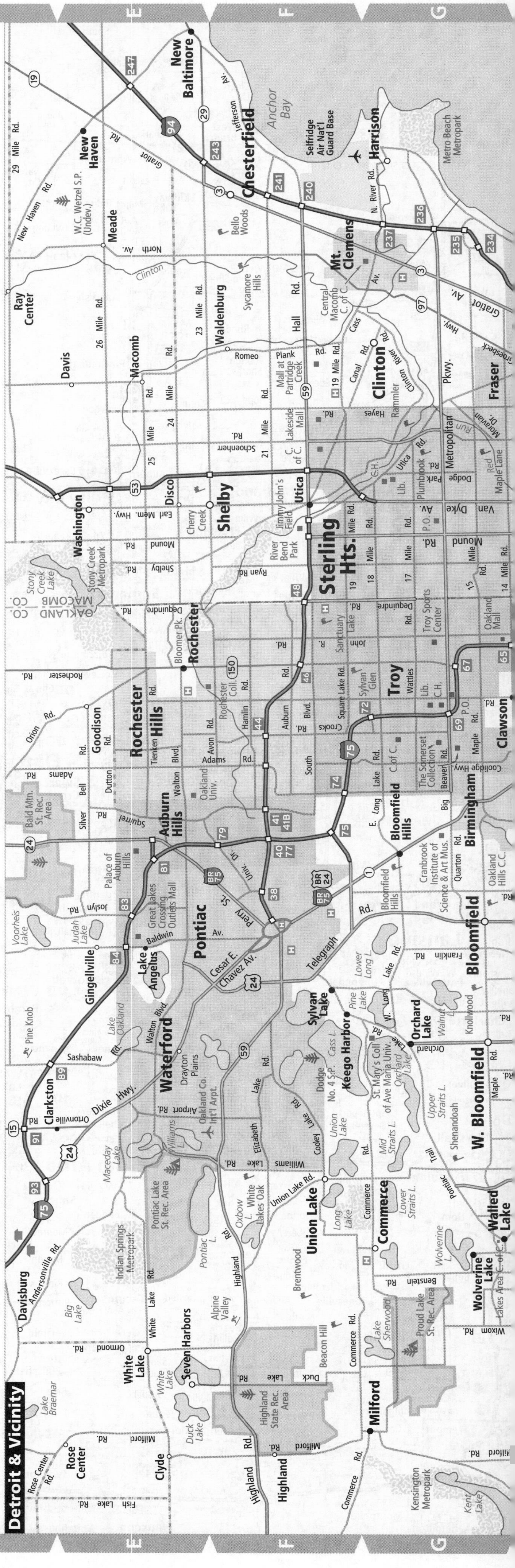

Ann Arbor

Flint

Grand Rapids

Detroit & Vicinity

Sights to see

© Rand McNally

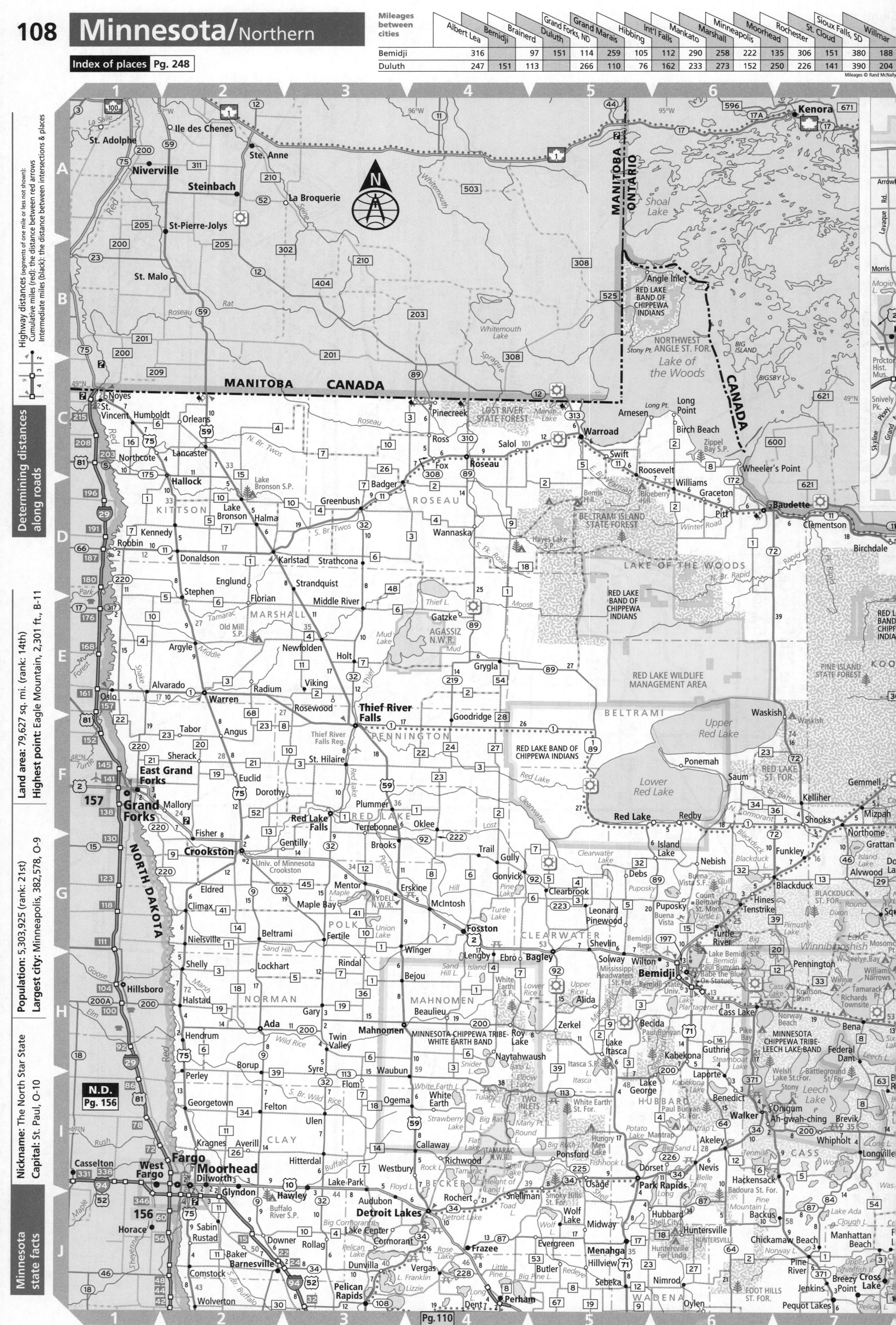

N.D. Pg. 156

Pg. 156

Pg. 110

Mileages between cities	Albert Lea	Bemidji	Brainerd	Grand Forks, ND	Grand Marais	Hibbing	Int'l Falls	Mankato	Marshall	Minneapolis	Moorhead	Rochester	St. Cloud	Sioux Falls, SD	Willmar
Minneapolis	96	222	130	152	314	262	208	293	80	153	233	86	65	236	93
Moorhead	328	135	136	250	82	361	212	249	303	206	233		321	170	244	172

Mileages © Rand McNally

continued p. 110

Total mileages through Minnesota
35 260 miles   94 260 miles
90 276 miles   2 255 miles
More mileages at www.randmcnally.com/MC

Duluth / Superior

One inch represents approx. 16 miles
0 5 10 15 20 25 mi
0 5 10 15 20 25 30 35 40 km

© Rand McNally

For continuation see main map
For continuation see map above
Wisconsin Pg. 228
Pg. 111

LAKE SUPERIOR

CANADA ONTARIO MICHIGAN

ISLE ROYALE NATIONAL PARK

BOUNDARY WATERS CANOE AREA

VOYAGEURS NAT'L PARK

Toll Road Information:
No toll roads

Road Conditions 511
& Construction:
511 296-3000, In MN: (800) 657-3774
www.511mn.org, www.dot.state.mn.us

Tourism Information:
Explore Minnesota Tourism
(888) 868-7476, (651) 296-5029, (651) 757-1845
www.exploreminnesota.com

Travel planning & on-the-road resources

Mileages between cities	Albert Lea	Bemidji	Brainerd	Duluth	Grand Forks, ND	Grand Marais	Hibbing	Int'l Falls	Mankato	Marshall	Minneapolis	Moorhead	Rochester	St. Cloud	Sioux Falls, SD	Willmar
Rochester	62	306	213	226	401	338	280	366	86	194	86	321		153	236	178
St. Cloud	160	151	63	141	251	253	173	251	135	130	65	170	153		220	62

Mileages © Rand McNally

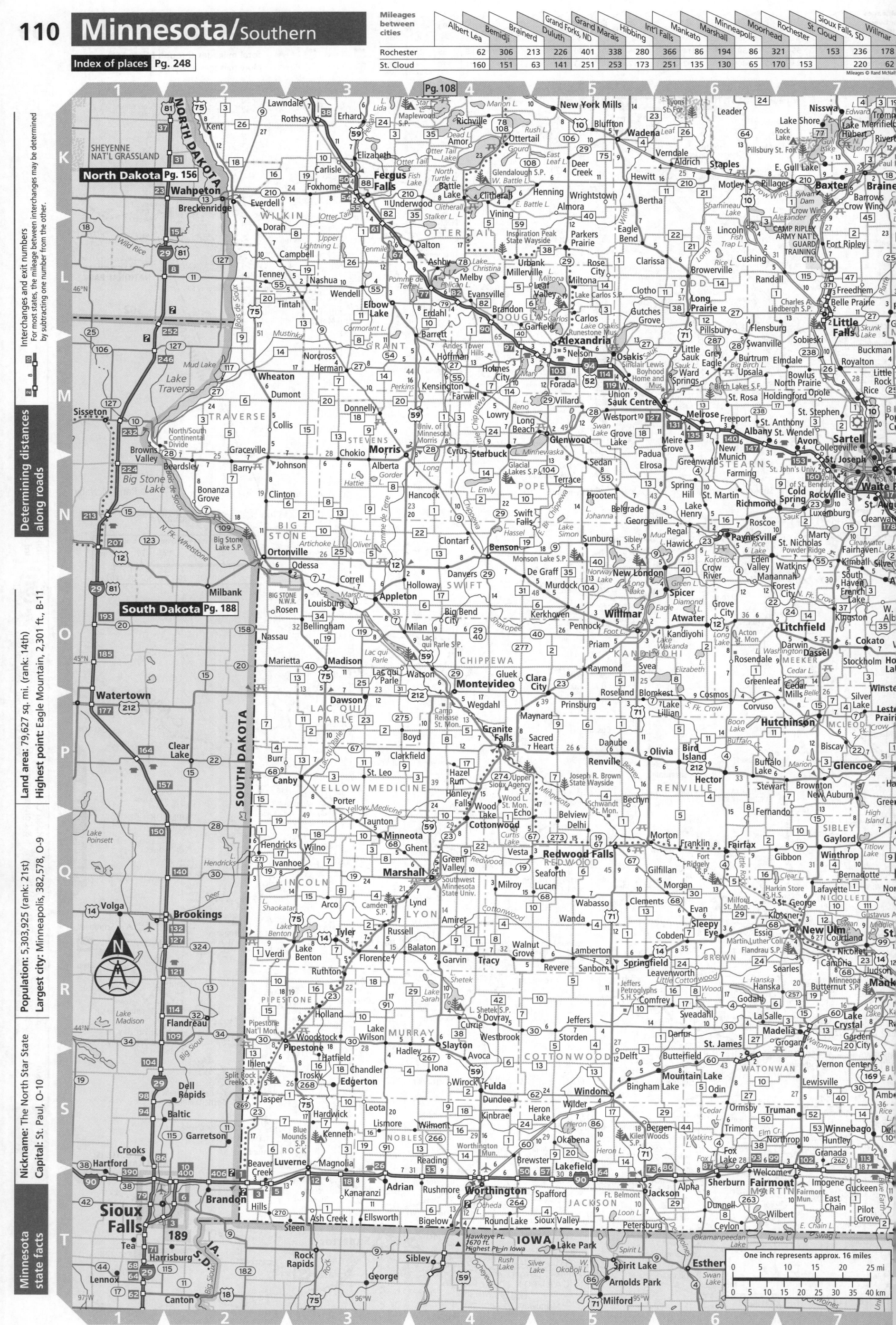

Pg. 108

North Dakota Pg. 156

South Dakota Pg. 188

Minnesota state facts

Nickname: The North Star State
Capital: St. Paul, O-10

Population: 5,303,925 (rank: 21st)
Largest city: Minneapolis, 382,578, O-9

Land area: 79,627 sq. mi. (rank: 14th)
Highest point: Eagle Mountain, 2,301 ft., B-11

Determining distances along roads

One inch represents approx. 16 miles

IOWA
Hawkeye Pt.
1670 ft.
Highest Pt. in Iowa

Mileages between cities	Albert Lea	Bemidji	Brainerd	Duluth	Grand Forks, ND	Grand Marais	Hibbing	Int'l Falls	Mankato	Marshall	Minneapolis	Moorhead	Rochester	St. Cloud	Sioux Falls, SD	Willmar
St. Paul	98	230	137	149	325	260	204	290	87	159	9	243	78	75	241	102
Sioux Falls, SD	176	380	281	390	319	500	456	494	155	91	236	244	236	220		158

Mileages © Rand McNally

Total mileages through Minnesota

| 35 | 260 miles | 94 | 260 miles |
| 90 | 276 miles | 2 | 255 miles |

More mileages at www.randmcnally.com/MC

St. Cloud

Rochester

© Rand McNally

No toll roads

Toll Road Information:

Road Conditions 511
(651) 296-3000, In MN: (800) 657-3774
& Construction: www.511mn.org, www.dot.state.mn.us

Tourism Information: Explore Minnesota Tourism
(888) 868-7476, (651) 296-5029, (651) 757-1845
www.exploreminnesota.com

Travel planning & on-the-road resources

Sights to see

Minneapolis / St. Paul & Vicinity

© Rand McNally

Sights to see

Mileages © Rand McNally

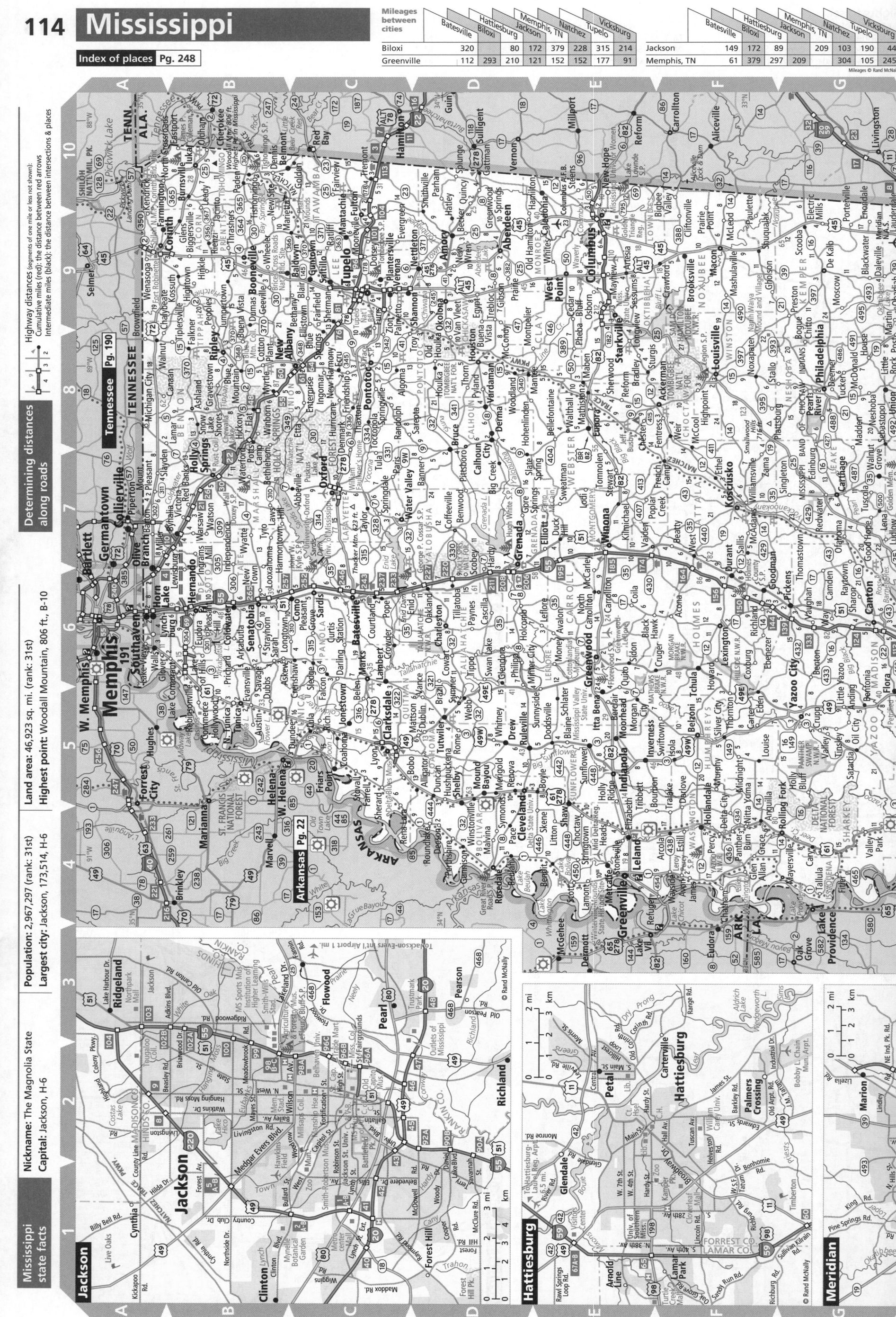

Mississippi state facts

Nickname: The Magnolia State
Capital: Jackson, H-6

Population: 2,967,297 (rank: 31st)
Largest city: Jackson, H-6

Land area: 46,923 sq. mi. (rank: 31st)
Highest point: Woodall Mountain, 806 ft., B-10

Determining distances along roads

Highway distances (segments of one mile or less not shown)
Cumulative miles (red): the distance between red arrows
Intermediate miles (black): the distance between intersections & places

Tennessee Pg. 190

Arkansas Pg. 22

	Batesville	Biloxi	Hattiesburg	Jackson	Memphis, TN	Natchez	Tupelo	Vicksburg
Meridian	176	172	89	91	234	194	142	134
New Orleans, LA	335	90	109	183	394	171	340	207

	Batesville	Biloxi	Hattiesburg	Jackson	Memphis, TN	Natchez	Tupelo	Vicksburg
Tupelo	74	315	232	190	105	283		225
Vicksburg	188	214	131	44	245	70	225	

Mileages © Rand McNally

Total mileages through Mississippi

10 77 miles	55 290 miles
20 169 miles	59 172 miles

More mileages at www.randmcnally.com/MC

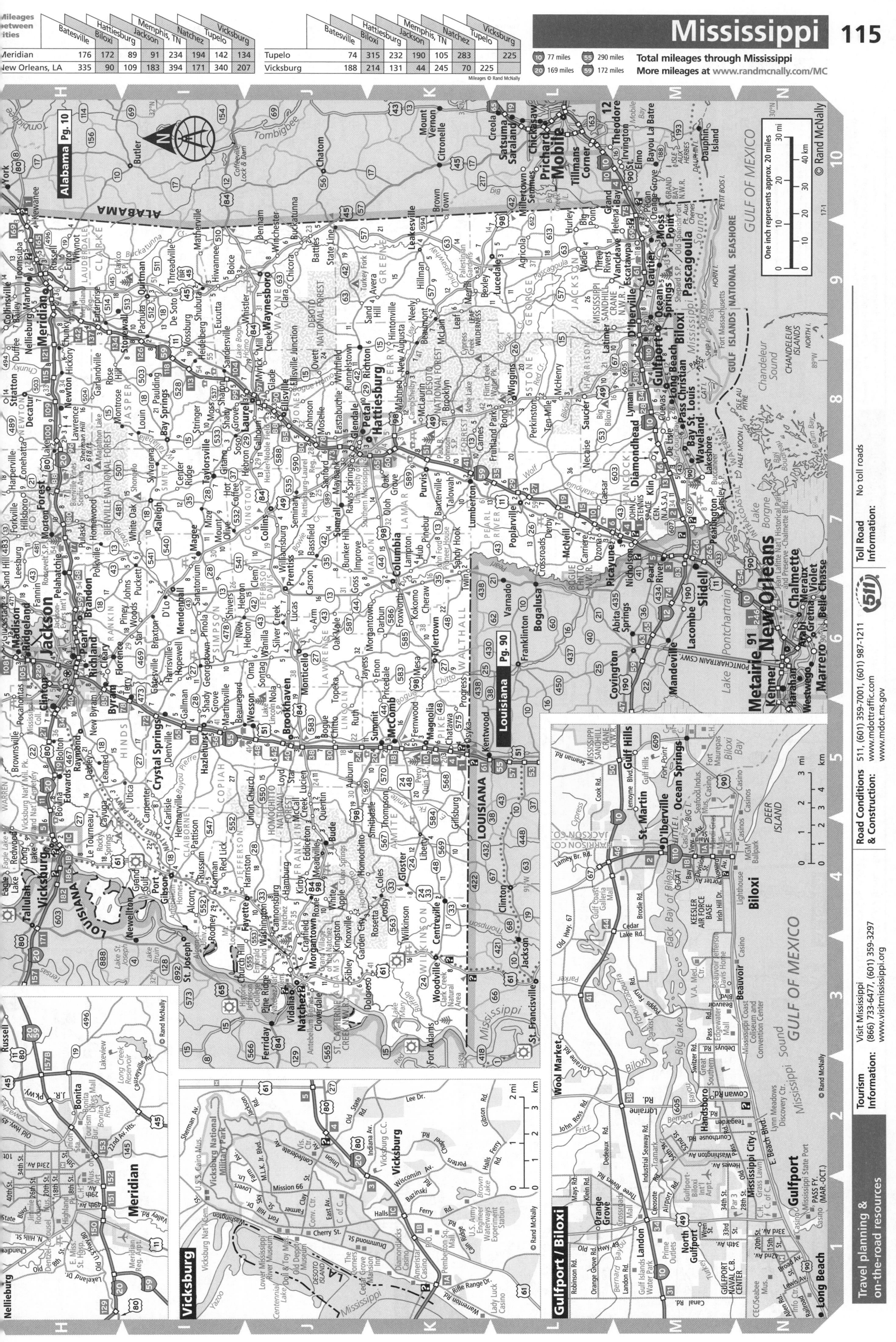

Travel planning & on-the-road resources

Tourism Information:	Visit Mississippi (866) 733-6477, (601) 359-3297 www.visitmississippi.org
Road Conditions & Construction:	511, (601) 359-7001, (601) 987-1211 www.mdottraffic.com www.mdot.ms.gov
511	
Toll Road Information:	No toll roads

© Rand McNally

Mileages between cities	Branson	Cape Girardeau	Columbia	Hannibal	Hayti	Jefferson City	Joplin	Kansas City	Kirksville	Maryville	Osage Beach	Poplar Bluff	Rolla	St. Louis	Springfield	West Plains
Cape Girardeau	295		225	218	80	216	336	348	313	445	218	82	158	114	270	182
Columbia	205	225		97	301	32	236	124	91	222	76	261	93	126	168	191

Mileages © Rand McNally

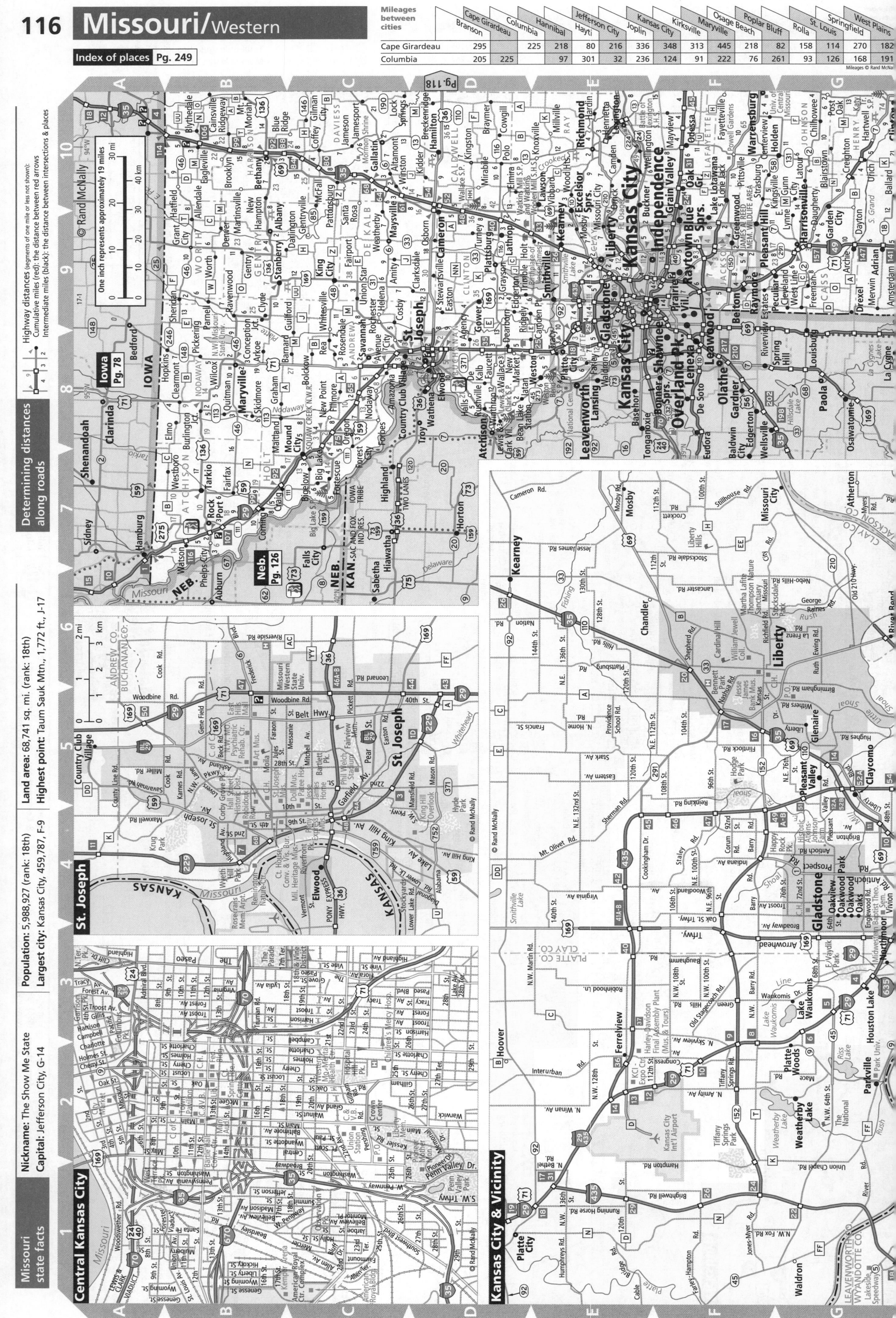

Missouri state facts

Nickname: The Show Me State

Capital: Jefferson City

Population: 5,988,927 (rank: 18th)

Largest city: Kansas City, 459,787, F-9

Land area: 68,741 sq. mi. (rank: 18th)

Highest point: Taum Sauk Mtn., 1,772 ft., J-17

Determining distances along roads

Highway distances (segments of one mile or less shown)
Cumulative miles (red): the distance between red arrows
Intermediate miles (black): the distance between intersections & places

One inch represents approximately 19 miles

Central Kansas City

St. Joseph

Kansas City & Vicinity

Mileages between cities	Branson	Cape Girardeau	Columbia	Hannibal	Hayti	Jefferson City	Joplin	Kansas City	Kirksville	Maryville	Osage Beach	Poplar Bluff	Rolla	St. Louis	Springfield	West Plains
Joplin	109	336	236	312	319	206		157	312	243	161	256	178	282	70	176
Kansas City	209	348	124	209	424	156	157		157	93	164	356	219	250	166	275

continued p. 118

Mileages © Rand McNally

continued p. 118

Total mileages through Missouri

35 · 115 miles   55 · 210 miles
44 · 290 miles   70 · 252 miles

More mileages at www.randmcnally.com/MC

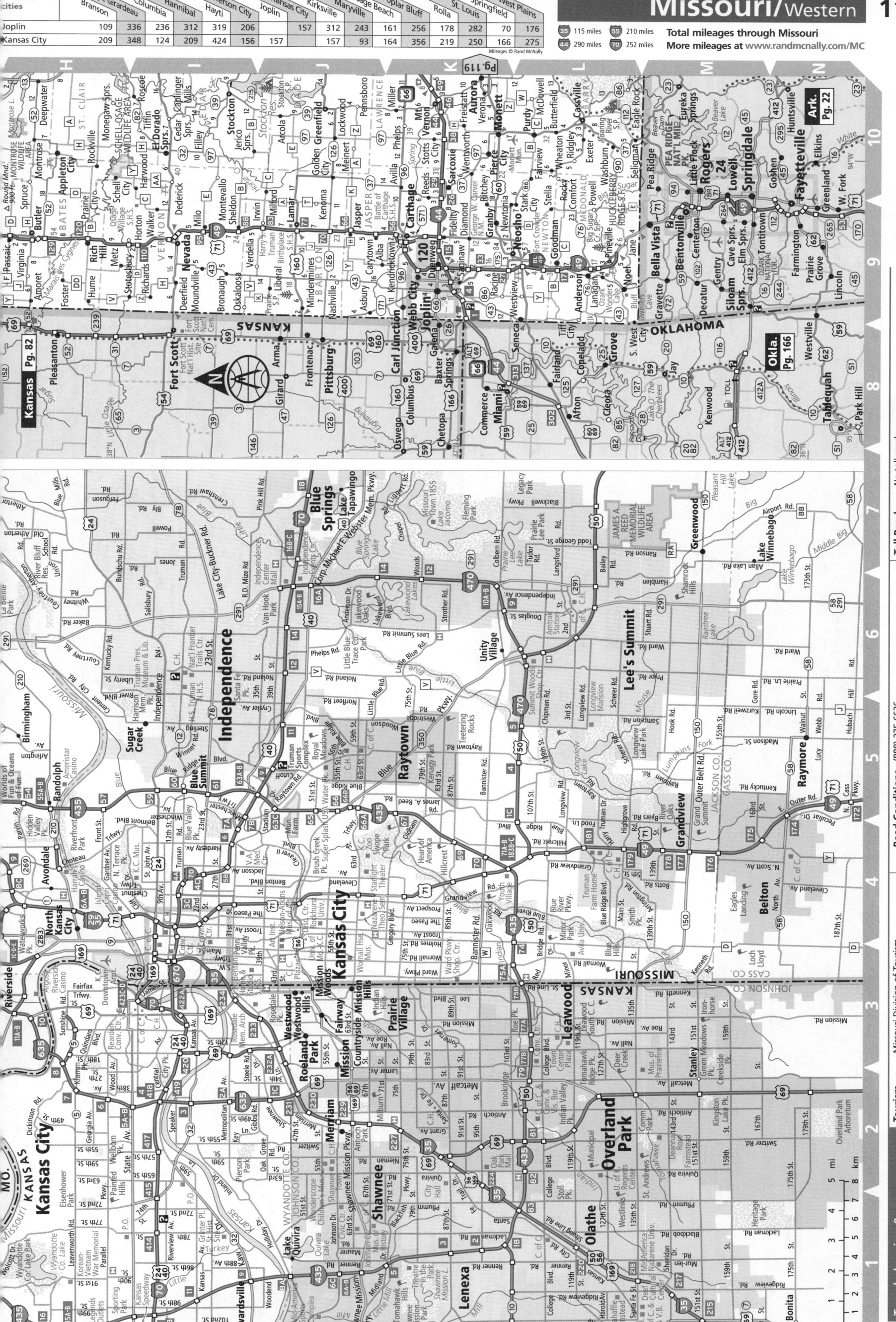

Travel planning & on-the-road resources

Tourism Information:
Missouri Division of Tourism
(573) 751-4133
www.visitmo.com

Road Conditions & Construction:
(888) 275-6636
(573) 751-2551
www.modot.org

Toll Road Information:
No toll roads

Index of places Pg. 249

Mileages between cities	Branson	Cape Girardeau	Columbia	Hannibal	Hayti	Jefferson City	Joplin	Kansas City	Kirksville	Maryville	Osage Beach	Poplar Bluff	Rolla	St. Louis	Springfield	West Plains
Poplar Bluff	215	82	261	255	62	223	256	356	350	457	224		147	151	191	98
St. Joseph	270	405	182	191	481	214	203	53	141	43	222	416	276	308	225	336

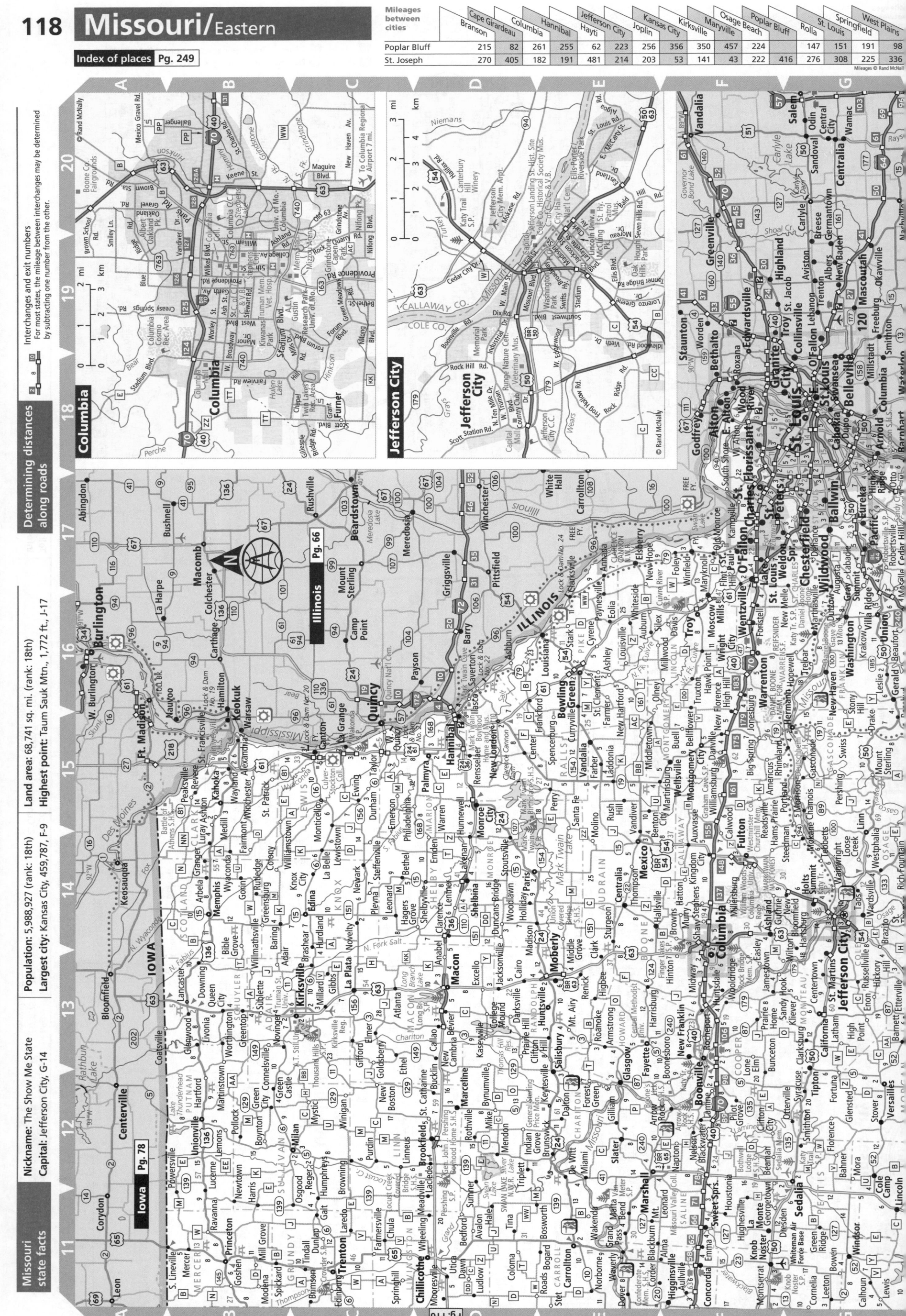

Mileages between cities

	Branson	Cape Girardeau	Columbia	Hannibal	Hayti	Jefferson City	Joplin	Kansas City	Kirksville	Maryville	Osage Beach	Poplar Bluff	Rolla	St. Louis	Springfield	West Plains
St. Louis	249	114	126	120	192	124	282	250	217	347	164	151	104		213	202
Springfield	42	270	168	242	253	136	70	166	259	266	91	191	108	213		108

Mileages © Rand McNally

	Total mileages through Missouri
35 — 115 miles	55 — 210 miles
44 — 290 miles	70 — 252 miles

More mileages at www.randmcnally.com/MC

Travel planning & on-the-road resources

Tourism Information: Missouri Division of Tourism (573) 751-4133 www.visitmo.com

Road Conditions & Construction: (888) 275-6636 (573) 751-2551 www.modot.org

Toll Road Information: No toll roads

One inch represents approximately 19 miles

Arkansas Pg. 22

Pg. 117

Pg. 190

Sights to see
- Andy Williams Moon River Theatre, Branson . . M-8
- Anheuser-Busch Brewery, St. Louis I-7
- Bass Pro Shops® Outdoor World®, Springfield C-3
- Dolly Parton's Dixie Stampede, Branson M-8
- Gateway Arch, St. Louis L-4
- Laumeier Sculpture Park, St. Louis J-4
- Magic House, Kirkwood. I-4

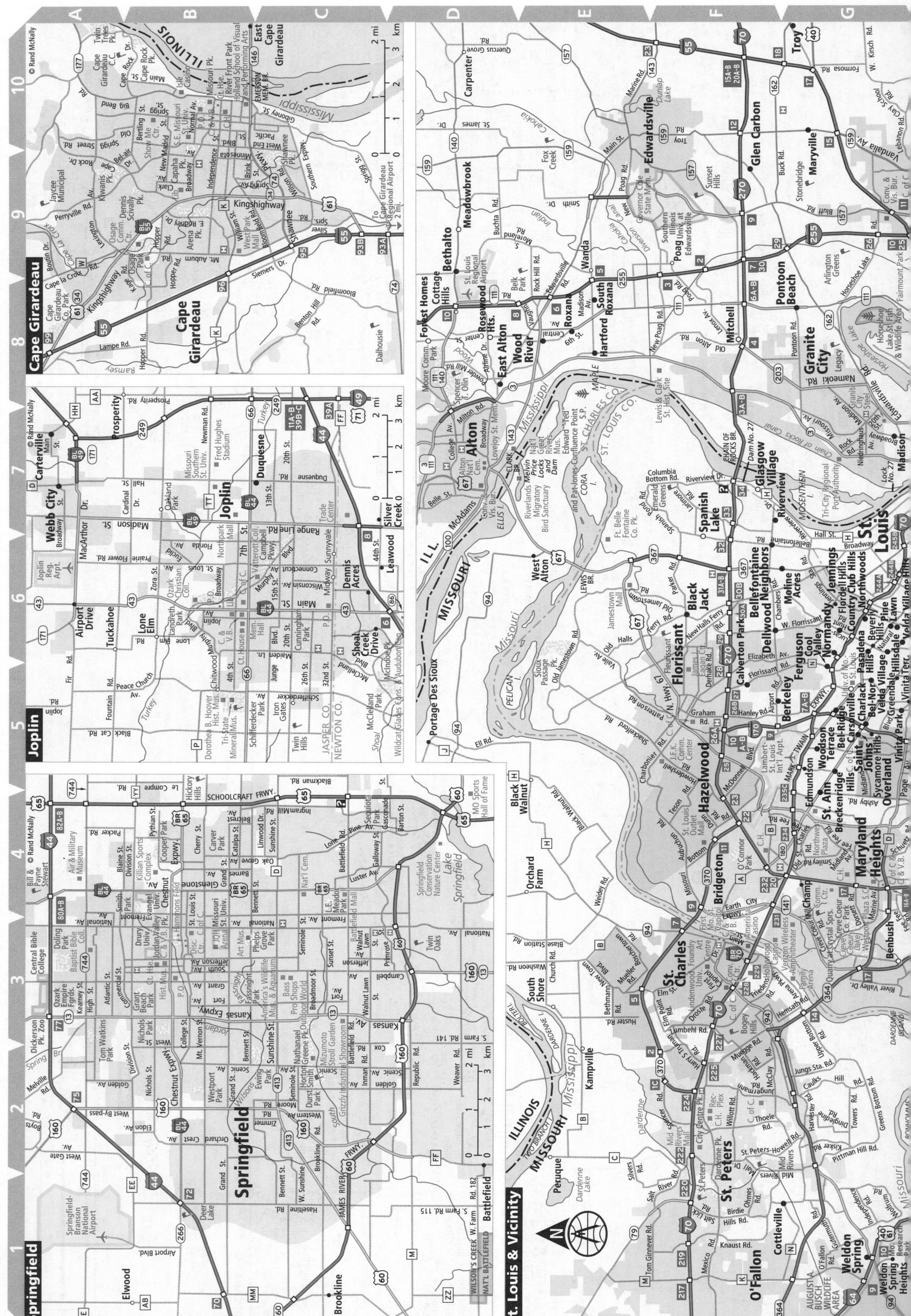

Sights to see

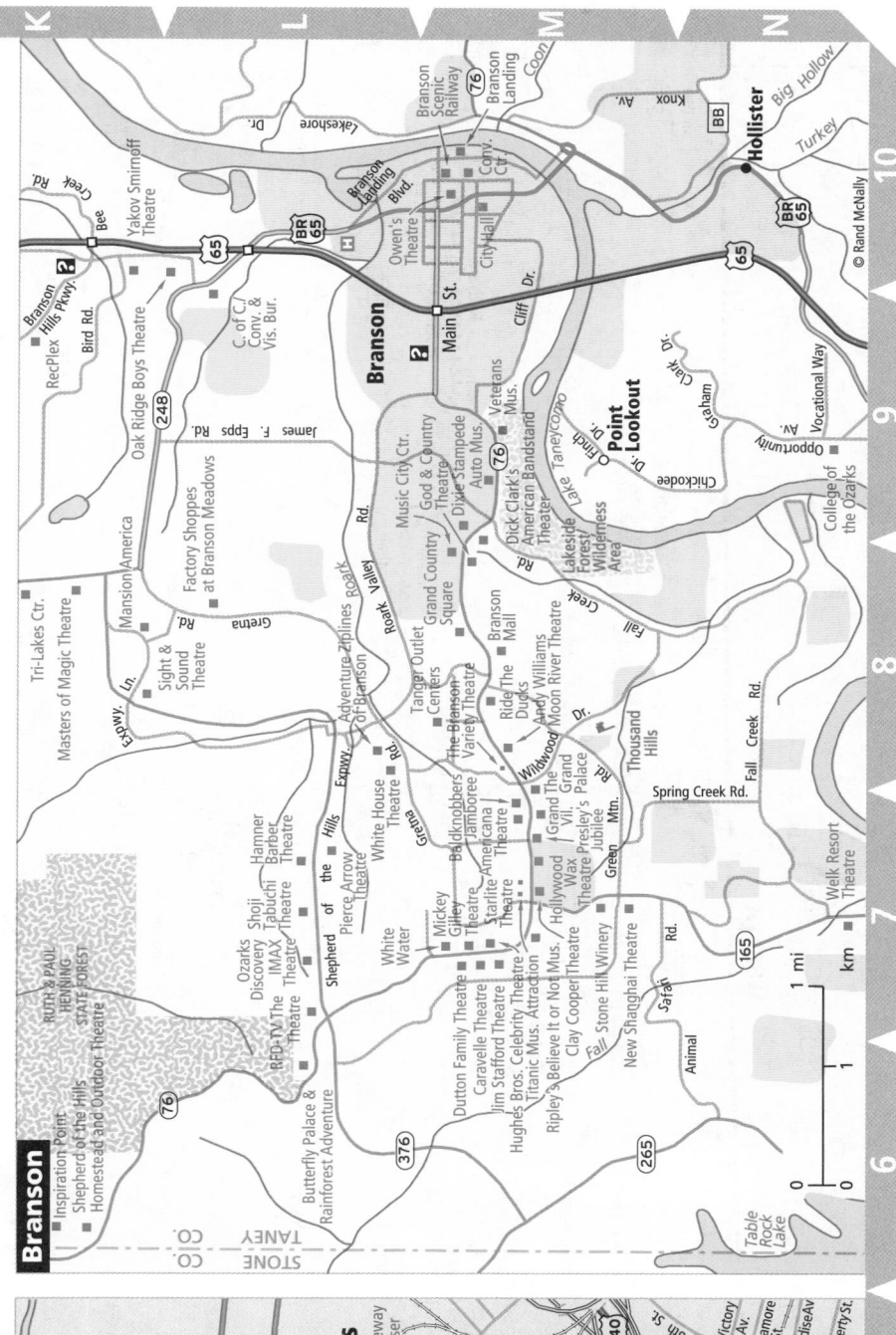

Branson

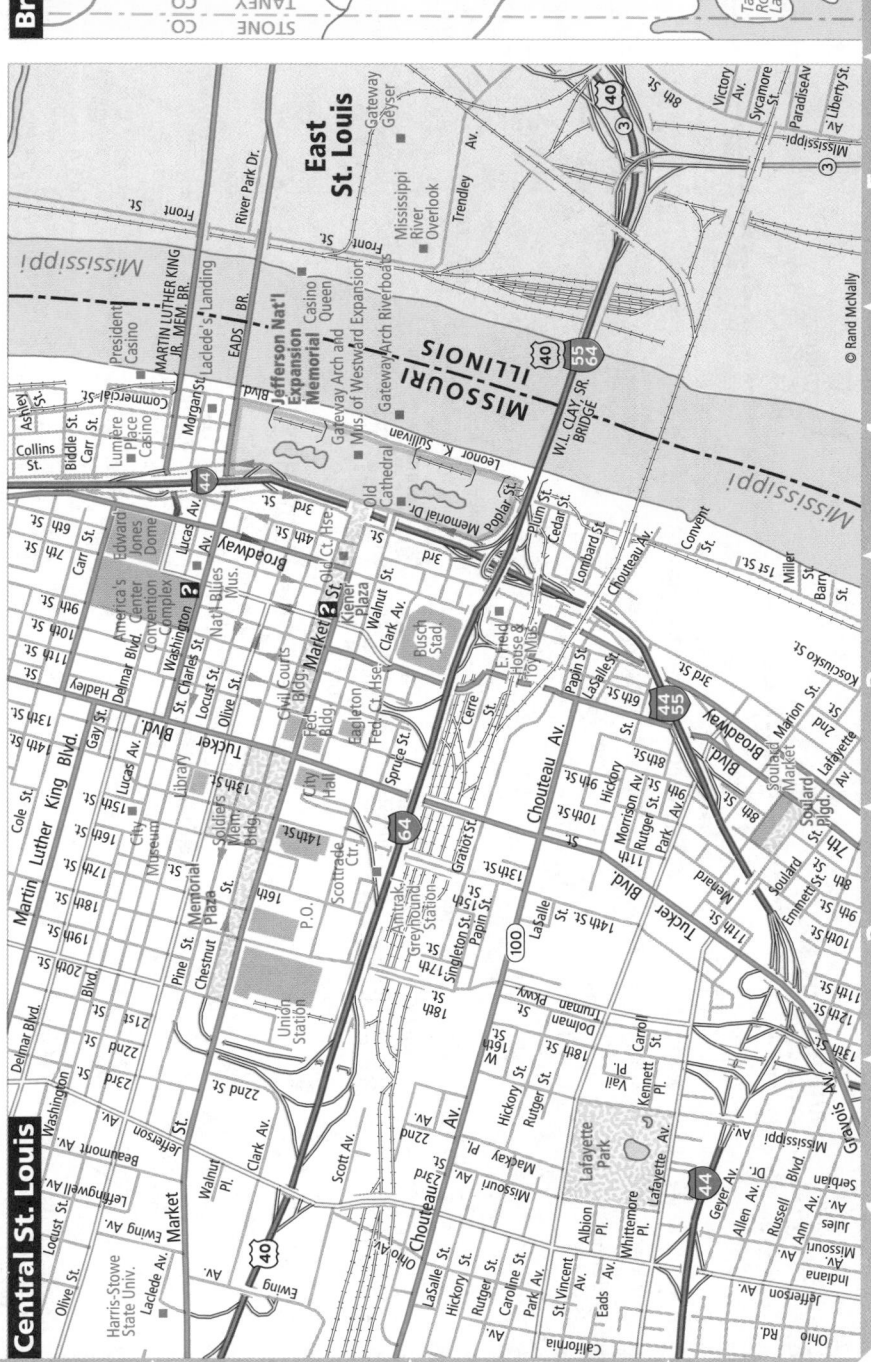

Central St. Louis

East St. Louis

Index of places Pg. 250

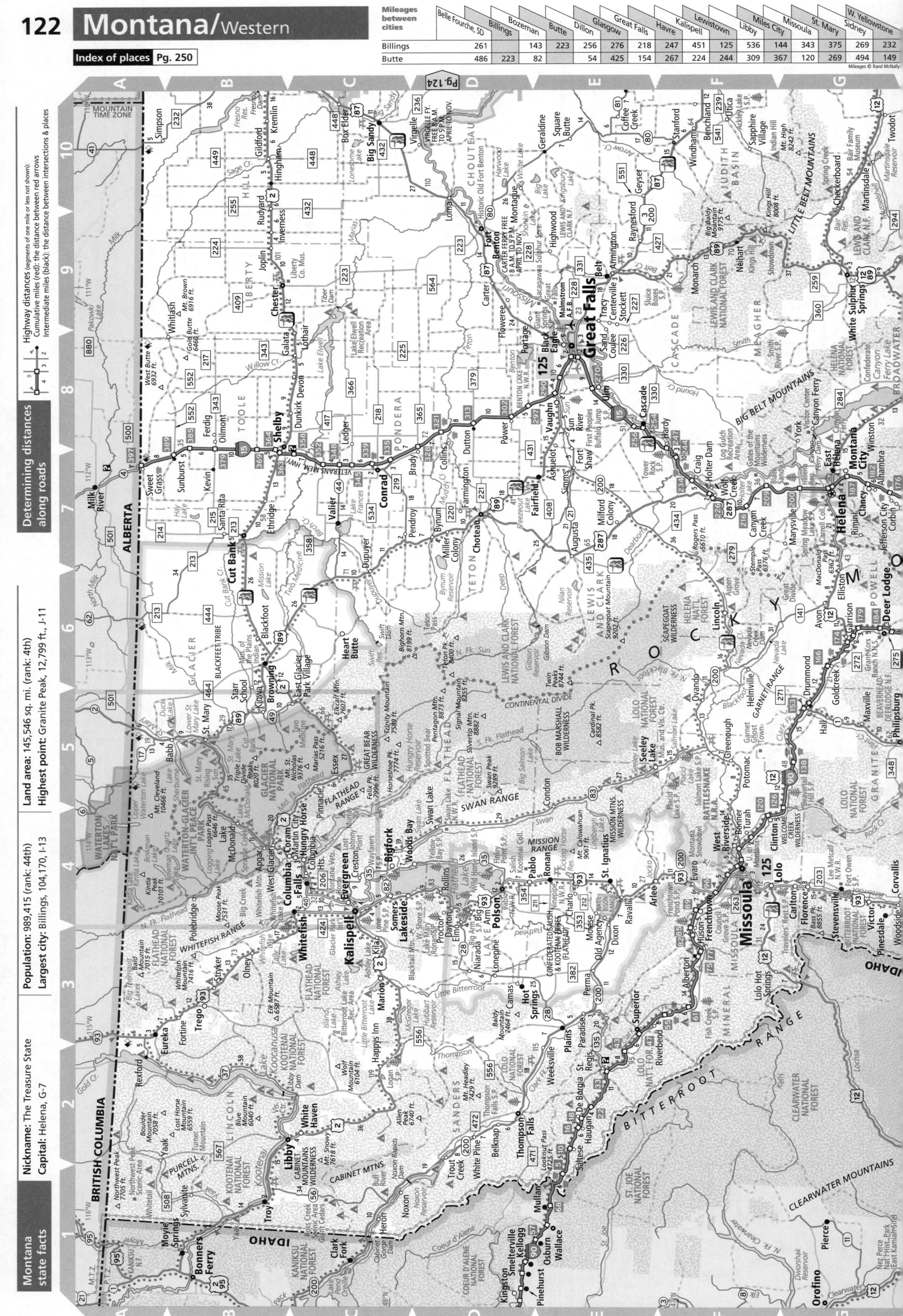

Montana state facts

Nickname: The Treasure State
Capital: Helena, G-7

Population: 989,415 (rank: 44th)
Largest city: Billings, 104,170, I-13

Land area: 145,546 sq. mi. (rank: 4th)
Highest point: Granite Peak, 12,799 ft., J-11

Determining distances along roads

Highway distances (segments of one mile or less not shown):
Cumulative miles (red); the distance between red arrows
Intermediate miles (black); the distance between intersections & places

Mileages between cities	Belle Fourche, SD	Billings	Bozeman	Butte	Dillon	Glasgow	Great Falls	Havre	Kalispell	Lewistown	Libby	Miles City	Missoula	St. Mary	Sidney	W. Yellowstone
Billings	261		143	223	256	276	218	247	451	125	536	144	343	375	269	232
Butte	486	223	82		54	425	154	267	224	244	309	367	120	269	494	149

Mileages © Rand McNally

Mileages between cities

	Belle Fourche, SD	Billings	Bozeman	Butte	Dillon	Glasgow	Great Falls	Havre	Kalispell	Lewistown	Libby	Miles City	Missoula	St. Mary	Sidney	W. Yellowstone
Great Falls	481	218	186	154	219	271		113	224	106	312	317	166	158	375	264
Helena	500	238	98	66	132	360	90	202	193	193	281	383	113	205	463	177

Mileages © Rand McNally

continued p. 124

Total mileages through Montana
15 396 miles 94 249 miles
90 552 miles

More mileages at www.randmcnally.com/MC

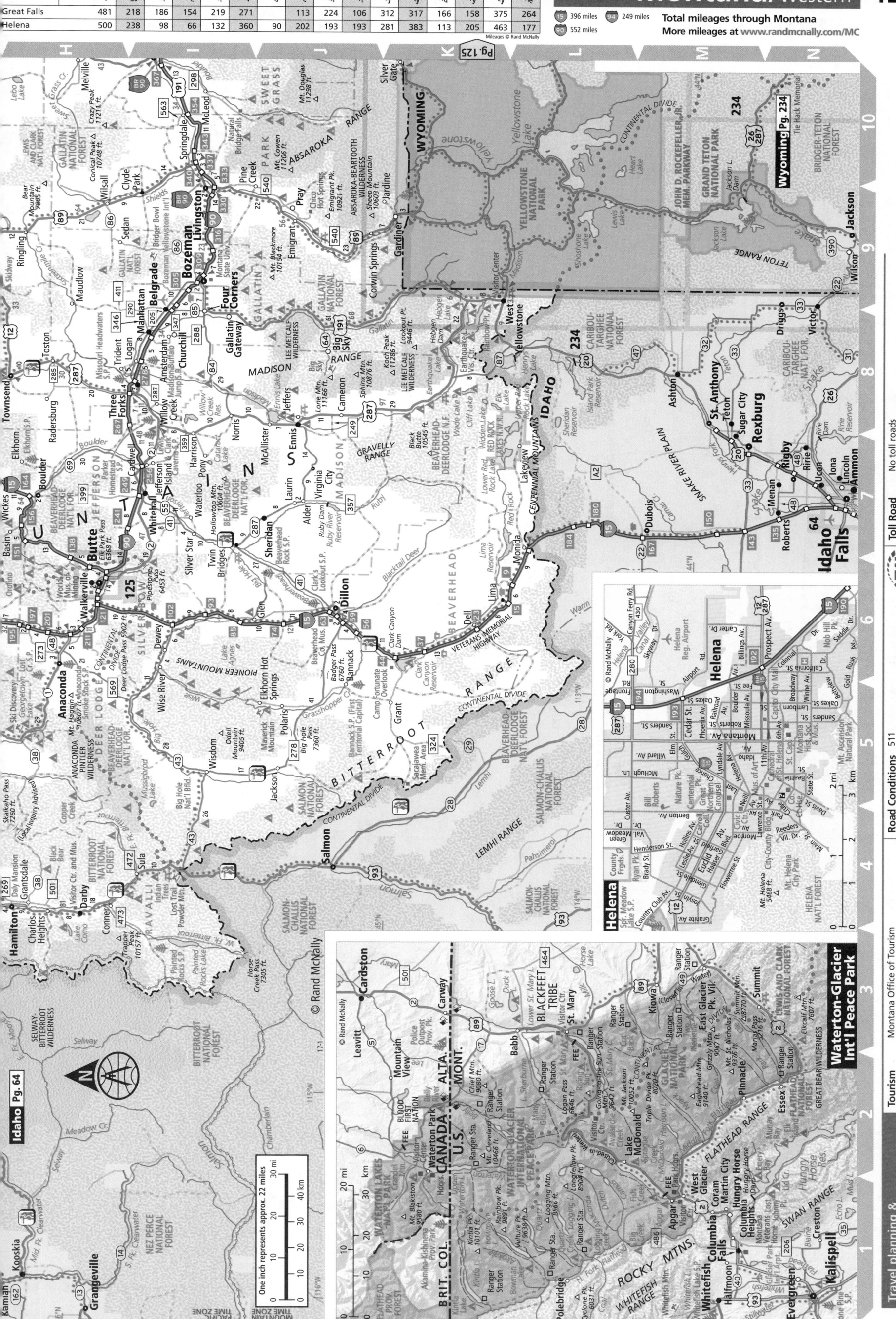

Idaho Pg. 64

Wyoming Pg. 234

Waterton-Glacier Int'l Peace Park

Helena

One inch represents approx. 22 miles

© Rand McNally

Travel planning & on-the-road resources

Tourism Information: Montana Office of Tourism (800) 847-4868 www.visitmt.com

Road Conditions & Construction: 511 (800) 226-7623, (406) 444-6200 www.mtd511.com, www.mdt.mt.gov

Toll Road Information: No toll roads

Mileages between cities	Belle Fourche, SD	Billings	Bozeman	Butte	Dillon	Glasgow	Great Falls	Havre	Kalispell	Lewistown	Libby	Miles City	Missoula	St. Mary	W. Yellowstone	Sidney
Kalispell	711	451	308	224	278	419	224	261		330	88	593	121	82	558	371
Miles City	174	144	285	367	399	195	317	333	593	211	678		487	473	126	375

Mileages © Rand McNally

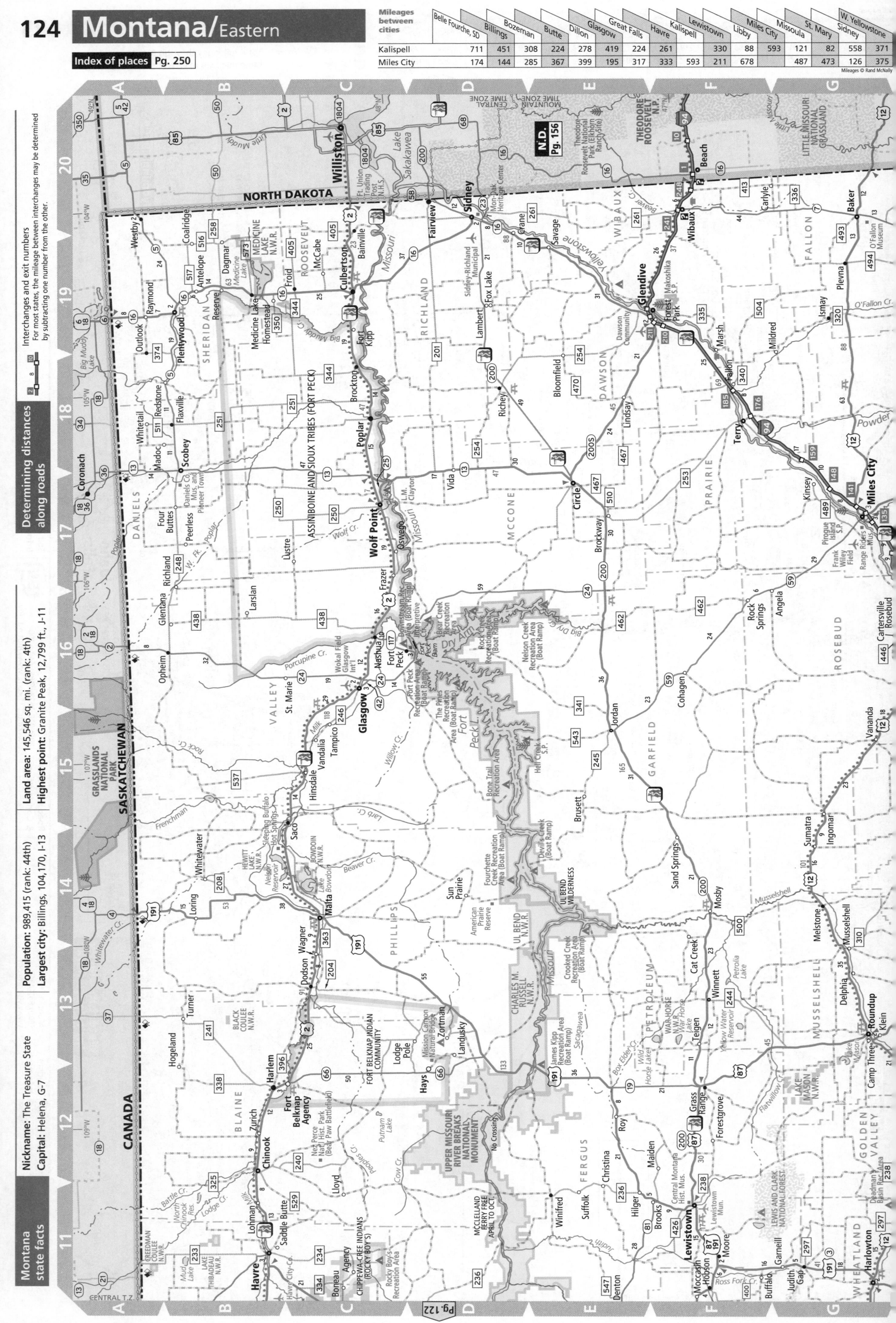

Montana state facts

Nickname: The Treasure State
Capital: Helena, G-7

Population: 989,415 (rank: 44th)
Largest city: Billings, 104,170, I-13

Land area: 145,546 sq. mi. (rank: 4th)
Highest point: Granite Peak, 12,799 ft., J-11

Determining distances along roads

Interchanges and exit numbers
For most states, the mileage between interchanges may be determined by subtracting one number from the other.

Mileages between cities	Belle Fourche, SD	Billings	Bozeman	Butte	Dillon	Glasgow	Great Falls	Havre	Kalispell	Lewistown	Libby	Miles City	Missoula	St. Mary	Sidney	W. Yellowstone
Missoula	606	343	202	120	172	437	166	280	121	272	191	487		203	614	267
Sidney	298	269	411	494	524	140	375	298	558	270	646	126	614	490		501

Mileages © Rand McNally

Total mileages through Montana
More mileages at www.randmcnally.com/MC

15 396 miles   94 249 miles
90 552 miles

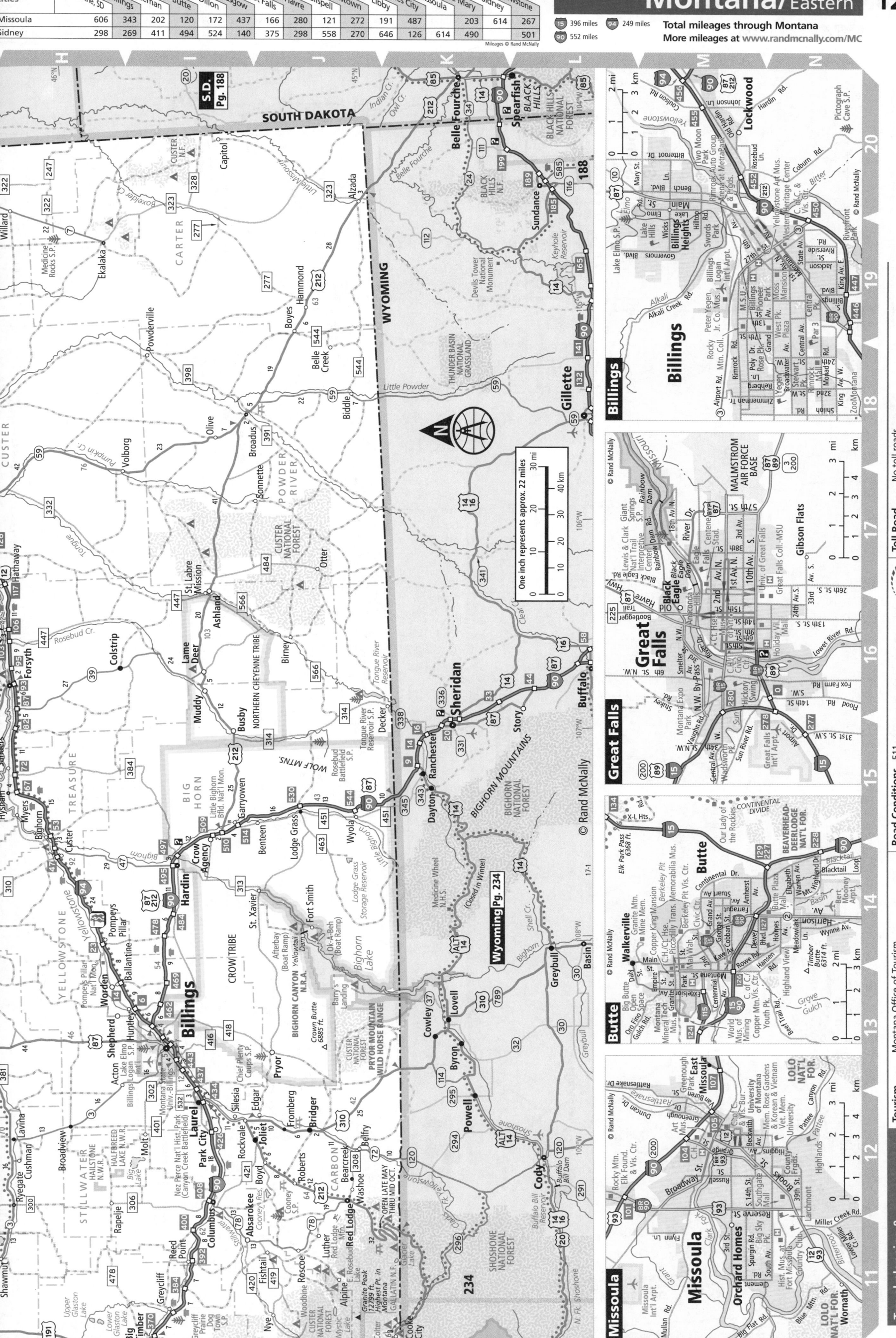

Travel planning &
on-the-road resources

Road Conditions
& Construction: 511
(800) 226-7623, (406) 444-6200
www.mtd511.com, www.mdt.mt.gov

Tourism
Information:
Montana Office of Tourism
(800) 847-4868
www.visitmt.com

Toll Road
Information:
No toll roads

Mileages between cities	Beatrice	Chadron	Columbus	Falls City	Grand Island	Kearney	Lincoln	McCook	Norfolk	North Platte	Ogallala	Omaha	O'Neill	Scottsbluff	Sioux City, IA	Valentine
Grand Island	131	326	64	196		50	93	152	105	145	194	147	112	323	187	210
Lincoln	41	450	79	102	93	129		232	124	224	274	55	208	402	151	304

Mileages © Rand McNally

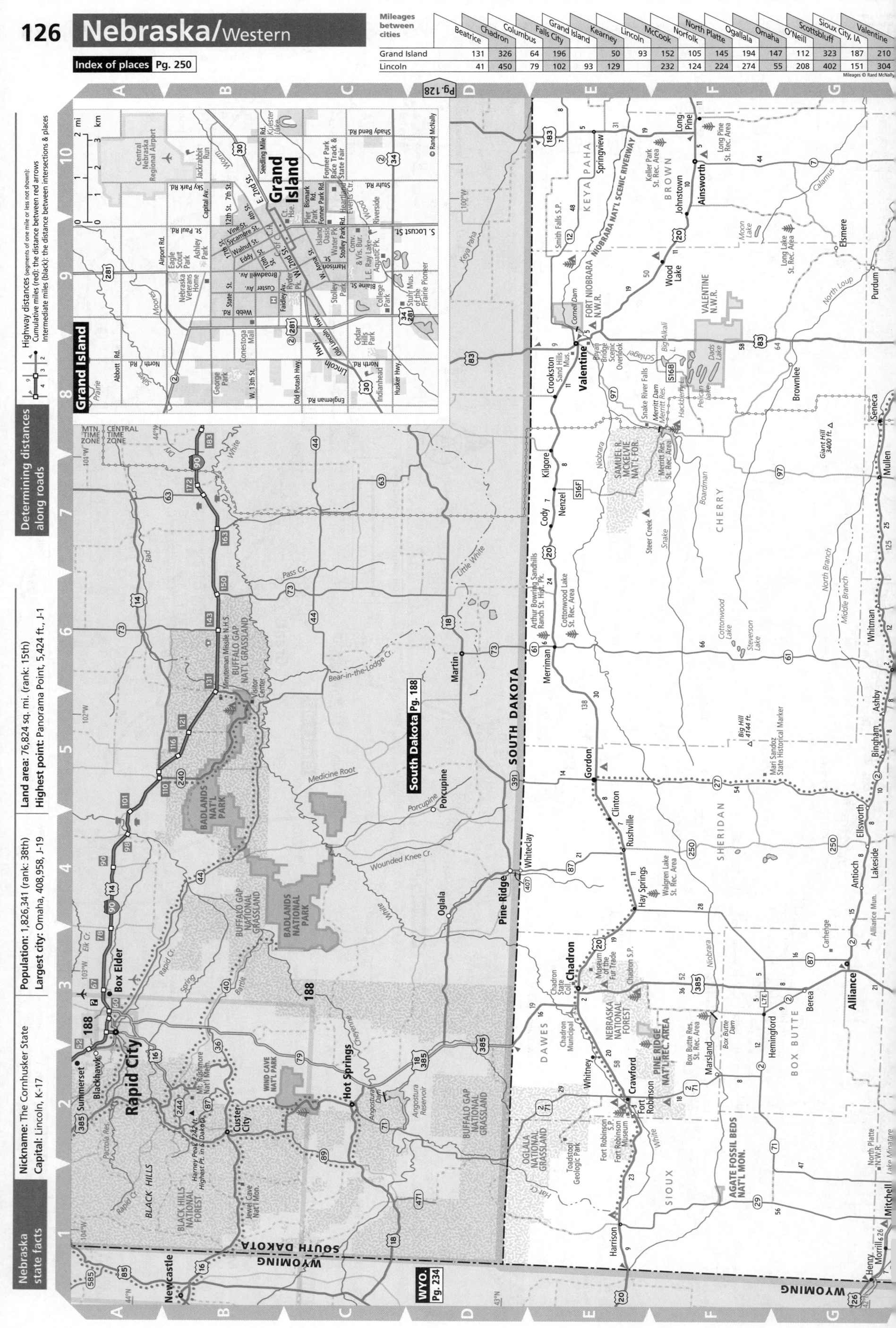

Pg. 128

South Dakota Pg. 188

WYO. Pg. 234

Nebraska state facts

Nickname: The Cornhusker State
Capital: Lincoln, K-17

Population: 1,826,341 (rank: 38th)
Largest city: Omaha, 408,958, J-19

Land area: 76,824 sq. mi. (rank: 15th)
Highest point: Panorama Point, 5,424 ft., J-1

Mileages between cities	Beatrice	Chadron	Columbus	Falls City	Grand Island	Kearney	Lincoln	McCook	Norfolk	North Platte	Ogallala	Omaha	O'Neill	Scottsbluff	Sioux City, IA	Valentine
Norfolk	162	322	45	218	105	155	124	259		250	300	109	75	417	82	186
North Platte	262	229	210	327	145	99	224	67	250		53	276	189	182	373	129

continued p. 128

Total mileages through Nebraska

| 80 | 455 miles | 83 | 226 miles |
| 81 | 219 miles | 20 | 436 miles |

More mileages at www.randmcnally.com/MC

Travel planning & on-the-road resources

Tourism Information: Nebraska Tourism (888) 444-1867 www.visitnebraska.com

Road Conditions & Construction: 511, (800) 906-9069 www.511nebraska.gov www.dor.state.ne.us

Toll Road Information: 511 — No toll roads

© Rand McNally

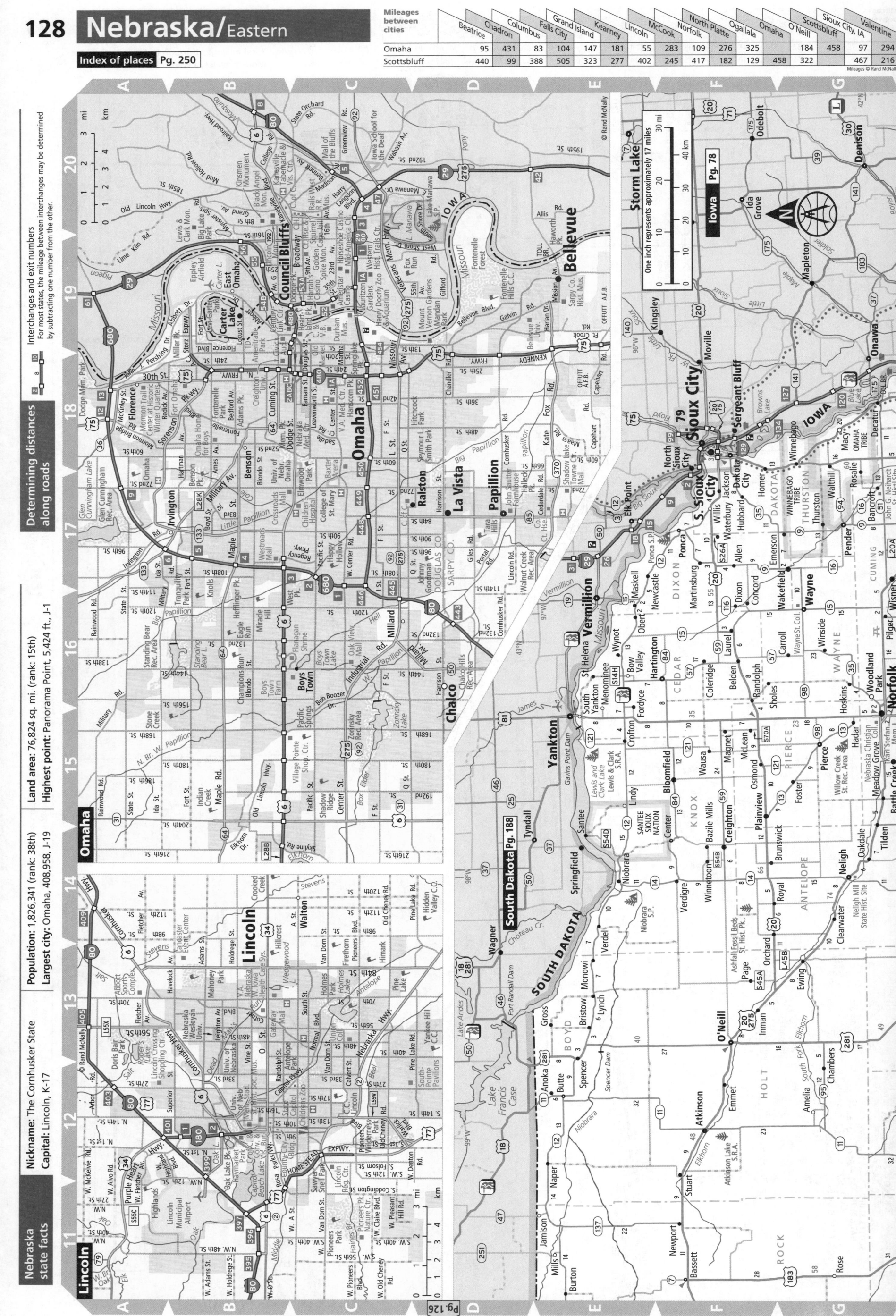

Nebraska state facts

Nickname: The Cornhusker State
Capital: Lincoln, K-17

Population: 1,826,341 (rank: 38th)
Largest city: Omaha, 408,958, J-19

Land area: 76,824 sq. mi. (rank: 15th)
Highest point: Panorama Point, 5,424 ft., J-1

Determining distances along roads

Interchanges and exit numbers
For most states, the mileage between interchanges may be determined by subtracting one number from the other.

Mileages between cities

	Beatrice	Chadron	Columbus	Falls City	Grand Island	Kearney	Lincoln	McCook	Norfolk	North Platte	Ogallala	Omaha	O'Neill	Scottsbluff	Sioux City, IA	Valentine
Sidney	381	131	329	445	263	218	343	186	369	122	71	394	311	77	492	251
Valentine	342	137	230	406	210	195	304	197	186	129	182	294	111	216	236	

Mileages © Rand McNally

Total mileages through Nebraska
- 80: 455 miles
- 83: 226 miles
- 81: 219 miles
- 20: 436 miles

More mileages at www.randmcnally.com/MC

Travel planning & on-the-road resources

Tourism Information: Nebraska Tourism (888) 444-1867 www.visitnebraska.com

Road Conditions & Construction: 511, (800) 906-9069, www.511nebraska.gov www.dor.state.ne.us

Toll Road Information: No toll roads

© Rand McNally

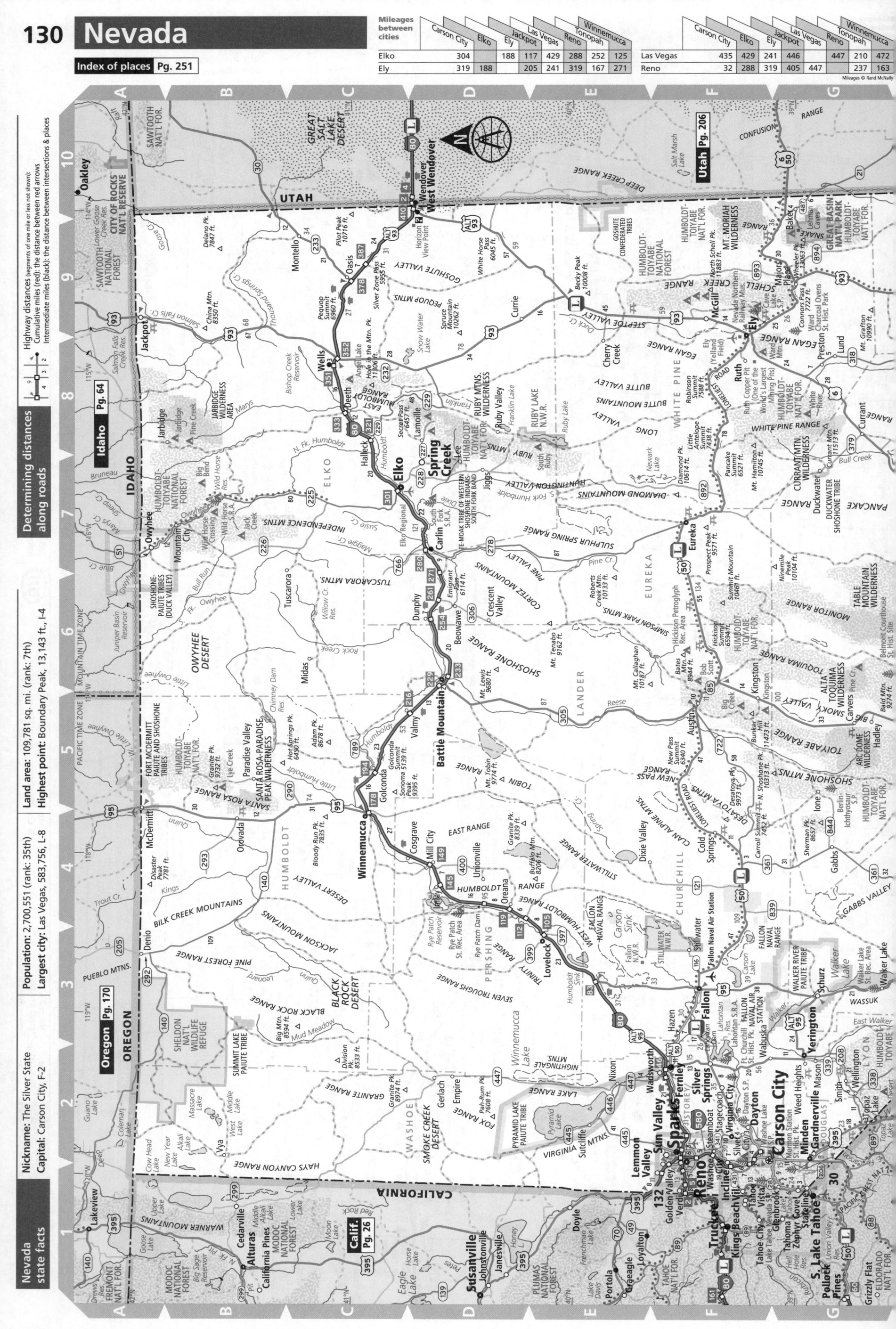

Nevada state facts

Nickname: The Silver State

Capital: Carson City, F-2

Population: 2,700,551 (rank: 35th)

Largest city: Las Vegas 583,756, L-8

Land area: 109,781 sq. mi. (rank: 7th)

Highest point: Boundary Peak, 13,143 ft., I-4

Determining distances along roads

Highway distances (segments of one mile or less not shown):

Cumulative miles (red): the distance between red arrows

Intermediate miles (black): the distance between intersections & places

Mileages between cities	Carson City	Elko	Ely	Jackpot	Las Vegas	Reno	Tonopah	Winnemucca
Elko	304		188	117	429	288	252	125
Ely	319	188		205	241	319	167	271
Las Vegas	435	429	241	446		447	210	472
Reno	32	288	319	405	447		237	163

Mileages © Rand McNally

Oregon Pg. 170

Idaho Pg. 64

Utah Pg. 206

Calif. Pg. 26

132

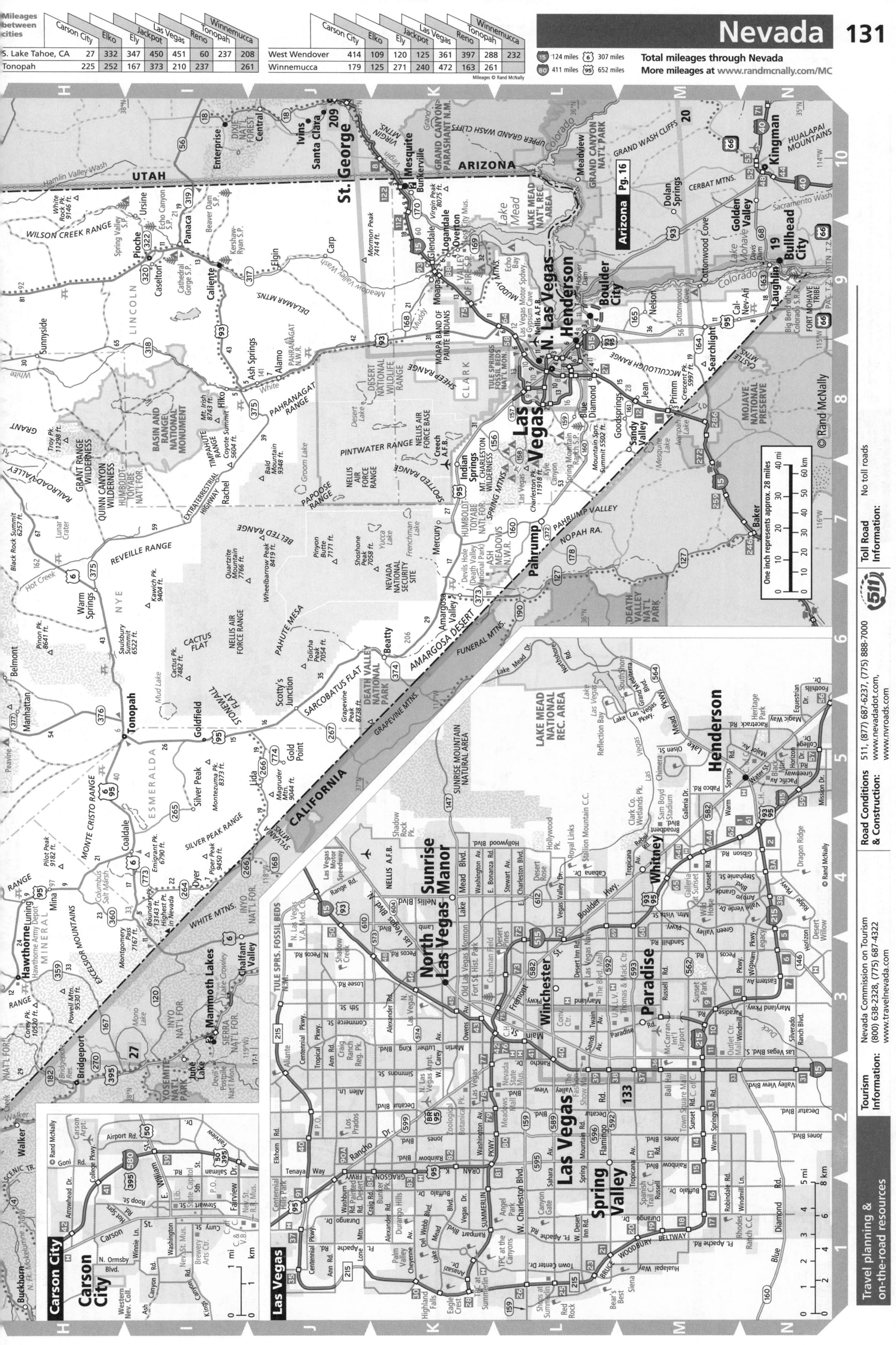

Mileages between cities	Carson City	Elko	Ely	Jackpot	Las Vegas	Reno	Tonopah	Winnemucca
S. Lake Tahoe, CA	27	332	347	450	451	60	237	208
Tonopah	225	252	167	373	210	237		261

	Carson City	Elko	Ely	Jackpot	Las Vegas	Reno	Tonopah	Winnemucca
West Wendover	414	109	120	125	361	397	288	232
Winnemucca	179	125	271	240	472	163	261	

Mileages © Rand McNally

Total mileages through Nevada
More mileages at www.randmcnally.com/MC

15: 124 miles   6: 307 miles
80: 411 miles   95: 652 miles

No toll roads

Toll Road Information:

Road Conditions & Construction: 511, (877) 687-6237, (775) 888-7000 www.nevadadot.com, www.nvroads.com

Tourism Information: Nevada Commission on Tourism (800) 638-2328, (775) 687-4322 www.travelnevada.com

Travel planning & on-the-road resources

© Rand McNally

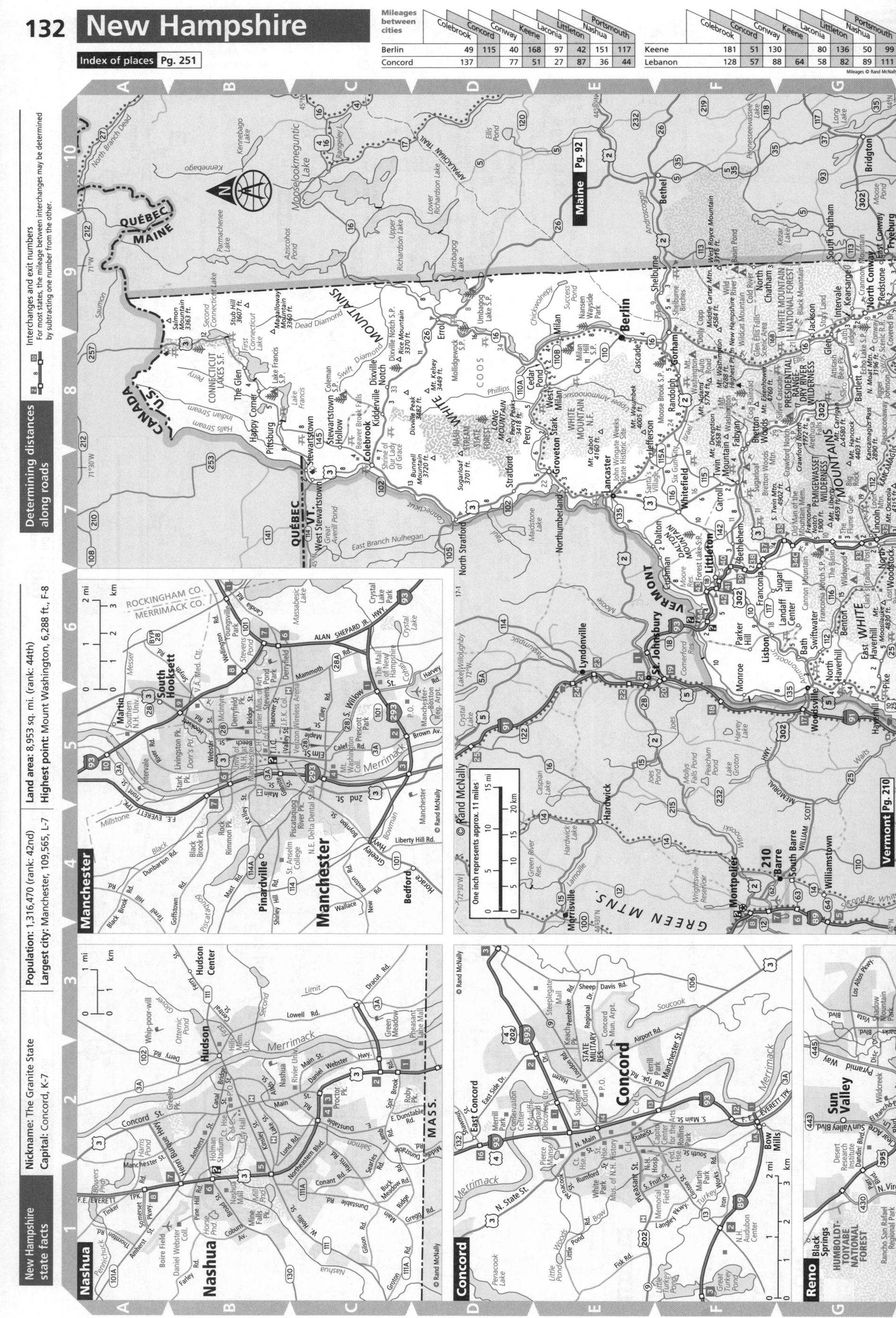

Mileages between cities	Colebrook	Concord	Conway	Keene	Laconia	Littleton	Nashua	Portsmouth
Berlin	49	115	40	168	97	42	151	117
Concord	137		77	51	27	87	36	44

	Colebrook	Concord	Conway	Keene	Laconia	Littleton	Nashua	Portsmouth
Keene	181	51	130		80	136	50	99
Lebanon	128	57	88	64	58	82	89	111

Mileages © Rand McNally

New Hampshire state facts

Nickname: The Granite State

Capital: Concord, K-7

Population: 1,316,470 (rank: 42nd)

Largest city: Manchester, 109,565, L-7

Land area: 8,953 sq. mi. (rank: 44th)

Highest point: Mount Washington, 6,288 ft., F-8

Determining distances along roads

For most states, the mileage between interchanges may be determined by subtracting one number from the other.

Interchanges and exit numbers

Mileages between cities	Colebrook	Concord	Conway	Keene	Laconia	Littleton	Nashua	Portsmouth
Littleton	56	87	54	136	66		121	129
Manchester	155	18	95	55	45	105	18	43

	Colebrook	Concord	Conway	Keene	Laconia	Littleton	Nashua	Portsmouth
Nashua	172	36	113	50	63	121		54
Portsmouth	180	44	77	99	57	129	54	

Mileages © Rand McNally

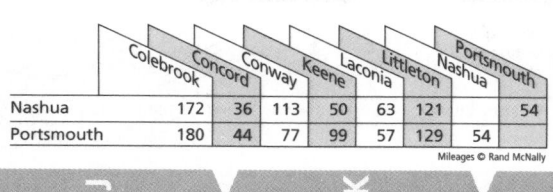

89 61 miles   95 16 miles
93 132 miles   2 36 miles

Total mileages through New Hampshire
More mileages at www.randmcnally.com/MC

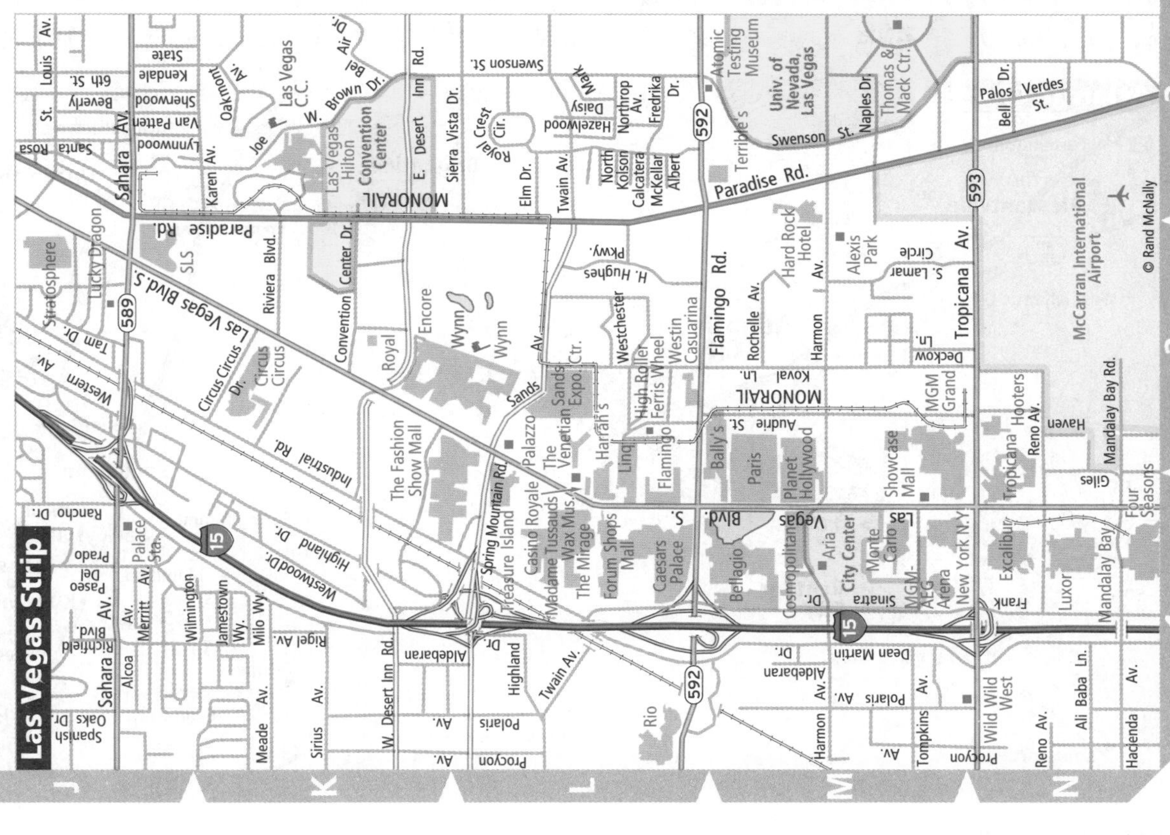

Travel planning & on-the-road resources

Tourism Information: New Hampshire Division of Travel & Tourism (603) 271-2665 www.visitnh.com

Road Conditions & Construction: 511, (603) 271-6862 www.nhtmc.com www.nh.gov/dot

Toll Road Information: Bureau of Turnpikes (E-ZPass) (877) 643-9727, (603) 485-3806 www.nh.gov/dot/org/operations/turnpikes/turnpikesindex.htm

Mileages between cities	Atlantic City	Camden	Cape May	Jersey City	Long Branch	Newark	New Brunswick	New York, NY	Paterson	Phillipsburg	Port Jervis, NY	Princeton	Toms River	Trenton	Vineland	Wilmington, DE
Atlantic City		58	47	120	82	115	94	126	129	138	182	99	52	90	36	82
Camden	58		88	86	76	80	61	96	94	80	143	45	55	34	36	31

Mileages © Rand McNally

New Jersey state facts

Nickname: The Garden State
Capital: Trenton, J-8

Population: 8,791,894 (rank: 11th)
Largest city: Newark, 277,140, F-12

Land area: 7,354 sq. mi. (rank: 46th)
Highest point: High Point, 1,803 ft., A-9

Determining distances along roads

Highway distances (segments of one mile or less shown)
Cumulative miles (red): the distance between red arrows
Intermediate miles (black): the distance between intersections & places

Newark & Vicinity

Atlantic City

Pennsylvania Pg. 174

© Rand McNally

Mileages between cities	Atlantic City	Camden	Cape May	Jersey City	Long Branch	Newark	New Brunswick	New York, NY	Paterson	Phillipsburg	Port Jervis, NY	Princeton	Toms River	Trenton	Vineland	Wilmington, DE
Cape May	47	88		151	114	147	126	157	161	170	214	131	84	121	48	98
Newark	115	80	147	6	43		25	10	15	58	74	41	63	55	114	112

Mileages © Rand McNally

continued p. 136

78 68 miles   95 98 miles
80 68 miles

Total mileages through New Jersey
More mileages at www.randmcnally.com/MC

One inch represents approximately 6 miles
0   5   10 mi
0   5   10   15 km

New York Pg. 140

17-1 © Rand McNally

Pg. 137

Burlington Co. Bridge Commission: (856) 829-1900, (609) 387-1480; www.bcbridges.org
Del. River & Bay Authority (Delaware Memorial Bridge, Cape May/Lewes Ferry): (302) 571-6300; www.drba.net
Delaware River Port Authority (Philadelphia area bridges): (877) 567-3772; www.drpa.org
Delaware River Joint Toll Bridge Commission (other Delaware River bridges): (800) 363-0049; www.drjtbc.org

Toll Road Information (all use E-ZPass): 511

Road Conditions & Construction: 511, (866) 511-6538 www.511.nj.us www.state.nj.us/transportation

Tourism Information: New Jersey Travel & Tourism (609) 599-6540 www.visitnj.org

Travel planning & on-the-road resources

Continued on next page

Mileages between cities	Atlantic City	Camden	Cape May	Jersey City	Long Branch	Newark	New Brunswick	New York, NY	Paterson	Phillipsburg	Port Jervis, NY	Princeton	Toms River	Trenton	Vineland	Wilmington, DE
New Brunswick	94	61	126	30	34	25		36	39	48	92	16	43	26	95	93
Phillipsburg	138	80	170	64	81	58	48	68	67		74	54	101	54	118	95

Mileages © Rand McNally

Mileages between cities	Atlantic City	Camden	Cape May	Jersey City	Long Branch	Newark	New Brunswick	New York, NY	Paterson	Phillipsburg	Port Jervis, NY	Princeton	Toms River	Trenton	Vineland	Wilmington, DE
Port Jervis, NY	182	143	214	89	110	74	92	95	73	74		94	130	122	180	158
Trenton	90	34	121	61	52	55	26	66	69	54	122	11	47		69	61

Total mileages through New Jersey
More mileages at www.randmcnally.com/MC

78 68 miles 95 98 miles
80 68 miles

Continued from previous page

N.J. Turnpike Authority (N.J. Turnpike, Gdn. St. Pkwy.) : (732) 750-5300; www.state.nj.us/turnpike; www.panynj.gov
Port Authority of N.Y. & N.J. (NYC area inter-state bridges & tunnels); (800) 221-9903; www.panynj.gov
South Jersey Transportation Authority (Atlantic City Expressway): (609) 965-6060; www.sjta.com

Toll Road Information: (all use E-ZPass)

511
www.511-nj.org

Road Conditions & Construction: 511, (866) 511-6538 www.511.nj.us www.state.nj.us/transportation

Tourism Information: New Jersey Travel & Tourism (609) 599-6540 www.visitnj.org

Travel planning & on-the-road resources

Trenton

© Rand McNally

One inch represents approximately 6 miles
0   5   10 mi
0   5   10   15 km

40°N
39°30'N
74°W
74°30'W
39°N

ATLANTIC OCEAN

Determining distances along roads

Highway distances (segments of one mile or less not shown)

Cumulative miles (red): the distance between arrows

Intermediate miles (black): the distance between intersections & places

Mileages between cities	Albuquerque	Carlsbad	Clayton	Gallup	Las Cruces	Socorro	Taos	Tucumcari		Albuquerque	Carlsbad	Clayton	Gallup	Las Cruces	Socorro	Taos	Tucumcari
Albuquerque		277	270	137	222	78	128	173	Clayton	270	374		407	415	347	163	111
Carlsbad	277		374	412	206	241	336	263	Clovis	219	180	168	356	292	248	246	83

Mileages © Rand McNally

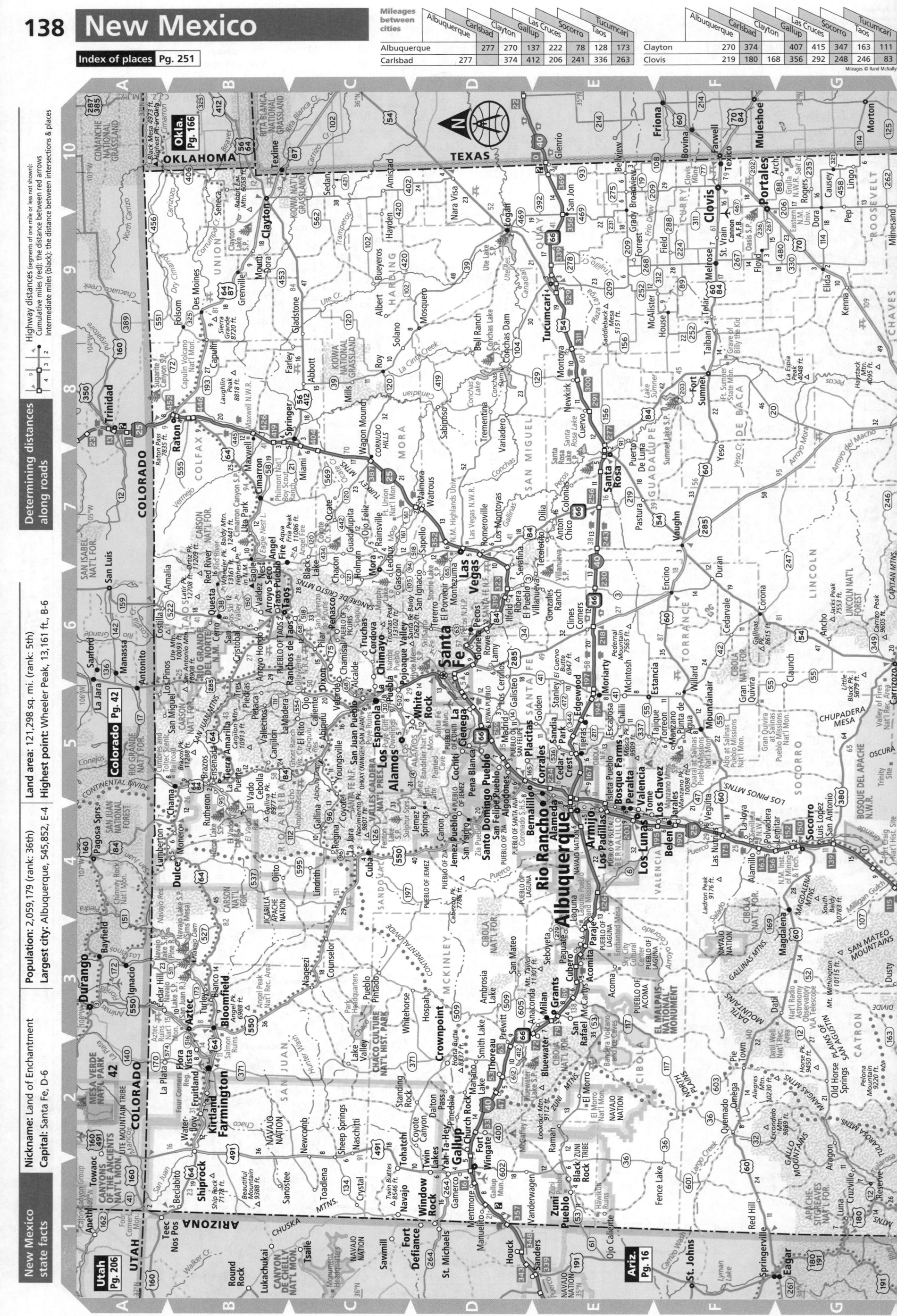

Mileages between cities

	Albuquerque	Carlsbad	Clayton	Gallup	Las Cruces	Socorro	Tucumcari	Taos
Farmington	180	455	418	121	404	258	202	354
Las Cruces	222	206	415	338		146	351	303
Roswell	199	76	293	336	184	165	260	182
Santa Fe	58	268	215	197	282	136	68	166

Mileages © Rand McNally

Total mileages through New Mexico

10 — 164 miles 40 — 374 miles 25 — 462 miles

More mileages at www.randmcnally.com/MC

Travel planning & on-the-road resources

Tourism Information:
New Mexico Tourism Department
(505) 827-7400, (505) 827-7336
www.newmexico.org

Road Conditions & Construction:
511
(800) 432-4269, (505) 827-5100
www.nmroads.com, www.dot.state.nm.us

Toll Road Information: No toll roads

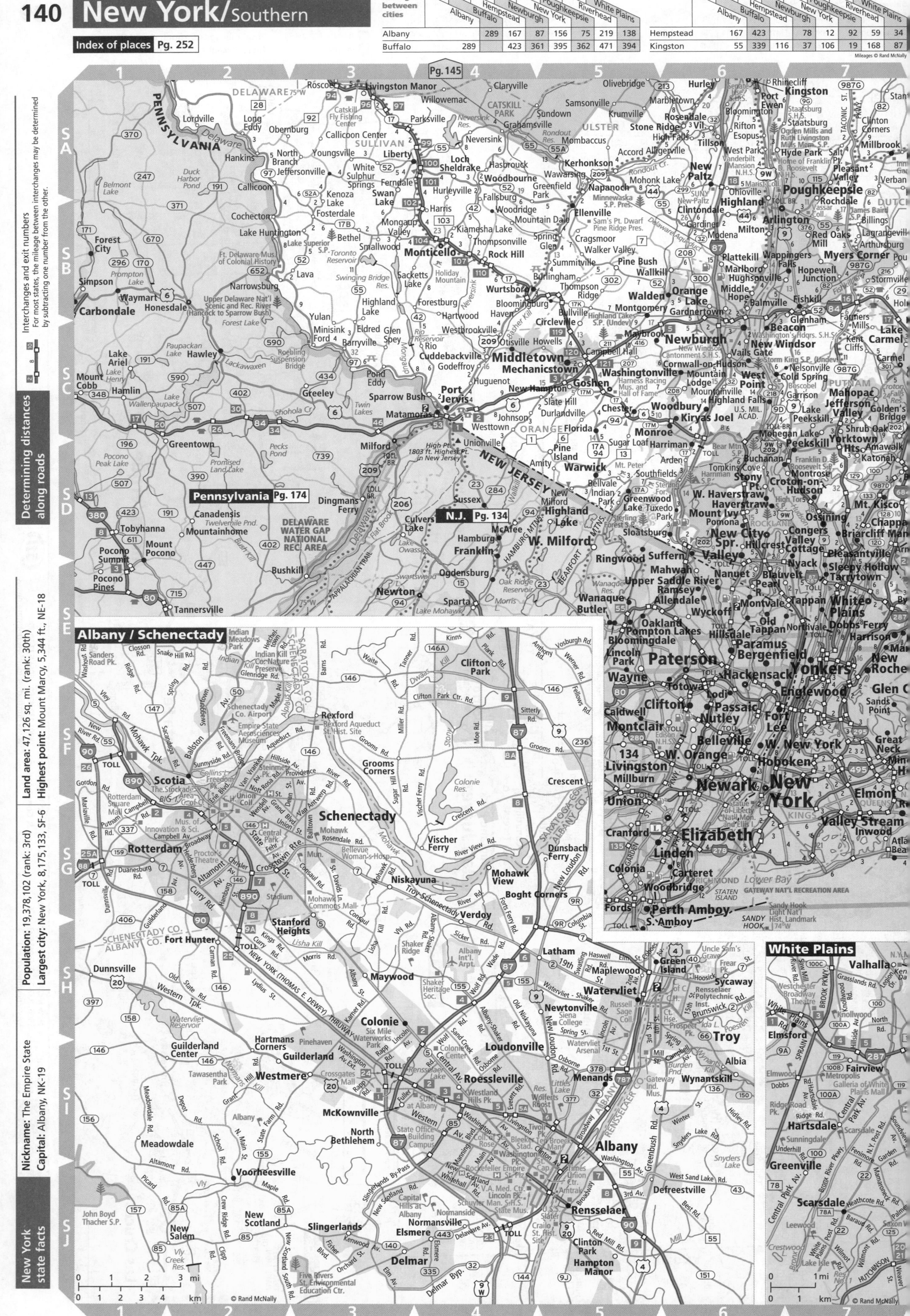

New York State facts

Nickname: The Empire State
Capital: Albany, NK-19

Population: 19,378,102 (rank: 3rd) | Largest city: New York, 8,175,133, SF-6

Land area: 47,126 sq. mi. (rank: 30th) | Highest point: Mount Marcy, 5,344 ft., NE-18

Determining distances along roads

Interchanges and exit numbers
For most states, the mileage between interchanges may be determined by subtracting one number from the other.

Albany / Schenectady

White Plains

Mileages between cities

	Albany	Buffalo	Hempstead	Newburgh	New York	Poughkeepsie	Riverhead	White Plains
Montauk	260	513	97	172	107	184	42	126
Newburgh	87	361	78		72	19	130	49

	Albany	Buffalo	Hempstead	Newburgh	New York	Poughkeepsie	Riverhead	White Plains
New York	156	395	12	72		84	66	26
Poughkeepsie	75	362	92	19	84		143	60

Mileages © Rand McNally

Total mileages through New York

84	72 miles	95	24 miles
87	334 miles	495	66 miles

More mileages at www.randmcnally.com/MC

One inch represents approximately 10 miles

MTA (N.Y. City in-state bridges & tunnels); 511, say "Bridges & Tunnels"; www.mta.info/bandt
N.Y. State Bridge Authority (Hudson R. bridges): (845) 691-7245; www.nysba.state.ny.us
Port Authority of N.Y. and N.J. (N.Y.C. inter-state bridges & tunnels): (800) 221-9903; www.panynj.gov

Toll Road Information: (all use E-ZPass)

Road Conditions & Construction: 511, (888) 465-1169 www.511ny.org; www.dot.ny.gov Thruway: (800) 847-8929; www.thruway.ny.gov

Tourism Information: New York State Division of Tourism (800) 225-5697 www.iloveny.com

Travel planning & on-the-road resources

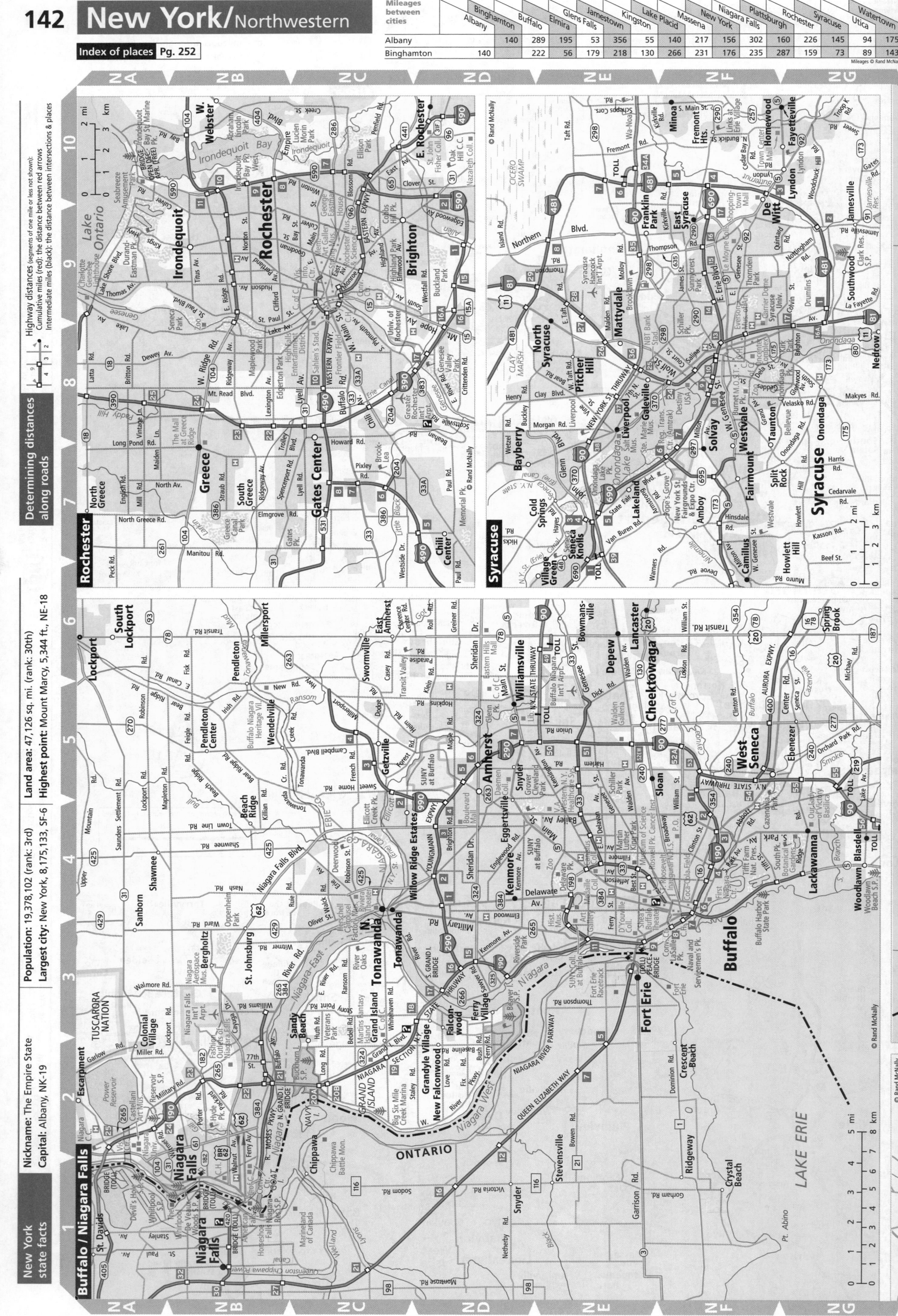

Mileages between cities	Albany	Binghamton	Buffalo	Elmira	Glens Falls	Jamestown	Kingston	Lake Placid	Massena	New York	Niagara Falls	Plattsburgh	Rochester	Syracuse	Utica	Watertown
Albany		140	289	195	53	356	55	140	217	156	302	160	226	145	94	175
Binghamton	140		222	56	179	218	130	266	231	176	235	287	159	73	89	143

Mileages © Rand McNally

New York state facts

Nickname: The Empire State
Capital: Albany, NK-19

Population: 19,378,102 (rank: 3rd)
Largest city: New York, 8,175,133, SF-6

Land area: 47,126 sq. mi. (rank: 30th)
Highest point: Mount Marcy, 5,344 ft., NE-18

Buffalo / Niagara Falls

Rochester

Syracuse

Determining distances along roads

Highway distances (segments of one mile or less not shown)
Cumulative miles (red): the distance between red arrows
Intermediate miles (black): the distance between intersections & places

© Rand McNally

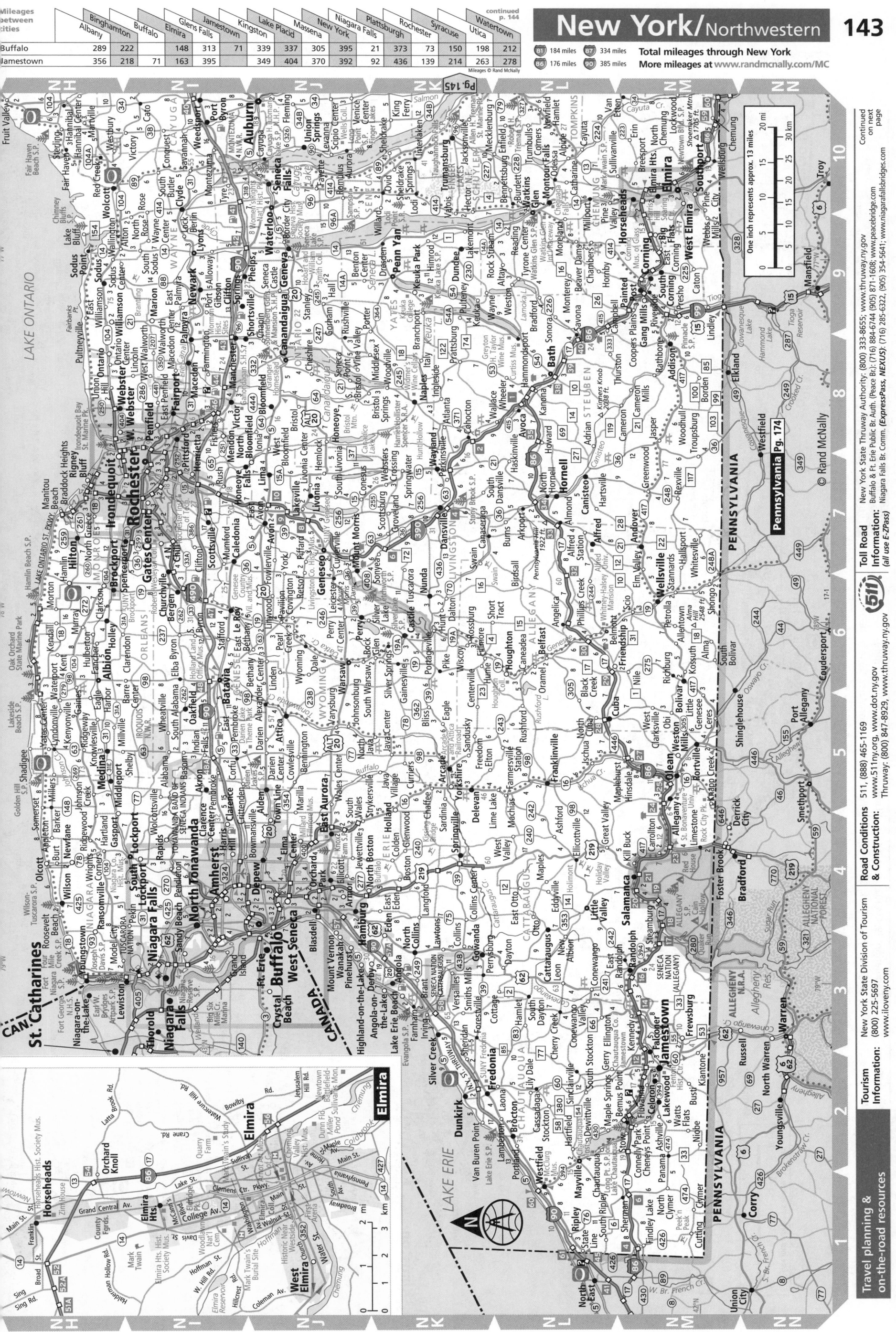

Mileages between cities	Albany	Binghamton	Buffalo	Elmira	Glens Falls	Jamestown	Kingston	Lake Placid	Massena	New York	Niagara Falls	Plattsburgh	Rochester	Syracuse	Utica	Watertown	continued p. 144
Buffalo	289	222		148	313	71	339	337	305	395	21	373	73	150	198	212	
Jamestown	356	218	71	163	395		349	404	370	392	92	436	139	214	263	278	

Mileages © Rand McNally

Total mileages through New York
81 184 miles   87 334 miles
86 176 miles   90 385 miles
More mileages at www.randmcnally.com/MC

New York state facts

Nickname: The Empire State
Capital: Albany, NK-19

Population: 19,378,102 (rank: 3rd)
Largest city: New York, 8,175,133, SF-6

Land area: 47,126 sq. mi. (rank: 30th)
Highest point: Mount Marcy, 5,344 ft., NE-18

Determining distances along roads

Interchanges and exit numbers
For most states, the mileage between interchanges may be determined by subtracting one number from the other.

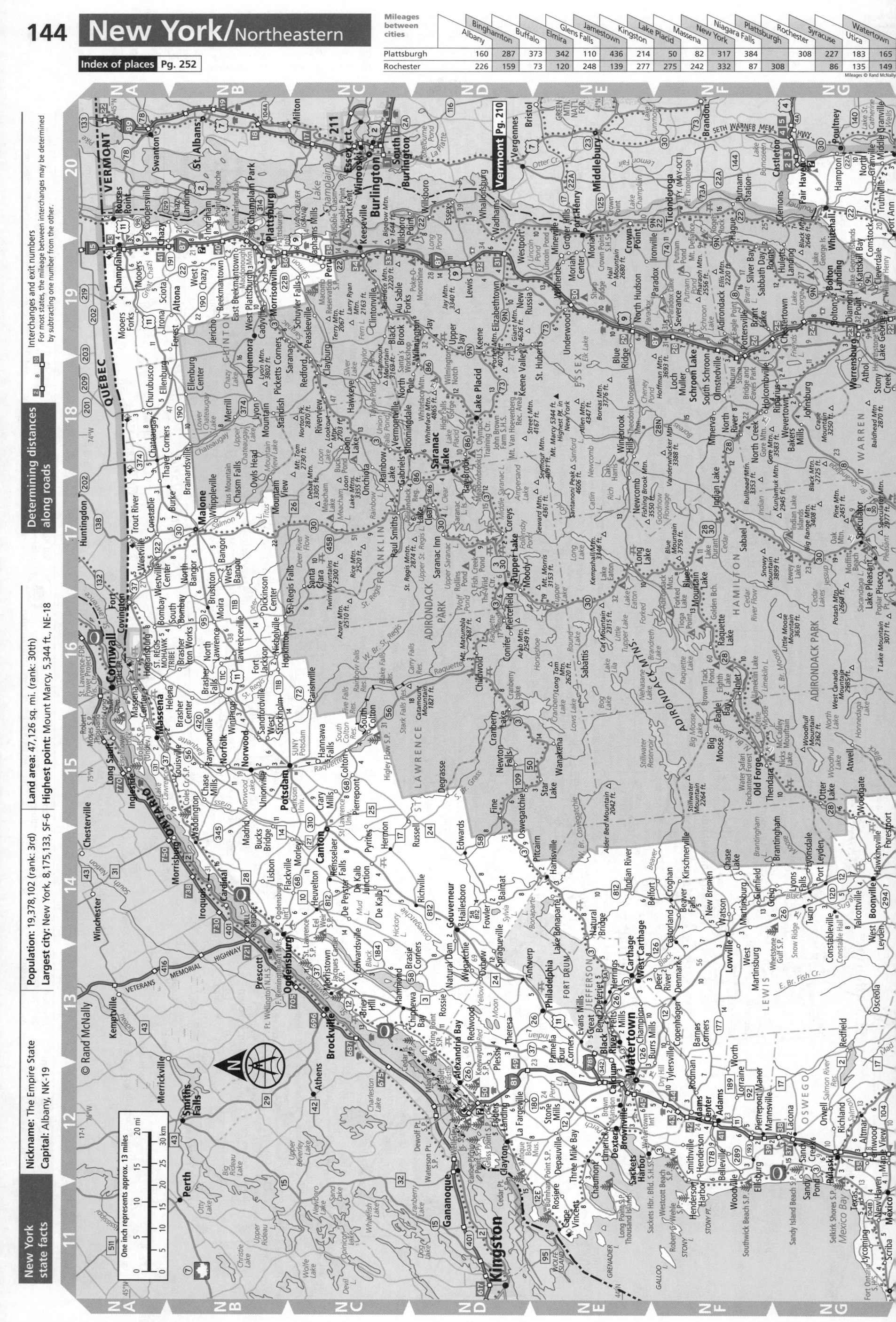

Mileages between cities	Albany	Binghamton	Buffalo	Elmira	Glens Falls	Jamestown	Kingston	Lake Placid	Massena	New York	Niagara Falls	Plattsburgh	Rochester	Syracuse	Utica	Watertown
Syracuse	145	73	150	90	160	214	195	195	159	246	162	227	86		53	70
Watertown	175	143	212	160	179	278	226	125	89	316	225	165	149	70	80	

Mileages © Rand McNally

81 184 miles 87 334 miles
86 176 miles 90 385 miles

Total mileages through New York
More mileages at www.randmcnally.com/MC

Toll Road Information:
Ogdensburg Br. & Port Auth. (Commuter Card): (315) 393-4080; www.ogdensport.com
Seaway Int'l Bridge Corp. (Seaway Transit Card): (613) 932-6601; www.sibc.ca
Thousand Islands Bridge Authority (Alexandria Bay): (315) 482-2501; www.tibridge.com

Road Conditions & Construction:
511, (888) 465-1169
www.511ny.org, www.dot.ny.gov
Thruway: (800) 847-8929, www.thruway.ny.gov

Tourism Information:
New York State Division of Tourism
(800) 225-5697
www.iloveny.com

Travel planning & on-the-road resources

Mass. Pg. 98
Conn. Pg. 48
Pennsylvania Pg. 174
Pennsylvania Pg. 143
Pg. 140

Sights to see

continued p.148

Sights to see

- Guggenheim Museum, Manhattan A-5
- Intrepid Sea-Air Space Mus., Manhattan C-2
- Lincoln Center, Manhattan B-3
- Madison Square Garden, Manhattan. D-2
- Meadowlands Sports Complex, East Rutherford, N.J. F-8
- Metropolitan Museum of Art, Manhattan B-5

(located on pages 146-149)

Sights to see

ATLANTIC OCEAN

QUEENS

BROOKLYN

NASSAU CO.

QUEENS CO.

KINGS CO.

GATEWAY NATIONAL RECREATION AREA

GATEWAY NAT'L RECREATION AREA

John F. Kennedy Int'l Airport

Jamaica Bay

Levittown
North Massapequa
Plainedge
Seaford
Wantagh
East Meadow
North Bellmore
Bellmore
North Merrick
Merrick
Uniondale
Hempstead
Roosevelt
Freeport
S. Hempstead
Baldwin Harbor
Baldwin
Garden City
West Hempstead
Rockville Centre
Oceanside
Point Lookout
Garden City South
Garden City Park
Franklin Square
Lakeview
Malverne
Lynbrook
East Rockaway
Bay Park
Island Park
Harbor Isle
Long Beach
Lido Beach
New Hyde Park
South Floral Park
Bellerose
Elmont
Alden Manor
North Valley Stream
Valley Stream
Hewlett
Hewlett Bay Park
Hewlett Neck
Woodsburgh
Woodmere
Cedarhurst
Lawrence
Inwood
Atlantic Beach
Hicksville
Jamaica
Howard Beach
Cross Bay Blvd.
Rockaway Beach
Breezy Point
Coney Island

© Rand McNally

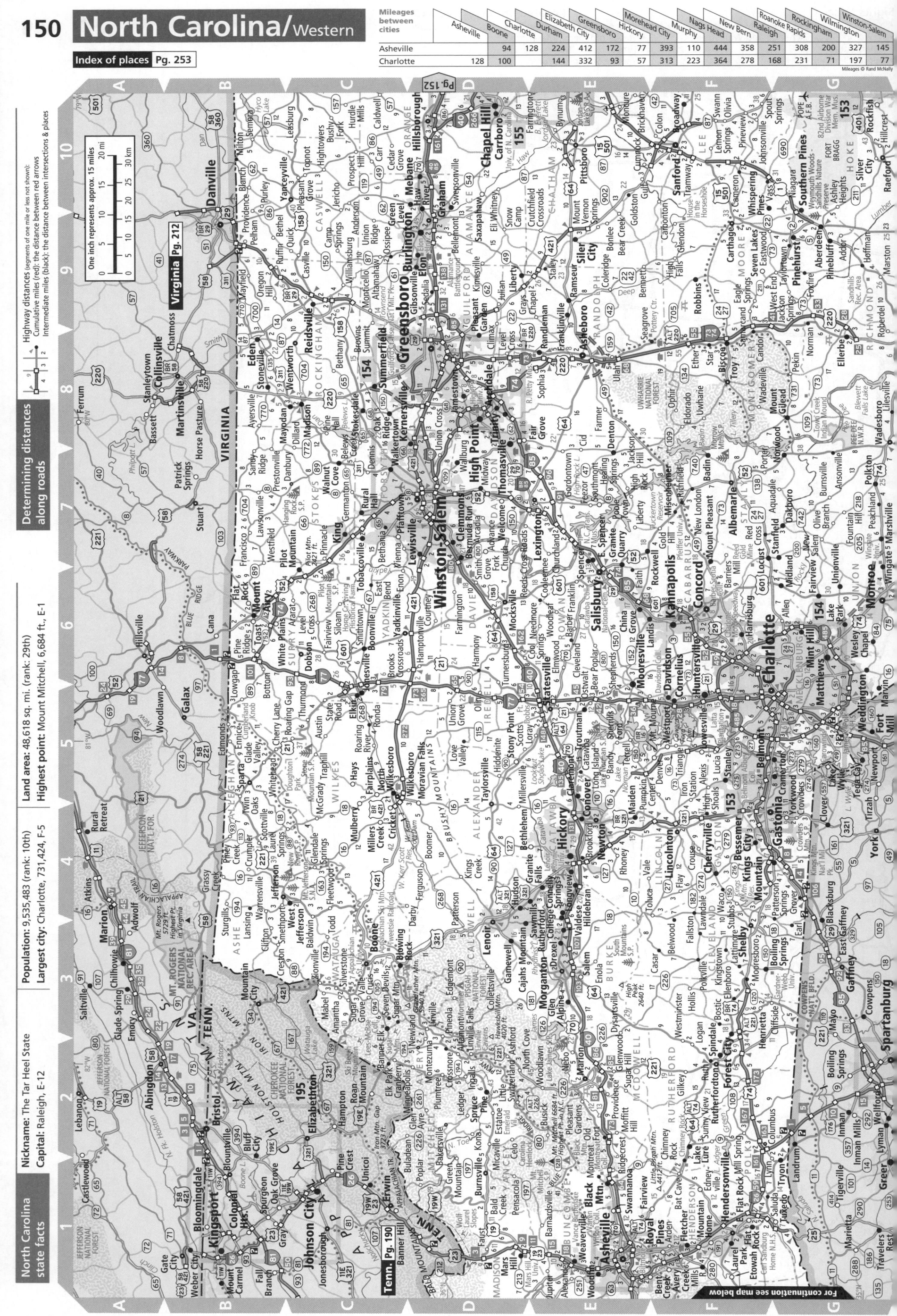

Mileages between cities	Asheville	Boone	Charlotte	Durham	Elizabeth City	Greensboro	Hickory	Morehead City	Murphy	Nags Head	New Bern	Raleigh	Roanoke Rapids	Rockingham	Wilmington	Winston-Salem
Asheville		94	128	224	412	172	77	393	110	444	358	251	308	200	327	145
Charlotte	128	100		144	332	93	57	313	223	364	278	168	231	71	197	77

Mileages © Rand McNally

North Carolina state facts

Nickname: The Tar Heel State
Capital: Raleigh, E-12

Population: 9,535,483 (rank: 10th)
Largest city: Charlotte, 731,424, F-5

Land area: 48,618 sq. mi. (rank: 29th)
Highest point: Mount Mitchell, 6,684 ft., E-1

Determining distances along roads

Virginia Pg. 212

Tenn. Pg. 190

For continuation see map below

			Total mileages through North Carolina
40	419 miles	85	233 miles
77	102 miles	95	182 miles

More mileages at www.randmcnally.com/MC

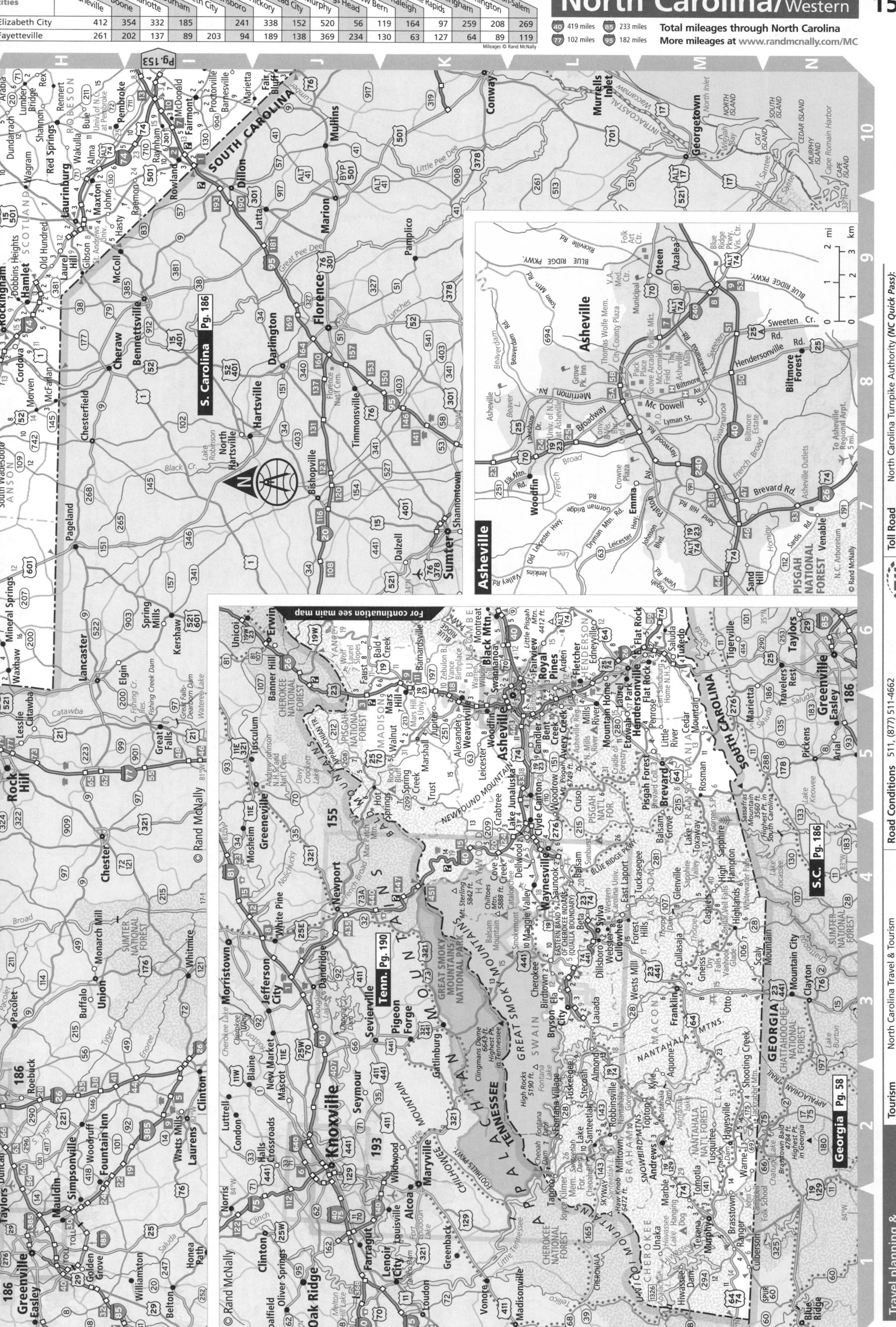

Pg.153
S. Carolina Pg. 186
S.C. Pg. 186
Tenn. Pg. 190
Georgia Pg. 58
For continuation see main map

Travel planning & on-the-road resources

Tourism Information:
North Carolina Travel & Tourism
(800) 847-4862
www.visitnc.com

Road Conditions & Construction:
511, (877) 511-4662
www.ncdot.gov/travel/511
www.ncdot.gov

Toll Road Information:
North Carolina Turnpike Authority (NC Quick Pass)
(877) 769-7277
www.ncdot.gov/turnpike

© Rand McNally

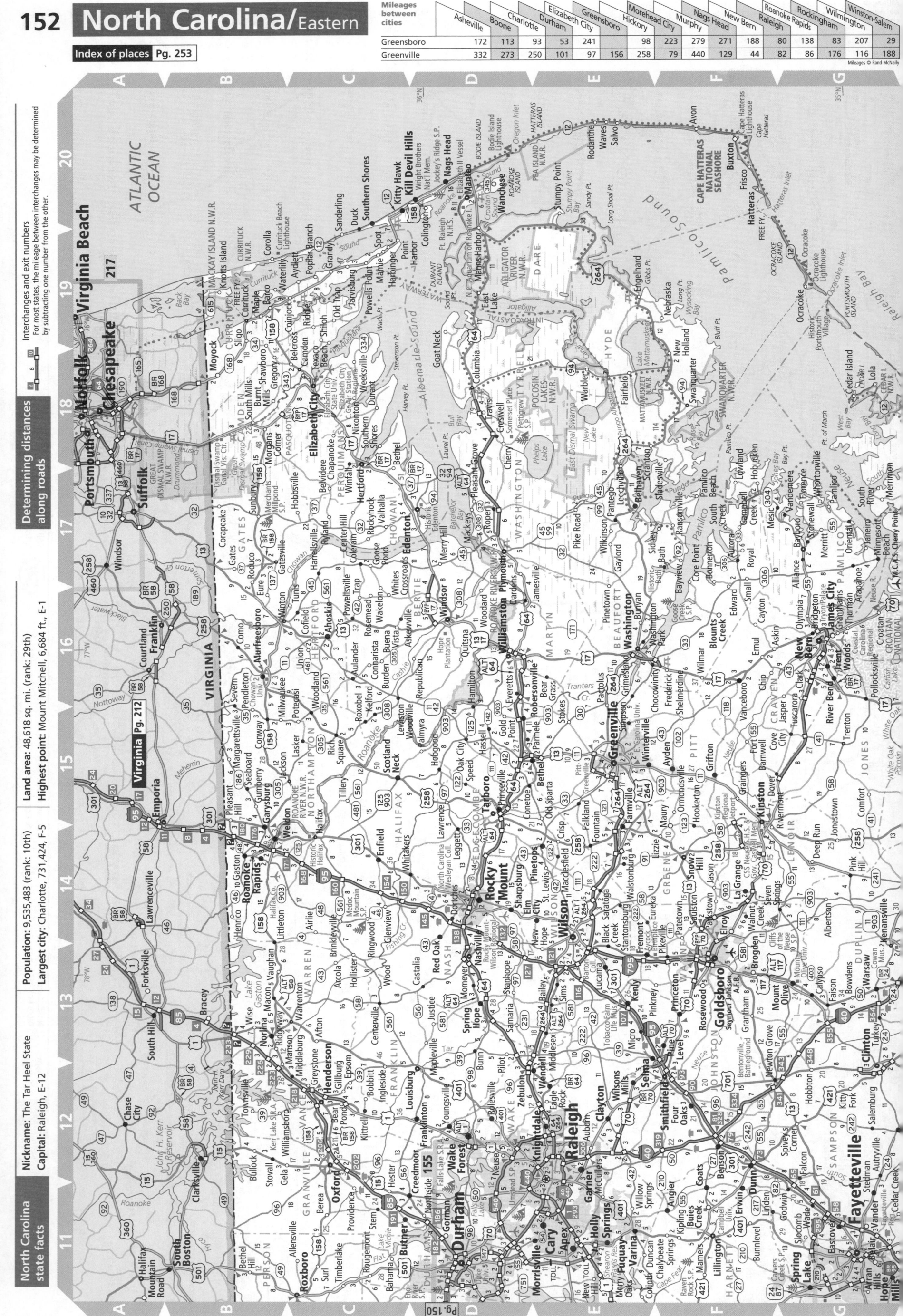

Mileages © Rand McNally

Mileages between cities	Asheville	Boone	Charlotte	Durham	Elizabeth City	Greensboro	Hickory	Morehead City	Murphy	Nags Head	New Bern	Raleigh	Roanoke Rapids	Rockingham	Wilmington	Winston-Salem
Greensboro	172	113	93	53	241		98	223	279	271	188	80	138	83	207	29
Greenville	332	273	250	101	97	156	258	79	440	129	44	82	86	176	116	188

North Carolina state facts

Nickname: The Tar Heel State
Capital: Raleigh, E-12

Population: 9,535,483 (rank: 10th)
Largest city: Charlotte, 731,424, F-5

Land area: 48,618 sq. mi. (rank: 29th)
Highest point: Mount Mitchell, 6,684 ft., E-1

Determining distances along roads

Interchanges and exit numbers
For most states, the mileage between interchanges may be determined by subtracting one number from the other.

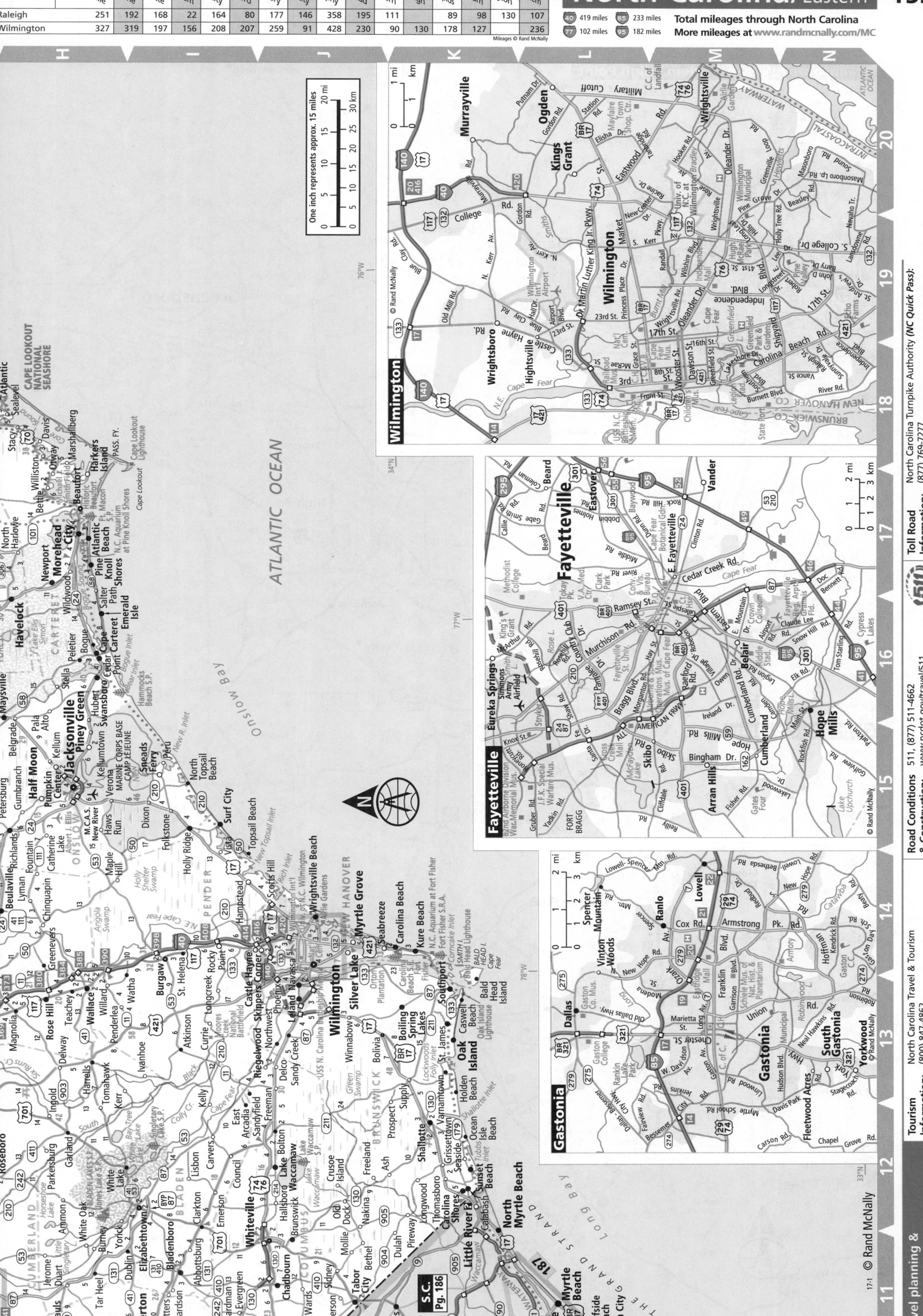

Mileages between cities	Asheville	Boone	Charlotte	Durham	Elizabeth City	Greensboro	Hickory	Morehead City	Murphy	Nags Head	New Bern	Roanoke Rapids	Rockingham	Wilmington	Winston-Salem
Raleigh	251	192	168	22	164	80	177	146	358	195	111	89	98	130	107
Wilmington	327	319	197	156	208	207	259	91	428	230	90	130	178	127	236

Mileages © Rand McNally

Total mileages through North Carolina
More mileages at www.randmcnally.com/MC

- 40 = 419 miles
- 85 = 233 miles
- 77 = 102 miles
- 95 = 182 miles

Travel planning & on-the-road resources

Tourism Information:	North Carolina Travel & Tourism (800) 847-4862 www.visitnc.com
Road Conditions & Construction:	511, (877) 511-4662 www.ncdot.gov/travel/511 www.ncdot.gov
Toll Road Information:	North Carolina Turnpike Authority (NC Quick Pass) (877) 769-7277 www.ncdot.gov/turnpike

© Rand McNally

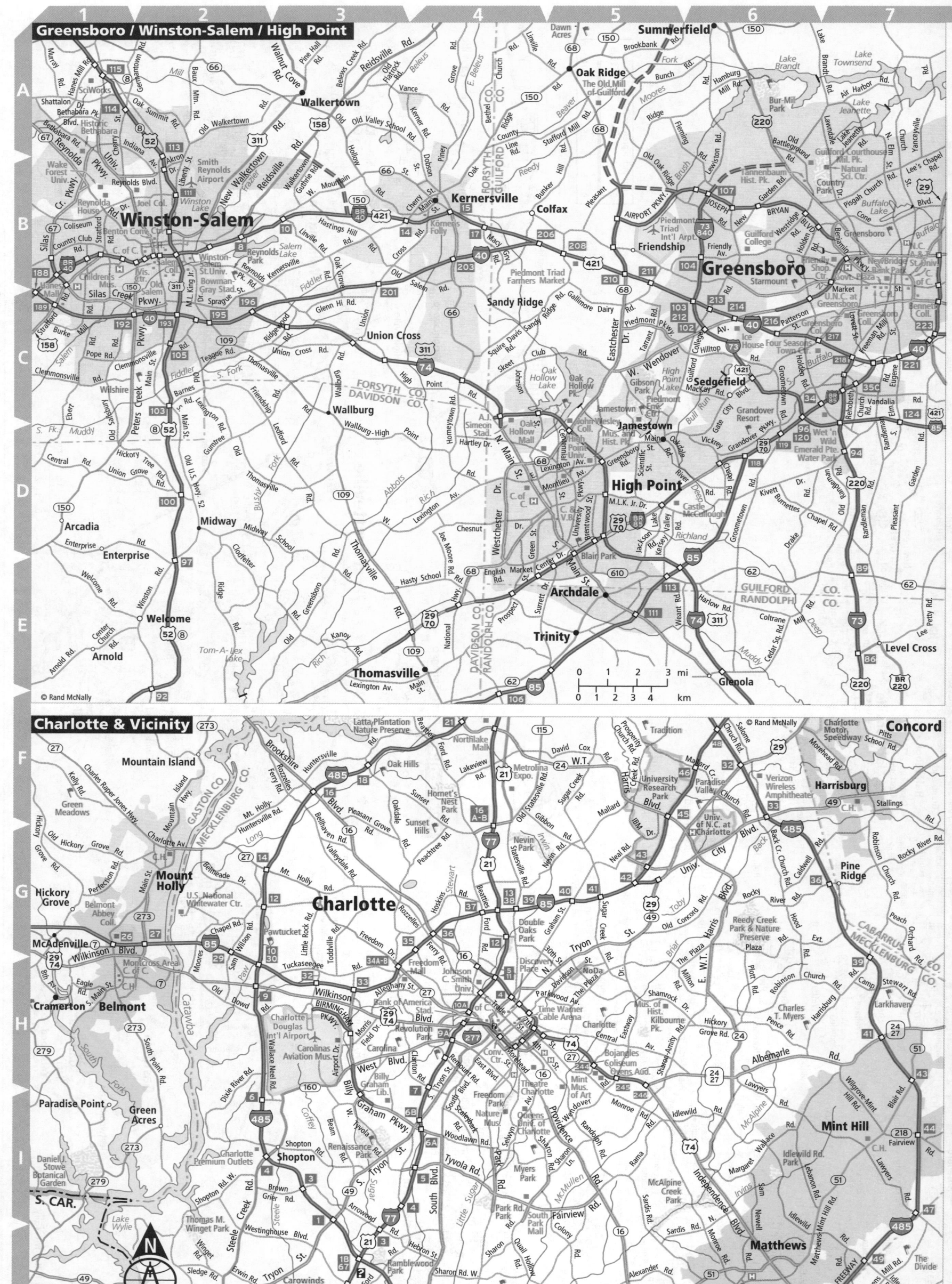

Greensboro / Winston-Salem / High Point

Charlotte & Vicinity

© Rand McNally

Sights to see

- Morehead Planetarium and Science Center, Chapel Hill H-8
- North Carolina Museum of Life and Science, Durham F-10
- North Carolina Museum of History, Raleigh . . I-12
- North Carolina State Capitol, Raleigh I-13
- Old Salem, Winston-Salem B-2
- Reynolda House, Winston-Salem B-1

Great Smoky Mountains National Park

© Rand McNally

Raleigh / Durham / Chapel Hill

© Rand McNally

Bismarck **Fargo**

Mandan

Bismarck

West Fargo   Fargo

Moorhead   Dilwo

Montana Pg. 122

Williston

Minot

Garrison

Watford City

Dickinson

Bismarck   **Mandan**

Bowman

Lemmon

SOUTH DAKOTA

S. Dakota Pg. 188

Interchanges and exit numbers
For most states, the mileage between interchanges may be determined by subtracting one number from the other.

Determining distances along roads

Land area: 69,000 sq. mi. (rank: 17th) | Highest point: White Butte, 3,506 ft., I-3

Population: 672,591 (rank: 48th) | Largest city: Fargo, 105,549, H-13

Nickname: The Peace Garden State | Capital: Bismarck, H-7

North Dakota state facts

© Rand McNally

Mileages between cities

	Bismarck	Bowman	Fargo	Garrison	Grand Forks	Jamestown	Williston	Winnipeg, MB
Grand Forks	272	444	80	256		171	334	146
Minot	110	260	268	47	210	170	124	299

	Bismarck	Bowman	Fargo	Garrison	Grand Forks	Jamestown	Williston	Winnipeg, MB
Wahpeton	243	416	54	315	131	142	470	273
Williston	228	170	422	144	334	293		424

Mileages © Rand McNally

Total mileages through North Dakota

29	218 miles	2	359 miles
94	352 miles	83	265 miles

More mileages at www.randmcnally.com/MC

One inch represents approx. 22 miles
0 10 20 30 miles
0 10 20 30 40 km

Grand Forks (inset map)
Minot (inset map)

No toll roads

Toll Road Information: 511, (866) 696-3511, (855) 637-6237 www.dot.nd.gov

Road Conditions & Construction: 511 www.dot.nd.gov/travel-info-v2

Tourism Information: North Dakota Tourism (800) 435-5663, (701) 328-2525 www.ndtourism.com

Minnesota Pg. 108

© Rand McNally

Index of places Pg. 254

Mileages © Rand McNally

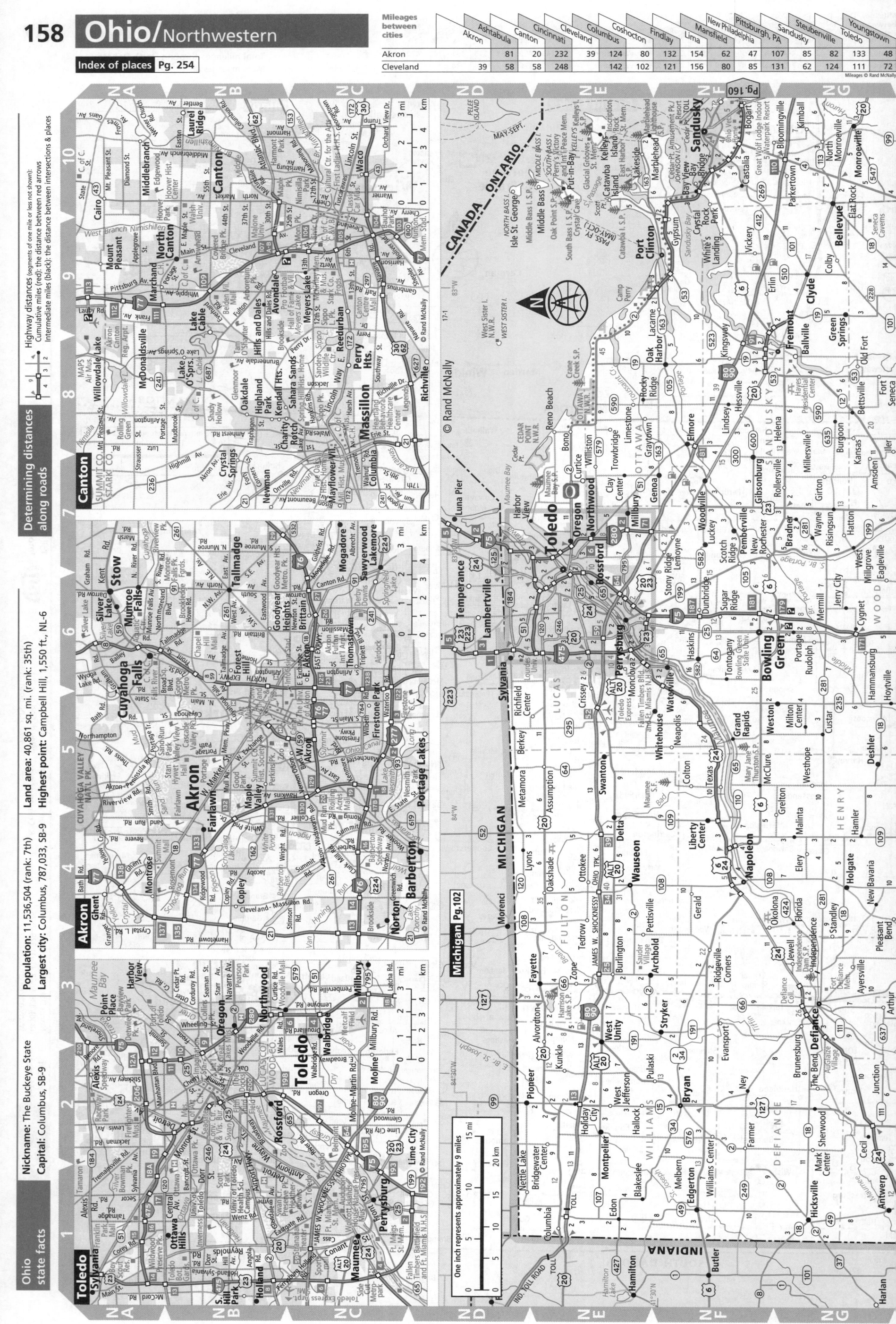

© Rand McNally

Ohio state facts

Nickname: The Buckeye State
Capital: Columbus, SB-9

Population: 11,536,504 (rank: 7th)
Largest city: Columbus, SB-9

Land area: 40,861 sq. mi. (rank: 35th)
Highest point: Campbell Hill, 1,550 ft., NL-6

Determining distances along roads

Highway distances (segments of one mile or less not shown)
Cumulative miles (red): the distance between red arrows
Intermediate miles (black): the distance between intersections & places

One inch represents approximately 9 miles

Pg. 160
Michigan Pg. 102

Mileages between cities	Akron	Ashtabula	Canton	Cincinnati	Cleveland	Columbus	Coshocton	Findlay	Lima	Mansfield	New Philadelphia	Pittsburgh, PA	Sandusky	Steubenville	Toledo	Youngstown (continued p. 160)
Columbus	124	194	126	106	142		71	96	91	66	118	184	112	150	142	172
Defiance	180	214	185	169	157	135	177	51	44	123	190	274	98	246	57	214

Mileages © Rand McNally

Total mileages through Ohio

- 71: 248 miles
- 75: 211 miles
- 80: 237 miles
- 90: 245 miles

More mileages at www.randmcnally.com/MC

Toll Road Information: Ohio Turnpike and Infrastructure Commission (E-ZPass): (888) 876-7453; www.ohioturnpike.org

Road Conditions & Construction: (614) 466-7170, www.buckeyetraffic.org, www.dot.state.oh.us Ohio Turnpike: (888) 876-7453, (440) 234-2030, (440) 234-2081 www.ohioturnpike.org

Tourism Information: Tourism Ohio (800) 282-5393 www.discoverohio.com

Travel planning & on-the-road resources

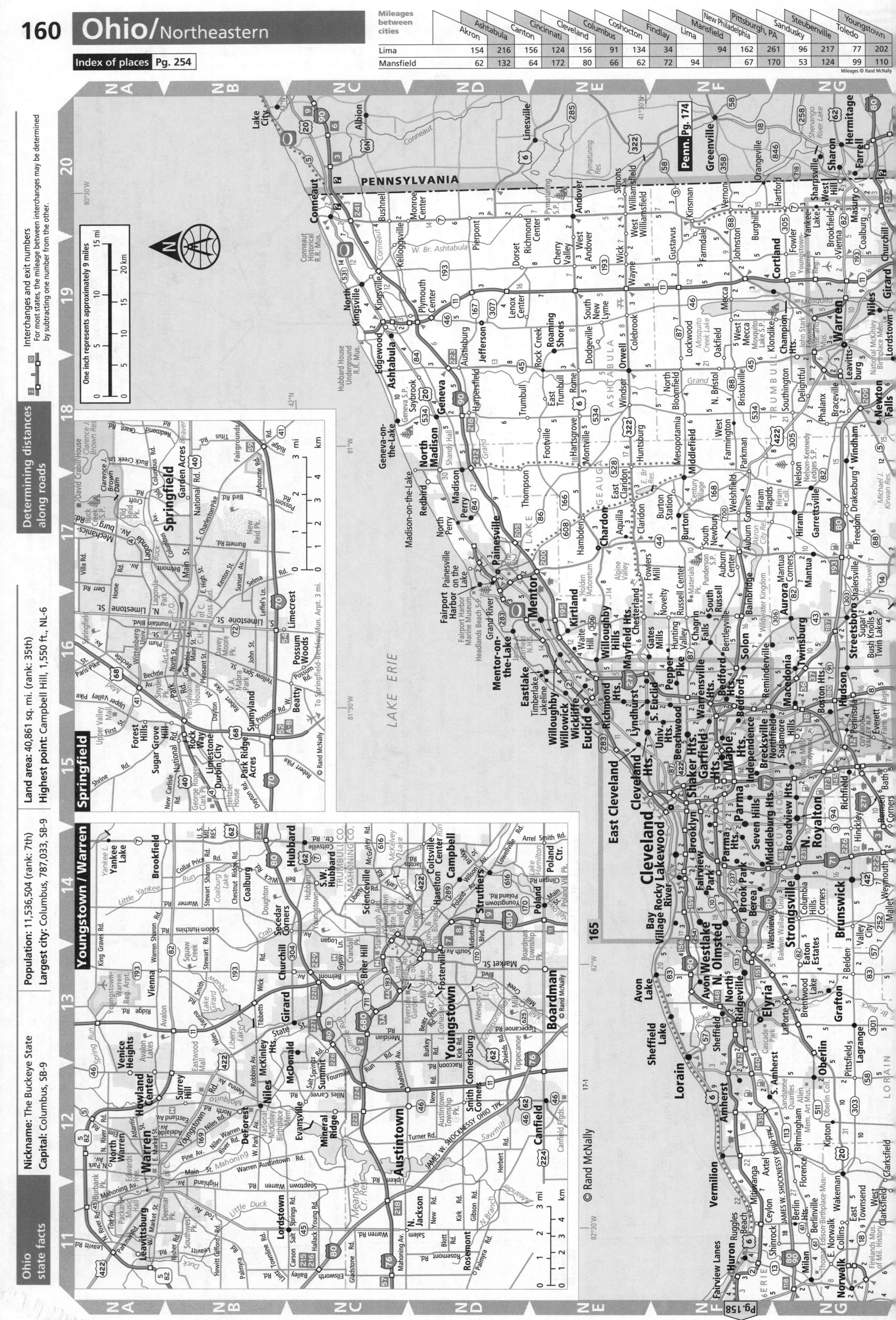

Mileages between cities	Akron	Ashtabula	Canton	Cincinnati	Cleveland	Columbus	Coshocton	Findlay	Lima	Mansfield	New Philadelphia	Pittsburgh, PA	Sandusky	Steubenville	Toledo	Youngstown
Lima	154	216	156	124	156	91	134	34		94	162	261	96	217	77	202
Mansfield	62	132	64	172	80	66	62	72	94		67	170	53	124	99	110

Mileages © Rand McNally

Ohio state facts

Nickname: The Buckeye State
Capital: Columbus, SB-9

Population: 11,536,504 (rank: 7th)
Largest city: Columbus, 787,033, SB-9

Land area: 40,861 sq. mi. (rank: 35th)
Highest point: Campbell Hill, 1,550 ft., NL-6

Determining distances along roads

Interchanges and exit numbers
For most states, the mileage between interchanges may be determined by subtracting one number from the other.

One inch represents approximately 9 miles

Springfield

Youngstown / Warren

LAKE ERIE

PENNSYLVANIA

© Rand McNally

Penn. Pg. 174

165

Pg. 158

Mileages between cities	Akron	Ashtabula	Canton	Cincinnati	Cleveland	Columbus	Coshocton	Findlay	Lima	Mansfield	New Philadelphia	Pittsburgh, PA	Sandusky	Steubenville	Toledo	Youngstown
Toledo	133	171	152	200	111	142	152	44	77	99	179	228	58	221		169
Youngstown	48	57	57	279	72	172	117	180	202	110	84	67	122	66	169	

Mileages © Rand McNally

Total mileages through Ohio
- 71 248 miles
- 75 211 miles
- 80 237 miles
- 90 245 miles

More mileages at www.randmcnally.com/MC

Road Conditions & Construction: (614) 466-7170, www.buckeyetraffic.org, www.dot.state.oh.us
Ohio Turnpike: (888) 876-7453, (440) 234-2030, (440) 234-2081

Toll Road Information: Ohio Turnpike and Infrastructure Commission
(E-ZPass): (888) 876-7453; www.ohioturnpike.org

Tourism Information: Tourism Ohio (800) 282-5393 www.discoverohio.com

Travel planning & on-the-road resources

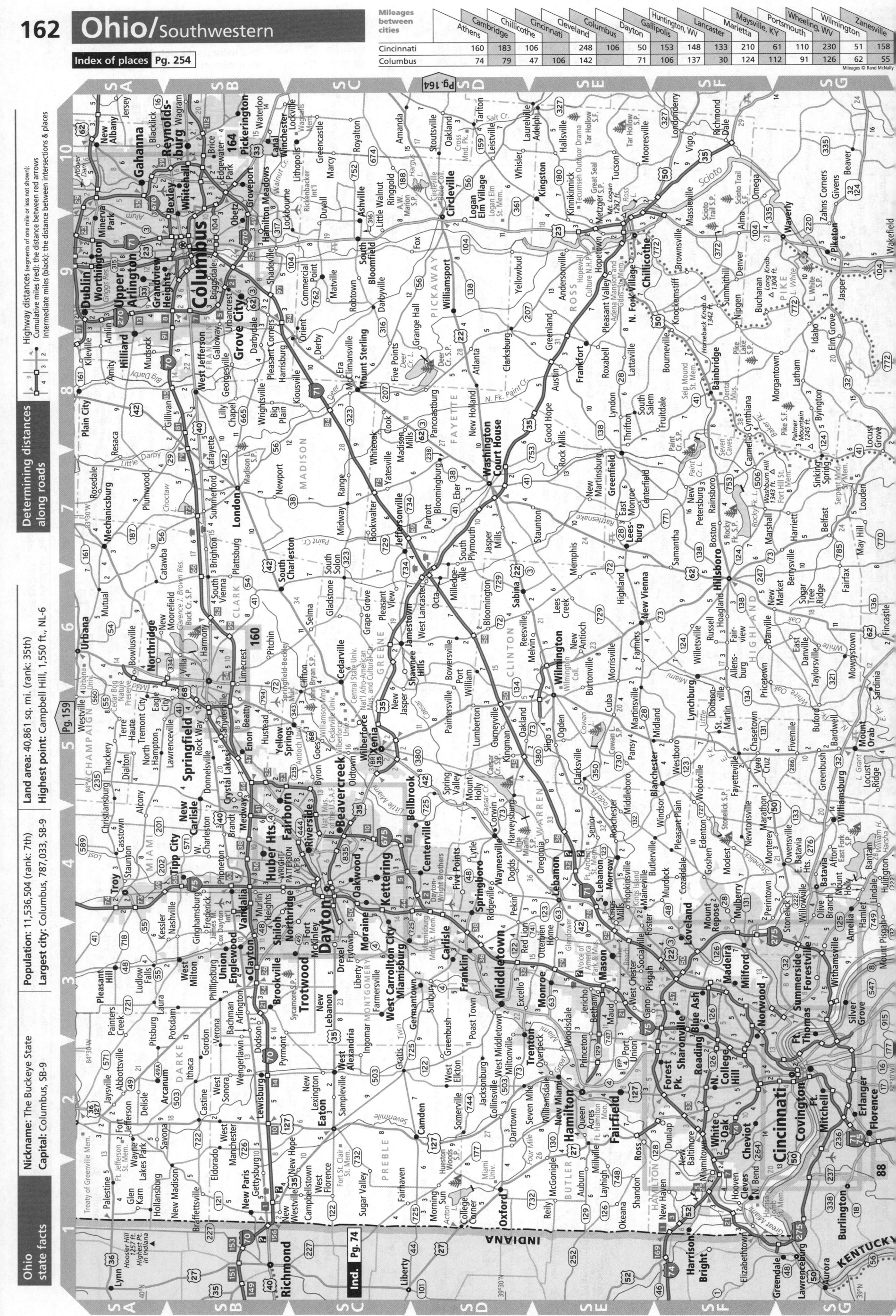

	Athens	Cambridge	Chillicothe	Cincinnati	Cleveland	Columbus	Dayton	Gallipolis	Huntington, WV	Lancaster	Marietta	Maysville, KY	Portsmouth	Wheeling, WV	Wilmington	Zanesville
Cincinnati	160	183	106		248	106	50	153	148	133	210	61	110	230	51	158
Columbus	74	79	47	106	142		71	106	137	30	124	112	91	126	62	55

Mileages © Rand McNally

Ohio state facts

Nickname: The Buckeye State
Capital: Columbus, SB-9

Population: 11,536,504 (rank: 7th)
Largest city: Columbus, 787,033, SB-9

Land area: 40,861 sq. mi. (rank: 35th)
Highest point: Campbell Hill, 1,550 ft., NL-6

continued p. 164

Mileages between cities	Athens	Cambridge	Chillicothe	Cincinnati	Cleveland	Columbus	Dayton	Gallipolis	Huntington, WV	Lancaster	Marietta	Maysville, KY	Portsmouth	Wheeling, WV	Wilmington	Zanesville
Dayton	134	149	77	50	212	71		137	168	101	195	108	122	197	34	126
Gallipolis	42	114	60	153	235	106	137		39	86	66	111	55	162	112	94

Mileages © Rand McNally

Total mileages through Ohio
70 226 miles   75 211 miles
71 248 miles   77 160 miles
More mileages at www.randmcnally.com/MC

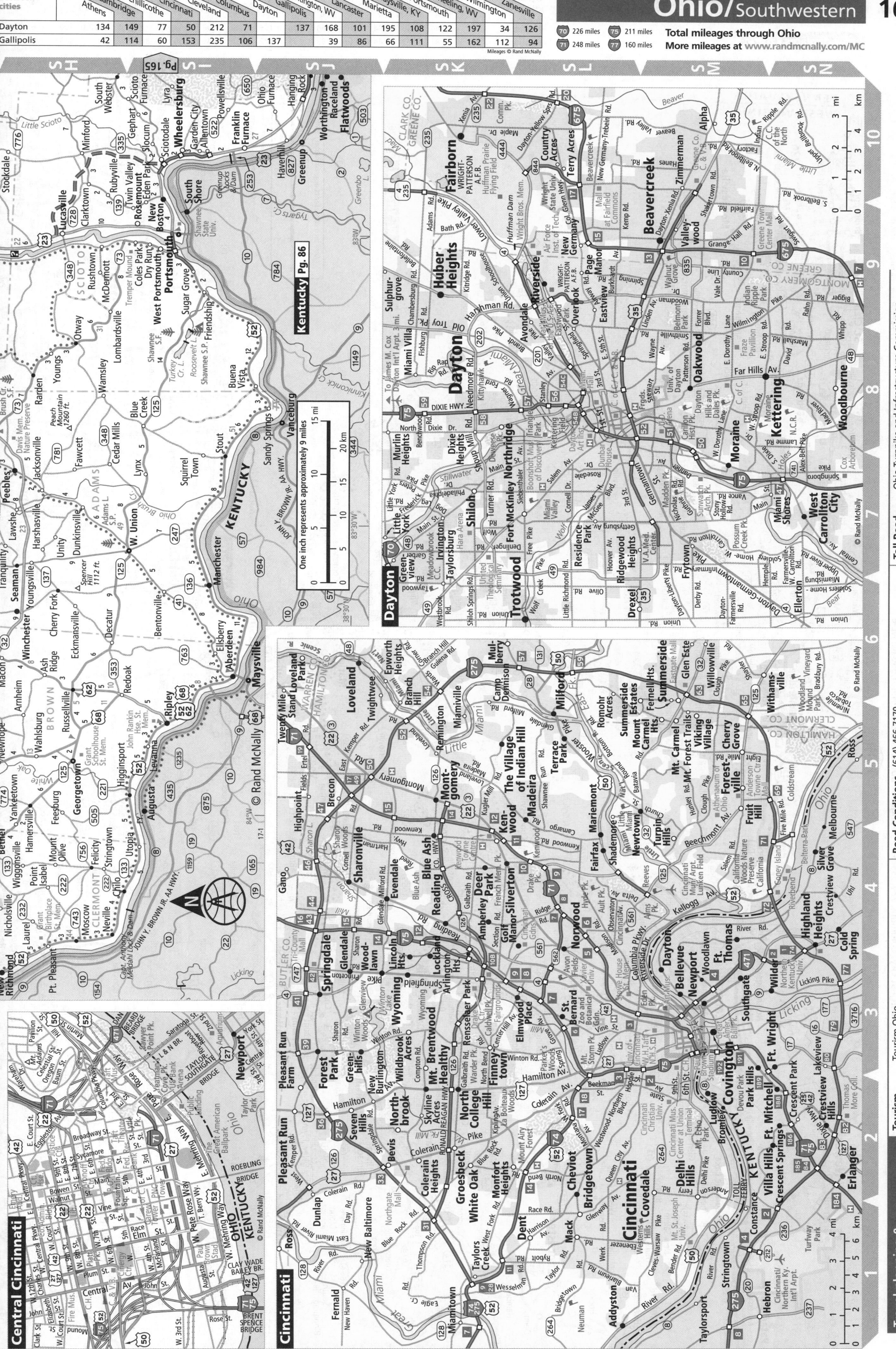

Kentucky Pg. 86

Central Cincinnati

Cincinnati

Dayton

Travel planning & on-the-road resources

Tourism Information: Tourism Ohio (800) 282-5393 www.discoverohio.com

Road Conditions & Construction: (614) 466-7170 www.buckeyetraffic.org, www.dot.state.oh.us Cincinnati metro area: 511

Toll Road Information: Ohio Turnpike and Infrastructure Commission (E-ZPass): (888) 876-7453; www.ohioturnpike.org

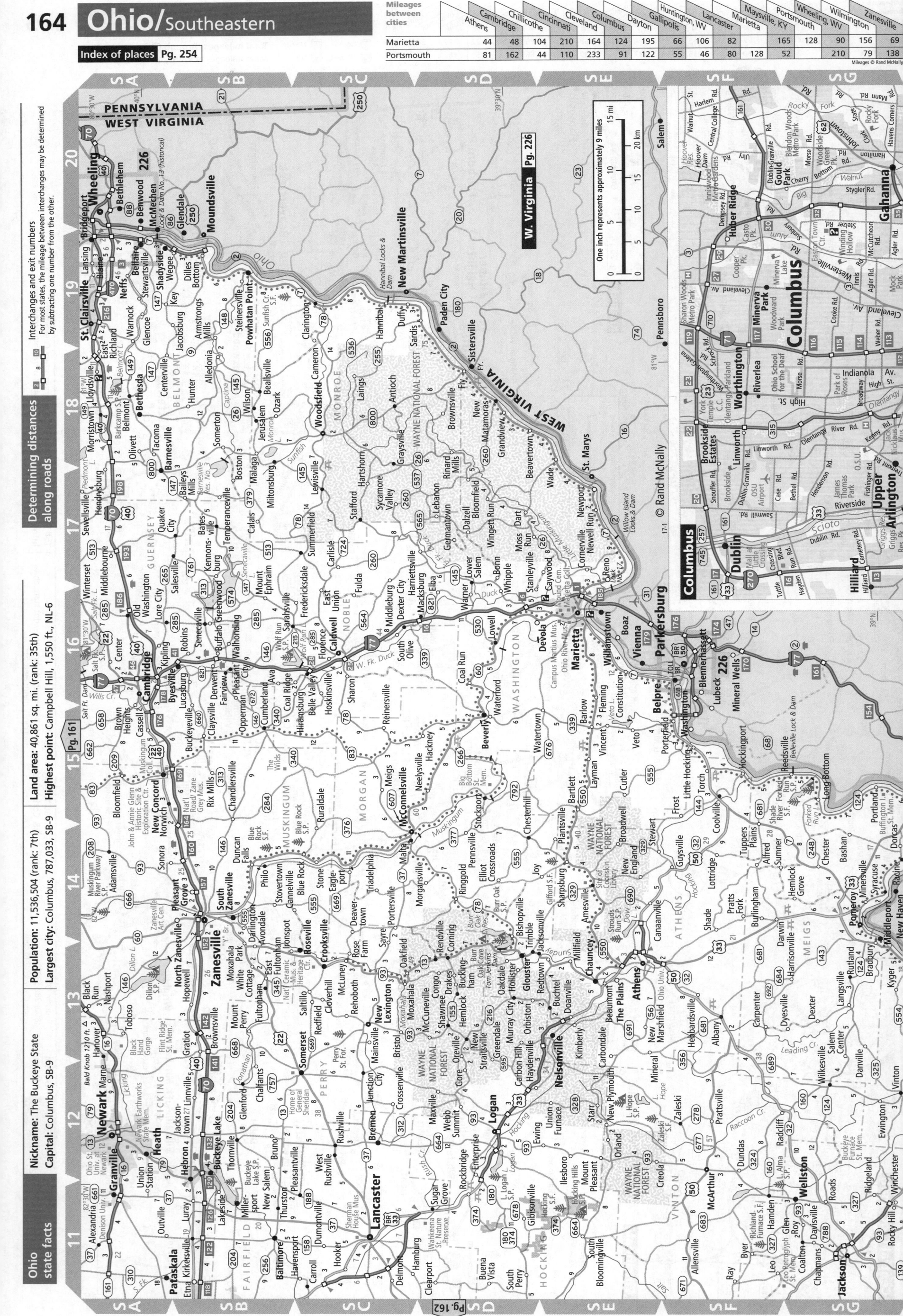

Mileages between cities	Athens	Cambridge	Chillicothe	Cincinnati	Cleveland	Columbus	Dayton	Gallipolis	Huntington, WV	Lancaster	Marietta	Maysville, KY	Portsmouth	Wheeling, WV	Wilmington	Zanesville
Marietta	44	48	104	210	164	124	195	66	106	82		165	128	90	156	69
Portsmouth	81	162	44	110	233	91	122	55	46	80	128	52		210	79	138

Mileages © Rand McNally

Ohio state facts

Nickname: The Buckeye State
Capital: Columbus, SB-9

Population: 11,536,504 (rank: 7th)
Largest city: Columbus, SB-9

Land area: 40,861 sq. mi. (rank: 35th)
Highest point: Campbell Hill, 1,550 ft., NL-6

Determining distances along roads

Interchanges and exit numbers
For most states, the mileage between interchanges may be determined by subtracting one number from the other.

One inch represents approximately 9 miles

15 mi

20 km

Mileages between cities

	Athens	Cambridge	Chillicothe	Cincinnati	Cleveland	Columbus	Dayton	Gallipolis	Huntington, WV	Lancaster	Marietta	Maysville, KY	Portsmouth	Wheeling, WV	Wilmington	Zanesville
Springfield	118	123	69	77	185	45	27	129	160	74	168	102	114	171	38	99
Zanesville	52	24	94	158	145	55	126	94	134	45	69	164	138	72	114	

Mileages © Rand McNally

Total mileages through Ohio

70 — 226 miles 75 — 211 miles
71 — 248 miles 77 — 160 miles

More mileages at www.randmcnally.com/MC

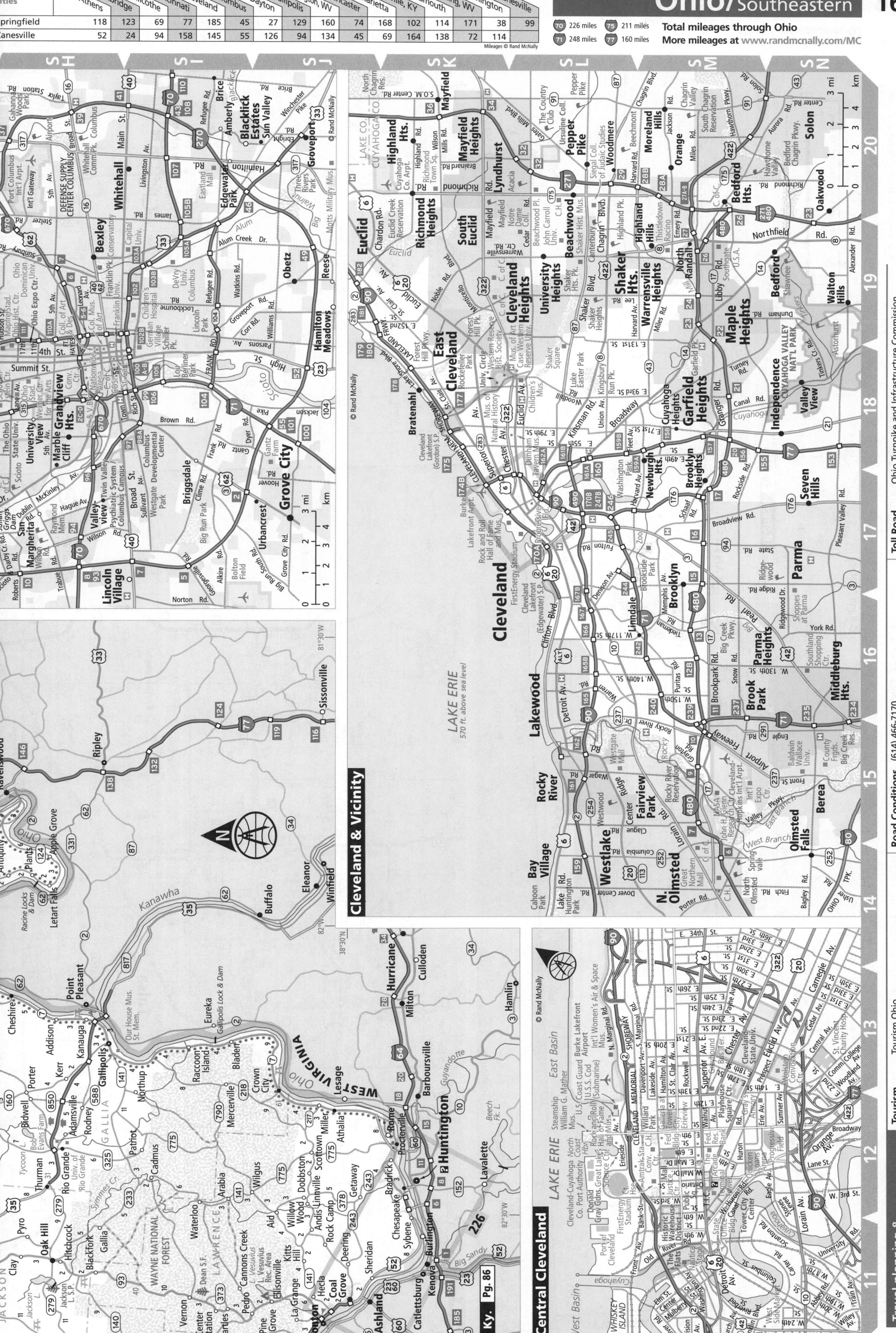

Cleveland & Vicinity

Central Cleveland

LAKE ERIE 570 ft. above sea level

Ky. – Pg. 86

Pg. 163

Travel planning & on-the-road resources

Tourism Information: Tourism Ohio (800) 282-5393 www.discoverohio.com

Road Conditions & Construction: (614) 466-7170 www.buckeyetraffic.org, www.dot.state.oh.us Cincinnati metro area: 511

Toll Road Information: Ohio Turnpike and Infrastructure Commission (E-ZPass): (888) 876-7453; www.ohioturnpike.org

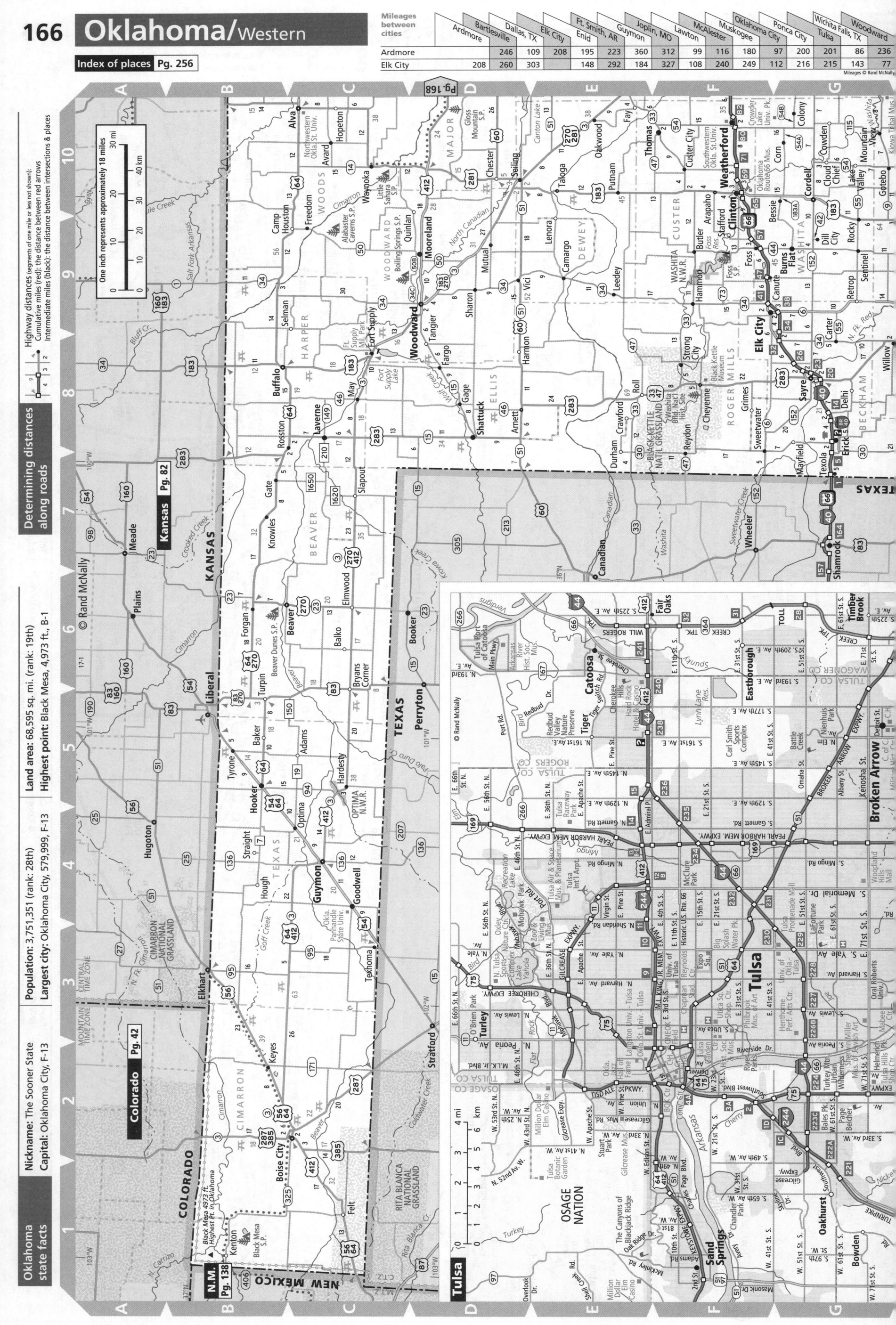

Oklahoma state facts

Nickname: The Sooner State
Capital: Oklahoma City, F-13

Population: 3,751,351 (rank: 28th)
Land area: 68,595 sq. mi. (rank: 19th)

Largest city: Oklahoma City, 579,999, F-13
Highest point: Black Mesa, 4,973 ft., B-1

Determining distances along roads

Highway distances (segments of one mile or less not shown!)
Cumulative miles (red): the distance between red arrows
Intermediate miles (black): the distance between intersections & places

One inch represents approximately 18 miles
30 mi
0 10 20 30 40 km

© Rand McNally

Mileages between cities	Ardmore	Bartlesville	Dallas, TX	Elk City	Enid	Ft. Smith, AR	Guymon	Joplin, MO	Lawton	McAlester	Muskogee	Oklahoma City	Ponca City	Tulsa	Wichita Falls, TX	Woodward
Ardmore		246	109	208	195	223	360	312	99	116	180	97	200	201	86	236
Elk City	208	260	303		148	292	184	327	108	240	249	112	216	215	143	77

Mileages © Rand McNally

Mileages between cities	Ardmore	Bartlesville	Dallas, TX	Elk City	Enid	Ft. Smith, AR	Guymon	Joplin, MO	Lawton	McAlester	Muskogee	Oklahoma City	Ponca City	Tulsa	Wichita Falls, TX	Woodward
Enid	195	134	302	148		232	211	227	142	204	164	99	67	114	196	87
Guymon	360	344	459	184	211	443		438	294	391	375	263	278	326	317	124

continued p. 168

Mileages © Rand McNally

Total mileages through Oklahoma
More mileages at www.randmcnally.com/MC

35 236 miles   44 329 miles
40 331 miles   75 227 miles

Pg.169
Texas Pg. 198

Oklahoma City & Vicinity

Norman

Travel planning & on-the-road resources

Tourism Information: Oklahoma Tourism & Recreation Department (800) 652-6552 www.travelok.com

Road Conditions & Construction: (877) 403-7623 (405) 425-2385 www.okladot.state.ok.us

Toll Road Information: Oklahoma Turnpike Authority (PIKEPASS) (800) 745-3727, (405) 425-3600 www.pikepass.com

© Rand McNally

Mileages between cities	Ardmore	Bartlesville	Dallas, TX	Elk City	Enid	Ft. Smith, AR	Guymon	Joplin, MO	Lawton	McAlester	Muskogee	Oklahoma City	Ponca City	Tulsa	Wichita Falls, TX	Woodward
Idabel	149	248	171	352	316	136	504	295	245	116	180	240	293	203	238	380
Muskogee	180	91	236	249	164	70	375	117	218	65		137	142	50	272	251

Mileages © Rand McNally

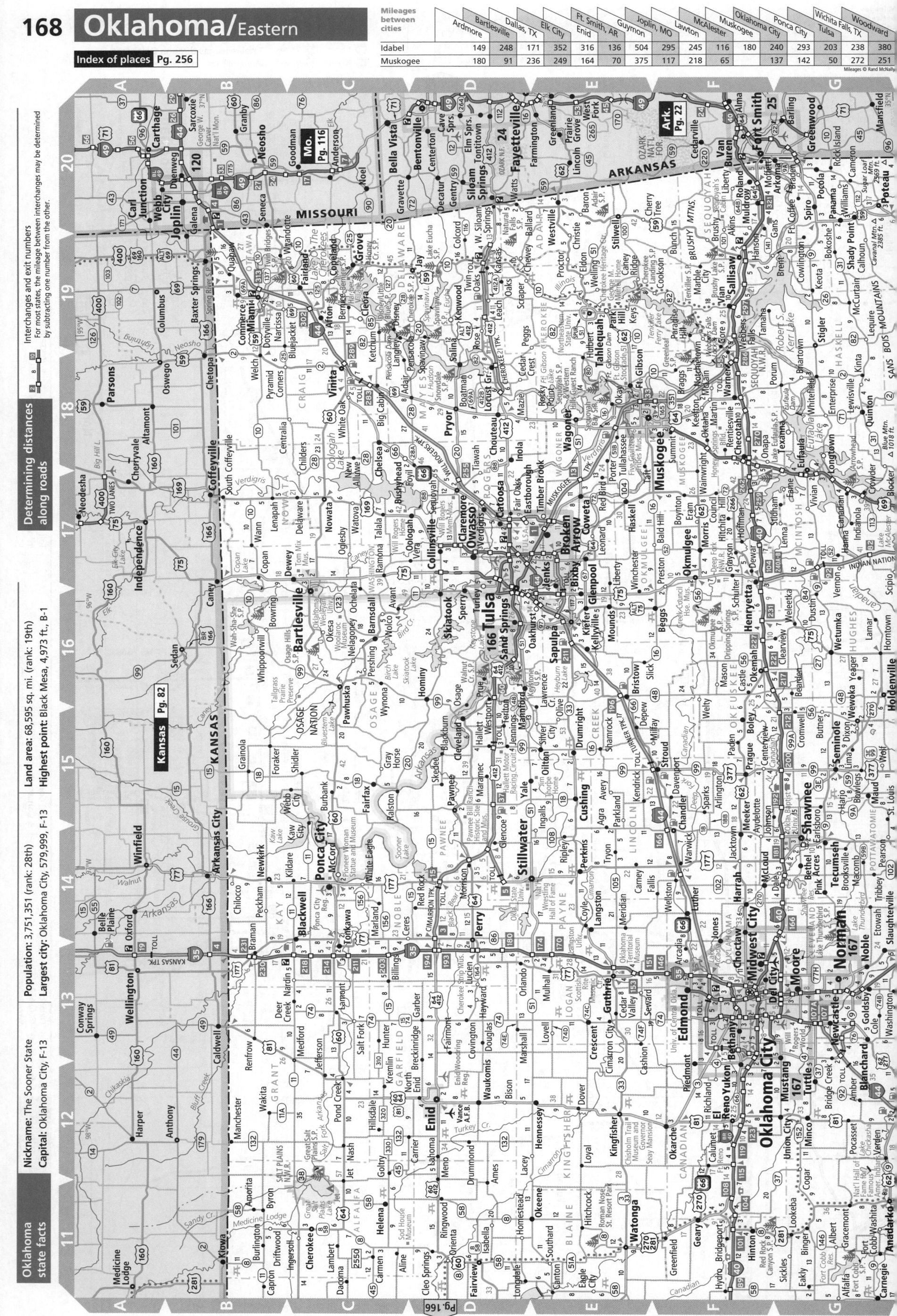

Mileages between cities	Ardmore	Bartlesville	Dallas, TX	Elk City	Ft. Smith, AR	Enid	Guymon	Joplin, MO	Lawton	McAlester	Muskogee	Oklahoma City	Ponca City	Tulsa	Wichita Falls, TX	Woodward
Oklahoma City	97	149	204	112	99	180	263	216	86	128	137		105	104	140	139
Tulsa	201	45	258	215	114	118	326	113	191	91	50	104	91		244	202

Mileages © Rand McNally

Total mileages through Oklahoma

35	236 miles	44	329 miles
40	331 miles	75	227 miles

More mileages at www.randmcnally.com/MC

Muskogee

Lawton — FORT SILL

Edmond

Travel planning & on-the-road resources

Tourism Information: Oklahoma Tourism & Recreation Department (800) 652-6552 www.travelok.com

Road Conditions & Construction: (877) 403-7623 (405) 425-2385 www.okladot.state.ok.us

Toll Road Information: Oklahoma Turnpike Authority (PIKEPASS) (800) 745-3727, (405) 425-3600 www.pikepass.com

one inch represents approximately 18 miles

Mileages between cities	Astoria	Bend	Brookings	Burns	Coos Bay	Crater Lake N.P.	Eugene	Gov't Camp	John Day	Lakeview	Medford	Ontario	Pendleton	Portland	Salem	The Dalles
Bend	250		287	130	228	107	115	106	151	175	172	260	242	161	131	129
Corvallis	166	127	280	257	132	187	47	126	260	284	210	387	290	82	37	165

Mileages © Rand McNally

Oregon state facts

Nickname: The Beaver State
Capital: Salem, E-4

Population: 3,831,074 (rank: 27th)
Largest city: Salem, E-4

Land area: 95,988 sq. mi. (rank: 10th)
Highest point: Mount Hood, 11,239 ft., D-7

Determining distances along roads

Highway distances (segments of one mile or less not shown):
Cumulative miles (red): the distance between red arrows
Intermediate miles (black): the distance between intersections & places

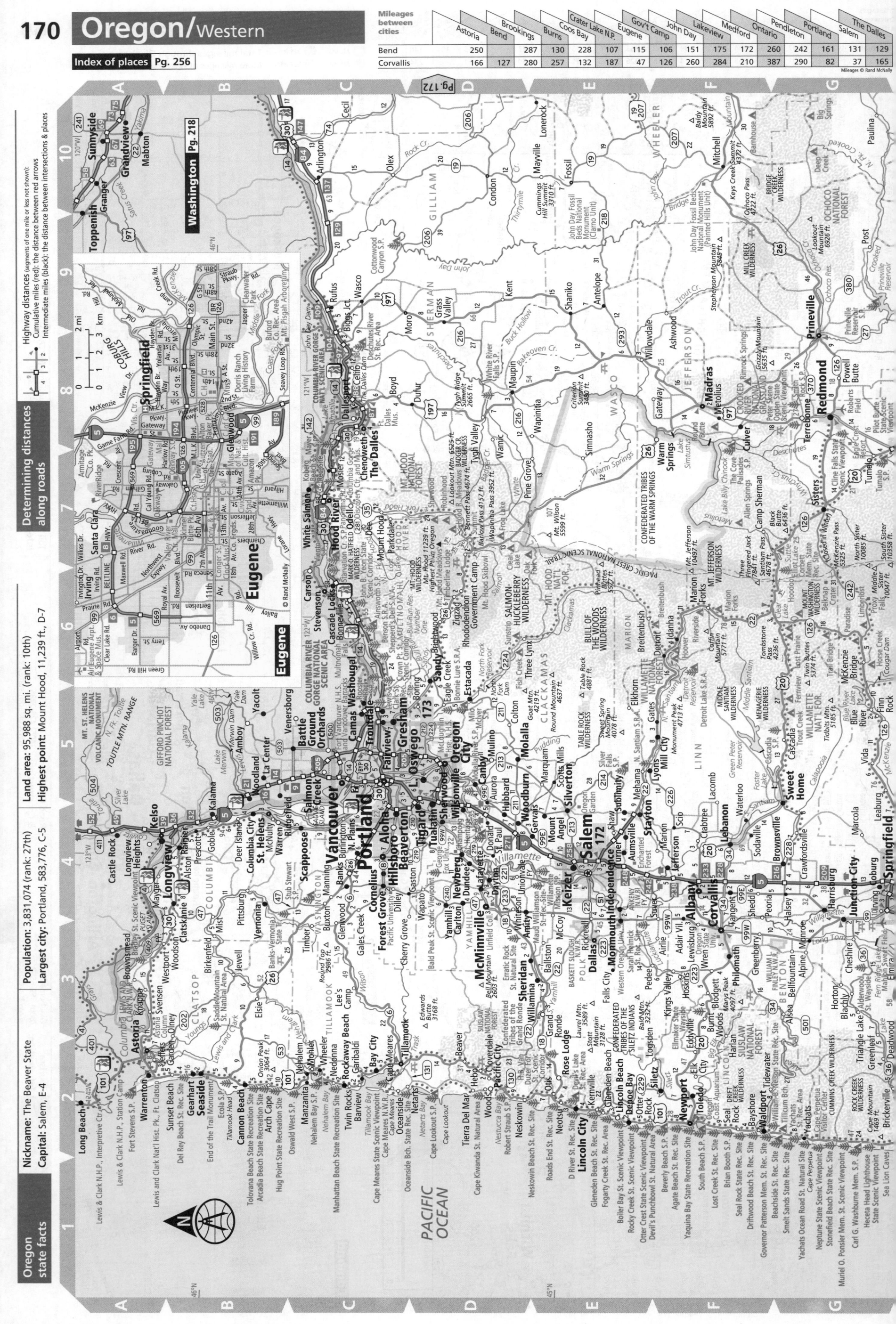

Mileages between cities

	Astoria	Bend	Brookings	Burns	Coos Bay	Crater Lake N.P.	Eugene	Gov't Camp	John Day	Lakeview	Medford	Ontario	Pendleton	Portland	Salem	The Dalles (continued p. 172)
Eugene	193	115	234	245	109	142		154	249	241	166	375	318	110	66	193
McDermitt, NV	525	277	525	147	505	356	392	380	218	222	400	187	354	436	408	405

Mileages © Rand McNally

Total mileages through Oregon
- 5 — 308 miles
- 84 — 375 miles
- 82 — 11 miles
- 101 — 348 miles

More mileages at www.randmcnally.com/MC

Bridge of the Gods (Cascade Locks): (541) 374-8619; portofcascadelocks.org/bridge-of-the-gods/
Hood River Bridge (BreezeBy): (541) 386-1645; www.portofhoodriver.com/bridge/index.php

Toll Road Information: 511 — www.oregon.gov/odot, www.tripcheck.com

Road Conditions & Construction: 511 — (800) 977-6368, (503) 588-2941

Tourism Information: Travel Oregon — (800) 547-7842 — www.traveloregon.com

Travel planning & on-the-road resources

California Pg. 26

Mileages between cities	Astoria	Bend	Brookings	Burns	Coos Bay	Crater Lake N.P.	Eugene	Gov't Camp	John Day	Lakeview	Medford	Ontario	Pendleton	Portland	Salem	The Dalles
Medford	356	172	125	305	169	74	166	317	328	171		432	481	273	228	356
Ontario	464	260	547	130	488	367	375	354	131	269	432		167	374	420	291

Mileages © Rand McNally

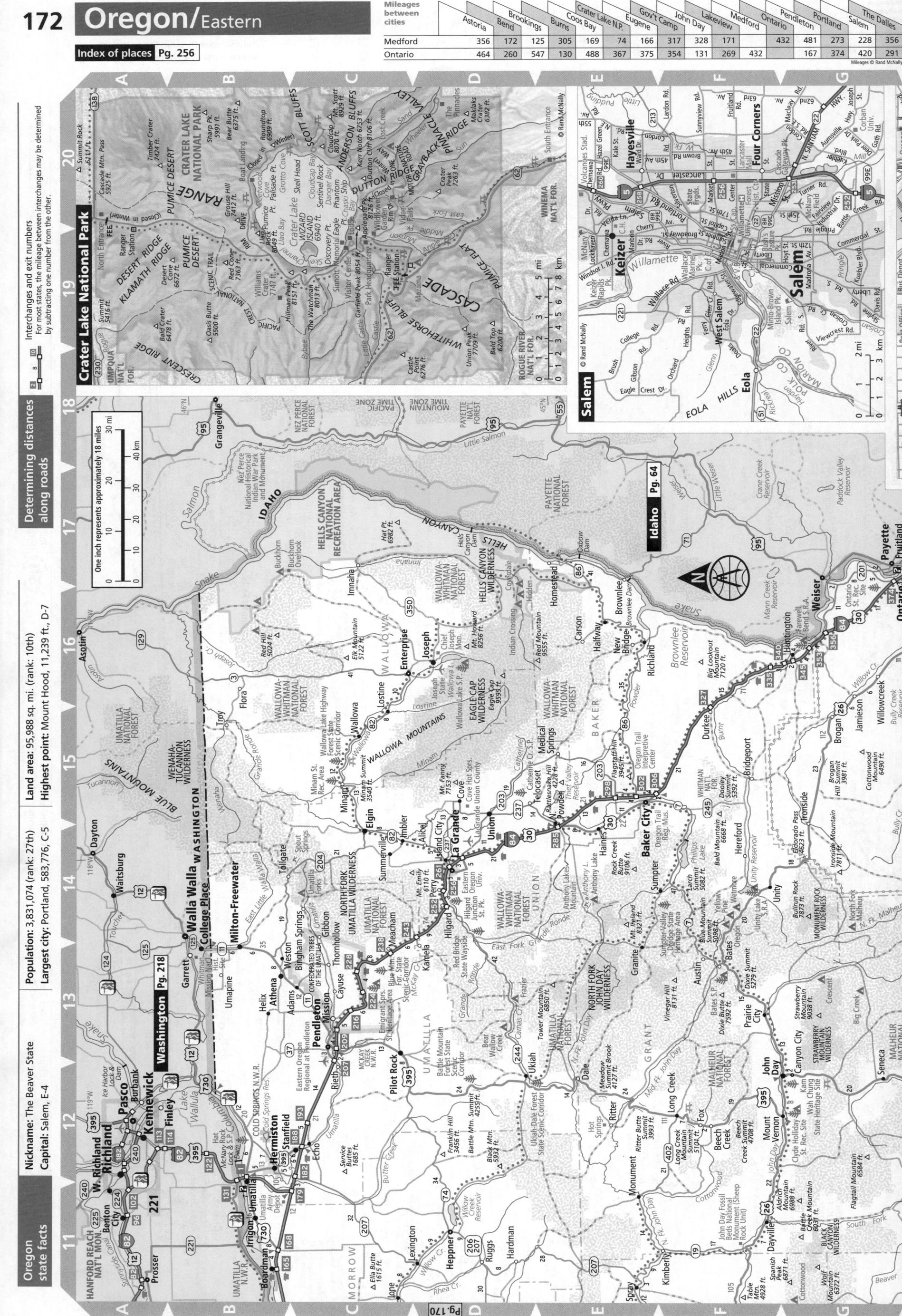

Mileages between cities

	Astoria	Bend	Brookings	Burns	Coos Bay	Crater Lake N.P.	Eugene	Gov't Camp	John Day	Lakeview	Medford	Ontario	Pendleton	Portland	Salem	The Dalles
Pendleton	298	242	550	196	428	349	318	188	126	335	481	167		208	254	125
Portland	96	161	342	281	220	250	110	55	265	336	273	374	208		47	83

Mileages © Rand McNally

5	308 miles	84	375 miles	**Total mileages through Oregon**
82	11 miles	101	348 miles	More mileages at www.randmcnally.com/MC

Central Portland

Portland & Vicinity

IDAHO

NEVADA

Nevada Pg. 130

MOUNTAIN T.Z.
PACIFIC T.Z.

Nevada Pg. 171

© Rand McNally

Travel planning & on-the-road resources

Tourism Information:	Travel Oregon (800) 547-7842 www.traveloregon.com
Road Conditions & Construction:	511 (800) 977-6368, (503) 588-2941 www.oregon.gov/odot, www.tripcheck.com
Toll Road Information:	Bridge of the Gods (Cascade Locks): (541) 374-8619; portofcascadelocks.org/bridge-of-the-gods/bridge/index.php Hood River Bridge (BreezeBy): (541) 386-1645; www.portofhoodriver.com

Mileages between cities	Altoona	Chambersburg	Cumberland, MD	Du Bois	Erie	Galeton	Harrisburg	Johnstown	Kittanning	Meadville	New Castle	Philadelphia	Pittsburgh	State College	Uniontown	Warren
Altoona		90	66	71	202	135	134	46	79	165	127	234	96	41	112	130
Chambersburg	90		87	153	282	215	54	94	160	246	206	157	160	101	149	218

Mileages © Rand McNally

© Rand McNally

One inch represents approx. 9 miles

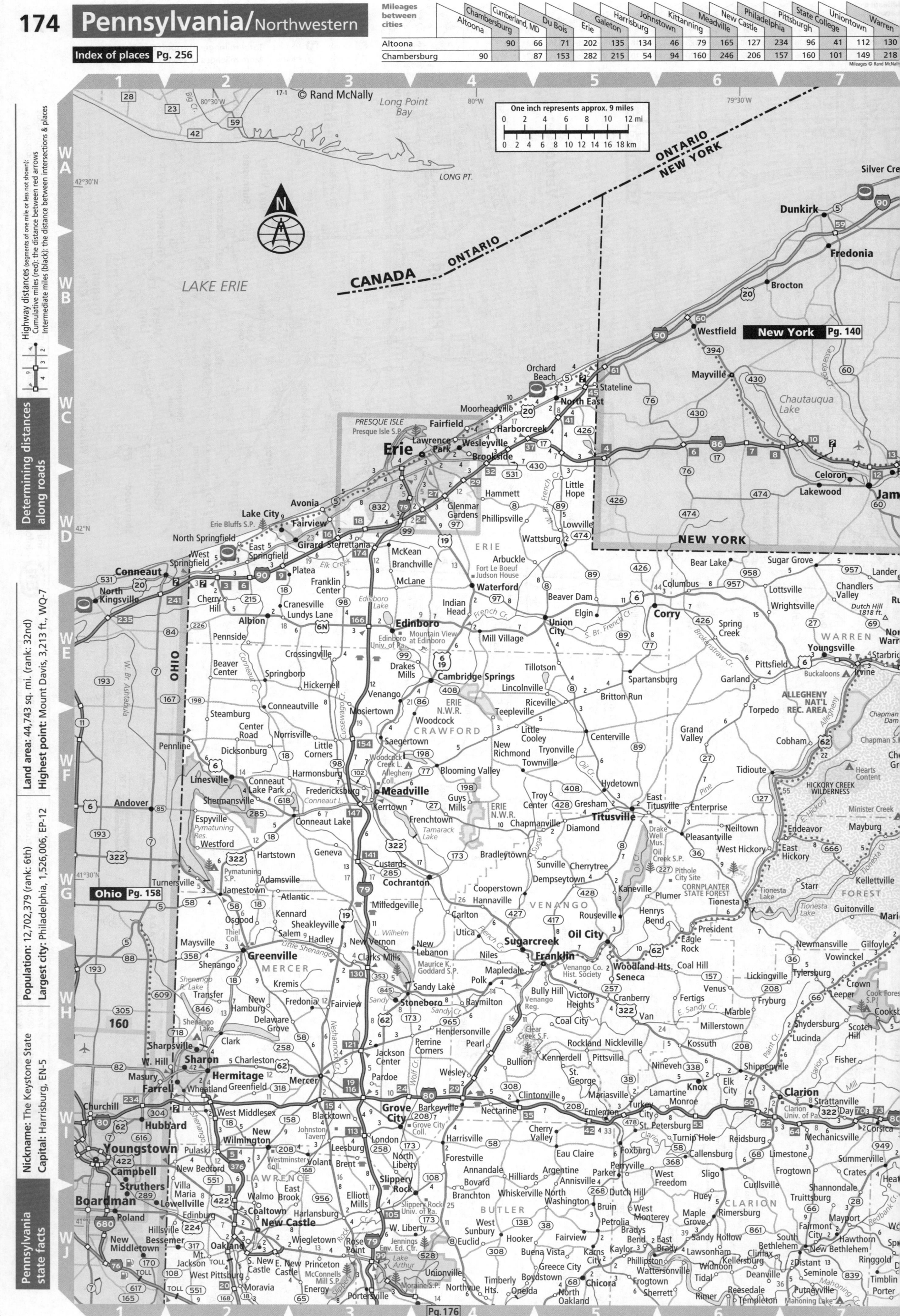

Pennsylvania state facts

Nickname: The Keystone State
Capital: Harrisburg, EN-5

Population: 12,702,379 (rank: 6th)
Largest city: Philadelphia, 1,526,006, EP-12

Land area: 44,743 sq. mi. (rank: 32nd)
Highest point: Mount Davis, 3,213 ft., WQ-7

New York Pg. 140

Ohio Pg. 158

Pg. 176

Mileages between cities	Altoona	Chambersburg	Cumberland, MD	Du Bois	Erie	Galeton	Harrisburg	Johnstown	Kittanning	Meadville	New Castle	Philadelphia	Pittsburgh	State College	Uniontown	Warren
Erie	202	282	232	148		159	297	177	123	41	88	419	127	208	184	66
Johnstown	46	94	70	77	177	179	137		53	141	102	238	67	85	80	135

Mileages © Rand McNally

continued p. 176

Total mileages through Pennsylvania
70 — 168 miles 79 — 183 miles
80 — 311 miles 90 — 46 miles
More mileages at www.randmcnally.com/MC

Erie (inset map, scale 0–3 mi / 0–4 km)

Altoona (inset map, scale 0–3 mi / 0–4 km)

Side panel:

Toll Road Information (all use E-ZPass):
Del. River Port Authority (Philadelphia area bridges): (877) 567-3772; www.drpa.org
Del. River Joint Toll Bridge Comm. (other Del. River bridges): (800) 363-0049; www.drjtbc.org
Pennsylvania Turnpike Commission: (800) 331-3414; www.paturnpike.com

511

Road Conditions & Construction:
511
(888) 783-6783
www.dot.state.pa.us

Tourism Information:
Pennsylvania Tourism Office
(800) 847-4872
www.visitpa.com

Travel planning & on-the-road resources

Mileages between cities	Altoona	Chambersburg	Cumberland, MD	Du Bois	Erie	Galeton	Harrisburg	Johnstown	Kittanning	Meadville	New Castle	Philadelphia	Pittsburgh	State College	Uniontown	Warren
New Castle	127	206	156	110	88	197	250	102	48	52		350	52	171	108	120
Pittsburgh	96	160	111	101	127	200	203	67	42	91	52	304		135	51	148

Mileages © Rand McNally

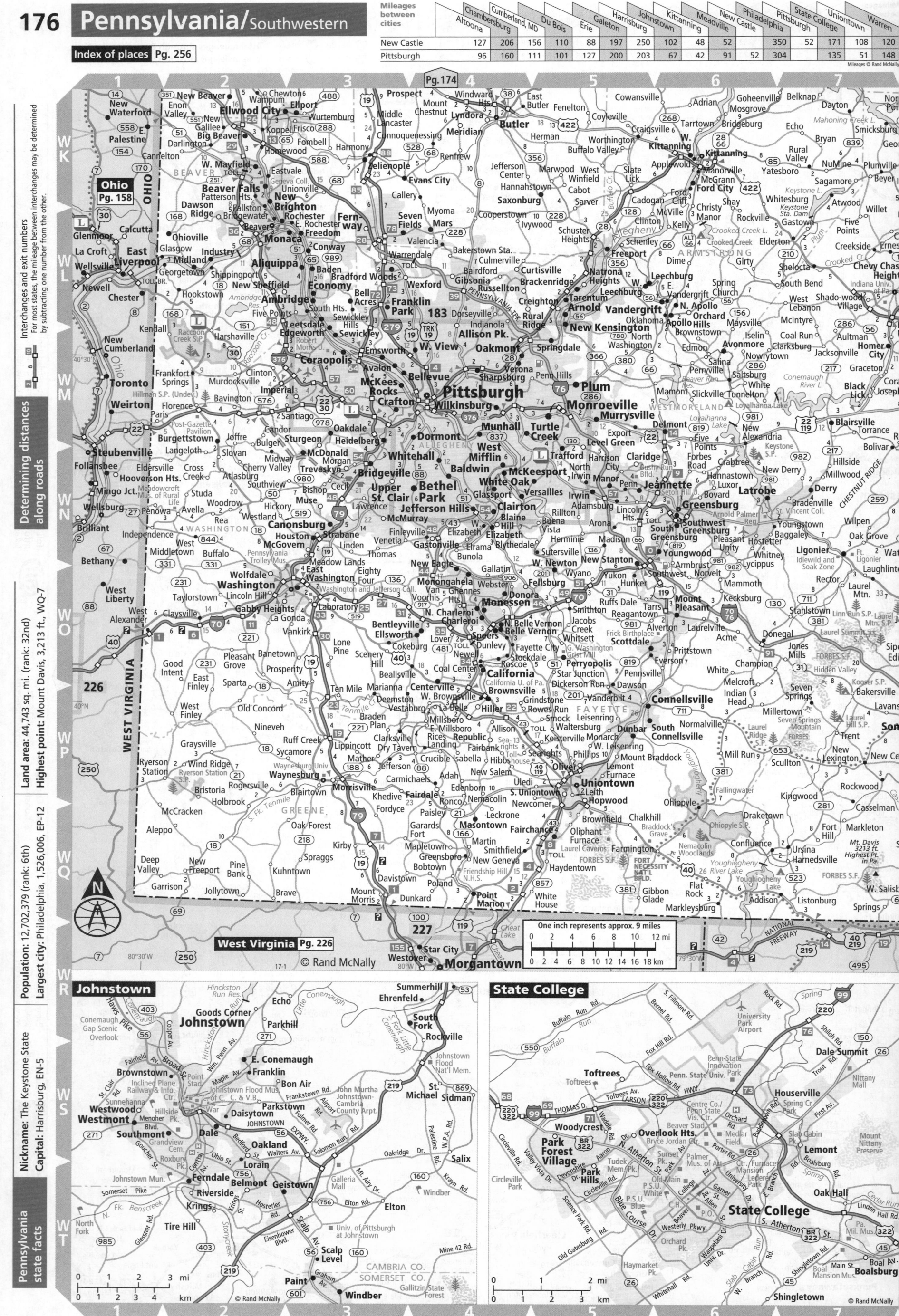

Pennsylvania state facts

Nickname: The Keystone State
Capital: Harrisburg, EN-5

Population: 12,702,379 (rank: 6th)
Largest city: Philadelphia, 1,526,006, EP-12

Land area: 44,743 sq. mi. (rank: 32nd)
Highest point: Mount Davis, 3,213 ft., WQ-7

Determining distances along roads

Interchanges and exit numbers
For most states, the mileage between interchanges may be determined by subtracting one number from the other.

One inch represents approx. 9 miles

© Rand McNally

Johnstown

State College

Mileages between cities

	Altoona	Chambersburg	Cumberland, MD	Du Bois	Erie	Galeton	Harrisburg	Johnstown	Kittanning	Meadville	New Castle	Philadelphia	Pittsburgh	State College	Uniontown	Warren
State College	41	101	106	61	208	100	87	85	120	173	171	193	135		152	119
Williamsport	100	132	166	110	257	72	83	146	168	220	219	176	196	63	212	171

Mileages © Rand McNally

	168 miles		183 miles	**Total mileages through Pennsylvania**
	311 miles		46 miles	More mileages at www.randmcnally.com/MC

Pennsylvania/Southwestern — regional road map

Gettysburg / Gettysburg National Military Park

York

Toll Road Information: (all use E-ZPass) Del. River Port Authority (Philadelphia area bridges): (877) 567-3772; www.drpa.org — Del. River Joint Toll Bridge Comm. (other Del. River bridges): (800) 363-0049; www.drjtbc.org — Pennsylvania Turnpike Commission: (800) 331-3414; www.paturnpike.com

511 — www.dot.state.pa.us

Road Conditions & Construction: 511 (888) 783-6783

Tourism Information: Pennsylvania Tourism Office (800) 847-4872 www.visitpa.com

Travel planning & on-the-road resources

© Rand McNally

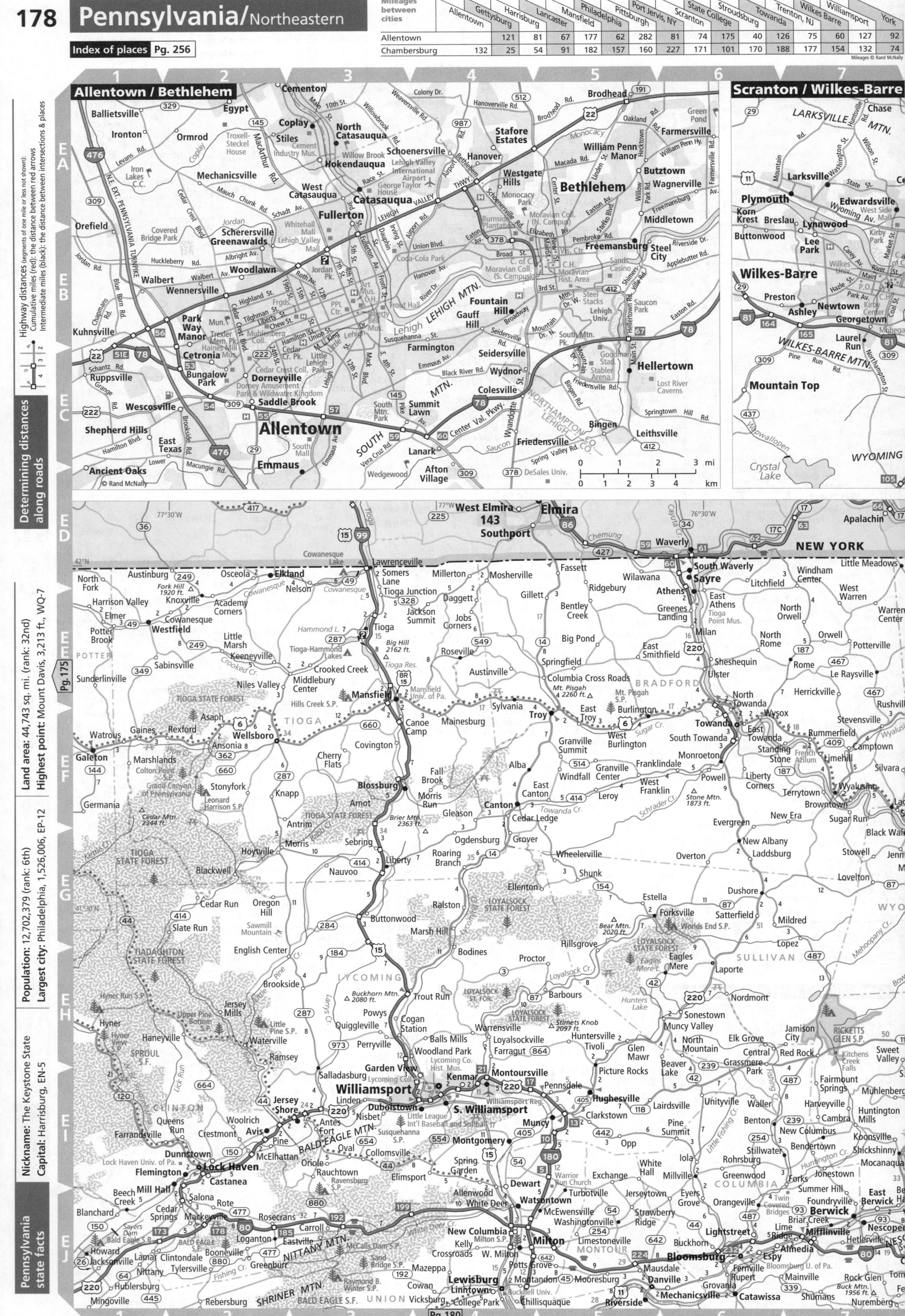

Allentown / Bethlehem

Scranton / Wilkes-Barre

Pennsylvania state facts

Nickname: The Keystone State
Capital: Harrisburg, EN-5

Population: 12,702,379 (rank: 6th)
Largest city: Philadelphia, 1,526,006, EP-12

Land area: 44,743 sq. mi. (rank: 32nd)
Highest point: Mount Davis, 3,213 ft., WQ-7

Determining distances along roads

Highway distances (segments of one mile or less not shown)
Cumulative miles (red): the distance between red arrows
Intermediate miles (black): the distance between intersections & places

Mileages between cities	Allentown	Gettysburg	Harrisburg	Lancaster	Mansfield	Philadelphia	Pittsburgh	Port Jervis, NY	Scranton	State College	Stroudsburg	Towanda	Trenton, NJ	Wilkes Barre	Williamsport	continued p. 180 York
Harrisburg	81	38		39	133	107	203	176	120	87	119	139	127	104	83	26
Philadelphia	62	138	107	78	226		304	140	124	193	100	175	32	109	176	101

Mileages © Rand McNally

76	350 miles	81	232 miles		**Total mileages through Pennsylvania**
80	311 miles	95	51 miles		**More mileages at** www.randmcnally.com/MC

© Rand McNally

Del. River Port Authority (Philadelphia area bridges): (877) 567-3772; www.drpa.org
Del. River Joint Toll Bridge Comm. (other Del. River bridges): (800) 363-0049; www.drjtbc.org
Pennsylvania Turnpike Commission: (800) 331-3414; www.paturnpike.com

Toll Road Information: (all use E-ZPass)

Road Conditions & Construction: 511 (888) 783-6783 www.dot.state.pa.us

Tourism Information: Pennsylvania Tourism Office (800) 847-4872 www.visitpa.com

Travel planning & on-the-road resources

New York Pg. 140

New Jersey Pg. 134

Pg. 181

One inch represents approx. 9 miles

Index of places **Pg. 256**

Mileages between cities	Allentown	Gettysburg	Harrisburg	Lancaster	Mansfield	Philadelphia	Pittsburgh	Port Jervis, NY	Scranton	State College	Stroudsburg	Towanda	Trenton, NJ	Wilkes Barre	Williamsport	York
Reading	37	96	64	34	175	62	261	118	100	150	76	152	82	86	126	56
Scranton	74	160	120	132	102	124	279	59		150	46	64	137	16	101	146

Mileages © Rand McNally

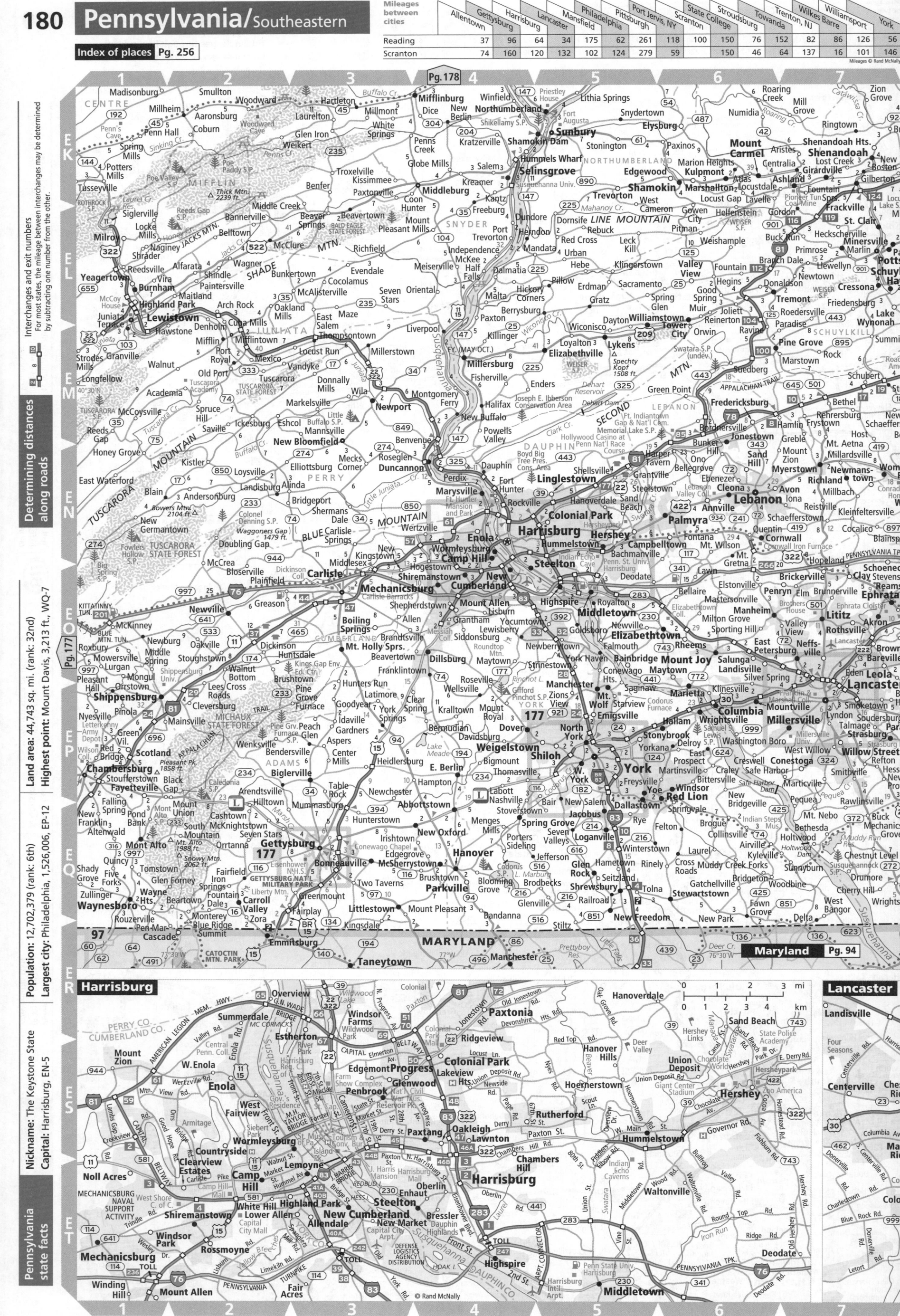

Mileages between cities	Allentown	Gettysburg	Harrisburg	Lancaster	Mansfield	Philadelphia	Pittsburgh	Port Jervis, NY	Scranton	State College	Stroudsburg	Towanda	Trenton, NJ	Wilkes Barre	Williamsport	York
State College	175	129	87	126	107	193	135	205	150		162	134	213	132	63	118
Williamsport	127	126	83	123	50	176	196	157	101	63	113	67	189	84		115

Total mileages through Pennsylvania
76 — 350 miles   81 — 232 miles
80 — 311 miles   95 — 51 miles
More mileages at www.randmcnally.com/MC

New Jersey Pg. 134

One inch represents approx. 9 miles
0 2 4 6 8 10 12 mi
0 2 4 6 8 10 12 14 16 18 km

Reading (inset map)
Lancaster (inset map)

Del. River Port Authority (Philadelphia area bridges): (877) 567-3772; www.drpa.org
Del. River Joint Toll Bridge Comm. (other Del. River bridges): (800) 363-0049; www.drjtbc.org
Pennsylvania Turnpike Commission: (800) 331-3414; www.paturnpike.com

Toll Road Information: 511 (all use E-ZPass)

Road Conditions & Construction: 511 (888) 783-6783 www.dot.state.pa.us

Tourism Information: Pennsylvania Tourism Office (800) 847-4872 www.visitpa.com

Travel planning & on-the-road resources

© Rand McNally

Sights to see

- Adventure Aquarium, Camden, N.J.......... E-5
- The Andy Warhol Museum, Pittsburgh L-2
- Betsy Ross House, Philadelphia............. F-10
- Carnegie Science Center, Pittsburgh........ L-1
- Duquesne & Monongahela Inclines, Pittsburgh .... M-1 & N-2
- Franklin Institute Science Museum, Philadelphia F-6

Philadelphia & Vicinity

Central Philadelphia

Sights to see

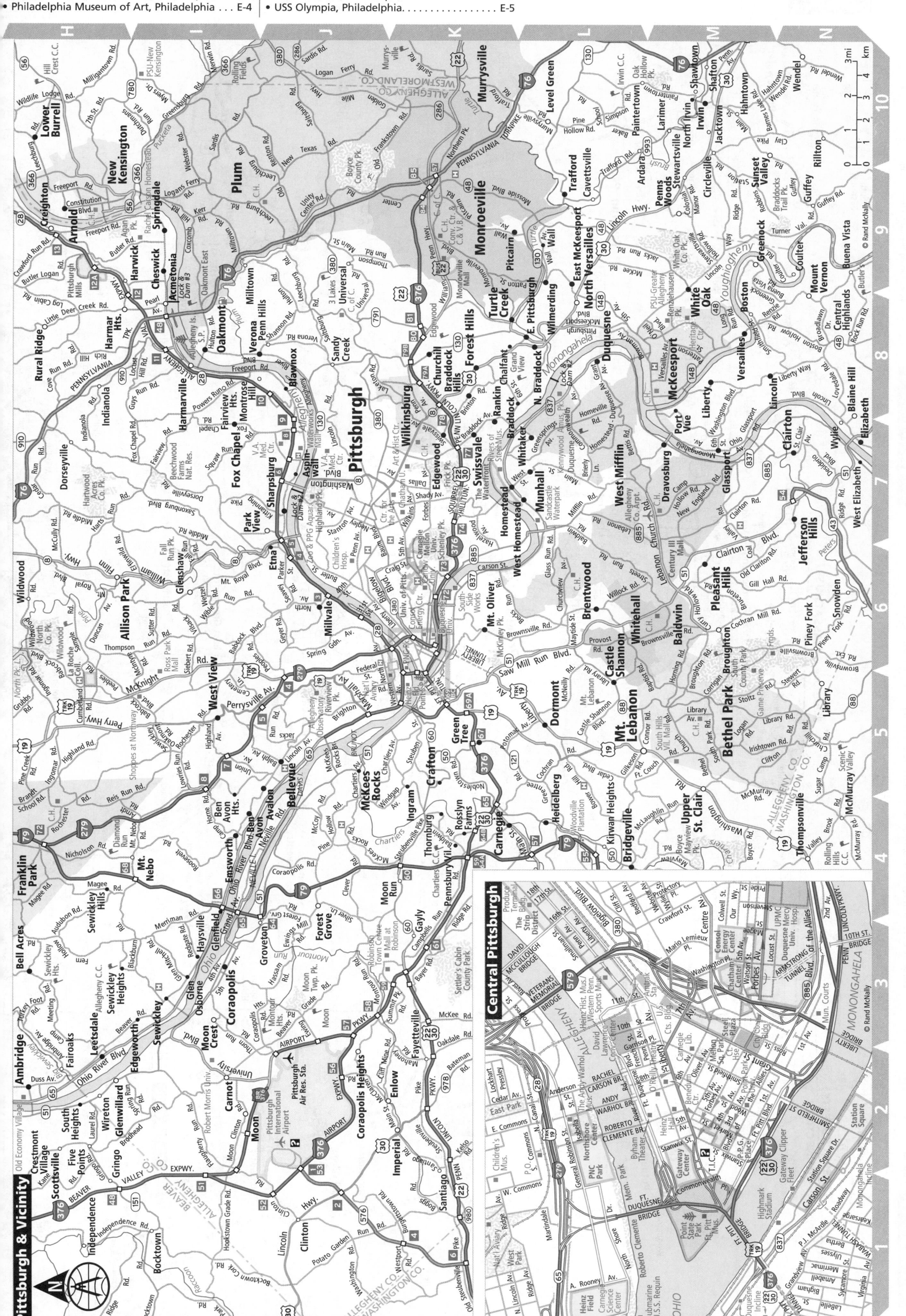

Mileages between cities

	Fall River, MA	Kingston	Newport	Providence	Warwick	Westerly	Woonsocket	Worcester, MA			Fall River, MA	Kingston	Newport	Providence	Warwick	Westerly	Woonsocket	Worcester, MA
Chepachet	35	41	45	19	23	54	13	37		Newport	20	16		33	26	39	47	72
Fall River, MA		35	20	16	25	58	31	56		Providence	16	29	33		10	42	14	40

Mileages © Rand McNally

Rhode Island state facts

Nickname: The Ocean State
Capital: Providence, D-6

Population: 1,052,567 (rank: 43rd)
Largest city: Providence, 178,042, D-6

Land area: 1,034 sq. mi. (rank: 50th)
Highest point: Jerimoth Hill, 812 ft, C-3

Determining distances along roads

Interchanges and exit numbers
For most states, the mileage between interchanges may be determined by subtracting one number from the other.

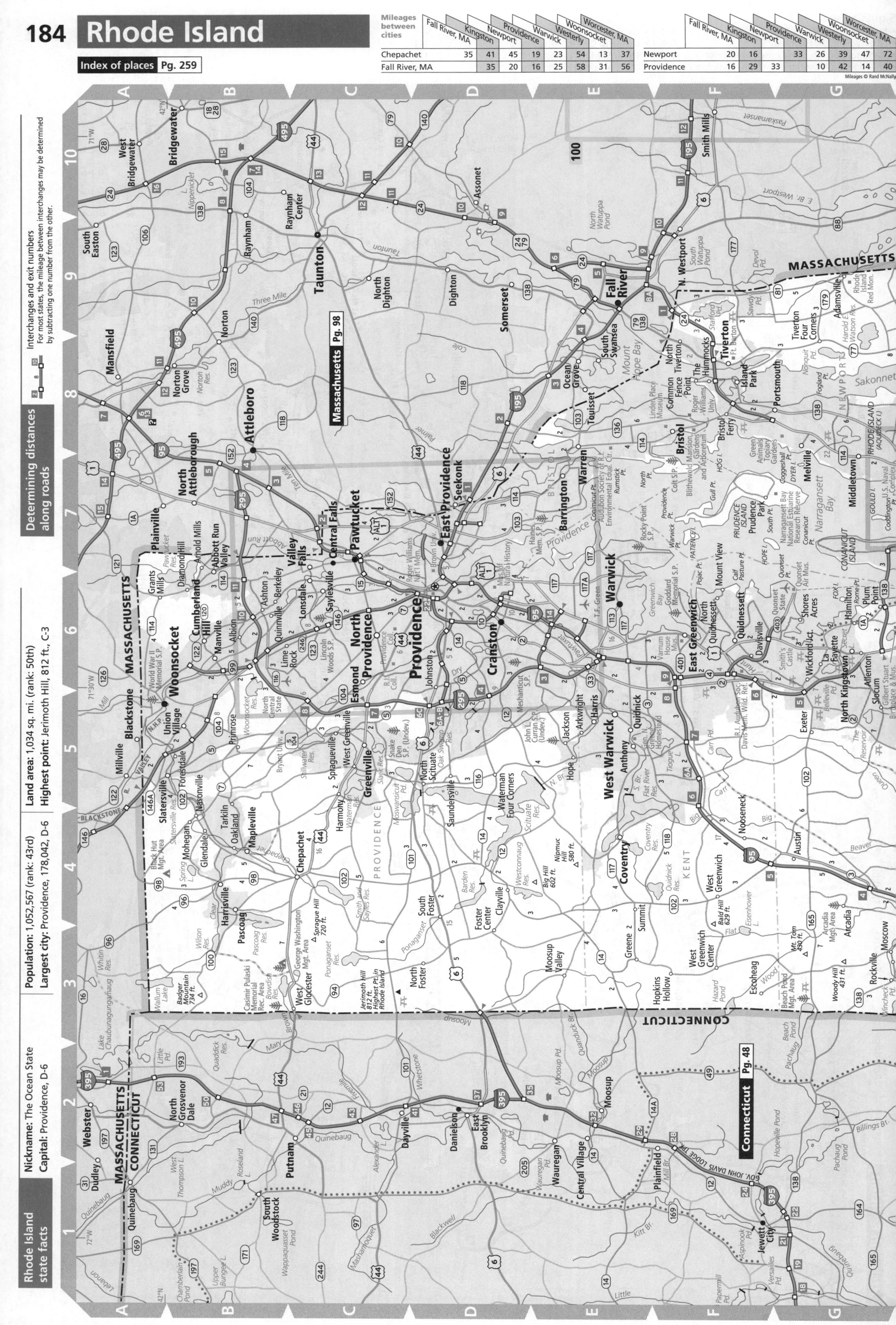

Mileages between cities	Fall River, MA	Kingston	Newport	Providence	Warwick	Westerly	Woonsocket	Worcester, MA
Warwick	25	23	26	10		37	24	50
Westerly	58	23	39	42	37		56	82

	Fall River, MA	Kingston	Newport	Providence	Warwick	Westerly	Woonsocket	Worcester, MA
Woonsocket	31	43	47	14	24	56		27
Worcester, MA	56	68	72	40	50	82	27	

Mileages © Rand McNally

Total mileages through Rhode Island
95 42 miles   6 31 miles
1 60 miles

More mileages at www.randmcnally.com/MC

© Rand McNally

Tourism Information: Rhode Island Tourism Division (401) 278-9100 www.visitrhodeisland.com

Road Conditions & Construction: 511 (888) 401-4511, (401) 222-2450 www.dot.ri.gov/travel

Toll Road Information: R.I. Turnpike & Bridge Authority (E-ZPass) (877) 743-9727 www.ritba.org

Travel planning & on-the-road resources

Index of places Pg. 259

Mileages between cities

	Anderson	Augusta, GA	Charleston	Charlotte, NC	Columbia	Hilton Head I.	Myrtle Beach	Spartanburg
Augusta, GA	92		175	160	72	151	216	120
Charleston	238	175		207	112	104	95	201
Charlotte, NC	128	160	207		93	253	176	72
Columbia	117	72	112	93		158	148	93

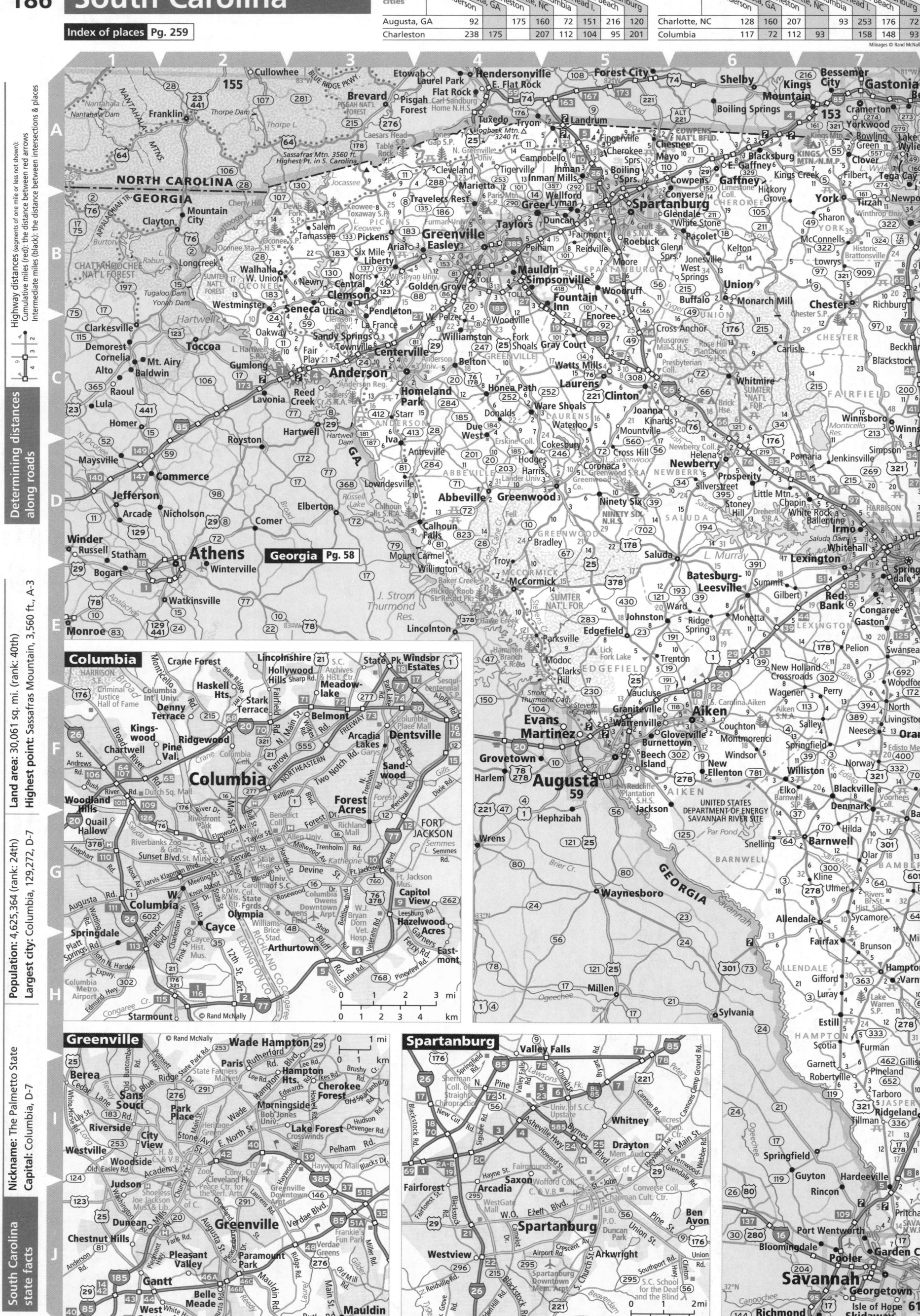

	Anderson	Augusta, GA	Charlotte, NC	Columbia	Hilton Head I.	Myrtle Beach	Spartanburg
Florence	206	148	130	104	81	177	67	169
Myrtle Beach	273	216	95	176	148	200		237

	Anderson	Augusta, GA	Charlotte, NC	Columbia	Hilton Head I.	Myrtle Beach	Spartanburg
Savannah, GA	282	134	106	251	156	34	202	246
Spartanburg	60	120	201	72	93	247	237	

Mileages © Rand McNally

Total mileages through South Carolina
20 142 miles   85 106 miles
26 221 miles   95 199 miles
More mileages at www.randmcnally.com/MC

Charleston
Hilton Head Island
Myrtle Beach

One inch represents approximately 17 miles
0 5 10 15 20 25 mi
0 5 10 15 20 25 30 35 40 km

Cross Island Pkwy. (Hilton Head I.) (*Palmetto Pass*): (843) 342-6718; www.crossislandparkway.org
Southern Connector (Greenville) (*Palmetto Pass*): (855) 725-7277; www.southernconnector.com

Toll Road Information:

Road Conditions & Construction: 511 (877) 511-4672, (855) 467-2368 www.511sc.org, www.dot.state.sc.us

Tourism Information: South Carolina Dept. of Parks, Rec. & Tourism (803) 734-1700 www.discoversouthcarolina.com

Travel planning & on-the-road resources

© Rand McNally
17-1

Index of places Pg. 259

Mileages between cities	Aberdeen	Mobridge	Pierre	Pine Ridge	Rapid City	Sioux Falls	Watertown	Yankton
Aberdeen		100	160	360	333	203	96	236
Belle Fourche	312	212	206	172	60	403	362	421

	Aberdeen	Mobridge	Pierre	Pine Ridge	Rapid City	Sioux Falls	Watertown	Yankton
Mobridge	100		108	308	243	303	196	332
Pierre	160	108		200	173	224	188	242

Mileages © Rand McNally

South Dakota state facts

Nickname: The Mount Rushmore State | Capital: Pierre, D-7

Population: 814,180 (rank: 46th) | Largest city: Sioux Falls, 153,888, F-13

Land area: 75,811 sq. mi. (rank: 16th) | Highest point: Harney Peak, 7,242 ft., E-2

Determining distances along roads

Interchanges and exit numbers — For most states, the mileage between interchanges may be determined by subtracting one number from the other.

One inch represents approx. 25 miles

Montana Pg. 122
Wyo. Pg. 234
Nebraska Pg. 126

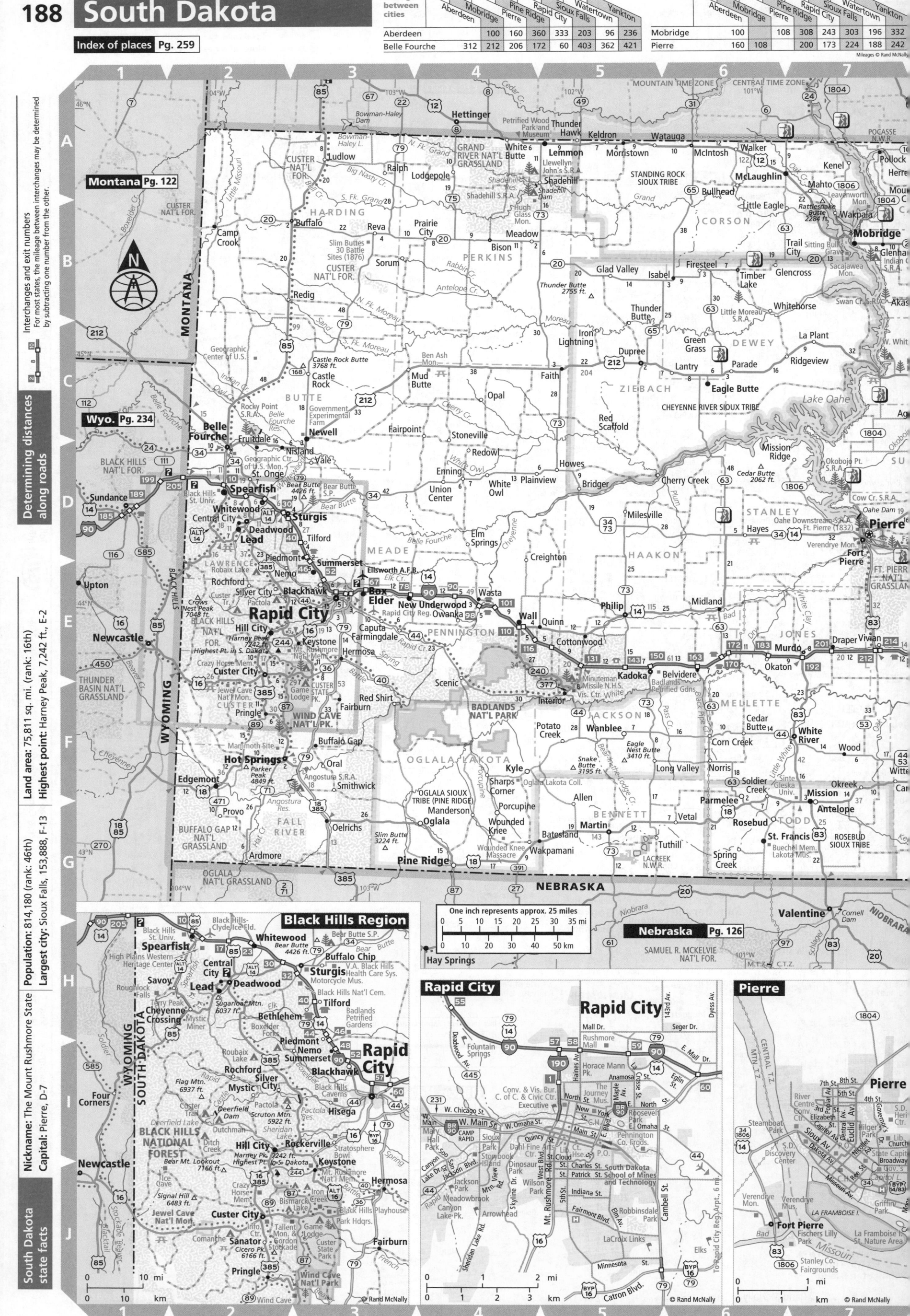

Black Hills Region

Rapid City

Pierre

© Rand McNally

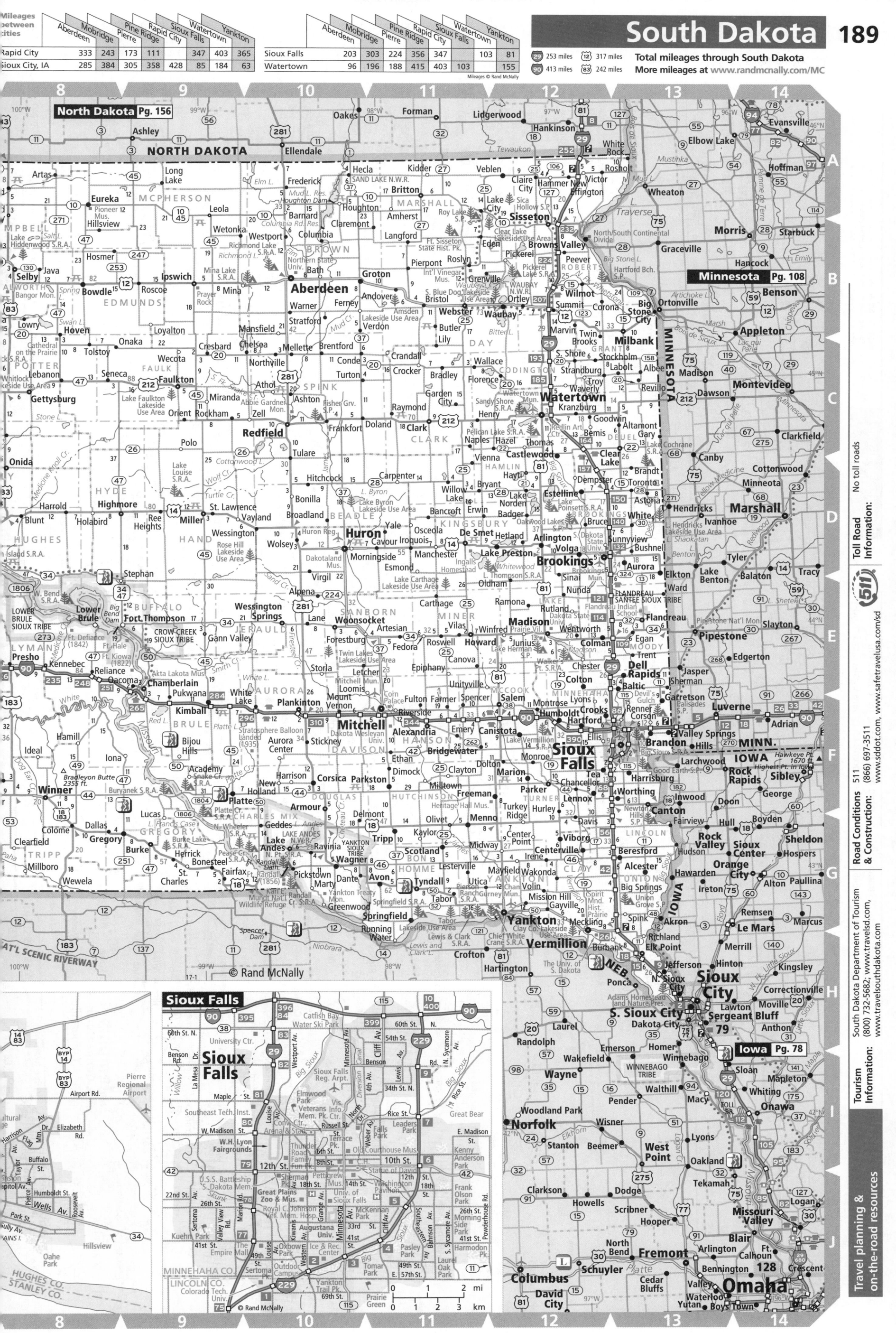

Mileages between cities	Aberdeen	Mobridge	Pierre	Pine Ridge	Rapid City	Sioux Falls	Watertown	Yankton
Rapid City	333	243	173	111		347	403	365
Sioux City, IA	285	384	305	358	428	85	184	63

	Aberdeen	Mobridge	Pierre	Pine Ridge	Rapid City	Sioux Falls	Watertown	Yankton
Sioux Falls	203	303	224	356	347		103	81
Watertown	96	196	188	415	403	103		155

Mileages © Rand McNally

29	253 miles
90	413 miles
12	317 miles
83	242 miles

Total mileages through South Dakota
More mileages at www.randmcnally.com/MC

North Dakota Pg. 156

Minnesota Pg. 108

Iowa Pg. 78

© Rand McNally

Sioux Falls

© Rand McNally

Tourism Information: South Dakota Department of Tourism (800) 732-5682; www.travelsd.com; www.travelsouthdakota.com

Road Conditions & Construction: 511 (866) 697-3511 www.sddot.com, www.safetravelusa.com/sd

Toll Road Information: No toll roads

Travel planning & on-the-road resources

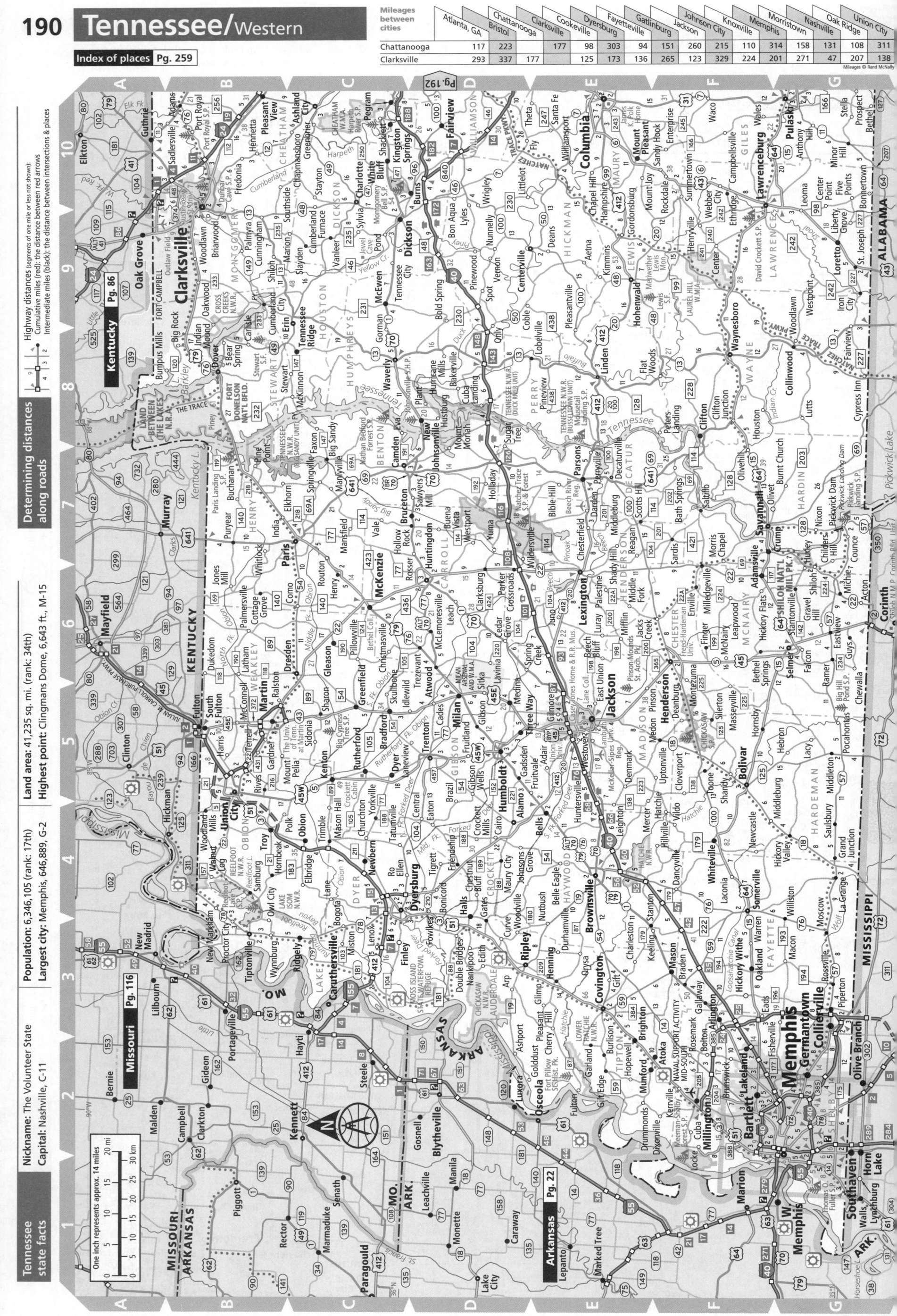

Determining distances along roads

Highway distances (segments of one mile or less not shown):
Cumulative miles (red): the distance between red arrows
Intermediate miles (black): the distance between intersections & places

Mileages between cities	Atlanta, GA	Bristol	Chattanooga	Clarksville	Cookeville	Dyersburg	Fayetteville	Gatlinburg	Jackson	Johnson City	Knoxville	Memphis	Morristown	Nashville	Oak Ridge	Union City
Dyersburg	418	463	303	173	252		229	392	47	455	351	76	398	172	334	34
Fayetteville	211	317	94	136	109	229		246	167	308	204	243	252	90	189	224

continued p. 192

Mileages © Rand McNally

40 455 miles	75 161 miles
65 121 miles	81 76 miles

Total mileages through Tennessee
More mileages at www.randmcnally.com/MC

Travel planning & on-the-road resources

Tourism Information: Tennessee Department of Tourist Development (615) 741-2159 www.tnvacation.com

Road Conditions & Construction: 511 (877) 244-0065 www.tn511.com, www.tdot.state.tn.us

Toll Road Information: No toll roads

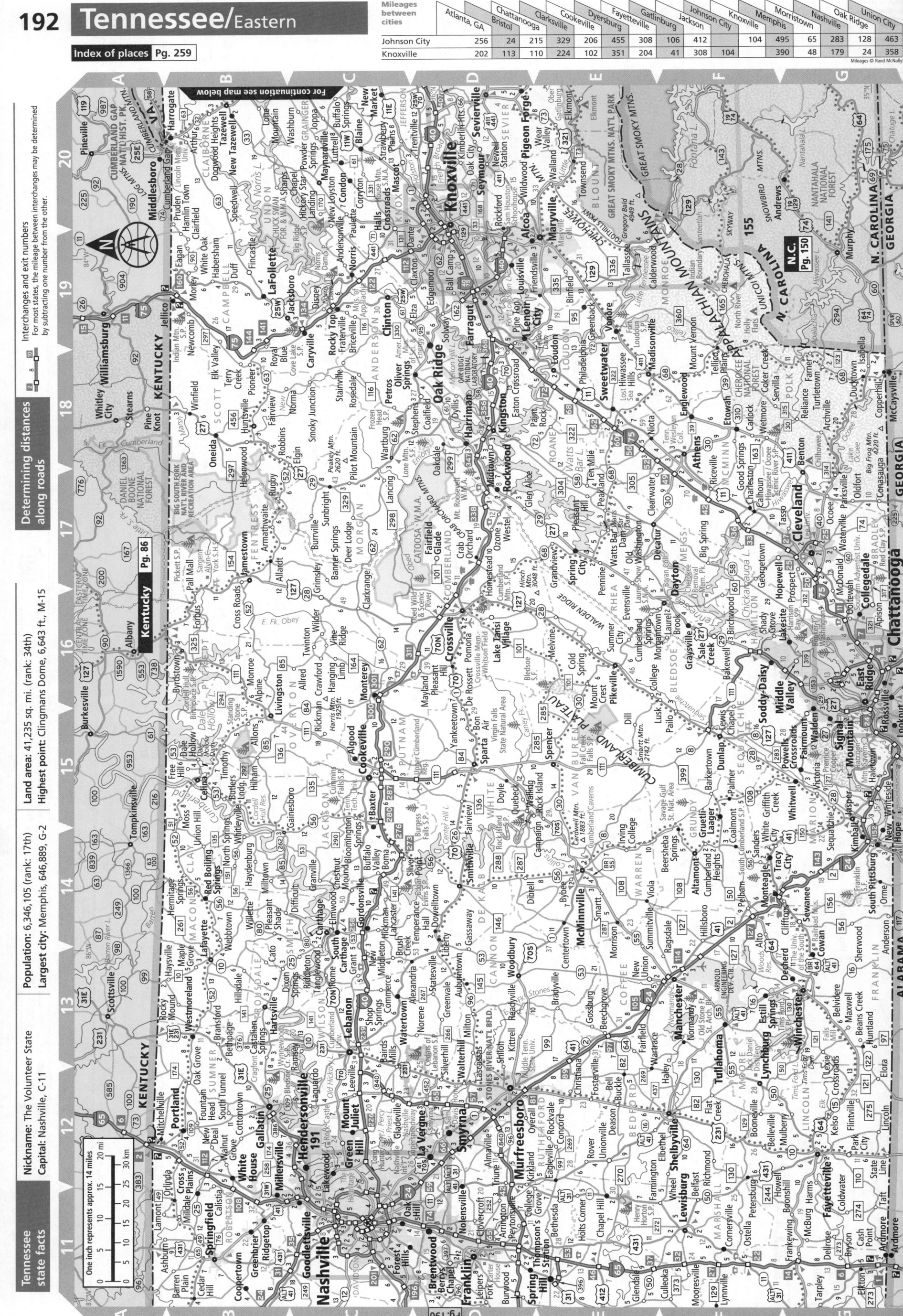

Tennessee state facts

Nickname: The Volunteer State
Capital: Nashville, C-11

Population: 6,346,105 (rank: 17th)
Largest city: Memphis, 646,889, G-2

Land area: 41,235 sq. mi. (rank: 34th)
Highest point: Clingmans Dome, 6,643 ft., M-15

Determining distances along roads
For most states, the mileage between interchanges may be determined by subtracting one number from the other.

Interchanges and exit numbers

One inch represents approx. 14 miles

For continuation see map below

Kentucky Pg. 86

Kentucky Pg. 190

N.C. Pg. 150

Total mileages through Tennessee

40 455 miles   75 161 miles
65 121 miles   81 76 miles

More mileages at www.randmcnally.com/MC

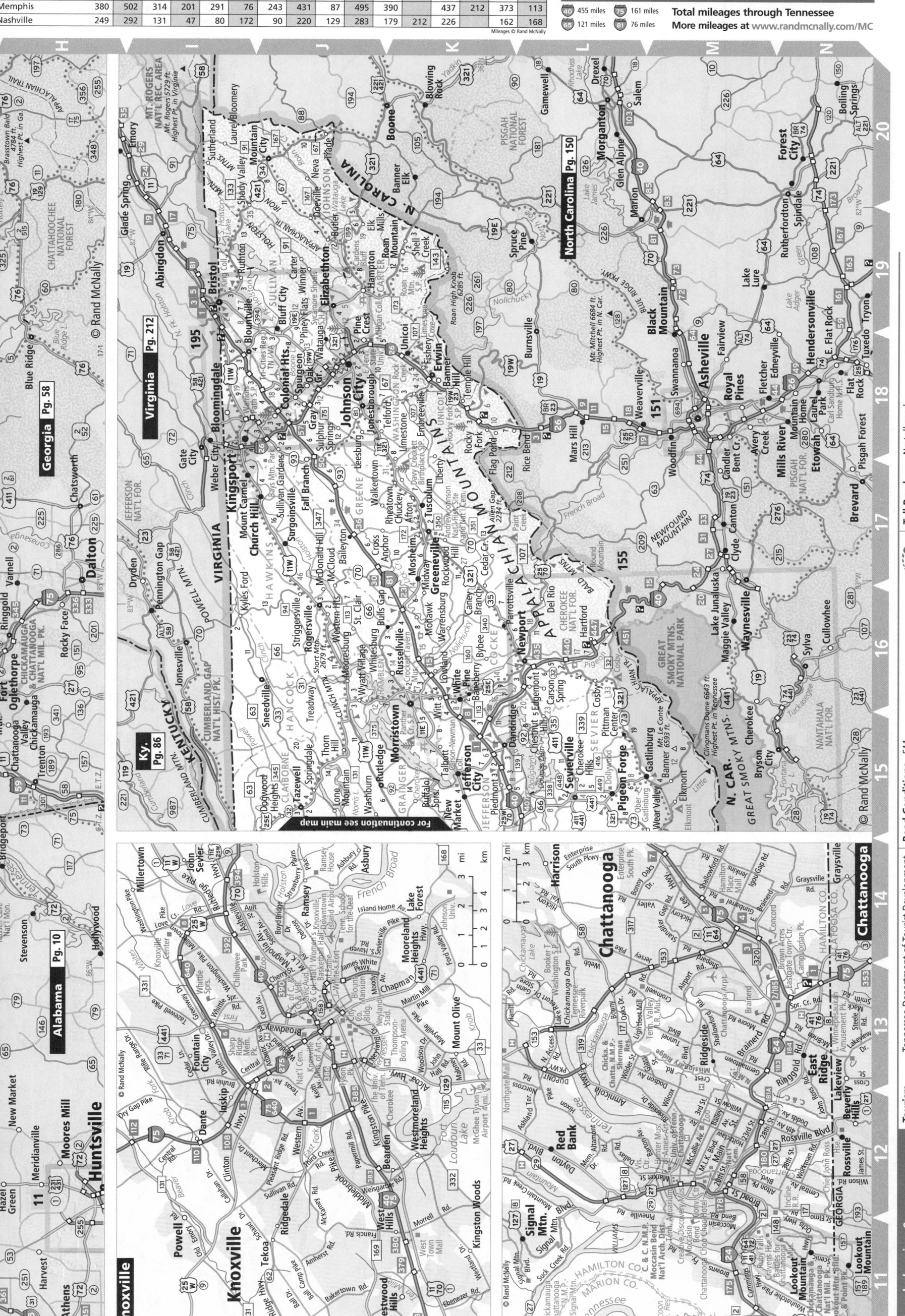

Travel planning & on-the-road resources

Tourism Information: Tennessee Department of Tourist Development (615) 741-2159 www.tnvacation.com

Road Conditions & Construction: 511 (877) 244-0065 www.tn511.com, www.tdot.state.tn.us

Toll Road Information: No toll roads

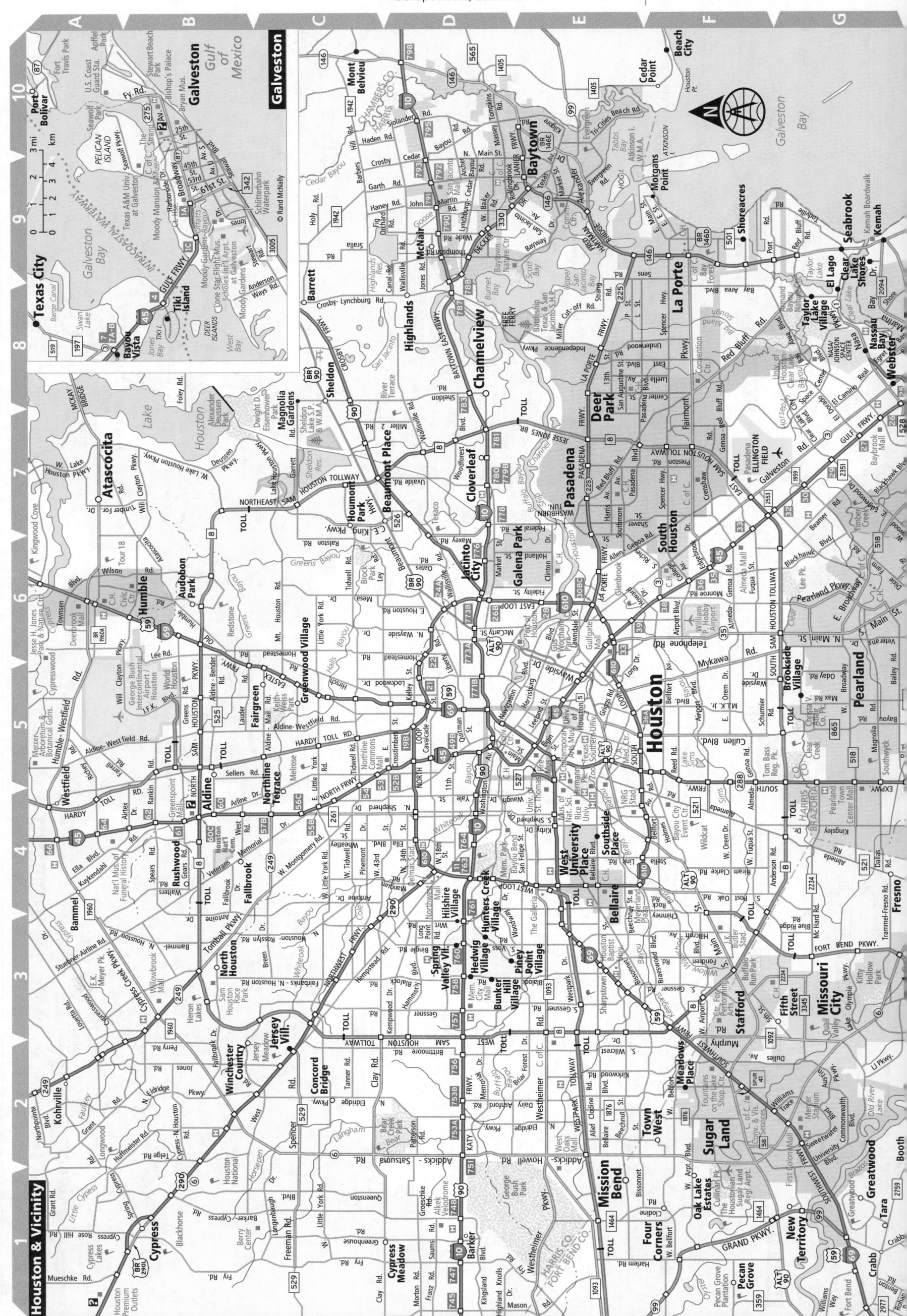

Galveston

Houston & Vicinity

Sights to see

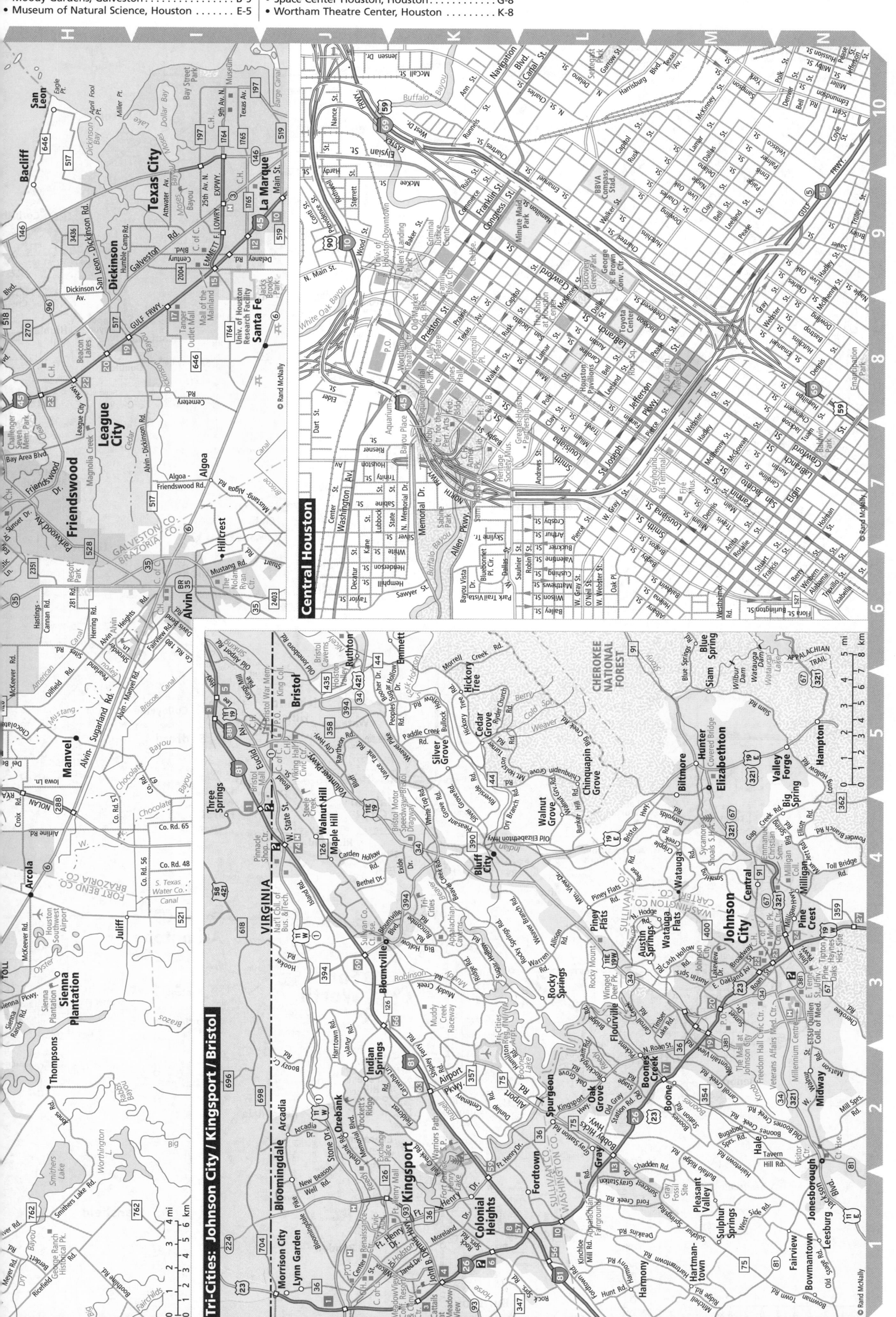

Sights to see

Central Dallas

Central Fort Worth

© Rand McNally

Sights to see

- Ripley's Believe It or Not! & Louis Tussaud's Palace of Wax, Grand Prairie G-8
- The Sixth Floor Museum at Dealey Plaza, Dallas B-1
- Stockyards Historic District, Fort Worth G-4
- Sundance Square, Fort Worth E-1
- Texas Civil War Museum, Fort Worth G-2
- Will Rogers Memorial Center, Fort Worth H-3

Dallas / Fort Worth & Vicinity

© Rand McNally

Mileages © Rand McNally

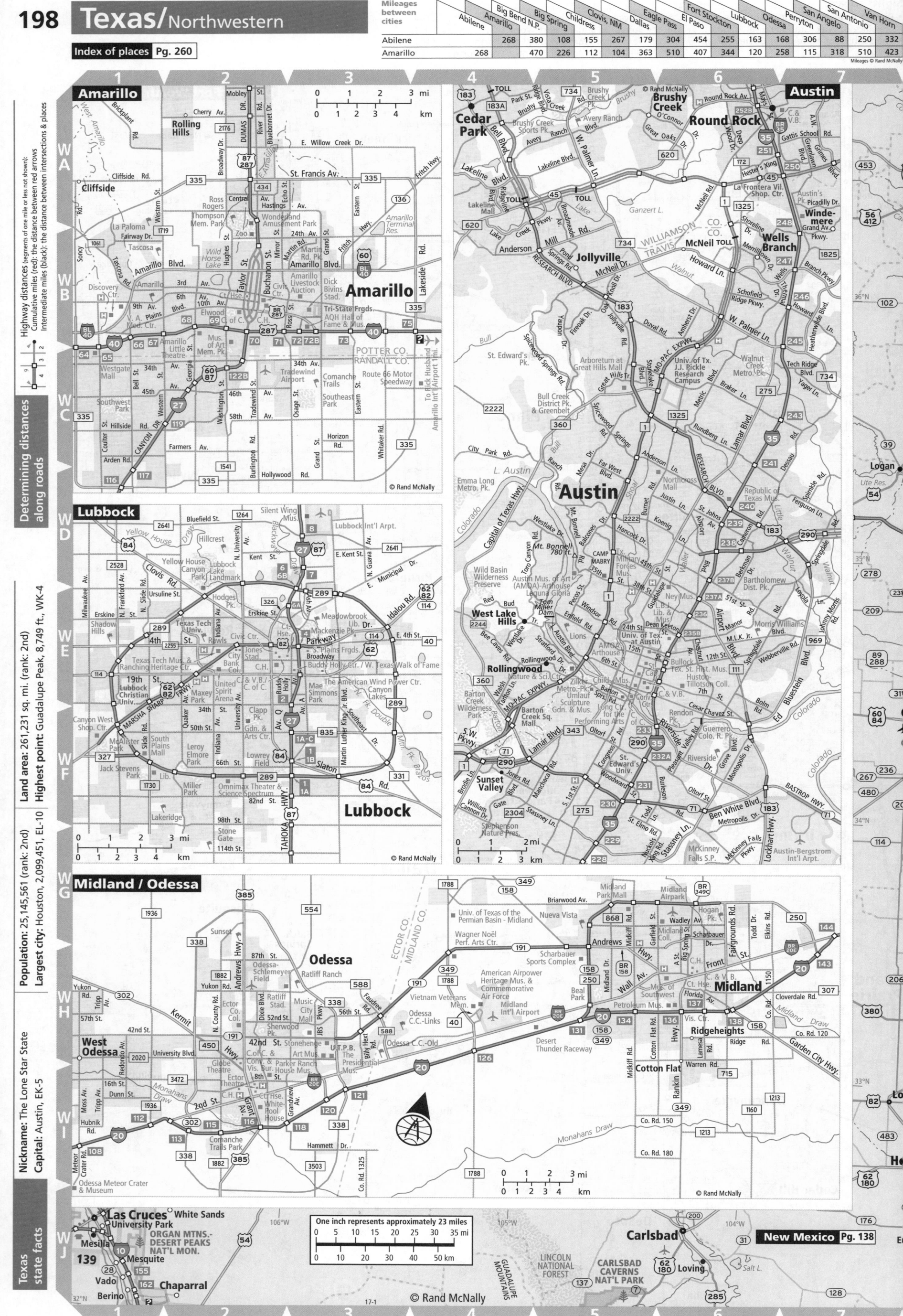

© Rand McNally

One inch represents approximately 23 miles

Texas state facts

Nickname: The Lone Star State
Capital: Austin, EK-5

Population: 25,145,561 (rank: 2nd)
Largest city: Houston, 2,099,451, EL-10

Land area: 261,231 sq. mi. (rank: 2nd)
Highest point: Guadalupe Peak, 8,749 ft., WK-4

Determining distances along roads

Highway distances (segments of one mile or less not shown); Cumulative miles (red): the distance between red arrows; Intermediate miles (black): the distance between intersections & places

New Mexico Pg. 138

139

17-1

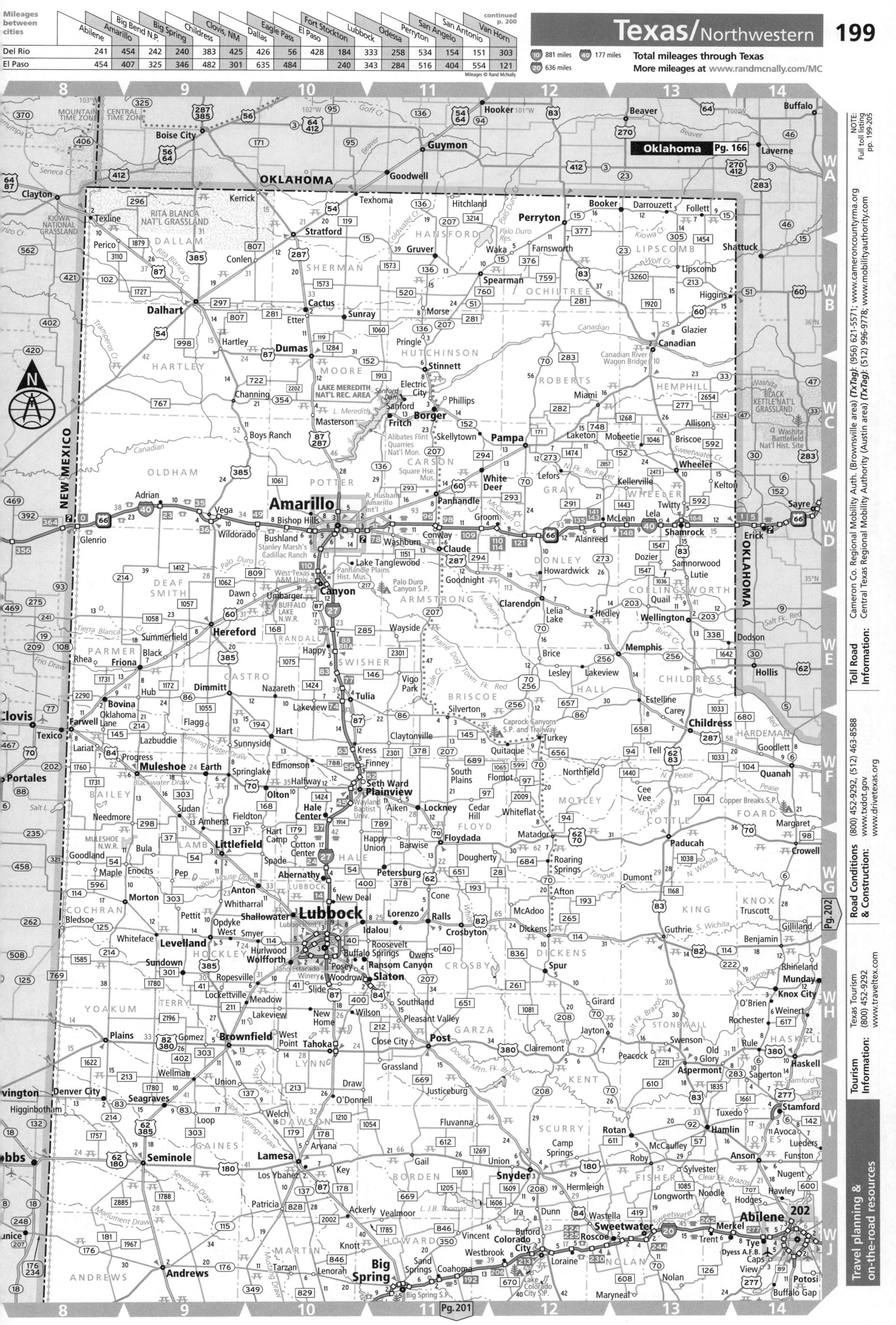

Mileages between cities	Abilene	Amarillo	Big Bend N.P.	Big Spring	Childress	Clovis, NM	Dallas	Eagle Pass	El Paso	Fort Stockton	Lubbock	Odessa	Perryton	San Angelo	San Antonio	Van Horn continued p. 200
Del Rio	241	454	242	240	383	425	426	56	428	184	333	258	534	154	151	303
El Paso	454	407	325	346	482	301	635	484		240	343	284	516	404	554	121

Mileages © Rand McNally

Total mileages through Texas
10 881 miles   40 177 miles
20 636 miles
More mileages at www.randmcnally.com/MC

NOTE: Full toll listing pp. 199-205

Toll Road Information:
Cameron Co. Regional Mobility Auth. (Brownsville area) (TxTag) (956) 621-5571; www.cameroncountyrma.org
Central Texas Regional Mobility Authority (Austin area) (TxTag) (512) 996-9778; www.mobilityauthority.com

Road Conditions & Construction:
(800) 452-9292, (512) 463-8588
www.txdot.gov
www.drivetexas.org

Tourism Information:
Texas Tourism (800) 452-9292
www.traveltex.com

Travel planning & on-the-road resources

Oklahoma Pg. 166

Pg. 202

Pg. 201

Nickname: The Lone Star State
Capital: Austin, EK-5

Population: 25,145,561 (rank: 2nd)
Largest city: Houston, 2,099,451, EL-10

Land area: 261,231 sq. mi. (rank: 2nd)
Highest point: Guadalupe Peak, 8,749 ft., WK-4

Determining distances along roads

Interchanges and exit numbers
For most states, the mileage between interchanges may be determined by subtracting one number from the other.

One inch represents approximately 23 miles

Texas state facts

© Rand McNally

Mileages between cities	Abilene	Amarillo	Big Bend N.P.	Big Spring	Childress	Clovis, NM	Dallas	Eagle Pass	El Paso	Fort Stockton	Lubbock	Odessa	Perryton	San Angelo	San Antonio	Van Horn
San Angelo	88	318	290	86	226	296	269	212	404	162	194	132	377		213	282
San Antonio	250	510	404	299	408	493	276	143	554	315	390	352	556	213		434

Total mileages through Texas
10 881 miles   40 177 miles
20 636 miles
More mileages at www.randmcnally.com/MC

NOTE: Full toll listing pp. 199-205

Toll Road Information:
Fort Bend County Toll Road Authority (Houston area) (TxTag, EZTAG, TollTag): (281) 242-9740; www.fbctra.com
Harris County Toll Road Authority (Houston area) (TxTag, EZTAG, TollTag): (281) 875-3279; www.hctra.org

Road Conditions & Construction:
(800) 452-9292, (512) 463-8588
www.txdot.gov
www.drivetexas.org

Tourism Information:
Texas Tourism
(800) 452-9292
www.traveltex.com

Travel planning & on-the-road resources

© Rand McNally

Mileages between cities	Abilene	Austin	Beaumont	Brownsville	Dallas	Houston	Laredo	Lufkin	Paris	San Angelo	San Antonio	Shreveport, LA	Texarkana	Tyler	Waco	Wichita Falls
Abilene		221	449	524	179	377	396	363	285	88	250	368	358	280	183	151
Austin	221		242	353	193	157	237	224	296	208	81	325	366	224	99	299

Mileages © Rand McNally

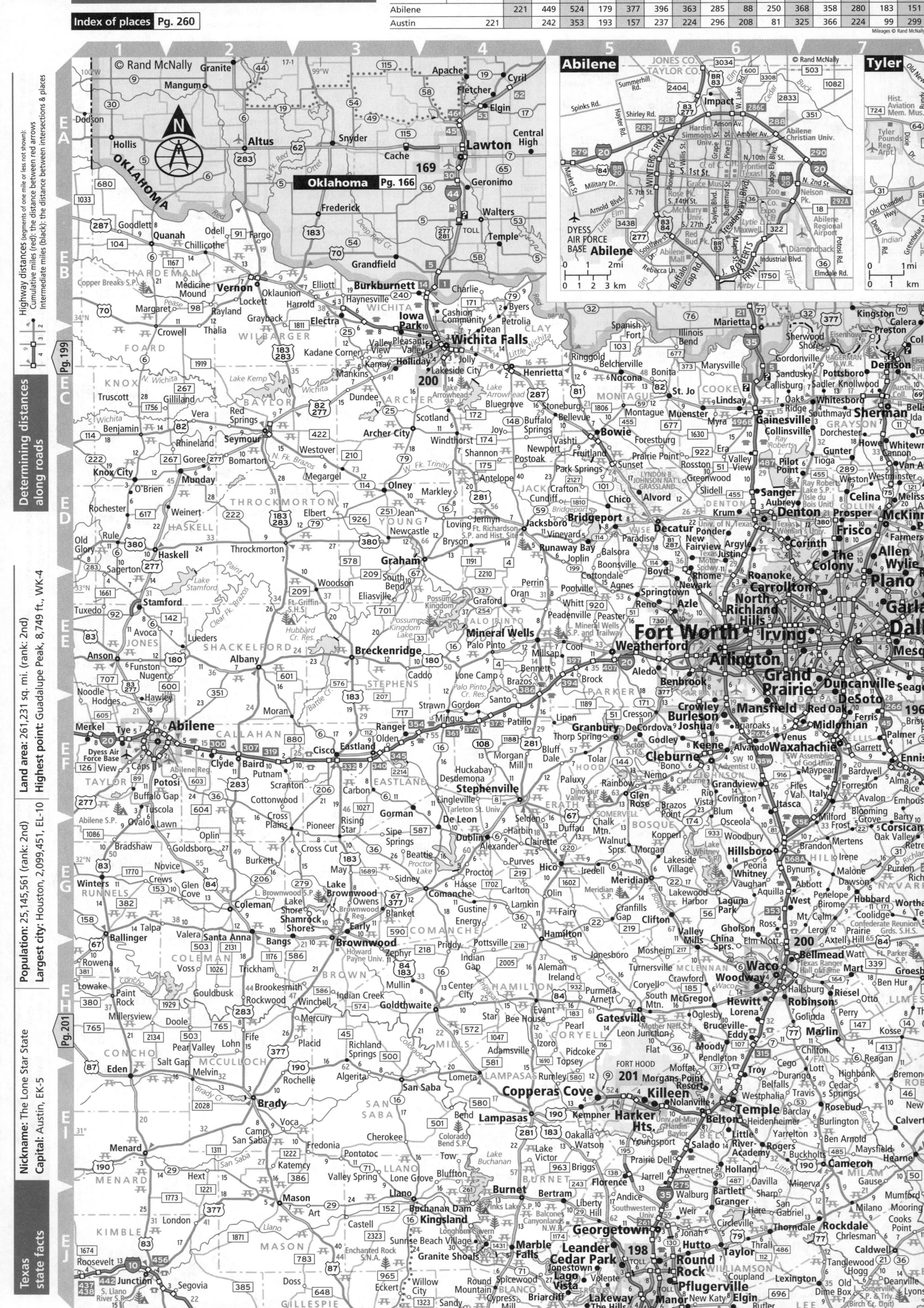

Pg.199

Pg.201

Texas state facts

Nickname: The Lone Star State
Capital: Austin, EK-5

Population: 25,145,561 (rank: 2nd)
Largest city: Houston, 2,099,451, EL-10

Land area: 261,231 sq. mi. (rank: 2nd)
Highest point: Guadalupe Peak, 8,749 ft., WK-4

Determining distances along roads

Highway distances (segments of one mile or less not shown):
Cumulative miles (red): the distance between red arrows
Intermediate miles (black): the distance between intersections & places

continued p. 204

Mileages between cities	Abilene	Austin	Beaumont	Brownsville	Dallas	Houston	Laredo	Lufkin	San Angelo	Paris	San Antonio	Shreveport, LA	Texarkana	Tyler	Waco	Wichita Falls
Brownsville	524	353	439		547	354	204	473	622	491	274	596	650	530	435	614
Corpus Christi	387	217	292	156	410	207	138	328	496	355	138	449	504	392	316	477

Mileages © Rand McNally

Total mileages through Texas
10 881 miles   30 223 miles
20 636 miles   35 504 miles
More mileages at www.randmcnally.com/MC

Mileages between cities	Abilene	Austin	Beaumont	Brownsville	Dallas	Houston	Laredo	Lufkin	Paris	San Angelo	San Antonio	Shreveport, LA	Texarkana	Tyler	Waco	Wichita Falls
Dallas	179	193	282	547		228	428	183	106	269	276	187	177	100	96	139
Houston	377	157	85	354	228		348	118	299	368	197	242	295	199	184	375

Mileages © Rand McNally

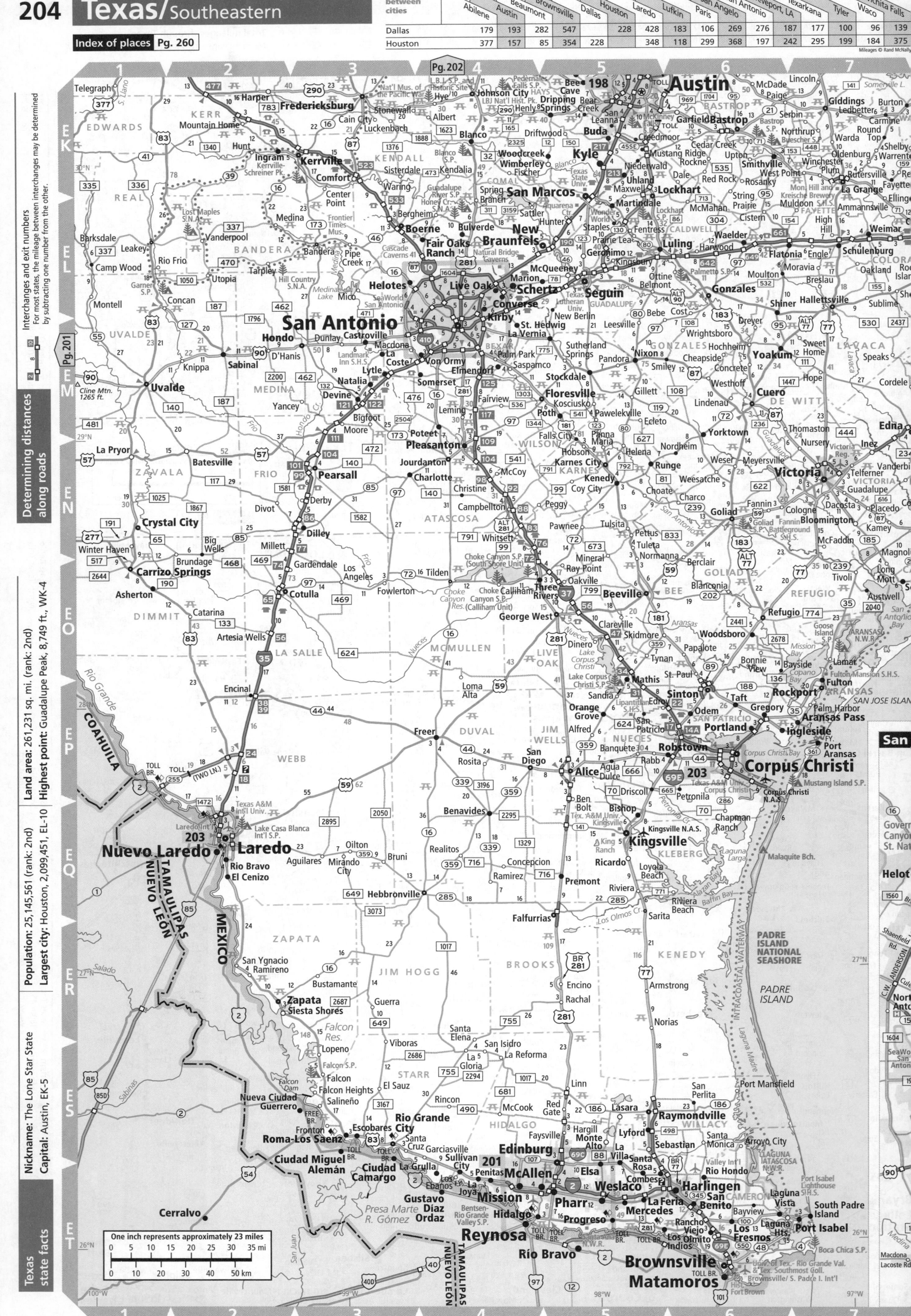

One inch represents approximately 23 miles

0 5 10 15 20 25 30 35 mi

0 10 20 30 40 50 km

Texas state facts

Nickname: The Lone Star State
Capital: Austin, EK-5

Population: 25,145,561 (rank: 2nd)
Largest city: Houston, 2,099,451, EL-10

Land area: 261,231 sq. mi. (rank: 2nd)
Highest point: Guadalupe Peak, 8,749 ft., WK-4

Determining distances along roads

Interchanges and exit numbers
For most states, the mileage between interchanges may be determined by subtracting one number from the other.

Mileages between cities	Abilene	Austin	Beaumont	Brownsville	Dallas	Houston	Laredo	Lufkin	Paris	San Angelo	San Antonio	Shreveport, LA	Texarkana	Tyler	Waco	Wichita Falls
San Antonio	250	81	280	274	276	197	154	314	380	213		406	451	309	180	341
Shreveport, LA	368	325	206	596	187	242	565	120	154	455	406		72	98	226	324

Mileages © Rand McNally

10 881 miles   30 223 miles
20 636 miles   35 504 miles

Total mileages through Texas

More mileages at www.randmcnally.com/MC

NOTE: Full route listing pp. 199-205

© Rand McNally

Central San Antonio

Bryan / College Station

Beaumont / Port Arthur

San Antonio

GULF OF MEXICO

Louisiana Pg. 90

Pg. 203

Toll Road Information: SH 130 Concession Co. (TX 130) (TxTag): (888) 468-9824; www.mysh130.com — Texas Department of Transportation (all other toll roads in Texas) (TxTag): (888) 468-9824; www.txtag.org

Road Conditions & Construction: (800) 452-9292, (512) 463-8588 — www.txdot.gov — www.drivetexas.org

Tourism Information: Texas Tourism (800) 452-9292 — www.traveltex.com

Travel planning & on-the-road resources

Mileages between cities	Blanding	Cedar City	Grand Jct., CO	Las Vegas, NV	Logan	Moab	Ogden	Page, AZ	Park City	Price	Provo	Richfield	St. George	Salt Lake City	Vernal	Wendover
Grand Junction, CO	186	335		506	363	112	319	380	286	164	240	224	389	283	140	401
Logan	388	330	363	499		313	46	457	113	199	124	239	385	82	252	199

Mileages © Rand McNally

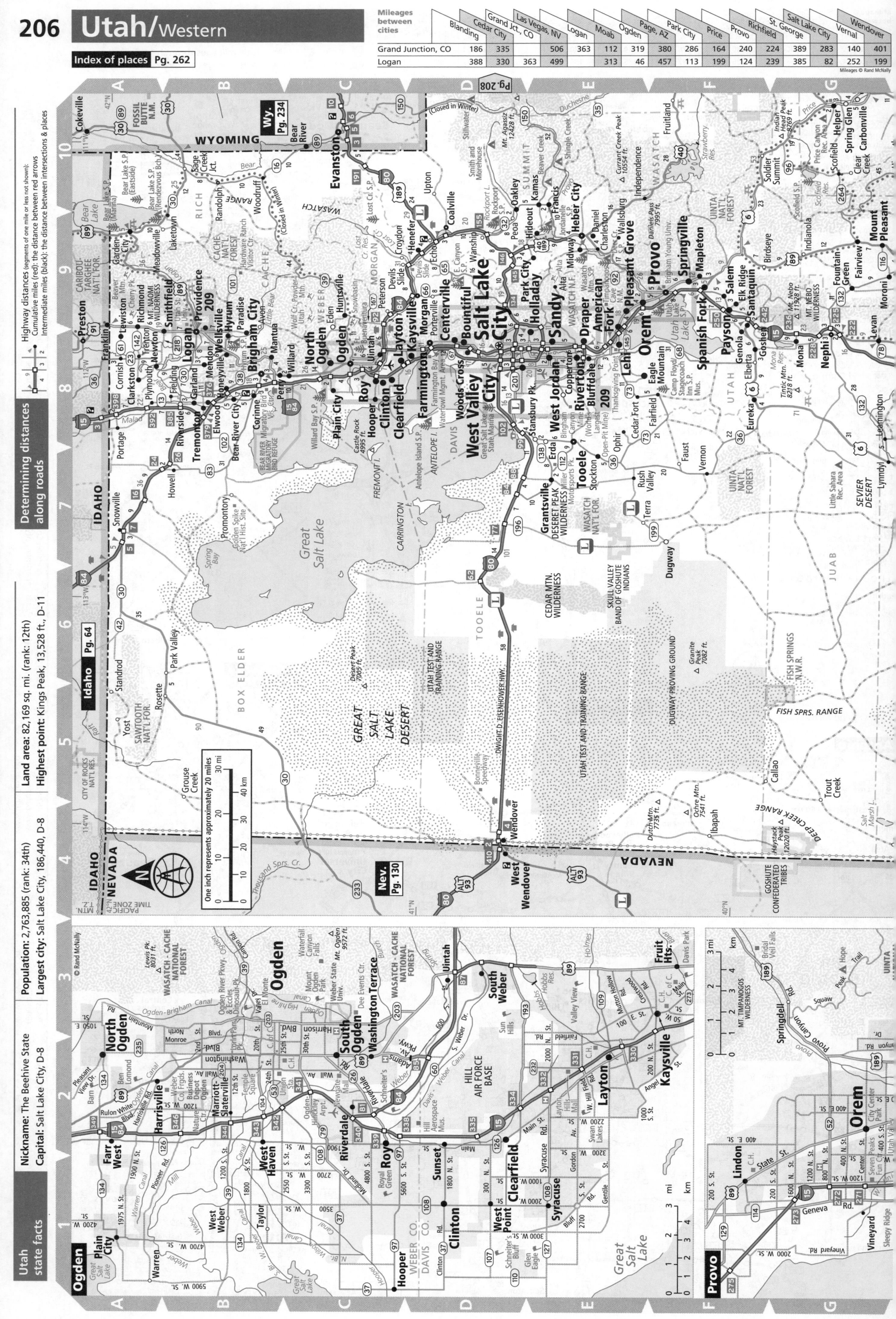

Wy. Pg. 234
Idaho Pg. 64
Nev. Pg. 130
Pg. 208

Utah state facts

Nickname: The Beehive State
Capital: Salt Lake City, D-8

Population: 2,763,885 (rank: 12th)
Largest city: Salt Lake City, 186,440, D-8

Land area: 82,169 sq. mi. (rank: 34th)
Highest point: Kings Peak, 13,528 ft., D-11

Determining distances along roads

Highway distances (segments of one mile or less not shown)
Cumulative miles (red): the distance between red arrows
Intermediate miles (black): the distance between intersections & places

One inch represents approximately 20 miles
30 mi / 40 km

© Rand McNally

Mileages between cities	Blanding	Cedar City	Grand Jct., CO	Las Vegas, NV	Logan	Moab	Ogden	Page, AZ	Park City	Price	Provo	Richfield	Salt Lake City	St. George	Vernal	Wendover
Moab	74	287	112	456	313		269	268	238	115	190	174	341	234	207	352
Richfield	249	114	224	282	239	174	194	219	166	121	115		169	159	232	270

Mileages © Rand McNally

Total mileages through Utah		More mileages at www.randmcnally.com/MC
15 401 miles	80 196 miles	
70 232 miles	84 119 miles	

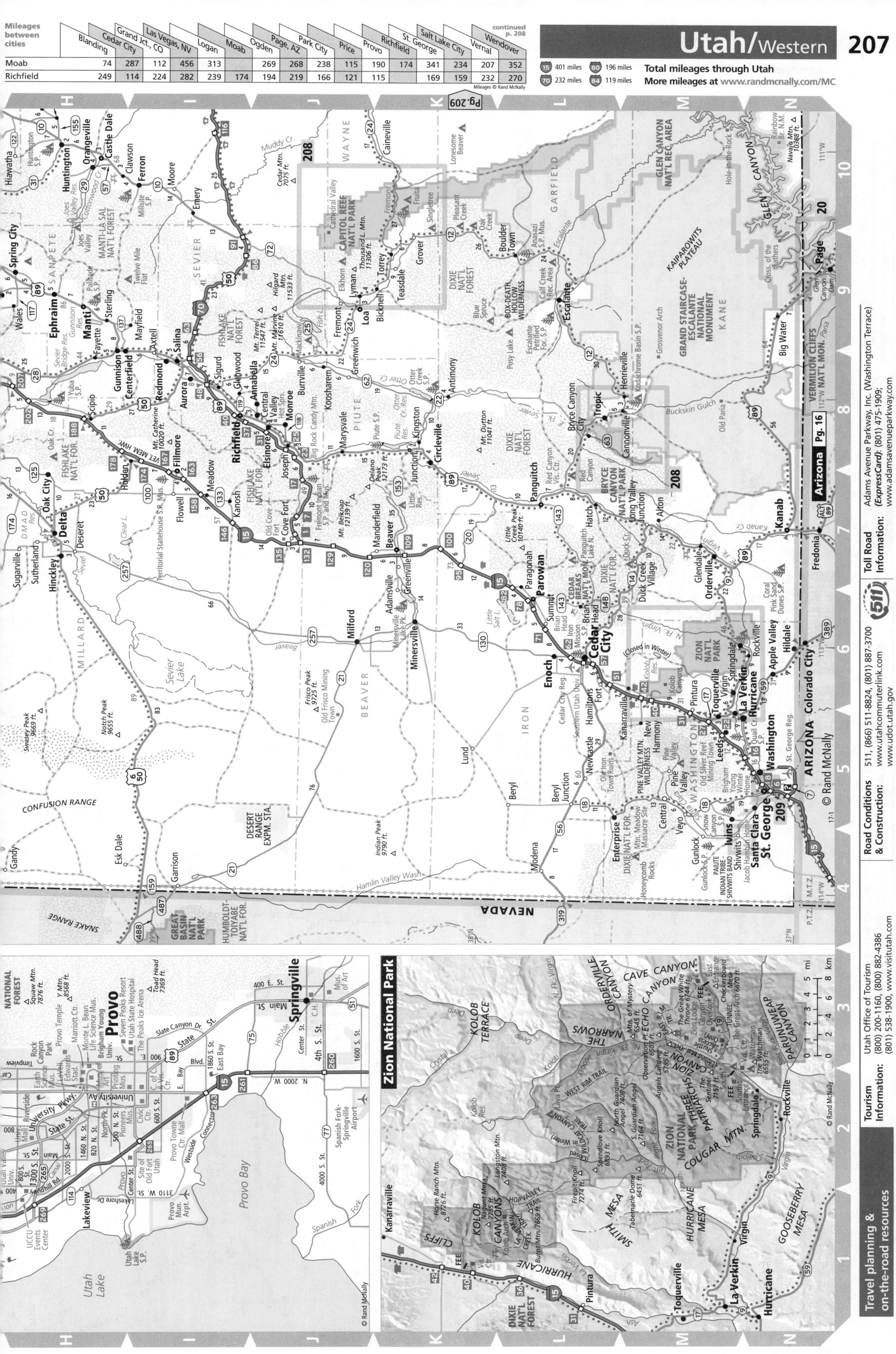

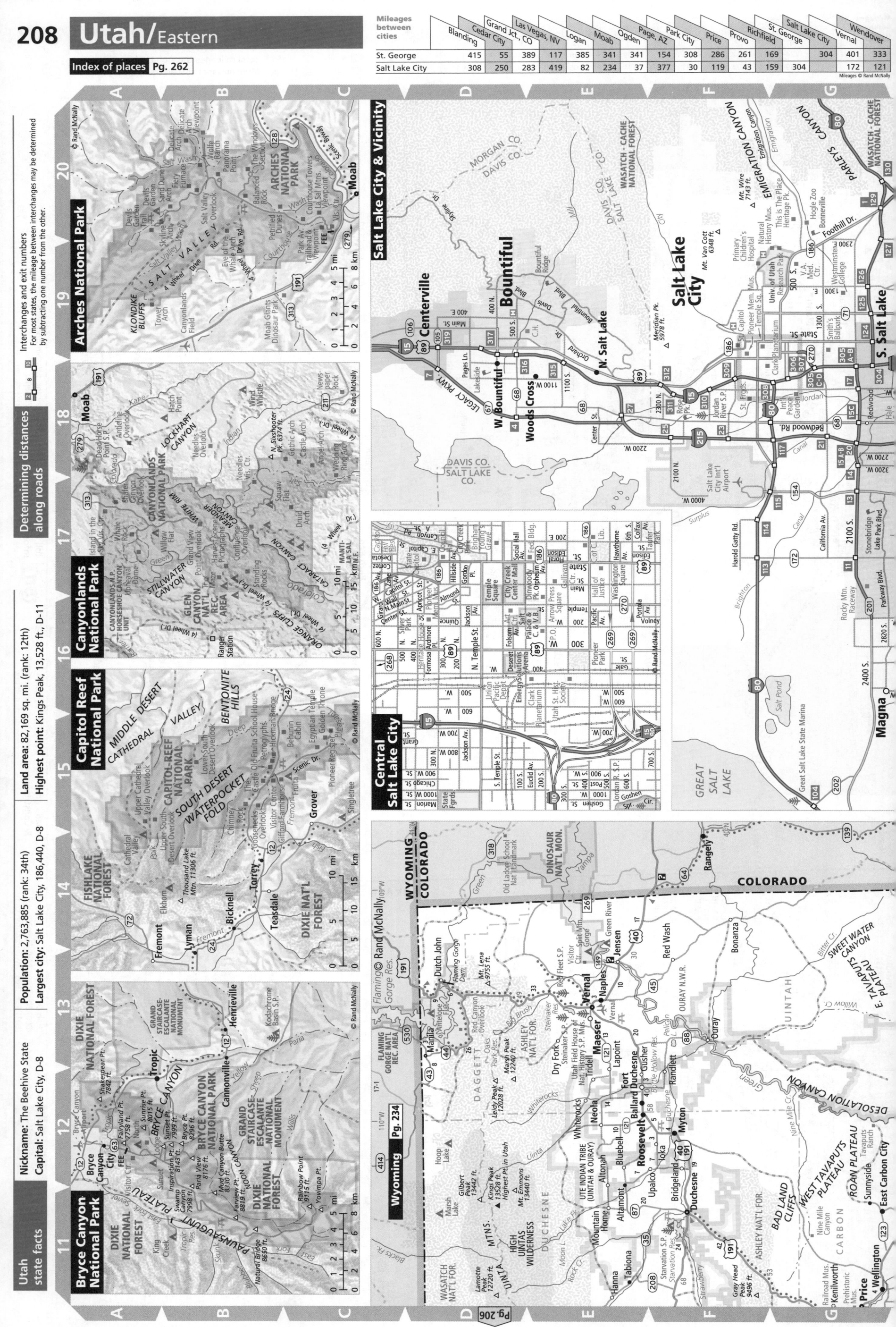

Index of places Pg. 262

Utah state facts

Nickname: The Beehive State
Capital: Salt Lake City, D-8

Population: 2,763,885 (rank: 34th)
Largest city: Salt Lake City, D-8

Land area: 82,169 sq. mi. (rank: 12th)
Highest point: Kings Peak, 13,528 ft., D-11

Interchanges and exit numbers
For most states, the mileage between interchanges may be determined by subtracting one number from the other.

Determining distances along roads

Mileages between cities	Blanding	Cedar City	Grand Jct., CO	Las Vegas, NV	Logan	Moab	Ogden	Page, AZ	Park City	Price	Provo	Richfield	St. George	Salt Lake City	Vernal	Wendover
St. George	415	55	389	117	385	341	341	154	308	286	261	169		304	401	333
Salt Lake City	308	250	283	419	82	234	37	377	30	119	43	159	304		172	121

Mileages © Rand McNally

Arches National Park

Canyonlands National Park

Capitol Reef National Park

Bryce Canyon National Park

Salt Lake City & Vicinity

Central Salt Lake City

Wyoming Pg. 234

Mileages between cities

	Blanding	Cedar City	Grand Jct., CO	Las Vegas, NV	Logan	Moab	Ogden	Page, AZ	Park City	Price	Provo	Richfield	St. George	Salt Lake City	Vernal	Wendover
Vernal	281	345	140	514	252	207	207	450	145	112	154	232	401	172		291
Wendover	426	317	401	361	199	352	154	503	150	237	161	270	333	121	291	

Mileages © Rand McNally

Total mileages through Utah
More mileages at www.randmcnally.com/MC

- 15 = 401 miles
- 80 = 196 miles
- 70 = 232 miles
- 84 = 119 miles

Mileages between cities	Albany, NY	Brattleboro	Burlington	Montpelier	Newport	Rutland	St. Johnsbury	White River Jct.		Albany, NY	Brattleboro	Burlington	Montpelier	Newport	Rutland	St. Johnsbury	White River Jct.
Albany, NY		78	151	156	230	90	187	128	Burlington	151	151		39	76	67	75	90
Brattleboro	78		151	115	164	73	121	62	Montpelier	156	115	39		78	66	37	54

Mileages © Rand McNally

Vermont state facts

Nickname: The Green Mountain State

Capital: Montpelier, E-5

Population: 625,741 (rank: 49th)

Largest city: Burlington, 42,417, D-2

Land area: 9,217 sq. mi. (rank: 43rd)

Highest point: Mount Mansfield, 4,393 ft., D-4

Determining distances along roads

Highway distances (segments of one mile or less not shown):

Cumulative miles (red): the distance between red arrows

Intermediate miles (black): the distance between intersections & places

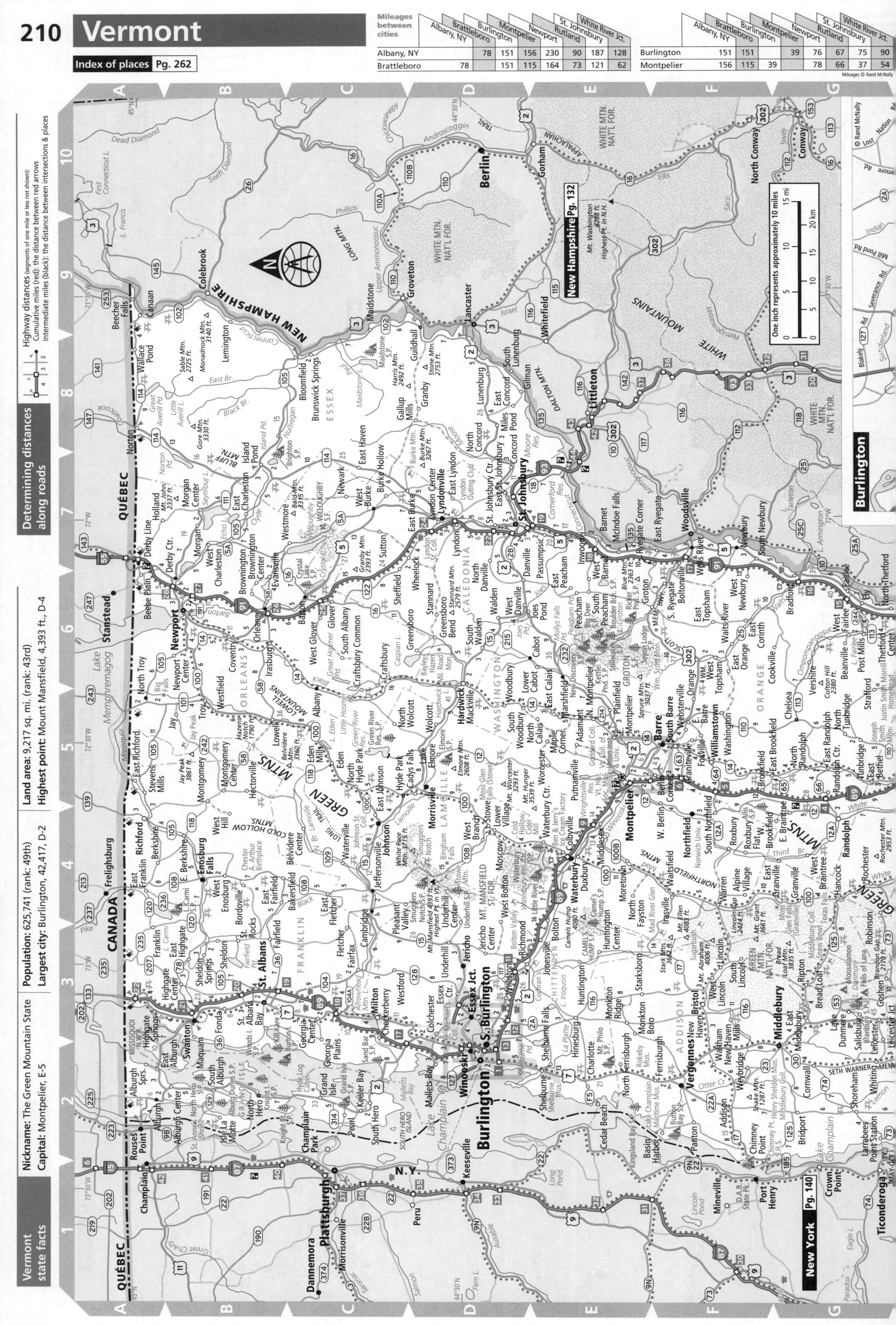

Mileages between cities	Albany, NY	Brattleboro	Burlington	Montpelier	Newport	Rutland	St. Johnsbury	White River Jct.
Newport	230	164	76	78		147	43	102
Rutland	90	73	67	66	147		105	45

Mileages between cities	Albany, NY	Brattleboro	Burlington	Montpelier	Newport	Rutland	St. Johnsbury	White River Jct.
St. Johnsbury	187	121	75	37	43	105		60
White River Jct.	128	62	90	54	102	45	60	

Mileages © Rand McNally

Total mileages through Vermont

| 89 | 130 miles | 93 | 11 miles |
| 91 | 177 miles | 4 | 64 miles |

More mileages at www.randmcnally.com/MC

Montpelier / Barre

Tourism Information: Vermont Department of Tourism and Marketing (800) 837-6668, (802) 828-3237 www.vermontvacation.com

Road Conditions & Construction: 511 www.511vt.com www.aot.state.vt.us

Toll Road Information: No toll roads

Travel planning & on-the-road resources

© Rand McNally

Mileages between cities	Chincoteague / Bristol	Danville	Emporia	Fredericksburg	Harrisonburg	Lynchburg	Manassas	Norfolk	Richmond	Roanoke	Virginia Beach	Washington, DC	Williamsburg	Winchester	Wytheville
Bristol	510	192	341	323	242	200	347	407	321	145	423	377	370	310	67
Charlottesville	253	260	131	136	66	61	65	81	157	71	117	174	116	121	128	183

Mileages © Rand McNally

Virginia state facts

Nickname: Old Dominion
Capital: Richmond, J-14

Population: 8,001,024 (rank: 12th)
Largest city: Virginia Beach, J-18

Land area: 39,490 sq. mi. (rank: 36th)
Highest point: Mount Rogers, 5,729 ft., M-1

One inch represents approximately 13 miles

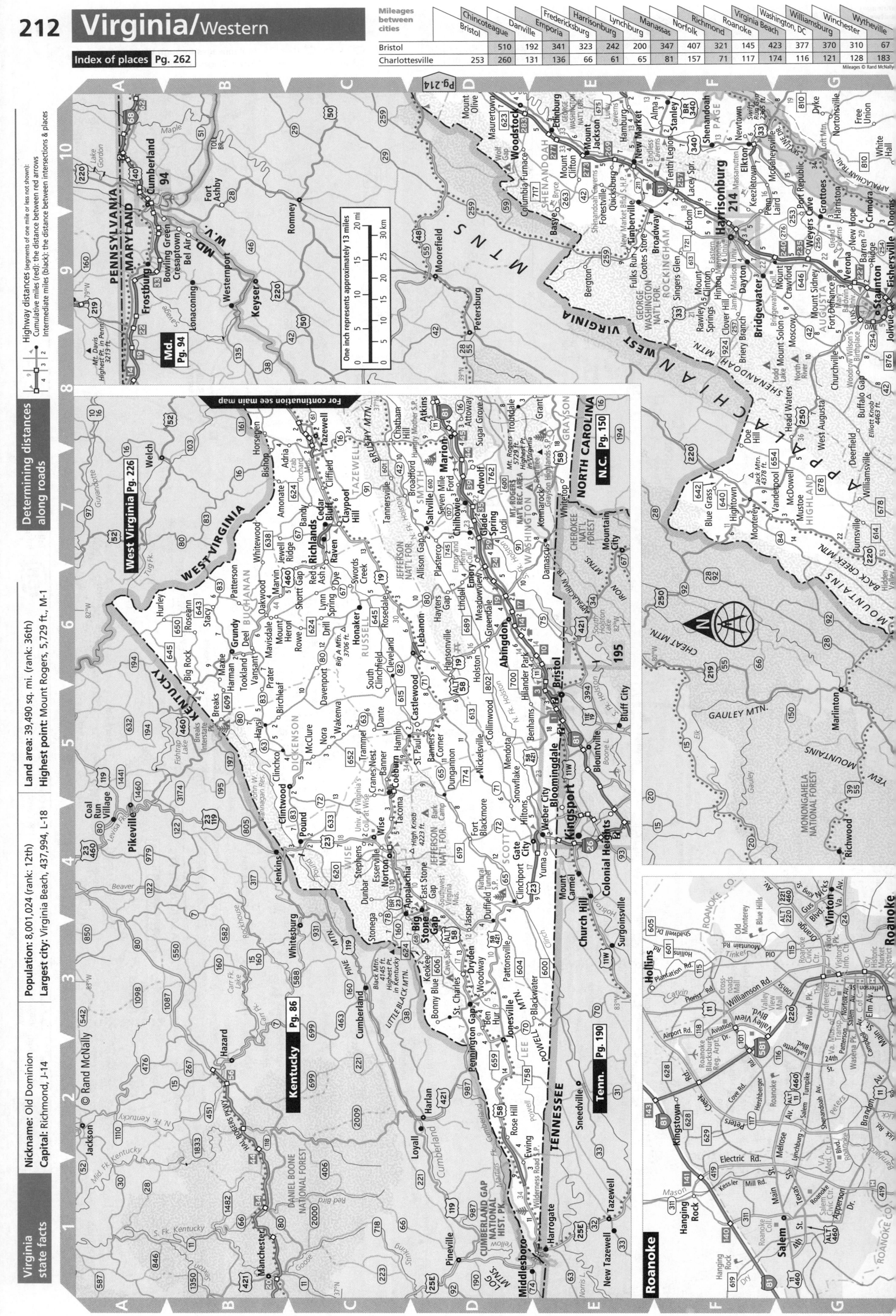

Mileages between cities	Chincoteague	Bristol	Danville	Emporia	Fredericksburg	Harrisonburg	Lynchburg	Manassas	Norfolk	Richmond	Roanoke	Virginia Beach	Washington, DC	Williamsburg	Winchester	Wytheville
Danville	192	300		115	197	163	68	215	191	144	89	206	247	199	230	124
Norfolk	407	104	191	78	139	216	189	177		91	276	17	189	41	222	340

continued p. 214

Total mileages through Virginia

64 298 miles | 85 69 miles | 81 325 miles | 95 179 miles

More mileages at www.randmcnally.com/MC

© Rand McNally

Travel planning & on-the-road resources

Tourism Information: Virginia Tourism (800) 847-4882 www.virginia.org

Road Conditions & Construction: 511, (800) 578-4111, (800) 367-7623 www.511virginia.org www.virginiadot.org/travel

Toll Road Information: (all use E-ZPass) Chesapeake Bay Bridge-Tunnel: (757) 331-2960; www.cbbt.com Chesapeake Expressway (VA 168): (757) 204-0100; www.chesapeakeexpressway.com Dulles Greenway: (703) 707-8870; www.dullesgreenway.com

N. Carolina Pg. 150

Continued on next page

Pg. 215

West Virginia Pg. 226

For continuation see map above

Mileages between cities

	Bristol	Chincoteague	Danville	Emporia	Fredericksburg	Harrisonburg	Lynchburg	Manassas	Norfolk	Richmond	Roanoke	Virginia Beach	Washington, DC	Williamsburg	Winchester	Wytheville
Richmond	321	190	144	66	56	130	114	96	91		187	105	107	50	135	253
Roanoke	145	378	89	176	192	111	53	214	276	187		292	241	238	178	77

Mileages © Rand McNally

Virginia state facts

Nickname: Old Dominion
Capital: Richmond, J-14
Population: 8,001,024 (rank: 12th)
Largest city: Virginia Beach, 437,994, L-18
Land area: 39,490 sq. mi. (rank: 36th)
Highest point: Mount Rogers, 5,729 ft., M-1

Determining distances along roads

Interchanges and exit numbers
For most states, the mileage between interchanges may be determined by subtracting one number from the other.

© Rand McNally

Mileages between cities	Chincoteague	Danville	Emporia	Fredericksburg	Harrisonburg	Lynchburg	Manassas	Norfolk	Richmond	Roanoke	Virginia Beach	Washington, DC	Williamsburg	Winchester	Wytheville
Bristol															
Washington, DC	377	168	247	174	53	132	182	32	189	107	241	205		153	76	307
Winchester	310	244	230	200	83	68	164	54	222	135	178	236	76		181	244

Mileages © Rand McNally

Total mileages through Virginia
64 298 miles 85 69 miles
81 325 miles 95 179 miles
More mileages at www.randmcnally.com/MC

Sights to see
- Agecroft Hall and Gardens, Richmond C-7
- Children's Museum of Virginia, Portsmouth M-6
- Chrysler Museum of Art, Norfolk L-6
- Colonial Williamsburg, Williamsburg F-2
- Edgar Allan Poe Museum, Richmond C-8
- First Landing State Park, Virginia Beach L-9
- Hermitage Foundation Museum, Norfolk K-5

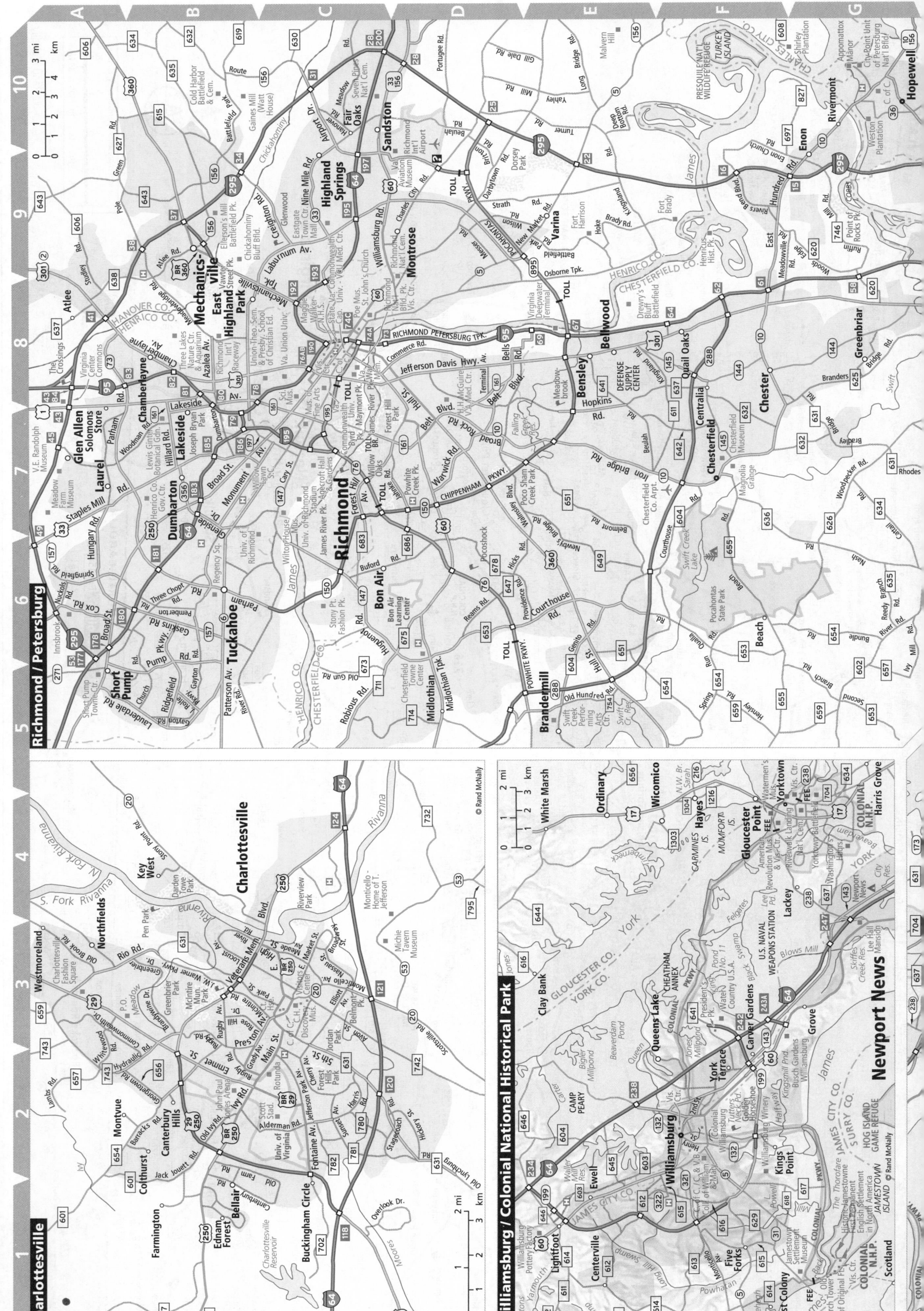

Sights to see

Hampton Roads: Norfolk / Virginia Beach / Newport News

Determining distances along roads

Highway distances (segments of one mile or less not shown):
Cumulative miles (red): the distance between red arrows
Intermediate miles (black): the distance between intersections & places

Mileages between cities

	Aberdeen	Bellingham	Colville	Kennewick	Longview	Olympia	Omak	Port Angeles	Portland, OR	Seattle	Spokane	Tacoma	The Dalles, OR	Vancouver, BC	Wenatchee	Yakima
Lewiston, ID	402	396	173	124	381	353	237	431	339	313	102	325	256	449	228	204
Portland, OR	141	261	422	213	48	113	377	228		172	351	141	83	313	291	185

Mileages © Rand McNally

continued p. 220

Total mileages through Washington

| 5 | 277 miles | 90 | 297 miles |
| 82 | 133 miles | 101 | 373 miles |

More mileages at www.randmcnally.com/MC

Oregon Pg. 170

One inch represents approx. 14 miles

0 5 10 15 20 mi
0 10 20 30 km

© Rand McNally

Travel planning & on-the-road resources

Tourism Information: Washington Tourism (800) 544-1800 www.experiencewa.com

Road Conditions & Construction: 511 (800) 695-7623 www.wsdot.wa.gov/traffic

Toll Road Information: Washington State Department of Transportation (Good to Go!) www.wsdot.wa.gov/tolling (Tacoma Narrows Bridge & SR 520 Bridge): (866) 936-8246; www.wsdot.wa.gov

511

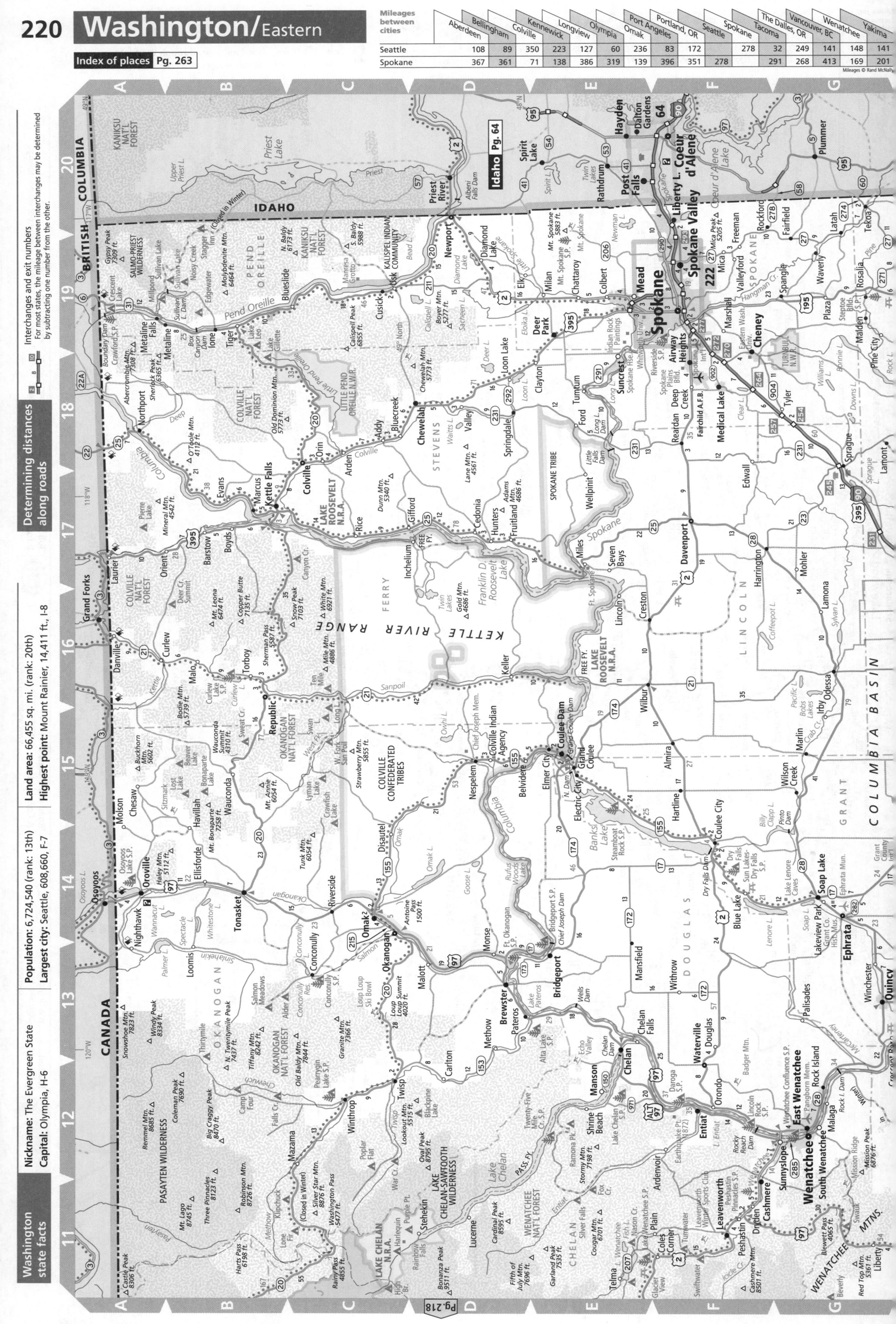

Mileages between cities	Aberdeen	Bellingham	Colville	Kennewick	Longview	Olympia	Omak	Port Angeles	Portland, OR	Seattle	Spokane	Tacoma	The Dalles, OR	Vancouver, BC	Wenatchee	Yakima
Seattle	108	89	350	223	127	60	236	83	172		278	32	249	141	148	141
Spokane	367	361	71	138	386	319	139	396	351	278		291	268	413	169	201

Mileages © Rand McNally

Washington state facts

Nickname: The Evergreen State
Capital: Olympia, H-6

Population: 6,724,540 (rank: 13th)
Largest city: Seattle, 608,660, F-7

Land area: 66,455 sq. mi. (rank: 20th)
Highest point: Mount Rainier, 14,411 ft., I-8

Determining distances along roads

Interchanges and exit numbers
For most states, the mileage between interchanges may be determined by subtracting one number from the other.

Mileages between cities

	Aberdeen	Bellingham	Colville	Kennewick	Longview	Olympia	Omak	Port Angeles	Portland, OR	Seattle	Spokane	Tacoma	The Dalles, OR	Vancouver, BC	Wenatchee	Yakima
Tacoma	77	121	362	235	96	28	248	106	141	32	291		217	174	160	153
Yakima	230	224	272	82	166	181	192	259	185	141	201	153	102	276	106	

Mileages © Rand McNally

Total mileages through Washington
More mileages at www.randmcnally.com/MC

- ⑤ 277 miles
- ⑨⓪ 297 miles
- ⑧② 133 miles
- ⑩① 373 miles

Tri-Cities: Kennewick / Pasco / Richland

Yakima

Oregon Pg. 170

One inch represents approx. 14 miles

© Rand McNally

Toll Road Information: Washington State Department of Transportation (Good to Go!)
(Tacoma Narrows Bridge & SR 520 Bridge): (866) 936-8246; www.wsdot.wa.gov/tolling

511

Road Conditions & Construction: 511
(800) 695-7623
www.wsdot.wa.gov/traffic

Tourism Information: Washington Tourism
(800) 544-1800
www.experiencewa.com

Travel planning & on-the-road resources

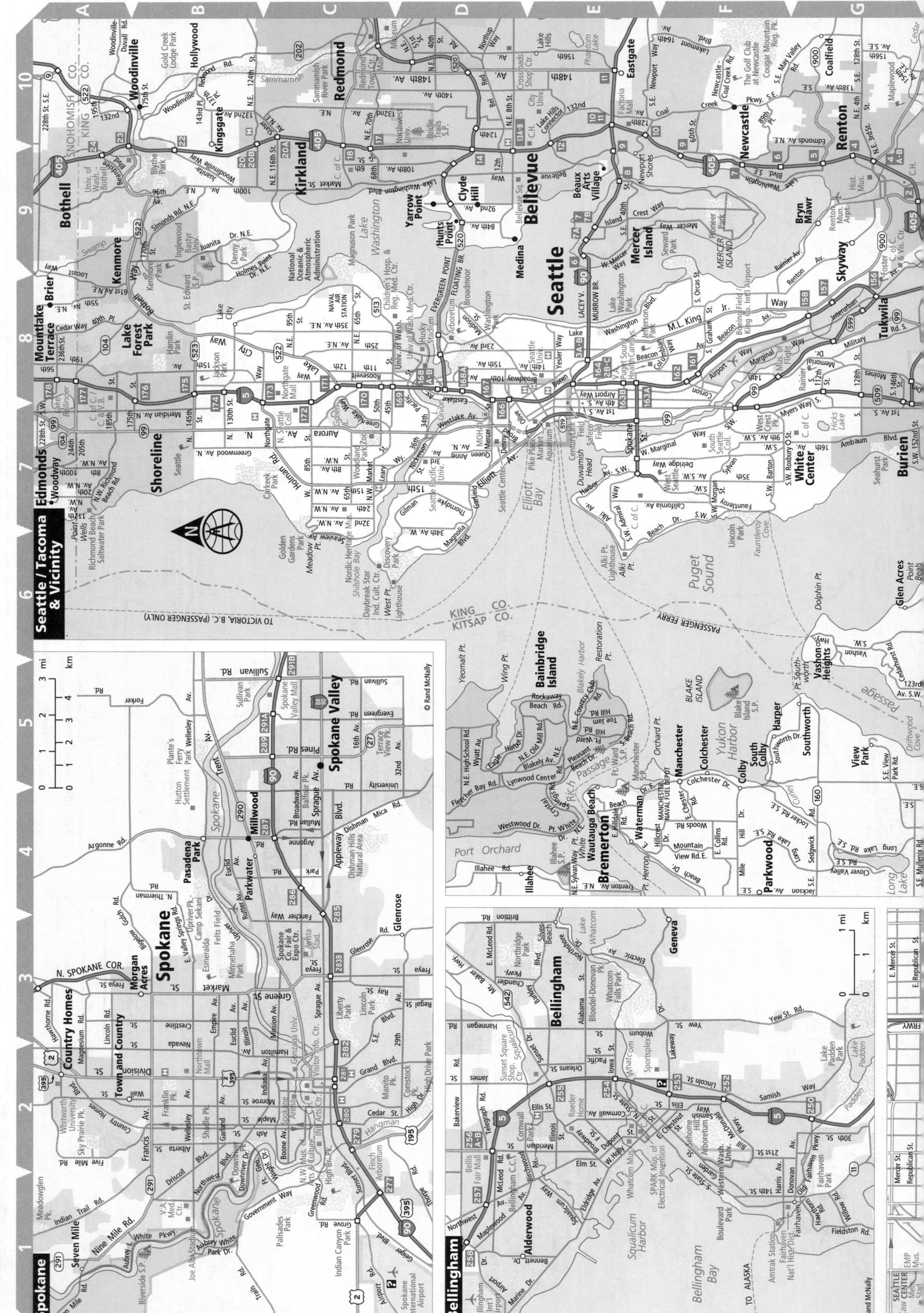

Seattle / Tacoma & Vicinity

Spokane

Bellingham

© Rand McNally

Sights to see

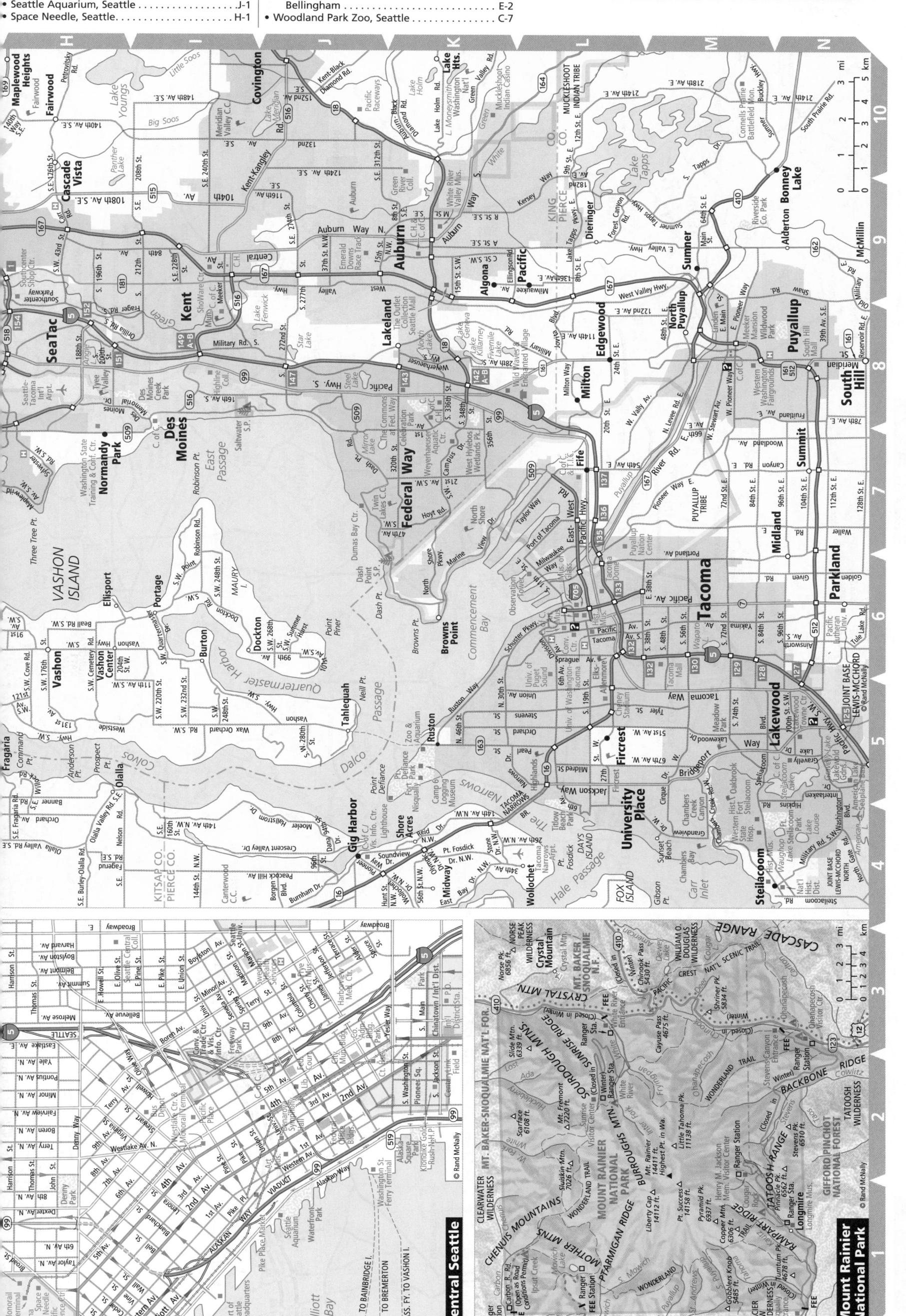

Sights to see

- Arlington National Cemetery, Arlington, Va. G-6
- Frederick Douglass National Historic Site G-7
- Freedom Park, Arlington, Va. G-5
- John F. Kennedy Ctr. for the Performing Arts .. K-3
- Martin Luther King Jr. Memorial M-4
- National Arboretum.........................F-7
- National Mall................................M-7

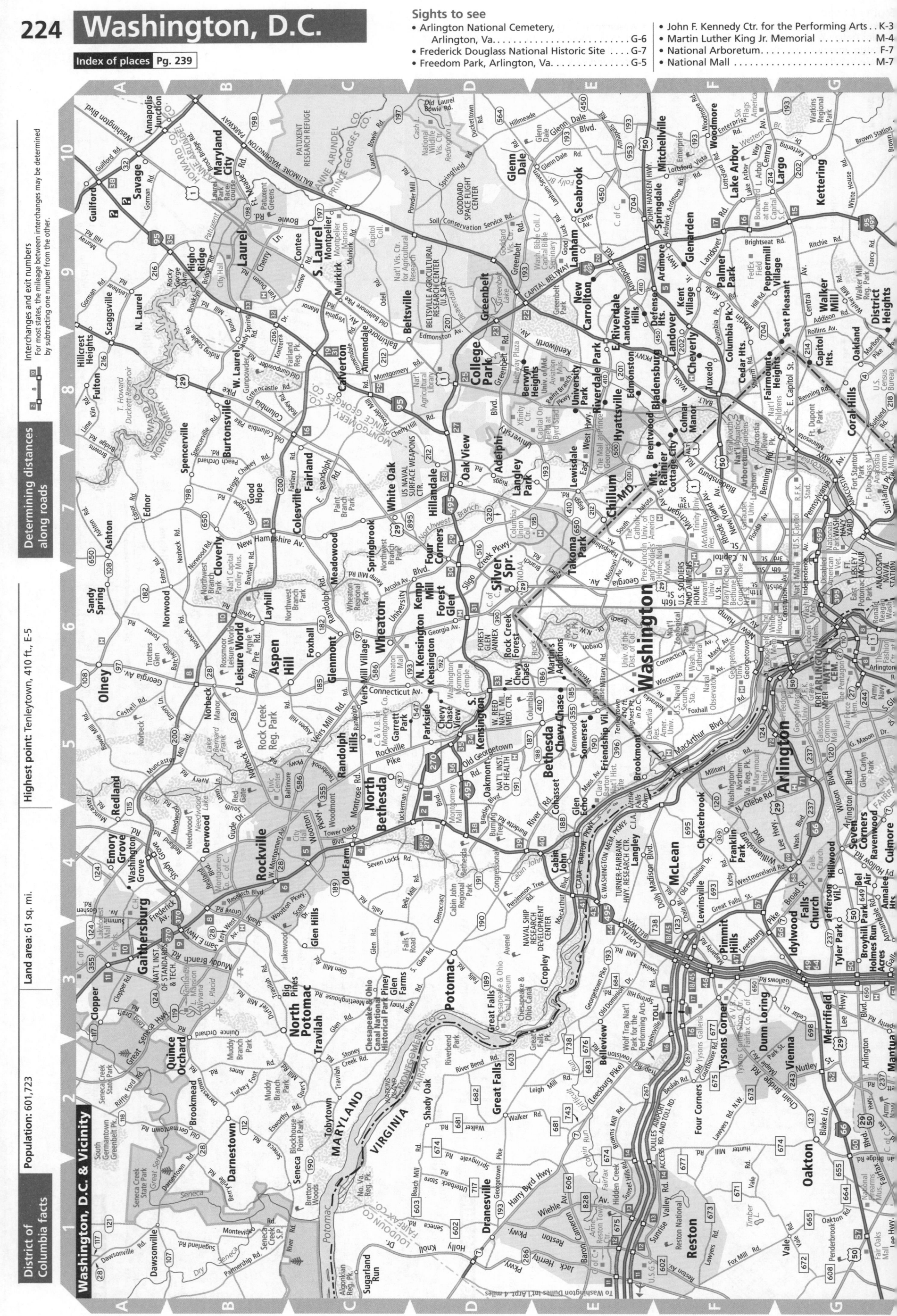

Sights to see
- National Zoological Park F-6
- Patuxent Research Refuge National Wildlife
  Visitor Center, Laurel, Md. D-10
- The Pentagon, Arlington, Va. G-6
- Supreme Court of the United States M-10
- United States Botanic Garden M-8
- Wolf Trap National Park for the Performing
  Arts, Vienna, Va. E-2

Central Washington, D.C.

The following places are identified only by a letter-number key.
- A-1 American Pharmaceutical Assoc.
- A-2 American Red Cross-D.C. Chapter
- A-3 American Red Cross-Nat'l Hdqtrs.
- A-4 Arts and Industries Bldg.
- C-1 Chamber of Commerce (U.S.)
- C-2 Commerce Department
- C-3 Continental Hall
- C-4 Constitution Hall
- C-5 Corcoran Gallery of Art
- C-6 Customs Service
- D-1 Department of Agriculture
- D-2 Department of the Interior South
- F-1 Federal Office Bldg.
- F-2 Freer Gallery of Art
- G-1 General Services Admin. Bldg.
- G-2 G.S.A. Regional Office
- H-1 Hirshhorn Museum & Sculpture Garden
- H-2 House Office Building
- H-3 Housing & Urban Development
- J-1 Judiciary Square
- J-2 Justice Department
- L-1 Library of Congress
- L-2 L'Enfant Plaza
- M Metro Station Locations
- N-1 National Academy of Sciences
- N-2 National Collection of Fine Arts
- N-3 Nat'l Museum of African Art
- N-4 Nat'l Museum of the American Indian
- N-5 National Portrait Gallery
- O-1 Office of Personnel Management
- R-1 Old Post Office
- R-1 Ripley Center
- S-1 Securities & Exchange Comm.
- S-2 Senate Office Building
- S-3 Sewall-Belmont House
- S-4 Smithsonian Discovery Theater
- S-5 Sackler Gallery of Asian Art
- U-1 U.S. Holocaust Memorial Museum
- U-2 U.S. Navy Memorial

Tourism Information: Destination DC (800) 422-8644, (202) 789-7000 www.washington.org

Road Conditions & Construction: 311 (202) 737-4404, (202) 673-6813 ddot.dc.gov

Toll Road Information: No toll roads in D.C.; see Maryland and Virginia for toll road information

Travel planning & on-the-road resources

© Rand McNally

West Virginia state facts

Nickname: The Mountain State
Capital: Charleston, J-3

Population: 1,852,994 (rank: 37th)
Largest city: Charleston, 51,400, J-3

Land area: 24,038 sq. mi. (rank: 41st)
Highest point: Spruce Knob, 4,863 ft., I-9

Determining distances along roads

Highway distances (segments of one mile or less shown):
Cumulative miles (red): the distance between red arrows
Intermediate miles (black): the distance between intersections & places

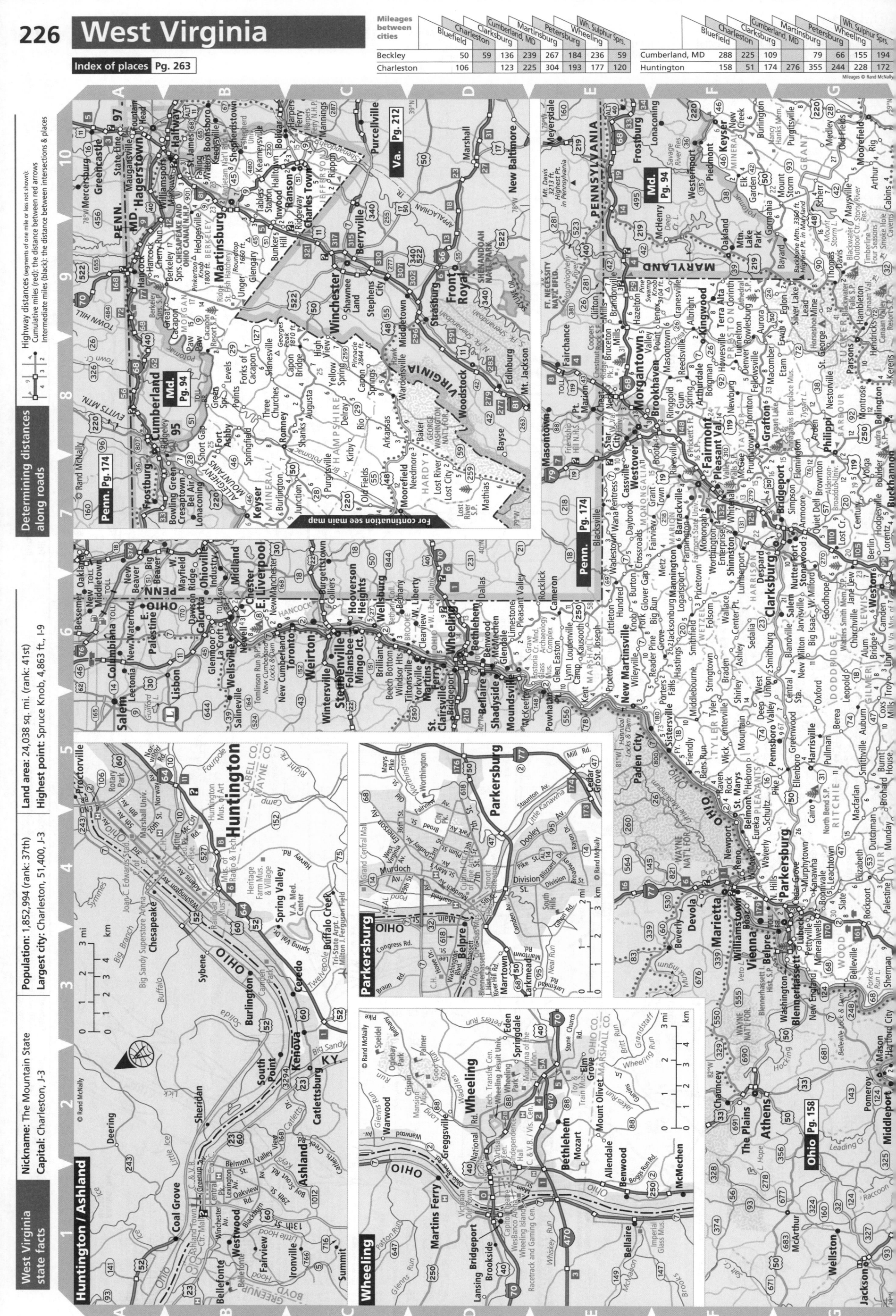

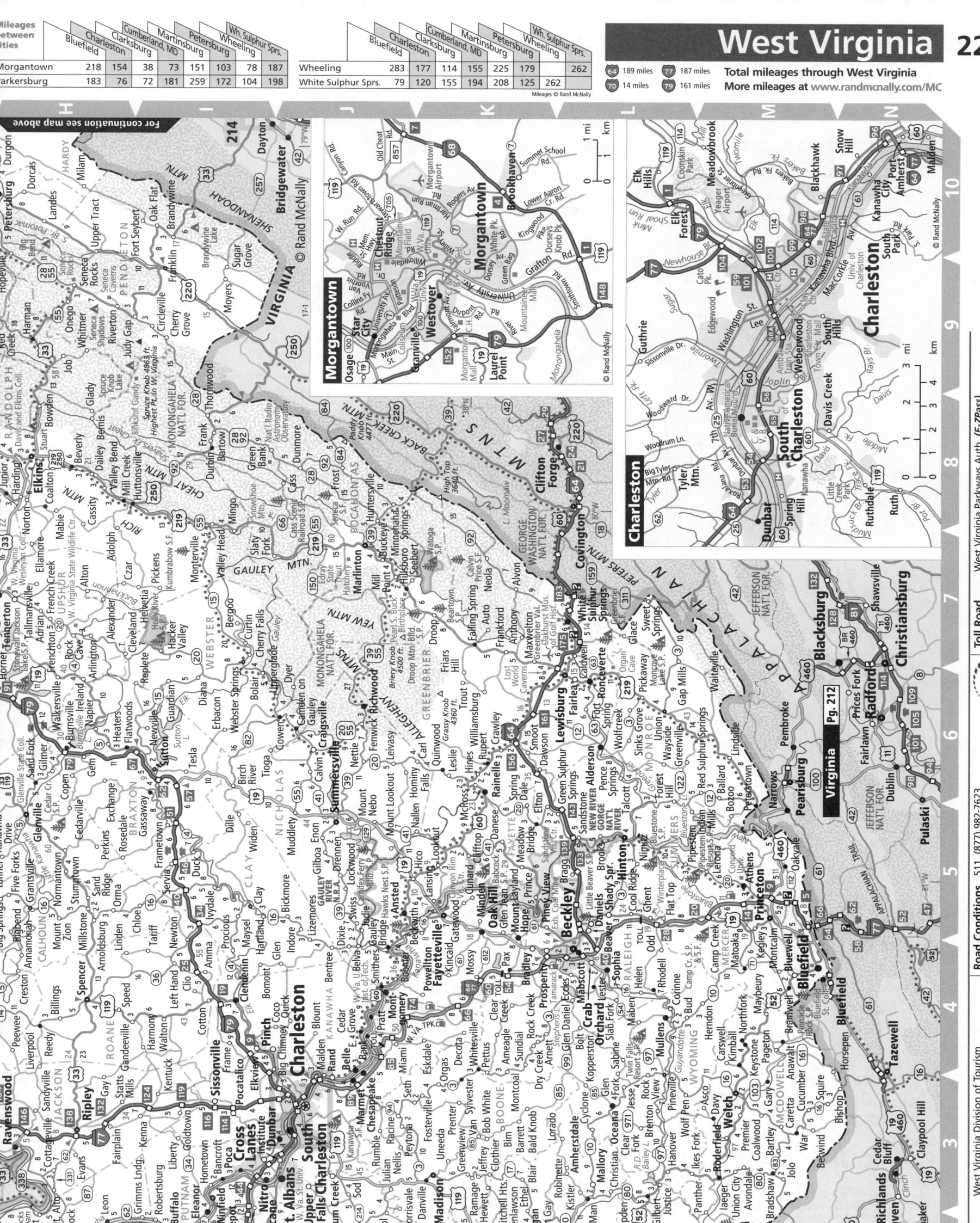

Travel planning & on-the-road resources

Tourism Information:
West Virginia Division of Tourism
(800) 225-5982, (304) 558-2200
www.wvtourism.com, gotowv.com

Road Conditions & Construction:
511, (877) 982-7623
www.511.org
www.transportation.wv.gov

Toll Road Information:
West Virginia Parkways Auth. (E-ZPass)
(304) 926-1900
www.transportation.wv.gov/turnpike

Mileages between cities	Beloit	Chicago, IL	Dubuque, IA	Eau Claire	Green Bay	Hayward	La Crosse	Madison	Milwaukee	Oshkosh	Rhinelander	Sheboygan	Sturgeon Bay	Superior	Wausau	Wisconsin Dells
Chicago, IL	96		177	315	206	420	281	146	90	175	338	145	245	462	281	195
Eau Claire	223	315	192		192	106	86	177	243	181	155	228	237	149	98	124

Mileages © Rand McNally

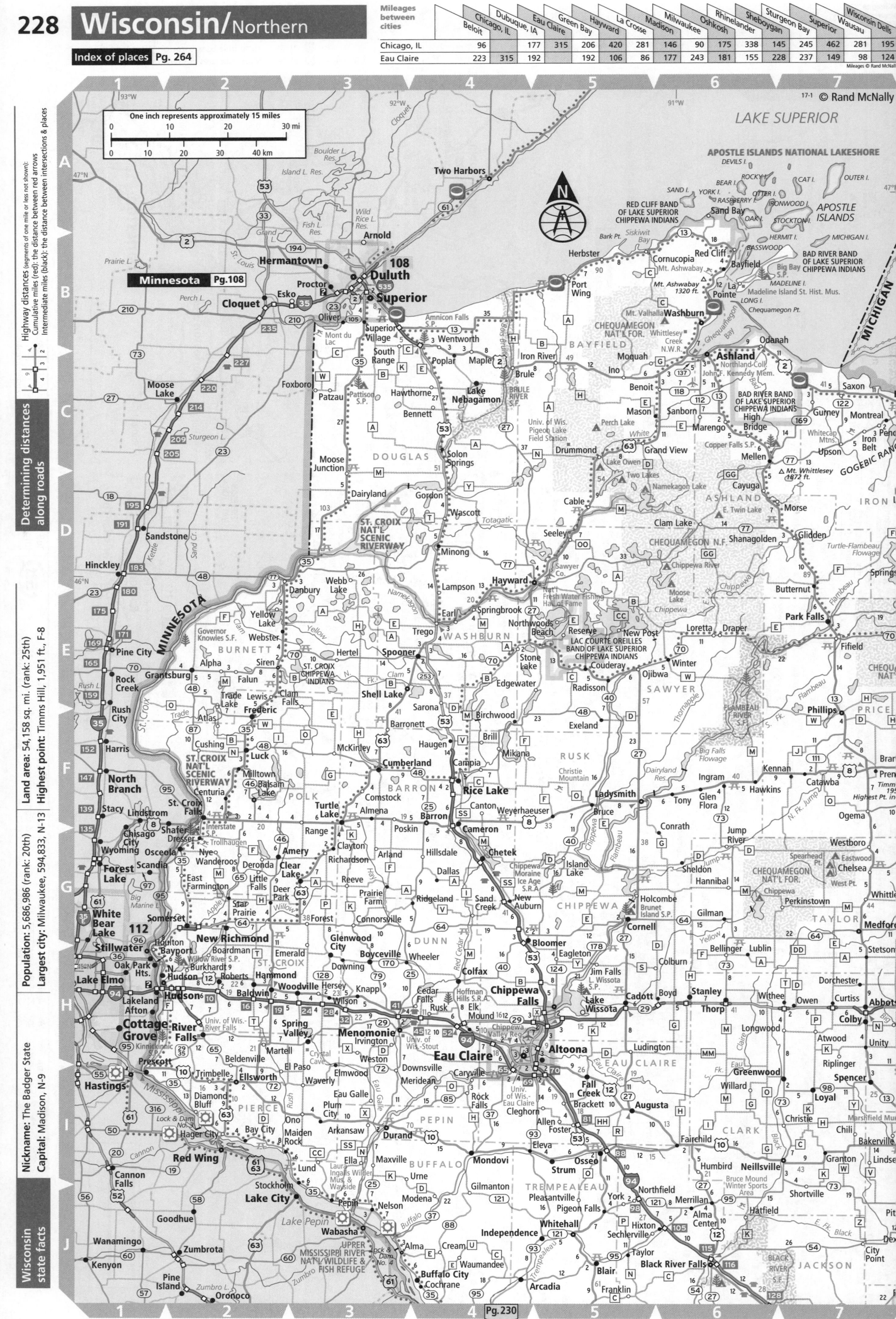

17-1 © Rand McNally

Pg.108

Pg. 230

Mileages between cities	Beloit	Chicago, IL	Dubuque, IA	Eau Claire	Green Bay	Hayward	La Crosse	Madison	Milwaukee	Oshkosh	Rhinelander	Sheboygan	Sturgeon Bay	Superior	Wisconsin Dells	Wausau
Green Bay	184	206	233	192		283	203	138	116	52	136	64	44	326	96	132
La Crosse	188	281	119	86	203	190		143	209	153	214	195	248	233	170	90

Mileages © Rand McNally

continued p. 230

39 182 miles   90 189 miles   **Total mileages through Wisconsin**
43 192 miles   94 341 miles   More mileages at www.randmcnally.com/MC

© Rand McNally

Index of places Pg. 264

Mileages between cities	Beloit	Chicago, IL	Dubuque, IA	Eau Claire	Green Bay	Hayward	La Crosse	Madison	Milwaukee	Oshkosh	Rhinelander	Sheboygan	Sturgeon Bay	Superior	Wausau	Wisconsin Dells
Madison	54	146	93	177	138	282	143		78	87	200	117	185	325	143	57
Milwaukee	74	90	171	243	116	348	209	78		86	244	54	155	390	187	123

Mileages © Rand McNally

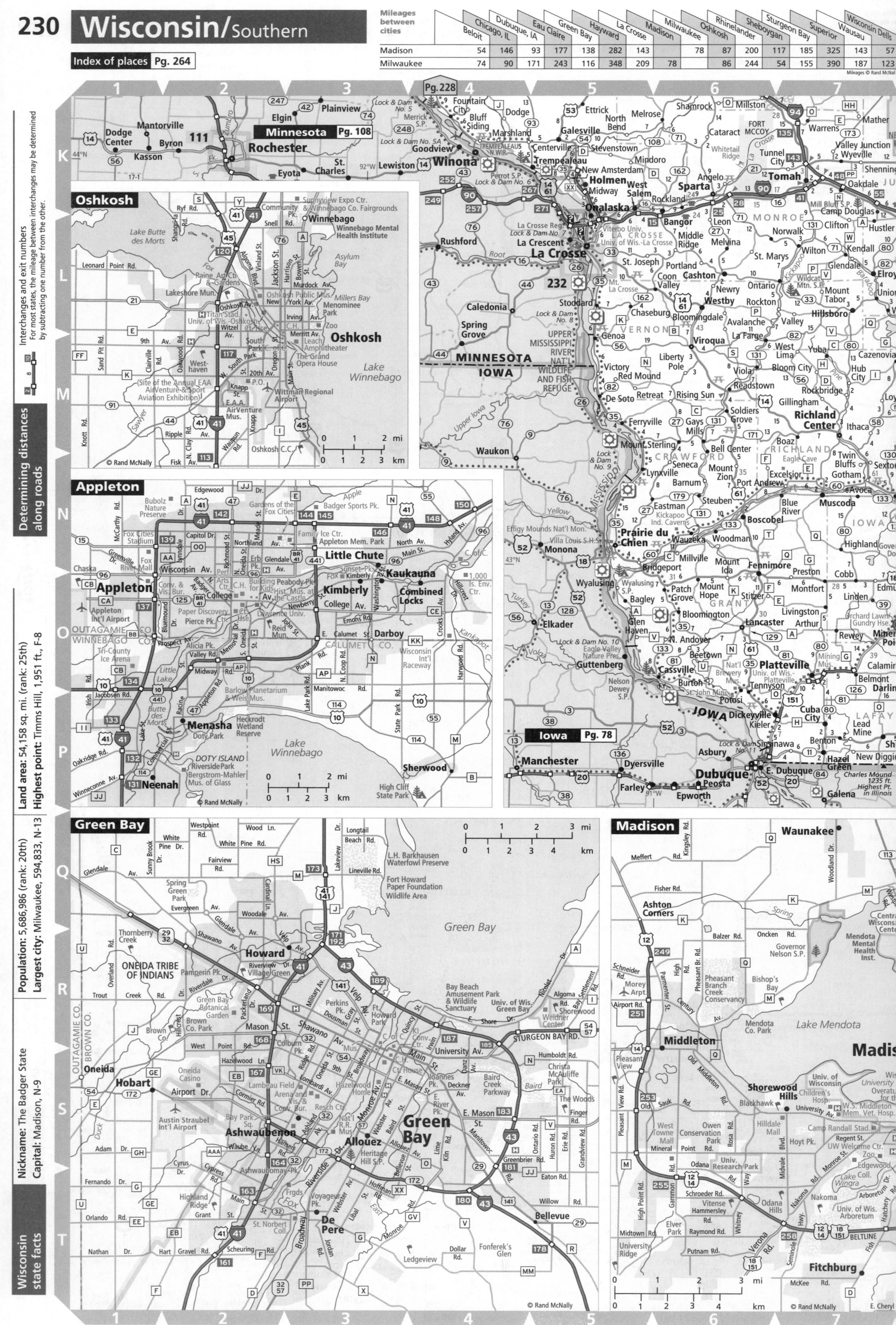

Determining distances along roads

Interchanges and exit numbers
For most states, the mileage between interchanges may be determined by subtracting one number from the other.

Land area: 54,158 sq. mi. (rank: 25th)
Highest point: Timms Hill, 1,951 ft, F-8
Population: 5,686,986 (rank: 20th)
Largest city: Milwaukee, 594,833, N-13

Wisconsin state facts
Nickname: The Badger State
Capital: Madison, N-9

Mileages between cities		Chicago, IL	Dubuque, IA	Eau Claire	Green Bay	Hayward	La Crosse	Madison	Milwaukee	Oshkosh	Rhinelander	Sheboygan	Sturgeon Bay	Superior	Wausau	Wisconsin Dells
	Beloit															
Superior		370	462	339	149	326	70	233	325	390	332	182	388	370	232	271
Wausau		189	281	239	98	96	189	170	143	187	103	59	158	141	232	112

Mileages © Rand McNally

39	182 miles	90	189 miles	Total mileages through Wisconsin
43	192 miles	94	341 miles	More mileages at www.randmcnally.com/MC

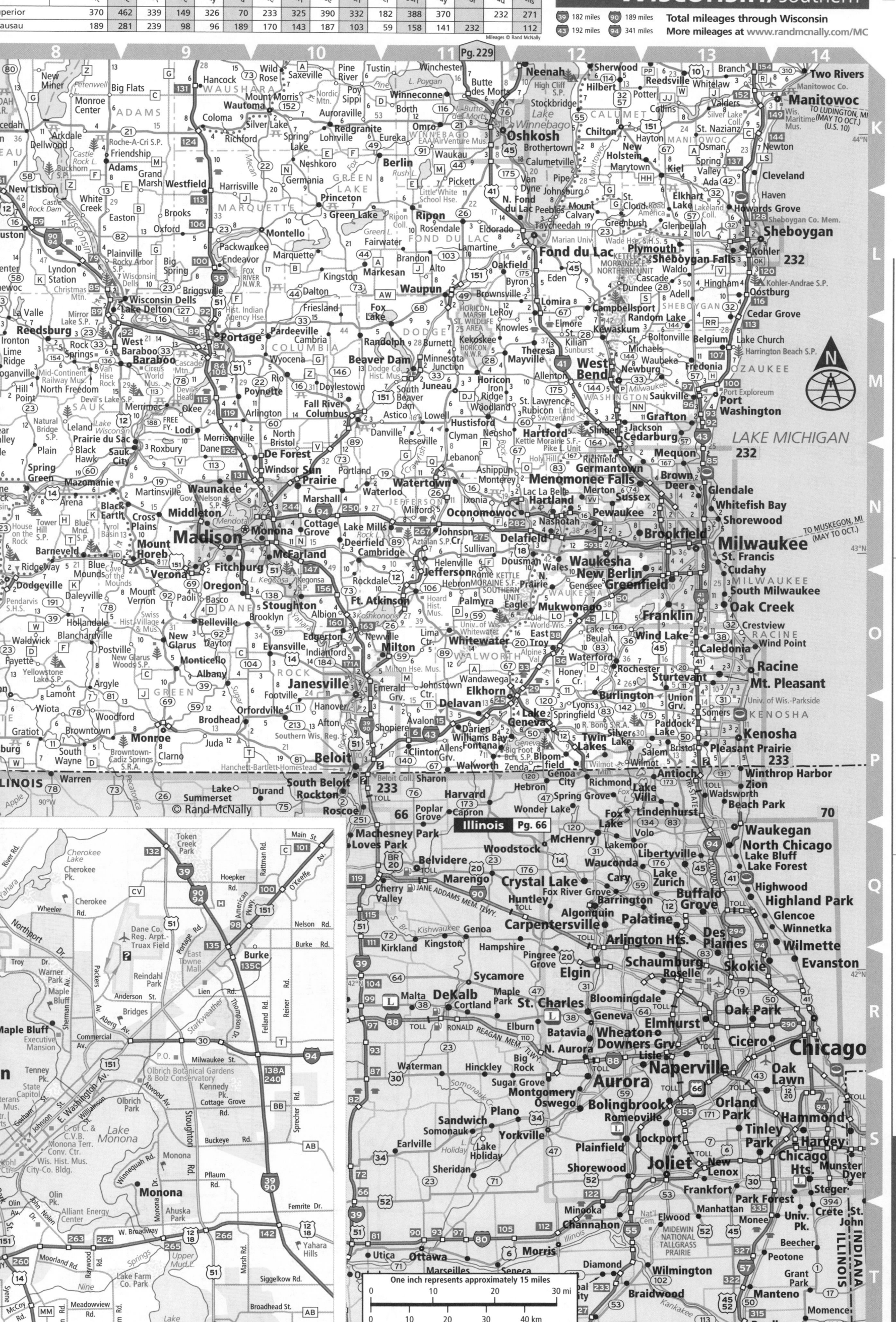

One inch represents approximately 15 miles

0   10   20   30 mi
0 10 20 30 40 km

© Rand McNally

Sights to see

- Angel Museum, Beloit N-6
- Betty Brinn Children's Museum, Milwaukee L-3
- Golden Rondelle Theatre, Racine J-10
- Harley Davidson Museum, Milwaukee M-2
- Henry Maier Festival Park, Milwaukee M-3
- J.M. Kohler Arts Center, Sheboygan F-10
- Kenosha History Center, Kenosha L-10

La Crosse

Sheboygan

Milwaukee & Vicinity

© Rand McNally

Sights to see
- Miller Brewery, Milwaukee E-5
- Milwaukee Art Museum & War Memorial, Milwaukee L-3
- Milwaukee Public Museum, Milwaukee L-2
- Mitchell Park Horticultural Conservatory, Milwaukee F-5
- Petit National Ice Center, Milwaukee F-4

Kenosha / Racine

Janesville / Beloit

Central Milwaukee

Mileages between cities	Cheyenne Casper	Evanston Cody	Gillette	Laramie	Spearfish, SD Sheridan		
Casper	178	213	325	126	147	148	219
Cheyenne	178		392	357	244	49	324	290

Mileages between cities	Cheyenne Casper	Evanston Cody	Gillette	Laramie	Spearfish, SD Sheridan		
Cody	213	392		376	250	363	148	344
Jackson	283	432	177	190	411	383	325	504

Mileages © Rand McNally

Wyoming state facts

Nickname: The Equality State
Capital: Cheyenne, M-9

Population: 563,626 (rank: 50th)
Largest city: Cheyenne, 59,466, M-9

Land area: 97,093 sq. mi. (rank: 9th)
Highest point: Gannett Peak, 13,804 ft., I-3

Determining distances along roads

Highway distances (segments of one mile or less not shown):
Cumulative miles (red): the distance between red arrows
Intermediate miles (black): the distance between intersections & places

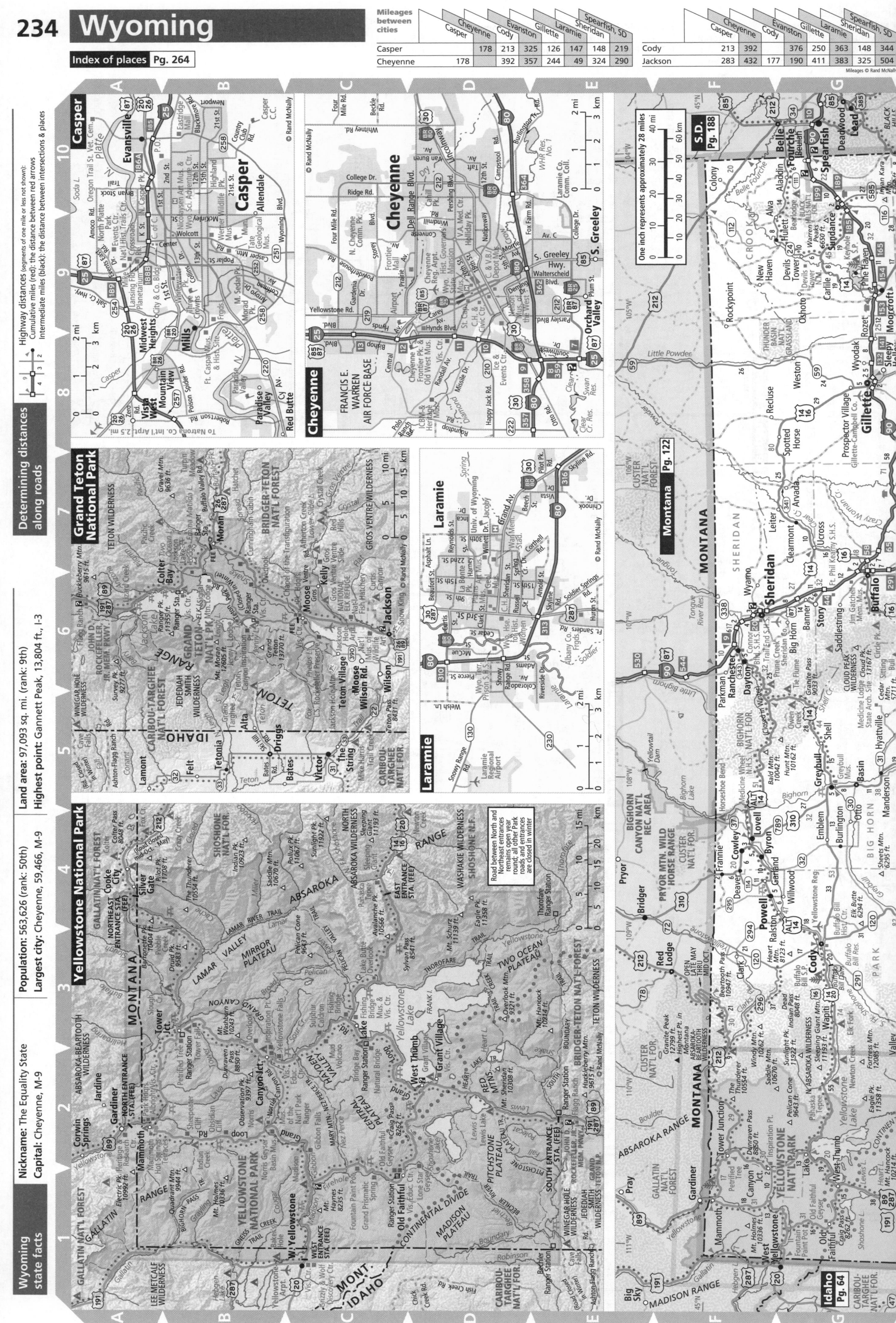

Mileages between cities	Casper	Cheyenne	Cody	Evanston	Gillette	Laramie	Sheridan	Spearfish, SD
Riverton	119	272	138	238	248	222	213	341
Rock Springs	225	257	278	100	351	207	373	444

	Casper	Cheyenne	Cody	Evanston	Gillette	Laramie	Sheridan	Spearfish, SD
Sheridan	148	324	148	473	103	294		196
Spearfish, SD	219	290	344	544	93	296	196	

Mileages © Rand McNally

Total mileages through Wyoming
25 301 miles 90 209 miles
80 403 miles 80 505 miles
More mileages at www.randmcnally.com/MC

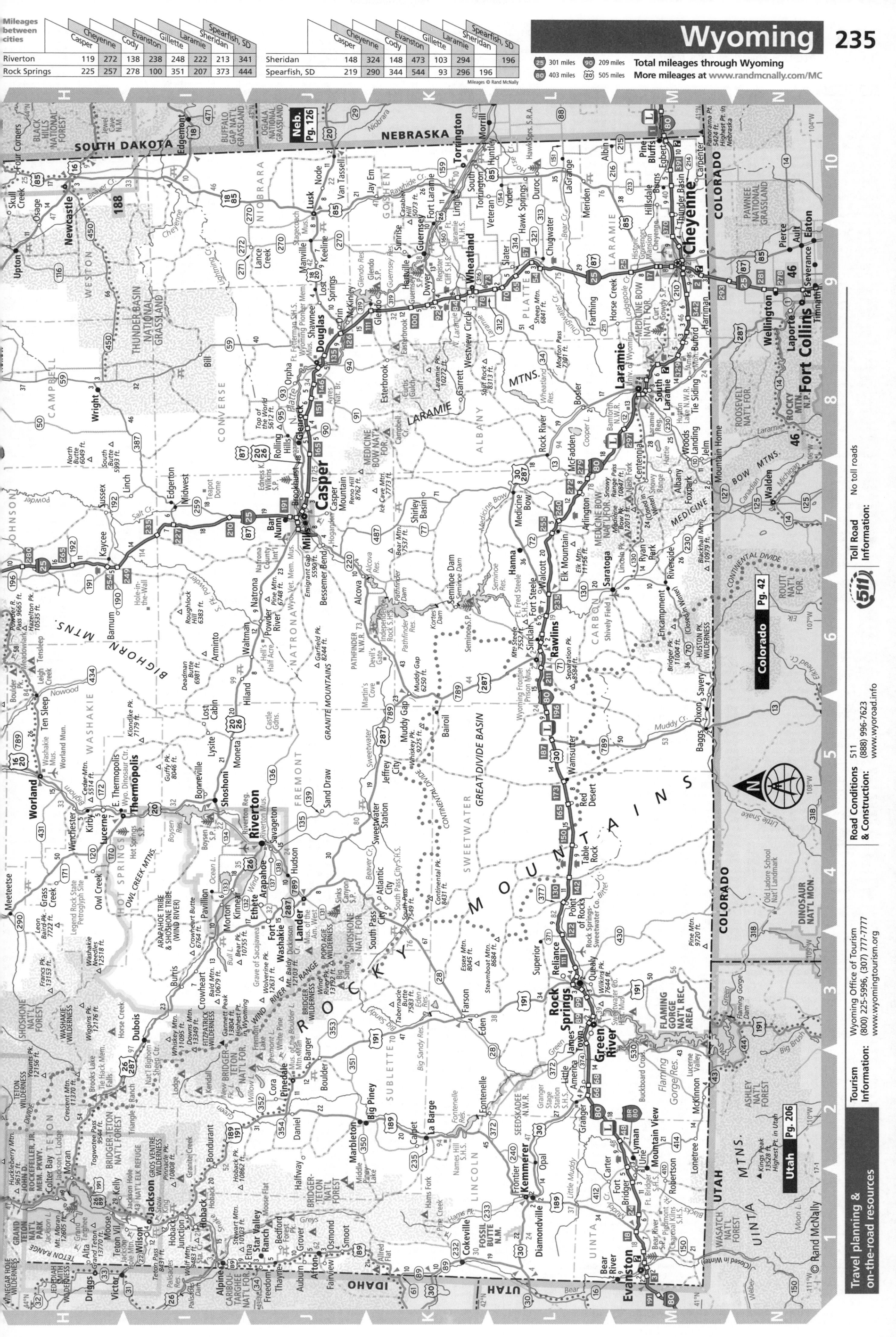

Travel planning & on-the-road resources

Tourism Information: Wyoming Office of Tourism (800) 225-5996, (307) 777-7777 www.wyomingtourism.org

Road Conditions & Construction: 511 (888) 996-7623 www.wyoroad.info

Toll Road Information: No toll roads

Colorado Pg. 42
Utah Pg. 206

© Rand McNally

United States Counties, cities, towns & places
Populations are from the 2010 U.S. Census or are Rand McNally estimates

*, †, ‡, §, ◊   See explanation under state title in this index.
County and parish names are listed in capital letters & boldface type.
Independent cities (not included in a county) are listed in italics.

*, †, ‡, §, ◊   See explanation under state title in this index.
County and parish names are listed in capital letters & boldface type.
Independent cities (not included in a county) are listed in italics.

238 California–Colorado

Freedom, 3070 ... SB-3
Freeport, 38 ... *J-2
Fremont, 214089 ... NM-6
French Camp, 3376 ... NM-7
French Gulch, 346 ... NE-5
Freshwater, 300 ... ND-2
Fresno, 494665 ... SC-8
FRESNO CO., 930450 ... SC-7
Friant, 509 ... SB-8
Fruitridge Manor ... *I-3
Fruto ... NH-5
Fullerton, 135161 ... SJ-12
Fulton, 541 ... NK-4
Furnace Creek, 24 ... SC-14
Galt, 23647 ... NL-7
Garberville, 913 ... NF-2
Garden Acres, 10648 ... *L-10
Garden Grv., 170883 ... SK-12
Garden Valley, 700 ... NJ-8
Gardena, 58829 ... ‡H-6
Garey, 68 ... SH-6
Gas Pt., 30 ... NF-5
Gasquet, 661 ... NA-2
Gaviota, 70 ... SI-7
Gazelle, 70 ... NC-5
Genesee, 150 ... NG-9
Georgetown, 2367 ... NJ-8
Gerber, 1060 ... NG-6
Geyserville, 862 ... NJ-4
Gilroy, 48821 ... SB-4
Glamis ... SM-18
Glen Ellen, 784 ... NK-5
Glencoe, 300 ... NK-9
Glendale, 191719 ... SJ-11
Glendora, 50073 ... §D-12
Glenhaven, 360 ... NI-4
Glenn, 110 ... NH-6
GLENN CO., 28122 ... NH-5
Glennville, 210 ... SE-10
Glenview, 160 ... ‡D-3
Goffs ... SG-18
Gold River, 7912 ... *G-5
Gold Run, 200 ... NI-8
Golden Hills, 8656 ... SG-10
Goleta, 29888 ... SI-7
Gonzales, 8187 ... SC-4
Goodyears Bar, 68 ... NH-8
Gorman, 50 ... SH-10
Goshen, 3006 ... SD-8
Graeagle, 737 ... NG-9
Granada Hills ... ‡B-4
Grand Ter., 12040 ... §E-18
Grangeville, 469 ... SD-8
Granite Bay, 20402 ... *E-6
Granite Hills, 3035 ... †I-7
Graniteville, 11 ... NH-9
Grass Valley, 12860 ... NI-8
Graton, 1707 ... NK-4
Grayson, 952 ... NM-8
Greeley Hill, 915 ... NM-10
Green Brae, 3400 ... ND-12
Greenacres, 5566 ... SL-5
Greenfield, 16330 ... SD-4
Greenview, 201 ... NB-4
Greenville, 1129 ... NF-8
Greenwood, 600 ... NJ-8
Grenada, 367 ... NB-5
Gridley, 6584 ... NH-7
Grimes, 391 ... NI-6
Grizzly Flat, 1066 ... NK-9
Groveland, 601 ... NM-10
Grover Bch., 13156 ... SG-6
Guadalupe, 7080 ... SG-6
Gualala, 1500 ... NJ-3
Guasti ... §E-15
Guerneville, 4534 ... NK-4
Guernsey ... SD-8
Guinda, 254 ... NJ-6
Gustine, 5520 ... SA-5
Hacienda Hts., 54038 ... ‡F-10
Half Moon Bay, 11324 ... NN-5
Hamburg, 140 ... NB-4
Hamilton Branch, 537 ... NF-8
Hamilton City, 1759 ... NG-6
Hammond ... SM-1
Hanford, 53967 ... SD-8
Happy Camp, 1190 ... NB-3
Harbor City ... ‡I-6
Hardwick, 138 ... SC-8
Harmony ... SF-5
Harris ... NF-3
Harvard ... SG-15
Hat Creek, 309 ... ND-7
Havasu Lake, 410 ... SH-20
Havilah ... SF-10
Hawaiian Gdns., 14254 ... ‡H-9
Hawkinsville, 20 ... NB-5
Hawthorne, 84293 ... ‡G-6
Hayfork, 2368 ... NE-4
Hayward, 144186 ... NM-6
Healdsburg, 11254 ... NJ-4
Heber, 4275 ... SM-17
Helena ... NE-4
Helendale, 700 ... SH-13
Helm ... SC-7
Hemet, 78657 ... SK-14
Henderson Vil., 200 ... NL-7
Herald, 1184 ... NK-8
Hercules, 24060 ... NC-15
Herlong, 298 ... NF-10
Hermosa Bch., 19506 ... ‡H-5
Herndon ... SA-17
Hesperia, 90173 ... SI-13
Hi Vista ... SH-12
Hickman, 641 ... NM-9
Hidden Hills, 1856 ... ‡D-2
Hidden Valley, 1400 ... NJ-8
Hidden Valley Lake, 5579 ... NJ-5
Highgrove, 3988 ... §F-18
Highland, 53104 ... SJ-13
Highway City ... SB-17
Hillsborough, 10825 ... NI-14
Hilt, 30 ... NA-5
Hinkley, 1000 ... SG-13
Hobart Mills ... NH-10
Hodge ... SH-13
Hollister, 34928 ... SB-4
Hollywood ... ‡E-6
Hollywood by the Sea ... †C-8
Holt ... NL-7
Holtville, 5939 ... SM-18
Home Gdns., 11570 ... §H-16
Homewood, 350 ... NI-10
Honcut, 370 ... NI-7
Honeydew, 80 ... NF-2
Hooker ... NF-5
Hoopa, 1200 ... ND-3
Hope Ranch, 1600 ... †B-3
Hopeton ... NN-9
Hopland, 756 ... NI-4
Hornbrook, 248 ... NA-5
Hornitos, 75 ... NN-10
Horse Creek ... NB-4
Hughson, 6640 ... NM-8
HUMBOLDT CO., 134623 ... NE-2
Humboldt Hill, 3414 ... NE-2
Hume ... SB-10
Humphreys Sta. ... SB-8
Huntington Bch., 189992 ... SK-12
Huntington Pk., 58114 ... ‡F-7
Huron, 6754 ... SD-7
Hyampom, 241 ... NE-3
Hydesville, 1237 ... NE-2
Idlewild, 43 ... SE-10
Idria ... SC-6
Idyllwild, 2200 ... SK-15
Igo ... NE-5
Imperial, 14758 ... SM-17
Imperial Bch., 26324 ... SN-14
IMPERIAL CO., 174528 ... SM-18
Incline, 60 ... NM-1
Independence, 669 ... SB-11
Indian Wells, 4958 ... SK-16
Indio, 76036 ... SK-16
Indio Hills, 972 ... SG-2
Industry, 219 ... §F-11
Inglenook, 50 ... NH-2
Inglewood, 109673 ... SJ-11
Ingot ... NE-6
Inverness, 1304 ... NL-4
INYO CO., 18546 ... SC-13
Inyokern, 1099 ... SF-12
Ione, 7918 ... NK-8
Iowa Hill ... NI-8
Irvine, 212375 ... SK-12
Irwin, 1050 ... NN-8
Irwindale, 1422 ... §D-11
Isla Vista, 23096 ... SI-7
Island Mtn. ... NG-3
Isleton, 804 ... NL-7
Ivanhoe, 4495 ... SD-9
Ivanpah ... SF-18
Jackson, 4651 ... NK-9
Jacumba, 561 ... SN-16
Jamesburg ... SC-4
Jamestown, 3433 ... NL-9
Jamul, 6163 ... SN-14
Janesville, 1408 ... NF-9
Jenner, 136 ... NK-3
Johannesburg, 172 ... SF-12
Johnsondale ... SE-10
Johnstonville, 1024 ... NF-9
Johnsville, 20 ... NG-9
Jonesville ... NF-7
Joshua Tree, 7414 ... SJ-16
Julian, 1502 ... SM-15
Junction City, 680 ... NE-4
June Lake, 629 ... NM-12
Jurupa Valley, 94235 ... §F-16
Kaweah ... SM-1
Keddie, 66 ... NG-8
Keeler, 66 ... SC-12
Keene, 431 ... SG-10
Kelsey, 250 ... NJ-8
Kelseyville, 3353 ... NI-4
Kelso ... SG-17
Kennedy, 3254 ... *M-10
Kensington, 5077 ... ND-14
Kentfield, 6485 ... ND-11
Kenwood, 1028 ... NK-5
Kerman, 13544 ... SC-7
KERN CO., 839631 ... SF-10
Kernville, 1395 ... SE-11
Keswick, 451 ... NE-5
Kettleman City, 1439 ... SE-7
Keyes, 5601 ... NM-8
King City, 12874 ... SD-5
Kings Bch., 3796 ... NI-10
KINGS CO., 152982 ... SD-7
Kingsburg, 11382 ... SC-8
Kirkville ... NJ-6
Kirkwood, 158 ... NJ-10
Kirkwood, 100 ... NG-6
Kit Carson ... NJ-10
Klamath, 779 ... NB-2
Klamath Glen, 290 ... NB-2
Klamath River ... NB-4
Kneeland, 30 ... ND-2
Knights Ferry, 700 ... NM-9
Knights Lndg., 995 ... NJ-7
Knightsen, 1568 ... NL-7
Kramer Jct., 200 ... SG-13
Kyburz, 150 ... NJ-10
La Cañada Flintridge, 20246 ... ‡C-7
La Crescenta, 13000 ... ‡C-7
La Grange ... NM-9
La Habra, 60239 ... §G-11
La Habra Hts., 5325 ... §G-11
La Honda, 928 ... SA-2
La Jolla ... †H-1
La Mesa, 57065 ... †I-5
La Mirada, 48527 ... ‡G-10
La Palma, 15568 ... ‡H-10
La Porte, 26 ... NH-8
La Presa, 34169 ... †J-5
La Puente, 39816 ... ‡E-10
La Quinta, 37467 ... SK-16
La Riviera, 10802 ... *H-4
La Verne, 31063 ... SJ-12
Ladera, 1426 ... NL-16
Ladera Hts., 6498 ... ‡F-6
Ladera Ranch, 350 ... §L-15
Lafayette, 23893 ... ND-16
Laguna Bch., 22723 ... SK-12
Laguna Hills, 30344 ... §L-14
Laguna Niguel, 62979 ... §M-14
Laguna Woods, 16192 ... §L-13
L. Alpine ... NK-10
L. Arrowhead, 12424 ... §B-20
Lake City, 61 ... NB-10
LAKE CO., 64665 ... NI-4
L. Elsinore, 51821 ... SK-13
L. Forest, 77264 ... SK-12
L. Hughes, 649 ... SH-11
L. Isabella, 3466 ... SF-11
L. Los Angeles, 12328 ... SH-12
L. Nacimiento, 2411 ... SE-5
Lake of the Pines, 3917 ... NI-8
Lake View Ter. ... ‡B-5
L. Wildwood, 4991 ... NI-8
Lakehead, 461 ... ND-5
Lakeland Vil., 11541 ... §K-18
Lakeport, 4753 ... NI-4
Lakeshore ... SA-9
Lakeside, 20648 ... SM-14
Lakeview, 2104 ... SJ-14
Lakewood, 80048 ... ‡H-9
Lamont, 15120 ... SG-10
Lanare, 589 ... SC-7
Lancaster, 156633 ... SH-11
Landers, 2300 ... SI-15
Larkspur, 11926 ... ND-11
Las Cruces, 70 ... SI-7
Las Flores, 5971 ... §L-15
LASSEN CO., 34895 ... NE-9
Lathrop, 18023 ... NM-7
Laton, 1824 ... SC-8
Lawndale, 32769 ... ‡H-5
Laytonville, 1227 ... NG-3
Le Grand, 1659 ... SA-7
Lebec, 1468 ... SH-10
Lee Vining, 222 ... NL-12
Leggett, 122 ... NG-2
Lemon Cove, 308 ... SC-9
Lemon Cove ... SN-1
Lemon Grv., 25320 ... †J-5
Lemon Hts., 2800 ... §I-13
Lemoore, 24531 ... SD-8
Lennox, 22753 ... ‡G-6
Lenwood, 3543 ... SH-14
Leona Valley, 1607 ... ‡M-6
Lewiston, 1193 ... NE-4
Likely, 63 ... NC-9
Lincoln, 42819 ... NJ-7
Lincoln Acres, 1650 ... †K-4
Lincoln Vil., 4381 ... *K-9
Linda, 17773 ... NI-7
Linden, 1784 ... NL-8
Lindsay, 11768 ... SD-9
Litchfield, 195 ... NF-9
Little Lake, 50 ... SE-12
Little River, 117 ... NI-2
Little Valley ... ND-8
Littlerock, 1377 ... SI-12
Live Oak, 8392 ... NI-7
Live Oak Sprs., 240 ... SN-16
Livermore, 80968 ... NM-6
Livingston, 13058 ... NN-9
Loch Lomond, 300 ... NJ-4
Lockeford, 3233 ... NL-8
Lockwood, 379 ... SE-5
Lodgepole ... SL-2
Lodi, 62134 ... NL-7
Lodoga, 197 ... NI-5
Logan Hts. ... †J-3
Loleta, 783 ... NE-1
Loma Linda, 23261 ... SJ-13
Loma Rica, 2368 ... NI-7
Lomita, 20256 ... ‡I-6
Lompoc, 42434 ... SH-6
London, 1869 ... SC-8
Lone Pine, 2035 ... SC-11
Long Barn, 155 ... NL-10
Long Bch., 462257 ... SK-11
Longvale, 50 ... NH-3
Lookout, 84 ... NC-8
Loomis, 6430 ... NJ-8
Loraine ... SF-11
Los Alamitos, 11449 ... ‡I-9
Los Alamos, 1890 ... SH-6
Los Altos, 28976 ... NN-6
Los Altos Hills, 7922 ... NL-16
Los Angeles, 3792621 ... SJ-11
LOS ANGELES CO., 9818605 ... SI-12
Los Banos, 35972 ... SB-5
Los Gatos, 29413 ... SA-3
Los Molinos, 2037 ... NG-6
Los Nietos, 8200 ... ‡F-9
Los Olivos, 1132 ... SH-7
Los Osos, 14276 ... SF-5
Los Ranchitos, 425 ... NC-11
Los Serranos ... §F-14
Lost Hills, 2412 ... SF-8
Lost Lake, 110 ... SJ-20
Lotus, 700 ... NJ-8
Lower Lake, 1294 ... NJ-5
Loyalton, 769 ... NH-10
Loyola, 3261 ... NL-17
Lucas Valley, 4000 ... NC-11
Lucerne, 3067 ... NI-4
Lucerne Valley, 5811 ... SI-14
Ludlow ... SH-16
Lynwood, 69772 ... ‡G-7
Lytle Creek, 701 ... §B-16
Macdoel, 133 ... NB-6
Mad River, 420 ... NE-3
Madeline ... ND-9
Madera, 61416 ... SB-7
Madera Acres, 9163 ... SB-7
MADERA CO., 150865 ... SB-7
Madison, 503 ... NJ-6
Magalia, 11310 ... NG-7
Malibu, 12645 ... SJ-10
Mammoth Lakes, 8234 ... NM-12
Manchester, 195 ... NI-2
Manhattan Bch., 35135 ... SJ-11
Manteca, 67096 ... NM-8
Manton, 347 ... NF-6
Maricopa, 1154 ... SG-8
Marin City, 2666 ... NE-12
MARIN CO., 252409 ... NL-4
Marina, 19718 ... SC-3
Marina del Rey, 8866 ... ‡F-5
Marinwood, 2300 ... NB-11
Mariposa, 2173 ... NN-10
MARIPOSA CO., 18251 ... SA-7
Markleeville, 210 ... NJ-11
Marshall ... NL-4
Martell, 282 ... NK-9
Martinez, 35824 ... NL-6
Marysville, 12072 ... NI-7
Massack ... NG-8
Maxwell, 1103 ... NI-6
Maywood, 27395 ... ‡F-8
McArthur, 338 ... ND-7
McCloud, 1101 ... NC-6
McFarland, 12707 ... SE-9
McKinleyville, 15177 ... ND-2
McKittrick, 115 ... SF-8
Mead Valley, 18510 ... §H-19
Meadow Valley, 464 ... NG-8
Meadow Vista, 3217 ... NI-8
Mecca, 8577 ... SK-16
Meeks Bay ... NI-10
Meiners Oaks, 3571 ... SI-9
Mendocino, 894 ... NH-2
MENDOCINO CO., 87841 ... NH-3
Mendota, 11014 ... SB-6
Menifee, 77519 ... SK-14
Menlo Pk., 32026 ... NN-5
Merced, 78958 ... SA-6
MERCED CO., 255793 ... SA-6
Meridian, 358 ... NI-6
Mesa Verde, 1023 ... SK-19
Mettler, 136 ... SG-9
Middletown, 1323 ... NJ-5
Midpines, 1204 ... NN-10
Midway City, 8485 ... ‡J-10
Milford, 167 ... NF-9
Mill Creek, 20 ... NF-7
Mill Valley, 13903 ... NL-5
Millbrae, 21532 ... NI-13
Millville, 727 ... NE-6
Milo ... SD-10
Milpitas, 66790 ... NN-6
Milton ... NL-8
Mineral, 123 ... NF-7
Mineral King ... SC-10
Minkler, 1003 ... SC-8
Mira Mesa ... †F-3
Mira Monte, 6854 ... SI-9
Miracle Hot Sprs. ... SF-10
Miranda, 520 ... NF-2
Mission Bch. ... †I-1
Mission Hills ... ‡B-4
Mission Viejo, 93305 ... SK-12
Mi-Wuk Vil., 941 ... NL-10
Moccasin ... NM-10
Modesto, 201165 ... NM-8
Modjeska, 500 ... §J-15
MODOC CO., 9686 ... NB-8
Mojave, 4238 ... SG-11
Mokelumne Hill, 646 ... NK-9
Mono City, 170 ... NL-12
MONO CO., 14202 ... NL-13
Mono Hot Sprs. ... SA-9
Mono Vil. ... NK-2
Monrovia, 36590 ... ‡D-10
Montague, 1443 ... NB-5
Montalvin Manor, 2876 ... NC-14
Montalvo ... †B-9
Montara, 2909 ... NJ-12
Montclair, 36664 ... §E-14
Monte Nido, 850 ... ‡E-2
Monte Rio, 1152 ... NK-4
Monte Sereno, 3341 ... NN-18
Montebello, 62500 ... ‡F-9
Montecito, 8965 ... SI-8
Monterey, 27810 ... SC-3
MONTEREY CO., 415057 ... SD-4
Monterey Pk., 60269 ... ‡E-8
Montgomery Creek, 163 ... ND-6
Montrose, 4100 ... ‡C-7
Moorpark, 34421 ... SI-10
Morada, 3828 ... *K-10
Moraga, 16016 ... NE-16
Moreno Valley, 193365 ... SJ-14
Morgan Hill, 37882 ... SA-3
Mormon Bar, 130 ... NN-10
Morongo Valley, 3552 ... SJ-15
Morro Bay, 10234 ... SF-5
Moss Bch., 3103 ... NJ-12
Mt. Baldy, 200 ... §B-14
Mt. Bullion ... NN-10
Mt. Hebron, 95 ... NB-6
Mt. Helix, 6400 ... †I-6
Mt. Shasta, 3394 ... NC-6
Mountain Ctr., 63 ... SK-15
Mountain Gate, 943 ... NE-5
Mountain Mesa, 777 ... SF-11
Mountain Pass ... SF-17
Mountain Ranch, 1628 ... NL-9
Mountain View, 74066 ... NL-17
Mountain View, 1500 ... NC-16
Mugginsville, 50 ... NB-4
Murphys, 2213 ... NL-9
Murrieta, 103466 ... SK-14
Murrieta Hot Sprs., 2948 ... §L-20
Muscoy, 10644 ... §D-18
Myers Flat, 146 ... NF-2
Napa, 76915 ... NK-5
NAPA CO., 136484 ... NK-5
National City, 58582 ... SN-14
Navarro, 250 ... NI-3
Needles, 4844 ... SH-19
Nelson, 150 ... NH-6
Nevada City, 3068 ... NI-8
NEVADA CO., 98764 ... NH-9
New Cuyama, 517 ... SG-8
New Pine Creek, 98 ... NA-10
Newark, 42573 ... NM-6
Newberry Sprs., 1500 ... SH-15
Newcastle, 1224 ... NJ-8
Newell, 449 ... NB-7
Newman, 10224 ... SA-5
Newport Bch., 85186 ... SK-12
Newville ... NG-5
Nicasio, 96 ... NL-4
Nice, 2731 ... NI-4
Nicolaus, 211 ... NJ-7
Niland, 1006 ... SL-17
Nipomo, 16714 ... SG-6
Nipton, 25 ... SF-18
Norco, 27063 ... SJ-13
Nord, 320 ... NG-6
Norden ... NI-9
N. Bloomfield ... NH-8
N. Edwards, 1058 ... SG-12
N. Fair Oaks, 14687 ... NK-15
N. Fork, 500 ... SA-8
N. Highlands, 42694 ... *F-4
N. Hills ... ‡C-4
N. Hollywood ... ‡D-6
N. Richmond, 3717 ... ND-13
N. San Juan, 269 ... NH-8
N. Shore, 3477 ... SK-16
N. Tustin, 24044 ... §I-13
Northridge ... ‡C-4
Norwalk, 105549 ... ‡H-9
Novato, 51904 ... NL-5
Nubieber, 50 ... ND-8
Nuevo, 6447 ... §I-20
Nyland, 2200 ... †B-9
Oak Grv., 100 ... SL-14
Oak Hills, 8879 ... SI-13
Oak Pk., 13811 ... ‡C-1
Oak Run, 250 ... NE-6
Oak View, 4066 ... SI-9
Oakdale, 20675 ... NM-8
Oakhurst, 2829 ... NN-11
Oakland, 390724 ... NM-5
Oakley, 35432 ... NL-6
Oakville, 71 ... NK-5
Oasis, 6890 ... SK-16
O'Brien, 30 ... ND-5
Occidental, 1115 ... NK-4
Ocean Bch. ... †J-1
Oceano, 7286 ... SG-6
Oceanside, 167086 ... SL-13
Ocotillo, 266 ... SM-16
Ocotillo Wells, 200 ... SL-16
Oildale, 32684 ... SF-9
Ojai, 7461 ... SI-9
Olancha, 192 ... SD-12
Old River, 200 ... SG-9
Old Sta., 51 ... NE-7
Olinda ... NE-5
Olinda ... §G-12
Olive ... §H-12
Olivehurst, 13656 ... NI-7
Olympic Valley ... *F-8
Omo Ranch ... NK-9
O'Neals ... SA-8
Ono, 60 ... NE-5
Ontario, 163924 ... SJ-12
Onyx, 475 ... SE-11
Orange, 136416 ... §I-12
ORANGE CO., 3010232 ... SK-12
Orange Cove, 9078 ... SC-9
Orange Pk. Acres ... §I-13
Orangevale, 33960 ... *F-6
Orcutt, 28905 ... SH-6
Ordbend, 80 ... NH-6
Oregon House, 300 ... NI-8
Orick, 357 ... NC-2
Orinda, 17643 ... NE-16
Orland, 7291 ... NG-6
Orleans, 375 ... NC-3
Oro Fino, 30 ... NB-4
Oro Grande, 310 ... SH-13
Orosi, 8770 ... SC-9
Oroville, 15546 ... NH-7
Otay ... †M-4
Outingdale, 400 ... NK-9
Oxnard, 197899 ... SJ-9
Pacheco, 3685 ... NC-17
Pacific ... NJ-9
Pacific Bch. ... †H-1
Pacific Grv., 15041 ... SC-3
Pacific Palisades ... ‡E-4
Pacifica, 37234 ... NM-5
Pacoima ... ‡B-5
Paicines ... SB-4
Pajaro, 3070 ... SB-3
Pala, 1050 ... SL-14
Palermo, 5382 ... NH-7
Palm City ... †M-4
Palm Desert, 48445 ... SK-15
Palm Sprs., 44552 ... SJ-15
Palmdale, 152750 ... SH-11
Palo Alto, 64403 ... NN-5
Palo Cedro, 1269 ... NE-6
Palo Verde, 171 ... SK-19
Paloma, 300 ... NL-9
Palomar Pk., 530 ... NJ-15
Palos Verdes Estates, 13438 ... ‡I-5
Paradise, 26218 ... NG-7
Paramount, 54098 ... ‡H-8
Park Vil., 100 ... SC-14
Parkfield ... SE-6
Parkway, 14670 ... *I-2
Parkwood, 2268 ... SB-7
Parlier, 14494 ... SC-8
Pasadena, 137122 ... SJ-11
Paskenta, 112 ... NG-5
Paso Robles, 29793 ... SF-6
Patrick Creek ... NA-2
Patterson, 20413 ... NN-8
Pauma Valley, 800 ... SL-14
Paxton, 14 ... NG-8
Paynes Creek, 57 ... NF-6
Paynesville ... NJ-11
Peanut ... NE-4
Pearblossom, 700 ... SI-12
Pearland ... ‡M-9
Pearsonville, 17 ... SE-12
Pebble Bch. ... SC-3
Penn Valley, 1621 ... NI-8
Penngrove, 2522 ... NK-4
Pennington ... NI-6
Penryn, 831 ... NJ-8
Pepperwood, 60 ... NE-2
Perris, 68386 ... SK-13
Pescadero, 643 ... SA-2
Petaluma, 57941 ... NL-4
Peters, 672 ... NL-8
Petrolia ... NF-1
Phelan, 14304 ... SI-13
Phillipsville, 140 ... NF-2
Philo, 349 ... NI-3
Piñon Hills, 7272 ... SI-12
Pico Rivera, 62942 ... ‡F-9
Piedmont, 10667 ... NE-15
Piedra, 270 ... SB-8
Piercy ... NG-2
Pilot Hill, 800 ... NJ-8
Pine Grv., 2219 ... NK-9
Pine Hills, 3131 ... ND-2
Pine Mtn. Club, 2315 ... SH-9
Pine Valley, 1510 ... SM-15
Pinehurst, 150 ... SC-9
Pineridge, 200 ... SB-9
Pinole, 18390 ... NC-14
Pioneer Pt. ... SE-13
Piru, 2063 ... SI-10
Pismo Bch., 7655 ... SG-6
Pittsburg, 63264 ... NL-6
Pittville ... ND-7
Pixley, 3310 ... SE-9
Placentia, 50533 ... §H-12
PLACER CO., 348432 ... NI-9
Placerville, 10389 ... NJ-9
Plainview, 945 ... SD-9
Planada, 4584 ... SA-6
Plantation, 65 ... NJ-3
Plaster City, 60 ... SM-17
Platina, 100 ... NF-4
Playa Del Rey ... ‡G-5
Pleasant Grv., 250 ... NJ-7
Pleasant Hill, 33152 ... NL-6
Pleasanton, 70285 ... NM-6
PLUMAS CO., 20007 ... NF-9
Plymouth, 1005 ... NK-8
Point Arena, 449 ... NJ-2
Point Reyes Sta., 848 ... NL-4
Pollock Pines, 6871 ... NJ-9
Pomona, 149058 ... SJ-12
Pond, 200 ... SE-9
Pondosa ... NC-7
Pope Valley, 250 ... NK-5
Port Costa, 190 ... NB-16
Port Hueneme, 21723 ... SJ-9
Porter Ranch ... ‡B-3
Porterville, 54165 ... SD-9
Portola, 2104 ... NG-9
Portola Hills, 6391 ... §K-15
Portola Valley, 4353 ... NL-15
Potrero, 656 ... SN-15
Potter Valley, 646 ... NH-4
Poway, 47811 ... SM-14
Pozo ... SF-6
Prather ... SB-8
Princeton, 303 ... NH-6
Proberta, 267 ... NF-6
Prunedale, 17560 ... SB-3
Pulga, 30 ... NG-7
Pumpkin Ctr., 520 ... SG-9
Quartz Hill, 10912 ... SH-11
Quincy, 1728 ... NG-8
Rackerby, 350 ... NH-7
Rail Road Flat, 475 ... NK-9
Rainbow, 1832 ... SL-14
Raisin City, 380 ... SC-7
Ramona, 20292 ... SM-14
Ranchita, 300 ... SL-15
Rancho Calaveras, 5325 ... NL-8
Rancho Cordova, 64776 ... NK-7
Rancho Cucamonga, 165269 ... §D-15
Rancho Mirage, 17218 ... SK-15
Rancho Murieta, 5488 ... NK-8
Rancho Palos Verdes, 41643 ... ‡J-6
Rancho Rinconada ... NM-18
Rancho San Diego, 21208 ... †J-6
Rancho Santa Fe, 3117 ... SM-14
Rancho Santa Margarita, 47853 ... §K-16
Randsburg, 69 ... SF-12
Ravendale ... NE-10
Raymond, 200 ... SA-7
Red Bank ... NF-5
Red Bluff, 14076 ... NF-6
Red Hill, 2800 ... §J-13
Red Mtn., 100 ... SF-12
Redcrest, 89 ... NE-2
Redding, 89861 ... NE-5
Redlands, 68747 ... SJ-14
Redondo Bch., 66748 ... SJ-11
Redway, 1225 ... NF-2
Redwood City, 76815 ... NN-5
Redwood Valley, 1729 ... NI-3
Reedley, 24194 ... SC-8
Requa, 180 ... NB-2
Rescue, 1200 ... NJ-8
Reseda ... ‡C-4
Rialto, 99171 ... SJ-13
Rice ... SJ-19
Richardson Sprs., 100 ... NG-6
Richfield, 306 ... NG-6
Richgrove, 2882 ... SE-9
Richmond, 103701 ... ND-13
Richvale, 244 ... NH-7
Ridgecrest, 27616 ... SF-12
Rimforest, 700 ... §B-19
Rio del Mar, 9216 ... SB-3
Rio Dell, 3368 ... NE-2
Rio Linda, 15106 ... *F-3
Rio Oso, 356 ... NJ-7
Rio Vista, 7360 ... NL-7
Ripley, 692 ... SK-19
Ripon, 14297 ... NM-8
Ripperdan, 350 ... SB-7
River Pines, 379 ... NK-9
Riverbank, 22678 ... NM-8
Riverdale, 3153 ... SC-7
Riverdale Pk., 1128 ... *J-8
Riverside, 303871 ... SJ-13
RIVERSIDE CO., 2189641 ... SJ-16
Robbins, 323 ... NJ-7
Rocklin, 56974 ... NJ-8
Rodeo, 8679 ... NB-15
Rohnert Pk., 40971 ... NK-4
Rolinda, 200 ... SC-7
Rolling Hills, 1860 ... ‡I-6
Rolling Hills Estates, 8067 ... ‡I-6
Rollingwood, 2969 ... NC-14
Romoland, 1684 ... §I-20
Rosamond, 18150 ... SH-11
Rosedale, 14058 ... SF-9
Roseland, 6325 ... *L-6
Rosemead, 53764 ... ‡E-9
Rosemont, 22681 ... *H-4
Rosemont, 800 ... †E-6
Roseville, 118788 ... NJ-7
Ross, 2415 ... NC-11
Rossmoor, 10244 ... ‡I-9
Rough And Ready, 963 ... NI-8
Round Mtn., 155 ... NE-6
Rovana ... NN-13
Rowland Hts., 48993 ... §F-11
Rumsey, 200 ... NJ-5
Running Sprs., 4862 ... SI-14
Ruth, 195 ... NF-3
Rutherford, 164 ... NK-5
Ryde, 200 ... NL-7
Sacramento, 466488 ... NK-7
SACRAMENTO CO., 1418788 ... NK-8
Sage ... SK-14
St. Helena, 5814 ... NK-5
Salida, 13722 ... NM-8
Salinas, 150441 ... SC-3
Salmon Creek, 86 ... NK-4
Salton City, 3763 ... SL-16
Salton Sea Bch., 422 ... SL-16
Salyer, 500 ... ND-3
Samoa, 258 ... ND-2
San Andreas, 2783 ... NL-9
San Anselmo, 12336 ... NC-11
San Antonio Hts., 3371 ... §D-14
San Ardo, 517 ... SD-5
SAN BENITO CO., 55269 ... SC-5
San Bernardino, 209924 ... SJ-13
SAN BERNARDINO CO., 2035210 ... SG-16
San Bruno, 41114 ... NM-5
San Carlos, 28406 ... NN-5
San Clemente, 63522 ... SL-13
San Diego, 1307402 ... SN-14
SAN DIEGO CO., 3095313 ... SM-15
San Dimas, 33371 ... §D-12
San Fernando, 23645 ... SI-11
San Francisco, 805235 ... NM-5
SAN FRANCISCO CO., 805235 ... NE-12
San Gabriel, 39718 ... ‡E-9
San Gregorio, 200 ... NN-5
San Jacinto, 44199 ... SK-14
San Joaquin, 4001 ... SC-7
SAN JOAQUIN CO., 685306 ... NL-8
San Jose, 945942 ... NN-6
San Juan Bautista, 1862 ... SB-4
San Juan Capistrano, 34593 ... SK-12
San Leandro, 84950 ... NM-6
San Lorenzo, 23452 ... NH-16
San Lucas, 269 ... SD-5
San Luis Obispo, 45119 ... SG-6
SAN LUIS OBISPO CO., 269637 ... SG-6
San Luis Rey ... †H-8
San Marcos, 83781 ... SL-14
San Marino, 13147 ... ‡D-9
San Martin, 7027 ... SB-4
San Mateo, 97207 ... NI-14
SAN MATEO CO., 718451 ... SA-2
San Miguel, 2336 ... SE-6
San Pablo, 29139 ... NL-5
San Pedro ... ‡J-7
San Quentin, 100 ... ND-12
San Rafael, 57713 ... NL-5
San Ramon, 72148 ... NM-6
San Simeon, 462 ... SE-4
San Ysidro ... †N-4
Sand City, 334 ... *M-2
Sanger, 24270 ... SC-8
Santa Ana, 324528 ... SK-12
Santa Barbara, 88410 ... SI-8
SANTA BARBARA CO., 423895 ... SH-8
Santa Clara, 116468 ... NL-18
SANTA CLARA CO., 1781642 ... SA-4
Santa Clarita, 176320 ... SI-10
Santa Cruz, 59946 ... SB-3
SANTA CRUZ CO., 262382 ... SB-3
Santa Fe Sprs., 16223 ... ‡G-9
Santa Margarita, 1259 ... SF-6
Santa Maria, 99553 ... SG-6
Santa Monica, 89736 ... SJ-11
Santa Nella Vil., 1380 ... SB-5
Santa Paula, 29321 ... SI-9
Santa Rita Pk., 170 ... SB-6
Santa Rosa, 167815 ... NK-4
Santa Susana, 1037 ... ‡B-2
Santa Venetia, 4292 ... NC-12
Santa Ynez, 4418 ... SH-7
Santa Ysabel, 100 ... SL-15
Santee, 53413 ... SM-14
Saranap, 5202 ... NE-17
Saratoga, 29926 ... SA-3
Saticoy, 1029 ... †A-9
Sattley, 49 ... NH-9
Sausalito, 7061 ... NE-12
Sawyers Bar, 100 ... NC-4
Schellville, 200 ... NK-5
Scotia, 850 ... NE-2
Scotland, 285 ... §B-16
Scott Bar, 150 ... NB-4
Scotts Valley, 11580 ... SB-3
Sea Ranch, 1305 ... NJ-3
Seal Bch., 24168 ... ‡J-9
Searles Valley, 1739 ... SE-13
Seaside, 33025 ... SC-3
Sebastopol, 7379 ... NK-4
Sedco Hills, 3078 ... §K-19
Seeley, 1739 ... SM-17
Seiad Valley, 270 ... NB-4
Selma, 23219 ... SC-8
Seneca ... NF-8
Seven Pines ... SK-4
Shackelford, 3371 ... *J-9
Shafter, 16988 ... SF-9
Shandon, 1295 ... SF-6
Shasta, 1771 ... NE-5
SHASTA CO., 177223 ... NE-6
Shasta Lake, 10164 ... NE-5
Shaver Lake, 634 ... SB-9
Sheep Ranch, 110 ... NL-9
Shelter Cove, 693 ... NF-2
Sheridan, 1238 ... NJ-7
Sherman Oaks ... ‡D-5
Sherwood Forest, 2600 ... ND-14
Shingle Sprs., 4432 ... NJ-8
Shingletown, 2283 ... NE-6
Shively, 110 ... NE-2
Shore Acres, 4000 ... NB-18
Shoshone, 31 ... SE-15
Sierra City, 221 ... NH-9
SIERRA CO., 3240 ... NH-9
Sierra Madre, 10917 ... ‡D-9
Sierraville, 200 ... NH-9
Signal Hill, 11016 ... ‡I-8
Silver City ... SM-2
Silver Strand, 1200 ... †C-8
Silverado, 800 ... §J-15
Simi Valley, 124237 ... SI-10
Simmler ... SF-7
SISKIYOU CO., 44900 ... NC-5
Sisquoc, 183 ... SH-6
Sites ... NI-5
Sky Valley, 2406 ... SG-1
Skyforest, 750 ... §B-20
Sleepy Hollow ... §G-13
Sloat, 100 ... NG-9
Sloughhouse, 350 ... NK-8
Smartville, 177 ... NI-7
Smith River, 866 ... NA-2
Smithflat, 250 ... NJ-9
Snelling, 231 ... NN-9
Soda Sprs., 81 ... NI-9
Solana Bch., 12867 ... SM-13
SOLANO CO., 413344 ... NK-6
Soledad, 25738 ... SC-4
Solvang, 5245 ... SH-7
Somerset, 160 ... NK-9
Somes Bar, 150 ... NC-3
Somis, 1000 ... SI-9
Sonoma, 10648 ... NK-5
SONOMA CO., 483878 ... NJ-3
Sonora, 4903 ... NL-9
Soquel, 9644 ... SB-3
Sorensens, 50 ... NJ-10
Soulsbyville, 2215 ... NL-10
S. Dos Palos, 1620 ... SB-6
S. El Monte, 20116 ... ‡E-10
S. Fontana ... §E-16
S. Gate, 94396 ... ‡G-8
S. Laguna ... §M-13
S. L. Tahoe, 21403 ... NJ-10
S. Los Angeles ... ‡G-7
S. Pasadena, 25619 ... ‡D-8
S. San Francisco, 63632 ... NM-5
S. San Gabriel, 8070 ... ‡E-9
S. San Jose Hills, 20551 ... §F-11
S. Taft, 2169 ... SG-8
S. Whittier, 57156 ... ‡G-10
Spalding Tract, 178 ... NE-9
Spanish Ranch, 170 ... NG-8
Spreckels, 673 ... *N-5
Spring Gdn., 16 ... NG-9
Spring Valley, 28205 ... SN-14
Springville, 934 ... SD-10
Squaw Valley, 3162 ... SC-9
Stallion Sprs., 2488 ... SG-10
Standish, 180 ... NF-9
STANISLAUS CO., 514453 ... SA-4
Stanton, 38186 ... ‡I-10
Stevinson, 313 ... NN-8
Stewarts Pt., 100 ... NJ-3
Stinson Bch., 632 ... NL-4
Stirling City, 295 ... NG-7
Stockton, 291707 ... NL-7
Stonyford, 149 ... NH-5
Storrie, 4 ... NG-7
Stovepipe Wells, 30 ... SC-13
Stratford, 1277 ... SD-7
Strathmore, 2819 ... SD-9
Strawberry, 5393 ... ND-12
Strawberry, 86 ... NL-10
Strawberry Valley, 100 ... NH-8
Studio City ... ‡D-5
Suisun City, 28111 ... NL-6
Sultana, 775 ... SC-9
Summerland, 1448 ... SI-8
Sun Valley ... ‡C-6
Sunfair ... SF-2
Sunland ... ‡B-6
Sunnyside, 4235 ... SC-20
Sunnyside, 1000 ... †K-5
Sunnyvale, 140081 ... NL-17
Sunol, 913 ... NI-19
Sunset Bch., 971 ... ‡J-9
Surf ... SH-6
Surfside ... ‡J-9
Susanville, 17947 ... NF-9
Sutter, 2904 ... NI-6
SUTTER CO., 94737 ... NI-6
Sutter Creek, 2501 ... NK-8
Swanton ... SB-2
Sycamore ... NI-6
Sylmar ... ‡B-4
Sylvia Pk., 600 ... ‡D-3
Taft, 9327 ... SG-8
Taft Hts., 1949 ... SG-8
Tahoe City, 700 ... NI-10
Tahoe Pines, 110 ... NI-10
Tahoe Vista, 1433 ... NI-10
Tahoma, 1191 ... NI-10
Talmage, 1130 ... NI-3
Tamalpais Valley, 7000 ... NE-12
Tara Hills, 5126 ... NC-14
Tarpey Vil., 3888 ... SB-20
Tarzana ... ‡D-4
Tassajara Hot Sprs. ... SD-4
Taylorsville, 140 ... NG-8
Tecopa, 150 ... SE-16
Tecopa Hot Sprs., 50 ... SE-16
Tehachapi, 14414 ... SG-11
Tehama, 418 ... NG-6
TEHAMA CO., 63463 ... NG-5
Temecula, 100097 ... SK-14
Temescal Valley, 22535 ... §I-16
Temple City, 35558 ... ‡E-9
Templeton, 7674 ... SF-6
Tennant, 41 ... NB-6
Terminous, 381 ... NL-7
Termo ... ND-9
Terra Bella, 3310 ... SE-9
Thermal, 2865 ... SK-16
Thermalito, 6646 ... NH-7
Thornton, 1131 ... NL-7
Thousand Oaks, 126683 ... SJ-10
Thousand Palms, 7715 ... SJ-15
Three Rivers, 2182 ... SC-10
Three Rocks, 246 ... SC-6
Tiburon, 8962 ... NM-5
Tionesta, 30 ... NB-8
Tipton, 2543 ... SD-9
Tollhouse, 400 ... SB-8
Tomales, 204 ... NK-4
Toms Place, 170 ... NM-13
Topanga, 8289 ... ‡E-3
Topanga Pk., 600 ... ‡D-2
Topaz, 50 ... NK-11
Torrance, 145438 ... SK-11
Trabuco Canyon, 800 ... §K-15
Tracy, 82922 ... NM-7
Tranquillity, 799 ... SC-7
Traver, 713 ... SC-8
Tres Pinos, 476 ... SB-4
Trimmer ... SB-9
Trinidad, 367 ... ND-2
Trinity Ctr., 267 ... ND-5
TRINITY CO., 13786 ... NE-4
Trinity Vil., 297 ... ND-3
Truckee, 16180 ... NI-10
Tujunga ... ‡B-7
Tulare, 59278 ... SD-9
TULARE CO., 442179 ... SD-9
Tulelake, 1010 ... NA-7
Tuolumne, 1779 ... NL-10
TUOLUMNE CO., 55365 ... NM-9
Turlock, 68549 ... NN-8
Tustin, 75540 ... §J-12
Tuttle, 103 ... SA-6
Tuttletown, 668 ... NL-9
Twain, 82 ... NG-8
Twain Harte, 2226 ... NL-10
Twentynine Palms, 25048 ... SJ-16
Twin Bridges ... NJ-10
Twin Peaks, 2100 ... §B-19
Ukiah, 16075 ... NI-3
Union City, 69516 ... NI-16
University City ... †G-2
Upland, 73732 ... SJ-12
Upper Lake, 1052 ... NI-4
Vacaville, 92428 ... NK-6
Valinda, 22822 ... §E-11
Valle Vista, 14578 ... SK-14
Vallecito, 442 ... NL-9
Vallejo, 115942 ... NL-5
Valley Acres, 527 ... SG-8
Valley Ctr., 9277 ... SL-14
Valley Ford, 147 ... NK-4
Valley Home, 228 ... NM-8
Valley Sprs., 3553 ... NL-8
Valyermo, 100 ... SI-12
Van Nuys ... ‡C-5
Vandenberg Vil., 6497 ... SH-6
Venice ... ‡F-4
Ventucopa, 50 ... SH-8
Ventura, 106433 ... SI-9
VENTURA CO., 823318 ... SH-9
Verdemont ... §C-18
Vernalis ... NM-7
Vernon, 112 ... ‡F-7
Victor, 293 ... NL-8
Victorville, 115903 ... SI-13
Vidal ... SI-20
Vidal Jct. ... SI-19
View Pk., 5500 ... ‡F-6
Villa Pk., 5812 ... §I-12
Vina, 237 ... NG-6
Vincent, 15922 ... SI-11
Vine Hill, 3761 ... NC-16
Vineyard, 24836 ... *J-4
Vinton, 155 ... NG-10
Viola, 30 ... NE-7
Visalia, 124442 ... SD-9
Vista, 93834 ... SL-13
Volcano, 115 ... NK-9
Volta, 246 ... SB-5
Vorden ... NK-7
Walker, 721 ... NK-11
Wallace, 403 ... NL-8
Walnut, 29172 ... §E-12
Walnut Creek, 64173 ... NL-6
Walnut Grv., 1542 ... NL-7
Walnut Pk., 15966 ... ‡F-7
Warner Sprs. ... SL-15
Wasco, 25545 ... SF-9
Washington, 185 ... NI-9
Waterford, 8456 ... NM-9
Waterloo, 572 ... NL-8
Watsonville, 51199 ... SB-3
Watts ... ‡G-7
Wawona, 169 ... NN-11
Weaverville, 3600 ... NE-4
Weed, 2967 ... NC-5
Weimar, 850 ... NI-8
Weitchpec, 30 ... NC-3
Weldon, 2642 ... SE-11
Wendel ... NF-10
Weott, 288 ... NF-2
W. Athens, 8729 ... ‡G-7
W. Carson, 21699 ... ‡I-7
W. Covina, 106098 ... §E-11
W. Hollywood, 34399 ... ‡E-6
W. Los Angeles ... ‡E-5
W. Menlo Pk., 3659 ... NK-15
W. Park, 1157 ... SC-18
W. Point, 674 ... NK-9
W. Puente Valley, 22636 ... §E-11
W. Sacramento, 48744 ... NK-7
Westhaven, 370 ... ND-2
WestL. Vil., 8270 ... SJ-10
Westley, 603 ... NN-8
Westminster, 89701 ... ‡J-10
Westmorland, 2225 ... SM-17
Westport, 160 ... NH-2
Westwood, 1647 ... NF-8
Wheatland, 3456 ... NI-7
Whiskeytown, 100 ... NE-5
Whispering Pines, 100 ... NJ-4
White River ... SE-10
White Water ... SJ-15
Whitethorn, 300 ... NF-2
Whitley Gdns., 285 ... SE-6
Whitmore, 100 ... NE-6
Whittier, 85331 ... SJ-12
Wilbur Sprs. ... NI-5
Wildomar, 32176 ... SK-13
Wildwood, 50 ... NF-4
Williams, 5123 ... NI-6
Willits, 4888 ... NH-3
Willow Creek, 1710 ... ND-3
Willow Ranch ... NB-10
Willows, 6166 ... NH-6
Wilmington ... ‡I-7
Wilseyville, 350 ... NK-9
Wilsonia, 5 ... SK-1
Wilton, 5363 ... NK-7
Winchester, 2534 ... SK-14
Windsor, 26801 ... NK-4
Windsor Hills, 5000 ... ‡F-6
Winter Gdns., 20631 ... †H-6
Winterhaven, 394 ... SM-20
Winters, 6624 ... NK-6
Winton, 10613 ... NN-9
Wofford Hts., 2200 ... SE-11
Woodcrest, 14347 ... §H-18
Woodfords, 100 ... NJ-11
Woodlake, 7279 ... SC-9
Woodland, 55468 ... NJ-6
Woodland Hills ... ‡D-3
Woodside, 5287 ... NK-15
Woodville, 1740 ... SD-9
Woody ... SE-10
Wrightwood, 4525 ... SI-12
Wyandotte, 110 ... NH-7
Yermo, 1000 ... SH-14
Yettem, 211 ... SC-9
Yolano ... NK-7
Yolo, 450 ... NJ-6
YOLO CO., 200849 ... NJ-6
Yorba Linda, 64234 ... §G-13
Yorkville, 130 ... NJ-3
Yosemite Forks, 210 ... NN-11
Yosemite Lakes, 4952 ... SA-8
Yosemite Vil., 1035 ... NM-11
Yountville, 2933 ... NK-5
Yreka, 7765 ... NB-5
Yuba City, 64925 ... NI-7
YUBA CO., 72155 ... NI-7
Yucaipa, 51367 ... SJ-14
Yucca Valley, 20700 ... SJ-15
Zamora, 100 ... NJ-6
Zenia, 40 ... NF-3

Colorado

Page locator

Map keys	Atlas pages
1–10	42–43
11–20	44–45

* City keyed to pp. 46–47

ADAMS CO., 441603 ... E-15
Agate, 80 ... F-16
Aguilar, 538 ... L-14
Akron, 1702 ... D-17
Alamosa, 8780 ... L-11
ALAMOSA CO., 15445 ... L-11
Allenspark, 528 ... D-12
Allison, 110 ... N-7
Alma, 270 ... G-11
Almont, 70 ... I-9
Amherst, 58 ... B-20
Anton, 40 ... E-17
Antonito, 781 ... M-11
Arapahoe, 100 ... H-20
ARAPAHOE CO., 572003 ... F-14
Arboles, 280 ... N-7
ARCHULETA CO., 12084 ... M-8
Arlington, 40 ... J-17
Aroya ... H-18
Arriba, 193 ... G-17
Arriola, 240 ... L-4
Arvada, 106433 ... E-13
Aspen, 6658 ... G-9
Atwood, 133 ... C-17
Ault, 1519 ... C-14
Aurora, 325078 ... E-14
Avon, 6447 ... F-10
Avondale, 674 ... J-15
BACA CO., 3788 ... L-19
Bailey, 150 ... F-12
Barnesville ... C-14
Barr Lake, 100 ... *F-9
Bartlett ... L-20
Basalt, 3857 ... F-8
Bayfield, 2333 ... M-7
Bedrock ... J-4
Beecher Island ... E-20
Bellvue, 400 ... C-13
Bennett, 2308 ... E-15
BENT CO., 6499 ... K-18
Berthoud, 5105 ... D-13
Bethune, 237 ... G-19
Beulah, 280 ... J-13
Black Forest, 13116 ... H-14
Black Hawk, 118 ... E-12
Blakeland, 700 ... *L-6
Blanca, 385 ... L-12
Blende, 878 ... J-14
Blue Mtn., 15 ... D-4
Blue River, 849 ... F-11
Bonanza, 16 ... J-10
Boncarbo, 70 ... M-14
Bond ... E-9
Bondad ... M-6
Boone, 339 ... J-15
Boulder, 97385 ... D-13
BOULDER CO., 294567 ... D-12
Bow Mar, 866 ... *K-6
Bowie, 40 ... H-7
Boyero ... H-17
Brandon, 21 ... I-19
Branson, 74 ... N-16
Breckenridge, 4540 ... F-11
Breen ... M-6
Briggsdale, 110 ... C-15
Brighton, 33352 ... E-14
Bristol, 130 ... J-20
Broadmoor ... *I-1
Brookvale, 280 ... F-12
Broomfield, 55889 ... E-13
BROOMFIELD CO., 55889 ... *E-6
Brush, 5463 ... D-16
Buena Vista, 2617 ... H-11
Buffalo Creek ... F-13
Buford ... E-7
Burlington, 4254 ... G-20
Burns ... E-9
Byers, 1160 ... E-15
Caddoa ... J-18
Cahone, 50 ... L-4
Calhan, 780 ... H-15
Camp Bird ... K-7
Campion, 1830 ... D-13
Campo, 109 ... M-19
Cañon City, 16400 ... I-13
Capulin, 200 ... M-11
Carbondale, 6427 ... F-8
Carr, 60 ... B-13
Cascade, 500 ... H-13
Castle Pines North, 12390 ... *M-8
Castle Rock, 48231 ... F-14
Cattle Creek, 641 ... F-8
Cedaredge, 2253 ... H-6
Centennial, 100377 ... F-13
Center, 2230 ... K-11
Central City, 663 ... E-12
CHAFFEE CO., 17809 ... I-11
Chama, 245 ... M-12
Cheraw, 252 ... J-17
Cherry Creek, 11120 ... *J-8
Cherry Hills Vil., 5987 ... *J-7
CHEYENNE CO., 1836 ... H-19
Cheyenne Wells, 846 ... H-20
Chimney Rock ... M-8
Chipita Pk., 465 ... H-13
Chivington, 40 ... I-19
Chromo ... N-9
Cimarron ... I-7
Clark ... B-9
Clarkville ... C-19
CLEAR CREEK CO., 9088 ... F-12
Clifton, 19889 ... G-5
Coal Creek, 343 ... J-13
Coaldale, 255 ... J-11
Coalmont, 50 ... C-10
Cokedale, 129 ... M-14
Collbran, 708 ... G-6
Colona, 30 ... J-7
Colorado City, 2193 ... K-14
Colorado Sprs., 416427 ... H-14
Columbine ... B-9
Columbine Valley, 1256 ... *K-6
Commerce City, 45913 ... *H-7
Como ... G-11
Conejos, 58 ... M-11
CONEJOS CO., 8256 ... M-10
Conifer, 200 ... F-12
Cope, 100 ... F-18
Cortez, 8482 ... L-5
COSTILLA CO., 3524 ... M-12
Cotopaxi, 47 ... J-12
Cowdrey, 100 ... B-10
Craig, 9464 ... C-7
Crawford, 431 ... H-7
Creede, 290 ... K-9
Crested Butte, 1487 ... H-8
Crestone, 127 ... K-11
Cripple Creek, 1189 ... H-13
Crook, 110 ... B-18
Crowley, 176 ... J-16
CROWLEY CO., 5823 ... J-16
Crystola, 160 ... H-13
Cuchara ... M-13
CUSTER CO., 4255 ... J-12
Dacono, 4152 ... D-13
Dailey ... C-18
De Beque, 504 ... F-6
Deckers ... G-13
Deer Trail, 546 ... F-15
Del Norte, 1686 ... L-10
Delhi ... L-16
Delta, 8915 ... H-6
DELTA CO., 30952 ... H-6
Denver, 600158 ... E-13
DENVER CO., 600158 ... *H-8
Devine ... J-15
Dillon, 904 ... F-11
Dinosaur, 339 ... D-4
Divide, 127 ... H-13
Dolores, 936 ... L-5
DOLORES CO., 2064 ... K-5
DOUGLAS CO., 285465 ... G-13
Dove Creek, 735 ... K-4
Doyleville ... I-9
Drake ... C-12
Dupont, 3650 ... *G-7
Durango, 16887 ... M-6
Eads, 609 ... I-19
Eagle, 6508 ... F-9
EAGLE CO., 52197 ... E-9
E. Portal ... E-12
Eastlake ... *F-7
Eaton, 4365 ... C-14
Eckley, 257 ... D-19
Edgewater, 5170 ... *I-6
Edwards, 10266 ... F-9
Egnar ... K-4
El Jebel, 3801 ... F-8
El Moro, 221 ... M-15
EL PASO CO., 622263 ... H-14
Elbert, 230 ... G-14
ELBERT CO., 23086 ... F-15
Eldora, 142 ... E-12
Eldorado Sprs., 585 ... E-13
Elizabeth, 1358 ... G-14
Elk Sprs., 25 ... C-5
Ellicott, 1131 ... H-15
Empire, 282 ... E-12
Englewood, 30255 ... F-13
Erie, 18135 ... D-13
Estes Pk., 5858 ... C-12
Estrella ... M-11
Evans, 18537 ... C-14
Evergreen, 9038 ... F-12
Fairplay, 679 ... G-11
Falcon, 255 ... H-14
Falfa, 100 ... M-6
Farisita ... K-13
Federal Hts., 11467 ... *G-6
Ferncliff, 70 ... D-12
Firestone, 10147 ... D-13
Flagler, 561 ... G-18
Fleming, 408 ... B-18
Florence, 3881 ... J-13
Florissant, 104 ... H-13
Ft. Carson, 13813 ... *I-2
Ft. Collins, 143986 ... C-13
Ft. Garland, 433 ... L-12
Ft. Lupton, 7377 ... D-14
Ft. Lyon ... J-18
Ft. Morgan, 11315 ... D-16
Fountain, 25846 ... I-14
Fowler, 1182 ... J-16
Foxfield, 685 ... F-14
Foxton ... F-13
Franktown, 395 ... F-14
Fraser, 1224 ... E-11
Frederick, 8679 ... D-13
FREMONT CO., 46824 ... I-12
Frisco, 2683 ... F-11
Fruita, 12646 ... G-4
Fruitvale, 7675 ... G-5
Galeton, 225 ... C-14
Garcia, 110 ... N-12
Garden City, 234 ... F-2
Gardner, 100 ... K-13
GARFIELD CO., 56389 ... F-6
Gateway ... H-4
Gem Vil. ... M-7
Genoa, 139 ... G-17
Georgetown, 1034 ... E-12
Gilcrest, 1034 ... D-14
Gilman ... F-10
GILPIN CO., 5441 ... E-12
Glade Pk., 40 ... G-4
Glen Haven, 130 ... C-12
Glendale, 4184 ... *I-7
Glendevey ... B-11
Glenwood Sprs., 9614 ... F-8
Golden, 18867 ... E-13
Goldfield, 49 ... H-13
Goodnight, 1400 ... I-1
Goodrich, 35 ... D-15
Gould, 50 ... C-11
Granada, 517 ... J-20
Granby, 1864 ... D-11
GRAND CO., 14843 ... D-10
Grand Jct., 58566 ... G-5
Grand Lake, 471 ... D-11
Grand Mesa, 30 ... G-6
Grand View Estates, 528 ... *L-9
Granite ... H-10
Grant ... F-12
Greeley, 92889 ... C-14
Green Mtn. Camp ... E-10
Green Mtn. Falls, 640 ... H-13
Greenwood, 140 ... J-13
Greenwood Vil., 13925 ... *K-7
Grover, 137 ... B-15
Guffey, 98 ... H-12
Gulnare, 100 ... M-14
Gunbarrel, 9263 ... *A-7
Gunnison, 5854 ... I-9
GUNNISON CO., 15324 ... H-8
Gypsum, 6477 ... F-9
Hahns Peak, 40 ... B-9
Hale ... F-20
Hamilton, 30 ... C-7
Hardin ... D-15
Harris Pk., 200 ... F-12
Hartman, 81 ... J-20
Hartsel, 80 ... H-11
Hasty, 144 ... J-18
Haswell, 68 ... I-18
Hawley ... K-16
Haxtun, 946 ... C-19
Hayden, 1810 ... C-8
Heeney, 76 ... E-10
Henderson, 600 ... *F-8
Hereford, 60 ... B-15
Hermosa, 260 ... L-6
Hesperus ... M-6
Hiawatha, 10 ... A-5
Highland Pk., 300 ... F-12
Highlands Ranch, 96713 ... *L-7
Hillrose, 264 ... D-17
Hillside ... J-12
HINSDALE CO., 843 ... K-7
Hoehne, 111 ... M-15
Holly, 802 ... J-20
Holyoke, 2313 ... C-19
Homelake, 260 ... L-11
Hooper, 103 ... K-11
Hot Sulphur Sprs., 663 ... D-11
Hotchkiss, 944 ... H-7
Howard, 723 ... I-11
Hoyt, 30 ... E-15
Hudson, 2356 ... D-14
HUERFANO CO., 6711 ... L-13
Hugo, 730 ... G-17
Hygiene, 400 ... D-13
Idaho Sprs., 1717 ... E-12
Idalia, 88 ... E-20
Ignacio, 697 ... M-7
Iliff, 266 ... B-18
Indian Hills, 1280 ... F-13
Irondale ... *G-8
Ivywild ... *H-2
JACKSON CO., 1394 ... B-10
Jamestown, 274 ... D-12
Jansen, 112 ... M-14
Jaroso, 60 ... N-12
Jefferson, 40 ... F-11
JEFFERSON CO., 534543 ... F-12
Joes, 80 ... F-19
Johnson Vil., 246 ... H-11
Johnstown, 9887 ... D-13
Julesburg, 1225 ... B-20
Karval, 65 ... H-17
Kassler ... *M-5
Keenesburg, 1127 ... D-14
Kelim, 90 ... C-13
Keota ... B-15
Kersey, 1454 ... C-14
Kim, 74 ... M-17
Kiowa, 723 ... G-14
KIOWA CO., 1398 ... I-18
Kirk, 59 ... F-19
Kit Carson, 233 ... H-18
KIT CARSON CO., 8270 ... F-19
Knob Hill ... *H-2
Kremmling, 1444 ... D-10
La Garita ... K-10
La Jara, 818 ... M-11
La Junta, 7077 ... K-17
LA PLATA CO., 51334 ... L-6
La Salle, 1955 ... D-14
La Valley, 160 ... M-12
La Veta, 800 ... L-13
Lafayette, 24453 ... *D-5
Laird, 47 ... D-20
Lake City, 408 ... K-8
LAKE CO., 7310 ... G-10
L. George, 120 ... H-12
Lakeside, 8 ... *H-6
Lakewood, 142980 ... *I-5
Lamar, 7804 ... J-19
Laporte, 2450 ... *A-8
LARIMER CO., 299630 ... C-12
Larkspur, 183 ... G-13
Las Animas, 2410 ... J-17
LAS ANIMAS CO., 15507 ... M-15
Las Mesitas, 60 ... N-10
Last Chance, 25 ... E-17
Lawson, 320 ... E-12
Lay ... C-7
Lazear, 140 ... H-7
Leadville, 2602 ... G-10
Lebanon, 160 ... L-5
Lewis, 302 ... L-4
Limon, 1880 ... G-16
LINCOLN CO., 5467 ... H-17
Lincoln Pk., 3546 ... I-13
Lindon, 120 ... E-17
Littleton, 41737 ... F-13
Livermore, 60 ... B-13
Lochbuie, 4726 ... *E-10
Log Lane Vil., 873 ... D-16
LOGAN CO., 22709 ... B-17
Loma, 1293 ... G-4
Lombard Vil., 600 ... I-2
Lone Tree, 10218 ... *L-8
Longmont, 86270 ... D-13
Louisville, 18376 ... E-13
Louviers, 269 ... F-13
Loveland, 66859 ... C-13
Lucerne, 160 ... C-14
Ludlow ... M-14
Lyons, 2033 ... D-13
Mack, 240 ... G-4
Maher, 100 ... I-7
Manassa, 991 ... M-11
Mancos, 1336 ... M-5
Manitou Sprs., 4992 ... H-13
Manzanola, 434 ... J-16
Marble, 131 ... G-8
Marvel, 65 ... M-6
Masonville, 140 ... C-13
Matheson ... G-16
Maybell, 72 ... C-6
Maysville, 135 ... I-10
McClave, 190 ... J-18
McCoy, 24 ... E-9
Mead, 3405 ... D-13
Meeker, 2475 ... D-6
Meeker Pk., 120 ... D-12
Meredith ... F-9
Merino, 284 ... C-17
Mesa, 240 ... G-6
MESA CO., 146723 ... H-5
Mesita, 50 ... M-12
Milliken, 5610 ... D-14
Milner, 200 ... C-9
MINERAL CO., 712 ... L-8
Minturn, 1027 ... F-10
Model, 110 ... M-15
Moffat, 116 ... K-11
MOFFAT CO., 13795 ... C-6
Mogote, 85 ... N-11
Molina, 90 ... G-6
Monte Vista, 4444 ... L-10
Montezuma, 65 ... F-11
MONTEZUMA CO., 25535 ... M-4
Montrose, 19132 ... I-6
MONTROSE CO., 41276 ... I-6
Monument, 5530 ... G-13
MORGAN CO., 28159 ... D-16
Morrison, 428 ... F-13
Mosca, 130 ... L-11
Mt. Crested Butte, 801 ... H-9
Mountain View, 1700 ... *B-8
Mountain View, 507 ... *H-6
Mountain Vil., 1320 ... K-6
Nathrop, 200 ... H-11
Naturita, 546 ... J-5
Nederland, 1445 ... E-12
New Castle, 4518 ... F-7
Ninaview ... L-17
Niwot, 4006 ... D-13
N. Avondale, 50 ... J-15
Northglenn, 35789 ... *F-7
Norwood, 518 ... J-5
Nucla, 711 ... J-5
Nunn, 416 ... B-14
Oak Creek, 884 ... D-9
Oak Grv., 175 ... I-6
Ohio, 40 ... I-9
Olathe, 1849 ... I-6
Olney Sprs., 345 ... J-16
Ophir, 159 ... K-6
Orchard, 90 ... D-15
Orchard City, 3119 ... H-6
Orchard Mesa, 6836 ... G-5
Ordway, 1080 ... J-16
Ortiz, 60 ... N-11
OTERO CO., 18831 ... K-16
Otis, 475 ... D-18
Ouray, 1000 ... K-7
OURAY CO., 4436 ... J-6
Ovid, 318 ... B-19
Oxford, 90 ... M-7
Padroni, 76 ... B-17
Pagosa Jct., 25 ... N-8
Pagosa Sprs., 1727 ... M-8
Palisade, 2692 ... G-5
Palmer Lake, 2420 ... G-13
Pandora ... K-
Paoli, 34 ... C-19
Paonia, 1451 ... H-7
Parachute, 1085 ... F-6
Paradox, 70 ... I-4
Paragon Estates, 380 ... *D-
PARK CO., 16206 ... G-1
Parker, 45297 ... F-14
Parlin, 50 ... I-
Parshall, 47 ... D-1
Pearl ... B-1
Peckham, 135 ... D-14
Peetz, 238 ... B-18
Penrose, 3582 ... I-13
Peyton, 250 ... H-14
PHILLIPS CO., 4442 ... C-19
Phippsburg, 204 ... D-9
Pierce, 834 ... C-1
Pikeview ... *F-
Pine Grv., 150 ... F-1
Pitkin, 66 ... I-1
PITKIN CO., 17148 ... G-
Placerville, 250 ... K-
Platner, 35 ... D-1
Platoro, 100 ... M-
Platteville, 2485 ... D-1
Pleasant View, 80 ... L-

*, †, ‡, §, ◊ See explanation under state title in this index.
County and parish names are listed in capital letters & boldface type.
Independent cities (not included in a county) are listed in italics.

Colorado (continued)

Poncha Sprs., 737 ...I-11
Poudre Park, 100 ...C-13
Powder Wash, 55 ...B-6
Powderhorn ...J-8
Pritchett, 140 ...M-18
Proctor ...K-19
Prospect Valley, 70 ...D-15
Prowers ...J-19
PROWERS CO., 12551 ...K-14
Pryor ...L-16
Pueblo, 106595 ...J-14
PUEBLO CO., 159063 ...J-14
Pueblo Ctr., 29637 ...J-14
Punkin Ctr. ...H-16
Purcell ...J-17
Ramah, 123 ...G-15
Rand ...C-10
Rangely, 2365 ...D-4
Raymer, 96 ...C-16
Raymond, 60 ...D-12
Red Cliff, 267 ...F-10
Red Feather Lakes, 343 ...B-12
Red Wing, 40 ...K-13
Redlands, 8685 ...G-5
Redmesa, 40 ...M-5
Redstone, 130 ...G-8
Redvale, 236 ...J-5
Rico, 265 ...K-6
Ridgway, 924 ...J-7
Rifle, 9172 ...F-7
RIO BLANCO CO., 6666 ...E-6
RIO GRANDE CO., 11982 ...L-10
Rockvale, 487 ...J-13
Rocky Ford, 3957 ...K-16
Roggen, 130 ...D-15
Rollinsville, 181 ...E-12
Romeo, 404 ...M-11
Roswell ...*G-2
ROUTT CO., 23509 ...C-8
Rush, 80 ...H-15
Rustic ...B-12
Rye, 153 ...K-13
SAGUACHE CO., 6108 ...K-9
St. Petersburg ...J-8
Salida, 5236 ...I-11
Salt Creek, 587 ...J-14
San Acacio, 40 ...M-12
San Antonio, 190 ...N-11
San Isabel, 50 ...K-13
SAN JUAN CO., 699 ...L-7
San Luis, 629 ...M-12
SAN MIGUEL CO., 7359 ...K-5
San Pablo, 170 ...M-11
Sanford, 879 ...M-12
Sapinero ...J-8
Sargents, ...I-10
Sawpit, 40 ...K-6
Security, 4400 ...*I-3
Sedalia, 206 ...F-13
Sedgwick, 146 ...B-19
SEDGWICK CO., 2379 ...B-19
Segundo, 98 ...M-14
Seibert, 180 ...F-18
Severance, 3165 ...C-14
Shawnee, 100 ...F-12
Sheridan, 5664 ...*J-6
Sheridan Lake, 88 ...J-20
Silt, 2930 ...F-7
Silver Cliff, 587 ...J-12
Silver Plume, 170 ...F-12
Silverthorne, 3887 ...E-11
Silverton, 637 ...K-7
Simla, 616 ...G-15
Singleton, 40 ...L-6
Slater, 50 ...A-8
Slick Rock ...J-5
Snowmass ...G-9
Snowmass Vil., 2826 ...G-9
Snyder, 132 ...D-16
Somerset ...H-7
S. Fork, 386 ...L-9
S. Platte ...F-12
Springfield, 1451 ...L-19
Starkville ...*M-14
Steamboat Sprs., 12088 ...C-8
Sterling, 14777 ...C-17
Stoner, ...K-6
Stonewall, 80 ...M-13
Stonington, 30 ...M-20
Strasburg, 2447 ...E-14
Stratmoor Hills, 2350 ...*I-2
Stratton, 658 ...G-19
Stratton Meadows ...*I-2
Stringtown, 140 ...J-8
Sugar City, 258 ...J-16
SUMMIT CO., 27994 ...F-11
Sunbeam ...C-6
Superior, 12483 ...D-13
Swink, 617 ...K-17
Tabernash, 417 ...E-11
TELLER CO., 23350 ...H-13
Telluride, 2325 ...K-6
Texas Creek ...J-12
Thatcher ...L-15
Thornton, 118772 ...E-13
Thurman ...N-7
Tiffany ...N-5
Timnath, 625 ...C-13
Timpas ...L-16
Tincup ...H-10
Toonerville ...K-17
Toponas ...D-9
Torres ...L-15
Towaoc, 1087 ...M-4
Towner, 22 ...J-20
Trinchera, 80 ...N-16
Trinidad, 9096 ...M-14
Twin Lakes, 171 ...H-10
Two Buttes, 43 ...L-19
Tyrone ...L-15
Uravan ...J-4
Vail, 5305 ...F-10
Vancorum ...J-5
Vernon, 20 ...E-19
Victor, 397 ...I-13
Viejo San Acacio ...M-12
Vigil, 40 ...M-13
Villa Grv., 40 ...J-11
Villegreen, 80 ...L-17
Vineland, 251 ...J-15
Virginia Dale ...B-13
Vona, 106 ...G-19
Walden, 608 ...C-10
Walsenburg, 3068 ...L-14
Walsh, 546 ...L-20
Ward, 150 ...D-12

WASHINGTON CO., 4814 ...D-17

Watkins, 653 ...E-14
Wattenberg, 330 ...E-14
Waverly, 300 ...B-13
WELD CO., 252825 ...B-15
Weldona, 139 ...D-16
Wellington, 6289 ...B-13
Westcliffe, 568 ...J-12
Western Hills, 2600 ...*G-6
Westminster, 106114 ...E-13
Weston, 55 ...M-14
Wetmore, 60 ...J-13
Wheat Ridge, 30166 ...*H-5
Whitepine ...i-10
Whitewater, 200 ...H-5
Widefield, 4200 ...*J-4
Wiggins, 893 ...D-15
Wild Horse, 25 ...H-18
Wiley, 405 ...J-19
Willard, 40 ...C-17
Williamsburg, 662 ...J-13
Windsor, 18644 ...C-13
Winter Pk., 999 ...E-11
Wolcott, 15 ...E-9
Woodland Pk., 7200 ...H-13
Woodrow, 20 ...E-17
Woody Creek, 263 ...G-9
Wray, 2342 ...D-20
Yampa, 429 ...D-9
Yellow Jacket, 60 ...L-5
Yoder ...H-15
Yuma, 3524 ...D-19
YUMA CO., 10043 ...D-19

Connecticut

Page locator / Map keys A–J / Atlas pages 48–49

Abington, 750 ...B-13
Addison, 80 ...C-9
Allingtown ...I-9
Almyville, ...B-13
Amenia Union, 100 ...B-4
Amesville, 120 ...A-4
Amston, 780 ...D-11
Andover, 600 ...C-11
Ansonia, 19249 ...F-6
Ashford, 330 ...B-12
Ashford Ctr., 280 ...C-12
Attawaugan, 660 ...B-13
Atwoodville, 200 ...C-12
Avon, 1800 ...C-8
Baileyville, 460 ...B-6
Ball Pond, 2400 ...E-3
Ballouville, 400 ...B-13
Baltic, 1250 ...D-12
Bantam, 759 ...C-5
Barkhamsted, ...A-7
Bashan ...E-10
Beacon Falls, 1650 ...E-6
Berkshire Estates, 220 ...F-5
Berlin, 1230 ...D-8
Bethany, 1280 ...F-7
Bethel, 9549 ...E-4
Bethlehem, 2021 ...D-5
Birch Hill, 230 ...C-4
Birchwood, 380 ...B-8
Black Pt., 20 ...G-12
Bloomfield, 7500 ...B-8
Blue Hills, 2901 ...H-13
Boardman Br., 100 ...D-4
Bolton, 230 ...C-10
Botsford, 490 ...E-5
Bozrah Street ...E-12
Branchville, 360 ...E-4
Branford, 5819 ...G-8
Branford Ctr., 5819 ...J-11
Bridgeport, 144229 ...H-5
Bridgewater, 500 ...D-4
Bristol, 60477 ...D-7
Broad Brook, 4069 ...B-9
Brookfield, 1650 ...D-4
Brookfield Ctr., 1550 ...E-4
Brooklyn, 980 ...C-13
Buckingham, 200 ...C-10
Bulls Bridge, 100 ...D-3
Bunker Hill ...A-2
Burlington, 500 ...C-7
Burnside ...H-14
Byram, 4146 ...I-3
Canaan, 1212 ...A-5
Candlewood Isle, 1260 ...E-3
Candlewood Knolls, 560 ...E-3
Candlewood Shores, 1800 ...E-3
Cannondale, 141 ...G-4
Canterbury, 200 ...C-13
Canton, 480 ...B-7
Canton Ctr., 380 ...B-7
Cedar Bch. ...J-7
Centerbrook, 1000 ...F-10
Centerville ...H-10
Central Vil., 1800 ...C-13
Chaplin, 230 ...C-12
Cheshire, 5865 ...D-8
Chester, 1558 ...F-10
Chesterfield ...F-11
Clarks Corner ...B-13
Clarks Falls, 170 ...E-14
Clinton, 3368 ...G-10
Cobalt, 500 ...E-9
Colchester, 4781 ...D-11
Colebrook, 60 ...A-6
Collinsville, 3746 ...C-7
Columbia, 800 ...C-11
Cornwall, 330 ...B-5
Cornwall Bridge, 100 ...B-4
Cos Cob, 6770 ...I-1
Coventry, 600 ...C-11
Cromwell, 2500 ...D-9
Crystal Lake, 1945 ...B-10
Danbury, 80893 ...E-4
Danielson, 4051 ...C-13
Darien, 20732 ...H-4
Dayville, 1650 ...B-13
Deep River, 1700 ...F-10
Derby, 12902 ...F-6
Devon, 80 ...G-6
Dodgingtown, 300 ...E-4
Double Bch., 1100 ...G-8
Durham, 2933 ...E-9
Eagleville, 460 ...C-11
E. Berlin, 1900 ...D-9
E. Bridgeport ...H-4
E. Brooklyn, 1638 ...C-13
E. Canaan, 1060 ...A-5
E. Farmington Hts. ...C-7
450 ...B-3

E. Glastonbury, 300 ...C-10

E. Granby, 1300 ...A-8
E. Haddam, 800 ...E-10
E. Hampton, 2691 ...D-10
E. Hartford, 51252 ...C-9
E. Hartland, 1200 ...A-7
E. Haven, 29257 ...G-7
E. Litchfield, 180 ...C-6
E. Morris ...D-6
E. Mountain ...B-3
E. River, 3800 ...G-9
E. Thompson, 640 ...A-14
E. Village, 100 ...F-6
E. Willington, ...B-11
E. Windsor Hill, 450 ...B-9
E. Woodstock, 470 ...A-13
Eastford, 1020 ...B-12
Easton, 480 ...B-5
Ebbs Corner, 620 ...A-8
Ellington, 1700 ...B-10
Ellsworth ...C-4
Elmwood ...C-8
Essex, 1270 ...F-11
Fabyan, 520 ...A-13
Fair Haven ...H-4
Fair Haven East ...H-4
Fair Lawn ...B-3
Fairfield, 57300 ...H-5
FAIRFIELD CO., 916829 ...F-4
Fairmount ...A-2
Falls Vil., 538 ...A-4
Farmington, 3100 ...C-8
Fenwick, 43 ...G-11
Firetown, 160 ...B-8
Fitchville, 300 ...E-12
Flanders, 1330 ...F-11
Flanders, 170 ...C-4
Forest Hts. ...B-8
Fort Hill, 100 ...E-14
Foxon ...H-7
Franklin, 140 ...D-12
Gales Ferry, 1162 ...F-12
Gaylordsville, 330 ...D-3
Georgetown, 1805 ...G-4
Giants Neck, 1330 ...G-11
Gilead, 170 ...D-11
Gilman, 40 ...D-12
Glasgo, 520 ...D-13
Glastonbury, 7387 ...C-9
Glenbrook ...D-3
Golden Spur, 130 ...F-12
Good Hill, 300 ...D-5
Goshen, 890 ...B-5
Granby, 700 ...A-8
Greenfield Hill ...H-5
Greenwich, 12942 ...I-3
Greystone, 160 ...D-6
Grosvenor Dale ...A-13
850 ...A-13
Groton, 10389 ...F-12
Groton Long Pt., 518 ...G-12
Grove Bch. ...G-10
Guilford, 2597 ...G-9
Gurleyville, 130 ...C-11
Haddam, 1300 ...E-10
Haddam Neck, 270 ...E-10
Hadlyme, 640 ...F-10
Hallville, 80 ...E-13
Hamburg, 110 ...F-11
Hamden, 56900 ...F-7
Hampton, 600 ...C-12
Hanover, 500 ...D-12
Happyland, 320 ...C-12
Harrisville, 90 ...B-13
Hartford, 124775 ...C-9
HARTFORD CO., 894014 ...B-8
Hartland ...A-7
Harwinton, 400 ...C-6
Hawleyville, 100 ...E-4
Hayden, 110 ...D-8
Hazardville, 4599 ...A-9
Hebron, 800 ...D-11
Higganum, 1660 ...E-10
Honeypot Glen, 1200 ...E-5
Hopeville ...D-13
Hopewell ...D-9
Hotchkissville, 350 ...D-5
Huntington, ...F-6
Hydeville, 250 ...A-14
Indian Neck, 2500 ...G-8
Ivoryton, 2600 ...F-10
Jewett City, 3487 ...D-13
Jordan Vil., 400 ...G-12
Kensington, 8459 ...D-8
Kent, 300 ...C-4
Kent Furnace ...C-4
Killingly Ctr., 110 ...B-14
Killingworth, 300 ...F-9
Kings Corner, 270 ...B-9
Knollcrest, 400 ...E-9
Knollwood, 500 ...C-9
Lakeside, 1340 ...C-5
Lakeside, 550 ...D-5
Lakeview Ter., 100 ...E-4
Lakeville, 820 ...A-4
Laurel Bch. ...G-7
Laysville, 400 ...G-11
Lebanon, 440 ...D-12
Ledyard Ctr., 1800 ...C-13
Leesville, 160 ...E-10
Leetes Island, 260 ...G-9
Liberty Hill, 260 ...D-12
Lime Rock, 160 ...A-4
LITCHFIELD CO., 189927 ...A-5
Litchfield, 4205 ...F-3
Long Hill ...F-6
Long Hill, 400 ...G-6
Lords Pt., 350 ...F-14
Lordship ...H-6
Lyme Sta., 530 ...G-11
Lyons Plains, 350 ...G-5
Macedonia, 300 ...B-7
Madison, 2290 ...G-9
Manchester, 30577 ...C-10
Manchester Htt., 947 ...C-12
300 ...C-12
Mansfield Depot, 300 ...C-11
Mansfield ...C-11
Marble Dale, 220 ...D-4
Marion, 450 ...D-7
Marlborough, 200 ...D-9
Mechanicsville, 160 ...A-13
Meriden, 60868 ...E-8
Merrow, 260 ...B-11
Mianus ...I-2
Middle Haddam ...E-9
450 ...E-9
MIDDLESEX CO., 165676 ...E-9
Middlefield, 4200 ...E-9
Middletown, 47648 ...E-9
Milford, 51271 ...G-6

Millbrook ...H-10

Milldale, 900 ...E-7
Millington, 50 ...E-11
Millville ...C-2
Milton, 150 ...C-5
Minortown ...D-6
Mixville, 1400 ...A-7
Mohegan, 460 ...E-12
Momauguin ...J-10
Monroe, 8500 ...F-5
Montowese ...F-8
Moodus, 1413 ...E-10
Morris, 300 ...D-5
Morris Cove ...H-7
Mt. Hope, 200 ...B-12
Mystic, 4205 ...F-13
Naugatuck, 31862 ...E-6
Nepaug, 300 ...B-7
New Britain, 73206 ...D-8
New Canaan, 17900 ...H-4
New Fairfield, 5200 ...E-4
New Hartford, 620 ...B-7
New Haven, 129779 ...G-7
NEW HAVEN CO., 862477 ...E-7
New London, 27620 ...F-12
NEW LONDON CO., 274055 ...E-13
New Milford, 6523 ...D-4
New Preston, 1182 ...D-5
Newent, 230 ...D-13
Newington, 30562 ...C-8
Newtown, 1941 ...F-5
Niantic, 3114 ...F-12
Nichols ...F-6
Noank, 1796 ...F-13
Norfolk, 553 ...A-5
N. Ashford ...A-13
N. Branford, 7400 ...F-8
N. Canton, 280 ...B-7
N. Granby, 1944 ...A-8
N. Grosvenor Dale, 1530 ...A-13
N. Guilford ...F-9
N. Haven, 24093 ...F-8
N. Kent, 170 ...C-4
N. Madison ...F-9
N. Stonington, 350 ...F-14
N. Westchester, 300 ...D-10
N. Wilton, 500 ...G-4
N. Windham, 1000 ...C-12
N. Woodstock ...A-13
Northfield, 650 ...C-6
Northford, 3600 ...F-8
Northville, 400 ...D-4
Norwalk, 85603 ...H-4
Norwich, 40493 ...E-12
Oakdale, 910 ...E-12
Oakdale Manor, 400 ...E-5
Oakland Gdns., 300 ...I-11
Oakville, 9047 ...D-6
Old Greenwich, 6611 ...I-3
Old Lyme, 480 ...G-11
Old Lyme Shores, 300 ...G-11
Old Mystic, 3554 ...F-13
2039 ...E-11
Oneco, 750 ...C-14
Orange, 13956 ...G-7
Orcutts, 240 ...A-11
Oronoque ...I-7
Oswegatchie, 150 ...F-12
Oxford, 2100 ...F-6
Pachaug ...D-13
Palmertown, 610 ...E-12
Pawcatuck, 5624 ...F-14
Pequabuck ...D-7
Phoenixville, 80 ...B-12
Pine Bridge, 1000 ...E-5
Pine Meadow, 800 ...B-7
Pine Orchard, 950 ...G-8
Pine Rock Pk. ...I-7
Plainfield, 2557 ...D-13
Plainville, 17400 ...D-8
Plantsville, 6000 ...D-8
Platts Mills ...E-6
Pleasant Valley, 460 ...B-7
Plymouth, 1200 ...D-7
Point O'Woods, 740 ...F-12
Pomfret, 670 ...B-13
Pomfret Ctr., 390 ...B-13
Pomfret Lndg., 110 ...B-13
Ponset, 500 ...E-10
Poquetanuck, 220 ...E-13
Poquonock, 1150 ...C-9
Poquonock Bridge, 1727 ...F-12
Portland, 5862 ...D-9
Preston City, 210 ...D-13
Prospect, 7770 ...E-7
Putnam, 7214 ...B-13
Putnam Hts., 210 ...B-14
Quaddick, 540 ...A-14
Quaker Hill, 500 ...F-12
Quarryville, 400 ...E-10
Quinebaug, 1133 ...A-13
Redding, 1500 ...F-4
Redding Ridge, 550 ...F-5
Ridgebury, 220 ...E-4
Ridgefield, 7645 ...G-4
Riverclift ...I-2
Riverside, 8416 ...I-3
Riverton, 580 ...A-7
Robertsville, 280 ...A-6
Rockfall, 980 ...E-9
ROCKVILLE, 7474 ...B-10
Rogers, 660 ...B-13
Roxbury, 350 ...D-4
Roxbury Falls, 130 ...C-5
Sachem Head, 500 ...G-8
Salem, 40 ...E-11
Salisbury ...A-4
Sandy Hook, 1200 ...E-5
Saybrook Manor, 1052 ...G-10
Saybrook Pt., 300 ...G-11
Scantic, 400 ...B-9
Scotland, 900 ...C-12
Seymour, 14300 ...F-6
Shady Rest, 270 ...C-13
Shailerville ...E-10
Sharon, 729 ...A-4
Sharon Valley, 300 ...A-4
Shelton, 39559 ...G-6
Sherman, 150 ...D-3
Short Bch., 2600 ...G-8
Simsbury, 5836 ...B-8
Slades, 1241 ...A-4
Somers, 1789 ...A-10
Somersville, 1300 ...A-10
Sound View, 1200 ...G-11
S. Britain, 1060 ...E-5
S. Canaan ...A-5
S. Coventry ...C-11
S. End ...H-3
S. Glastonbury, 2000 ...D-9

S. Killingly, 220 ...C-14

S. Lyme, 320 ...G-11
S. Norfolk ...B-5
S. Willington, 320 ...B-11
S. Windham, 1421 ...D-12
S. Windsor, 14000 ...C-9
S. Woodstock, 1291 ...A-13
Southbury, 3400 ...E-5
Southington ...D-7
Southport, 1585 ...H-5
Spring Glen ...H-10
Spring Hill, 200 ...C-11
Stafford, 720 ...A-11
Stafford Sprs., 4988 ...A-11
Staffordville, 720 ...A-11
Stamford, 122643 ...I-3
Stepney, 750 ...C-13
Sterling, 660 ...C-14
Sterling Hill ...C-14
Stevenson, 1150 ...F-5
Stonington, 929 ...F-13
Stony Creek, 830 ...G-8
Storrs, 15344 ...C-11
Straitsville ...C-2
Stratfield ...H-5
Stratford, 51384 ...G-6
Suffield Depot, 1325 ...A-9
Taconic, 350 ...A-4
Tariffville, 1324 ...B-8
Terryville, 5387 ...D-7
Thomaston, 1910 ...D-6
Thompson, 260 ...A-14
Thompsonville, 8577 ...A-9
Tolland, 800 ...B-11
TOLLAND CO., 152691 ...B-10
Torrington, 36383 ...C-6
Trumbull, 36018 ...G-5
Twin Lakes, 380 ...A-4
Uncasville, 1420 ...F-12
Union, 60 ...A-12
Union City ...E-6
Unionville, 4400 ...C-7
Upper Stepney, 1000 ...F-5
Vernon, 28100 ...B-10
Versailles, 580 ...D-12
Voluntown, 520 ...D-14
Wallingford, 18209 ...E-8
Warehouse Pt., 2100 ...B-9
Warren, 240 ...C-4
Warrenville, 180 ...B-12
Washington, 700 ...D-5
Washington Depot, 500 ...D-4
Waterbury, 110366 ...E-6
Waterford, ...F-12
Watertown, 3574 ...D-6
Wauregan, 1205 ...C-13
Wequetequock, 850 ...F-14
W. Avon, 100 ...C-8
W. Cornwall, 330 ...B-4
W. Goshen, 700 ...B-6
W. Granby, 700 ...A-8
W. Hartford, 63268 ...C-8
W. Hartland, 400 ...A-7
W. Haven, 55564 ...G-7
W. Mystic ...F-13
W. Norfolk ...A-5
W. Redding, 200 ...F-4
W. Side Hill ...B-2
W. Simsbury, 2447 ...B-8
W. Stafford, 600 ...A-11
W. Suffield, 860 ...A-9
W. Thompson, 210 ...A-13
W. Woodstock ...A-12
Westbrook, 2413 ...G-10
Westchester, 200 ...D-10
Westford, 100 ...B-12
Weston, 1460 ...G-4
Westport, 26391 ...H-4
Westville ...H-9
Wethersfield, 26668 ...C-9
Whigville, 450 ...C-7
Whitneyville ...H-10
Wildemere Bch. ...J-7
Willimantic, 17737 ...C-11
Willington ...B-11
Wilsonville, 640 ...A-13
Wilton, 732 ...G-4
Winchester Ctr., 200 ...B-6
Windham, 1150 ...C-12
WINDHAM CO., 118428 ...C-13
Windsor, 18800 ...B-9
Windsor Locks, 12498 ...B-9
Winnecasset, 350 ...D-10
Winsted, 7712 ...B-6
Winthrop, 490 ...F-10
Wolcott, 6400 ...D-7
Woodbridge, 7860 ...F-7
Woodbury, 1294 ...E-5
Woodmont, 1488 ...G-7
Woodstock, 350 ...A-12
Woodstock Valley, 350 ...A-12
Woodtick, 540 ...D-7
Woodville ...C-5

Delaware

Page locator / Map keys A–N / Atlas pages 50–51

Adamsville ...J-2
Andrewville ...J-2
Angola by the Bay, 11217 ...C-6
Arden, 439 ...C-3
Ardentown, 264 ...A-10
Argos Corner, 50 ...J-5
Ashland ...A-7
Atlanta, 65 ...B-2
Bayard ...K-5
Bay View Bch., 60 ...F-8
Bear, 19371 ...D-2
Bayside ...J-5
Bellefonte, 1193 ...A-14
Bellevue, 200 ...C-8
Berrydale, 441 ...J-3
Bethel, 171 ...L-3
Big Stone Bch., 15 ...J-4
Blackbird ...D-2
Blackiston ...D-2
Blades, 1241 ...K-4
Bowers Bch., 335 ...H-4
Boxwood, 50 ...B-9
Brandywine, 3600 ...A-3
Bridgeville, 2048 ...K-2
Broadkill Bch., 60 ...J-5
Brookside, 14353 ...D-8
Shortly, ...C-6
22711 ...D-5
Slaughter Bch., 207 ...J-4

Bryans Store ...L-3

Camden, 3464 ...H-3
Cannon, 100 ...K-3
Canterbury, 150 ...H-3
Capitol Pk., 600 ...G-9
Carlisle Vil., 200 ...F-7
Carpenter, 1300 ...A-10
Castle Vil., 200 ...F-7
Centerville, 300 ...A-2
Cheswold, 1380 ...G-2
Christiana, 500 ...D-2
Clarksville, 200 ...L-5
Claymont, 8253 ...C-3
Clayton, 2918 ...F-2
Concord, 250 ...K-2
Cool Spr., 50 ...K-4
Corner Ketch ...C-6
Coverdale Crossroads, ...K-2
Dagsboro, 805 ...L-4
Delaware City, 1695 ...D-2
Delmar, 1597 ...M-3
Dewey Bch., 341 ...L-5
Dover, 36047 ...G-2
Downs Chapel, 25 ...G-1
Dublin Hill, 40 ...J-1
Dupont Manor, 300 ...G-3
Edgemoor, 5677 ...B-9
Ellendale, 381 ...J-3
Elsmere, 6131 ...C-2
Farmington, 110 ...J-3
Farnhurst ...C-8
Faulkland, 150 ...B-8
Felton, 1298 ...H-2
Fieldsboro ...L-2
Frankford, 847 ...L-4
Frederica, 774 ...J-3
Georgetown, 6422 ...K-3
Glasgow, 14303 ...D-1
Granogue ...A-8
Gravel Hill, 75 ...K-4
Greenback ...C-7
Greenville, 2326 ...C-2
Greenwood, 973 ...J-2
Guyencourt, 100 ...A-8
Hanby Cors., ...A-10
Harbeson, 400 ...K-4
Hares Corner, 40 ...C-8
Harmony ...D-1
Harrington, 3562 ...J-3
Hartly, 74 ...G-1
Hazlettville ...H-2
Hearns Crossroads ...B-8
Hearns Mill, 10 ...K-4
Henlopen Acres, 122 ...K-5
Henry Clay ...B-8
Hitchens Crossroads ...L-3
Hockessin, 13527 ...C-2
Hollyville ...K-4
Houston, 374 ...H-3
Huntley, 100 ...H-5
Indian Bch., 10 ...K-5
Iron Hill, 500 ...D-5
Jimtown, 45 ...K-4
Johnson, 35 ...L-5
Keen-Wik, 400 ...M-5
Kent Acres, 1890 ...H-8
KENT CO., 162310 ...H-2
Kenton, 261 ...G-2
Kirkwood, 150 ...D-2
Kitts Hummock, 300 ...H-3
Lake Pines, 125 ...M-8
Laurel, 3708 ...L-2
Lebanon, 120 ...H-3
Leipsic, 183 ...G-3
Lewes, 2747 ...J-5
Lincoln, 500 ...J-3
Little Creek, 224 ...G-3
Little Heaven, 250 ...H-3
Long Neck, 1850 ...K-5
Lynch Hts., 125 ...J-3
Magnolia, 125 ...H-3
Marshallton, 800 ...K-5
Masseys Lndg., 80 ...K-5
Mastens Corner, 60 ...I-2
McClellanville, 125 ...C-1
Mechanicsville, 150 ...L-2
Middleford, 150 ...K-3
Middletown, 18871 ...E-1
Midway, 400 ...A-13
Midway, 9559 ...L-5
Milford Crossroads, 100 ...J-3
Millsboro, 3877 ...L-4
Milton, 2576 ...J-4
Mt. Cuba ...B-8
Mt. Pleasant, 100 ...E-1
Nanticoke Acres, 50 ...K-3
Nassau, 400 ...K-5
New Castle, 5285 ...D-2
NEW CASTLE CO., 538479 ...E-2
Newark, 31454 ...C-1
Newport, 1055 ...C-2
North Shores, 100 ...K-5
N. Star, 7980 ...C-1
Oak Orchard, 500 ...L-5
Oakley ...J-3
Ocean View, 1882 ...L-5
Odessa, 364 ...E-2
Ogletown, 600 ...C-1
Omar, ...L-4
Pearsons Corner, 100 ...H-2
Pepper ...J-1
16323 ...L-4
Pike Creek, 7898 ...C-6
Pine Tree Cors., ...K-5
Pinetown ...L-3
Plainfield ...L-3
Port Penn, 250 ...E-2
Porters Corner, 50 ...J-5
Prices Corner, 1500 ...C-8
Red Lion ...D-2
Reeves Crossing ...J-4
Rehoboth Bch., 1327 ...K-5
Rising Sun, 250 ...H-3
Riverdale, 500 ...L-5
Robbins Bch., 1060 ...L-5
Rodney Vil., 1487 ...H-3
Rodric Vil., 100 ...H-8
Rogers Cors., ...C-9
Roxana, 100 ...L-5
St. Georges, 150 ...E-2
Sandtown, 60 ...G-2
Scotts Corner ...J-1
Seaford, 6928 ...K-3
Selbyville, 2167 ...M-4
Shaft Ox Corner ...L-3
Shawnee Acres, 150 ...H-2
Bloomingdale ...H-4

Smyrna, 10023 ...F-2

S. Bethany, 449 ...L-5
S. Bowers, 50 ...H-4
Stanton, 3100 ...C-2
Staytonville, 40 ...J-3
Summit Bridge, 60 ...E-1
Sussex Gdns., 1215 ...L-4
SUSSEX CO., 197145 ...K-3
Sussex Shores, 10 ...L-5
Sycamore, 20 ...L-3
Talleys Corner ...A-8
Talleyville, 800 ...A-2
Thompsonville ...A-8
Townsend, 2049 ...F-1
Vernon ...J-3
Viola, 157 ...H-3
Ward ...L-4
Warwick, 100 ...L-4
Ways Corner, 800 ...A-9
Whaleys Crossroads, ...L-3
Whitesville, 50 ...M-3
Williamsville, 75 ...M-5
Williamsville ...L-2
Willow Grv., 75 ...G-3
Wilmington, 70851 ...C-2
Wilmington Manor, 7889 ...D-8
Winterthur, 100 ...B-8
Woodale ...D-1
Woodenhawk ...L-2
Woodland ...L-2
Woodland Bch., 150 ...F-3
Woodside, 181 ...H-3
Wyoming, 1313 ...H-2
Yorklyn, 300 ...C-2

District of Columbia

Page locator / Map keys A–N / Atlas pages 224–225

Georgetown ...E-6
Washington, 601723 ...E-6

Florida

Page locator / Map keys A–J / Atlas pages 52–53 / K–T 54–55
*City keyed to p. 51
†City keyed to pp. 56–57

Adamsville, 280 ...D-7
Alachua, 9059 ...D-7
Alafaya, 78113 ...H-10
Alford, 489 ...R-7
Allentown, 884 ...Q-3
Altamonte Sprs., 41496 ...H-10
Altha, 536 ...R-7
Alton, 100 ...Q-9
Altoona, 89 ...G-9
Alturas, 4185 ...J-9
Alva, 2596 ...N-9
Amelia City, 730 ...B-10
Anclote, 260 ...A-6
Angiers Pk., 980 ...R-13
Ankona, 280 ...L-13
Anna Maria, 1503 ...K-6
Anthony, 1150 ...F-8
Apalachicola, 2231 ...T-8
Apopka, 41542 ...H-9
Arcadia, 7637 ...L-9
Archer, 1118 ...E-7
Aripeka, 300 ...H-5
Armstrong, 300 ...C-10
Arran ...Q-7
Asbury Lake, 8700 ...C-9
Astatula, 1810 ...H-9
Astor, 1556 ...F-9
Astor Pk., 150 ...F-9
Athena, 60 ...J-3
Atlantic Bch. ...B-8
12655 ...B-8
Atlantis, 2005 ...N-14
Auburndale, 13507 ...I-9
Aucilla, 900 ...O-4
Avalon Bch., 679 ...R-3
Ave Maria, 30 ...O-10
Aventura, 35762 ...P-14
Avon Pk., 8836 ...K-10
Azalea Pk., 12556 ...N-4
Babson Pk., 1356 ...J-10
Bagdad, 3761 ...R-3
Baker, 300 ...Q-4
Bal Harbour, 2513 ...K-9
Bakers Mill ...C-5
Balm, 1457 ...J-8
Barberville, 165 ...F-10
Bartow, 17298 ...J-9
Bascom, 120 ...R-7
BAY CO., 168852 ...S-6
Bay Pk. Islands, 5628 ...K-2
Bay Lake, 130 ...I-5
Bay Lake, 20 ...I-9
Bay Pines, 2931 ...J-5
Bay Sprs., 50 ...Q-2
Bayonet Pt., 24376 ...H-5
Bayou George, 230 ...S-6
Bayport, 43 ...H-5
Bayshore, 300 ...N-9
Baywood Vil., 1300 ...A-9
Bee Ridge, 9598 ...L-7
Belair, 400 ...*N-8
Belcher, 400 ...A-5
Belle Isle, 5988 ...O-4
Belleair, 3869 ...A-6
Belleair Bluffs, 2031 ...C-1
Belleair Shores, 100 ...C-1
Belleview, 4492 ...F-8
Bellview, 23355 ...R-2
Berrydale, 441 ...Q-3
Beulah, 400 ...*R-7
Beverly Bch., 400 ...F-11
Beverly Hills, 8445 ...G-7
Big Coppitt Key, 2458 ...T-9
Big Pine Key, 4252 ...T-10
Biscayne Pk., 3055 ...K-9
Bithlo, 8268 ...H-11
Blackman, 200 ...Q-2
Blountstown, 2514 ...R-7

Bloxham, 200 ...B-1

Bluff Sprs., 220 ...Q-2
Boca Del Mar, 21800 ...†F-9
Boca Grande, 700 ...N-8
Boca Pointe, 3300 ...†F-9
Boca Raton, 84392 ...O-14
Boca West, 2100 ...†E-9
Bokeelia, 1780 ...N-8
Bonifay, 2793 ...Q-6
Bonita Sprs., 43914 ...O-9
Bostwick, 300 ...D-9
Boulogne, 260 ...A-8
Bowden ...I-3
Bowling Green, 2930 ...K-9
Boyette, 5890 ...*D-5
Boynton Bch., 68217 ...N-14
Bradenton, 49546 ...K-7
Bradenton Bch., 1171 ...K-6
BRADFORD CO., 28520 ...D-8
Bradfordville, 470 ...B-2
Bradley Jct., 686 ...J-8
Brandon, 103483 ...J-7
Branford, 712 ...D-6
Bratt, 200 ...Q-2
Brent, 21804 ...*I-9
BREVARD CO., 543376 ...J-12
Briny Breezes, 601 ...†D-10
Bristol, 996 ...R-7
Broadview Pk., 7125 ...†I-8
Bronson, 1113 ...E-7
Brooker, 338 ...D-7
Brookridge, 4420 ...H-7
Brooksville, 7719 ...H-7
Bryant, 180 ...M-13
Bryceville, 550 ...B-8
Buchanan ...R-8
Buckhead Ridge, 1450 ...L-11
Buckingham, 4036 ...N-9
Buenaventura Lakes, 26079 ...I-10
Bunnell, 2676 ...E-10
Bushnell, 2418 ...H-8
Callahan, 1123 ...B-9
Callaway, 14405 ...S-6
Cameron City, 180 ...K-5
Campbell, 2479 ...I-10
Campbellton, 230 ...Q-7
Campton, 125 ...Q-4
Campville, 200 ...D-8
Canal Pt., 367 ...M-12
Candler, 370 ...F-8
Canova Bch. ...J-13
Cantonment, 2800 ...R-2
Cape Canaveral, 9912 ...H-12
Cape Coral, 154305 ...N-8
Cape Haze, 400 ...M-8
Capitola, 165 ...B-3
Capps, 20 ...B-3
Captiva, 583 ...N-8
Carrabelle, 2778 ...T-1
Carrollwood, 33365 ...*B-3
Carters Cor., 250 ...†J-3
Caryville, 411 ...Q-6
Casselberry, 26241 ...I-4
Cassia, 90 ...G-10
Cedar Grv., 3397 ...S-6
Cedar Key, 702 ...F-5
Center Hill, 988 ...H-8
Century, 1698 ...Q-2
Chaires, 100 ...B-3
Chapman, 500 ...*A-4
Chassahowitzka, 850 ...G-6
Chattahoochee, 3652 ...R-8
Cherry Lake ...B-4
Chester, 370 ...A-9
Chiefland, 2245 ...E-6
Chipley, 3605 ...Q-6
Chipola ...P-7
Chokoloskee, 359 ...P-10
Christmas, 1146 ...H-11
Chuluota, 2483 ...H-11
Chumuckla, 850 ...Q-2
Citra, 950 ...F-8
CITRUS CO., 141236 ...G-7
Citrus Pk., 24252 ...*A-3
Citrus Ridge, 12015 ...*I-1
Citrus Sprs., 8622 ...G-7
Clair-Mel City, 7500 ...*C-4
Clarcona, 2990 ...M-3
Clearwater, 107685 ...J-6
Clermont, 28742 ...H-9
Cleveland, 2990 ...M-9
Clewiston, 7155 ...M-11
Cloud Lake, 135 ...J-10
Cocoa, 17140 ...I-12
Cocoa Bch., 11231 ...I-12
Coconut Creek, 52909 ...†C-8
Coconut Grv. ...†I-8
Codys Cor., 110 ...F-10
Coleman, 703 ...H-8
Collier City ...P-9
COLLIER CO., 321520 ...O-10
COLUMBIA CO., 67531 ...B-7
Combee Settlement, 5628 ...*I-9
Conch Key, 140 ...S-12
Concord, 125 ...B-2
Conway, 13467 ...N-10
Cooper City, 28547 ...†J-8
Copeland, 30 ...P-10
Coral Cove, 1160 ...J-13
Coral Gables, 46780 ...Q-14
Coral Sprs., 121096 ...O-13
Coral Ter., 24376 ...†I-7
Cortez, 4241 ...K-6
Cottage Hill, 1050 ...R-2
Cottondale, 933 ...Q-6
Crawfordville, 3702 ...C-2
Crescent Bch., 931 ...D-10
Crescent City, 1577 ...E-10
Crestview, 20978 ...Q-4
Cross City, 1728 ...D-5
Cross Creek, 300 ...E-8
Crystal Bch., 1350 ...†A-1
Crystal River, 3108 ...G-7
Crystal Sprs., 1327 ...I-8

Cudjoe Key, 1763 ...T-10

Curlew, 780 ...*B-1
Ft. Ogden, 300 ...M-8
Curlew Bch., 40286 ...Q-13
Cypress, 250 ...R-6
Cypress Gdns., 8917 ...*K-5
Cypress Quarters, 1300 ...M-12
Dade City, 6437 ...I-8
Dalkeith ...*L-7
Dania Bch., 29639 ...P-13
Darby, 375 ...I-7
Darsey, 300 ...A-2
Davenport, 2888 ...I-9
Davie, 91992 ...P-13
Daytona Bch., 61005 ...F-11
Daytona Bch. Shores, 4247 ...A-14
De Funiak Sprs., 5177 ...R-5
De Leon Sprs., 2614 ...F-10
De Soto City, 600 ...K-10
DE SOTO CO., 34862 ...L-9
DeBary, 19320 ...G-10
Deer Pk. ...I-11
Deerfield Bch., 75018 ...O-14
DeLand, 27031 ...F-10
Dellwood, 75 ...Q-7
Delray Bch., 60522 ...N-14
Deltona, 85182 ...G-10
Denaud ...N-9
Destin, 12305 ...R-4
Dinsmore ...*L-7
Dixie ...*J-7
DIXIE CO., 16422 ...E-5
Dixie Ranch Acres, 335 ...L-11
Doctors Inlet, 1800 ...C-9
Doral, 45704 ...†I-7
Dorcas ...Q-4
Dover, 3702 ...A-3
Dowling Pk., 500 ...C-5
Drifton, 25 ...B-3
Duette, 200 ...K-8
Dukes, 200 ...D-7
Dundee, 3717 ...J-9
Dunedin, 35321 ...J-6
Dunnellon, 1733 ...F-7
Durant, 225 ...J-8
DUVAL CO., 864263 ...B-8
Eagle Lake, 2255 ...J-9
Earleton, 320 ...D-8
E. Lake Weir, 140 ...G-8
E. Naples, 2050 ...O-9
E. Palatka, 1654 ...C-9
E. Tampa, 750 ...*C-4
Eastpoint, 2337 ...T-8
Eaton Pk., 900 ...*K-2
Ebro, 270 ...R-6
Edgar, 50 ...A-8
Edgewater, 20750 ...G-11
Edgewood, 2503 ...N-4
Egypt Lake, 3500 ...*B-3
El Destinado, 550 ...*L-8
El Jobean, 600 ...M-8
El Portal, 2325 ...*K-8
Elfers, 13986 ...I-6
Elkton, 300 ...D-9
Ellaville ...B-5
Ellenton, 4275 ...*L-1
Ellzey ...E-6
Eloise, 250 ...K-4
Emporia, 100 ...F-10
Englewood, 14863 ...M-7
Ensley, 20602 ...R-2
Enterprise, 600 ...G-10
Eridu, 60 ...C-4
Escambia Farms ...*K-5
ESCAMBIA CO., 297619 ...Q-2
Espanola, 100 ...E-10
Estero, 22612 ...N-9
Estifanulga, 120 ...R-8
Esto, 364 ...Q-5
Eureka, 130 ...F-8
Eustis, 18558 ...G-9
Eva ...I-9
Everglades City, 400 ...P-10
Evergreen, 130 ...A-9
Evinston, 240 ...E-8
Fairbanks, 300 ...D-8
Fairfield, 45 ...F-8
Fairview Shores, 10239 ...M-3
Fanning Sprs., 764 ...E-6
Federal Pt., 260 ...D-9
Felda, 200 ...N-10
Fellsmere, 5197 ...J-12
Fenholloway ...C-4
Fernandina Bch., 11487 ...B-10
Ferndale, 472 ...H-9
Ferry Pass, 28921 ...R-2
Fidelis, 156 ...*J-5
Fish Lake, 570 ...I-6
Fisher Island, 132 ...*M-9
Five Points, 1065 ...C-7
Flagler Bch., 4484 ...E-11
FLAGLER CO., 95696 ...E-10
Flamingo, 9054 ...N-10
Flamingo Bay, 880 ...N-8
Flemington, 400 ...F-8
Florahome, 430 ...D-9
Floral City, 5217 ...G-7
Florida City, 11245 ...Q-13
Floridana Bch., 500 ...J-12
Fiorosa, 1000 ...R-4
Forest, 300 ...F-9
Forest Hills ...*B-3
Forest Mills, 550 ...Q-5
Ft. Drum, 140 ...K-12
Ft. Green, 101 ...K-9
Ft. Green Sprs., 231 ...K-8
3700 ...A-3
Ft. Lonesome ...J-8
Ft. McCoy, 900 ...F-8
Ft. Meade, 5626 ...J-9
Ft. Myers, 68190 ...N-9
Ft. Myers Bch., 6277 ...N-8

Ft. Myers Villas, 5600 ...N-2

Ft. Pierce, 41590 ...L-13
Ft. Walton Bch., 19507 ...R-4
Ft. White, 567 ...D-6
Fountainbleu ...*L-7
Fowlers Bluff, 90 ...E-6
Fox Town, 300 ...*I-2
Franklin, 100 ...*M-2
FRANKLIN CO., 11549 ...T-8
Franklinton, 500 ...B-9
Freeport, 1787 ...R-5
Frink ...R-7
Frontenac, 680 ...H-12
Frostproof, 2992 ...J-10
Fruit Cove, 29362 ...C-9
Fruitland, 500 ...F-10
Fruitland Pk., 4078 ...G-8
Fruitville, 13224 ...L-7
Fuller Hts., 8758 ...J-8
GADSDEN CO., 46389 ...B-1
Gainesville, 124354 ...E-7
Galloway, 150 ...*J-1
Garden City, 150 ...Q-4
Garden Grv., 674 ...*I-9
Gardner, 463 ...L-9
Gaskin, 150 ...Q-5
Gateway, 8401 ...N-9
Geneva, 2990 ...G-11
Georgetown, 400 ...E-9
Gibsonia, 4507 ...*I-1
Gibsonton, 14234 ...J-7
Gifford, 9590 ...K-13
GILCHRIST CO., 16939 ...E-6
Gilmore ...H-3
Gladeview, 11535 ...*L-8
Glen Ridge, 219 ...*B-10
Glendale, 100 ...Q-5
Glenvar Hts., 16898 ...*M-7
Glenwood, 600 ...F-10
Golden Bch., 919 ...*J-9
Golden Gate, 23961 ...O-9
Golden Gate, 2650 ...L-13
Golden Glades, 630 ...I-10
Goldenrod, 12039 ...M-4
Golf, 230 ...†C-9
Gonzalez, 13273 ...R-2
Goodbys ...I-3
Goodland, 300 ...P-9
Gordonville, 1500 ...*K-4
Goulds, 1915 ...N-10
Grace ...*J-9
Graceville, 2278 ...Q-6
Graham, 200 ...D-8
Grand Island, 1200 ...G-9
Grand Ridge, 892 ...R-7
21362 ...C-10
Grandin, 400 ...D-9
Grant-Valkaria, 3850 ...J-12
Green Cove Sprs., 6908 ...C-9
Greenacres City, 37573 ...†B-8
Greenland, 600 ...*B-1
Greensboro, 602 ...B-1
Greenville, 843 ...B-4
Greenway, 686 ...Q-3
Gretna, 1460 ...B-1
Griffin ...†J-8
Gritney, 200 ...Q-3
Grove City, 1804 ...M-7
Grove Pk., 140 ...E-8
Gulf Bch. Hts., 1600 ...*K-7
Gulf Breeze, 5763 ...R-3
Gulf Gate ...†E-1
Gulf Hammock, 250 ...F-6
Gulf Stream, 786 ...†D-10
Gulfport, 12029 ...J-6
Hacienda Village ...I-6
Hague, 400 ...E-7
Haines City, 20535 ...I-9
Hallandale Bch., 37113 ...P-13
Halls City, 145 ...M-10
Hampton, 500 ...D-8
Hampton Sprs. ...C-4
Hague ...A-9
Hanson ...B-4
Harbinwood Estates, ...*L-7
Hardaway, 240 ...C-6
HARDEE CO., 27115 ...K-8
Harlem, 2658 ...M-11
Harold, 823 ...R-3
Hastings, 580 ...D-10
Havana, 1754 ...B-1
Hawthorne, 1417 ...E-8
Haynes City ...I-9
Hedges, 800 ...R-9
Hernando, 9054 ...G-7
HERNANDO CO., 172778 ...H-7
Hesperides ...J-10
Hialeah, 224669 ...†I-3
Hialeah Gdns., 21744 ...P-9
High Sprs., 5350 ...D-7
Highland, 140 ...E-7
Highland City, 10834 ...*J-9
Highland View, 450 ...T-7
Highlands Pk. Estates ...*B-3
HIGHLANDS CO., 98786 ...L-10
Highpoint, 2300 ...K-5

Hildreth ...D-6

Hilliard, 3086 ...A-8
Hillsboro Bch., 1875 ...†F-10
Hillsboro Pines, 446 ...†I-8
HILLSBOROUGH CO., 1229226 ...J-8
Hinson, 150 ...Q-6
Hobe Sound, 11521 ...L-13
Holder, 200 ...G-7
Holiday, 22423 ...I-6
Holley, 1630 ...R-3
Hollister, 900 ...D-9
Holly Hill, 11659 ...F-11
Hollywood, 140768 ...P-13
Holmes Bch., 3836 ...K-6
HOLMES CO., 19927 ...Q-6
Holopaw, 240 ...I-11
Holt, 300 ...Q-4
Homeland, 360 ...J-9
Homestead, 60512 ...Q-13
Homosassa, 2578 ...G-7
Homosassa Sprs., 13791 ...G-7
Horseshoe Bch., 169 ...E-5
Hosford, 650 ...R-8
Houston, 200 ...D-5
Howey-in-the-Hills, 1098 ...G-9
Hudson, 12158 ...I-6
Hull ...D-7
Hypoluxo, 2588 ...*C-10
Immokalee, 24154 ...N-10
Indialantic, 2720 ...J-12
Indian Creek Vil., 86 ...*J-9
Indian Harbour Bch., 8225 ...I-12
Indian Lake Estates, 400 ...J-10
Indian River Shores, 3901 ...K-13
Indian Rocks Bch., 4113 ...J-6
Indialantic ...J-12
Indiantown, 6083 ...M-12
Indio, 330 ...K-13
Inglis, 1325 ...G-6
Inlet Bch., 400 ...S-5
Intercession City, 630 ...I-10
Interlachen, 1403 ...D-9
Inverness, 7210 ...G-7
Inwood, 6403 ...*I-9
Islamorada, 6119 ...S-12
Island Grv., 100 ...E-8
Isleworth, 700 ...N-2
Iva, 1915 ...H-4
Ives Estates, 19525 ...*J-9
Jacksonville, 821784 ...C-9
Jacksonville Bch., 21362 ...C-10
JACKSON CO., 49746 ...Q-7
MADISON CO., 19224 ...C-4
Jan Phyl Vil., 5573 ...*K-4
Jasper, 4546 ...B-5
Jay, 533 ...Q-3
Jennings, 878 ...E-5
Jensen Bch., 11707 ...L-13
Jerome ...P-10
Jobe, 2013 ...A-10
June Bch., 4094 ...I-12
Juno Bch., 3176 ...M-14
Jupiter, 55156 ...M-14
Jupiter Inlet Bch., ...M-14
Jupiter Island, 817 ...M-14
Kathleen, 6332 ...I-8
Keaton Bch., 25 ...D-5
Kendale Lakes, 56148 ...Q-13
Kendall, 75371 ...Q-13
Kendrick ...F-8
Kenneth City, 4980 ...J-6
Key Biscayne, 10507 ...Q-14
Key Colony Bch., 797 ...S-12
Key Haven, 800 ...T-9
Key Largo, 10433 ...R-13
Key West, 24649 ...T-9
Keystone, 10453 ...*A-2
Keystone Hts., 1350 ...D-8
Killarney ...N-1
Kinard, 50 ...S-7
Kings Ferry ...A-9
Kings Pt., 12000 ...†D-9
Kissimmee, 59682 ...I-10
Kissimmee Pk., 160 ...I-10
Knights ...I-8
Kolin ...R-8
Korona, 75 ...E-10
Kossuthville, 400 ...*J-3
Kuhlman, 50 ...A-8
Labelle, 4640 ...N-10
Lacoochee, 1714 ...H-8
La Crosse, 360 ...D-7
La Grange ...C-12
Lake Alfred, 5015 ...*I-9
L. Bird, 50 ...D-4
L. Brantley, 3000 ...I-4
L. Buena Vista, 16 ...N-1
L. Butler, 1897 ...D-7
L. Cain Hills, 1600 ...N-1
Lake City, 12046 ...C-7
L. Clarke Shores, 3400 ...*B-10
Lake Como, 500 ...E-9
L. Geneva, 200 ...D-8
L. Hamilton, 1231 ...I-9
L. Harbor, 45 ...M-11
L. Helen, 2624 ...G-10
L. Jem, 340 ...G-9
L. Lorraine, 4006 ...R-4
L. Mann Highlands, 370 ...N-2
L. Mary, 13822 ...H-10
L. Monroe, 150 ...G-10
LAKE CO., 297052 ...H-9

Lake Pk., 8155 ...M-14

L. Placid, 2223 ...L-10
L. Shore, ...J-1
L. Suzy, 1040 ...M-8
L. Wales, 14225 ...J-9
L. Worth, 34910 ...N-14
Lakeland, 97422 ...I-8
Lakeport, 300 ...L-11
Lakewood Pk., ...K-13
Lamont, 178 ...B-3
Lanark Vil., 400 ...T-1
Land O' Lakes, 31996 ...I-7
Lantana, 10423 ...N-14
Largo, 77648 ...J-6
Lauderdale Lakes, 32593 ...†I-8
Lauderdale-by-the-Sea, 6056 ...†G-10
Lauderhill, 66887 ...†I-8
Laurel, 8171 ...L-7
Laurel Hill, 537 ...Q-4
Lawtey, 730 ...C-8
Layton, 184 ...S-12
Lazy Lake, 24 ...†I-8
Lealman, 19879 ...*C-1
Lebanon Sta., 30 ...D-9
Lecanto, 5882 ...G-7
Lee, 352 ...B-4
LEE CO., 618754 ...N-9
Leesburg, 20117 ...G-9
Lehigh Acres, 86784 ...N-9
Leisure City, 22655 ...Q-13
Lemon Grv., 657 ...K-9
Leonia, 150 ...Q-5
LEON CO., 275487 ...B-3
LEVY CO., 40801 ...E-6
Liberty, 100 ...Q-5
LIBERTY CO., 8365 ...S-8
Lighthouse Pt., 10344 ...O-14
Limestone, 132 ...L-9
Linden, 120 ...H-9
Lisbon, 260 ...G-9
Lithia ...J-8
Little Havana ...*L-8
Live Oak, 6899 ...C-6
Lloyd, 215 ...B-3
Lochloosa, 360 ...E-8
Lockhart, 13060 ...M-3
Lokosee ...J-11
Long Bch. ...D-8
Longboat Key, 6888 ...L-6
Longwood, 13657 ...I-4
Lorida, 100 ...K-10
Loughman, 880 ...I-10
Lowell, 220 ...F-8
Loxahatchee Groves, 3180 ...N-13
Lulu, 100 ...C-7
Lumberton, 250 ...Q-4
Luraville ...C-5
Lutz, 19344 ...I-7
Lynn Haven, 18493 ...S-6
Lynne, 200 ...F-8
Macclenny, 6374 ...C-8
Madeira Bch., 4263 ...J-6
Madison, 2843 ...B-4
21362 ...C-10
Maitland, 15751 ...M-4
Malabar, 2757 ...J-12
Malone, 2088 ...Q-7
Manalapan, 406 ...*C-10
Manasota, 540 ...M-7
MANATEE CO., 322833 ...K-7
Mandarin ...*M-7
Mango, 11313 ...*B-5
Mangonia Bch., 1888 ...*A-10
Manhattan, 80 ...*B-3
Marathon, 8297 ...S-11
Marco Island, 16413 ...P-9
Margate, 53284 ...O-13
Marianna, 6102 ...Q-7
Marineland, 16 ...E-10
Marion Oaks, 4200 ...G-8
Martel, 200 ...F-8
McAlpin, 150 ...C-6
McDavid, 100 ...Q-2
McIntosh, 452 ...E-8
Medart, 150 ...C-2
Medley, 838 ...*I-6
Medulla, 8892 ...*J-8
Melbourne, 76068 ...I-12
Melbourne Bch., 3101 ...I-12
Melbourne Shores, ...J-12
Melbourne Vil., 662 ...I-12
Melrose, 1100 ...D-8
Memphis, 7848 ...J-6
Merritt Island, 34743 ...I-12
Mexico Bch., 1072 ...*J-7
Micanopy, 658 ...E-8
Micco, 9092 ...J-12
Miccosukee, 285 ...A-3
Middleburg, 13008 ...C-9
Midway, 3004 ...A-3
Midway, 1705 ...G-10
Migliano, 100 ...R-4
Millgrove ...F-8
Milligan, 0 ...Q-4
Milliview, 1100 ...*J-1
Milton, 8826 ...R-3
Mims, 9147 ...H-12
Minneola, 9403 ...H-9
Miramar, 122041 ...†J-7
Miramar Bch., 6146 ...R-4
Mission Bay ...†E-9
Mission City, 1700 ...*I-1
MONROE CO., 73090 ...R-11

Montbrook ...E-7

Monticello, 2506 ...B-3
Montverde, 1463 ...M-1
Moore Haven, 1680 ...M-11
Morningside Pk., ...O-3
Morriston, 164 ...F-7
Morse Shores, 3300 ...*L-3
Moss Bluff, 120 ...F-9
Mossy Head, 250 ...Q-5
Mt. Carmel, 227 ...Q-3
Mt. Dora, 12378 ...G-9
Mt. Pleasant, 75 ...Q-6
Mt. Plymouth, 4011 ...G-9
Mulberry, 3817 ...J-8
Munson, 372 ...Q-3
Murdock ...M-8
Myakka City, 170 ...L-8
Myakka Head, 100 ...K-8
Myrtle Grv., 15870 ...R-2
Naalcrest, 500 ...*K-5
Naples, 21537 ...O-9
Naples Manor, 5562 ...P-9
Naples Pk., 5967 ...O-9
Naranja, 8303 ...Q-13
Narcoossee, 200 ...I-10
NASSAU CO., 73314 ...B-9
Nassauville, 1900 ...B-9
National Gdns., 400 ...F-11
Navarre, 31378 ...R-3
Neptune Bch., 7037 ...C-10
New Berlin ...*L-7
New Hope, 110 ...R-8
New Port Richey, 14911 ...I-6
New Smyrna Bch., 22464 ...G-11
Newberry, 4950 ...E-7
Newburn ...E-7
Newport ...C-2
Niceville, 12749 ...R-4
Nobleton, 282 ...H-8
Nocatee, 4524 ...L-9
Nokomis, 3167 ...L-7
Noma, 211 ...Q-6
N. Bay Vil., 7137 ...*K-9
N. Fort Myers, 39407 ...N-9
N. Key Largo, 244 ...R-13
N. Lauderdale, 41023 ...†I-8
N. Miami, 58786 ...P-13
N. Miami Bch., 41523 ...P-13
N. Palm Bch., 12015 ...M-14
N. Port, 57357 ...M-8
N. Redington Bch., 1417 ...*D-1
N. River Shores, ...L-13
Northdale, 22079 ...*A-2
Oak Grv., 300 ...*I-1
Oak Hill, 1792 ...G-11
Oakdale, 2538 ...N-1
Oakland Pk., ...†I-8
41363 ...O-14
O'Brien, 200 ...C-6
Ocala, 56315 ...F-8
Ocean Ridge, 1786 ...*C-10
Ocklawaha, 860 ...F-8
Ocoee, 35579 ...M-2
Odessa, 7267 ...I-7
Ojus, 18036 ...*J-9
Okahumpka, 267 ...G-9
OKALOOSA CO., 180822 ...R-4
Okeechobee, 5621 ...L-11
OKEECHOBEE CO., 39996 ...K-11
Old Myakka, 200 ...*L-7
Old Town, 250 ...E-6
Oldsmar, 13591 ...I-6
Olustee, 260 ...C-7
Olympia Hts., 13488 ...*I-7
Ona, 210 ...K-9
Oneco, 3200 ...K-7
Opa-locka, 15219 ...P-13
Orange City, 10599 ...G-10
ORANGE CO., 1145956 ...H-11
Orange Hts., 130 ...D-8
Orange Lake, 700 ...E-8
Orange Mills, 200 ...D-9
Orange Pk., 8412 ...C-9
Orangedale, 250 ...C-9
Orangedale, 400 ...C-9
Orchid, 415 ...J-13
Oriole Bch., 1420 ...*J-10
Orlando, 238300 ...H-11
Orlovista, 6123 ...N-3
Ormond Bch., 38137 ...F-11
Ormond-By-The-Sea, 7406 ...F-11
Ortega ...*M-7
OSCEOLA CO., 268685 ...I-11
Osprey, 6100 ...L-7
Otter Creek, 134 ...E-6
Overstreet, 70 ...T-7
Oviedo, 33342 ...H-10
Oxford, 360 ...H-8
Ozona, 700 ...I-6
Pahokee, 5649 ...M-12
Painters Hill, 50 ...E-10
Paisley, 818 ...G-9
Palatka, 10558 ...D-9
Palm Bay, 103190 ...J-11
PALM BCH. CO., 1320134 ...N-13
Palm Bch., 8348 ...N-14
Palm Bch. Gdns., 48452 ...M-14
Palm City, 23100 ...L-13
Palm Coast, 75180 ...E-10
Palm Harbor, 59249 ...I-6
Palm River, 18928 ...*B-10
Palm Shores, 5253 ...I-12
Palm Valley, 20019 ...C-10
Palma Sola, 3100 ...*I-2
Palmdale, 50 ...M-10

*, †, ‡, §, ◊   See explanation under state title in this index.
County and parish names are listed in capital letters & boldface type.
Independent cities (not included in a county) are listed in italics.

Hawaii–Illinois 241

Koloa, 2144 I-2
Kualapu'u, 2027 J-6
Kukuihaele, 336 L-9
Kuli'ou'ou, 370 N-5
Kunia Camp, 580 L-2
Kurtistown, 1298 M-10
Lahaina, 11704 K-7
Lā'ie, 6138 J-4
Lāna'i City, 3102 K-6
Laupāhoehoe, 581 L-9
Līhu'e, 6455 I-2
Lower Paia, 220 I-9
Mā'alaea, 352 I-8
Mā'ili, 9488 M-1
Mākaha, 8278 L-1
Makakilo City, 18248 M-2
Makawao, 7184 I-9
Mākena, 99 J-9
Mānā I-2
MAUI CO., 154834 J-7
Maunalani Hts., 700 G-10
Maunaloa, 376 J-6
Maunawili, 2040 M-5
Mililani Town, 27629 L-3
Miloli'i N-8
Mountain View, 3924 M-9
Nā'ālehu, 866 N-9
Nānākuli, 12666 J-4
Niu, 570 N-5
Olowalu, 80 I-8
Ō'ōkala, 150 L-9
Pā'auhau, 270 L-9
Pa'auilo, 595 L-9
Pacific Hts., 650 F-8
Pacific Palisades, 5600 M-3
Pāhala, 1356 N-9
Pāhoa, 945 M-10
Paia, 2668 I-9
Pāpā N-8
Pāpa'aloa, 320 L-9
Pāpa'ikou, 1314 M-10
Pa'uwela, 500 K-7
Pearl City, 47698 J-5
Pepe'ekeo, 1789 M-10
Poamoho L-3
Pukalani, 7574 K-7
Punalu'u K-4
Pu'uanahulu M-8
Pu'uiki J-10
Pu'ukoli'i, 200 I-8
Pu'unēnē I-8
Pu'uwai I-1
St. Louis Hts., 1000 G-10
Spreckelsville I-9
Sunset Bch., 660 J-3
'Ulupalakua, 75 K-7
Volcano, 2575 M-9
Wahiawā, 17821 J-5
Waiakoa, 900 J-9
Waialua, 3860 J-7
Wai'anae, 13177 J-4
Waiehu, 600 I-8
Waikapu, 2965 K-7
Waikīkī, 3000 H-9
Wailua, 2254 I-2
Wailua, 120 I-10
Wailuku, 15313 K-7
Waimānalo, 5451 J-5
Waimānalo Bch., 4481 M-6
Waimea, 9212 L-9
Waimea, 1855 I-2
Waimea, 650 J-2
Waipahu, 38216 M-3
Waipi'o Acres L-3
Whitmore Vil., 4499 L-3
Woodlawn, 1200 F-9

Idaho

Page locator
Map keys Atlas pages
A–N 64–65

Aberdeen, 1994 L-6
Acequia, 124 M-5
ADA CO., 392365 K-2
ADAMS CO., 3976 H-1
Ahsahka, 150 F-2
Albion, 267 M-5
Almo N-5
American Falls, 4457 L-6
Ammon, 13816 K-7
Arbon, 35 M-7
Arco, 995 K-6
Arimo, 355 M-7
Ashton, 1127 J-8
Athol, 692 C-1
Atlanta K-3
Atomic City, 29 K-6
Bancroft, 377 M-8
Banida, 125 M-8
Banks, 17 J-2
BANNOCK CO., 82839 M-7
Basalt, 394 K-7
Bayview, 350 C-2
BEAR LAKE CO., 5986 N-9
Bellevue, 2287 K-4
BENEWAH CO., 9285 E-1
Bennington, 190 M-8
Bern, 60 M-8
Big Creek H-3
BINGHAM CO., 45607 L-6
Blackfoot, 11899 L-7
BLAINE CO., 21376 K-5
Blanchard, 261 C-1
Bliss, 318 L-4
Bloomington, 206 M-8
Boise, 205671 K-2
BOISE CO., 7028 J-2
Bone K-8
BONNER CO., 40877 C-2
Bonners Ferry, 2543 B-2
BONNEVILLE CO., 104234 K-8
BOUNDARY CO., 10972 B-2
Bovill, 260 E-2
Bowmont, 150 K-1
Bruneau, 100 L-2
Buhl, 4122 M-4
Burgdorf H-2
Burley, 10345 M-5
Butte City, 74 K-6
BUTTE CO., 2891 K-6
Cabinet C-2
Calder D-2
Caldwell, 46237 K-1
CAMAS CO., 1117 K-4
Cambridge, 328 I-1
CANYON CO., 188923 K-1
Carey, 604 K-5
Careywood C-2
CARIBOU CO., 6963 L-7
Carmen, 25 H-5
Cascade, 939 I-2
CASSIA CO., 22952 M-5
Castleford, 226 M-4
Cataldo, 260 D-2
Cavendish, 30 F-2
Challis, 1081 I-4
Chatcolet D-1
Chester, 350 J-8
Chilco C-1
Chubbuck, 13922 L-7
CLARK CO., 982 J-7
Clark Fork, 536 C-2
Clarkia, 80 E-2
Clayton, 7 J-4
Clearwater, 50 G-2
CLEARWATER CO., 8761 E-3
Clifton, 259 M-7
Cobalt H-4
Cocolalla, 140 C-2
Coeur d'Alene, 44137 D-1
Colburn, 100 B-2
Conda L-8
Coolin, 200 B-1
Corral K-4
Cottonwood, 900 G-2
Council, 839 I-2
Craigmont, 501 F-2
Crouch, 162 J-2
Culdesac, 380 F-1
CUSTER CO., 4368 J-4
Dalton Gdns., 2335 C-1
Darlington, 50 K-6
Dayton, 463 N-7
Deary, 506 E-2
Declo, 343 M-5
Dietrich, 332 L-4
Dingle, 200 M-8
Dixie, 25 G-3
Donnelly, 152 I-2
Dover, 556 C-2
Downey, 625 M-7
Driggs, 1660 K-9
Drummond, 16 J-8
Dubois, 677 J-7
Eagle, 19908 K-2
E. Hope, 210 C-2
Eastport A-2
Eden, 405 M-4
Elba M-5
Elk City, 200 G-3
Elk River, 125 E-2
Ellis, 40 I-5
Elmira B-2
ELMORE CO., 27038 L-3
Emida, 100 E-2
Emmett, 6557 J-2
Fairfield, 416 K-4
Featherville K-3
Felt J-8
Fenn, 30 G-2
Ferdinand, 159 F-2
Fernan Lake Vil., 169 D-1
Fernwood, 425 E-2
Filer, 2508 M-4
Firth, 477 L-7
Fish Haven, 50 N-8
Franklin, 641 N-8
FRANKLIN CO., 12786 M-8
FREMONT CO., 13242 J-8
Fruitland, 4684 J-1
Fruitvale, 100 I-2
Gannett K-5
Garden City, 10972 B-6
Garden Valley, 394 J-2
GEM CO., 16719 J-2
Genesee, 955 F-1
Georgetown, 476 M-8
Gibbonsville G-5
Gifford F-2
Givens Hot Sprs., 120 K-1
Glenns Ferry, 1319 L-3
Golden G-3
Gooding, 3567 L-4
GOODING CO., 15464 L-4
Grace, 915 M-8
Grand View, 452 L-2
Grangeville, 3141 G-2
Grasmere M-2
Greencreek, 30 F-2
Greenleaf, 846 K-1
Greer F-2
Hagerman, 872 L-4
Hailey, 7960 K-4
Hamer, 48 J-7
Hammett, 300 L-3
Hansen, 1144 M-4
Harpster, 50 G-2
Harrison, 203 D-1
Harvard, 55 E-1
Hayden, 13294 C-1
Hayden Lake, 574 C-1
Hazelton, 753 M-5
Headquarters, 35 F-3
Heise K-8
Helmer E-2
Henry L-8
Heyburn, 3089 M-5
Hill City L-3
Holbrook N-7
Hollister, 272 M-4
Homedale, 2633 K-1
Hope, 86 C-2
Horseshoe Bend, 707 J-2
Howe, 80 K-6
Hoyt, 40 D-2
Huetter, 100 E-9
Idaho City, 485 K-2
IDAHO CO., 16267 G-2
Idaho Falls, 56813 K-7
Indian Valley, 75 I-2
Inkom, 854 L-7
Iona, 1803 K-7
Irwin, 219 K-8
Island Pk., 286 I-8
JEFFERSON CO., 26140 K-7
Jerome, 10890 M-4
JEROME CO., 22374 L-4
Joel, 100 E-1
Juliaetta, 579 F-1
Kamiah, 1295 F-2
Kellogg, 2120 D-2
Kendrick, 303 F-1
Ketchum, 2689 K-4
Kilgore I-7
Kimberly, 3264 M-4
King Hill, 100 L-3
Kingston, 800 D-2
Kooskia, 607 F-2
Kootenai, 678 B-2
KOOTENAI CO., 138494 C-1
Kuna, 15210 K-2
Laclede, 400 C-1
L. Fork, 120 I-2
Lakeview, 40 C-2
Lapwai, 1137 F-1
LATAH CO., 37244 E-2
Lava Hot Sprs., 407 M-7
Leadore, 105 I-6
Lemhi, 30 I-5
LEMHI CO., 7936 H-4
Lenore F-2
Leslie J-5
Letha, 240 J-1
LEWIS CO., 3821 F-2
Lewiston, 31894 F-1
Lewisville, 458 K-7
Liberty M-8
Lincoln, 3647 K-7
LINCOLN CO., 5208 L-5
Lorenzo, 100 K-8
Lost River, 68 K-5
Lowell, 25 F-3
Lowman, 42 J-3
Lucile, 100 G-2
Mackay, 517 J-5
MADISON CO., 37536 K-8
Magic City L-4
Malad City, 2095 M-7
Malta, 193 M-6
Marley, 100 L-4
Marsing, 1031 K-1
Marysville, 180 J-8
May, 50 I-5
McCall, 2991 I-2
McCammon, 809 M-7
McGuires E-7
Meadows, 190 I-2
Medimont D-2
Melba, 513 K-1
Menan, 741 K-7
Meridian, 75092 K-2
Mesa, 65 I-2
Middleton, 5524 K-1
Midvale, 171 I-1
Minidoka, 112 L-5
MINIDOKA CO., 20069 L-5
Mink Creek M-8
Monteview J-7
Montpelier, 2597 M-8
Moore, 189 K-6
Moreland, 1278 L-7
Moscow, 23800 E-1
Mt. Idaho G-2
Mountain Home, 14206 L-3
Moyie Sprs., 718 B-2
Mud Lake, 358 K-7
Mullan, 692 D-3
Murphy, 97 L-1
Murray, 75 D-2
Murtaugh, 115 M-5
Nampa, 81557 K-1
Naples, 450 B-2
New Centerville J-2
New Meadows, 496 H-2
New Plymouth, 1538 J-1
Newdale, 323 J-8
NEZ PERCE CO., 39265 F-1
Nezperce, 466 F-2
Nordman B-1
N. Fork H-5
Oakley, 763 M-5
Ola J-2
Onaway, 187 E-1
ONEIDA CO., 4286 N-6
Oreana L-2
Orofino, 3142 F-2
Orogrande G-3
Osburn, 1555 D-2
Ovid M-8
OWYHEE CO., 11526 M-2
Oxford, 48 M-7
Palisades, 100 K-8
Paris, 513 M-8
Parker, 305 J-8
Parma, 1983 K-1
Patterson, 5 I-5
Paul, 1169 M-5
Payette, 7433 J-1
PAYETTE CO., 22623 J-1
Peck, 197 F-2
Picabo, 100 K-5
Pierce, 508 F-3
Pine K-3
Pinehurst, 1619 D-2
Pingree, 150 L-7
Pioneerville J-2
Placerville, 53 J-2
Pleasant View F-6
Pleasantview, 220 N-7
Plummer, 1044 D-1
Pocatello, 54255 L-7
Pollock, 140 H-2
Ponderay, 1137 B-2
Porthill A-2
Post Falls, 27574 C-1
Potlatch, 804 E-1
POWER CO., 7817 M-6
Preston, 5204 N-8
Prichard D-2
Priest River, 1751 C-1
Princeton, 148 E-1
Rathdrum, 6826 C-1
Red River Hot Sprs. G-3
Reubens, 71 F-2
Rexburg, 25484 K-8
Reynolds L-1
Richfield, 482 L-5
Rigby, 3945 K-7
Riggins, 419 H-2
Ririe, 656 K-8
Riverside, 838 L-7
Roberts, 580 K-7
Rockland, 295 M-6
Rocky Bar K-3
Rogerson, 100 M-4
Rose Lake D-2
Rupert, 5554 M-5
St. Anthony, 3542 J-8
St. Charles, 131 N-8
St. Joe D-2
St. Maries, 2402 D-2
Salmon, 3112 H-5
Samaria, 100 N-7
Samuels, 150 B-2
Sanders E-1
Sandpoint, 7365 C-2
Santa, 100 E-2
Shelley, 4409 K-7
Shoshone, 1461 L-4
SHOSHONE CO., 12765 D-2
Shoup, 60 H-4
Silver City L-1
Silverton, 300 D-2
Smelterville, 627 D-2
Smiths Ferry, 75 J-2
Soda Sprs., 3058 M-8
Southwick, 40 F-2
Spalding F-1
Spencer, 37 J-7
Spirit Lake, 1945 C-1
Springfield, 100 L-7
Stanley, 63 J-4
Star, 5793 K-2
Sterling L-6
Stites, 221 G-2
Stone N-6
Sugar City, 1514 J-8
Sun Valley, 1406 K-4
Sunbeam, 40 J-4
Swan Valley, 204 K-8
Swanlake M-7
Sweet, 200 J-2
Syringa, 30 F-3
Tendoy I-5
Tensed, 123 E-1
Terreton K-7
Teton, 735 J-8
TETON CO., 10170 K-8
Tetonia, 269 K-8
Thatcher M-8
The String, 100 K-9
Thornton, 100 K-8
Triumph K-4
Troy, 862 E-1
Twin Falls, 44125 M-4
TWIN FALLS CO., 77230 M-4
Tyhee, 1123 L-7
Ucon, 1108 K-7
Ustick B-5
VALLEY CO., 9862 I-3
Victor, 1928 K-9
Viola, 150 E-1
Virginia M-7
Waha F-1
Wallace, 784 D-2
Warm Lake I-3
Warm River, 3 J-8
Warren, 45 H-3
WASHINGTON CO., 10198 I-1
Wayan, 35 L-8
Weippe, 441 F-2
Weiser, 5507 J-1
Wendell, 2782 L-4
Weston, 437 N-7
White Bird, 91 G-2
Whitney, 200 N-8
Wilder, 1533 K-1
Winchester, 340 F-1
Worley, 257 D-1
Yellow Pine, 32 I-3

Illinois

Page locator
Map keys Atlas pages
A–J 66–67
K–T 68–69
* City keyed to pp. 70–71
† City keyed to pp. 72–73
‡ City keyed to pp. 120–121
§ City keyed to p. 233

Abingdon, 3319 G-6
Adair, 210 H-5
Adams, 50 J-3
ADAMS CO., 67103 J-3
Addieville, 252 O-8
Addison, 36942 *H-5
Adeline, 85 B-8
Aden P-11
Adrian, 60 H-4
Akin, 110 Q-10
Albany, 891 C-6
Albers, 1190 O-8
Albion, 1988 P-12
Alden, 250 A-11
Aledo, 3640 E-5
Alexander, 300 K-7
ALEXANDER CO., 8238 T-8
Alexis, 831 F-5
Algonquin, 30046 B-11
Alhambra, 681 N-7
Allendale, 475 O-13
Allenville, 148 K-11
Allerton, 291 J-12
Alma, 320 N-10
Alorton, 2002 ‡I-8
Alpha, 671 E-6
Alsey, 227 K-5
Alsip, 19277 *K-8
Alta, 400 G-8
Altamont, 2319 M-10
Alto Pass, 391 R-9
Alton, 27865 N-6
Altona, 531 F-6
Alvin, 279 I-13
Amboy, 2500 D-9
Anchor, 146 H-11
Ancona, 80 F-10
Andalusia, 1178 E-5
Andover, 578 E-6
Anna, 4442 S-9
Annapolis, 55 M-13
Annawan, 878 E-7
Antioch, 14430 A-12
Apple Canyon Lake, 558 A-6
Apple River, 366 A-7
Aptakisic *D-6
Arbury Hills, 1770 *M-7
Archer †M-15
Arcola, 2916 K-11
Arenzville, 409 J-6
Argenta, 947 J-10
Argo Fay, 100 C-7
Argyle, 100 A-10
Arlington, 193 D-9
Arlington Hts., 75101 B-12
Armington, 343 I-9
Armstrong, 200 I-12
Aroma Pk., 743 F-13
Arrowsmith, 294 H-10
Arthur, 2288 K-11
Ashburn *J-8
Ashkum, 761 G-12
Ashland, 1333 J-7
Ashley, 536 P-9
Ashmore, 785 K-12
Ashton, 972 C-9
Assumption, 1168 K-9
Astoria, 1141 I-6
Athens, 1988 J-7
Athensville, 50 L-6
Atkinson, 972 E-7
Atlanta, 1692 I-9
Atlas, 50 K-4
Atterberry, 120 J-7
Atwater, 100 L-7
Atwood, 1224 J-11
Auburn, 4771 K-7
Augusta, 587 I-4
Aurora, 197899 C-11
Austin *H-8
Ava, 654 Q-8
Aviston, 1945 O-8
Avon, 799 G-6
Avondale *G-9
Balcom, 70 S-9
Baldwin, 373 P-7
Banner, 189 H-7
Bannockburn, 1583 *D-7
Bardolph, 251 H-5
Barnhill, 80 P-11
Barrington, 10327 B-12
Barrington Hills, 4209 *E-3
Barry, 1318 K-4
Barstow, 140 S-6
Bartelso, 595 O-8
Bartlett, 41208 *G-3
Bartonville, 6471 H-8
Basco, 98 H-3
Batavia, 26045 C-11
Batchtown, 214 M-5
Bath, 333 I-6
Bay City T-11
Baylis, 205 K-4
Beach Pk., 13638 A-12
Beardstown, 6123 J-6
Beason, 189 I-9
Beaucoup, 80 P-9
Beaverville, 362 F-13
Bedford Pk., 580 *J-7
Beecher, 4359 E-13
Beecher City, 463 M-10
Beecreek L-5
Belgium, 404 I-13
Belknap, 104 S-10
Bellair, 25 M-12
Belle Prairie City, 54 P-11
Belle Rive, 361 P-10
Belleview, 25 L-4
Belleville, 44478 O-7
Bellevue, 1978 G-8
Bellflower, 357 I-11
Bellmont, 276 O-12
Belltown, 40 L-6
Bellwood, 19071 *H-7
Belvidere, 25585 B-10
Bement, 1730 J-11
Benld, 1556 M-7
Bensenville, 18352 *G-6
Benson, 423 G-9
Bentley, 35 H-4
Benton, 7087 Q-10
Berdan, 50 L-6
Berkeley, 5209 *H-6
Berlin, 180 K-7
Bernadotte, 100 H-6
Berry, 70 K-8
Berryville, 30 O-12
Berwick, 160 G-5
Berwyn, 56657 *I-8
Bethalto, 9521 N-7
Bethany, 1352 K-10
Beverly, 30 J-4
Beverly *K-9
Bible Grv., 100 N-11
Big Foot Prairie, 75 A-10
Big Rock, 1126 C-11
Biggsville, 304 G-4
Bingham, 83 M-9
Birds, 50 N-13
Bishop Hill, 128 E-6
Bismarck, 579 I-13
Bissell †L-17
Blackstone, 100 F-10
Blandinsville, 651 H-4
Bloomfield S-10
Bloomingdale, 22018 C-12
Bloomington, 76610 H-9
Blue Island, 23706 *K-9
Blue Mound, 1158 K-9
Blue Ridge I-11
Bluff City, 300 M-9
Bluff Sprs., 120 J-6
Bluffs, 715 K-5
Bluford, 688 P-10
Blyton, 25 H-6
Boaz S-10
Boden, 100 E-5
Bogota, 60 N-12
Bolingbrook, 73366 D-12
BOND CO., 17768 N-8
Bondville, 443 I-11
Bone Gap, 246 O-12
Bonfield, 382 F-12
Bonnie, 397 P-10
Boody, 276 K-9
BOONE CO., 54165 B-10
Boos N-12
Borton, 60 K-12
Boskydell, 30 R-9
Boulder, 100 N-9
Bourbon, 140 K-11
Bourbonnais, 18631 F-12
Bowen, 494 I-4
Braceville, 793 E-11
Bradford, 768 F-8
Bradley, 15895 F-13
Braidwood, 6191 E-12
Breese, 4442 O-8
Bremen, 50 Q-7
Bridgeport, 1886 N-13
Bridgeport *I-9
Bridgeview, 16446 *J-7
Brighton, 2254 M-6
Brighton Pk. *I-9
Brimfield, 868 G-7
Bristol, 500 D-11
Broadlands, 349 J-12
Broadview, 7932 *I-7
Broadwell, 145 I-8
Brocton, 322 K-12
Brookfield, 18978 *I-7
Brooklyn, 749 ‡H-7
Brooklyn, 100 I-5
Brookport, 984 T-10
Brookville, 80 B-8
Broughton, 194 Q-11
BROWN CO., 6937 J-5
Brownfield, 75 S-11
Browning, 137 I-6
Browns, 134 O-12
Brownstown, 759 M-10
Brownsville, 50 Q-12
Bruce, 50 K-11
Brussels, 141 M-5
Bryant, 220 H-6
Buckingham, 300 F-12
Buckley, 600 H-12
Buckner, 462 Q-9
Buda, 538 E-8
Buffalo, 503 J-8
Buffalo Grv., 41496 B-12
Buffalo Hart, 25 J-8
Bull Valley, 1077 *B-2
Buncombe, 203 S-9
Bungay, 45 P-11
Bunker Hill, 1774 M-7
Burbank, 28925 *J-8
BUREAU CO., 34978 E-8
Burgess, 50 F-5
Burksville, 80 P-6
Burlington, 618 B-11
Burnham, 4206 *L-10
Burnt Prairie, 52 P-11
Burr Ridge, 10559 *J-6
Burtons Br., 700 *B-3
Bushnell, 3117 H-5
Bushton, 100 K-12
Butler, 180 M-8
Butterfield, 3750 *I-5
Byron, 3753 B-9
Cabery, 266 F-12
Cable, 120 E-5
Cache, 50 T-9
Cahokia, 15241 O-6
Cairo, 2831 T-9
Caledonia, 197 A-10
Calhoun, 172 O-12
CALHOUN CO., 5089 L-5
Calumet City, 37042 *L-10
Calumet Pk., 7835 *L-9
Calvin, 30 P-12
Camargo, 445 J-12
Cambria, 1228 R-9
Cambridge, 2160 E-6
Camden, 86 I-5
Cameron, 200 G-5
Camp Grv., 120 F-8
Camp Pt., 1132 J-4
Campbell Hill, 336 Q-8
Campton Hills, 11131 *H-1
Campus, 166 F-11
Canton, 14704 H-7
Cantrall, 139 J-8
Capron, 1376 A-10
Carbon Cliff, 2134 S-5
Carbondale, 25902 R-9
Carlinville, 5917 L-7
Carlock, 552 H-9
Carlyle, 3281 O-8
Carman, 100 G-4
Carmi, 5240 Q-12
Carol Stream, 39711 *H-4
Carpenter, 100 ‡D-10
Carpentersville, 37691 B-11
Carrier Mills, 1653 R-10
CARROLL CO., 15387 C-7
Carrollton, 2484 L-6
Carterville, 5496 R-9
Carthage, 2605 H-4
Cary, 18271 B-11
Casey, 2769 L-12
Caseyville, 4245 ‡H-9
Casner, 50 J-10
CASS CO., 13642 J-6
Castleton, 130 F-7
Catlin, 2040 I-13
Cave-In-Rock, 318 S-12
Cazenovia, 100 G-9
Cedar Pt., 277 E-9
Cedarville, 741 A-8
Centerville, 50 P-12
Central City, 1172 O-9
Centralia, 13032 O-9
Centreville, 5309 ‡I-8
Cerro Gordo, 1403 J-10
Chadwick, 551 C-7
Chambersburg, 100 J-5
Champaign, 81055 I-11
CHAMPAIGN CO., 201081 J-12
Chana, 200 C-9
Chandlerville, 553 J-6
Channahon, 12560 E-11
Chapin, 512 K-6
Charleston, 21838 L-12
Charlotte, 25 G-11
Chatham, 11500 K-7
Chatham *J-10
Chatsworth, 1205 G-11
Chauncey, 80 N-13
Chebanse, 1062 F-12
Chemung, 308 A-10
Cheneyville, 80 H-13
Chenoa, 1785 G-10
Cherry, 482 E-9
Cherry Valley, 3162 B-10
Chester, 8586 Q-7
Chesterfield, 188 L-6
Chesterville, 110 K-11
Chestnut, 246 J-9
Chicago, 2695598 C-13
Chicago Hts., 30276 D-13
Chicago Lawn *J-9
Chicago Ridge, 14305 *K-8
Chillicothe, 6097 F-8
Chrisman, 1343 J-13
CHRISTIAN CO., 34800 K-8
Christopher, 2382 Q-9
Cicero, 83891 C-13
Cisco, 261 J-10
Cisne, 672 O-11
Cissna Pk., 846 H-12
Clare, 75 C-10
Claremont, 176 N-12
Clarence, 80 H-12
Clarendon Hills, 8427 *I-6
CLARK CO., 16335 L-13
Clarksburg, 50 L-10
Clarksville, 100 L-13
Clay City, 959 N-11
CLAY CO., 13815 N-11
Clayton, 709 J-4
Claytonville, 130 H-13
Clear Lake, 229 †L-17
Clearing *J-8
Cleveland, 188 D-6
Clifton, 1468 F-12
Clinton, 7225 I-10
CLINTON CO., 37762 N-8
Coal City, 5587 E-11
Coal Valley, 3743 E-6
Coalton, 304 L-9
Coatsburg, 147 J-4
Cobden, 1157 S-9
Coello, 608 Q-9
Coffeen, 685 M-8
Colchester, 1401 H-5
COLES CO., 53873 K-11
Coleta, 164 C-7
Colfax, 1061 H-10
Collinsville, 25579 N-7
Collison, 100 I-13
Colmar, 70 H-4
Colona, 5099 T-6
Columbia, 9707 O-6
Columbus, 99 J-4
Compton, 303 D-9
Concord, 167 J-6
Congerville, 474 H-9
COOK CO., 5194675 C-13
Cooks Mills, 200 K-11
Cooksville, 182 H-10
Cora, 25 Q-8
Cordova, 672 D-6
Corinth, 30 R-10
Cornell, 467 F-10
Cornland, 93 J-8
Cortland, 4270 C-10
Cottage Hills, 980 ‡D-8
Coulterville, 945 P-8
Country Club Hills, 16541 *M-8
Countryside, 5895 *J-7
Cowden, 629 L-10
Cowling, 120 P-12
Crab Orchard, 333 R-10
Cragin *H-8
CRAWFORD CO., 19817 M-13
Creal Sprs., 543 R-10
Crescent City, 615 G-13
Crest Hill, 20837 *M-4
Creston, 662 C-10
Crestwood, 10950 *L-8
Crete, 8259 E-13
Creve Coeur, 5451 G-8
Cropsey, 120 H-11
Crossville, 745 P-12
Crystal Lake, 40743 B-11
Cuba, 1294 H-6
Cullom, 555 G-11
CUMBERLAND CO., 11048 L-11
Curran, 212 K-7
Custer Pk., 300 E-12
Cutler, 441 Q-8
Cypress, 234 S-9
Dahinda, 150 F-6
Dahlgren, 525 P-10
Dakota, 506 A-8
Dale, 150 Q-11
Dallas City, 945 G-4
Dalton City, 544 K-10
Dalzell, 717 E-9
Dana, 159 F-10
Danforth, 604 G-12
Danvers, 1154 H-9
Danville, 33027 I-13
Darien, 22086 *J-5
Darmstadt, 68 P-7
Darwin, 60 L-13
Davis, 677 A-8
Davis Jct., 2373 B-9
Dawson Pk. G-13
Daysville, 150 C-9
Dayton, 537 E-10
De Land, 446 I-10
De Soto, 1590 R-9
De Witt, 184 I-10
DE WITT CO., 16561 I-9
Decatur, 76122 J-10
Deer Creek, 704 G-9
Deer Grv., 48 D-8
Deer Pk., 3200 *D-4
Deer Plain, 80 N-5
Deerfield, 18225 *D-7
DeKalb, 43862 C-10
DEKALB CO., 105160 B-10
Del Mar Woods, 120 *D-7
Delafield, 40 P-11
Delavan, 1689 H-8
Delwood R-11
Dennison, 100 L-13
Denver, 120 I-4
Depue, 1838 E-9
Des Plaines, 58364 B-12
Deselm E-12
Detroit, 83 K-5
Devereux Hts. †K-17
Dewey, 150 I-11
Diamond, 2527 E-11
Diamond Lake, 1500 *C-5
Dieterich, 617 M-11
Dillon, 60 H-8
Divernon, 1172 K-8
Dix, 461 O-10
Dixmoor, 3644 *L-9
Dixon, 15733 C-8
Dixon Sprs., 50 S-10
Dolton, 23153 *L-10
Dongola, 726 S-9
Donnellson, 210 M-8
Donovan, 304 G-13
Dorsey, 200 M-7
DOUGLAS CO., 19980 K-12
Dover, 168 E-8
Dowell, 408 Q-9
Downers Grv., 47833 C-12
Downs, 1005 H-10
Druce Lake, 200 *A-5
Du Bois, 205 P-9
Du Quoin, 6109 Q-9
Duck Lake Woods, 400 *A-4
Duncans Mills, 60 I-6
Dundas, 250 N-12
Dunfermline, 300 H-7
Dunlap, 1386 G-8
Dunning *G-7
DUPAGE CO., 916924 C-12
Dupo, 4138 O-6
Durand, 1443 A-9
Dwight, 4260 F-11
Eagerville, 127 M-7
Earlville, 1701 D-10
E. Alton, 6301 N-6
E. Cape Girardeau, 385 S-8
E. Carondelet, 499 ‡J-7
E. Clinton C-6
E. Dubuque, 1704 A-5
E. Dundee, 2860 *E-2
E. Galesburg, 812 F-6
E. Hannibal, 35 K-3
E. Hardin, 30 M-5
E. Hazel Crest, 1543 *M-9
E. Lynn, 200 H-13
E. Moline, 21302 D-6
E. Peoria, 23402 G-8
E. St. Louis, 27006 O-6
Easton, 321 I-7
Eastwood Manor, 950 *A-3
Eaton, 100 M-13
Echo Lake, 550 *C-4
Eddyville, 101 S-11
Edelstein, 160 F-8
Eden, 220 P-8
Edgar, 40 K-13
EDGAR CO., 18576 K-13
Edgewood, 440 N-10
Edgington, 450 E-5
Edinburg, 1078 K-8
Edison Pk. *F-7
Edwards, 350 G-7
EDWARDS CO., 6721 O-12
Edwardsville, 24293 N-7
Effingham, 12328 M-11
EFFINGHAM CO., 34242 M-11
Egan, 50 B-8
El Dara, 78 K-4
El Paso, 2810 G-9
Elbridge, 80 K-13
Elburn, 5602 C-11
Elco, 150 S-9
Eldorado, 4122 R-11
Eldred, 201 L-5
Eleroy, 120 A-7
Elgin, 108188 B-11
Elizabeth, 761 A-6
Elizabethtown, 299 S-11
Elk Grove Vil., 33127 *F-5
Elkhart, 405 J-8
Elkville, 928 Q-9
Ellery, 50 P-12
Elliott, 295 H-11
Ellis Grv., 363 Q-7
Ellisville, 96 G-6
Ellsworth, 195 H-10
Elmhurst, 44121 C-12
Elmira, 50 F-7
Elmwood, 2097 G-7
Elmwood Pk., 24883 *H-7
Elsah, 673 M-6
Elvaston, 165 H-3
Elwin, 150 K-9
Elwood, 2279 E-12
Emden, 485 I-8
Emerald Pk., 400 *A-3
Emington, 117 F-11
Emma, 90 Q-12
Energy, 1146 R-9
Enfield, 596 P-11
Englewood *J-9
Enterprise, 40 O-11
Eola, 100 *J-3
Equality, 595 R-11
Erie, 1602 D-7
Essex, 802 F-12
Etna, 60 L-11
Eureka, 5295 G-9
Evanston, 74486 B-13
Evansville, 701 Q-7
Evergreen Pk., 19852 *K-8
Ewing, 307 Q-10
Exeter, 65 K-5
Fair Haven, 30 C-7
Fairbury, 3757 G-11
Fairdale, 200 B-10
Fairfield, 5154 P-11
Fairmont, 2459 *M-4
Fairmont City, 2635 ‡H-8
Fairmount, 642 J-13
Fairview, 522 G-6
Fairview Hts., 17078 ‡I-9
Fall Creek, 40 J-3
Fancher, 75 L-10
Fancy Prairie, 100 J-8
Fandon, 60 H-5
Farina, 518 N-10
Farmer City, 2037 I-10
Farmersville, 724 L-8
Farmington, 2448 G-7
FAYETTE CO., 22140 M-9
Fayetteville, 366 P-7
Fenton, 170 D-7
Ferris, 156 H-4
Fiatt, 200 H-6
Fieldon, 239 M-5
Fillmore, 330 M-9
Findlay, 683 K-10
Fisher, 1881 I-11
Fishhook, 30 J-4
Fithian, 485 I-12
Five Islands Pk., 220 *G-2
Flag Ctr., 100 C-9
Flanagan, 1110 G-10
Flat Rock, 331 N-13
Flatville, 60 I-12
Flora, 5070 N-11
Floraville, 53 P-6
Florence, 100 B-8
Florence, 38 K-5
Flossmoor, 9464 *M-9
Foosland, 101 H-11
FORD CO., 14081 H-12
Ford Hts., 2763 *N-10
Forest City, 246 H-7
Forest Homes, 1700 ‡D-8
Forest Lake, 1659 *C-5
Forest Pk., 14167 *I-7
Forest View, 698 *I-7
Forrest, 1220 G-11
Forreston, 1446 B-8
Forsyth, 3490 J-10
Fosterburg, 250 M-6
Fountain Green, 120 H-4
Fowler, 400 J-3
Fox Lake, 10579 A-12
Fox River Grv., 4854 B-11
Frankfort, 17782 D-12
Franklin, 610 K-7
FRANKLIN CO., 39561 Q-10
Franklin Grv., 1021 C-9
Franklin Pk., 18333 *G-7
Frederick, 100 I-5
Freeburg, 4354 O-7
Freeman Spur, 287 Q-9
Freeport, 25638 B-8
Fulton, 3481 C-6
FULTON CO., 37069 H-6
Fults, 26 P-6
Funks Grv. H-9
Future City, 150 T-9
Gage Pk. *J-9
Galatia, 933 Q-11
Gale T-8
Galena, 3429 A-6
Galesburg, 32195 F-6
GALLATIN CO., 5589 R-12
Galt, 210 C-7
Galton, 20 K-11
Galva, 2589 F-7
Ganntown, 35 S-10
Garden of Eden, 140 F-13
Garden Plain, 80 C-6
Garden Prairie, 352 B-10
Gardner, 1463 F-11
Garrett, 162 J-11
Gays, 281 L-11
Geff, 367 O-11
Geneseo, 6586 E-6
Geneva, 21495 C-11
Genoa, 5193 B-10
Georgetown, 3474 J-13
Gerlaw, 150 F-5
German Valley, 463 B-8
Germantown, 1269 O-8
Germantown Hills, 3438 G-8
Gibson City, 3407 H-11
Gibsonia R-12
Gifford, 975 I-12
Gila, 35 M-11
Gilberts, 6879 *E-1
Gilead, 30 M-5
Gillespie, 3319 M-7
Gilman, 1814 G-12
Gilson, 190 G-6
Girard, 2103 L-7
Gladstone, 281 G-4
Glasford, 1022 H-7
Glasgow, 141 K-5
Glen Carbon, 12934 ‡F-9
Glen Ellyn, 27450 *H-5
Glenarm, 200 K-8
Glencoe, 8723 B-13
Glendale, 50 S-10
Glendale Hts., 34208 *G-4
Glenview, 44692 *E-7
Glenwood, 8969 *M-9
Godfrey, 17982 M-6
Godley, 601 E-11
Golconda, 668 S-11
Golden, 644 I-4
Golden Eagle, 50 N-5
Golden Gate, 68 P-12
Golf, 500 *F-8
Good Hope, 396 H-5
Goodenow, 140 E-13
Goodfield, 860 G-9
Goodwine, 80 H-13
Gordon, 20 M-13
Goreville, 1049 R-9
Gorham, 236 R-8
Grafton, 674 M-5
Grand Detour, 429 C-8
Grand Ridge, 560 E-10
Grand Tower, 605 R-8
Grandview, 1441 †L-17
Grandview, 110 K-13
Granite City, 29849 N-6
Grant Pk., 1331 E-13
Grantfork, 337 N-8
Grantsburg, 150 S-10
Granville, 1427 E-9
Graymont, 130 G-10
Grayslake, 20957 *B-5
Grayville, 1666 P-12
Green Oaks, 3866 *B-6
Green Valley, 709 H-8
Greenbush, 100 G-5
GREENE CO., 13886 L-5
Greenfield, 1071 L-6
Greenup, 1513 L-12
Greenview, 778 I-7
Greenville, 7000 N-8
Gridley, 1432 G-10
Griggsville, 1226 K-5
Grimsby R-8
Groveland, 500 H-8
GRUNDY CO., 50063 E-11
Gulfport, 54 G-4
Gurnee, 31295 *A-6
Hagarstown, 100 M-9
Hainesville, 3597 *A-5
Half Day *C-6
Hallsville, 80 I-9
Hamburg, 128 L-5
Hamburg N-9
Hamel, 816 N-7
Hamilton, 2951 H-3
HAMILTON CO., 8457 P-11
Hammond, 509 J-10
Hampshire, 5563 B-11
Hampton, 1863 R-5
HANCOCK CO., 19104 H-3
Hanna City, 1225 G-7
Hanover, 844 B-6
Hanover Pk., 37973 *F-4
Harco, 100 R-10
Hardin, 967 M-5
HARDIN CO., 4320 S-11
Harding, 120 D-10
Hardinville N-13
Harmon, 120 D-8
Harper, 30 B-8
Harrisburg, 9017 R-11
Harrison, 160 A-9
Harrisonville P-6
Harristown, 1367 J-9
Hartford, 1429 ‡E-8
Hartsburg, 314 I-8
Harvard, 9447 A-10
Harvel, 223 L-8
Harvey, 25282 D-13
Harwood Hts., 8612 *G-7
Havana, 3301 I-7
Hawthorn Woods, 7663 *C-5
Hayes J-11
Hazel Crest, 14100 *M-9
Hazel Dell, 100 M-12
Hebron, 1216 A-11
Hecker, 481 P-7
Hegeler, 1900 I-13
Hegewisch *L-10
Henderson, 255 F-6
HENDERSON CO., 7331 G-4
Hennepin, 757 E-9
Henning, 251 I-13
Henry, 2464 F-8
HENRY CO., 50486 E-6
Herald, 80 Q-12
Herbert, 100 B-10
Hermon, 50 G-6
Herod, 70 R-11
Herrick, 436 M-9
Herrin, 12501 R-9
Herscher, 1591 F-12
Hersman, 80 J-5
Hettick, 181 L-7
Hewittville, 450 K-9
Heyworth, 2841 I-9
Hickory Grv., 400 J-3
Hickory Hills, 14049 *J-7
Hidalgo, 106 M-12
Highland, 9919 N-8
Highland Hills *I-5
Highland Lake *A-5
Highland Pk., 29763 B-13
Highway Vil. †J-17
Highwood, 5405 B-13
Hillcrest, 1326 C-9
Hillerman, 35 T-10
Hillsboro, 6207 M-8
Hillsdale, 523 D-6
Hillside, 8157 *H-6
Hillview, 193 L-5
Hinckley, 2070 C-10
Hindsboro, 313 K-12
Hinsdale, 16816 *J-6
Hodgkins, 1897 *J-7
Hoffman, 508 O-9
Hoffman Estates, 51895 *F-4
Holcomb, 270 B-9
Holder, 60 H-10
Holiday Hills, 610 *B-3
Hollywood Hts., 1060 ‡H-9
Homer, 1193 J-12
Homer Glen, 24220 *L-6
Hometown, 4349 *J-8
Homewood, 19323 *M-9
Hoopeston, 5351 H-13
Hooppole, 204 D-7
Hopedale, 865 H-8
Hopewell, 410 F-8
Hopkins Pk., 603 F-13
Hord, 175 N-11
Hoyleton, 531 O-9
Hudson, 1838 H-9
Huey, 169 O-9
Hull, 461 K-3
Humboldt, 437 K-11
Hume, 380 J-13
Humm Wye, 25 S-11
Hunt City, 90 M-12
Huntley, 24291 B-11
Hurst, 795 Q-9
Hutsonville, 554 M-13
Hutton, 50 L-12
Hyde Pk. *J-10
Illinois City, 250 E-4
Illiopolis, 891 J-9
Ina, 2338 P-10
Indian Creek, 462 *C-6
Indian Head Pk., 3809 *J-6
Indian Oaks, 500 E-13
Indianola, 276 J-13
Industry, 478 I-5
Ingalls Pk., 3314 *N-5
Ingleside, 1700 *A-4
Ingraham, 150 N-11
Inverness, 7399 *E-5
Iola, 141 N-10
Ipava, 470 H-6
Irene B-10
Iroquois, 154 G-13
IROQUOIS CO., 29718 G-12
Irving, 495 M-8
Irving Pk. *G-8
Irvington, 659 O-9
Irwin, 74 F-12
Island Lake, 8080 *B-3
Itasca, 8649 *G-5
Iuka, 489 O-10
Ivanhoe, 100 *B-5
Ivesdale, 267 J-11
JACKSON CO., 60218 Q-8
Jacksonville, 19446 K-6
Jamestown, 120 N-8
Janesville, 150 L-11
JASPER CO., 9698 M-12
JEFFERSON CO., 38827 O-10
Jefferson Pk. *G-8
Jerome, 1656 †M-16
JERSEY CO., 22985 M-6
Jerseyville, 8465 M-6
Jewett, 223 M-12
JO DAVIESS CO., 22678 B-6
JOHNSON CO., 12582 S-10
Johnsonville, 77 O-11
Johnston City, 3543 R-10
Joliet, 147433 D-12
Jonesboro, 1821 S-9
Joppa, 360 T-10
Joslin, 100 D-6
Joy, 417 E-4
Junction, 129 R-12
Junction City, 482 O-9
Justice, 12926 *J-7
Kampsville, 328 L-5
Kane, 438 M-6
KANE CO., 515269 C-11
Kaneville, 484 C-11
Kangley, 251 F-10
Kankakee, 27537 F-12
KANKAKEE CO., 113449 F-12
Kansas, 787 K-12
Kappa, 227 G-9
Karbers Ridge, 45 R-11
Karnak, 499 S-10
Kasbeer, 85 D-8
Kaskaskia, 14 Q-7
Keenes, 83 P-10
Keeneyville, 300 *G-4
Keensburg, 210 P-13
Keithsburg, 609 F-4
Kell, 219 O-10
Kellerville, 30 J-4
Kemper, 70 M-6
Kempton, 231 F-11
KENDALL CO., 114736 D-11
Kenilworth, 2513 *E-8
Kenney, 326 I-9
Kent, 100 A-7
Keptown, 45 M-10
Kewanee, 12916 E-7
Keyesport, 421 N-9
Kickapoo, 400 G-7
Kilbourne, 302 I-7
Kildeer, 3968 *D-5
Kincaid, 1505 K-8
Kinderhook, 216 K-3
Kings, 250 C-9
Kingston, 1164 B-10
Kingston, 30 J-4
Kingston Mines, 302 H-7
Kinmundy, 796 N-10
Kinsman, 99 E-11
Kirkland, 1744 B-10
Kirksville, 50 K-10
Kirkwood, 714 G-5
Knollwood, 1747 *B-7
KNOX CO., 52919 F-6
Knoxville, 2911 F-6
La Clede, 100 N-10
La Fox, 250 *H-1
La Grange, 15550 *I-7
La Grange Highlands, 3650 *J-6
La Grange Pk., 13579 *I-7
La Harpe, 1235 H-4
La Hogue, 30 G-12
La Moille, 726 D-9
La Prairie, 47 I-4
La Rose, 144 F-9
La Salle, 9609 E-9
LA SALLE CO., 113924 E-10
Lacon, 1937 F-8
Ladd, 1295 E-9
Lafayette, 223 F-7
L. Barrington, 4973 *C-4
L. Bluff, 5722 B-12
Lake City, 110 K-10
LAKE CO., 703462 B-12
L. Forest, 19375 B-13
L. Fork, 100 J-8
L. Holiday, 4761 D-10
Lake in the Hills, 28965 *D-2
L. Killarney, 700 *C-3
L. Lawrence, 150 N-13
L. Mattoon, 1000 L-11
L. Summerset, 2048 A-8
L. Villa, 8741 A-12
L. Wildwood, 500 F-9
L. Zurich, 19631 B-12
Lakemoor, 6017 A-11
Lakeview *G-9
Lakewood, 3811 *C-1
Lakewood, 100 L-10
Lanark, 1457 B-7
Lancaster, 150 O-13
Landes N-13
Lane, 130 I-10
Langleyville, 432 K-8
Lansing, 28331 *M-10
LaPlace, 259 J-10
Larchland G-5
Latham, 380 J-9
Laura, 150 F-7
Lawndale, 150 I-9
Lawndale *I-8
Lawrence, 200 A-10
LAWRENCE CO., 16833 N-13
Lawrenceville, 4348 N-13
Le Roy, 3560 H-10
Leaf River, 443 B-8
Lebanon, 4418 O-7
Lee, 337 C-10
Lee Ctr., 250 C-9
LEE CO., 36031 D-8
Leesville, 100 F-13
Leland, 977 D-10
Leland Grv., 1503 †M-16
Lemont, 16000 *K-5
Lena, 2912 A-7
Lenzburg, 521 P-7
Leonore, 130 E-9
Lerna, 286 L-11
Lewistown, 2384 H-6
Lexington, 2060 G-10
Liberty, 516 J-4
Libertyville, 20315 B-12
Lick Creek, 60 S-9
Lily Lake, 993 C-11
Lilymoor, 450 *A-3
Lima, 163 I-3
Lincoln, 14504 I-8
Lincolnshire, 7275 *D-6
Lincolnwood, 12590 *F-8
Lindenhurst, 14462 A-12
Lindenwood, 300 B-9
Lis M-11
Lisbon, 285 D-11
Lisbon Ctr. *M-1
Lisle, 22390 C-12
Litchfield, 6939 M-8
Literberry, 100 J-6
Little America, 200 H-7
Little York, 331 F-5
Littleton, 181 I-5
Lively Grv., 45 P-8
Liverpool, 129 H-7
Livingston, 858 M-7
LIVINGSTON CO., 38950 F-11
Loami, 745 K-7
Lockport, 24839 D-12
Loda, 407 H-12
Lodge, 100 I-11
Logan, 327 Q-10
Logan K-13
LOGAN CO., 30305 I-8
Logan Sq. *H-9
Lomax, 454 G-4
Lombard, 43165 *H-5
London Mills, 392 G-6
Long Creek, 1328 J-10
Long Grv., 8043 *D-5
Long Lake, 3515 *A-4
Long Pt., 226 F-10
Longview, 153 J-12
Loogootee, 70 N-10
Loop *H-9
Loraine, 313 I-3
Loran, 40 B-7
Lostant, 498 F-9
Louisville, 1139 N-11
Loves Pk., 23996 A-9
Lovington, 1130 K-10
Low Pt., 200 G-9
Lowder, 100 K-7
Lowell, 50 E-9
Ludlow, 371 H-12
Lyndon, 648 D-7
Lynn Ctr., 150 E-6
Lynnville, 117 K-6
Lynwood, 9007 *M-10
Lyons, 10729 *I-7
Macedonia, 63 Q-10
Machesney Pk., 23499 A-9
Mackinaw, 1950 H-8
Macomb, 19288 H-5
Macon, 1138 K-9
MACON CO., 110768 J-9
MACOUPIN CO., 47765 L-7
Madison, 3891 ‡G-7
MADISON CO., 269282 N-7
Maeystown, 157 P-6
Magnolia, 260 F-9
Mahomet, 7258 I-11
Makanda, 561 R-9
Malta, 1164 C-10
Manchester, 292 K-6
Manhattan, 7051 E-12
Manito, 1642 H-7
Manlius, 359 E-8
Mansfield, 906 I-11
Manteno, 9204 E-13
Manville, 50 F-10
Maple Pk., 1310 C-10
Mapleton, 270 H-7
Maquon, 284 G-6
Marblehead, 100 J-3
Marcelline, 100 I-3
Marengo, 7648 B-10
Marietta, 112 H-6
Marine, 960 N-7
Marion, 17193 R-10
MARION CO., 39437 O-10
Marissa, 1979 P-7
Markham, 12508 *L-9
Marley, 100 *M-6
Maroa, 1801 J-10
Marseilles, 5094 E-10
Marshall, 3933 L-13
MARSHALL CO., 12640 F-9
Martinsville, 1167 L-13
Martinton, 381 F-13
Maryville, 7487 ‡G-10
Mascoutah, 7483 O-7
Mason, 345 N-10
Mason City, 2343 I-8
MASON CO., 14666 I-7
MASSAC CO., 15429 T-10
Matherville, 723 E-5
Matteson, 19009 *N-8
Mattoon, 18555 L-11
Maunie, 139 Q-12
Maywood, 24090 *H-7
Mazon, 1015 E-11
McClure, 402 S-8
McConnell, 250 A-7
McCook, 228 *J-7
McCormick R-10
McCullom Lake, 1049 *A-2
MCDONOUGH CO., 32612 I-5
McHenry, 26992 A-11
MCHENRY CO., 308760 A-11
McLean, 830 I-9
MCLEAN CO., 169572 H-10
McLeansboro, 2883 Q-11
McNabb, 285 F-9
Meadowbrook, 1000 ‡D-9
Meadows, 300 G-10
Mechanicsburg, 590 J-8
Media, 107 G-4
Medinah *G-5
Medora, 419 M-6
Melrose L-13
Melrose Pk., 25411 *H-7
Melvin, 452 H-11
MENARD CO., 12705 I-7
Mendon, 953 I-3
Mendota, 7372 D-9
Menominee, 248 A-5
Meppen, 60 M-5
MERCER CO., 16434 E-5
Meredosia, 1044 J-5
Meriden, 50 D-9
Mermet S-10
Merna, 40 H-10
Merrionette Pk., 1900 *K-9
Metamora, 3636 G-8
Metcalf, 189 J-13
Metropolis, 6537 T-10
Mettawa, 547 *C-6
Meyer, 50 I-3
Michael, 50 L-5
Middletown, 324 I-8
Midlothian, 14819 *L-8
Midway, 330 H-8
Midway, 25 T-10
Milan, 5099 T-3
Milford, 1306 G-13
Mill Creek, 65 S-9
Mill Shoals, 215 P-11
Milledgeville, 1032 C-7
Millersburg, 100 E-5
Millersville, 65 L-9
Millington, 665 D-10
Millstadt, 4011 O-6
Milton, 271 K-5
Mineral, 237 E-7
Minier, 1252 H-9
Minonk, 2078 G-9
Minooka, 10924 E-11
Mitchell, 1356 ‡F-8
Mitchellsville, 100 R-11
Modesto, 189 L-7
Modoc, 100 Q-6
Moecherville *J-2
Mokena, 18740 *M-7
Moline, 43483 D-5
Momence, 3310 F-13
Monee, 5148 E-13
Monica, 80 F-7
Monmouth, 9444 F-5
Monroe Ctr., 471 B-9
MONROE CO., 32957 P-6
Montgomery, 18438 D-11
MONTGOMERY CO., 30104 L-8
Monticello, 5548 J-11
Montrose, 201 M-11
Mooseheart, 100 *I-2
MORGAN CO., 35547 J-6
Morgan Pk. *K-9
Morris, 13636 E-11
Morrison, 4188 C-7
Morrisonville, 1056 L-8
Morton, 16267 H-8
Morton Grv., 23270 *F-7
MOULTRIE CO., 14846 K-10
Mound City, 588 T-9
Mounds, 810 T-9
Mt. Auburn, 480 K-9
Mt. Carmel, 7284 O-13
Mt. Carroll, 1717 B-7
Mt. Erie, 88 O-12
Mt. Greenwood *K-8
Mt. Morris, 2998 B-8
Mt. Olive, 2099 M-7
Mt. Pleasant, 50 S-9
Mt. Prospect, 54167 *E-6
Mt. Pulaski, 1566 J-9
Mt. Sterling, 2025 J-5
Mt. Vernon, 15277 P-10
Mt. Zion, 5833 K-10
Moweaqua, 1831 K-9
Mozier, 50 L-5
Muddy, 68 R-11
Mulberry Grv., 634 N-9
Mulkeytown, 175 Q-9
Mundelein, 31064 *C-5
Murdock, 150 J-12
Murphysboro, 7970 R-8
Murrayville, 587 K-6
Nachusa, 270 C-8
Naperville, 141853 C-12
Naplate, 496 E-10
Naples, 130 K-5
Nashville, 3258 P-8
Nason, 236 P-9
National City ‡H-7
Nauvoo, 1149 H-3
Near North Side *H-9
Nebo, 340 L-5
Nekoma, 30 F-6
Nelson, 170 C-8
Neoga, 1636 L-11
Neponset, 473 E-7
Neunert, 25 R-8
New Athens, 2054 P-7
New Baden, 3349 O-7
New Bedford, 75 D-7
New Berlin, 1346 K-7
New Boston, 683 F-4
New Burnside, 211 R-10
New Canton, 359 K-4
New Columbia, 150 S-10
New Delhi, 40 M-6
New Douglas, 319 M-8
New Grand Chain, 210 T-9
New Hanover, 60 O-6
New Haven, 433 Q-12
New Hebron, 50 M-13
New Holland, 269 I-8
New Lenox, 24394 D-12
New Liberty, 70 T-11
New Memphis, 300 O-8
New Milford, 697 B-9
New Minden, 215 O-8
New Philadelphia, 100 H-5
New Salem, 137 K-4
New Windsor, 748 E-6
Newark, 992 D-11
Newbern, 100 M-6
Newman, 865 J-12
Newton, 2849 M-12
Niantic, 707 J-9
Niles, 29803 *F-7
Nilwood, 239 L-7
Niota, 300 G-3
Noble, 677 N-12
Nokomis, 2256 L-9
Nora, 121 A-7
Normal, 52497 H-9
Normandy, 30 D-8
Norridge, 14572 *G-7
Norris, 213 G-7
Norris City, 1275 Q-11
N. Aurora, 16760 C-11
N. Barrington, 3047 *C-4
N. Chicago, 32574 A-12
N. Dupo, 1380 ‡J-7
N. Glen Ellyn, 1400 *H-5
N. Henderson, 187 F-5
N. Riverside, 6672 *I-7
Northbrook, 33170 *E-7
Northfield, 5420 *E-8
Northlake, 12323 *H-6
Nortonville, 50 K-6
Norway, 300 E-10
Norwood Pk. *G-7
Nutwood, 120 M-5
Oak Brook, 7883 *I-6
Oak Forest, 27962 *L-8
Oak Grv., 396 E-5
Oak Hill, 100 G-7
Oak Hills, 1150 ‡H-9
Oak Lawn, 56690 D-13
Oak Pk., 51878 C-13
Oak Run, 547 F-6
Oakbrook Ter., 2134 *I-6
Oakdale, 221 P-8
Oakford, 286 I-7
Oakland, 880 K-12
Oakwood, 1595 I-13
Oakwood Hills, 2083 *C-3
Oblong, 1466 M-12
Oconee, 180 L-9
Odell, 1046 F-11
Odin, 1076 O-9
O'Fallon, 28281 O-7
Ogden, 810 I-12
OGLE CO., 53497 B-8
Oglesby, 3791 E-9
Ohio, 513 D-8
Ohlman, 135 L-9
Oilfield L-12
Okawville, 1434 O-8
Old Kane M-6
Old Ripley, 108 N-8
Old Shawneetown, 193 R-12
Olive Branch, 864 T-8
Oliver, 110 L-13
Olmsted, 333 T-9
Olney, 9115 N-12
Olympia Fields, 4988 *N-9
Omaha, 266 Q-11
Omega, 50 N-10
Onarga, 1368 G-12
Oneco, 50 A-8
Oneida, 700 F-6
Ontarioville *G-4

***, †, ‡, §, ◊ See explanation under state title in this index.**
County and parish names are listed in capital letters & boldface type.
Independent cities (not included in a county) are listed in italics.

Opdyke, 254 P-10
Ophiem, 170 E-6
Oquawka, 1371 F-4
Orange Prairie †H-15
Orangeville, 793 A-8
Oraville, 100 Q-8
Orchardville, 100 O-10
Oreana, 875 J-10
Oregon, 3721 C-9
Orient, 358 Q-9
Orion, 1861 E-6
Orland Hills, 7149 *M-7
Orland Pk., 56767 D-12
Osceola, 50 E-7
Oskaloosa N-10
Oswego, 30355 D-11
Ottawa, 18768 E-10
Otterville, 126 M-6
Owaneco, 239 L-9
Oxville, 30 K-5
Ozark, 110 S-10
Palatine, 68557 B-12
Palestine, 1369 M-13
Palmer, 229 L-8
Palmyra, 698 L-7
Palos Hts., 12515 *L-8
Palos Hills, 17484 *K-7
Palos Pk., 4847 *K-7
Pana, 5847 L-9
Panama, 343 M-8
Pankeyville, 200 R-11
Panola, 45 G-9
Papineau, 171 F-13
Paris, 8837 K-13
Park City, 7570 *A-7
Park Forest, 21975 D-13
Park Ridge, 37480 *F-7
Parkersburg, 199 O-12
Passport, 30 N-12
Patoka, 584 N-9
Patterson, 142 L-5
Patton, 90 O-13
Paw Paw, 870 D-9
Pawnee, 2739 K-8
Paxton, 4473 H-12
Payson, 1026 J-3
Pearl, 138 L-5
Pearl City, 838 B-7
Pecatonica, 2195 A-8
Pekin, 34094 H-8
Penfield, 193 I-12
Peoria, 115007 G-8
PEORIA CO., 186494 G-7
Peoria Hts., 6156 G-8
Peotone, 4142 E-13
Percy, 970 Q-8
Perry, 397 J-5
PERRY CO., 22350 P-8
Peru, 10295 E-9
Pesotum, 551 J-11
Peters Creek S-12
Petersburg, 2260 J-7
Petrolia, 90 N-13
Philadelphia, 60 J-6
Phillipstown, 44 P-12
Philo, 1466 J-12
Phoenix, 1964 *L-9
Piasa, 200 M-6
PIATT CO., 16729 J-10
Pierron, 600 N-8
Pike, 30 L-4
PIKE CO., 16430 K-4
Pinckneyville, 5648 Q-8
Pingree Grv., 4532 B-11
Pinkstaff, 150 N-13
Piper City, 826 G-12
Pittsburg, 572 R-10
Pittsfield, 4576 K-4
Plainfield, 39581 D-12
Plainview, 150 M-7
Plainville, 264 J-3
Plano, 10856 D-11
Plato Ctr., 120 *F-1
Plattville, 242 D-11
Pleasant Hill, 966 L-4
Pleasant Mound, 100 N-9
Pleasant Plains, 802 J-7
Plymouth, 505 I-4
Poag, 60 ‡F-9
Pocahontas, 784 N-8
Polo, 2355 C-8
Pontiac, 11931 G-10
Pontoon Bch., 5836 ‡G-8
Pontoosuc, 146 G-3
POPE CO., 4470 S-11
Poplar Grv., 5023 A-10
Port Barrington, 1517 *C-3
Port Byron, 1647 D-6
Portage Pk. *G-8
Posen, 5987 *L-9
Posey, 75 O-8
Potomac, 750 I-13
Pottstown, 70 †I-15
Prairie City, 379 G-5
Prairie du Rocher, 604 Q-6
Prairie Grv., 1904 *C-3
Prairie View *D-6
Preemption, 350 E-5
Prentice, 30 J-7
Preston Hts., 2575 *N-4
Princeton, 7660 E-8
Princeville, 1738 F-7
Prophetstown, 2080 D-7
Prospect Hts., 16256 *E-6
Pulaski, 206 T-9
PULASKI CO., 6161 T-9
Pulleys Mill, 60 R-9
Pullman *K-10
Putnam, 200 F-8
PUTNAM CO., 6006 E-8
Quincy, 40633 J-3
Radford K-9
Radom, 220 P-9
Raleigh, 350 Q-11
Ramsey, 1037 M-9
RANDOLPH CO., 33476 Q-7
Rankin, 561 H-12
Ransom, 384 F-10
Rantoul, 12941 I-12
Rapatee, 80 G-6
Rapids City, 959 D-6
Rardin, 160 K-12
Raritan, 138 G-4
Raymond, 1006 L-8
Red Bud, 3698 P-7
Reddick, 163 F-11
Redmon, 173 K-13
Reevesville, 160 S-10
Renault, 200 P-6
Reynolds, 539 E-5
Reynoldsville S-8
Rice, 100 P-8
RICHLAND CO., 16233 N-12
Richmond, 1874 A-11
Richton Pk., 13646 *N-8
Richview, 253 P-9
Ridge Farm, 882 J-13
Ridgefield, 120 *B-1
Ridgway, 869 R-12
Ridott, 164 B-8
Riggston, 40 K-5
Rinard, 110 O-11
Ringwood, 836 A-11
Rio, 220 F-6
Ripley, 86 J-5
Rising Sun, 35 Q-12
Ritchie, 60 E-12
River Forest, 11172 *H-7
River Grv., 10227 *H-7
Riverdale, 13549 *L-9
Riverside, 8875 *I-7
Riverton, 3455 J-8
Riverview, 200 B-6
Riverwoods, 3660 *D-7
Roanoke, 2065 G-9
Robbins, 5337 *L-9
Roberts, 362 H-12
Robinson, 7713 M-13
Roby, 80 K-8
Rochelle, 9574 C-9
Rochester, 3689 K-8
Rock City, 315 A-8
Rock Falls, 9266 C-8
Rock Grv., 150 A-8
Rock Island, 39018 D-5
ROCK ISLAND CO., 147546 E-4
Rock River Ter., 230 B-9
Rockbridge, 169 L-6
Rockdale, 1976 *N-4
Rockford, 152871 B-9
Rockport, 200 K-4
Rockton, 7685 A-9
Rockwood, 42 Q-7
Rogers Pk. *F-9
Rolling Meadows, 24099 *E-5
Rome, 1738 G-8
Romeoville, 39680 D-12
Rondout *B-7
Roodhouse, 1814 L-6
Rosamond, 200 L-9
Roscoe, 10785 A-9
Rose Hill, 80 M-12
Rosedale, 40 M-5
Roseland *K-9
Roselle, 22763 C-12
Rosemont, 4202 *G-7
Roseville, 989 G-5
Rosewood Hts., 4038 ‡D-8
Rosiclare, 1160 S-11
Rossville, 1331 H-13
Round Knob, 50 T-10
Round Lake, 18289 *A-4
Round Lake Bch., 28175 *A-4
Round Lake Hts., 2676 *A-4
Round Lake Pk., 7505 *A-4
Roxana, 1542 N-6
Royal, 293 I-12
Royal Lake, 197 M-7
Royalton, 1151 Q-9
Ruma, 317 P-7
Rushville, 3192 I-5
Russell, 130 §N-8
Russellville, 94 N-13
Rutland, 318 F-9
Sadorus, 416 J-11
Sailor Sprs., 95 N-11
St. Anne, 1257 F-13
St. Augustine, 120 G-6
St. Charles, 32974 C-11
ST. CLAIR CO., 270056 O-7
St. David, 589 H-7
St. Elmo, 1426 M-10
St. Francisville, 697 O-13
St. Jacob, 1098 N-7
St. Johns, 219 Q-9
St. Joseph, 3967 I-12
St. Libory, 615 P-7
St. Peter, 359 N-10
St. Rose, 250 N-8
Ste. Marie, 244 N-12
Salem, 7485 O-10
SALINE CO., 24913 R-11
Saline Mines, 25 R-12
Salisbury, 160 J-7
Sammons Pt., 279 F-12
Samsville O-12
San Jose, 642 I-8
Sandoval, 1274 O-9
Sandusky, 250 T-9
Sandwich, 7421 D-10
SANGAMON CO., 197465 K-7
Saratoga, 50 S-9
Sauget, 159 ‡I-7
Sauk Vil., 10506 *N-10
Saunemin, 420 G-11
Savanna, 3062 B-6
Savoy, 7280 J-11
Saybrook, 693 H-11
Scales Mound, 376 A-6
Schapville, 50 A-6
Schaumburg, 74227 B-12
Schiller Pk., 11793 *G-7
Schram City, 586 M-8
SCHUYLER CO., 7544 I-5
Sciota, 61 H-5
Scotland, 110 J-13
SCOTT CO., 5355 K-5
Scottville, 116 L-6
Seaton, 222 F-5
Seatonville, 314 E-9
Secor, 373 G-9
Seneca, 2371 E-10
Serena, 250 D-10
Sesser, 1931 Q-9
Seward, 300 B-8
Seymour, 303 I-11
Shabbona, 925 C-10
Shangrila, 400 C-9
Shannon, 757 B-7
Shattuc, 220 O-9
Shawneetown, 1239 R-12
Sheffield, 926 E-7
SHELBY CO., 22363 K-10
Shelbyville, 4700 L-10
Sheldon, 1070 G-13
Sherburnville, 80 E-13
Sheridan, 2137 D-10
Sherman, 4148 J-8
Sherrard, 640 E-5
Shiloh, 12651 ‡I-10
Shipman, 624 M-7
Shirland, 200 A-9
Shirley, 150 H-9
Shobonier, 250 N-9
Shorewood, 15615 D-12
Shumway, 202 M-10
Sibley, 272 H-11
Sidell, 617 J-13
Sidney, 1233 J-12
Sigel, 373 L-11
Signal Hill ‡I-8
Silver Lake, 800 *C-3
Silvis, 7479 S-5
Simpson, 60 S-10
Sims, 252 P-11
Skokie, 64784 B-13
Sleepy Hollow, 3304 *E-2
Smithfield, 230 H-6
Smithshire, 200 G-5
Smithton, 3693 O-7
Somonauk, 1893 D-10
Sorento, 498 M-8
S. Barrington, 4565 *E-4
S. Beloit, 7892 A-9
S. Chicago *J-10
S. Chicago Hts., 4139 *N-9
S. Deering *K-10
S. Elgin, 21985 *G-2
S. Holland, 22030 *M-10
S. Jacksonville, 3331 K-6
S. Pekin, 1146 H-8
S. Roxana, 2053 ‡E-8
S. Shore *J-10
S. Wilmington, 681 F-11
Southern View, 1642 †M-16
Sparland, 406 F-8
Sparta, 4302 P-7
Spaulding, 873 J-8
Speer, 100 F-8
Spring Bay, 452 G-8
Spring Gdn., 50 P-10
Spring Grv., 5778 A-11
Spring Hill, 50 D-7
Spring Valley, 5558 E-9
Springerton, 110 P-11
Springfield, 116250 J-8
Standard City, 152 L-7
Stanford, 596 H-9
STARK CO., 5994 F-7
State Park Pl., 2600 ‡H-9
Staunton, 5139 M-7
Steel City, 150 Q-10
Steeleville, 2083 Q-8
Steger, 9570 D-13
Stelle, 100 F-12
STEPHENSON CO., 47711 A-8
Sterling, 15370 C-8
Steward, 256 C-9
Stewardson, 734 L-10
Stickney, 6786 *I-8
Stillman Valley, 1120 B-9
Stillwell, 80 I-3
Stockland, 150 H-13
Stockton, 1862 A-7
Stone Pk., 4946 *H-7
Stonefort, 297 R-10
Stonington, 932 K-9
Stoy, 104 M-13
Strasburg, 467 L-10
Stratford, 50 C-8
Strawn, 100 G-11
Streamwood, 39858 *F-3
Streator, 13710 F-10
Stronghurst, 883 G-4
Sublette, 449 D-9
Sugar Grv., 8997 C-11
Sullivan, 4440 K-10
Summer Hill, 100 K-4
Summerfield, 451 O-7
Summit, 11054 *J-7
Summum, 150 I-6
Sumner, 3174 N-13
Sun River Ter., 528 F-13
Sunfield, 220 Q-9
Sunny Hill, 400 E-6
Sunnyland †J-18
Swan Creek, 90 G-5
Swansea, 13430 O-7
Swanwick, 100 P-8
Sycamore, 17519 C-10
Sylvan Lake, 430 *C-5
Symerton, 87 E-12
Table Grv., 416 H-6
Tallula, 488 J-7
Tamalco, 40 N-9
Tamaroa, 638 P-9
Tamms, 632 T-9
Tampico, 790 D-7
Taylor Ridge, 200 E-5
Taylor Sprs., 690 M-8
Taylorville, 11246 K-9
TAZEWELL CO., 135394 H-8
Temple Hill, 35 S-10
Tennessee, 115 H-4
Terre Haute, 150 G-4
Teutopolis, 1530 M-11
Texas City Q-11
Texico, 160 O-10
Thackeray, 50 P-11
Thawville, 241 G-12
Thayer, 693 K-7
Thebes, 436 T-8
Third Lake, 1182 *A-5
Thomasboro, 1126 I-12
Thompsonville, 543 Q-10
Thomson, 590 C-6
Thornton, 2338 *M-10
Tilden, 934 P-7
Tilton, 2724 I-13
Timberlane, 934 A-10
Timewell, 122 J-4
Tinley Pk., 56703 D-13
Tioga, 100 I-3
Tiskilwa, 829 E-8
Toledo, 1238 L-12
Tolono, 3447 J-11
Toluca, 1414 F-9
Tonica, 768 E-9
Topeka, 76 H-7
Toulon, 1292 F-7
Tovey, 512 K-8
Towanda, 480 H-10
Tower Hill, 611 L-10
Tower Lake, 1283 *C-4
Tremont, 2236 H-8
Trenton, 2715 O-8
Trilla, 250 L-11
Triumph, 150 D-9
Trivoli, 450 G-7
Trout Valley, 537 *C-3
Trowbridge, 50 L-11
Troy, 9888 N-7
Troy Grv., 250 E-9
Tuscola, 4480 J-11
Udina, 120 *F-1
Ullin, 463 S-9
Union, 580 B-11
UNION CO., 17808 S-9
Union Hill, 58 F-12
Unionville, 200 C-7
Unionville, 70 T-11
Unity, 200 T-9
University Pk., 7129 E-13
Uptown *G-9
Urbana, 41250 I-12
Urbandale, 200 T-9
Ursa, 626 I-3
Utica, 1352 E-9
Valier, 669 Q-9
Valley City, 13 K-5
Valley View, 2100 *G-2
Valmeyer, 1263 P-6
Van Burensburg, 50 M-9
Van Orin, 120 D-8
Vandalia, 7042 M-9
Varna, 384 F-9
Venedy, 138 O-8
Venice, 1890 ‡H-7
Vera, 100 M-9
Vergennes, 298 Q-8
Vermilion, 225 K-13
VERMILION CO., 81625 J-13
Vermont, 667 I-6
Vernon, 129 N-9
Vernon Hills, 25113 *C-6
Verona, 215 E-11
Versailles, 478 J-5
Victoria, 316 F-6
Vienna, 1434 S-10
Villa Grv., 2537 J-12
Villa Hills, 1410 ‡J-8
Villa Pk., 21904 *H-5
Villa Ridge, 500 T-9
Viola, 955 E-5
Virden, 3425 L-7
Virgil, 329 C-11
Virginia, 1611 J-6
Volo, 2929 A-12
WABASH CO., 11947 O-13
Wacker, 50 B-7
Waddams Grv., 60 A-7
Wadsworth, 3815 A-12
Waggoner, 266 L-8
Wakefield, 50 N-12
Walnut, 1416 D-8
Walnut Grv., 50 H-5
Walnut Hill, 108 O-9
Walpole, 50 Q-11
Walsh, 140 Q-7
Walshville, 64 M-8
Waltonville, 434 P-9
Wamac, 1185 O-9
Wanda, 80 ‡E-9
Wapella, 558 I-10
Ware, 260 S-8
Warren, 1428 A-7
WARREN CO., 17707 G-5
Warrensburg, 1210 J-9
Warrenville, 13140 *I-3
Warsaw, 1607 H-3
Wasco, 300 *G-1
Washburn, 1155 F-9
Washington, 15134 G-8
WASHINGTON CO., 14716 P-8
Washington Pk., 4196 ‡H-8
Wasson, 200 R-11
Wataga, 843 F-6
Waterloo, 9811 P-6
Waterman, 1506 C-10
Watseka, 5255 G-13
Watson, 754 M-11
Wauconda, 13603 B-12
Waukegan, 89078 A-12
Waverly, 1307 K-7
Wayne, 2431 *G-3
Wayne City, 1032 P-11
WAYNE CO., 16760 O-11
Waynesville, 434 I-9
Wedron, 300 E-10
Weldon, 429 I-10
Wellington, 242 H-13
Wendelin, 60 N-11
Wenona, 1056 F-9
Wenonah, 37 L-9
W. Brooklyn, 142 D-9
W. Chicago, 27086 *H-3
W. City, 661 Q-10
W. Dundee, 7331 *E-2
W. End Q-10
W. Frankfort, 8182 Q-10
W. Jersey, 50 F-7
W. Liberty, 180 N-12
W. Peoria, 4458 †I-15
West Pt., 178 I-3
W. Salem, 897 O-12
W. Union, 288 M-13
W. Vienna, 90 S-9
W. York, 129 M-13
Westchester, 16718 *I-7
Western Sprs., 12975 *I-6
Westervelt, 128 L-10
Westfield, 601 L-12
Westmont, 24685 *J-5
Weston, 100 G-10
Westville, 3202 J-13
Wetaug, 50 S-9
Wheaton, 52894 C-12
Wheeler, 147 M-11
Wheeling, 37648 *E-6
White City, 232 M-7
WHITE CO., 14665 P-11
White Hall, 2520 L-6
White Heath, 290 I-11
WHITESIDE CO., 58498 C-7
Whittington, 200 Q-10
Wildwood *A-5
WILL CO., 677560 E-12
Williamsfield, 578 F-7
WILLIAMSON CO., 66357 R-10
Williamsville, 1476 J-8
Willisville, 633 Q-8
Willow Hill, 230 M-12
Willow Sprs., 5524 *J-7
Willowbrook, 8540 *J-6
Wilmette, 27087 B-13
Wilmington, 5724 E-12
Wilsonville, 586 M-7
Wilton Ctr., 100 E-12
Winchester, 1593 K-5
Windsor, 1187 L-11
Winfield, 9080 *H-4
Winnebago, 3101 B-9
WINNEBAGO CO., 295266 A-9
Winnetka, 12187 B-13
Winslow, 338 A-7
Winterrowd N-11
Winthrop Hbr., 6742 A-13
Witt, 903 L-8
Wolf Lake, 300 S-8
Womac L-7
Wonder Lake, 4026 A-11
Wood Dale, 13770 *G-6
Wood River, 10657 N-6
Woodbine, 140 A-6
Woodburn, 170 M-7
Woodbury, 70 M-11
WOODFORD CO., 38664 G-9
Woodhull, 811 F-6
Woodland, 324 G-13
Woodlawn, 698 P-9
Woodridge, 32971 *J-5
Woodson, 512 K-6
Woodstock, 24770 A-11
Woodworth, 100 G-13
Woosung, 180 C-8
Worden, 1044 N-7
Worth, 10789 *K-8
Wrights, 100 L-6
Wyanet, 991 E-8
Wynoose, 40 O-12
Wyoming, 1429 F-7
Xenia, 391 O-10
Yale, 86 M-12
Yates City, 693 G-7
York, 100 M-13
York Ctr. *I-5
Yorkfield *H-6
Yorktown, 100 D-7
Yorkville, 16921 D-11
Yuton E-1
Zeigler, 1801 Q-9
Zion, 24413 A-13

Indiana

Page locator

Map keys	Atlas pages
A–J	74–75
K–T	76–77

* City keyed to pp. 72–73

Aberdeen, 90 O-13
Abington, 80 K-13
Aboite, 50 D-12
Abydel, 30 P-7
Acme, 30 N-9
Adams, 175 L-11
Adams, 150 L-8
ADAMS CO., 34387 E-13
Adams Lake, 500 B-12
Adamsboro E-8
Ade, 20 E-4
Advance, 477 I-7
Aetna *M-13
Ainsworth *N-14
Akron, 1167 D-9
Alamo, 66 I-5
Albany, 2165 H-12
Albion, 2349 B-11
Alert, 90 M-10
Alexandria, 5145 H-10
Alford, 90 Q-5
Alfordsville, 101 P-6
Algiers, 50 Q-5
ALLEN CO., 355329 D-12
Allendale, 250 L-4
Allisonville *A-19
Alpine, 40 K-12
Alquina, 130 K-13
Alta J-4
Alton, 55 R-8
Altona, 197 C-12
Alvarado B-14
Ambia, 239 G-4
Amboy, 384 F-10
Americus, 423 G-6
Amity, 225 L-9
Amo, 401 K-7
Anderson, 56129 I-10
Andersonville, 250 L-12
Andrews, 1149 E-11
Angola, 8612 A-13
Annapolis, 100 J-5
Anoka, 60 F-8
Antioch, 150 H-7
Arba, 40 I-14
Arcadia, 1666 H-9
Arcola, 180 D-12
Ardmore, 2200 *I-18
Argos, 1691 C-8
Ari, 30 C-12
Arlington, 433 K-11
Armstrong S-3
Arthur, 75 Q-4
Ashland, 80 J-12
Ashley, 983 B-13
Athens, 130 D-9
Atherton, 45 K-4
Atlanta, 725 H-9
Attica, 3245 H-5
Atwood, 300 C-9
Auburn, 12731 C-13
Augusta, 50 *B-17
Aultshire I-2
Aurora, 3750 N-13
Austin, 4295 O-10
Avilla, 2401 C-12
Avoca, 583 O-7
Avon, 12446 J-8
Avondale, 500 F-10
Azalia, 140 N-10
Bainbridge, 746 J-6
Bakers Cor., 70 I-9
Banquo, 50 F-11
Barbee, 900 C-10
Bargersville, 4013 L-9
Barnard, 30 J-7
BARTHOLOMEW CO., 76794 M-9
Bartlettsville N-8
Bartonia, 30 I-14
Bass Lake, 1195 C-7
Batesville, 6520 M-12
Bath, 100 L-14
Battle Ground, 1334 G-6
Beanblossom, 200 M-8
Beardstown, 50 D-7
Beaver City E-4
Beaver Dam, 250 D-9
Becks Mill P-9
Bedford, 13413 O-7
Beech Grv., 14192 K-9
Beechwood R-8
Belle Union, 90 K-7
Bellefountain, 40 G-14
Belleville, 400 K-7
Bellmore, 140 J-5
Belmont, 10 M-8
Belshaw, 40 C-4
Ben Davis *E-16
Bengal, 30 L-10
Bennetts Switch, 90 F-9
Bennington, 70 O-13
Benton, 150 B-10
BENTON CO., 8854 F-4
Bentonville, 65 K-12
Berne, 3999 F-13
Bethany, 81 L-8
Bethany, 25 M-9
Bethel, 90 I-14
Bethlehem, 100 P-11
Beverly Shores, 613 A-6
Bicknell, 2915 O-4
Bippus, 200 E-11
Birdseye, 416 R-7
BLACKFORD CO., 12766 G-12
Blackhawk, 80 M-4
Blaine, 10 G-13
Blairsville, 250 S-2
Blanford, 342 K-4
Blocher, 200 P-11
Bloomfield, 2405 N-6
Blooming Grv., 75 L-13
Bloomingdale, 335 J-5
Bloomingport, 60 I-13
Bloomington, 80405 M-7
Blountsville, 134 I-12
Blue Lake, 300 C-12
Blue Ridge, 250 L-11
Bluffton, 9897 F-12
Boggstown, 400 K-10
Bono, 25 P-8
BOONE CO., 56640 I-8
Boone Grv., 175 C-5
Boonville, 6246 S-4
Borden, 808 Q-9
Boston, 138 K-14
Boswell, 778 G-4
Boundary City, 20 H-13
Bourbon, 1810 C-9
Bowling Green, 300 L-5
Bowman Q-4
Boxley, 100 I-9
Boyleston, 90 H-8
Bradford, 150 Q-9
Branchville, 70 R-7
Brazil, 7912 L-5
Bremen, 4588 B-9
Brems, 50 C-7
Bretzville, 50 R-6
Brewersville, 50 N-11
Brick Chapel, 40 K-6
Bridgeport *E-15
Bridgeton, 150 K-5
Bright, 5693 M-14
Brighton, 125 A-12
Brimfield, 150 B-11
Bringhurst, 125 G-7
Bristol, 1602 A-10
Bristow, 120 R-6
Brook, 997 E-4
Brooklyn, 1598 L-8
Brooksburg, 81 O-12
Brookston, 1554 F-6
Brookville, 2596 L-13
BROWN CO., 15242 M-8
Browns Valley, 90 J-6
Brownsburg, 21285 J-8
Brownstown, 2947 O-9
Brownsville, 250 K-13
Bruce Lake, 100 D-8
Bruceville, 478 O-4
Brunswick, 200 C-4
Brushy Prairie, 30 A-12
Bryant, 252 G-13
Bryantsburg, 50 O-12
Buck Creek, 207 G-6
Buckskin, 120 R-4
Bucktown, 20 N-4
Buddha, 40 O-8
Buena Vista, 80 L-12
Buffalo, 692 E-6
Buffaloville, 40 S-6
Bunker Hill, 888 F-9
Bunker Hill, 500 P-3
Burket, 195 D-9
Burlington, 603 G-8
Burlington Bch., 900 B-5
Burnettsville, 346 F-7
Burney, 130 M-11
Burns Hbr., 1156 A-5
Burnsville, 60 M-10
Burr Oak, 100 C-8
Burrows, 240 F-7
Busseron O-4
Butler, 2684 B-13
Butler Ctr., 35 C-13
Butlerville, 282 N-11
Byrneville, 40 Q-9
Cadiz, 150 J-11
Cale, 35 O-6
Cambria, 100 H-7
Cambridge City, 1870 J-12
Camby *G-15
Camden, 611 F-7
Cammack, 180 H-11
Campbellsburg, 585 P-8
Canaan, 90 O-12
Cannelburg, 135 P-5
Cannelton, 1563 T-6
Canton, 175 P-9
Carbon, 397 K-5
Carbondale, 15 H-4
Cardonia, 90 K-5
Carefree, 25 R-8
Carlisle, 692 N-4
Carlos, 80 I-13
Carmel, 79191 I-9
Carp L-6
Carpentersville, 40 J-6
CARROLL CO., 20155 G-7
Carthage, 927 K-11
Cass, 100 N-4
CASS CO., 38966 F-8
Cassville, 120 G-9
Castleton *A-20
Cataract, 50 L-6
Cates, 125 I-4
Catlin, 100 K-5
Cato, 30 Q-5
Cayuga, 1162 J-4
Cedar Grv., 156 L-13
Cedar Lake, 11560 C-4
Celestine, 250 Q-6
Center, 250 G-9
Center Pt., 242 L-5
Center Sq., 20 O-13
Centerton, 200 L-8
Centerville, 2552 J-13
Central, 35 S-9
Central Barren, 120 Q-9
Ceylon, 60 F-13
Chalmers, 508 F-6
Chambersburg, 50 Q-8
Chandler, 2887 S-4
Chapel Creek, 400 Q-10
Chapel Hill *E-15
Charlestown, 7585 Q-11
Charlottesville, 450 J-11
Chelsea, 125 P-11
Chester, 50 J-13
Chesterfield, 2547 I-11
Chesterton, 13068 A-5
Chili, 150 E-9
China O-12
Chrisney, 481 S-5
Churubusco, 1796 C-12
Cicero, 4812 I-9
Cincinnati, 90 N-7
Circleville, 300 K-11
CLARK CO., 110232 Q-10
Clarks Hill, 611 H-7
Clarksburg, 149 L-12
Clarksville, 21724 R-10
Clarksville, 150 I-10
Clay City, 861 M-5
CLAY CO., 26890 L-5
Claypool, 431 D-10
Clayton, 972 K-7
Clear Creek, 1200 N-7
Clear Lake, 339 A-13
Clear Spr., 75 O-8
Clermont, 1356 J-8
Clifford, 233 M-10
Clinton, 4893 K-4
CLINTON CO., 33224 H-7
Clinton Falls, 100 K-6
Clover Vil., 200 K-10
Cloverdale, 2172 L-6
Cloverland, 100 L-5
Clunette, 75 C-10
Clymers, 120 F-8
Coal City, 270 M-5
Coal Creek, 10 I-4
Coalmont, 402 M-5
Coatesville, 523 K-7
Coesse, 100 D-11
Colburn, 193 G-7
Cold Sprs., 180 B-13
Colfax, 691 H-7
Collamer, 50 D-10
Collegeville, 330 E-5
Collett G-13
Collins, 60 C-11
Coloma, 80 J-4
Columbia City, 8750 D-11
Columbus, 44061 M-10
Commiskey, 100 O-11
Connersville, 13481 K-12
Converse, 1265 F-10
Cornettsville, 20 O-5
Cortland, 175 N-9
Corunna, 254 B-12
Cory, 135 L-5
Corydon, 3122 R-9
Country Club Hts., 79 G-2
Country Vil., 1100 H-11
Covington, 2645 I-4
Cowan, 250 I-12
Craigville, 135 E-13
Crandall, 152 R-9
Crane, 184 O-6
CRAWFORD CO., 10713 Q-7
Crawfordsville, 15915 I-6
Creston, 80 C-4
Cromwell, 512 B-11
Crooked Lake, 300 A-13
Cross Plains, 150 N-12
Crothersville, 1591 O-10
Crown Ctr., 30 K-7
Crown Pt., 27317 B-4
Crows Nest, 73 *C-18
Crumstown, 120 A-8
Crystal, 100 Q-6
Culver, 1353 C-8
Cumberland, 5169 J-9
Cunot, 100 L-6
Curtisville, 150 H-10
Cutler, 125 G-7
Cuzco, 50 Q-7
Cyclone, 20 H-8
Cynthiana, 545 R-3
Dabney, 50 N-12
Dale, 1593 R-5
Daleville, 1647 I-11
Dalton, 40 I-12
Dana, 608 J-4
Danville, 9001 J-7
Darlington, 843 I-6
Darmstadt, 1407 S-3
DAVIESS CO., 31648 O-5
Daylight, 200 S-4
Dayton, 1420 G-6
De Camp Gdns., 150 D-3
De Gonia, 40 S-5
DE KALB CO., 42223 B-13
Deacon F-8
DEARBORN CO., 50047 M-13
Decatur, 9405 E-13
DECATUR CO., 25740 M-11
Decker, 249 Q-3
Deedsville, 95 E-9
Deer Creek, 160 F-8
Deerfield, 50 H-13
Delaware, 150 M-12
DELAWARE CO., 117671 H-11
Delong, 140 D-8
Delp, 100 G-6
Delphi, 2893 F-7
Demotte, 3814 C-5
Denham, 150 D-7
Denver, 482 E-9
Depauw, 120 Q-8
Deputy, 86 O-11
Derby, 100 S-7
Desoto, 180 H-12
Diamond, 120 K-5
Dillman, 25 F-11
Dillsboro, 1327 N-13
Disko, 80 D-9
Dixon, 100 E-14
Dodd S-7
Dogwood, 30 S-9
Dolan, 50 M-7
Domestic F-13
Donaldson, 125 C-8
Doolittle Mills R-7
Dover, 100 M-13
Dover, 60 I-7
Dover Hill, 114 P-6
Dublin, 790 J-12
Dubois, 488 Q-6
DUBOIS CO., 41889 Q-6
Dudleytown, 60 O-10
Dugger, 920 N-4
Dune Acres, 182 A-5
Dunfee, 40 D-12
Dunkirk, 2362 G-12
Dunlap, 6235 A-10
Dunlapsville, 45 K-13
Dunnington, 30 G-4
Dunns Br., 70 C-6
Dunreith, 177 J-11
Dupont, 339 O-11
Dyer, 16390 B-4
Eagle Vil., 120 J-8
Eagletown, 300 I-9
Earl Pk., 348 F-4
E. Chicago, 29698 A-4
E. Enterprise, 148 O-13
E. Germantown, 410 J-13
E. Mt. Carmel Q-3
Eaton, 1805 H-12
Eckerty, 150 R-7
Economy, 187 I-13
Eden, 80 J-10
Edgerton, 100 D-14
Edgewood, 1913 I-10
Edinburgh, 4480 L-9
Edna Mills, 40 G-7
Edwardsport, 303 O-4
Edwardsville, 600 R-10
Ege, 30 C-12
Ekin, 60 H-9
Elberfeld, 625 R-4
Elizabeth, 162 R-9
Elizabethtown, 504 N-10
Elizaville, 80 I-8
Elkhart, 50949 A-9
ELKHART CO., 197559 B-9
Ellettsville, 6378 M-7
Elnora, 640 O-5
Elrod, 60 N-12
Elston, 100 F-2
Elwood, 8614 H-10
Elwren, 30 N-7
Eminence, 180 L-7
Emison, 154 O-4
Emma, 150 A-11
Emporia, 50 I-11
Enchanted Hills, 600 B-11
English, 645 Q-7
English Lake, 30 C-6
Enos D-4
Enterprise T-5
Epsom, 30 O-5
Etna Green, 586 C-9
Eureka, 80 T-5
Evansville, 117429 S-3
Everton, 600 K-13
Fair Oaks, 145 D-5
Fairbanks, 125 M-3
Fairland, 315 K-10
Fairmount, 2954 G-11
Fairview, 100 H-12
Fairview O-13
Fairview Pk., 1386 K-4
Falmouth, 100 K-12
Farmers M-6
Farmers Retreat, 60 N-13
Farmersburg, 1118 M-4
Farmersville, 50 S-2
Farmland, 1333 H-13
Fayette, 100 J-8
FAYETTE CO., 24277 K-12
Fayetteville, 60 O-7
Ferdinand, 2157 R-6
Ferguson Hill, 160 L-1
Fiat, 30 G-12
Fillmore, 533 K-6
Fincastle, 30 J-6
Fish Lake, 1016 B-7
Fishers, 76794 J-9
Fishersburg, 120 I-10
Five Points, 125 K-8
Flat Rock, 250 L-10
Fletcher Lake, 40 E-8
Flint, 90 A-13
Flora, 2036 G-7
Florence, 80 O-13
Florida, 100 I-10
FLOYD CO., 74578 Q-9
Floyds Knobs, 800 Q-10
Folsomville, 50 R-5
Fontanet, 423 K-5
Foraker, 80 B-10
Foresman, 25 E-4
Forest, 350 H-8
Forest Hill, 100 M-11
Ft. Branch, 2771 R-3
Ft. Ritner, 80 O-8
Ft. Wayne, 253691 D-12
Fortville, 3929 J-10
Foster, 30 I-4
Fountain, 80 H-4
Fountain City, 796 J-13
FOUNTAIN CO., 17240 I-4
Fountaintown, 150 K-10
Fowler, 2317 F-4
Fowlerton, 261 G-11
Francesville, 879 E-6
Francisco, 469 Q-4
Frankfort, 16422 H-7
Franklin, 23712 L-9
FRANKLIN CO., 23087 L-13
Frankton, 1862 H-10
Fredericksburg, 85 Q-9
Fredonia, 40 R-8
Freedom, 160 M-6
Freeland Pk., 50 F-4
Freelandville, 643 O-4
Freetown, 385 N-9
Fremont, 2138 A-13
French Lick, 1807 P-7
Frenchtown, 30 R-8
Friendship, 100 N-12
Fritchton, 100 P-4
Fulda, 130 S-6
Fulton, 333 E-8
FULTON CO., 20836 D-8
Gadsden, 30 I-8
Galena, 1818 Q-10
Galveston, 1311 F-9
Garden Vil., 4000 C-3
Garrett, 6286 C-12
Gary, 80294 B-4
Gas City, 5965 G-11
Gaston, 871 H-11
Gatchel S-7
Gem J-10
Geneva, 1293 F-13
Geneva, 120 L-10
Gentryville, 268 S-5
Georgetown, 2876 R-9
Georgetown, 50 F-7
Georgia P-7
Gessie, 80 I-4
GIBSON CO., 33503 R-3
Gifford, 45 D-5
Gilead, 35 E-9
Gilman, 20 H-11
Gingrich, 150 F-7
Gings K-12
Glen Pk., 30 *M-13
Glendale, 40 P-5
Glenwood, 250 K-12
Glezen, 100 Q-4
Gnaw Bone, 125 M-9
Goblesville, 75 D-11
Goldsmith, 225 H-9
Goodland, 1043 F-4
Goshen, 31719 B-10
Gosport, 826 L-7
Grabill, 1053 C-13
Grammer, 160 M-10
Grandview, 749 S-5
Grandview G-1
Granger, 30465 A-9
GRANT CO., 70061 G-10
Grantsburg, 130 R-7
Grass Creek, 80 E-8
Gravelton, 30 B-10
Grayford, 100 N-11
Graysville, 135 N-3
Green Hill, 125 G-5
Greencastle, 10326 K-6
Greendale, 4520 N-14
GREENE CO., 33165 N-6
Greenfield, 20602 J-10
Greens Fork, 423 J-13
Greensboro, 143 J-11
Greensburg, 11492 M-11
Greentown, 2415 G-9
Greenville, 595 Q-9
Greenwood, 49791 K-9
Griffin, 172 R-2
Griffith, 16893 B-4
Groveland, 75 J-7
Grovertown, 150 C-7
Guilford, 100 M-13
Guion, 30 J-5
Guthrie, 25 N-7
Gwynneville, 250 K-11
Hackleman, 40 G-10
Hadley, 60 K-7
Hagerstown, 1787 J-12
Hall, 100 L-7
Hamburg, 100 L-12
Hamilton, 1532 B-13
HAMILTON CO., 274569 I-9
Hamlet, 800 C-7
Hammond, 80830 A-4
Hancock Chapel Q-9
HANCOCK CO., 70002 J-10
Handy, 125 N-7
Hanna, 463 B-6
Hanover, 3546 P-11
Hardinsburg, 248 Q-8
Harlan, 1634 C-13
Harmony, 656 L-5
Harrisburg, 50 K-12
HARRISON CO., 39364 R-9
Harrisville, 50 H-13
Harrodsburg, 691 N-7
Hartford, 40 N-13
Hartford City, 6220 G-12
Hartsville, 362 M-10
Hartzel, 200 B-12
Harveysburg, 30 I-4
Haskell, 25 B-6
Hatfield, 813 T-5
Haubstadt, 1577 R-3
Hayden, 521 N-10
Haysville, 300 Q-6
Hazelwood, 250 K-7
Hazleton, 263 Q-3
Headlee, 45 E-7
Heath G-7
Hebron, 3724 C-5
Hedrick, 55 H-4
Heilman R-5
Helmer, 120 B-12
Helmsburg, 130 M-8
Heltonville, 500 O-8
Hemlock, 150 G-9
Henderson, 40 K-11
HENDRICKS CO., 145448 K-7
Hendricksville, 40 N-7
HENRY CO., 49462 J-11
Henryville, 1905 P-10
Herbst, 112 G-10
Heritage Lake, 1300 K-7
Heusler, 150 S-3
Highland, 23727 *M-11
Highland, 4489 S-12
Hillham, 50 Q-7
Hillisburg, 180 H-8
Hillsboro, 538 I-5
Hillsboro, 140 I-12
Hillsdale, 250 S-3
Hillsdale, 180 J-4
Hindustan M-7
Hitchcock P-9
Hoagland, 821 E-13
Hobart, 29059 *M-13
Hobbieville, 100 N-7
Hobbs, 170 H-9
Holland, 626 R-5
Hollandsburg, 40 J-5
Holton, 480 N-12
Home Pl., 1300 J-9
Homer, 175 K-11
Honey Creek, 120 I-11
Honeyville, 100 B-11
Hoosier Highlands, 100 L-6
Hoover, 40 E-9
Hope, 2102 M-10
Hortonville, 200 I-9
Houston, 60 N-9
HOWARD CO., 82752 G-8
Howe, 807 A-11
Howell T-12
Howesville, 30 M-5
Hudson, 518 B-13
Hudson Lake, 1297 A-7
Huntertown, 4810 C-12
Huntingburg, 6057 R-6
Huntington, 17391 E-11
HUNTINGTON CO., 37124 E-11
Huntsville, 200 I-10
Huntsville, 60 I-13
Huron, 300 P-7
Hyde Pk., 200 J-3
Hymera, 801 M-4
Idaville, 461 F-7
Ijamsville, 70 E-10
Independence, 120 H-5
Indian Hts., 3011 G-9
Indian Sprs., 60 O-6
Indian Vil., 30 *I-19
Indiana Bch., 80 E-6
Indianapolis, 820445 J-9
Ingalls, 2394 J-10
Inwood, 100 C-9
Iona, 30 P-4
Ireland, 450 Q-5
Irvington J-2
JACKSON CO., 42376 O-9
Jacksonburg, 100 J-13
Jalapa, 171 F-10
Jamestown, 958 J-7
Jamestown, 500 A-13
Jamestown, 300 A-9
Jasonville, 2222 M-5
Jasper, 15038 Q-6
JASPER CO., 33478 D-5
JAY CO., 21253 G-13
JEFFERSON CO., 32428 O-11
Jeffersonville, 44953 R-10
JENNINGS CO., 28525 N-10
Jerome, 100 G-10
Jessup, 40 K-5
Jewell Vil., 700 M-10
Johnson, 75 R-3
JOHNSON CO., 139654 L-9
Johnstown, 60 O-4
Jolietville, 225 I-8
Jonesboro, 1756 G-11
Jonesville, 177 N-10
Jordan, 75 L-6
Judah N-7
Judyville, 60 H-4
Kasson, 150 S-3
Kempton, 335 H-8
Kendallville, 9862 B-12
Kennard, 471 J-11
Kent, 70 O-11
Kentland, 1748 F-4
Kewanna, 613 D-8
Keystone, 150 F-12
Kilmore, 45 H-7
Kimmell, 422 B-11
Kingman, 511 I-4
Kingsbury, 242 B-7
Kingsford Hts., 1435 B-7
Kingsland, 75 E-12
Kirklin, 788 H-8
Kirkpatrick H-6
Kirksville N-7
Kitchel, 25 K-14
Klondike E-1
Knightstown, 2182 J-11
Knightsville, 872 L-5
Kniman, 75 D-5
Knob Hill S-13
Knox, 3704 C-7
KNOX CO., 38440 P-4
Kokomo, 45468 G-9
Koleen, 60 N-6
Koontz Lake, 1557 B-7
KOSCIUSKO CO., 77358 C-10
Kossuth P-9
Kouts, 1879 C-5
Kramer, 90 H-5
Kurtz, 125 N-8
Kyana, 30 R-6
La Crosse, 551 C-6
La Fontaine, 875 F-10
La Paz, 561 B-8
Laconia, 50 S-9
Ladoga, 985 J-6
Lafayette, 67140 G-6
Lagrange, 2625 A-11
LAGRANGE CO., 37128 B-11
Lagro, 415 E-10
L. Bruce, 150 D-8
L. Cicott, 100 F-7
LAKE CO., 496005 C-4
L. Dalecarlia, 1355 C-4
L. Eliza, 600 B-5
L. Holiday, 750 I-6
L. James, 800 A-13
Lake of the Woods, 700 B-8
Lake on the Green N-9
Lake Sta., 12572 *M-14
Lake Village, 765 D-4
Lakes of the Four Seasons, 7033 B-5
Laketon, 623 E-10
Lakeville, 786 B-8
Lamar, 100 S-6
Lancaster, 100 F-11
Lancaster O-11
Landess, 188 F-11
Lanesville, 564 R-9
Laotto, 250 C-12
Lapel, 2068 I-10
LaPorte, 22053 A-7
LAPORTE CO., 111467 B-7
Larwill, 283 D-11
Laud, 100 D-11
Laurel, 512 L-12
Lawrence, 46001 J-9
LAWRENCE CO., 46134 O-8
Lawrenceburg, 5042 N-14
Lawrenceport, 100 O-8
Lawrenceville, 70 M-13
Lawton, 30 D-7
Leases Cor. E-8
Leavenworth, 238 R-8
Lebanon, 15792 I-7
Lee, 25 E-6
Leesburg, 555 C-10
Leesville, 60 O-8
Leipsic, 50 P-8
Leisure, 30 H-10
Leiters Ford, 200 D-8
Lena, 70 K-5
Leo-Cedarville, 3603 C-13
Leopold, 100 S-7
Leota, 40 P-10
Leroy, 200 C-5
Letts, 150 M-11
Lewis, 175 M-4
Lewis Creek, 30 L-10
Lewisville, 366 J-12
Lewisville, 25 L-7
Lexington, 450 P-11
Liberty, 2133 K-13
Liberty Ctr., 200 F-12
Liberty Mills, 200 D-10
Libertyville, 80 K-4
Ligonier, 4405 B-11
Lincoln, 90 F-8
Lincoln City, 120 R-5
Lincolnville, 150 F-10
Linden, 759 H-6
Linkville, 30 B-8
Linn Grv., 200 F-13
Linton, 5413 N-5
Linwood, 170 H-10
Lisbon, 50 B-12
Little York, 192 P-10
Livonia, 128 P-8
Lizton, 488 J-7
Locke, 80 B-9
Lockport, 20 F-7
Lodi, 85 J-4
Logansport, 18396 F-8
Lomax, 30 C-6
London, 100 K-10
Long Bch., 1179 A-6
Loogootee, 2751 P-6
Lookout M-12
Loon Lake, 400 C-11
Lorane C-11
Losantville, 237 I-12
Lovett, 65 O-11
Lowell, 9276 C-4
Lower Sunset Pk., 120 F-6
Lucerne, 130 E-8
Lydick, 800 A-8
Lyford, 400 K-4
Lynn, 1097 I-13
Lynnville, 888 R-4
Lyons, 742 N-5
Mace, 150 I-6
Mackey, 106 R-4
Macy, 209 E-9
Madison, 11967 O-12
MADISON CO., 131636 H-10
Magnet, 40 S-7
Majenica, 75 F-11
Malden, 120 C-5
Manchester, 120 M-13
Manhattan, 50 K-6
Manilla, 267 K-11
Mansfield, 30 K-5
Manson, 35 H-7
Maple Lane *I-20
Maples, 100 D-13
Maplewood, 50 J-7
Marco, 100 N-5
Marengo, 828 Q-8
Mariah Hill, 500 R-6
Marietta, 200 L-10
Marion, 29948 G-11
MARION CO., 903393 J-9
Marion Hts., 220 K-1
Markland, 30 O-13
Markle, 1095 E-12
Markleville, 528 I-11
Mars Hill *F-17
Marshall, 324 J-5
MARSHALL CO., 47051 C-8
Marshfield, 60 H-4
MARTIN CO., 10334 P-6
Martinsburg, 100 Q-9
Martinsville, 11828 L-8
Maryland, 800 M-2
Marysville, 150 P-11
Marywood, 600 M-2
Matthews, 596 G-11
Mauckport, 81 S-9
Max, 50 I-7
Maxinkuckee C-8
Maxwell, 200 J-10
Mays, 175 K-11
Maysville, 100 P-5
Maywood *F-17
McCordsville, 4797 J-10
McCoysburg, 40 E-5
McCutchanville, 300 S-3
McGrawsville, 70 F-9
Meadowbrook, 250 E-3
Meadowbrook H-2
Mecca, 335 K-4
Mechanicsburg, 150 I-11
Mechanicsburg, 100 I-7
Medaryville, 614 D-6
Medford, 30 I-12
Medora, 693 O-9
Mellott, 197 H-5
Melody Hill, 3628 S-13
Mentone, 1001 D-9
Mentor R-7
Meridian Hills, 1616 *B-18
Merom, 228 N-3
Merriam, 80 C-11
Merrillville, 35246 B-4
Metamora, 974 L-13
Metea, 60 E-8
Metz, 90 A-13
Mexico, 836 E-9
Miami, 325 F-9
MIAMI CO., 36903 F-9
Michiana Shores, 313 A-6
Michigan City, 31479 A-6
Michigantown, 467 H-8
Middleboro, 50 J-14
Middlebury, 3420 A-10
Middlebury, 100 M-5
Middlefork, 70 G-8
Middletown, 2322 I-11
Middletown, 100 L-11
Middletown Pk., 850 J-1
Midland, 300 N-5
Mier, 78 G-10
Milan, 1899 N-13
Milford, 1562 B-10
Milford, 120 L-11
Milledgeville I-7
Miller *L-13
Millersburg, 903 B-10
Millersburg P-8
Millersville *C-19
Millgrove, 150 G-12
Millhousen, 127 M-11
Milligan, 35 J-5
Millport O-9
Milltown, 818 Q-8
Millville, 90 J-12
Milroy, 604 L-11
Milton, 490 J-12
Milton, 20 N-13
Mishawaka, 48252 A-9
Mitchell, 4350 P-7
Mixersville, 20 L-14
Modoc, 196 I-13
Mongo, 200 A-12
Monitor G-6
Monmouth, 60 E-13
Monon, 1777 E-6
Monroe, 842 F-13
Monroe, 40 H-7
Monroe City, 545 P-4
MONROE CO., 137974 M-7
Monroeville, 1235 E-13
Monrovia, 1063 K-7
Monterey, 218 D-7
Montezuma, 1022 J-4
Montgomery, 343 P-5
MONTGOMERY CO., 38124 I-6
Monticello, 5378 F-6
Montmorenci, 243 G-5
Montpelier, 1805 G-12
Moorefield, 50 O-12
Mooreland, 375 I-12
Moores Hill, 597 N-13
Mooresville, 9326 K-8
Moran, 75 G-7
MORGAN CO., 68894 L-7
Morgantown, 986 L-8
Morocco, 1129 E-4
Morris, 300 M-12
Morristown, 1218 K-10
Morton, 100 J-6
Moscow, 100 L-11
Mt. Auburn, 117 J-12
Mt. Auburn, 45 L-10
Mt. Ayr, 122 E-4
Mt. Carmel, 86 L-14
Mt. Comfort, 100 J-10
Mt. Etna, 94 F-11
Mt. Meridian, 50 K-6
Mt. Pleasant, 70 I-12
Mt. Pleasant R-7
Mt. Sterling, 25 O-13
Mt. Summit, 352 I-12
Mt. Vernon, 6687 S-2
Mt. Zion, 30 F-12
Mulberry, 1254 H-7
Muncie, 70085 H-12
Munster, 23603 B-4
Murray, 110 E-12
Nabb, 150 P-11
Napoleon, 234 M-12
Nappanee, 6648 B-9
Nashville, 803 M-8
Nebraska, 90 N-11
Needham, 80 L-9
Needmore, 100 O-7
Needmore, 30 M-8
Nevada Mills, 50 A-13
New Albany, 36372 R-10
New Alsace, 150 M-13
New Amsterdam, 27 S-8
New Augusta *B-16
New Boston, 40 S-6
New Boston S-9
New Brunswick, 30 J-7
New Carlisle, 1861 A-7
New Castle, 18114 J-12
New Chicago, 2035 *M-13
New Columbus, 125 I-11
New Corydon, 100 G-14
New Elliott, 800 *N-12
New Frankfort, 20 O-10
New Goshen, 390 K-4
New Harmony, 789 R-2
New Haven, 14794 D-13
New Lebanon, 120 N-4
New Lisbon, 200 J-12
New London, 200 G-8
New Marion, 120 N-12
New Market, 636 J-6
New Maysville, 60 J-7
New Middletown, 93 R-9
New Mt. Pleasant, 20 H-13
New Palestine, 2055 K-10
New Paris, 1494 B-10
New Pekin, 1401 Q-9
New Philadelphia, 60 P-9
New Pittsburg, 35 H-13
New Pt., 331 M-12
New Richmond, 333 H-6
New Ross, 347 I-7
New Salem, 200 L-12
New Salisbury, 613 R-9
New Trenton, 252 M-13
New Washington, 566 P-11
New Waverly, 150 F-9
New Whiteland, 5472 K-9
New Winchester, 70 J-7
Newark, 75 N-6
Newbern, 200 M-10
Newberry, 193 O-5
Newburgh, 3325 S-4
Newport, 515 J-4
NEWTON CO., 14244 D-4
Newtonville, 90 S-6
Newtown, 256 H-5
Newville, 120 C-13
Nineveh, 250 L-9
NOBLE CO., 47536 C-12
Noblesville, 51969 I-9
Nora *A-18
Norman, 100 N-8
Norristown, 40 L-10
N. Crows Nest, 45 *B-18
N. Grove, 120 F-9
N. Hayden C-4
N. Judson, 1772 C-6
N. Liberty, 1896 B-8
N. Manchester, 6112 D-10
N. Salem, 518 J-7
N. Terre Haute, 4305 L-4
N. Vernon, 6728 N-11
N. Webster, 1146 C-10
Norway, 386 F-6
Notre Dame, 5973 *I-19
Nulltown, 60 K-12
Numa, 35 K-4
Oak Forest L-13
Oakford, 225 G-9
Oakland City, 2429 Q-4
Oaktown, 608 O-4
Oakville, 225 I-12
Ober, 100 C-7
Ockley, 80 G-7
Odell, 30 H-5
Odon, 1354 O-5
Ogden, 120 J-11
Ogden Dunes, 1110 *L-14
Ogilville N-9
OHIO CO., 6128 N-13
Oldenburg, 674 M-12
Omega, 40 H-9
Ontario, 230 A-12
Onward, 100 F-9
Oolitic, 1184 O-7
Ora, 200 D-7
Orange, 80 K-12
ORANGE CO., 19840 P-7
Orangeville, 40 P-7
Orestes, 414 H-10
Oriole R-7
Orland, 434 A-12
Orleans, 2142 P-8
Ormas, 30 C-11
Osceola, 2463 A-9
Osgood, 1624 N-12
Ossian, 3289 E-12
Oswego, 150 C-10
Otis, 80 A-6
Otisco, 400 P-11
Otterbein, 1262 G-5
Otwell, 434 Q-5
Owasco, 45 G-7
OWEN CO., 21575 M-6
Owensburg, 406 O-6
Owensville, 1284 R-3
Oxford, 1162 G-5
Packerton, 90 D-10
Palestine, 300 D-9
Palmyra, 930 Q-9
Paoli, 3677 P-7
Paragon, 659 L-7
Paris Crossing, 100 O-11
PARKE CO., 17339 J-5
Parker City, 1419 H-12
Parkersburg, 75 J-6
Parr, 150 D-5
Patoka, 735 Q-3
Patricksburg, 275 M-6
Patriot, 209 O-14
Patronville, 30 T-5
Paxton, 300 N-4
Paynesville, 60 P-11
Peabody, 25 D-11
Pelzer, 60 S-4
Pence, 85 H-4
Pendleton, 4253 I-10
Penntown, 120 M-13
Pennville, 701 G-12
Pennville, 100 J-13
Peoga, 100 M-9
Peoria, 50 F-9
Peppertown, 20 L-12
Perkinsville, 100 I-10
PERRY CO., 19338 S-7
Perrysburg, 50 E-9
Perrysville, 456 I-4
Perth, 45 K-5
Peru, 11417 F-9
Petersburg, 2383 Q-4
Petersville, 220 M-10
Petroleum, 150 F-12
Pheasant Run, 1200 *N-19
Philadelphia, 300 J-10
Philomath, 35 K-13
Phlox, 120 G-10
Pickard, 60 H-8
Pierceton, 1015 C-10
Pike I-7
PIKE CO., 12845 Q-5
Pimento, 125 M-4
Pine Lake, 1700 A-7
Pine Vil., 217 G-5
Pinhook, 40 B-6
Pinola, 50 B-6
Pittsboro, 2928 J-8
Pittsburg, 300 F-7
Plainfield, 27631 K-8
Plainville, 476 O-5
Plato, 20 A-12
Pleasant, 25 O-12
Pleasant Lake, 500 B-13
Pleasant Mills, 150 E-14
Pleasant View, 300 K-10
Pleasantville, 100 N-5
Plevna, 70 G-9
Plum Tree, 25 F-11
Plymouth, 10033 C-8
Poe, 110 E-13
Pt. Isabel, 91 G-10
Poland, 150 L-6
Poneto, 166 F-12
Portage, 36828 B-5
Porter, 4858 A-5
PORTER CO., 164343 C-5
Portersville, 120 Q-6
Portland, 6223 G-13
POSEY CO., 25910 S-2
Poseyville, 1045 R-2
Prairie Creek, 250 M-4
Prairieton, 175 L-4
Preble, 140 E-13
Princes Lakes, 1312 L-9
Princeton, 8644 Q-3
Progress, 40 I-11
Prospect, 100 P-7
Providence, 75 L-9
Pulaski, 150 E-7
PULASKI CO., 13402 D-7
PUTNAM CO., 37963 K-6
Putnamville, 150 K-6
Pyrmont, 220 G-7
Queensville, 100 N-10
Quercus Grv., 50 O-13
Quincy, 150 L-7
Raccoon, 35 J-6
Radnor, 75 G-7
Raglesville, 141 O-6
Ragsdale, 129 O-4
Rainsville, 50 G-4
Raleigh, 80 K-12
Ramsey, 200 Q-9
RANDOLPH CO., 26171 I-13
Raub, 100 F-4
Ravenswood *B-18
Ray, 60 A-13
Rays Crossing, 60 K-11
Reddington, 200 N-10
Redkey, 1353 H-12
Reelsville, 150 K-6
Reiffsburg, 40 F-12
Remington, 1185 F-5
Rensselaer, 5859 E-5
Reynolds, 533 F-6
Richland, 50 L-12
Richland City, 425 S-5
Richmond, 36812 J-13
Richvalley, 120 F-10
Ridgeville, 803 H-13
Rigdon, 60 G-10

*, †, ‡, §, ◊ See explanation under state title in this index.
County and parish names are listed in capital letters & boldface type.
Independent cities (not included in a county) are listed in italics.

Wiota, 116 J-6
Wiscotta, 40 I-8
Woden, 229 C-9
Wood E-16
Woodbine, 1459 H-3
Woodburn, 202 K-10
WOODBURY CO., 102172 F-3
Woodland M-10
Woodward, 1024 H-9
Woolstock, 168 E-9
WORTH CO., 7598 B-11
Worthington, 401 F-17
Wright, 50 J-13
WRIGHT CO., 13229 E-9
Wyman, 30 K-16
Wyoming, 515 G-17
Yale, 246 H-7
Yarmouth, 120 K-16
Yetter, 34 F-6
Yorktown, 85 L-5
Zaneta F-13
Zearing, 554 G-11
Zwingle, 91 F-18

Kansas

Page locator
Map keys 1–10: Atlas pages 82–83
Map keys 11–20: Atlas pages 84–85
* City keyed to p. 117

Abbyville, 87 H-11
Abilene, 6844 E-13
Ada, 100 D-11
Adams, 20 I-11
Admire, 156 F-16
Agenda, 68 B-12
Agra, 267 B-8
Agricola F-17
Akron J-13
Alamota, 25 F-6
Albert, 175 F-9
Alden, 148 G-10
Alexander, 65 F-7
Aliceville, 40 G-17
Allen, 177 E-15
ALLEN CO., 13371 H-17
Alma, 832 D-15
Almena, 408 B-7
Alta Vista, 444 E-15
Altamont, 1080 J-18
Alton, 103 C-9
Altoona, 414 I-17
Americus, 894 F-15
Ames, 40 C-12
Amy F-5
Andale, 928 H-12
ANDERSON CO., 8102 G-17
Andover, 11791 H-13
Angelus, 45 D-5
Angola, 50 J-17
Anson, 30 I-12
Antelope F-14
Anthony, 2269 J-11
Antonino, 50 E-8
Arcadia, 310 H-19
Argonia, 501 J-12
Arkansas City, 12415 J-13
Arlington, 473 H-11
Arma, 1481 I-19
Arnold, 50 F-6
Arrington, 40 C-17
Ash Grv. D-10
Asherville, 28 C-11
Ashland, 867 J-7
Ashton, 25 J-13
Assaria, 413 E-12
Atchison, 11021 C-18
ATCHISON CO., 16924 C-17
Athol, 44 B-9
Atlanta, 195 I-14
Attica, 626 J-11
Atwood, 1194 B-4
Aubry, 100 E-19
Auburn, 1227 E-16
Augusta, 9274 H-13
Aulne, 50 G-13
Aurora, 60 C-12
Axtell, 406 B-15
Baileyville, 181 B-15
Bala, 30 D-13
Baldwin City, 4515 E-18
Bancroft C-16
BARBER CO., 4861 J-9
Barnard, 70 D-11
Barnes, 159 B-14
Bartlett, 80 J-18
BARTON CO., 27674 F-9
Basehor, 4613 D-18
Bassett, 14 H-17
Bavaria, 90 E-12
Baxter Sprs., 4238 J-19
Bazaar, 25 G-15
Bazine, 334 F-7
Beagle, 70 F-18
Beardsley B-3
Beattie, 200 B-15
Beaumont, 200 I-15
Beaver, 40 F-9
Beeler, 45 F-6
Bel Aire, 6769 H-13
Bellaire B-9
Belle Plaine, 1681 I-13
Belleville, 1991 B-12
Belmont, 35 I-11
Beloit, 3835 C-11
Belpre, 84 H-8
Belvidere, 25 I-8
Belvue, 205 D-15
Bendena, 117 B-18
Benedict, 73 I-16
Bennington, 672 D-12
Bentley, 530 H-12
Benton, 880 H-13
Bern, 166 B-16
Berryton, 400 E-17
Berwick B-16
Beulah, 60 I-19
Beverly, 162 D-11
Big Bow, 95 I-2
Big Sprs., 75 D-17
Bird City, 447 B-3
Bison, 255 F-8
Blaine, 80 C-15
Blair, 40 B-18
Blakeman B-4
Bloom, 75 I-6
Bloomington, 60 C-9
Blue Mound, 275 G-18
Blue Rapids, 1019 B-14
Bluff City, 65 J-11
Bogue, 143 C-7
Boicourt, 30 G-19
Bolton, 40 J-16
Bonita *N-1
Bonner Sprs., 7314 D-18
BOURBON CO., 15173 H-18
Boyle, 30 C-17
Brainerd, 70 H-13
Brazilton, 80 I-18
Bremen, 80 B-14
Brenham I-8
Brewster, 305 C-3
Bridgeport, 75 F-12
Bronson, 323 H-18
Brookville, 262 E-11
BROWN CO., 9984 B-17
Brownell, 29 F-7
Bucklin, 794 I-7
Bucyrus, 193 E-19
Buffalo, 232 H-17
Buhler, 1327 G-12
Bunker Hill, 95 E-9
Burden, 535 J-14
Burdett, 247 G-7
Burdick, 75 F-14
Burlingame, 934 E-16
Burlington, 2674 G-16
Burns, 228 G-14
Burr Oak, 174 B-10
Burrton, 901 G-12
Bush City G-18
Bushong, 34 F-15
Bushton, 279 F-10
BUTLER CO., 65880 H-14
Byers, 35 H-9
Cadmus F-18
Cairo, 20 I-10
Caldwell, 1068 J-12
Calista I-10
Calvert, 25 B-7
Cambridge, 82 J-14
Canada, 75 F-13
Caney, 2203 J-16
Canton, 748 F-12
Capaldo I-19
Carbondale, 1437 E-16
Carlton, 42 E-13
Carlyle, 100 G-17
Carneiro E-11
Cassoday, 129 G-14
Castleton, 25 H-11
Catharine, 104 E-8
Cawker City, 469 C-10
Cedar, 14 C-9
Cedar Bluffs, 35 A-5
Cedar Pt., 28 G-14
Cedar Vale, 579 J-15
Centerville, 100 G-18
Centralia, 512 B-15
Centropolis, 170 E-17
Chanute, 9119 H-17
Chapman, 1393 E-13
Charleston, 25 H-5
Chase, 477 F-10
CHASE CO., 2790 G-14
Chautauqua, 111 J-15
CHAUTAUQUA CO., 3669 J-15
Cheney, 2094 I-12
Cherokee, 714 I-19
CHEROKEE CO., 21603 J-18
Cherryvale, 2367 J-17
Chetopa, 1125 J-18
CHEYENNE CO., 2726 B-2
Cimarron, 2184 H-5
Circleville, 170 C-16
Claflin, 645 F-10
CLARK CO., 2215 J-6
Claudell B-9
Clay Ctr., 4334 C-13
CLAY CO., 8535 D-13
Clayton, 59 B-6
Clearwater, 2481 I-12
Clements G-14
Clifton, 554 C-13
Climax, 72 H-15
Clinton, 40 E-17
Clonmel I-12
CLOUD CO., 9533 C-11
Clyde, 716 C-12
Coats, 83 I-9
Codell, 75 D-8
COFFEY CO., 8601 G-16
Coffeyville, 10295 J-17
Colby, 5387 C-4
Coldwater, 828 J-8
Collyer, 109 D-6
Colony, 408 G-17
Columbus, 3312 J-19
Colwich, 1327 H-12
COMANCHE CO., 1891 J-8
Concordia, 5395 C-12
Conway F-12
Conway Sprs., 1272 I-12
Coolidge, 95 G-1
Copeland, 310 I-5
Corbin, 100 J-12
Corning, 157 B-16
Corwin, 25 J-10
Cottonwood Falls, 903 F-15
Council Grv., 2182 E-15
Countryside, 295 *J-2
Courtland, 285 B-11
COWLEY CO., 36311 J-14
Coyville, 46 H-16
CRAWFORD CO., 39134 I-18
Crestline, 110 J-19
Croweburg, 75 I-19
Cuba, 156 B-12
Cullison, 101 I-9
Culver, 121 E-12
Cummings, 70 C-17
Cunningham, 454 I-10
Dalton J-13
Damar, 132 D-7
Danville, 38 J-11
De Graff H-14
De Soto, 5720 D-18
Dearing, 431 J-17
DECATUR CO., 2961 B-5
Deerfield, 700 H-3
Delavan, 25 F-14
Delia, 169 D-16
Delphos, 359 D-12
Denison, 187 C-17
Denmark D-10
Dennis, 150 I-17
Densmore, 35 C-7
Denton, 148 B-17
Derby, 22158 I-13
Detroit, 114 E-13
Devon, 30 H-19
Dexter, 278 J-14
Diamond Sprs. F-14
DICKINSON CO., 19754 E-13
Dighton, 1038 F-5
Dodge City, 27340 H-6
Doniphan B-18
DONIPHAN CO., 7945 B-18
Dorrance, 185 E-10
DOUGLAS CO., 110826 E-17
Douglass, 1700 I-13
Dover, 140 E-16
Downs, 900 C-10
Dresden, 41 C-5
Duluth, 25 C-15
Dundee, 60 G-9
Dunlap, 30 F-15
Duquoin I-11
Durham, 112 F-13
Dwight, 272 E-14
Earlton, 55 I-17
Eastborough, 773 M-9
Easton, 253 C-18
Edgerton, 1671 E-18
Edmond, 49 C-7
Edna, 442 J-17
Edson, 40 C-3
EDWARDS CO., 3037 H-8
Edwardsville, 4340 *I-1
Effingham, 546 C-17
El Dorado, 13021 H-14
Elbing, 229 G-13
Elgin, 89 K-15
Elk City, 325 J-16
ELK CO., 2882 I-15
Elk Falls, 107 I-15
Elkhart, 2205 J-2
Ellinwood, 2131 F-10
Ellis, 2062 E-7
ELLIS CO., 28452 D-8
Ellsworth, 3120 E-10
ELLSWORTH CO., 6497 E-11
Elmdale, 55 F-14
Elmo, 30 E-13
Elmont, 100 D-16
Elsmore, 77 H-18
Elwood, 1224 B-18
Elyria, 75 G-12
Emmett, 191 C-16
Emporia, 24916 F-15
Englevale, 25 I-19
Englewood, 77 J-6
Ensign, 187 I-6
Enterprise, 855 E-13
Erie, 1150 I-18
Esbon, 99 B-10
Eskridge, 534 E-16
Eudora, 6136 E-18
Eureka, 2633 H-15
Everest, 284 B-17
Fairmount, 100 D-18
Fairview, 260 B-16
Fairway, 3882 *J-3
Fall River, 162 I-16
Falun, 87 F-12
Farlington, 75 I-19
Farlinville G-19
Faulkner, 30 J-18
Fellsburg, 20 H-8
FINNEY CO., 36776 G-5
Floral, 40 I-14
Florence, 465 G-14
Fontana, 224 F-19
Ford, 216 I-7
FORD CO., 33848 I-6
Formoso, 93 B-11
Ft. Dodge, 165 H-6
Ft. Scott, 8087 H-19
Fostoria, 70 C-14
Fostoria, 35 E-16
Fowler, 590 I-6
Frankfort, 726 B-15
Franklin, 375 I-19
FRANKLIN CO., 25992 F-17
Frederick, 18 F-10
Fredonia, 2482 I-16
Freeport, 5 J-11
Friend, 30 G-4
Frontenac, 3437 I-19
Fulton, 163 G-19
Furley, 100 H-13
Galatia, 39 F-9
Galena, 3085 J-19
Galesburg, 126 I-17
Galva, 870 F-12
Garden City, 26658 H-4
Garden Plain, 849 I-12
Gardner, 19123 E-18
Garfield, 190 G-8
Garland, 100 H-19
Garnett, 3415 G-18
Gas, 564 H-17
Gaylord, 114 C-9
GEARY CO., 34362 E-14
Gem, 88 C-4
Geneseo, 267 F-11
Geuda Sprs., 185 J-13
Girard, 2789 I-19
Glade, 96 B-8
Glasco, 498 C-11
Glen Elder, 445 C-10
Glendale, 35 E-11
Goddard, 4344 I-12
Goessel, 539 G-13
Goff, 126 B-16
Goodland, 4489 C-2
Goodrich, 40 G-18
Gorham, 334 E-9
Gove, 80 E-5
GOVE CO., 2695 E-5
GRAHAM CO., 2597 D-6
Grainfield, 277 D-5
Grandview Plaza, 1560 D-14
GRANT CO., 7829 I-3
Grantville, 180 D-17
GRAY CO., 6006 H-5
Great Bend, 15995 F-9
Greeley, 302 F-18
GREELEY CO., 1247 F-2
Green, 128 C-13
Greenleaf, 331 B-13
Greensburg, 777 I-8
Greenwich, 80 K-10
Greenwich Hts., 960 M-10
GREENWOOD CO., 6689 H-15
Grenola, 216 I-15
Gretna B-8
Gridley, 341 G-16
Grigston F-5
Grinnell, 259 D-5
Gross, 50 I-19
Grove D-16
Groveland G-12
Gypsum, 405 E-12
Hackney, 25 J-13
Haddam, 104 B-13
Half Mound C-17
Hallowell, 200 J-18
Halls Summit F-17
Halstead, 2085 H-12
Hamilton, 268 H-15
HAMILTON CO., 2690 G-2
Hamlin, 46 B-17
Hammond H-19
Hanover, 682 B-14
Hanston, 206 G-7
Harding G-19
Hardtner, 172 K-9
Harlan, 25 C-9
Harper, 1473 J-11
HARPER CO., 6034 J-11
Harris, 51 F-17
Hartford, 371 G-16
HARVEY CO., 34684 G-12
Harveyville, 236 E-16
HASKELL CO., 4256 I-4
Havana, 104 J-16
Haven, 1237 H-12
Havensville, 133 C-16
Haverhill, 50 H-14
Haviland, 701 I-8
Hays, 20510 E-8
Haysville, 10826 I-13
Hazelton, 93 J-10
Healy, 234 F-5
Hedville, 50 E-12
Heizer, 125 F-9
Hepler, 132 H-18
Herington, 2526 E-14
Herkimer, 50 B-14
Herndon, 129 B-4
Hessdale E-15
Hesston, 3709 G-12
Hewins, 40 J-15
Hiattville, 60 H-19
Hiawatha, 3172 B-17
Hickok, 80 I-3
Highland, 1012 B-17
Highland Pk. M-16
Hill City, 1474 C-7
Hillsboro, 2993 F-13
Hillsdale, 229 E-19
Hitschmann, 20 F-10
HODGEMAN CO., 1916 G-6
Hoisington, 2706 F-9
Holcomb, 2094 H-4
Holland E-13
Hollenberg, 21 B-13
Hollis C-12
Holton, 3329 C-16
Holyrood, 447 F-10
Home, 160 B-14
Homewood, 30 F-17
Hope, 368 E-13
Hopewell H-9
Horace, 70 F-2
Horton, 1776 B-17
Howard, 687 I-15
Hoxie, 1201 C-5
Hoyt, 669 D-16
Hudson, 129 G-9
Hugoton, 3904 J-3
Humboldt, 1953 H-17
Hunnewell, 67 K-12
Hunter, 57 D-10
Huron, 54 B-17
Hutchinson, 42080 G-11
Idana, 70 C-13
Independence, 9483 J-17
Industry D-13
Ingalls, 306 H-5
Inman, 1377 G-12
Iola, 5704 H-17
Ionia, 80 C-10
Iowa Pt., 35 B-17
Isabel, 90 I-10
Iuka, 163 H-9
JACKSON CO., 13462 C-16
Jamestown, 286 C-11
Jarbalo, 100 D-18
Jefferson, 50 J-17
JEFFERSON CO., 19126 D-17
Jennings, 96 B-6
Jetmore, 867 G-6
Jewell, 432 B-11
JEWELL CO., 3077 B-11
Johnson, 1495 I-2
JOHNSON CO., 544179 E-18
Junction City, 23353 D-14
Kackley, 25 B-11
Kalvesta, 40 G-6
Kanopolis, 492 E-11
Kanorado, 153 C-1
Kansas City, 145786 D-19
KEARNY CO., 3977 G-3
Keats, 170 D-14
Kelly, 40 B-16
Kendall, 250 H-2
Kensington, 473 B-9
Kimball H-18
Kincaid, 122 G-18
Kingman, 3177 I-11
KINGMAN CO., 7858 I-11
Kingsdown, 200 I-7
Kinsley, 1457 H-8
Kiowa, 1026 K-10
KIOWA CO., 2553 I-8
Kipp, 59 E-12
Kiro D-16
Kirwin, 171 B-8
Kismet, 459 J-4
La Crosse, 1342 F-8
La Cygne, 1149 F-19
La Harpe, 578 H-18
Labette, 78 J-18
LABETTE CO., 21607 J-18
Lafontaine, 100 I-16
Lake City, 50 J-9
L. Quivira, 906 *J-1
L. Wabaunsee, 250 E-15
Lakin, 2216 H-3
Lamont, 45 G-16
Lancaster, 298 C-17
Lane, 225 F-18
LANE CO., 1750 F-5
Langdon, 42 H-10
Langley F-11
Lansing, 11265 D-18
Larkinburg, 30 C-17
Larned, 4054 G-8
Latham, 139 I-14
Latimer, 20 E-14
Lawrence, 87643 D-18
Lawton, 90 J-19
Le Loup, 50 E-18
Le Roy, 561 G-17
Leavenworth, 35251 C-18
LEAVENWORTH CO., 76227 D-18
Leawood, 31867 D-19
Lebanon, 218 B-10
Lebo, 940 F-16
Lecompton, 625 D-17
Lehigh, 175 F-13
Lenexa, 48190 D-19
Lenora, 250 C-6
Leon, 704 H-14
Leona, 48 B-17
Leonardville, 449 C-14
Leoti, 1534 F-3
Leoville, 50 C-5
Levant, 61 C-3
Lewis, 451 H-8
Liberal, 20525 J-4
Liberty, 123 J-17
Liebenthal, 103 F-8
Lillis C-15
Lincoln, 1297 D-11
LINCOLN CO., 3241 D-11
Lincolnville, 203 F-13
Lindsborg, 3458 F-12
Linn, 410 B-13
LINN CO., 9656 G-18
Linn Valley, 804 F-19
Linwood, 375 D-18
Little River, 557 F-11
Logan, 589 B-7
LOGAN CO., 2756 E-3
Lone Elm, 25 G-18
Lone Star E-17
Long Island, 134 B-7
Longford, 79 D-13
Longton, 348 I-16
Loretta, 30 F-8
Lorraine, 138 F-10
Lost Sprs., 70 F-13
Louisburg, 4315 E-19
Louisville, 188 D-15
Lovewell, 25 B-11
Lowemont C-18
Lucas, 393 D-10
Ludell, 100 B-4
Luray, 194 D-9
Lyndon, 1052 F-17
LYON CO., 33690 F-15
Lyons, 3739 G-11
Macksville, 549 H-9
Madison, 701 G-15
Mahaska, 83 A-12
Maize, 3420 H-12
Manchester, 95 D-13
Manhattan, 52281 D-14
Mankato, 869 B-10
Manning F-5
Manter, 171 I-2
Maple City, 20 J-14
Maple Hill, 620 D-16
Mapleton, 84 G-19
Marienthal, 71 F-3
Marion, 1927 F-13
MARION CO., 12660 G-13
Marquette, 641 F-11
MARSHALL CO., 10117 B-14
Marysville, 3294 B-14
Matfield Green, 47 G-14
Mayetta, 341 C-16
Mayfield, 113 J-12
McCracken, 190 F-7
McCune, 405 I-18
McDonald, 160 B-3
McFarland, 256 D-15
McLouth, 880 D-18
McPherson, 13155 F-12
MCPHERSON CO., 29180 F-11
Meade, 1721 J-5
MEADE CO., 4575 J-5
Medicine Lodge, 2009 J-10
Medora, 50 G-11
Melrose, 50 J-18
Melvern, 385 F-17
Menlo, 61 C-5
Mentor, 100 E-12
Mercier, 25 B-17
Meriden, 813 D-17
Merriam, 11003 *J-2
MIAMI CO., 32787 F-18
Michigan Valley, 150 E-17
Midway I-11
Milan, 82 J-12
Milberger, 25 E-9
Mildred, 28 G-18
Milford, 530 D-14
Miller, 50 F-16
Milton, 155 I-12
Miltonvale, 539 C-12
Mingo, 40 D-4
Minneapolis, 2032 D-12
Minneola, 745 I-6
Mission, 9323 *J-3
Mission Hills, 3498 *J-3
Mission Woods, 178 *J-3
Mitchell F-11
MITCHELL CO., 6373 D-11
Modoc, 35 F-4
Moline, 371 I-15
Monmouth I-18
Mont Ida, 50 G-17
Montana, 55 J-18
Montezuma, 966 I-5
MONTGOMERY CO., 35471 I-16
Montrose B-11
Monument, 75 D-4
Moran, 558 H-18
Morehead, 50 I-17
Morganville, 192 C-13
Morland, 154 C-6
Morrill, 230 B-16
MORRIS CO., 5923 F-14
Morrowville, 155 B-13
MORTON CO., 3233 J-2
Moscow, 310 I-3
Mound City, 694 G-19
Mound Valley, 407 J-17
Moundridge, 1737 G-12
Mt. Hope, 813 H-12
Mulberry, 520 I-19
Mullinville, 255 I-7
Mulvane, 6111 I-13
Munden, 100 B-12
Munjor, 213 E-8
Murdock, 75 I-11
Muscotah, 176 C-17
Narka, 94 B-12
Nashville, 64 I-10
Natoma, 335 D-9
Navarre, 75 E-13
Neal, 65 H-16
Nekoma, 80 F-8
NEMAHA CO., 10178 B-16
Neodesha, 2486 I-17
NEOSHO CO., 16512 I-17
Neosho Falls, 141 G-17
Neosho Rapids, 265 F-16
Ness City, 1449 F-6
NESS CO., 3107 F-7
Netawaka, 143 C-16
Neutral J-19
New Albany, 56 I-16
New Almelo, 50 C-6
New Cambria, 126 E-12
New Lancaster, 25 F-19
New Salem, 80 J-14
New Strawn, 394 G-16
Newman, 40 D-17
Newton, 19132 G-13
Nickerson, 1070 G-11
Nicodemus, 60 C-7
Niles, 40 E-12
Niotaze, 82 J-16
Norcatur, 151 B-6
N. Newton, 1759 G-13
N. Topeka L-16
Northbranch, 25 B-10
Norton, 2928 B-7
NORTON CO., 5671 B-6
Nortonville, 637 C-17
Norway, 40 B-12
Norwich, 491 I-11
Oak Hill, 24 D-13
Oak Valley, 25 I-16
Oakland L-16
Oaklawn, 3000 N-9
Oakley, 2045 D-4
Oberlin, 1788 B-5
Ocheltree, 100 E-19
Odin, 101 F-10
Offerle, 199 H-7
Ogallah, 90 E-7
Ogden, 2087 D-14
Oketo, 66 B-14
Olathe, 125872 E-19
Olivet, 67 F-16
Olmitz, 114 F-9
Olpe, 546 G-15
Olsburg, 219 C-14
Onaga, 702 C-15
Oneida, 75 B-16
Opolis, 130 I-19
Osage City, 2943 F-16
OSAGE CO., 16295 E-16
Osawatomie, 4447 F-18
Osborne, 1431 C-9
OSBORNE CO., 3858 C-9
Oskaloosa, 1113 D-17
Oswego, 1829 J-18
Otis, 282 F-8
Ottawa, 12649 F-18
OTTAWA CO., 6091 D-12
Overbrook, 1058 E-17
Overland Pk., 173372 D-19
Oxford, 1049 J-13
Ozawkie, 645 D-17
Page City, 40 D-4
Palco, 277 D-7
Palmer, 111 C-13
Paola, 5602 F-18
Paradise, 49 D-9
Park, 126 D-5
Park City, 7297 H-13
Parker, 277 F-18
Parkerfield, 426 J-14
Parkerville, 59 E-14
Parsons, 10500 I-18
Partridge, 248 H-11
Pauline N-15
PAWNEE CO., 6973 G-7
Pawnee Rock, 252 G-9
Paxico, 221 D-15
Peabody, 1210 G-13
Pearl E-13
Peck, 110 I-13
Penalosa, 17 H-10
Penokee, 150 C-6
Peoria, 40 F-18
Perry, 929 D-17
Perth, 50 J-12
Peru, 139 J-16
Petrolia, 85 H-17
Pfeifer, 80 E-8
PHILLIPS CO., 5642 B-8
Phillipsburg, 2581 B-8
Pickrell Cor., 40 H-14
Piedmont, 250 I-15
Pierceville, 100 H-5
Pilsen, 200 F-13
Piqua, 107 H-17
Pittsburg, 20233 I-19
Plains, 1146 J-5
Plainville, 1903 D-8
Pleasant Grv. E-17
Pleasanton, 1216 G-19
Plevna, 98 H-10
Plymouth, 50 F-15
Pomona, 832 F-17
Portis, 103 C-9
POTTAWATOMIE CO., 21604 C-15
Potter, 100 C-18
Potwin, 449 H-13
Powhattan, 77 B-17
Prairie View, 134 B-7
Prairie Vil., 21447 D-19
Pratt, 6835 I-9
PRATT CO., 9656 I-9
Prescott, 264 G-19
Preston, 158 H-10
Pretty Prairie, 680 H-11
Princeton, 277 F-18
Prospect, 500 H-14
Protection, 514 J-7
Purcell B-17
Quenemo, 388 F-17
Quincy H-16
Quinter, 918 D-6
Radium, 25 G-9
Radley, 200 I-19
Rago, 30 I-11
Ramona, 187 F-13
Randall, 65 C-11
Randolph, 163 C-14
Ransom, 294 F-6
Rantoul, 184 F-18
RAWLINS CO., 2519 B-4
Raymond, 79 G-10
Reading, 231 F-16
Redfield, 146 H-19
Redwing, 20 F-9
Reece, 140 H-15
RENO CO., 64511 H-11
Republic, 116 B-11
REPUBLIC CO., 4980 B-12
Reserve, 84 A-17
Rexford, 232 C-5
Rice C-12
RICE CO., 10083 F-10
Richfield, 43 J-2
Richmond, 464 F-18
Richter, 20 F-17
Riley, 939 D-14
RILEY CO., 71115 C-14
Riverdale, 60 I-13
Riverton, 929 J-19
Robinson, 234 B-17
Rock, 80 I-13
Rock Creek, 50 D-17
Rocky Ford D-14
Roeland Pk., 6731 *J-3
Rolla, 442 J-2
Rome J-12
ROOKS CO., 5181 D-8
Roper H-17
Rosalia, 171 H-14
Rose H-17
Rose Hill, 3931 I-13
Roseland, 77 J-19
Rossville, 1151 D-16
Roxbury, 104 F-12
Rozel, 156 G-8
Ruleton, 30 C-2
Rush Ctr., 170 F-8
RUSH CO., 3307 F-8
Russell, 4506 E-9
RUSSELL CO., 6970 D-9
Russell Sprs., 24 E-3
Sabetha, 2571 B-16
St. Benedict, 70 B-15
St. Clere C-16
St. Francis, 1329 B-2
St. George, 639 D-15
St. John, 1295 H-9
St. Joseph, 55 C-12
St. Leo, 25 I-10
St. Mark, 100 H-12
St. Marys, 2627 D-16
St. Paul, 629 I-18
St. Peter, 30 D-6
Salina, 47707 E-12
SALINE CO., 55606 E-11
Sanford G-8
Satanta, 1133 I-4
Savonburg, 109 H-18
Sawyer, 124 I-9
Saxman, 25 G-11
Scammon, 482 J-19
Scandia, 372 B-11
Schoenchen, 207 E-8
Schulte, 50 I-12
Scipio F-18
Scott City, 3816 F-4
SCOTT CO., 4936 F-4
Scottsville, 25 C-11
Scranton, 710 E-16
Sedan, 1124 J-15
Sedgwick, 1695 H-12
SEDGWICK CO., 498365 I-12
Seguin, 25 C-5
Selden, 219 C-5
Selkirk, 35 F-3
Selma G-18
Seneca, 1991 B-16
Severance, 94 B-17
Severy, 259 I-15
Seward, 64 G-9
SEWARD CO., 22952 J-4
Shallow Water, 40 F-4
Sharon, 158 J-10
Sharon Sprs., 748 E-2
Sharpe G-17
Shaw I-18
Shawnee, 62209 D-19
SHAWNEE CO., 177934 E-16
SHERIDAN CO., 2556 D-5
Sherman, 50 J-18
SHERMAN CO., 6010 C-2
Sherwin, 40 J-18
Shields, 30 F-5
Silver Lake, 1439 D-16
Silverdale, 50 J-14
Simpson, 86 C-11
Sitka J-7
Skiddy E-14
Smith Ctr., 1665 B-9
SMITH CO., 3853 B-9
Smolan, 215 E-12
Soldier, 136 C-16
Solomon, 1095 E-13
Somerset, 40 F-19
S. Haven, 363 J-12
S. Hutchinson, 2457 G-11
S. Mound I-18
Sparks, 50 B-18
Spearville, 773 H-7
Speed, 37 B-8
Spivey, 78 I-11
Spring Hill, 5437 E-19
Springdale, 30 D-18
Stafford, 1042 H-10
STAFFORD CO., 4437 G-9
Stanley *M-2
STANTON CO., 2235 H-1
Stark, 72 H-18
Sterling, 2328 G-11
STEVENS CO., 5724 J-3
Stilwell, 250 E-19
Stippville, 30 J-19
Stockton, 1329 C-8
Strauss I-18
Strong City, 485 F-15
Studley, 50 C-6
Stull, 45 D-17
Stuttgart, 75 B-8
Sublette, 1453 I-4
Summerfield, 156 A-15
SUMNER CO., 24132 J-12
Sun City, 53 I-9
Suppesville, 75 I-12
Susank, 34 F-9
Sycamore, 200 J-17
Sylvan Grv., 279 D-10
Sylvia, 218 H-10
Syracuse, 1812 G-2
Talmage, 99 D-13
Talmo, 50 B-12
Tampa, 112 F-13
Tasco C-6
Tecumseh, 650 M-17
Terra Hts. N-15
Tescott, 319 D-11
Thayer, 497 I-17
THOMAS CO., 7900 C-3
Thrall G-15
Timken, 76 F-8
Tipton, 210 C-10
Tonganoxie, 4996 D-18
Topeka, 127473 D-16
Toronto, 281 H-16
Towanda, 1450 H-13
Trading Post G-19
Traer, 25 B-5
Trego Ctr. E-6
TREGO CO., 3001 E-6
Tribune, 741 F-2
Trousdale H-8
Troy, 1010 B-18
Turon, 387 H-10
Tyro, 220 J-16
Udall, 746 I-13
Ulysses, 6161 I-3
Uniontown, 272 H-18
Upland, 25 D-13
Urbana, 30 I-17
Utica, 158 F-6
Valeda, 70 J-17
Valley Ctr., 6822 H-13
Valley Falls, 1192 C-17
Varner H-11
Vassar, 530 E-17
Venango, 100 F-11
Verdi E-12
Vermillion, 112 B-15
Vernon H-17
Vesper, 25 D-10
Victoria, 1214 E-8
Vilas H-17
Vine Creek D-12
Vining, 45 C-13
Vinland, 30 E-18
Viola, 130 I-12
Virgil, 71 H-16
Vliets, 35 B-15
Voda D-6
Wabaunsee, 110 D-15
WABAUNSEE CO., 7053 E-15
Wagstaff, 25 E-19
Wakarusa, 260 E-16
WaKeeney, 1862 D-7
Wakefield, 980 D-13
Waldo, 30 D-9
Waldron, 11 K-11
Walker, 60 E-9
Wallace, 57 E-2
WALLACE CO., 1485 D-2
Walnut, 220 I-18
Walton, 235 G-13
Wamego, 4372 D-15
Washington, 1131 B-13
WASHINGTON CO., 5799 B-13
Waterloo, 30 I-11
Waterville, 680 B-14
Wathena, 1364 B-18
Wauneta J-15
Waverly, 592 F-17
Wayne B-12
Wayside, 65 J-16
Webber, 25 B-11
Weir, 686 I-19
Welda, 129 G-18
Wellington, 8172 J-12
Wells, 40 D-12
Wellsford, 25 I-9
Wellsville, 1857 E-18
Weskan, 161 E-2
W. Mineral, 185 J-19
Westfall, 40 E-11
Westmoreland, 778 C-15
Westphalia, 163 G-17
Westwood, 1506 *J-3
Westwood Hills, 359 *J-3
Wetmore, 368 B-16
Wheaton, 95 C-15
Wheeler, 50 B-2
White City, 618 E-14
White Cloud, 176 A-17
Whitewater, 718 H-13
Whiting, 187 C-17
Wichita, 382368 H-13
WICHITA CO., 2234 F-3
Wilburton J-2
Willard, 92 D-16
Williamsburg, 397 F-17
Williamstown, 75 D-17
Willis, 38 B-17
Willowbrook, 87 G-11
Willowdale, 20 I-10
Wilmore, 53 J-8
Wilmot, 30 I-14
Wilroads Gdns., 609 H-6
Wilsey, 153 F-14
Wilson, 781 E-10
WILSON CO., 9409 I-16
Winchester, 551 C-17
Windom, 130 F-11
Windthorst, 15 H-7
Winfield, 12301 J-13
Winifred, 25 B-15
Winona, 162 D-3
Womer B-9
Woodbine, 170 E-13
Woodruff, 25 A-8
WOODSON CO., 3309 H-16
Woodston, 136 C-8
Worden E-17
Wright, 163 H-6
WYANDOTTE CO., 157505 D-19
Xenia, 25 G-18
Yates Ctr., 1417 H-16
Yoder, 194 H-11
Zeandale, 50 D-15
Zenda, 90 I-10
Zenith H-10
Zook G-8
Zurich, 99 D-8

Kentucky

Page locator
Map keys 1–10: Atlas pages 86–87
Map keys 11–20: Atlas pages 88–89
* City keyed to p. 163
† City keyed to p. 226

Aaron, 70 M-10
Aberdeen, 200 K-5
Acton, 125 K-10
ADAIR CO., 18656 L-10
Adairville, 852 N-5
Adamson K-18
Adolphus, 150 N-7
Ages, 500 M-16
Airport Gdns., 700 K-17
Akersville N-8
Albany, 2033 M-10
Alexandria, 8477 D-13
Allegre, 100 L-4
Allen City, 193 J-18
ALLEN CO., 19956 M-7
Allensville, 157 M-4
Almo, 100 M-1
Alpha, 25 M-11
Alpine, 50 M-12
Alton, 300 H-11
Alton Sta., 450 H-11
Altro, 35 K-16
Alvaton, 80 M-6
Amandaville M-10
Amos, 50 N-7
Anchorage, 2348 B-10
Anco, 360 K-17
ANDERSON CO., 21421 H-11
Anna L-6
Annville, 1095 K-14
Anthoston, 250 I-3
Anton, 200 K-3
Argillite, 50 F-18
Argo J-20
Arjay, 600 M-15
Arlington, 324 F-2
Artemus, 590 M-15
Ary, 60 K-17
Ashbyburg, 40 J-3
Ashcamp, 150 K-19
Asher, 100 L-16
Ashland, 21684 F-18
Athertonville, 75 J-9
Athol, 75 J-15
Auburn, 1340 M-5
Audubon Pk., 1473 C-7
Augusta, 1190 E-14
Aurora, 200 M-1
Austin, 150 M-8
Auxier, 669 I-18
Avawam, 250 K-16
Axtel, 60 J-6
Bagdad, 220 G-11
Baizetown, 25 K-5
Bakerton, 35 M-10
BALLARD CO., 8249 E-2
Ballardsville, 200 G-10
Balltown, 80 I-9
Bandana, 203 E-3
Bandy K-12
Banner, 100 J-18
Barbourmeade, 1218 A-9
Barbourville, 3165 M-14
Bardstown, 11700 I-9
Bardstown Jct. I-9
Bardwell, 723 F-2
Barlow, 675 E-2
BARREN CO., 42173 M-8
Barrier, 75 M-12
Baskett, 300 I-3
BATH CO., 11591 G-15
Battletown, 150 H-7
Baxter, 800 M-16
Bays, 25 J-16
Bear Branch, 80 L-15
Beattyville, 1307 J-15
Beaumont, 100 M-9
Beauty, 600 I-19
Beaver, 200 K-18
Beaver Dam, 3409 K-5
Beaverlick, 75 E-12
Beda J-5
Bedford, 599 F-10
Bee Spr., 150 K-7
Beech Creek, 250 L-4
Beech Grv., 243 J-3
Beechmont, 689 L-4
Beechwood G-12
Beechwood Vil., 1324 B-8
Belcher, 150 K-19
Belfry, 600 J-19
BELL CO., 28691 M-15
Bellefonte, 888 †B-1
Bellemeade, 865 B-9
Belleview, 343 D-11
Bellevue, 5955 A-20
Belmont, 100 I-9
Belton, 250 L-4
Bengal K-9
Benham, 500 L-17
Bennettstown, 35 M-2
Benton, 4349 F-4
Berea, 13561 J-13
Berkley, 125 F-2
Berlin, 45 E-13
Berry, 264 F-13
Bethany, 65 J-16
Bethel, 200 G-14
Bethelridge, 30 K-12
Bethlehem, 260 G-11
Betsy Layne, 688 J-18
Beulah, 50 K-2
Beulah Hts., 50 M-13
Beverly, 30 L-15
Bewleyville, 100 I-7
Big Clifty, 300 J-7
Big Creek, 300 L-15
Big Eddy, 150 B-12
Big Laurel, 120 L-16
Big Spr., 90 I-7
Bighill, 200 J-13
Bimble, 200 M-15
Birdsville E-4
Black Gnat, 50 K-9
Black Snake, 200 M-16
Blackey, 120 L-17
Blackford, 100 J-2
Blackmont, 300 M-16
Blaine, 47 H-18
Blandville, 90 F-2
Bledsoe, 50 L-16
Bloomfield, 838 I-10
Blue Licks Spr. G-14
Blue Ridge Mnr., 767 B-9
Blue River, 30 J-18
Bluehole L-15
Board Tree, 50 J-20
Boaz, 20 F-4
Bohon, 30 I-11
Boldman, 130 J-18
Bond, 90 K-14
Bondville I-11
Bonnieville, 255 K-8
Boone J-13
BOONE CO., 118811 E-11
Boonesborough I-13
Booneville, 81 J-15
Boons Camp, 125 I-18
Boston, 266 I-9
Boston, 80 E-13
BOURBON CO., 19985 H-13
Bow, 25 M-10
Bowen, 35 I-15
Bowling Green, 58067 L-6
BOYD CO., 49542 G-18
BOYLE CO., 28432 J-11
Bracht E-12
BRACKEN CO., 8488 F-13
Bradfordsville, 294 J-10
Brainard J-17
Brandenburg, 2643 H-7
BREATHITT CO., 13878 J-16
Breckinridge G-13
BRECKINRIDGE CO., 20059 I-6
Breeding, 60 L-9
Bremen, 197 K-4
Brewers, 125 F-4
Briarwood, 435 B-9
Bridgeport, 200 H-11
Briensburg, 250 F-4
Brinkley, 125 K-17
Broad Fields, 250 B-8
Broadwell G-13
Brodhead, 1211 K-13
Bromley, 763 B-19
Bronston, 400 L-12
Brooks, 2401 H-9
Brooksville, 642 F-14
Broughtentown, 50 K-12
Browder, 300 K-4
Brownsboro Farm, 648 A-9
Brownsboro Vil., 319 B-8
Brownsville, 836 K-7
Bruin, 60 G-17
Brush Grv. I-10
Bryantsville, 130 I-12
Buchanan, 50 G-18
Buckeye I-12
Buckhorn, 162 K-16
Buckner, 5837 G-9
Buechel, 7272 C-8
Buffalo, 498 J-9
Buford, 75 J-5
Bulan, 600 K-17
BULLITT CO., 74319 H-9
Burgin, 965 I-12
Burkesville, 1521 M-10
Burkhart, 30 I-16
Burlington, 15926 D-12
Burna, 257 D-4
Burnaugh, 175 G-18
Burning Sprs., 100 K-15
Burnside, 611 L-12
Burton, 70 K-18
Burtonville, 60 F-15
Bush, 15 L-14
Buskirk, 150 J-20
Butler, 612 E-13
BUTLER CO., 12690 K-6
Bybee, 150 I-14
Cadiz, 2558 M-2
Cairo, 150 I-2
CALDWELL CO., 12984 K-1
Calhoun, 763 J-4
California, 90 E-13
Callaway, 300 M-15
CALLOWAY CO., 37191 N-1
Calvary, 60 J-10
Calvert City, 2566 E-4
Calvin, 150 M-15
Camargo, 1081 H-14
Cambridge, 175 C-9
Camp Dix, 30 F-16
Camp Kennedy, 30 I-12
Camp Nelson, 40 I-12
CAMPBELL CO., 90336 E-13
Campbellsburg, 813 F-10
Campbellsville, 9108 K-10
Campton, 441 I-15
Canada, 400 J-19
Cane Valley, 150 L-10
Caney, 100 I-16
Caneyville, 608 K-6
Canmer, 140 K-8
Cannel City, 250 I-16
Cannon, 150 M-14
Cannonsburg, 856 G-18
Canton, 75 M-1
Carlisle, 2010 G-14
CARLISLE CO., 5104 F-2
Carrie, 80 K-17
CARROLL CO., 10811 F-11
Carrollton, 3938 F-10
Carrsville, 50 D-4
Carter, 50 F-17
CARTER CO., 27720 G-17
Cartwright, 40 M-11
CASEY CO., 15955 K-11
Casey Creek, 50 K-10
Caseyville, 40 J-1
Catlettsburg, 1856 G-18
Causey L-16
Cave City, 2240 L-8
Cawood, 731 M-16
Cayce, 123 G-2
Cecil, 125 E-3
Cecilia, 572 J-8
Center, 125 L-9
Centertown, 423 K-4
Centerville, 120 G-13
Central City, 5978 K-4
Cerulean, 314 L-2
Chalybeate, 50 L-7
Chapel Hill, 50 M-7
Chaplin, 418 I-10
Chappell, 50 L-16
Charleston, 200 K-2
Charters F-16
Chatham, 40 E-14
Chavies, 170 K-16
Cherokee B-8
Cherrywood Vil., 327 B-8
Chestnut Grv., 60 G-10
Chloe, 150 J-19
Choateville, 200 A-11
CHRISTIAN CO., 73955 L-3
Cinda, 60 L-16
CLARK CO., 35613 I-13
Clark Hill, 300 G-16
Clarkson, 875 J-7
Clay, 1181 J-2
Clay City, 1077 I-14
CLAY CO., 21730 K-15
Claymour M-4
Claypool M-7
Claysville, 50 F-13
Clearfield, 1300 H-16
Cleaton, 500 K-4
Clementsville, 75 K-10
Clermont, 250 I-9
Clifford, 40 H-19
Clifton, 200 H-11
Clifty, 275 L-4
Clinton, 1388 G-2
CLINTON CO., 10272 N-11
Closplint, 150 M-17
Cloverport, 1152 I-6
Coal Run Vil., 1706 J-19
Cobb, 30 L-2
Coburg K-10
Cold Spr., 5912 C-20
Coldstream, 1100 A-10
Coldwater, 125 G-4
Coleman J-20
Colemansville, 40 F-13
Colesburg, 90 I-8
College Hill I-14
Colonial Ter. B-9
Colson K-18
Columbia, 4452 L-10
Columbus, 170 F-2
Colville G-13
Combs, 900 K-16
Comer J-3
Concord, 35 F-15
Confederate L-1
Confluence, 20 K-16
Connersville, 35 G-13
Constance, 100 B-17
Constantine, 40 J-7
Conway, 50 J-13
Cool Sprs., 50 K-5
Co-Operative, 180 M-12
Coopersville, 80 M-12
Coral Ridge E-7
Corbin, 7304 L-14
Corinth, 232 F-12
Corinth M-5
Cornettsville, 90 L-17
Cornishville, 90 I-11
Corydon, 720 I-2
Cottle I-16
Covington, 40640 D-12
Cowan, 150 G-14
Coxs Creek, 50 I-9
Crab Orchard, 841 J-12
Cranks, 120 M-17
Crayne, 173 K-1
Craynor, 85 J-18
Crescent Pk. C-18
Crescent Sprs., 3801 B-18
Crestview, 475 C-20
Crestview Hills, 3148 C-18
Crestwood, 4531 G-9
Crider, 60 L-1
Crittenden, 3815 E-12
CRITTENDEN CO., 9315 K-1
Crockett, 40 H-17
Crofton, 749 L-3
Cromona, 400 K-18
Cromwell, 240 K-5
Cropper, 150 G-10
Crossland, 50 G-4
Crown, 50 L-18
Crutchfield, 110 G-3
Crystal, 20 J-15
Cub Run, 125 K-7
Cuba, 125 G-3
Culver, 30 H-17
Cumberland, 2237 L-17
CUMBERLAND CO., 6856 M-9
Cundiff L-10
Cunningham, 400 F-3
Curdsville, 150 I-3
Custer, 125 I-7
Cutshin, 100 L-16
Cynthiana, 6402 G-13
Daisy, 200 L-17
Danville, 16218 J-12
Davella I-18
David, 300 J-17
DAVIESS CO., 96656 J-4
Davis G-12
Dawson Sprs., 2764 L-2
Day L-18
Daysville, 75 M-4
Dayton, 5338 A-20
Deane, 80 K-18
Deatsville, 80 I-9
Debord, 30 I-18
Decoy, 20 J-17
Defoe, 50 G-11
Dekoven, 125 J-1
Delphia, 100 L-17
Demossville, 60 E-13
Denniston, 75 I-15
Denton, 30 G-17
Depoy, 70 K-4
Dermont, 75 B-2
Devon, 50 D-12
Dexter, 277 G-5
Diablock, 453 K-17
Diamond, 150 K-2
Dice, 20 K-16
Dixie, 100 I-2
Dixon, 786 J-2
Dizney, 250 M-17
Dog Walk K-12
Dongola L-18
Dorton, 250 K-18
Douglass Hills, 5484 B-9
Dover, 252 E-14
Draffenville, 300 F-4
Drakesboro, 515 K-4
Dreyfus, 150 J-13
Drift, 300 J-18
Dry Ridge, 2191 F-12
Dublin, 50 G-3
Dubre, 60 M-9
Duckers H-11
Dukedom, 50 G-3
Dukes I-5
Dunbar, 75 K-5
Duncan I-11
Dundee, 150 J-5
Dunmor, 200 L-4
Dunnville, 225 K-11
Dwale, 329 J-18
Dwarf, 100 K-17
Dycusburg, 26 K-1
Dyer, 125 I-7
Earlington, 1413 K-3
E. Bernstadt, 716 K-14
E. Union G-14
Eastview, 60 J-7
Echols, 50 K-5
Eddyville, 2554 L-1
Edgewood, 8575 C-18
EDMONSON CO., 12161 K-6
Edmonton, 1595 L-9
Egypt, 30 K-14
Eighty Eight, 75 M-8
Ekron, 135 I-7
Elba, 30 J-3
Eli, 100 L-11
Elihu, 100 L-12
Elizabethtown, 28531 I-8
Elizaville, 181 G-14
Elk Creek, 20 H-10
Elk Horn, 50 K-10
Elkatawa, 50 J-16
Elkfork, 1539 H-17
Elkhorn City, 982 K-19
Elkton, 2062 M-4
Ella L-10
ELLIOTT CO., 7852 H-17
Elliottville, 40 G-16
Elmburg, 75 G-11
Elsie, 25 I-17
Elsmere, 8451 C-18
Emerson, 25 G-16
Eminence, 2498 G-10
Emlyn, 427 M-14
Emmalena, 100 K-17
English, 150 F-10
Ensor I-5
Eolia, 300 L-18
Epleys, 75 M-5
Epworth F-15
Erlanger, 18082 D-12
Ermine, 300 L-18
ESTILL CO., 14672 I-14
Ethridge E-11
Etty, 100 K-18
Eubank, 319 K-12
Evanston J-17
Evarts, 962 M-17
Ewing, 264 G-14
Exie L-9
Ezel, 235 I-16
Fairdale E-7
Fairdealing, 100 M-1
Fairfield, 113 I-10
Fairplay, 20 L-10
Fairview, 286 M-3
Fairview, 40 F-14
Fairview †B-1
Falcon, 120 I-17
Fall Rock, 90 K-15
Falls of Rough, 75 J-6
Fallsburg, 125 G-18
Falmouth, 2169 F-13
Fancy Farm, 458 F-3
Farmers, 284 H-15
Farmersville, 40 K-2
Farmington, 245 G-4
Farristown J-13
Faubush, 80 L-11
FAYETTE CO., 295803 H-12
Faywood, 100 H-12
Fearsville, 60 L-3
Fedscreek, 175 J-20
Ferguson, 924 L-12
Fern Creek, 17870 D-9
Ferndale, 200 M-15
Fincastle, 817 A-10
Finchville, 200 H-10
Finley, 20 J-10
Finney M-7
Firebrick, 350 E-17
Fisty, 125 K-17
Flaherty, 250 I-7
Flat Lick, 960 M-15
Flatgap, 100 H-17
Flatwoods, 7423 F-18
FLEMING CO., 14348 G-14
Fleming-Neon, 770 K-18
Flemingsburg, 2658 G-15
Flippin, 35 M-8
Florence, 29951 D-12
FLOYD CO., 39451 J-18
Folsom, 40 E-12
Folsomdale, 150 F-3
Fonde, 75 N-14
Foraker, 40 J-17
Ford, 140 I-13
Fords Branch, 200 J-19
Fordsville, 524 J-5
Forest Grv., 125 H-13
Forest Hills, 444 C-9
Forest Hills, 300 J-19
Forks of Elkhorn, 150 A-13
Ft. Mitchell, 8207 D-12
Ft. Thomas, 16325 D-12
Ft. Wright, 5723 B-19
Foster, 40 E-13
Fount L-15
Fountain Run, 217 M-8
Four Oaks, 140 F-13
Fourmile, 450 M-15
Foxport, 50 F-15
Frakes, 125 N-14
Frances, 50 K-1
Frankfort, 25527 G-11
Franklin, 8408 M-6
FRANKLIN CO., 49285 G-11
Franklin Cross Roads, 60 J-8
Frazer, 35 L-12
Fredericktown, 150 I-10
Fredonia, 401 K-1
Freeburn, 399 J-20
Freedom M-10
Frenchburg, 486 H-15
Fruit Hill L-3
Fulgham, 60 G-3
Fulton, 2445 G-3
FULTON CO., 6813 G-2
Future City, 200 E-3
Gage, 40 E-3
GALLATIN CO., 8589 E-11
Gamaliel, 376 N-8
Gano, 300 M-17
Gap in Knob, 180 H-9
Garden Vil., 100 J-19
Gardenside B-14
Gardnersville, 50 E-12
Garfield, 150 I-7
Garner, 150 K-17
Garrard, 65 L-15
GARRARD CO., 16912 J-12
Garrett, 500 J-18
Garrett, 150 I-7
Garrison, 866 F-16
Gascon L-9
Gasper L-5
Gatliff, 60 M-14
Gays Creek, 80 K-16
Geneva, 150 I-2
Georgetown, 29098 G-12
Germantown, 154 F-14
Gest, 50 G-11
Ghent, 323 E-11
Gilbertsville, 458 E-5
Gilley, 50 L-17
Gilpin, 50 K-11
Girdler, 250 L-14
Glasgow, 14028 L-8
Gleanings J-9
Glen Dean, 50 J-6
Glencoe, 360 E-11
Glendale, 350 J-8
Glens Fork, 100 L-10
Glensboro, 130 H-11
Glenview, 531 A-8
Glenview Hills, 319 A-8
Glenville, 20 J-4
Globe, 250 G-16
Goddard G-15
Gold City M-6
Goldbug, 100 M-13
Goose Rock, 200 L-15
Gordon, 100 L-17
Goshen, 909 G-9
Gracey, 138 M-2
Gradyville, 75 L-9
Graham, 700 K-4
Grahamville, 200 E-3
Grahn, 550 G-17
Grange City, 75 G-15
Grangertown, 100 J-1
GRANT CO., 4662 F-12
Grants Lick, 100 E-13
Grassy Creek I-16
Gratz, 78 F-11
Gravel Switch, 75 J-11
GRAVES CO., 37121 F-4
Gray, 750 L-14
Gray Hawk, 100 K-14
Graymoor-Devondale, 2870 B-9
Grays Branch, 125 F-17
Grays Knob, 300 M-16
Grayson, 4217 G-17
GRAYSON CO., 25746 J-7
Grayson Sprs. J-7
GREEN CO., 11258 K-9
Green Spr., 715 A-9
Greensburg, 2163 K-9
Greenup, 1188 F-18
GREENUP CO., 36910 F-17
Greenville, 4312 K-4
Greenwood, 95 M-12
Grethel, 100 J-18
Grider, 50 M-9
Grove Ctr., 70 J-1
Guffie J-4
Gulnare J-19
Gum Sulphur K-13
Gunlock, 20 J-17
Guston, 200 I-7
Guthrie, 1419 N-4
Habit, 100 I-5
Haddix, 150 J-16
Hadley, 25 L-6
Hagerhill, 150 I-18
Haldeman, 250 G-16
Halfway, 35 M-7
Halls Gap, 90 J-12
Halo, 150 K-18
Hamlin, 175 N-1
Hammonville, 30 K-8
Hampton, 100 D-4
HANCOCK CO., 8565 I-5
Hanson, 742 K-3
Hardin, 615 F-5
HARDIN CO., 105543 I-8
Hardin Sprs. J-7
Hardinsburg, 2343 I-6
Hardshell, 15 J-16
Hardy, 650 J-19
Hardyville, 156 K-8
Hargett I-14
Harlan, 1745 M-16
HARLAN CO., 29278 L-17
Harned, 140 I-6
Harold, 400 J-18
HARRISON CO., 18846 F-12
Harrisonville, 75 H-11
Harrods Creek A-8
Harrodsburg, 8340 I-11
HART CO., 18199 K-8
Hartford, 2672 J-5
Hatcher, 60 K-10
Hawesville, 945 I-5
Hays, 30 L-7
Haywood L-8
Hazard, 4456 K-17
Hazel, 410 G-4
Hazel Green, 228 I-16
Headquarters G-14
Hebbardsville, 125 I-3
Hebron, 5929 B-16
Heflin J-4
Heidelberg, 300 J-15
Heidrick, 700 M-14
Helechawa, 25 I-16
Helena, 50 F-15
Hellier, 400 K-19
Helton, 30 L-16
Hemphill, 500 K-18
Henderson, 28757 I-3

*, †, ‡, §, ◊ See explanation under state title in this index.
County and parish names are listed in capital letters & boldface type.
Independent cities (not included in a county) are listed in italics.

HENDERSON CO., 46250 ....I-2
Hendricks, 60 ....I-17
Hendron, 4687 ....E-4
HENRY CO., 15416 ....F-11
Henshaw, 100 ....J-1
Heritage Creek, 1435 ....
Herndon, 150 ....M-3
Hesler, 60 ....F-11
Hestand, 25 ....N-9
Hi Hat, 250 ....K-18
Hickman, 2395 ....G-2
HICKMAN CO., 4902 ....F-3
Hickory, 150 ....F-3
High Br., 242 ....I-12
High Pt., 100 ....L-16
Highgrove H-9
Highland Hts., 6923 ....C-20
Highland Pk. ....
Highview, 15161 ....D-9
Hilda G-15
Hillcrest, 300 ....I-13
Hillsboro, 150 ....G-15
Hillview, 8172 ....H-9
Hima, 250 ....L-15
Himyar, 100 ....L-16
Hindman, 777 ....K-17
Hinton Hills, 400 ....I-6
Hiram, 100 ....L-17
Hiseville, 240 ....L-8
Hitchins, 350 ....G-17
Hodgenville, 3206 ....J-8
Holland, 75 ....M-7
Hollow Creek, 783 ....D-8
Hollyvilla, 537 ....H-6
Holmes Mill, 75 ....M-17
Holy Cross, 70 ....J-9
Hooktown G-13
Hope, 90 ....L-16
HOPKINS CO., 46920 ....K-2
Hopkinsville, 31577 ....M-3
Hopson L-2
Horse Branch, 200 ....J-6
Horse Cave, 2311 ....L-8
Hoskinston, 150 ....L-16
Houston Acres, 507 ....C-9
Howardstown, 100 ....J-9
Huddy, 450 ....J-19
Hudson, 50 ....J-7
Hueysville, 200 ....J-18
Huff, 40 ....K-6
Hunter, 150 ....J-17
Hunters Trace D-6
Huntsville, 100 ....L-6
Hurstbourne, 4216 ....B-9
Hurstbourne Acres, 1811 ....
Hustonville, 405 ....J-11
Hyattsville L-16
Hyden, 365 ....L-16
Idle Hour T-C1
Ilsley, 150 ....K-3
Independence, 24757 ....E-12
Indian Hills, 2868 ....B-8
Indian Hills, 200 ....L-11
Indian Hills, 80 ....F-10
Inez, 717 ....J-19
Ingram, 250 ....M-15
Ironville, 600 ....T-C1
Irvine, 2715 ....I-14
Irvington, 1181 ....I-7
Island, 458 ....J-4
Island City, 25 ....K-15
Isom, 150 ....K-17
Isonville, 100 ....H-17
Iuka L-1
Ivel, 150 ....J-18
Ivyton, 30 ....I-17
Jabez J-12
Jackson, 2231 ....J-16
JACKSON CO., 13494 ....J-14
Jacksontown, 40 ....G-11
Jacktown I-17
Jacobs, 25 ....G-16
Jamboree, 100 ....J-20
Jamestown, 1794 ....L-11
Jeff, 323 ....K-17
JEFFERSON CO., 741096 ....H-9
Jeffersontown, 26595 ....H-9
Jeffersonville, 1506 ....H-14
Jenkins, 2203 ....K-18
Jeremiah, 100 ....K-17
JESSAMINE CO., 48586 ....I-12
Jett, 180 ....H-13
Jett, 100 ....H-19
JOHNSON CO., 23356 ....I-17
Johnsville K-13
Jonancy, 125 ....K-18
Jonesville, 35 ....K-8
Jordan, 20 ....G-2
Judy H-14
Junction City, 2241 ....J-11
Kajay, 100 ....M-14
Keaton, 70 ....I-17
Keavy, 125 ....L-13
Keene, 300 ....H-12
Kehoe H-18
Kelat, 85 ....L-16
Kelly, 100 ....L-3
Kenton, 175 ....E-12
KENTON CO., 159720 ....E-12
Kenton Vale, 110 ....B-16
Kentontown F-14
Kenvir, 297 ....M-17
Kerby Knob, 15 ....J-14
Kessinger, 125 ....K-8
Kettle, 50 ....M-10
Kevil, 376 ....E-3
Keysburg, 50 ....N-4
Kimper, 75 ....J-19
Kings Creek L-17
Kings Mtn., 125 ....K-12
Kingsley, 381 ....C-8
Kingston, 130 ....J-13
Kingswood, 200 ....K-12
Kinniconick, 75 ....F-16
Kirbyton, 70 ....L-1
Kirkmansville, 50 ....L-3
Kirksey, 150 ....G-4
Kirksville, 150 ....J-13
Kite, 150 ....K-17
Kniffley, 75 ....K-10
Knob Lick, 40 ....L-8
KNOTT CO., 16346 ....J-17
Knottsville, 400 ....I-6
KNOX CO., 31883 ....L-15

Knoxville, 75 ....E-12
Kona, 200 ....K-18
Korea H-16
Krypton, 120 ....K-16
Kuttawa, 649 ....L-1
La Center, 1009 ....E-2
La Fayette, 165 ....N-4
La Grange, 8082 ....G-10
Lackey, 250 ....J-18
Lair, 80 ....G-13
Lake City, 300 ....L-1
Lakeside Pk., 2668 ....C-18
Lakeview C-19
Lamasco, 100 ....L-1
Lamb, 50 ....M-8
Lambric, 20 ....K-16
Lamero, 20 ....K-16
Lamont K-16
Lancaster, 3442 ....J-12
Langley, 400 ....J-18
LARUE CO., 14193 ....J-9
LAUREL CO., 58849 ....L-14
Lawrenceburg, 10505 ....H-11
Leander, 80 ....J-18
Leatherwood, 140 ....L-17
Lebanon, 5539 ....J-10
Lebanon Jct., 1813 ....I-8
Leburn, 250 ....K-17
Lecta, 80 ....L-8
Ledbetter, 1683 ....E-4
Lee City, 100 ....I-16
LEE CO., 7887 ....J-15
Leesburg, 75 ....G-13
Leitchfield, 6699 ....J-7
Lenox, 20 ....J-18
Lerose, 100 ....J-15
LESLIE CO., 11310 ....L-16
Letcher, 150 ....K-17
LETCHER CO., 24519 ....L-17
Levee L-18
Level Green K-13
Levi J-14
LEWIS CO., 13870 ....F-16
Lewisburg, 810 ....L-5
Lewisburg, 125 ....F-15
Lewisport, 1670 ....I-5
Lexington, 295803 ....H-12
Liberty, 2168 ....K-11
Lida L-14
Liggett, 180 ....M-16
Lily, 500 ....L-14
Limaburg, 200 ....C-16
LINCOLN CO., 24742 ....J-12
Lindseyville, 200 ....K-7
Linefork, 125 ....L-17
Linton, 40 ....M-2
Linwood, 50 ....K-8
Littcarr, 50 ....K-17
Little, 40 ....L-17
Little Mount, 60 ....H-10
Little Rock, 75 ....G-14
Little Sandy, 50 ....H-16
Littleton, 275 ....L-15
Livermore, 1365 ....J-4
Livia, 15 ....J-4
Livingston, 226 ....K-13
LIVINGSTON CO., 9519 ....D-4
Lloyd, 900 ....G-17
Load G-16
Lockport, 100 ....G-11
Logana, 200 ....I-12
LOGAN CO., 26835 ....L-5
Lola, 200 ....K-1
Lombard I-15
Loretta, 50 ....J-17
London, 7993 ....L-14
Lone Oak, 450 ....E-3
Lone Ridge L-11
Lookout, 150 ....K-19
Loretto, 713 ....J-10
Lost Creek, 40 ....J-16
Louellen L-17
Louisa, 2467 ....H-18
Louisville, 597337 ....G-8
Lovelaceville, 148 ....F-3
Lovely, 700 ....J-19
Lowes, 98 ....F-3
Lowmansville, 50 ....H-18
Loyall, 1461 ....M-16
Lucas, 120 ....M-8
Ludlow, 4407 ....B-19
Lusby's Mill, 50 ....F-12
Lynch, 747 ....L-17
Lyndale, 450 ....H-13
Lyndon, 11002 ....B-9
Lynn F-11
Lynn Grv., 250 ....G-4
Lynnview, 914 ....C-7
LYON CO., 8314 ....L-1
Lyons, 60 ....J-9
Lytten H-16
Macedonia L-2
Maceo, 413 ....I-4
MADISON CO., 82916 ....J-13
Madisonville, 19591 ....K-3
Madrid, 50 ....J-7
MAGOFFIN CO., 13333 ....J-17
Majestic, 400 ....J-20
Mallie, 50 ....K-17
Malone, 100 ....K-16
Maloneton, 200 ....F-17
Mammoth Cave M-20
Manchester, 1255 ....L-15
Manitou, 181 ....K-3
Mannington, 125 ....L-3
Mannsville, 700 ....K-10
Manton, 20 ....K-10
Marcum K-19
Mariba, 60 ....I-15
Marion, 3039 ....K-1
MARION CO., 19820 ....J-10
Marrowbone, 400 ....K-19
Marrowbone, 217 ....M-9
MARSHALL CO., 31448 ....F-4
Marshes Siding, 700 ....M-12
Martha, 20 ....H-17
Martin, 634 ....J-18
MARTIN CO., 12929 ....I-19
Mary Alice, 250 ....M-16
Mary Helen, 160 ....M-16
Mason, 90 ....F-12
MASON CO., 17490 ....F-15
Masonville, 1014 ....I-4
Massac, 4505 ....E-3
Mattoon K-8
Maud, 40 ....I-10

Mayfield, 10024 ....F-3
Mayking, 487 ....L-18
Mayo H-14
Maysville, 9011 ....F-15
Maytown, 243 ....I-16
Mazie, 30 ....H-17
McAfee, 50 ....I-11
McAndrews, 450 ....J-19
McDaniels, 200 ....I-6
McDowell, 400 ....J-18
McHenry, 388 ....J-5
McKee, 800 ....K-14
McKinney, 275 ....J-11
McQuady, 75 ....I-6
McRoberts, 784 ....K-18
McVeigh, 250 ....J-19
McVille, 85 ....D-11
MEADE CO., 28602 ....I-7
Meadow Vale, 736 ....A-9
Meadowthorpe B-14
Meadowview Estates, 363 ....
Means, 150 ....H-15
Melber, 300 ....F-3
Melbourne, 401 ....*SN-4
Meldrum, 150 ....K-18
Melvin, 250 ....K-18
Memphis Jct., 250 ....C-3
Menifee E-12
MENIFEE CO., 6306 ....I-15
Mentor, 193 ....E-13
MERCER CO., 21331 ....I-11
Meredith K-7
Merry Oaks, 150 ....L-8
Meta, 250 ....J-19
METCALFE CO., 10099 ....L-9
Mexico, 30 ....L-18
Middleburg, 200 ....K-11
Middlesboro M-16
Middletown, 7218 ....Q-9
Midland, 175 ....H-15
Midway, 1641 ....H-12
Midway, 45 ....G-4
Milburn, 250 ....F-3
Milford, 90 ....I-7
Mill Sprs., 50 ....M-12
Millersburg, 792 ....G-13
Millerstown, 150 ....K-8
Millstone, 117 ....K-18
Milltown, 25 ....K-10
Millville, 200 ....H-11
Millwood, 200 ....J-6
Milton, 574 ....E-10
Minerva, 50 ....E-14
Minorsville, 50 ....G-12
Mintonville K-11
Mitchellsburg, 350 ....J-11
Mize, 10 ....I-16
Molus, 130 ....M-16
Monroe, 50 ....K-9
Monterey, 180 ....G-11
MONTGOMERY CO., 26499 ....H-14
Monticello, 6188 ....M-11
Mooleyville, 80 ....I-6
Moon, 10 ....I-17
Mooresville, 75 ....I-8
Mooresville, 45 ....I-10
Moorland, 431 ....B-9
Moorman, 175 ....K-4
Moranburg F-14
Morehead, 6845 ....G-16
Moreland, 150 ....J-11
Morgan, 30 ....F-13
MORGAN CO., 13923 ....H-16
Morganfield, 3285 ....I-2
Morgantown, 2394 ....K-5
Morning View, 100 ....E-12
Morrill, 100 ....J-13
Mortons Gap, 863 ....K-3
Mortonsville, 90 ....H-12
Moscow, 42 ....F-1
Moseleyville, 200 ....I-4
Mt. Carmel, 100 ....G-16
Mt. Eden, 200 ....H-10
Mt. Hermon, 40 ....M-8
Mt. Olivet, 390 ....F-14
Mt. Sherman, 250 ....J-9
Mt. Sterling, 6895 ....H-14
Mt. Vernon, 2477 ....K-13
Mt. Victory L-12
Mt. Washington, 9117 ....H-9
Mountain Ash, 200 ....N-14
Mousie, 400 ....J-18
Mouthcard, 150 ....J-19
Mozelle, 150 ....L-16
Mud Lick L-9
MUHLENBERG CO., 31499 ....L-4
Muldraugh, 947 ....I-8
Munfordville, 1615 ....K-8
Murray, 17741 ....G-4
Murray Hill, 582 ....A-9
Muses Mills, 80 ....G-15
Myers, 50 ....G-18
Myra, 100 ....J-19
Nancy, 400 ....K-12
Napoleon, 50 ....G-12
Natural Br., 10 ....I-15
Nebo, 236 ....K-3
Nerinx, 300 ....J-10
Nevada, 30 ....L-6
New Castle, 912 ....G-10
New Columbus, 75 ....F-12
New Concord, 100 ....H-4
New Haven, 855 ....I-9
New Hope, 129 ....I-9
New Liberty, 115 ....G-11
New Market, 50 ....J-10
New Zion, 120 ....I-10
Newburg D-8
Newfoundland, 150 ....H-17
Newman, 100 ....J-14
Newport, 15273 ....B-20
Newtown, 60 ....G-13
Niagara D-11
Nicholasville, 28015 ....I-12
Nippa, 150 ....K-18
Noctor, 40 ....J-16
Norbourne Estates, 441 ....B-8

N. Corbin, 1773 ....L-14
N. Middletown, 643 ....H-14
Northfield, 1020 ....B-8
Nortonville, 1204 ....K-3
Norwood, 370 ....B-9
Nuckols, 60 ....I-7
Oak Grv., 7489 ....N-3
Oakdale, 1900 ....C-4
Oakland, 225 ....L-7
Oakton, 125 ....G-2
Oddville F-13
OHIO CO., 23842 ....J-5
Oil Sprs., 150 ....I-17
Okolona, 17807 ....D-8
Oldtown, 60 ....G-17
Olga, 15 ....L-10
Olive, 100 ....M-1
Olive Hill, 1599 ....G-16
Olmstead, 125 ....M-4
Olympia, 15 ....H-15
Olympia Sprs. H-15
Omaha K-18
Oneida, 410 ....K-15
Onton, 141 ....J-3
Orville G-11
Oscar, 50 ....E-2
Oven Fork, 170 ....L-18
Owensboro, 57265 ....I-4
Owenton, 1327 ....F-11
Owingsville, 1530 ....H-15
Rochester, 152 ....K-5
ROCKCASTLE CO., 17056 ....K-13
Rockfield, 70 ....M-6
Rockholds, 390 ....M-14
Rockhouse, 200 ....K-19
Rockport, 266 ....K-4
Rocky Hill, 160 ....L-7
Rolling Fields, 646 ....B-8
Rolling Hills, 959 ....B-9
Rome, 150 ....C-1
Rosewood L-6
Rosewood J-4
Rosine, 20 ....J-6
Rowand, 75 ....K-19
Rowdy, 100 ....J-16
Rowletts, 300 ....K-8
Roxana, 150 ....L-17
Royalton, 200 ....I-17
Royville, 50 ....L-10
Ruddels Mills, 40 ....G-13
Rumsey, 200 ....J-4
Rush, 200 ....G-18
RUSSELL CO., 17565 ....L-11
Russell Sprs., 2441 ....L-11
Russellville, 6960 ....M-5
Ryland, 200 ....D-11
Sacramento, 468 ....K-4
Sadieville, 300 ....F-12
Salem, 752 ....K-1
Salmons, 40 ....M-14
Salol G-4
Salt Gum, 20 ....L-15
Salt Lick, 303 ....H-15
Salvisa, 420 ....I-11
Samuels, 60 ....I-8
Sandgap, 300 ....J-14
Sandy Hook, 675 ....H-17
Sardis, 100 ....F-14
Sassafras, 950 ....K-17
Saul, 30 ....K-16
Savoyard J-16
Saxton, 120 ....M-14
Scalf, 30 ....M-15
Schochoh, 60 ....M-5
Science Hill, 693 ....L-12
Scottsville, 834 ....G-10
Scottsville, 4226 ....M-7
Se Ree, 100 ....K-5
Sebree, 1603 ....J-3
Sedalia, 295 ....G-4
Sextons Creek, 30 ....K-15
Shady Grv., 35 ....K-2
Shady Grv. K-2
Shannon F-14
Sharkey, 150 ....G-15
Sharon Grv., 175 ....M-4
Sharpe, 300 ....F-4
Sharpsburg, 323 ....G-14
Shawhan, 140 ....G-13
Shawnee Estates B-8
Shelbiana, 350 ....J-19
Shelby City, 250 ....J-11
SHELBY CO., 42074 ....G-10
Shelbyville, 14045 ....G-10
Shepherdsville, 11222 ....H-9
Sherburne, 60 ....G-15
Sheridan, 90 ....K-17
Sherman, 150 ....E-12
Shively, 15264 ....C-8
Shopville L-12
Short Creek, 45 ....I-7
Shoulderblade J-15
Shrewsbury, 30 ....I-8
Sideview H-14
Sidney, 100 ....J-19
Siler, 300 ....M-14
Siler, 300 ....I-11
Siloam, 175 ....H-17
Silver Grv., 1102 ....C-20
SIMPSON CO., 17327 ....M-6
Simpsonville, 2484 ....G-10
Sitka, 150 ....I-18
Sizerock, 40 ....L-16
Skylight, 90 ....G-9
Slade, 100 ....I-15
Slate Valley H-15
Slaughters, 216 ....J-3

Raven, 75 ....K-18
Ravenna, 605 ....I-14
Rawick, 134 ....J-9
Ready K-10
Rectorville, 150 ....F-15
Redbush, 60 ....I-17
Redfox, 150 ....K-17
Redhouse I-13
Reed, 100 ....I-4
Reeds Crossing, 150 ....I-3
Reid Vil., 150 ....H-14
Reidland, 4491 ....E-4
Reynolds Sta., 100 ....I-5
Rhoda, 100 ....L-7
Rhodelia, 30 ....H-6
Riceville I-17
Rich Pond, 300 ....M-6
Richardsville, 300 ....L-6
Richelieu L-5
Richland, 75 ....K-3
Richmond, 31364 ....I-13
Richwood C-16
Rineyville, 400 ....I-8
Ringos Mills, 45 ....G-15
River Bluff, 403 ....G-9
Riverside Gdns. C-5
Riverwood, 446 ....A-8
Roark, 75 ....L-16
Robards, 515 ....J-3
Robinson Creek, 400 ....
Rockcastle Co. ....
Sloans Valley, 200 ....L-12
Smilax, 100 ....L-16
Smith, 150 ....M-16
Smith Mills, 450 ....I-2
Smithfield, 106 ....G-10
Smithland, 301 ....K-4
Smiths Grv., 714 ....L-7
Smyrna D-8
Snow M-10
Soft Shell, 30 ....K-17
Soldier, 200 ....G-16
Somerset, 11196 ....L-12
Sonora, 513 ....J-8
Sorgho, 500 ....J-4
South, 25 ....K-6
S. Carrollton, 184 ....K-4
S. Irvine, 400 ....I-14
S. Park E-7
S. Park View, 7 ....C-8
S. Portsmouth, 180 ....F-17
S. Shore, 1122 ....E-17
S. Union, 75 ....M-6
S. Wallins, 859 ....M-16
S. Williamson, 600 ....J-20
Southgate, 3803 ....B-20
Southville H-10
Spa L-4
Sparksville, 50 ....L-9
Sparta, 231 ....F-11
Speedwell J-13
Spottsville, 325 ....I-3
Spring Grv., 60 ....I-1
Spring Lick, 40 ....J-6
Spring Mill, 287 ....D-8
Spring Valley, 654 ....A-9
Springfield, 2519 ....J-10
Springlee, 426 ....B-8
Stab, 20 ....L-13
Stacy, 50 ....K-16
Staffordsville, 200 ....I-18
Stamping Ground, 643 ....G-12
Stanford, 3487 ....J-12
Stanley, 300 ....I-4
Stanton, 2733 ....I-14
Stanville, 125 ....J-18
State Line, 10 ....G-2
Static N-11
Stearns, 1416 ....M-12
Steff, 10 ....K-6
Stella G-4
Stephens, 15 ....I-17
Stephensburg, 150 ....I-8
Stephensport, 200 ....I-6
Steubenville, 150 ....K-11
Stinnett, 125 ....L-16
Stonewall L-12
Stoney Fork, 25 ....L-16
Straight Creek, 50 ....M-15
Strathmoor Vil., 648 ....C-8
Stringtown, 40 ....B-17
Strunk, 70 ....N-13
Sturgis, 1898 ....J-1
Sublett L-17
Sublimity City, 800 ....L-14
Sugar Grv. H-15
Sugar Sta., 25 ....L-11
Sugar Grv., 80 ....L-6
Sugartit D-12
Sullivan, 300 ....J-2
Sulphur Lick M-8
Sulphur Sprs., 150 ....J-5
Sulphur, 80 ....G-10
Sulphur Well, 60 ....L-9
Summer Shade, 307 ....M-9
Summersville, 568 ....K-9
Summit, 900 ....I-18
Summit, 700 ....J-8
Sunfish, 90 ....K-6
Sunrise, 45 ....F-13
Sunshine, 350 ....M-16
Swamp Branch, 10 ....I-18
Swampton I-17
Sweeden, 125 ....K-7
Sylvania D-5
Symsonia, 615 ....F-4
Talbert, 75 ....K-6
Talcum, 300 ....K-17
Tallega, 30 ....J-15
Tateville, 100 ....L-12
TAYLOR CO., 24512 ....K-10
Taylor Mill, 6604 ....C-19
Taylorsport, 100 ....B-18
Taylorsville, 763 ....H-10
Temple Hill, 75 ....M-8
Terrapin L-17
Texas, 60 ....I-17
Thealka, 400 ....I-18
Thousandsticks, 70 ....K-16
Three Sprs., 80 ....C-4
Three Sprs., 30 ....I-2
Thruston, 50 ....I-4
Tilden, 40 ....J-2
Tilford K-6
Tiline, 75 ....K-1
Tilton, 50 ....G-15
Timsley, 100 ....M-7
TODD CO., 12460 ....M-4
Tolls Pt. G-10
Tollesboro, 600 ....F-15
Tolu, 88 ....J-1
Tomahawk, 150 ....J-18
Tompkinsville, 2402 ....M-9
Tompkinsville M-8
Totz, 250 ....L-17
Touristville M-12
Tracy M-7
Tram, 125 ....J-18
Trapp, 30 ....I-14
Trenton, 384 ....M-4
Tress City, 100 ....M-14
TRIGG CO., 14339 ....M-2
TRIMBLE CO., 8809 ....F-10
Trosper, 120 ....L-15
Troy F-11
Tyner, 150 ....K-14
Tyrone, 100 ....I-11
Ulvah, 75 ....L-17
Ulysses, 30 ....I-18
Union, 5379 ....C-16
Union Star, 50 ....I-7
Uniontown, 1002 ....I-2
Upper Tygart G-16
Upton, 603 ....J-8
Utica, 300 ....I-4
Valley J-17
Valley Sta. C-8
Valley View, 150 ....I-13

Slemp, 50 ....L-17
Sligo, 60 ....F-10
Van Lear, 1050 ....I-18
Vanceburg, 1518 ....F-16
Vancleve, 80 ....J-16
Verda, 800 ....M-16
Verona, 1455 ....C-12
Versailles, 8568 ....H-12
Vertrees I-7
Vest, 100 ....K-17
Vicco, 334 ....K-17
Victory K-14
Villa Hills, 7489 ....B-18
Vincent, 30 ....J-16
Vine Grv., 4520 ....I-8
Viper, 100 ....K-17
Virgie, 250 ....K-18
Visalia, 110 ....E-13
Volga, 50 ....I-17
Waco, 200 ....I-13
Waddy, 220 ....H-11
Wakefield, 30 ....N-10
Waldo E-7
Walker, 75 ....M-15
Wallingford, 100 ....G-15
Wallins Creek, 156 ....M-16
Wallonia, 60 ....L-2
Walnut Grv., 10 ....A-8
Walton, 3635 ....C-12
Waneta, 75 ....J-14
Warfield, 269 ....I-19
WARREN CO., 113792 ....L-7
Warsaw, 1615 ....E-11
WASHINGTON CO., 11717 ....I-10
Water Valley, 279 ....G-3
Waterford, 90 ....H-9
Watergap J-18
Waterview, 40 ....M-9
Watterson Pk., 976 ....C-8
Waverly, 308 ....I-2
Waverly Hills D-5
Wax K-7
Wayland, 426 ....J-18
WAYNE CO., 20813 ....M-12
Waynesburg, 200 ....K-12
Webbs Cross Roads, 50 ....L-11
Webbville, 80 ....G-17
Webster, 120 ....I-7
WEBSTER CO., 13621 ....J-2
Wedonia, 10 ....F-15
Weeksbury, 800 ....K-18
Weir, 70 ....J-4
Welchs Creek, 65 ....K-6
Wellington, 565 ....G-8
Wellington, 50 ....H-15
Wesco, 250 ....K-3
W. Buechel, 1230 ....C-8
W. Irvine, 500 ....I-14
W. Liberty, 3435 ....I-16
W. Louisville, 100 ....I-4
W. Paducah, 100 ....E-3
W. Point, 797 ....H-8
W. Van Lear, 600 ....I-18
Westbend, 300 ....J-4
Westport, 268 ....F-9
Westview, 4746 ....*B-5
Westwood, 634 ....B-9
Wheatcroft, 160 ....I-2
Wheatley, 50 ....F-11
Wheeler M-15
Wheelersburg, 60 ....I-17
Wheelwright, 780 ....K-18
White City, 50 ....I-17
White Mills, 150 ....J-8
White Oak, 75 ....I-16
White Plains, 884 ....K-3
Whitesburg, 2139 ....L-18
Whitesville, 552 ....I-5
Whitley City, 1170 ....M-13
WHITLEY CO., 35637 ....M-13
Wiborg, 100 ....M-13
Wickliffe, 688 ....F-2
Wilder, 3035 ....B-20
Wildie, 150 ....K-13
Willard, 150 ....G-17
Williamsburg, 5245 ....M-14
Williamsport, 200 ....I-18
Williamstown, 3925 ....F-12
Willisburg, 282 ....I-10
Wilmore, 3686 ....I-12
Wilton H-14
Winchester, 18368 ....H-13
Winding Falls ....
Windsor, 50 ....L-11
Windy, 75 ....M-13
Windy Hills, 2385 ....B-8
Wingo, 620 ....G-3
Winston, 120 ....I-17
Wittensville, 200 ....I-18
Wofford, 200 ....M-15
Wolf Creek, 40 ....I-16
WOLFE CO., 7355 ....I-15
Wonnie I-17
Woodbine, 500 ....M-14
Woodburn, 355 ....M-6
Woodbury, 90 ....K-5
WOODFORD CO., 24939 ....I-11
Woodland Hills, 696 ....B-10
Woodlawn, 229 ....*SN-4
Woodlawn Pk., 942 ....B-8
Woollum, 20 ....L-14
Wooton, 200 ....K-16
Worthington, 1609 ....F-18
Worthington Hills, 1446 ....A-10
Worthville, 185 ....F-11
Wrigley, 50 ....H-16
Wurtland, 995 ....F-18
Yeaddiss, 50 ....L-16
Yeaman I-7
Yelvington, 175 ....I-5
Yerkes, 140 ....K-16
Yosemite, 250 ....K-11
Younger Creek, 150 ....M-9
Zebulon, 200 ....K-18
Zion, 350 ....I-17
Zoe J-16
Zula M-11

Algiers E-14
ALLEN PAR., 25764 ....F-4
Alluvial City, 520 ....I-10
Alto, 380 ....C-6
Alton, 380 ....G-10
Amelia, 2459 ....I-7
Amite, 4141 ....F-8
Anacoco, 869 ....E-3
Angie, 251 ....F-9
Arabi, 3635 ....H-9
Arcadia, 2919 ....B-3
Archibald, 230 ....C-6
Arnaudville, 1057 ....G-5
ASCENSION PAR., 107215 ....H-7
Ashland, 269 ....C-3
ASSUMPTION PAR., 23421 ....H-7
Athens, 249 ....B-3
Atlanta, 163 ....D-4
Avery Island, 350 ....H-5
Avondale, 4954 ....C-12
AVOYELLES PAR., 42073 ....E-5
Aycock A-3
Bains, 60 ....F-7
Baker, 13895 ....G-7
Baldwin, 2436 ....I-6
Ball, 4000 ....D-4
Basile, 1821 ....G-4
Baskin, 254 ....C-6
Bastrop, 11365 ....A-5
Baton Rouge, 229493 ....G-7
Bawcomville, 3588 ....B-5
Bayou Blue, 12352 ....I-8
Bayou Chicot, 150 ....F-5
Bayou Current F-5
Bayou Goula, 612 ....H-7
Bayou Sorrel, 420 ....H-7
Bayou Vista, 4652 ....I-7
Baywood, 100 ....G-7
BEAUREGARD PAR., 35654 ....D-3
Beaver C-2
Beekman, 200 ....A-5
Beggs C-5
Belcher, 263 ....A-2
Bell City, 350 ....H-4
Belle Chasse, 12679 ....I-9
Belle Rose, 1902 ....H-7
Bellevue, 70 ....B-2
Bellwood D-4
Belmont, 361 ....D-2
Benson, 130 ....C-2
Bentley, 300 ....D-4
Benton, 1948 ....B-2
Bernice, 1689 ....A-4
Berwick, 4946 ....I-7
Bethany, 150 ....C-1
Bienville, 218 ....C-3
BIENVILLE PAR., 14353 ....B-3
Big Bend, 60 ....F-6
Big Cane, 50 ....F-5
Blanchard, 2899 ....B-1
Bogalusa, 12232 ....F-10
Bohemia, 40 ....I-10
Bolinger, 200 ....A-2
Bonita, 284 ....A-6
Bonnabel Pl. C-12
Boothville, 854 ....J-11
Bordelonville, 525 ....F-5
Borodino, 240 ....F-5
Bosco, 50 ....C-5
Bossier City, 61315 ....B-2
BOSSIER PAR., 116979 ....A-2
Bourg, 2579 ....I-8
Boyce, 1064 ....D-4
Branch, 388 ....G-5
Breaux Br., 8139 ....H-5
Brittany F-7
Broadmoor B-13
Broussard, 8197 ....H-5
Brusly, 2589 ....G-7
Bryceland, 108 ....B-3
Buckeye, 100 ....D-5
Bunkie, 4171 ....F-5
Buras, 945 ....J-10
Burr Ferry, 120 ....E-2
Bush, 300 ....G-10
CADDO PAR., 254969 ....B-1
Cade, 1723 ....H-5
Cadeville B-5
Calhoun, 679 ....B-5
Calvin, 230 ....C-4
Cameron, 406 ....I-3
CAMERON PAR., 6839 ....H-2
Campti, 1050 ....C-3
Cankton, 484 ....G-5
Carencro, 7526 ....G-5
Carlisle, 50 ....C-6
Caroline H-8
Carrollton, 70 ....C-12
Carterville C-4
Caspiana, 60 ....C-2
Castor, 258 ....C-3
Catahoula, 1094 ....H-6
CATAHOULA PAR., 10407 ....D-6
Cecilia, 1900 ....H-6
Cedar Grv. B-10
Center, 70 ....E-2
Centerville, 700 ....I-6
Central, 26854 ....G-7
Chacahoula, 150 ....I-8
Chackbay, 5177 ....I-8
Chalmette, 16751 ....H-10
Chambers, 200 ....F-5
Charenton, 1903 ....I-6
Chase, 170 ....C-6
Chataignier, 364 ....G-5
Chatham, 557 ....C-4
Chauvin, 2912 ....I-8
Cheneyville, 625 ....E-5
Chestnut, 40 ....C-3
Chipola F-8
Choctaw G-7
Choudrant, 845 ....B-4
Church Pt., 4560 ....G-5
Claiborne, 11507 ....B-5
CLAIBORNE PAR., 17195 ....A-3
Clarence, 499 ....D-3
Clarks, 1017 ....C-5
Clay, 120 ....B-5
Clayton, 711 ....D-6
Clifton A-2
Clinton, 1653 ....F-7
Colfax, 1558 ....D-4
College Town C-12
Collinston, 337 ....A-6
Colyell G-8
Columbia, 390 ....C-5
CONCORDIA PAR., 20822 ....E-6

Convent, 711 ....H-8
Converse, 440 ....D-2
Cotton Valley, 1009 ....B-2
Cottonport, 2006 ....F-5
Couchwood, 60 ....C-2
Coushatta, 1964 ....C-3
Covington, 8765 ....G-9
Creole, 213 ....I-4
Creston, 70 ....D-3
Crew Lake, 140 ....B-6
Cross Roads, 50 ....C-2
Crowley, 13265 ....H-5
Crown Pt., 980 ....I-9
Crowville, 250 ....C-6
Crozier, 1250 ....I-8
Cullen, 1163 ....A-2
Cut Off, 5976 ....I-9
Cypremort H-6
Cypress, 150 ....D-3
Dalcour, 140 ....I-10
Darlington F-7
Darnell, 300 ....C-5
Darrow, 460 ....H-7
Davant, 110 ....I-10
DE SOTO PAR., 26656 ....D-2
Deer Pk., 50 ....E-6
Delacroix, 450 ....I-10
Delcambre, 1866 ....H-5
Delhi, 2919 ....B-6
Delmont Pl. A-12
Delta, 284 ....C-7
Denham Sprs., 10215 ....G-8
DeQuincy, 3235 ....G-2
DeRidder, 10578 ....F-3
Derry, 30 ....D-4
Des Allemands, 2505 ....I-8
Deville, 1764 ....D-5
Diamond, 180 ....I-10
Dixie, 100 ....B-2
Dixie Gdns., 500 ....B-10
Dixie Inn, 273 ....B-3
Dodson, 337 ....C-4
Donaldsonville, 7436 ....H-7
Donner, 260 ....I-7
Downsville, 140 ....B-4
Doyline, 818 ....B-2
Dry Creek, 300 ....G-3
Dry Prong, 436 ....D-4
Dubach, 961 ....B-4
Dubberly, 273 ....B-3
Dulac, 1463 ....I-8
Dunn, 180 ....B-6
Duplessis, 350 ....H-7
Duson, 1716 ....H-5
E. BATON ROUGE PAR., 440101 ....G-7
E. CARROLL PAR., 7759 ....B-7
E. FELICIANA PAR., 20267 ....F-7
East Point, 90 ....C-2
Easton, 170 ....F-4
Eastwood, 4093 ....B-2
Echo, 300 ....E-5
Edgard, 2441 ....H-8
Edgefield, 230 ....C-5
Edgerly, 400 ....H-2
Effie, 200 ....E-5
Egan, 631 ....H-4
Elizabeth, 532 ....F-4
Elm Grv., 230 ....B-2
Elmwood, 4635 ....C-12
Elton, 1128 ....G-4
Empire, 993 ....J-10
Enterprise, 130 ....D-6
Epps, 854 ....B-6
Erath, 2114 ....H-5
Eros, 155 ....C-4
Erwinville, 2192 ....G-7
Estelle, 16377 ....I-9
Esther I-5
Estherwood, 889 ....H-4
Ethel, 300 ....F-7
Eunice, 10398 ....G-4
Eva F-5
Evangeline, 340 ....G-4
Evans, 250 ....F-3
Evelyn, 50 ....C-2
Evergreen, 310 ....F-5
Extension, 100 ....C-4
Fairbanks, 280 ....B-5
Farmerville, 3860 ....B-4
Felixville, 50 ....F-7
Fenton, 379 ....G-3
Ferriday, 3511 ....D-6
Fields, 40 ....G-2
Fisher, 230 ....D-3
Fishville D-4
Flatwoods, 200 ....C-2
Flora, 130 ....D-3
Florien, 633 ....D-3
Fluker, 300 ....F-8
Folsom, 716 ....G-9
Fordoche, 908 ....G-6
Forest, 355 ....B-6
Forest Hill, 818 ....E-4
Forest Oaks B-14
Forked Island, 300 ....I-5
Ft. Jesup, 509 ....D-3
Ft. Necessity, 190 ....C-6
Franklin, 7660 ....I-6
FRANKLIN PAR., 20767 ....C-6
Franklinton, 3857 ....F-9
French Settlement, 1116 ....G-8
Frierson, 143 ....C-2
Frogmore, 80 ....D-6
Frost F-7
Fullerton, 50 ....F-3
Galbraith, 200 ....D-4
Galliano, 7676 ....I-9
Garden City, 300 ....I-6
Gardner, 150 ....D-4
Garyville, 2811 ....H-8
Gayles, 2 ....B-3
Geismar, 250 ....H-7
Georgetown, 327 ....D-4
Gibsland, 979 ....B-3
Gibson, 150 ....I-8
Gilalrt, 100 ....B-7
Gilbert, 521 ....C-6
Gilliam, 154 ....A-1
Gillis, 657 ....G-3
Glencoe, 211 ....I-6
Glenmora, 1342 ....F-4
Gloster, 94 ....C-2

Golden Meadow, 2101 ....J-9
Goldman, 60 ....D-7
Goldonna, 430 ....C-3
Gonzales, 9781 ....H-8
Goodwill, 200 ....B-6
Gordon A-3
Gorum, 150 ....D-4
Grambling, 4949 ....B-4
Gramercy, 3613 ....H-8
Grand Cane, 242 ....C-2
Grand Chenier, 500 ....I-3
Grand Coteau, 947 ....G-5
Grand Ecore, 150 ....C-3
Grand Isle, 1296 ....J-10
Grand Lake, 300 ....H-3
Grangeville, 100 ....F-8
Grant, 100 ....F-5
GRANT PAR., 22309 ....D-4
Gray, 5584 ....I-8
Grayson, 532 ....C-5
Greensburg, 708 ....F-8
Greenwood, 3219 ....B-1
Gretna, 17736 ....H-9
Grosse Tete, 647 ....G-6
Guegue, 1398 ....H-4
Hackberry, 1261 ....H-2
Hackley D-3
Hagewood, 150 ....D-3
Hahnville, 3344 ....H-9
Haile, 130 ....A-4
Hall Summit, 300 ....C-3
Hamburg, 280 ....F-5
Hammond, 20019 ....G-8
Happy Jack, 200 ....I-10
Harahan, 9277 ....H-9
Harisonburg, 348 ....D-6
Harvey, 20348 ....F-13
Hathaway G-4
Haughton, 3454 ....B-2
Hayes, 780 ....H-3
Haynesville, 2377 ....A-3
Head of Island, 250 ....H-8
Hebert, 200 ....C-5
Heflin, 244 ....B-3
Henderson, 1674 ....G-5
Henry, 350 ....I-5
Hermitage, 250 ....G-7
Hessmer, 802 ....F-5
Hicks, 50 ....F-3
Hico, 100 ....B-4
Hineston, 350 ....E-4
Hodge, 470 ....C-4
Holden, 60 ....G-8
Holloway, 70 ....D-4
Holly Ridge, 50 ....C-6
Hollywood B-10
Holum, 50 ....C-3
Homer, 3237 ....A-3
Hornbeck, 480 ....D-3
Hosston, 318 ....A-2
Houma, 33727 ....I-8
Hudson C-4
Hughes, 110 ....B-6
Husser, 70 ....G-9
ICBM PAR., 23240 ....H-6
IBERVILLE PAR., 33387 ....G-6
Ida, 221 ....A-1
Independence, 1665 ....G-8
Indian Vil., 320 ....G-3
Innis, 250 ....F-6
Inniswold, 6180 ....C-13
Iota, 1500 ....H-4
Iowa, 2996 ....H-3
Ironton, 230 ....I-10
Jackson, 3842 ....F-7
Jamestown, 139 ....C-3
Jarreau, 520 ....G-6
Jean Lafitte, 1903 ....I-9
Jeanerette, 5530 ....H-6
Jefferson, 11193 ....C-12
JEFFERSON DAVIS PAR., 31594 ....G-3
JEFFERSON PAR., 432552 ....H-9
Jena, 3398 ....D-5
Jennings, 10383 ....H-4
Jigger, 180 ....C-6
Johnson's Bayou, 150 ....I-2
Jones, 250 ....A-5
Jonesboro, 4704 ....C-4
Jonesville, 2452 ....D-6
Jordan Hill, 211 ....B-3
Junction City, 582 ....A-4
Kaplan, 4896 ....H-4
Keatchie, 295 ....C-2
Kelly, 200 ....C-5
Kentwood, 2198 ....F-8
Kilbourne, 416 ....A-7
Killian, 1206 ....G-8
Kinder, 2477 ....G-3
Kisatchie, 80 ....D-3
Kraemer, 934 ....I-8
Krotz Sprs., 1198 ....G-6
Kurthwood, 70 ....E-3
LA SALLE PAR., 14890 ....D-5
Labadieville, 1854 ....I-7
Lacamp, 100 ....D-4
Lacombe, 8679 ....G-10
Lafayette, 120623 ....H-5
LAFAYETTE PAR., 221578 ....H-5
LAFOURCHE PAR., 96318 ....I-9
L. Arthur, 2894 ....H-4
L. Charles, 71993 ....H-3
L. Providence, 3991 ....B-7
Lakeland, 350 ....G-6
Lakeshore, 1930 ....B-5
Lakeview, 948 ....C-6
Lakeview D-13
Lamourie, 300 ....E-4
Laplace, 29872 ....H-8
Larose, 7400 ....I-9

Larto, 120 ....E-5
Latanier, 50 ....E-5
Laurel Hill, 50 ....F-7
Lawtell, 1198 ....G-5
Le Blanc, 200 ....B-6
Le Moyen, 200 ....F-5
Lecompte, 1227 ....E-4
Lees, 150 ....G-5
Leesville, 6612 ....E-3
Leeville, 200 ....J-9
Legonier, 230 ....F-4
Lena, 350 ....D-4
Leonville, 1084 ....G-5
Leroy, 150 ....N-6
Letton A-3
Lettsworth, 200 ....F-6
Lewisburg, 260 ....G-5
Liberty Hill, 50 ....A-4
Lillie, 118 ....A-4
LINCOLN PAR., 46735 ....B-4
Lindsay, 20 ....C-6
Linville, 150 ....A-3
Little Creek, 130 ....D-5
Live Oak Mnr., 1900 ....E-11
Livingston, 1769 ....G-8
LIVINGSTON PAR., 128026 ....G-8
Livonia, 1442 ....G-6
Lockhart, 30 ....A-4
Lockport, 2578 ....I-8
Log Cabin, 300 ....A-3
Logansport, 1555 ....C-1
Lone Pine F-2
Longleaf, 300 ....F-4
Longstreet, 157 ....C-1
Longville, 635 ....G-3
Loranger, 670 ....G-9
Loreauville, 887 ....H-6
Lottie, 450 ....G-6
Lucky, 272 ....C-3
Luling, 1374 ....H-8
Luna, 50 ....C-5
Lunita, 50 ....C-2
Lutcher, 3559 ....H-8
Lydia, 952 ....H-6
MADISON PAR., 12093 ....C-6
Madisonville, 748 ....G-9
Mamou, 3242 ....G-4
Mandeville, 11560 ....G-9
Mangham, 672 ....C-6
Manifest, 120 ....D-5
Many, 2853 ....D-2
Maringouin, 1098 ....G-6
Marion, 765 ....A-5
Marksville, 5702 ....F-5
Marrero, 33141 ....H-9
Martin, 594 ....C-3
Mathews, 2209 ....I-8
Maurepas, 150 ....G-8
Maurice, 964 ....H-5
Maxie, 100 ....G-4
Mayna, 100 ....B-6
McManus, 300 ....D-5
McNary, 211 ....F-4
Melder, 70 ....D-4
Melrose, 150 ....D-3
Melville, 1041 ....G-6
Mer Rouge, 628 ....A-6
Meraux, 5816 ....H-10
Mermentau, 661 ....H-4
Merryville, 1103 ....F-2
Metairie, 138481 ....H-9
Midway, 1291 ....D-5
Midway B-2
Milton, 3030 ....H-5
Minden, 13082 ....B-3
Mira, 100 ....A-1
Mitchell, 100 ....D-2
Mittie, 120 ....G-3
Monroe, 48815 ....B-5
Montegut, 1540 ....I-8
Monterey, 439 ....E-6
Montgomery, 730 ....C-3
Monticello, 5172 ....A-14
Montpelier, 266 ....G-8
Mooringsport, 793 ....B-1
Mora D-4
Moreauville, 929 ....F-5
MOREHOUSE PAR., 27979 ....A-6
Morgan City, 12404 ....I-7
Morganza, 650 ....F-6
Morrow, 50 ....F-5
Morse, 812 ....H-4
Moss Bluff, 11557 ....G-3
Mt. Hermon, 300 ....F-8
Mt. Lebanon, 80 ....B-3
Mt. Olive G-4
Mt. Zion, 130 ....A-4
Myrtle Grv., 40 ....I-10
Nairn, 110 ....J-10
Napoleonville, 660 ....H-7
Natchez, 597 ....D-3
Natchitoches, 18323 ....D-3
NATCHITOCHES PAR., 39566 ....D-3
Nebo, 150 ....D-5
Negreet, 150 ....D-2
New Era, 20 ....A-4
New Iberia, 32531 ....H-6
New Llano, 2504 ....E-3
New Orleans, ...H-9
New Roads, 4831 ....G-6
Newellton, 1137 ....C-6
Nibletts Bluff H-2
Noble, 252 ....D-2
Norco, 3074 ....H-9
Norwood, 322 ....F-7
Oak Grv., 1727 ....A-7
Oak Manor C-8
Oak Ridge, 144 ....B-6
Oakdale, 7780 ....F-4
Oakville, 150 ....I-10
Oberlin, 1774 ....G-4
Oil City, 1008 ....A-1
Old Jefferson, 6980 ....C-13
Olla, 1385 ....C-5
Opelousas, 16634 ....G-5
Oretta, 80 ....F-3
ORLEANS PAR., 343829 ....H-9
Oscar, 200 ....G-6
Spencer, 100 ....B-5
Spokane, 442 ....C-6
Spring Ridge B-2

Palmetto, 164 ....G-5
Paradis, 1298 ....H-9
Parks, 653 ....H-6
Patterson, 6112 ....I-7
Pearl River, 2506 ....G-10
Pecan Island, 400 ....I-4
Pelican, 200 ....D-2
Perry, 200 ....H-5
Perryville, 90 ....C-9
Phoenix, 500 ....I-10
Pickering, 50 ....E-3
Pierre Part, 3169 ....H-7
Pigeon, 600 ....H-7
Pilottown, 170 ....J-11
Pine, 120 ....F-9
Pine Grv., 180 ....F-8
Pine Prairie, 1616 ....F-4
Pineville, 14555 ....E-4
Pioneer, 156 ....A-6
Pitkin, 576 ....F-4
Plain Dealing, 1015 ....A-2
Plaquemine, 7119 ....H-7
PLAQUEMINES PAR., 23042 ....I-10
Plattenville, 390 ....H-7
Plauchville, 248 ....F-5
Pleasant Hill, 723 ....D-2
Pt. Blue, 140 ....D-5
Pointe a la Hache, 187 ....I-10
POINTE COUPEE PAR., 22802 ....G-6
Pollock, 469 ....D-4
Ponchatoula, 6559 ....G-9
Poplar Grv., 200 ....A-12
Port Allen, 5180 ....G-7
Port Barre, 2055 ....G-5
Port Fourchon, 150 ....J-10
Port Sulphur, 1760 ....I-10
Port Vincent, 741 ....G-8
Powhatan, 135 ....D-3
Prairieville, 26895 ....H-7
Prien, 7810 ....H-3
Princeton, 150 ....C-6
Provencal, 611 ....D-3
Quitman, 181 ....C-4
Raceland, 10193 ....I-8
Ragley, 100 ....G-3
Ramah G-6
RAPIDES PAR., 131613 ....F-4
Rayne, 7953 ....H-5
Rayville, 3695 ....B-6
Red Chute, 6261 ....B-2
RED RIVER PAR., 9091 ....D-3
Reddell, 733 ....G-4
Reeves, 232 ....G-3
Reggio, 150 ....I-10
Reserve, 9766 ....H-8
RICHLAND PAR., 20725 ....C-5
Richmond, 577 ....C-7
Richwood, 3392 ....B-5
Ridgecrest, 694 ....D-6
Ringgold, 1495 ....C-3
River Ridge, 13494 ....C-11
Riverton, 80 ....C-6
Robeline, 174 ....D-3
Robert, 400 ....G-9
Rocky Branch, 200 ....B-5
Rocky Mount, 100 ....B-2
Rodessa, 274 ....A-1
Rogers A-6
Rosa C-5
Rosedale, 793 ....G-6
Rosefield, 30 ....D-5
Roseland, 1123 ....F-8
Rosepine, 1692 ....F-3
Roy, 80 ....C-5
Ruston, 21859 ....B-4
SABINE PAR., 24233 ....E-2
Sadie C-4
St. Amant, 300 ....H-8
St. Bernard, 830 ....H-10
ST. BERNARD PAR., 35897 ....H-10
ST. CHARLES PAR., 52780 ....H-8
St. Francisville, 1765 ....F-7
St. Gabriel, 6677 ....H-7
ST. HELENA PAR., 11203 ....F-8
ST. JAMES PAR., 22102 ....H-8
ST. JOHN THE BAPTIST PAR., 45924 ....H-8
St. Joseph, 1176 ....D-7
St. Landry, 600 ....G-5
ST. LANDRY PAR., 83384 ....G-5
ST. MARTIN PAR., 52160 ....H-6
St. Martinville, 6114 ....H-6
ST. MARY PAR., 54650 ....I-6
St. Maurice, 323 ....D-3
ST. TAMMANY PAR., 233740 ....G-9
Saline, 277 ....C-3
Sandy Hill, 300 ....F-6
Sarepta, 891 ....A-2
Schriever, 6853 ....I-8
SCOTLANDVILLE G-7
Scott, 8614 ....H-5
Seymourville, 3000 ....H-7
Shaw Hills, 900 ....A-3
Shelburn, 117 ....C-6
Sheridan G-9
Shongaloo, 182 ....A-3
Shreveport, 199311 ....B-2
Sibley, 1123 ....B-3
Sicily Island, 526 ....D-6
Sieper, 100 ....E-4
Sikes, 119 ....C-4
Simmesport, 2161 ....F-6
Simpson, 638 ....E-3
Simsboro, 841 ....B-4
Singer, 287 ....F-3
Slagle, 300 ....E-3
Slaughter, 997 ....F-7
Slidell, 27068 ....H-10
Somerset C-6
Sorrel, 766 ....H-7
Spearsville, 137 ....A-4

Springville, 840 ....C-9
Stanley, 107 ....D-1
Starks, 664 ....G-2
Start, 905 ....B-6
Sterlington, 1594 ....B-5
Stonewall, 1814 ....C-2
Sugartown, 54 ....F-3
Sulphur, 20410 ....H-2
Summer Grv. C-9
Summerfield, 180 ....A-4
Summerville, 150 ....D-5
Sun, 400 ....G-9
Sunnybrook, 800 ....A-13
Sunrise, 400 ....B-12
Sunset, 2897 ....G-5
Swartz, 4536 ....B-5
Talisheek, 400 ....G-9
Talla Bena, 50 ....B-7
Tallulah, 7335 ....C-7
Tangipahoa, 748 ....F-8
TANGIPAHOA PAR., 121097 ....G-8
Taylortown C-4
TENSAS PAR., 5252 ....D-6
TERREBONNE PAR., 111860 ....I-7
Terry, 150 ....F-14
Terrytown, 23319 ....F-14
Theriot, 200 ....J-8
Thibodaux, 14566 ....I-8
Thornwell, 190 ....H-4
Tickfaw, 694 ....G-8
Tioga, 1300 ....D-4
Toomey, 50 ....H-2
Toro E-2
Transylvania, 180 ....B-7
Trees, 160 ....B-1
Triumph, 216 ....J-11
Trout, 200 ....D-5
Tullos, 385 ....D-5
Tunica, 230 ....F-6
Turkey Creek, 441 ....F-4
UNION PAR., 22721 ....A-4
Urania, 1313 ....D-5
Varnado, 1461 ....F-10
Venice, 202 ....J-11
Verda, 150 ....D-4
VERMILION PAR., 57999 ....I-4
Vernon, 30 ....C-3
VERNON PAR., 52334 ....E-3
Vidalia, 4299 ....D-6
Vidrine, 150 ....G-4
Vienna, 386 ....B-4
Ville Platte, 7430 ....G-5
Vinton, 3212 ....H-2
Violet, 4973 ....H-10
Vivian, 3671 ....A-1
Vixen, 30 ....C-5
Vowells Mill, 30 ....D-3
W. BATON ROUGE PAR., 20767 ....C-5
W. CARROLL PAR., 11604 ....A-7
W. FELICIANA PAR., 15625 ....F-7
Waggaman, 10015 ....E-11
Wakefield, 110 ....F-7
Walker, 6138 ....G-8
Walters, 50 ....C-5
Warden, 90 ....B-6
Wardville, 1200 ....C-4
Warnerton F-9
Washington, 964 ....G-5
WASHINGTON PAR., 47168 ....F-9
Waterproof, 688 ....D-7
Watson, 1047 ....G-8
Waverly A-6
WEBSTER PAR., 41207 ....A-2
Welcome, 800 ....H-8
Welsh, 3226 ....H-4
W. Monroe, 13065 ....B-5
Westgate D-11
Westlake, 4568 ....H-3
Westminster, 3008 ....C-13
Westport C-4
Westwego, 8534 ....H-9
Weyanoke, 150 ....F-6
White Castle, 1883 ....H-7
Whitehall, 90 ....D-5
Whitehall, 500 ....D-12
Whiteville, 30 ....C-5
Wickland Ter. D-12
Wildsville, 500 ....D-6
Williana, 50 ....C-4
Willow Glen, 500 ....C-4
Willowdale D-12
Wilson, 595 ....F-7
Winfield, 4840 ....D-4
Winnfield, 4840 ....D-4
Winnsboro, 4910 ....C-6
WINN PAR., 15313 ....D-4
Wisner, 964 ....C-6
Woodlawn, 250 ....H-3
Woodworth, 1096 ....E-4
Wyatt C-5
Youngsville, 8105 ....H-5
Zachary, 14960 ....G-7
Zion F-7
Zwolle, 1759 ....D-2
Zylks, 60 ....A-1

Michigan

Page locator

Map keys	Atlas pages
A–J	102–103
K–T	104–105

* City keyed to pp. 106–107

***, †, ‡, §, ◊ See explanation under state title in this index.**
County and parish names are listed in capital letters & boldface type.
Independent cities (not included in a county) are listed in italics.

Pinconning, 1307...M-10
Pine Creek...S-7
Pine Run, 660...O-11
Piney Woods, 500...L-8
Pinnebog, 620...L-12
Pittsburg...P-9
Pittsford, 530...T-9
Plainfield, 40...Q-10
Plainwell, 3804...R-9
Pleasant Ridge, 2526...*H-6
Pleasant Valley...*J-2
Plymouth, 9132...*J-7
Pokagon, 140...S-5
Pompeii, 200...Q-9
Pontiac, 59515...Q-12
Port Austin, 664...L-12
Port Hope, 267...L-13
Port Huron, 30184...P-14
Port Sanilac, 623...N-14
Port Sheldon, 180...P-5
Portage, 46292...R-6
Portland, 3883...Q-9
Posen, 234...H-11
Poseyville, 100...N-9
Potterville, 2617...Q-8
Powers, 621...G-1
Prairieville, 180...Q-6
Prattville, 200...T-9
Prescott, 266...L-10
Presque Isle, 120...H-11

PRESQUE ISLE CO., 13376...H-9
Princeton, 180...E-1
Prudenville, 1682...L-8
Pulaski, 100...S-8
Pullman, 600...Q-5
Quanicassee, 130...N-11
Quincy, 1652...S-8
Quinnesec, 1191...D-13
Raco, 50...B-9
Ralph, 60...E-1
Ramsay, 1080...C-10
Rankin, 220...P-11
Ransom, 130...P-8
Rapid City, 1352...J-7
Rapid River, 60...O-5
Ravenna, 1219...O-5
Ray, 60...T-8
Ray Ctr....*D-9
Reading, 1078...T-8
Red Oak, 50...*J-4
Redford, 51622...*J-4
Reed City, 2425...M-6
Reeman, 110...N-5
Reese, 1454...N-11
Remus, 480...N-7
Republic, 570...C-13
Rexton, 160...E-7
Rhodes, 130...M-9
Richland, 751...R-6
Richmond, 5735...P-13
Richmondville, 30...N-13
Richville, 30...N-11
Ridgeway, 200...S-10
Riga, 400...T-11
Riley Ctr., 60...*P-13
River Rouge, 7903...*K-6
Riverdale, 400...N-8
Riverside, 290...S-4
Riverview, 12486...*M-6
Rives Jct., 450...P-9
Roberts, 50...Q-14
Rochester, 12711...Q-12
Rochester Hills, 70995...Q-12
Rock, 440...E-2
Rockford, 5719...O-6
Rockland, 270...B-12
Rockwood, 3289...S-13
Rodney, 160...M-7
Rogers City, 2827...G-10
Rollin, 110...S-9
Romeo, 3596...P-12
Romulus, 23989...R-12
Roosevelt Pk., 3831...O-4
Roscommon, 1075...L-8
ROSCOMMON CO., 24449...K-8
Rose Ctr., 170...*E-1
Rose City, 653...K-10
Roseburg, 30...M-8
Rosebush, 368...M-8
Rosedale...L-8
Roseville, 47299...Q-13
Rothbury, 432...N-4
Royal Oak, 57236...*H-6
Rudyard, 1100...C-8
Rumely, 90...D-3
Russellville, 220...O-11
Ruth, 230...M-13
Saginaw, 51508...N-11
SAGINAW CO., 200169...O-10
Sagola, 180...D-13
St. Charles, 2054...O-10
St. Clair, 5485...P-13
ST. CLAIR CO., 163040...P-13
St. Clair Shores, 59715...Q-13
St. Helen, 2668...K-9
St. Ignace, 2452...F-8
St. James, 205...F-6
St. Johns, 7865...O-9
St. Joseph, 8365...S-4
ST. JOSEPH CO., 61295...T-6
St. Louis, 7482...N-8
Salem, 350...*I-1
Saline, 8810...R-11
Samaria, 480...T-11
Sand Creek, 110...T-10
Sand Lake, 500...O-6
Sand River, 80...D-2
Sands, 60...D-2
Sandusky, 2613...N-13
Sanford, 859...M-9
SANILAC CO., 43114...N-13
Saranac, 1325...P-7
Saugatuck, 925...Q-5
Sault Ste. Marie, 14144...D-9
Sawyer, 780...S-4
Schaffer, 50...F-2
Schoolcraft, 1525...*K-9
SCHOOLCRAFT CO., 8485...E-4
Scofield, 5-11
Scotts, 350...R-6
Scottville, 1214...M-4
Sears, 90...M-7
Sebewaing, 1759...M-11

Selkirk, 40...K-10
Seney, 200...D-5
Seven Harbors, 4700...*E-1
Shabbona, 90...N-10
Shady Shores, 350...K-10
Shaftsburg, 270...*E-7
Shelby, 65159...*E-7
Shelby, 2065...N-4
Shelbyville, 160...Q-6
Sheldon, 590...*I-1
Shepardsville, 70...P-9
Shepherd, 1515...N-8
Sheridan, 649...O-7
Sherman, 30...M-5
Sherman City, 30...N-7
Sherwood, 309...S-7
SHIAWASSEE CO., 70648...P-10
Shiawasseetown...P-10
Shields, 6587...N-10
Shingleton, 320...D-4
Shoreham, 862...S-4
Sidnaw, 300...C-12
Sidney, 120...O-7
Silver City, 60...B-11
Silverwood, 170...N-12
Six Lakes, 420...N-7
Skandia, 300...D-2
Skanee, 100...B-13
Skeels...L-8
Skidway Lake, 3392...L-10
Snover, 448...N-13
Sodus, 180...S-4
Somerset, 140...S-9
Somerset Ctr., 440...S-9
S. Boardman, 536...J-7
S. Branch, 150...K-10
S. Haven, 4403...R-4
S. Ionia, 100...P-7
S. Lyon, 11327...Q-11
S. Range, 758...A-12
S. Rockwood, 1675...S-12
Southfield, 71739...Q-12
Southgate, 30047...*M-5
Spalding, 590...E-2
Sparlingville...P-14
Sparr, 30...J-9
Sparta, 4140...O-6
Spratt...H-10
Spring Arbor, 2881...R-9
Spring Lake, 2323...O-5
Springfield, 5260...R-7
Springport, 800...R-8
Springville, 60...L-9
Spruce, 120...I-11
Stalwart, 60...D-8
Standish, 1509...L-10
Stanton, 1417...O-7
Stanwood, 211...N-6
Stephenson, 862...H-1
Sterling, 530...L-10
Sterling Hts., 129699...Q-12
Steuben, 70...D-4
Stevensville, 1142...S-4
Stockbridge, 1218...R-10
Stonington...E-3
Stony Lake, 50...N-4
Stronach, 162...L-4
Strongs, 380...D-7
Sturgis, 10994...T-7
Sumner, 170...O-8
Sumnerville, 180...S-5
Sunfield, 578...Q-8
Sunrise Lake, 1350...R-7
Suttons Bay, 618...I-6
Swartz Creek, 5758...P-10
Sylvan Lake, 1720...*F-4
Tallmadge...P-6
Tallman, 70...M-6
Tawas City, 1827...K-11
Taylor, 63131...R-12
Tecumseh, 8521...S-10
Tekonsha, 717...S-8
Temperance, 8517...T-11
Temple, 300...L-8

Isabella, 1681...N-8
Virginia Pk., 1800...Q-5
Vogel Ctr., 110...L-7
Volinia, 40...S-5
Vriesland, 50...P-5
Vulcan, 100...D-14
Wacousta, 1440...P-8
Wadhams, 550...P-14
Wakefield, 1851...C-10
Wakelee, 80...S-5
Waldenburg, 110...*F-8
Waldron, 538...T-9
Walhalla, 380...M-5
Walker, 23537...*B-1
Walkerville, 247...M-5
Wallace, 150...H-1
Walled Lake, 6999...*G-2
Walloon Lake, 290...H-8
Waltz, 500...*N-3
Warren, 134056...Q-13
Washington, 1850...Q-12
Washtenaw CO.
Waterford, 71981...Q-12
Waterloo, 190...R-10
Waters, 150...I-8
Watersmeet, 428...C-11
Watertown, 100...N-13
Watervliet, 1735...R-4
Watrousville, 200...N-11
Watson, 30...Q-6
Watton, 150...C-12
Waucedah, 60...F-1
Wayland, 4079...Q-6
Wayne, 17593...*K-3

Brownfield, 250 .... A-8
Brownsville, 40 .... H-5
Bruce, 1939 .... D-8
Buckatunna, 516 .... J-9
Bude, 1063 .... J-4
Buena Vista, 70 .... D-5
Buena Vista B-8
Bunker Hill, 150 .... F-7
Burnsville, 936 .... B-10
Byhalia, 1302 .... B-7
Byram, 11489 .... H-6
Caesar, 250 .... L-7
Caledonia, 1041 .... C-9
Calhoun, 250 .... J-8
Calhoun City, 1774 .... C-8
CALHOUN CO.,
  14962 .... D-8
Camden, 700 .... G-6
Canaan, 80 .... J-8
Cannonsburg, 130 .... J-4
Canton, 13189 .... G-6
Carlisle, 90 .... I-4
Carnes, 150 .... K-8
Carpenter, 110 .... I-5
Carriere, 880 .... L-7
CARROLL CO.,
  10597 .... E-6
Carrollton, 190 .... E-6
Carson, 500 .... J-7
Carter, 80 .... F-5
Carterville F-7
Carthage, 5075 .... G-7
Cary, 311 .... G-4
Cascilla, 250 .... D-6
Cayuga, 40 .... I-5
Cedar Bluff, 450 .... E-9
Center Ridge I-7
Centreville, 1684 .... K-4
Chalybeate, 320 .... A-8
Charleston, 2193 .... D-6
Chatawa, 150 .... J-5
Chatham, 40 .... F-4
Cheraw K-6
Chester, 250 .... E-8
CHICKASAW CO.,
  17392 .... D-8
Chicora, 40 .... C-4
Choctaw, 250 .... E-4
CHOCTAW CO.,
  8547 .... F-8
Chunky, 326 .... H-8
Church Hill, 40 .... J-3
CLAIBORNE CO.,
  9604 .... I-4
Clara, 410 .... J-9
CLARKE CO.,
  16732 .... H-9
Clarksdale, 17962 .... C-5
CLAY CO., 20634 .... E-8
Cleary, 1150 .... H-6
Clem, 50 .... J-7
Cleveland, 12334 .... D-5
Cliftonville, 90 .... F-9
Clinton, 25216 .... H-5
Cloverdale, 645 .... J-3
Coahoma, 177 .... C-5
COAHOMA CO.,
  26151 .... D-5
Coffeeville, 905 .... D-7
Coila, 50 .... E-6
Coldwater, 1677 .... B-6
Coles, 60 .... K-4
Collins, 2586 .... I-7
Collinsville, 1948 .... H-9
Columbia, 6582 .... K-6
Columbus, 23640 .... E-9
Commerce B-5
Como, 1279 .... C-6
Conehatta, 1342 .... H-8
COPIAH CO., 29449 .... I-5
Corinth, 14573 .... A-9
Cotton Plant, 40 .... D-6
Courtland, 511 .... C-6
COVINGTON CO.,
  19568 .... I-7
Cowart D-6
Coxburg, 30 .... F-6
Cranfield, 140 .... J-4
Crawford, 641 .... F-9
Crenshaw, 885 .... C-6
Crosby, 318 .... K-4
Crossroads C-7
Crowder, 712 .... C-6
Cruger, 80 .... E-6
Crupp, 80 .... G-5
Crystal Sprs., 5044 .... I-5
Cuevas, 170 .... M-8
Curtis Sta., 140 .... L-6
Cynthia A-1
Darbun, 40 .... K-6
Darling, 226 .... C-6
Darlove F-5
De Kalb, 1164 .... G-9
De Lisle, 1147 .... M-8
De Soto, 200 .... I-9
Courtland, 511 .... C-6
DE SOTO CO.,
  161252 .... B-6
Decatur, 1841 .... H-8
Deemer, 90 .... G-8
Derma, 1025 .... D-8
Diamondhead, 8425 .... M-8
D'Iberville, 9486 .... M-9
D'Lo, 452 .... I-6
Doddsville, 98 .... E-5
Doloroso, 95 .... K-3
Drew, 1927 .... D-5
Dubbs B-5
Dublin, 160 .... D-6
Duck Hill, 732 .... E-7
Duffee, 110 .... H-9
Dumas, 40 .... B-9
Duncan, 423 .... D-5
Durant, 2673 .... F-6
Eagle Lake, 200 .... H-4
Eastabuche, 210 .... I-8
Eastport, 300 .... B-10
Ecru, 895 .... C-8
Eddiceton, 150 .... J-4
Eden, 103 .... F-5
Edinburg, 110 .... G-7
Edwards, 1034 .... I-5
Egypt, 80 .... D-9
Electric Mills, 50 .... G-9
Elliott E-7
Elliott, 990 .... E-7
Ellisville, 4448 .... I-8
Ellisville Jct., 10 .... I-8
Enid, 140 .... D-7
Enon K-6
Enondale, 90 .... G-9

Enterprise, 526 .... H-9
Enterprise, 200 .... H-8
Enzor, 150 .... D-8
Escatawpa, 3722 .... M-9
Estill F-4
Ethel, 418 .... F-7
Etta C-8
Eucutta, 120 .... I-9
Eudora, 200 .... B-6
Eupora, 2197 .... E-8
Evansville, 35 .... C-9
Evergreen, 80 .... C-9
Fairfield, 90 .... C-9
Fairview, 200 .... C-8
Falcon, 167 .... C-6
Falkner, 514 .... A-8
Fannin H-6
Farmington, 2186 .... A-9
Farrell, 218 .... C-5
Fayette, 1614 .... J-4
Fentress, 90 .... C-8
Fernwood, 400 .... K-5
Fitler, 30 .... G-4
Flora, 1886 .... G-5
Florence, 4141 .... H-6
Flowood, 7823 .... C-3
Forest, 5684 .... H-7
Forest Hill D-1
Forkville, 150 .... H-7
FORREST CO.,
  74934 .... K-8
Ft. Adams, 80 .... K-3
Foxworth, 603 .... K-6
FRANKLIN CO.,
  8118 .... J-4
French Camp, 174 .... F-7
Friars Pt., 1200 .... C-5
Friendship, 200 .... C-8
Fruitland Pk. I-3
Fulton, 3961 .... C-9
Furrs, 150 .... C-9
Gallman, 400 .... I-4
Garden City J-4
Garlandville H-8
Gattman, 90 .... D-10
Gautier, 18572 .... M-9
Geeville B-9
GEORGE CO.,
  22578 .... L-9
Georgetown, 286 .... I-6
Gholson G-8
Gibson, 100 .... D-9
Gillsburg K-5
Gitano I-8
Glade, 140 .... I-8
Glen Allan, 500 .... F-4
Glendale, 1657 .... I-8
Glendora, 151 .... D-6
Glen, 412 .... B-9
Gloster, 960 .... K-4
Glover, 50 .... A-6
Gluckstadt, 210 .... H-6
Golden, 191 .... C-10
Good Hope, 110 .... G-8
Goodman, 1386 .... F-6
Gore Sprs., 110 .... D-7
Goss, 100 .... J-6
Grace, 270 .... F-4
Grand Gulf, 60 .... I-4
Gravestown, 200 .... B-8
GREENE CO.,
  14400 .... K-9
Greenville, 34400 .... E-4
Greenwood, 15205 .... E-6
Greenwood Sprs.,
  260 .... D-10
Grenada, 13092 .... D-7
GRENADA CO.,
  21906 .... D-7
Gulf Hills, 7144 .... M-5
Gulfport, 67793 .... M-8
Gunnison, 452 .... D-4
Guntown, 2083 .... C-9
Hamburg, 120 .... J-4
Hamilton, 457 .... D-9
HANCOCK CO.,
  43929 .... M-7
Handsboro M-2
Hardy, 80 .... C-8
Harmontown, 200 .... B-7
Harperville, 170 .... H-7
HARRISON CO.,
  187105 .... L-8
Harriston, 340 .... J-4
Harrisville, 380 .... I-6
Hatley, 482 .... D-9
Hattiesburg, 45989 .... K-8
Hatten, 640 .... K-8
Heads E-4
Hebron, 40 .... I-7
Hebron, 30 .... J-7
Heidelberg, 718 .... I-8
Helena, 1184 .... M-9
Hermanville, 400 .... I-4
Hernando, 14090 .... B-6
Hickory, 530 .... H-8
Hickory Flat, 601 .... B-8
Highpoint F-8
Highway, 150 .... B-9
Hillsboro, 1130 .... H-7
HINDS CO.,
  245285 .... I-5
Hintonville, 340 .... K-8
Hiwannee I-9
Hohenlinden E-8
Holcomb, 40 .... E-6
Hollandale, 2702 .... F-4
Holly Bluff, 300 .... G-5
Holly Ridge, 100 .... E-5
Holly Sprs., 7699 .... B-7
HOLMES CO.,
  19198 .... F-6
Homerstown H-6
Homestead H-6
Hopewell, 30 .... H-6
Horn Lake, 26066 .... A-6
Horton K-6
House, 100 .... G-8
Houlka, 626 .... D-8
Houston, 3623 .... D-8
Howard, 80 .... K-7
Hub K-7
HUMPHREYS CO.,
  9375 .... F-5
Hurley, 1551 .... L-9
Hurricane, 200 .... C-8
Hushpuckena, 60 .... D-5
Improve, 40 .... I-7
Independence, 80 .... B-7
Indianola, 10683 .... C-5
Ingomar, 250 .... C-8
Ingrams Mill, 50 .... B-8
Inverness, 1019 .... E-5
Iola, 713 .... F-5
ISSAQUENA CO.,
  1406 .... G-4
ITAWAMBA CO.,
  23401 .... C-9

Itta Bena, 2049 .... E-5
Iuka, 3028 .... B-10
Jacinto, 220 .... B-9
Jackson, 173514 .... H-6
JACKSON CO.,
  139668 .... L-9
James F-4
JASPER CO., 17062 .... I-8
Jayess, 110 .... J-5
JEFFERSON CO.,
  7726 .... J-4
JEFFERSON DAVIS
  CO., 12487 .... J-6
Johns J-6
Johnson, 30 .... J-8
JONES CO., 67761 .... J-8
Jonestown, 1298 .... C-5
Jumpertown, 480 .... B-9
KEMPER CO.,
  10456 .... G-9
Kendrick, 200 .... A-9
Kewanee, 60 .... H-9
Kilmichael, 699 .... E-7
Kiln, 2238 .... M-7
Kingston, 390 .... J-3
Kirby J-6
Knoxville, 100 .... J-4
Kokomo, 210 .... K-6
Kosciusko, 7402 .... F-7
Kossuth, 209 .... B-9
LAFAYETTE CO.,
  47351 .... C-7
Lake, 324 .... H-8
L. Cormorant, 270 .... B-6
Lake of Hills, 200 .... B-6
L. View, 200 .... A-6
Lakeshore, 1200 .... M-7
Lamar, 150 .... A-8
LAMAR CO.,
  55658 .... K-7
Lamar Pk. J-4
Lambert, 1638 .... C-6
Lamont, 70 .... F-4
Lampton, 150 .... K-6
Landon M-1
Latimer, 6079 .... M-9
Lauderdale, 442 .... G-9
LAUDERDALE CO.,
  80261 .... H-9
Laurel, 18540 .... I-8
Lawrence, 200 .... H-8
LAWRENCE CO.,
  12929 .... J-6
Laws Hill, 170 .... B-7
Le Tourneau, 200 .... H-4
Leaf, 120 .... K-8
LEAKE CO., 23805 .... G-7
Leakesville, 898 .... K-9
Learned, 94 .... I-5
LEE CO., 82910 .... C-9
Leedy, 100 .... B-10
Leesburg H-7
Leflore, 50 .... D-6
LEFLORE CO.,
  32317 .... E-6
Leland, 4481 .... E-5
Lena, 148 .... G-7
Lewisburg, 120 .... B-6
Lexington, 1731 .... F-6
Liberty, 728 .... K-4
LINCOLN CO.,
  34869 .... J-5
Little Rock, 230 .... G-8
Little Yazoo, 110 .... G-5
Litton E-7
Lodi, 50 .... E-7
Long Bch., 14792 .... M-8
Long Lake, 100 .... H-4
Longtown, 250 .... C-6
Longview, 390 .... F-8
Looxahoma, 170 .... C-7
Lorman, 560 .... I-4
Louin, 277 .... H-8
Louise, 199 .... F-5
Louisville, 6631 .... F-8
LOWNDES CO.,
  59779 .... E-9
Loyd Star, 30 .... J-5
Lucas, 30 .... A-8
Lucedale, 2923 .... L-9
Lucien, 50 .... J-5
Ludlow, 240 .... G-7
Lula, 298 .... C-5
Lumberton, 2086 .... K-7
Lyman, 1277 .... M-8
Lynchburg, 2437 .... A-6
Lyon, 350 .... C-5
MADISON CO.,
  95203 .... G-6
Magee, 4408 .... I-7
Magnolia, 2400 .... K-5
Mahned, 150 .... K-8
Malvina, 30 .... D-4
Mantachie, 1144 .... C-9
Mantee, 232 .... E-8
Marietta, 256 .... C-9
Marion, 1479 .... H-9
MARION CO.,
  27088 .... K-7
Marks, 1735 .... C-6
MARSHALL CO.,
  37144 .... B-7
Martin, 110 .... C-8
Martinsville I-6
Mashulaville, 60 .... F-9
Matherville, 50 .... I-9
Mathiston, 698 .... E-8
Mattson, 150 .... D-5
Maybank, 30 .... F-5
Mayersville, 547 .... G-4
Mayhew, 110 .... E-9
McAdams, 250 .... F-7
McCall Creek, 140 .... J-5
McCarley, 150 .... E-6
McComb, 12790 .... K-5
McCool, 135 .... F-7
McDonald, 50 .... H-7
McHenry, 160 .... L-8
McLain, 441 .... K-9
McLaurin, 530 .... K-8
McLeod K-9
McNeill, 1000 .... L-7
Meadville, 449 .... J-4
Mendenhall, 2504 .... I-6
Meridian, 41148 .... H-9
Merigold, 439 .... D-5
Merrill, 90 .... L-9
Mesa H-6
Metcalfe, 1067 .... E-4
Michigan City, 250 .... A-8
Midnight, 240 .... F-5
Mill Creek C-8
Miller, 80 .... H-7
Minter City, 200 .... D-6
Mize, 340 .... I-7
Money, 120 .... E-6

Quito, 60 .... E-6
Raleigh, 1462 .... I-7
Randolph, 400 .... C-8
RANKIN CO.,
  141617 .... H-6
Ratliff, 120 .... C-9
Rawls Sprs., 1254 .... J-7
Raymond, 1933 .... H-5
Raytown, 140 .... G-7
Red Banks, 580 .... B-7
Red Lick, 150 .... I-4
Redwater, 633 .... G-7
Redwood, 200 .... H-4
Reform, 110 .... G-8
Refuge G-4
Rena Lara, 270 .... C-5
Renova, 668 .... D-5
Rich, 100 .... C-5
Richland, 6912 .... H-6
Richland, 30 .... I-8
Ridgeland, 24047 .... H-6
Rienzi, 317 .... B-9
Ripley, 5395 .... B-8
Robinsonville, 260 .... B-5
Rodney, 90 .... I-3
Rolling Fork, 2143 .... G-4
Rome, 180 .... D-5
Rose Hill, 250 .... H-8
Rosedale, 1873 .... D-4
Roundlake, 50 .... D-4
Roxie, 497 .... J-4
Ruleville, 3007 .... D-5
Runnelstown J-8
Russell, 110 .... H-9
Russum, 90 .... I-4
Sallis, 134 .... F-7
Saltillo, 4752 .... C-9
Sanatorium, 500 .... I-7
Sand Hill, 30 .... H-6
Sand Hill, 250 .... H-6
Sandersville, 731 .... I-8
Sandy Hook, 60 .... K-7
Sanford, 150 .... J-7
Sarah, 230 .... B-6
Sardis, 1703 .... C-6
Sarepta, 50 .... C-8
Satartia, 55 .... G-5
Saucier, 1342 .... L-8
Savage, 160 .... H-6
Schlater, 310 .... E-5
Scobey, 90 .... D-6
Scooba, 732 .... G-9
Scott, 300 .... E-4
SCOTT CO., 28264 .... H-7
Sebastopol, 272 .... G-8
Seminary, 314 .... J-7
Sessums, 170 .... E-9
Shady Grv., 420 .... I-8
Shady Grv., 30 .... J-6
Shannon, 1925 .... C-9
West, 185 .... F-7
Sharon, 1406 .... I-8
Sharon, 30 .... G-6
Shaw, 1952 .... E-5
Shelby, 2229 .... D-5
Sherard, 150 .... C-5
Sherman, 650 .... C-9
Sherwood, 30 .... E-8
Shivers I-6
Shubuta, 441 .... I-9
Shuqualak, 501 .... F-9
Sibley, 290 .... J-3
Sidon, 509 .... E-6
Silver City, 337 .... F-5
Silver Creek, 200 .... J-6
Simpson, 50 .... G-7
Singleton C-7
Skene, 200 .... D-5
Slate Spr., 110 .... D-7
Slayden, 120 .... A-7
Sledge, 545 .... C-6
SMITH CO., 16491 .... I-7
Smithdale, 100 .... J-5
Smithville, 942 .... D-10
Snow Lake Shores,
  319 .... B-8
Sontag, 220 .... J-6
Soso, 408 .... I-8
Southaven, 48982 .... A-6
Springdale C-7
Springville C-7
St. Martin, 7730 .... M-5
Stallo G-8
Star, 550 .... H-6
Starkville, 23888 .... E-9
State Line, 565 .... I-9
Steens, 210 .... E-10
Stewart, 280 .... E-8
STONE CO., 17786 .... L-8
Stoneville, 250 .... E-4
Stonewall, 1088 .... H-9
Stovall, 30 .... C-5
Stratton, 1250 .... H-8
Stringer, 430 .... I-8
Sturgis, 250 .... F-8
Summit, 1705 .... K-5
Sumner, 316 .... D-6
Sumrall, 1421 .... J-7
Sunflower, 1159 .... E-5
SUNFLOWER CO.,
  29450 .... E-5
Sunnyside M-8
Swan Lake, 80 .... D-6
Sweatman E-7
Swiftown, 110 .... E-6
Sylvarena, 110 .... I-7
Symonds, 100 .... A-7
TALLAHATCHIE CO.,
  15378 .... D-6
Tallula, 100 .... G-4
Talowah, 150 .... K-7
Tate, 100 .... B-6
TATE CO., 28886 .... B-6
Taylor, 322 .... C-7
Taylorsville, 1353 .... I-7
Tchula, 2096 .... F-6
Ten Mile I-8
Terry, 1063 .... H-6
Thaxton, 643 .... C-8
Thomastown, 200 .... G-7
Thompson, 30 .... A-7
Thornton, 200 .... F-6
Thrasher, 250 .... B-9
Threadville, 30 .... D-9
Three Rivers, 40 .... C-9
Tillatoba, 90 .... D-7
Tinsley, 260 .... G-5
Tiplersville, 120 .... A-8
Tippo, 120 .... D-6
Tishomingo, 339 .... B-10
TISHOMINGO CO.,
  19593 .... B-10

Oak Grv., 7795 ... F-10
Oak Grove Vil., 509 ... H-16
Oak Ridge, 243 ... J-19
Oakland, 1381 ... *I-5
Oakland Pk. ... *B-7
Oaks, 129 ... G-4
Oakview, 375 ... G-4
Oakville, 36143 ... *K-6
Oakwood, 185 ... G-4
Oakwood Pk., 188 ... G-4
Oates ... J-16
Odessa, 5300 ... F-10
Odin ... J-13
O'Fallon, 79329 ... F-17
Old Appleton, 85 ... J-19
Old Mines, 200 ... H-17
Old Monroe, 265 ... F-17
Olden, 80 ... L-14
Olivette, 7737 ... *H-5
Olney ... F-16
Olympian Vil., 774 ... H-17
Oran, 1294 ... K-19
Orchard Farm, 300 ... *E-4
Oregon, 857 ... C-8
OREGON CO., 10881 ... L-16
Orrick, 837 ... E-10
Osage Bch., 4351 ... H-13
OSAGE CO., 13878 ... G-14
Osborn, 423 ... D-9
Osceola, 947 ... H-11
Osgood, 48 ... C-11
Oskaloosa ... I-9
Otterville, 454 ... G-12
Otto, 500 ... G-17
Overland, 16062 ... *G-4
Owensville, 2676 ... H-15
Oxly, 200 ... L-17
Ozark, 17820 ... K-12
OZARK CO., 9723 ... L-13
Ozark View, 1000 ... *I-4
Pacific, 7002 ... G-17
Pagedale, 3304 ... *H-5
Painton, 50 ... K-19
Palmyra, 3595 ... D-15
Paris, 1220 ... D-14
Park Hills, 8759 ... I-17
Parkdale, 170 ... *K-3
Parkville, 5554 ... G-2
Parma, 713 ... L-19
Parnell, 191 ... B-9
Pasadena Hills, 930 ... *G-6
Pascola, 108 ... M-19
Passaic, 34 ... H-9
Patterson, 250 ... K-17
Patton, 120 ... J-18
Patton Jct., 90 ... J-18
Pattonsburg, 348 ... C-10
Paynesville, 77 ... E-16
Peace Valley ... L-15
Peach Orchard ... M-19
Peaksville, 30 ... B-15
Peculiar, 4608 ... F-9
PEMISCOT CO., 18296 ... M-19
Pennsboro, 30 ... J-10
Perry, 693 ... E-15
PERRY CO., 18971 ... I-19
Perryville, 8225 ... I-19
Pershing ... G-15
Peruque, 80 ... *E-2
PETTIS CO., 42201 ... G-11
Pevely, 5484 ... H-18
Phelps, 80 ... K-10
Phelps City, 24 ... B-7
PHELPS CO., 45156 ... J-14
Philadelphia, 265 ... D-15
Phillipsburg, 202 ... J-13
Pickering, 160 ... B-8
Piedmont, 1977 ... K-17
Pierce City, 1292 ... K-10
PIKE CO., 18516 ... E-16
Pilot Grv., 768 ... F-12
Pilot Knob, 746 ... I-17
Pine Crest, 40 ... K-15
Pine Lawn, 3275 ... *G-6
Pineville, 791 ... L-9
Pittsburg, 200 ... I-11
Pittsville, 80 ... F-10
Plad ... I-12
Plato, 109 ... J-14
Platte City, 4691 ... E-8
PLATTE CO., 89322 ... E-8
Platte Woods, 385 ... G-2
Plattsburg, 2319 ... D-9
Pleasant Hill, 8113 ... F-9
Pleasant Hope, 614 ... I-11
Pleasant Valley, 2961 ... G-5
Plevna, 21 ... C-14
Pocahontas, 114 ... *J-19
Pt. Lookout, 1200 ... *M-6
Pt. Pleasant ... M-20
POLK CO., 31137 ... I-11
Pollock, 89 ... B-12
Polo, 575 ... D-10
Pomona, 511 ... L-14
Pontiac, 175 ... M-13
Poplar Bluff, 17023 ... L-18
Portage Des Sioux, 328 ... *D-5
Portageville, 3228 ... M-19
Portland, 130 ... G-15
Post Oak ... G-10
Potosi, 2660 ... I-17
Pottersville ... L-14
Powe, 110 ... L-18
Powell, 85 ... L-9
Powersville, 60 ... B-12
Poynor, 100 ... L-17
Prairie City ... H-10
Prairie Hill, 90 ... D-13
Prairie Home, 280 ... F-13
Preston, 223 ... I-12
Princeton, 1166 ... B-11
Prosperity, 120 ... *A-8
PULASKI CO., 52274 ... I-14
Purdin, 190 ... C-12
Purdy, 1098 ... L-10
PUTNAM CO., 4979 ... B-12
Puxico, 881 ... K-18
Queen City, 598 ... B-13
Quincy ... H-11
Quitman, 45 ... B-8
Qulin, 458 ... L-18
Racine, 200 ... K-9
RALLS CO., 10167 ... E-15
Randles, 130 ... K-19
Randolph, 52 ... H-5
RANDOLPH CO., 25414 ... D-13
Ravanna, 98 ... B-11
Ravenwood, 440 ... B-9
RAY CO., 23494 ... E-10
Raymondville, 363 ... J-15
Raymore, 19206 ... F-9
Raytown, 29526 ... F-9
Rea, 50 ... C-8
Readsville ... F-15
Redford, 100 ... J-17
Reeds, 95 ... K-10
Reeds Spr., 913 ... L-11
Reger, 80 ... C-12
Renick, 172 ... E-13
Rensselaer, 228 ... D-15
Republic, 14751 ... K-11
Revere, 79 ... B-15
Reynolds, 100 ... J-16
REYNOLDS CO., 6696 ... J-16
Rhineland, 142 ... G-15
Rhyse ... J-15
Rich Fountain, 220 ... G-14
Rich Hill, 1396 ... H-9
Richards, 96 ... I-9
Richland, 1863 ... I-13
Richmond, 5797 ... E-10
Richmond Hts., 8603 ... *H-5
Richwoods, 300 ... H-17
Ridgedale, 450 ... M-12
Ridgely, 104 ... D-9
Ridgeway, 464 ... B-10
Ridgley, 120 ... L-10
RIPLEY CO., 14100 ... L-17
Risco, 346 ... L-19
Ritchey, 82 ... K-9
River Aux Vases, 110 ... I-18
River Bend, 10 ... G-6
Riverside, 2937 ... H-3
Riverview, 2856 ... *F-7
Riverview Estates, 82 ... F-9
Rives, 63 ... N-19
Roach, 200 ... I-12
Roads ... I-11
Roanoke, 30 ... E-13
Robertsville, 250 ... G-17
Roby, 150 ... J-14
Rocheport, 239 ... F-13
Rochester, 200 ... C-9
Rock Hill, 4635 ... *I-5
Rock Port, 1318 ... B-7
Rockbridge ... L-13
Rockville, 166 ... H-10
Rocky Comfort, 190 ... L-10
Rocky Mount, 130 ... H-13
Rogersville, 3073 ... K-12
Rolla, 19559 ... I-15
Roscoe, 124 ... I-10
Rosebud, 409 ... G-15
Roselle, 60 ... J-17
Rosendale, 143 ... C-8
Rothville, 99 ... D-12
Round Spr. ... J-15
Rover ... L-15
Rush Hill, 151 ... E-15
Rushville, 303 ... D-8
Russellville, 807 ... G-13
Rutledge, 109 ... B-14
Sabula, 50 ... J-17
Saginaw, 297 ... K-9
St. Ann, 13020 ... *G-4
St. Anthony, 130 ... H-14
St. Catharine, 90 ... C-12
St. Charles, 65794 ... F-17
ST. CHARLES CO., 360485 ... G-16
St. Clair, 4724 ... H-16
ST. CLAIR CO., 9805 ... H-10
St. Clement, 78 ... E-16
St. Elizabeth, 336 ... H-14
ST. FRANCOIS CO., 65359 ... I-18
St. Francisville, 179 ... B-15
St. George, 1337 ... *J-5
St. James, 4216 ... H-15
St. Johns, 6517 ... *G-5
St. Joseph, 76780 ... D-8
St. Louis, 319294 ... G-18
ST. LOUIS CO., 998954 ... G-17
St. Martins, 1140 ... G-13
St. Mary, 360 ... I-19
St. Patrick, 30 ... B-15
St. Paul, 1829 ... F-17
St. Peters, 52575 ... F-17
St. Robert, 4340 ... I-14
St. Thomas, 263 ... G-14
Ste. Genevieve, 4410 ... H-18
STE. GENEVIEVE CO., 18145 ... I-18
Salcedo, 90 ... K-19
Salem, 4950 ... I-15
SALINE CO., 23370 ... F-11
Salisbury, 1618 ... E-12
Sandy Hook ... F-13
Santa Fe, 100 ... E-15
Santa Rosa ... C-10
Sappington, 7580 ... *J-5
Sarcoxie, 1330 ... K-10
Savannah, 5057 ... C-8
Saverton, 80 ... D-16
Schell City, 249 ... H-10
SCHUYLER CO., 4431 ... B-13
Scopus, 160 ... J-19
SCOTLAND CO., 4843 ... B-14
Scott City, 4565 ... J-20
SCOTT CO., 39191 ... K-20
Sedalia, 21387 ... G-12
Sedgewickville, 173 ... J-19
Seligman, 851 ... L-10
Senath, 1767 ... M-18
Seneca, 2336 ... L-9
Seymour, 1921 ... K-13
SHANNON CO., 8441 ... K-15
Shaw, 80 ... F-14
Shelbina, 1704 ... D-14
SHELBY CO., 6373 ... D-14
Shelbyville, 552 ... D-14
Sheldon, 543 ... I-9
Shell Knob, 1379 ... L-11
Sheridan, 195 ... B-9
Shirley, 120 ... I-17
Shoal Creek Drive, 337 ... *C-6
Shrewsbury, 6254 ... *I-5
Sikeston, 16318 ... K-19
Silex, 187 ... E-16
Silva, 300 ... K-18
Silver Creek, 623 ... *C-7
Silver Lake, 30 ... I-19
Simmons, 30 ... K-14
Skidmore, 284 ... B-8
Slater, 1856 ... E-12
Sleeper, 100 ... I-13
Smithton, 570 ... G-12
Smithville, 8425 ... E-9
S. Fork, 241 ... L-14
S. Lineville, 28 ... B-11
S. Shore, 200 ... F-17
South West City, 970 ... L-9
Spanish Lake, 19650 ... *F-6
Sparta, 1756 ... K-12
Spencerburg ... E-15
Spickard, 254 ... B-11
Spokane, 177 ... L-11
Springfield, 159498 ... K-11
Springhill ... C-11
Spruce, 80 ... H-10
Squires, 110 ... L-13
Stanberry, 1185 ... B-9
Stanton, 200 ... H-16
Stark ... E-16
Stark City, 139 ... L-9
Steedman, 135 ... G-15
Steele, 2172 ... N-19
Steelville, 1642 ... I-16
Steffenville, 30 ... C-14
Stella, 158 ... L-9
Stephens, 140 ... F-14
Stet, 30 ... E-11
Stewartsville, 750 ... D-9
Stockton, 1819 ... I-10
STODDARD CO., 29968 ... L-19
STONE CO., 32202 ... L-11
Stony Hill, 90 ... G-16
Stotesbury, 18 ... I-9
Stotts City, 220 ... K-10
Stoutland, 192 ... I-13
Stoutsville, 36 ... D-14
Stover, 1094 ... G-12
Strafford, 2358 ... J-12
Strain ... H-16
Strasburg, 141 ... F-10
Sturdivant, 100 ... K-18
Sturgeon, 872 ... E-14
Sublette, 30 ... B-13
Success ... J-14
Sugar Creek, 3345 ... I-5
Sullivan, 7081 ... H-16
SULLIVAN CO., 6714 ... B-12
Summersville, 502 ... K-15
Sumner, 102 ... D-12
Sunnyvale ... *C-6
Sunrise Bch., 431 ... H-13
Sunset Hills, 8496 ... *J-4
Swedeborg, 200 ... I-13
Sweet Sprs., 1484 ... F-11
Swiss ... G-15
Sycamore Hills, 668 ... *G-5
Syracuse, 172 ... G-12
Tallapoosa, 168 ... L-19
TANEY CO., 51675 ... L-12
Taneyville, 396 ... L-12
Taos, 878 ... G-14
Tarkio, 1583 ... B-7
Taylor, 150 ... C-15
Tebbetts, 170 ... G-14
Tecumseh, 100 ... L-14
Teresita, 100 ... K-15
TEXAS CO., 26008 ... K-14
Thayer, 2243 ... L-15
Theodosia, 243 ... L-13
Thomasville, 68 ... L-15
Thompson, 200 ... E-14
Thornfield, 80 ... L-13
Tiff City, 120 ... L-9
Tiffin, 80 ... I-10
Tightwad, 69 ... H-11
Tina, 157 ... D-11
Tindall, 77 ... C-11
Tipton, 3262 ... G-13
Town & Country, 10815 ... *H-3
Tracy, 208 ... E-8
Treloar, 130 ... G-16
Trenton, 6001 ... C-11
Trimble, 646 ... D-9
Triplett, 41 ... D-12
Troy, 10540 ... F-16
Truxton, 91 ... F-16
Tuckahoe, 90 ... *A-6
Tunas ... I-12
Turney, 148 ... D-9
Tuscumbia, 203 ... H-13
Twin Oaks, 392 ... *I-3
Udall, 120 ... L-14
Union, 10204 ... G-16
Union City ... K-11
Union Star, 437 ... C-9
Unionville, 1865 ... B-12
Unity Vil., 99 ... K-6
University City, 35371 ... *H-5
Urbana, 417 ... I-12
Urich, 505 ... G-10
Utica, 270 ... D-11
Valles Mines, 500 ... H-17
Valley Pk., 6942 ... *J-3
Valley View, 300 ... K-11
Van Buren, 819 ... K-16
Vandalia, 3899 ... E-15
Vandiver, 71 ... E-15
Vanduser, 267 ... K-19
Vanzant, 80 ... K-14
Velda Vil., 1420 ... *G-6
Velda Vil. Hills, 1055 ... *G-6
Verdella ... I-9
VERNON CO., 21159 ... I-9
Verona, 619 ... K-10
Versailles, 2482 ... G-12
Vibbard, 210 ... E-10
Viburnum, 693 ... I-16
Vichy, 220 ... H-15
Vienna, 610 ... H-14
Villa Ridge, 2636 ... G-17
Vineland, 120 ... H-17
Vinita Pk., 1880 ... *G-5
Vinita Ter., 277 ... *G-5
Viola ... L-11
Virginia ... H-9
Vista, 54 ... H-11
Wainwright, 85 ... G-14
Wakenda ... E-11
Waldron, 200 ... E-8
Walker, 270 ... I-9
Wallace, 115 ... D-8
Walnut Grv., 665 ... J-11
Walnut Shade, 300 ... L-12
Wappapello, 150 ... K-18
Wardell, 427 ... M-19
Wardsville, 1506 ... G-14
Warren ... D-15
WARREN CO., 32513 ... F-16
Warrensburg, 18838 ... F-10
Warrenton, 7880 ... F-16
Warsaw, 2127 ... H-11
Warson Woods, 1962 ... *I-4
Washburn, 435 ... L-10
Washington, 13982 ... G-16
WASHINGTON CO., 25195 ... H-16
Wasola, 113 ... L-13
Watson, 100 ... B-7
Waverly, 849 ... E-11
Wayland, 533 ... B-15
WAYNE CO., 13521 ... K-18
Waynesville, 4830 ... I-14
Weatherby, 107 ... C-9
Weatherby Lake, 1723 ... G-2
Weaubleau, 418 ... I-11
Webb City, 10996 ... K-9
WEBSTER CO., 36202 ... J-12
Webster Groves, 22995 ... *I-5
Weingarten, 133 ... I-18
Weldon Spr., 5443 ... F-17
Weldon Spr. Hts., 91 ... *G-1
Wellington, 812 ... E-10
Wellston, 2313 ... *H-6
Wellsville, 1217 ... F-15
Wentworth, 147 ... K-10
Wentzville, 29070 ... F-17
Wesco ... I-15
W. Alton, 522 ... F-18
W. Line, 97 ... G-9
W. Plains, 11986 ... L-15
W. Quincy, 30 ... C-15
Westboro, 141 ... B-7
Weston, 1641 ... E-8
Westphalia, 389 ... G-14
Westview, 110 ... L-9
Westwood, 278 ... *H-4
Wheatland, 371 ... I-11
Wheaton, 696 ... L-10
Wheeling, 271 ... D-11
Whitakerville, 100 ... H-11
White Church ... L-15
White Oak, 50 ... M-19
Whiteside, 75 ... E-16
Whitesville, 80 ... C-9
Whitewater, 125 ... J-19
Whiting, 150 ... M-12
Wilbur Pk., 471 ... *I-6
Wilcox, 70 ... B-8
Wilderness ... L-16
Wildwood, 35517 ... G-17
Willard, 5288 ... J-11
Williamsburg, 100 ... F-15
Williamstown ... B-15
Williamsville, 342 ... K-17
Willmathsville ... B-13
Willow Sprs., 2184 ... K-14
Wilson City, 115 ... K-20
Wilton, 80 ... F-13
Winchester, 1547 ... *I-3
Winchester, 110 ... B-15
Windsor, 2901 ... G-11
Windyville ... I-12
Winfield, 1404 ... F-17
Winigan, 44 ... C-12
Winona, 1335 ... K-16
Winston, 259 ... C-10
Winthrop, 60 ... D-8
Wishart ... J-11
Wittenberg, 60 ... I-20
Wolf Island, 30 ... M-20
Wood Hts., 717 ... E-10
Woodlawn ... D-14
Woodson Ter., 4063 ... *G-5
Wooldridge, 61 ... F-13
Worth, 63 ... B-9
WORTH CO., 2171 ... B-9
Worthington, 81 ... B-13
Wright City, 3119 ... F-16
WRIGHT CO., 18815 ... J-13
Wyaconda, 227 ... B-14
Wyatt, 319 ... K-20
Yukon, 60 ... J-15
Zalma, 122 ... K-18

Montana

Page locator

Map keys	Atlas pages
1–10	122–123
11–20	124–125

Absarokee, 1150 ... I-11
Acton, 60 ... H-13
Agency, 355 ... C-11
Alberton, 420 ... F-3
Alder, 103 ... J-7
Alhambra ... G-7
Alpine ... I-11
Alzada, 29 ... J-20
Amsterdam, 180 ... H-8
Anaconda, 9298 ... H-6
Angela, 10 ... G-16
Antelope, 51 ... B-19
Arlee, 636 ... E-4
Armington, 75 ... E-9
Ashland, 824 ... I-17
Ashuelot, 40 ... E-8
Augusta, 309 ... E-7
Avon, 111 ... G-6
Babb, 174 ... B-5
Bainville, 208 ... C-20
Baker, 1741 ... G-20
Ballantine, 320 ... H-13
Bannack, 25 ... J-5
Basin, 212 ... H-7
Bearcreek, 79 ... J-12
BEAVERHEAD CO., 9246 ... K-6
Belfry, 218 ... J-12
Belgrade, 7389 ... I-8
Belknap, 158 ... D-2
Belle Creek, 20 ... J-18
Belt, 597 ... E-9
Benchland, 10 ... F-10
Benteen, 30 ... J-15
Biddle, 41 ... J-18
Big Arm, 177 ... D-4
BIG HORN CO., 12865 ... I-15
Big Sandy, 598 ... C-10
Big Sky, 2308 ... J-8
Big Timber, 1641 ... I-10
Bigfork, 4270 ... C-4
Bighorn, 15 ... H-15
Billings, 104170 ... I-13
Billings Hts., 6000 ... M-20
Birney, 137 ... J-16
Black Eagle, 904 ... E-8
Blackfoot, 80 ... B-6
BLAINE CO., 6491 ... B-12
Bloomfield, 15 ... E-18
Boneau, 380 ... C-11
Bonner, 200 ... F-4
Boulder, 1183 ... H-7
Box Elder, 87 ... C-10
Boyd, 35 ... J-12
Boyes, 25 ... J-19
Bozeman, 37280 ... I-9
Brady, 140 ... D-7
Bridger, 708 ... J-12
Broadus, 468 ... I-18
Broadview, 192 ... H-12
BROADWATER CO., 5612 ... G-8
Brockton, 255 ... C-18
Brockway, 35 ... E-17
Brooks ... F-11
Browning, 1016 ... B-6
Brusett ... E-15
Buffalo, 10 ... F-11
Busby, 745 ... I-15
Butte, 33525 ... H-6
Bynum, 31 ... D-7
Camas, 58 ... D-3
Cameron, 10 ... I-8
Camp Three, 173 ... G-13
Canyon Creek, 250 ... F-7
Canyon Ferry ... G-8
Capitol ... I-20
CARBON CO., 10078 ... J-12
Cardwell, 50 ... I-7
Carlton, 694 ... G-4
Carlyle ... F-20
Carter, 58 ... D-9
CARTER CO., 1160 ... I-19
Cartersville ... F-16
Cascade, 685 ... E-8
CASCADE CO., 81327 ... F-8
Cat Creek ... F-14
Centerville, 25 ... E-9
Charlo, 379 ... E-4
Charlos Hts., 120 ... H-4
Checkerboard, 20 ... G-10
Chester, 847 ... B-9
Chinook, 1203 ... B-12
Choteau, 1684 ... D-7
CHOUTEAU CO., 5813 ... D-10
Christina, 20 ... E-11
Churchill, 902 ... I-8
Circle, 615 ... E-17
Clancy, 1661 ... G-7
Clinton, 1052 ... F-4
Clyde Pk., 288 ... I-9
Coalridge ... B-19
Coffee Creek, 65 ... E-10
Cohagen, 15 ... F-16
Collins ... D-8
Colstrip, 2214 ... H-16
Columbia Falls, 4688 ... C-4
Columbia Hts., 110 ... C-4
Columbus, 1893 ... I-12
Condon, 343 ... E-5
Conner, 216 ... H-4
Conrad, 2570 ... C-7
Cooke City, 75 ... K-11
Coram, 539 ... C-4
Corbin ... G-7
Corvallis, 976 ... G-4
Corwin Sprs., 109 ... J-9
Craig, 43 ... F-7
Crane, 102 ... D-20
Creston, 70 ... C-4
Crow Agency, 1616 ... I-15
Culbertson, 714 ... C-19
Cushman ... H-12
Custer, 159 ... H-14
CUSTER CO., 11699 ... H-18
Cut Bank, 2869 ... B-7
Dagmar, 50 ... B-19
DANIELS CO., 1751 ... A-17
Darby, 720 ... H-4
DAWSON CO., 8966 ... E-18
Dayton, 84 ... D-4
De Borgia, 78 ... E-2
Decker, 20 ... K-16
Deer Lodge, 3111 ... G-6
DEER LODGE CO., 9298 ... H-5
Dell, 25 ... K-6
Delphia, 20 ... G-13
Denton, 255 ... E-10
Devon ... C-8
Dewey, 50 ... I-6
Dillon, 4134 ... I-6
Dixon, 203 ... E-4
Dodson, 124 ... C-13
Drummond, 309 ... G-5
Dunkirk, 10 ... C-8
Dupuyer, 86 ... C-6
Dutton, 316 ... D-8
E. Glacier Pk. Vil., 363 ... C-5
E. Helena, 1984 ... G-7
E. Missoula ... M-13
Edgar, 114 ... J-12
Ekalaka, 332 ... H-19
Elkhorn, 10 ... H-7
Elkhorn Hot Sprs., 60 ... J-5
Elliston, 219 ... G-6
Elmo, 180 ... D-4
Emigrant, 488 ... J-9
Ennis, 838 ... J-8
Essex, 30 ... C-5
Ethridge, 15 ... B-7
Eureka, 1037 ... A-3
Evaro, 322 ... F-4
Evergreen, 7616 ... C-4
Fairfield, 708 ... E-7
Fairview, 840 ... D-20
Fallon, 164 ... F-18
FALLON CO., 2890 ... G-19
Farmington ... D-7
Ferdig ... B-8
FERGUS CO., 11586 ... E-12
Fishtail, 85 ... J-11
FLATHEAD CO., 90928 ... D-5
Flaxville, 71 ... B-18
Florence, 765 ... G-4
Floweree, 25 ... D-9
Forest Pk. ... F-9
Forestgrove, 60 ... F-12
Forsyth, 1777 ... H-16
Ft. Belknap Agency, 1293 ... C-12
Ft. Benton, 1464 ... D-9
Ft. Kipp, 40 ... C-19
Ft. Peck, 233 ... C-16
Ft. Shaw, 280 ... E-8
Ft. Smith, 161 ... J-14
Fortine, 325 ... B-3
Four Buttes, 20 ... B-17
Four Corners, 3146 ... I-8
Fox Lake, 158 ... D-19
Frazer, 362 ... C-17
Frenchtown, 1825 ... F-4
Froid, 185 ... C-19
Fromberg, 438 ... J-12
Galata, 25 ... C-8
GALLATIN CO., 89513 ... J-8
Gallatin Gateway, 856 ... I-8
Gardiner, 875 ... K-9
GARFIELD CO., 1206 ... F-15
Garneill, 10 ... G-11
Garrison, 96 ... G-6
Garryowen, 60 ... I-15
Geraldine, 261 ... E-10
Geyser, 87 ... E-10
Gibson Flats, 100 ... N-17
Gildford, 179 ... B-10
GLACIER CO., 13399 ... B-6
Glasgow, 3250 ... C-16
Glen, 30 ... I-6
Glendive, 4935 ... F-19
Glentana, 10 ... B-16
Goldcreek, 10 ... G-6
GOLDEN VALLEY CO., 884 ... G-12
GRANITE CO., 3079 ... G-5
Grant, 25 ... K-5
Grantsdale, 175 ... H-4
Grass Range, 110 ... F-12
Great Falls, 58505 ... E-8
Greenough ... F-5
Greycliff, 112 ... I-11
Halfmoon, 100 ... M-1
Hall, 100 ... G-5
Hamilton, 4348 ... H-4
Hammond, 15 ... J-19
Happys Inn, 164 ... C-2
Hardin, 3505 ... I-14
Hardy ... F-8
Harlem, 808 ... B-12
Harlowton, 997 ... G-11
Harrison, 137 ... I-7
Hathaway, 30 ... H-17
Haugan, 90 ... E-2
Havre, 9310 ... B-11
Hays, 843 ... D-12
Heart Butte, 582 ... C-6
Helena, 28190 ... G-7
Helmville, 80 ... F-6
Heron, 282 ... C-1
Highwood, 176 ... E-9
Hilger, 40 ... E-11
HILL CO., 16096 ... B-10
Hingham, 118 ... B-10
Hinsdale, 217 ... C-15
Hobson, 215 ... F-11
Hogeland, 60 ... B-12
Holter Dam ... F-7
Homestead, 50 ... B-19
Hot Sprs., 544 ... D-3
Hungry Horse, 826 ... C-4
Huntley, 446 ... I-13
Huson, 210 ... F-3
Hysham, 312 ... H-15
Ingomar, 20 ... G-15
Inverness, 55 ... B-9
Ismay, 19 ... G-19
Jackson, 50 ... J-5
Jardine, 57 ... K-9
Jeffers, 80 ... J-8
Jefferson City, 472 ... G-7
JEFFERSON CO., 11406 ... H-7
Jefferson Island ... I-7
Joliet, 595 ... J-12
Joplin, 157 ... B-9
Jordan, 343 ... E-15
JUDITH BASIN CO., 2072 ... F-10
Judith Gap, 126 ... G-11
Kalispell, 19927 ... C-4
Kevin, 154 ... B-7
Kila, 392 ... C-3
Kinsey, 25 ... G-17
Kiowa ... B-5
Klein, 168 ... G-13
Kremlin, 98 ... B-10
LAKE CO., 28746 ... D-3
L. McDonald ... B-4
Lakeside, 2669 ... C-4
Lakeview, 10 ... L-7
Lambert, 160 ... D-19
Lame Deer, 2052 ... I-16
Landusky ... D-13
Larslan, 25 ... B-16
Laurel, 6718 ... I-12
Laurin, 60 ... J-7
Lavina, 187 ... H-12
Ledger, 25 ... C-8
LEWIS & CLARK CO., 63395 ... E-6
Lewistown, 5901 ... F-11
Libby, 2628 ... B-2
LIBERTY CO., 2339 ... B-9
Lima, 221 ... K-6
Lincoln, 1013 ... F-6
LINCOLN CO., 19687 ... B-2
Lindsay, 50 ... E-18
Livingston, 7044 ... I-9
Lloyd, 10 ... C-11
Lockwood, 6797 ... M-20
Lodge Grass, 428 ... J-15
Lodge Pole, 265 ... D-13
Logan, 99 ... I-8
Lohman ... B-11
Lolo, 3892 ... F-4
Lolo Hot Sprs., 10 ... F-3
Loma, 85 ... D-10
Lonepine, 162 ... D-3
Loring, 10 ... B-14
Lothair, 15 ... C-8
Lustre, 25 ... C-17
Luther ... J-11
MADISON CO., 7691 ... J-7
Madoc, 15 ... B-18
Maiden ... F-12
Malta, 1997 ... C-14
Manhattan, 1520 ... I-8
Marion, 886 ... C-3
Marsh ... F-19
Martin City, 500 ... C-4
Martinsdale, 64 ... G-10
Marysville, 80 ... G-7
Maudlow ... H-9
Maxville, 130 ... G-5
McAllister, 100 ... J-8
McCabe, 20 ... C-19
MCCONE CO., 1734 ... D-17
McLeod, 10 ... I-10
MEAGHER CO., 1891 ... F-8
Medicine Lake, 225 ... B-19
Melstone, 96 ... G-14
Melville, 20 ... H-10
Mildred, 30 ... G-19
Miles City, 8410 ... G-17
Milford Colony, 130 ... E-7
Miller Colony, 70 ... D-7
MINERAL CO., 4223 ... F-3
Missoula, 66788 ... F-4
MISSOULA CO., 109299 ... F-3
Moccasin, 35 ... F-11
Moiese, 10 ... E-4
Molt, 20 ... I-12
Monarch, 80 ... F-9
Monida, 10 ... L-7
Montague, 15 ... D-10
Montana City, 2715 ... G-7
Moore, 193 ... F-11
Mosby, 15 ... F-14
Muddy, 617 ... I-16
Musselshell, 60 ... G-13
MUSSELSHELL CO., 4538 ... G-13
Myers ... H-15
Nashua, 290 ... C-16
Neihart, 51 ... F-9
Niarada, 27 ... D-3
Norris, 60 ... I-8
Noxon, 218 ... C-1
Nye, 30 ... J-11
Oilmont, 35 ... B-8
Old Agency, 107 ... E-4
Olive ... I-18
Olney, 191 ... B-3
Opheim, 85 ... B-16
Orchard Homes, 5197 ... M-11
Oswego, 30 ... C-17
Otter ... J-17
Outlook, 47 ... A-19
Ovando, 81 ... F-5
Pablo, 2254 ... D-4
Paradise, 163 ... E-3
Park City, 983 ... I-12
PARK CO., 15636 ... J-10
Peerless, 70 ... B-17
Pendroy, 35 ... C-7
Perma ... E-3
PETROLEUM CO., 494 ... E-13
Philipsburg, 820 ... G-5
PHILLIPS CO., 4253 ... C-13
Pine Creek ... J-9
Pinesdale, 917 ... G-4
Pinnacle, 15 ... C-5
Plains, 1048 ... E-3
Plentywood, 1734 ... B-19
Plevna, 162 ... G-19
Polaris, 10 ... J-5
Polebridge, 30 ... B-4
Polson, 4488 ... D-4
Pompeys Pillar, 70 ... H-14
PONDERA CO., 6153 ... C-8
Pony, 118 ... I-7
Poplar, 810 ... C-18
Portage ... D-9
Potomac, 30 ... F-5
POWDER RIVER CO., 1743 ... J-17
Powderville, 10 ... I-18
POWELL CO., 7027 ... G-6
Power, 179 ... D-8
PRAIRIE CO., 1179 ... F-17
Pray, 681 ... J-9
Proctor, 75 ... D-4
Pryor, 618 ... J-13
Radersburg, 60 ... H-8
Rapelje, 225 ... H-12
Ravalli, 76 ... E-4
RAVALLI CO., 40212 ... I-4
Raymond, 10 ... A-19
Raynesford, 50 ... E-9
Red Lodge, 2125 ... J-12
Redstone, 50 ... B-18
Reed Pt., 193 ... I-11
Reserve, 23 ... B-19
Rexford, 105 ... A-2
Richey, 177 ... D-18
Richland, 60 ... B-17
RICHLAND CO., 9746 ... D-19
Rimini ... G-7
Ringling, 60 ... H-9
Riverbend, 484 ... E-3
Roberts, 361 ... J-12
Rock Sprs., 20 ... F-16
Rockvale ... I-12
Rollins, 209 ... D-4
Ronan, 1871 ... E-4
ROOSEVELT CO., 10425 ... C-19
Roscoe, 15 ... J-11
Rosebud, 111 ... H-16
ROSEBUD CO., 9233 ... G-16
Roundup, 1788 ... G-13
Roy, 108 ... E-12
Rudyard, 258 ... B-10
Ryegate, 245 ... H-12
Saco, 197 ... C-15
Saddle Butte, 128 ... B-11
St. Ignatius, 842 ... E-4
St. Labre Mission, 400 ... I-16
St. Marie, 264 ... C-16
St. Mary, 20 ... B-5
St. Regis, 319 ... E-2
St. Xavier, 83 ... J-14
Saltese, 40 ... E-2
Sand Coulee, 212 ... E-8
Sand Sprs., 20 ... F-14
Sanders, 20 ... H-15
SANDERS CO., 11413 ... D-2
Santa Rita, 113 ... B-7
Sapphire Vil., 50 ... F-10
Savage, 320 ... E-19
Scobey, 1017 ... B-18
Sedan, 99 ... H-9
Seeley Lake, 1659 ... E-5
Shawmut, 42 ... H-11
Shelby, 3376 ... B-8
Shepherd, 516 ... H-13
Sheridan, 642 ... J-7
SHERIDAN CO., 3384 ... B-19
Sidney, 5191 ... D-20
Silesia, 96 ... I-12
SILVER BOW CO., 34200 ... H-6
Silver Gate, 20 ... K-10
Silver Star, 100 ... I-7
Simms, 354 ... E-7
Simpson ... A-10
Somers, 1109 ... C-4
Sonnette ... J-17
Springdale, 42 ... I-10
Square Butte, 25 ... E-10
Stanford, 401 ... F-10
Starr School, 252 ... B-6
Stevensville, 1809 ... G-4
STILLWATER CO., 9117 ... H-12
Stockett, 169 ... E-9
Stryker, 26 ... B-3
Suffolk, 15 ... E-11
Sula, 37 ... I-4
Sumatra ... G-14
Summit ... M-3
Sun Prairie ... D-14
Sun River, 124 ... E-8
Sunburst, 375 ... B-7
Superior, 812 ... E-3
Swan Lake, 113 ... D-4
Sweet Grass, 58 ... A-7
SWEET GRASS CO., 3651 ... J-10
Sylvanite, 103 ... B-1
Tampico, 15 ... C-15
Teigen, 10 ... F-13
Terry, 605 ... F-18
TETON CO., 6073 ... D-6
Thompson Falls, 1313 ... D-2
Three Forks, 1869 ... I-8
TOOLE CO., 5324 ... B-8
Toston, 108 ... H-8
Townsend, 1878 ... H-8
Tracy, 225 ... E-9
TREASURE CO., 718 ... H-15
Trego, 541 ... B-3
Trident, 15 ... H-8
Trout Creek, 242 ... D-2
Troy, 938 ... B-1
Turah, 306 ... F-4
Turner, 61 ... B-13
Twin Bridges, 375 ... I-7
Twodot, 35 ... G-10
Ulm, 738 ... E-8
Valier, 509 ... C-7
VALLEY CO., 7369 ... B-15
Vananda ... G-15
Vandalia, 20 ... C-15
Vaughn, 658 ... E-8
Victor, 745 ... G-4
Vida, 50 ... D-18
Virgelle ... D-10
Virginia City, 190 ... J-7
Volborg ... H-17
Wagner ... C-13
Walkerville, 675 ... H-6
Washoe ... J-12
Waterloo, 50 ... I-7
Weeksville, 83 ... E-2
W. Glacier, 227 ... B-4
W. Riverside, 800 ... F-4
W. Yellowstone, 1271 ... K-9
Westby, 168 ... A-20
WHEATLAND CO., 2168 ... G-11
White Haven, 577 ... C-2
White Pine ... D-2
White Sulphur Sprs., 939 ... G-9
Whitefish, 6357 ... C-4
Whitehall, 1038 ... I-7
Whitetail, 110 ... A-18
Whitewater, 64 ... B-14
Whitlash, 35 ... B-8
Wibaux, 589 ... F-20
WIBAUX CO., 1017 ... E-20
Wickes, 30 ... G-7
Willard ... H-20
Willow Creek, 210 ... I-8
Wilsall, 178 ... H-9
Windham, 35 ... F-10
Winifred, 208 ... E-11
Winnett, 182 ... F-13
Winston, 147 ... G-8
Wisdom, 98 ... I-5
Wise River, 60 ... I-6
Wolf Creek, 150 ... F-7
Wolf Pt., 2621 ... C-17
Woods Bay, 661 ... D-4
Woodside ... G-4
Worden, 577 ... H-13
Wornath, 5197 ... N-11
Wyola, 215 ... J-15
Yaak, 248 ... A-2
YELLOWSTONE CO., 147972 ... H-13
York ... G-8
Zortman, 69 ... D-13
Zurich, 50 ... B-12

Nebraska

Page locator

Map keys	Atlas pages
1–10	126–127
11–20	128–129

Abie, 69 ... I-17
Adams, 573 ... L-18
ADAMS CO., 31364 ... L-13
Agnew, 60 ... J-17
Ainsworth, 1728 ... F-10
Albion, 1650 ... H-14
Alda, 642 ... K-13
Alexandria, 177 ... M-16
Allen, 377 ... F-17
Alliance, 8491 ... G-3
Alma, 1133 ... M-11
Almeria ... H-11
Aloys ... H-17
Alvo, 132 ... K-18
Amelia, 30 ... G-12
Ames, 24 ... I-17
Amherst, 248 ... K-11
Angora, 20 ... H-3
Angus, 40 ... M-14
Anoka, 6 ... E-12
Anselmo, 145 ... I-10
Ansley, 441 ... J-11
ANTELOPE CO., 6685 ... G-14
Antioch ... G-4
Arapahoe, 1026 ... M-10
Arcadia, 311 ... I-12
Archer, 81 ... J-14
Arlington, 1243 ... I-18
Arnold, 597 ... I-9
Arthur, 117 ... I-6
ARTHUR CO., 460 ... I-5
Ashby, 100 ... G-5
Ashland, 2453 ... J-18
Ashton, 194 ... J-12
Assumption, 30 ... L-13
Atkinson, 1245 ... F-12
Atlanta, 131 ... L-11
Auburn, 3460 ... L-19
Aurora, 4479 ... K-14
Avoca, 242 ... K-19
Axtell, 726 ... L-12
Ayr, 94 ... L-13
Bancroft, 495 ... G-17
BANNER CO., 690 ... I-1
Barada, 24 ... M-20
Barneston, 116 ... M-18
Bartlett, 117 ... H-13
Bartley, 283 ... M-9
Bassett, 619 ... F-11
Battle Creek, 1207 ... G-15
Bayard, 1209 ... H-2
Bazile Mills, 29 ... F-14
Beatrice, 12459 ... M-17
Beaver City, 609 ... M-10
Beaver Crossing, 403 ... K-16
Bee, 191 ... J-16
Beemer, 678 ... H-17
Belden, 115 ... F-16
Belgrade, 126 ... I-14
Bellevue, 50137 ... J-19
Bellwood, 435 ... I-16
Belvidere, 48 ... M-15
Benedict, 234 ... J-15
Benkelman, 953 ... M-6
Bennet, 719 ... K-18
Bennington, 1458 ... I-18
Benson ... B-18
Berea, 41 ... G-3
Bertrand, 750 ... L-11
Berwyn, 83 ... I-11
Big Sprs., 400 ... J-5
Bingham, 40 ... G-5
Bladen, 237 ... M-13
BLAINE CO., 478 ... H-9
Blair, 7990 ... I-18
Bloomfield, 1028 ... F-15
Bloomington, 103 ... M-12
Blue Hill, 936 ... M-13
Blue Sprs., 331 ... M-17
Boelus, 189 ... J-13
Boone, 20 ... I-14
BOONE CO., 5505 ... H-14
Bow Valley, 116 ... E-16
BOX BUTTE CO., 11308 ... G-2
BOYD CO., 2099 ... E-13
Boys Town, 745 ... J-18
Bradshaw, 273 ... K-15
Brady, 428 ... J-9
Brainard, 330 ... J-16
Brandon, 10 ... K-5
Brewster, 17 ... H-10
Bridgeport, 1545 ... H-3
Bristow, 65 ... E-13
Broadwater, 128 ... I-3
Brock, 112 ... L-19
Broken Bow, 3559 ... I-10
BROWN CO., 3145 ... F-10
Brownlee, 15 ... G-8
Brownson, 20 ... J-3
Brownville, 132 ... L-20
Brule, 326 ... J-5
Bruning, 279 ... L-15
Bruno, 99 ... J-17
Brunswick, 138 ... F-14
BUFFALO CO., 46102 ... K-12
Burchard, 82 ... M-18
Burr, 57 ... L-18
BURT CO., 6858 ... H-18
Burton, 10 ... E-11
Burwell, 1210 ... H-12
Bushnell, 124 ... J-1
BUTLER CO., 8395 ... J-16
Butte, 326 ... E-12
Byron, 83 ... M-15
Cairo, 785 ... K-13
Callaway, 539 ... J-10
Cambridge, 1063 ... M-9
Campbell, 347 ... M-13
Carleton, 91 ... M-15
Carroll, 229 ... G-16
CASS CO., 25241 ... K-19
Cedar Bluffs, 610 ... I-17
CEDAR CO., 8852 ... F-16
Cedar Creek, 390 ... J-19
Cedar Rapids, 382 ... I-14
Center, 94 ... F-14
Central City, 2934 ... J-14
Ceresco, 889 ... J-17
Chadron, 5851 ... E-3
Chalco, 10994 ... D-16
Chambers, 268 ... G-12
Champion, 103 ... L-6
Chapman, 287 ... J-14
Chappell, 929 ... J-4
CHASE CO., 3966 ... L-5
CHERRY CO., 5713 ... F-7
Chester, 232 ... M-15
CHEYENNE CO., 9998 ... J-3
Clarks, 369 ... J-15
Clarkson, 658 ... H-16
Clatonia, 231 ... L-17
Clay Ctr., 760 ... L-14
CLAY CO., 6542 ... L-14
Clearwater, 419 ... G-14
Clinton, 41 ... E-4
Cody, 154 ... E-7
Coleridge, 473 ... F-16
COLFAX CO., 10515 ... I-16
Colon, 110 ... J-17
Colton ... J-3
Columbus, 22111 ... I-16
Comstock, 93 ... I-11
Concord, 166 ... F-16
Cook, 321 ... L-18
Cordova, 137 ... K-16
Cornlea, 36 ... H-15
Cortland, 482 ... L-17
Cotesfield, 46 ... I-13
Cowles, 30 ... M-13
Cozad, 3977 ... K-10
Crab Orchard, 38 ... L-18
Craig, 199 ... H-18
Crawford, 997 ... E-2
Creighton, 1154 ... F-14
Creston, 203 ... H-16
Crete, 6960 ... L-17
Crofton, 726 ... E-15
Crookston, 69 ... E-8
Crowell ... H-17
Culbertson, 595 ... M-8
CUMING CO., 9139 ... G-17
Curtis, 939 ... L-8
Cushing, 32 ... J-13
CUSTER CO., 10939 ... J-10
Dakota City, 1919 ... F-18
DAKOTA CO., 21006 ... F-17
Dalton, 315 ... I-3
Danbury, 101 ... M-9
Dannebrog, 303 ... J-13
Darr ... K-10
Davenport, 294 ... M-15
Davey, 154 ... J-17
David City, 2906 ... J-16
DAWES CO., 9182 ... E-2
Dawson, 146 ... M-19
DAWSON CO., 24326 ... K-10
Daykin, 166 ... L-16
De Soto, 30 ... I-19
De Witt, 513 ... L-17
Decatur, 481 ... G-18
Denton, 190 ... K-17
Deshler, 747 ... M-15
DEUEL CO., 1941 ... J-4
Deweese, 67 ... L-14
Dickens ... K-7
Diller, 260 ... M-17
Dix, 255 ... J-2
Dixon, 87 ... F-16
DIXON CO., 6000 ... F-16
Dodge, 612 ... H-17
DODGE CO., 36691 ... I-17
Doniphan, 829 ... K-13
Dorchester, 586 ... K-16
Douglas, 173 ... L-18
DOUGLAS CO., 517110 ... I-18
Du Bois, 147 ... M-19
Dunbar, 187 ... K-19
Duncan, 351 ... I-15
DUNDY CO., 2008 ... M-6
Dunning, 103 ... H-9
Dwight, 204 ... J-16
Eagle, 1024 ... K-18
E. Omaha ... B-19
Eddyville, 97 ... K-10
Edgar, 498 ... L-14
Edison, 133 ... M-10
Elba, 215 ... J-13
Elgin, 661 ... H-14
Elk City, 50 ... I-18
Elk Creek, 98 ... M-19
Ellis, 70 ... M-17
Ellsworth, 30 ... G-5
Elm Creek, 901 ... K-11
Elmwood, 634 ... K-18
Elsie, 106 ... K-6
Elsmere, 30 ... G-9
Elwood, 707 ... L-10
Elyria, 51 ... H-12
Emerald, 170 ... K-17
Emerson, 840 ... G-17
Emmet, 48 ... F-12
Enders, 42 ... L-6
Endicott, 132 ... M-16
Enola, 40 ... H-15
Ericson, 92 ... H-13
Eustis, 401 ... L-10
Ewing, 387 ... G-13
Exeter, 591 ... L-15
Fairbury, 3942 ... M-16
Fairfield, 387 ... L-14
Fairmont, 560 ... L-15
Falls City, 4325 ... M-20
Farnam, 171 ... K-9
Farwell, 122 ... J-13
Filley, 132 ... M-18
FILLMORE CO., 5890 ... L-15
Firth, 590 ... L-17
Florence ... A-18
Fontanelle, 54 ... I-18
Fordyce, 139 ... E-16
Ft. Calhoun, 908 ... I-19
Ft. Robinson, 60 ... E-2
Foster, 51 ... G-15
Franklin, 1000 ... M-12
FRANKLIN CO., 3225 ... M-12
Fremont, 26397 ... I-18
Friend, 1027 ... K-16
FRONTIER CO., 2756 ... L-8
Fullerton, 1307 ... I-14
Funk, 194 ... L-11
FURNAS CO., 4959 ... M-9
GAGE CO., 22311 ... L-17
Gandy, 32 ... J-9
GARDEN CO., 2057 ... I-4
GARFIELD CO., 2049 ... H-12
Garland, 216 ... K-17
Garrison, 54 ... I-16
Gates ... I-10
Geneva, 2217 ... L-15
Genoa, 1003 ... I-15
Gering, 8500 ... H-1
Gibbon, 1833 ... K-12
Gilead, 39 ... M-16
Giltner, 352 ... K-14
Gladstone, 30 ... M-16
Glenvil, 310 ... L-14
Glenwood Pk., 250 ... K-12
Goehner, 154 ... K-16
Gordon, 1612 ... E-5
GOSPER CO., 2044 ... L-10
Gothenburg, 3574 ... K-9
Grafton, 126 ... L-15
Grainton, 25 ... K-7
Grand Island, 48520 ... K-13
Grant, 1165 ... K-6
GRANT CO., 614 ... H-5
Greeley, 466 ... I-13
GREELEY CO., 2538 ... I-13
Greenwood, 568 ... J-18
Gresham, 223 ... J-16
Gretna, 4441 ... J-18
Gross, 2 ... E-13
Guide Rock, 225 ... M-14
Gurley, 214 ... J-3
Hadar, 293 ... G-15
Haigler, 158 ... M-5
HALL CO., 58607 ... J-13
Hallam, 213 ... L-17
Halsey, 76 ... H-9
HAMILTON CO., 9124 ... K-14
Hamlet, 57 ... L-7
Hampton, 423 ... K-14
Hansen, 50 ... K-13
Harbine, 49 ... M-17
Hardy, 159 ... M-14
HARLAN CO., 3423 ... M-11
Harrisburg, 100 ... I-1
Harrison, 251 ... E-1
Hartington, 1554 ... F-16
Harvard, 1013 ... L-14
Hastings, 24907 ... L-13
Hay Sprs., 570 ... E-4
Hayes Ctr., 214 ... L-7
HAYES CO., 967 ... L-7
Hazard, 70 ... K-11
Heartwell, 71 ... L-12
Hebron, 1579 ... M-15
Hemingford, 803 ... F-3
Henderson, 991 ... K-15
Hendley, 24 ... M-10
Henry, 106 ... G-1
Herman, 268 ... H-18
Hershey, 665 ... J-7
Hickman, 1657 ... L-17
Hildreth, 378 ... M-12
HITCHCOCK CO., 2908 ... M-7
Holbrook, 207 ... M-10
Holdrege, 5495 ... L-11
Holmesville, 51 ... M-17
Holstein, 214 ... L-13
HOLT CO., 10435 ... F-12
Homer, 549 ... F-18
HOOKER CO., 736 ... H-7
Hooper, 830 ... I-17
Hordville, 144 ... J-14
Hoskins, 285 ... G-16
HOWARD CO., 6274 ... J-13
Howe, 30 ... L-19
Howells, 561 ... H-16
Hubbard, 236 ... F-17
Hubbell, 68 ... M-15
Humboldt, 877 ... M-19
Humphrey, 760 ... H-15
Huntley, 44 ... M-11
Hyannis, 182 ... G-6
Imperial, 2071 ... L-6
Inavale, 117 ... M-13
Indianola, 584 ... M-9
Inglewood, 325 ... I-18
Inland, 62 ... L-14
Inman, 129 ... F-13
Irvington, 150 ... B-17
Ithaca, 148 ... J-18
Jackson, 223 ... F-17
Jamison ... E-11
Jansen, 118 ... M-16
JEFFERSON CO., 7547 ... M-16
Johnson, 328 ... L-19
JOHNSON CO., 5217 ... L-18
Johnstown, 64 ... F-10
Julian, 59 ... L-19
Juniata, 755 ... L-13
Kearney, 30787 ... K-12
KEARNEY CO., 6489 ... L-12
KEITH CO., 8368 ... J-6
Kenesaw, 880 ... L-13
Kennard, 361 ... I-18
KEYA PAHA CO., 824 ... E-10
Keystone, 59 ... J-6
Kilgore, 77 ... E-8
Kimball, 2496 ... J-1
KIMBALL CO., 3821 ... J-1
KNOX CO., 8701 ... F-15
Kramer, 60 ... L-17
La Platte, 114 ... J-19
La Vista, 15758 ... D-17
Lakeside, 30 ... G-4
Lamar, 23 ... L-5
LANCASTER CO., 285407 ... K-17
Lanham, 30 ... M-17
Laurel, 964 ... F-16
Lawrence, 304 ... M-14
Lebanon, 80 ... M-9
Leigh, 405 ... H-16
Lemoyne, 82 ... J-6
Leshara, 112 ... I-18
Lewellen, 224 ... I-5
Lewiston, 68 ... M-18
Lexington, 10230 ... K-10
Liberty, 76 ... M-18
Lincoln, 258379 ... K-17
LINCOLN CO., 36288 ... K-8
Lindsay, 255 ... H-15
Lindy, 13 ... E-15
Linwood, 88 ... I-17
Lisco, 64 ... I-4
Litchfield, 262 ... J-12
Lodgepole, 318 ... J-4
LOGAN CO., 763 ... I-8
Loma, 30 ... J-17
Long Pine, 305 ... F-11
Loomis, 382 ... L-11
Lorenzo, 58 ... J-3
Loretto, 42 ... H-14
Lorton, 41 ... L-19
Louisville, 1106 ... J-18
Loup City, 1029 ... J-12
LOUP CO., 632 ... H-11
Lowell, 30 ... L-12
Lushton, 30 ... K-15
Lyman, 341 ... H-1
Lynch, 245 ... E-13
Lyons, 851 ... H-18
Macon, 30 ... M-12
Macy, 1023 ... G-18
Madison, 2438 ... H-15
MADISON CO., 34876 ... H-15
Madrid, 231 ... K-6
Magnet, 57 ... F-15
Malcolm, 382 ... K-17
Malmo, 120 ... I-17
Manley, 178 ... K-18
Marion, 40 ... M-9
Marquette, 229 ... J-14
Marsland, 10 ... F-2
Martell, 100 ... K-17
Martinsburg, 94 ... F-17
Mascot ... M-11
Maskell, 76 ... E-16
Mason City, 171 ... J-11
Max, 57 ... M-6
Maxwell, 312 ... J-8
Maywood, 261 ... L-8
McCook, 7698 ... M-8
McCool Jct., 409 ... K-15
McGrew, 105 ... H-2
McLean, 36 ... F-15
MCPHERSON CO., 539 ... I-7
Mead, 569 ... J-18
Meadow Grv., 301 ... G-15
Melbeta, 112 ... H-2
Memphis, 114 ... J-18
Menominee, 30 ... E-15
Merna, 363 ... I-10
MERRICK CO., 7845 ... J-14
Merriman, 128 ... E-6
Milburn ... H-10
Milford, 2090 ... K-16
Millard ... C-16
Miller, 136 ... K-11
Milligan, 285 ... L-16
Mills ... E-11
Minatare, 816 ... H-2
Minden, 2923 ... L-12
Mitchell, 1702 ... H-1
Monowi, 1 ... E-13
Monroe, 284 ... I-15
Moorefield, 32 ... K-9
Morrill, 921 ... G-1
MORRILL CO., 5042 ... H-3
Morse Bluff, 135 ... I-17
Mullen, 509 ... G-7
Murdock, 236 ... K-18
Murray, 463 ... K-19
Mynard, 60 ... J-19
NANCE CO., 3735 ... I-14
Naper, 84 ... E-12
Naponee, 106 ... M-12
Nebraska City, 7289 ... K-19
Nehawka, 204 ... K-19
Neligh, 1599 ... G-14
Nelson, 488 ... M-14
Nemaha, 149 ... L-20
NEMAHA CO., 7248 ... L-19
Nenzel, 20 ... E-7
Newcastle, 325 ... E-17
Newman Grv., 721 ... H-15
Newport, 97 ... F-11
Nickerson, 369 ... I-18
Niobrara, 370 ... E-14
Nora, 21 ... M-14
Norfolk, 24210 ... G-15
Norman, 43 ... L-12
N. Bend, 1177 ... I-17
N. Loup, 297 ... I-12
N. Platte, 24733 ... J-8
Northport, 80 ... H-3
NUCKOLLS CO., 4500 ... M-14
Oak, 66 ... M-15
Oakdale, 322 ... G-14
Oakland, 1244 ... H-18
Obert, 23 ... E-16
Oconto, 151 ... J-10
Octavia, 127 ... I-16
Odell, 307 ... M-17
Odessa, 130 ... K-11
Ogallala, 4737 ... J-6
Ohiowa, 115 ... L-16
Omaha, 408958 ... J-19
O'Neill, 3705 ... F-13
Ong, 63 ... L-15
Orchard, 379 ... F-14
Ord, 2112 ... I-12
Orleans, 386 ... M-11
Orum, 30 ... I-18
Osceola, 880 ... J-15
Oshkosh, 884 ... I-4
Osmond, 783 ... F-15
Otoe, 171 ... K-19
OTOE CO., 15740 ... K-18
Overton, 594 ... K-11
Oxford, 779 ... M-10
Page, 166 ... F-13
Palisade, 351 ... L-7
Palmer, 472 ... J-14
Palmyra, 545 ... K-18
Panama, 256 ... L-18
Papillion, 18894 ... J-19
Parks, 23 ... M-6
Paul ... L-19
Pauline, 60 ... L-13
Pawnee City, 878 ... M-19
PAWNEE CO., 2773 ... M-18
Paxton, 523 ... J-7
Pender, 1002 ... G-17
PERKINS CO., 2970 ... K-6
Peru, 865 ... L-19
Petersburg, 333 ... H-14
PHELPS CO., 9188 ... L-11
Phillips, 287 ... K-14
Pickrell, 199 ... L-17
Pierce, 1767 ... G-15
PIERCE CO., 7266 ... G-15
Pilger, 352 ... G-16
Plainview, 1246 ... F-15
Platte Ctr., 336 ... I-15
PLATTE CO., 32237 ... I-15
Plattsmouth, 6502 ... J-19
Pleasant Dale, 205 ... K-17
Pleasanton, 341 ... K-12
Plymouth, 409 ... M-17
Polk, 322 ... J-15
POLK CO., 5406 ... J-15
Ponca, 961 ... F-17
Poole, 19 ... K-12
Potter, 337 ... J-2
Powell, 20 ... M-16
Prague, 303 ... I-17
Prairie Home, 70 ... K-18
Preston, 28 ... M-20
Primrose, 61 ... I-14
Princeton, 50 ... L-17
Prosser, 66 ... K-13
Purdum, 20 ... G-9
Raeville, 22 ... H-14
Ragan, 38 ... M-11
Ralston, 5943 ... C-17
Randolph, 944 ... F-16
Ravenna, 1360 ... J-12
Raymond, 167 ... K-17
Red Cloud, 1020 ... M-13
RED WILLOW CO., 11055 ... M-8
Redington, 30 ... I-2
Republican City, 150 ... M-11
Reynolds, 69 ... M-16
RICHARDSON CO., 8363 ... M-20
Richland, 73 ... I-16
Ringgold ... I-8
Rising City, 374 ... J-16
Riverdale, 182 ... K-12
Riverton, 89 ... M-13
Roca, 220 ... K-17
ROCK CO., 1526 ... G-11
Rockford ... M-17
Rockville, 106 ... J-12
Rogers, 95 ... I-17
Rosalie, 160 ... G-17
Roscoe, 63 ... J-6
Rose, 10 ... G-11
Roseland, 235 ... L-13
Rosemont, 20 ... M-13
Royal, 63 ... F-14
Rulo, 172 ... M-20
Rushville, 890 ... E-4
Ruskin, 123 ... M-15
St. Bernard, 30 ... H-15
St. Edward, 705 ... I-14
St. Helena, 96 ... E-16
St. Libory, 264 ... J-13
St. Mary, 50 ... L-18
St. Paul, 2290 ... J-13
Salem, 112 ... M-20
SALINE CO., 14200 ... L-16
Santee, 346 ... E-14
Sarben, 31 ... J-7
Sargent, 525 ... I-11
Saronville, 47 ... L-14
SARPY CO., 158840 ... J-18
SAUNDERS CO., 20780 ... J-17
Schuyler, 6211 ... I-16
Scotia, 318 ... I-13
SCOTTS BLUFF CO., 36970 ... H-1
Scottsbluff, 15039 ... H-1
Scribner, 857 ... H-17
Seneca, 33 ... G-8
Seward, 6964 ... K-16
SEWARD CO., 16750 ... J-16
Shelby, 714 ... J-16
Shelton, 1059 ... K-13
SHERIDAN CO., 5469 ... F-4
SHERMAN CO., 3152 ... J-12
Shickley, 341 ... L-15
Sholes, 21 ... F-16
Shubert, 150 ... M-20
Sidney, 6757 ... J-3
Silver Creek, 362 ... J-15
SIOUX CO., 1311 ... F-1
Smithfield, 54 ... L-10
Snyder, 300 ... H-17
S. Bend, 99 ... J-18
S. Sioux City, 13353 ... F-18
S. Yankton, 50 ... E-15
Spalding, 487 ... H-13
Spencer, 455 ... E-13
Sprague, 142 ... L-17
Springfield, 1529 ... J-18
Springview, 242 ... E-10
Stamford, 183 ... M-11
Stanton, 1577 ... H-16
STANTON CO., 6129 ... H-16
Staplehurst, 242 ... K-16
Stapleton, 305 ... I-8
Steele City, 61 ... M-17
Steinauer, 75 ... M-18
Stella, 152 ... M-19
Sterling, 476 ... L-18
Stockham, 44 ... K-14
Stockville, 25 ... L-9
Strang, 29 ... L-15
Stratton, 343 ... M-7
Stromsburg, 1171 ... J-15
Stuart, 590 ... F-12
Sumner, 236 ... K-11
Sunol, 73 ... J-3
Superior, 1957 ... M-14
Surprise, 43 ... I-16
Sutherland, 1286 ... J-7
Sutton, 1502 ... L-15
Swanton, 94 ... L-16
Swedeburg, 40 ... J-17
Syracuse, 1942 ... K-18
Table Rock, 269 ... M-19
Talmage, 233 ... L-19
Tamora, 58 ... K-16
Tarnov, 46 ... I-15
Taylor, 190 ... H-11
Tecumseh, 1677 ... L-18
Tekamah, 1736 ... H-18
Telbasta ... I-18
Terrytown, 1198 ... H-1
Thayer, 62 ... K-15
THAYER CO., 5228 ... M-15
Thedford, 188 ... H-8
THOMAS CO., 647 ... H-8
Thompson ... M-16
Thurston, 132 ... G-17
THURSTON CO., 6940 ... G-17
Tilden, 953 ... G-15
Tobias, 106 ... L-16
Touhy, 30 ... J-17
Trenton, 560 ... M-7
Trumbull, 205 ... K-14
Tryon, 157 ... I-7
Uehling, 230 ... H-18
Ulysses, 171 ... J-16
Unadilla, 311 ... K-18
Union, 233 ... K-19
Upland, 143 ... M-12
Utica, 861 ... K-16
Valentine, 2737 ... E-8
Valley, 1875 ... I-18
VALLEY CO., 4260 ... I-12
Valparaiso, 570 ... I-17
Venango, 164 ... K-5
Venice, 75 ... I-18
Verdel, 30 ... E-14
Verdigre, 575 ... F-14
Verdon, 172 ... M-20
Virginia, 60 ... M-18
Waco, 236 ... K-15
Wahoo, 4508 ... J-17
Wakefield, 1451 ... G-17
Wallace, 366 ... K-7
Walthill, 780 ... G-18
Walton, 306 ... K-18
Wann, 86 ... I-18
Washington, 150 ... I-18
WASHINGTON CO., 20234 ... H-18
Waterbury, 73 ... F-17
Waterloo, 848 ... I-18
Wauneta, 577 ... L-6
Wausa, 634 ... F-15
Waverly, 3277 ... K-18
Wayne, 5660 ... G-16
WAYNE CO., 9595 ... G-16
WEBSTER CO., 3812 ... M-13
Weeping Water, 1050 ... K-18
Weissert, 30 ... I-11
Wellfleet, 78 ... K-8
Western, 235 ... L-16
Westerville, 39 ... I-11
Weston, 324 ... I-17
WHEELER CO., 818 ... H-13
Whiteclay, 10 ... D-4
Whitman, 140 ... G-6
Whitney, 77 ... E-2
Wilber, 1855 ... L-17

*, †, ‡, §, ◊ See explanation under state title in this index.
County and parish names are listed in capital letters & boldface type.
Independent cities (not included in a county) are listed in italics.

Nevada
Page locator
Map keys — Atlas pages
A–N 130–131
* City keyed to p. 30
† City keyed to pp. 132–133

New Hampshire
Page locator
Map keys — Atlas pages
A–N 132–133

New Jersey
Page locator
Map keys — Atlas pages
A–J 134–135
K–T 136–137
* City keyed to page 50
† City keyed to pp. 146–147
‡ City keyed to p. 148
§ City keyed to p. 182

New Mexico
Page locator
Map keys — Atlas pages
A–N 138–139

Glorieta, 430 .... D-6
Golden, 37 .... E-5
Gonzales Ranch, 40 .... E-6
Grady, 107 .... E-9
Gran Quivira F-5
GRANT CO., 29514 .... I-1
Grants, 9182 .... E-3
Greenfield, 150 .... H-8
Grenville, 38 .... B-9
GUADALUPE CO., 4687 .... E-7
Guadalupita, 250 .... C-7
Hachita, 49 .... K-2
Hagerman, 1257 .... H-8
Hanover, 167 .... I-2
HARDING CO., 695 .... C-9
Hatch, 1648 .... I-4
Hayden C-9
HIDALGO CO., 4894 .... K-1
High Rolls, 834 .... I-6
Hillsboro, 124 .... I-3
Hobbs, 34122 .... I-10
Holman, 250 .... C-6
Hondo, 250 .... H-7
Hope, 105 .... I-7
Hospah, 160 .... D-3
House, 68 .... F-9
Humble City, 50 .... I-10
Hurley, 1297 .... I-2
Ilfeld, 100 .... D-6
Isleta Pueblo E-4
Jal, 2047 .... J-10
Jarales, 2475 .... F-4
Jemez Pueblo, 1788 .... D-4
Jemez Sprs., 250 .... D-4
Kenna, 30 .... G-9
Kingston, 32 .... I-3
Kirtland, 7875 .... B-2
La Cienega, 3819 .... D-5
La Jara, 207 .... C-4
La Joya, 82 .... F-4
La Luz, 1697 .... I-6
La Mesa, 728 .... J-4
La Plata, 612 .... A-2
La Puebla, 1186 .... C-5
La Puente, 80 .... B-5
La Union, 1106 .... K-4
Laguna, 1241 .... E-3
L. Arthur, 436 .... I-8
L. Valley, 64 .... C-2
Lakewood, 100 .... I-8
LaMadera, 154 .... B-5
Lamy, 218 .... D-6
Las Cruces, 97618 .... J-4
Las Nutrias, 149 .... F-4
Las Palomas, 173 .... I-4
Las Vegas, 13753 .... D-7
LEA CO., 64727 .... H-9
Ledoux, 180 .... C-6
Lemitar, 330 .... G-4
Lincoln, 130 .... H-6
LINCOLN CO., 20497 .... G-6
Lindrith, 50 .... C-4
Lingo, 20 .... G-10
Loco Hills, 126 .... I-9
Logan, 1042 .... D-9
Lordsburg, 2797 .... J-1
Los Alamos, 12019 .... C-5
LOS ALAMOS CO., 17950 .... C-5
Los Cerrillos, 321 .... D-5
Los Chavez, 5446 .... F-4
Los Lunas, 14835 .... E-4
Los Montoyas D-7
Los Padillas, 2500 .... E-4
Los Pinos, 30 .... A-5
Los Ranchos de Albuquerque, 6024 .... L-8
Loving, 1413 .... J-8
Lovington, 11009 .... I-10
Luis Lopez, 107 .... G-4
Lumberton, 73 .... B-4
Luna, 158 .... G-1
LUNA CO., 25095 .... J-2
Madrid, 204 .... D-5
Magdalena, 938 .... G-4
Malaga, 147 .... J-8
Maljamar, 200 .... I-9
Manuelito D-1
Manzano, 29 .... F-5
Mariano Lake D-2
Maxwell, 254 .... B-8
Mayhill, 75 .... I-6
McAlister, 60 .... F-9
McCartys, 48 .... E-3
McDonald, 50 .... H-10
McIntosh, 1484 .... E-5
MCKINLEY CO., 71492 .... D-3
Melrose, 651 .... F-9
Mentmore, 200 .... D-1
Mescalero, 1338 .... H-6
Mesilla, 2196 .... J-4
Mesquite, 1112 .... J-4
Miami, 100 .... C-7
Midway, 971 .... H-8
Milan, 3245 .... E-3
Mills, 50 .... C-8
Milnesand, 30 .... G-10
Mimbres, 667 .... I-2
Mogollon, 60 .... H-1
Monero B-4
Montezuma, 200 .... D-7
Monticello, 60 .... H-3
Montoya, 30 .... E-8
Monument, 206 .... I-10
Mora, 656 .... C-6
MORA CO., 4881 .... C-7
Moriarty, 1910 .... E-5
Mosquero, 93 .... D-9
Mt. Dora, 100 .... B-9
Mountainair, 928 .... F-5
Mule Creek, 30 .... H-1
Nadine, 376 .... I-10
Nageezi, 286 .... C-3
Nara Visa, 95 .... D-10
Naschitti, 301 .... C-2
Navajo, 1645 .... C-1
Newcomb, 339 .... C-2
Newkirk, 7 .... E-8
Nogal, 96 .... H-6
Ocate, 50 .... C-7
Oil Ctr. I-10
Ojito B-4
Ojo Caliente, 350 .... C-5
Ojo Caliente E-1
Ojo Feliz, 80 .... C-7
Old Albuquerque M-8
Old Horse Sprs. G-2
Old Picacho, 200 .... M-1
Omega, 30 .... F-2
Organ, 323 .... J-5
Orogrande, 52 .... J-5
OTERO CO., 63797 .... I-6
Otis, 150 .... J-8
Paguate, 421 .... E-3
Paradise Hills, 4256 .... K-7
Paraje, 777 .... E-3
Pastura, 23 .... E-7
Pecos, 1392 .... D-6
Pena Blanca, 709 .... D-5
Penasco, 589 .... C-6
Pep, 30 .... G-10
Peralta, 3660 .... E-4
Petaca, 90 .... B-5
Picacho, 100 .... H-7
Pie Town, 186 .... F-2
Pilar, 80 .... C-6
Pinedale D-2
Pinon, 25 .... I-6
Pinos Altos, 198 .... I-2
Placitas, 4977 .... D-5
Playas, 74 .... J-1
Pleasanton, 106 .... H-1
Pojoaque Valley, 1907 .... C-5
Polvadera, 269 .... F-4
Portales, 12280 .... F-10
Prewitt, 460 .... D-2
Pueblo Pintado, 192 .... C-3
Puerto De Luna, 141 .... E-8
Punta de Agua, 30 .... F-5
QUAY CO., 9041 .... E-9
Quemado, 228 .... F-2
Questa, 1770 .... B-6
Radium Sprs., 1699 .... J-4
Rainsville, 150 .... C-7
Ramah, 370 .... E-2
Ranchos de Taos, 2518 .... C-6
Raton, 6885 .... B-8
Red Hill, 80 .... F-1
Red River, 477 .... B-6
Redrock, 50 .... I-1
Regina, 105 .... C-4
Reserve, 289 .... G-1
Ribera, 416 .... D-6
Rincon, 271 .... I-4
RIO ARRIBA CO., 40246 .... B-4
Rio Rancho, 87521 .... E-4
Riverside, 80 .... I-8
Rodeo, 101 .... K-1
Rogers, 50 .... G-10
Romeroville D-7
ROOSEVELT CO., 19846 .... G-9
Roswell, 48366 .... H-8
Rowe, 415 .... D-6
Roy, 234 .... C-8
Ruidoso, 8029 .... H-6
Ruidoso Downs, 2815 .... H-6
Rutheron, 100 .... B-5
Sabinoso D-8
Sacramento, 58 .... I-6
St. Vrain, 30 .... F-9
Salem, 942 .... I-4
San Antonio, 165 .... G-4
San Cristobal, 273 .... B-6
San Felipe Pueblo, 2404 .... D-5
San Ignacio D-6
San Jon, 216 .... E-9
San Juan I-3
SAN JUAN CO., 130044 .... B-2
San Juan Pueblo, 1143 .... C-5
San Lorenzo, 97 .... I-3
San Mateo, 161 .... D-3
San Miguel A-5
SAN MIGUEL CO., 29393 .... D-7
San Patricio, 200 .... H-7
San Rafael, 933 .... E-3
San Ysidro, 193 .... D-4
Sandia Pk., 237 .... E-5
SANDOVAL CO., 131561 .... C-4
Sanostee, 371 .... B-1
Santa Clara, 1686 .... I-2
Santa Fe, 67947 .... D-6
SANTA FE CO., 144170 .... D-5
Santa Rosa, 2848 .... E-7
Santa Teresa, 4258 .... K-4
Santo Domingo Pueblo, 2456 .... D-5
Sapello, 120 .... D-7
Seboyeta, 179 .... E-3
Sedan, 50 .... C-10
Seneca, 30 .... B-10
Serafina, 60 .... D-7
Seton Vil., 100 .... N-5
Sheep Sprs., 245 .... C-2
Shiprock, 8295 .... B-2
SIERRA CO., 11988 .... I-4
Silver City, 10315 .... I-2
Smith Lake, 200 .... D-2
Socorro, 9051 .... G-4
SOCORRO CO., 17866 .... G-5
Solano, 30 .... C-8
Springer, 1047 .... C-8
Standing Rock D-2
Stanley, 130 .... E-6
Sunland Pk., 14106 .... K-5
Sunspot, 70 .... I-6
Taiban, 40 .... F-8
Tajique, 130 .... E-5
Taos, 5716 .... B-6
TAOS CO., 32937 .... B-6
Taos Pueblo, 1135 .... B-6
Tatum, 798 .... H-10
Tecolotito, 232 .... E-7
Tererro, 80 .... D-6
Texico, 1130 .... F-10
Thoreau, 1865 .... D-2
Tierra Amarilla, 382 .... B-5
Tijeras, 541 .... E-5
Tinnie, 140 .... H-7
Toadlena, 200 .... C-1
Tohatchi, 808 .... C-1
Tolar F-9
Tome, 1867 .... E-4
TORRANCE CO., 16383 .... F-6
Torreon, 237 .... F-5
Tortugas, 500 .... N-2
Trementina, 80 .... D-8
Tres Piedras, 200 .... B-6
Truchas, 560 .... C-6
Truth or Consequences, 6475 .... H-4
Tucumcari, 5363 .... E-9
Tularosa, 2842 .... I-5
Turley B-3
Twin Lakes, 1052 .... D-1
Tyrone, 637 .... I-2
UNION CO., 4549 .... B-9
University Pk., 4192 .... J-4
Ute Pk., 71 .... B-7
Vado, 3194 .... J-4
Valdez, 180 .... B-6
Valencia, 2192 .... E-4
VALENCIA CO., 76569 .... F-4
Vallecitos, 140 .... B-5
Valmora, 30 .... D-7
Vanadium, 100 .... I-2
Vanderwagen, 300 .... D-1
Variadero, 50 .... D-8
Vaughn, 446 .... F-7
Veguita, 232 .... F-4
Velarde, 502 .... C-6
Villanueva, 229 .... E-6
Virden, 152 .... I-1
Wagon Mound, 314 .... C-7
Waterflow, 1670 .... B-2
Watrous, 135 .... D-7
Weed, 63 .... I-6
White Rock, 5725 .... D-5
White Sands, 1651 .... J-5
White Signal, 181 .... I-2
Whitehorse D-3
Whites City, 7 .... J-8
Willard, 253 .... F-5
Williamsburg, 449 .... H-4
Wimsatt, 150 .... I-6
Winston, 61 .... H-3
Yah-Ta-Hey, 590 .... D-1
Yeso, 10 .... F-8
Youngsville, 56 .... C-5
Zuni Pueblo, 6302 .... E-1

New York

Page locator

Map keys	Atlas pages
SA1–SJ14	140–141
NA1–NN10	142–143
NA11–NN20	144–145

* City keyed to pp. 146–147
† City keyed to pp. 148–149

Accord, 562 .... NN-17
Acra, 575 .... NL-18
Adams, 1775 .... NF-12
Adams Ctr., 1568 .... NF-12
Addison, 1763 .... NM-8
Adirondack, 200 .... NF-19
Adrian, 95 .... NL-8
Afton, 822 .... NL-14
Akron, 2868 .... NI-5
Alabama, 300 .... NI-5
Albany, 97856 .... NK-19
ALBANY CO., 304204 .... NK-18
Albertson, 5182 .... †G-17
Albia SI-6
Albion, 6056 .... NH-6
Alcove, 220 .... NK-18
Alden, 2605 .... NJ-5
Alden Manor .... †I-16
Alder Creek, 450 .... NH-14
Alexander, 509 .... NJ-5
Alexandria Bay, 1078 .... ND-12
Alfred, 4174 .... NL-7
Alfred Sta., 350 .... NL-7
Allegany, 1816 .... NM-5
ALLEGANY CO., 48946 .... NL-6
Allentown, 350 .... NM-6
Alligerville, 135 .... NN-18
Alloway, 100 .... NI-9
Alma, 225 .... NM-6
Almond, 466 .... NL-7
Alpine, 250 .... NL-10
Alps, 100 .... NK-20
Altamont, 1720 .... NJ-18
Altay, 100 .... NL-9
Altmar, 407 .... NG-12
Alton, 550 .... NH-9
Altona, 730 .... NB-19
Amagansett, 1165 .... SE-13
Amawalk, 1390 .... SD-7
Amber, 350 .... NJ-11
Amboy, 600 .... NF-7
Amboy Ctr. NH-12
Amenia, 955 .... NN-20
Ames, 145 .... NJ-16
Amherst, 45800 .... NI-4
Amity, 60 .... SD-5
Amityville, 9523 .... SJ-10
Amsterdam, 18620 .... NI-18
Ancram, 450 .... NM-19
Ancramdale, 500 .... NM-19
Andes, 252 .... NM-16
Andover, 1042 .... NM-7
Angelica, 869 .... NL-6
Angola, 2127 .... NK-3
Angola-on-the-Lake, 1675 .... NK-3
Annadale *M-6
Annandale-on-Hudson, 100 .... NM-18
Antwerp, 686 .... ND-13
Apalachin, 1131 .... NM-12
Appleton, 200 .... NH-4
Apulia Sta., 300 .... NJ-12
Arcade, 2071 .... NK-5
Arden, 100 .... SD-6
Argyle, 306 .... NH-20
Arkport, 844 .... NL-7
Arkville, 500 .... NM-16
Arlington, 4061 .... SB-7
Armonk, 4330 .... SD-7
Armor, 1550 .... NJ-4
Arthursburg, 215 .... SB-7
Arverne .... †L-14
Asharoken, 654 .... SE-9
Ashford, 70 .... NL-4
Ashville, 800 .... NM-2
Astoria .... †G-11
Athens, 1668 .... NL-19
Athol, 250 .... NG-18
Atlanta, 700 .... NK-8
Atlantic Bch., 1891 .... SG-7
Attica, 2547 .... NJ-5
Atwell, 20 .... NG-15
Au Sable Forks, 559 .... NC-19
Auburn, 27687 .... NJ-10
Auburndale .... †G-14
Augusta, 150 .... NI-14
Aurora, 724 .... NJ-10
Austerlitz, 400 .... NL-20
Ava, 300 .... NH-14
Averill Pk., 1693 .... NK-19
Avoca, 946 .... NL-8
Avon, 3394 .... NJ-7
Babylon, 12166 .... SJ-11
Bainbridge, 1355 .... NL-14
Baiting Hollow, 1642 .... SE-11
Bakers Mills, 280 .... NG-18
Baldwin, 24033 .... †J-18
Baldwin Hbr., 8102 .... †J-18
Baldwinsville, 7378 .... NI-11
Ballston Spa, 5409 .... NI-19
Balmat, 100 .... ND-14
Balmville, 3178 .... SB-6
Bangor, 300 .... NB-17
Barker, 533 .... NH-5
Barnes Cors., 150 .... NF-13
Barneveld, 284 .... NH-14
Barre Ctr., 160 .... NI-6
Barryville, 600 .... SC-3
Barton, 300 .... NM-11
Basom, 200 .... NI-5
Batavia, 15465 .... NI-6
Batchellerville, 70 .... NH-18
Bath, 5786 .... NL-8
Bath Bch. *K-10
Baxter Estates, 999 .... †E-16
Bay Pk., 2212 .... †J-17
Bay Ridge *K-9
Bay Shore, 26337 .... SF-9
Bayberry, 6200 .... ND-7
Baychester .... †D-13
Bayport, 8896 .... SJ-14
Bayside .... †G-15
Bayville, 6669 .... SE-8
Beach Ridge NB-4
Beacon, 15541 .... SC-6
Bearsville, 550 .... NM-18
Beaver Dams, 600 .... NL-9
Beaver Falls, 700 .... NF-14
Beaver Meadow, 100 .... NK-13
Bedford, 1834 .... SD-8
Bedford Hills, 3001 .... SD-7
Bedford-Stuyvesant .... †I-11
Beechhurst .... †F-14
Beekmantown, 300 .... NB-19
Belfast, 837 .... NL-6
Belfort, 50 .... NF-14
Belgium, 115 .... NI-11
Belle Terre, 792 .... SE-10
Bellerose, 1193 .... †H-16
Bellerose Ter., 2198 .... †H-16
Belleville, 226 .... NF-12
Bellmore, 16218 .... †I-20
Bellport, 2084 .... SF-10
Bellvale, 200 .... SD-5
Belmont, 969 .... NL-6
Bemis Hts., 115 .... NI-19
Bemus Pt., 364 .... NM-2
Bennettsburg, 110 .... NL-10
Bennington, 200 .... NJ-5
Benson, 100 .... NH-17
Benton Ctr., 220 .... NJ-9
Bergen, 1176 .... NI-6
Bergholtz, 700 .... NB-3
Berkshire, 350 .... NL-12
Berlin, 1200 .... NJ-20
Berne, 600 .... NK-18
Bernhards Bay, 400 .... NH-12
Bethany Ctr., 200 .... NJ-6
Bethel, 350 .... SB-3
Bethpage, 16429 .... †G-20
Big Flats, 5277 .... NM-9
Big Indian, 350 .... NM-17
Big Moose, 75 .... NF-15
Billings, 480 .... SB-7
Binghamton, 47376 .... NM-12
Birdsall, 50 .... NL-6
Black Brook, 200 .... NC-19
Black Creek, 250 .... NL-5
Black River, 1348 .... NE-13
Blasdell, 2553 .... NJ-4
Blauvelt, 5689 .... SE-7
Bleecker, 115 .... NI-17
Bliss, 527 .... NK-5
Blodgett Mills, 303 .... NK-12
Bloomfield, 1361 .... NJ-8
Bloomingburg, 420 .... SB-5
Bloomingdale, 600 .... ND-18
Bloomington, 800 .... NN-18
Bloomville, 213 .... NL-16
Blossvale, 300 .... NH-13
Blue Mtn. Lake, 220 .... NF-17
Blue Pt., 4773 .... SI-14
Blue Ridge NE-19
Boardwalk .... †L-13
Boght Cors., 1150 .... SG-5
Bohemia, 10180 .... SI-13
Boiceville, 800 .... NM-17
Bolivar, 1047 .... NM-6
Bolton, 300 .... NG-19
Bolton, 513 .... NG-19
Bombay, 300 .... NA-16
Boonville, 2072 .... NG-14
Borden, 40 .... NM-8
Border City, 250 .... NJ-9
Borodino, 100 .... NJ-11
Boston, 500 .... NK-4
Bouckville, 450 .... NJ-13
Bovina Ctr., 200 .... NL-16
Bowmansville, 600 .... NI-4
Braddock Hts., 700 .... NH-7
Bradford, 200 .... NL-9
Brainardsville, 250 .... NB-18
Branchport, 400 .... NK-9
Brant, 600 .... NK-3
Brant Lake, 850 .... NF-19
Brantingham, 500 .... NF-14
Brasher Ctr., 85 .... NB-16
Brasher Falls, 669 .... NB-16
Brasher Iron Works, 175 .... NB-16
Brasie Cors., 30 .... ND-13
Breakabeen, 80 .... NK-17
Breesport, 626 .... NM-10
Breezy Pt. .... †L-11
Brentwood, 60664 .... SF-9
Brewerton, 4029 .... NH-12
Brewster, 2390 .... SC-8
Briarcliff Mnr., 7867 .... SD-7
Bridgehampton, 1756 .... SE-13
Bridgeport, 1490 .... NI-12
Bridgewater, 470 .... NJ-14
Brier Hill, 400 .... NC-13
Brighton, 36609 .... NC-9
Brighton Bch. *L-10
Brightwaters, 3103 .... SJ-12
Brisben, 100 .... NL-13
Bristol, 100 .... NJ-8
Bristol Sprs., 120 .... NJ-8
Broad Channel .... †K-14
Broadacres, 1280 .... SA-11
Broadalbin, 1327 .... NI-17
Brockport, 8366 .... NH-6
Brocton, 1486 .... NL-2
BRONX CO., 1385108 .... *D-11
Bronxville, 6323 .... †B-13
Brookfield, 600 .... NJ-14
Brooktondale, 500 .... NL-11
Brookville, 3465 .... †E-19
BROOME CO., 200600 .... NM-12
Brownsville .... †J-12
Brownville, 1119 .... NE-12
Brunswick, 800 .... NJ-19
Brushton, 474 .... NB-16
Buchanan, 2230 .... SD-6
Bucks Br., 40 .... NB-15
Buffalo, 261310 .... NJ-4
Bullville, 900 .... SB-5
Burdett, 340 .... NL-10
Burke, 211 .... NB-17
Burlingham, 500 .... SB-5
Burlington Flats, 100 .... NJ-15
Burns, 150 .... NL-7
Burnt Hills, 1620 .... NJ-18
Burrs Mills, 100 .... NF-13
Burt, 400 .... NH-4
Burtonsville, 100 .... NJ-17
Bushnellsville, 200 .... NM-17
Bushwick .... †I-12
Busti, 391 .... NM-2
Byron, 400 .... NI-6
Cadosia, 300 .... NM-14
Cadyville, 900 .... NB-19
Cairo, 1402 .... NL-18
Calcium, 3491 .... NE-13
Caledonia, 2201 .... NI-7
Callicoon, 167 .... SA-2
Callicoon Ctr., 430 .... NN-15
Calverton, 6510 .... SE-11
Cambria Hts. .... †I-15
Cambridge, 1870 .... NI-20
Camden, 2231 .... NH-13
Cameron, 200 .... NM-8
Cameron Mills, 125 .... NM-8
Camillus, 1213 .... NI-11
Campbell, 713 .... NL-9
Campbell Hall, 650 .... SC-5
Campville, 350 .... NM-12
Canaan, 450 .... NL-20
Canajoharie, 2229 .... NJ-16
Canandaigua, 10545 .... NJ-8
Canarsie .... †J-12
Canaseraga, 550 .... NK-7
Canastota, 4804 .... NI-13
Candor, 851 .... NL-11
Caneadea, 500 .... NL-6
Canisteo, 2270 .... NL-7
Canton, 6314 .... NC-14
Cape Vincent, 726 .... NE-11
Cardiff, 150 .... NJ-12
Carle Pl., 4981 .... †G-18
Carlisle, 700 .... NJ-17
Carmel, 3600 .... SC-7
Caroga Lake, 518 .... NI-17
Caroline, 70 .... NL-11
Carrollton, 100 .... NM-4
Carthage, 3747 .... NE-13
Cassadaga, 634 .... NL-2
Cassville, 250 .... NJ-14
Castile, 1015 .... NK-6
Castle Creek, 400 .... NL-12
Castleton Corners *K-7
Castleton-on-Hudson, 1473 .... NK-19
Castorland, 351 .... NF-14
Catharine, 100 .... NL-10
Cato, 532 .... NI-10
Caton, 150 .... NM-9
Catskill, 4081 .... NL-19
Cattaraugus, 1002 .... NL-4
CATTARAUGUS CO., 80317 .... NL-4
Caughdenoy, 150 .... NH-12
Cayuga, 549 .... NJ-10
CAYUGA CO., 80026 .... NI-10
Cayuga Hts., 3729 .... NK-11
Cayuta, 200 .... NL-10
Cazenovia, 2835 .... NJ-13
Cedar Hill, 300 .... NK-19
Cedarhurst, 6592 .... †K-16
Cedarville, 200 .... NJ-15
Celoron, 1112 .... NM-2
Center Moriches, 7580 .... SF-11
Centereach, 31578 .... SF-10
Centerport, 5508 .... SE-9
Centerville, 250 .... NK-5
Central Br., 593 .... NJ-17
Central Islip, 34450 .... SF-9
Central Sq., 1848 .... NH-12
Centre Island, 410 .... †C-20
Ceres, 400 .... NM-5
Chadwicks, 1506 .... NI-14
Chaffee, 350 .... NK-5
Chambers, 550 .... NL-9
Champion, 100 .... NE-13
Champlain, 1101 .... NA-19
Champlain Pk., 1200 .... NB-20
Chapin, 180 .... NJ-8
Chappaqua, 1436 .... SD-7
Charleston *M-5
Charleston Four Cors., 200 .... NJ-17
Charlotteville, 250 .... NK-16
Charlton, 320 .... NI-18
Chase Lake, 75 .... NF-14
Chase Mills, 250 .... NB-15
Chasm Falls NB-17
Chateaugay, 833 .... NA-18
Chatham, 1770 .... NL-19
Chaumont, 624 .... NE-12
Chautauqua, 191 .... NL-2
CHAUTAUQUA CO., 134905 .... NL-2
Chazy, 565 .... NB-19
Chazy Lndg., 100 .... NB-20
Cheektowaga, 75178 .... NE-5
Chemung, 600 .... NM-10
CHEMUNG CO., 88830 .... NL-9
Chenango Br., 2883 .... NM-12
CHENANGO CO., 50477 .... NK-13
Chenango Forks, 500 .... NL-13
Cheneys Pt., 250 .... NM-2
Cherry Creek, 461 .... NL-3
Cherry Valley, 520 .... NJ-16
Cherryplain, 300 .... NK-20
Cheshire, 250 .... NJ-8
Chester, 3969 .... SC-5
Chestertown, 677 .... NG-19
Childwold, 100 .... ND-16
Chili Ctr., 4350 .... ND-7
Chippewa Bay, 350 .... NC-13
Chittenango, 5081 .... NI-13
Choconut Ctr., 250 .... SB-11
Churchtown, 300 .... NM-19
Churchville, 1961 .... NI-7
Churubusco, 200 .... NA-18
Cicero, 1100 .... NI-12
Cincinnatus, 400 .... NK-12
Circleville, 1350 .... SC-5
Clarence, 2646 .... NI-4
Clarence Ctr., 2257 .... NI-4
Clarendon, 350 .... NH-6
Clark Mills, 1905 .... NI-14
Clarks Mills, 130 .... NI-19
Clarkson, 4358 .... NH-6
Clarksville, 800 .... NK-18
Claryville, 100 .... NN-16
Claverack, 1000 .... NL-19
Clay, 700 .... NI-12
Clayburg, 100 .... NC-18
Clayton, 1978 .... ND-12
Clayville, 350 .... NI-14
Clemons, 100 .... NG-20
Clermont, 500 .... NM-19
Cleveland, 750 .... NH-12
Cleverdale, 500 .... NG-19
Clifton, 150 .... NI-7
Clifton *K-8
Clifton Pk., 1200 .... NJ-19
Clifton Sprs., 2127 .... NI-9
Climax, 165 .... NL-19
Clinton, 1942 .... NI-14
CLINTON CO., 82128 .... NB-19
Clinton Cors., 450 .... NN-19
Clinton Pk., 880 .... SJ-5
Clintondale, 1452 .... SB-6
Clintonville, 200 .... NC-19
Clyde, 2093 .... NI-10
Clymer, 600 .... NM-1
Cobleskill, 4678 .... NK-17
Cochecton, 200 .... SB-2
Coeymans Hollow, 550 .... NK-18
Cohocton, 838 .... NK-8
Cohoes, 16168 .... NJ-19
Cold Brook, 329 .... NH-15
Cold Spr., 2013 .... SC-6
Cold Spr. Hbr., 5070 .... SH-10
Cold Sprs., 650 .... NE-7
Colden, 550 .... NK-4
College Pt. .... †F-13
Colliersville, 150 .... NK-15
Collins, 500 .... NK-3
Collins Ctr., 480 .... NK-4
Colonial Vil. NA-2
Colonie, 7793 .... NJ-19
Colosse, 120 .... NH-12
Colton, 345 .... NC-15
COLUMBIA CO., 63096 .... NM-19
Columbus, 150 .... NK-14
Commack, 36124 .... SF-9
Comstock, 350 .... NG-20
Conesus, 400 .... NJ-7
Conesville, 150 .... NL-17
Conewango, 150 .... NL-3
Conewango Valley, 300 .... NL-3
Coney Island *L-10
Congers, 8363 .... SD-7
Conifer, 75 .... ND-16
Conklin, 1800 .... NM-13
Connelly Pk., 100 .... NM-2
Conquest, 75 .... NI-10
Constable, 350 .... NA-17
Constableville, 242 .... NG-14
Constantia, 1182 .... NH-12
Cooks Falls, 200 .... NN-15
Coopers Plains, 598 .... NM-9
Cooperstown, 1852 .... NK-15
Coopersville, 210 .... NA-20
Copake, 1200 .... NM-20
Copake Falls, 500 .... NM-20
Copenhagen, 801 .... NF-13
Coram, 39113 .... SF-10
Corbett, 150 .... NM-15
Corbettsville, 460 .... NM-13
Coreys, 130 .... ND-17
Corfu, 709 .... NI-5
Corinth, 2559 .... NH-19
Corning, 11183 .... NM-9
Cornwall-on-Hudson, 3018 .... SC-6
Cornwallville, 130 .... NL-18
Corona .... †G-13
Cortland, 19204 .... NK-12
CORTLAND CO., 49336 .... NK-12
Cossayuna, 350 .... NH-20
Cottage, 110 .... NL-3
Cove Neck, 286 .... †D-20
Coventry, 250 .... NL-13
Coventryville, 85 .... NL-13
Covington, 180 .... NJ-6
Cowlesville, 500 .... NJ-5
Coxsackie, 2813 .... NL-19
Cragsmoor, 449 .... SB-5
Cranberry Creek, 225 .... NI-17
Cranberry Lake, 200 .... ND-16
Crary Mills, 120 .... NC-15
Craryville, 600 .... NM-19
Crescent, 530 .... SF-5
Crittenden, 250 .... NI-5
Croghan, 618 .... NF-14
Cropseyville, 200 .... NJ-19
Cross River, 980 .... SD-8
Croton Falls, 970 .... SC-8
Croton-on-Hudson, 8070 .... SD-7
Crown Pt., 1000 .... NE-20
Cuba, 1575 .... NL-5
Cuddebackville, 1100 .... SC-4
Curriers, 110 .... NK-5
Cutchogue, 3349 .... SE-12
Cutting, 90 .... NM-1
Cuyler, 150 .... NJ-12
Cuylerville, 297 .... NJ-7
Dale, 100 .... NJ-6
Dalton, 362 .... NK-6
Damascus, 200 .... NM-13
Danby, 250 .... NL-11
Dannemora, 3936 .... NB-19
Dansville, 4719 .... NK-7
Darien, 300 .... NJ-5
Darien Ctr., 700 .... NJ-5
Davenport, 400 .... NK-16
Davenport Ctr., 349 .... NL-15
Davis Pk. SJ-14
Dayton, 350 .... NL-3
De Kalb, 100 .... NC-14
De Kalb Jct., 519 .... NC-14
De Lancey, 110 .... NL-15
De Peyster, 300 .... NC-14
De Witt NI-12
Deansboro, 500 .... NI-14
Deer Pk., 27745 .... SF-9
Deer River, 300 .... NF-13
Deferiet, 294 .... NE-13
Defreestville, 960 .... NK-19
Degrasse, 140 .... ND-15
Delanson, 377 .... NJ-18
DELAWARE CO., 47980 .... NM-15
Delevan, 1089 .... NK-5
Delhi, 3087 .... NL-15
Delmar, 8300 .... NK-19
Delphi Falls, 500 .... NJ-12
Denmark, 150 .... NF-13
Depauville, 577 .... NE-12
Depew, 15303 .... NJ-4
Deposit, 1663 .... NM-14
Derby, 1200 .... NK-3
DeRuyter, 558 .... NJ-12
Dewittville, 350 .... NL-2
Dexter, 1052 .... NE-12
Diamond Pt., 400 .... NG-19
Dickinson Ctr., 300 .... NB-16
Dix Hills, 26892 .... SI-11
Dobbs Ferry, 10875 .... SE-7
Dolgeville, 2206 .... NI-16
Dorloo, 450 .... NJ-16
Dormansville, 100 .... NK-18
Douglaston .... †G-15
Dover Furnace SB-8
Dover Plains, 1323 .... SA-8
Downsville, 617 .... NM-15
Dresden, 308 .... NK-9
Dryden, 1890 .... NK-11
Duanesburg, 391 .... NJ-18
Dundee, 1725 .... NK-9
Dunkirk, 12563 .... NK-2
Dunnsville SH-1
Dunsbach Ferry, 650 .... SG-5
Durham, 150 .... NL-18
Durhamville, 584 .... NI-13
Durlandville, 160 .... SC-5
DUTCHESS CO., 297488 .... NN-19
Eagle, 150 .... NK-5
Eagle Bay, 200 .... NF-16
Eagle Br., 350 .... NI-20
Eagle Hbr., 250 .... NH-5
Eagleville, 60 .... NI-20
Earlton, 255 .... NL-18
Earlville, 872 .... NJ-13
E. Amherst, 700 .... NC-6
E. Aurora, 6236 .... NJ-4
E. Avon, 608 .... NJ-7
E. Beekmantown, 125 .... NB-19
E. Berne, 200 .... NK-18
E. Bethany, 150 .... NJ-6
E. Branch, 400 .... NM-15
E. Chatham, 500 .... NL-20
E. Corning, 650 .... NM-9
E. Durham, 600 .... NL-18
E. Eden, 300 .... NK-4
E. Elmhurst .... †G-12
E. Glenville, 6616 .... NJ-18
E. Greenbush, 4487 .... NK-19
E. Greenwich, 220 .... NI-20
E. Hampton, 1083 .... SE-13
E. Hills, 6955 .... SF-8
E. Homer, 200 .... NK-12
E. Islip, 14475 .... SJ-12
E. Marion, 926 .... SD-12
E. Meadow, 38132 .... SF-8
E. Meredith, 200 .... NL-15
E. Nassau, 587 .... NK-20
E. New York .... †I-12
E. Northport, 20217 .... SF-9
E. Norwich, 2709 .... †E-19
E. Otto, 300 .... NL-4
E. Palmyra, 135 .... NI-9
E. Pembroke, 600 .... NI-5
E. Penfield, 200 .... NI-8
E. Pharsalia, 160 .... NK-13
E. Quogue, 4757 .... SF-12
E. Randolph, 620 .... NM-3
E. Rochester, 6587 .... ND-10
E. Rockaway, 9818 .... †J-17
E. Schodack, 500 .... NK-19
E. Springfield, 220 .... NJ-16
E. Syracuse, 3084 .... NF-9
E. Williamson, 500 .... NH-9
E. Williston, 2556 .... †G-17
E. Windsor, 50 .... NM-13
E. Worcester, 300 .... NK-16
Eastchester, 19554 .... †B-14
Eastport, 1831 .... SF-11
Eaton, 500 .... NJ-13
Ebenezer NG-5
Eddyville, 55 .... NL-4
Eden, 3516 .... NK-3
Edgemere .... †K-15
Edinburg, 300 .... NH-18
Edmeston, 657 .... NK-14
Edwards, 439 .... ND-14
Edwardsville, 110 .... NC-13
Eggertsville, 15019 .... ND-5
Elba, 676 .... NI-6
Elbridge, 1058 .... NI-11
Eldred, 750 .... SC-3
Elizabethtown, 754 .... ND-19
Elizaville, 600 .... NM-19
Ellenburg, 600 .... NB-18
Ellenburg Ctr., 400 .... NB-18
Ellenville, 4135 .... SB-5
Ellicott, 550 .... NJ-4
Ellicottville, 376 .... NL-4
Ellington, 500 .... NL-3
Ellisburg, 244 .... NF-12
Elm Valley, 75 .... NM-7
Elma Ctr., 2571 .... NJ-4
Elmhurst .... †G-13
Elmira, 29200 .... NM-10
Elmira Hts., 4097 .... NM-10
Elmont, 33198 .... SF-7
Elmsford, 4664 .... SH-7
Elsmere, 4200 .... NK-19
Eltingville *M-6
Elton, 110 .... NK-5
Emmons, 150 .... NK-15
Endicott, 13392 .... NM-12
Endwell, 11446 .... NM-12
Enfield, 200 .... NL-10
Ephratah, 160 .... NI-16
ERIE CO., 919040 .... NK-4
Erieville, 400 .... NJ-13
Erin, 483 .... NM-10
Escarpment, 1200 .... NA-2
Esopus, 650 .... NN-18
Esperance, 345 .... NJ-17
Essex, 400 .... ND-20
ESSEX CO., 39370 .... NE-18
Etna, 550 .... NK-11
Euclid, 180 .... NI-11
Evans Mills, 621 .... NE-13
Fabius, 352 .... NJ-12
Fair Haven, 745 .... NH-10
Fairfield, 150 .... NI-15
Fairmount, 10224 .... NI-11
Fairport, 5353 .... NI-8
Fairview, 3099 .... SI-7
Falconer, 2420 .... NM-2
Falconwood, 1500 .... ND-3
Fallsburg, 800 .... SB-4
Fancher, 300 .... NH-6
Far Rockaway .... †K-15
Farmers Mills, 375 .... SC-7
Farmersville Sta., 300 .... NL-5
Farmingdale, 8189 .... SJ-10
Farmington, 100 .... NI-8
Farmingville, 15481 .... SF-10
Farnham, 382 .... NK-3
Fayette, 430 .... NJ-10
Fayetteville, 4373 .... NI-12
Felts Mills, 372 .... NE-13
Ferndale, 850 .... SA-4
Fernwood, 200 .... NG-12
Ferry Vil., 200 .... ND-3
Fillmore, 603 .... NK-6
Findley Lake, 800 .... NM-1
Fine, 300 .... ND-15
Fire Island Pines, 900 .... SG-10
Fishers, 400 .... NI-8
Fishers Island, 236 .... SD-14
Fishers, 89 .... ND-12
Fishkill, 2171 .... SB-7
Fishs Eddy, 350 .... NN-15
Flackville, 110 .... NC-14
Flanders, 4472 .... SE-11
Flatbush .... †J-11
Fleischmanns, 351 .... NM-17
Fleming, 220 .... NJ-10
Floral Pk., 15863 .... †H-16
Florence, 130 .... NH-13
Florida, 2833 .... SC-5
Flower Hill, 4665 .... †F-16
Floyd, 300 .... NH-14
Flushing .... †G-13
Fluvanna, 900 .... NM-2
Fly Creek, 350 .... NJ-15
Fonda, 795 .... NI-17
Forest, 40 .... NB-19
Forest Hills .... †H-13
Forestburg, 100 .... SB-4
Forestport, 900 .... NH-14
Forestville, 697 .... NK-3
Ft. Ann, 484 .... NG-20
Ft. Covington, 1200 .... NA-16
Ft. Edward, 3375 .... NH-19
Ft. Hunter, 1250 .... SH-2
Ft. Jackson, 135 .... NB-16
Ft. Johnson, 490 .... NI-17
Ft. Plain, 2322 .... NJ-16
Ft. Salonga, 10008 .... SG-11
Fosterdale, 150 .... SB-3
Fourth Lake, 300 .... NH-19
Fowler, 300 .... ND-14
Fowlerville, 227 .... NJ-7
Fox Hills *K-8
Frankfort, 2598 .... NI-15
Franklin, 374 .... NL-15
FRANKLIN CO., 51599 .... NC-17
Franklin Pk., 2600 .... NE-9
Franklin Sprs., 300 .... NI-14
Franklin Sq., 29320 .... †H-17
Franklinville, 1740 .... NL-5
Fraser, 30 .... NL-15
Fredonia, 11230 .... NK-2
Freedom, 200 .... NK-5
Freehold, 500 .... NL-18
Freeport, 42860 .... SG-8
Freeville, 520 .... NK-11
Fremont Hts., 150 .... NF-10
Fresh Meadows .... †H-14
Frewsburg, 1906 .... NM-3
Friendship, 1218 .... NL-6
Fruit Valley, 50 .... NH-10
Fulton, 11896 .... NH-11
FULTON CO., 55531 .... NI-17
Fultonham, 400 .... NK-17
Fultonville, 784 .... NJ-17
Gabriels, 250 .... NC-17
Gaines, 200 .... NH-6
Gainesville, 229 .... NK-6
Galeville, 4617 .... NE-8
Gallupville, 325 .... NK-17
Galway, 200 .... NI-18
Gang Mills, 4185 .... NM-9
Gansevoort, 600 .... NH-19
Garden City, 22371 .... †H-18
Garden City Pk., 7806 .... †H-17
Garden City South, 4024 .... †H-17
Gardiner, 950 .... SB-6
Gardnertown, 4373 .... SB-6
Garrattsville, 150 .... NK-15
Garrison, 800 .... SC-6
Gasport, 1248 .... NH-4
Gates Ctr., 4910 .... NI-7
GENESEE CO., 60079 .... NI-6
Geneseo, 8031 .... NJ-7
Geneva, 13261 .... NJ-9
Genoa, 500 .... NK-11
Georgetown, 500 .... NJ-13
German, 60 .... NK-13
Germantown, 845 .... NM-18
Gerritsen .... †L-11
Gerry, 800 .... NL-2
Getzville, 2300 .... NC-5
Ghent, 564 .... NL-19
Gilbertsville, 399 .... NK-14
Gilboa, 200 .... NL-17
Glasco, 2099 .... NM-18
Glen, 180 .... NJ-17
Glen Aubrey, 485 .... NL-12
Glen Castle, 300 .... SA-11
Glen Cove, 26964 .... SF-8
Glen Head, 4697 .... †E-18
Glen Oaks .... †G-16
Glen Spey, 500 .... SC-3
Glendale .... †I-13
Glenfield, 430 .... NF-14
Glenford, 550 .... NM-18
Glenham, 2000 .... SB-7
Glenmont, 1200 .... NK-19
Glens Falls, 14700 .... NH-19
Glenwood, 500 .... NK-4
Glenwood, 3779 .... †E-17
Gloversville, 15665 .... NI-17
Godeffroy, 550 .... SC-4
Golden's Br., 1630 .... SC-7
Gorham, 617 .... NJ-9
Goshen, 5454 .... SC-5
Gouverneur, 3949 .... ND-14
Gowanda, 2709 .... NK-3
Grafton, 600 .... NJ-20
Grahamsville, 700 .... NN-17
Granby Ctr., 100 .... NH-11
Grand Gorge, 1000 .... NL-17
Grand Island, 800 .... NI-3
Grandyle Vil., 4629 .... ND-3
Graniteville *K-7
Granville, 2543 .... NG-20
Gravesend .... †K-11
Gravesville, 120 .... NH-15
Gray, 75 .... NH-15
Great Bend, 843 .... NE-13
Great Neck, 9989 .... SF-7
Great Neck Estates, 2761 .... †F-15
Great Neck Plaza, 6707 .... †F-16
Great Valley, 250 .... NL-4
Greece, 65000 .... NB-7
Green Island, 2620 .... SH-5
Green River, 200 .... NL-20
Greene, 1580 .... NL-13
GREENE CO., 49221 .... NL-18
Greenfield Ctr., 700 .... NI-18
Greenfield Pk., 500 .... SB-4
Greenlawn, 13742 .... SH-11
Greenpoint .... †H-11
Greenport, 2197 .... SD-12
Greenvale, 1094 .... †F-18
Greenville, 7116 .... SJ-7
Greenville, 688 .... NL-18
Greenwich, 1777 .... NI-20
Greenwood, 520 .... NM-7
Greenwood Lake, 3154 .... SD-5
Greig, 300 .... NG-14
Groom Cors., 370 .... SF-3
Groton, 2363 .... NK-11
Groveland, 650 .... NK-7
Grover Hills, 300 .... NE-19
Grymes Hill *K-8
Guilderland, 1900 .... SI-2
Guilderland Ctr., 860 .... NJ-18
Guilford, 362 .... NL-14
Gurn Spr., 145 .... NH-19
Hadley, 1009 .... NH-18
Hagaman, 1292 .... NI-18
Hague, 450 .... NF-19
Hailesboro, 624 .... ND-14
Haines Falls, 700 .... NL-18
Halcottsville, 240 .... NL-16
Halesite, 2498 .... SH-10
Half Hollow Hills, 4950 .... SI-11
Hall, 216 .... NJ-9
Hallsport, 110 .... NM-7
Hamburg, 9409 .... NJ-4
Hamden, 250 .... NM-15
Hamilton, 4239 .... NJ-13
HAMILTON CO., 4836 .... NF-16
Hamlet, 80 .... NL-3
Hamlin, 5521 .... NH-6
Hammond, 280 .... NC-13
Hammondsport, 661 .... NL-8
Hampton, 400 .... NG-20
Hampton Bays, 13603 .... SE-12
Hampton Mnr., 2417 .... SJ-5
Hancock, 1031 .... NN-14
Hankins, 400 .... NN-15
Hannawa Falls, 1042 .... NC-15
Hannibal, 555 .... NH-10
Hannibal Ctr., 115 .... NH-10
Harbor Hills, 575 .... †F-15
Harbor Isle, 1301 .... †K-17
Harford, 200 .... NL-11
Harford Mills, 180 .... NL-12
Harlem .... †F-11
Harpersfield, 110 .... NL-16
Harpursville, 500 .... NM-13
Harriman, 2424 .... SD-6
Harris, 600 .... SB-4
Harris Hill, 5508 .... NI-4
Harrison, 13620 .... †A-16
Harrisville, 628 .... NE-14
Hartfield, 100 .... NL-2
Hartford, 500 .... NH-20
Hartland, 200 .... NH-4
Hartmans Cors., 100 .... SI-2
Hartsdale, 5293 .... SI-7
Hartsville, 200 .... NL-7
Hartwick, 629 .... NK-15
Hartwick Seminary, 100 .... NK-15
Hartwood, 50 .... SB-4
Hasbrouck, 220 .... NN-16
Haskinville, 100 .... NL-7
Hastings, 350 .... NH-12
Hauppauge, 20882 .... SH-12
Haven, 70 .... SB-4
Haverstraw, 11910 .... SD-6
Hawkeye, 100 .... NC-18
Hawkinsville, 100 .... NG-14
Head of the Harbor, 1472 .... SG-13
Hector, 300 .... NK-10
Helena, 350 .... NA-16
Hemlock, 557 .... NJ-7
Hempstead, 53891 .... SF-8
Henderson, 224 .... NF-12
Henderson Hbr., 350 .... NF-12
Henrietta, 1200 .... NI-7
Hensonville, 600 .... NL-17
Herkimer, 7743 .... NI-15
HERKIMER CO., 64519 .... NH-15
Hermon, 422 .... NC-14
Herricks, 4295 .... †G-17
Herrings, 90 .... NE-13
Heuvelton, 714 .... NC-14
Hewlett, 6819 .... †J-16
Hewlett Bay Pk., 404 .... †K-16
Hewlett Hbr., 1263 .... †K-17
Hewlett Neck, 445 .... †K-16
Hicksville, 41547 .... SF-8
Higgins Bay, 50 .... NH-16
Higginsville, 50 .... NI-13
High Falls, 627 .... NN-18
Highland, 5647 .... SB-6
Highland Falls, 3900 .... SC-6
Highland Lake, 450 .... SB-3
Highland-on-the-Lake, 1800 .... NJ-3
Highmount, 300 .... NM-17
Hillcrest, 7558 .... SD-6
Hillside .... †H-14
Hilton, 5886 .... NH-7
Himrod, 300 .... NK-9
Hinckley, 250 .... NH-15
Hinsdale, 900 .... NM-5
Hobart, 441 .... NL-16
Hoffmeister, 45 .... NH-16
Hogansburg, 100 .... NA-16
Holbrook, 27195 .... SI-13
Holcombville, 200 .... NF-18
Holland, 1206 .... NK-5
Holland Patent, 458 .... NH-14
Holley, 1811 .... NH-6
Hollis .... †H-15
Holmes, 460 .... SB-8
Holmesville, 150 .... NK-14
Holtsville, 19714 .... SI-14
Homer, 3291 .... NK-12
Homewood, 1450 .... NG-10
Honeoye, 579 .... NJ-8
Honeoye Falls, 2674 .... NI-7
Hoosick, 400 .... NJ-20
Hoosick Falls, 3501 .... NJ-20
Hope Falls, 80 .... NH-17
Hope Farm, 300 .... SA-7
Hopewell Jct., 376 .... SB-7
Hopkinton, 200 .... NB-16
Hornby, 300 .... NL-9
Hornell, 8563 .... NL-7
Horseheads, 6461 .... NM-10
Houghton, 1693 .... NL-6
Howard, 200 .... NL-8
Howard Bch. .... †J-13
Howells, 500 .... SC-5
Howlett Hill, 650 .... NG-7
Hubbardsville, 250 .... NJ-14
Hudson, 6713 .... NL-19
Hudson Falls, 7281 .... NH-19
Hughsonville, 1400 .... SB-7
Huguenot, 800 .... SC-4
Huguenot *M-6
Hulberton, 100 .... NH-6
Huletts, 200 .... NG-19
Hume, 400 .... NK-6
Hunt, 78 .... NK-6
Hunter, 502 .... NL-18
Huntington, 18046 .... SH-10
Huntington Bay, 1425 .... SH-10
Huntington Sta., 33029 .... SF-9
Hurley, 3458 .... NN-18
Hurleyville, 750 .... SA-4
Hyde Pk., 1908 .... NN-18
Hyde Pk., 100 .... NK-15
Hyndsville, 200 .... NK-16
Ilion, 8053 .... NI-15
Indian Falls, 170 .... NI-5
Indian Lake, 600 .... NF-17
Indian Pk., 600 .... SD-5
Indian River, 45 .... NE-14
Indian Vil., 700 .... NJ-12
Ingleside, 90 .... NK-8
Ingraham, 110 .... NB-19
Inlet, 400 .... NF-16
Interlaken, 602 .... NK-10
Inwood, 9792 .... SG-7
Ionia, 300 .... NJ-8
Irona, 300 .... NA-19
Irondequoit, 51692 .... NH-7
Ironville, 100 .... NE-19
Irving, 600 .... NK-3
Ischua, 200 .... NL-5
Island Pk., 4655 .... †K-17
Islandia, 3335 .... SI-13
Islip, 18689 .... SF-9
Islip Ter., 5389 .... SI-12
Italy, 120 .... NK-8
Ithaca, 30014 .... NL-11
Jacks Reef, 500 .... NI-11
Jackson Hts. .... †G-12
Jacksonville, 670 .... NK-10
Jamaica .... †H-14
Jamesport, 1710 .... SE-12
Jamestown, 31146 .... NM-2
Jamesville, 700 .... NI-12
Jasper, 500 .... NM-8
Java Ctr., 200 .... NK-5
Java Vil., 300 .... NK-5
Jay, 500 .... ND-19
Jefferson, 500 .... NK-16
JEFFERSON CO., 116229 .... NE-13
Jefferson Valley, 6700 .... SC-7
Jeffersonville, 359 .... NN-15
Jericho, 13567 .... SF-8
Jericho, 100 .... NB-19
Jewell, 100 .... NH-13
Jewettville, 100 .... NJ-4
Johnsburg, 300 .... NG-18
Johnson, 500 .... SC-4
Johnson City, 15174 .... NM-12
Johnson Creek, 280 .... NH-5
Johnsonburg, 120 .... NJ-5
Johnsonville, 380 .... NJ-20
Johnstown, 8743 .... NI-17
Jonesville, 420 .... NJ-19
Jordan, 1368 .... NI-11
Jordanville, 250 .... NJ-15
Kanona, 450 .... NL-8
Katonah, 1679 .... SD-7
Kattskill Bay, 500 .... NG-19
Keene, 450 .... ND-19
Keene Valley, 350 .... ND-19
Keeseville, 1815 .... NC-19
Kelsey, 70 .... NM-14
Kendall, 500 .... NH-6
Kenmore, 15423 .... ND-4
Kennedy, 465 .... NM-3
Kenoza Lake, 400 .... SB-3
Kensington, 1161 .... †F-15
Kensington .... †J-11
Kent, 125 .... NH-6
Kent Cliffs, 110 .... SC-7
Kenyonville, 110 .... NH-5
Kerhonkson, 1684 .... NN-17
Keuka, 150 .... NK-9
Keuka Pk., 1137 .... NK-9
Kew Gdns. .... †H-13
Kiamesha Lake, 850 .... SB-4
Kiantone, 120 .... NM-2
Kill Buck, 650 .... NM-4
Killawog, 300 .... NL-12
Kinderhook, 1211 .... NL-19
King Ferry, 300 .... NK-10
KINGS CO., 2504700 .... SG-7
Kings Pk., 17282 .... SE-9
Kings Pt., 5005 .... †F-15
Kingsbury, 200 .... NH-19
Kingston, 23893 .... NN-18
Kirkville, 500 .... NI-12
Kirschnerville, 40 .... NF-14
Kiryas Joel, 20175 .... SC-6
Knapp Creek, 150 .... NM-5
Knowlesville, 300 .... NH-5
Knox, 400 .... NK-18
Knoxboro, 150 .... NI-14
Kossuth, 60 .... NM-6
Krumville, 150 .... NN-17
La Fargeville, 608 .... ND-12
Lackawanna, 18141 .... NG-4
Lacona, 582 .... NG-12
LaFayette, 600 .... NJ-12
Lagrangeville, 500 .... SB-7
L. Bluff, 50 .... NH-9
L. Bonaparte NE-14
L. Carmel, 8282 .... SC-7
L. Clear, 400 .... ND-17
L. Delta, 2020 .... NH-14
L. Erie Bch., 3872 .... NK-3
L. George, 906 .... NG-19
L. Grove, 11163 .... SH-13
L. Hill, 400 .... NM-18
L. Huntington, 600 .... SB-3
L. Katrine, 2397 .... NM-18
L. Luzerne, 1150 .... NH-19
L. Peekskill, 2150 .... SC-7
L. Placid, 2521 .... ND-18
L. Pleasant, 350 .... NG-17
L. Ronkonkoma, 20155 .... SH-13
L. Success, 2934 .... †G-16
Lakeland, 2786 .... NE-7
Lakemont, 250 .... NK-9
Lakeport, 500 .... NI-12
Lakeview, 5615 .... †I-17
Lakeville, 756 .... NJ-7
Lakewood, 3002 .... NM-2
Lamberton, 130 .... NL-2
Lancaster, 10352 .... NE-6
Lanesville, 350 .... NM-17
Langford, 230 .... NK-4
Lansing, 3529 .... NK-11
Laona, 250 .... NL-2
Laphams Mills, 120 .... NC-19
Larchmont, 5864 .... †B-15
Lassellsville, 300 .... NI-16
Latham, 4200 .... SH-5
Lattingtown, 1739 .... †D-18
Laurel, 1394 .... SE-12
Laurel Hollow, 1952 .... SH-10
Laurelton .... †I-15
Laurens, 263 .... NK-15
Lava, 50 .... SB-3
Lawrence, 6483 .... †K-16
Lawrenceville, 230 .... NB-16
Lawtons, 460 .... NK-3
Lawyersville, 200 .... NJ-17
Le Roy, 4391 .... NI-6
Lebanon, 200 .... NJ-13
Lebanon Sprs., 500 .... NK-20
Lee, 200 .... NH-13
Lee Ctr., 620 .... NH-14
Leeds, 377 .... NL-18
Leicester, 468 .... NJ-6
Leon, 350 .... NL-3
Leonardsville, 500 .... NJ-14
Levanna, 50 .... NJ-10
Levittown, 51881 .... SF-8
Lewbeach, 200 .... NM-16
Lewis, 450 .... ND-19
LEWIS CO., 27087 .... NF-13
Lewiston, 2701 .... NI-3
Lexington, 500 .... NL-17
Liberty, 4392 .... NN-16
Lido Bch., 2897 .... SG-8
Lily Dale, 500 .... NL-2
Lima, 2139 .... NJ-7
Lime Lake, 867 .... NL-5
Limerick, 170 .... NE-12
Limestone, 389 .... NM-4
Lincklaen, 50 .... NK-12
Lincoln, 140 .... NI-8
Linden, 110 .... NJ-6
Lindenhurst, 27253 .... SF-9
Lindley, 400 .... NM-9
Linwood, 74 .... NJ-6
Lisbon, 500 .... NB-14
Lisle, 320 .... NL-12
Little Falls, 4946 .... NI-16
Little Genesee, 270 .... NM-5
Little Neck .... †G-15
Little Valley, 1143 .... NL-4
Little York, 400 .... NK-12
Liverpool, 2347 .... NE-8
LIVINGSTON CO., 65393 .... NK-7
Livingston Manor, 1221 .... NN-16
Livingstonville, 110 .... NK-17
Livonia, 1409 .... NJ-7
Livonia Ctr., 421 .... NJ-7
Lloyd Hbr., 3660 .... SE-8
Loch Muller, 100 .... NF-18
Loch Sheldrake, 1050 .... NN-16
Lock Berlin, 125 .... NI-9
Locke, 550 .... NK-11
Lockport, 21165 .... NI-4
Lockwood, 300 .... NM-10
Locust Grv., 9700 .... †F-20
Locust Manor .... †I-15
Locust Valley, 3406 .... SF-8
Lodi, 291 .... NK-10
Long Bch., 33275 .... SG-8
Long Eddy, 400 .... NN-15
Long Island City .... †G-11
Long Lake, 547 .... NE-17
Loon Lake, 100 .... NC-18
Lordville, 100 .... NN-14
Lorraine, 174 .... NF-12
Loudonville SI-5
Louisville, 500 .... NB-15
Lowville, 3470 .... NF-14
Ludlowville, 440 .... NK-11
Lycoming, 650 .... NG-11
Lynbrook, 19427 .... †J-17
Lyndon NG-10
Lyndonville, 838 .... NH-5
Lyon Mtn., 423 .... NB-18
Lyons, 3619 .... NI-9
Lyons Falls, 566 .... NG-14
Lyonsdale, 50 .... NG-14
Lysander, 275 .... NH-11
Mabbettsville, 65 .... NN-19
Macedon, 1523 .... NI-8
Macedon Ctr., 200 .... NI-8
Machias, 471 .... NL-5
Madison, 305 .... NJ-14
MADISON CO., 73442 .... NJ-13
Madrid, 757 .... NB-15
Mahopac, 8369 .... SC-7
Maine, 1110 .... NM-12
Mallory, 350 .... NH-12
Malone, 5911 .... NB-17
Malta, 450 .... NI-19
Malta Ridge, 130 .... NI-19
Malverne, 8514 .... †I-17
Mamaroneck, 18929 .... SE-7
Manchester, 1709 .... NI-8
Manhasset, 8080 .... †F-16
Manhattan Bch. .... †L-11
Manitou Bch., 250 .... NH-7
Manlius, 4704 .... NI-12
Mannsville, 354 .... NF-12
Manorhaven, 6556 .... †E-16
Manorville, 14314 .... SE-11
Maple Sprs., 400 .... NL-2
Maple View, 280 .... NG-12
Maplecrest, 150 .... NL-18
Maplehurst, 200 .... NM-5
Maples, 60 .... NL-4
Maplewood, 800 .... SH-5
Marathon, 919 .... NL-12
Marbletown, 200 .... NN-18
Marcellus, 1813 .... NI-11
Margaretville, 596 .... NM-16
Marietta, 80 .... NJ-11
Marilla, 375 .... NJ-4
Mariners Hbr. *J-6
Marion, 1511 .... NI-9
Marlboro, 3669 .... SB-6
Martinsburg, 400 .... NF-14
Martville, 110 .... NH-10
Maryland, 165 .... NK-15
Masonville, 600 .... NL-14
Maspeth .... †H-12
Massapequa, 21685 .... SG-8
Massapequa Pk., 17008 .... SJ-10
Massena, 10936 .... NA-15
Massena Ctr., 50 .... NA-15
Mastic, 15481 .... SF-11
Mastic Bch., 12930 .... SF-11
Matinecock, 810 .... †D-18
Mattituck, 4219 .... SE-12
Mattydale, 6446 .... NE-8
Maybrook, 2958 .... SC-5
Mayfield, 832 .... NI-17
Mayville, 1711 .... NL-2
Maywood, 3400 .... SH-3
McConnellsville, 500 .... NH-13
McDonough, 300 .... NK-13
McGraw, 1053 .... NK-12
McKownville, 4850 .... SI-3
McLean, 600 .... NK-11
Meadowdale SI-1
Mechanicstown, 6858 .... SC-5
Mechanicville, 5196 .... NJ-19
Mecklenburg, 280 .... NL-10
Meco, 150 .... NI-17
Medford, 24142 .... SF-10
Medina, 6065 .... NH-5
Medusa, 350 .... NL-18
Medway, 285 .... NL-18
Melrose, 350 .... NJ-19
Melrose Pk., 2294 .... NJ-11
Melville, 18985 .... SI-10
Menands, 3990 .... NJ-19
Mendon, 1000 .... NI-8
Meridale, 250 .... NL-15
Meridian, 309 .... NI-11
Merrick, 22097 .... †J-19
Merrill, 450 .... NB-18
Mexico, 1624 .... NG-11
Middle Falls, 270 .... NI-19
Middle Granville, 600 .... NG-20
Middle Grv., 620 .... NI-18
Middle Hope, 3000 .... SB-6
Middle Island, 10483 .... SE-10
Middle Vil. .... †H-13
Middleburgh, 1500 .... NK-17
Middlefield, 350 .... NK-16
Middleport, 1840 .... NH-5
Middlesex, 400 .... NK-8
Middletown, 28086 .... SC-5
Middleville, 1400 .... SH-11
Middleville, 512 .... NI-15
Midland Bch. *L-8
Milford, 415 .... NK-15
Mill Neck, 997 .... †D-19
Millbrook, 1452 .... NN-19
Miller Pl., 12339 .... SE-10
Millers, 150 .... NH-5
Millersport NB-6
Millerton, 958 .... NM-20
Millport, 312 .... NL-10
Millville, 120 .... NH-5
Milton, 1403 .... SB-6
Minaville, 220 .... NJ-17
Mineola, 18799 .... SF-8
Minerva, 300 .... NF-18
Minetto, 1069 .... NH-11
Mineville, 1269 .... NE-19
Minisink Ford, 200 .... SC-3
Minoa, 3449 .... NI-12
Model City, 300 .... NH-3
Modena, 900 .... SB-6
Mohawk, 2731 .... NI-15
Mohawk View SG-4
Mohegan Lake, 3600 .... SC-7
Mohonk Lake, 300 .... NN-18
Moira, 500 .... NB-16
Mombaccus, 150 .... NN-17
Mongaup Valley, 750 .... SB-3
Monroe, 8364 .... SC-6
MONROE CO., 744344 .... NH-7
Montauk, 3326 .... SE-14
Monterey, 215 .... NL-9
Montezuma, 450 .... NI-10
Montgomery, 3814 .... SB-5
MONTGOMERY CO., 50219 .... NJ-16
Monticello, 6726 .... SB-4
Montour Falls, 1711 .... NL-10
Montrose, 2731 .... SD-7
Moody, 200 .... ND-17
Mooers, 442 .... NA-19
Mooers Forks, 600 .... NA-19
Moravia, 1282 .... NJ-11
Moreland, 100 .... NL-9
Moriah, 400 .... NE-19
Moriah Ctr., 400 .... NE-19
Morley, 120 .... NC-14
Morris, 583 .... NK-14
Morrisonville, 1545 .... NB-19
Morristown, 395 .... NC-13
Morrisville, 2199 .... NJ-13
Morton, 200 .... NH-6
Mottville, 350 .... NI-11
Mt. Ivy, 6878 .... SD-6
Mt. Kisco, 10877 .... SD-7
Mt. Morris, 2986 .... NJ-7
Mt. Tremper, 650 .... NM-17
Mt. Upton, 570 .... NL-14
Mt. Vernon, 67292 .... †C-13
Mt. Vernon, 2800 .... NJ-3
Mt. Vision, 225 .... NK-15
Mountain Dale, 200 .... SB-4
Mountain Lodge, 1000 .... SC-6
Mountain View, 150 .... NB-17
Mountainville, 600 .... SC-6
Mumford, 800 .... NI-7
Munnsville, 474 .... NI-13
Munsey Pk., 2693 .... †F-16
Munsons Corners, 2728 .... NK-11
Murray, 100 .... NH-6
Muttontown, 3497 .... †E-19
Myers Corner, 6790 .... SB-7
Nanuet, 17882 .... SE-6
Napanoch, 1174 .... SA-5
Naples, 1041 .... NK-8
Narrowsburg, 431 .... SB-2
Nassau, 1133 .... NK-19
NASSAU CO., 1339532 .... SF-7
Natural Br., 365 .... NE-14
Natural Dam, 65 .... ND-14
Nedrow, 2244 .... NI-12
Nelliston, 596 .... NJ-16
Nelson, 300 .... NJ-13
Nelsonville, 628 .... SC-7
Neponsit .... †L-13
Nesconset, 13387 .... SH-13
Neversink, 350 .... NN-16
New Albion, 200 .... NL-3
New Baltimore, 960 .... NK-19
New Berlin, 1028 .... NK-14
New Bremen, 200 .... NF-14
New Brighton *J-8
New Cassel, 14059 .... †G-19
New City, 33559 .... SD-6
New Dorp *L-7
New Dorp Bch. *L-8
New Falconwood, 1200 .... ND-2
New Hampton, 1200 .... SC-5
New Hartford, 1847 .... NI-14
New Haven, 400 .... NG-11
New Hope, 80 .... NJ-11
New Hyde Pk., 9712 .... †H-16
New Kingston, 150 .... NL-16
New Lebanon, 950 .... NK-20
New Lisbon, 100 .... NK-15
New Milford, 600 .... SD-5
New Paltz, 6818 .... SA-6
New Rochelle, 77062 .... SE-7
New Russia, 160 .... ND-19
New Salem, 450 .... NK-18
New Scotland, 200 .... SJ-2
New Spr.ville *K-6
New Suffolk, 349 .... SE-12
New Utrecht *K-10
New Windsor, 8922 .... SC-6
New Woodstock, 500 .... NJ-13
New York, 8175133 .... SF-6
NEW YORK CO., 1585873 .... *D-11
New York Mills, 3327 .... SA-12
Newark, 9145 .... NI-9
Newark Valley, 997 .... NL-12
Newburgh, 28866 .... SC-6
Newcomb, 300 .... NE-17
Newfane, 3822 .... NH-4
Newfield Hamlet, 759 .... NL-10
Newport, 640 .... NI-15
Newton Falls, 400 .... ND-15
Newtonville, 2300 .... SH-5
NIAGARA CO., 216469 .... NH-4
Niagara Falls, 50193 .... NI-3
Nichols, 512 .... NM-11
Nicholville, 370 .... NB-16
Nile, 250 .... NM-6
Nimmonsburg, 900 .... NM-12
Nineveh, 400 .... NM-13
Niobe, 150 .... NM-2
Niskayuna, 4859 .... NJ-19
Nissequogue, 1749 .... SH-12
Niverville, 1662 .... NK-19
Norfolk, 1327 .... NB-15
Normansville SJ-4
N. Argyle, 250 .... NH-20
N. Bangor, 600 .... NB-17
N. Bay, 800 .... NH-13
N. Bellmore, 19941 .... †I-19
N. Bethlehem, 400 .... SI-3
N. Blenheim, 200 .... NK-17
N. Bloomfield, 2260 .... NJ-7
N. Boston, 2521 .... NJ-4
N. Branch, 500 .... NN-15
N. Broadalbin, 65 .... NI-18
N. Brookfield, 250 .... NJ-14
N. Chemung, 200 .... NM-10
N. Chili, 2300 .... NI-7
N. Clymer, 120 .... NM-1
N. Collins, 1232 .... NK-3
N. Creek, 616 .... NF-18
N. Cuba, 60 .... NL-5
N. Granville, 500 .... NG-20
N. Greece, 500 .... NH-7
N. Harpersfield, 100 .... NK-16
N. Haven, 833 .... SE-13
N. Hills, 5075 .... †F-17
N. Hillsdale, 200 .... NL-20
N. Hoosick, 350 .... NI-20
N. Hornell, 778 .... NL-7
N. Hudson, 100 .... NE-19
N. Java, 250 .... NK-5
N. Lawrence, 400 .... NB-16
N. Lynbrook, 793 .... †I-17
N. Massapequa, 17886 .... †H-20
N. Merrick, 12272 .... †I-19

***, †, ‡, §, ◊ See explanation under state title in this index.**
County and parish names are listed in capital letters & boldface type.
Independent cities (not included in a county) are listed in italics.

Column 1

N. New Hyde Pk., 14899 ....†G-16
N. Norwich, 600 ....NM-14
N. Petersburg, 250 ...NJ-20
N. Pharsalia, 130 ....NK-13
N. Pitcher, 170 ....NK-13
N. Pole, 70 ....ND-18
N. River, 365 ....NE-9
N. Rose, 636 ....NI-9
N. Salem, 930 ....SC-8
N. Sea, 4458 ....SE-12
N. Syracuse, 6800 ......NI-12
N. Tonawanda, 31568 ....NI-4
N. Valley Stream, 16628 ....†I-16
N. Western, 500 ....NH-14
Northport, 7401 ....SE-9
Northumberland, 250 ....NI-19
Northville, 1099 ....NH-18
Norton Hill, 385 ....NL-18
Norway, 150 ....NH-15
Norwich, 7190 ....NK-14
Norwood, 1657 ....NB-15
Noyack, 3568 ....SE-12
Nunda, 1377 ....NK-6
Nyack, 6765 ....SD-7
Oak Bch., 100 ....SE-9
Oakdale, 7974 ....SJ-13
Oakfield, 1813 ....NI-5
Oakland Gdns. ....†G-15
Oakwood *L-7
Oakwood Bch. NM-15
Oberburg, 200 ....NM-15
Oceana, 591 ....NL-10
Ogdensburg, 11128 ....NB-14
Ohio, 70 ....NH-15
Ohioville, 250 ....SA-6
Olcott, 1241 ....NH-4
Old Brookville, 2134 ....†E-18
Old Field, 918 ....SE-10
Old Forge, 756 ....NF-15
Old Westbury, 4671 ....†F-18
Olean, 14452 ....NM-5
Olivebridge, 400 ....NN-17
Oliverea, 150 ....NM-17
Olmstedville, 400 ....NF-18
Onchiota, 85 ....NC-18
Oneida, 11393 ....NI-13

ONEIDA CO.,
234878 ....NH-13
Oneonta, 13901 ....NK-15

ONONDAGA CO.,
467026 ....NI-12
Onondaga Hill, 2000 ....NG-8
Ontario, 2160 ....NH-8
Ontario Ctr., 600 ....NH-8

ONTARIO CO.,
107931 ....NJ-8
Oppenheim, 500 ....NI-16
Oramel, 150 ....NL-6

ORANGE CO.,
372813 ....SC-4
Orange Lake, 6982 .....SB-6
Orchard Knol, 250 ......NH-1
Orchard Pk., 3246 ......NJ-4
Orient, 743 ....SD-13
Oriskany, 1400 ....NI-14
Oriskany Falls, 732 ....NJ-14

ORLEANS CO.,
42883 ....NI-6
Orwell, 400 ....NG-12
Osceola, 200 ....NG-13
Ossining, 25060 ....SD-7
Oswegatchie, 300 ......ND-15
Oswego, 18142 ....NG-11

OSWEGO CO.,
122109 ....NG-12
Otego, 1010 ....NL-15
Otisco, 250 ....NJ-11
Otisville, 1068 ....SC-4

OTSEGO CO.,
62259 ....NK-15
Otselic, 400 ....NJ-13
Otter Lake, 460 ....NG-15
Otto, 550 ....NL-4
Ouaquaga, 400 ....NM-14
Ovid, 602 ....NK-10
Owasco, 400 ....NJ-11
Owego, 3896 ....NM-11
Owls Head, 360 ....NB-17
Oxbow, 108 ....ND-13
Oxford, 1450 ....NL-13
Oyster Bay, 6707 ....SF-8
Oyster Bay Cove, 2197 ....†D-20
Ozone Pk. ....†-13
Painted Post, 1809 .....NM-9
Palatine Br., 737 ....NI-16
Palenville, 1037 ....NM-18
Palermo, 20 ....NH-11
Palmyra, 3536 ....NI-8
Pamelia Four Cors., 250 ....NE-12
Panama, 479 ....NM-2
Panther Lake, 190 ....NG-12
Paradox, 100 ....NF-19
Paris, 200 ....NI-14
Parish, 450 ....NG-11
Parishville, 647 ....NC-16
Park Ter., 200 ....SC-11
Parkchester ....†E-13
Parksville, 700 ....NN-16
Parkville SE-12
Patchogue, 11798 ....SF-10
Pattersonville, 600 ......NJ-18
Paul Smiths, 671 ....NC-17
Pavilion, 646 ....NJ-6
Pawling, 2347 ....SB-8
Pearl Creek, 150 ....NJ-6
Pearl River, 15876 ......SC-6
Peasleeville, 800 ....NC-19
Peconic, 683 ....SE-12
Peekskill, 23583 ....SD-7
Pelham, 250 ....NK-17
Pelham Manor, 5486 .†C-14
Pembroke, 200 ....NI-5
Pendleton, 300 ....NH-4
Penfield, Ctr., 120 ......NB-5
Penfield, 6300 ....NH-8
Penn Yan, 5159 ....NK-9
Perkinsville, 400 ....NK-7
Perry, 3673 ....NK-6
Perry Ctr., 100 ....NJ-6
Perrysburg, 401 ....NK-3
Perryville, 100 ....NI-13
Peru, 1591 ....NC-19
Peterboro, 400 ....NI-13
Petersburg, 600 ....NJ-20

Column 2

Petrolia, 70 ....NM-6
Phelps, 1989 ....NI-9
Philadelphia, 1252 ......NE-13
Phillips Creek, 70 ....NL-6
Philmont, 1379 ....NL-19
Phoenicia, 309 ....NM-17
Phoenix, 2382 ....NH-11
Picketts Cors., 200 .....NB-19
Piercefield, 200 ....ND-16
Pierrepont, 100 ....NC-15
Pierrepont Manor, 228 ....NF-12
Piffard, 220 ....NJ-7
Pike, 371 ....NK-6
Pine Bush, 1780 ....SB-5
Pine City, 420 ....NM-10
Pine Island, 1500 ....SD-5
Pine Lake, 25 ....NH-16
Pine Plains, 1353 ....NM-19
Pine Valley, 813 ....NL-10
Pinehurst, 850 ....NJ-3
Piseco, 200 ....NG-16
Pitcaim, 125 ....NC-14
Pitcher, 200 ....NK-13
Pitcher Hill, 5000 ....NE-8
Pittsfield, 601 ....NK-14
Pittsford, 1355 ....NI-8
Pittstown, 100 ....NJ-20
Plainedge, 8817 ....†I-17
Plainview, 26217 ....†I-18
Plandome, 1349 ....†F-16
Plandome Hts. ....†F-16
Plandome Manor, 872 ....NI-6
Plattekill, 1260 ....SB-6
Plattsburgh SH-13
Pleasant Plains *M-5
Pleasant Valley, 1145 ....SA-7
Pleasantville, 7019 ....SD-7
Plessis, 164 ....ND-13
Plymouth, 400 ....NK-14
Poestenkill, 1061 ....NJ-19
Point Lookout, 1219 ..*K-19
Poland, 508 ....NH-15
Pomona, 3103 ....SD-6
Pompey, 500 ....NJ-12
Pond Eddy, 350 ....SC-3
Poplar Ridge, 150 ......NJ-10
Poquott, 953 ....SE-10
Port Byron, 1290 ....NI-10
Port Chester, 28967 ..SC-8
Port Dickinson, 1641 ....NM-13
Port Ewen, 3546 ....NM-18
Port Gibson, 453 ....NI-9
Port Henry, 1194 ....NE-20
Port Jefferson, 7750 ....SE-10
Port Jervis, 8828 ....SC-4
Port Kent, 250 ....NC-20
Port Leyden, 672 ....NG-14
Port Richmond *J-7
Port Washington, 15846 ....SF-7
Port Washington North, 3154 ....†E-16
Portageville, 300 ....NK-6
Porter Cors., 350 ....NI-18
Portland, 950 ....NL-2
Portlandville, 300 ....NK-15
Portville, 1014 ....NM-5
Potsdam, 9428 ....NC-15
Pottersville, 424 ....NF-19
Poughkeepsie, 32736 ....SB-6
Poughquag, 450 ....SB-7
Pratts Hollow, 70 ......NJ-13
Prattsburg, 950 ....NK-8
Prattsville, 355 ....NL-17
Preble, 250 ....NJ-12
Presho, 150 ....NM-9
Preston, 125 ....NK-13
Preston Hollow, 250 ..NJ-17
Princes Bay *M-6
Prospect, 291 ....NH-15
Pulaski, 2365 ....NG-12
Pulteney, 400 ....NK-8
Pumpville, 698 ....NH-9
Purdys, 970 ....SC-8

PUTNAM CO.,
99710 ....SC-7
Putnam Lake, 3844 ...SC-8
Putnam Sta., 300 ......NF-20
Pyrites, 200 ....NC-15
Quaker Hill, 150 ....SB-8
Quarry Hts., 600 ....SH-8
Queens Vil. ....†-15

QUEENS CO.,
2230722 ....SG-7
Queensbury, 967 ......SF-11
Rainbow Lake, 50 .....NC-17
Randall, 250 ....NI-17
Sandy Pond NG-11
Ransomville, 1419 ....NH-4
Rapids, 1636 ....NI-4
Raquette Lake, 170 ..NF-16
Rathbone, 100 ....NM-8
Ravena, 3268 ....NK-19
Ray Brook, 400 ....ND-18
Raymertown, 500 .....NJ-19
Raymondville, 500 ....NB-15
Reading Ctr., 175 .....NL-9
Red Creek, 532 ....NH-10
Red Hook, 1961 ....NM-19
Red Oaks Mill, 3613 .SB-7
Redfield, 600 ....NG-13
Redford, 477 ....NC-18
Redwood, 863 ....ND-13
Rego Pk. ....†H-13
Remsen, 508 ....NH-15
Rensselaer, 9392 ......NJ-19

RENSSELAER CO.,
159429 ....NJ-20
Rensselaer Falls, 330 ....NC-14
Rensselaerville, 300 ..NK-18
Rexford, 340 ....NJ-7
Rexville, 90 ....NM-7
Rhinebeck, 2657 ....NN-18
Rhinecliff, 450 ....NN-18
Richburg, 450 ....NM-6
Richfield, Sprs., 1264 ....NJ-15
Richford, 350 ....NL-12
Richland, 200 ....NG-11

RICHMOND CO.,
468730 ....SG-6
Richmond Hill ....†H-14
Richmond Valley *N-5
Richmondville, 918 ....NK-16

Column 3

Richville, 323 ....ND-14
Ridge, 13336 ....SE-10
Ridgeway, 100 ....NH-5
Ridgewood, 210 ....NH-4
Ridgewood ....†-12
Rifton, 456 ....NM-18
Rigney Bluff, 1090 .....NH-7
Rio, 180 ....SC-4
Riparius, 200 ....NF-18
Riverdale, 3559 ....†C-12
Riverhead, 13299 ......SE-11
Riverside, 497 ....NM-9
Riverside, 250 ....NM-13
Riverview, 200 ....NE-13
Roaring Brook, 250 ...NE-9
Rochdale, 1800 ....SB-5
Rochester, 210565 ....NI-7
Rock City Falls, 700 ....NI-18
Rock Glen, 120 ....NK-6
Rock Hill, 1742 ....SB-4
Rock Stream, 100 ......NK-9
Rockaway Pk. ....†-13
Rockaway Pt., 112 ....NL-14
Rockland, 100 ....NL-14
Rockland, 300 ....NN-15

ROCKLAND CO.,
311687 ....SD-6
Rockville Centre, 24023 ....SG-8
Rockwood, 300 ....NI-17
Rocky Pt., 4140 ....SE-10
Rodman, 153 ....NF-12
Roessleville SI-4
Rome, 33725 ....NH-14
Romulus, 400 ....NJ-10
Ronkonkoma, 19082 ....SH-13
Roosevelt, 16258 ......†I-17
Roosevelt Bch., 200 ....NI-3
Roscoe, 541 ....NN-15
Rose, 400 ....NI-10
Rosebank *K-8
Roseboom, 200 ....NJ-16
Rosedale ....†-15
Rosendale Vil., 1349 ....NN-18
Rosiere, 60 ....NE-11
Roslyn, 2770 ....†F-17
Roslyn Estates, 1251 ....†F-17
Roslyn Hbr., 1051 .....†F-17
Roslyn Hts., 6577 .....†F-17
Ross Cors., 800 ....NM-12
Rossburg, 80 ....NK-6
Rossie, 150 ....ND-13
Rossville *M-5
Rotterdam, 20652 .....NJ-18
Rotterdam Jct., 1000 ....NJ-18
Round Lake, 623 ......NI-19
Round Top, 600 ....NL-18
Rouses Point, 2209 ..NA-20
Roxbury, 700 ....NL-16
Roxbury *L-12
Rural Grv., 200 ....NJ-17
Rush, 500 ....NI-7
Rushford, 363 ....NL-5
Rushville, 677 ....NJ-8
Russell, 300 ....NC-15
Russell Gdns., 945 ....†F-16
Russia, 80 ....NH-15
Rye, 15720 ....SC-8
Rye Brook, 9347 ....SI-9
Sabael, 200 ....NF-17
Sabattis, 30 ....NE-17
Sabbath Day Pt., 160 ....NF-19
Sackets Hbr., 1450 ...NE-12
Sackets Lake, 800 .....SB-4
Saddle Rock, 830 ......†F-15
Sag Hbr., 2169 ....SE-13
Sagaponack, 313 ....SE-13
St. Albans ....†I-15
St. George *J-8
St. Huberts, 30 ....NE-19
St. James, 13268 ......SH-13
St. Johnsburg, 525 ...NB-3
St. Johnsville, 1732 ....NI-16
St. Bonaventure NM-5
Sanborn, 1645 ....NA-3
Sandy Creek, 850 .....NG-12
Sandwood, 200 ....NB-15
Sands Pt., 2675 ....†E-17
Sandusky, 450 ....NK-5
Sandy Bch., 2350 .....NI-3
Sandy Creek, 771 .....NG-12
Sandy Pond NG-11
Sanford, 500 ....NM-14

SARATOGA CO.,
219607 ....NH-18
Saratoga Sprs., 26586 ....NI-19
Sardinia, 550 ....NK-5
Saugerties, 3971 ....NM-18
Sauquoit, 930 ....NI-14
Savannah, 508 ....NI-10
Savona, 827 ....NM-8
Sayville, 16853 ....SF-10
Scarsdale, 17166 ......†A-14
Schaghticoke, 592 ....NI-19
Schenectady, 66135 ....NJ-18

SCHENECTADY CO.,
154727 ....NJ-18
Schenevus, 531 ....NK-16
Schoharie, 922 ....NK-17
Schroon Lake, 833 ....NF-19
Schuyler Falls, 500 ...NC-19
Schuylerville, 1386 ...NI-19
Scio, 609 ....NM-6
Sciota, 180 ....NB-19
Scipio Ctr., 120 ....NJ-10
Scotia, 7729 ....NJ-18
Scott, 150 ....NJ-12
Scottsburg, 150 ....NK-7
Scottsville, 2001 ....NI-8

Column 4

Sea Cliff, 4995 ....†E-17
Seaford, 15294 ....†I-20
Seagate *L-10
Searingtown, 4915 ....†G-17
Selden, 19851 ....SH-14
Sempronius, 100 ....NJ-11
Seneca Castle, 550 ...NJ-9
Seneca Falls, 6681 ...NJ-10
Seneca Knolls, 2011 ....NE-7
Seneca Pt., 200 ....NJ-8
Sennett, 300 ....NI-11
Severance, 200 ....NF-19
Shadigee, 100 ....NH-5
Shandaken, 500 ....NM-17
Sharon Sprs., 558 .....NJ-16
Shawnee NA-4
Sheds, 70 ....NJ-13
Shelby, 300 ....NH-5
Sheldrake, 300 ....NJ-10
Sheldrake Sprs., 150 ....NJ-10
Shelter Island, 1333 ....SD-12
Shelter Island Hts., 1048 ....SD-12
Sherburne, 1367 ....NK-14
Sherman, 730 ....NM-1
Sherrill, 3071 ....NI-13
Shinnecock Hills, 2188 ....SE-12
Shirley, 27854 ....SF-11
Shokan, 1183 ....NM-18
Shongo, 125 ....NM-6
Shoreham, 531 ....SE-10
Short Tract, 500 ....NL-6
Shortsville, 1439 ......NI-8
Shrub Oak, 2011 ......SC-7
Sidney, 3900 ....NL-14
Sidney Ctr., 800 ....NL-14
Silver Bay, 250 ....NF-19
Silver Creek, 2656 ...NK-3
Silver Lake, 600 ....NJ-6
Silver Sprs., 782 ....NK-6
Sinclairville, 588 ....NL-2
Skaneateles, 2450 ....NJ-11
Skaneateles Falls, 850 ....NI-11
Slate Hill, 800 ....SC-5
Slaterville Sprs., ...NL-12
Sleepy Hollow, 9870 ..SC-7
Slingerlands, 2100 ....SJ-3
Sloan, 3661 ....NE-5
Sloansville, 200 ....NI-17
Sloatsburg, 3039 ......SD-6
Smallwood, 580 ....SB-3
Smiths Mills, 700 ......NL-3
Smithtown, 26470 .....SH-12
Smithville Ctr., 200 ...NM-12
Smithville Flats, 351 ....NL-13
Smyrna, 213 ....NK-13
Snyder ND-5
Sodus, 1819 ....NH-9
Sodus Ctr., 200 ....NH-9
Sodus Pt., 900 ....NH-9
Solon, 50 ....NK-12
Solvay, 6584 ....NI-11
Somerset, 70 ....NH-5
Sonora, 70 ....NL-9
Sonyea, 350 ....NK-7
Sound Bch., 7612 ....SE-10
Soundview ....†E-13
S. Alabama, 100 ....NI-5
S. Amenia, 100 ....NN-20
S. Apalachin, 200 .....NM-12
S. Argyle, 230 ....NH-20
S. Beach *L-8
S. Berne NK-18
S. Bethlehem, 550 ....NK-19
S. Bolivar, 75 ....NM-6
S. Bombay NB-16
S. Brooklyn *I-10
S. Butler, 250 ....NI-10
S. Cairo, 950 ....NL-18
S. Colton, 400 ....NC-15
S. Columbia, 100 ......NJ-14
S. Corning, 1145 ....NM-9
S. Dansville, 125 ....NK-7
S. Dayton, 620 ....NL-3
S. Edmeston, 120 .....NK-14
S. Floral Pk., 1764 ....†I-16
S. Glens Falls, 3518 ....NI-19
S. Granville NH-20
S. Greece NH-20
S. Hannibal, 35 ....NH-11
S. Hartford, 100 ....NH-20
S. Hempstead, 3243 ....†I-18
S. Huntington, 9422 ....SI-10
S. Jamesport, 600 ....SE-12
S. Kortright, 180 ....NL-16
S. Livonia, 250 ....NJ-7
S. Lockport, 8324 .....NI-4
S. New Berlin, 135 ....NK-14
S. Nyack, 600 ....SD-6
S. Onondaga, 650 ....NJ-11
S. Otselic, 506 ....NK-13
S. Ozone Pk. ....†-14
S. Ripley NL-1
S. Salem, 12300 ......SD-8
S. Schroon, 200 ....NF-19
S. Sodus, 130 ....NH-9
S. Stockton NL-2
S. Valley, 50 ....NM-3
S. Wales, 450 ....NJ-4
S. Warsaw, 200 ....NJ-6
S. Worcester, 150 .....NK-16
3109 ....NH-19
University Gdns. ....†G-16
Unadilla, 1138 ....NL-15
Unadilla Forks, 50 ....NJ-15
Underwood, 55 ....NE-19
Union Ctr., 1900 ....NM-13
Union Sprs., 1174 .....NJ-10
Union Vil. NH-19
Upper Brookville, 1698 ....†E-18
Upper Jay, 500 ....NE-19
Utica, 62235 ....NI-14
Vail Mills, 150 ....NI-17
Vails Gate, 3369 ....SC-6
Valatie, 1819 ....NL-19

Column 5

Springfield Gdns. ....†I-15
Springs, 6592 ....SE-13
Springville, 4296 ....NK-4
Springwater, 650 ......NK-7
Staatsburg, 377 ....NN-18
Stafford, 500 ....NI-6
Stamford, 1119 ....NL-16
Standish, 190 ....NB-18
Stanford Hts., 1050 ....NJ-18
Standfordville, 630 ....NN-19
Stanley, 300 ....NJ-9
Stannards, 798 ....NM-6
Star Lake, 809 ....NE-15
Starkville, 125 ....NJ-16
State Line, 100 ....NL-1
Steamburg, 900 ....NM-3
Stephentown, 750 ....NK-20
Sterling, 300 ....NH-10
Steuben, 100 ....NH-15

STEUBEN CO.,
98990 ....NL-8
Stewart Manor, 1896 ....†H-17
Stilesville, 85 ....NM-14
Stillwater, 1738 ....NI-19
Stittville, 700 ....NH-14
Stockbridge, 100 ......NI-13
Stockport, 400 ....NL-19
Stockton, 450 ....NL-2
Stone Mills, 45 ....NE-12
Stone Ridge, 1173 ....NN-18
Stony Brook, 13740 ....SE-10
Stony Creek, 600 ......NG-18
Stony Pt., 12147 ....SD-6
Stormville, 700 ....SB-7
Stottville, 1375 ....NL-19
Stow, 300 ....NM-2
Stratford, 800 ....NI-16
Strykersville, 647 ......NJ-5
Stuyvesant, 550 ....NL-19
Suffern, 10723 ....SD-6
Sugar Loaf, 400 ....SC-5

SULLIVAN CO.,
77547 ....NN-15
Sullivanville, 120 ......NM-10
Summer Hill, 100 .....NJ-11
Summit, 200 ....NK-16
Summitville, 700 ....SB-5
Sundown, 200 ....NN-17
Surprise, 200 ....NL-18
Swain, 200 ....NK-7
Swan Lake, 1200 .....SA-3
Swormville, 550 ....NC-6
Sycaway, 1950 ....NH-5
Sylvan Bch., 897 ......NH-13
Syosset, 18829 ....SF-8
Syracuse, 145170 .....NI-12
Taberg, 150 ....NH-13
Taborton, 200 ....NK-20
Taghkanic, 120 ....NM-19
Talcottville, 100 ....NG-14
Tannersville, 539 ......NL-18
Tappan, 6613 ....SE-7
Tarrytown, 11277 .....SC-7
Taunton, 1050 ....NF-7
Taylor, 200 ....NK-12
Terryville, 11849 ......SG-14
Texas, 175 ....NG-11
Texas Valley, 75 ....NL-12
Thayer Corners, ...NJ-17
Thendara, 230 ....NF-15
Theresa, 863 ....ND-13
Thomaston, 2617 .....†F-16
Thompson Ridge, ...SB-5
Three Mile Bay, 227 ....NE-12
Three Rivers, 200 .....NI-11
Throop's Neck ....†-14
Ticonderoga, 3382 ...NF-20
Tillson, 1586 ....NN-18
Tioga Ctr., 600 ....NM-11
Titusville SG-15
Tivoli, 1125 ....NM-19
Todd Hill *K-7
Tomkins Cove, 850 ...SD-6
Tonawanda, 15130 ...NC-4
Tottenville *N-5
Towaco, 65 ....ND-13
Town Line, 2367 ....NJ-4
Towners, 150 ....SC-8
Travis *L-6
Treadwell, 200 ....NL-16
Triangle, 350 ....NM-13
Trumbulls Corners, ...NL-11
2012 ....NE-13
Truthville, 350 ....NH-20
Truxton, 500 ....NJ-12
Tuckahoe, 6486 ....†B-13
Tuckahoe, 1373 ....SE-12
Tully, 873 ....NJ-12
Tunnel, 200 ....NM-13
Tupper Lake, 3667 ...ND-17
Turin, 232 ....NG-14
Tuscarora, 76 ....NN-8
Tuxedo Pk., 623 ....SD-6
Twin Orchards, 1600 ....SC-10
Tyrrellville, 100 ....NF-13
Tyre, 180 ....NI-10
Tyrone, 500 ....NL-9

ULSTER CO.,
182493 ....NN-17
Unadilla, 1140 ....NL-15
Unadilla Forks, ...NJ-15

Column 6

Valley Cottage, 9107 ....SD-6
Valley Falls, 466 ....NJ-19
Valley Stream, 37511 ....SG-7
Valois, 350 ....NK-9
Van Buren Pt., 300 ...NK-2
Van Etten, 537 ....NM-10
Van Hornesville, 1050 ....NJ-15
Varna, 500 ....NL-11
Varysburg, 360 ....NJ-5
Venice Ctr., 135 ....NJ-10
Verbank, 400 ....SA-7
Verdoy, 1000 ....SH-4
Vernon, 1172 ....NI-13
Vernon Ctr., 300 ......NI-13
Verona, 461 ....NI-13
Versailles, 280 ....NL-3
Vesper, 180 ....NJ-12
Vestal, 500 ....NM-12
Vestal Ctr., 800 ....NM-12
Veteran, 200 ....NM-10
Victor, 2696 ....NI-8
Victory, 140 ....NI-10
Victory Mills, 605 .....NI-19
Vienna, 600 ....NH-13
Vilage Green, 3891 ....NE-6
Village of the Branch, SH-12
Vine Valley, 200 ....NJ-9
Virgil, 300 ....NK-12
Vischer Ferry, 330 ....SG-4
Vista, 750 ....SD-8
Volney, 150 ....NH-11
Voorheesville, 2789 ....NK-18
Wading River, 7719 ....SE-11
Waddington, 972 ......NB-14
Wadhams, 125 ....NE-19
Wading River, 550 ....NE-11
Wainscott, 650 ....SE-13
Wakefield ....†C-13
Walden, 6978 ....SB-6
Walker Valley, 853 ...SB-5
Wallace, 200 ....NJ-3
Wallington, 110 ....NH-9
Wallkill, 2288 ....NN-18
Walton, 3088 ....NM-15
Walworth, 850 ....NH-8
Wampsville, 543 ......NI-13
Wanakah, 3199 ....NJ-3
Wanakena, 250 ....NE-15
Wantagh, 18871 ......†I-20
Wappingers Falls, 5522 ....SB-7
Warners, 500 ....NI-11
Warnerville, 1000 .....NK-17

WARREN CO.,
65707 ....NG-18
Warrensburg, 3103 ....NG-19
Warsaw, 3473 ....NJ-6
Warwick, 6731 ....SD-5

WASHINGTON CO.,
63216 ....NH-20
Washington Ctr., ...†E-11
Washington Mills, 1183 ....SC-12
Washingtonville, 5899 ....SC-6
Wassaic, 700 ....NN-20
Water Island SJ-14
Waterford, 1990 ....NJ-19
Waterloo, 5171 ....NJ-10
Waterport, 400 ....NH-5
Watertown, 27023 ....NE-12
Waterville, 1583 ....NJ-14
Watervliet, 10000 .....NJ-19
Watkins Glen, 1859 ....NL-10
Watson, 100 ....NF-14
Watts Flats, 100 ......NM-2
Waverly, 4444 ....NM-11
Wawarsing, 800 ....SA-5
Wayland, 1865 ....NK-7
Wayne, 550 ....NK-9
Webb NF-15
Webbs Mills, 300 .....NM-10
Webster, 5399 ....NH-8
Websters Crossing, ..NK-7
Weedsport, 1815 ......NI-10
Wegatchie, 65 ....ND-13
Wells Br., 300 ....NL-14
Wells, 600 ....NH-17
Wellsboro, 380 ....NM-10
Wellsburg, 847 ....SB-4
Wellsville, 4679 ....NM-6
Wendelville, 100 ....NI-4
W. Amboy, 125 ....NH-12
W. Babylon, 43213 ...SF-9
W. Bangor, 296 ....NB-17
W. Bloomfield, 600 ...NJ-8
W. Branch, 100 ....NG-14
W. Burlington, 100 ...NK-15
W. Camp, 400 ....NM-18
W. Carthage, 3109 ...NF-13
W. Chazy, 529 ....NB-19
W. Chenango, 350 ...NM-13
W. Clarksville, 300 ...NM-5
W. Corners, 1800 .....SB-9
W. Danby, 200 ....NL-11
W. Davenport, 250 ...NL-15
W. Eaton, 500 ....NJ-14
W. Edmeston, 125 ...NK-14
W. Elmira, 4967 ....NM-10
W. Exeter, 100 ....NJ-15
W. Falls, 1510 ....NJ-4
W. Fulton, 200 ....NK-17
W. Galway, 150 ....NH-17
W. Glens Falls, 7071 ....NH-19
W. Groton, 60 ....NL-11
W. Haverstraw, 10165 ....SD-6
W. Hebron, 175 ....NH-20
W. Hempstead, 18862 ....†I-17
W. Hills, 5592 ....SI-10
W. Hurley, 900 ....NM-18
W. Islip, 28335 ....SI-11
W. Kill, 200 ....NL-17
W. Laurens, 150 ......NK-15
W. Lebanon, 450 .....NK-20
W. Leyden, 500 ....NG-14
W. Martinsburg, 60 ....NG-14
W. Milton, 350 ....NI-19
W. Monroe, 400 ......NH-12
W. New Brighton *J-8
W. Oneonta, 600 .....NK-15
W. Park, 850 ....NN-18
W. Plattsburgh, 150 ....NB-19
W. Point, 6763 ....SC-6

Column 7

W. Sand Lake, 2660 ....NK-19
W. Sayville, 5011 .....SJ-13
W. Schuyler, 240 .....NI-15
W. Seneca, 44711 ....NJ-4
W. Shokan, 350 ....NM-17
W. Stephentown, 330 ....NK-20
W. Stockholm, 300 ....NB-15
W. Taghkanic, 200 ....NM-19
W. Valley, 518 ....NL-4
W. Walworth, 150 ....NI-8
W. Webster, 8700 ....NH-8
W. Windsor, 850 .....NM-13
W. Winfield, 826 ......NJ-15
Westbrookville, 500 .SC-4
Westbury, 15146 .....SG-18
Westbury South, 9500 ....†G-19
Westdale, 400 ....NH-13
Westerleigh *K-7
Westerlo, 680 ....NK-18
Westernville, 600 .....NH-14
Westfield, 3224 ....NL-1
Westhampton, 3079 ....SF-11
Westhampton Bch., 1721 ....SF-11
Westmere, 7284 ......NJ-18
Westmoreland, 427 ....NI-14
Weston, 90 ....NL-9
Weston Mills, 1472 ....NM-5
Westport, 518 ....ND-20
Westtown, 700 ....SC-4
Westvale, 4963 ....NF-7
Westville, 100 ....NA-17
Westville Ctr., 120 ...NA-17
Wevertown, 200 ......NF-18
Whallonsburg, 200 ....ND-20
Wheatley Hts., 5130 ....SI-10
Wheatville, 150 ....NI-5
Wheeler, 130 ....NL-8
Whipplesville, 300 ...NM-17
White Creek, 300 .....NK-20
White Plains, 56853 ..SK-7
White Sulphur Sprs., 600 ....NM-16
Whitehall, 2614 ....NG-20
Whitesboro, 3772 ....SA-12
Whitestone ....†C-14
Whitesville, 800 ....NM-7
Whitney Pt., 964 ......NL-12
Willard, 600 ....NK-10
Willet, 400 ....NK-13
Williams Br. ....†D-13
Williamson, 2495 ....NH-9
Williamstown, 5300 ....ND-5
Williston Pk. ....†G-17
Willow Pt., 1700 ......SB-10
Willow Ridge Estates, 4800 ....NC-4
Willowemoc, 70 ....NN-16
Willsboro, 753 ....ND-20
Willsboro Pt., 500 ....NC-20
Willseyville, 330 ......NL-11
Wilmington, 937 ......NE-18
Wilson, 1264 ....NH-3
Windham, 367 ....NL-18
Windsor, 916 ....NM-13
Winebrook Hills, ...NE-18
Wingdale, 650 ....SB-8
Winthrop, 530 ....NB-15
Wiscoy, 165 ....NK-6
Witherbee, 347 ....NE-19
Wolcott, 1701 ....NH-10
Wolcottsville, 600 ....NI-5
Wood Haven ....†I-13
39772 ....NI-9
Webbs Mills, 300 .....NM-10
Woodbourne, 1200 ..SA-4
Woodbury, 10686 ....SC-6
Woodburgh, 778 ......†K-16
Woodgate, 450 ....NG-15
Woodhull, 350 ....NM-8
Woodland, 200 ....NC-17
Woodlawn, 900 ....NJ-3
Woodmere, 17121 ...†J-16
Woodridge, 847 ......SB-4
Woodrow *M-6
Woodsburg, 778 ......†K-16
Woodstock, 2088 .....NM-18
Woodville, 250 ....NM-17
Woodworth NB-12
Worcester, 1113 ....NK-16
Worth, 25 ....NF-12
Wright's Cors., 200 ...NH-4
Wurtsboro, 1246 ......SB-4
Wyandanch, 11647 ..SI-11
Wyanttskill, 3376 ....NJ-19
Wyoming, 434 ....NJ-6
Yaphank, 5945 ....SF-10
Yonkers, 195976 .....SE-7
York, 650 ....NJ-6
Yorkshire, 600 ....NK-5
Yorktown Hts., 1781 ..SD-7
Yorkville, 2689 ....NI-14
Youngstown, 1935 ...NH-3
Youngsville, 800 ......NN-16
Yulan, 750 ....SC-3

Column 8 — North Carolina

Alexis, 600 ....F-5

ALLEGHANY CO.,
11155 ....B-4
Allen G-6
Allensville, 80 ....C-11
Alliance, 776 ....G-17
Alma, 50 ....H-10
Almond, 150 ....J-2
Altamahaw, 347 ....C-9
Altamont, 50 ....D-2
Amantha, 50 ....D-3
Ammon, 30 ....H-12
Anderson, 60 ....C-10
Andrews, 1781 ....M-2
Angier, 4350 ....E-11
Ansonville, 631 ....G-7
Antioch, 80 ....H-10

ANSON CO.,
26948 ....H-7
Apex, 37476 ....E-11
Aquadale, 397 ....G-7
Aquone, 220 ....M-2
Arabia, 110 ....H-10
Ararat, 50 ....B-6
Arcadia, 130 ....D-7
Archdale, 11415 ....D-8
Arcola, 60 ....C-13
Arden, 800 ....F-1
Arnold *E-1
Aran Hills, 2240 ....M-15
Ash, 250 ....J-12
Asheboro, 25012 ....E-8
Asheville, 83393 ....E-1
Ashford D-2
Ashley Hts., 380 ....G-10
Askewville, 241 ....C-16
Askin, 200 ....F-11
Atkinson, 299 ....I-13
Atlantic, 543 ....H-18
Atlantic Bch., 1495 ....H-17
Aulander, 895 ....C-16
Aurora, 520 ....F-17
Austin C-5
Autryville, 196 ....G-12
Avery Creek, 1950 .....F-1
Avon, 776 ....F-20
Ayden, 4932 ....F-15
Aydlett, 240 ....C-19
Ayersville, 120 ....B-8
Azalea M-4
Badin, 1974 ....F-7
Bahama, 500 ....C-11
Bailey, 569 ....E-13
Bakersville, 464 ....D-2
Bald Creek, 110 ....D-1
Bald Head Island, 158 ....K-13
Baldwin C-4
Balsam, 400 ....L-4
Balsam Grv., 120 ....M-5
Banner Elk, 1028 ....C-3
Barber, 80 ....E-6
Barco, 300 ....B-19
Barkers Creek, 50 .....*E-12
Barnardsville, 160 .....D-1
Barnesville, 130 ....I-10
Barriers Mill, 30 ....H-8
Bat Cave, 600 ....F-1
Bath, 249 ....F-17
Bayboro, 1263 ....G-17
Bayleaf, 800 ....G-13
Bayview, 346 ....F-17
Bear Creek, 110 ....E-10
Bear Grass, 75 ....E-16
Bear Poplar C-6
Beaufort, 4039 ....H-17
Belair, 1120 ....M-16
Belcross, 147 ....C-18
Belgrade, 270 ....H-16
Belhaven, 1688 ....F-17
Bellamont, 220 ....D-9
Belmont, 10076 ....G-5
Belvoir, 950 ....E-15
Belwood, 950 ....F-4
Benson, 3311 ....F-12
Bent Creek, 1287 ....E-1
Berea, 140 ....C-12
Bermuda Run, 1725 ...D-7
Bessemer City, 5340 ..F-4
Beta, 130 ....L-4
Bethania, 450 ....C-7
Bethel, 1577 ....D-15
Bethel, 60 ....B-9
Bethel, 80 ....J-11
Bethel Hill B-11
Bethesda *G-11
Bethlehem, 4214 ....E-4
Bettie, 170 ....H-17
Beulaville, 1296 ....H-14
Biltmore Forest, 1343 ....E-1
Birdtown, 400 ....L-3
Biscoe, 1700 ....F-8
Black Creek, 769 ....E-13
Black Mtn., 7848 ....E-1
Bladenboro, 1750 ......I-11
Blanch, 100 ....B-10
Blounts Creek, 1150 ..F-16
Blowing Rock, 1241 ...C-3
Boardman, 157 ....I-11
Bobbitt, 100 ....C-12
Bogue, 684 ....H-16
Boiling Spr. Lakes, 5372 ....K-13
Boiling Sprs., 4647 ....F-3
Bolivia, 143 ....J-12
Bolton, 691 ....J-12
Bonlee, 320 ....E-9
Bonnerton, 30 ....F-17
Boomer, 500 ....D-4
Boone, 17122 ....C-3
Bostic, 386 ....F-3
Bottom F-5
Bowdens, 270 ....G-13
Bowie B-4
Braggtown, 90 ....C-11
Brandywine, 350 ....J-3
Brasstown, 300 ....M-1
Brevard, 7609 ....M-5
Brickhaven, 60 ....E-10
Bridgeton, 454 ....G-16
Brinkleyville, 50 ....C-13
Broadway, 1229 ....F-10
Brogden, 2633 ....G-13
Brookford, 442 ....E-4
Brooks Crossroads, 320 ....D-6
Browns Summit, 340 ..C-9

Column 9

Brunswick, 1119 ....J-11

BRUNSWICK CO.,
107431 ....J-12
Bryson City, 1424 ....L-3
Buena Vista, 30 ....C-15
Buie, 110 ....H-10
Buies Creek, 2942 .....F-11
Buladean, 180 ....C-2
Bullock, 250 ....B-12
Bunn, 344 ....D-13

BUNCOMBE CO.,
238318 ....E-1
Bunnlevel, 552 ....F-11
Bunyan, 40 ....G-16
Burden, 30 ....C-16
Burgaw, 3872 ....I-14
Burlington, 49963 ....D-9
Burney, 70 ....H-11
Burnsville, 1693 ....D-1
Burnsville, 50 ....G-7
Bushy Fork, 50 ....B-10
Butner, 7591 ....C-11
Butters, 294 ....I-11
Buxton, 1273 ....F-20
Bynum, 490 ....E-10

CABARRUS CO.,
178011 ....F-6
Cajahs Mtn., 2823 ....D-3
Calabash, 1786 ....K-12
Caldwell C-10

CALDWELL CO.,
83029 ....D-3
Calypso, 538 ....G-13
Camden, 599 ....C-18

CAMDEN CO.,
9980 ....B-18
Cameron, 285 ....F-10
Camp Sprs., 40 ....C-9
Campbell Creek, ...F-17
Candler, 1000 ....E-1
Candor, 840 ....F-8
Canton, 4227 ....L-4
Cape Carteret, 1970 ..H-16
Carbonton, 60 ....F-10
Carolina Bch., 5706 ...K-14
Carolina Shores, 3048 ....K-12
Carpenter, 300 ....*I-10
Carr, 50 ....C-10
Carrboro, 19582 ....D-10
Carthage, 2205 ....F-9
Carvers, 70 ....I-12
Cary, 135234 ....E-11
Casar, 297 ....F-3
Cashiers, 157 ....M-4
Castalia, 320 ....D-13
Castle Hayne, 1202 ...I-14
Caswell Bch., 398 ......K-13

CASWELL CO.,
23719 ....C-9
Catawba, 603 ....E-5

CATAWBA CO.,
154358 ....E-4
Catherine Lake, ...H-15
Cayton, 70 ....F-15
Cedar Creek, 210 ....G-11
Cedar Grv., 150 ....C-10
Cedar Island, 150 ......G-18
Cedar Mtn., 200 ....M-5
Cedar Pt., 1279 ....H-16
Celo D-1
Center Hill, 50 ....C-17
Centerville, 89 ....C-13
Cerro Gordo, 207 ....J-11
Chadbourn, 1856 ....J-11
E. Fayetteville, ...*H-11
E. Flat Rock, 4995 .....F-1
E. Lake, 100 ....D-19
E. Laport, 100 ....L-4
Eastover, 3628 ....G-11
Eastwood, 30 ....F-9
Eborn's Crossroads, ...F-16
Eden, 15527 ....B-8
Edenton, 5004 ....D-17
Edgemont D-3

EDGECOMBE CO.,
57244 ....D-14
Edmonds, 80 ....D-15
Edneyville, 2367 ....F-1
Edward, 300 ....F-17
Efland, 650 ....D-10
Elberson, 300 ....I-10
Eldorado, 250 ....F-8
Eli Whitney, 50 ....D-10
Elizabeth City, 18683 ....C-18
Elizabethtown, 3583 ..I-12
Elk Pk., 452 ....C-2
Elkin, 4001 ....C-5
Ellenboro, 873 ....F-3
Ellerbe, 1032 ....G-8
Elm City, 1298 ....C-14
Elmwood E-6
Eloy, 2933 ....H-12
Emerald Isle, 3655 ....H-16
Emerson, 30 ....H-11
Emerson, 80 ....H-12
Emma, 1100 ....M-7
Engelhard, 650 ....F-19
Enfield, 2532 ....C-14
Enka, 150 ....D-1
Ennice B-5
Enola, 50 ....I-12
Enterprise, 70 ....*D-1
Eron, 250 ....B-16
Erwin, 4597 ....G-11
Eubanks, 110 ....*D-10
Eure, 240 ....B-16
Eureka, 197 ....E-14
Eureka Sprs., 2910 ....K-16
Evergreen, 421 ....J-11
Everetts, 180 ....E-16
Fair Bluff, 951 ....J-10
Fairfield, 250 ....E-19
Fairmont, 2630 ....I-10
Fairview, 2620 ....F-1
Fairview, 80 ....D-5
Faison, 961 ....G-13
Faith, 807 ....E-6
Falcon, 258 ....G-12

Column 10

Cordova, 1775 ....H-8
Core Pt., 120 ....F-17
Corinth, 170 ....E-11
Cornelius, 24866 ....F-5
Corolla, 150 ....B-19
Council, 80 ....I-12
Courtney, 550 ....D-6
Cove City, 399 ....G-15
Cove Creek, 260 ....K-4
Crabtree, 50 ....K-4
Cramerton, 4165 ....G-5
Cranberry, 250 ....C-2
Creedmoor, 4124 ....C-11
Creston, 70 ....B-3
Creswell, 276 ....D-18
Cricket, 1855 ....C-4
Crisp, 120 ....E-14
Croatan, 130 ....G-16
Crossnore, 192 ....C-2
Crouse, 900 ....F-4
Crowders G-4
Crumpler, 100 ....B-3
Cruso, 200 ....L-4
Cruse Island, 120 ....L-12
Crutchfield Crossroads, F-4
Cullasaja, 500 ....M-3
Cullowhee, 6228 ....L-4
Cumberland, ...M-15

CUMBERLAND CO.,
319431 ....H-11
Cumnock, 250 ....E-10
Currie, 300 ....I-13
Currituck, 60 ....B-19

CURRITUCK CO.,
23547 ....B-19
Curritack, 340 ....C-6
Dabney, 70 ....C-12
Dallas, 4488 ....L-13
Dana, 120 ....M-5
Danbury, 189 ....C-7
Dardens, 150 ....D-17
Davenport, 80 ....F-16
Davidson, 10944 ....F-5

DAVIDSON CO.,
162878 ....D-7

DAVIE CO., 41240.....D-6
Davis, 422 ....H-18
Deep Run, 300 ....G-14
Delco, 348 ....J-13
Dellwood, 200 ....L-4
Delway, 203 ....H-13
Dennis, 200 ....C-7
Denton, 1636 ....E-7
Denver, 2309 ....F-5
Dillard, 80 ....C-8
Dillsboro, 232 ....L-3
Dobbins Hts., 866 ......H-9
Dobson, 1495 ....B-6
Dortches, 935 ....D-14
Dover, 401 ....F-15
Drexel, 1858 ....E-3
Dublin, 338 ....I-11
Dudley, 320 ....G-13
Duck, 369 ....C-19
Dunn, 9263 ....F-12
Durham, 228330 ....D-11

DURHAM CO.,
267587 ....D-11
Dysartsville, 130 ....E-3
Eagle Rock, 100 ....E-12
Eagle Sprs., 350 ....F-9
Earl, 260 ....G-3
East Arcadia, 487 ....I-12
E. Bend, 612 ....C-6
Gibsonville, 6410 ....D-9
Germanton, 827 ....C-7
Gibson, 540 ....H-9
Glade Valley, 100 ......B-4
Glen Alpine, 1517 ......E-3
Glen Ayre, 60 ....D-2
Glen Raven, 2837 .....C-9
Glendale Spr. B-4
Glenola E-8
Glenview, 30 ....D-14
Glenwood, 150 ....*E-6
Gliden C-2
Gloucester, 150 ....H-17
Gneiss M-3
Goat Neck, 80 ....D-19
Godwin, 139 ....G-11
Gold Hill, 370 ....F-7
Gold Pt., 90 ....D-15
Goldsboro, 36437 ......F-13
Goldston, 637 ....E-10
Goose Pond, 30 ....*C-7
Gordon C-5
Gordontown, 130 ......C-11
Gorman, 1011 ....D-11
Goshen, 150 ....I-13
Grahamtown, ...L-4

GRAHAM CO.,
8861 ....L-2
Graingers, 50 ....F-14
Grandy, 950 ....C-19
Granite Falls, 4722 ....E-4
Granite Quarry, 2930 ..E-7
Grantham, 400 ....G-13
Grantsboro, 688 ....G-17
Grassy Creek, 60 ....B-4
Grassy Chapel E-9
Graysville, 140 ....D-9
Green Hill, 350 ....L-3
Green Level, 210 ....D-10
Green Level *D-10
Green Mtn., 150 ....D-1
Green Sea, 40 ....J-11
Greenevers, 634 ....H-14
Greensboro, 269666 ..D-8
Greenville, 84554 ......E-15
Gregory, 60 ....B-18
Greystone, 150 ....C-12
Grifton, 2617 ....F-15
Grimesland, 441 ....E-16
Grissom, 60 ....C-11
Grover, 708 ....G-4
Kyle L-4

Column 11

Falkland, 96 ....E-15
Falls, 110 ....G-13
Fallston, 607 ....F-4
Farmer, 50 ....E-8
Farmington, 300 ....D-6
Farmville, 4654 ....E-14
Faust D-1
Fayetteville, ...G-11
Fearrington, 903 ....*J-8
Feezor, 150 ....D-7
Ferguson, 170 ....D-4
Fig, 150 ....C-2
Fig, 150 ....*L-2
Fletcher, 7187 ....F-1
Florence, 170 ....G-3
Folkstone, 150 ....I-15
Fontana Vil., 80 ....L-2
Forest City, 7476 ....F-3
Forest Hills, 365 ....L-4
Forestville *F-14
Forsyth Co. D-7

FORSYTH CO.,
350670 ....C-7
Ft. Barnwell, 350 ....F-15
Fountain, 427 ....E-14
Fountain, 100 ....F-14
Four Oaks, 1921 ....F-12
Foxfire, 902 ....G-9
Francisco B-7
Franklin, 3845 ....M-3

FRANKLIN CO.,
60619 ....C-12
Franklinton, 2023 ......C-12
Franklinville, 1164 .....E-9
Frederick, 30 ....*I-10
Freeland, 60 ....J-12
Freeman, 150 ....J-13
Fremont, 1255 ....E-13
Friendship *B-5
Frisco, 200 ....F-20
Fuquay-Varina, 17937 ....E-11
Gamewell, 4051 ....D-3
Garland, 625 ....H-12
Garner, 25745 ....E-12
Garysburg, 1050 ....B-14
Gaston, 1152 ....B-14
Gastonia, ...G-4

GASTON CO.,
206086 ....F-4
Gaston, 370 ....B-17
Gatesville, 321 ....B-17

GATES CO.,
12197 ....B-17
Gatesville, 321 ....B-17
Jackson, 513 ....C-15

JACKSON CO.,
40271 ....M-4
Jackson Hill E-7
Jackson Sprs., 300 ...G-9
Jacksonville, 70145 ...H-15
James City, 5899 ......G-16
Jamestown, 3382 ......D-8
Jamesville, 491 ....D-16
Janeiro, 40 ....G-17
Jarvisburg, 450 ....C-19
Jason, 100 ....F-14
Jasper, 130 ....C-18
Jefferson, 1611 ....B-4
Jericho, 30 ....D-11
Jerome, 80 ....H-11
Johns, 50 ....D-11

JOHNSTON CO.,
168878 ....F-12
Jonathan, 590 ....*D-14
Jones, ...G-16

JONES CO.,
10153 ....G-15
Jonesboro, ...F-10
Jonesville, 2285 ....C-5
Joyland *G-10
Julian, 400 ....D-9
Jupiter, 30 ....D-1
Kannapolis, 42625 .....F-6
Kelford, 251 ....C-16
Kelly, 544 ....I-13
Kenansville, 856 ....H-13
Kenly, 1339 ....E-13
Kernersville, 23123 ....D-8
Kerr, 30 ....H-12

Column 12

Haws Run, 200 ....H-15
Hayesville, 311 ....M-2
Hays, 1851 ....C-5

HAYWOOD CO.,
59036 ....K-4
Healing Sprs. *E-7
Hemby Br., 1520 ......*J-7
Hendersonville, 11368 ....L-12

HENDERSON CO.,
106740 ....F-1
Hendersonville F-1
Hertford, 2143 ....C-18
Henrietta, 961 ....F-3
Hester C-11
Hickory, 40010 ....E-4
Hickory Grv., 862 .....*G-1
Hiddenite, 536 ....D-5
High Falls, 220 ....F-9
High Hampton, 50 .....M-4
High Rock, 30 ....E-7
Highlands, 924 ....M-4
Hightowers C-9
Hightsville, 739 ....L-19
Hildebran, 2023 ....E-4
Hillcrest, 440 ....G-10
Hillsborough, 6087 ....D-10
Hiwassee Dam, 300 ..M-1
Hobbsville, 110 ....C-17
Hobbton, 40 ....G-12
Hobgood, 348 ....D-15
Hoffman, 588 ....G-9

HOKE CO., 46952 ....G-10
Holden Bch., 575 ......K-13
Hollis, 50 ....F-3
Hollister, 674 ....C-13
Holly Ridge, 1268 ......I-15
Holly Sprs., 24661 .....E-11
Hookerton, 409 ....F-14
Hope Mills, 15176 ......G-11
Hot Sprs., 560 ....C-1
Hubert, 330 ....H-16
Hudson, 3776 ....D-4
Huntersville, 46773 ...F-5
Hurdle Mills, 50 ....C-10

HYDE CO., 5810 ......E-18
Indian Trail, 33518 ....*J-7
Ingalls, 200 ....C-2
Ingleside, 50 ....C-12
Ingold, 471 ....H-12

IREDELL CO.,
159437 ....D-5
Iron Sta., 755 ....F-5
Ivanhoe, 264 ....I-13
Jackson, 513 ....C-15

Column 13 — North Carolina county list

LENOIR CO.,
59495 ....G-14
Level Cross, 350 ....D-8
Level Cross C-6
Lewiston Woodville, 549 ....C-16
Lewisville, 12639 ......D-7
Lexington, 18931 ......E-7
Liberty, 2656 ....D-9
Liberty, 100 ....F-2
Lilesville, 536 ....G-8
Lillington, 3194 ....F-11

LINCOLN CO.,
78265 ....F-4
Lincolnton, 10486 ......F-4
Linden, 100 ....D-3
Linville, 300 ....C-3
Linville Falls, 350 ......D-2
Lisbon, 100 ....H-12
Little River, 350 ....*F-1
Little Switzerland, 300 ....D-2
Littleton, 674 ....B-14
Lizzie, 100 ....E-14
Locust, 2930 ....F-7
Logan F-4
Lola, 40 ....G-18
Long Island, 200 ....E-5
Longcreek, 220 ....I-13
Longview, 4871 ....E-4
Longwood, 430 ....K-12
Loray, 190 ....E-5
Louisburg, 3359 ....D-12
Love Valley, 90 ....D-5
Lowell, 3526 ....M-14
Lowes Grv. *H-10
Lowesville, 2945 ....F-5
Lowgap, 324 ....B-5
Lowland, 450 ....F-17
Lucama, 1108 ....E-13
Lucia, 160 ....F-5
Luther, Br., 94 ....H-10
Lumberton, 21542 .....I-11
Lyman, 100 ....H-4
Lynn, 530 ....F-1
Mabel, 90 ....C-3
Macclesfield, 471 ......E-14
Macedonia *J-12
Mackeys, 150 ....D-17
Macon, 119 ....B-13

MACON CO.,
33922 ....M-3
Madison, 2246 ....C-8

MADISON CO.,
20764 ....D-1
Maggie Valley, 1150 ..L-4
Magnolia, 939 ....H-13
Maiden, 3310 ....E-4
Mamers, 826 ....F-11
Mamie, 60 ....C-19
Manns Hbr., 821 ....D-20
Manson, 200 ....B-12
Manteo, 1434 ....D-20
Maple, 250 ....B-19
Maple Hill, 390 ....H-14
Mapleville, 30 ....D-13
Marble, 321 ....M-2
Margarettsville, 240 ..B-15
Marietta, 175 ....J-11
Marion, 7838 ....E-2
Mars Hill, 1869 ....D-1
Marshall, 872 ....K-5
Marshallberg, 403 .....H-18
Marshville, 2402 ....G-7
Marston, 200 ....H-9
Martin, 280 ....J-11

MARTIN CO.,
24505 ....E-16
Marvin, 1579 ....G-5
Matthews, 27198 ......G-6
Maury, 1685 ....F-14
Maxton, 2426 ....H-10
Mayfield, 130 ....*J-7
Maynard, 278 ....C-8
Maysville, 1019 ....H-16
McAdenville, 651 .....*G-1
McCullers *F-11
McDonald, 113 ....I-10

McDOWELL CO.,
44996 ....E-2
McFarlan, 117 ....H-8
McGrady, 220 ....C-4
Mebane, 11393 ....D-10

MECKLENBURG CO.,
919628 ....E-6
Merrimon, 130 ....G-17
Merritt, 90 ....G-17
Merry Hill, 80 ....D-17
Merry Oaks, 150 ....E-11
Mesic, 220 ....F-17
Micaville, 200 ....D-1
Micro, 441 ....E-13
Middleburg, 133 ....C-12
Middlesex, 822 ....E-13
Midland, 3073 ....G-6
Midway, 4679 ....*D-2
Mill Spr., 500 ....F-2
Millers Creek, 2112 ..C-4
Millersville, 220 ....C-2
Mills River, 6802 ....F-1
Milltown, 150 ....C-2
Milton, 166 ....B-10
Milwaukee, 285 ....B-16
Mineral Sprs., 2639 ..H-6
Minneapolis, 250 ......D-2
Minnesott Bch., 440 ....G-17
Mint Hill, 22722 ....G-6
Misenheimer, 728 .....F-7

MITCHELL CO.,
15579 ....D-1
Mocksville, 5051 ....D-6
Moffitt Hill, 170 ....E-2
Mollie, 30 ....H-11
Momeyer, 224 ....D-13
Moncure, 711 ....E-10
Monroe, 32797 ....G-6
Montezuma, 250 ......D-2

MONTGOMERY CO.,
27798 ....F-8
Monticello, 130 ....D-9
Montreat, 723 ....E-1
Mooresboro, 311 ......F-3
Mooresville, 18931 ...E-5
Moravian Falls, 1901 ..D-5
Morehead City, 8661 ....H-17
Morgans Cor., 30 .....B-18
Morganton, 16918 ....E-3
Morrisville, 18576 .....E-11
Morven, 511 ....H-8
Mt. Airy, 10388 ....B-6
Mt. Gilead, 1181 ......G-8
Mt. Holly, 13656 ....*G-1

North Carolina (continued)

NASH CO., 95840..D-13 · NEW HANOVER CO., 202667..J-14 · NORTHAMPTON CO., 22099..C-15 · ONSLOW CO., 177772..H-14 · ORANGE CO., 133801..C-10 · PAMLICO CO., 13144..G-17 · PASQUOTANK CO., 40661..C-18 · PENDER CO., 52217..J-14 · PERQUIMANS CO., 13453..C-17 · PERSON CO., 39464..B-11 · PITT CO., 168148..F-15 · POLK CO., 20510..F-1 · RANDOLPH CO., 141752..E-8 · RICHMOND CO., 46639..G-8 · ROBESON CO., 134168..H-10 · ROCKINGHAM CO., 93643..C-8 · ROWAN CO., 138428..E-6 · RUTHERFORD CO., 67810..G-2 · SAMPSON CO., 63431..G-12 · SCOTLAND CO., 36157..H-9 · STANLY CO., 60585..F-7 · STOKES CO., 47401..C-7 · SURRY CO., 73673..C-6 · SWAIN CO., 13981..L-3 · TRANSYLVANIA CO., 33090..M-5 · TYRRELL CO., 4407..D-18 · UNION CO., 201292..G-6 · VANCE CO., 45422..C-12 · WAKE CO., 900993..D-12 · WARREN CO., 20972..C-13 · WASHINGTON CO., 13228..D-17 · WATAUGA CO., 51079..C-3 · WAYNE CO., 122623..F-13 · WILKES CO., 69340..C-5 · WILSON CO., 81234..E-14 · YADKIN CO., 38406..C-6 · YANCEY CO., 17818..D-1

North Dakota

Page locator

	Map keys	Atlas pages
	A–J	156–157

ADAMS CO., 2343..J-4 · BARNES CO., 11066..H-11 · BENSON CO., 6660..E-9 · BILLINGS CO., 783..G-2 · BOTTINEAU CO., 6429..D-7 · BOWMAN CO., 3151..J-2 · BURKE CO., 1968..D-4 · BURLEIGH CO., 81308..H-7 · CASS CO., 149778..H-12 · CAVALIER CO., 3993..D-10 · DICKEY CO., 5289..J-10 · DIVIDE CO., 2071..D-3 · DUNN CO., 3536..G-4 · EDDY CO., 2385..F-9 · EMMONS CO., 3550..J-8 · FOSTER CO., 3343..G-9 · GOLDEN VALLEY CO., 1680..G-2 · GRAND FORKS CO., 66861..F-12 · GRANT CO., 2394..J-5 · GRIGGS CO., 2420..G-11 · HETTINGER CO., 2477..J-4 · KIDDER CO., 2435..G-8 · LA MOURE CO., 4139..J-10 · LOGAN CO., 1990..J-9 · MCHENRY CO., 5395..E-7 · MCINTOSH CO., 2809..J-9 · MCKENZIE CO., 6360..F-2 · MCLEAN CO., 8962..F-6 · MERCER CO., 8424..G-5 · MORTON CO., 27411..I-5 · MOUNTRAIL CO., 7673..E-4 · NELSON CO., 3126..F-11 · OLIVER CO., 1846..G-5 · PEMBINA CO., 7413..D-11 · PIERCE CO., 4357..D-8 · RAMSEY CO., 11451..E-10 · RANSOM CO., 5457..I-11 · RENVILLE CO., 2470..D-6 · RICHLAND CO., 16321..I-12 · ROLETTE CO., 13937..C-8 · SARGENT CO., 3829..J-12 · SHERIDAN CO., 1321..F-7 · SIOUX CO., 4153..J-6 · SLOPE CO., 727..I-2 · STARK CO., 24199..H-4 · STEELE CO., 1975..F-11 · STUTSMAN CO., 21100..H-9 · TOWNER CO., 2246..D-9 · TRAILL CO., 8121..F-12 · WALSH CO., 11119..E-11 · WARD CO., 61675..E-5 · WELLS CO., 4207..G-8 · WILLIAMS CO., 22398..D-3

Ohio

Page locator

	Map keys	Atlas pages
	NA1–NN10	158–159
	NA11–NN20	160–161
	SA1–SN10	162–163
	SA11–SN20	164–165
*City keyed to p. 226		

ADAMS CO., 28550..SH-7 · ALLEN CO., 106331..NJ-4 · ASHLAND CO., 53139..NJ-12 · ASHTABULA CO., 101497..NE-18 · ATHENS CO., 64757..SF-14 · AUGLAIZE CO., 45949..NK-4 · BELMONT CO., 70400..NN-17 · BROWN CO., 44846..SH-5 · BUTLER CO., 368130..SE-1 · CARROLL CO., 28836..NK-17 · CHAMPAIGN CO., 40097..NN-5 · CLARK CO., 138333..SB-6 · CLERMONT CO., 197363..SH-4 · CLINTON CO., 42040..SD-6 · COLUMBIANA CO., 107841..NL-19 · COSHOCTON CO., 36901..NM-13 · CRAWFORD CO., 43784..NK-9 · CUYAHOGA CO., 1280122..NG-14 · DARKE CO., 52959..NM-1 · DEFIANCE CO., 39037..NG-2 · DELAWARE CO., 174214..NM-9

E. Canton, 1591 ....NJ-17
E. Claridon, 260 ....NE-17
E. Cleveland, 17843 ....NE-15
E. Danville, 100 ....SG-6
E. Fairfield, 100 ....NJ-19
E. Fultonham, 335 ....SB-13
E. Greenville, 180 ....NJ-15
E. Liberty, 366 ....NM-6
E. Liverpool, 11195 ....NK-20
E. Monroe, 120 ....SE-7
E. Norwalk, 80 ....NG-11
E. Palestine, 4721 ....NI-20
E. Richland, 300 ....NN-18
E. Rochester, 231 ....NJ-18
E. Sparta, 819 ....NJ-16
E. Springfield, 350 ....NL-19
E. Townsend, 80 ....NI-11
E. Trumbull, 80 ....NE-18
E. Union, 30 ....SC-16
Eastlake, 18577 ....NE-16
Easton, 200 ....NI-15
Eastview SL-9
Eaton, 8407 ....SC-2
Eaton Estates, 1222 ....NG-13
Eber, 300 ....SD-7
Eckmansville SH-6
Eden Pk., 430 ....SI-9
Edenton, 300 ....SF-4
Edgerton, 2012 ....NF-1
Edgewater Pk., 700 ....SB-10
Edgewood, 4432 ....NC-19
Edinburg, 250 ....NH-17
Edison, 437 ....NK-10
Edon, 834 ....NE-1
Elba, 70 ....SD-16
Eldorado, 509 ....SB-2
Elery, 25 ....NG-4
Elgin, 57 ....NJ-4
Elida, 1905 ....NJ-4
Elizabethtown, 350 ....SF-1
Elkton, 80 ....NJ-19
Ellerton SN-6
Elliot Crossroads SD-14
Ellisonville, 50 ....SJ-11
Ellsberry, 60 ....SI-6
Ellsworth, 260 ....NH-18
Elm Grv., 35 ....SG-8
Elmore, 1410 ....NF-8
Elmwood Pl., 2188 ....SL-3
Elroy, 35 ....NM-1
Elyria, 54533 ....NF-13
Empire, 299 ....NK-20
Englewood, 13465 ....SB-3
Enon, 2415 ....SB-5
Enterprise, 170 ....SD-12
Epworth NI-11
Epworth Hts., 150 ....SK-6
Era, 130 ....SC-8
ERIE CO., 77079 ....NF-11
Eris, 25 ....NN-5
Erlin, 80 ....NF-9
Espyville, 80 ....NK-8
Essex, 90 ....NL-7
Etna, 1215 ....SB-11
Euclid, 48920 ....NE-15
Eureka, 100 ....SI-13
Evansport, 300 ....NF-3
Evansville, 200 ....NC-12
Evendale, 2767 ....SK-4
Everett, 25 ....NG-15
Ewing, 30 ....SE-12
Ewington, 65 ....SG-12
Excello, 50 ....SJ-3
Fairborn, 32352 ....SB-5
Fairfax, 1699 ....SL-4
Fairfax, 40 ....SG-7
Fairfield, 42510 ....SE-2
Fairfield, 50 ....NL-19
FAIRFIELD CO., 146156 ....SB-11
Fairhaven, 200 ....SC-1
Fairhope, 1720 ....NJ-17
Fairlawn, 7437 ....NH-15
Fairpoint, 500 ....NN-18
Fairport Hbr., 3109 ....ND-17
Fairview, 83 ....SB-16
Fairview, 50 ....SF-6
Fairview Lanes, 1000 ....NF-10
Fairview Pk., 16826 ....NF-14
Fallsburg, 80 ....NM-12
Farmdale, 200 ....NF-20
Farmer, 120 ....NF-2
Farmers, 45 ....SE-6
Farmerstown, 330 ....NL-15
Farmersville, 1009 ....SC-3
Fawcett SH-7
Fayette, 1283 ....NE-3
FAYETTE CO., 29030 ....SD-8
Fayetteville, 330 ....SF-5
Feesburg, 500 ....SH-5
Felicity, 818 ....SH-4
Fernald, 25 ....SJ-1
Fernell Hts., 330 ....SM-6
Fincastle, 85 ....SG-6
Findlay, 41202 ....NH-6
Finneytown, 12741 ....SK-3
Firestone Pk. NC-5
Fitchville, 350 ....NH-11
Five Points, 1824 ....SD-4
Five Points, 120 ....SC-8
Fivemile SG-5
Flat Rock, 233 ....NG-9
Fleming, 40 ....SE-16
Fletcher, 473 ....NN-4
Florence, 200 ....NG-12
Florence, 150 ....NN-19
Florence, 100 ....SC-16
Florida, 232 ....NG-4
Flushing, 879 ....NN-18
Fly, 80 ....SD-18
Footville NE-18
Foraker, 130 ....NJ-6
Forest, 1461 ....NJ-7
Forest Hill NB-6
Forest Hills, 200 ....NA-15
Forest Pk., 18720 ....SF-2
Forestville, 10532 ....SG-3
Ft. Jefferson, 80 ....SA-2
Ft. Jennings, 485 ....NJ-3
Ft. Loramie, 1478 ....NL-3
Ft. McKinley, 3989 ....SL-7
Ft. Recovery, 1430 ....NL-1
Ft. Seneca, 254 ....NG-8
Ft. Shawnee, 3726 ....NJ-4
Foster SE-3
Fosterville ND-13
Fostoria, 13441 ....NH-7
Fowler, 250 ....NG-19
Fowlers Mill, 320 ....NE-17
Fox, 25 ....SD-9
Frankfort, 1064 ....SE-8
Franklin, 11771 ....SD-3
FRANKLIN CO., 1163414 ....NN-10
Franklin Furnace, 1660 ....SI-10
Franklin Sq., 240 ....NI-19
Frazeysburg, 1326 ....NN-13
Frederick, 150 ....SB-3
Fredericksburg, 423 ....NJ-14
Fredericksdale SC-16
Fredericktown, 2493 ....NL-11
Fredericktown, 200 ....NJ-20
Freeburg, 90 ....NI-17
Freedom, 90 ....NG-17
Freeport, 369 ....NM-17
Fremont, 16734 ....NG-8
Frenchtown, 60 ....NM-2
Fresno, 140 ....NL-15
Friendship, 351 ....SI-9
Frost, 25 ....SF-15
Fruit Hill, 3755 ....SM-5
Fruitdale, 50 ....SF-8
Fryburg, 150 ....NK-4
Frytown, 45 ....SC-13
Fulda, 40 ....SC-16
Fulton, 258 ....NL-10
FULTON CO., 42698 ....NE-3
Fultonham, 176 ....SB-13
Funk, 110 ....NJ-13
Gahanna, 33248 ....SA-10
Galena, 653 ....NM-9
Galion, 10512 ....NJ-10
Gallia SH-11
GALLIA CO., 30934 ....SH-12
Gallipolis, 3641 ....SH-13
Galloway, 250 ....SB-9
Gambier, 2391 ....NL-12
Ganges, 120 ....NI-11
Gano, 200 ....SF-3
Garden Acres, 250 ....NB-17
Garden City, 300 ....SI-10
Garfield, 120 ....NI-18
Garfield Hts., 28849 ....NF-15
Garrettsville, 2325 ....NG-17
Gates Mills, 2270 ....NE-16
GEAUGA CO., 93389 ....NE-17
Geneva, 6215 ....ND-18
Geneva-on-the-Lake, 1288 ....NC-18
Genoa, 2336 ....NF-7
Georges Run, 400 ....NM-20
Georgesville, 160 ....SB-8
Georgetown, 4331 ....SH-5
Georgetown, 150 ....NM-18
Gephart SI-10
Gerald, 50 ....NF-4
Germano, 200 ....NL-18
Germantown, 5547 ....SD-3
Germantown, 35 ....SD-17
Getaway, 100 ....SJ-12
Gettysburg, 513 ....NN-2
Gettysburg, 80 ....SE-1
Geyer, 50 ....NK-4
Ghent, 1600 ....NH-15
Gibisonville, 130 ....SD-11
Gibsonburg, 2581 ....NF-7
Gilboa, 184 ....NH-5
Gillivan SB-8
Gilmore, 85 ....NM-16
Ginghamsburg, 250 ....SB-4
Girard, 9958 ....NH-19
Girton, 50 ....NG-7
Givens, 75 ....SG-10
Gladstone, 30 ....SC-6
Glandorf, 1001 ....NH-4
Glasgow, 40 ....NJ-19
Glasgow NM-15
Glen Este, 350 ....SM-6
Glen Karn, 40 ....SA-1
Glen Roy, 100 ....SG-11
Glencoe, 310 ....SA-19
Glendale, 2155 ....SJ-3
Glenford, 173 ....SB-12
Glenmont, 272 ....NK-13
Glenmoor, 1987 ....NJ-20
Glenmore, 50 ....NJ-1
Glouster, 1791 ....SD-13
Gnadenhutten, 1288 ....NL-16
Goes, 100 ....SC-5
Golf Manor, 3611 ....SL-4
Gomer, 350 ....NI-4
Good Hope, 234 ....SE-8
Goodyear Hts. NB-6
Gordon, 212 ....SB-2
Gore, 240 ....SD-12
Goshen, 730 ....SF-4
Goshen, 200 ....NL-16
Gould Pk. SG-20
Grafton, 6636 ....NG-13
Grand Rapids, 965 ....NF-5
Grand River, 399 ....ND-17
Grandview, 60 ....SD-18
Grandview Hts., 6536 ....SB-9
Grandview Hts., 170 ....NM-4
Grange Hall, 20 ....SD-8
Granger, 90 ....NH-15
Grant, 60 ....NJ-6
Granville, 5646 ....NN-11
Grape Grv., 35 ....SC-6
Gratiot, 221 ....SB-13
Gratis, 881 ....SC-2
Graysville, 76 ....SC-18
Graytown, 180 ....NE-8
Green, 25699 ....NI-16
Green Camp, 374 ....NK-8
Green Sprs., 1368 ....NG-9
Greenbush SD-2
Greenbush SG-5
Greencastle SC-10
Greendale, 30 ....SD-13
GREENE CO., 161573 ....SC-6
Greenfield, 4639 ....SE-7
Greenford, 700 ....NI-19
Greenhills, 3615 ....SJ-3
Greenland SF-9
Greensburg, 600 ....NI-16
Greentown, 3804 ....NI-16
Greenview SK-7
Greenville, 13227 ....NM-2
Greenwich, 1476 ....NH-11
Greenwood, 40 ....SB-16
Greer, 50 ....NL-13
Grelton, 110 ....NG-4
Groesbeck, 6788 ....SK-2
Grove City, 35575 ....SB-9
Groveport, 5363 ....SJ-20
Grover Hill, 402 ....NH-2
Guerne, 250 ....NJ-14
Guernsey, 50 ....NM-15
GUERNSEY CO., 40087 ....NM-16
Guilford, 320 ....NJ-18
Gurneyville SD-5
Gustavus NF-19
Gutman, 35 ....NK-4
Guysville, 250 ....SF-14
Gypsum, 200 ....NF-9
Hackney, 40 ....SD-15
Hallock, 100 ....NE-2
Hallsville, 230 ....SE-10
Hambden, 180 ....NE-17
Hamburg SC-11
Hamden, 879 ....SF-11
Hamersville, 546 ....SH-5
Hamilton, 62477 ....SE-2
HAMILTON CO., 802374 ....SF-1
Hamilton Meadows, 2100 ....SB-9
Hamler, 576 ....NG-4
Hamlet, 160 ....SG-4
Hammansburg, 100 ....NG-6
Hammondsville, 400 ....NK-19
HANCOCK CO., 74782 ....NI-5
Hanging Rock, 221 ....SJ-10
Hanley Vil. NJ-11
Hannibal, 411 ....SC-19
Hanover, 921 ....NN-12
Hanover NL-18
Hanoverton, 408 ....NJ-18
Harbor View, 123 ....ND-7
Hardin, 80 ....NM-3
HARDIN CO., 32058 ....NJ-6
Harlem, 150 ....NN-10
Harlem Sprs., 300 ....NK-18
Harmon, 50 ....NJ-15
Harmony, 250 ....SB-6
Harper, 70 ....NL-6
Harpersfield ND-18
Harpster, 204 ....NJ-8
Harriett, 30 ....SG-7
Harriettsville, 60 ....SD-17
Harrisburg, 320 ....SC-8
Harrisburg, 100 ....NI-17
Harrison, 9897 ....SF-1
HARRISON CO., 15864 ....NM-17
Harrisonville, 150 ....SG-13
Harrisville, 235 ....NM-18
Harrod, 417 ....NJ-5
Harshasville SH-7
Hartford, 350 ....NG-20
Hartland NH-11
Hartsgrove, 300 ....NE-18
Hartshorn SC-17
Hartville, 2944 ....NI-16
Harveysburg, 546 ....SD-5
Haselton ND-14
Haskins, 1188 ....NF-6
Hatton, 50 ....NG-7
Havana, 110 ....NH-10
Havensport, 60 ....SC-11
Haverhill, 120 ....SJ-10
Haviland, 215 ....NH-2
Haydenville, 381 ....SD-12
Hayesville, 448 ....NJ-12
Heath, 10310 ....SA-12
Hebbardsville, 50 ....SF-13
Hebron, 2336 ....SB-12
Hecla, 200 ....SJ-11
Helena, 224 ....NG-8
Hemlock, 155 ....SD-13
Hemlock Grv., 70 ....SG-14
Hendrysburg, 150 ....NN-17
HENRY CO., 28215 ....NG-4
Hepburn, 100 ....NK-7
Hessville, 214 ....NF-8
Hicksville, 3581 ....NG-1
Higginsport, 251 ....SJ-5
Highland, 254 ....SE-6
HIGHLAND CO., 43589 ....SF-6
Highland Hts., 8345 ....SK-20
Highland Hills, 1130 ....SM-19
Highland Pk., 700 ....NJ-15
Highlandtown, 100 ....NK-19
Highpoint, 1503 ....SJ-5
Hill Grv., 100 ....NM-1
Hilliard, 28435 ....SA-8
Hills & Dales, 221 ....NB-9
Hillsboro, 6605 ....SE-6
Hinckley, 500 ....NG-14
Hiram, 1406 ....NG-17
Hiram Rapids, 250 ....NF-17
Hiramsburg SC-16
Hitchcock SH-11
Hoagland, 50 ....SF-6
HOCKING CO., 29380 ....SE-11
Hockingport, 212 ....SF-15
Holgate, 1109 ....NG-4
Holiday City, 52 ....NE-2
Holland, 1764 ....NB-1
Hollansburg, 227 ....SA-1
Hollister, 300 ....SD-13
Holloway, 338 ....NM-17
HOLMES CO., 42366 ....NK-13
Holmesville, 372 ....NK-14
Homer, 250 ....NM-11
Homerville, 80 ....NH-13
Homeworth, 481 ....NI-18
Honeytown, 40 ....NJ-14
Hooker SC-11
Hooven, 534 ....SF-1
Hopedale, 950 ....NM-18
Hopetown, 50 ....SE-9
Hopewell, 250 ....SB-13
Hopkinsville SE-4
Hoskinsville SC-16
Houcktown, 180 ....NI-6
Houston, 220 ....NM-3
Howard, 242 ....NL-12
Howenstein, 160 ....NK-16
Howland Ctr., 6351 ....NA-12
Hoytville, 303 ....NG-5
Hubbard, 7874 ....NH-20
Huber Hts., 38101 ....SB-4
Huber Ridge, 4604 ....SF-19
Hudson, 22262 ....NG-16
Hulington, 100 ....SG-4
Hume, 135 ....NK-3
Hunter SB-18
Hunting Valley, 705 ....NF-16
Huntington, 220 ....NH-12
Huntsburg, 300 ....NE-18
Huntsville, 431 ....NL-5
Huron, 7149 ....NF-11
HURON CO., 59626 ....NH-11
Hustead, 120 ....SB-5
Hyatts, 50 ....NM-8
Iberia, 452 ....NK-10
Idaho, 50 ....SG-9
Iler NG-8
Ilesboro SE-12
Independence, 7133 ....NF-15
Independence, 100 ....NG-3
Ingomar, 60 ....SC-2
Irondale, 387 ....NK-19
Ironspot, 150 ....SB-13
Ironton, 11129 ....SJ-11
Irvington SK-7
Irwin, 150 ....NN-7
Island View, 300 ....NK-5
Isle St. George, 50 ....ND-10
Isleta NM-15
Ithaca, 136 ....SB-2
Jackson, 6397 ....SG-10
Jackson Ctr., 1462 ....NL-4
JACKSON CO., 33225 ....SH-11
Jacksonburg, 63 ....SD-2
Jacksontown, 350 ....SB-12
Jacksonville, 481 ....SE-13
Jacksonville, 75 ....SH-7
Jacobsburg, 200 ....SB-19
Jamestown, 1993 ....SC-6
Jasper, 250 ....SG-9
Jasper Mills, 40 ....SD-7
Jaysville, 30 ....NN-2
Jefferson, 3120 ....ND-19
Jefferson, 200 ....NJ-13
JEFFERSON CO., 69709 ....NK-19
Jeffersonville, 1203 ....SC-7
Jelloway, 90 ....NK-12
Jenera, 221 ....NI-6
Jericho, 200 ....SE-3
Jerome, 200 ....NN-8
Jeromesville, 562 ....NI-13
Jerry City, 427 ....NG-6
Jersey, 250 ....NN-10
Jerusalem, 161 ....SB-18
Jewell, 100 ....NG-3
Jewett, 692 ....NL-18
Johnston, 250 ....NF-19
Johnstown, 4632 ....NN-10
Jonestown, 80 ....NJ-2
Joy SE-14
Junction, 100 ....NG-2
Junction City, 819 ....SC-12
Justus, 100 ....NJ-15
Kalida, 1542 ....NI-4
Kanauga, 175 ....SH-13
Kansas, 179 ....NG-8
Keene, 100 ....NL-14
Kelleys Island, 312 ....NE-10
Kelloggsville, 200 ....NC-19
Kemp, 70 ....NJ-3
Kendall Hts., 850 ....NB-8
Kennard, 40 ....NM-6
Kennonsburg, 50 ....SB-17
Kensington, 320 ....NJ-18
Kent, 28904 ....NH-16
Kenton, 8262 ....NK-6
Kenwood, 6981 ....SK-4
Kerr, 90 ....SH-13
Kessler, 100 ....SB-3
Kettering, 56163 ....SC-4
Kettlersville, 179 ....NL-3
Key SA-19
Kidron, 944 ....NJ-15
Kieferville, 40 ....NH-4
Kilbourne, 139 ....NM-9
Kileville, 25 ....NN-8
Kilgore, 100 ....NL-18
Killbuck, 817 ....NL-13
Kimball, 110 ....NG-10
Kimberly, 40 ....SE-13
Kimbolton, 144 ....NN-15
Kingman SD-5
Kings Creek, 300 ....NN-6
Kings Mills, 1319 ....SE-3
Kingston, 1032 ....SE-10
Kingsville, 650 ....NC-19
Kingsway NF-8
Kinnikinnick, 65 ....SE-9
Kinsman, 600 ....NF-20
Kiousville SC-8
Kipling, 180 ....SA-16
Kipton, 243 ....NG-12
Kirby, 118 ....NJ-7
Kirkersville, 525 ....SB-11
Kirkpatrick, 80 ....NJ-9
Kirkwood, 60 ....NM-4
Kirtland, 6866 ....NE-16
Kitts Hill, 200 ....SJ-11
Klondike, 250 ....NG-19
Knockemstiff SF-9
KNOX CO., 60921 ....NM-12
Knoxville, 180 ....NK-19
Kossuth, 80 ....NK-3
Kunkle, 246 ....NE-2
Kyger, 60 ....SG-13
La Croft, 1144 ....NK-20
La Grange, 70 ....SJ-11
La Rue, 747 ....NK-7
Lacarne, 200 ....NF-9
Lafayette, 445 ....NJ-5
Lafayette, 202 ....SB-7
Lafayette, 120 ....NH-14
Lafferty, 304 ....NN-18
Lagrange, 2103 ....NG-13
Laings, 30 ....SC-18
L. Cable, 2500 ....NB-9
LAKE CO., 230041 ....ND-17
L. Fork NJ-13
L. Milton, 1100 ....NH-18
L. O'Springs, 600 ....NB-8
Lakeline, 226 ....NE-16
Lakemore, 3068 ....NH-16
Lakeside, 694 ....NE-10
Lakeside, 600 ....NN-4
Lakeview, 1072 ....NL-5
Lakeville, 130 ....NK-13
Lakewood, 52131 ....NF-14
Lancaster, 38780 ....SC-11
Landeck, 100 ....NJ-3
Langsville, 80 ....SG-13
Lansing, 634 ....NN-19
LaPorte, 400 ....NG-13
Latham, 230 ....SG-8
Lattasburg, 100 ....NI-13
Lattaville, 60 ....SE-8
Latty, 193 ....NH-2
Laura, 474 ....SA-3
Laurel, 150 ....SH-4
Laurel Ridge, 2350 ....NI-16
Laurelville, 527 ....SE-10
LAWRENCE CO., 62450 ....SI-11
Lawrenceville, 300 ....SA-5
Lawshe, 60 ....SH-7
Layhigh, 60 ....SE-1
Layland, 50 ....NL-14
Layman SE-15
Leavittsburg, 1973 ....NG-18
Leavittsville, 100 ....NK-17
Lebanon, 20033 ....SE-4
Lebanon, 50 ....SD-17
Lees Creek, 160 ....SE-6
Leesburg, 1314 ....SE-7
Leesville, 200 ....NL-10
Leesville, 158 ....NL-17
Leetonia, 1959 ....NI-19
Leipsic, 2093 ....NH-5
Leistville, 40 ....SD-10
Lemert, 30 ....NJ-8
Lemoyne, 300 ....NF-7
Lena, 100 ....NN-4
Lenox Ctr., 60 ....ND-19
Leo SF-11
Leonardsburg NL-9
Letart Falls, 180 ....SH-14
Levanna, 80 ....SI-5
Lewis Ctr., 350 ....NM-9
Lewisburg, 1820 ....SB-2
Lewistown, 222 ....NL-5
Lewisville, 176 ....SC-17
Lexington, 4822 ....NJ-11
Liberty, 240 ....SC-3
Liberty Ctr., 1180 ....NF-4
LICKING CO., 166492 ....NN-11
Lightsville, 30 ....NM-1
Lilly Chapel, 200 ....SB-8
Lima, 38771 ....NJ-4
Limaville, 151 ....NI-17
Lime City, 120 ....ND-2
Limecrest, 400 ....SB-6
Limestone, 50 ....NE-8
Limestone City, 40 ....NB-15
Lincoln Hts., 3286 ....SK-3
Lincoln Vil., 9032 ....SI-17
Lindale, 200 ....SG-4
Lindsey, 446 ....NF-8
Linndale, 179 ....SM-16
Linnville, 90 ....SJ-12
Linnville, 60 ....SB-12
Linworth SF-18
Lisbon, 2821 ....NJ-19
Litchfield, 400 ....NH-13
Lithopolis, 1106 ....SC-10
Little Hocking, 263 ....SF-15
Little Sandusky, 50 ....NJ-8
Little Walnut, 80 ....SC-9
Little Washington NJ-11
Little York, 400 ....SK-7
Lloydsville, 150 ....NN-18
Lock NM-11
Lockbourne, 237 ....SC-9
Lockington, 141 ....NM-3
Lockland, 3449 ....SK-3
Lockville, 90 ....SC-10
Lockwood, 30 ....NF-18
Locust Grv., 220 ....SG-7
Locust Ridge SG-5
Lodi, 2746 ....NH-13
Logan, 7152 ....SD-12
LOGAN CO., 45858 ....NL-5
Logan Elm Vil., 1118 ....SD-9
Loganville, 55 ....NL-5
Lombardsville, 40 ....SH-9
London, 9904 ....SB-7
Londonderry, 400 ....SF-10
Londonderry, 40 ....NN-17
Long Bottom, 70 ....SG-15
Lorain, 64097 ....NF-13
LORAIN CO., 301356 ....NG-12
Lordstown, 3417 ....NH-18
Lore City, 325 ....SA-16
Lottridge SF-14
Louden SG-7
Loudonville, 2641 ....NK-12
Louisville, 9186 ....NI-17
Loveland, 12081 ....SF-3
Loveland Pk., 1523 ....SJ-6
Lowell, 549 ....SD-16
Lowellville, 1155 ....NH-20
Lower Salem, 86 ....SD-17
Lucas, 615 ....NJ-12
LUCAS CO., 441815 ....NE-5
Lucasburg SB-16
Lucasville, 2757 ....SH-9
Luckey, 1012 ....NF-7
Ludlow Falls, 208 ....SA-3
Lumberton, 150 ....SD-5
Luray, 110 ....SB-11
Lykens, 70 ....NI-9
Lynchburg, 1499 ....SF-6
Lyndhurst, 14001 ....NE-16
Lyndon, 200 ....SE-8
Lynx, 220 ....SI-7
Lyons, 562 ....ND-4
Lyra, 40 ....SI-10
Lytle, 200 ....SD-4
Macedon, 70 ....NL-1
Macedonia, 11188 ....NG-16
Mack, 11585 ....SL-1
Macksburg, 186 ....SD-16
Macon, 140 ....SH-6
Madeira, 8726 ....SF-3
Madison, 3184 ....ND-18
MADISON CO., 43435 ....NN-7
Madison Mills, 60 ....SC-8
Madison-on-the-Lake, 950 ....ND-18
Magnetic Sprs., 268 ....NL-8
Magnolia, 978 ....NK-17
MAHONING CO., 238823 ....NI-18
Mainesville, 975 ....SE-4
Mainsville, 30 ....SC-13
Malaga, 180 ....SB-18
Malinta, 265 ....NG-4
Mallet Creek, 300 ....NH-14
Malta, 671 ....SC-14
Malvern, 1189 ....NJ-17
Manchester, 4000 ....NI-15
Manchester, 2023 ....SI-6
Mandale, 50 ....NH-3
Mansfield, 47821 ....NJ-11
Mantua, 1043 ....NG-17
Mantua Cors., 80 ....NG-17
Maple Hts., 23138 ....NF-15
Maple Valley NB-5
Mapleton, 90 ....NJ-17
Maplewood, 230 ....NL-4
Marathon, 300 ....SF-5
Marble Cliff, 573 ....SH-18
Marblehead, 903 ....NE-10
Marchand NA-9
Marcy SC-10
Marengo, 342 ....NL-10
Maria Stein, 300 ....NL-2
Mariemont, 3403 ....SL-4
Marietta, 14085 ....SE-16
Marion, 36837 ....NK-8
MARION CO., 66501 ....NK-7
Mark Ctr., 200 ....NG-2
Marlboro, 500 ....NI-17
Marne, 783 ....NN-12
Marseilles, 112 ....NJ-7
Marshall, 110 ....SF-7
Marshallville, 756 ....NI-15
Martel, 250 ....NK-9
Martins Ferry, 6915 ....NN-19
Martinsburg, 237 ....NM-12
Martinsville, 463 ....SE-5
Marysville, 22094 ....NM-7
Massieville, 400 ....SF-9
Massillon, 32149 ....NJ-16
Masury, 2064 ....NG-20
Matville SC-9
Maud, 500 ....SE-3
Maumee, 14286 ....NC-1
Maximo, 200 ....NI-17
Maxville, 100 ....SD-12
May Hill, 50 ....SG-7
Mayfield, 3460 ....SK-20
Mayfield Hts., 19155 ....NE-16
Mayflower Vil. NC-7
Maynard, 400 ....NN-19
Maysville, 100 ....NJ-14
Maysville, 50 ....NJ-5
McArthur, 1701 ....SF-12
McCartyville, 160 ....NL-3
McClimansville, 60 ....SC-8
McClure, 725 ....NF-5
McComb, 1648 ....NH-5
McConnelsville, 1784 ....SC-14
McCuneville, 90 ....SD-13
McCutchenville, 400 ....NI-8
McDermott, 434 ....SH-9
McDonald, 3263 ....NH-19
McDonaldsville, 180 ....NI-16
McGill, 20 ....NH-1
McGonigle, 130 ....SE-2
McGuffey, 501 ....NJ-5
McKinley Hts., 1060 ....NB-13
McLuney, 75 ....SC-13
McZena, 40 ....NJ-13
Mecca, 60 ....NF-19
Mechanicsburg, 1644 ....NN-6
Mechanicstown, 280 ....NK-18
Medina, 26678 ....NH-14
MEDINA CO., 172332 ....NH-13
Medway, 2000 ....SB-5
Meeker, 150 ....NK-8
Meigs, 40 ....SC-15
MEIGS CO., 23770 ....SG-13
Melbern, 200 ....NF-2
Melmore, 153 ....NH-8
Melrose, 275 ....NH-3
Melvin, 90 ....SE-6
Memphis SE-6
Mendon, 662 ....NJ-2
Mentor, 47159 ....NE-16
Mentor-on-the-Lake, 7443 ....ND-16
Mercer, 50 ....NK-2
MERCER CO., 40814 ....NK-1
Mercerville, 100 ....SI-13
Mermill NG-6
Mesopotamia, 300 ....NF-18
Metamora, 627 ....ND-5
Metzger, 200 ....SE-9
Mexico, 60 ....NI-8
Meyers Lake, 569 ....NC-9
MIAMI CO., 102506 ....NN-3
Miami Shores SN-7
Miami Villa SK-8
Miamisburg, 20181 ....SD-3
Miamitown, 1259 ....SE-1
Miamiville, 242 ....SK-5
Middle Bass, 100 ....NE-10
Middle Pt., 576 ....NI-2
Middleboro, 50 ....SE-4
Middlebourne, 80 ....NN-16
Middlebranch, 220 ....NI-16
Middleburg, 220 ....NM-6
Middleburg, 50 ....SC-17
Middleburg Hts., 15946 ....NF-14
Middlebury, 30 ....NI-1
Middlefield, 2694 ....NF-17
Middleport, 2530 ....SG-14
Middleton, 80 ....NI-19
Middletown, 48694 ....SD-3
Middletown, 25 ....NM-6
Midland, 315 ....SF-5
Midvale, 754 ....NL-16
Midway, 322 ....SC-7
Mifflin, 137 ....NJ-12
Milan, 1367 ....NG-11
Milford, 6709 ....SF-3
Milford Ctr., 792 ....NM-7
Millbrook, 60 ....NJ-13
Millbury, 1200 ....NE-7
Milledgeville, 112 ....SD-7
Miller, 200 ....SJ-12
Miller City, 137 ....NH-4
Millersburg, 3025 ....NK-14
Millersport, 1044 ....SB-11
Millerstown, 90 ....NN-5
Millersville, 150 ....NG-8
Millfield, 341 ....SE-13
Millport, 110 ....NJ-18
Millville, 708 ....SE-2
Millwood, 200 ....NL-12
Milton Ctr., 144 ....NG-5
Miltonsburg, 43 ....SB-18
Miltonville, 170 ....SD-3
Mineral SE-14
Mineral City, 727 ....NK-16
Mineral Ridge, 3892 ....NH-19
Minersville, 70 ....SG-14
Minerva, 3720 ....NJ-17
Minerva Pk., 1272 ....NN-9
Minford, 693 ....SH-10
Mingo, 100 ....NM-6
Mingo Jct., 3454 ....NL-20
Minster, 2805 ....NL-3
Mitiwanga, 130 ....NF-11
Modest SF-4
Mogadore, 3853 ....NH-16
Mohicanville, 100 ....NJ-13
Moline, 470 ....NC-2
Monclova, 120 ....NE-6
Monfort Hts., 11948 ....SL-2
Monnett, 60 ....NJ-9
Monroe, 12442 ....SE-3
Monroe Ctr., 100 ....ND-20
MONROE CO., 14642 ....SC-18
Monroeville, 1400 ....NG-10
Monroeville, 50 ....NK-19
Monterey, 120 ....SG-4
Montezuma, 165 ....NL-2
Montgomery, 10251 ....SK-5
MONTGOMERY CO., 535153 ....SC-3
Monticello, 40 ....NJ-2
Montpelier, 4072 ....NE-2
Montra, 100 ....NL-4
Montrose, 350 ....NH-15
Montville, 330 ....NE-18
Moorefield, 100 ....NM-17
Mooresville SE-10
Moraine, 6307 ....SC-4
Moreland, 100 ....NJ-14
Moreland Hills, 3320 ....SM-20
MORGAN CO., 15054 ....SC-15
Morganville, 25 ....SD-14
Morgantown, 50 ....SG-8
Morning Sun, 200 ....SD-1
Morral, 399 ....NJ-8
Morristown, 303 ....NN-18
Morrisville, 70 ....SE-6
Morrow, 1188 ....SE-4
MORROW CO., 34827 ....NK-9
Moscow, 185 ....SH-4
Moss Run SD-17
Moulton, 130 ....NK-3
Mt. Air, 300 ....NN-9
Mt. Blanchard, 492 ....NI-6
Mt. Carmel, 4741 ....SM-5
Mt. Carmel Hts., 1200 ....SM-5
Mt. Cory, 204 ....NI-5
Mt. Eaton, 241 ....NJ-15
Mt. Ephraim, 80 ....SB-16
Mt. Forest Trails, 450 ....SM-5
Mt. Gilead, 3660 ....NK-10
Mt. Healthy, 6098 ....SK-2
Mt. Holly, 250 ....SG-4
Mt. Holly SD-5
Mt. Hope, 200 ....NK-14
Mt. Jefferson, 100 ....NM-3
Mt. Liberty, 250 ....NL-11
Mt. Olive SH-4
Mt. Orab, 3664 ....SG-5
Mt. Perry, 220 ....SB-13
Mt. Pisgah, 100 ....SG-4
Mt. Pleasant, 478 ....NM-19
Mt. Pleasant, 70 ....SE-12
Mt. Pleasant NA-9
Mt. Repose, 4672 ....SF-4
Mt. Sterling, 1782 ....SC-8
Mt. Vernon, 16990 ....NL-11
Mt. Victory, 627 ....NK-7
Mowrystown, 360 ....SG-6
Moxahala, 300 ....SC-13
Moxahala Pk., 200 ....SB-13
Mudsock, 25 ....SA-8
Mulberry, 3323 ....SF-4
Munroe Falls, 5012 ....NA-6
Murdock SF-4
Murlin Hts., 550 ....SB-4
Murray City, 449 ....SD-13
MUSKINGUM CO., 86074 ....NN-14
Mutual, 104 ....NN-6
Nankin, 400 ....NI-12
Napoleon, 8749 ....NF-4
Nashport, 260 ....NN-13
Nashville, 197 ....NK-13
Nashville, 100 ....SB-3
Navarre, 1957 ....NJ-16
Neapolis, 423 ....NF-5
Neelysville, 40 ....SD-15
Neffs, 993 ....NN-19
Negley, 281 ....NJ-20
Nellie, 131 ....NL-13
Nelson, 80 ....NG-18
Nelsonville, 5392 ....SE-13
Neptune, 130 ....NK-2
Nettle Lake, 200 ....ND-1
Nevada, 760 ....NI-8
Neville, 100 ....SH-4
New Albany, 7724 ....NN-10
New Albany, 75 ....NI-19
New Alexander, 50 ....NJ-18
New Alexandria, 272 ....NM-19
New Antioch, 220 ....SE-6
New Athens, 320 ....NM-18
New Baltimore, 661 ....SF-2
New Baltimore, 250 ....NI-17
New Bavaria, 99 ....NG-4
New Bedford, 220 ....NL-14
New Bloomington, 515 ....NK-7
New Boston, 2272 ....SI-9
New Bremen, 2978 ....NL-3
New Burlington, 5069 ....SJ-2
New California, 1411 ....NN-8
New Carlisle, 5785 ....SB-5
New Concord, 2491 ....SA-15
New Cumberland, 150 ....NK-17
New Dover, 130 ....NM-8
New England, 50 ....SE-14
New Franklin, 230 ....NJ-17
New Gdn., 100 ....NJ-18
New Germany SL-9
New Guilford, 30 ....NM-13
New Hagerstown, 40 ....NL-17
New Hampshire, 174 ....NK-5
New Harrisburg, 100 ....NK-17
New Harrison, 50 ....NN-2
New Haven, 583 ....SF-1
New Haven, 399 ....NH-10
New Holland, 801 ....SD-8
New Hope, 150 ....SC-1
New Jasper, 100 ....SC-5
New Knoxville, 879 ....NL-3
New Lebanon, 3995 ....SC-3
New Lexington, 4731 ....SC-13
New Lexington, 100 ....SC-2
New London, 2461 ....NH-12
New Madison, 892 ....SB-1
New Market, 50 ....SG-6
New Marshfield, 326 ....SE-13
New Martinsburg, 150 ....SE-7
New Matamoras, 896 ....SD-18
New Miami, 2249 ....SE-2
New Middletown, 1621 ....NI-20
New Moorefield, 300 ....SA-6
New Moscow, 35 ....NM-14
New Paris, 1629 ....SB-1
New Petersburg, 150 ....SF-7
New Philadelphia, 17288 ....NL-16
New Pittsburg, 388 ....NJ-13
New Plymouth, 120 ....SE-12
New Richland, 100 ....NL-5
New Richmond, 2582 ....SH-3
New Riegel, 249 ....NH-7
New Rochester, 75 ....NF-7
New Rumley, 140 ....NL-18
New Salem, 130 ....SB-12
New Somerset, 150 ....NK-19
New Springfield, 600 ....NI-20
New Stark, 70 ....NJ-6
New Straitsville, 722 ....SD-13
New Vienna, 1224 ....SE-6
New Washington, 967 ....NI-10
New Waterford, 1238 ....NI-20
New Weston, 136 ....NL-1
New Westville, 90 ....SB-1
New Winchester, 40 ....NJ-9
Newark, 47573 ....NN-12
Newburgh Hts., 2167 ....SM-18
Newcastle, 100 ....NL-13
Newcomerstown, 3822 ....NM-15
Newell Run SE-17
Newhope, 150 ....SH-5
Newman, 300 ....NJ-15
Newport, 1003 ....SE-17
Newport, 200 ....NL-16
Newport, 198 ....NM-3
Newport, 180 ....SB-7
Newton Falls, 4795 ....NG-18
Newtonsville, 392 ....SF-4
Newtown, 2672 ....SM-5
Ney, 354 ....NF-2
Nicholsville, 200 ....SH-4
Niles, 19266 ....NG-19
Nipgen, 100 ....SF-9
NOBLE CO., 14645 ....SC-16
N. Auburn, 40 ....NI-10
N. Baltimore, 3432 ....NH-6
N. Bend, 857 ....SF-1
N. Benton, 280 ....NH-18
N. Bloomfield, 500 ....NF-18
N. Bristol, 160 ....NF-18
N. Canton, 17488 ....NI-16
N. College Hill, 9397 ....SF-2
N. Creek, 80 ....NH-3
N. Fairfield, 560 ....NH-11
N. Fork Vil., 1700 ....SE-9
N. Georgetown, 150 ....NI-18
N. Hampton, 478 ....SA-5
N. Industry, 2700 ....NJ-16
N. Jackson, 900 ....NH-18
N. Kingsville, 2923 ....NC-19
N. Lawrence, 268 ....NI-15
N. Lewisburg, 1490 ....NM-6
N. Liberty, 80 ....NK-12
N. Lima, 900 ....NI-19
N. Madison, 8547 ....ND-18
N. Monroeville, 40 ....NG-10
N. Olmsted, 32718 ....NF-14
N. Perry, 893 ....ND-17
N. Randall, 1027 ....SM-19
N. Ridgeville, 29465 ....NF-13
N. Robinson, 205 ....NJ-10
N. Royalton, 30444 ....NG-15
N. Salem, 100 ....NN-15
N. Star, 236 ....NM-2
N. Warren NA-12
N. Woodbury, 90 ....NK-10
N. Zanesville, 2816 ....SB-14
Northbrook, 10668 ....SK-2
Northfield, 3677 ....NG-15
Northridge, 8500 ....SB-4
Northridge, 7572 ....SA-6
Northup, 100 ....SI-13
Northwood, 5265 ....NE-7
Northwood, 80 ....NL-6
Norton, 12085 ....NH-15
Norton, 50 ....NL-9
Norwalk, 17012 ....NG-11
Norwich, 102 ....SA-15
Norwood, 19207 ....SF-3
Nova, 430 ....NH-12
Novelty, 500 ....NF-16
Oak Hbr., 2759 ....NF-8
Oak Hill, 1551 ....SH-11
Oakdale, 570 ....NB-8
Oakdale SD-13
Oakfield, 100 ....SE-13
Oakfield, 40 ....NF-18
Oakland, 120 ....SD-10
Oakland SD-5
Oakshade, 100 ....NE-4
Oakwood, 9202 ....SC-4
Oakwood, 3667 ....SN-20
Oakwood, 608 ....NH-3
Oberlin, 8286 ....NG-12
Obetz, 4532 ....SB-9
Oceola, 190 ....NI-8
Octa, 59 ....SD-6
Ogden, 100 ....SE-5
Ohio City, 705 ....NJ-2
Ohio Furnace, 150 ....SJ-10
Okeana, 240 ....SE-1
Okolona, 140 ....NF-4
Old Fort, 186 ....NG-8
Old Washington, 279 ....NN-16
Oldtown, 80 ....SC-5
Olena, 350 ....NH-11
Olive Branch, 200 ....SG-4
Olive Green, 65 ....NM-10
Olivesburg, 80 ....NI-11
Olivett, 80 ....SA-18
Olmsted Falls, 9024 ....SN-14
Omega, 130 ....SF-10
Oneida, 150 ....NJ-17
Ontario, 6225 ....NJ-11
Opperman, 30 ....SE-16
Oran, 50 ....NM-3
Orange, 3323 ....SM-20
Orange, 35 ....NM-15
Orangeville, 197 ....NF-20
Orbiston, 40 ....SD-13
Orchard Island, 300 ....NL-5
Oregon, 20291 ....NE-7
Oregonia, 300 ....SE-4
Oreville, 150 ....SD-13
Orient, 270 ....SC-9
Orland, 50 ....SE-12
Orrville, 8380 ....NI-14
Orwell, 1660 ....NE-18
Osgood, 302 ....NL-2
Ostrander, 643 ....NM-8
Otsego, 50 ....NN-14
Ottawa, 4460 ....NH-4
OTTAWA CO., 41428 ....NE-7
Ottawa Hills, 4517 ....NB-1
Otterbien Home, 700 ....SE-3
Ottokee, 35 ....NE-4
Ottoville, 976 ....NI-3
Otway, 87 ....SH-8
Outville, 110 ....SA-11
Overlook SL-8
Overpeck, 300 ....SE-2
Overton, 140 ....NI-13
Owensville, 794 ....SG-4
Oxford, 21371 ....SD-1
Ozark, 40 ....SB-18
Padua, 70 ....NK-1
Page Manor SL-9
Pagetown, 40 ....NL-10
Painesville, 19563 ....ND-17
Painesville on the Lake, 850 ....ND-17
Painters Creek, 150 ....NN-2
Paintersville, 70 ....SD-5
Palestine, 200 ....NN-1
Palmyra, 240 ....NH-18
Pancoastburg, 87 ....SD-8
Pandora, 1153 ....NI-5
Pansy SE-5
Paris, 220 ....NJ-17
Park Ridge Acres, 300 ....NB-15
Parkertown, 25 ....NG-10
Parkman, 600 ....NF-18
Parma, 81601 ....NF-15
Parma Hts., 20718 ....NF-14
Parral, 218 ....NK-16
Parrott SD-7
Pasco, 50 ....NM-4
Pataskala, 14962 ....SA-11
Patmos NI-18
Patriot, 140 ....SI-12
Patterson, 139 ....NJ-7
Pattersonville, 30 ....NI-18
Paulding, 3605 ....NH-2
PAULDING CO., 19614 ....NH-1
Pavonia, 100 ....NJ-11
Payne, 1194 ....NH-1
Pedro, 110 ....SJ-11
Peebles, 1782 ....SH-7
Pekin, 250 ....SD-4
Pekin, 100 ....NK-17
Pemberton, 350 ....NM-4
Pemberville, 1371 ....NF-7
Penfield, 100 ....NH-13
Peninsula, 565 ....NG-15
Pennsville, 150 ....SD-14
Peoli, 30 ....NM-16
Peoria, 230 ....NM-7
Pepper Pike, 5979 ....NF-16
Perintown, 150 ....SF-4
Perry, 1663 ....ND-17
PERRY CO., 36058 ....SC-12
Perry Hts., 8441 ....NC-8
Perrysburg, 20623 ....NE-6
Perrysville, 735 ....NK-12
Perrysville, 60 ....NL-17
Perryton, 100 ....NN-12
Peru, 70 ....NH-10
Petersburg, 950 ....NI-20
Pettisville, 498 ....NE-3
Pfeiffer Sta., 30 ....NK-7
Phalanx NG-18
Pharisburg, 50 ....NL-8
Phillipsburg, 557 ....SB-3
Philo, 733 ....SB-14
Philothea, 120 ....NL-1
Phoneton, 220 ....SB-4
PICKAWAY CO., 55698 ....SD-9
Pickerington, 18291 ....SB-10
Pickrelltown, 60 ....NM-6
Piedmont, 200 ....NM-17
Pierpont, 420 ....ND-20
Pigeon Run, 250 ....NJ-15
PIKE CO., 28709 ....SG-9
Piketon, 2181 ....SG-9
Pikeville, 40 ....NM-2
Pine Grv., 50 ....SJ-11
Piney Fork, 350 ....NM-19
Pioneer, 1380 ....ND-2
Piqua, 20522 ....NN-3
Pisgah, 1000 ....SE-3
Pitchin, 150 ....SB-6
Pitsburg, 388 ....SA-2
Pittsfield, 200 ....NG-12
Plain City, 4225 ....NN-8
Plainfield, 157 ....NM-15
Plants, 150 ....SH-14
Plantsville, 25 ....SE-14
Plattsburg, 160 ....SB-6
Plattsville, 100 ....NM-4
Pleasant Bend, 50 ....NG-4
Pleasant City, 447 ....SB-16
Pleasant Cors., 80 ....SB-9
Pleasant Grv., 1742 ....SB-14
Pleasant Grv., 130 ....NM-19
Pleasant Hill, 1200 ....NN-3
Pleasant Home, 200 ....NI-13
Pleasant Plain, 154 ....SF-4
Pleasant Ridge SK-4
Pleasant Run, 4953 ....SJ-2
Pleasant Run Farm, 4654 ....SJ-2
Pleasant Valley, 500 ....SF-9
Pleasant View, 35 ....SC-6
Pleasantville, 960 ....SC-11
Plumwood, 319 ....SA-7
Plymouth, 1857 ....NI-10
Plymouth Ctr., 50 ....ND-19
Poast Town, 150 ....SD-3
Pt. Isabel, 45 ....SH-4
Point Pl. NA-3
Pt. Pleasant, 35 ....SH-4
Poland, 2555 ....NH-20
Poland Ctr., 250 ....NE-14
Polk, 336 ....NI-12
Pomeroy, 1852 ....SG-14
Port Clinton, 6056 ....NF-9
Port Jefferson, 371 ....NM-4
Port Union, 100 ....SE-3
Port Washington, 569 ....NM-16
Port William, 254 ....SD-6
Portage, 438 ....NG-6
PORTAGE CO., 161419 ....NH-17
Portage Lakes, 6968 ....NI-15
Porter, 150 ....SH-13
Porterfield, 130 ....SF-15
Portersville, 85 ....SC-14
Portland, 120 ....SG-15
Portsmouth, 20226 ....SI-9
Possum Woods, 200 ....NC-16
Potsdam, 288 ....SB-3
Powell, 11500 ....NN-9
Powellsville, 50 ....SI-10
Powhatan Pt., 1592 ....SB-19
Pratts Fork SF-14
Prattsville, 30 ....SF-12
PREBLE CO., 42270 ....SC-1
Pricetown, 60 ....SF-6
Princeton, 120 ....SE-3
Proctorville, 574 ....SK-12
Prospect, 1112 ....NL-8
Pulaski, 132 ....NF-2
Pulaskiville, 50 ....NK-10
Put-in-Bay, 138 ....NE-10
PUTNAM CO., 34499 ....NI-4
Pyrmont, 120 ....SB-3
Pyro, 150 ....SH-11
Quaker City, 502 ....SB-17
Queen Acres, 650 ....SE-2
Quincy, 706 ....NM-5
Raccoon Island SI-13
Racine, 675 ....SG-14
Radcliff, 150 ....SF-12
Radnor, 201 ....NL-8
Ragersville, 150 ....NL-15
Rainsboro, 280 ....SF-7
Randolph, 750 ....NH-17
Range, 40 ....SC-7
Rarden, 159 ....SH-8
Ravenna, 11724 ....NH-17
Rawson, 570 ....NI-5
Ray, 100 ....SF-11
Rayland, 417 ....NM-19
Raymond, 257 ....NM-7
Reading, 10385 ....SF-3
Red Lion, 200 ....SD-3
Redbird, 2000 ....ND-17
Redfield, 50 ....SC-13
Redhaw, 50 ....NI-13
Redoak SH-6
Redtown SE-13
Reedsburg, 150 ....NJ-13
Reedsville, 300 ....SG-15
Reedtown, 50 ....NH-10
Reedurban, 4400 ....NJ-16
Reese, 400 ....SJ-19
Reesville, 250 ....SD-6
Rehoboth, 100 ....SC-13
Reily, 200 ....SE-1
Reinersville, 100 ....SC-15
Reminderville, 3404 ....NF-16
Remington, 328 ....SK-5
Remsen Cors., 75 ....NG-15
Rendville, 36 ....SD-13
Reno, 1293 ....SE-17
Reno Bch., 430 ....NE-8
Rensselaer Pk., 850 ....SK-3
Republic, 549 ....NH-9
Resaca, 40 ....NN-7
Residence Pk. SL-7
Reynoldsburg, 35893 ....SB-10
Rice NH-3
Richland, 200 ....NJ-14
Rich Hill, 75 ....NM-10
Richfield, 3648 ....NG-15
Richfield Ctr., 110 ....NE-5
RICHLAND CO., 124475 ....NI-11
Richmond, 481 ....NL-19
Richmond Ctr., 100 ....ND-20
Richmond Dale, 377 ....SF-10
Richmond Hts., 10546 ....NE-16
Richville, 3324 ....NI-16
Richwood, 2229 ....NL-8
Ridgeland, 50 ....SG-11
Ridgeton, 20 ....NJ-9
Ridgeville, 200 ....SD-4
Ridgeville Corners, 435 ....NF-3
Ridgeway, 338 ....NK-6
Ridgewood Hts. SM-7
Rimer, 50 ....NI-3
Rinard Mills, 30 ....SD-18
Ringgold, 200 ....SC-10
Ringgold, 25 ....NN-15
Rio Grande, 830 ....SH-12
Ripley, 1750 ....SI-5
Risingsun, 606 ....NG-7
Rittman, 6491 ....NI-14
River Cors., 60 ....NH-13
Riverlea, 545 ....SF-18
Riverside, 25201 ....SC-4
Rix Mills, 40 ....SB-15
Roads, 160 ....SG-11
Roaming Shores, 1508 ....NE-19
Robertsville, 331 ....NJ-17
Robins, 90 ....SB-16
Robtown SC-9
Rochester, 182 ....NH-12
Rock Camp, 80 ....SJ-11
Rock Creek, 529 ....NE-18
Rock Mills, 30 ....SE-7
Rock Way, 160 ....SB-5
Rockbridge, 182 ....SD-11
Rockford, 1120 ....NJ-2
Rockport, 90 ....NI-4
Rocky Hill SG-11
Rocky Ridge, 417 ....NE-8
Rocky River, 20213 ....NF-14
Rodney, 250 ....SH-12
Rogers, 237 ....NJ-20
Rollersville, 40 ....NG-7
Rome, 1450 ....SK-12
Rome, 200 ....NE-18
Rome, 90 ....NI-11
Romohr Acres, 300 ....SL-6
Rootstown, 650 ....NH-17
Rose Farm, 200 ....SC-13
Rosedale, 180 ....NN-7
Roseland, 2150 ....NJ-11
Rosemont, 90 ....ND-11
Rosemount, 2112 ....SI-9
Roseville, 1852 ....SC-13
Rosewood, 257 ....NM-5
Ross, 3417 ....SE-2
ROSS CO., 78064 ....SE-9
Rossburg, 201 ....NM-2
Rossford, 6293 ....NE-6
Roswell, 219 ....NL-16
Roundhead, 300 ....NK-5
Rowsburg, 90 ....NI-13
Roxabell, 200 ....SE-8
Royalton, 260 ....SC-10
Rubyville SH-10
Rudolph, 458 ....NG-6
Ruggles, 40 ....NH-12
Ruggles Bch., 50 ....NF-11
Ruraldale, 60 ....SC-14
Rush Run, 250 ....NM-19
Rushsylvania, 516 ....NL-6
Rushtown SH-9
Rushville, 302 ....SC-12
Russell, 50 ....SF-6
Russell Ctr., 200 ....NF-16
Russells Pt., 1391 ....NL-5
Russellville, 561 ....SH-6
Russia, 640 ....NM-3
Rutland, 393 ....SG-13
Sabina, 2564 ....SD-6
Sagamore Hills, 1930 ....NG-15
Sahara Sands, 650 ....NB-8
St. Bernard, 4368 ....SL-3
St. Clairsville, 5184 ....NN-18
St. Henry, 2427 ....NL-2
St. Johns, 185 ....NK-4
St. Louisville, 373 ....NM-12
St. Martin, 129 ....SF-5
St. Marys, 8332 ....NK-3
St. Paris, 2089 ....NN-5
Salem, 12303 ....NI-18
Salem Ctr., 80 ....SG-13
Salesville, 129 ....SB-17
Salineville, 1311 ....NK-19
Saltillo, 110 ....SC-13
Samantha, 130 ....SE-6
Sampleville, 200 ....SC-2
San Margherita, 300 ....SH-17
Sandusky, 25793 ....NF-10
SANDUSKY CO., 60944 ....NF-8
Sandy Sprs. SJ-8
Sandyville, 368 ....NK-16
Santa Fe, 100 ....NL-6
Sarahsville, 166 ....SB-16
Sardinia, 980 ....SG-5
Sardis, 559 ....SD-19
Savannah, 413 ....NI-12
Savona, 50 ....SA-2
Sawyerwood, 1540 ....NC-6
Saybrook ND-18
Sayre SC-13
Schoenbrunn, 700 ....NL-16
Schumm, 25 ....NJ-1
Scienceville NC-14
Scio, 763 ....NL-18
SCIOTO CO., 79499 ....SH-9
Scioto Furnace, 250 ....SI-10
Sciotodale, 1081 ....SI-10
Scotch Ridge, 90 ....NF-7
Scott, 286 ....NI-2
Scottown, 100 ....SJ-12
Seal, 25 ....NI-8
Seaman, 944 ....SH-7
Sebring, 4420 ....NI-18
Secedar Corners, 300 ....NC-14
Selma, 130 ....SC-6
SENECA CO., 56745 ....NH-8
Senecaville, 457 ....SB-16
Senior SE-4
Seven Hills, 11804 ....NF-15
Seven Mile, 751 ....SD-2
Seventeen, 120 ....NL-16
Sewellsville, 35 ....NN-17
Shade, 120 ....SF-14
Shademore, 40 ....SL-5
Shadeville, 100 ....SB-9
Shadyside, 3785 ....SA-19
Shaker Hts., 28448 ....NF-15
Shalersville, 220 ....NG-17
Shandon, 400 ....SE-1
Sharon, 90 ....SC-16
Sharon Ctr., 350 ....NH-15
Sharonville, 13560 ....SF-3
Sharpsburg, 50 ....SE-14
Shauck, 200 ....NK-10
Shawnee, 655 ....SD-13
Shawnee Hills, 2171 ....SC-6
Shawnee Hills, 681 ....NN-8
Sheffield, 3982 ....NF-13
Sheffield Lake, 9137 ....NF-13
Shelby, 9317 ....NI-10
SHELBY CO., 49423 ....NM-3
Shenandoah, 100 ....NI-11
Sheridan, 500 ....SJ-11
Sherrodsville, 304 ....NK-17
Sherwood, 827 ....NG-2
Shiloh, 11000 ....SB-4
Shiloh, 649 ....NI-11
Shinrock NG-11
Shreve, 1514 ....NJ-13
Sidney, 21229 ....NM-4
Signal, 40 ....NJ-19
Silver Lake, 2519 ....NH-16
Silverton, 4788 ....SK-4
Simons, 70 ....NE-20
Sinking Spr., 133 ....SG-7
Skyline Acres, 1717 ....SK-2
Sligo, 300 ....SE-5
Slocum SI-10
Smith Corners ND-12
Smithfield, 869 ....NM-19
Smithville, 1252 ....NI-14
Smyrna, 40 ....NM-17
Snyderville, 200 ....SB-5
Socialville SE-3
Solon, 23348 ....NF-16
Somerdale, 320 ....NK-16
Somerset, 1481 ....SC-12
Somerton, 180 ....SB-18
Somerville, 281 ....SD-2
Sonora, 250 ....SA-14
S. Amherst, 1688 ....NF-12
S. Bloomfield, 1744 ....SC-9
S. Bloomingville, 40 ....SE-11
S. Charleston, 1693 ....SB-6
S. Condit, 110 ....NM-10
S. Euclid, 22295 ....NE-15
S. Hill Pk., 1040 ....NB-1
S. Lebanon, 4115 ....SE-4
S. New Lyme, 120 ....NE-19
S. Newbury, 70 ....NF-17
S. Olive, 40 ....SC-16
S. Perry, 140 ....SD-11
S. Plymouth, 20 ....SD-7
South Point, 3958 ....*B-2
S. Russell, 3810 ....NF-16
S. Salem, 204 ....SE-8
S. Solon, 355 ....SC-6
S. Vienna, 384 ....SB-6
S. Webster, 866 ....SH-10
S. West Hubbard NC-14
S. Woodbury, 30 ....NL-10
S. Zanesville, 1989 ....SB-14
Southington, 400 ....NG-18
Sparta, 161 ....NL-10
Spencer, 753 ....NH-13
Spencerville, 2223 ....NJ-3
Spring Mill, 150 ....NJ-11
Spring Mtn., 80 ....NL-13
Spring Valley, 479 ....SD-5
Springboro, 17409 ....SD-4
Springdale, 11223 ....SJ-3
Springfield, 60608 ....SB-6
Springhills, 150 ....NM-5
Springville, 40 ....SJ-13
Squirrel Town SI-7
Stafford, 81 ....SC-17
Standley NG-3
Stanleyville, 40 ....SD-16
Stanwood, 30 ....NJ-15
STARK CO., 375586 ....NJ-17
Starr, 25 ....SE-12
Staunton, 120 ....NN-4
Staunton, 100 ....SE-7
Steam Cors. NJ-10
Steinersville, 200 ....SB-19
Stelvideo, 90 ....NN-2
Sterling, 457 ....NI-14
Steuben, 60 ....NH-10
Steubenville, 18659 ....NL-20
Stewart, 247 ....SE-14
Stewartsville, 200 ....SA-19
Stillwater, 150 ....NM-17
Stockdale, 135 ....SH-10
Stockport, 503 ....SD-15
Stone SC-14
Stone Creek, 177 ....NL-15
Stonelick, 100 ....SG-4
Stony Ridge, 411 ....NF-7
Stout, 94 ....SI-7
Stoutsville, 560 ....SD-10
Stovertown, 35 ....SB-14
Stow, 34837 ....NH-16
Strasburg, 2608 ....NK-16
Stratford, 80 ....NM-9
Stratton, 294 ....NK-20
Streetsboro, 16028 ....NG-16
Stringtown, 50 ....SH-4
Strongsville, 44750 ....NG-14
Struthers, 10713 ....NH-20
Stryker, 1335 ....NF-3
Suffield, 500 ....NH-16
Sugar Bush Knolls, 177 ....NG-16
Sugar Grv., 426 ....SD-11
Sugar Grv., 160 ....NK-19
Sugar Grv., 150 ....SI-9
Sugar Grv. Hill, 300 ....NB-15
Sugar Ridge, 130 ....NF-6
Sugar Tree Ridge, 110 ....SG-6
Sugar Valley, 25 ....SC-1
Sugarcreek, 2220 ....NK-15
Sullivan, 450 ....NH-12
Sulphur Sprs., 194 ....NI-9
Sulphurgrove SK-9
Summerfield, 254 ....SC-17
Summerford, 250 ....SB-7
Summerside, 5083 ....SG-3
Summerside Estates, 1700 ....SM-6
Summersville, 80 ....NJ-7
Summit, 700 ....NC-13
SUMMIT CO., 541781 ....NH-15
Summithill, 20 ....SF-9
Summitville, 135 ....NJ-18
Sumner SF-14
Sun Valley SJ-20
Sunbury, 4389 ....NM-10
Sunbury, 110 ....SD-3
Sunnyland, 250 ....NB-15
Surrey Hill, 700 ....NB-12
Swanders, 80 ....NL-4
Swanton, 3690 ....NE-5
Sybene, 200 ....SK-12
Sycamore, 861 ....NI-8
Sycamore Valley, 25 ....SC-17
Sylvania, 18965 ....ND-6
Syracuse, 826 ....SG-14
Tacoma, 100 ....SA-18
Tallmadge, 17537 ....NH-16
Tarlton, 282 ....SD-10
Tawawa, 100 ....NM-4
Taylors Creek, 660 ....SK-1
Taylorsburg SG-6
Taylorsville SE-6
Tedrow, 173 ....NE-4
Temperanceville, 80 ....SB-17
Terrace Pk., 2251 ....SL-5
Terre Haute, 180 ....NN-5
Terry Acres, 165 ....SL-10
Texas, 130 ....NF-5
Thackery, 120 ....NN-5
The Bend, 100 ....NG-2
The Plains, 3080 ....SE-13
The Vil. of Indian Hill, 5785 ....SK-5
Thomastown NC-6
Thompson, 370 ....ND-18
Thornville, 991 ....SB-12
Thrifton, 40 ....SF-8
Thurman, 103 ....SH-12
Thurston, 604 ....SB-11
Tiffin, 17963 ....NH-8
Tiltonsville, 1372 ....NM-19
Timberlake, 675 ....NE-16
Tipp City, 9689 ....SB-4
Tippecanoe, 121 ....NM-17
Tipton, 25 ....NH-1
Tiro, 280 ....NI-10
Tiverton, 80 ....NL-13
Toboso, 200 ....NN-12
Toledo, 287208 ....NE-7
Tontogany, 367 ....NF-6
Torch, 300 ....SF-15
Toronto, 5091 ....NL-20
Townwood, 25 ....NH-5
Trail NK-15
Tranquility, 30 ....SH-7
Tremont City, 375 ....SA-5
Trenton, 11869 ....SD-3
Triadelphia, 40 ....SC-14
Trimble, 390 ....SD-13
Trinway, 365 ....NN-13
Trotwood, 24431 ....SC-3
Trowbridge, 50 ....NE-8
Troy, 25058 ....NN-3
Trumbull, 200 ....ND-18
TRUMBULL CO., 210312 ....NG-18
Tucson SE-10
Tuppers Plains, 465 ....SF-14
Turpin Hills, 5099 ....SM-4
Tuscarawas, 1056 ....NL-16
TUSCARAWAS CO., 92582 ....NM-16
Twenty Mile Stand, 300 ....SJ-6
Twightwee SJ-6
Twin Lakes, 300 ....NG-16
Twin Valley, 300 ....SI-9
Twinsburg, 18795 ....NG-16
Tymochtee, 25 ....NI-8
Tyndall, 150 ....NM-14
Uhrichsville, 5413 ....NL-16
Union, 6419 ....SB-3
Union City, 1666 ....NM-1
UNION CO., 52300 ....NL-7
Union Furnace, 430 ....SE-12
Union Sta. SA-11
Unionport, 150 ....NL-19
Uniontown, 3309 ....NI-16
Uniontown, 230 ....NN-18
Unionvale, 90 ....NM-18
Unionville Ctr., 233 ....NN-7
Unopolis, 222 ....NK-4
Unity, 100 ....NJ-19
Unity, 30 ....SH-7
University Hts., 13539 ....NF-15
University View, 500 ....SH-18
Upper Arlington, 33771 ....SA-9
Upper Sandusky, 6596 ....NJ-8
Urbana, 11793 ....NN-5
Urbancrest, 960 ....SB-9
Utica, 2132 ....NM-11
Utopia, 70 ....SI-4
Valley City, 400 ....NG-14
Valley Hi, 212 ....NM-6
Valley View, 2034 ....SN-18
Valley View, 620 ....SH-17
Valleywood SM-9
Van Buren, 328 ....NH-6
Van Wert, 10846 ....NI-2
VAN WERT CO., 28744 ....NJ-2
Vanatta, 130 ....NN-11
Vandalia, 15246 ....SB-4
Vanlue, 359 ....NI-7
Vaughnsville, 262 ....NI-4
Venedocia, 124 ....NJ-2
Venice Hts., 1300 ....NA-12
Vera Cruz SF-5
Vermilion, 10594 ....NF-12
Vernon, 100 ....NF-20
Vernon SI-11
Verona, 494 ....SB-2
Versailles, 2687 ....NM-2
Veto, 110 ....SE-15
Vickery, 121 ....NF-9
Vienna, 600 ....NG-19
Vigo, 120 ....SF-10
Viking Vil., 1230 ....SM-5
Villa, 120 ....SB-6
Villa Nova, 800 ....NK-3
Vincent, 339 ....SE-15
Vinton, 222 ....SG-12
VINTON CO., 13435 ....SF-11
Wabash, 70 ....NK-1
Waco, 380 ....NJ-16
Wade SE-18
Wadsworth, 21567 ....NH-14
Wagram, 125 ....SB-10
Wahlsburg, 30 ....SH-5
Wainwright, 250 ....NL-16
Waite Hill, 471 ....NE-16
Wakatomika, 40 ....NM-13
Wakefield, 140 ....SH-9
Wakeman, 1047 ....NG-12
Walbridge, 3019 ....NC-9
Waldo, 338 ....NL-9
Walhonding, 100 ....SB-16
Walhonding, 90 ....NL-13
Walnut Creek, 878 ....NK-15
Walton Hills, 2281 ....SN-19
Wamsley, 90 ....SH-8
Wapakoneta, 9867 ....NK-4
Warner, 130 ....SD-16
Warnock, 200 ....SA-19
Warren, 41557 ....NG-19
WARREN CO., 212693 ....SE-4
Warrensburg NM-8
Warrensville Hts., 13542 ....NF-15
Warrenton, 50 ....NM-19
Warsaw, 682 ....NL-13
WASHINGTON CO., 61778 ....SD-16
Washington Court House, 14192 ....SD-7
Washingtonville, 801 ....NI-19
Waterford, 450 ....SD-15
Waterford, 70 ....NK-11
Waterloo, 170 ....SB-10
Waterloo, 150 ....SJ-12
Watertown, 220 ....SE-15
Waterville, 5523 ....NE-5
Watkins, 130 ....NM-8
Wauseon, 7332 ....NE-4
Waverly, 4408 ....SG-9
Wayland, 200 ....NH-18
Wayne, 887 ....NG-7
Wayne, 100 ....NE-19

*, †, ‡, §, ◊ See explanation under state title in this index.
County and parish names are listed in capital letters & boldface type.
Independent cities (not included in a county) are listed in *italics*.

Allen, 375 ... EO-3
Allenport, 648 ... WN-13
Allens Mills ... WI-9
Allensville, 503 ... WM-13
Allentown, 118032 ... EL-10
Allenwood, 321 ... EI-4
Allison, 625 ... WP-4
Allison Pk., 21552 ... WL-4
Allport, 264 ... WJ-12
Almedia, 1078 ... EJ-6
Almont, 75 ... EN-11
Alsace Mnr., 478 ... ER-14
Altenwald, 40 ... EQ-1
Altoona, 46320 ... WM-11
Alum Bank, 198 ... WO-10
Alverda, 400 ... WL-9
Alverton, 350 ... WO-5
Ambler, 6417 ... EO-12
Ambridge, 7050 ... WL-3
Amity, 400 ... WO-3
Amityville, 250 ... EN-9
Amsbry, 65 ... WM-10
Analomink, 200 ... EJ-12
Ancient Oaks, 6661 ... EM-10
Andalusia, 3500 ... ‡B-8
Andersonburg, 50 ... EN-2
Andreas, 200 ... EK-9
Andrews Settlement, 40 ... WE-13
Angelica, 100 ... EN-8
Angels ... EH-11
Anita, 600 ... WJ-8
Annandale, 275 ... WI-4
Annisville, 35 ... WI-5
Annville, 4767 ... EN-6
Ansonia, 50 ... EF-2
Ansonville, 100 ... WK-10
Antes Fort, 400 ... EI-3
Antrim, 400 ... EF-2
Apollo, 1647 ... WL-6
Appenzell, 150 ... EJ-11
Applebachsville, 120 ... EM-11
Applewold, 310 ... WK-6
Ararat ... EE-10
Arbuckle, 50 ... WD-4
Arcadia, 220 ... WK-9
Arch Rock, 100 ... EL-2
Archbald, 6984 ... EG-10
Ardara, 300 ... ‡L-10
Ardenheim, 25 ... WM-13
Ardmore, 12455 ... ‡D-2
Ardsley, 4500 ... ‡A-4
Arendtsville, 952 ... EP-2
Argentine, 60 ... WI-5
Aristes, 311 ... EK-7
Armagh, 122 ... WM-8
Armbrust, 230 ... WN-6
ARMSTRONG CO., 68941 ... WL-6
Arnold, 5157 ... WL-5
Arnot, 332 ... EF-3
Arona, 370 ... WN-5
Asaph, 100 ... EF-2
Asbury ... WB-9
Ashfield, 300 ... EK-9
Ashland, 2817 ... EK-7
Ashland, 60 ... WK-11
Ashley, 2790 ... EI-9
Ashtola, 150 ... WO-9
Ashville, 227 ... WM-10
Aspers, 350 ... EP-3
Aspinwall, 2801 ... ‡J-7
Atco, 200 ... EF-12
Atglen, 1406 ... EP-8
Athens, 3367 ... EE-6
Atlantic, 77 ... WG-2
Atlantic ... WK-11
Atlas, 809 ... EK-6
Atlasburg, 401 ... WN-2
Atwood, 107 ... WK-7
Auburn, 741 ... EL-8
Auburn Ctr., 50 ... EF-8
Auburn Four Corners, 60 ... EF-8
Audubon, 8433 ... EO-11
Aultman, 225 ... WM-7
Austin, 562 ... WF-12
Austinburg, 60 ... ED-2
Austinville, 150 ... EE-4
Avalon, 4705 ... WM-3
Avella, 804 ... WN-2
Avis, 1484 ... EI-2
Avoca, 2661 ... EB-10
Avon, 1667 ... EN-6
Avondale, 1265 ... EQ-9
Avonia, 1205 ... WD-3
Avonmore, 1011 ... WM-6
Axemann, 150 ... WK-14
Bachmanville, 200 ... EN-6
Baden, 4135 ... WL-3
Baggaley, 600 ... WN-6
Bainbridge, 1355 ... EO-5
Bair, 400 ... EP-5
Bairdford, 698 ... WL-4
Bakers Summit, 110 ... WN-11
Bakerstown Sta., 400 ... WL-4
Bakersville, 200 ... WP-7
Bakerton, 900 ... WL-9
Bala-Cynwyd, 8000 ... ‡D-3
Bald Eagle, 250 ... WL-12
Baldwin, 19767 ... WN-4
Ballietsville, 250 ... EA-1
Balls Mills, 60 ... EH-4
Bally, 1090 ... EM-10
Bandanna, 225 ... EQ-4
Banetown, 100 ... WO-3
Bangor, 5273 ... EK-12
Bannerville, 110 ... EL-2
Barbours, 120 ... EH-5
Bard, 50 ... WP-10
Bareville, 1250 ... EO-8
Barkeyville, 207 ... WI-4
Barnes, 200 ... WF-8
Barnesville, 300 ... EK-8
Barnsley, 100 ... EQ-8
Barree, 70 ... WL-12
Barto, 180 ... EN-10
Bath, 2693 ... EL-11
Baumstown, 422 ... EN-9
Bausman, 300 ... ET-8
Bavington, 50 ... WM-2
Baxter ... WI-8
Beach Haven, 500 ... EJ-7
Beach Lake, 320 ... EG-12
Beallsville, 466 ... WO-4
Bear Creek Vil., 257 ... EI-9
Bear Lake, 164 ... WD-6
Beartown, 200 ... EQ-2
Beartown ... EO-8
Beaumont, 200 ... EH-8
Beaver, 4531 ... WL-2
Beaver Brook, 400 ... EJ-8
Beaver Ctr., 40 ... WE-2
BEAVER CO., 170539 ... WK-2
Beaver Dam, 130 ... WE-5
Beaver Falls, 8987 ... WK-2
Beaver Lake ... EH-6
Beaver Meadows, 869 ... EJ-9
Beaver Sprs., 674 ... EL-3
Beaverdale, 1035 ... WN-9
Beavertown, 965 ... EL-3
Beavertown, 90 ... EO-4
Beavertown, 40 ... WN-11
Beccaria, 175 ... WK-11
Bechtelsville, 942 ... EN-10
Beckersville, 200 ... EO-9
Bedford, 2841 ... WP-10
BEDFORD CO., 49762 ... WO-10
Bedminster, 500 ... EM-12
Beech Creek, 701 ... EJ-1
Beechwood ... WG-11
Beersville, 250 ... EK-10
Belair, 1310 ... ER-8
Belden ... WO-10
Belfast, 1257 ... EK-11
Belknap, 40 ... WK-7
Bell Acres, 1388 ... WL-3
Bellaire ... EO-6
Belle Vernon, 1093 ... WO-4
Bellefonte, 6187 ... WK-14
Bellegrove, 300 ... EN-6
Belleville, 1827 ... WL-14
Bellevue, 8370 ... WM-3
Bells, 75 ... WK-10
Belltown, 60 ... EL-2
Bellwood, 1828 ... WL-11
Belmont, 2784 ... WT-2
Belmont Hills, 1500 ... ‡C-2
Belsano, 400 ... WM-9
Ben Avon, 1781 ... ‡I-4
Ben Avon Hts., 371 ... ‡I-5
Bendersville, 641 ... EP-3
Bendertown, 50 ... EI-7
Benezette, 200 ... WH-11
Benfer, 100 ... EK-3
Bensalem, 3000 ... ‡A-8
Benson, 191 ... WO-8
Bentley Creek, 160 ... EE-5
Bentleyville, 2581 ... WO-4
Benton, 824 ... EI-6
Benvenue, 25 ... EN-4
Berkley, 200 ... EM-8
Berkleys Mill, 60 ... WQ-8
BERKS CO., 411442 ... EM-8
Berlin, 2104 ... WP-8
Berlinsville, 200 ... EK-10
Bermudian, 40 ... EP-4
Berne, 130 ... EM-8
Bernville, 955 ... EM-8
Berrysburg, 368 ... EL-5
Berwick, 10477 ... EJ-7
Berwyn, 3631 ... EP-11
Bessemer, 1111 ... WJ-2
Bethany, 246 ... EF-11
Bethel, 499 ... EM-7
Bethel Pk., 32313 ... WN-4
Bethesda, 45 ... EQ-7
Bethlehem, 74982 ... EL-11
Bethlehem, 25 ... WK-9
Betula ... WF-11
Beyer, 100 ... WK-7
Big Beaver, 1970 ... WK-2
Big Cove Tannery, 200 ... WQ-12
Big Pond, 100 ... EE-5
Big Run, 624 ... WJ-9
Bigler, 398 ... WJ-11
Biglerville, 1200 ... EP-3
Bigmount, 100 ... EP-4
Bingen, 350 ... EC-5
Bingham, 40 ... WE-10
Bingham Ctr. ... WE-14
Birchardville, 40 ... EE-8
Bird in Hand, 402 ... EP-7
Birdsboro, 5163 ... EN-9
Birmingham, 90 ... WL-12
Bishop, 800 ... WN-3
Bittersville, 150 ... EP-6
Black Gap ... EP-1
Black Lick, 1462 ... WM-7
Black Walnut, 150 ... EF-8
Blacktown, 50 ... WI-3
Blackwell, 80 ... EG-2
Blain, 263 ... EN-1
Blain City, 250 ... WK-10
Blaine Hill, 1100 ... WN-4
Blainsport, 110 ... EN-8
BLAIR CO., 127089 ... WN-11
Blairs Mills, 100 ... WN-14
Blairsville, 3412 ... WM-7
Blairtown, 60 ... WP-3
Blakely, 6564 ... EG-10
Blakeslee, 300 ... EI-10
Blanchard, 740 ... EJ-1
Blandburg, 402 ... WL-11
Blandon, 7152 ... EM-9
Blawnox, 1432 ... ‡J-8
Blooming Glen, 650 ... EN-12
Blooming Grv., 200 ... EH-12
Blooming Grv., 100 ... EQ-4
Blooming Valley, 337 ... WF-4
Bloomingdale, 2100 ... ES-9
Bloomington, 80 ... WJ-10
Bloomsburg, 14855 ... EJ-6
Bloserville, 200 ... EO-2
Blossburg, 1538 ... EF-3
Blough, 80 ... WO-8
Blue Ball, 1031 ... EO-8
Blue Bell, 6067 ... EO-11
Blue Knob ... WN-10
Blue Ridge Summit, 891 ... ER-2
Blythedale, 250 ... WN-5
Boalsburg, 3722 ... WK-13
Boardman, 35 ... WK-11
Bobtown, 757 ... WQ-4
Bocktown ... ‡I-1
Bodines, 50 ... EG-4
Boiling Sprs., 3225 ... EO-3
Bolivar, 465 ... WN-7
Bolivar Run, 350 ... WD-10
Boltz, 160 ... WM-8
Bon Air, 600 ... WS-2
Bonneauville, 1800 ... EQ-3
Booneville, 75 ... EJ-2
Booths Cor., 200 ... EQ-10
Boothwyn, 4933 ... *B-10
Bordnersville ... EM-6
Bossardsville ... EJ-11
Boston, 545 ... ‡M-8
Boswell, 1277 ... WO-8
Bovard, 700 ... WN-6
Bovard, 40 ... WJ-4
Bowmanstown, 937 ... EK-10
Bowmansville, 2077 ... EO-8
Boyds Mills, 85 ... EF-12
Boydstown, 50 ... WJ-4
Boyertown, 4055 ... EN-10
Boynton, 200 ... WQ-8
Brackenridge, 3260 ... WL-5
Brackney, 200 ... ED-8
Braddock, 2159 ... ‡L-8
Braddock Hills, 1880 ... ‡K-8
Braden Plan, 250 ... WP-3
Bradenville, 545 ... WN-7
Bradford, 8770 ... WD-10
BRADFORD CO., 62622 ... EE-5
Bradford Woods, 1171 ... WL-3
Bradleytown, 50 ... WG-4
Bradys Bend, 150 ... WJ-5
Branch Dale, 388 ... EL-7
Branchton, 80 ... WJ-4
Branchville ... WD-3
Brandamore, 300 ... EP-9
Brandonville, 197 ... EK-7
Brandtsville ... EO-3
Brandy Camp, 200 ... WH-10
Brandywine Manor, 200 ... EO-9
Brave, 201 ... WQ-2
Breezewood, 300 ... WP-11
Breinigsville, 4138 ... EM-10
Brent, 90 ... WI-3
Brentwood, 9643 ... ‡L-6
Breslau, 500 ... EA-7
Bressler, 1437 ... ET-4
Briar Creek, 660 ... EJ-7
Brickerville, 1309 ... EO-7
Bridesburg ... ‡D-6
Bridgeburg ... WK-6
Bridgeport, 4554 ... ‡A-1
Bridgeport, 40 ... EN-2
Bridgeton ... EQ-6
Bridgeville, 5148 ... WN-3
Bridgewater, 704 ... WL-2
Bridgewater, 250 ... ‡B-9
Brisbin, 411 ... WK-11
Bristol, 9726 ... EO-13
Bristoria, 40 ... WP-2
Britton Run ... WE-5
Broad Top City, 452 ... WO-12
Brockport, 300 ... WI-9
Brockton, 500 ... EL-8
Brockway, 2072 ... WI-9
Brodbecks ... EQ-5
Brodhead, 100 ... EA-5
Brodheadsville, 1800 ... EJ-11
Brogue, 200 ... EQ-6
Brookdale, 60 ... ED-9
Brookhaven, 8006 ... EQ-11
Brookland, 15 ... WE-13
Brooklyn, 250 ... EF-9
Brookside, 2200 ... WC-4
Brookside ... EH-3
Brookston, 90 ... WF-8
Brookville, 3924 ... WI-8
Broomall, 10789 ... EP-11
Brotherton, 60 ... WP-8
Broughton, 3000 ... ‡M-6
Browndale, 525 ... EF-10
Brownfield, 400 ... WQ-5
Brownstown, 2816 ... EO-7
Brownstown, 744 ... WN-8
Brownstown, 30 ... WM-6
Brownsville, 2331 ... WP-4
Browntown, 1418 ... EB-9
Browntown, 90 ... EF-7
Bruin, 524 ... WJ-5
Brunnerville, 250 ... EO-7
Brush Valley, 300 ... WM-8
Brushtown, 340 ... EQ-4
Brushtown ... EO-2
Bryan, 30 ... WK-7
Bryn Athyn, 1375 ... EO-12
Bryn Mawr, 3779 ... ‡C-1
Buck, 120 ... EQ-7
Buck Hill Falls, 950 ... EI-11
Buck Mtn., 70 ... EJ-9
Buck Run, 176 ... EL-7
Buck Run, 150 ... EP-9
Buck Valley ... WQ-11
Buckhorn, 318 ... EJ-6
Buckhorn, 130 ... WM-10
Buckingham, 2000 ... EN-12
BUCKS CO., 625249 ... EM-11
Bucktown, 60 ... EO-10
Buena Vista, 600 ... WN-5
Buena Vista, 60 ... WJ-5
Buffalo, 120 ... WN-2
Buffalo Mills, 100 ... WP-10
Buffalo Run, 75 ... WK-13
Buffalo Valley, 120 ... WK-5
Bulger, 407 ... WM-2
Bullion, 40 ... WI-4
Bullis Mills ... WD-11
Bully Hill, 150 ... WH-5
Bungalow Pk., 200 ... EC-2
Bunker Hill, 170 ... EN-6
Bunkertown, 60 ... EL-3
Bunola, 300 ... WN-4
Burgettstown, 1388 ... WM-2
Burlington, 156 ... EF-5
Burnham, 2054 ... EL-1
Burning Well ... WF-10
Burnside, 234 ... WK-9
Burnt Cabins, 125 ... WO-13
Burtville ... WF-12
Bushkill, 1200 ... EI-12
Bustleton ... ‡B-7
Butler, 13757 ... WK-4
BUTLER CO., 183862 ... WJ-4
Buttonwood, 620 ... EB-6
Buttonwood ... EG-3
Butztown, 1500 ... EA-5
Byrnedale, 427 ... WH-10
Byromtown ... WG-8
Cabot, 400 ... WK-5
Cadogan, 400 ... WK-6
Cairnbrook, 520 ... WO-9
Caledonia, 200 ... WH-11
California, 6795 ... WO-4
Callensburg, 207 ... WI-6
Callery, 394 ... WK-4
Caln, 1519 ... EP-9
Calvin, 90 ... WN-12
Cambra, 70 ... EI-7
CAMBRIA CO., 143679 ... WL-10
Cambridge, 140 ... EO-8
Cambridge Sprs., 2595 ... WE-4
Cameron, 50 ... WG-12
CAMERON CO., 5085 ... WG-11
Camp Hill, 7888 ... EN-4
Campbelltown, 3616 ... EN-6
Camptown, 180 ... EF-7
Canadensis, 1200 ... EI-11
Canan, 140 ... WB-12
Candor, 60 ... WM-2
Cannelton, 100 ... WK-2
Canoe Camp, 150 ... EF-3
Canoe Creek, 250 ... WM-11
Canonsburg, 8992 ... WN-3
Canton, 1976 ... EF-4
CARBON CO., 65249 ... EJ-9
Carbondale, 8891 ... EG-10
Carlisle, 18682 ... EO-3
Carlisle Sprs. ... EN-3
Carlton, 80 ... WG-4
Carmichaels, 483 ... WP-4
Carnegie, 7972 ... ‡K-4
Carnot, 4500 ... ‡I-2
Carroll ... EJ-3
Carroll Valley, 3876 ... EQ-2
Carrolltown, 853 ... WL-9
Carter Camp, 20 ... WF-14
Carversville, 400 ... EN-12
Carverton, 500 ... EA-9
Casanova, 90 ... WJ-12
Cashtown, 459 ... EQ-2
Cassandra, 147 ... WM-10
Casselman, 94 ... WP-7
Cassville, 143 ... WN-12
Castanea, 1125 ... EI-2
Castle Gdn., 45 ... WH-12
Castle Shannon, 8316 ... ‡L-5
Catasauqua, 6436 ... EL-11
Catawissa, 1552 ... EJ-6
Cavettsville, 120 ... ‡L-9
Cecil, 900 ... WN-3
Cedar Hts., 800 ... ‡B-2
Cedar Ledge, 25 ... EF-4
Cedar Run, 100 ... EG-2
Cedar Sprs., 90 ... EJ-2
Cedarbrook, 2800 ... ‡B-4
Cementon, 1538 ... EL-10
Center Mills, 80 ... EP-3
Center Moreland ... EH-8
Center Road ... WF-2
Center Valley, 900 ... EM-11
Centerport, 387 ... EM-8
Centerville, 3263 ... WO-4
Centerville, 1700 ... ES-7
Centerville, 218 ... WF-5
Centerville, 125 ... WQ-10
Central, 100 ... EH-6
Central City, 1124 ... WO-9
Central Highlands, 700 ... ‡N-8
Centralia, 10 ... EK-7
CENTRE CO., 153990 ... EK-1
Centre Hall, 1265 ... WK-14
Cessna, 60 ... WO-10
Cetronia ... EC-2
Chadds Ford, 1200 ... EQ-10
Chalfant, 800 ... ‡K-8
Chalfont, 4009 ... EN-12
Chalkhill, 141 ... WQ-5
Challenge ... WH-10
Chambers Hill, 1500 ... ES-4
Chambersburg, 20268 ... EP-1
Chambersville, 100 ... WL-7
Champion, 300 ... WO-6
Chandlers Valley, 250 ... WE-7
Chaneysville, 80 ... WQ-10
Chapman, 199 ... EK-11
Chapmanville, 90 ... WG-5
Charleroi, 4120 ... WO-4
Charleston, 100 ... WI-2
Charlesville ... WP-10
Chase, 978 ... EA-7
Chatham, 300 ... EQ-9
Chatwood, 1000 ... EP-10
Chelsea, 160 ... EQ-11
Cheltenham ... ‡B-5
Cherry Flats, 250 ... EF-3
Cherry Grv. ... WF-8
Cherry Hill, 300 ... EK-11
Cherry Hill, 60 ... WE-2
Cherry Hill, 35 ... EQ-7
Cherry Tree, 364 ... WL-9
Cherry Valley, 200 ... WN-2
Cherry Valley, 66 ... WI-5
Cherrytown, 120 ... WN-11
Cherrytree ... WG-5
Cherryville, 1580 ... EK-10
Chest Sprs., 149 ... WL-10
Chester, 33972 ... EQ-11
CHESTER CO., 498886 ... EP-9
Chester Hts., 2531 ... EP-11
Chester Hill, 883 ... WK-12
Chester Sprs., 450 ... EO-10
Chestnut Grv., 100 ... WJ-10
Chestnut Level, 200 ... EQ-7
Chestnut Ridge, 100 ... ES-7
Cheswick, 1746 ... ‡I-9
Chevy Chase Hts., 1502 ... WL-8
Chewton, 488 ... WK-2
Cheyney, 150 ... EP-10
Chicora, 1043 ... WJ-5
Childs, 450 ... EG-10
Chillisquaque, 400 ... EJ-4
Chinchilla, 2098 ... EA-13
Choconut, 50 ... ED-8
Christiana, 1168 ... EP-8
Christmans, 100 ... EJ-10
Christy Mnr., 75 ... WK-6
Chrome ... EQ-8
Churchill, 3011 ... ‡K-8
Churchtown, 470 ... EO-8
Churchville, 60 ... WO-10
Circleville, 450 ... ‡M-10
Cito, 20 ... WQ-13
Clairton, 6796 ... WN-4
Clappertown, 110 ... WN-11
Clarence, 626 ... WJ-13
Clarendon, 450 ... WF-8
Claridge, 1200 ... WN-5
Clarington, 125 ... WH-8
Clarion, 5276 ... WI-6
CLARION CO., 39988 ... WJ-6
Clark, 640 ... WH-2
Clarks Green, 1476 ... EA-13
Clarks Mills, 120 ... WH-3
Clarks Summit, 5116 ... EG-9
Clarksburg, 180 ... WM-6
Clarkstown, 200 ... EI-5
Clarksville, 230 ... WP-3
Claussville, 40 ... EL-10
Clay, 1559 ... EO-7
Claylick ... WQ-13
Claysburg, 1625 ... WN-10
Claysville, 829 ... WO-2
Clear Ridge, 30 ... WO-13
Clear Run, 350 ... WI-9
Clear Spr., 40 ... EP-3
Clearfield, 6215 ... WJ-11
Clearfield, 200 ... EK-11
CLEARFIELD CO., 81642 ... WI-11
Clearview Estates, 2500 ... ET-2
Clearville, 200 ... WP-11
Cleona, 2080 ... EN-6
Clermont, 100 ... WF-10
Cleversburg, 100 ... EP-2
Clifford, 500 ... EF-10
Clifton, 300 ... EI-10
Clifton Hts., 6652 ... ‡F-2
Climax, 40 ... WJ-6
Clinton, 434 ... WM-2
Clinton, 75 ... WL-6
CLINTON CO., 39238 ... EI-1
Clintondale, 100 ... EJ-1
Clintonville, 508 ... WI-4
Cloe, 250 ... WJ-8
Clover Creek, 170 ... WN-11
Clyde, 50 ... WM-8
Clymer, 1357 ... WL-8
Coal Ctr., 139 ... WO-4
Coal City, 25 ... WH-5
Coal Glen, 25 ... WI-9
Coal Hill, 120 ... WH-6
Coal Run, 310 ... WM-7
Coaldale, 2281 ... EK-9
Coaldale, 161 ... WO-12
Coalmont, 106 ... WO-12
Coalport, 523 ... WL-10
Coaltown, 1200 ... WJ-2
Coatesville, 13100 ... EP-9
Cobham ... WF-7
Coburn, 236 ... EK-2
Cocalico ... EN-7
Cochranton, 1136 ... WG-4
Cochranville, 668 ... EP-9
Cocolamus, 50 ... EL-3
Cogan Sta., 600 ... EH-3
Cokeburg, 630 ... WO-3
Colebrookdale, 130 ... EN-10
Colegrove ... WF-11
Colesburg ... WE-13
Colesville, 150 ... EC-4
Coleville, 250 ... WK-13
College Hts., 550 ... ES-13
College Pk., 160 ... EJ-4
Collegeville, 5089 ... EO-11
Collingdale, 8786 ... ‡F-2
Collinsville, 150 ... EQ-6
Collomsville, 200 ... EI-3
Colmar, 800 ... EN-12
Colonial Mnr., 550 ... ET-8
Colonial Pk., 13229 ... EN-5
Colony Pk., 1076 ... ET-11
Columbia, 10400 ... EP-6
COLUMBIA CO., 67295 ... EI-6
Columbia Cross Roads, 220 ... EE-5
Columbus, 824 ... WE-6
Colver, 959 ... WM-9
Colwyn, 2546 ... ‡F-3
Commodore, 331 ... WL-8
Compass, 140 ... EP-8
Concord, 135 ... WN-14
Conestoga, 1258 ... EP-7
Coneville ... WE-12
Conewago Hts., 900 ... EO-5
Confluence, 780 ... WQ-6
Conneaut Lake, 653 ... WF-3
Conneaut Lake Pk., 200 ... WF-2
Conneautville, 774 ... WE-2
Connellsville, 7637 ... WP-5
Connoquenessing, 528 ... WK-4
Conrad ... WG-13
Conshohocken, 7833 ... EO-11
Conway, 2176 ... WL-3
Conyngham, 1914 ... EJ-8
Cookport, 75 ... WL-9
Cooksburg, 20 ... WH-7
Coolspring, 180 ... WJ-8
Coon Hunter, 40 ... EK-3
Coopersburg, 2386 ... EM-11
Cooperstown, 460 ... WG-4
Cooperstown, 200 ... WL-4
Coplay, 3192 ... EL-10
Coral, 325 ... WM-7
Coraopolis, 5677 ... WM-3
Coraopolis Hts., 1400 ... ‡J-2
Cork Lane, 700 ... EB-10
Cornwall, 4112 ... EN-6
Cornwells Hts., 1391 ... ‡B-8
Corry, 6605 ... WE-5
Corsica, 357 ... WI-7
Cortez, 350 ... EG-10
Coryville, 70 ... WE-11
Costello, 50 ... WG-12
Coudersport, 2546 ... WF-12
Coulter, 300 ... ‡N-9
Countryside, 2500 ... ES-2
Coupon, 275 ... WM-10
Courtdale, 732 ... EA-8
Cove Gap, 60 ... WQ-13
Coventryville, 350 ... EO-10
Covington, 650 ... EF-3
Covode, 75 ... WK-8
Cowan ... EJ-4
Cowanesque, 150 ... EE-2
Cowansville, 140 ... WK-6
Coyleville ... WK-5
Crabtree, 277 ... WN-6
Crafton, 5951 ... WM-3
Craigsville, 150 ... WK-5
Craley, 300 ... EP-6
Cramer, 100 ... WM-8
Cranberry, 300 ... WH-5
Cranesville, 638 ... WE-2
Crates ... WI-7
CRAWFORD CO., 88765 ... WF-4
Creekside, 309 ... WL-7
Creighton, 1500 ... WL-5
Crenshaw, 468 ... WI-9
Cresco, 500 ... EI-11
Cresson, 1711 ... WM-10
Cressona, 1651 ... EL-7
Crestmont, 90 ... EI-2
Crestmont Vil., 700 ... ‡H-1
Creswell ... EP-6
Croft, 60 ... WJ-11
Crooked Creek, 50 ... EE-3
Crosby, 225 ... WF-11
Cross Creek, 137 ... WN-2
Cross Fork, 60 ... WG-13
Cross Keys, 200 ... WM-11
Cross Keys, 70 ... WN-14
Cross Roads, 512 ... EQ-6
Crossingville, 60 ... WE-3
Crosswicks, 540 ... ‡B-5
Crown, 183 ... WH-7
Croydon, 9950 ... ‡B-9
Crucible, 725 ... WP-4
Crystal Spr., 100 ... WP-11
Cuba Mills, 90 ... EL-2
Culmerville, 600 ... WL-4
CUMBERLAND CO., 235406 ... EO-3
Cumbola, 443 ... EL-8
Curllsville, 110 ... WI-6
Curry Run, 45 ... WK-10
Curryville, 200 ... WN-11
Curtisville, 1064 ... WL-4
Curwensville, 2542 ... WJ-10
Custards, 30 ... WG-3
Custer City, 300 ... WE-10
Cyclone, 450 ... WE-10
Daggett, 50 ... EE-4
Dagus Mines, 400 ... WH-10
Daguscahonda, 120 ... WH-10
Daisytown, 326 ... WS-2
Dale, 1234 ... WN-8
Dale Summit, 180 ... WS-7
Daleville, 420 ... EH-10
Dallas, 2804 ... EH-8
Dallastown, 4049 ... EP-5
Dalmatia, 488 ... EL-4
Dalton, 1234 ... EG-9
Damascus, 365 ... EF-12
Danboro, 500 ... EN-12
Danielsville, 750 ... EK-10
Danville, 4699 ... EJ-5
Darby, 10687 ... EP-12
Darlington, 254 ... WK-2
Darlington Cors. ... EP-10
Dauberville, 848 ... EM-8
Dauphin, 791 ... EN-4
DAUPHIN CO., 268100 ... EN-4
Davidsburg, 25 ... EP-4
Davidsville, 1130 ... WO-8
Davistown, 60 ... WQ-3
Dawson, 367 ... WO-5
Dawson Ridge, 1200 ... WL-2
Day, 40 ... WI-7
Dayton, 553 ... WK-7
Dayton, 100 ... EM-5
Dean, 90 ... WL-10
Deanville, 65 ... WJ-6
Deckers Pt., 50 ... WK-8
Deemston, 722 ... WP-3
Deep Valley, 75 ... WQ-1
Deer Lake, 687 ... EL-8
Defiance, 239 ... WO-12
Degolia ... WE-10
Delano, 342 ... EK-8
DELAWARE CO., 558979 ... EP-11
Delaware Grv., 25 ... WH-3
Delaware Water Gap, 746 ... EJ-12
Delmont, 2686 ... WM-6
Delroy, 200 ... EP-6
Delta, 728 ... EQ-7
Dempseytown, 200 ... WG-5
Denholm, 75 ... EL-2
Dents Run ... WH-11
Denver, 3861 ... EO-8
Deodate, 80 ... EO-5
Derrick City, 1000 ... WD-10
Derry, 2688 ... WN-7
Desire, 90 ... WJ-9
Devault, 100 ... EO-10
Devon, 1515 ... EP-11
Dewart, 1471 ... EI-4
Diamond, 50 ... WF-5
Diamondville, 100 ... WL-8
Dice ... EK-4
Dickerson Run, 400 ... WP-5
Dickinson, 100 ... EO-2
Dickson City, 6070 ... EG-10
Dicksonburg ... WF-2
Dillsburg, 2563 ... EO-4
Dilltown, 250 ... WM-8
Dime ... WL-6
Dimock, 300 ... EF-8
Dingmans Ferry, 1000 ... EI-13
Distant, 750 ... WJ-7
Dixonville, 600 ... WL-8
Doe Run, 100 ... EP-9
Dolington, 250 ... EN-13
Donaldson, 328 ... EL-6
Donegal, 120 ... WO-6
Donnally Mills, 80 ... EM-3
Donora, 4781 ... WO-4
Dora, 50 ... WJ-7
Dormont, 8593 ... WM-4
Dorneyville, 4406 ... EC-2
Dornsife, 100 ... EL-5
Dorrance, 50 ... EI-8
Dorseyville, 650 ... WL-4
Dott, 40 ... WQ-12
Doubling Gap ... EN-2
Douglassville, 448 ... EN-9
Dover, 2007 ... EP-4
Downingtown, 7891 ... EP-10
Doylesburg, 150 ... WO-14
Doylestown, 8380 ... EN-12
Drakes Mills, 40 ... WE-4
Draketown, 60 ... WQ-6
Dravosburg, 1792 ... ‡M-7
Drehersville, 40 ... EL-8
Drexel Hill, 28043 ... EP-11
Drifting, 150 ... WJ-12
Drifton, 800 ... EJ-9
Driftwood, 67 ... WH-12
Drumore, 115 ... EQ-7
Drums, 600 ... EJ-8
Drury Run, 100 ... WH-14
Dry Run, 200 ... WO-14
Dry Tavern, 697 ... WP-4
Dryville, 398 ... EM-9
Dublin, 2158 ... EN-12
DuBois, 7794 ... WI-9
Duboistown, 1205 ... EI-4
Dudley, 184 ... WO-12
Duke Ctr., 850 ... WE-11
Dunbar, 1042 ... WP-5
Duncannon, 1522 ... EN-4
Duncansville, 1233 ... WM-11
Dundaff, 175 ... EF-10
Dundore, 30 ... EL-4
Dunkard, 150 ... WQ-4
Dunlevy, 381 ... WO-4
Dunlo, 342 ... WN-9
Dunmore, 14057 ... EH-10
Dunnstown, 1360 ... EI-2
Dupont, 2711 ... EC-10
Duquesne, 5565 ... ‡L-8
Durham, 200 ... EL-12
Duryea, 4917 ... EB-10
Dushore, 608 ... EG-6
Dutch Hill, 110 ... WJ-5
Dysart, 120 ... WL-10
Eagle, 130 ... EO-10
Eagle Rock, 60 ... WG-6
Eagles Mere, 120 ... EH-6
Earlston, 1122 ... WP-11
Earlville, 500 ... EN-9
E. Altoona, 200 ... WM-11
E. Athens, 400 ... EE-6
E. Bangor, 1172 ... EK-12
E. Benton, 175 ... EG-10
E. Berlin, 1521 ... EP-4
E. Berwick, 2007 ... EJ-7
E. Brady, 942 ... WJ-5
E. Brook, 300 ... WJ-3
E. Butler, 732 ... WK-4
E. Canton, 25 ... EF-5
E. Conemaugh, 1220 ... WN-9
E. Earl, 1144 ... EO-8
E. Finley ... WP-2
E. Freedom, 972 ... WN-11
E. Greenville, 2951 ... EM-10
E. Hickory, 150 ... WG-6
E. Kane, 135 ... WF-9
E. Lansdowne, 2668 ... ‡E-2
E. Lemon, 400 ... EG-9
E. McKeesport, 2126 ... ‡L-9
E. Millsboro, 400 ... WP-4
E. New Castle, 250 ... WJ-2
E. Petersburg, 4506 ... EO-7
E. Pittsburgh, 1822 ... ‡L-8
E. Prospect, 905 ... EP-6
E. Rochester, 567 ... WL-3
E. Salem, 186 ... EL-3
E. Sharpsburg, 110 ... WN-11
E. Side, 317 ... EJ-9
E. Smethport, 500 ... WE-11
E. Smithfield, 500 ... EE-5
E. Springfield, 400 ... WD-2
E. Stroudsburg, 9840 ... EJ-12
E. Texas, 450 ... EC-2
E. Titusville, 60 ... WF-5
E. Towanda, 400 ... EF-6
E. Troy, 140 ... EF-5
E. Vandergrift, 674 ... WL-6
E. Washington, 2234 ... WO-3
E. Waterford, 190 ... EN-1
E. York, 8777 ... WS-14
Eastland Hills, 550 ... ES-9
Easton, 26800 ... EL-12
Eastvale, 225 ... WK-2
Eastville, 80 ... EJ-3
Eatonville, 200 ... EG-8
Eau Claire, 316 ... WI-5
Ebenezer, 200 ... EN-6
Ebensburg, 3351 ... WM-9
Echo, 150 ... WR-3
Echo, 30 ... WK-7
Echo Lake, 80 ... EJ-12
Eckley, 30 ... EJ-9
Eckville ... EL-8
Economy, 8970 ... WL-3
Eddington, 1906 ... ‡B-8
Eddington Gdns., 800 ... ‡A-8
Eddystone, 2410 ... ‡G-1
Eden, 700 ... EO-7
Edenborn, 294 ... WP-4
Edenburg, 681 ... EM-8
Edendale, 100 ... WK-11
Edenville, 150 ... WP-13
Edgegrove, 500 ... EQ-4
Edgemont, 900 ... ES-3
Edgewood, 3118 ... ‡K-7
Edgewood, 2384 ... EK-6
Edgeworth, 1680 ... WM-3
Edie, 83 ... WO-8
Edinboro, 6438 ... WE-3
Edinburg, 200 ... WJ-2
Edmon, 120 ... WM-6
Edwardsville, 4816 ... EA-7
Effort, 2269 ... EJ-11
Egypt, 2391 ... EA-2
Ehrenfeld, 228 ... WN-9
Eighty Four, 657 ... WO-3
Elam, 200 ... EQ-10
Elberta, 180 ... WM-11
Elbon ... WH-10
Eldersville, 200 ... WN-2
Elderton, 356 ... WL-7
Eldred, 825 ... WE-11
Elgin, 218 ... WE-5
Elimsport, 65 ... EI-4
Elizabeth, 1493 ... WN-4
Elizabethtown, 11545 ... EO-6
Elizabethville, 1510 ... EM-5
Elk City, 80 ... WI-6
ELK CO., 31946 ... WG-10
Elk Grv., 45 ... EH-6
Elk Lake, 100 ... EF-8
Elkins Pk., 4700 ... ‡B-5
Elkland, 1821 ... ED-2
Ellenton, 25 ... EG-5
Ellerslie, 550 ... ‡A-9
Elliott Mills ... WJ-3
Elliottsburg, 220 ... EN-2
Ellisburg, 55 ... WE-13
Ellport, 1180 ... WK-3
Ellsworth, 1027 ... WO-4
Ellwood City, 7921 ... WK-2
Elm, 150 ... EO-7
Elmer ... EE-1
Elmhurst, 830 ... EH-10
Elrama, 307 ... WN-4
Elstonville, 60 ... EO-6
Elton, 600 ... WN-9
Elverson, 1225 ... EO-9
Elysburg, 2194 ... EK-6
Embreeville, 90 ... EP-9
Emeigh, 400 ... WL-9
Emerald, 240 ... EL-10
Emerickville, 150 ... WI-8
Emigsville, 2672 ... EP-5
Emlenton, 625 ... WI-5
Emmaus, 11211 ... EM-10
Emmaville, 40 ... WP-11
Emporium, 2073 ... WG-12
Emsworth, 2449 ... WM-3
Endeavor, 200 ... WG-7
Enders, 65 ... EM-4
Energy, 50 ... WJ-3
English Ctr., 60 ... EH-2
Enhaut, 1007 ... ET-4
Enid ... WO-12
Enlow, 1013 ... ‡K-2
Ennisville ... WL-13
Enola, 6111 ... EN-4
Enon Valley, 306 ... WK-2
Enterprise, 50 ... WF-6
Entriken, 125 ... WN-12
Ephrata, 13394 ... EO-7
Equinunk, 130 ... EE-11
Ercildoun, 100 ... EP-9
Erdenheim ... ‡B-3
Erdman, 200 ... EL-5
Erie, 101786 ... WC-4
ERIE CO., 280566 ... WD-4
Erlen, 800 ... ‡B-4
Ernest, 462 ... WL-7
Erwinna, 140 ... EM-12
Eshcol ... EM-2
Espy, 1642 ... EJ-6
Espyville, 300 ... WF-2
Essington ... ‡G-2
Estella, 50 ... EG-5
Estherton, 1200 ... ER-3
Etna, 3451 ... ‡J-6
Euclid, 90 ... WJ-4
Evans City, 1833 ... WK-3
Evans Falls, 270 ... EG-8
Evansburg, 2129 ... EO-11
Evendale, 165 ... EL-3
Everett, 1834 ... WP-11
Evergreen, 70 ... EF-6
Everson, 793 ... WO-5
Ewingsville, 400 ... ‡L-4
Exchange, 100 ... EI-5
Exeter, 5652 ... EH-9
Export, 917 ... WM-5
Exton, 4842 ... EP-10
Eyers Grv., 105 ... EJ-6
Factoryville, 1158 ... EG-9
Fair Acres, 500 ... ET-3
Fairbank, 600 ... WP-4
Fairbrook, 225 ... WL-13
Fairchance, 1975 ... WQ-5
Fairdale, 2059 ... WP-4
Fairdale, 40 ... EE-8
Fairfield, 1100 ... WC-4
Fairfield, 507 ... EQ-2
Fairhope, 50 ... WQ-9
Fairless Hills, 8466 ... EO-13
Fairmont City, 300 ... WJ-7
Fairmount Sprs., 40 ... EI-7
Fairoaks, 800 ... ‡H-2
Fairplay ... EQ-2
Fairview, 2348 ... WD-3
Fairview, 250 ... WJ-8
Fairview, 198 ... WJ-5
Fairview, 50 ... WH-3
Fairview Hts., 600 ... ‡I-8
Fairville, 150 ... *A-7
Fall Brook, 200 ... EF-4
Fallentimber, 150 ... WL-10
Falling Spr., 200 ... EP-1
Falls, 230 ... EG-9
Falls Creek, 1037 ... WI-9
Fallsington, 1300 ... †T-12
Fallston, 266 ... WK-2
Falmouth, 420 ... EO-5
Fannettsburg, 950 ... WO-13
Farmers Valley, 120 ... WE-11
Farmersville, 991 ... EO-7
Farmersville, 50 ... EA-6
Farmington, 800 ... EB-4
Farmington, 767 ... WQ-6
Farragut, 60 ... EH-4
Farrandsville, 120 ... EI-2
Farrell, 5111 ... WI-2
Farwell, 350 ... WH-14
Fassett, 175 ... ED-5
Fawn Grv., 452 ... EQ-6
Fayette City, 596 ... WO-4
FAYETTE CO., 136606 ... WP-5
Fayetteville, 3128 ... EP-1
Fayetteville, 300 ... ‡K-2
Fellsburg, 1180 ... WO-4
Felton, 506 ... EQ-6
Feltonville ... ‡C-5
Fenelton, 110 ... WK-5
Fern Brook, 550 ... EH-8
Fern Glen, 350 ... EJ-7
Ferndale, 1636 ... WN-8
Ferndale, 400 ... EM-12
Fernridge ... EJ-10
Fernville, 556 ... EJ-6
Fernway, 12414 ... WL-3
Fertigs, 65 ... WH-6
Finleyville, 461 ... WN-4
Fisher, 130 ... WH-7
Fishertown, 400 ... WO-10
Fisherville, 60 ... EM-4
Five Forks, 50 ... EQ-1
Five Points, 600 ... WL-3
Five Points, 100 ... ES-14
Five Points, 20 ... WL-7
Five Points ... WM-6
Fivepointville, 1156 ... EO-8
Flat Rock, 140 ... WQ-6
Fleetville, 350 ... EG-9
Fleetwood, 4085 ... EM-9
Flemington, 1330 ... EI-2
Flicksville, 100 ... EK-12
Flinton, 250 ... WL-10
Florence, 250 ... WM-2
Flourtown, 4538 ... ‡A-3
Fogelsville, 950 ... EL-10
Folcroft, 6606 ... ‡F-2
Folsom, 8323 ... ‡F-1
Fombell, 100 ... WK-3
Fontana, 150 ... EN-6
Foot of Ten, 672 ... WC-12
Forbes Road, 650 ... WN-6
Force, 253 ... WI-10
Ford City, 2991 ... WK-6
Ford Cliff, 371 ... WK-6
Fordyce, 20 ... WQ-3
Forest City, 1911 ... EF-10
FOREST CO., 7716 ... WG-7
Forest Grv., 2600 ... ‡J-4
Forest Hills, 6518 ... ‡K-8
Forest Lake, 100 ... EE-8
Forest Pk., 300 ... EI-9
Forestville, 100 ... WI-4
Forks ... EI-7
Forkston, 70 ... EG-8
Forksville, 145 ... EG-5
Ft. Hill, 35 ... WQ-7
Ft. Hunter, 150 ... EN-4
Ft. Littleton, 100 ... WP-13
Ft. Loudon, 886 ... WP-13
Ft. Washington, 5446 ... EO-12
Forty Fort, 4214 ... EH-9
Foster Brook, 1251 ... WD-10
Fostoria, 40 ... WL-11
Foundryville, 256 ... EJ-7
Fountain, 250 ... EL-6
Fountain Dale, 150 ... EQ-2
Fountain Hill, 4597 ... EL-11
Fountain Sprs., 278 ... EK-7
Foustown, 200 ... WR-12
Fox Chapel, 5388 ... ‡I-7
Fox Chase ... ‡B-6
Fox Hill, 125 ... EC-8
Foxburg, 183 ... WI-5
Frackville, 3805 ... EK-7
Franconia, 430 ... EN-11
Frankford ... ‡C-6
Frankfort Sprs., 130 ... WM-2
Franklin, 6545 ... WH-5
Franklin, 323 ... WN-9
Franklin Ctr., 30 ... WD-3
FRANKLIN CO., 149618 ... WP-13
Franklin Forks, 110 ... EE-9
Franklin Pk., 13470 ... WL-3
Franklindale, 100 ... EF-6
Franklintown, 489 ... EO-4
Franklinville, 75 ... WL-12
Frankstown, 200 ... WM-11
Frazer, 2000 ... EP-10
Frederick, 120 ... EN-10
Fredericksburg, 1357 ... EM-6
Fredericksburg, 733 ... WF-3
Fredonia, 502 ... WH-3
Freeburg, 575 ... EK-4
Freedom, 1569 ... WL-3
Freeland, 3531 ... EJ-9
Freemansburg, 2636 ... EB-5
Freeport, 1813 ... WL-5
Frenchtown, 60 ... WF-4
Frenchville, 200 ... WI-12
Freysville, 400 ... EP-6
Friedens, 1523 ... WP-8
Friedensburg, 858 ... EL-7
Friedensville, 800 ... EC-4
Friendsville, 111 ... EE-8
Frisco, 850 ... WK-3
Fritztown, 200 ... EN-8
Frogtown, 70 ... WJ-5
Frogtown, 40 ... WI-7
Frostburg, 120 ... WJ-8
Fryburg, 375 ... WH-6
Frystown, 380 ... EM-7
Fullerton, 14925 ... EL-10
FULTON CO., 14845 ... WP-12
Furlong, 700 ... EN-12
Gabby Hts., 1200 ... WO-2
Gaines, 120 ... EF-1
Galeton, 1149 ... EF-1
Galilee, 180 ... EF-12
Gallatin, 250 ... WO-4
Gallitzin, 1668 ... WM-10
Ganister, 85 ... WM-12
Gap, 1931 ... EP-8
Gapsville ... WP-11
Garards Fort, 100 ... WQ-3
Garden City ... ‡G-1
Garden View, 2503 ... EI-4
Gardenville, 250 ... EN-12
Gardners, 150 ... EP-3
Garland, 300 ... WE-6
Garrett, 456 ... WQ-8
Garrett Hill ... ‡C-1
Garrison, 50 ... WQ-2
Gastonville, 2818 ... WN-4
Gastown, 150 ... WL-7
Gatchellville, 60 ... EQ-6
Gatesburg, 100 ... WL-13
Gauff Hill, 350 ... EB-4
Gayly, 300 ... ‡K-3
Geeseytown, 100 ... WM-11
Geiger, 90 ... WP-8
Geigertown, 500 ... EO-9
Geistown, 2467 ... WN-9
Gelatt, 50 ... EE-10
Genesee, 300 ... WD-13
Geneva, 109 ... WG-3
Georgetown, 1640 ... EB-7
Georgetown, 1022 ... EP-8
Georgetown, 200 ... EL-11
Georgetown, 174 ... WL-2
Georgeville, 30 ... WK-8
Germania, 130 ... EF-1
Germansville, 250 ... EL-9
Germantown ... ‡C-4
Geryville ... EM-11
Gettysburg, 7620 ... EQ-3
Ghennes Hts., 900 ... WO-4
Gibbon Glade, 65 ... WQ-5
Gibraltar, 680 ... EN-9
Gibson, 200 ... EE-10
Gibsonia, 2733 ... WL-4
Gifford, 500 ... WE-10
Gilbert, 700 ... EK-11
Gilberton, 769 ... EK-7
Gilbertsville, 4832 ... EN-10
Gilfoyle, 20 ... WG-7
Gillett, 300 ... EE-5
Ginter, 120 ... WK-11
Ginther, 75 ... EK-8
Gipsy, 125 ... WK-9
Girard, 3104 ... WD-3
Girardville, 1519 ... EK-7
Girty, 30 ... WL-6
Glade City, 130 ... WQ-8
Gladwyne, 4000 ... ‡C-2
Glasgow, 250 ... WL-11
Glasgow, 60 ... WL-1
Glassport, 4483 ... WN-4
Gleason ... EF-4
Gleasonton ... WH-14
Glen Campbell, 245 ... WK-9
Glen Forney, 120 ... EQ-2
Glen Hazel ... WG-10
Glen Hope, 142 ... WK-10
Glen Iron, 150 ... EK-3
Glen Lyon, 1873 ... EI-8
Glen Mawr, 100 ... EH-5
Glen Moore, 1000 ... ES-9
Glen Osborne, 547 ... ‡I-3
Glen Richey, 270 ... WJ-10
Glen Rock, 2025 ... EQ-5
Glen Roy ... EQ-8
Glen Savage, 15 ... WP-9
Glen Summit, 250 ... EI-9
Glenburn, 953 ... EG-9
Glencoe, 15 ... WQ-9
Glendale, 75 ... EC-10
Glendon, 440 ... EL-11
Glenfield, 205 ... ‡I-4
Glenmar Gdns., 200 ... WD-4
Glenmoore, 900 ... EO-9
Glenolden, 7153 ... ‡F-2
Glenshaw, 8981 ... ‡I-6
Glenside, 8384 ... ‡A-4
Glenville, 100 ... EQ-5
Glenwillard, 1100 ... ‡H-2
Glenwood, 3000 ... ES-3
Glenwood, 50 ... EF-9
Globe Mills, 45 ... EK-4
Goheenville, 50 ... WK-7
Gold, 50 ... WE-13
Goldsboro, 952 ... EO-5
Good Intent, 25 ... WO-2
Good Spr., 90 ... EL-6
Goods Cor., 500 ... WR-2
Goodtown, 20 ... WP-8
Goodville, 482 ... EO-8
Goodyear, 100 ... EP-3
Gordon, 763 ... EL-7
Gordonville, 508 ... EP-8
Goshenville, 150 ... EP-10
Gouldsboro, 890 ... EI-11
Gowen City, 220 ... EL-6
Graceton, 257 ... WM-7
Graceville, 50 ... WP-11
Gradyville, 500 ... EP-11
Grampian, 356 ... WJ-10
Grand Valley, 175 ... WF-6
Grandview Hts., 2050 ... ES-9
Grantham, 500 ... EO-4
Grantville, 230 ... EN-5
Granville, 440 ... EM-1
Granville Ctr., 110 ... EF-5
Granville Summit, 85 ... EF-5
Grassflat, 511 ... WJ-12
Grassmere Pk., 50 ... EH-6
Graterford, 900 ... EO-11
Gratz, 765 ... EL-5
Gray, 275 ... WO-8
Graysville, 160 ... WP-2
Grazierville, 665 ... WL-11
Greason, 150 ... EO-2
Great Bend, 734 ... ED-9
Greble, 100 ... EM-7
Greece City, 40 ... WJ-5
Greeley, 1000 ... EH-12
Green Lane, 508 ... EN-11
Green Pt., 75 ... EM-6
Green Tree, 4432 ... ‡K-5
Green Vil., 400 ... EP-1
Greenawalds, 1200 ... EB-2
Greenburr, 130 ... EJ-2
Greencastle, 3996 ... WQ-14
Greendale ... WF-9
GREENE CO., 38686 ... WQ-3
Greenes, 894 ... EE-6
Greenfield, 40 ... WI-2
Greenfields, 1170 ... ES-12
Greenmount, 70 ... EQ-3
Greenock, 2195 ... ‡M-9
Greensboro, 260 ... WQ-4
Greensburg, 14892 ... WN-6
Greentown, 1000 ... EH-11
Greenville, 5919 ... WH-2
Greenwood, 2458 ... WM-11
Greenwood, 30 ... EI-6
Gresham, 75 ... WF-5
Grill, 1468 ... ET-12
Grindstone, 498 ... WP-4
Gringo, 600 ... ‡H-1
Grovania ... EJ-6
Grove City, 8322 ... WI-3
Grover, 200 ... EG-4
Groveton, 500 ... ‡J-3
Guffey, 100 ... ‡N-9
Guitonville, 50 ... WG-7
Gulph Mills, 450 ... ‡B-1
Guys Mills, 124 ... WF-4
Gwynedd, 600 ... EO-11
Hadley, 180 ... WH-3
Hahntown, 400 ... ‡M-10
Halifax, 841 ... EM-4
Hallam, 2673 ... EP-6
Hallstead, 1303 ... ED-9
Hallton, 30 ... WH-8
Hamburg, 4289 ... EM-8
Hametown, 80 ... EQ-5
Hamilton, 125 ... WJ-8
Hamilton Pk., 3500 ... ES-8
Hamlin, 1100 ... EH-11
Hamlin, 85 ... EM-6
Hammett ... WD-4
Hamorton, 100 ... *A-7
Hampton, 632 ... EP-4
Haneyville ... EH-2
Hannahstown, 80 ... WK-5
Hannastown, 350 ... WN-6
Hannaville, 176 ... WG-4
Hanover, 15289 ... EQ-4
Hanover, 800 ... EA-4
Hanover Hills, 160 ... ES-5
Hanoverdale ... EN-5
Harborcreek, 1500 ... WC-4
Harding, 400 ... EA-10
Harford, 250 ... EF-9
Harlansburg, 300 ... WJ-3
Harleigh, 1104 ... EJ-8
Harleysville, 9286 ... EN-11
Harmar Hts., 1050 ... ‡H-8
Harmarville, 1100 ... ‡I-8
Harmonsburg, 401 ... WF-3
Harmonville, 1500 ... ‡B-2
Harmony, 890 ... WK-3
Harnedsville, 90 ... WQ-7
Harper Tavern, 50 ... EN-6
Harrisburg, 49528 ... EN-4
Harrison City, 134 ... WN-5
Harrison Valley, 250 ... EE-1
Harrisonville, 50 ... WP-12
Harrisville, 897 ... WI-4
Harshaville ... WM-2
Hartleton, 283 ... EK-3
Hartstown, 201 ... WG-2
Hartsville, 700 ... EN-12
Harveys Lake, 2791 ... EH-8
Harveyville, 50 ... EI-7
Harwick, 899 ... ‡H-9
Harwood, 420 ... EJ-8
Hastings, 1278 ... WL-9
Hatboro, 7360 ... EO-12
Hatfield, 3290 ... EN-11
Haverford, 6000 ... ‡D-2
Havertown, 30000 ... ‡D-1
Hawk Run, 534 ... WK-12
Hawley, 1211 ... EG-12
Hawstone, 60 ... EM-2
Hawthorn, 494 ... WJ-7
Haydentown, 120 ... WQ-5
Haysville, 70 ... ‡I-3
Hayti, 950 ... EP-9
Hazel Hurst, 300 ... WF-10
Hazen, 125 ... WI-8
Hazleton, 25340 ... EJ-8
Heart Lake, 130 ... EE-9
Heathville, 15 ... WI-7
Hebe, 70 ... EL-5
Hebron Ctr. ... WE-13
Heckscherville, 220 ... EL-7
Hecktown, 1200 ... EL-11
Hecla, 100 ... EL-8
Hegins, 812 ... EL-6
Heidelberg, 1244 ... WM-3
Heidlersburg, 707 ... EP-3
Heilwood, 711 ... WL-9
Helfenstein, 100 ... EL-6
Helixville ... WO-9
Hellertown, 5898 ... EL-11
Helvetia, 90 ... WJ-9
Hemlock ... WE-8
Hendersonville ... WH-4
Henrietta, 100 ... WN-11
Henrys Bend, 60 ... WG-6
Henryville, 300 ... EI-11
Hepburnia, 140 ... WJ-10
Hereford, 930 ... EM-10
Herman, 400 ... WK-5
Herminie, 789 ... WN-5
Hermitage, 16220 ... WI-2
Herndon, 324 ... EL-4
Herrick Ctr., 125 ... EF-10
Herrickville, 75 ... EE-7
Hershey, 14257 ... EN-5
Heshbon, 50 ... WM-8
Hessdale, 100 ... EP-7
Hesston, 175 ... WM-12
Hetlerville ... EJ-7
Hibbs, 200 ... WP-4
Hickernell, 50 ... WE-3
Hickory, 740 ... WN-2
Hickory Cors., 60 ... EL-4
Hickory Grv., 30 ... ED-9
Highland Pk., 1900 ... ET-2
Highland Pk., 1380 ... EL-1
Highspire, 2399 ... EO-5
Hilldale, 1246 ... EB-9
Hiller, 1155 ... WP-4
Hilliards, 120 ... WI-5
Hillsdale, 250 ... WK-9
Hillsgrove, 200 ... EH-5
Hillside, 200 ... WN-7
Hillsville, 600 ... WJ-2
Hilltown, 800 ... EN-12
Hilltown, 60 ... EE-12
Hilltown ... EQ-2
Hinkletown, 175 ... EO-8
Hoadleys, 110 ... EG-11
Hobbie, 350 ... EJ-8
Hoernerstown, 50 ... ES-5
Hogestown, 300 ... EN-4
Hokendauqua, 3378 ... EA-3
Holbrook, 40 ... WQ-2
Holland, 5300 ... EO-13
Hollidaysburg, 5791 ... WM-11
Hollisterville ... EH-11
Hollsopple, 500 ... WO-8
Hollywood, 800 ... ‡B-5
Holmes, 2800 ... ‡F-2
Holmesburg ... ‡C-7
Holtwood, 200 ... EQ-7
Home, 400 ... WL-8
Home Camp ... WI-10
Homer City, 1707 ... WM-7
Homestead, 3165 ... ‡K-7
Hometown, 1349 ... EK-8
Homeville, 50 ... EQ-8
Homewood, 109 ... WK-2
Honeoye, 20 ... WD-12
Honesdale, 4480 ... EG-11
Honey Brook, 1713 ... EO-9
Honey Grv., 200 ... EN-1
Hooker, 100 ... WJ-5
Hookstown, 147 ... WL-2
Hooversville, 645 ... WO-8
Hop Bottom, 337 ... EF-9
Hopeland, 738 ... EO-7
Hopewell, 230 ... WO-11
Hopwood, 2090 ... WP-5
Horsham, 14842 ... EO-12
Hosensack ... EM-10
Host, 25 ... EM-7
Hostetter, 740 ... WN-6
Houserville, 1814 ... WK-13
Houston, 1296 ... WN-3
Houtzdale, 797 ... WK-11
Howard, 720 ... EJ-1
Hoytville, 40 ... EG-2
Hublersburg, 104 ... EJ-1
Hudson, 1443 ... EB-8
Hudsondale, 100 ... EK-9
Huey, 125 ... WJ-6
Huffs Church, 150 ... EM-10
Hughestown, 1392 ... EB-10
Hughesville, 2128 ... EI-5
Humboldt, 120 ... EJ-8
Hummels Wharf, 1353 ... EK-4
Hummelstown, 4538 ... EN-5
Hunker, 291 ... WO-5
Hunlock Creek, 300 ... EI-8
Hunters Run, 60 ... EO-3
Hunterstown, 547 ... EQ-3
Huntersville, 50 ... EH-5
Huntingdon, 7093 ... WM-12
HUNTINGDON CO., 45913 ... WN-12
Huntingdon Valley, 10000 ... ‡A-6
Huntington Mills, 175 ... EI-7
Huntsdale, 300 ... EO-2
Huntsville, 100 ... EH-8
Husband ... WP-8
Hustontown, 450 ... WP-12
Hyde, 1399 ... WJ-11
Hyde Pk., 2528 ... ES-13
Hydetown, 526 ... WF-5
Hyndman, 910 ... WQ-9
Hyner, 150 ... EH-1
Ickesburg, 280 ... EM-2
Idamar, 30 ... WL-8
Idaville, 177 ... EP-3
Imler, 150 ... WO-10
Imperial, 2541 ... WM-3
Independence, 110 ... WN-1
Independence, 100 ... ‡H-1
Independence, 70 ... EL-4
Indian Crossing, 20 ... WD-11
Indian Head, 175 ... WP-6
Indian Head ... WE-4
Indian Lake, 394 ... WP-9
Indian Orchard, 300 ... EG-11
Indiana, 13975 ... WL-7
INDIANA CO., 88880 ... WK-8
Indianola, 900 ... WL-4
Industry, 1835 ... WL-2
Ingram, 3330 ... ‡K-5
Inkerman, 1819 ... EB-9
Intercourse, 1274 ... EP-8
Iola, 144 ... EI-6
Iona, 800 ... EN-7
Irishtown, 430 ... EQ-4
Iron Sprs., 200 ... EQ-2
Ironton, 300 ... EA-1
Irvine, 200 ... WE-7
Irvona, 647 ... WK-10
Irwin, 3973 ... WN-5
Isabella, 275 ... WP-4
Iselin, 275 ... WM-6
Ithan ... ‡C-1
Ivyland, 1041 ... EO-12
Ivywood, 40 ... WL-4
Jackson, 90 ... EE-10
Jackson Ctr., 224 ... WH-3
Jackson Summit ... EE-4
Jacksonville, 637 ... WM-7
Jacksonville, 100 ... EL-11
Jacksonville, 95 ... EJ-1
Jacksonwald, 3393 ... ET-14
Jacktown, 200 ... ‡M-10
Jacobs Creek, 275 ... WO-5
Jacobus, 1841 ... EQ-5
James City, 287 ... WF-9
Jamestown, 617 ... WG-2
Jamestown, 400 ... WN-10
Jamison, 850 ... EN-12
Jamison City, 134 ... EH-7
Janesville, 600 ... WK-11
Jeannette, 9654 ... WN-5
Jeddo, 98 ... EJ-9
Jefferson, 733 ... EQ-4
Jefferson, 270 ... WP-3
Jefferson Ctr., 80 ... WK-4
JEFFERSON CO., 45200 ... WH-8
Jefferson Hills, 10619 ... WN-4
Jenkintown, 4422 ... EO-12
Jenners, 250 ... WO-8
Jennerstown, 695 ... WO-8
Jennersville, 45 ... EQ-9
Jenningsville, 100 ... EG-7
Jericho, 20 ... WH-12
Jermyn, 2169 ... EG-10
Jerome, 1017 ... WO-8
Jersey Mills, 55 ... EH-2
Jersey Shore, 4361 ... EI-3
Jerseytown, 184 ... EJ-6
Jessup, 4676 ... EG-10
Jim Thorpe, 4781 ... EK-9
Joanna, 80 ... EO-9
Jobs Corners ... EE-4
Joffre, 536 ... WM-2
Johnsonburg, 2483 ... WG-10
Johnstown, 20978 ... WN-8
Joliett, 275 ... EL-6
Jollytown, 25 ... WQ-2
Jonas, 60 ... EJ-10
Jones Mills, 300 ... WO-7
Jonestown, 1905 ... EM-6
Jonestown, 64 ... EI-7
Josephine, 300 ... WM-7
Julian, 152 ... WK-13
Juneau, 30 ... WK-8
Junedale, 200 ... EK-8
JUNIATA CO., 24636 ... EM-2
Juniata Gap, 1100 ... WA-12
Juniata Ter., 542 ... EM-1
Justus ... EB-14
Kane, 3730 ... WF-9
Kanesholm ... WF-9
Kaneville ... WG-5
Kantner, 80 ... WO-8
Kantz, 35 ... EK-4
Kaolin, 150 ... EQ-9
Karns City, 209 ... WJ-5
Karthaus, 250 ... WI-12
Kasiesville, 30 ... WQ-13
Kauffman, 150 ... WQ-14
Kaylor, 200 ... WJ-5
Kearney ... WO-12
Kearsarge ... WB-10
Keating ... WI-13
Keating Summit, 100 ... WF-12
Kecksburg, 140 ... WO-6
Keelersville, 100 ... EM-11
Keeneyville, 100 ... EE-2
Keewaydin ... WI-12
Keisterville, 300 ... WP-5
Kelayres, 533 ... EK-8
Kellersburg, 100 ... WJ-6
Kellettville, 100 ... WG-7
Kelly, 70 ... WL-6
Kelly Crossroads, 70 ... EJ-4
Kelton, 140 ... EQ-9
Kemblesville, 125 ... EQ-9
Kempton, 169 ... EL-9
Kendall ... WM-2
Kenhorst, 2877 ... ET-12
Kenilworth, 1907 ... EO-10
Kenmar, 4124 ... EI-4
Kennard, 20 ... WG-2
Kennerdell, 247 ... WH-5
Kennett Sq., 6072 ... EQ-10
Kensington ... ‡D-5
Kenwick Vil., 200 ... ER-9
Kenwood, 25 ... WL-8
Kerr, 250 ... WJ-11
Kerrmoor, 25 ... WK-10
Kerrtown, 305 ... WF-3
Kersey, 937 ... WH-10
Khedive, 40 ... WP-3
Killinger, 75 ... EM-4
Kimberton, 450 ... EO-10
Kimmelton, 80 ... WO-8
King ... WN-10
King of Prussia, 19936 ... EO-11
Kings Manor, 650 ... ‡B-1
Kingsdale, 200 ... ER-3
Kingsley, 200 ... EF-9
Kingston, 13182 ... EI-9
Kingwood, 120 ... WP-7
Kintnersville, 100 ... EM-12
Kinzers, 450 ... EP-8
Kirby, 35 ... WQ-3
Kirkwood, 396 ... EQ-8
Kirwan Hts., 500 ... ‡L-4
Kissimmee, 100 ... EK-3
Kistler, 320 ... WN-13
Kistler, 40 ... EN-2
Kittanning, 4044 ... WK-6
Klecknersville, 300 ... EK-11
Kleinfeltersville, 250 ... EN-7
Klinesville, 100 ... EM-9
Klinesville, 60 ... EP-6
Klingerstown, 127 ... EL-5
Knapp ... EF-2
Knauers ... EN-8
Knobsville, 100 ... WP-13
Knox, 1146 ... WI-6
Knox Dale, 300 ... WJ-8
Knoxville, 629 ... EE-2
Koonsville, 200 ... EI-7
Koppel, 762 ... WK-2
Korn Krest, 850 ... EB-6
Kossuth, 150 ... WH-6
Kralltown, 75 ... EP-4
Kratzerville, 383 ... EK-4
Kreamer, 822 ... EK-4
Kreidersville, 270 ... EL-10
Kremis, 20 ... WH-2
Kresgeville, 400 ... EK-10
Krings, 150 ... WT-2
Krumsville, 140 ... EL-9
Kuhnsville, 500 ... EB-1
Kuhntown, 30 ... WQ-2
Kulpmont, 2924 ... EK-6
Kulpsville, 8194 ... EN-11
Kunkle, 150 ... EH-8
Kunkletown, 200 ... EK-11
Kushequa, 60 ... WF-10
Kutztown, 5012 ... EM-9
Kylertown, 340 ... WJ-12
Kyleville, 25 ... EQ-7
La Anna ... EI-11
La Belle, 350 ... WP-4
La Gonda, 70 ... WO-2
La Plume, 400 ... EG-9
Laboratory, 850 ... WO-3
Labott, 50 ... EP-4
Laceyville, 379 ... EF-7
LACKAWANNA CO., 214437 ... EH-10
Lackawaxen, 600 ... EG-12
Laddsburg, 60 ... EG-6
Lafayette, 40 ... WE-10
Lafayette Hill, 6700 ... ‡B-3
Laflin, 1487 ... EB-9
Lahaska, 200 ... EN-12
Lairdsville, 120 ... EI-5
L. Ariel, 1250 ... EG-11
L. Carey, 400 ... EG-8
Lake City, 3031 ... WD-2
L. Como, 280 ... EE-11
L. Harmony, 850 ... EJ-10
L. Winola, 748 ... EG-9
L. Wynonah, 2640 ... EL-7
Lakemont, 1868 ... WM-11
Lakeside, 200 ... EE-10
Lakeview Hts., 600 ... ES-4
Lakeville, 500 ... EG-11
Lakewood, 300 ... EE-11
Lamar, 562 ... EJ-1
Lamartine, 200 ... WI-5
Lambertsville, 70 ... WO-8
Lamott, 800 ... ‡B-5
Lampeter, 1669 ... ET-10
Lanark, 400 ... EC-4
Lancaster, 59322 ... EP-7
LANCASTER CO., 519445 ... EP-8
Landenberg, 100 ... EQ-9
Lander, 150 ... WD-7
Landingville, 159 ... EL-8
Landis Valley, 800 ... ER-9
Landisburg, 218 ... EN-2
Landisville, 1893 ... EO-6
Lanes Mills, 30 ... WI-9
Lanesboro, 506 ... ED-10
Langdondale, 100 ... WO-11
Langeloth, 717 ... WN-2
Lansdale, 16269 ... EN-11
Lansdowne, 10620 ... ‡E-2
Lanse, 450 ... WJ-12
Lansford, 3941 ... EK-9
Lantz Cors., 40 ... WF-10
Laporte, 316 ... EH-6
Larabee ... WE-11
Larimer, 750 ... ‡M-10
Larksville, 4480 ... EI-8
Latimore, 60 ... EP-3
Latrobe, 8338 ... WN-6
Latta Grv. ... WN-13
Lattimer, 600 ... EJ-8
Laughlintown, 950 ... WO-7
Laurel, 25 ... EQ-6
Laurel Lake, 300 ... EE-8
Laurel Mtn., 167 ... WO-7
Laurel Run, 500 ... EI-9
Laureldale, 3911 ... EN-9
Laurelton, 221 ... EK-3
Laurelville, 150 ... WO-6
Laurys Sta., 1243 ... EL-10
Lavansville, 150 ... WP-7
Lavelle, 742 ... EK-6
Laverock, 1100 ... ‡B-4
Lawn, 300 ... EO-6
Lawndale ... ‡C-6
Lawnton, 3813 ... ES-4
Lawrence, 540 ... WN-3
LAWRENCE CO., 91108 ... WI-2
Lawrence Pk., 3982 ... WC-4
Lawrenceville, 581 ... ED-3
Lawsonham, 50 ... WJ-6
Lawsville Ctr., 75 ... EE-9
Lawton, 85 ... EF-8
Le Raysville, 290 ... EE-7
Leaders Hts., 1200 ... WT-13
Leamersville, 80 ... WN-11
Lebanon, 25477 ... EN-6
LEBANON CO., 133568 ... EM-6
Leck Kill, 200 ... EL-5
Leckrone, 250 ... WQ-4
Lecontes Mills, 125 ... WJ-11
Lee Pk., 3600 ... EI-8
Leechburg, 2156 ... WL-5
Leeper, 200 ... WH-7
Lees Cross Roads, 200 ... EP-2
Leesburg, 100 ... WI-3
Leesport, 1918 ... EM-8
Leetsdale, 1218 ... WL-3
Lehigh, 100 ... EH-10
LEHIGH CO., 349497 ... EL-10
Lehighton, 5500 ... EK-9
Lehman, 250 ... EH-8

***, †, ‡, §, ◊ See explanation under state title in this index.**
County and parish names are listed in capital letters & boldface type.
Independent cities (not included in a county) are listed in *italics*.

Leinbachs, 150 .... ES-11
Leisenring, 600 .... WP-5
Leith, 900 .... WP-5
Leithsville, 300 .... EM-11
Lemasters, 250 .... WQ-13
Lemon EP-8
Lemont, 2270 .... WK-13
Lemont Furnace, 827 .... WP-5
Lemoyne, 4553 .... ET-3
Lenape, 200 .... EP-10
Lenhartsville, 165 .... EM-9
Lenoxville, 130 .... EF-10
Leola, 7214 .... EO-7
Leroy, 90 .... WJ-3
Lester *G-2
Level Green, 4020 .... WN-5
Levittown, 52983 .... EO-13
Lewis Run, 617 .... WE-10
Lewisberry, 362 .... EO-4
Lewisburg, 5792 .... EL-4
Lewistown, 8338 .... EL-1
Lewisville, 225 .... EQ-9
Liberty, 2551 .... *M-8
Liberty, 249 .... EG-3
Liberty Cors., 100 .... EF-8
Library, 6000 .... WN-7
Lickingville, 60 .... WH-9
Lightner, 1400 .... WR-13
Lightstreet, 1093 .... EJ-6
Ligonier, 1573 .... WM-7
Lilly, 968 .... WM-10
Lima, 2735 .... EP-11
Lime Ridge, 890 .... EJ-7
Limehill EF-7
Limeport, 250 .... EM-11
Limerick, 800 .... EN-10
Limestoneville, 70 .... EK-5
Lincoln, 1072 .... *M-8
Lincoln Hts, 300 .... WN-5
Lincoln Pk., 1615 .... ET-11
Lincolnville, 96 .... WF-8
Lincolnway, 1900 .... WS-12
Linconia, 950 .... *A-8
Linden, 270 .... EK-3
Linden, 100 .... WN-3
Linesville, 1040 .... WF-7
Linfield, 650 .... EO-10
Linglestown, Elena EN-5
Linntown, 1489 .... EL-4
Linwood, 3281 .... *O-4
Lionville, 6189 .... EO-10
Lippincott, 40 .... WP-3
Lisburn, 400 .... ET-3
Listie, 700 .... WM-8
Listonburg WQ-7
Litchfield, 80 .... EK-5
Lithia Sprs., 90 .... EK-5
Lititz, 9369 .... EO-7
Little Cooley, 50 .... WF-8
Little Cors., 45 .... WF-3
Little Gap, 80 .... EK-10
Little Hope, 60 .... WD-5
Little Marsh, 80 .... EE-2
Little Meadows, 273 .... ED-7
Littlestown, 4434 .... EQ-3
Liverpool, 955 .... EM-4
Llewellyn, 800 .... EL-7
Llewellyn Cors. EC-8
Loag, 200 .... WR-9
Lobachsville EM-9
Lock Haven, 9772 .... EI-2
Locke Mills EL-1
Locust EL-8
Locust Gap, 450 .... EK-6
Locust Run, 100 .... EK-3
Locustdale, 177 .... EK-7
Loganton, 468 .... EJ-2
Loganville, 1240 .... EQ-5
London WJ-3
London Grv., 250 .... EQ-9
Lone Pine, 50 .... WO-3
Long Pond, 900 .... EJ-10
Longfellow, 215 .... EM-1
Longstown, 100 .... WS-14
Longswamp, 300 .... EM-10
Loop, 60 .... WC-13
Lopez, 180 .... EG-7
Lorain, 759 .... WS-2
Lorane, 4236 .... EN-9
Lords Valley, 70 .... EH-12
Loretto, 1302 .... WM-10
Lost Creek, 500 .... EK-7
Lottsville, 100 .... WD-10
Lovejoy, 50 .... WL-8
Loveton, 100 .... EQ-2
Lover WO-4
Lower Allen, 6694 .... ET-3
Lower Burrell, 11761 .... *H-10
Lowville, 130 .... WD-4
Loyalsockville, 400 .... EH-4
Loyalton, 450 .... EM-5
Loysburg, 330 .... WQ-11
Loysville, 200 .... EN-2
Lucerne Mines, 937 .... WM-7
Lucinda, 300 .... WH-9
Luciusboro, 100 .... WH-9
Ludlow, 500 .... WF-8
Lumber City, 76 .... WJ-10
Lumberville, 200 .... EM-12
Lundys Lane, 180 .... WE-2
Lurgan, 90 .... EO-1
Luthersburg, 325 .... WJ-9
Luxor, 750 .... WN-6
Luzerne, 2845 .... EH-9
LUZERNE CO., 320918 .... EH-8
Lycippus, 90 .... WN-6
LYCOMING CO., 116111 .... EH-3
Lykens, 1779 .... EM-5
Lyleville, 135 .... WL-10
Lynch WG-8
Lyndell, 400 .... EO-10
Lyndon, 750 .... EP-7
Lyndora, 1300 .... WK-4
Lynn, 130 .... EM-7
Lynnport, 200 .... EL-9
Lynnville, 55 .... EL-9
Lynnwood, 330 .... EB-7
Lyons, 478 .... EM-9
Macdonaldton, 130 .... WP-8
Mackeyville, 250 .... EJ-2
Macungie, 3074 .... EM-10
Maddensville WO-13
Madera, 1000 .... WK-10
Madisonburg, 168 .... EK-1

Madisonville, 150 .... EH-10
Madley EH-10
Mahaffey, 368 .... WK-9
Mahanoy City, 4162 .... EK-8
Maiden Creek, 200 .... EM-9
Mainesburg, 200 .... EF-4
Mainland, 2000 .... EN-10
Mainsville, 300 .... EP-1
Mainville, 132 .... EJ-6
Maitland, 357 .... EL-2
Malta EI-6
Malvern, 2998 .... EO-10
Mammoth, 525 .... WO-6
Mamont WM-6
Manatawny, 200 .... EN-9
Manchester, 2763 .... EP-5
Mandata, 60 .... EL-5
Manheim, 4858 .... EO-6
Manns Choice, 300 .... WP-10
Mannsville, 25 .... EM-3
Manor, 3239 .... WN-5
Manorville, 410 .... WK-6
Mansfield, 3625 .... EE-3
Mantz, 300 .... EL-6
Maple Bch., 100 .... *B-10
Maple Grv., 135 .... WJ-6
Maple Lake EH-10
Mapledale, 200 .... EO-1
Mapleglen, 441 .... WN-13
Mapletown, 130 .... WQ-4
Maplewood WK-2
Maplewood Pk., 1700 .... ‡F-1
Marble, 130 .... WH-8
Marchand WK-8
Marcus Hook, 2397 .... EQ-11
Margo Gdns., 300 .... *L-10
Marianna, 494 .... WP-3
Mariasville WL-5
Marienville, 3137 .... WG-8
Marietta, 2588 .... EP-6
Marion, 953 .... WQ-14
Marion, Ctr., 451 .... WK-8
Marion Hts., 611 .... EK-6
Markesburg, 204 .... WN-13
Markleton, 40 .... WQ-7
Markleysburg, 284 .... WQ-6
Markton WJ-8
Marlin, 661 .... EL-7
Mars, 1699 .... WL-4
Marsh EO-9
Marshall WK-4
Marshallton, 1441 .... EK-6
Marshallton, 600 .... EP-10
Marsburg, 50 .... WF-9
Marshlands, 50 .... EL-7
Marstown, 150 .... EM-6
Martha Furnace, 25 .... WK-13
Marticville, 400 .... EP-7
Martin, 110 .... WQ-4
Martindale, 180 .... EO-8
Martindale, 140 .... WN-13
Martins Creek, 631 .... EK-12
Martinsburg, 1958 .... WN-11
Martinsville, 100 .... EH-14
Marwood, 60 .... WK-5
Marysville, 2534 .... EN-4
Masontown, 3450 .... WQ-4
Mastersonville, 185 .... EO-6
Masthope, 685 .... EG-12
Matamoras, 2469 .... EH-14
Mather, 737 .... WP-3
Mattawana, 276 .... WM-14
Mausdale, 75 .... EJ-5
Maxatawny, 250 .... EM-10
Mayburg WG-7
Mayfield, 1807 .... EG-10
Mayport, 80 .... WJ-7
Maysville, 60 .... WM-8
Maysville WK-8
Maytown, 3824 .... EO-6
Maytown EO-4
Maze EL-3
Mazeppa, 225 .... EK-4
McAdoo, 2300 .... EK-8
McAlevys Fort, 70 .... WL-13
McAlisterville, 971 .... EL-3
McCartney, 70 .... WK-10
McClure, 941 .... EL-3
McConnellsburg, 1220 .... WP-14
McConnellstown, 1194 .... WM-12
McCoysville, 100 .... EM-1
McCracken, 60 .... EM-2
McCrea EN-2
McDonald, 2149 .... WN-3
McElhattan, 598 .... EI-2
McEwensville, 279 .... EJ-5
McGees Mills, 100 .... WK-9
McGovern, 2742 .... WN-3
McGrann, 700 .... WK-6
McIntyre, 200 .... EH-3
McKean, 388 .... WD-3
McKEAN CO., 43450 .... WF-10
McKeansburg, 163 .... EL-8
McKee, 200 .... WP-11
McKee Half Falls, 130 .... EL-4
McKees Rocks, 6104 .... WM-3
McKeesport, 24386 .... *J-10
McKinney EO-1
McKnightstown, 226 .... EQ-2
McLane, 75 .... WD-3
McMichael, 50 .... EJ-11
McMurray, 4647 .... WN-3
McSherrystown, 3038 .... EQ-4
McVeytown, 342 .... WM-14
McVille WD-2
Meadow Lands, 822 .... WN-3
Meadowbrook, 1000 .... *A-5
Meadville, 13388 .... WF-3
Mechanics Grv., 120 .... EP-7
Mechanicsburg, 8981 .... EN-3
Mechanicsville, 3100 .... EJ-6
Mechanicsville, 500 .... EN-12

Mechanicsville, 120 .... EA-2
Mechanicsville, 35 .... WI-7
Mechanicsville, 25 .... EJ-10
Mecks Corner EN-3
Media, 5327 .... EP-11
Mehoopany, 350 .... EG-8
Meiserville, 100 .... EL-4
Melcroft, 250 .... WP-6
Melrose Pk., 6500 .... *B-5
Mendenhall, 600 .... EQ-10
Menges Mills, 200 .... EP-5
Menno, 80 .... WM-14
Mentcle, 100 .... WL-9
Mercer, 2002 .... WI-3
Mercersburg, 1561 .... WQ-13
Meridian, 3881 .... WK-4
Merion Sta., 700 .... ‡D-3
Merrittown, 664 .... EM-10
Meshoppen, 563 .... EG-8
Metal, 100 .... WP-13
Mexico, 472 .... EM-2
Meyersdale, 2184 .... WQ-8
Middle Creek, 100 .... WK-3
Middle Lancaster, ... WK-3
Middle Spr., 80 .... EO-1
Middleburg, 1309 .... EK-4
Middlebury, 90 .... EJ-9
Middleport, 405 .... EL-8
Middlesex, 250 .... EO-3
Middleton, 8901 .... EO-5
Middletown, 7378 .... EA-5
Midland, 2635 .... WL-2
Midvale EB-8
Midway, 913 .... WN-2
Mifflin, 642 .... EM-2
MIFFLIN CO., 46682 .... EK-2
Mifflinburg, 3540 .... EK-4
Mifflintown, 936 .... EM-2
Mifflinville, 1253 .... EJ-7
Milan, 300 .... EE-6
Milanville, 175 .... EF-12
Mildred, 200 .... EG-6
Milesburg, 1123 .... WJ-13
Milford, 1021 .... EH-13
Milford Sq., 897 .... EM-11
Mill City, 650 .... EG-9
Mill Creek, 328 .... WM-13
Mill Grv., 40 .... EK-7
Mill Hall, 1613 .... EI-2
Mill Run, 400 .... WP-6
Mill Run, 250 .... WM-11
Mill Vil., 412 .... WE-4
Millardsville, 140 .... EN-7
Millbach EN-7
Millbourne, 1159 .... ‡E-2
Milledgeville, 60 .... WG-4
Millersburg, 2557 .... EM-4
Millerstown, 673 .... EM-3
Millerstown, 40 .... WP-3
Millersville, 8168 .... EP-7
Millerton, 316 .... ED-4
Millertown, 200 .... WP-6
Millheim, 904 .... EK-2
Millmont, 150 .... EK-4
Millport, 80 .... WE-12
Millrift, 170 .... EH-14
Mills, 125 .... WE-14
Millsboro, 666 .... WP-4
Milltown, 170 .... EP-10
Milltown .... ‡I-9
Millvale, 3744 .... ‡J-6
Millville, 948 .... EI-6
Millwood, 566 .... WN-7
Milroy, 1498 .... EL-1
Milton, 7042 .... EJ-4
Milton Grv., 100 .... EO-6
Mineral Sprs., 300 .... WJ-11
Minersville, 4397 .... EL-7
Mingoville, 503 .... EJ-1
Minisink Hills, 350 .... EJ-12
Miquon, 300 .... *B-2
Mocanaqua, 646 .... EI-8
Modena, 535 .... EP-9
Mogeetown, 1400 .... *A-1
Mohnton, 3043 .... EN-8
Mohrsville, 383 .... EM-8
Monaca, 5737 .... WL-3
Monarch, 200 .... WP-5
Monessen, 7720 .... WO-4
Mongul, 60 .... EO-1
Monongahela, 4300 .... WO-4
Monroe, 90 .... WI-6
MONROE CO., 169842 .... EJ-11
Monroeton, 554 .... EF-6
Monroeville, 28386 .... *I-9
Mont Alto, 1705 .... EQ-1
Mont Clare, 1800 .... EO-10
Montandon, 903 .... EJ-4
Montdale, 400 .... EG-10
Montello, 30 .... EF-11
Monterey, 100 .... ‡D-9
Monterey EQ-2
Montgomery, 1579 .... EI-4
MONTGOMERY CO., 799874 .... EN-10
Montgomery Ferry, 50 .... EM-4
Montgomeryville, 12624 .... EN-12
Montoursville, 4615 .... EI-4
Montrose, 1617 .... EE-9
Montrose Hill, 1600 .... ‡J-8
Monument, 50 .... EI-2
Moon, 1000 .... ‡I-2
Moon Crest, 2100 .... ‡I-3
Moon Run, 400 .... *K-4
Mooresburg, 80 .... EJ-5
Moorestown, 250 .... EK-11
Moorhead WD-2
Moorheadville WC-4
Moosic, 5719 .... EH-9
Morann, 400 .... WK-12
Moravia, 200 .... WJ-2
Morea, 80 .... WK-9
Morganton, 826 .... EO-9
Morris, 250 .... EG-2
Morris Run, 400 .... EF-4
Morrisdale, 754 .... WJ-12
Morrisville, 8728 .... EO-14
Morrisville, 1265 .... WN-3
Morrisville, 200 .... ‡F-1
Moscow, 2026 .... EH-10

Moselem, 150 .... EM-9
Moselem Sprs., 70 .... EM-9
Mosgrove WK-6
Moshannon, 281 .... WJ-13
Moshersville, 200 .... EG-8
Mosierstown, 35 .... WE-3
Mostoller, 30 .... WO-8
Mt. Aetna, 354 .... EM-7
Mt. Allen, 2000 .... EO-3
Mt. Alton WE-10
Mt. Bethel, 65 .... EK-12
Mt. Carmel, 5893 .... EK-6
Mt. Chestnut, 100 .... WK-4
Mt. Cobb, 1799 .... EH-10
Mt. Eagle, 103 .... EJ-1
Mt. Gretna, 196 .... EN-6
Mt. Holly Sprs., 2030 .... EO-3
Mt. Jackson, 300 .... WJ-2
Mt. Jewett, 919 .... WF-10
Mt. Joy, 7410 .... EO-6
Mt. Lebanon, 33100 .... *L-5
Mt. Morris, 737 .... WQ-3
Mt. Nebo, 1500 .... *L-4
Mt. Nebo, 300 .... EQ-7
Mt. Oliver, 3463 .... *K-6
Mt. Penn, 3106 .... EN-9
Mt. Pleasant, 4454 .... WO-6
Mt. Pleasant, 200 .... EN-8
Mt. Pleasant, 65 .... EJ-9
Mt. Pleasant Mills, 464 .... EL-4
Mt. Pocono, 3170 .... EI-11
Mt. Royal, 150 .... EM-4
Mt. Union, 2447 .... WN-13
Mt. Union, 100 .... WP-2
Mt. Vernon, 2200 .... *N-8
Mt. Vernon WK-9
Mt. Wilson, 200 .... EN-6
Mt. Wolf, 1393 .... EP-5
Mt. Zion, 350 .... EN-6
Mt. Zion, 100 .... ES-1
Mt. Zion EA-10
Mountain Top, 10982 .... EI-9
Mountainhome, 1182 .... EI-11
Mountville, 2802 .... EP-6
Mowersville, 40 .... EO-1
Muddy Creek Forks, 650 .... EH-11
Muhlenberg, 200 .... EI-7
Muhlenberg Pk., 1420 .... ES-12
Muir, 451 .... EL-6
Muncy, 2477 .... EI-5
Muncy Valley, 270 .... EH-6
Mundys Corner, 205 .... WN-9
Munhall, 11406 .... *M-4
Munson, 275 .... WJ-12
Munster, 300 .... WM-10
Murdocksville, 11300 .... ‡K-1
Murrell EO-7
Murrysville, 15268 .... *I-11
Muse, 2504 .... WN-3
Myerstown, 3062 .... EN-7
Myobeach, 65 .... EG-8
Myoma, 100 .... WK-8
Myrtle WD-12
Naginey, 120 .... EL-1
Nanticoke, 10465 .... EI-8
Nantmel Vil., 650 .... EO-10
Nanty Glo, 2734 .... WM-9
Narberth, 4282 .... EP-12
Nashville, 200 .... EM-8
Natrona Hts., 2800 .... *G-5
Nazareth, 5746 .... EL-11
Nectarine WK-8
Needmore, 170 .... WQ-12
Neelyton, 80 .... WO-13
Neffs, 60 .... EL-10
Neffsville, 1000 .... EO-7
Neilton, 25 .... WF-6
Nelson, 300 .... ED-3
Nemacolin, 937 .... WP-4
Nescopeck, 1583 .... EJ-7
Nesquehoning, 3349 .... EK-9
Nassau Vil., 1500 .... *G-5

Oakland, 1569 .... WJ-2
Oakland, 616 .... EE-10
Oaks, 110 .... EL-2
Oakleigh, 1000 .... EE-10
Oakmont, 6303 .... WM-4
Oaks, 856 .... EO-11
Oakville, 150 .... EO-2
Oberlin, 588 .... ET-4
Ogdensburg, 75 .... EG-4
Ogletown, 150 .... WO-9
Ohiopyle, 59 .... WQ-6
Ohioville, 3533 .... WL-2
Oil, 75 .... WN-2
Oil City, 10557 .... WG-5
Oklahoma, 809 .... WL-6
Oklahoma, 782 .... WN-6
Olanta, 100 .... WK-10
Old Boston, 200 .... EC-9
Old Concord, 30 .... WP-2
Old Forge, 8313 .... EH-9
Old Port, 90 .... EM-2
Oley, 1282 .... EN-9
Oliphant Furnace, 250 .... WQ-5
Oliveburg, 150 .... WJ-8
Oliver, 2535 .... WP-5
Olney .... ‡C-5
Olyphant, 5151 .... EG-10
Oneida, 200 .... EK-8
Oneida, 100 .... WK-9
Ono, 300 .... EN-6
Opp EM-9
Orange, 300 .... EH-9
Orangeville, 508 .... EI-6
Orbisonia, 428 .... WN-13
Orchard Bch., 11 .... EM-9
Orchard Hills, 1952 .... WL-6
Ore Hill, 95 .... WN-11
Ore Valley, 200 .... WT-14
Orefield, 750 .... EB-1
Oregon, 250 .... EO-7
Oregon Hill, 100 .... EG-2
Oreland, 5678 .... *A-4
Oriental, 100 .... EL-3
Oriole, 100 .... EO-7
Ormrod, 300 .... EA-2
Ormsby, 100 .... WE-10
Orrstown, 262 .... EP-1
Orrtanna, 173 .... EQ-2
Orson, 125 .... EE-10
Orviston, 95 .... WI-14
Orwell, 100 .... EE-7
Orwigsburg, 3099 .... EL-8
Orwin, 314 .... EM-6
Osceola, 400 .... ED-2
Osceola Mills, 1141 .... WK-11
Osgood, 40 .... WO-10
Osterburg, 250 .... WO-10
Osterhout, 30 .... EI-8
Oswayo, 139 .... WE-13
Ottsville, 250 .... EM-12
Oval, 361 .... EH-3
Overbrook, 200 .... ES-9
Overlook, 200 .... ES-9
Overlook Hts, 1200 .... WS-5
Overton, 85 .... EG-6
Overview, 50 .... EL-7
Oxford, 5077 .... EQ-8
Packerton, 200 .... EK-9
Paint, 1023 .... WN-9
Painterville WO-10
Paintertown, 120 .... ‡L-10
Paisley, 100 .... WQ-4
Palm, 370 .... EM-10
Palmer Hts, 3762 .... EL-11
Palmerton, 5414 .... EK-10
Palmyra, 7320 .... EN-6
Palo Alto, 1032 .... EL-7
Panic, 80 .... WJ-8
Paoli, 5575 .... EO-10
Paradise, 1129 .... EP-8
Paradise, 250 .... WN-8
Paradise Valley, 150 .... EI-11
Pardoe, 50 .... WL-3
Paris, 732 .... WM-1
Park Forest Vil., 9660 .... WS-5
Park Hills, 2000 .... EO-5
Park View, 1300 .... ‡J-7
Park Way Manor, 2000 .... EB-2
Parker, 840 .... WJ-5
Parker Ford, 800 .... EO-10
Parkesburg, 3593 .... EP-9
Parkhill, 300 .... WN-9
Parkside, 2328 .... EQ-11
Parkstown, 75 .... WS-2
Parkville, 6706 .... EQ-5
Parryville, 525 .... EK-10
Patchinville, 30 .... WN-10
Patterson Hts., 636 .... WK-2
Patton, 1769 .... WM-10
Paupack, 600 .... EH-12
Pavia, 90 .... WO-10
Paxinos, 500 .... EK-6
Paxtang, 1561 .... ES-4
Paxton, 100 .... EL-4
Paxtonia, 5412 .... ER-4
Paxtonville, 265 .... EK-3
Peach Glen, 100 .... EP-3
Pearl, 50 .... WH-4
Pecks Pond EH-12
Pen Argyl, 3595 .... EK-11
Pen Mar, 900 .... EQ-1
Penbrook, 3008 .... ES-3
Penfield, 650 .... WI-10
Penn, 475 .... WN-5
Penn Hall, 60 .... EK-1
Penn Hills EE-8
Penn Lake Pk., 308 .... EI-9
Penn Pines, 650 .... WL-8
Penn Valley, 6000 .... ‡C-2
Penndel, 2328 .... EO-13
Penline, 40 .... WF-2
Penns Creek, 715 .... EK-3
Penns Pk., 500 .... EN-13
Penns Woods, 2600 .... *M-9
Pennsburg, 3843 .... EN-10
Pennsbury Vil., 661 .... *K-4
Pennsdale, 110 .... EI-5
Pennside, 4215 .... ET-13
Pennside, 90 .... EO-7
Pennsville, 280 .... WO-5
Pennsville, 200 .... ‡C-2
Pennsylvania Furnace, 150 .... WL-13
Pennwyn, 780 .... EC-12
Penowa, 20 .... WN-1
Penryn, 1024 .... EO-6
Pequea, 300 .... EP-7
Perdix, 90 .... EN-4
Perkasie, 8511 .... EN-11
Perkiomen Hts., 70 .... EN-10
Perrine Cors. EO-1
PERRY CO., 45969 .... EN-3
Perryopolis, 1784 .... WO-5

Perryville, 180 .... WI-5
Perryville, 70 .... WM-6
Perryville, 25 .... WM-6
Petersburg, 480 .... WM-12
Petrolia, 212 .... WJ-5
Pharethel, 150 .... WI-9
Philadelphia, 1526006 .... EP-12
PHILADELPHIA CO., 1526006 .... EO-12
Philipsburg, 2770 .... WK-12
Phillips, 225 .... WP-5
Phillipston, 45 .... WJ-6
Phillipsville WM-2
Phoenixville, 16440 .... EO-10
Picture Rocks, 678 .... EH-5
Pigeon, 20 .... WG-8
PIKE CO., 57369 .... EH-12
Pilgrim Gdns., 1650 .... ‡E-1
Pillow, 298 .... EL-5
Pine, 80 .... EI-2
Pine Bank, 20 .... WQ-2
Pine Glen, 190 .... WJ-14
Pine Grv., 2186 .... EM-6
Pine Grv. Furnace, 25 .... EP-3
Pine Grv. Mills, 1502 .... WL-13
Pine Summit, 55 .... EI-6
Pinecroft, 100 .... WM-11
Pineville, 950 .... EN-13
Piney Fork, 400 .... *N-6
Pinola, 20 .... EL-5
Pipersville, 600 .... EM-12
Pitcairn, 3294 .... *K-9
Pitman, 300 .... EL-6
Pittsburgh, 305704 .... WM-4
Pittsfield, 500 .... WE-7
Pittston, 7739 .... EH-9
Pittsville, 35 .... WN-5
Plain, 1096 .... WN-4
Plains, 4335 .... EI-8
Plainsville, 350 .... EI-8
Platea, 430 .... WD-3
Pleasant Gap, 2879 .... WK-14
Pleasant Grv., 50 .... WQ-2
Pleasant Hall, 150 .... EP-1
Pleasant Hills, 8268 .... *M-6
Pleasant Mount, 125 .... EE-11
Pleasant Unity, 600 .... WN-6
Pleasant Valley, 200 .... EM-1
Pleasantville, 892 .... WG-6
Plum, 27126 .... WM-5
Plumer, 150 .... WG-6
Plumsteadville, 2637 .... EN-12
Plumville, 307 .... WK-7
Plymouth, 5951 .... EI-8
Plymouth Meeting, 6177 .... ‡A-2
Pocahontas, 135 .... WP-8
Pocono Lake, 750 .... EI-10
Pocono Mnr., 300 .... EI-11
Pocono Pines, 1409 .... EI-11
Pocono Summit, 1500 .... EI-11
Point WO-10
Pt. Marion, 1159 .... WQ-4
Pt. Pleasant, 800 .... EM-12
Poland, 75 .... WN-2
Polk, 816 .... WH-5
Pomeroy, 401 .... EP-9
Pond Bank, 200 .... EQ-1
Pond Eddy, 50 .... EG-13
Pond Hill, 200 .... EI-8
Port Allegany, 2157 .... WE-11
Port Carbon, 1889 .... EL-7
Port Clinton, 325 .... EM-8
Port Griffith, 1350 .... EB-9
Port Matilda, 606 .... WK-13
Port Royal, 925 .... EM-2
Port Trevorton, 769 .... EL-4
Port Vue, 3798 .... *M-8
Portage, 2638 .... WN-10
Porter, 25 .... WJ-7
Porters Sideling, 100 .... EQ-4
Portersville, 235 .... WJ-3
Portland Mills, 40 .... WH-9
Portland, 519 .... EJ-12
Potter Brook, 200 .... WD-11
Potters Mills, 180 .... EK-1
Pottersdale, 20 .... WJ-12
Pottersville, 75 .... EF-11
Potts Grv., 140 .... EJ-5
Pottstown, 22377 .... EN-10
Pottsville, 14324 .... EL-7
Powell, 150 .... EF-6
Powells Valley, 600 .... EM-4
Powys, 100 .... EN-3
Prescott, 50 .... WI-8
Prescottville, 550 .... EO-7
Presidnet, 100 .... WH-7
Preston, 240 .... EE-11
Preston Pk., 200 .... EE-11
Pricetown, 180 .... EN-9
Primos, 900 .... ‡F-2
Primrose, 600 .... EL-7
Princeton, 150 .... WI-2
Pringle, 979 .... EA-8
Prittstown WP-8
Proctor, 50 .... EH-3
Progress, 9765 .... ES-3
Prompton, 250 .... EG-11
Prospect, 1169 .... WK-4
Prospect, 250 .... WH-5
Prospect Pk., 6454 .... EP-11
Prospect Pk., 327 .... WG-12
Prospectville, 550 .... EO-11
Prosperity, 175 .... WO-3
Pulaski, 300 .... WI-2
Punxsutawney, 5962 .... WJ-8
Purcell, 25 .... WO-11
Purchase Line, 40 .... WL-8
Putneyville, 140 .... WJ-7
Puzzletown WO-10
Quakake, 300 .... EK-8
Quaker Hills, 50 .... EP-7
Quaker Lake, 70 .... ED-8
Quakertown, 8979 .... EN-11
Quarryville, 2576 .... EP-7
Quecreek, 150 .... WO-8
Queen, 100 .... WN-10
Queens Run, 50 .... EI-2
Quentin, 594 .... EN-6
Quicktown, 50 .... EN-13
Quiggleville, 50 .... EH-4
Quincy, 400 .... EQ-1
Radnor .... ‡C-1
Railroad, 278 .... EQ-5
Rainsburg, 133 .... WP-10

Ralston, 400 .... EG-4
Ramey, 451 .... WK-11
Ramsey, 45 .... WK-2
Rankin, 2122 .... *K-7
Ransom, 250 .... EH-9
Rauh, 100 .... EF-8
Raubsville, 1088 .... EL-12
Rauchtown, 726 .... EI-3
Ravine, 662 .... EM-6
Rawlinsville, 150 .... EQ-7
Raymilton WG-4
Raymond, WE-13 .... WE-13
Rea, 50 .... WN-2
Reading, 88082 .... EN-9
Reamstown, 3361 .... EO-8
Reamstown, 300 .... EO-8
Rebuck, 150 .... EL-5
Rector, 400 .... WN-7
Red Bn., 200 .... EP-1
Red Cross, 70 .... EL-3
Red Lion, 6373 .... EP-5
Red Rock, 30 .... EH-7
Redclyffe, 20 .... WN-8
Redeers, 350 .... EJ-11
Reedsville, 350 .... EL-1
Reeds Gap, 30 .... EM-1
Reedsville, 641 .... EL-1
Reels Cors., 25 .... WO-9
Reese, 80 .... WM-11
Reesedale, 50 .... WJ-6
Refton, 298 .... EP-7
Rehrersburg, 319 .... EM-7
Reidsburg, 40 .... WJ-6
Reiffton, 4178 .... ET-13
Reinerton, 424 .... EL-6
Reinholds, 1803 .... EN-8
Reistville, 100 .... EN-7
Renfrew, 350 .... WK-4
Renovo, 1228 .... WH-14
Republic, 1096 .... WP-4
Revere, 600 .... EM-12
Reynoldsville, 2759 .... WI-9
Rhawns, 1598 .... EO-6
Rices, 463 .... WM-8
Riceville, 68 .... WE-5
Rich Hill, 150 .... WO-12
Richardsville, 40 .... WI-8
Richboro, 6563 .... EO-13
Richfield, 549 .... EL-3
Richland, 1519 .... EN-7
Richlandtown, 1327 .... EM-11
Richmond, 100 .... EK-12
Richmond Furnace, ... WP-13
Ridgebury, 170 .... ED-5
Ridgeview, 800 .... ER-4
Ridgewood, 300 .... EB-9
Ridgway, 4078 .... WH-9
Ridley Farms, 1500 .... ‡F-1
Ridley Pk., 7002 .... ‡G-1
Riegelsville, 868 .... EL-12
Rillton, 900 .... WN-5
Rimer, 40 .... WJ-6
Rimersburg, 951 .... WJ-6
Rinely EQ-6
Ringgold, 250 .... WH-7
Ringtown, 818 .... EK-7
River View Pk., 3380 .... ES-12
Riverside, 1932 .... EJ-5
Riverside, 381 .... WT-2
Rixford, 400 .... WE-10
Roaring Branch, 100 .... EG-4
Roaring Creek, 156 .... EK-6
Roaring Spr., 2585 .... WN-11
Robertsdale, 240 .... WO-12
Robesonia, 2061 .... EN-8
Robinson, 614 .... WN-7
Rochester, 3657 .... WL-2
Rochester Mills, 250 .... WK-8
Rock, 60 .... EM-8
Rock Glen, 300 .... EJ-7
Rock Lebanon Hills, ... WO-9
Rockhill, 371 .... WO-13
Rockingham, 60 .... WN-9
Rockland, 30 .... WH-5
Rockledge, 2543 .... EO-12
Rockport, 85 .... EJ-9
Rockspring WL-13
Rockton, 200 .... WJ-10
Rockville, 170 .... WM-4
Rockville, 85 .... EN-4
Rockville WL-8
Rockwood, 890 .... WP-7
Roddersville, 200 .... EI-11
Rogersville, 140 .... WP-3
Rogertown, 140 .... WH-5
Rohrerstown, 1200 .... ES-8
Rohrsburg, 45 .... EI-6
Rome, 441 .... EE-7
Ronco, 256 .... WP-4
Roscoe, 812 .... WO-4
Rose Pt., 90 .... WJ-3
Rose Valley, 913 .... ‡E-1
Rosebud, 40 .... WO-10
Rosecrans EJ-2
Roseglen, 110 .... EN-3
Rosemont, 75 .... *C-1
Roseto, 1567 .... EK-11
Roseville, 189 .... EE-4
Roslyn, 10000 .... *A-5
Rossiter, 646 .... WK-9
Roseville Junc. .... ‡K-4
Rossyln Farms, 427 .... ‡K-4
Rossmoyne, 1100 .... ET-2
Rote, 507 .... EI-2
Rothsville, 3044 .... EO-7
Roulette, 779 .... WF-11
Round Top, 115 .... WO-9
Rouseville, 523 .... WG-5
Rouzerville, 917 .... EQ-1
Rowes Run, 564 .... WP-4
Roxbury, 275 .... EO-1
Roxbury, 50 .... EL-7
Royal, 100 .... EL-5
Royalton, 907 .... EO-5
Royer, 45 .... WN-11
Royersford, 4752 .... EO-10
Ruff Creek, 50 .... WP-3
Ruffs Dale, 60 .... WO-5
Rummel, 600 .... WO-8
Rummerfield, 35 .... EF-7
Rural Ridge, 1000 .... WL-4
Rural Valley, 876 .... WK-7

Rush, 100 .... EF-8
Rushland, 350 .... EN-13
Rushville, 45 .... EF-8
Russell, 1408 .... WE-8
Russell City, 60 .... WG-9
Russell Hill EG-8
Russellton, 1440 .... WL-4
Russellville, 125 .... EQ-8
Rutherford, 4303 .... ES-4
Rutledge, 784 .... ‡F-1
Rydal, 1800 .... *A-5
Ryde, 70 .... WM-14
Rye EO-5
Ryerson Sta., 80 .... WP-2
Ryot, 30 .... WO-11
Sabinsville, 300 .... EE-1
Sabula, 200 .... WI-10
Sacramento, 300 .... EL-6
Saddle Brook, 1160 .... EC-2
Sadsburyville, 700 .... EP-9
Saegersville, 150 .... ED-11
Saegertown, 997 .... WF-3
Safe Hbr., 150 .... EP-7
Sagamore, 450 .... WK-7
Saginaw, 200 .... EP-5
St. Augustine, 200 .... WL-10
St. Benedict, 450 .... WL-9
St. Boniface, 120 .... WL-9
St. Clair, 3004 .... EL-7
St. Clairsville, 78 .... WO-10
St. George, 50 .... WI-5
St. Johns, 300 .... EI-8
St. Joseph, 150 .... EE-8
St. Lawrence, 1809 .... EN-9
St. Lawrence, 400 .... WE-13
St. Marys, 13070 .... WH-10
St. Michael, 480 .... WN-9
St. Paul, 75 .... WO-8
St. Peters, 400 .... EO-9
St. Petersburg, 400 .... WI-5
St. Thomas, 900 .... WP-13
Salem, 150 .... EK-4
Salem, 30 .... WG-2
Salemville, 50 .... WO-11
Salina, 500 .... WM-6
Salisbury, 727 .... WQ-8
Salix, 1149 .... WN-9
Saltsburg, 238 .... EI-3
Shumans, 140 .... EJ-7
Shunk, 45 .... EG-5
Siddonsburg, 110 .... EO-4
Sidman, 431 .... WN-9
Sigel, 250 .... WI-9
Siglerville, 106 .... EL-1
Silkworth, 820 .... EH-8
Silvara, 80 .... EF-7
Silver Lake, 150 .... ED-9
Silver Spr., 300 .... EP-6
Silverdale, 871 .... EN-11
Simpson, 1275 .... EG-10
Sinking Spr., 4008 .... EN-8
Sinnemahoning, 350 .... WH-12
Sipesville, 350 .... WO-8
Sizerville, 35 .... WG-12
Skelp, 60 .... WL-11
Skinners Eddy, 40 .... EF-7
Skippack, 3758 .... EN-11
Skytop, 200 .... EI-11
Slate Lick, 150 .... WK-6
Slate Run, 60 .... EG-2
Slatedale, 455 .... EL-10
Slateford, 250 .... EJ-12
Slatington, 4232 .... EL-10
Slickville, 388 .... WM-6
Sligo, 720 .... WI-6
Slippery Rock, 3625 .... WJ-4
Slocum Cors., 150 .... EI-8
Slovan, 555 .... WN-2
Smethport, 1655 .... WE-11
Smicksburg, 46 .... WK-8
Smithfield, 4180 .... WM-12
Smithfield, 875 .... WQ-5
Smithport, 100 .... WK-8
Smithton, 399 .... WO-5
Smithville EP-7
Smock, 583 .... WP-5
Smoke Run, 150 .... WK-11
Smoketown, 357 .... EP-7
Smullton, 125 .... EJ-2
Snow Shoe, 765 .... WJ-13
School Lane Hills, ... EC-8
SNYDER CO., 39702 .... EL-4
Snydersburg, 100 .... WH-7
Snydertown, 339 .... EK-5
Studa, 100 .... WI-10
Stump Creek, 300 .... WI-9
Sturgeon, 1710 .... WN-3
Suedberg, 200 .... EM-6
Sugar Grv., 614 .... WD-7
Sugar Notch, 989 .... EI-8
Sugar Run, 100 .... EF-7
Sugarcreek, 5294 .... WH-4
Sunbury, 9905 .... EK-5
Sunderlinville, 55 .... EE-1
Sunnybrook, 300 .... EO-7
Sunnyburn, 80 .... EQ-5
Sunset Valley, 2700 .... *M-10
Sunville, 300 .... WG-4
Surveyor, 35 .... WL-10
Suscon, 700 .... EH-9
SUSQUEHANNA CO., 43356 .... EF-8
Susquehanna Depot, 1643 .... ED-10
Sutersville, 605 .... WN-5
Swanville, 500 .... EM-12
Swanville, 100 .... *B-3
Swarthmore, 6194 .... ‡F-1
Swedeland, 300 .... *B-1
Sweden Valley, 223 .... WF-13
Sweet Valley, 500 .... EH-7
Swiftwater, 600 .... EI-11
Swineford WL-4
Swiss Vale, 8983 .... *K-7
Swoyersville, 5062 .... EH-9
Sybertsville, 200 .... EI-8
Sycamore, 60 .... WP-3
Sykesville, 1157 .... WJ-9
Sylvan, 20 .... WQ-14
Sylvania, 219 .... EE-5
Table Rock, 62 .... EP-3
Tacony .... ‡C-6
Tafton, 600 .... EH-12

Talmage, 325 .... ET-10
Tamaqua, 7107 .... EK-8
Tamiment, 125 .... EI-12
Van, 60 .... WH-1
Van Voorhis, 166 .... WO-4
Vandergrift, 5205 .... WL-6
Vanderling, 751 .... EF-12
Vandyke, 80 .... EM-2
Varden, 150 .... EG-11
Venetia, 450 .... WN-4
VENANGO CO., 54984 .... WG-5
Venus, 150 .... WH-6
Verona, 2474 .... WM-4
Vera Cruz, 250 .... EM-10
Versailles, 1515 .... *M-8
Vestaburg, 350 .... WP-4
Vicksburg, 261 .... EJ-4
Victory Hts., 250 .... WN-13
Villa Maria, 150 .... WI-2
Villanova .... ‡C-1
Vinco, 1305 .... WM-9
Vinemont, 100 .... EN-8
Vintondale, 414 .... WM-8
Vira, 150 .... ‡C-1
Virginville, 309 .... EM-9
Volant, 168 .... WI-3
Vosburg EG-8
Vowinckel, 135 .... WH-8
Wagner, 128 .... EL-2
Wagontown, 400 .... EO-9
Wakefield, 500 .... EQ-7
Walbert, 200 .... EB-1
Wall, 580 .... *L-9
Wallaceton, 313 .... WJ-11
Waller, 48 .... EH-8
Wallingford .... ‡E-1
Walls Cors., 30 .... EG-8
Walnut, 115 .... EM-8
Walnut Bottom, ... EO-2
Walnutport, 2076 .... EL-10
Walnuttown, 484 .... EM-9
Walston, 275 .... WJ-8
Waltersburg, 275 .... WP-5
Waltonville, 125 .... ET-6
Wampum, 714 .... WJ-3
Wanamakers, 55 .... ‡C-3
Wamanie, 612 .... EI-8
Wapwallopen, 145 .... EI-8
Warfordsburg, ... WQ-12
135 .... WQ-12
Warminster, 31400 .... EO-12
Warren, 9710 .... WE-8
Warren Ctr., 100 .... EE-7
WARREN CO., 41815 .... WE-7
Warrendale, 500 .... WL-3
Warrensville, 300 .... EH-4
Warrington, 7000 .... EN-12
Warrior Run, 584 .... EI-8
Warriors Mark, 200 .... WL-12
Warwick, 200 .... EO-9
Washington, 13663 .... WO-3
Washington Boro, 729 .... EP-6
WASHINGTON CO., 207820 .... WN-2
Washington Crossing, 850 .... EN-13
Washingtonville, 273 .... EJ-5
Wassergass, 201 .... EL-11
Water Street, 15 .... WM-12
Waterford, 1510 .... WD-4
Waterford, 1517 .... WO-4
Waterloo, 300 .... WN-14
Waterman, 140 .... WM-8
Waterside, 50 .... WO-11
Waterville, 150 .... EH-1
Watrous, 150 .... EF-1
Watsontown, 2351 .... EJ-4
Wattsonville, 150 .... WJ-6
Wattsburg, 403 .... WD-5
Waverly, 604 .... EG-9
Wayland, 1341 .... EG-11
WAYNE CO., 52822 .... EF-11
Waynesboro, 10568 .... EQ-1
Waynesburg, 4176 .... WP-3
Weatherly, 2525 .... EJ-9
Webster, 250 .... WO-5
Webster Mills, 25 .... WQ-12
Weedville, 542 .... WI-10
Weigelstown, 12875 .... EP-4
Weikert, 215 .... EK-2
Weishample, 100 .... EK-6
Weissport, 412 .... EK-9
Weldbank, 100 .... WF-8
Weldon .... ‡A-5
Wellersburg, 181 .... WQ-9
Wells Tannery, 175 .... WO-12
Wellsboro, 3263 .... EF-2
Wellsville, 242 .... EP-4
Welsh Run, ... WQ-13
Wendel, 150 .... WN-5
Wernersville, 750 .... EN-8
Wescosville, 2494 .... EN-13
Wescosville, 5872 .... EC-1
Wesley, 90 .... EL-2
Wesleyville, 3341 .... WC-4
W. Alexander, 604 .... WO-1
W. Auburn, 100 .... EF-8
W. Bangor, 300 .... EK-11
W. Brownsville, 992 .... WP-4
W. Cameron, 165 .... EL-5
W. Catasauqua, 700 .... EA-1
W. Chester, 18461 .... EP-10
W. Clifford, 50 .... EF-9
W. Conshohocken, 1320 .... ‡A-1
W. Decatur, 533 .... WJ-11
W. Elizabeth, 518 .... WN-4
W. Enola, 800 .... ES-2
W. Fairfield, 60 .... WN-6
W. Fairview, 1282 .... ES-1
W. Finley, 100 .... WP-2
W. Franklin, 40 .... ‡A-5
W. Freedom, 240 .... WI-5
W. Grove, 2854 .... EQ-9
W. Hazleton, 3609 .... EI-8

*, †, ‡, § ◊ See explanation under state title in this index.
County and parish names are listed in capital letters & boldface type.
Independent cities (not included in a county) are listed in italics.

Pennsylvania–Tennessee 259

W. Hickory, 300 ... WG-6
W. Homestead, 1929 ... ‡L-7
W. Kittanning, 1175 ... WK-6
W. Lancaster, 800 ... ES-8
W. Lawn, 1775 ... ET-11
W. Lebanon, 125 ... WL-7
W. Leechburg, 1294 ... WL-5
W. Leisenring, 600 ... WP-5
W. Liberty, 343 ... WJ-4
W. Liberty, 70 ... WJ-9
W. Mayfield, 1239 ... WK-2
W. Middlesex, 863 ... WI-2
W. Middletown, 139 ... WN-4
W. Mifflin, 20313 ... WN-4
W. Milton, 900 ... EJ-4
W. Monterey, 75 ... WJ-5
W. Nanticoke, 749 ... EI-8
W. Newton, 2633 ... WO-5
W. Pike, 20 ... WF-14
W. Pittsburg, 808 ... WJ-4
W. Pittston, 4868 ... EB-9
W. Reading, 4212 ... ET-12
W. Renovo ... WH-14
W. Salisbury, 85 ... WQ-8
W. Springfield, 300 ... WD-2
W. Sunbury, 192 ... WJ-4
W. View, 6771 ... WM-4
W. Warren, 50 ... EE-7
W. Willow, 300 ... EP-7
W. Winfield, 30 ... WK-5
W. Wyoming, 2725 ... EA-9
W. Wyomissing, 3407 ... ET-12
W. York, 4617 ... EP-5
Westfield, 1064 ... EE-1
Westford, 150 ... WG-2
Westgate Hills ... EA-4
Westland, 167 ... WN-2
Westline, 75 ... WF-9
Westminster, 100 ... EC-9
Westmont, 5181 ... WN-8
WESTMORELAND CO., 365169 ... WM-6
Weston, 321 ... EF-8
Westover, 390 ... WK-10
Westport, 80 ... WH-13
Westtown, 500 ... EP-10
Westville, 40 ... WI-9
Westwood, 1000 ... WS-1
Wetmore ... WF-9
Wexford, 1100 ... WL-3
Wharton, 25 ... WG-12
Wheatland, 632 ... WI-2
Wheelerville ... EG-5
Whiskerville, 110 ... WJ-4
Whitaker, 1271 ... ‡L-7
White, 400 ... WO-6
White, 40 ... WM-6
White Deer, 500 ... EJ-4
White Hall ... EI-5
White Haven, 1097 ... EJ-9
White Hill, 580 ... ET-2
White Horse, 130 ... EP-8
White House, 80 ... WQ-4
White Mills, 659 ... EG-12
White Oak, 7862 ... WN-5
White Sprs., 550 ... EK-3
Whitehall, 13944 ... WN-4
Whites Valley, 60 ... EF-11
Whitesburg, 90 ... WK-6
Whitney, 400 ... WN-6
Whitsett, 200 ... WO-5
Wiconisco, 921 ... EM-5
Widnoon, 90 ... WK-6
Wiegletown, 100 ... WJ-3
Wila, 75 ... EM-8
Wilawana, 50 ... ED-5
Wilbur, 140 ... WO-8
Wilcox, 383 ... WG-10
Wildwood, 600 ... ‡H-6
Wilkes-Barre, 41498 ... EI-9
Wilkinsburg, 15930 ... WM-4
Willet, 30 ... WL-7
William Penn Manor, 350 ... EA-5
Williamsburg, 1254 ... WM-12
Williamson, 200 ... WQ-13
Williamsport, 29381 ... EI-4
Williamstown, 1387 ... EM-5
Willow Grv., 15726 ... EO-12
Willow Hill, 100 ... WO-13
Willow Street, 7578 ... EP-7
Willowdale ... EQ-9
Wilmerding, 2190 ... ‡L-9
Wilmore, 225 ... WN-9
Wilpen, 320 ... WN-7
Wilson, 7896 ... EL-11
Wimmers, 250 ... EH-10
Winburne, 550 ... WJ-12
Wind Gap, 2720 ... EK-11
Wind Ridge, 215 ... WP-2
Windber, 4138 ... WO-9
Windfall, 90 ... EF-5
Windham Ctr. ... ED-7
Winding Hill, 370 ... ET-1
Windsor, 1319 ... EP-6
Windsor Castle, 100 ... EM-8
Windsor Farms, 500 ... EP-3
Windsor Pk., 1100 ... ET-1
Windward Hts., 800 ... WJ-4
Winfield, 900 ... EK-4
Wingate, 100 ... WJ-13
Winterdale, 250 ... ED-11
Winterstown, 632 ... EQ-5
Wireton, 600 ... ‡H-2
Wissinoming ... ‡C-6
Wittenberg, 15 ... WQ-8
Wolfdale, 2888 ... WO-2
Wolfsburg, 220 ... WP-10
Womelsdorf, 2810 ... EN-7
Wood, 265 ... WO-12
Woodbine, 50 ... EQ-6
Woodbury, 284 ... WO-11
Woodcock, 157 ... WF-4
Woodland, 400 ... WI-11
Woodland Hts., 1261 ... WH-5
Woodland Pk., 950 ... EH-9
Woodlawn, 1850 ... EL-10
Woodlyn, 9485 ... EQ-11
Woodrow ... WN-2
Woodside, 2425 ... ‡S-11
Woodward, 110 ... EK-2
Woodycrest, 500 ... WS-5
Woolrich, 800 ... EI-2
Worleytown ... WQ-14
Wormleysburg, 3070 ... EN-4
Worthington, 639 ... WK-5
Worthville, 67 ... WJ-8
Wrights ... WF-12
Wrights Corners ... WE-10
Wrightsdale, 25 ... EQ-8
Wrightstown, 400 ... EN-13
Wrightsville, 2310 ... EP-6
Wrightsville, 70 ... WE-6
Wurtemburg, 400 ... WK-3
Wyalusing, 596 ... EF-7
Wyano, 484 ... WO-5
Wycombe, 600 ... EN-13
Wydnor, 630 ... EC-4
Wylie, 100 ... ‡N-7
Wyncote, 3044 ... ‡B-4
Wyndmoor, 5498 ... ‡B-4
Wynnewood, 7800 ... ‡D-2
Wyoming, 3073 ... EB-9
WYOMING CO., 28276 ... EG-7
Wyomissing, 10461 ... EN-8
Wysox, 400 ... EF-6
Yardley, 2434 ... EN-13
Yarnell ... WJ-13
Yatesboro, 450 ... WK-7
Yatesville, 607 ... EB-9
Yeadon, 11762 ... ‡E-3
Yeagertown, 1050 ... EL-1
Yellow Creek, 60 ... WO-11
Yellow House, 200 ... EN-9
Yocumtown, 200 ... EO-5
Yoe, 1018 ... EP-5
York, 43718 ... EP-5
YORK CO., 434972 ... EP-4
York Haven, 709 ... EO-5
York Sprs., 833 ... EP-3
Yorkana, 229 ... EP-6
Yorkshire, 1700 ... WS-14
Yostville ... EH-10
Youngstown, 326 ... WN-6
Youngsville, 1729 ... WE-7
Youngwood, 3050 ... WN-6
Yukon, 677 ... WO-5
Zelienople, 3812 ... WK-3
Zieglersville, 900 ... EN-11
Zion, 2030 ... WK-14
Zion Grv., 200 ... EK-7
Zionhill, 100 ... EM-11
Zions View, 250 ... EP-5
Zionsville, 300 ... EM-10
Zooks Corner, 700 ... ES-9
Zora ... EQ-2
Zullinger, 250 ... EQ-1

Rhode Island

Page locator
Map keys Atlas pages
A–N 184–185

Abbott Run Valley, 1800 ... B-7
Adamsville, 600 ... G-9
Albion, 170 ... B-6
Allenton, 650 ... G-6
Alton, 400 ... I-3
Anthony, 3400 ... E-5
Arcadia, 120 ... G-4
Arkwright, 220 ... E-5
Arnold Mills, 640 ... B-7
Ashaway, 1485 ... I-3
Ashton, 910 ... B-6
Austin, 150 ... G-4
Avondale, 230 ... J-2
Barrington, 16300 ... E-7
Berkeley, 910 ... B-6
Bonnet Shores, 1500 ... H-6
Bradford, 1406 ... I-3
Bridgetown, 2200 ... H-6
Bristol, 22400 ... E-8
BRISTOL CO., 49875 ... E-7
Bristol Ferry, 180 ... F-8
Burdickville, 500 ... I-3
Canonchet, 210 ... I-3
Carolina, 970 ... H-4
Centerville, 80 ... E-3
Central Falls, 19376 ... C-7
Charlestown, 2000 ... I-4
Chepachet, 1675 ... C-4
Clayville, 300 ... D-4
Common Fence Pt., 900 ... F-8
Coventry, 8600 ... E-4
Cranston, 80387 ... D-6
Cumberland Hill, 7934 ... B-6
Davisville, 550 ... F-6
Diamond Hill, 910 ... B-6
Dunns Cors., 170 ... I-3
E. Greenwich, 11800 ... F-6
E. Providence, 47037 ... D-7
Escoheag, 120 ... F-3
Esmond, 5000 ... C-6
Exeter, 310 ... G-5
Forestdale, 550 ... B-5
Foster Ctr., 355 ... D-3
Galilee, 560 ... I-5
Glendale, 860 ... B-4
Grants Mills ... A-6
Green Hill, 300 ... I-5
Greene, 888 ... E-3
Greenville, 8658 ... C-5
Hamilton, 270 ... G-6
Harmony, 985 ... C-5
Harris, 1250 ... E-5
Harrisville, 1605 ... B-4
Haversham, 170 ... I-3
Hope, 350 ... E-5
Hope Valley, 1612 ... H-4
Hopkins Hollow ... E-3
Hopkinton, 590 ... H-3
Indian L. Shores, 250 ... H-6
Island Pk., 1550 ... F-8
Jackson, 200 ... E-5
Jamestown, 5000 ... H-7
Jerusalem, 100 ... I-5
Johnston ... D-6
KENT CO., 166158 ... F-4
Kenyon, 550 ... H-4
Kingston, 6974 ... H-5
La Fayette, 760 ... G-6
Lime Rock, 300 ... B-6
Little Compton, 550 ... H-9
Lonsdale, 4200 ... C-6
Manville, 3200 ... B-6
Mapleville, 1600 ... B-4
Matunuck, 580 ... I-5
Melville, 1320 ... G-8
Middletown, 3800 ... G-7
Misquamicut, 390 ... J-3
Mohegan, 310 ... I-4
Moosup Valley, 220 ... E-3
Moscow, 30 ... G-3
Mt. View, 700 ... F-6
Narragansett Pier, 3409 ... I-6
Nasonville, 430 ... B-4
New Shoreham, 830 ... L-5
Newport, 24672 ... H-7
NEWPORT CO., 82888 ... G-8
Nooseneck ... F-4
N. Foster ... D-3
N. Kingstown, 3000 ... G-6
N. Providence, 32000 ... C-6
N. Quidnessett, 330 ... F-6
N. Scituate, 410 ... D-5
N. Tiverton ... F-8
Oakland, 600 ... B-4
Pascoag, 4577 ... B-4
Pawtucket, 71148 ... C-7
Peace Dale, 3400 ... H-5
Perryville, 50 ... I-5
Pettaquamscutt Lake Shores, 750 ... H-6
Plum Pt., 380 ... G-6
Point Judith, 430 ... I-6
Portsmouth, 4200 ... F-8
Potter Hill, 300 ... I-3
Primrose, 530 ... B-5
Providence, 178042 ... D-6
PROVIDENCE CO., 626667 ... C-4
Prudence Pk. ... F-7
Quidnessett, 2000 ... F-6
Quidnick, 2700 ... E-5
Quinnville, 370 ... B-6
Quonochontaug, 333 ... J-4
Rockville, 320 ... G-3
Sakonnet, 200 ... H-8
Saunderstown, 430 ... H-6
Saundersville, 170 ... D-5
Saylesville, 3800 ... C-6
Shannock, 1100 ... H-4
Shelter Hbr., 120 ... J-3
Shores Acres, 490 ... G-6
Slatersville, 2400 ... A-5
Slocum, 110 ... G-5
Snug Hbr., 600 ... I-5
S. Foster, 130 ... D-4
S. Hopkinton, 500 ... I-3
Spragueville ... C-5
Summit, 100 ... E-4
Tarkiln, 370 ... B-5
The Hummocks, 220 ... F-8
Tiverton, 7557 ... F-8
Tiverton Four Corners, 160 ... G-8
Union Vil., 2300 ... B-5
Usquepaug, 530 ... H-4
Valley Falls, 11547 ... C-7
Wakefield, 300 ... I-6
Warren, 10600 ... E-8
Warwick, 82672 ... E-6
WASHINGTON CO., 126979 ... H-4
Watch Hill, 154 ... J-2
Waterman Four Corners, 120 ... D-5
Weekapaug, 425 ... J-3
W. Glocester, 200 ... C-3
W. Greenville ... C-5
W. Greenwich ... F-4
W. Greenwich Ctr. ... F-3
W. Kingston, 1400 ... H-5
W. Warwick, 29100 ... E-5
Westerly, 17936 ... J-2
White Rock, 410 ... J-2
Wickford Jct., 100 ... G-6
Wood River Jct., 270 ... I-4
Woodville, 60 ... H-4
Woonsocket, 41186 ... A-5
Wyoming, 270 ... H-4

South Carolina

Page locator
Map keys Atlas pages
A–J 186–187
* City keyed to p. 59

Abbeville, 5237 ... D-4
ABBEVILLE CO., 25417 ... D-4
Adams Run, 600 ... H-9
Aiken, 29524 ... F-6
AIKEN CO., 160099 ... F-6
Alcolu, 429 ... E-9
Allendale, 3482 ... G-7
ALLENDALE CO., 10419 ... H-6
Anderson, 26686 ... C-3
ANDERSON CO., 187126 ... C-3
Andrews, 2861 ... F-11
Antreville, 140 ... D-4
Arcadia, 2634 ... I-4
Arcadia Lakes, 861 ... F-3
Arial, 2543 ... B-3
Arkwright ... J-5
Arthurtown, 1450 ... H-3
Atlantic Bch., 334 ... E-13
Awendaw, 1294 ... G-11
Aynor, 560 ... D-12
Ballentine, 730 ... D-7
Bamberg, 3607 ... G-7
BAMBERG CO., 15987 ... G-7
Barnwell, 4750 ... G-7
BARNWELL CO., 22621 ... G-6
Batesburg-Leesville, 5362 ... E-6
Beaufort, 12361 ... I-8
BEAUFORT CO., 162233 ... I-8
Beckhamville, 360 ... C-8
Beech Island, 1500 ... F-5
Belle Meade, 1900 ... J-2
Belmont, 2400 ... F-3
Belton, 4134 ... C-4
Belvedere, 5792 ... *A-13
Ben Avon, 1700 ... J-6
Bennettsville, 9069 ... C-11
Berea, 14295 ... H-1
BERKELEY CO., 177843 ... G-10
Bethune, 334 ... C-9
Beverly Hills, 1500 ... G-10
Bishopville, 3471 ... D-9
Blacksburg, 1848 ... A-6
Blackstock, 200 ... C-7
Blackville, 2406 ... F-7
Blenheim, 154 ... C-11
Blue Brick, 100 ... B-6
Bluffton, 12530 ... J-8
Blythewood, 2034 ... D-8
Boiling Sprs., 8219 ... A-5
Bonneau, 487 ... G-10
Bonneau Bch., 1929 ... F-10
Bowling Green, 500 ... A-7
Bowman, 968 ... F-8
Bradley, 170 ... D-4
Bradleyville ... *B-13
Branchville, 1024 ... G-8
Briarcliffe Acres, 457 ... E-13
Brittons Neck, 600 ... E-12
Brunson, 554 ... H-7
Bucksport, 876 ... E-12
Buffalo, 1266 ... B-6
Burnettown, 2673 ... F-5
Burton, 6976 ... I-8
Cades, 300 ... E-10
CALHOUN CO., 15175 ... E-8
Calhoun Falls, 2004 ... D-4
Camden, 6838 ... D-8
Cameron, 424 ... F-8
Campobello, 502 ... A-5
Canadys, 200 ... G-8
Capitol View, 4000 ... E-8
Carlisle, 436 ... C-6
Cartersville, 110 ... D-10
Catawba, 1343 ... B-8
Cayce, 12528 ... G-2
Centenary, 500 ... D-12
Centerville, 6586 ... C-3
Centerville, 4400 ... H-10
Central, 5159 ... B-3
Chaparral Ranches, 5000 ... G-10
Chapin, 1445 ... D-7
Charleston, 120083 ... H-10
CHARLESTON CO., 350209 ... H-10
Chartwell, 500 ... F-1
Cheraw, 5851 ... B-10
CHEROKEE CO., 55342 ... B-6
Cherokee Forest, 2100 ... I-3
Cherokee Sprs., 110 ... A-5
Chesnee, 868 ... A-5
Chester, 5607 ... B-7
CHESTER CO., 33140 ... C-7
Chesterfield, 1472 ... B-10
CHESTERFIELD CO., 46734 ... C-9
Chestnut Hills, 1400 ... J-1
City View, 1345 ... I-1
CLARENDON CO., 34971 ... F-9
Clarks Hill, 381 ... E-5
Clearwater, 4370 ... *B-14
Clemson, 13905 ... B-3
Cleveland, 220 ... A-4
Clinton, 8490 ... C-5
Clio, 726 ... C-11
Clover, 5094 ... A-7
Cokesbury, 215 ... D-5
COLLETON CO., 38892 ... H-8
Columbia, 129272 ... D-7
Converse, 608 ... B-5
Conway, 17103 ... E-12
Coosawhatchie, 300 ... I-8
Cope, 77 ... F-7
Cordova, 169 ... F-8
Coronaca, 191 ... D-5
Cottageville, 762 ... H-9
Couchton, 500 ... F-6
Coward, 752 ... E-11
Cowpens, 2162 ... A-6
Crane Forest, 700 ... E-2
Cross, 300 ... F-10
Cross Anchor, 126 ... C-5
Cross Hill, 507 ... D-5
Dale, 150 ... I-8
Dalzell, 3059 ... D-9
Darlington, 6289 ... D-10
DARLINGTON CO., 68681 ... C-10
Davis Sta., 150 ... F-9
Denmark, 3538 ... F-7
Denny Ter., 1750 ... F-2
Dentsville, 14062 ... F-3
Dillon, 6788 ... C-11
DILLON CO., 32062 ... C-12
Donalds, 348 ... C-4
Dorchester, 450 ... G-9
DORCHESTER CO., 136555 ... G-9
Dovesville, 200 ... C-10
Drayton, 1400 ... I-5
Drayton, 700 ... A-11
Due West, 1247 ... C-4
Duncan, 3181 ... B-5
Duncan, 361 ... I-6
Early Branch, 150 ... H-8
Easley, 19993 ... B-4
E. Gaffney, 3085 ... A-6
Eastmont, 500 ... H-4
Eastover, 813 ... E-8
Edgefield, 4750 ... E-5
EDGEFIELD CO., 26985 ... E-5
Edgemoor, 350 ... B-7
Edisto Bch., 414 ... I-9
Effingham, 230 ... D-11
Ehrhardt, 545 ... G-7
Elgin, 2607 ... B-8
Elgin, 1311 ... D-8
Elko, 193 ... F-7
Elliott, 650 ... D-10
Elloree, 692 ... F-9
Enoree, 665 ... C-5
Estill, 2040 ... H-7
Eutawville, 315 ... F-9
Evergreen, 120 ... D-11
Fair Play, 687 ... C-3
Fairfax, 2025 ... H-7
FAIRFIELD CO., 23956 ... C-7
Fairforest, 1693 ... J-4
Fairmont, 250 ... I-5
Filbert, 300 ... A-7
Fingerville, 134 ... A-5
Florence, 37056 ... D-10
FLORENCE CO., 136885 ... D-10
Floydale, 250 ... C-11
Folly Bch., 2617 ... H-10
Folly Field ... J-11
Forest Acres, 10361 ... G-3
Forest Bch. ... J-10
Forestbrook, 4612 ... I-12
Fork, 280 ... C-11
Fork Shoals, 180 ... C-4
Ft. Lawn, 895 ... B-8
Ft. Mill, 10811 ... B-8
Ft. Motte, 150 ... E-8
Fountain Inn, 7799 ... B-5
Frogmore, 300 ... I-9
Furman, 239 ... H-7
Gable, 200 ... E-10
Gadsden, 1632 ... E-8
Gaffney, 12414 ... A-6
Galivants Ferry, 180 ... D-12
Gantt, 14229 ... J-1
Garden City Bch. ... F-12
Garnett, 110 ... I-7
Gaston, 1645 ... E-7
Georgetown, 9163 ... F-12
GEORGETOWN CO., 60158 ... F-11
Gifford, 288 ... H-7
Gilbert, 565 ... E-6
Gillisonville, 200 ... I-7
Givhans, 200 ... G-9
Glendale, 307 ... B-5
Glenn Sprs., 110 ... B-5
Golden Grv., 2467 ... B-4
Goose Creek, 35938 ... G-10
Goretown, 110 ... D-13
Grace, 300 ... B-8
Grahamville, 250 ... I-8
Graniteville, 2614 ... F-5
Graves, 200 ... F-11
Gray Court, 795 ... C-5
Great Falls, 1979 ... C-8
Greeleyville, 438 ... F-10
Green Pond, 200 ... H-8
Green Sea, 200 ... D-12
Greenville, 58409 ... B-4
GREENVILLE CO., 451225 ... C-4
Greenwood, 23222 ... D-5
GREENWOOD CO., 69661 ... D-5
Greer, 25515 ... B-4
Gresham, 200 ... E-11
Grover, 180 ... G-8
Hamer, 500 ... C-12
Hampton, 2808 ... H-7
HAMPTON CO., 21090 ... H-7
Hampton Hts., 1600 ... I-2
Hanahan, 17997 ... H-10
Harbour Town ... J-9
Hardeeville, 2952 ... J-7
Harleyville, 677 ... G-9
Harris, 350 ... D-5
Hartsville, 7764 ... C-10
Haskell Hts., 1000 ... E-2
Hazelwood Acres, 1000 ... G-4
Heath Sprs., 790 ... C-8
Helena, 300 ... D-6
Hemingway, 459 ... E-11
Hendersonville, 240 ... H-8
Hickory Grv., 440 ... B-6
Hickory Grv., 250 ... E-12
Hilda, 447 ... G-7
Hilton Head Island, 37099 ... J-8
Hodges, 155 ... D-4
Holly Hill, 1277 ... F-9
Hollywood, 4714 ... H-9
Hollywood Hills, 950 ... F-2
Homeland Pk., 6296 ... C-3
Homewood, 300 ... E-12
Honea Path, 3597 ... C-4
Honey Hill, 110 ... G-11
Hopkins, 2882 ... E-8
Horatio, 300 ... D-9
HORRY CO., 269291 ... D-13
Inman, 2321 ... A-5
Inman Mills, 1050 ... A-5
Irmo, 11097 ... D-7
Isle of Palms, 4133 ... H-10
Iva, 1218 ... D-3
Jackson, 1700 ... F-6
Jacksonboro, 478 ... H-9
JASPER CO., 24777 ... I-7
Jedburg, 200 ... G-9
Jefferson, 753 ... C-9
Jenkinsville, 46 ... D-7
Joanna, 1539 ... C-5
Johnsonville, 1480 ... E-11
Johnston, 2362 ... E-5
Jonesville, 911 ... B-6
Judson, 2050 ... J-1
Kellytown, 200 ... C-10
Kelton, 150 ... B-6
Kensington, 600 ... F-12
Kershaw, 1803 ... C-8
KERSHAW CO., 61697 ... C-8
Kiawah Island, 1626 ... I-10
Kinards, 250 ... C-6
Kings Creek, 200 ... A-6
Kingstree, 3328 ... E-10
Kingswood, 2100 ... F-1
Kline, 197 ... G-7
La France, 900 ... C-3
Ladson, 13790 ... G-10
Lake City, 6675 ... E-11
L. Forest, 1000 ... I-3
L. View, 807 ... C-12
L. Wylie, 8841 ... A-7
Lamar, 989 ... D-10
Lancaster, 8526 ... B-8
LANCASTER CO., 76652 ... C-5
Lando, 300 ... B-7
Landrum, 2376 ... A-5
Lane, 508 ... F-10
Latta, 1379 ... C-11
Laurel Bay, 5891 ... I-8
Laurens, 9139 ... C-5
LAURENS CO., 66537 ... B-8
LEE CO., 19220 ... D-9
Leesville, 3112 ... B-8
Lexington, 17870 ... E-7
LEXINGTON CO., 262391 ... E-7
Liberty, 3269 ... B-3
Liberty Hill, 160 ... C-8
Lincoln Shire, 1400 ... E-2
Litchfield Bch., 500 ... F-12
Little Mtn., 291 ... D-6
Little River, 8960 ... E-13
Little Rock, 500 ... C-11
Livingston, 136 ... F-7
Lobeco, 400 ... I-8
Lodge, 120 ... G-8
Lone Star, 200 ... F-8
Long Bay Estates, 200 ... J-14
Longcreek, 200 ... B-2
Longs, 300 ... E-13
Loris, 2396 ... D-13
Lowndesville, 128 ... D-3
Lowrys, 200 ... B-7
Lugoff, 7434 ... D-8
Luray, 127 ... H-7
Lydia, 642 ... D-10
Lyman, 3243 ... B-5
Lynchburg, 373 ... D-10
Manning, 4108 ... E-9
Marietta, 1200 ... A-4
Marion, 6939 ... D-11
MARION CO., 33062 ... D-11
MARLBORO CO., 28933 ... C-11
Mauldin, 22889 ... B-4
Mayesville, 731 ... D-9
Mayo, 1592 ... A-5
McBee, 867 ... C-9
McClellanville, 499 ... G-11
McColl, 2174 ... B-11
McConnells, 255 ... B-7
McCormick, 2783 ... E-4
MCCORMICK CO., 10233 ... E-4
Meadowlake, 2700 ... F-3
Meggett, 1226 ... H-9
Miley, 120 ... H-7
Modoc, 218 ... E-4
Monarch Mill, 1811 ... B-6
Moncks Cor., 7885 ... G-10
Monetta, 236 ... E-6
Montmorenci, 900 ... F-6
Moore, 200 ... B-5
Morningside, 750 ... I-2
Morris Acres, 450 ... H-10
Mt. Carmel, 216 ... D-4
Mt. Croghan, 195 ... B-9
Mt. Pleasant, 67843 ... C-13
Mountville, 108 ... C-5
Mullins, 4663 ... D-12
Murrells Inlet, 7547 ... F-12
Myrtle Bch., 27109 ... E-13
Neeses, 374 ... F-7
New Ellenton, 2052 ... F-6
New Holland Crossroads, 200 ... E-6
New Zion, 140 ... E-10
Newberry, 10277 ... D-6
NEWBERRY CO., 37508 ... D-5
Newport, 4136 ... B-7
Newry, 172 ... B-3
Nichols, 368 ... D-12
Ninety Six, 1998 ... D-5
Nixons Crossroads, 250 ... E-13
Norris, 813 ... B-3
North, 754 ... F-7
N. Augusta, 21348 ... *B-13
N. Charleston, 97471 ... A-12
N. Hartsville, 3251 ... C-10
N. Myrtle Bch., 13752 ... E-13
N. Santee, 300 ... G-11
Norway, 337 ... F-7
Oak Grv., 150 ... C-11
Oakway, 200 ... C-3
Oatland, 150 ... F-12
OCONEE CO., 74273 ... B-2
Olanta, 563 ... E-10
Olar, 257 ... G-7
Olympia, 1200 ... G-2
Orangeburg, 13964 ... F-8
ORANGEBURG CO., 92501 ... F-8
Osborn, 150 ... H-9
Pacolet, 2235 ... B-6
Pageland, 2760 ... B-9
Pamplico, 1226 ... D-11
Paramount Pk., 700 ... J-2
Paris, 1950 ... I-2
Park Pl., 1500 ... I-2
Parksville, 117 ... E-4
Patrick, 351 ... C-10
Pawleys Island, 103 ... F-12
Paxville, 185 ... E-9
Pee Dee, 250 ... D-11
Pelham, 500 ... B-5
Pelion, 674 ... E-7
Pendleton, 2964 ... C-3
Perry, 233 ... F-7
Pickens, 3126 ... B-3
PICKENS CO., 119224 ... B-3
Pierpont, 2700 ... A-11
Pine Island, 30 ... I-13
Pine Ridge, 400 ... C-10
Pine Valley, 1400 ... F-1
Pineland, 200 ... I-7
Pineville, 500 ... F-10
Pinewood, 538 ... E-9
Pinopolis, 948 ... G-10
Plantersville, 150 ... F-12
Pleasant Valley, 1200 ... J-2
Pomaria, 179 ... D-6
Pontiac, 250 ... D-8
Port Royal, 10678 ... I-8
Port Royal Plantation ... J-12
Poston, 150 ... E-11
Pritchardville, 150 ... J-8
Prosperity, 1180 ... D-6
Quail Hollow, 600 ... G-3
Quinby, 932 ... D-11
Rains, 500 ... D-12
Ravenel, 2465 ... H-9
Red Bank, 9617 ... E-7
Reevesville, 196 ... G-8
Reidville, 601 ... B-5
Rembert, 306 ... D-9
Richburg, 275 ... B-7
RICHLAND CO., 384504 ... E-8
Ridge Spr., 737 ... E-6
Ridgeland, 4036 ... I-7
Ridgeville, 1979 ... G-9
Ridgeway, 319 ... D-8
Ridgewood, 1600 ... F-2
Rimini, 200 ... E-9
Riverside, 2350 ... I-1
Robertville, 120 ... I-7
Rock Hill, 66154 ... B-7
Rockville, 134 ... I-9
Roebuck, 2200 ... B-5
Rowesville, 304 ... F-8
Ruby, 360 ... B-9
Ruffin, 300 ... G-8
Russellville, 488 ... F-10
St. Andrews ... B-12
St. George, 2084 ... G-9
St. Matthews, 2021 ... E-8
St. Stephen, 1697 ... F-10
Salem, 135 ... B-3
Salley, 398 ... F-7
Salters, 270 ... F-10
Saluda, 3565 ... D-6
SALUDA CO., 19875 ... D-6
Sampit, 150 ... F-11
Sandwood, 2400 ... F-3
Sandy Sprs., 1200 ... C-3
Sans Souci, 7869 ... I-1
Santee, 961 ... F-9
Santee Circle, 350 ... G-10
Sardinia, 250 ... E-10
Saxon, 3424 ... I-4
Schultz Hill ... *B-13
Scotia, 215 ... H-7
Scranton, 932 ... E-11
Sea Pines ... J-10
Seabrook Island, 1714 ... I-10
Sellers, 219 ... D-11
Seneca, 8102 ... B-3
Shannontown, 1500 ... E-9
Sharon, 494 ... B-7
Sheldon, 200 ... I-8
Shiloh, 214 ... E-10
Shulerville, 350 ... G-11
Silverstreet, 162 ... D-6
Simpson, 150 ... E-7
Simpsonville, 18238 ... B-4
Six Mile, 675 ... B-3
Smoaks, 126 ... G-8
Snelling, 274 ... G-6
Socastee, 19952 ... E-12
Society Hill, 563 ... C-10
S. Congaree, 2306 ... E-7
S. For. Estates, 1000 ... J-2
Spartanburg, 37013 ... B-5
SPARTANBURG CO., 284307 ... B-5
Spring Mills, 1400 ... C-8
Springdale, 2636 ... E-7
Springfield, 524 ... F-7
Stark Ter., 370 ... F-2
Starmount, 600 ... H-2
Starr, 173 ... C-3
State Pk., 50 ... E-3
Stateburg, 1380 ... E-9
Stoney Hill, 150 ... D-6
Stuckey, 245 ... E-11
Sullivans Island, 1791 ... H-10
Summer Hill ... *B-13
Summerton, 1000 ... F-9
Summerville, 43392 ... G-10
Summit, 402 ... E-6
Sumter, 40524 ... E-9
SUMTER CO., 107456 ... E-9
Surfside Bch., 3837 ... F-12
Swansea, 827 ... E-7
Sycamore, 180 ... G-7
Tamassee, 200 ... B-3
Tarboro, 180 ... I-7
Taylors, 21617 ... B-4
Tega Cay, 7620 ... A-7
Tigerville, 1312 ... A-4
Tillman, 300 ... I-7
Timmonsville, 2320 ... D-10
Tirzah, 2150 ... B-7
Townville, 500 ... C-3
Travelers Rest, 4576 ... B-4
Trenton, 196 ... E-5
Trio, 250 ... F-10
Troy, 93 ... D-4
Turbeville, 766 ... E-10
Ulmer, 88 ... G-7
Union, 8393 ... B-6
UNION CO., 28961 ... B-6
Utica, 1489 ... B-3
Valley Falls, 6299 ... A-4
Van Wyck, 350 ... B-8
Vance, 170 ... F-9
Varnville, 2162 ... H-7
Vaucluse, 500 ... F-5
Wade Hampton, 20461 ... H-3
Wadmalaw Island, 300 ... H-9
Wagener, 797 ... E-7
Walhalla, 4263 ... B-2
Wallace, 892 ... B-10
Walterboro, 5398 ... H-8
Wampee, 200 ... E-13
Ward, 91 ... E-6
Ware Shoals, 2170 ... C-4
Warrenville, 1233 ... F-5
Waterloo, 166 ... C-5
Watts Mills, 1635 ... C-5
Wedgefield, 1615 ... E-9
Wellford, 2378 ... B-5
W. Columbia, 14988 ... G-2
W. Gantt, 3050 ... J-2
W. Pelzer, 880 ... C-4
W. Springs, 160 ... B-6
W. Union, 291 ... B-2
Westminster, 2418 ... B-2
Westview, 2000 ... J-4
Westville, 2200 ... C-8
White Rock, 440 ... D-7
White Stone, 200 ... B-6
Whitehall ... D-7
Whitmire, 1441 ... C-6
Whitney, 1500 ... I-5
Williams, 117 ... G-8
WILLIAMSBURG CO., 34423 ... F-11
Williamston, 3934 ... C-4
Willington, 142 ... E-4
Williston, 3139 ... F-6
Windsor, 121 ... F-6
Windsor Estates, 2200 ... E-4
Winnsboro, 3550 ... C-7
Winnsboro Mills, 1898 ... C-7
Woodford, 185 ... E-7
Woodland Hills, 2700 ... I-2
Woodruff, 4090 ... B-5
Woodside, 180 ... I-1
Woodville, 160 ... C-4
Yemassee, 1027 ... H-8
York, 7736 ... B-7
YORK CO., 226073 ... B-7

South Dakota

Page locator
Map keys Atlas pages
A–J 188–189

Aberdeen, 26091 ... B-10
Academy, 10 ... F-9
Agar, 76 ... C-8
Akaska, 42 ... B-8
Albee, 16 ... C-13
Alcester, 807 ... G-13
Alexandria, 615 ... F-11
Allen, 420 ... G-5
Alpena, 286 ... E-10
Altamont, 34 ... C-13
Amherst, 70 ... A-11
Andover, 91 ... B-11
Antelope, 826 ... G-7
Ardmore ... E-2
Arlington, 915 ... D-12
Armour, 699 ... F-10
Artas, 9 ... A-8
Artesian, 138 ... E-11
Ashton, 122 ... C-10
Astoria, 139 ... D-13
Athol, 50 ... C-10
Aurora, 532 ... D-13
Aurora Ctr., 12 ... F-10
AURORA CO., 2710 ... E-10
Avon, 590 ... G-11
Badger, 107 ... D-12
Baltic, 1089 ... E-13
Bancroft, 19 ... D-11
Barnard, 60 ... A-10
Batesland, 108 ... G-4
Bath, 172 ... B-10
BEADLE CO., 17398 ... D-10
Belle Fourche, 5594 ... D-2
Belvidere, 49 ... E-6
Bemis, 40 ... C-12
BENNETT CO., 3431 ... G-5
Beresford, 2005 ... G-13
Bethlehem, 10 ... H-3
Big Sprs., 10 ... G-13
Big Stone City, 467 ... B-13
Bijou Hills, 6 ... F-9
Bison, 333 ... B-4
Blackhawk, 2892 ... E-3
Blunt, 354 ... D-8
BON HOMME CO., 7070 ... G-11
Bonesteel, 275 ... G-9
Bonilla, 30 ... D-10
Bowdle, 502 ... B-8
Box Elder, 7800 ... E-3
Bradley, 72 ... C-11
Brandon, 8785 ... F-13
Brandt, 107 ... D-13
Brentford, 77 ... C-10
Bridger, 50 ... D-5
Bridgewater, 492 ... F-11
Bristol, 341 ... B-11
Britton, 1241 ... A-11
Broadland, 31 ... D-10
Brookings, 22056 ... D-12
BROOKINGS CO., 31965 ... D-12
BROWN CO., 36531 ... B-10
Bruce, 204 ... D-12
BRULE CO., 5255 ... F-9
Bryant, 456 ... D-11
Buffalo, 330 ... B-3
BUFFALO CO., 1912 ... E-9
Buffalo Gap, 126 ... F-3
Bullhead, 348 ... A-6
Burbank, 90 ... H-13
Burke, 604 ... G-9
Bushnell, 65 ... D-13
Butler, 17 ... B-11
BUTTE CO., 10110 ... C-3
Camp Crook, 63 ... B-2
CAMPBELL CO., 1466 ... B-8
Canistota, 656 ... F-12
Canova, 105 ... E-11
Canton, 3057 ... F-13
Caputa, 40 ... E-3
Carpenter, 30 ... D-11
Carter, 10 ... F-7
Carthage, 144 ... E-11
Castle Rock ... C-3
Castlewood, 627 ... C-12
Cavour, 114 ... D-11
Cedar Butte ... F-6
Center Pt., 20 ... G-12
Centerville, 882 ... G-12
Central City, 134 ... D-2
Chamberlain, 2387 ... E-9
Chancellor, 264 ... F-12
CHARLES MIX CO., 9129 ... G-10
Chelsea, 27 ... C-10
Cherry Creek, 300 ... D-5
Chester, 261 ... E-12
Cheyenne Crossing ... E-2
Claire City, 76 ... A-12
Claremont, 127 ... B-11
Clark, 1139 ... C-11
CLARK CO., 3691 ... C-11
CLAY CO., 13864 ... G-12
Clayton ... F-11
Clear Lake, 1273 ... C-13
Clearfield, 10 ... G-8
CODINGTON CO., 27227 ... C-12
Colman, 594 ... E-12
Colome, 296 ... G-8
Colton, 687 ... E-12
Columbia, 136 ... B-10
Conde, 140 ... C-10
Corn Creek, 105 ... F-6
Corona, 109 ... B-12
Corsica, 592 ... F-10
Corson, 70 ... F-13
CORSON CO., 4050 ... B-6
Cottonwood, 9 ... E-5
Crandall ... C-11
Creighton, 10 ... E-4
Cresbard, 104 ... C-9
Crocker, 19 ... C-11
Crooks, 1269 ... F-12
Custer, 2067 ... E-2
CUSTER CO., 8216 ... F-2
Dallas, 120 ... G-8
Dante, 84 ... G-10
Davis, 85 ... F-12
DAVISON CO., 19504 ... F-10
DAY CO., 5710 ... C-11
De Smet, 1089 ... D-11
Deadwood, 1270 ... D-2
Dell Rapids, 3633 ... E-13
Delmont, 234 ... G-10
Dempster, 70 ... D-12
DEUEL CO., 4364 ... C-13
DEWEY CO., 5301 ... C-6
Dimock, 125 ... F-11
Doland, 180 ... C-10
Dolton, 37 ... F-12
DOUGLAS CO., 3002 ... F-10
Draper, 82 ... E-7
Dupree, 525 ... C-5
Eagle Butte, 1318 ... C-6
Eden, 89 ... B-11
Edgemont, 774 ... F-2
EDMUNDS CO., 4071 ... B-8
Egan, 278 ... E-13
Elk Pt., 1963 ... H-13
Elkton, 736 ... D-13
Ellis, 90 ... F-12
Elm Sprs., 20 ... D-4
Emery, 447 ... F-11
Enning, 30 ... D-4
Epiphany, 50 ... E-11
Erwin, 45 ... D-11
Esmond ... D-11
Estelline, 768 ... D-12
Ethan, 331 ... F-11
Eureka, 868 ... A-8
Fairburn, 85 ... F-3
Fairfax, 115 ... G-9
Fairpoint ... C-4
Fairview, 60 ... G-13
Faith, 421 ... C-5
FALL RIVER CO., 7094 ... G-2
Farmer, 10 ... F-11
Farmingdale ... E-3
FAULK CO., 2364 ... C-9
Faulkton, 736 ... C-9
Fedora, 37 ... E-11
Ferney, 43 ... B-10
Firesteel, 20 ... B-6
Flandreau, 2341 ... E-13
Florence, 374 ... C-12
Forestburg, 73 ... E-11
Ft. Pierre, 2078 ... D-7
Ft. Thompson, 1282 ... E-9
Frankfort, 149 ... C-10
Frederick, 199 ... A-10
Freeman, 1306 ... F-12
Fruitdale, 64 ... D-2
Fulton, 91 ... F-11
Gann Valley, 14 ... E-9
Garden City, 53 ... C-11
Garretson, 1166 ... F-13
Gary, 227 ... C-13
Gayville, 407 ... G-12
Geddes, 208 ... G-10
Gettysburg, 1162 ... C-8
Glad Valley, 10 ... B-5
Glencross, 40 ... B-6
Glenham, 105 ... B-7
Goodwin, 146 ... C-12
GRANT CO., 7356 ... C-12
Green Grass, 35 ... C-6
Greenwood, 100 ... G-10
Gregory, 1295 ... G-9
GREGORY CO., 4271 ... G-9
Grenville, 54 ... B-11
Groton, 1458 ... B-10
HAAKON CO., 1937 ... D-5
Hamill, 11 ... F-8
HAMLIN CO., 5903 ... D-12
Hammer ... A-12
HAND CO., 3431 ... D-9
HANSON CO., 3331 ... F-11
HARDING CO., 1255 ... B-3
Harrisburg, 4089 ... F-13
Harrison, 52 ... F-10
Harrold, 124 ... D-8
Hartford, 2534 ... F-12
Hayes, 40 ... D-6
Hayti, 381 ... D-12
Hazel, 91 ... C-12
Hecla, 227 ... A-10
Henry, 267 ... C-11
Hermosa, 398 ... E-3
Herreid, 438 ... A-8
Herrick, 105 ... G-9
Hetland, 46 ... D-12
Highmore, 795 ... D-9
Hill City, 948 ... E-2
Hillsview, 3 ... B-8
Hisega ... I-3
Hitchcock, 91 ... D-10
Holabird, 20 ... D-8
Hosmer, 208 ... B-8
Hot Sprs., 3711 ... F-2
Houghton, 60 ... A-10
Hoven, 406 ... B-8
Howard, 858 ... E-11
Howes, 20 ... D-5
Hudson, 296 ... G-13
HUGHES CO., 17022 ... D-8
Humboldt, 589 ... F-12
Hurley, 415 ... F-12
Huron, 12592 ... D-10
HUTCHINSON CO., 7343 ... F-11
HYDE CO., 1420 ... D-8
Ideal, 60 ... F-8
Interior, 94 ... F-5
Iona, 10 ... F-9
Ipswich, 954 ... B-9
Irene, 420 ... G-12
Iron Lightning, 40 ... C-5
Iroquois, 266 ... D-11
Isabel, 135 ... B-6
JACKSON CO., 3031 ... F-5
Java, 129 ... B-8
Jefferson, 547 ... H-13
JERAULD CO., 2071 ... E-10
JONES CO., 1006 ... E-6
Junius, 50 ... E-12
Kadoka, 654 ... E-5
Kaylor, 47 ... G-11
Keldron, 10 ... A-5
Kenel, 50 ... A-7
Kennebec, 240 ... E-8
Keystone, 337 ... E-3
Kidder, 57 ... A-11
Kimball, 703 ... F-9
KINGSBURY CO., 5148 ... D-11
Kranzburg, 172 ... C-12
Kyle, 846 ... F-4
La Plant, 171 ... C-7
Labolt, 68 ... C-13
L. Andes, 879 ... G-10
Lake City, 51 ... A-11
LAKE CO., 11200 ... E-12
L. Norden, 467 ... D-12
L. Preston, 599 ... D-12
Lane, 59 ... E-10
Langford, 313 ... B-11
Lantry, 40 ... C-6
LAWRENCE CO., 24097 ... E-2
Lead, 3124 ... D-2
Lebanon, 47 ... C-8
Lemmon, 1227 ... A-5
Lennox, 2111 ... F-12
Leola, 457 ... A-9
Lesterville, 127 ... G-11
Letcher, 173 ... E-10
Lily, 4 ... C-11
LINCOLN CO., 44828 ... G-13
Little Eagle, 319 ... B-7
Lodgepole, 60 ... A-4
Long Lake, 31 ... A-9
Long Valley, 20 ... F-5
Loomis, 34 ... E-10
Lower Brule, 613 ... E-8
Lowry, 6 ... B-8
Loyalton ... B-9
Lucas ... G-9
Ludlow, 10 ... A-3
LYMAN CO., 3755 ... E-8
Lyons, 100 ... E-12
Madison, 6474 ... E-12
Mahto, 20 ... A-7
Manchester, 10 ... D-11
Manderson, 180 ... G-4
Mansfield, 93 ... B-10
Marion, 784 ... F-12
MARSHALL CO., 4656 ... A-11
Martin, 1071 ... G-5
Marty, 402 ... G-10
Marvin, 34 ... B-12
Mayfield, 20 ... G-12
MCCOOK CO., 5618 ... E-12
McIntosh, 173 ... A-6
McLaughlin, 663 ... A-6
MCPHERSON CO., 2459 ... A-9
MEADE CO., 25434 ... D-3
Meadow, 30 ... B-4
Meckling, 90 ... G-12
Mellette, 210 ... C-10
MELLETTE CO., 2048 ... F-6
Menno, 608 ... G-11
Midland, 129 ... E-6
Midway, 30 ... G-12
Milbank, 3353 ... B-13
Milesville, 30 ... D-5
Millboro, 10 ... G-8
Miller, 1489 ... D-9
Milltown, 10 ... F-11
Mina, 30 ... B-9
MINER CO., 2389 ... E-11
MINNEHAHA CO., 169468 ... E-12
Miranda, 20 ... C-9
Mission, 1182 ... G-7
Mission Hill, 177 ... G-12
Mission Ridge ... D-7
Mitchell, 15254 ... F-11
Mobridge, 3465 ... B-7
Monroe, 160 ... F-12
Montrose, 472 ... F-12
MOODY CO., 6486 ... E-13
Morningside, 105 ... D-10
Morristown, 67 ... A-5
Mound City, 71 ... A-8
Mt. Vernon, 462 ... F-10
Mud Butte, 10 ... C-3
Murdo, 488 ... E-7
Mystic ... I-2
Naples, 41 ... C-11
Nemo, 50 ... E-2
New Effington, 256 ... A-12
New Holland, 76 ... F-10
New Underwood, 660 ... E-3
Newell, 603 ... C-3
Nisland, 232 ... D-2
Norris, 152 ... F-6
N. Sioux City, 2530 ... H-13
Northville, 143 ... C-10
Nunda, 43 ... E-12
Oacoma, 451 ... E-9
Oelrichs, 126 ... G-3
Oglala, 1290 ... G-4
OGLALA LAKOTA CO., 13586 ... F-4
Okaton, 36 ... E-6
Okreek, 269 ... F-7
Oldham, 133 ... E-12
Olivet, 74 ... G-11
Onaka, 15 ... B-8
Onida, 658 ... D-8
Opal, 30 ... C-4
Oral, 60 ... F-3
Orient, 63 ... C-9
Ortley, 65 ... B-12
Osceola, 30 ... D-11
Owanka, 20 ... E-4
Parade, 20 ... C-6
Parker, 1022 ... F-12
Parkston, 1508 ... F-11
Parmelee, 562 ... F-6
Peever, 168 ... B-12
PENNINGTON CO., 100948 ... E-4
PERKINS CO., 2982 ... B-4
Philip, 779 ... E-5
Pickerel, 30 ... B-12
Pickstown, 201 ... G-10
Piedmont, 222 ... D-3
Pierpont, 135 ... B-11
Pierre, 13646 ... D-7
Pine Ridge, 3308 ... G-4
Plainview, 20 ... D-4
Plankinton, 707 ... F-10
Platte, 1230 ... F-9
Pollock, 241 ... A-7
Polo, 40 ... C-9
Porcupine, 1062 ... G-4
Potato Creek, 50 ... F-5
POTTER CO., 2329 ... C-8
Prairie City, 23 ... B-4
Presho, 497 ... E-8
Pringle, 112 ... F-2
Provo, 80 ... G-2
Pukwana, 285 ... F-9
Quinn, 54 ... E-4
Ralph, 10 ... A-3
Ramona, 174 ... E-12
Rapid City, 67956 ... E-3
Ravinia, 61 ... G-10
Raymond, 50 ... C-11
Red Scaffold, 100 ... C-5
Red Shirt, 40 ... F-3
Redfield, 2333 ... C-10
Redig, 10 ... B-2
Redowl, 10 ... D-4
Ree Hts., 62 ... D-9
Reliance, 191 ... E-8
Renner, 305 ... F-13
Reva, 10 ... B-3
Revillo, 119 ... C-13
Richland, 89 ... H-13
Ridgeview, 90 ... C-7
Riverside, 30 ... F-11
ROBERTS CO., 10149 ... B-12
Rochford, 50 ... E-2
Rockerville ... I-3
Rockham, 33 ... C-9
Roscoe, 329 ... B-9
Rosebud, 1587 ... G-6
Rosholt, 423 ... A-12
Roslyn, 183 ... B-11
Roswell, 15 ... E-11
Running Water, 36 ... H-11
Rutland, 80 ... E-12
St. Charles, 11 ... G-9
St. Francis, 709 ... G-6
St. Lawrence, 198 ... D-9
St. Onge, 191 ... D-2
Salem, 1347 ... F-12
Sanator ... J-2
SANBORN CO., 2355 ... E-10
Savoy ... H-2
Scenic, 80 ... E-4
Scotland, 841 ... G-11
Selby, 642 ... B-8
Seneca, 38 ... C-8
Shadehill, 20 ... A-5
Sharps Corner, 60 ... F-4
Sherman, 78 ... E-13
Silver City, 60 ... E-2
Sinai, 120 ... D-12
Sioux Falls, 153888 ... F-13
Sisseton, 2470 ... B-12
Smithwick, 30 ... F-3
Soldier Creek, 227 ... F-6
Sorum ... B-3
S. Shore, 225 ... C-12
Spearfish, 10494 ... D-2
Spencer, 154 ... F-11
Spink, 40 ... G-13
SPINK CO., 6415 ... C-10
Spring Creek, 268 ... G-6
Springfield, 1989 ... G-11
STANLEY CO., 2966 ... D-6
Stephan, 30 ... E-9
Stickney, 284 ... F-10
Stockholm, 108 ... C-12
Stoneville, 20 ... D-4
Storla, 6 ... E-10
Strandburg, 72 ... C-12
Stratford, 72 ... B-10
Sturgis, 6627 ... D-2
SULLY CO., 1373 ... D-7
Summerset, 1814 ... E-3
Summit, 288 ... B-12
Sunnyview, 50 ... D-12
Tabor, 423 ... G-11
Tea, 3806 ... F-12
Thomas ... C-12
Thunder Butte, 70 ... C-5
Thunder Hawk, 30 ... A-5
Tilford, 40 ... D-3
Timber Lake, 443 ... B-6
TODD CO., 9612 ... G-6
Tolstoy, 36 ... C-8
Toronto, 212 ... D-13
Trail City, 130 ... B-7
Trent, 232 ... E-13
Tripp, 647 ... G-11
TRIPP CO., 5644 ... G-8
Troy, 10 ... C-12
Tulare, 207 ... D-10
Turkey Ridge, 10 ... G-12
TURNER CO., 8347 ... F-12
Turton, 48 ... C-10
Tuthill, 30 ... G-5
Twin Brooks, 69 ... B-12
Tyndall, 1067 ... G-11
Union Ctr., 80 ... D-4
UNION CO., 14399 ... G-13
Unityville, 20 ... E-11
Utica, 65 ... G-11
Vale, 136 ... D-3
Valley Sprs., 759 ... F-13
Vayland ... D-9
Veblen, 531 ... A-12
Verdon, 5 ... B-10
Vermillion, 10571 ... G-12
Vetal ... G-6
Viborg, 782 ... G-12
Victor, 20 ... A-12
Vienna, 45 ... D-11
Vilas, 20 ... E-11
Virgil, 16 ... D-10
Vivian, 119 ... E-7
Volga, 1768 ... D-12
Volin, 161 ... G-12
Wagner, 1566 ... G-10
Wakonda, 321 ... G-12
Wakpala, 200 ... B-7
Wakpamani, 30 ... G-4
Walker, 10 ... A-6
Wall, 766 ... E-4
Wallace, 85 ... C-11
WALWORTH CO., 5438 ... B-8
Wanblee, 725 ... F-5
Ward, 48 ... E-13
Warner, 457 ... B-10
Wasta, 80 ... E-4
Watauga, 30 ... A-5
Watertown, 21482 ... C-12
Waubay, 576 ... B-12
Waverly, 37 ... C-12
Webster, 1886 ... B-11
Wecota, 20 ... C-9
Wentworth, 171 ... E-12
Wessington, 170 ... D-10
Wessington Sprs., 956 ... E-10
Westport, 133 ... B-10
Wetonka, 8 ... B-9
Wewela, 20 ... G-8
White, 485 ... D-13
White Butte, 20 ... A-4
White Lake, 372 ... F-10
White Owl, 30 ... D-4
White River, 581 ... F-7
White Rock, 3 ... A-13
Whitehorse, 141 ... B-6
Whitewood, 927 ... D-2
Willow Lake, 263 ... D-11
Wilmot, 492 ... B-13
Winfred, 52 ... E-12
Winner, 2897 ... F-8
Witten, 79 ... F-8
Wolsey, 376 ... D-10
Wood, 62 ... F-7
Woonsocket, 655 ... E-10
Worthing, 877 ... F-13
Wounded Knee, 382 ... G-4
Yale, 108 ... D-11
Yankton, 14454 ... G-12
YANKTON CO., 22438 ... G-12
Zell, 30 ... C-10
ZIEBACH CO., 2801 ... C-5

Tennessee

Page locator
Map keys Atlas pages
1–10 190–191
11–20 192–193
* City keyed to p. 155
† City keyed to p. 195

Acton, 100 ... G-6
Adair, 70 ... E-5
Adams, 633 ... B-10
Adamsville, 2207 ... F-6
Aetna, 100 ... E-9
Afton, 250 ... K-17
Alamo, 2461 ... D-4
Alcoa, 8449 ... D-19
Alexandria, 966 ... C-15
Algood, 3495 ... C-15
Allardt, 634 ... B-15
Allons, 190 ... B-15
Allred, 100 ... C-16
Almaville, 170 ... D-12
Alpine, 200 ... B-16
Altamont, 1045 ... F-14
Alto, 50 ... G-14
Anderson, 150 ... G-14
ANDERSON CO., 75129 ... C-18
Andersonville, 472 ... C-19
Anthony Hill, 200 ... G-10
Apison, 2469 ... G-16
Arcadia, 30 ... †J-2
Archville, 120 ... G-18
Ardmore, 1213 ... G-11
Arlington, 11517 ... F-3
Armathwaite, 140 ... B-17
Arp, 290 ... D-3
Arrington, 150 ... D-11
Arthur, 400 ... B-20
Asbury, 300 ... J-14
Ashburn, 100 ... A-11
Ashland City, 4541 ... C-10
Ashport, 200 ... D-2
Athens, 13458 ... F-18
Atoka, 8387 ... F-2
Atwood, 938 ... D-6
Auburntown, 269 ... D-13
Austin Sprs., 250 ... †M-3
Baileyton, 431 ... J-17
Bairds Mills, 40 ... C-12
Bakerville, 30 ... D-8
Bakewell, 250 ... F-16
Ball Camp, 240 ... D-19
Baneberry, 482 ... K-16
Banner, 200 ... M-15
Banner Hill, 1497 ... K-18
Banner Sprs., 180 ... C-17
Barkertown, 240 ... F-15
Barren Plain, 100 ... B-11
Bartlett, 54613 ... F-2
Bath Sprs., 70 ... F-7
Baxter, 1365 ... C-15
Beans Creek ... G-13
Bear Spr., 70 ... B-8
Bearden ... K-16
BEDFORD CO., 45058 ... E-12
Beech Bluff, 250 ... E-6
Beechgrove, 190 ... E-13
Beersheba Sprs., 477 ... F-14
Belfast, 230 ... F-11
Bell Buckle, 500 ... E-12
Belle Eagle ... E-4
Belle Meade, 2912 ... L-7
Belleville, 60 ... F-12
Bells, 2437 ... E-4
Belvidere, 180 ... G-13
Benton, 1385 ... G-17
BENTON CO., 16489 ... C-7
Berry Hill, 537 ... L-8
Berrys Chapel, 3000 ... D-11
Bethel, 150 ... G-10
Bethel Sprs., 718 ... F-6
Bethesda, 50 ... E-11
Bethpage, 288 ... B-13
Bible Hill, 30 ... E-7
Big Rock, 350 ... B-8
Big Sandy, 557 ... C-7
Big Spr., 270 ... †N-4
Big Spr., 100 ... F-17
Biltmore, 1800 ... †M-5
Binfield, 140 ... E-19
Birchwood, 480 ... F-16
Blaine, 1856 ... C-20
BLEDSOE CO., 12876 ... F-16
Bloomingdale, 9888 ... I-18
Bloomington Sprs., 270 ... C-15
BLOUNT CO., 123010 ... E-20
Blountville, 3074 ... I-18
Blue Spr., 200 ... †M-6
Bluff City, 1733 ... J-19
Bogota, 200 ... C-3
Bold Spr., 30 ... D-9
Bolivar, 5417 ... F-5
Bolton, 350 ... F-2
Boma, 30 ... C-14
Bon Air, 200 ... D-15
Bon Aqua, 200 ... D-10
Bonicord ... D-4
Bonnertown, 100 ... G-10
Boone, 80 ... †M-2
Boones Creek ... †L-2
Booneville, 60 ... F-12
Boonshill, 50 ... G-11
Bordeaux ... J-7
Bowmantown, 60 ... †N-1
Boyds Creek, 120 ... *A-10
Braden, 282 ... F-3
Bradford, 1048 ... C-5
BRADLEY CO., 98963 ... G-17
Bradyville, 200 ... E-13
Bransford, 170 ... B-13
Brazil, 200 ... D-5
Brentwood, 37060 ... D-11
Briarwood, 590 ... B-9
Briceville, 800 ... C-19
Bridgeport, 30 ... *A-13
Brighton, 2735 ... E-2
Bristol, 26702 ... I-19
Brownsville, 10292 ... E-4
Bruceton, 1478 ... D-7
Brunswick, 240 ... F-2
Brush Creek, 300 ... C-13
Bryson, 30 ... G-11
Buchanan, 300 ... B-7
Buena Vista, 150 ... D-7
Buffalo Sprs., 30 ... K-15
Buffalo Valley, 100 ... C-14
Bulls Gap, 738 ... K-16
Bumpus Mills, 300 ... A-8
Burlison, 425 ... E-2
Burns, 1468 ... D-10
Burnt Church, 100 ... G-7
Burrville ... C-17
Butler, 500 ... J-19
Butlers, 30 ... B-15
Bybee, 450 ... K-16
Bybee, 300 ... E-14
Byrdstown, 803 ... B-16
Cades, 50 ... D-5
Cades Cove, 30 ... *C-9
Cairo, 60 ... D-4
Calderwood, 820 ... E-19
Calhoun, 490 ... F-17
Calistia, 70 ... D-13
Camden, 3582 ... C-7
Campaign, 500 ... E-15
CAMPBELL CO., 40716 ... B-19
Campbellsville, 100 ... F-10
Caney Branch ... K-16
CANNON CO., 13801 ... D-13
Carlisle, 150 ... B-8
Carlock, 200 ... F-18
CARROLL CO., 28522 ... D-6
Carson Spr., 700 ... *A-13
Carter, 500 ... J-19
CARTER CO., 57424 ... J-19
Carthage, 2306 ... C-14
Caryville, 2297 ... C-19
Cash Pt., 100 ... G-11
Castalian Sprs., 556 ... B-13
Catlettsburg ... *A-11
Cato, 50 ... B-13
Cedar Creek, 300 ... K-17
Cedar Grv., 115 ... D-6
Cedar Grv. ... †K-5
Cedar Hill, 314 ... B-11
Celina, 1495 ... B-15
Center ... F-9
Center Point ... G-10
Centertown, 243 ... E-14
Centerville, 3644 ... D-9
Central, 2279 ... †M-4
Central, 50 ... D-4
Chapel Hill, 1445 ... E-11
Chapel Hill, 120 ... E-10
Chapmansboro, 220 ... C-10
Charleston, 651 ... F-17
Charleston, 150 ... E-3
Charlotte, 1235 ... C-10
Chattanooga, 167674 ... G-16
CHEATHAM CO., 39105 ... B-10
Cherokee Hills, 600 ... L-15
Cherry, 40 ... E-3
CHESTER CO., 17131 ... F-6
Chesterfield, 469 ... E-7
Chestnut Bluff, 80 ... E-4
Chestnut Hill, 400 ... L-15
Chestnut Mound, 150 ... C-14
Chewalla, 200 ... G-6
Childers Hill ... G-7
Chinquapin Grv., 300 ... †L-5
Christiana, 350 ... E-12
Christmasville, 100 ... C-6
Chuckey, 360 ... K-17
Church Hill, 6737 ... J-17
Churchton, 100 ... C-4
CLAIBORNE CO., 32213 ... J-15
Clairfield, 200 ... B-19
Clarkrange, 575 ... C-16
Clarksburg, 393 ... D-6
Clarksville, 132929 ... B-10
Claxton, 250 ... D-19
CLAY CO., 7861 ... B-14
Clearwater, 30 ... E-17
Cleveland, 41285 ... G-17
Clifftops, 200 ... G-14
Clifton, 2694 ... F-8
Clifton Jct., 220 ... F-8
Clinton, 9841 ... C-19
Clovercroft, 30 ... D-11
Cloverport, 80 ... E-5
Coalfield, 2463 ... D-18
Coalmont, 841 ... F-14
Coble, 100 ... D-9
COCKE CO., 35662 ... K-16
COFFEE CO., 52796 ... E-13
Coker Creek, 130 ... F-19
Cold Spr., 200 ... E-16
Coldwater, 30 ... G-11
College, 100 ... E-16
College Grv., 650 ... D-11
Collegedale, 8282 ... G-16
Collierville, 43965 ... G-3
Collinwood, 982 ... G-8
Colonial Hts., 6934 ... J-18
Columbia, 34681 ... E-10
Commerce, 60 ... C-13
Como, 200 ... C-6
Conasauga, 250 ... G-17
Concord, 100 ... E-12
Condon, 2125 ... C-20
Cookeville, 30435 ... C-15
Coopertown, 4278 ... B-11
Copperhill, 354 ... G-18
Cornersville, 1194 ... F-11
Corryton, 100 ... C-20
Cosby, 400 ... L-16
Cottage Grv., 88 ... B-6
Cottontown, 367 ... B-12
Counce, 700 ... G-7
Cove Creek Cascades, 90 ... *B-10
Covington, 9038 ... E-3
Cowan, 1737 ... G-13
Crab Orchard, 752 ... D-17
Crawford, 100 ... C-16
Crestwood Hills, 1600 ... K-11
CROCKETT CO., 14586 ... D-4
Crockett Mills, 400 ... D-4
Cross Anchor, 100 ... I-17
Cross Plains, 1714 ... B-11
Cross Roads, 180 ... B-17
Crossville, 10795 ... D-16
Crump, 1428 ... F-7
Cuba, 50 ... F-4
Cuba, 20 ... D-10
Culleoka, 360 ... F-11
Cumberland City, 311 ... B-9
CUMBERLAND CO., 56053 ... D-17
Cumberland Furnace, 300 ... C-10
Cumberland Gap, 494 ... B-20
Cumberland Hts., 210 ... F-14
Cumberland Sprs., 60 ... E-16
Cunningham, 60 ... B-9
Curve, 350 ... D-3
Cypress Inn, 350 ... G-8
Dale Hollow, 200 ... B-15
Dancyville, 50 ... F-4
Dandridge, 2812 ... K-15
Dante, 260 ... D-19
Darden, 399 ... E-7
DAVIDSON CO., 626681 ... C-11
Dayton, 7191 ... F-16

*, †, ‡, §, ◊ See explanation under state title in this index.
County and parish names are listed in capital letters & boldface type.
Independent cities (not included in a county) are listed in italics.

Texas 261

Garden Ridge, 3259 ... EP-12
Garden Valley, 120 ... EF-9
Gardendale ... EO-2
Gardendale, 1574 ... WK-9
Garfield, 1698 ... EK-6
Garland, 226876 ... EE-7
Garrett, 806 ... EF-7
Garrison, 895 ... EG-11
Garwood, 850 ... EL-8
Gary, 311 ... EF-11
GARZA CO., 6461 ... WH-11
Gatesville, 15751 ... EH-5
Gause, 500 ... EI-7
Gay Hill ... EK-8
Geneva, 100 ... EH-12
George West, 2445 ... EO-5
Georgetown, 47400 ... EJ-5
Geronimo, 1032 ... EL-5
Gholson, 1061 ... EG-6
Giddings, 4881 ... EK-7
Gilchrist, 750 ... EL-12
Gill ... EF-11
GILLESPIE CO., 24837 ... EJ-2
Gillett, 100 ... EM-5
Gilliland ... WG-14
Gilmer, 4905 ... EE-10
Girard, 50 ... WH-12
Girvin, 30 ... WM-9
Gladewater, 6441 ... EE-10
GLASSCOCK CO., 1226 ... WK-11
Glazier, 50 ... WB-13
Glen Cove, 40 ... WK-14
Glen Flora, 300 ... EM-8
Glen Rose, 2444 ... EF-5
Glendale, 125 ... EI-10
Glenn Hts., 11278 ... †J-10
Glenrio ... WD-8
Glidden, 661 ... EL-8
Godley, 1009 ... EF-6
Golden, 500 ... EE-9
Goldsboro, 40 ... WK-14
Goldsmith, 257 ... WK-9
Goldthwaite, 1878 ... EH-4
Goliad, 1908 ... EN-6
GOLIAD CO., 7210 ... EO-6
Golinda, 559 ... EH-6
Gomez ... WH-9
Gonzales, 7237 ... EL-6
GONZALES CO., 19807 ... EM-5
Goodland ... WG-8
Goodlett, 50 ... WF-14
Goodlow, 200 ... EF-8
Goodnight, 25 ... WD-11
Goodrich, 271 ... EJ-11
Gordon, 478 ... EF-4
Gordonville, 150 ... EC-7
Goree, 203 ... ED-2
Gorman, 1083 ... EF-3
Gouldbusk, 70 ... EH-2
Graford, 584 ... EE-4
Graham, 8903 ... ED-4
Granbury, 7978 ... EF-5
Grand Bluff, 95 ... EF-12
Grand Prairie, 175396 ... EE-7
Grand Saline, 3136 ... EE-9
Grandfalls, 360 ... WL-8
Grandview, 1561 ... EF-6
Granger, 1419 ... EJ-6
Granite Shoals, 4910 ... EJ-4
Granjeno, 293 ... WT-9
Grape Creek, 3154 ... WL-13
Grapeland, 1489 ... EH-9
Grapevine, 46334 ... †E-6
Grassland ... WH-11
GRAY CO., 22535 ... WD-12
Grayback, 15 ... EB-2
Grayburg, 250 ... EK-12
Grays Prairie, 337 ... EF-8
GRAYSON CO., 120877 ... EC-7
Greatwood, 11538 ... *G-1
Greenville, 25557 ... ED-8
Greenvine, 30 ... EK-8
Greenwood ... WK-10
Greenwood, 90 ... ED-6
Greenwood Vil., 4000 ... *C-5
GREGG CO., 121730 ... EF-10
Gregory, 1907 ... EP-6
Grey Forest, 483 ... EP-8
GRIMES CO., 26604 ... EJ-8
Groesbeck, 4328 ... EH-7
Groom, 574 ... WD-12
Groves, 16144 ... EK-13
Groveton, 1057 ... EI-10
Gruver, 1194 ... WB-11
Guadalupe, 90 ... EN-7
GUADALUPE CO., 131533 ... EL-5
Guerra, 6 ... ER-3
Gun Barrel City, 5672 ... EF-8
Gunter, 1498 ... ED-7
Gustine, 476 ... EG-4
Guthrie, 160 ... WG-13
Guy, 75 ... EM-9
Hackberry, 968 ... †B-9
Hagansport, 70 ... ED-10
Hainesville, 100 ... EE-10
Hale Ctr., 2252 ... WF-10
HALE CO., 36273 ... WG-10
Halfway, 60 ... WF-10
HALL CO., 3353 ... WE-12
Hallettsville, 2550 ... EL-7
Hallsburg, 507 ... EH-7
Hallsville, 3577 ... EE-11
Haltom City, 42409 ... †G-4
Hamilton, 3095 ... EG-4
HAMILTON CO., 8517 ... EH-4
Hamlin, 2124 ... WI-13
Hamshire, 600 ... EK-12
Hankamer, 600 ... EK-11
HANSFORD CO., 5613 ... WA-11
Happy, 678 ... WE-10
Happy Union ... WG-10
Harbin ... EG-4
HARDEMAN CO., 4139 ... WF-14
Hardin, 819 ... EK-11
HARDIN CO., 54635 ... EJ-12
Hare ... EJ-6
Hargill, 877 ... ES-5
Harker Hts., 26700 ... EI-5
Harleton, 300 ... EE-11
Harlingen, 64849 ... ET-6
Harper, 1192 ... EK-2
HARRIS CO., 4092459 ... EK-9
HARRISON CO., 65631 ... EF-12
Harrold, 115 ... EB-3
Hart, 1114 ... WF-10
Hart Camp ... WF-10
Hartley, 540 ... WB-9
HARTLEY CO., 6062 ... WC-9
Harwood, 130 ... EL-6
Haskell, 3322 ... WH-14
HASKELL CO., 5899 ... WH-14
Hasse, 100 ... EG-4
Hawkins, 1278 ... EE-10
Hawley, 634 ... WJ-14
Haynesville, 100 ... EB-3
HAYS CO., 157107 ... EK-4
Hearne, 4459 ... EI-7
Hebbronville, 4558 ... EQ-4
Hebron, 415 ... †D-9
Hedley, 329 ... WE-12
Hedwig Vil., 2557 ... *D-3
Heidenheimer, 300 ... EI-6
Helena, 30 ... EN-5
Helotes, 7341 ... EL-3
Hemphill, 1198 ... EH-13
HEMPHILL CO., 3807 ... WC-13
Hempstead, 5770 ... EK-8
Henderson, 13712 ... EF-11
HENDERSON CO., 78532 ... EF-9
Henly, 40 ... EK-4
Henrietta, 3141 ... EC-4
Hereford, 15370 ... WE-9
Hermleigh, 345 ... WJ-12
Hewitt, 13549 ... EH-6
Hext, 70 ... EI-2
Hickory Creek, 3247 ... †B-7
Hico, 1379 ... EG-5
Hidalgo, 11198 ... ET-4
HIDALGO CO., 774769 ... ES-4
Hideaway, 3083 ... EF-9
Higginbotham ... WI-8
Higgins, 397 ... WB-13
High Hill, 30 ... EL-7
High Island, 500 ... EL-12
Highbank ... EI-7
Highland Pk., 8564 ... †F-10
Highland Vil., 15056 ... †C-7
Highlands, 7522 ... EK-10
HILL CO., 35089 ... EG-7
Hill Country Vil., 985 ... EQ-10
Hillcrest, 730 ... *I-6
Hillister, 300 ... EJ-12
Hillje, 70 ... EM-8
Hillsboro, 8456 ... EG-6
Hilltop Lakes, 1101 ... EI-8
Hilshire Vil., 746 ... *D-3
Hitchcock, 6961 ... EL-11
Hitchland ... WA-11
Hobson, 150 ... EN-5
Hochheim, 80 ... EM-6
HOCKLEY CO., 22935 ... WH-9
Hodges ... WJ-14
Hogg ... EJ-7
Holland, 1121 ... EI-6
Holliday, 1758 ... EC-3
Holly, 40 ... EI-10
Holly Sprs. ... EI-13
Hollywood Pk., 3062 ... EQ-10
Homer, 350 ... EH-11
Hondo, 8803 ... EM-3
Honey Grv., 1668 ... EC-8
Honey Island, 300 ... EJ-12
HOOD CO., 51182 ... EF-5
Hooks, 2769 ... EC-11
Hope ... EM-7
HOPKINS CO., 35161 ... ED-9
Horizon City, 16735 ... WK-2
Houmont Pk., 2500 ... *C-7
Houston, 2099451 ... EL-10
HOUSTON CO., 23732 ... EH-9
HOWARD CO., 35012 ... WJ-11
Howardwick, 402 ... WD-12
Howe, 2600 ... EC-7
Howland, 50 ... EC-9
Hub, 25 ... WE-9
Hubbard, 1423 ... EG-7
Huckabay, 150 ... EF-4
Hudson, 4731 ... EH-11
HUDSPETH CO., 3476 ... WL-3
Huffman, 3000 ... EK-10
Hughes Sprs., 1760 ... ED-11
Hull, 669 ... EK-11
Humble, 15133 ... EK-10
Hungerford, 347 ... EL-9
Hunt, 650 ... EK-2
HUNT CO., 86129 ... ED-8
Hunter, 40 ... EL-5
Hunters Creek Vil., 4367 ... *D-3
Huntington, 2118 ... EH-11
Huntsville, 38548 ... EI-9
Hurlwood, 130 ... WG-10
Hurst, 37337 ... †G-6
Hutchins, 5338 ... †I-11
HUTCHINSON CO., 22150 ... WB-11
Hutto, 14698 ... EJ-6
Huxley, 385 ... EG-12
Hye, 70 ... EK-4
Iago, 161 ... EM-9
Ida, 25 ... EC-7
Idalou, 2250 ... WG-10
Illinois Bend ... EC-6
Impact, 35 ... EA-6
Imperial, 278 ... WL-8
Independence, 125 ... EJ-8
Indian Creek ... EH-3
Indian Gap ... EH-4
Indianola, 50 ... EN-8
Industry, 304 ... EK-8
Inez, 2098 ... EN-7
Ingleside, 9387 ... EP-6
Ingram, 1804 ... EK-2
Iola, 401 ... EI-8
Iowa Pk., 6355 ... EC-3
Ira, 300 ... WJ-12
Iraan, 1229 ... WM-10
Iredell, 339 ... EG-5
Ireland, 30 ... EH-5
Irene, 150 ... EG-7
IRION CO., 1599 ... WL-12
Irving, 216290 ... EE-7
Italy, 1863 ... EF-7
Itasca, 1644 ... EF-6
Ivanhoe, 100 ... EC-8
Ivanhoe, 538 ... EI-12
Izoro, 25 ... EH-5
Jacinto City, 10553 ... *D-6
JACK CO., 9044 ... ED-4
Jacksboro, 4511 ... ED-4
Jackson ... EF-9
JACKSON CO., 14075 ... EN-8
Jacksonville, 14544 ... EG-10
Jamaica Bch., 983 ... EM-11
Jamestown ... EI-13
Jarrell, 984 ... EI-5
Jasper, 7590 ... EI-12
JASPER CO., 35710 ... EJ-12
Jayton, 534 ... WH-12
Jean, 100 ... ED-3
JEFF DAVIS CO., 2342 ... WM-6
Jefferson, 2106 ... EE-11
JEFFERSON CO., 252273 ... EL-12
Jermyn, 100 ... ED-4
Jersey Vil., 7620 ... EK-9
Jewett, 1167 ... EH-8
JIM HOGG CO., 5300 ... ER-3
JIM WELLS CO., 40838 ... EP-4
Joaquin, 824 ... EG-12
Johnson City, 1656 ... EK-4
JOHNSON CO., 150934 ... EF-6
Johntown, 180 ... ED-10
Jolly, 172 ... EC-4
Jollyville, 16151 ... WB-5
Jonah, 100 ... EJ-6
JONES CO., 20202 ... WI-14
Jones Creek, 2020 ... EM-10
Jonesboro, 150 ... EH-5
Jonestown, 1834 ... EJ-5
Jonesville, 150 ... EE-12
Joplin ... ED-5
Josephine, 812 ... ED-8
Joshua, 5910 ... EF-6
Jourdanton, 3871 ... EN-4
Joy ... EC-4
Judson, 500 ... EE-11
Juliff, 100 ... EL-10
Junction, 2574 ... WN-14
Juno, 10 ... WO-11
Justiceburg, 80 ... WI-11
Justin, 3246 ... ED-6
Kadane Corner, 90 ... EC-3
Kamay, 300 ... EC-3
Kamey ... EN-7
Kanawha, 40 ... EC-10
Karnack, 300 ... EE-12
Karnes City, 3042 ... EN-5
KARNES CO., 14824 ... EN-5
Katemcy, 90 ... EI-2
Katy, 14102 ... EL-9
Kaufman, 6703 ... EE-8
KAUFMAN CO., 103350 ... EF-8
Keene, 6106 ... EF-6
Keller, 39627 ... †E-5
Kellerville ... WD-13
Kellyville ... EE-11
Kelton, 40 ... WD-13
Kemah, 1773 ... *G-9
Kemp, 1154 ... EF-8
Kempner, 1089 ... EI-5
Kendalia, 100 ... EK-4
KENDALL CO., 33410 ... EK-3
Kendleton, 380 ... EL-9
Kenedy, 3296 ... EN-5
KENEDY CO., 416 ... ER-6
Kenefick, 563 ... EK-11
Kennard, 337 ... EH-10
Kennedale, 6763 ... †I-5
Kenney, 200 ... EK-8
Kent, 50 ... WM-6
KENT CO., 808 ... WI-12
Kerens, 1573 ... EF-8
Kermit, 5708 ... WK-8
KERR CO., 49625 ... EK-2
Kerrick, 50 ... WA-10
Kerrville, 22347 ... EK-3
Key ... WI-10
Kildare, 60 ... ED-12
Kildare Jct., 50 ... EE-12
Kilgore, 12975 ... EF-10
Killeen, 127921 ... EI-5
KIMBLE CO., 4607 ... WN-14
KING CO., 286 ... WG-13
Kingsbury, 782 ... EL-5
Kingsland, 6030 ... EJ-4
Kingston, 140 ... ED-8
Kingsville, 26213 ... EQ-5
KINNEY CO., 3598 ... WQ-13
Kirby, 8000 ... EL-4
Kirbyville, 2142 ... EI-13
Kirvin, 129 ... EG-8
KLEBERG CO., 32061 ... EQ-5
Klondike, 175 ... ED-9
Knickerbocker, 170 ... WM-12
Knippa, 689 ... WQ-14
Knollwood, 226 ... EC-7
Knott, 150 ... WJ-10
Knox City, 1130 ... WH-14
KNOX CO., 3719 ... WG-14
Kohrville, 400 ... *A-2
Kopperl, 250 ... EG-6
Kosciusko, 100 ... EM-5
Kosse, 464 ... EH-7
Kountze, 2123 ... EJ-12
Kress, 715 ... WF-10
Krum, 4157 ... ED-6
Kurten, 398 ... EI-8
Kyle, 28016 ... EK-5
La Blanca ... WR-11
La Feria, 7302 ... ET-5
La Gloria ... ES-4
La Grange, 4641 ... EK-7
La Grulla, 1622 ... ET-4
La Homa, 11985 ... WR-8
La Joya, 3985 ... ET-4
La Marque, 14509 ... EL-11
La Porte, 33800 ... EL-11
La Pryor, 1643 ... WR-14
La Reforma ... ES-4
La Salle, 200 ... EN-7
LA SALLE CO., 6886 ... EO-2
La Vernia, 1034 ... EM-5
La Villa, 1957 ... ES-5
La Ward, 213 ... EN-8
LaCoste, 1119 ... EM-3
Lacy-Lakeview, 6489 ... WR-7
Ladonia, 612 ... ED-8
LaFayette, 80 ... EE-10
Lago Vista, 6041 ... EJ-5
Laguna Hts., 3488 ... ET-6
Laguna Pk., 1276 ... EG-6
Laguna Vista, 3117 ... ET-6
Laird Hill, 400 ... EF-10
Lajitas, 80 ... WQ-6
L. Brownwood, 1532 ... EG-3
L. Creek, 75 ... EC-9
L. Dallas, 7105 ... †B-8
L. Jackson, 26849 ... EM-10
L. Shore, 300 ... EG-3
L. Tanglewood, 796 ... WD-10
L. Victor, 50 ... EI-4
L. Worth, 4584 ... †G-3
Lakeport, 974 ... EF-11
Lakeside, 1307 ... †G-2
Lakeside City, 997 ... EC-4
Lakeside Vil., 600 ... EG-6
Laketon ... WC-12
Lakeview, 25 ... WE-10
Lakeview, 35 ... WH-10
Lakeview, 107 ... WE-12
Lakeway, 11391 ... EJ-5
Lakewood Harbor, 40 ... EG-6
Lakewood Vil., 545 ... †B-8
Lamar, 636 ... EO-7
LAMAR CO., 49793 ... EC-9
Lamasco, 35 ... EC-8
LAMB CO., 13977 ... WG-9
Lamesa, 9422 ... WI-10
Lamkin, 50 ... EG-4
Lampasas, 6681 ... EI-4
LAMPASAS CO., 19677 ... EI-4
Lancaster, 36361 ... †J-10
Lane City, 300 ... EM-9
Laneville, 250 ... EG-11
Langtry, 30 ... WP-11
Lannius, 90 ... EC-8
Lantana, 6874 ... †C-6
Laredo, 236091 ... EQ-2
Lariat, 60 ... WF-8
LaRue, 160 ... EF-9
Lasara, 1039 ... ES-5
Lassater, 50 ... EE-11
Latexo, 322 ... EH-9
LAVACA CO., 19263 ... EM-7
Lawn, 314 ... WK-14
Lawrence, 300 ... EE-8
Lazbuddie, 250 ... WF-9
League City, 83560 ... EL-10
Leakey, 425 ... WP-14
Leander, 26521 ... EJ-5
Ledbetter, 80 ... EK-7
LEE CO., 16612 ... EJ-6
Leesburg, 120 ... ED-10
Leesville, 180 ... EM-5
Lefors, 497 ... WC-12
Leggett, 350 ... EI-11
Leigh, 75 ... EE-12
Lela, 80 ... WD-13
Lelia Lake, 130 ... WE-12
Leming, 946 ... EM-4
Lenorah, 80 ... WJ-10
LEON CO., 16801 ... EI-8
Leon Jct., 50 ... EH-5
Leon Valley, 10151 ... ER-8
Leona, 175 ... EI-9
Leonard, 1990 ... ED-8
Leroy, 337 ... EG-7
Lesley, 10 ... WE-12
Levelland, 13542 ... WG-9
Lewisville, 95290 ... †C-8
Lexington, 1177 ... EJ-7
Liberty, 250 ... EI-13
Liberty, 8397 ... EK-11
LIBERTY CO., 75643 ... EJ-11
Liberty Grv., 50 ... †E-14
Liberty Hill, 967 ... EJ-5
Lilbert, 70 ... EG-11
LIMESTONE CO., 23384 ... EH-7
Lincoln, 120 ... EK-7
Lincoln Pk., 308 ... †A-8
Lindale, 4818 ... EF-9
Linden, 1988 ... ED-11
Lindenau, 50 ... EM-6
Lindsay, 1018 ... EC-6
Lingleville, 100 ... EF-4
Linn, 801 ... ES-5
Linwood, 40 ... EG-10
Lipan, 430 ... EF-5
Lipscomb, 37 ... WB-13
LIPSCOMB CO., 3302 ... WB-13
Lissie, 150 ... EL-8
Little River-Academy, 1961 ... EI-6
Littlefield, 6372 ... WG-9
Live Oak, 13131 ... EL-4
LIVE OAK CO., 11531 ... EO-4
Liverpool, 482 ... EM-10
Livingston, 5335 ... EI-11
Llano, 3232 ... EJ-3
LLANO CO., 19301 ... EI-3
Lobo ... WM-5
Lockett ... EB-2
Lockettville, 25 ... WH-9
Lockhart, 12698 ... EL-5
Lockney, 1842 ... WF-11
Lodi, 200 ... EE-12
Log Cabin, 714 ... EF-8
Lohn, 150 ... EH-2
Lolita, 555 ... EN-8
Loma Alta, 25 ... WP-12
Loma Alta, 100 ... EO-4
Lometa, 856 ... EI-4
London, 200 ... EJ-2
Lone Camp, 100 ... EE-4
Lone Grv. ... EI-4
Lone Oak, 598 ... EE-8
Lone Star, 1581 ... EE-11
Long Branch, 120 ... EF-11
Long Lake, 50 ... EG-9
Long Mott, 125 ... EO-7
Longview, 80455 ... EE-11
Longworth ... WJ-13
Loop, 225 ... WI-9
Lopeño, 174 ... ES-3
Lopezville, 4333 ... WS-10
Loraine, 602 ... WJ-12
Lorena, 1691 ... EH-6
Lorenzo, 1147 ... WG-11
Los Angeles ... EO-3
Los Campos, 100 ... WQ-12
Los Ebanos, 335 ... ET-4
Los Fresnos, 5542 ... ET-6
Los Indios, 1083 ... ET-5
Los Ybanez, 19 ... WI-10
Lott, 759 ... EI-7
Louise, 995 ... EM-8
Lovelady, 649 ... EI-10
Loving, 250 ... ED-4
LOVING CO., 82 ... WK-7
Lowake, 25 ... WL-13
Lowry Crossing, 1711 ... †A-13
Loyola Bch., 130 ... EQ-5
Lubbock, 229573 ... WH-10
LUBBOCK CO., 278831 ... WG-10
Lucas, 5166 ... †C-13
Luckenbach ... EK-3
Lueders, 346 ... WI-14
Lufkin, 35067 ... EH-11
Luling, 5411 ... EL-5
Lumberton, 11943 ... EJ-12
Lutie, 30 ... WD-13
Lydia, 75 ... EC-11
Lyford, 2611 ... ES-5
LYNN CO., 5915 ... WH-10
Lyons, 300 ... EJ-8
Lytle, 2492 ... EM-3
Mabank, 3035 ... EF-8
Macdona, 559 ... EM-3
MADISON CO., 13664 ... EI-8
Madisonville, 4396 ... EI-9
Magasco, 50 ... EH-12
Magnet, 80 ... EM-9
Magnolia, 1393 ... EK-9
Magnolia Bch., 200 ... EN-8
Magnolia Gdns. ... *C-8
Magnolia Sprs., 120 ... EI-12
Malakoff, 2324 ... EF-8
Malone, 269 ... EG-7
Malta, 150 ... EC-11
Manchester, 100 ... EC-10
Mankins, 20 ... EC-3
Manor, 5037 ... EJ-6
Mansfield, 56368 ... EF-6
Manvel, 5179 ... EL-10
Maple, 100 ... WG-8
Mapleton, 30 ... EI-9
Marathon, 430 ... WO-7
Marble Falls, 6077 ... EJ-4
Marfa, 1981 ... WN-6
Margaret, 40 ... WF-14
Marietta, 134 ... ED-11
Marion, 1066 ... EL-5
MARION CO., 10546 ... EE-11
Markham, 1082 ... EM-9
Markley, 30 ... ED-4
Marlin, 5967 ... EH-7
Marquez, 263 ... EH-8
Marshall, 23523 ... EE-11
Marshall Creek, 431 ... †D-5
Mart, 2209 ... EH-7
MARTIN CO., 4799 ... WJ-10
Martindale, 1116 ... EL-5
Martinez ... ES-12
Martinsville, 130 ... EG-11
Maryneal, 120 ... WJ-13
Marysville ... EC-6
Mason, 2114 ... EJ-2
MASON CO., 4012 ... EJ-2
Massey Lake, 75 ... EG-9
Masterson, 40 ... WC-10
Matador, 607 ... WG-12
Matagorda, 503 ... EN-9
MATAGORDA CO., 36702 ... EN-9
Mathis, 4942 ... EO-5
Maud, 1056 ... ED-11
Mauriceville, 3252 ... EJ-13
Maverick ... WK-13
MAVERICK CO., 54258 ... WR-13
Maxwell, 350 ... EL-5
May, 300 ... EG-3
Maydelle, 250 ... EG-10
Maypearl, 934 ... EF-6
Maysfield, 130 ... EI-7
McAdoo, 100 ... WG-12
McAllen, 129877 ... ET-4
McCamey, 1887 ... WM-9
McCaulley, 200 ... WI-13
McCook, 90 ... ES-4
McCoy, 20 ... EN-4
MCCULLOCH CO., 8283 ... EH-2
McDade, 685 ... EK-6
McFaddin, 175 ... EN-7
McGregor, 4987 ... EH-6
McKinney, 131117 ... ED-7
McLean, 778 ... WD-12
MCLENNAN CO., 234906 ... EH-6
McLeod, 250 ... ED-12
McMahan, 60 ... EL-6
MCMULLEN CO., 707 ... EO-4
McNair, 1400 ... *D-9
McNeil, 30 ... WB-6
McQueeney, 2545 ... EL-5
Meadow, 593 ... WH-10
Meadows Pl., 4660 ... *F-2
Medicine Mound, 30 ... EB-2
Medina, 450 ... EL-2
MEDINA CO., 46006 ... EM-2
Megargel, 203 ... ED-3
Melissa, 4695 ... ED-7
Melrose ... EH-11
Melvin, 178 ... EI-2
Memphis, 2290 ... WE-13
Menard, 1471 ... WM-14
MENARD CO., 2242 ... WN-14
Mentone, 19 ... WK-7
Mercedes, 15570 ... ET-5
Mercury, 50 ... EH-3
Mereta, 200 ... WL-13
Meridian, 1493 ... EG-5
Merkel, 2590 ... WJ-13
Mertens, 125 ... EG-7
Mertzon, 781 ... WM-12
Mesquite, 139824 ... EE-7
Mexia, 7459 ... EG-8
Meyersville, 120 ... EN-6
Miami, 597 ... WC-12
Mico, 100 ... EL-3
Middleton ... EH-9
Midfield, 150 ... EM-8
Midkiff, 180 ... WL-10
Midland, 111147 ... WK-10
MIDLAND CO., 136872 ... WK-10
Midlothian, 18037 ... EF-7
Midway, 228 ... EI-9
Mila Doce, 6222 ... WS-12
Milam, 1480 ... EH-13
MILAM CO., 24757 ... EI-7
Milano, 428 ... EJ-7
Mildred, 368 ... EG-8
Miles, 829 ... WL-13
Milford, 728 ... EG-7
Miller Grv., 125 ... ED-9
Millersview, 100 ... WL-14
Millett, 40 ... EN-2
Millican, 240 ... EJ-8
MILLS CO., 4936 ... EH-4
Millsap, 403 ... EE-5
Minden, 300 ... EG-11
Mineola, 4515 ... EE-9
Mineral, 60 ... EN-5
Mineral Wells, 16788 ... EE-4
Minerva, 60 ... EJ-7
Mingus, 235 ... EF-4
Minter ... EC-9
Mirando City, 375 ... EQ-3
Mission, 77058 ... ET-4
Mission Bend, 36501 ... *E-1
Missouri City, 67358 ... EL-10
MITCHELL CO., 9403 ... WK-12
Mobeetie, 101 ... WC-13
Moffat, 200 ... EI-6
Monahans, 6953 ... WL-8
Monkstown, 35 ... EC-8
Monroe City, 90 ... EK-11
Mont Belvieu, 3835 ... EK-11
Montague, 304 ... EC-5
MONTAGUE CO., 19719 ... EC-5
Montalba, 150 ... EG-9
Monte Alto, 1924 ... ES-5
Montell ... WP-14
Montgomery, 621 ... EJ-9
MONTGOMERY CO., 455746 ... EJ-9
Moody, 1371 ... EH-6
Moore, 475 ... EM-3
MOORE CO., 21904 ... WC-10
Moore Sta., 201 ... EF-9
Mooring ... EJ-7
Moran, 270 ... EF-2
Moravia ... EL-7
Morgan, 490 ... EG-5
Morgan Mill, 200 ... EF-4
Morgan's Pt., 339 ... *F-9
Morgan's Pt. Resort, 4170 ... EI-6
MORRIS CO., 12934 ... ED-11
Morse, 147 ... WB-11
Morton, 2006 ... WG-9
Moscow, 300 ... EI-11
Mosheim, 100 ... EH-5
Moss Hill, 150 ... EJ-11
MOTLEY CO., 1210 ... WF-12
Moulton, 886 ... EL-6
Mt. Calm, 320 ... EG-7
Mt. Enterprise, 447 ... EG-11
Mt. Pleasant, 15564 ... ED-10
Mt. Selman, 200 ... EF-10
Mt. Vernon, 2662 ... ED-10
Mountain Home, 90 ... EK-2
Muenster, 1544 ... EC-6
Muldoon, 80 ... EL-7
Muleshoe, 5158 ... WF-9
Mullin, 179 ... EH-3
Mumford, 200 ... EJ-7
Munday, 1300 ... WH-14
Muniz, 1370 ... WR-11
Murchison, 594 ... EF-9
Murphy, 17708 ... †D-13
Mustang Ridge, 861 ... EK-5
Myra, 250 ... EC-6
Myrtle Sprs., 828 ... EE-8
Nacogdoches, 32996 ... EG-11
NACOGDOCHES CO., 64524 ... EH-11
Nada, 170 ... EL-8
Naples, 1378 ... ED-11
Nash, 2960 ... EC-12
Nassau Bay, 4002 ... *G-8
Natalia, 1431 ... EM-3
NAVARRO CO., 47735 ... EG-7
Navasota, 7049 ... EJ-8
Nazareth, 311 ... WE-10
Neches, 300 ... EG-9
Nederland, 17547 ... EK-12
Needmore, 40 ... WF-9
Needville, 2823 ... EL-9
Negley ... EC-10
Nelsonville, 90 ... EK-8
Nemo, 60 ... EF-5
Nesbitt, 281 ... EE-11
Neuville, 70 ... EG-12
Nevada, 822 ... ED-8
New Baden, 120 ... EI-8
New Berlin, 511 ... EL-5
New Boston, 4550 ... EC-11
New Braunfels, 57740 ... EL-5
New Caney, 3000 ... EK-10
New Chapel Hill, 594 ... EF-10
New Deal, 794 ... WG-10
New Fairview, 1258 ... ED-6
New Home, 334 ... WH-10
New Hope ... EE-9
New Hope, 614 ... †A-13
New Katy, 60 ... EJ-6
New London, 998 ... EF-10
New Salem, 50 ... EG-10
New Summerfield, 1111 ... EG-10
New Taiton ... EM-8
New Territory, 15186 ... *G-1
New Ulm, 350 ... EK-8
New Waverly, 1032 ... EJ-10
New Willard, 100 ... EI-11
Newark, 1005 ... EE-6
Newcastle, 585 ... ED-3
Newgulf ... EM-9
Newport, 40 ... ED-5
Newton, 2478 ... EI-13
NEWTON CO., 14445 ... EI-13
Neylandville, 97 ... ED-8
Niederwald, 565 ... EK-5
Nixon, 2385 ... EM-5
Nobility ... ED-8
Nocona, 3033 ... EC-5
Nogalus, 100 ... EH-10
Nolan, 100 ... WJ-13
NOLAN CO., 15216 ... WJ-13
Nolanville, 4259 ... EI-5
Nome, 588 ... EK-12
Noodle, 50 ... WJ-13
Noonday, 777 ... EF-10
Nordheim, 307 ... EN-6
Norias, 50 ... ER-5
Normandy, 70 ... WR-12
Normangee, 685 ... EI-8
Normanna, 113 ... EO-5
N. Alamo, 3235 ... WS-10
N. Houston, 2000 ... *B-3
N. Richland Hills, 63343 ... EE-6
N. San Antonio Hills, 100 ... ER-7
N. Zulch, 550 ... EI-8
Northfield, 25 ... WF-12
Northlake, 1724 ... †C-5
Northline Ter., 2700 ... *C-4
Northrup, 50 ... EK-7
Norton, 75 ... WK-13
Norwood, 100 ... EH-12
Notrees, 125 ... WK-8
Novice ... EC-9
Novice, 139 ... WK-14
NUECES CO., 340223 ... EP-5
Nugent, 50 ... WI-14
Nurillo, 7344 ... WR-10
Nursery, 350 ... EN-7
Oak Grv., 90 ... EC-11
Oak Lake Estates, 2000 ... *F-1
Oak Pt., 2786 ... †A-8
Oak Ridge, 141 ... EC-6
Oak Ridge North, 3049 ... EK-10
Oak Valley, 368 ... EG-7
Oakalla, 80 ... EI-5
Oakhurst, 233 ... EI-10
Oakland, 85 ... EL-7
Oakville, 100 ... EO-5
Oakwood, 510 ... EH-9
O'Brien, 106 ... WH-14
OCHILTREE CO., 10223 ... WB-12
Odell, 95 ... EB-2
Odem, 2389 ... EP-6
Odessa, 99940 ... WK-9
O'Donnell, 831 ... WI-10
Oglesby, 484 ... EH-6
Oilton, 353 ... EQ-3
Oklahoma, 700 ... EK-9
Oklahoma Lane ... WF-8
Oklaunion, 150 ... EB-2
Old Boston, 170 ... EC-11
Old Dime Box ... EJ-7
Old Glory, 70 ... WH-13
Old Ocean, 950 ... EM-9
Old River-Winfree, 1245 ... EK-11
Olden, 500 ... EF-3
Oldenburg ... EK-7
OLDHAM CO., 2052 ... WC-9
Oletha ... EH-8
Olin ... EG-4
Olivarez, 3827 ... WS-12
Olivia, 250 ... EN-8
Olmito, 1210 ... ET-6
Olmos Pk., 2237 ... ER-10
Olney, 3285 ... ED-3
Olton, 2215 ... WF-10
Omaha, 1021 ... ED-11
Onalaska, 1764 ... EI-10
Opdyke West, 174 ... WG-9
Oplin, 75 ... EG-2
Oran, 60 ... EE-4
Orange, 18595 ... EK-13
ORANGE CO., 81837 ... EK-12
Orange Grv., 1318 ... EP-5
Orchard, 352 ... EL-9
Ore City, 1144 ... EE-11
Orla, 50 ... WK-6
Osceola, 100 ... EG-6
Ottine, 130 ... EL-6
Otto, 50 ... EH-7
Ovalo, 200 ... WK-14
Overton, 2554 ... EF-10
Ovilla, 3492 ... †J-9
Owens ... WH-11
Owens, 30 ... EG-3
Owentown, 120 ... EF-10
Oyster Creek, 1111 ... EM-10
Ozona, 3225 ... WN-11
Paducah, 1186 ... WG-13
Paige, 200 ... EK-6
Paint Rock, 273 ... WL-14
Palacios, 4718 ... EN-8
Palestine, 18712 ... EG-9
Palm Harbor, 125 ... EP-7
Palm Pk., 250 ... EM-4
Palmer, 2000 ... EF-7
Palmhurst, 2607 ... WS-9
Palmview, 5460 ... WS-8
Palo Pinto, 333 ... EE-4
PALO PINTO CO., 28111 ... EE-4
Paluxy, 55 ... EF-5
Pampa, 17994 ... WC-12
Pandora, 100 ... EM-5
Panhandle, 2452 ... WD-11
Panna Maria, 110 ... EN-5
Panola, 225 ... EF-12
PANOLA CO., 23796 ... EF-12
Pantego, 2394 ... †H-6
Panther Jct., 100 ... WQ-7
Papalote, 70 ... EO-6
Paradise, 441 ... ED-5
Paris, 25171 ... EC-9
Park Sprs., 80 ... ED-5
Parker, 3811 ... †C-13
PARKER CO., 116927 ... EE-5
PARMER CO., 10269 ... WE-8
Pasadena, 149043 ... EL-10
Patillo, 20 ... EF-4
Patricia, 60 ... WJ-10
Patroon, 60 ... EG-12
Pattonville, 220 ... EC-9
Pawelekville, 50 ... EM-5
Pawnee, 166 ... EN-5
Paxton, 120 ... EG-12
Payne Sprs., 767 ... EF-8
Peacock, 50 ... WH-13
Peadenville, 30 ... EE-4
Pear Valley, 40 ... EH-2
Pearl ... EH-5
Pearland, 91252 ... EL-10
Pearsall, 9146 ... EN-3
Peaster, 80 ... EE-5
Pecan Gap, 203 ... ED-9
Pecan Grv., 15963 ... *F-1
Pecos, 8780 ... WL-7
PECOS CO., 15507 ... WN-8
Peerless, 75 ... ED-9
Peggy, 10 ... EN-4
Pendleton, 200 ... EI-6
Penelope, 198 ... EG-7
Penitas, 4403 ... ET-4
Pennington, 125 ... EH-10
Penwell, 75 ... WK-9
Peoria, 100 ... EG-6
Pep, 50 ... WG-9
Perico ... WB-8
Perrin, 398 ... EE-4
Perry, 60 ... EH-7
Perryton, 8802 ... WA-12
Peters ... EK-8
Petersburg, 1202 ... WG-11
Petrolia, 686 ... EB-4
Petronila, 113 ... EP-6
Pettit, 80 ... WG-9
Pettus, 558 ... EN-5
Petty, 100 ... EC-9
Pflugerville, 46936 ... EJ-5
Pharr, 70400 ... ET-5
Phelps, 200 ... EJ-10
Phillips, 900 ... WC-11
Pickton, 150 ... ED-9
Pidcoke ... EH-5
Pierce, 125 ... EM-8
Pilot Pt., 3856 ... ED-7
Pine Forest, 487 ... EK-12
Pine Island, 988 ... EK-9
Pinehill, 40 ... EF-11
Pinehurst, 2097 ... EK-13
Pinehurst, 4624 ... EK-9
Pineland, 850 ... EH-12
Piney Pt. Vil., 3125 ... *D-3
Pioneer, 40 ... EG-3
Pipe Creek, 100 ... EL-3
Pittsburg, 4497 ... ED-10
Placedo, 692 ... EN-7
Placid, 30 ... EH-3
Plains, 1481 ... WH-8
Plainview, 22194 ... WF-10
Plano, 259841 ... EE-7
Plantersville, 200 ... EJ-9
Pleak, 1044 ... EL-9
Pleasant Farms, 110 ... WL-9
Pleasant Grv. ... EE-9
Pleasant Valley ... WH-11
Pleasant Valley, 336 ... EC-3
Pleasanton, 8934 ... EN-4
Pledger, 200 ... EM-9
Plum, 200 ... EK-7
Plum Grv., 600 ... EK-10
Point, 820 ... EE-9
Point Blank, 688 ... EI-10
Point Comfort, 737 ... EN-8
POLK CO., 45413 ... EI-11
Pollok, 300 ... EH-11
Ponder, 1395 ... ED-6
Ponta, 50 ... EG-10
Pontotoc, 130 ... EI-3
Poolville, 300 ... EE-5
Port Alto, 50 ... EN-8
Port Aransas, 3480 ... EP-7
Port Arthur, 53818 ... EK-13
Port Bolivar, 1300 ... EL-11
Port Isabel, 5006 ... ET-7
Port Lavaca, 12248 ... EN-8
Port Mansfield, 226 ... ES-6
Port Neches, 13040 ... EK-13
Port O'Connor, 1253 ... EO-8
Porter, 7000 ... EK-10
Porter Sprs., 100 ... EH-9
Portland, 15099 ... EP-6
Posey, 100 ... WH-10
Post, 5376 ... WH-11
Postoak, 50 ... ED-4
Poteet, 3260 ... EM-4
Poth, 1908 ... EM-5
Potosi, 2991 ... WJ-14
POTTER CO., 121073 ... WD-10
Pottsboro, 2160 ... EC-7
Pottsville, 100 ... EH-4
Powderly, 1178 ... EC-9
Powell, 136 ... EF-8
Poynor, 305 ... EG-9
Prairie Dell, 35 ... EI-6
Prairie Hill, 200 ... EH-7
Prairie Lea, 200 ... EL-5
Prairie Pt., 40 ... ED-6
Prairie View, 5576 ... EK-9
Prairieville ... EF-8
Premont, 2653 ... EQ-5
Presidio, 4426 ... WP-5
PRESIDIO CO., 7818 ... WO-5
Preston, 2096 ... EC-7
Price, 650 ... EF-10
Priddy, 180 ... EH-4
Princeton, 6807 ... ED-7
Pringle, 30 ... WB-11
Pritchett, 250 ... EE-10
Proctor, 200 ... EG-4
Progreso, 5507 ... ET-5
Progreso Lakes ... WT-12
Progress, 60 ... WF-8
Prosper, 9423 ... ED-7
Providence Vil., 4786 ... †A-8
Purdon, 130 ... EG-7
Purley, 120 ... ED-10
Purmela, 40 ... EH-5
Purves ... EG-4
Putnam, 94 ... EF-2
Pyote, 114 ... WL-8
Quail, 19 ... WE-13
Quanah, 2641 ... WF-14
Quarry ... EJ-8
Queen City, 1476 ... ED-12
Quemado, 230 ... WR-12
Quinlan, 1394 ... EE-8
Quintana, 56 ... EM-10
Quitaque, 411 ... WF-12
Quitman, 1809 ... EE-9
Rabb, 20 ... EP-5
Rachal, 35 ... ER-5
Rainbow, 80 ... EF-5
RAINS CO., 10914 ... EE-9
Ralls, 1944 ... WG-11
Ramireno, 35 ... ER-2
Ramirez, 50 ... EQ-4
Rancho Viejo, 2437 ... ET-6
RANDALL CO., 120725 ... WE-10
Randolph, 200 ... EC-8
Ranger, 2468 ... EF-3
Rankin, 778 ... WM-10
Ransom Canyon, 1096 ... WH-10
Ratcliff, 200 ... EH-10
Ravenna, 209 ... EC-8
Ray Pt. ... EO-5
Rayburn, 75 ... EJ-11
Rayland ... EB-2
Raymondville, 11284 ... ES-5
Raywood, 300 ... EK-11
Reagan, 220 ... EI-7
REAGAN CO., 3367 ... WL-11
REAL CO., 3309 ... WP-14
Realitos, 184 ... EQ-4
Red Bluff, 40 ... WK-6
Red Gate, 50 ... ES-5
Red Lick, 1008 ... EC-12
Red Oak, 10769 ... EF-7
RED RIVER CO., 12860 ... EC-10
Red Rock, 80 ... EK-6
Red Sprs., 40 ... EC-2
Redbank, 150 ... EC-11
Redford, 90 ... WP-5
Redland, 1047 ... EH-11
Redwater, 1057 ... ED-12
REEVES CO., 13783 ... WL-6
Refugio, 2890 ... EO-6
REFUGIO CO., 7383 ... EO-7
Reilly Sprs., 75 ... ED-9
Rek Hill, 40 ... EK-7
Reklaw, 379 ... EG-10
Rendon, 12552 ... †J-5
Reno, 2494 ... EE-5
Reno, 3166 ... EC-9
Retreat, 377 ... EG-8
Rhea, 50 ... WE-8
Rhineland, 80 ... WH-14
Rhome, 1522 ... ED-6
Rhonesboro, 50 ... EE-10
Ricardo, 1048 ... EQ-5
Rice, 923 ... EF-7
Richards, 300 ... EJ-9
Richardson, 99223 ... †E-11
Richland, 264 ... EG-8
Richland Hills, 7801 ... †G-5
Richland Sprs., 338 ... EH-3
Richmond, 11679 ... EL-9
Richwood, 3510 ... EM-10
Ridge ... EI-8
Ridgeheights, 200 ... WH-6
Ridgeway, 100 ... ED-9
Riesel, 1007 ... EH-7
Rincon ... ES-4
Ringgold, 200 ... EC-5
Rio Bravo, 4794 ... EQ-2
Rio Frio, 60 ... WP-14
Rio Grande City, 13834 ... ES-3
Rio Hondo, 2356 ... ET-6
Rio Vista, 873 ... EF-6
Rising Star, 835 ... EG-3
River Bend ... EH-13
River Oaks, 7427 ... †G-3
Riverside, 510 ... EI-10
Riviera, 689 ... EQ-5
Riviera Bch., 125 ... EQ-6
Roanoke, 5962 ... EE-6
Roans Prairie, 60 ... EJ-9
Roaring Sprs., 234 ... WG-12
Robert Lee, 1049 ... WK-13
ROBERTS CO., 929 ... WC-12
ROBERTSON CO., 16622 ... EI-7
Robinson, 10509 ... EH-6
Robstown, 11487 ... EP-6
Roby, 643 ... WI-13
Rochelle, 200 ... EI-2
Rochester, 324 ... WH-14
Rock Island, 200 ... EL-8
Rockdale, 5595 ... EJ-7
Rockland, 120 ... EI-12
Rockne, 60 ... EK-6
Rockport, 8766 ... EP-7
Rocksprings, 1182 ... WO-13
Rockwall, 37490 ... EE-7
ROCKWALL CO., 78337 ... EE-8
Rockwood, 100 ... EH-2
Rocky Mound, 75 ... ED-10
Roganville, 100 ... EI-13
Rogers, 1218 ... EI-6
Rolling Hills, 200 ... EK-9
Rolling Hills, 500 ... WA-2
Rollingwood, 1412 ... WE-5
Roma, 9765 ... ES-3
Romayor, 150 ... EJ-11
Roosevelt ... WG-11
Roosevelt, 20 ... WN-13
Ropesville, 434 ... WH-10
Rosalie, 80 ... EC-10
Rosanky, 180 ... EK-6
Roscoe, 1322 ... WJ-13
Rose City, 502 ... EQ-14
Rose Hill Acres, 441 ... EJ-12
Rosebud, 1412 ... EI-7
Rosenberg, 30618 ... EL-9
Rosevine, 100 ... EH-12
Rosewood ... EE-10
Rosharon, 1152 ... EM-10
Rosita ... EP-4
Ross, 283 ... EG-6
Rosser, 332 ... EF-8
Rosston, 60 ... ED-6
Rotan, 1508 ... WI-13
Round Mtn., 181 ... EJ-4
Round Rock, 99887 ... EJ-5
Round Top, 90 ... EK-7
Rowena, 450 ... WL-13
Rowlett, 56199 ... †E-13
Roxton, 650 ... EC-9
Royalty, 25 ... WL-8
Royse City, 9349 ... EE-8
Rugby, 10 ... EC-10
Ruidosa, 80 ... WO-5
Rule, 636 ... WH-14
Rumley ... EI-5
Runaway Bay, 1286 ... ED-5
Runge, 1031 ... EN-5
RUNNELS CO., 10501 ... WK-13
Rushwood, 3600 ... *B-4
Rusk, 5551 ... EG-10
RUSK CO., 53330 ... EG-11
Rutersville, 50 ... EK-7
Rye, 100 ... EJ-11
Sabinal, 1695 ... EM-2
SABINE CO., 10834 ... EG-12
Sachse, 20329 ... †D-13
Sacul, 170 ... EG-10
Sadler, 343 ... EC-7
Sagerton, 75 ... WI-14
St. Francis Vil., 500 ... †J-2
St. Hedwig, 2094 ... EM-4
St. Jo, 1043 ... EC-5
St. Paul, 584 ... EO-6
St. Paul, 1066 ... †C-13
Salado, 2126 ... EI-6
Salineño, 201 ... ES-3
Salmon ... EH-9
Salt Flat, 30 ... WK-4
Salt Gap ... EH-2
Saltillo, 200 ... ED-10
Samnorwood, 51 ... WD-13
San Angelo, 93200 ... WL-13
San Antonio, 1327407 ... EM-4
San Augustine, 2108 ... EH-12
SAN AUGUSTINE CO., 8865 ... EH-12
San Benito, 24250 ... ET-6
San Carlos, 3130 ... WR-11
San Diego, 4488 ... EP-4
San Elizario, 13603 ... WK-2
San Felipe, 747 ... EL-8
San Gabriel, 75 ... EJ-6
San Isidro, 240 ... ES-4
SAN JACINTO CO., 26384 ... EJ-10
San Juan, 33856 ... WS-10
San Leanna, 497 ... EK-5
San Leon, 4970 ... *H-10
San Marcos, 44894 ... EL-5
San Patricio, 395 ... EP-5
SAN PATRICIO CO., 64804 ... EP-6
San Perlita, 573 ... ES-6
San Saba, 3099 ... EI-3
SAN SABA CO., 6131 ... EI-3
San Ygnacio, 667 ... ER-2
Sand Flat, 100 ... EF-10
Sand Sprs., 835 ... WJ-11
Sanderson, 837 ... WO-9
Sandia, 379 ... EP-5
Sandusky, 20 ... EC-7
Sandy, 20 ... EJ-4
Sandy Pt., 150 ... EL-10
Sanford, 164 ... WC-11
Sanger, 6916 ... ED-6
Sansom Pk., 4686 ... †G-3
Santa Anna, 1099 ... EG-2
Santa Cruz, 54 ... ES-3
Santa Elena, 120 ... ER-4
Santa Fe, 12222 ... EL-10
Santa Monica, 83 ... ES-6
Santa Rosa, 2873 ... ET-5
Santo, 450 ... EF-4
Saragosa, 400 ... WM-7
Saratoga, 1200 ... EJ-11
Sargent, 400 ... EN-9
Sarita, 238 ... EQ-5
Saspamco, 200 ... EM-4
Sattler ... EL-4
Savoy, 831 ... EC-8
Sayers, 30 ... ET-12
Schertz, 31465 ... EL-4
Schicke Pt., 200 ... EN-8
SCHLEICHER CO., 3461 ... WM-13
Schulenburg, 2852 ... EL-7
Schwertner, 80 ... EI-6
Scissors, 3186 ... WT-11
Scotland, 501 ... EC-4
Scottsville, 376 ... EE-12
Scranton ... EF-3
Scroggins, 80 ... ED-10
Scurry, 681 ... EF-8
SCURRY CO., 16921 ... WI-12
Seabrook, 11952 ... EL-11
Seadrift, 1364 ... EO-7
Seagoville, 14835 ... EE-7
Seagraves, 2417 ... WI-9
Sealy, 6019 ... EL-8
Sebastian, 1917 ... ES-5
Sebastopol ... EI-10
Security, 30 ... EJ-10
Segno ... EJ-11
Segovia, 15 ... WN-14
Seguin, 25175 ... EL-5
Selden, 75 ... EG-4
Selma, 5540 ... EQ-12
Seminole, 6430 ... WI-9
Serbin, 60 ... EK-7
Seth Ward, 2025 ... WF-10
Seven Oaks, 111 ... EI-11
Seven Pts., 1455 ... EF-8
Seymour, 2740 ... EC-2
SHACKELFORD CO., 3378 ... EE-2
Shady Shores, 2612 ... †B-7
Shafter, 30 ... WP-5
Shallowater, 2484 ... WG-10
Shamrock, 1910 ... WD-13
Shamrock Shores, 1000 ... EG-3
Shannon ... ED-4
Sharp, 80 ... EJ-6
Shavano Pk., 3035 ... EQ-9
Sheffield, 450 ... WN-10
Shelby, 85 ... EK-7
SHELBY CO., 25448 ... EG-12
Shelbyville, 300 ... EG-12
Sheldon, 1990 ... EK-10
Shenandoah, 2134 ... EK-10
Shep ... WK-13
Shepherd, 2319 ... EJ-11
Sheridan, 500 ... EL-7
Sherman, 38521 ... EC-7
SHERMAN CO., 3034 ... WB-10
Sherwood, 100 ... WM-12
Sherwood Shores, 450 ... EC-7
Shiloh ... EK-11
Shiner, 2069 ... EL-6
Shiro, 200 ... EJ-9
Shoreacres, 1493 ... *F-9
Sidney, 200 ... EG-3
Sienna Plantation, 13721 ... *H-3
Sierra Blanca, 553 ... WL-4
Siesta Shores, 1382 ... ER-2
Silsbee, 6611 ... EJ-12
Silver Lake, 45 ... EE-9
Silverton, 731 ... WF-11
Simms, 275 ... ED-11
Singleton, 50 ... EJ-9
Sinton, 5665 ... EP-6
Sipe Sprs., 50 ... EG-3
Sisterdale, 40 ... EK-3
Skellytown, 473 ... WC-11
Skidmore, 925 ... EO-5
Slaton, 6121 ... WH-11
Slide, 40 ... WH-10
Slidell, 100 ... ED-6
Slocum, 225 ... EG-9
Smiley, 549 ... EM-6
SMITH CO., 209714 ... EF-9
Smith Hill ... EC-11
Smith Pt., 300 ... EL-11
Smithland ... EE-12
Smithville, 3817 ... EK-6
Smyer, 474 ... WG-10
Snook, 511 ... EJ-8
Snyder, 11202 ... WI-12
Socorro, 32013 ... WK-2
Somerset, 1631 ... EM-4
SOMERVELL CO., 8490 ... EF-5
Somerville, 1376 ... EJ-8
Sonora, 3027 ... WN-12
Sour Lake, 1813 ... EK-12
S. Alamo, 3361 ... WT-11
S. Bend, 125 ... EE-3
S. Haven, 100 ... WK-11
S. Houston, 16983 ... *F-6
S. Mountain, 384 ... EH-5
S. Padre Island, 2816 ... ET-7
S. Plains, 100 ... WF-11
Southlake, 26575 ... †E-6
Southland, 150 ... WH-11
Southmayd, 992 ... EC-7
Southside Pl., 1715 ... *E-4
Southton, 100 ... ET-11
Spade, 73 ... WG-10
Spanish Camp ... EL-8
Spanish Fort, 50 ... EC-5
Speaks, 60 ... EM-7
Spearman, 3368 ... WB-11
Spicewood, 200 ... EJ-4
Splendora, 1615 ... EK-10
Spofford, 95 ... WQ-13
Spring, 54298 ... EK-10
Spring Branch, 100 ... EL-4
Spring Hill, 60 ... EC-11
Spring Valley, 3611 ... *D-3
Springlake, 108 ... WF-9
Springtown, 2658 ... EE-5
Spur, 1318 ... WH-12
Spurger, 600 ... EI-12
Stafford, 17693 ... *F-3
Stamford, 3124 ... WI-14
Stanton, 2492 ... WK-10
Staples, 267 ... EL-5
Star, 100 ... EH-4
STARR CO., 60968 ... ES-3
STEPHENS CO., 9630 ... EE-3
Stephenville, 17123 ... EF-4
Sterling City, 888 ... WK-12
STERLING CO., 1143 ... WL-11
Stinnett, 1881 ... WC-11
Stockdale, 1442 ... EM-5
Stoneburg, 40 ... EC-5
Stonewall, 505 ... EK-3
STONEWALL CO., 1490 ... WH-13
Stony, 50 ... †J-1
Stowell, 1756 ... EK-12
Stratford, 2017 ... WA-10
Strawn, 653 ... EF-4
Streetman, 247 ... EG-8
String Prairie ... EK-6
Sublime, 125 ... EL-7
Sudan, 958 ... WF-9
Sugar Land, 78817 ... EL-9
Sullivan City, 4002 ... ET-4
Sulphur Bluff, 280 ... ED-9
Sulphur Sprs., 15449 ... ED-9
Summerfield, 70 ... WE-9
Sumner, 100 ... EC-9
Sundown, 1397 ... WH-9
Sunnyside, 70 ... WF-9
Sunnyvale, 5130 ... †G-13
Sunray, 1926 ... WB-10
Sunrise Beach Vil., 713 ... EJ-4
Sunset, 497 ... ED-5
Sunset Valley, 749 ... WF-4
Surfside Bch., 482 ... EM-10
Sutherland Sprs., 400 ... EM-5
SUTTON CO., 4128 ... WN-13
Swan, 350 ... EF-10
Sweeny, 3684 ... EM-9
Sweet Home, 250 ... EM-7
Sweetwater, 10906 ... WJ-13
Swenson, 50 ... WH-13
SWISHER CO., 7854 ... WE-10
Sylvester, 200 ... WI-13
Taft, 3048 ... EP-6
Tahoka, 2673 ... WH-10
Talco, 516 ... ED-10
Talpa, 100 ... WK-14
Tanglewood, 80 ... EJ-7
Tara, 1100 ... *G-1
Tarpley, 40 ... EL-2
TARRANT CO., 1809034 ... EE-6
Tarzan, 250 ... WJ-10
Tatum, 1385 ... EF-11
Taylor, 15191 ... EJ-6
TAYLOR CO., 131506 ... WK-14
Taylor Lake Vil., 3544 ... *G-8
Taylor Lndg., 228 ... EK-12
Teague, 3560 ... EH-8
Tehuacana, 283 ... EG-7
Telegraph, 15 ... WO-14
Telephone, 200 ... EC-8
Telferner, 700 ... EN-7
Tell, 75 ... WF-13
Temple, 66102 ... EI-6
Tenaha, 1160 ... EG-12
Tennessee Colony, 300 ... EG-9
Tennyson, 100 ... WL-13
Terlingua, 58 ... WQ-7
Terrell, 15816 ... EE-8
TERRELL CO., 984 ... WO-9
Terrell Hills, 4878 ... ER-10
TERRY CO., 12651 ... WH-9
Texarkana, 36411 ... EC-12
Texas City, 45099 ... EL-11
Texhoma, 346 ... WA-10
Texline, 507 ... WA-8
Texon, 25 ... WM-10
Thalia, 80 ... EC-2
The Colony, 36328 ... ED-7
The Hills, 2472 ... EK-5
Thicket, 300 ... EJ-11
Thomas ... EE-10
Thomaston, 85 ... EM-6
Thompsons, 246 ... EL-9
Thorndale, 1336 ... EJ-6
Thornton, 526 ... EH-7
Thorntonville, 476 ... WL-8
Thorp Spr., 200 ... EF-5
Thrall, 839 ... EJ-6
Three Rivers, 1848 ... EO-4
Throckmorton, 828 ... ED-2
THROCKMORTON CO., 1641 ... ED-2
Tigertown, 60 ... EC-9
Tilden, 261 ... EO-4
Timpson, 1155 ... EG-11
Tioga, 803 ... ED-7
Tira, 297 ... ED-9
TITUS CO., 32334 ... ED-10
Tivoli, 479 ... EO-7
Toco, 75 ... EC-9
Tolar, 681 ... EF-5
Tom Bean, 1045 ... EC-7
TOM GREEN CO., 110224 ... WM-13
Tomball, 10753 ... EK-9
Tool, 2240 ... EF-8
Topsey, 35 ... EI-5
Tornillo, 1568 ... WL-2
Tow, 300 ... EI-4
Town Bluff ... EI-12
Town West ... *F-2
Toyah, 90 ... WL-6
Toyahvale, 60 ... WM-6
Travis, 50 ... EI-7
TRAVIS CO., 1024266 ... EJ-5
Trent, 337 ... WJ-13
Trenton, 635 ... ED-8
Trickham, 30 ... EH-2
Trinidad, 886 ... EF-8
Trinity, 2697 ... EI-10
TRINITY CO., 14585 ... EI-10
Trophy Club, 8024 ... †D-5
Troup, 1869 ... EF-10
Trout Creek ... EJ-13
Troy, 1645 ... EI-6
Truscott, 60 ... WG-14
Tucker, 150 ... EG-9
Tuleta, 288 ... EN-5
Tulia, 4967 ... WE-10
Tulsita, 14 ... EN-5
Tunis, 150 ... EJ-8
Turkey, 421 ... WF-12
Turnersville, 100 ... EH-5
Turnertown, 250 ... EF-10
Turney ... EG-10
Tuscola, 742 ... WK-14
Tuxedo ... WI-14
Twitty ... WD-13
Tye, 1242 ... WJ-14
Tyler, 96900 ... EF-10
TYLER CO., 21766 ... EI-11
Tynan, 278 ... EO-5
Uhland, 1014 ... EK-5
Umbarger, 150 ... WD-10
Uncertain, 94 ... EE-12
Union ... WI-9
Union, 30 ... WI-12
Union Grv., 357 ... EE-10
Universal City, 18530 ... EQ-12
University Pk., 23068 ... †F-10
UPSHUR CO., 39309 ... EE-10
Upton ... EK-6
UPTON CO., 3355 ... WL-10
Utopia, 227 ... EL-2
Uvalde, 15751 ... WQ-14
UVALDE CO., 26405 ... WQ-14
VAL VERDE CO., 48879 ... WO-11
Valentine, 134 ... WN-5
Valera, 75 ... EG-2
Valley Mills, 1203 ... EH-6
Valley Spr., 80 ... EI-3
Valley View, 100 ... EC-3
Valley View, 757 ... ED-6
Van, 2632 ... EF-9
Van Alstyne, 3046 ... ED-7
Van Horn, 2063 ... WM-4
Van Vleck, 1844 ... EM-9
VAN ZANDT CO., 52579 ... EE-9
Vancourt, 125 ... WL-13
Vanderbilt, 395 ... EN-8
Vanderpool, 20 ... EL-2
Vashti, 70 ... EC-5
Vaughan, 20 ... EG-6
Vealmoor, 100 ... WJ-11
Vega, 884 ... WD-9
Venus, 2960 ... EF-6
Vera, 90 ... EC-2
Verhalen, 50 ... WM-7
Veribest, 40 ... WL-13
Vernon, 11002 ... EB-2
Viboras, 25 ... ER-3
Vick, 40 ... WL-13
Victoria, 62592 ... EN-7
VICTORIA CO., 86793 ... EN-7
Vidor, 10579 ... EK-12
View, 50 ... WJ-14
Vigo Pk., 50 ... WE-11
Village Mills, 300 ... EJ-12
Village of Tiki Island, 968 ... *B-8
Vincent, 100 ... WJ-11
Vineyard ... ED-5
Vinton, 1971 ... WK-1
Voca, 60 ... EI-2
Volente, 520 ... EJ-5
Von Ormy, 1085 ... EM-4
Voss, 20 ... EH-2
Votaw, 200 ... EJ-11
Waco, 124805 ... EH-6
Wadsworth, 300 ... EN-9
Waelder, 1065 ... EL-6
Waka, 100 ... WB-12
Wake Vil., 5492 ... EC-12
Wakefield ... EI-11
Walburg, 200 ... EJ-6
WALKER CO., 67861 ... EI-9
Wall, 200 ... WL-13
Waller, 2326 ... EK-9
WALLER CO., 43205 ... EK-9
Wallis, 1252 ... EL-9
Walnut Sprs., 827 ... EG-5
Walton, 90 ... EF-9
Wamba ... EC-12
WARD CO., 10658 ... WL-7
Warda, 100 ... EK-7
Waring, 100 ... EK-3
Warren, 757 ... EJ-12
Warrenton, 30 ... EK-7
Washburn, 160 ... WD-11
Washington, 300 ... EJ-8
WASHINGTON CO., 33718 ... EK-7
Waskom, 2160 ... EE-12
Wastella ... WJ-12
Watauga, 23497 ... †F-5
Water Valley, 200 ... WL-12
Watson ... EI-5
Watt ... EH-7
Waxahachie, 29621 ... EF-7
Wayside, 30 ... WE-11
Weatherford, 25250 ... EE-5
Weaver, 50 ... ED-9
WEBB CO., 250304 ... WT-14
Webster, 10400 ... *G-8
Weches, 30 ... EH-10
Weesatche, 170 ... EN-6
Weimar, 2151 ... EL-7
Weinert, 172 ... WH-14
Weir, 450 ... EJ-6
Welch, 222 ... WI-10
Weldon, 200 ... EI-9
Wellborn, 150 ... EJ-8
Wellington, 2189 ... WE-13
Wellman, 203 ... WI-9
Wells, 790 ... EH-10
Wells Branch, 12120 ... WB-6
Weser ... EN-6
Weslaco, 35670 ... ET-5
Wesley ... EK-8
West, 2807 ... EG-6
W. Columbia, 3905 ... EM-9
W. Lake Hills, 3063 ... WE-4
W. Orange, 3443 ... EK-13
W. Point ... WH-10
W. Point, 200 ... EK-7
W. Sharyland, 2309 ... WR-9
W. Tawakoni, 1576 ... EE-8
W. University Pl., 14787 ... *E-4
Westbrook, 253 ... WJ-12
Westfield, 800 ... *A-4
Westhoff, 300 ... EM-6
Westlake, 992 ... †D-6
Westminster, 861 ... ED-7
Weston, 563 ... ED-7
Weston Lakes, 2482 ... EL-9
Westover, 20 ... ED-3
Westover Hills, 682 ... †H-3
Westphalia, 150 ... EI-6
Westworth Vil., 2472 ... †H-3
Wharton, 8832 ... EM-8
WHARTON CO., 41280 ... EM-8
Wheeler, 1592 ... WC-13
WHEELER CO., 5410 ... WD-13
Wheelock, 150 ... EI-8
White Deer, 1000 ... WC-11
White Oak, 6469 ... EE-10
White Settlement, 16116 ... †G-2
Whiteface, 449 ... WG-9
Whiteflat, 5 ... WF-12
Whitehouse, 7660 ... EF-10
Whitesboro, 3793 ... EC-7
Whitewright, 1604 ... EC-8
Whitharral, 200 ... WG-9
Whitney, 2087 ... EG-6
Whitsett, 150 ... EN-4
Whitt, 150 ... EE-5
WICHITA CO., 131500 ... EB-3
Wichita Falls, 104553 ... EC-4
Wickett, 498 ... WL-8
Wiergate, 325 ... EI-13
WILBARGER CO., 13535 ... EC-2
Wildorado, 200 ... WD-10
Wildwood, 1235 ... EJ-12
Wilkinson ... ED-10
WILLACY CO., 22134 ... ES-6
WILLIAMSON CO., 422679 ... EJ-6
Willis, 5662 ... EJ-10
Willow City, 75 ... EJ-3
Wills Pt., 3524 ... EE-8
Wilmer, 3682 ... †J-12
Wilson, 489 ... WH-10
WILSON CO., 42918 ... EN-4
Wimberley, 2626 ... EK-5
Winchell, 40 ... EH-2
Winchester, 70 ... EK-7
Winchester Country, 2000 ... *B-2
Windcrest, 5364 ... ER-11
Windemere, 1037 ... WB-7
Windom, 199 ... EC-8
Windthorst, 409 ... EC-4
Winfield, 524 ... ED-10
Wingate, 150 ... WK-13
Wink, 940 ... WK-8
WINKLER CO., 7110 ... WK-8
Winnie, 3254 ... EK-12
Winnsboro, 3434 ... EE-10
Winona, 576 ... EF-10
Winter Haven, 25 ... WR-14
Winters, 2562 ... WK-14
WISE CO., 59127 ... ED-5
Wixon Valley, 254 ... EI-8
Woden, 250 ... EH-11
Wolfe City, 1412 ... ED-8
Wolfforth, 3670 ... WH-10
WOOD CO., 41964 ... EE-9
Woodbury, 40 ... EG-6
Woodcreek, 1457 ... EK-5
Woodlake, 120 ... EI-10
Woodlake, 800 ... ER-11
Woodland, 60 ... EC-10
Woodlawn, 250 ... EE-11
Woodrow, 120 ... WH-10
Woods, 100 ... EG-12
Woodsboro, 1512 ... EO-6
Woodson, 264 ... EE-3
Woodville, 2586 ... EI-12
Woodway, 8452 ... EH-6
Wortham, 1073 ... EG-8
Wrightsboro, 50 ... EM-6
Wylie, 41427 ... EE-7
Yancey, 200 ... EM-3
Yantis, 388 ... EE-9
Yarrelton, 30 ... EI-6
Yellowpine, 60 ... EH-13
Yoakum, 5815 ... EM-6

***, †, ‡, §, ◊ See explanation under state title in this index.**
County and parish names are listed in capital letters & boldface type.
Independent cities (not included in a county) are listed in italics.

262 Texas–Virginia

YOAKUM CO., 7879 WH-8
Yorktown, 2092 EM-6
YOUNG CO., 18550 ED-3
Youngsport, 90 EI-5
Zapata, 5089 ER-2
ZAPATA CO., 14018 ER-2
ZAVALA CO., 11677 WR-14
Zavalla, 713 EH-11
Zephyr, 300 EH-3

Utah

Page locator
Map keys Atlas pages
1–10 206–207
11–20 208–209

Adamsville, 50 K-6
Alta, 383 E-9
Altamont, 225 E-12
Alton, 119 M-7
Altonah, 40 E-12
American Fork, 26263 E-9
Aneth, 501 M-14
Annabella, 795 J-8
Antimony, 122 K-8
Apple Valley, 701 N-6
Aurora, 1016 I-8
Avon, 367 B-9
Axtell, 70 I-8
Ballard, 801 E-12
Bear River City, 853 B-8
Beaver, 3112 K-7
BEAVER CO., 6629 J-6
Beryl, 120 L-5
Beryl Jct., 197 L-5
Bicknell, 327 K-9
Big Water, 475 N-9
Birdseye, 50 F-9
Blanding, 3375 L-13
Bluebell, 293 E-12
Bluff, 258 M-13
Bluffdale, 7598 E-8
Bonanza, 1 F-14
Boulder Town, 226 L-9
Bountiful, 42552 D-8
BOX ELDER CO., 49975 B-5
Brian Head, 83 L-6
Bridgeland, 80 F-12
Brigham City, 17899 B-8
Bryce Canyon City, 198 L-8
Bullfrog, 200 M-11
Burrville, 40 J-8
CACHE CO., 112656 B-9
Caineville K-10
Callao F-5
Cannonville, 167 M-8
CARBON CO., 21403 G-11
Carbonville, 1567 G-10
Castle Dale, 1630 H-10
Castle Valley, 319 J-13
Cedar City, 28857 L-6
Cedar Fort, 368 E-8
Centerfield, 1367 H-8
Centerville, 15335 D-8
Central, 613 M-5
Central Valley, 528 J-8
Charleston, 415 E-9
Circleville, 547 K-8
Cisco I-14
Clarkston, 666 A-8
Clawson, 163 H-10
Clear Creek, 4 G-10
Clearfield, 30112 C-8
Cleveland, 464 H-10
Clinton, 20426 C-8
Coalville, 1363 D-9
Copperton, 826 E-8
Corinne, 685 B-8
Cornish, 288 A-8
Cottonwood H-19
Cottonwood Hts., 33433 I-19
Cove Fort J-7
Croydon, 50 C-9
DAGGETT CO., 1059 D-12
Daniel, 938 E-9
DAVIS CO., 306479 D-7
Delta, 3436 H-7
Deseret, 353 H-7
Devils Slide C-9
Draper, 42274 E-8
Dry Fork, 30 E-13
Duchesne, 1690 F-11
DUCHESNE CO., 18607 E-11
Duck Creek Vil., 400 M-7
Dugway, 795 F-7
Dutch John, 145 D-13
Eagle Mtn., 21415 E-8
E. Carbon City, 1301 G-11
Eastland, 90 L-14
Echo, 56 D-9
Eden, 600 C-9
Elberta, 256 F-8
Elk Ridge, 2436 F-9
Elmo, 418 H-10
Elsinore, 847 J-8
Elwood, 1034 B-8
Emery, 288 I-10
EMERY CO., 10976 H-11
Enoch, 5803 L-6
Enterprise, 1711 L-5
Ephraim, 6135 H-9
Erda, 4642 E-8
Escalante, 797 L-9
Esk Dale, 100 H-4
Eureka, 669 F-8
Fairfield, 119 F-8
Fairview, 1247 G-9
Farmington, 18275 D-8
Farr West, 5928 A-2
Faust F-7
Fayette, 242 H-8
Ferron, 1626 I-10
Fielding, 455 B-8
Fillmore, 2435 I-7
Flowell, 100 I-7
Ft. Duchesne, 714 E-12
Fountain Green, 1071 G-9
Francis, 1077 E-10
Fremont, 145 J-9
Fruit Hts., 4987 F-3
Fruitland, 40 F-10
Gandy H-4
Garden City, 562 A-9
GARFIELD CO., 5172 L-10
Garland, 2400 B-8
Garrison, 50 I-4
Genola, 1370 F-8
Glendale, 381 M-7
Glenwood, 464 I-8
Goshen, 921 F-8
GRAND CO., 9225 I-13
Granite, 1932 J-20
Grantsville, 8893 E-7
Green River, 952 I-12
Greenville, 110 K-7
Greenwich, 30 J-8
Grouse Creek, 80 B-5
Grover K-9
Gunlock, 150 M-4
Gunnison, 3285 H-8
Gusher, 160 E-12
Halchita, 266 N-12
Halls Crossing, 6 M-11
Hamiltons Fort, 100 L-6
Hanksville, 219 J-11
Hanna, 70 E-11
Harrisville, 5567 A-2
Hatch, 133 L-7
Heber City, 11362 E-9
Helper, 2201 G-10
Henefer, 766 D-9
Henrieville, 230 M-8
Herriman, 21785 K-17
Hiawatha, 50 H-10
Hideout, 656 E-9
Hildale, 2726 N-6
Hinckley, 696 H-7
Holden, 378 I-8
Holladay, 26472 E-8
Honeyville, 1441 B-8
Hooper, 7218 C-8
Howell, 245 B-7
Huntington, 2129 H-10
Huntsville, 608 C-9
Hurricane, 13748 N-5
Hyde Pk., 3833 L-20
Hyrum, 7609 B-8
Ibapah, 60 F-4
Independence, 164 E-10
Indianola, 30 G-9
Ioka, 50 F-12
IRON CO., 46163 L-5
Ivins, 6753 M-5
Jensen, 412 E-13
Joseph, 344 J-8
JUAB CO., 10246 G-6
Junction, 191 K-8
Kamas, 1811 E-10
Kanab, 4312 N-7
Kanarraville, 355 M-6
KANE CO., 7125 M-9
Kanosh, 474 I-7
Kaysville, 27300 D-8
Kearns, 35731 H-17
Kenilworth, 180 G-11
Kingston, 173 K-8
Koosharem, 327 J-8
La Sal, 395 K-14
La Sal Jct. K-13
La Verkin, 4060 M-5
Laketown, 248 B-9
Lakeview, 100 H-2
Lapoint, 350 E-12
Layton, 67311 C-8
Leamington, 226 G-8
Leeds, 820 M-5
Lehi, 47407 E-8
Levan, 841 G-8
Lewiston, 1766 A-8
Lindon, 10070 F-1
Loa, 572 J-9
Logan, 48174 B-8
Long Valley Jct. M-7
Lund K-5
Lyman, 258 J-9
Lynndyl, 106 G-7
Maeser, 3601 E-13
Magna, 26505 G-16
Manderfield K-7
Manila, 310 D-13
Manti, 3276 H-9
Mantua, 687 B-8
Mapleton, 7979 F-9
Marriott-Slaterville, 1701 B-2
Marysvale, 408 J-8
Mayfield, 496 I-9
Meadow, 310 I-7
Meadowville A-9
Mendon, 1282 B-8
Mexican Hat, 31 N-12
Midvale, 27964 I-19
Midway, 3845 E-9
Milford, 1409 J-6
MILLARD CO., 12503 H-6
Millcreek, 62139 H-19
Minersville, 907 K-6
Moab, 5046 J-13
Modena, 100 L-4
Mona, 1547 G-8
Monroe, 2256 J-8
Montezuma Creek, 335 M-14
Monticello, 1972 L-14
Moore I-10
Morgan, 3687 D-9
MORGAN CO., 9469 C-9
Moroni, 1423 G-9
Mt. Pleasant, 3260 G-9
Mountain Home, 120 E-11
Murray, 46746 H-19
Myton, 569 F-12
Naples, 1755 E-13
Navajo Mtn., 354 N-11
Neola, 461 E-12
Nephi, 5389 G-8
New Harmony, 207 M-5
Newcastle, 247 L-5
Newton, 789 A-8
N. Logan, 8269 M-20
N. Ogden, 17357 C-8
N. Salt Lake, 16322 E-18
Oak City, 578 H-7
Oakley, 1470 D-10
Ogden, 82825 C-8
Ophir, 38 E-8
Orangeville, 1470 H-10
Orderville, 577 M-7
Orem, 88328 E-9
Ouray, 40 F-13
Panguitch, 1520 L-7
Paradise, 904 B-8
Paragonah, 488 L-7
Park City, 7558 E-9
Park Valley, 60 B-6
Parowan, 2790 L-6
Payson, 18294 F-9
Peoa, 253 D-9
Perry, 4512 B-8
Peterson, 150 C-9
Pine Valley, 186 M-5
Pintura, 50 M-6
PIUTE CO., 1556 J-8
Plain City, 5476 C-8
Pleasant Grv., 33509 E-9
Plymouth, 414 A-8
Portage, 245 A-8
Porterville, 90 D-9
Price, 8715 G-11
Promontory B-7
Providence, 7075 B-9
Provo, 112488 F-9
Randlett, 220 F-12
Randolph, 464 B-10
Red Wash, 30 F-13
Redmond, 730 I-8
Redwood G-18
RICH CO., 2264 B-9
Richfield, 7551 I-8
Richmond, 2470 A-9
River Hts., 1734 N-20
Riverdale, 8426 C-2
Riverside, 760 B-8
Riverton, 38753 E-8
Rockville, 245 N-6
Roosevelt, 6046 E-12
Rosette B-5
Roy, 36884 C-8
Rush Valley, 447 E-7
Sage Creek Jct., 50 B-10
St. George, 72897 N-5
Salem, 6423 F-9
Salina, 2489 I-8
Salt Lake City 186440 D-8
SALT LAKE CO., 1029655 E-19
SAN JUAN CO., 14746 K-13
Sandy, 87461 E-8
SANPETE CO., 27822 H-9
Santa Clara, 6003 N-5
Santaquin, 9128 F-9
Scipio, 327 H-8
Scofield, 24 G-10
SEVIER CO., 20802 I-9
Shivwits, 30 M-4
Sigurd, 429 I-8
Smithfield, 9495 B-8
Snowville, 167 A-7
Soldier Summit F-10
S. Jordan, 50418 J-17
S. Ogden, 16532 C-2
S. Salt Lake, 23617 G-19
S. Weber, 6051 D-3
Spanish Fork, 34691 F-9
Spring City, 988 H-9
Spring Glen, 1126 G-10
Springdale, 529 M-6
Springdell, 120 G-3
Springville, 29466 F-9
Standrod A-5
Stansbury Pk., 5145 E-8
Sterling, 262 H-9
Stockton, 616 E-7
Sugarville, 30 H-7
Summit, 160 L-6
SUMMIT CO., 36324 D-10
Sunnyside, 377 G-11
Sunset, 5122 D-2
Sutherland, 165 H-7
Syracuse, 24331 E-1
Tabiona, 171 E-11
Taylor, 50 B-1
Taylorsville, 58652 H-17
Teasdale, 191 K-9
Terra, 50 E-7
Thompson Sprs., 39 I-13
Ticaboo, 50 L-11
Tooele, 31605 E-8
TOOELE CO., 58218 D-6
Toquerville, 1370 M-5
Torrey, 182 K-9
Tremonton, 7647 B-8
Trenton, 464 A-8
Tridell, 110 E-12
Tropic, 530 L-8
Trout Creek G-5
Ucolo L-14
Uintah, 1322 C-8
UINTAH CO., 32588 G-13
Union I-19
Upalco, 70 F-12
Upton D-10
UTAH CO., 516564 F-8
Vernal, 9089 E-13
Vernon, 243 F-7
Veyo, 483 M-5
Vineyard, 139 G-1
Virgin, 596 M-6
Wales, 302 H-9
Wallsburg, 250 E-9
Wanship, 400 D-9
Warren, 50 A-1
WASATCH CO., 23530 F-10
Washington, 18761 N-5
WASHINGTON CO., 138115 M-5
Washington Terrace, 9067 C-2
WAYNE CO., 2778 J-10
WEBER CO., 231236 C-9
Wellington, 1676 G-11
Wellsville, 3432 B-8
Wendover, 1400 D-4
W. Bountiful, 5265 D-18
W. Haven, 10272 B-2
W. Jordan, 103712 E-8
West Point, 9511 D-1
W. Valley City, 129480 D-8
W. Weber, 50 B-1
Whiterocks, 289 E-12
Willard, 1772 C-8
Woodruff, 180 B-10
Woods Cross, 9761 D-8
Yost A-5

Vermont

Page locator
Map keys Atlas pages
A–N 210–211

Adamant, 60 E-5
Addison, 110 F-2
ADDISON CO., 36821 F-3
Albany, 193 C-5
Alburgh, 497 A-2
Alburgh Ctr., 120 B-2
Alburgh Sprs., 110 A-2
Alpine Vil., 70 F-4
Amsden, 60 J-5
Andover, 130 J-4
Arlington, 1213 L-2
Ascutney, 540 J-5
Athens, 120 K-5
Bakersfield, 370 B-4
Barnard, 220 H-5
Barnet, 129 E-7
Barre, 9052 F-5
Barton, 737 C-6
Bartonsville, 200 K-5
Basin Hbr., 50 F-2
Beanville, 30 G-6
Beebe Plain, 200 A-6
Beecher Falls, 177 A-9
Bellows Falls, 3148 K-5
Belmont, 300 J-4
Belvidere Ctr., 60 C-4
Bennington, 9074 M-2
BENNINGTON CO., 37125 L-2
Benson, 308 H-2
Benson H-2
Berkshire, 130 A-4
Berlin Cors., 360 F-5
Bethel, 569 H-4
Blissville, 110 I-2
Bloomfield, 120 C-8
Bolton, 100 E-4
Boltonville F-7
Bomoseen, 250 I-2
Bondville, 150 K-4
Bordoville, 20 B-4
Bowlsville, 50 J-4
Bradford, 788 G-6
Brandon, 1648 H-3
Brattleboro, 7414 M-5
Bread Loaf G-3
Bridgewater, 300 I-5
Bridgewater Ctr., 60 I-4
Bridgewater Corners, 150 I-4
Bridport, 180 G-2
Bristol, 2030 F-3
Brookfield, 130 F-5
Brookside, 70 L-4
Brownington, 60 B-6
Brownington Ctr., 60 B-6
Brownsville, 100 I-5
Brunswick Sprs. C-8
Burke Hollow, 140 C-7
Burlington, 42417 D-2
Cabot, 233 D-6
Cadys Falls, 200 D-5
CALEDONIA CO., 31227 D-6
Cambridge, 236 C-4
Cambridgeport, 100 K-5
Canaan, 392 A-9
Castleton, 1485 I-2
Cavendish, 179 J-5
Cedar Bch. E-2
Center Rutland, 500 I-3
Charlotte, 350 E-2
Checkerberry, 120 C-3
Chelsea, 500 G-5
Chester, 1005 K-5
Chimney Pt. F-2
Chipmans Pt. H-2
Chippenhook, 190 I-3
Chiselville, 140 L-3
Chittenden, 270 H-3
CHITTENDEN CO., 156545 E-3
Clarendon, 270 I-3
Clarendon Sprs., 200 I-3
Colbyville E-4
Colchester, 450 D-3
Concord, 271 D-7
Cookville, 140 G-6
Cornwall, 100 G-2
Coventry, 97 B-6
Craftsbury, 160 C-6
Craftsbury Common, 180 C-5
Cuttingsville, 120 I-4
Danby, 350 J-3
Danby Four Cors., 80 J-3
Danville, 383 D-6
Derby Ctr., 597 B-6
Derby Line, 673 A-7
Dorset, 249 K-3
Dover, 100 L-4
Duxbury, 190 E-4
E. Alburgh, 70 A-2
E. Arlington, 620 L-3
E. Barnard, 30 H-5
E. Barre, 826 F-5
E. Berkshire, 100 B-4
E. Bethel, 200 G-5
E. Braintree, 50 G-4
E. Brookfield, 50 F-5
E. Burke, 132 C-7
E. Calais, 230 E-5
E. Charleston, 140 B-7
E. Concord, 150 D-8
E. Corinth, 150 F-6
E. Dorset, 350 K-3
E. Dover, 250 L-4
E. Dummerston, 200 L-5
E. Fairfield, 160 B-4
E. Fletcher, 20 C-4
E. Franklin, 80 A-4
E. Granville, 70 G-4
E. Haven, 80 C-7
E. Highgate, 130 B-3
E. Hubbardton, 70 H-3
E. Jamaica, 150 L-4
E. Johnson, 60 C-4
E. Lyndon, 120 D-7
E. Middlebury, 425 G-3
E. Montpelier, 80 E-5
E. Orange, 70 F-6
E. Peacham, 60 E-6
E. Poultney, 500 I-2
E. Randolph, 140 G-5
E. Richford, 100 A-5
E. Rupert, 30 J-3
E. Ryegate, 120 F-7
E. St. Johnsbury, 180 D-7
E. Topsham, 190 F-6
E. Wallingford, 280 J-4
Eden, 100 C-5
Eden Mills, 130 C-5
Ely, 50 G-6
Enosburg Falls, 1329 B-4
Essex Ctr., 850 D-3
ESSEX CO., 6306 C-8
Essex Jct., 9271 D-3
Evansville, 80 B-6
Fair Haven, 2269 I-2
Fairfax, 350 C-3
Fairfield, 130 B-3
Fairlee, 189 G-6
Felchville, 180 J-5
Ferrisburgh, 200 F-2
Fletcher, 60 C-3
Florence, 120 H-3
Fonda, 80 B-3
Forest Dale, 350 H-3
Foxville, 250 F-5
Franklin, 220 A-3
FRANKLIN CO., 47746 C-3
Gallup Mills, 20 D-8
Gassetts, 60 J-5
Gaysville, 250 H-4
Georgia Ctr., 150 C-3
Georgia Plains, 100 C-3
Gilman, 500 D-8
Glover, 303 C-6
Goshen, 50 G-3
Grafton, 300 K-5
Granby, 40 D-8
Grand Isle, 250 C-2
GRAND ISLE CO., 6970 B-2
Graniteville, 784 F-5
Granville, 200 G-4
Greensboro, 109 D-6
Greensboro Bend, 232 D-6
Groton, 437 F-6
Guildhall, 100 D-9
Guilford, 200 M-5
Halifax, 110 M-4
Hancock, 150 G-4
Hardwick, 1345 D-6
Hartford, 500 H-6
Hartland, 380 I-5
Hartland Four Corners, 200 I-5
Healdville J-4
Heartwellville, 60 M-3
Hectorville B-5
Hewitts Corners H-5
Highgate Ctr., 350 B-3
Highgate Sprs., 200 A-3
Hinesburg, 658 E-3
Holland, 100 A-7
Hortonia, 40 H-2
Houghtonville, 40 K-4
Hubbardton, 60 H-2
Huntington, 280 E-3
Huntington Ctr., 150 E-3
Hyde Pk., 462 C-5
Hydeville, 450 I-2
Inwood E-7
Ira, 100 I-3
Irasburg, 163 B-6
Irasville, 130 F-4
Island Pond, 821 B-7
Isle La Motte, 130 B-2
Jacksonville, 223 M-4
Jamaica, 230 K-4
Jay, 100 B-5
Jeffersonville, 729 C-4
Jericho, 1329 D-3
Jericho Ctr., 120 D-3
Joes Pond, 100 D-6
Johnson, 1443 C-4
Jonesville, 330 E-3
Keeler Bay C-2
Killington, 100 H-4
Kirby Corner, 50 I-10
L. Dunmore, 50 G-3
L. Elmore, 140 D-5
LAMOILLE CO., 24475 D-4
Larrabees Pt. Sta. G-2
Leicester, 50 G-3
Leicester Jct., 50 G-3
Lemington B-9
Lincoln, 150 F-3
Londonderry, 250 K-4
Lowell, 228 B-5
Lower Cabot, 60 E-6
Lower Vil., 300 D-4
Ludlow, 811 J-4
Lunenburg, 260 D-8
Lyndon, 450 D-7
Lyndon Ctr., 300 D-7
Lyndonville, 1207 D-7
Mackville, 100 D-6
Maidstone C-9
Mallets Bay D-2
Manchester, 749 K-3
Manchester Ctr., 2120 K-3
Maple Cor., 40 E-5
Maquam, 200 B-3
Marlboro, 230 M-4
Marshfield, 273 E-6
McIndoe Falls, 200 E-7
Mendon, 60 H-3
Middlebury, 6588 G-2
Middlesex, 200 E-4
Middletown Sprs., 200 I-3
Miles Pond, 30 D-8
Milton, 1861 C-3
Monkton Boro, 180 E-3
Monkton Ridge, 50 E-3
Montgomery, 220 B-5
Montgomery Ctr., 380 B-5
Montpelier, 7855 E-5
Moretown, 220 E-4
Morgan, 80 B-7
Morgan Ctr., 150 B-7
Morrisville, 1958 D-5
Moscow, 260 D-4
Mt. Holly, 200 J-4
Mt. Tabor, 100 J-3
New Haven, 140 F-3
New Haven Mills, 100 F-3
Newark, 70 C-7
Newbury, 365 F-7
Newfane, 118 L-4
Newport, 4589 B-6
Newport Ctr., 274 B-6
N. Bennington, 1643 L-2
N. Calais, 80 E-5
N. Clarendon, 550 I-3
N. Concord, 140 D-8
N. Danville, 110 D-7
N. Dorset J-3
N. Fayston E-4
N. Ferrisburgh, 150 E-2
N. Hartland, 302 I-6
N. Hero, 190 B-2
N. Hyde Pk., 380 C-5
N. Landgrove, 50 K-4
N. Montpelier, 150 E-5
N. Pownal, 350 M-2
N. Randolph, 50 G-5
N. Shrewsbury, 80 I-4
N. Springfield, 573 J-5
N. Thetford, 110 G-6
N. Troy, 620 A-5
N. Tunbridge, 70 G-5
N. Westminster, 247 K-5
N. Wolcott, 140 C-5
Northfield, 2101 F-4
Norton, 80 A-8
Norwich, 878 H-6
Orange, 70 F-5
ORANGE CO., 28936 F-5
Orleans, 818 B-6
ORLEANS CO., 27231 B-5
Orwell, 170 H-2
Panton, 50 F-2
Passumpsic, 200 E-7
Pawlet, 230 J-2
Peacham, 220 E-6
Pearl, 60 C-2
Perkinsville, 130 J-5
Peru, 150 K-3
Pittsfield, 140 H-4
Pittsford, 740 H-3
Plainfield, 401 E-5
Pleasant Valley C-4
Plymouth, 100 I-4
Plymouth Union I-4
Pomfret, 50 H-5
Post Mills, 220 G-6
Poultney, 1612 I-2
Pownal, 320 M-2
Pownal Ctr., 280 M-2
Proctor, 1740 H-3
Proctorsville, 454 J-5
Putnamville, 40 E-5
Putney, 523 L-5
Quechee, 656 I-5
Queen City Pk. J-8
Randolph, 1974 G-4
Randolph Ctr., 250 G-5
Rawsonville, 140 K-4
Readsboro, 321 M-3
Richford, 1361 A-4
Richmond, 723 D-3
Ripton, 130 G-3
Robinson G-4
Rochester, 299 G-4
Rockingham, 120 K-5
Roxbury, 300 F-4
Roxbury Flat, 40 F-4
Royalton, 100 H-5
Rupert, 140 K-2
Rutland, 16495 I-3
RUTLAND CO., 61642 I-2
Ryegate Corner, 90 F-7
St. Albans, 6918 B-3
St. Albans Bay, 500 B-3
St. Johnsbury, 6193 D-7
St. Johnsbury Ctr., 450 D-7
St. Rocks, 20 B-3
Salisbury, 200 G-3
Sandgate, 80 K-2
Saxtons River, 565 K-5
Searsburg, 50 M-3
Shaftsbury L-2
Sharon, 250 H-5
Sheffield, 230 C-7
Shelburne, 592 E-2
Shelburne Falls, 120 E-2
Sheldon, 320 B-3
Sheldon Sprs., 260 B-3
Shoreham, 100 G-2
Shrewsbury, 60 I-4
Simonsville, 80 K-4
S. Albany C-6
S. Alburgh, 100 B-2
S. Barre, 1219 F-5
S. Burlington, 17904 D-2
S. Dorset, 220 K-3
S. End, 40 J-3
S. Hero, 350 C-2
S. Lincoln, 70 F-3
S. Londonderry, 400 K-4
S. Lunenburg, 100 D-8
S. Newbury, 70 F-7
S. Newfane, 150 L-4
S. Northfield, 80 F-4
S. Peacham, 90 E-6
S. Pomfret, 160 H-5
S. Poultney, 110 I-2
S. Reading, 130 I-5
S. Royalton, 694 H-5
S. Ryegate, 450 F-6
S. Shaftsbury, 683 L-2
S. Sherburne, 80 I-4
S. Strafford, 150 H-6
S. Walden D-6
S. Wallingford, 230 J-3
S. Windham, 100 K-4
S. Woodbury, 70 D-5
S. Woodstock, 100 I-5
Springfield, 3979 J-5
Stamford, 400 M-3
Stannard, 30 D-6
Starksboro, 130 E-3
Stevens Mills, 30 A-5
Stockbridge, 100 H-4
Stowe, 495 D-4
Strafford, 70 G-5
Stratton L-3
Sudbury, 60 H-2
Sunderland, 220 K-3
Sutton, 130 C-7
Swanton, 2386 B-3
Tafts Corner, 50 J-10
Taftsville, 150 I-5
Tarbellville, 50 J-4
Thetford Ctr., 190 H-6
Thetford Hill, 130 H-6
Tinmouth, 80 J-3
Townshend, 180 L-4
Troy, 243 B-5
Tunbridge, 110 G-5
Tyson I-4
Underhill, 400 D-3
Underhill Ctr., 300 D-4
Union Vil., 50 H-6
Vergennes, 2588 F-2
Vernon, 250 M-5
Vershire, 120 G-6
Waits River, 70 F-6
Waitsfield, 164 F-4
Walden, 120 D-6
Wallace Pond, 100 A-8
Wallingford, 830 I-3
Waltham F-2
Wardsboro, 200 L-4
Warren, 370 F-4
Washington, 320 F-5
WASHINGTON CO., 59534 D-5
Waterbury, 1763 E-4
Waterbury Ctr., 500 E-4
Waterville, 110 C-4
Weathersfield Bow, 150 J-5
Websterville, 550 F-5
Wells, 397 J-2
Wells River, 399 F-7
W. Arlington, 50 K-2
W. Barnet, 80 E-6
W. Berlin, 150 F-5
W. Bolton D-4
W. Braintree, 110 G-4
W. Branch, 250 D-4
W. Brattleboro, 2740 M-5
W. Brookfield G-4
W. Burke, 343 C-7
W. Castleton H-2
W. Charleston, 220 B-7
W. Danville, 200 D-6
W. Dover, 350 L-4
W. Dummerston, 160 L-5
W. Enosburg, 60 B-4
W. Fairlee, 170 G-6
W. Glover, 50 C-6
W. Halifax, 160 M-4
W. Hartford, 340 H-5
W. Haven, 40 H-2
W. Hill, 30 B-4
W. Lincoln, 80 F-3
W. Newbury, 160 F-6
W. Pawlet, 300 J-2
W. Rupert, 180 K-2
W. Rutland, 2024 I-3
W. Topsham, 120 F-6
W. Townshend, 200 L-4
W. Wardsboro, 150 L-4
W. Woodstock, 150 I-5
Westfield, 100 B-5
Westford, 150 C-3
Westminster, 291 L-5
Westminster West, 80 L-5
Westmore, 100 C-7
Weston, 300 J-4
Weybridge, 140 F-2
Wheelock, 100 D-7
White River Jct., 2286 H-6
Whiting, 100 G-2
Whitingham, 330 M-4
Wilder, 1690 H-6
Williamstown, 1162 F-5
Williston, 450 D-3
Wilmington, 463 M-4
Windham, 70 K-4
WINDHAM CO., 44513 L-5
Windsor, 2066 I-5
WINDSOR CO., 56670 I-5
Winooski, 7267 D-2
Winooski Pk., 400 H-9
Wolcott, 180 D-5
Woodbury, 160 D-5
Woodford, 60 M-3
Woodford Hollow, 60 M-3
Woodstock, 900 I-5
Worcester, 112 E-5

Virginia

Page locator
Map keys Atlas pages
1–10 212–213
11–20 214–215
* City keyed to p. 195
† City keyed to pp. 216–217
‡ City keyed to pp. 224–225

Abbott J-5
Abingdon, 8191 D-6
Accomac, 519 I-19
ACCOMACK CO., 33164 I-20
Achilles, 650 K-17
Adkins Store J-15
Adner J-16
Adria, 260 K-1
Adwolf, 1530 M-1
Afton, 120 H-9
Aiken Summit, 60 M-7
ALBEMARLE CO., 98970 H-10
Alberta, 298 L-12
Albin, 300 C-11
Aldie, 330 D-13
Alexandria, 139966 E-15
Alleghany, 110 I-5
ALLEGHANY CO., 16250 I-5
Alleghany Spr., 140 K-5
Allison Gap, 700 D-7
Allisonia, 117 L-3
Alma, 130 F-10
Altavista, 3450 K-8
Alum Ridge, 80 L-4
Amburg, 280 J-17
AMELIA CO., 2690 J-12
Amelia Court House, 1099 K-12
Amherst, 2231 J-9
AMHERST CO., 32353 I-8
Amissville, 200 E-12
Amonate, 400 K-1
Andersonville, 70 J-10
Annalee Hts., 1800 ‡G-4
Annandale, 41008 E-14
Appalachia, 1754 C-4
Appomattox, 1733 K-9
APPOMATTOX CO., 14973 J-9
Aquia Hbr., 6727 F-14
Ararat, 350 M-4
Arcola, 233 D-13
Ark, 200 J-17
Arlington, 207627 D-15
ARLINGTON CO., 207627 ‡G-5
Armel, 130 D-11
Aroda, 100 G-11
Arrington, 708 I-9
Arvonia, 750 I-11
Ashburn, 43511 D-14
Ashland, 7225 I-14
Ashwood, 200 H-6
Atkins, 1143 L-1
Atlantic, 862 H-20
Atlee, 40 †A-8
Attoway, 250 M-1
AUGUSTA CO., 73750 G-9
Augusta Sprs., 257 H-8
Austinville, 850 L-3
Avon, 80 H-9
Axton, 300 M-7
Aylett, 200 I-15
Bacons Castle, 70 †I-1
Bacova, 70 H-6
Bailey's Crossroads, 23643 ‡H-5
Bakers Crossroads ‡J-3
Ballsville, 60 J-12
Bandy, 100 K-1
Banner, 250 C-5
Banners Corner, 300 D-5
Barbours Creek J-6
Barboursville, 150 G-11
Barhamsville, 150 J-16
Barley, 30 N-13
Barren Ridge, 110 G-9
Barren Sprs., 100 L-3
Bassett, 1100 M-6
Bastian, 420 K-2
Basye, 1253 E-9
Batesville, 200 H-10
BATH CO., 4731 H-7
Battery Pk. †K-3
Bavon, 150 J-17
Bay View, 180 K-18
Baywood M-2
Beach †F-6
Bealeton, 4435 F-13
Beaverdam, 170 H-13
Bedford, 6222 K-7
BEDFORD CO., 68676 K-7
Bel Air, 1500 ‡G-4
Bellair, 1400 †B-1
Belle Haven, 6518 ‡I-6
Belle Haven, 532 I-19
Belleview, 2300 ‡E-3
Bells Valley, 40 H-7
Bellwood, 6352 †E-8
Belspring, 256 K-4
Belvedere, 2200 ‡H-4
Ben Hur, 390 D-3
Benhams D-5
Benns Church, 872 L-17
Bensley, 5819 †E-8
Bent Creek, 50 J-9
Bent Mtn., 40 K-5
Bentonville, 380 E-11
Bergton, 100 E-9
Berryville, 4185 C-12
Bethel, 250 E-13
Big Island, 303 J-8
Big Rock, 650 B-6
Big Stone Gap, 5614 D-4
Birchleaf, 260 B-5
Birdsnest, 80 J-19
Bishop, 250 K-1
Blacksburg, 42620 K-4
Blackstone, 3621 L-12
Blackwater, 90 E-3
Blairs, 916 M-8
Blakes, 100 J-17
Bland, 409 K-2
BLAND CO., 6824 K-2
Blevinstown, 800 ‡H-1
Bloxom, 387 H-19
Blue Grass, 120 F-7
Blue Ridge, 3084 J-6
Bluefield, 5444 K-2
Bluemont, 200 C-12
Bocock, 80 G-20
Boissevain, 900 K-1
Bon Air, 16366 J-13
Bonny Blue, 100 D-3
Boones Mill, 239 K-6
Boonsboro E-17
Boston, 60 F-12
BOTETOURT CO., 33148 I-6
Bowers Hill †M-5
Bowlers Wharf, 120 I-16
Bowling Green, 1111 H-14
Boyce, 589 D-12
Boydton, 431 M-11
Boykins, 564 M-15
Bracey, 1554 M-12
Brambleton, 9845 D-13
Branchville, 114 M-14
Brandermill, 13173 ‡E-5
Brandon K-15
Brandy Sta., 360 F-12
Breaks, 150 B-5
Bremo Bluff, 190 I-11
Bridgewater, 5644 F-9
Bridle Creek, 30 M-2
Briery Branch, 160 F-9
Brightwood, 1001 F-11
Bristol, 17835 E-5
Broadford, 300 L-1
Broadway, 3691 E-9
Brodnax, 298 M-12
Brooke, 170 F-14
Brookneal, 1112 L-9
Brownsburg, 130 H-8
Browntown, 200 E-11
Broyhill Pk., 3700 ‡G-3
Bruington, 70 I-15
Brunswick M-13
BRUNSWICK CO., 17434 L-12
Buchanan, 1178 J-7
BUCHANAN CO., 24098 B-6
Buckingham, 350 J-10
Buckingham Circle, 900 †C-1
BUCKINGHAM CO., 17146 I-10
Bucknell Manor, 2350 ‡I-6
Buena Vista, 6650 I-8
Buffalo Gap, 100 G-8
Buffalo Sprs., 50 M-10
Bumpass, 80 H-13
Burgess, 80 H-17
Burke, 41055 ‡I-2
Burkes Gdn., 50 K-1
Burkeville, 432 K-11
Burnsville, 50 G-7
Burnt Chimney, 100 K-6
Burr Hill, 90 G-12
Burrowsville, 70 K-15
Butts Corner ‡I-1
Cabin Pt., 40 K-15
Caledonia I-12
Callaghan, 348 I-5
Callands, 150 M-7
Callao, 550 H-17
Callaway, 130 L-6
Calverton, 239 E-13
CAMPBELL CO., 54842 K-9
Cana, 1254 M-4
Canterbury Hills, 300 †B-2
Cape Charles, 1009 K-18
Capron, 166 M-15
Captains Cove, 1042 H-20
Caret, 60 H-15
Carloover, 70 H-6
CAROLINE CO., 28545 H-14
CARROLL CO., 30042 M-4
Carrollton, 4574 †K-3
Carrsbrook, 950 H-11
Carrsville, 359 M-16
Carson, 200 L-14
Cartersville, 380 I-12
Carver Gdns., 500 †F-2
Carysbrook, 30 I-11
Casanova, 190 E-13
Cascade, 170 N-7
Castlewood, 2045 D-5
Catalpa, 120 F-12
Catawba, 100 J-5
Catharpin, 670 D-13
Catlett, 296 E-13
Cave Spr., 24922 K-6
Cedar Bluff, 1137 C-7
Cedar Fork H-13
Cedarville, 450 D-11
Cedon, 150 H-13
Centenary, 30 I-10
Center Cross, 150 I-16
Centerville, 550 †E-1
Central Hill, 180 †L-1
Centralia, 200 †F-8
Centreville, 71135 E-14
Ceres, 50 L-1
Chamberlayne, 5456 †B-8
Chamblissburg, 80 K-7
Champlain, 150 H-15
Chantilly, 23039 D-14
Chapel K-3
Chapel Acres, 1200 ‡J-3
Charity, 50 M-5
Charles City, 133 J-15
CHARLES CITY CO., 7256 J-15
CHARLOTTE CO., 12586 L-10
Charlotte Court House, 543 L-10
Charlottesville, 43475 H-10
Chase City, 2351 M-11
Chatham, 1269 M-8
Chatham Hill, 30 L-1
Chatmoss, 1698 M-6
Check, 80 L-5
Cheriton, 487 K-18
Chesapeake, 222209 L-18
Chester, 20987 J-14
Chester Gap, 839 E-12
Chesterbrook, 1600 ‡F-4
Chesterfield, 3560 J-14
CHESTERFIELD CO., 316236 K-13
Chilesburg H-13
Chilhowie, 1781 M-1
Chincoteague, 2941 H-20
Christiansburg, 21041 K-4
Chuckatuck †L-3
Chula, 130 J-12
Church View, 70 I-16
Churchland †L-5
Churchville, 194 G-8
Claremont, 378 K-15
CLARKE CO., 14034 D-12
Clarksville, 1139 M-10
Claudville, 150 M-4
Clay Bank, 200 †E-3
Claypool Hill, 1776 C-7
Clayville, 80 J-13
Clear Brook, 190 C-12
Clearbrook, 550 K-6
Clearwater Pk., 140 I-6
Cleveland, 202 C-6
Cliffield, 150 K-1
Clifford, 180 I-9
Clifton Forge, 3884 I-6
Clinchco, 337 B-5
Clinchport, 70 D-4
Clintwood, 1414 C-5
Clover, 438 M-10
Clover Hill, 100 F-9
Cloverdale, 3119 J-6
Cluster Sprs., 811 M-9
Cobham Wharf, 80 †H-1
Cochran, 30 M-12
Cody L-9
Coeburn, 2139 C-5
Coleman Falls, 100 J-8
Coles Pt., 300 G-16
Colleen, 180 I-9
Collierstown, 70 I-7
Collinsville, 7335 M-6
Collinwood D-5
Colonial Bch., 3542 G-15
Colonial Hts., 17411 K-14
Colthurst, 470 †B-2
Columbia, 83 I-12
Columbia Furnace, 50 D-10
Comers Rock, 50 M-2
Concord, 1458 K-9
Cootes Store E-9
Copper Hill, 100 L-5
Copper Valley, 30 L-4
Courtland, 1284 M-15
Cove Creek K-2
Covesville, 240 H-10
Covington, 5961 I-6
CRAIG CO., 5190 J-5
Craigsville, 923 H-8
Crandon, 80 K-3
Cranes Nest, 200 C-5
Cresthill E-12
Crewe, 2326 K-12
Crimora, 2209 G-9
Critz, 160 M-5
Crockett, 330 L-2
Cross Jct., 50 C-11
Crows I-5
Crozet, 5565 H-10
Crozier, 140 I-13
Crystal Hill, 220 L-9
Cuckoo, 30 H-12
Cullen, 100 K-10
Culmore, 5200 ‡G-4
Culpeper, 16379 F-12
CULPEPER CO., 46689 F-12
Cumberland, 393 J-11
CUMBERLAND CO., 10052 J-11
Cunningham, 100 H-11
Dahlgren, 2653 F-15
Dale City, 65969 E-14
Daleville, 2557 J-6
Damascus, 814 E-7
Danieltown, 50 L-12
Dante, 649 C-5
Danville, 43055 N-8
Dare, 1500 †H-4
Darlington Hts., 30 K-10
Darvills, 80 L-13
Davenport, 100 C-6
Dawn I-14
Dayton, 1530 F-9
Deatonville, 50 K-12
Deel, 200 B-6
Deep Creek, 115 †N-5
Deerfield, 132 G-8
Delaplane, 200 D-12
Deltaville, 1119 J-17
Dendron, 272 L-15
Detrick, 40 E-11
DeWitt, 100 L-13
DICKENSON CO., 15903 C-5
Diggs, 80 J-17
Dillwyn, 447 J-11
Dinwiddie, 200 L-13
DINWIDDIE CO., 28001 L-13
Disputanta, 550 K-15
Dixie, 30 J-17
Dixie, 30 I-11
Doe Hill, 50 F-8
Dolphin, 80 M-13
Dooms, 1327 G-9
Doswell, 200 H-14
Drakes Branch, 530 L-10
Dranesville, 11921 ‡D-1
Draper, 320 L-3
Drewryville, 310 M-14
Drill C-6
Driver †M-4
Dry Fork, 150 M-8
Dryden, 1208 D-3
Dublin, 2534 K-4
Duffield, 91 D-3
Dugspur, 70 M-4
Dumbarton, 7879 †B-7
Dumfries, 4961 F-14
Dunbar, 130 C-4
Dundas, 150 L-12
Dungannon, 332 D-5
Dunn Loring, 8803 ‡F-3
Dunnsville, 150 H-16
Dutton, 270 J-17
Dye C-6
Dyke, 50 G-10
Eagle Rock, 350 I-6
Earls, 30 K-12
E. Highland Pk., 14796 †B-8
E. Lexington, 1463 I-8
E. Stone Gap, 500 D-4
Eastville, 305 J-19
Ebony, 161 N-12
Edgehill, 240 G-15
Edgerton M-13
Edinburg, 1041 E-10
Ednam Forest, 700 †B-1
Edom F-9
Eggleston, 270 K-4
Eheart, 90 G-11
Elberon, 50 K-16
Elk Creek, 150 M-2
Elkton, 2726 F-10
Elliston, 902 K-5
Elmo, 30 M-9
Elmont, 300 I-14
Elon, 200 J-8
Emory, 1251 D-7
Emporia, 5927 M-14
Enon, 3466 K-14
Esmont, 528 I-10
Esserville C-4
ESSEX CO., 11151 H-15
Etlan, 100 F-11
Ettrick, 6682 K-14
Evergreen, 170 K-10
Evington, 200 K-8
Ewell, 40 †E-1
Ewing, 439 D-1
Exmore, 1460 J-19
Faber, 150 I-10
Fair Oaks, 200 †C-10
Fair Port, 450 H-17
Fairfax, 22565 D-14
FAIRFAX CO., 22565 D-14
Fairfax Sta., 12030 ‡I-1
Fairfield, 600 H-8
Fairlawn, 2367 K-4
Fairview, 240 M-11
Fairview Bch., 391 G-14
Falling Spr., 150 H-6
Falls Church, 12332 D-14
Falls Mills, 450 K-2
Falmouth, 4274 G-14
Fancy Gap, 237 M-4
Farmington, 250 †B-1
Farmville, 8216 K-11
Farnham, 320 H-16
FAUQUIER CO., 65203 E-12
Favonia, 130 L-2
Ferncliff, 50 H-12
Ferrum, 2043 L-6
Ferry Farms, 4000 G-14
Fieldale, 879 M-6
Fife, 60 I-12
Figsboro M-6
Fincastle, 353 J-6
Finchley, 80 M-11
First Colony, 900 †F-1
Fishers Hill, 200 D-11
Fishersville, 7462 H-9
Five Forks, 200 K-16
Five Forks, 150 J-9
Five Mile Fork, 700 G-13
Flat Rock J-13
Flat Run, 30 F-13
Flint Hill, 209 E-12
Floyd, 425 L-5
FLOYD CO., 15279 L-5
FLUVANNA CO., 25691 I-11
Ford, 80 K-13
Forest, 9106 J-8
Forestville, 160 E-10
Fork Union, 400 I-11
Forksville, 1000 M-12
Ft. Blackmore, 250 D-4
Ft. Defiance, 120 G-9
Ft. Hunt, 16045 ‡J-6
Ft. Mitchell, 100 L-11
Four Corners ‡F-2
Four Mile Fork, 420 G-14
Franconia, 18245 ‡I-4
Franklin, 8582 M-15
FRANKLIN CO., 56159 L-6
Franklin Pk., 1800 ‡F-4
Franktown, 100 J-19
FREDERICK CO., 78305 C-11
Fredericksburg, 24286 G-14
Free Union, 193 G-10
Fries, 484 M-3
Front Royal, 14440 D-11
Fulks Run, 150 E-9
Gainesboro, 80 C-11
Gainesville, 11481 E-13
Gala, 30 I-6
Galax, 7042 M-3
Garrisonville, 300 F-14
Garysville, 60 K-15
Gasburg, 481 N-12
Gate City, 2034 E-4
Georges Tavern, 50 I-12
GILES CO., 17286 K-3
Glade Spr., 1456 D-7
Gladehill, 80 L-6
Gladstone, 50 J-9
Gladys, 250 K-9
Glasgow, 1133 I-7
Glen Allen, 14774 †A-7
Glen Lyn, 115 J-3
Glen Wilton, 200 I-6
Glenmore I-10
Glenns J-16
Glenvar, 976 K-5
Gloucester, 2951 J-17
GLOUCESTER CO., 36858 J-16
Gloucester Pt., 9402 K-17
Goldbond, 160 J-4
Goldvein, 200 F-13
Goochland, 861 I-12
GOOCHLAND CO., 21717 I-12
Goode, 170 K-8
Goodview, 70 K-7
Gordonsville, 1496 G-11
Gore, 160 C-11
Goshen, 361 H-7
Grafton, 1050 †H-4
Grant, 30 M-1
Gratton, 937 K-1
GRAYSON CO., 15533 M-2
Graysontown, 100 L-4
Great Falls, 15427 ‡D-2
Green Bay, 140 K-11
Greenbackville, 192 H-20
Greenbriar, 650 †G-8
Greendale, 100 D-6
GREENE CO., 18403 G-11
Greenfield, 60 H-9
GREENSVILLE CO., 12243 M-13
Greenville, 832 H-8
Gretna, 1267 L-8
Grizzard M-14
Grottoes, 2668 G-9
Grove, 680 †G-3
Groveton, 14598 ‡I-5
Grundy, 1021 B-6
Guinea, 80 G-14
Guinea Mills J-11
Gum Spr., 100 I-12
Gunton Pk., 30 L-3
Gwynn, 602 J-17
Hadensville, 80 I-12
Hague, 80 H-16
Halfway, 60 D-13
Halifax, 1309 M-9
HALIFAX CO., 36241 M-9
Hallwood, 206 H-20
Hamburg, 30 E-10
Hamilton, 506 C-13
Hamlin, 300 C-5
Hampden Sydney, 1450 K-11
Hampton, 137436 L-17
Hanging Rock F-1
Hanover, 252 I-14
HANOVER CO., 99863 I-13
Hansonville, 200 D-6
Harborton, 131 I-19
Harman, 600 B-5
Harmony, 60 N-9
Harris Grv., 170 †G-5
Harrisonburg, 48914 F-9
Harriston, 909 G-9
Hartfield, 150 J-17
Hartwood, 50 F-13
Hayes, 1000 †F-4
Hayfield, 130 C-11
Haymarket, 1782 E-13
Haynesville, 210 H-16
Haysi, 498 B-5
Hayters Gap D-6
Haywood, 100 F-11
Head Waters, 30 G-8
Healing Sprs., 100 H-6
Heathsville, 142 H-17
HENRICO CO., 306935 J-14
Henry, 220 M-6
HENRY CO., 54151 N-6
Henry Fork, 1234 L-6
Herndon, 23292 D-14
Hewlett H-13
HIGHLAND CO., 2321 G-7
Highland Sprs., 15711 J-14
Hightown, 50 F-7
Hilander Pk., 400 E-6
Hillsboro, 80 C-13
Hillsville, 2681 M-3
Hillwood, 1650 ‡G-4
Hiltons, 100 D-5
Hinton, 250 F-9
Hiwassee, 264 L-3
Hodges, 100 K-8
Hollins, 14673 K-6
Holly Brook K-3
Hollymead, 7690 G-11
Holmes Run Acres, 1400 ‡G-3
Holston, 50 D-6
Homeville L-15
Honaker, 1449 C-6
Hood, 90 G-11
Hopewell, 22591 K-14
Horse Pasture, 2227 M-6
Horsepen, 230 K-1
Hot Sprs., 738 H-6
Howardsville, 120 I-10
Huddleston, 100 K-7
Hudgins, 230 J-17
Hume, 160 E-12
Huntington, 11267 ‡I-6
Hurley, 600 A-6
Hurt, 1304 L-8
Hustle, 100 H-15
Hybla Valley, 15801 ‡J-5
Ida, 220 F-11
Idylwood, 17288 ‡G-3
Independence, 947 M-2
Independent Hill, 7419 E-14
Indian Sprs. ‡I-4
Indian Valley, 120 L-4
Indika †M-2
Ingram, 40 M-8
Iron Gate, 388 I-6
Ironto, 90 K-5
Irvington, 432 I-17
Isle of Wight, 70 L-16
ISLE OF WIGHT CO., 35270 L-16
Ivanhoe, 551 L-3
Ivor, 339 L-16
JAMES CITY CO., 67009 K-16
Jamesville, 80 J-19
Jarratt, 638 M-14
Jasper, 50 D-3
Java, 30 M-8
Jefferson I-12
Jefferson Vil., 2500 ‡G-4
Jeffersonton, 180 E-12
Jetersville, 200 K-12
Jewell Ridge, 350 B-7
Jolivue, 1129 G-9
Jonesville, 1034 D-2
Jordan Mines, 30 I-5
Keeling, 50 M-8
Keene, 200 H-10
Keezletown, 400 F-9
Keller, 178 I-19
Kempsville †M-7
Kenbridge, 1257 L-12
Kents Store, 50 H-12
Keokee, 416 D-3
Keswick, 200 H-11
Key West, 300 †B-4
Keysville, 832 L-11
Kilmarnock, 1487 I-17
KING & QUEEN CO., 6945 I-15
King & Queen Court House, 85 I-16
King George, 4457 G-15
KING GEORGE CO., 23584 G-15
King William, 252 I-15
KING WILLIAM CO., 15935 I-15
Kings Pk., 4333 ‡H-3
Kings Pt., 500 †F-2
Kingstown, 120 F-2
Kingsville, 50 K-11
Kinsale, 300 H-16
Konnarock, 200 M-1
La Crosse, 604 M-12
Lacey Spr., 150 F-10
Lackey, 500 †G-4
Ladd, 410 H-9
Ladysmith, 200 H-14
Lafayette, 449 K-5
Lahore G-12
L. Monticello, 9920 H-11
Lakeside, 11849 †B-7
Lakeside Vil., 80 I-11
Lambsburg, 190 N-3
Lancaster, 80 I-17
LANCASTER CO., 11391 I-17
Laneview, 30 I-16
Lanexa, 250 J-16
Langley, 1450 ‡E-4
Laurel, 16713 I-14
Laurel Fork, 80 M-4
Lawrenceville, 1438 M-13
Lawson, 150 L-16
Lebanon, 3424 D-6
Lebanon Church, 150 D-11
LEE CO., 25587 D-2
Leedstown, 50 G-15
Leesburg, 42616 C-13
Leesville, 50 K-8
Leon, 40 F-12
Lewinsville ‡F-3
Lewisetta, 250 H-17
Lexington, 7042 I-7
Lightfoot, 400 J-16
Lignum, 180 F-13
Lilian, 100 H-17
Lincolnia, 22855 ‡H-4
Lincolnia Hts., 1800 ‡H-4
Lindell D-6
Linden, 200 D-12
Linton Hall, 35725 E-13
Little Plymouth, 50 I-16
Littleton L-15
Lively, 300 I-17
Locust Creek, 50 H-13
Locust Dale, 40 G-12
Locust Grv., 60 G-13
Locust Hill, 150 I-17
Locustville, 100 I-19
Lodi D-7
London Bridge †M-9
Long Island, 70 L-9
Longdale Furnace, 150 I-7
Longview, 50 †L-3
Loretto, 30 H-15
Lorton, 18610 E-14
Lottsburg, 450 H-17
LOUDOUN CO., 312311 D-13
Louisa, 1555 H-12
LOUISA CO., 33153 H-12
Lovettsville, 1613 C-13
Lovingston, 520 I-9
Low Moor, 258 I-6
Lowesville, 120 I-9
Lucketts, 50 C-13
Lunenburg, 165 L-11
LUNENBURG CO., 12914 L-11
Luray, 4895 E-11
Lyells H-16
Lynch Sta., 500 K-8
Lynchburg, 75568 J-8
Lyndhurst, 1490 H-9
Lynn Spr. C-6
Lynnhaven †M-8
Macon, 40 J-12
Madison, 229 F-11
MADISON CO., 13308 F-11
Madison Hts., 11285 J-8
Madison Mills, 70 G-12
Madisonville, 50 K-10
Magnolia †N-3
Manakin, 300 I-13
Manassas, 37821 E-14
Manassas Pk., 14273 E-14
Mangohick, 90 I-14
Mannboro, 50 K-13
Manquin, 100 I-15
Manry L-15
Mantua, 7135 ‡G-3
Mappsville, 440 H-20
Marion, 5968 L-1
Markham, 190 D-12
Marshall, 1480 D-12
Martinsville, 13821 M-
Marumsco, 35036 E-14
Marvin, 130 B-6
Masonville ‡G-3
Massaponax, 210 G-14
Massies Mill, 120 I-9
Mathews, 555 J-17
MATHEWS CO., 8978 J-17
Matoaca, 2403 †H-
Mattaponi, 350 J-16
Maurertown, 770 D-1
Mavisdale, 450 B-6
Max Meadows, 562 L-
Maxie, 400 B-
Mayo, 30 N-
McClure, 350 C-
McCoy, 250 K-
McDonalds Mill K-
McDowell, 170 G-
McGaheysville, 550 F-1
McKenney, 483 L-1
McLean, 48115 ‡F-
Meadowview, 967 D-
Meadville, 30 M-
Mechanicsburg, 170 K-
Mechanicsville, 36348 I-1
MECKLENBURG CO., 32727 M-1
Meherrin, 190 K-1
Melfa, 408 I-1
Mendota, 160 D-
Merrifield, 15212 ‡G-
Middlebrook, 213 H-
Middleburg, 673 D-1
MIDDLESEX CO., 10959 J-1
Middletown, 1265 D-1
Midland, 218 F-1
Midlothian, 450 J-1
Mike K-
Milford, 500 H-1
Millboro, 450 H-
Millboro Sprs., 80 H-
Millenbeck I-1
Millers Tavern, 50 H-1
Millwood, 250 D-1
Mine Run, 30 G-1
Mineral, 467 H-1
Mint Spr., 150 H-
Mitchelltown, 200 H-
Mobjack, 250 J-1
Modest Town, 149 H-2
Mogarts Bch., 60 †J-
Mollusk, 120 I-1
Moneta, 220 K-
Monroe, 400 J-
Montclair, 19570 E-1
Montebello, 130 H-
Monterey, 147 F-
MONTGOMERY CO., 94392 K-
Montpelier, 150 I-1
Montpelier Sta., 120 G-1
Montrose, 7993 †D-
Montross, 384 G-1
Montvale, 698 J-
Montvue, 150 †A-
Morattico, 270 I-1
Morrisville, 190 F-1
Moscow G-
Moseley, 120 J-1
Motley, 1015 L-
Mt. Airy, 30 L-
Mt. Clifton, 70 E-1
Mt. Clinton, 80 F-
Mt. Crawford, 433 G-
Mt. Hermon, 3966 M-
Mt. Heron, 180 B-
Mt. Jackson, 1994 E-1
Mt. Laurel, 50 L-1
Mt. Olive, 90 D-1
Mt. Sidney, 663 G-
Mt. Solon, 200 G-
Mt. Vernon, 12416 E-1
Mountain Falls, 100 C-1
Mountain Grv. H-
Mountain Lake, 30 J-
Mountain Road, 1100 M-
Mountain Valley M-
Mouth of Wilson, 150 M-
Mustoe, 30 G-
Nain C-1
Narrows, 2029 K-
Naruna, 200 K-
Nasons, 30 G-1
Nassawadox, 499 J-1
Nathalie, 183 L-
Natural Bridge, 1500 I-
Natural Well, 30 H-
Naxera, 400 J-1
Nellysford, 1076 H-
NELSON CO., 15020 I-
Nelsonia, 523 H-2
New Alexandria, 950 ‡I-
New Baltimore, 8119 E-1
New Bohemia, 40 †I-1
New Canton, 70 I-1
New Castle, 153 J-
New Church, 205 H-2
New Glasgow, 50 I-
New Hope, 797 G-
New Kent, 239 J-1
NEW KENT CO., 18429 J-1
New London K-
New Market, 2146 E-1
New Pt., 300 J-1
Newbern, 300 L-
Newington, 12943 ‡J-
Newland H-1
Newport, 200 K-
Newport, 100 H-
Newport News, 180719 L-1
Newsoms, 321 M-1
Newtown, 200 F-1
Newtown, 100 H-1
Nicelytown, 160 I-
Nickelsville, 383 D-
Nineveh D-1
Nokesville, 1354 E-1
Nora, 150 C-
Norfolk, 242803 L-1
Norge, 1000 J-1
Norman, 70 F-1
North, 200 J-1
N. Garden, 900 H-1
N. Shore, 3094 L-
N. Springfield, 7274 ‡H-
N. View M-1
NORTHAMPTON CO., 12389 J-1
Northfields, 1400 †A-

*, †, ‡, §, ◊ See explanation under state title in this index.
County and parish names are listed in capital letters & boldface type.
Independent cities (not included in a county) are listed in italics.

Pipestem, 15	L-5	Spurlockville, 25	J-2
Pleasant Valley, 3149	F-7	Squire, 450	M-3
Pleasant Valley, 60	D-6	Star City, 1825	J-8
Pleasant View, 150	J-2	Statts Mills, 35	H-3
PLEASANTS CO.,		Steptown, 150	K-1
7605	F-5	Stonewood, 1806	J-7
Pliny, 100	J-3	Stringtown, 120	F-6
Poca, 974	J-3	Stumptown, 100	H-5
POCAHONTAS CO.,		Sugar Grv., 35	J-10
8719	J-8	**SUMMERS CO.,**	
Pocatalico, 1500	I-3	13927	L-5
Pt. Pleasant, 4350	H-2	Summersville, 3572	J-5
Points, 30	J-8	Sundial, 90	K-4
Port Amherst, 350	N-10	Sutton, 994	I-5
Porters Falls, 75	F-6	Sweet Sprs., 120	L-7
Powellton, 619	K-4	Swiss, 250	J-5
Pratt, 602	J-4	Switzer, 595	L-2
Premier, 90	M-3	Sylvester, 160	K-3
Prenter, 300	K-3	Tablers Sta., 100	B-10
PRESTON CO.,		Talcott, 400	L-6
33520	F-8	Tallmansville, 120	H-7
Pricetown, 85	F-6	Tanner, 100	H-5
Prichard, 527	J-1	Tariff, 20	I-4
Prince, 116	K-5	**TAYLOR CO., 16895**	F-8
Princeton, 6432	M-5	Taylorville, 300	J-5
Procious, 125	J-4	Tennerton, 1800	H-7
Proctor, 150	E-6	Terra Alta, 1477	F-9
Prosperity, 1498	K-4	Tesla, 40	I-5
Pruntytown, 150	F-7	Thomas, 586	G-9
Pullman, 154	G-5	Thornton, 550	F-8
Purgitsville, 50	C-7	Thornwood, 80	I-8
PUTNAM CO.,		Three Churches, 35	B-8
55486	I-3	Tioga, 98	I-6
Quick, 100	J-4	Trout, 40	L-6
Quiet Dell, 400	G-7	Troy, 125	G-6
Quinwood, 200	K-6	**TUCKER CO., 7141**	G-8
Racine, 256	J-3	Tunnelton, 294	F-8
Radnor, 60	K-1	Tyler, 70	I-5
Ragland, 400	L-2	**TYLER CO., 9208**	F-5
Rainelle, 1505	K-6	Tyler Mtn., 450	L-8
RALEIGH CO.,		Uneeda, 450	K-3
78859	L-4	Unger, 100	B-9
Ramage, 200	K-3	Union, 565	L-6
Rand, 1631	J-3	Union City, 150	M-3
RANDOLPH CO.,		Upper Falls, 3701	J-3
29405	H-8	Upper Tract, 90	H-10
Ranger, 180	J-2	Upperglade, 400	J-6
Ranson, 4440	C-10	**UPSHUR CO.,**	
Raven Rock, 40	F-5	24254	H-7
Ravenswood, 3876	H-3	Valley Bend, 485	H-8
Reader, 397	F-6	Valley Head, 267	I-8
Red Creek, 80	H-9	Valley Pt., 160	F-8
Red Jacket, 581	L-2	Van, 211	K-3
Red Sulphur Sprs.,		Varney, 250	L-2
Reedsville, 593	F-8	Verdunville, 687	K-2
Reedy, 182	H-4	Vienna, 10749	F-4
Replete,	I-6	Volga, 140	G-7
Rhodell, 173	L-4	Vulcan, 100	L-2
Richwood, 2051	J-6	Wadestown, 150	E-7
Ridgeley, 675	B-7	Waiteville, 40	M-6
Ridgeway, 350	C-9	Walkersville, 150	I-6
Rig, 125	G-10	Wallace, 475	F-6
Ringgold,	F-8	Walton, 350	H-4
Rio, 150	C-8	Wana, 130	E-7
Ripley, 3252	H-3	War, 862	M-3
Rippon, 50	C-10	Wardensville, 271	C-8
RITCHIE CO.,		Warwood	C-2
10449	G-4	Washington, 1175	G-3
Riverton, 100	H-9	Waverly, 395	F-4
Rivesville, 934	F-7	Wayne, 1413	J-1
ROANE CO., 14926	H-4	**WAYNE CO., 42481**	J-1
Robertsburg, 100	I-2	Wayside, 40	L-6
Robinette, 663	L-3	Weberwood	M-9
Rock Cave, 400	H-7	**WEBSTER CO., 9154**	I-7
Rock Creek, 200	K-4	Webster Sprs., 776	I-7
Rock View, 400	L-3	Weirton, 19746	C-3
Rocklick	E-6	Welch, 2406	M-3
Rockport, 50	G-4	Wellsburg, 2805	C-5
Roderfield, 188	M-3	W. Hamlin, 774	J-2
Romney, 1848	B-8	W. Liberty, 1542	D-6
Ronceverte, 1765	L-6	W. Logan, 424	K-2
Rosedale, 175	H-5	W. Milford, 630	G-7
Rowlesburg, 584	F-8	W. Union, 825	G-6
Rumble, 250	J-3	Weston, 4110	G-6
Rupert, 942	K-5	Westover, 3983	J-8
Ruth,	N-8	**WETZEL CO.,**	
Ruthdale, 65	N-8	16583	F-6
Sabine, 250	L-4	Wheeling, 28486	D-6
St. Albans, 11044	J-3	White Sulphur Sprs.,	
St. George, 60	G-8	2444	L-7
St. Joseph, 60	E-6	Whitehall, 648	F-7
St. Marys, 1860	F-4	Whitesville, 514	K-4
Salem, 1586	G-6	Whitman, 450	L-2
Salt Rock, 388	J-2	Whitmer, 106	H-9
Sand Fork, 159	H-6	Wick, 60	H-4
Sand Ridge, 150	H-4	Widen, 200	I-5
Sandstone, 250	L-5	Wileyville, 100	E-6
Sandyville, 100	H-3	Williamsburg, 225	L-6
Scherr, 25	G-10	Williamson, 3191	L-2
Scott, 25	F-5	Williamstown, 2908	F-4
Scott Depot, 1500	I-3	Willow Island	F-4
Sedalia, 60	J-4	Wilsondale, 40	K-1
Seebert, 30	J-7	Windsor Hts., 423	C-6
Seneca Rocks, 75	H-9	Winfield, 2301	I-3
Servia	J-5	**WIRT CO., 5717**	G-4
Seth, 75	K-3	Wolf Pen, 60	L-3
Shady Spr., 2998	L-5	Wolfcreek, 30	L-6
Shanks, 100	C-8	**WOOD CO., 86956**	G-3
Shepherdstown,		Worthington, 158	F-7
1734	B-10	**WYOMING CO.,**	
Sherman, 40	J-3	23796	L-4
Shinnston, 2201	F-7	Yawkey, 175	J-3
Shirley, 135	F-6	Yellow Spr., 100	C-8
Shoals, 70	J-1		
Short Gap, 500	B-7		
Sias, 35	J-2	**Wisconsin**	
Silver Lake, 120	G-9	Page locator	
Simpson, 250	G-7	Map keys	Atlas pages
Sinks Grv., 75	L-6	A–J	228–229
Sissonville, 4028	I-3	K–T	230–231
Sistersville, 1396	F-5	* City keyed to p. 109	
Slab Fork, 150	L-4	† City keyed to pp. 232–233	
Slanesville, 150	B-8		
Slate	G-4	Abbotsford, 2310	H-7
Slaty Fork, 100	I-7	Abrams, 340	C-11
Smithburg, 120	G-6	Ada, 130	L-13
Smithers, 813	J-4	Adams, 1967	K-8
Smithfield, 145	F-6	**ADAMS CO.,**	
Smithville, 200	G-5	20875	K-9
Smoot, 125	K-5	Adell, 516	L-13
Snow Hill, 275	N-10	Afton, 250	D-12
Sod, 150	J-3	Alaska, 30	D-12
Sophia, 1344	L-4	Albany, 1018	O-9
S. Charleston, 13450	J-3	Albion, 240	O-10
S. Hills	J-8	Algoma, 3167	J-14
S. Park	J-8	Allen, 30	O-11
Southside, 50	H-4	Allens Grv., 180	P-11
Speed	H-4	Allenton, 823	L-12
Spencer, 2322	H-4	Allouez, 13975	C-13
Spring Dale, 200	K-5	Alma, 781	I-3
Spring Hill	J-8	Alma Ctr., 503	I-6
Spring Valley, 900	D-3	Almena, 677	E-3
Springfield, 50	B-8	Almond, 448	J-9
Springfield, 477	B-8	Alpha, 50	O-11

*, †, ‡, §, ◊   See explanation under state title in this index.
County and parish names are listed in capital letters & boldface type.
Independent cities (not included in a county) are listed in italics.

Alto, 200	L-11	**BROWN CO.,**	
Altoona, 6706	H-5	248007	D-11
Alvin, 90	E-11	Brown Deer,	
Alverno, 180	F-13	11999	N-13
Amery, 2902	G-2	Brownsville, 581	L-12
Amherst, 1035	J-10	Browntown, 280	P-8
Amherst Jct., 377	J-10	Bruce, 779	F-5
Angelica, 92	I-3	Brule, 254	C-4
Angelo, 110	K-6	Brussels, 150	C-12
Anston, 80	I-12	Bryant, 100	G-9
Antigo, 8234	G-10	Buffalo City, 1023	J-4
Appleton, 72623	J-12	**BUFFALO CO.,**	
Arbor Vitae, 220	E-9	13587	J-4
Arcadia, 2925	J-4	Burke, 100	H-2
Arena, 834	N-8	Burkhardt, 60	H-2
Argonne, 160	F-11	Burlington, 10464	O-12
Argyle, 857	O-8	Burnett, 296	M-11
Arkansaw, 177	I-3	**BURNETT CO.,**	
Arkdale, 158	K-8	15457	E-2
Arland, 40	G-4	Burton, 30	O-6
Arlington, 819	M-9	Butler, 1841	D-3
Armstrong Creek,		Butte des Morts,	
200	F-12	962	K-11
Arnott, 50	J-9	Butternut, 375	D-7
Arpin, 333	I-8	Byron, 80	L-12
Arthur, 70	O-12	Cable, 206	D-5
Ashippun, 333	N-12	Caddy Vista, 900	J-6
Ashland, 8216	C-6	Cadott, 1437	H-5
ASHLAND CO.,		Calamine, 70	O-8
16157	D-6	Caledonia, 24705	O-13
Ashton Cors., 140	C-3	**CALUMET CO.,**	
Ashwaubenon,		48971	K-12
16963	C-13	Calumetville, 80	K-12
Astico, 40	M-11	Cambria, 767	M-10
Athelstane, 110	F-12	Cambridge, 1457	N-10
Athens, 1105	H-8	Cameron, 1783	F-4
Atlas, 70	J-8	Camp Douglas, 601	K-7
Atwood	H-7	Campbellsport,	
Auburndale, 703	I-8	2016	L-12
Augusta, 1550	I-5	Campia, 50	F-4
Aurora, 450	C-12	Canton, 100	F-4
Auroraville, 40	K-10	Carol Bch.	
Avalanche, 30	L-6	Estates	†M-13
Avalon, 20	P-11	Caroline, 270	H-11
Avoca, 637	N-7	Carter, 100	G-11
Babcock, 126	J-8	Carter, 100	O-11
Badger, 379	O-5	Caryville, 50	H-5
Baileys Hbr., 257	B-13	Cascade, 709	L-13
Bakerville, 50	I-7	Casco, 583	D-12
Baldwin, 3957	H-2	Cashton, 1102	L-6
Balsam Lake, 1009	F-2	Cascade, 947	O-6
Bancroft, 535	I-9	Cataract, 186	K-6
Bangor, 1459	K-6	Catawba, 110	F-7
Baraboo, 12048	M-9	Cazenovia, 318	M-7
Barneveld, 1231	N-8	Cecil, 570	H-12
Barnum, 30	N-6	Cedar Grv., 2113	M-13
Barron, 3423	F-4	Cedarburg, 11412	M-13
BARRON CO.,		Centerville, 150	K-4
45870	F-3	Centerville, 50	L-11
Barronett, 111	F-3	Centuria, 948	F-2
Basco, 60	O-9	Champion, 60	D-11
Bay City, 500	I-2	Chaseburg, 284	L-5
Bayfield, 487	B-6	Chelsea, 113	G-7
BAYFIELD CO.,		Cherokee	H-7
15014	B-5	Chetek, 2221	G-4
Bayside, 4389	†C-6	Chili, 226	I-7
Bear Creek, 448	J-11	Chilton, 3933	K-12
Bear Valley, 25	M-7	**CHIPPEWA CO.,**	
Beaver, 1413	J-1	62415	G-5
Beaver Dam,		Chippewa Falls,	
16214	M-11	13661	H-5
Beecher, 85	F-13	Christie, 30	J-1
Beetown, 150	O-6	City Pt., 40	J-7
Beldenville, 150	I-2	Clam Falls, 80	E-3
Belgium, 2245	M-13	Clam Lake, 50	D-6
Bell Ctr., 117	N-6	Clarno, 50	P-9
Belle Plaine, 50	I-11	**CLARK CO., 34690**	I-6
Belleville, 2385	O-9	Clayton, 571	F-3
Bellevue, 14570	J-13	Clear Lake, 1070	G-3
Bellinger		Clearwater Lake,	
Belmont, 986	O-7	150	E-10
Beloit, 36966	P-10	Cleghorn, 75	H-5
Bennett, 40	C-4	Cleveland, 1485	K-13
Benoit, 30	C-6	Clifton, 40	L-7
Benton, 973	P-7	Clinton, 2154	P-11
Berlin, 5524	K-10	Clintonville, 4559	I-11
Bethel, 100	O-8	Clyman, 422	M-11
Bevent, 110	I-9	Cobb, 458	O-7
Big Bend, 1290	†I-1	Cochrane, 450	J-4
Big Falls, 61	I-10	Colby, 1852	H-7
Big Flats	K-8	Coleman, 724	H-11
Big Spr., 40	L-9	Colfax, 1158	H-4
Billings Pk.	*C-9	Colgate, 90	†B-1
Birchwood, 442	F-4	Collins, 164	K-13
Birnamwood, 818	H-10	Coloma, 450	K-9
Biron, 839	I-8	**COLUMBIA CO.,**	
Black Creek, 1316	J-12	56833	M-10
Black Earth, 1338	N-9	Columbus, 4991	M-10
Black Hawk, 80	O-8	Combined Locks,	
Black River Falls,		3328	J-12
3622	J-6	Commonwealth,	
Blackwell, 90	F-11	240	E-12
Blair, 1366	J-5	Comstock, 100	F-3
Blanchardville, 825	O-9	Conover, 380	E-10
Blenker, 120	I-8	Conrath, 130	G-3
Bloom City, 80	M-7	Conover, 380	D-10
Bloomer, 3539	G-4	Coon Valley, 765	L-6
Bloomfield, 3722	P-12	Cooperstown, 50	J-13
Bloomingdale, 60	L-6	Cornell, 1467	G-5
Bloomington, 735	O-6	Cornucopia, 98	B-5
Bloomville, 25	G-6	Cottage Grv.,	
Blue Mounds, 855	N-8	6192	N-10
Blue River, 434	N-7	Cottage Grv., 4	N-10
Bluff Siding, 40	K-4	County Line, 40	K-5
Boaz, 156	M-7	Cranmoor, 120	J-7
Boltonville, 80	M-13	**CRAWFORD CO.,**	
Bonduel, 1478	I-12	16644	N-6
Borth, 35	K-11	Cream, 30	J-4
Boscobel, 3231	N-6	Crestview, 3500	J-13
Boulder Jct., 183	D-9	Crivitz, 984	G-12
Bowler, 302	H-10	Cross Plains, 3538	N-9
Boyceville, 1086	H-3	Cuba City, 2086	P-7
Boyd, 552	H-5	Cudahy, 18267	O-13
Brackett, 120	H-5	Cumberland, 2170	F-3
Bradley, 60	H-9	Curtiss, 216	H-7
Brandon, 879	L-11	Cushing, 100	F-2
Brantwood, 50	F-8	Custer, 170	I-9
Breed, 35	H-11	Dairyland, 20	D-3
Bridgeport, 60	N-5	Dalbo, 209	G-4
Briggsville, 380	L-9	Dalton, 272	L-10
Brill, 130	F-4	Dancy, 80	I-8
Bristol, 3148	P-13	Dane, 995	N-9
Brodhead, 3293	P-9	**DANE CO.,**	
Brokaw, 251	H-9	488073	O-9
Brookfield, 37920	N-12	Danbury, 350	E-3
Brooklyn, 1401	O-9	Darien, 1580	P-11
Brooks, 150	L-8	Darlington, 2451	P-8
Brookside, 75	J-13	De Forest, 8936	N-10
Brothertown, 200	K-12		

De Pere, 23800	J-13	Gillingham, 100	M-7
De Soto, 287	M-5	Gills Rock, 50	A-13
Deer Pk., 216	G-2	Gilman, 410	G-6
Deerbrook, 200	G-10	Gilmanton, 150	J-4
Deerfield, 2319	N-10	Gleason, 200	G-9
Delafield, 7085	N-12	Glen Flora, 92	F-6
Delavan, 8463	P-11	Glen Haven, 73	O-5
Dellwood, 563	K-8	Glenbeulah, 463	L-13
Denmark, 2123	J-13	Glendale, 12872	N-13
Deronda, 90	G-2	Glendale, 30	L-7
Detroit Hbr., 400	A-14	Glenwood City,	
Dexterville, 50	J-8	1242	H-3
Diamond Bluff, 194	I-2	Glidden, 507	D-7
Dickeyville, 1061	P-6	Goodman, 271	F-12
Dodge, 121	M-5	Goodrich, 40	G-8
DODGE CO.,		Gordon, 176	D-4
88759	M-11	Gotham, 191	N-7
Dodgeville, 4693	O-8	Grafton, 11459	M-13
Doering	N-7	Grand Marsh, 127	L-9
DOOR CO.,		Grand View, 150	C-6
27785	C-12	**GRANT CO.,**	
Dorchester, 876	H-7	51208	O-6
DOUGLAS CO.,		Granton, 355	I-7
44159	C-3	Grantsburg, 1341	E-2
Dousman, 2302	N-12	Gratiot, 236	P-8
Downing, 265	H-3	Green Bay, 104057	J-13
Downsville, 146	H-4	**GREEN CO.,**	
Doylestown, 297	M-10	36842	O-9
Draper, 30	E-6	Green Lake, 960	L-10
Dresser, 895	G-2	**GREEN LAKE CO.,**	
Drummond, 154	C-5	19051	K-10
Dunbar, 50	F-12	Green Valley, 133	H-12
Dundee, 140	L-12	Greenbush, 162	L-13
Duplainville	†E-2	Greendale, 14046	†G-5
Durand, 1931	I-3	Greenfield, 36720	O-13
Dyckesville, 50	C-12	Greenleaf, 607	J-12
Eagle, 1950	O-12	Greenville, 300	J-11
Eagle River, 1398	E-10	Greenwood, 1026	I-7
Eagleton, 40	H-5	Gresham, 586	H-11
Earl, 60	F-4	Gurney, 110	C-7
E. Farmington, 100	G-2	Hager City, 338	I-2
E. Troy, 4281	O-12	Halder, 40	H-8
Eastman, 428	N-5	Hales Cors., 7692	†G-4
Easton, 110	L-8	Hamburg	H-9
Eau Claire, 65883	H-4	Hammond, 1922	H-2
EAU CLAIRE CO.,		Hancock, 417	K-9
98736	H-5	Hannibal, 70	G-6
Eau Galle, 200	I-3	Hanover, 181	P-10
Eden, 875	L-12	Harmony, 35	B-11
Edgar, 1479	H-8	Harrison, 30	J-9
Edgerton, 5461	O-10	Harrisville, 200	K-9
Edgewater, 100	L-13	Hartford, 14223	M-12
Edmund, 173	O-7	Hartland, 9110	N-12
Egg Hbr., 201	B-13	Hatfield, 140	J-6
Eland, 202	H-10	Hatley, 574	H-10
Elcho, 339	F-10	Haugen, 287	F-4
Elderon, 179	H-10	Haven, 40	L-13
Eldorado, 250	L-11	Hawkins, 305	F-6
Eleva, 670	I-4	Hawthorne, 120	C-4
Elk Mound, 878	H-4	Hayes, 30	H-10
Elkhart Lake, 967	L-13	Hayton, 100	K-12
Elkhorn, 10084	P-12	Hayward, 2318	D-5
Ella	H-7	Hazel Green, 1256	P-7
Ellison Bay, 165	A-13	Hazelhurst, 500	E-9
Ellisville, 50	J-3	Heafford Jct., 200	F-9
Ellsworth, 3289	I-2	Hebron, 224	O-11
Elm Grv., 5934	†E-3	Helenville, 249	N-11
Elmhurst	H-10	Herbster, 165	B-5
Elmore, 80	M-12	Hersey, 85	H-3
Elmwood, 817	I-3	Hertel, 50	E-3
Elmwood Pk., 497	†J-10	Hewitt, 828	I-8
Elroy, 1442	L-7	High Br., 100	C-6
Elton, 130	G-11	Highland, 842	N-7
Embarrass, 400	I-11	Hilbert, 1132	K-12
Emerald, 161	G-3	Hiles, 100	E-10
Emerald Grv., 90	P-11	Hilbert, 1417	L-7
Endeavor, 468	L-9	Hillsboro, 1417	L-7
Enterprise, 90	F-11	Hillsdale, 180	G-4
Ephraim, 288	B-13	Hingham, 886	L-13
Erdman, 150	†E-8	Hixton, 433	J-6
Ettrick, 524	K-5	Hobart, 6182	J-12
Eureka, 220	K-11	Holcombe, 80	G-5
Euren, 40	D-12	Holland, 100	J-12
Evansville, 5012	O-10	Hollandale, 280	O-8
Exeland, 196	F-5	Hollister, 100	O-11
Fairchild, 550	I-6	Holmen, 9005	K-5
Fairwater, 371	L-11	Honey Creek, 400	O-12
Fall Creek, 1315	I-5	Horicon, 3655	M-11
Fall River, 1712	M-10	Hortonville, 2711	J-11
Falun, 100	F-2	Houlton, 386	H-1
Fayette, 40	P-9	Howard, 17399	J-13
Fence, 100	F-12	Howards Grv.,	
Fennimore, 2497	O-6	3188	L-13
Fenwood, 152	H-8	Hub City, 100	M-7
Ferryville, 176	M-5	Hubertus, 30	†B-1
Fifield, 330	F-7	Hudson, 12719	H-1
Fish Creek, 300	B-13	Humbird, 266	I-6
Fitchburg, 25260	N-9	Hurley, 1547	C-8
Flintville, 60	I-12	Hustisford, 1123	M-11
Florence, 592	E-12	Hustler, 194	L-7
FLORENCE CO.,		Independence, 1336	J-5
4423	E-12	Indianford, 250	O-10
Fond du Lac, 43021	L-12	Ingram, 76	G-6
FOND DU LAC CO.,		Institute, 50	C-13
101633	L-11	Iola, 1301	I-10
Fontana, 1760	P-11	**IOWA CO., 23687**	N-7
Footville, 808	P-10	Irma, 100	G-9
Forest, 50	G-3	Iron Belt, 173	C-7
FOREST CO.,		Iron Ridge, 929	M-11
9304	F-11	Iron River, 761	C-5
Forest Jct., 116	J-12	Ironton, 253	M-8
Forestville, 430	C-12	Irvington, 200	C-3
Ft. Atkinson,		Island Lake, 30	O-13
12368	O-11	Ives Grv., 50	†O-13
Foster, 90	L-7	Ixonia, 1640	N-11
Fountain City, 859	K-4	Jackson, 6753	M-13
Fountain Prairie	M-10	**JACKSON CO.,**	
Fox Lake, 1454	M-11	20449	J-7
Fox Pt., 6701	†C-6	Jacksonport, 60	B-13
Foxboro, 100	C-3	Janesville, 63575	P-10
Francis Creek, 669	J-13	Jefferson, 7973	N-11
Franklin, 35451	O-13	**JEFFERSON CO.,**	
Franklin, 50	J-1	83686	N-11
Franksville, 1789	†J-8	Jennings, 40	F-9
Frederic, 1137	F-2	Jim Falls, 237	H-5
Fredonia, 2160	M-13	Johnsburg, 180	L-12
Freedom, 400	J-12	Johnson Creek,	
French Island, 4410	†B-8	2738	N-11
Friendship, 735	K-9	Johnstown Ctr.,	
Friesland, 396	M-10	90	P-10
Galesville, 1481	K-5	Juda, 357	P-9
Gays Mills, 491	M-6	Jump River, 52	G-7
Genesee, 450	O-12	Junction City, 439	I-9
Genoa, 253	M-5	Juneau, 2814	M-11
Genoa City, 3042	P-12	**JUNEAU CO.,**	
Germania, 60	K-10	26664	K-7
Germantown,		Kaukauna, 15462	J-12
19749	N-13	Kekoskee, 161	M-11
Gillett, 1386	H-12	Kellner, 200	I-8
		Kellnersville, 332	J-13
		Kempster	G-10
		Kendall, 472	L-7
		Kennan, 135	F-7
		Kenosha, 99218	P-13
		KENOSHA CO.,	
		166426	P-13
		Keshena, 1262	H-11
		Kewaskum, 4004	M-12
		Kewaunee, 2952	J-14

KEWAUNEE CO.,		Merton, 3346	N-12
20574	C-12	Middle Inlet, 45	A-11
Kiel, 3738	K-13	Middle Ridge, 40	L-6
Kieler, 497	P-6	Middleton, 17442	N-9
Kimberly, 6468	J-12	Midway, 100	K-5
King, 1750	I-10	Milan, 130	H-8
Kingston, 310	L-10	Milford, 80	N-11
Klondike, 50	H-3	Milladore, 276	I-8
Knapp, 463	H-3	Millston, 125	K-6
Knowles, 160	M-12	Milltown, 917	F-2
Knowlton, 120	I-9	Milton, 5546	O-11
Kohler, 2120	L-13	Milwaukee,	
Kolberg	C-12	594833	N-13
Krakow, 354	I-12	**MILWAUKEE CO.,**	
Kronenwetter,		947735	O-13
7210	I-9	Minder, 100	K-7
La Crosse, 51320	L-5	Minocqua, 450	E-9
LA CROSSE CO.,		Minong, 540	E-4
114638	L-5	Minnesota Jct.,	
La Farge, 746	M-6	100	M-11
La Pointe, 100	B-6	Minocqua, 451	E-9
La Valle, 367	M-8	Mishicot, 1442	J-14
Lac du Flambeau,		Modena, 50	I-4
1969	E-9	Mole Lake, 435	F-10
Lac La Belle, 290	N-12	Mondovi, 2777	I-4
Ladysmith, 3414	F-5	Monico, 150	F-10
LAFAYETTE CO.,		Monona, 7533	N-10
16836	P-7	Monroe, 10827	P-9
L. Beulah, 300	O-12	**MONROE CO.,**	
L. Church, 100	M-13	44673	L-6
L. Delton, 2914	L-8	Montello, 1495	L-10
L. Geneva, 7651	P-12	Monterey, 120	N-12
L. Mills, 5708	N-11	Monticello, 1217	O-9
L. Nebagamon,		Montreal, 807	C-7
1069	C-4	Monticello, 1026	I-7
L. Tomahawk, 228	E-9	Mont Calvary, 762	L-12
L. Wissota, 2738	H-5	Mt. Hope, 225	O-6
Lakewood, 323	G-11	Mt. Horeb, 7009	N-9
Lamartine, 150	L-11	Mt. Ida, 45	O-6
Lamont, 30	O-8	Mt. Morris, 130	K-10
Lampson, 60	E-4	Mt. Pleasant,	
Lancaster, 3868	O-6	26197	O-13
L. of Lakes, 700	D-10	Mt. Sterling, 211	M-6
Langlade, 80	H-10	Mt. Tabor	L-7
Lannon, 1107	†C-2	Mt. Vernon, 180	O-9
Laona, 563	F-11	Mt. Zion	N-6
Larsen, 200	J-11	Mountain, 363	G-12
Lead Mine, 80	P-7	Mukwonago,	
Lebanon, 204	N-11	7355	O-12
Leland, 50	M-8	Muscoda, 1299	N-7
Lena, 564	B-11	Muskego, 24135	†H-2
Leon, 120	L-6	Myra, 100	D-10
Leopolis, 87	H-11	Namur, 30	C-12
LeRoy, 100	M-11	Nashotah, 1395	N-12
Lewis, 164	F-2	Navarino, 177	I-12
Liberty Pole, 50	M-6	Necedah, 916	K-8
Lily	G-11	Neenah, 25501	K-11
Lima Ctr., 200	O-11	Neillsville, 2463	I-7
Lime Ridge, 162	M-8	Nekoosa, 2580	J-8
Linden, 549	O-8	Nelma, 40	D-11
Lincoln, 160	C-8	Nelson, 374	J-3
LINCOLN CO.,		Nelsonville, 155	J-10
28743	G-8	Neopit, 690	H-11
Linden, 549	O-8	Neosho, 574	M-12
Lindsey, 50	J-7	Neshkoro, 434	K-9
Little Chicago, 50	H-8	New Amsterdam,	
Little Chute, 10449	J-12	150	K-5
Little Falls, 40	O-3	New Auburn, 548	G-4
Little Suamico, 180	C-11	New Berlin, 39584	N-13
Livingston, 664	O-7	New Diggings, 100	P-7
Lodi, 3050	M-9	New Franken, 250	D-11
Loganville, 300	M-8	New Glarus, 2172	O-9
Lohrville, 402	K-10	New Holstein,	
Lomira, 2430	L-12	3236	K-13
Lone Rock, 888	N-7	New Lisbon, 2554	L-8
Long Lake, 50	F-13	New London, 7295	I-11
Longwood, 40	H-7	New Miner, 45	K-8
Loretta, 100	E-6	New Post, 305	E-5
Lowell, 340	M-11	New Richmond,	
Loyal, 1261	I-7	8375	G-2
Loyd, 40	M-7	Newald, 95	E-11
Lublin, 118	H-6	Newburg, 1254	M-13
Lublin, 1119	H-6	Newry, 40	K-5
Luck, 1119	F-2	Newton, 80	K-13
Ludington, 25	K-8	Niagara, 1624	E-13
Lund, 45	I-3	Nichols, 273	I-12
Luxemburg, 2515	D-12	Norrie, 90	H-10
Lyndon Sta., 500	L-8	N. Andover, 50	O-8
Lynxville, 132	N-5	N. Bay, 241	†J-8
Lyons, 600	P-12	N. Bend, 110	J-5
Mackville, 200	J-12	N. Bristol, 100	O-13
Madison, 233209	N-9	N. Fond du Lac,	
Maiden Rock, 119	I-2	5014	L-12
Manawa, 1371	I-11	N. Freedom, 701	M-8
Manitowish, 80	D-8	N. Hudson, 3768	H-1
Manitowish Waters,		N. Prairie, 2141	O-12
400	D-8	Northfield, 80	J-5
Manitowoc, 33736	K-14	Northwoods Bch.,	
MANITOWOC CO.,		150	D-5
81442	K-13	Norwalk, 637	L-6
Maple, 200	C-4	**OCONTO CO.,**	
Maple Bluff, 1313	†R-8	37660	B-11
Maplewood, 225	C-12	Oconto Falls,	
Marathon, 1524	H-8	2891	H-12
MARATHON CO.,		Ogdensburg, 185	I-10
134063	H-9	Ojibwa, 100	E-7
Marengo, 35	D-6	Okee, 300	M-9
Maribel, 351	J-13	Oliver, 399	C-3
Marinette, 10968	B-12	Omro, 3517	K-11
MARINETTE CO.,		Onalaska, 17736	L-5
41749	A-11	Oneida, 1000	J-13
Marion, 1260	I-11	**ONEIDA CO.,**	
Markesan, 1476	L-10	35998	E-9
Marquette, 150	L-9	Ontario, 554	L-7
MARQUETTE CO.,		Oostburg, 2887	L-13
15404	L-9	Oregon, 9231	O-9
Marshall, 3862	N-10	Orfordville, 1442	P-10
Marshfield, 19118	I-8	Osceola, 2568	G-2
Marshland	J-4	Oshkosh, 66083	K-11
Martell, 150	I-2	Osseo, 1701	I-5
Marytown, 200	K-12	**OUTAGAMIE CO.,**	
Mason, 93	C-6	176695	J-11
Mather, 50	K-7	Owen, 940	H-7
Mattoon, 438	H-8	Oxford, 607	L-9
Mauston, 4423	L-8	**OZAUKEE CO.,**	
Maxville, 30	J-3	86395	M-13
Mayville, 5154	M-11	Packwaukee, 200	L-9
Mazomanie, 1652	N-8	Paddock Lake,	
McAllister, 50	A-12	2992	P-13
McFarland, 7808	N-10	Palmyra, 1781	O-11
McNaughton, 150	E-9	Pardeeville, 2115	M-10
Medford, 4326	G-7	Park Falls, 2462	E-7
Medina, 250	J-11	Park Ridge, 491	†I-9
Mellen, 731	C-7	Parrish, 30	G-9
Melrose, 500	J-5	Patch Grv., 198	O-6
Melvina, 104	L-6	Patzau, 50	C-3
Menasha, 17353	K-11	Pearson, 80	G-10
Menchalville, 80	J-13	Peebles, 100	L-12
Menomonee Falls,		Pelican Lake, 200	F-10
35626	N-13	Pella, 185	I-11
Menomonie, 16264	H-3	Pembine, 193	E-13
MENOMINEE CO.,		Pence, 131	C-7
4232	H-11	Pensaukee, 150	C-11
Mequon, 23132	M-13	Pepin, 837	J-3
Mercer, 516	D-8	**PEPIN CO., 7469**	J-4
Merrill, 9661	G-9	Perkinstown, 100	G-7
Merrillan, 542	I-6	Peru, 40	O-11
Merrimac, 420	M-9	Peshtigo, 3502	B-11

Pewaukee, 13195	N-12	St. Michaels, 110	M-12
Pewaukee, 8166	†D-1	St. Nazianz, 783	K-13
Phelps, 900	D-10	Salem, 1150	P-13
Phillips, 1478	F-7	Sampson, 25	J-1
Phlox, 150	H-10	Sanborn, 40	C-6
Pickerel, 300	G-11	Sand Bay	A-6
Pickett, 170	K-11	Sand Creek, 200	G-4
PIERCE CO., 41019	I-2	Sarona, 100	E-4
Pigeon Falls, 411	J-5	Sauk City, 3410	N-9
Pilsen, 50	J-13	**SAUK CO.,**	
Pine Lake, 130	O-3	61976	M-8
Pine River, 147	K-10	Saukville, 4451	M-13
Pipe, 100	K-12	**SAWYER CO.,**	
Pittsville, 874	J-8	16557	E-6
Plain, 773	N-8	Saxeville, 120	K-10
Plainfield, 905	K-9	Saxon, 90	C-7
Platteville, 11224	O-7	Sayner, 207	E-9
Pleasant Prairie,		Scandinavia, 363	I-10
19719	P-13	Schofield, 2169	H-9
Pleasantville, 45	K-7	Sechlerville, 50	J-5
Plover, 12123	I-9	Seeley, 80	D-5
Plum City, 599	I-3	Seneca, 200	N-6
Plymouth, 8445	L-13	Sextonville, 551	N-7
Poland, 80	J-13	Seymour, 3451	I-12
Polonia, 526	I-9	Shamrock	N-7
POLK CO., 44205	F-2	Shanagolden, 50	D-7
Poplar, 605	C-4	Sharon, 1605	P-11
Port Andrew, 40	N-7	Shawano, 9305	I-11
Port Edwards, 1818	J-8	**SHAWANO CO.,**	
Port Washington,		41949	H-10
11250	M-13	Sheboygan, 49288	L-13
Port Wing, 164	B-4	**SHEBOYGAN CO.,**	
Portage, 10324	M-9	115507	L-13
PORTAGE CO.,		Sheboygan Falls,	
70019	I-9	7775	L-13
Porterfield, 50	B-11	Sheldon, 237	G-6
Portland, 200	N-10	Shell Lake, 1347	E-3
Portland, 45	L-8	Shennington, 45	K-7
Poskin, 90	F-3	Sherry, 120	I-8
Post Lake, 374	F-10	Sherwood, 2713	K-12
Postville, 30	O-9	Shiocton, 921	J-11
Potosi, 688	P-6	Shopiere, 200	P-10
Pound, 377	B-11	Shorewood,	
Poy Sippi, 371	K-10	13162	N-13
Poynette, 2528	M-9	Shorewood Hills,	
Prairie du Chien,		1565	S-7
5911	N-5	Shortville	J-8
Prairie du Sac,		Shullsburg, 1226	P-7
3972	N-9	Silver Lake, 2411	P-12
Prairie Farm, 473	G-3	Silver Lake, 350	F-9
Prentice, 660	F-7	Sinsinawa, 250	P-6
Prescott, 4258	I-1	Siren, 806	E-2
Presque Isle, 260	D-9	Sister Bay, 876	A-13
PRICE CO., 14159	F-7	Slinger, 5068	M-12
Princeton, 1254	L-10	Slovan	D-12
Pulaski, 3539	I-12	Sobieski, 259	I-12
Pulcifer, 134	H-11	Soldiers Grv., 592	M-6
Radisson, 240	E-6	Solon Sprs., 600	C-4
RACINE CO.,		Somers, 530	P-13
195408	O-13	Somerset, 2635	G-1
Randolph, 1811	M-10	S. Beaver Dam, 60	M-11
Random Lake,		S. Milwaukee,	
1594	M-13	21156	O-13
Range, 100	C-3	S. Range, 120	B-3
Readstown, 415	M-6	S. Superior	*D-9
Redgranite, 2149	K-10	S. Wayne, 489	P-8
Reedsburg, 9200	M-8	Sparta, 9522	K-6
Reedsville, 1206	J-13	Spencer, 1925	I-7
Reeve, 50	G-3	Spirit, 35	G-8
Reeseville, 708	M-11	Spooner, 2682	E-4
Rewey, 292	O-7	Spread Eagle, 200	E-12
Rhinelander, 7798	F-9	Spring Green, 1628	N-8
Rib Lake, 890	G-7	Spring Lake, 130	K-10
RICHLAND CO.,		Spring Valley, 1352	H-3
18021	M-7	Springbrook, 120	E-5
Richfield, 11300	N-12	Springfield, 158	J-9
Richford, 50	K-9	Springstead, 100	D-8
Richland Ctr., 5184	M-7	Stangelville, 110	J-14
Ridgeland, 273	G-4	Stanley, 3608	H-6
Ridgeway, 653	N-8	Star Lake, 100	D-9
Ringle, 200	H-9	Star Prairie, 561	G-2
Rio, 1009	M-10	Starks, 50	F-11
Rio Creek, 100	D-12	Stephenville, 250	J-11
Ripon, 7733	L-11	Stetsonville, 541	H-7
RICHLAND CO.,		Steuben, 131	N-6
195408	O-13	Stevens Pt., 26717	I-9
Rising Sun, 30	M-6	Stevensville, 40	K-5
River Falls, 15000	H-2	Stiles, 100	C-11
River Hills, 1597	†C-6	Stitzer, 200	O-6
Roberts, 1651	H-2	Stockbridge, 636	K-12
Rochester, 3682	O-12	Stockholm, 66	J-3
ROCK CO.,		Stoddard, 774	L-5
160331	O-10	Stone Lake, 178	E-6
Rock Falls, 50	I-3	Stoughton, 12615	O-10
Rock Sprs., 362	M-8	Stratford, 1578	H-8
Rockbridge, 100	M-7	Strum, 1114	I-5
Rockdale, 214	O-10	Sturgeon Bay,	
Rockfield	†A-2	9144	C-13
Rockland, 594	K-6	Sturtevant, 6970	O-13
Rockton, 35	O-7	Suamico, 11346	D-11
Romeo, 689	O-11	Sugar Camp, 180	E-10
Rosendale, 1063	L-11	Sullivan, 659	N-11
Rosholt, 506	I-9	Summit Lake, 144	G-10
Rosiere, 60	C-12	Sun Prairie, 29364	N-10
Rothschild, 5269	H-9	Superior, 27244	B-3
Rowleys Bay, 70	A-13	Superior Vil., 664	B-3
Roxbury, 150	N-9	Suring, 544	H-12
Royalton, 250	I-11	Sussex, 10518	N-12
Rozellville, 200	H-8	Symco, 100	I-11
Rubicon, 170	M-12	Taycheedah, 704	L-12
Rudolph, 439	I-8	Taylor, 476	J-5
Rural, 150	I-10	**TAYLOR CO.,**	
Rusk, 150	H-4	20689	G-7
RUSK CO., 14755	F-5	Tennyson, 355	P-6
St. Cloud, 475	L-12	Theresa, 1262	M-11
ST. CROIX CO.,		Thiensville, 3235	†A-5
84345	H-2	Thompsonville	N-11
St. Croix Falls, 2133	F-2	Thornton, 65	H-11
St. Francis, 9365	N-13	Thorp, 1621	H-6
St. Germain, 400	E-9	Three Lakes, 600	E-10
St. Joseph, 400	F-9	Tigerton, 741	I-10
St. Kilian, 80	L-12	Tilleda, 91	H-11
St. Lawrence, 250	M-12	Tipler, 50	E-11
St. Marys, 25	L-6	Tisch Mills, 200	J-14
		Tomah, 9093	L-7
		Tomahawk, 3397	F-9
		Tomey, 100	C-3
		Townsend, 146	G-11
		Trade Lake, 60	E-2
		Trego, 227	E-4
		TREMPEALEAU CO.,	
		28816	J-5
		Trimbelle, 30	I-2
		Tripoli, 70	F-9
		Tunnel City, 60	L-7
		Turtle Lake, 1050	F-3
		Twin Bluffs, 80	M-8
		Twin Lakes, 5989	P-12
		Two Creeks, 50	J-14
		Two Rivers, 11712	K-14
		Underhill, 100	H-12
		Union Ctr., 100	L-8
		Union Grv., 4915	O-13
		Unity, 363	H-8
		Upson, 70	C-7
		Urne, 50	I-4
		Valders, 962	K-13
		Valley, 60	L-7

Valley Jct., 100	K-7	Bear River, 518	M-1
Valmy, 30	B-13	Bedford, 201	J-1
Van Dyne, 300	K-12	Bessemer Bend, 199	J-7
VERNON CO.,		Beulah, 73	G-6
29773	L-5	Big Horn, 80	G-6
Verona, 10619	N-9	**BIG HORN CO.,**	
Vesper, 584	I-8	11668	G-4
Victory, 120	M-5	Big Piney, 552	J-2
Viola, 696	M-6	Bill, 10	H-8
Viroqua, 4362	M-6	Bondurant, 93	I-2
Wabeno, 575	F-11	Bonneville	J-5
Waldo, 503	L-13	Bosler, 60	L-8
Wales, 2549	N-12	Boulder, 170	J-3
Walworth, 2816	P-11	Brookhurst, 185	J-7
WALWORTH CO.,		Buffalo, 4585	G-7
102228	O-11	Buford, 40	L-8
Wandawega, 50	O-12	Burlington, 288	G-4
Wanderoos, 110	G-2	Burns, 301	M-10
Warrens, 363	K-7	Byron, 593	F-4
WASHBURN CO.,		**CAMPBELL CO.,**	
15911	E-4	46133	H-8
WASHINGTON CO.,		Canyon Jct.	I-3
131887	M-12	**CARBON CO.,**	
Waterford, 5368	O-12	15885	L-6
Waterloo, 3333	N-10	Carlile, 30	G-9
Watertown, 23861	N-11	Carpenter, 94	M-10
Waukau, 45	K-11	Carter, 10	L-1
Waukesha, 70718	N-12	Casper, 49644	J-7
WAUKESHA CO.,		Casper Mtn., 401	J-7
389891	O-12	Centennial, 270	L-8
Waumandee, 68	J-4	Cheyenne, 59466	M-9
Waunakee, 12097	N-9	Chugwater, 212	L-9
Waupaca, 6069	J-10	Clark	G-3
WAUPACA CO.,		Clearmont, 142	G-7
52410	I-10	Cody, 9520	G-3
Waupun, 11340	L-11	Cokeville, 535	K-1
Wausau, 39106	H-9	Colony	F-10
Wausaukee, 575	A-11	Colter Bay	H-1
WAUSHARA CO.,		**CONVERSE CO.,**	
24496	K-9	13833	J-8
Wautoma, 2218	K-10	Cowley, 655	F-4
Wauwatosa, 46396	†E-4	Crawford, 681	†G-4
Wauzeka, 711	N-6	**CROOK CO., 7083**	F-9
Waverly	I-3	Crowheart, 145	I-4
Wayside, 200	J-13	Daniel, 150	I-2
Webb Lake, 60	D-3	Dayton, 757	F-6
Webster, 653	E-2	Devils Tower, 70	F-9
Wentworth, 100	B-4	Diamondville, 737	L-1
W. Allis, 60411	†F-4	Dixon, 97	M-6
W. Baraboo, 1414	M-9	Douglas, 6120	J-8
W. Bend, 31078	M-12	Dubois, 971	I-3
W. Bloomfield, 65	J-10	Dwyer	K-9
W. Lima, 40	M-7	E. Thermopolis, 254	H-5
W. Milwaukee,		Edden, 281	J-3
4206	†F-5	Edgerton, 195	I-7
W. Salem, 4799	K-5	Elk Mtn., 191	L-7
Westboro, 190	G-7	Emblem, 50	G-4
Westby, 2200	L-6	Encampment, 450	M-6
Westfield, 1254	L-9	Ethete, 1553	I-4
Weston, 14868	H-9	Etna, 164	J-1
Weston, 30	H-3	Evanston, 12359	M-1
Weyauwega, 1900	J-10	Evansville, 2544	A-10
Weyerhaeuser, 238	F-5	Fairview, 275	J-1
Wheeler, 348	H-3	Farson, 313	K-3
White Creek, 50	L-8	Farthing, 30	L-9
White Lake, 363	G-11	Ft. Bridger, 345	M-1
Whitefish Bay,		Ft. Laramie, 230	K-9
14110	N-13	Ft. Steele, 30	L-6
Whitefish Bay, 30	B-13	Ft. Washakie, 1759	I-4
Whitehall, 1558	J-5	Four Corners	H-9
Whitelaw, 757	J-13	Foxpark, 2	M-7
Whitewater,		Frannie, 157	F-4
14390	O-11	Freedom, 314	J-1
Whiting, 1724	I-9	**FREMONT CO.,**	
Whittlesey, 105	G-7	40123	J-5
Wild Rose, 725	K-9	Frontier, 40	L-1
Willard, 60	I-6	Garland, 115	F-4
Williams Bay, 2564	P-12	Garrett, 30	K-8
Wilmot, 442	P-12	Gillette, 29087	G-8
Wilson, 184	H-3	Glendo, 205	K-9
Wilton, 504	L-7	Glenrock, 2576	J-8
Winchester, 150	D-9	**GOSHEN CO.,**	
Winchester, 671	J-11	13249	K-10
Wind Lake, 5342	O-12	Granger, 139	L-2
Wind Pt., 1723	O-13	Grand Village	D-2
Windsor, 3573	N-10	Grass Creek, 50	H-5
Winnebago, 400	J-3	Greybull, 1847	G-5
WINNEBAGO CO.,		Grover, 147	J-1
166994	K-11	Guernsey, 1147	K-9
Winneconne, 2383	K-11	Halfway	J-2
Winter, 313	F-6	Hanna, 841	L-7
Wiota, 140	O-8	Harriman, 40	B-8
Wisconsin Dells,		Hartville, 62	K-9
2678	L-8	Hawk Sprs., 45	L-10
Wisconsin Rapids,		Hiland, 10	I-6
18367	J-8	Hillsdale, 47	M-10
Withee, 487	H-7	Hoback, 1176	I-1
Wittenberg, 1081	H-10	Hoback Jct., 200	I-1
Wonewoc, 816	L-7	**HOT SPRINGS CO.,**	
WOOD CO., 74745	J-8	4812	H-4
Woodboro, 50	F-9	Hudson, 458	I-4
Woodford, 50	P-9	Hulett, 383	G-9
Woodman, 130	N-6	Huntley, 30	L-10
Woodruff, 966	E-9	Hyattville, 75	G-6
Woodville, 1344	H-3	Jackson, 9577	I-1
Wrightstown, 2827	J-12	James Town, 536	J-7
Wyalusing, 80	O-5	Jay Em, 20	K-10
Wyeville, 147	K-7	Jeffrey City, 58	K-5
Wyocena, 768	M-10	Jelm, 30	M-8
Yellow Lake, 70	E-2	**JOHNSON CO.,**	
York, 40	J-5	8569	H-7
Yuba, 72	M-7	Kaycee, 263	H-7
Zachow, 150	I-12	Keeline, 10	J-9
Zenda, 200	P-11	Kelly, 138	H-1
Zittau, 60	K-11	Kemmerer, 2656	L-1
		Kinnear, 180	I-4
Wyoming		Kirby, 92	H-5
Page locator		La Barge, 551	K-2
Map keys	Atlas pages	LaGrange, 448	L-10
A–J	234–235	Lake	H-2
		Lance Creek, 43	J-9
Afton, 1911	J-1	Lander, 6867	I-4
Aladdin, 20	F-10	Laramie, 30816	M-8
Albany, 50	M-8	**LARAMIE CO.,**	
ALBANY CO.,		91738	M-9
36299	K-8	Leiter, 5	G-7
Albin, 181	M-10	Linch, 100	I-7
Alcova, 76	J-7	**LINCOLN CO.,**	
Allendale, 70	A-8	18106	K-1
Alpine, 828	I-1	Lingle, 468	K-10
Alta, 400	H-1	Little America, 68	L-2
Alva, 50	F-9	Lonetree, 49	M-2
Arapahoe, 1506	I-4	Lost Cabin, 30	I-6
Arlington, 25	L-7	Lost Sprs., 4	J-9
Arminto, 30	I-6	Lovell, 2360	F-4
Arvada, 43	G-8	Lucerne, 150	H-5
Atlantic City, 37	K-4	Lusk, 1567	J-10
Auburn, 328	J-1	Lyman, 2115	M-1
Baggs, 440	M-6	Lysite, 60	I-5
Bairoil, 106	K-6	Mammoth, 263	H-2
Banner, 40	G-7	Manderson, 114	G-5
Bar Nunn, 2213	J-7	Manville, 95	J-9
Barber	G-5	Marbleton, 1094	J-2
Basin, 1285	G-5		

McFadden, 80	L-
McKinley, 20	H-
Medicine Bow, 284	L-7
Meeteetse, 327	H-4
Meriden, 70	L-
Midwest, 404	I-7
Midwest Hts.	I-
Mills, 3461	J-3
Moneta	I-
Moorcroft, 1009	G-9
Moose, 180	H-1
Moose Wilson Road,	
1821	
Moran, 50	H-1
Morton,	
Mountain Home, 40	
Mountain View, 96	A-7
Muddy Gap, 20	
Natrona, 50	I-6
NATRONA CO.,	
75450	J-6
New Haven, 20	G-9
Newcastle, 3532	H-9
NIOBRARA CO.,	
484	J-9
Node, 20	J-9
Opal, 96	L-1
Orchard Valley, 80	M-
Orin, 46	J-
Orpha	J-
Osage, 208	H-9
Oshoto, 30	G-9
Osmond, 397	J-
Otto, 50	G-5
Owl Creek, 5	I-
Paradise Valley	J-3
PARK CO., 28205	G-3
Parkman, 151	F-6
Pine Bluffs, 1129	M-10
Pine Haven, 490	G-9
Pinedale, 2030	J-3
Point of Rocks,	
Powder River, 44	I-6
Powell, 6314	F-4
Prospector Vil., 200	H-
Quealy	L-
Ralston, 280	G-4
Ranchester, 855	F-7
Rawlins, 9259	L-6
Recluse, 30	G-8
Red Butte, 449	J-7
Red Desert, 30	L-
Reliance, 714	L-4
Riverside, 52	M-6
Riverton, 10615	I-4
Robertson, 99	L-1
Rock River, 245	L-8
Rockpoint	G-
Rockypoint	F-9
Rolling Hills, 440	J-8
Rozet, 40	G-9
Ryan Pk., 38	M-
Saddlestring, 15	G-7
Sand Draw	I-5
Saratoga, 1960	L-6
Savageton	J-7
Seminoe Dam, 40	K-6
Shawnee, 30	J-
Shell, 83	G-5
Sheridan, 17444	F-7
SHERIDAN CO.,	
27610	F-7
Shirley Basin, 100	K-7
Shoshoni, 649	I-5
Sinclair, 433	L-6
Skull Creek, 30	H-
Slater, 80	L-
Sleepy Hollow, 1308	G-
Smoot, 195	J-1
S. Greeley, 4217	M-
S. Laramie, 1560	M-
S. Pass City, 30	K-4
S. Torrington, 380	K-10
Spotted Horse	G-8
Star Valley Ranch,	
1503	J-1
SUBLETTE CO.,	
10247	J-2
Sundance, 1182	G-9
Sunrise, 30	J-
Superior, 244	L-4
Sussex	I-7
SWEETWATER CO.,	
43806	L-4
Table Rock,	L-
Ten Sleep, 260	H-6
TETON CO., 21294	H-1
Teton Vil., 330	H-1
Thayne, 366	J-1
Thermopolis, 3009	H-5
Thunder Basin, 100	G-
Tie Siding, 30	M-8
Torrington, 6501	K-10
Tower Jct.	H-
Ucross	G-7
UINTA CO., 21118	L-1
Upton, 960	H-9
Urie, 262	M-1
Valley	I-
Van Tassell, 15	J-10
Veteran, 80	K-10
Vista West, 951	A-10
Walcott, 30	L-6
Wamsutter, 451	L-5
WASHAKIE CO.,	
8533	H-5
W. Thumb, 80	H-2
Weston, 80	G-8
Westview Circle, 52	L-1
Wheatland, 3627	K-9
Wilson, 1482	H-1
Winchester, 60	H-5
Woods Lndg., 20	M-8
Worland, 5807	H-5
Wright, 1807	H-8
Wyarno, 40	F-7
Wyodak, 80	G-9
Yoder, 151	L-10